THE BEAT GOES ON!
Music as a Corps Ministry

THE BEAT GOES ON! *MUSIC AS A CORPS MINISTRY*
Copyright © 2017 by The Salvation Army

Published by Crest Books
Crest Books
The Salvation Army National Headquarters
615 Slaters Lane
Alexandria, VA 22313
Phone: 703/684-5523

Lt. Col. Allen Satterlee, Editor-in-Chief and National Literary Secretary
Roger Selvage, Art Director
Nick Holder, Editorial Assistant

Written by Harold Burgmayer
Edited by Linda Johnson, Dorothy Post, Beatrice Holz, William Carlson, JoAnn Shade
Designed by Keri Johnson
Illustrations and Front Cover by David Hulteen, Jr.

Scripture quotations are from the following sources:

The *Holy Bible, New International Version* (NIV), copyright © 1973, 1978, 1984, International Bible Society. Used by permission of the Zondervan Bible Publishers.

The *New American Standard Bible* ® (NASB) copyright © Copyright 1960, 1962, 1963, 1968, 1971, 1972, 1973, 1975, 1977, 1995 by the Lockman Foundation. Used by permission.

The Message Remix: The Bible in Contemporary Language by Eugene Peterson, Copyright © 1993, 1994, 1995, 1996, 2000, 2001, 2002. Used by permission of the NavPress Publishing Group.

The *King James Version* (KJV)

The *Living Bible Paraphrase* (TLB) copyright © 1971 Tyndale House Publishers, Wheaton, IL. All rights reserved.

The *Revised Standard Version* (RSV) copyright © 1946, 1971 by the Division of Christian Education of the National Council of Churches of Christ in the USA.

The *Holy Bible, New Living Translation* (NLT) copyright © 1996, Tyndale House Publishers, Inc., Wheaton, IL. All rights reserved.

Good News Bible: Today's English Version (TEV) © 1976, American Bible Society. Revised in 1992. Used with permission.

New Century Version ® (NCV®) Copyright © 2005 by Thomas Nelson. Used with permission All rights reserved.

Easy-To-Read Version (ERV) Copyright © 2006 by Bible League International. Used with permission.

Available in print from crestbooks.com

ISBN: 978-1-946709-02-8

Printed in the United States

All rights reserved. No part of this publication may be reproduced, stored in a retrieval system, or transmitted in any form or by any means without prior written permission of the publisher. Exceptions are brief quotations in printed reviews.

DEDICATION

To my loving partner
in life, mission, and ministry,
Priscilla Burgmayer.

ENDORSEMENTS
The Beat Goes On! *Music as a Corps Ministry*

The Beat Goes On! is an incredibly comprehensive resource for every avenue of music worship—from the theology behind the practice of Salvation Army music to the "nitty-gritty" of worship leadership—whether from the praise band, the piano, or the baton of a bandmaster, songster leader, youth band or singing company leader. This is a "must read" for *anyone* who wants to make a difference in Salvation Army musical worship. It is a powerful call to quality leadership and a remarkable educational tool from one of the best and most effective Salvation Army music leaders of our generation.

—Dr. Beatrice Hill Holz, OF
Territorial Songster Leader, USA South
Professor Emeritus of Music Education & Voice, Asbury University

The Beat Goes On! is not something to be read from cover to cover. It is a reference guide which provides practical instruction and resources for virtually every aspect of Salvation Army music and worship leadership. This comprehensive book will be especially helpful to any Salvationist who is unexpectedly thrust into a music leadership responsibility. In other words, just about everyone! This vital resource is a must for every corps library.

—William Himes, OF
Former *Territorial Music and Gospel Arts Secretary,* USA Central

A lifetime of practice, patience and prayer has eminently qualified Dr. Harold Burgmayer to author this compendium of helpful insights and strategies. His legacy of engagement in SA music-making is testimony in itself. And now we get to absorb some of what has been driving his efforts all these years.

If there is a more comprehensive examination of the way The Salvation Army has used, is using, and ought to use music as ministry…I haven't seen it! A must read for anybody who wants to make the most of this God-given and relevant ministry tool.

—Leonard Ballantine, Major
Songwriter and choral arranger, *Canadian Staff Songster Leader*

This is a valuable and practical resource for worship leaders and keyboardists in The Salvation Army. Harold (Dr. Burgmayer) has put together a comprehensive volume that will not only help to equip musicians to be their best in both musical and ministry preparation, but also better understand how all of the components of successful music ministry can fit together in a harmonious and Spirit-led way.

—Phil Laeger
Songwriter and worship leader

It is my pleasure to endorse this marvelous book, as it is well written, accessible and covers all the issues that corps musical leaders face. I have long admired Harold Burgmayer's pedagogical abilities, and this volume prompts us to be reflective about our practice, while giving a wealth of technical strategies.

Harold's emphasis on preparation, sound and communication sits alongside the spiritual sincerity that is required—if we are to challenge and inspire our listeners. The important mantra that we should always offer our best for the Highest comes through this book loud and clear, as is the encouragement to be bold, adventurous and tenacious to ensure that our ensembles transform from "minstrels to ministers."

—**Dorothy Nancekievill**
Leader, International Staff Songsters

Dr. Harold Burgmayer's *The Beat Goes On* provides valuable and time tested learnings to enhance and effectively develop corps music programs that strengthen the ongoing ministry of proclaiming the good news of Jesus Christ.

—**William B. Flinn, OF**
Bandmaster, Pasadena Tabernacle Band

Now here's a book whose time has come with Bandmaster Harold Burgmayer as the perfect leader and author to help us all. Make this required reading for yourself this year and recommend it to other corps music leaders as well. You'll be a better leader for it.

—**Jim Knaggs, Commissioner**
Former Territorial Commander, USA West and Australia East

While written from a very practical perspective in easily accessible language, this is the definitive textbook for Salvationist musicians, worship leaders and corps officers. Harold's many years of hands-on music-making at the corps, divisional and territorial levels, combined with his scholarly approach to research, makes this the go-to resource book for music leaders for years to come.

—**Craig Lewis**
Territorial Music and Gospel Arts Secretary, Canada and Bermuda Territory

This book takes a homogeneous approach to Salvation Army music-making. Spiritual, musical and leadership blocks are set out by Dr. Harold Burgmayer for leaders and musicians within the movement to lay foundations and build music ministry within their own corps setting. With online resources and training included, this is a vital tool for all those who want to develop, grow and improve in this unique ministry.

—**Andrew Blyth**
Head of Music Editorial, UK Territory

The Beat Goes On! is a wonderful gift for those passionate about utilizing song for the glory of God. Within these pages, Harold Burgmayer has creatively and comprehensively captured the power of song as a ministry tool, the essentials of vocal training and performance for every age group, and the ins and outs of effective worship team leadership. With this manual in hand, corps leaders will have the necessary tools to advance the wonderful legacy of Salvation Army music ministry into the future.

—**Margaret Davis, Major**
Soprano Soloist and Voice Specialist

The Beat Goes On! Music as a Corps Ministry
Table of Contents

Introduction
Foreword by General André Cox 1
Preface by Ronald Waiksnoris 3
About the Author/Acknowledgements/Special Thanks by Harold Burgmayer 5
How to Use This Book by Harold Burgmayer 11

Prelude
THE LOVE LANGUAGE OF MUSIC
Streams of Living Water
    The Beat Goes On... 13
    Make the World with Music Ring! 15
    Seeing Is Believing! 16
    The Hidden Vigor of Winter 19
    Sheep Without a Shepherd 20

Part One:
MUSIC MINISTERS

Chapter One
FROM MINSTRELS TO MINISTERS
Daring to Draw Near
    Minstrels or Ministers? 27
    Daring to Draw Near 29
    From Spectator to Participant 31
    Music for Evangelism 35
    The Music Minister's Toolbox—Getting it Right with
      our Music Offerings 37
    Ideas to Enhance Worship and Communication 39
    Music Ministry Resources 42

Chapter Two
SUNDAY MORNING
A Lifeline to the Church
    A Call to Worship 43
    What Word, What Song? 45
    What Plan? 50
    What Offering? 55
    Who Makes This Happen?—Ministry as a Partnership 58
    The Rehearsal Leader's Toolbox—Working the Plan 62
    Worship Design Resources 66

TABLE OF CONTENTS

Chapter Three
HAND ME DOWN *MY* SILVER TRUMPET
Making Things Happen at *Your* Corps

Luther and the People's Song	69
Moses and the Handmade Trumpets	70
Sallie Salvos	71
Music and Arts School Models	75
Preparation Is Everything!	78
The Youth Leader's Toolbox—You Get More with a Kind Word … and Consistency	80
Youth Music Leader's Resources	82

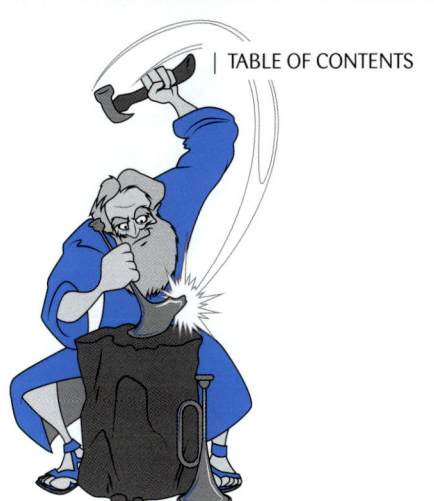

Chapter Four
WORKERS TOGETHER
The Corps Leadership Team

In the Valley of Dry Bones	83
People of Purpose	84
Better Young Than Never	86
Adults at the Kids' Table	91
Come and Dine at the Adult Table (Well, maybe?)	96
Corps Dynamics Resources	100

Chapter Five
THEN SINGS MY SOUL!
The Song Leader

Dear Sun Day Song	101
We Need a Song Leader	103
Our Treasury of Salvation Army Song	104
The Evolution of Hymns, Gospel Songs, and Worship Choruses	107
Finding and Projecting the Right Words	108
Finding the Right Tune—The Metrical Index	111
Before Introducing a Song	114
A Script for Song Leading	116
Food, Glorious Food—Sing a New Song (Occasionally!)	117
The Song Leader's Toolbox—Everybody Can Learn Simple Beat Patterns/Christmas Carols	119
Song Leader Resources	124

Part Two:
YOUTH MUSIC MINISTRY

Chapter Six
LET THE CHILDREN SING!
Training Young Singers through Small Group Instruction

From the Mouths of Children…	127
Goal #1 Experience Unison Pitch	128
Goal #2 Experience High, Low, and Middle	129
Goal #3 Recognize and Sing Stepwise Pitches	130
Goal #4 Establish the Basics with the Intermediate Vocal Group	132
Goal #5 Read Stepwise Melodies	136
Children's Vocal Resources	142

The Beat Goes On

If you cannot teach me to fly, teach me to sing.
—J.M. Barrie, author of Peter Pan

Chapter Seven
THE RIGHT SONG FOR YOUR KIDS
Bit By Bit, Putting It Together

The Halcyon Days of Singing Company	145
Goal #6 Develop Unison and Two-Part Singing	146
Goal #7 Introduce More Advanced Concepts	147
The Singing Company Leader's Toolbox—Approaching a New Children's Song	150
Win Them One by One	151
A Six-Week Rehearsal Plan: *They Should Know*	154
Singing Company Leader's Resources	164

Chapter Eight
ALL HAIL TO DANIEL'S BAND!
Building an Instrumental Program from the Bottom Up

Jimmy Gets Junior Band	165
What, Me? The Youth Band Leader?	168
Drip, Drip, Drip! Short and Long Term Goals	169
The Trumpet Shall Sound! Building a Beginner Instrumental Program	170
The Youth Band Rehearsal	175
The New Piece/Learning to Troubleshoot—*This Little Light of Mine*	177
Beginner Brass and Youth Band Repertoire	181

Chapter Nine
GOD'S SPECIAL INSTRUMENTS
The Brass and Drum Instructor's Toolbox

Two Lessons Ahead/Who Me, Teach?	183
Getting Started on a Brass Instrument	185
Trombone Pointers	187
Twelve Tips for Giving a Beginner Brass Lesson	188
To Infinity and Beyond—Helps for Advancing Brass Players	189
Getting Started on the Snare Drum	191
Establishing a Snare Drum Routine	192
Brass and Percussion Instruction	194

Part Three:
ADULT MUSIC MINISTRY

Chapter Ten
WHAT'S THE SCORE?
How to "Hear" a Vocal or Brass Score

Scores of Meanings!	201
How Can We "Hear" a Score?	203
Why Do We Read?	203
How Did You Learn to Read?	204
Unraveling the "Mystery of The Five Lines"	205
Scene 1: The Five Lines Case begins ... With Our Eyes/Seeing Rhythmic Movement and Pitch Profiles	205

| TABLE OF CONTENTS

Scene 2: The Five Lines Case Continues With Our Ears/Hearing Harmonic
   Combinations, Color, Dynamics and Expression 206
Scene 3: There's More to The Five Lines Case
   In Our Inner Ear/Hearing Vocal Colors 208
   What's the Vocal Score? Seven Steps to Learning a New Song—*Come Home* . . . 209
   What's the Band Score?—*What A Friend*. 214
Scene 4: More Clues ... Using Our Inner Ear 214
Scene 5: The Case of Coloring Outside "The Five Lines" ... With Our Eyes. 219
Score-Reading Resources 219

Chapter Eleven
FROM SCORE READING TO SCORE STUDY
Marking a Vocal or Brass Score

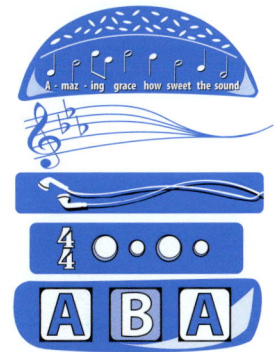

The Investigation Unearths More! 223
A Tapestry of Layers—*God's Children* 223
Marks on a Score 231
Seven Steps and Marking a New Song—*Come Home*. 238
Score Study Resources 241

Chapter Twelve
AWAKE MY VOICE AND SING!
The Songster Leader

Moment by Moment 243
The Worshiping Choir 244
Linking Hearts and Voices 247
It's All in the Warm-Up! (Well, almost all) 249
A Nine-Step Choral Warm-Up 254
Diction Helps/Vowels 258
To "R" or Not to "R," That is the Question 259
Consonants. 261
Other Suggestions on Diction 262
Choral Training Resources. 263

Chapter Thirteen
THE EFFECTIVE SONGSTER REHEARSAL
The Songster Leader's Toolbox

Carol's Secret 265
Building Beautiful Sound 267
Setting a Spiritual Standard 271
From Vocal Score to Rehearsal Preparation—A Strategy for *Only This I Ask* . 272
It's Just a Hymn! 277
Ways to Re-Voice Hymns for Brigades 279
For the Beauty of the Earth 282
There is Music Everywhere—Salvation Army Choral Publications 284
Songster Leadership Resources. 285

The Beat Goes On

Chapter Fourteen
STRIKE UP THE BAND!
The Bandmaster's Rehearsal and Sunday Preparation

Booth and the Birth of The Salvation Army Band 287
The Brass Band Today—Dynamo or Dinosaur? 288
The Instruments of the Brass Band 290
Band Training—"No Uncertain Sound" Revisited 293
Not All Notes Are Created Equal—Tuning 298
Scales Require Tuning 300
Working Other Angles 303
Dan Rather Interviews Stokowski 305
Salvation Army Brass Publications 307
Brass Level Guidelines 310
The Bandmaster's Resources 311

Chapter Fifteen
SCORE STUDY TO REHEARSAL STRATEGY
The Bandmaster's Toolbox

From Songster Anthem to Brass Transcription—*How Sweet the Name* (French),
   Original Choral/Organ Version 313
From Layers to Rehearsal Tactics—*How Sweet the Name*, Brass Band Version 317
From Band Score to Piano Reduction 322
Stella by Piano Reduction 328
Score Preparation Resources 336

Part Four:
WORSHIP LEADERSHIP

Chapter Sixteen
PLAY ME A SONG, YOU'RE THE PIANO-MAN!
Keyboard Basics

Getting Acquainted with the Piano 339
Chording and Playing By Ear 342
Scales Expand into Triads 345
Chords Can Be Inverted 348
Inversions Help Us "Voice-Lead" 350
The Dominant Seventh (V7) Chord 353
Piano Instruction Resources 355

Chapter Seventeen
KEYBOARD WORSHIP
The Meeting Pianist

Piano Worship 357
Hands On! Elaborating on the Piano Tune Book 360
The Circle of Fifths and You! 363
Applying the Circle of Fifths at the Keyboard 366
Modulation 368
Less is More!—Accompanying Soloists and Songsters 371
Meeting Pianist Resources 375

| TABLE OF CONTENTS

Chapter Eighteen
MORE THAN A SONG
Leading the Worship Team

Flow, River, Flow 377
Another Sunday ... On Our Toes 378
Praying a Playlist 379
Creating the Playlist 380
Locating the Music and Words 384
Arranging the Playlist 386
Creating Seamless Transitions 390
The Worship Leader's Rehearsal Prep 393
Worship Team Resources 397

Chapter Nineteen
THE HOLY HASSLE OF ANOTHER SUNDAY
The Worship Leader's Toolbox

Worship ... Another Sunday? 399
Location, Location, Location—Positioning the Worship Band 401
Sound, Sound, Sound—The Effective Sound Check 404
Sing, Sing, Sing—Making Adjustments on Stage 405
Chords, Chords, and More Chords! 407
Chording on Guitar 412
How to Sing Harmonies 415
Knowing When to Subtract (–) from or Add (+) to Chords 420
More Worship Team Resources 423

Part Five:
THE CONDUCTOR'S TOOLBOX

Chapter Twenty
WHERE'S THE BEAT?
Conducting Fundamentals

Why You Worry? ... Just Do This! 427
Handling Traffic or Making Music? 429
The Four Basic Beat Patterns—4, 3, 2, and 6 431
The Conducting Language 439
The Beat Gesture 444
Conducting Fundamentals Resources 447

Chapter Twenty-One
STICKS, STARTS AND STOPS
More Conducting Fundamentals

From Aural to Visual—A Brief History of Conducting 449
To Baton or Not to Baton? 450
Starts and Entrance Cues 454
Pauses and Cut-offs 461

The Beat Goes On

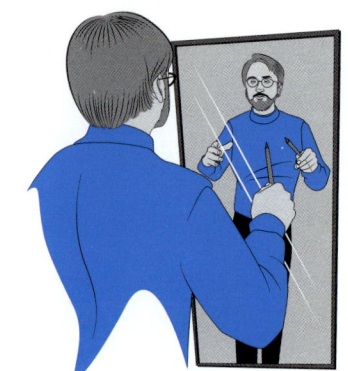

Chapter Twenty-Two
GESTURE AND EXPRESSION
Expanding the Conductor's Toolbox

What's In the Beat?	467
Tempo	468
The Expressive Beat Gesture	476
Use of the Left Hand	483
Exploring Dynamics	492
The Art of Phrasing	496

Chapter Twenty-Three
LISTEN AND RESPOND
Making the Rehearsal Work ... 501

A Tale of Two Conductors	502
Lessons in Rehearsal Routine	503
Listen and ... Respond—Cappuccino and the Fine Art of Listening	505
From the Inside Out ...	507
Listen and ... Respond—Connecting Over a Second Cup	510
Lessons in Rehearsal Mechanics	511
How Do I Get Performers to Watch Me?	512
How Do I Know When and How to Stop?	513
Is It Okay to Allow Questions?	515
How Can I Get My Ensemble "Inside" the Music?	517
From Snapshots to Slideshows—Rehearsal Strategies	524
Rehearsal Leaders' Resources	527

Postlude
PASSING THE BATON
The Beat Goes On!

A Race into the Future!	529
Passing the Baton to the Next Generation	530
Searching for Eagles	533
Assimilating the How, When and Why	534
The Emerging Leader's Toolbox—Paul Passes the Baton	540
Leaders, Not Helpers	540
From Cross Training to Empowerment	541
Establish High Standards of Excellence	543
Discover Your Group's Identity ... Together	544
Body Building	545
Quiet Strength	545
Finishing Well	546
Salvation Heroes	552

Endnotes	553
Online Appendix and Audio Resources	565
Scripture Index	571
Music Index	573
Topic Index	577

| TABLE OF CONTENTS

FOREWORD
by General André Cox

From the time when David was put in charge of music at the Tabernacle (1 Chronicles 6:31-32), through the Psalms, to one of the earliest Christian hymns (Philippians 2:5-11), to the encouragement to "speak to one another with psalms, hymns and spiritual songs" as we "sing and make music in our hearts to the Lord" (Ephesians 5:19) until the time we join the great multitude in white robes (Revelation 7:9-12) music has been and will continue to be an important aspect of our worship.

Music has the potential to transcend barriers of language and culture. Music achieves so much—it calms the troubled soul, comforts the distressed, brings joy, expresses hope and communicates emotion when often words fail us.

There is a unique partnership between music and The Salvation Army. Ever since William Booth saw the opportunity that brass bands provided for open air ministry, music has been a central component of Salvation Army life. God is a creative God and when He created us He placed within us something of His own creative nature. From that creative spark, Salvationists have been involved in music-making, seeking to continually give praise to God as we communicate the Gospel of Jesus Christ and help bring people into a living relationship with Him.

Music is powerful in and of itself, but when imbued with the Holy Spirit it enters a whole new dimension. As Salvationist worshipers and musicians, it is important to ensure we give "our utmost for His Highest" as Oswald Chambers would say. Our music-making is not performance, it is worship. Our music is not about perfection, but about giving all that we have and are to God. Our music-making is not about us, but about God.

I wholeheartedly commend Dr. Harold Burgmayer's book to you. This book expertly blends the why and how of Salvationist musicianship so that we give of our best to God, and He is glorified in all that we do. With a wealth of experience and a deep spirituality, Dr. Burgmayer is well placed to author this work. This book will be a useful resource to the leader as well as the participant, to the novice as well as to the experienced and to the officer as well as the soldier.

May God bless and meet with you in your moments of music and worship.

— **André Cox**
December 2016
GENERAL
International Leader of The Salvation Army

PREFACE
by Ronald Waiksnoris

Dr. Harold Burgmayer has led a life immersed in learning and teaching. As a young man, God led him to study architecture at the prestigious Cooper Union in Greenwich Village, New York City. I have known Harold since those days and have long-felt that those studies prepared him to design one of the finest divisional music programs in the United States. After his studies at Cooper Union, he started his musical path that eventually led to a Doctorate in Music Composition from Temple University in Philadelphia.

As we worked together on various projects and programs from Star Lake Musicamp to musical convocations and councils, I came to admire his skill and passion for music, worship and people. He was the "modern" Salvation Army music leader before we knew that there would be one. He has valued music ministry to young people so much that he structured detailed curricula to help them develop their skills on various instruments and voice.

As you read this book, you will understand that his experience has allowed him to address just about every aspect of Salvation Army music-making that can be considered. Even with all that detail, this is not a history book or a philosophy book. This is a "how to" book that gives clear guidance for what you, the important reader, hope to accomplish in your corps situation.

God very clearly gave The Salvation Army a tremendous gift of music along with a heart for souls. From the earliest days, music was used to reach the masses. And, importantly, God gave the Army inspired composers to create the music that would be used in building the Kingdom. This book offers a look into those early days with photographs that tell a story all their own. This book gives technical and practical advice from the mind and heart of a man who has lived the book.

You don't need to read this from cover to cover, although you would be better for it, but you do need to keep it handy. Every Sunday your corps has worship. Use the worship leader's toolbox. Many of us dream of having music in every Salvation Army corps. Keyboard players are a big part of that. Look for instruction in those pages. If you have suddenly found yourself in a leadership position and you're not quite sure what to do, this book will help you prepare. In our history we have had Orders and Regulations for just about everything. Now we have a practical book to help and guide.

As I have watched this book evolve, I have become more aware that music is one of the strong influences that holds us together in The Salvation Army. So, read this book, digest it, use it and share it with others. In my thirty-two years in this walk of music and faith as Territorial Music Secretary, I have become convinced of one thing in particular… the beat goes on!

—*Ronald Waiksnoris*
December 2016
Former *Territorial Music Secretary*, USA Eastern Territory
and *New York Staff Bandmaster*

ABOUT THE AUTHOR
by Harold Burgmayer

Harold Burgmayer assumed the role of Music and Gospel Arts Secretary for The Salvation Army USA Central Territory in August of 2015. Previously Harold served for thirty-four years as Divisional Music Director for The Salvation Army in Eastern Pennsylvania and Delaware (Pendel). This included leadership of the Pendel Brass and Singers, who recorded sixteen albums and traveled to South America, Canada, South Africa, Scandinavia, the Caribbean, and throughout the United States, including participation in the Rose Parade. Harold headed up the corps music programs of the Philadelphia Pioneer Corps from 1985–2015, and before that served as bandmaster and songster leader at the Philadelphia Citadel Corps from 1977–1985.

At age fourteen, Harold began conducting and arranging music for a small Salvation Army corps band in Levittown, Pennsylvania, while benefiting from the music program of the Pendel Division under the leadership of Bandmaster Kenneth Strehle and later, Bandmaster Ivor and Songster Leader Janette Bosanko. In the fall of 1973, Harold began architectural studies at the prestigious Cooper Union and was invited to join the New York Staff Band under Bandmaster Derek Smith. Harold's desire to pursue music composition coincides with a commitment to Jesus Christ made in the spring of 1977.

Harold completed a Master's degree and a Doctor of Musical Arts degree in music composition from Temple University, and has produced over 400 arrangements and compositions ranging from simple children's songs to a symphony for full orchestra. Harold, along with his wife Priscilla, have appeared as guest clinicians, specializing in the training of singers and instrumentalists. Numerous articles and instructional materials, including the Music Arts Proficiency (M.A.P.) curriculum reflect the intent to develop music leaders.

Harold's life verse, Psalm 27:4, expresses his heart-felt desire to dwell in God's presence:

> One thing have I desired of the Lord, that will I seek after;
> that I may dwell in the house of the Lord all the days of my life,
> to behold the beauty of the Lord and to enquire in his temple. —KJV

ACKNOWLEDGING MENTORS

The teaching expressed in this book represents, in great part, what others have poured into me over the years. It is therefore important that I share with you, the reader, influences on my own life and calling as a music minister in The Salvation Army.

A SALVATIONIST-TRAINED MUSICIAN...

The journey begins with frequent cornet lessons, every morning outside our summer cottage from my father, **Harold George Burgmayer**.

Harold (seated on the left) with his brother Paul Burgmayer in 1963.

Pendel Brass 50th Anniversary, 2014. In the front row are former conductors Bill Flinn, Janette and Ivor Bosanko and Harold Burgmayer.

From early on, I sat next to him at band practices, and as I grew, aspired to start new beginners as he did season after season. My mother **Naomi Burgmayer** made it to every performance I had. In 1969 I heard the Pendel Brass for the first time, led by then divisional music director **Bandmaster Ken Strehle**. I never imagined being a conductor and composer. I just knew I wanted to be part of a band like that. Bandmaster Strehle proved a valuable model of consistency as a divisional music director over thirty plus years. He was unrelenting in effective soft-playing of hymn tunes, and taught a reverence for the devotional music of Erik Leidzén and Dean Goffin.

A young, enthusiastic **Bill Flinn** led the Pendel Brass and Singers, followed by **Ivor and Janette Bosanko** for four years. Ivor, in particular, mentored me in my early writing and as a fledgling corps bandmaster at the Philadelphia Citadel corps. Bill, Ivor and Janette continued to encourage and support me, even after they moved on to ministries on the West Coast.

An end-of-summer highlight was the annual pilgrimage to Star Lake Musicamp, where I would observe the Star Lake Band rehearsing with the likes of Eric Ball, Ray Steadman-Allen, and Bernard Adams. In particular, the band training by four-time guest **Jim Williams** made an indelible impression, as well as what developed into the life-long mentorship by **Robert Redhead**, who used and even recorded my early band pieces with the Canadian Staff Band. My first real composition lessons were twice-a-day sessions with **Leslie Condon** at Star Lake in 1976. Bandmasters Ronald Waiksnoris, Charles Baker and Dr. Ronald Holz, also Star Lake alumni, were early models of leadership, and have remained life-long encouragers of my leadership and writing.

When I headed to Manhattan to attend architecture school in 1973, I thought I would have to abandon my passion for music. Hardest was relinquishing leadership of our small corps band in Levittown, PA, where I was making my first arrangements and transcriptions for small brass ensemble. After the first semester I was invited by then **Staff Bandmaster Derek Smith** to play in the New York Staff Band. In time I found the Wednesday afternoon rehearsals away from school a much needed respite from a rigorous architecture school curriculum.

A few years later when I assumed leadership of the Philadelphia Citadel Band and Songsters and eventually the Pendel Brass and Singers for thirty-five seasons, most of the band training concepts (and even expressions) can be traced back to my four years of playing under Derek Smith. In the process, I was exposed to the very finest and most recent Salvation Army compositions, and I began to study how these pieces were put together, making piano reductions of the then new pieces by **Bill Himes**, **Bruce Broughton**, and **Jim Curnow**.

Pendel Brass, 1989.

Pendel Brass and Timbrelists, 2000.

A FRIEND OF SINGERS

In August of 1981, I assumed the position of divisional music director for the Pendel Division, vacated as Ivor Bosanko headed West to serve as Territorial Music Secretary. While in Pendel, Ivor often introduced a new hymn tune on a Sunday morning or for a united Salvation Army meeting. Following his example, I began to arrange new tunes to words in *The Song Book of The Salvation Army*, out of which emerged a life-long love of writing for voices. I had a good choir background as a boy soprano soloist in a Lutheran church choir, and later in high school and college. I aspired to be able to work effectively with voices of all ages. I was a late bloomer in this regard and sought out concerts, conferences and weekend seminars on choral topics.

Pendel Singers: *Face to Face* recording, 1998.

To this day, I consistently utilize the engaging techniques of **Helen Kemp** when working with children's voices (and even with adults). Through my own university education at Temple, I became exposed to methodologies for allowing singers, from young ages, to effectively read music notation. This emerged as one of my priorities in developing choral expression and a high standard in our Salvation Army vocal ensembles. **Dr. Beatrice Holz** has been so helpful over the years as a sounding board for sight-singing curriculum, and has used a number of my songster pieces with her ensembles.

I was also influenced by two Australian Salvationists, **Dr. Ronald Smart** and **Graeme Press**, through ground-breaking recording projects, where I learned about presentation and achieving blend. They paved the way, along with **Len Ballantine**, for bridging Salvation Army singing to the emerging contemporary Christian music scene.

Select Children's Chorus, *King's Kids* recording, 1992.

The most enduring education I received was from the piano bench week-to-week supporting my wife **Priscilla Burgmayer** as she would train singers, young and old, at the Philadelphia Pioneer Corps. I would take note of what really worked for voices, and as an arranger try to apply what I was observing to the line, voicing, tessitura, and pulse of my next piece. Priscilla had a knack for instinctively bringing musical or lyrical ideas to a higher level, either in the rehearsal or on the way home. I conducted choirs of every variety over many summers including choruses at Star Lake Musicamp from 1979 to 2013. For most of those years, I was associated with the Star Lake Vocal School where much of the voice-related material in this volume was first field tested.

A TEACHER'S HEART

For as long as I can remember I wanted to teach music. I admire the elevated position given to teachers in Eastern cultures, after our parent-caregivers, as the most influential people in society. As I approached high school years, family economics demanded that I make a choice between lessons on either piano or trumpet. I chose the latter and most of how I approach private lessons emanates from trumpet lessons with Al Wargo. I made an embouchure change in my college years with Bill Grandy. Experiencing this process proved invaluable in later years as a private lesson teacher. High school band director Ron Daggett gave me my first opportunities in jazz playing and arranging, and his counterpart, choir director Ted Kloos, made rehearsals and concerts relational and enjoyable.

Cornet trio of the Burgmayer brothers—David, Paul, and Harold, 1969.

Cornet trio of three former students—Derek Lance, Jon Knaggs, and Jason Knaggs, 1991.

A personal breakthrough with music theory and harmony occurred in graduate music school with Dr. Stimson Carrow. Some of his mantras are included in this book. **Dr. Gail Poch** was my first formal conducting teacher, and the one who helped me break a lot of bad habits, acquired from years of exaggerated gestures cajoling beginner bands. Two composition teachers at Temple University, **Dr. Clifford Taylor** and **Dr. Maurice Wright**, shared an infectious fascination for how music is put together, benefiting not only my own writing and score study, but something I have endeavored to share with another generation of conductors and composers.

Summer music interns, 2015.

EXPERIENCE IS THE BEST TEACHER

Early in my tenure as a divisional music director, I began to look for opportunities to train leaders, even replace myself in certain roles. I initially followed the format of the legendary Leidzén leadership courses that had made a real impact on music-making across the USA Eastern Territory in the 1950s. With ever-increasing calendar demands, the idea of meeting weekly over six weeks proved difficult, so we began to find opportunities for leadership workshop weekends, evenings given over for teacher talk during music camp, consultations with local leaders and corps officers, and days set aside for professional development within the music department. Perhaps most successful was the multi-tiered summer music intern training which took place over seven weeks at Camp Ladore each summer. Each music intern/instructor has initial intense training and progressively takes on more and more instructional roles as the summer progresses, with the expectation that these skills will be applied to one's corps in the coming season.

Harold and Priscilla Burgmayer, 1997.

Looking back, I also made a commitment to corps music ministry as a local officer to set an example of what could happen. That meant that I did everything possible to keep inviable weekly music activities and worship at the Philadelphia Pioneer Corps. For thirty years my wife Priscilla and I walked through the ups and downs of a transient population, numerous officer moves and an intense upheaval in the demographics around the corps. Many of the stories and illustrations within these chapters emanate from our experience maintaining a strong influence and musical presence in that troubled neighborhood.

SPECIAL THANKS

A portion of my leadership instruction first took form as a TEAM seminar (TEAM being Teaching, Equipping, Affirming, Multiplying), released online with outlines, written narratives of each lesson, supporting slides and handouts put together by **Amber Medin** and **Doug Berry**. Some years later, a meeting was convened which included **Ron Waiksnoris**, then the USA East Territorial Music Secretary, and **Chip Kelly**, the USA East Discipleship Training Specialist, to discuss how these materials could be expanded into book form to reach a broader Salvationist audience, including use at the training colleges with cadets. The concept was enthusiastically endorsed and supported by **Colonel Kenneth Maynor**, then territorial program secretary, and his wife **Colonel Cheryl Maynor**, who eventually oversaw publications in the USA Eastern Territory. My gratitude extends to Colonel Janice Howard (former Communications Head in the USA East) and to The Salvation Army National Publications (under Major Allen Satterlee) for coordinating the publication of this book.

Central Territory Worship Arts Seminar, 2017.

Thus began a six year journey working beside some wonderful, dedicated partners. We set out to make a comprehensive resource for present and future officers and lay leaders involved in worship planning, brass and praise bands, songsters and singing company, and for those teaching learners on piano, guitar, brass and percussion. Attention is given to lesson and rehearsal preparation, as well as conducting at all levels of corps music-making. The Bars Rest questions and activities extend use of this book to class and small group settings.

EDITORIAL TEAM

The editors for the manuscript were **Linda Johnson** and **Dorothy Post**, both Salvationists with an eye for keeping the material accessible and practical for a wide range of readers—from non-musicians and first-generation Salvationists to lifelong Salvation Army musicians from corps with a rich musical heritage. Sharing their expertise to specific chapters were Drs. Beatrice and Ronald Holz, Paul Scott, Kim Garreffa, Peggy Thomas, Hollie Ruthberg, Rick and Cathy Hayes, Eric Dina, Ronda Atwater, Chuck Goodin, Priscilla Burgmayer, Margaret Davis, Meghan Pierson, Mark Bender, and Joe Caddy. Additional conceptual feedback was received from Peter Farthing, Derek Lance, William Himes, Dorothy Nancekievill, Len Ballantine, Aaron Harris and Robert Redhead, while **Beatrice Holz**, **William Carlson** and **JoAnn Shade** patiently proofread the full production of twenty-five chapters.

PRODUCTION TEAM

From the outset, the search was on for the most illuminating cartoons, charts, photos and diagrams, as well as annotated music examples to illustrate concepts and teaching points. My design partner throughout the project has been **Keri Johnson**, from the USA Eastern Territory Communications team, supported by **Reggie Raines**. Keri was uncompromising in making every page spread attractive and informative. **David Hulteen, Jr.** provided cartoons to fit a variety of scenarios, always with an attractive consistency of style. **Rose Harris** and **Lisa Collier** added to the graphic appeal of most chapters with diagrams, annotations and photos.

The musical excerpts and scores were typeset by Brian Bowen, Joel Collier and Harold Burgmayer, with annotations applied by **Douglas Berry**. Brindley Venables, Eric Dina, and Derek Lance set up the Online Appendix and Audio Resources, providing the online audio examples. Lisa Collier and Josh Turner assisted with the Online Appendix.

The Beat Goes On

Harold with Colonel Henry Gariepy, 2008.

The photographers are identified on a number of photos. Others were generously shared from the International, National and USA–East archives (Jack Kerr), or expertly taken by Jonathan Knaggs, Joe Pritchard, Dave Hulteen Jr., Katie Laidlaw, Stephany Suarez, Aaron and Rose Harris, Siran Farrar, Andrew Grey and Scott Thomas. My appreciation is extended to those who consented to pose or be included in photos. Special thanks to a few individuals featured in series of photos for specific chapters: Ryan McCarthy (Chapter 6), Abigail Pastin (7), Jamie Colon, Marissa Riley and Bill Quick (9), Erin Burgmayer-Morgan and the Pendel Singers (12), Hannah Park (16), Bram Rader (17), Jane Lamm (20), Bea Holz (21 & 22), Ronda Atwater and the Pendel Youth Chorus (23).

FROM ONE GENERATION TO ANOTHER...

I would be remiss not to thank and acknowledge several generations of youngsters and leaders who have taught me much as I have prepared and sought to minister as their leader. These valuable lessons are being passed on to yet another generation. Besides my own parents, I am also greatly indebted to my in-laws, **Colonels Henry and Marjorie Gariepy**, who not only provided valued insight and direction, but taught me much about the writing process. Finally to my immediate family, daughters **Sarah**, **Katie**, **Carissa**, **Erin**, and wife **Priscilla**, thanks for being an integral part of our family's musical ministry at the Philadelphia Pioneer Corps, within the Pendel Division, and each summer at Camp Ladore. Much of that journey is chronicled in this volume.

—**Harold Burgmayer**
August, 2017
West Dundee, Illinois

The Burgmayer Family in Australia, 1997.

The Burgmayer Girls—Sarah, Carissa, Erin and Katie, 2015.

HOW TO USE THIS BOOK
Beyond These Pages

The things you have heard me say ... entrust to reliable people who will also be qualified to teach others. —2 Timothy 2:2

The Beat Goes On! – Music in Corps Ministry is designed to be a comprehensive overview of music ministries within the corps setting. A significant segment of Salvation Army life—from present and future lay leaders to cadets and officers—will benefit from some portion of this instructive resource.

Emerging and present music leaders are encouraged to explore chapters outside their expertise. The relationship of officers to their musicians is addressed primarily in Part One (Chapters One through Five). There is much that non-musical officers can glean from the music leadership chapters, especially those relating to worship design and song leading.

PART ONE: MUSIC MINISTERS

Chapters One through Five address our intentionality in planning and implementing weekly music programs and worship services, including the fundamentals of song-leading.

PART TWO: YOUTH MUSIC MINISTRY

Chapters Six through Nine seek to equip and encourage the training of youth choruses and youth bands.

PART THREE: ADULT MUSIC MINISTRY

Chapters Ten through Fifteen systematically unravel the mystery of learning to read a musical score, and take a thorough look at leadership of songsters and bands.

PART FOUR: WORSHIP LEADERSHIP

Chapters Sixteen through Nineteen will profit meeting pianists, worship team members and song leaders—whether novice or seasoned veterans—with insights on music and chord selection.

PART FIVE: THE CONDUCTOR'S TOOLBOX

Chapters Twenty through Twenty-Three concentrate on communicating through effective conducting patterns and gestures, as well as facilitating effective rehearsals.

The **Prelude** and **Postlude** consider significant challenges to accepting and passing on the mantle of leadership in the corps. Most chapters begin with specific aims, include a situational story, and conclude with a resource listing. Several sets of questions in each chapter, identified as Bars Rest, allow for further personal reflection or group discussion.

To help address a specific topic or question, peruse the **Table of Contents** listing or search the **Topic** or **Scripture Index**. A separate **Music Index** catalogs explanations of musical terms and concepts found throughout the book.

Sidebar **Cross References** allow for further inquiry into a topic.

THE TOOLBOX

The approach to most topics is two-fold, often distributed over two chapters. The main thrust and content is presented in the first portion, while more hands-on, technical nuts–and–bolts instruction, including lesson plans for successful rehearsals, make up the concluding Toolbox section.

The online **Appendix and Audio Resources** supplement the Toolbox topics for instrumentalists, singers, pianists, guitarists, percussionists, conductors and worship leaders alike. These can be accessed at **www.music.saconnects.org**, permitting the reader to reference supporting materials and/or audio demonstrations of musical examples while studying a chapter. In the course of the reading, these are indicated either in the body text or in the sidebar as helpful cross references:

> Additional **Home Practice Suggestions** are found in Appendix 8.4

To aid the reader, the online appendix and audio files are organized in order of appearance within each chapter. These are cataloged at the back of the book following the **Endnotes**. The Appendix reference materials are identified by number. For instance, Appendix 8.5 is the fifth appendix reference for Chapter Eight. These titles appear in **bold**:

> Appendix 8.5   **Major and Minor Scale** sheets - Correlated by number for youth bands

Audio demonstrations of musical examples are indicated sequentially by title, with the page(s) on which the printed music appears noted on the left margin. These titles appear in ***bolded italics***:

> *Chapter Eight* online audio demonstration:
> pp. 178–179   ***This Little Light of Mine*** (arr. Hollie Ruthberg) from *38 Sunday School Choruses for Young Bands*

Over twenty-five chapters, we explore many marvelous avenues of corps ministry through which we can speak the love language of music. From the youngest child in the singing company to an eager teen in the worship band to the seasoned bandsman or songster, all need guidance. We pray that this teaching proves practical and instructive for the novice music leader, and uplifting and invigorating for the veteran. **So let the beat go on!** …

PRELUDE

THE LOVE LANGUAGE OF MUSIC
Streams of Living Water

Whoever believes in me, as the Scripture has said, streams of living water will flow from within him. —John 7:38

I wept at the beauty of your hymns and canticles, and was powerfully moved at the sweet sound of your Church singing. These sounds flowed into my ears, and the truth streamed into my heart. —St. Augustine of Hippo

Have you ever noticed how much music is involved in our daily lives? Walk onto an elevator, into a store, or make a call and get put on hold—you'll hear music. Car radios, headphones, and ringtones inundate our ears with music. It is hard to imagine a TV drama or film without swelling musical strains. The whole world makes music. Throughout history, military and church leaders alike have understood that corporate singing is unparalleled for bringing people together. Song permeates celebrations, revolutions, and solemn occasions. Songs tell our story. Music is one of God's ways of allowing us to express our emotions. For centuries, the central beliefs of the Church have been carried on the wings of song.

Music in the Church is a universal language that unites worshipers across diverse cultures. Today, the heart-throbbing pulse of Salvation Army music-making beats across the globe. Could our Salvationist forebears have imagined the worldwide magnitude of the Spirit's outpouring of music on The Salvation Army? *And the beat goes on! ...* Join me in a sampling of the ongoing "mighty moving of the Spirit" in Salvation Army centers across today's global community.

THE BEAT GOES ON ...

We travel first along a dusty road to the **Khubvi (South Africa) Corps** hall packed with neatly uniformed South African Salvationists. During worship that spans nearly four hours, one falls into a sense of timelessness, surrounded by warm smiles, pulsing movement, and nearly uninterrupted song. Yes, the band marches its way to the corps and the effervescent songsters swoon with vitality, undergirded by the pulsating beat of hand-drums. The hallmark is *"joy, joy, joy!"*

Khubvi (South Africa) Corps

Soldiers wrap themselves in blankets as they huddle on a chilly autumn Sunday morning in the outdoor parking lot of the **Philadelphia Pioneer Corps**. The singing, keyboard, and drums echo off the neighboring brownstones. Curious neighbors hear the sounds and come to see what is being celebrated. One muses that this is how 17-year-old Eliza Shirley birthed this corps—in the open air! As the praise and worship segment climaxes, a deeply felt warmth of the Spirit hovers over the crowd. We are reminded, "To love the Lord our God is the heartbeat of our mission. The spring from which our service overflows."[1]

In one of the youngest divisions across The Salvation Army world, musicians from **Ecuador** navigate the hilly terrain in vibrant witness to a loving God. The steady beat subsides as the bass drum is transformed into a makeshift altar.

25th Anniversary Parade, Ecuador

Montclair Citadel (New Jersey) Corps

As we enter **Montclair Citadel**, New Jersey, the soothing tones of the band drift into the lobby, wooing us to "come and dine." The banquet includes a touching testimony of God's faithfulness, songster and piano offerings, and a challenge from the corps officer, followed by a warm corps family fellowship time. With each succeeding downbeat, the music refreshes and nourishes the soul.

Ascending the steps of the London Tube, the martial strains of the **Regent Hall Band** vigorously reverberate against the shop

Buenos Aires Central Songsters

windows on a busy sunlit Sunday afternoon. Coaxed by the booming pulse of the bass drum, our hearts swell with pride as salvation's story is told amid hundreds of onlookers. The music brings the message!

Crisp lines of wood, tile, and glass in the **Buenos Aires Central Corps** hall can scarcely contain the warm, sincere expressions of the handsomely uniformed songsters sharing their message of *amor*. Pulsating Latin beats uniquely blend with praise and worship offerings.

Prelude | THE LOVE LANGUAGE OF MUSIC

A storefront window with a large Salvation Army shield conceals the inner walls lined with Girl Guard projects, banners, and framed Junior and Senior Soldier pledge certificates at **Sussex Chapel**, Delaware. There is a sense of anticipation as the 13-piece youth band, supporting parents, and Haitian congregation gather to celebrate worship in their makeshift one-room chapel. And so the beat of Salvation Army music goes on! ...

Sussex Chapel, Delaware Youth Band

MAKE THE WORLD WITH MUSIC RING!

Our Salvationist forefathers declared without equivocation:

> Make the world with music ring,
> While with heart and voice we sing
> Praises to our God and King
> ... Tell with no uncertain sound
> ... Of the Savior we have found.
> —Charles Coller

Open-air march in Soweto, South Africa

From the dusty byways of Soweto to the austere courtyards of Buckingham Palace, salvation songs have resounded with vigorous vitality through the years. Salvation Army musicians of today continue that ministry, as the most recent *Orders and Regulations for Band and Songster Brigades in the United States* affirms:

New York Staff Band at Buckingham Palace

Supreme Purposes: Salvation Army music organizations exist to proclaim the Army's message: salvation from sin through Jesus Christ; and to accomplish the Army's purposes: the glorification of God and the salvation of souls.

Value of Music: All members of the Army's music organizations should be alive to the value of the judicious use of instrumental and vocal music. Music, of course, can often cheer the spirit but, when associated with the truths of the Christian religion, can be greatly used to lead sinners to God and to confirm saints in their faith.[2]

Over the years Salvation Army music has evolved in many ways, but the central purposes, "to bring glory to God and the salvation of souls" have remained unaltered and universally honored. People's lives change when they hear, and especially when they participate in, beautiful music. It is a gift of God, available to young and old. Music, perhaps more than any other arm of The Salvation Army, has for generations sustained folks within our ranks. Numerous officers and soldiers speak of the allure of Salvation Army music-making that kept them involved until God won their hearts.

Richard Slater, Father of Salvation Army music.

General John Larsson at the piano.

We remind ourselves that "This is how God showed His love among us: He sent His one and only Son into the world that we might live through Him ... We know that we live in Him and He in us, because He has given us of His Spirit." (1 John 4:9,13) Army music pioneer Richard Slater witnessed to his own firsthand experience when he wrote:

> Round us flows the cleansing river,
>   The holy, mighty, wonder-working river,
> That can make a saint of a sinner.

Robert Robinson understood the Holy Spirit streaming through our song when he wrote over a century before the birth of William Booth's Army:

> Come, thou Fount of every blessing,
>   Tune my heart to sing Thy grace;
> Streams of mercy never ceasing,
>   Call for songs of loudest praise.
> Teach me some melodious sonnet,
>   Sung by flaming tongues above;
> Praise His name—I'm fixed upon it—
>   Name of God's redeeming love.

To this day Salvationists continue to discover their "love language" through music and the arts. As one youngster challenged General John Larsson, "The Army needs more music. Not less. God has given the Army an enormous advantage by entrusting it with the gift of music. It has a ready-made road into everyone's heart and mind. It has been given a universal language."[3]

SEEING IS BELIEVING!

> *Faith is the substance of things hoped for,*
> *the evidence of things not seen.*
>   —Hebrews 11:1, *KJV*

Allow me to borrow a short dialogue between the Queen and Alice in *Through the Looking Glass* by Lewis Carroll:

'I can't believe that,' said Alice.

'Can't you?' the Queen said, in a pitying tone.
  'Try again. draw a long breath and shut your eyes.'

Alice laughed. 'There's no use trying,' she said:
  'One can't believe impossible things.'

'I daresay you haven't had much practice,' said
  the Queen. 'When I was your age, I always did it
  for half an hour a day. Why, sometimes I've believed
  as many as six impossible things before breakfast.'

What do you **see** when you look at your corps? If you pause long enough, you will **see** and **even believe!** Consider the young boys and girls coming through the corps building for summer day camp. See them holding instruments in a young people's band under the watchful eye of admiring parents. A choir made up of recovering addicts declares the Gospel message as they sing together. See God using their music to change lives. A guitarist and drummer "jam" in the corps hall between meetings. See the beginnings of a praise band. A youngster can't seem to stay away from the corps piano, endlessly repeating basic block chords. See her as a future songwriter. Some boys and girls seem to move their bodies naturally to music. See a vibrant dance team painting vivid pictures of redemption and restoration.

"Faith is the substance of things hoped for, the evidence of things not seen." (Hebrews 11:1, *KJV*) If you are a leader who has served for years, imagine a musical section in your corps remade into another vessel. "So the potter formed it into another pot, shaping it as seemed best to him." (Jeremiah 18:4b) What might it look like?

Start small

Reggie McNeal, in the preface to his challenging *The Present Future* reminds us that too often we think of the present in terms of the past behind us, rather than in light of a future that is speeding toward us.[4] One person who **sees**—and **believes**—represents the "present future" of Salvation Army music-making. Even in established corps music programs like those in Regent Hall, Montclair, Soweto, and Buenos Aires, one discovers a leader who sees and believes beyond the moment.

Usually this starts small, with simple first steps. "Do not despise this small beginning, for the eyes of the Lord rejoice to see the work begin." (Zechariah 4:10, *TLB*) Although first steps in leadership require patience and focus, remember that every musician or artist starts somewhere. The missing cog is often the encourager-leader who sees and believes in another's potential for the future. *How many young people and adults, for want of a leader, have been denied the privilege and high calling to be included in the musical arts of the Church?*

Mother Teresa once said, "We ourselves feel that what we are doing is just a drop in the ocean. But if that drop was not in the ocean, I think the ocean would be less because of that missing drop. I do not agree with the *big* way of doing things." Perhaps it is a blessing when Salvationists are forced to take our energy and resources off the big events, and put our zeal back into doing our small part in the harvest at home in our local corps. We don't necessarily need a big toolbox but rather a big heart to do our small part.

A small beginning for a future songwriter-General. The Palermo, Argentina Corps Band, 1953, includes the youthful John Larsson (to the left of the conductor on horn). Larsson at 17 assumed leadership and began writing his first arrangements for this small ensemble.

> "I think the ocean would be less because of that missing drop."
> —Mother Teresa

The Beat Goes On

> "We will NOT wage war using Salvation Army tactics!"
> —Adolf Hitler

What do we need in our toolbox?

Paul implores us, "to walk in a manner worthy of the calling with which you have been called." How? "With all humility and gentleness, with patience, showing tolerance for one another in love, being diligent to preserve the unity of the Spirit in the bond of peace." Why? Paul continues, "For the equipping of the saints for the work of service, to the building up of the body of Christ." (Ephesians 4:2–3,12, *NASB*)

Adolf Hitler once thundered, "We will not wage war using Salvation Army tactics!"[5] And it would be impossible to imagine the Nazi regime "building one another up, avoiding unwholesome talk, remaining kind, tenderhearted and forgiving of each other." (Ephesians 4:29, 32, paraphrase) "We don't pretend to love others … We really love them … Working happily together, as much as is possible." (Romans 12:9–10, 18, paraphrase) In the words of Meredith Willson, the Salvationist is "to love the unloved … That's the creed of a God-fearing Army!"[6] Songwriters Getty and Townend understood this militarism, too, when they wrote, "An Army bold, whose battle cry is love!"[7]

Your calling—a divine treasure

We can reminisce about glorious music-making in days past, but our tomorrows are dependent on those willing to step up and assume leadership in the local corps today. The future rests with those who commit to love people, to love music, and most importantly, to love the Lord. In *Called to Conquer*, Derek Prince says, "There are two great moments in a person's life. The first is the moment you were born and the second is the moment you discover why you were born." He asserts that at the moment you embrace the second seminal revelation, your "life calling" starts to take shape. "Yet many miss this," Prince laments:

You need to discover Your Calling like it is a Treasure.

> We forget, deny or never take the time to realize what we were really born to do. We turn to parents, family, popular culture, want ads or maybe even the path of least resistance to tell us what would make our lives valuable. We wait for a divine voice to boom from the clouds, 'You there! Yes, you! This is what I am calling you to do!' But that is not how it works. You need to take action. And when you do your life will never be the same … You need to discover Your Calling like it is a Treasure.

My "ah-ha" moment

In my own life, this "ah-ha" moment came late on a Wednesday evening after conducting a rehearsal of a band in need of a bandmaster. I was 21 years of age and engaged in rigorous architectural studies in Manhattan. I had set my mind on putting music behind me to pursue academic goals. The rehearsal visit was the rare exception, and it required a rail commute of several hours. A member from the band picked me up and provided a quick supper before we headed into an intense evening of rehearsal.

On that sleepless Wednesday night, God spoke to me, "This is the way you will go. Take this band." I struggled with God over this as the obstacles seemed insurmountable. I knew it would not be an easy task. I was younger than most of the band members and rightly regarded as a novice.

Philadelphia Citadel Band, 1978

www.music.saconnects.org

Many, including my parents, would see this as too costly an investment of time. The exceptions were the divisional music director and corps officer at the time, who sat in the chapel pews and observed that rehearsal. Over the initial months, they stood by and believed in me.

I obeyed the voice of God and led that band for nine years. During those years I learned much of what I know about conducting. My journey as leader of that group, although bumpy and fraught with numerous errors in judgment, prepared me well for over thirty years as a divisional music director. My principal task, as I see it now, is to awaken that kind of passion for corps music leadership. It is a calling. Many are called, but too few keep their eye on that Divine Treasure and stay the course "come what may."[8]

Pendel Brass preparing for the dedication of the Camp Ladore Performing Arts Recreation Center (PARC), 2009.

THE HIDDEN VIGOR OF WINTER

A remnant will survive. . .whose stump still lives to grow again.
—Isaiah 6:13, *TLB*

When we speak of a divine calling, we are reminded of Isaiah's dramatic vision of the throne of God. In answer to God's question, he cried out, "Here am I. Send me!" (Isaiah 6:8) This oft-cited mantra precedes a stern message pleading for God's people to "hear, understand, return, and be healed." Isaiah, in verse 11 of that same chapter, inquires, "Lord, how long?" God answers, "Until all cities are devastated, houses are without people and the land is utterly desolate ... Only a tenth portion will remain, subject to burning, like an oak whose stump remains when felled." The passage concludes, *"The holy seed is its stump."*

John Calvin uses an analogy of the seasons of trees to explain how this remnant of the Church will be restored. "The leaves wither in the autumn, then blossom in the spring. This could not happen, did they not *retain some vigor during the winter,* though to outward appearance they are dead."[9] How many of us picture our movement in decline? Calvin insists the Church endures "numerous afflictions and appears utterly ruined, but there is still some concealed energy, which, though it be not immediately manifest to our eyes, will at length yield its fruit." We are not the last one standing, as Elijah thought, when there are, in fact, "seven thousand who have not bowed to Baal." (1 Kings 19:14,18) Referring to Elijah's appeal to God, Paul reminds us that the existence of a faithful remnant is not dependent on good works, but on those "chosen by grace." (Romans 11:5–7)

Will banding survive?

For generations, naysayers have questioned the relevance of Salvationist music-making, particularly banding. One reason for the decline of Salvation Army music-making in the Western world is a lack of commitment to musical training through young people's sections, such as singing company and youth band.[10] In some places, music-making has been relegated to the push of a button. An increasing number of empty seats for Sunday meetings further suggests a Salvation Army worship community in decline.

Could it be that God, instead, may be preserving the life of His church? A *Newsweek* article written in 1941 estimated there "were perhaps a thousand Salvation Army corps bands in the United States, the majority of which had between eight and fourteen members."[11] Now over seven decades later, an ongoing decline in Salvation Army church attendance has affected banding across the four United States territories. At the close of 2013 there were an average of eight men and women playing in 311 senior band units across the country.[12] Ironically, while the number of bandsmen and songsters in America peaked generations back, most acknowledge that a number of today's music sections are the finest in our history. The variety and compass of our musical and artistic expressions have expanded significantly. One of the Army's best-guarded secrets may be the remnant of fine players and leaders carrying on Salvation Army musical culture with great imagination—*a hidden vigor in what appears to be winter.*

SHEEP WITHOUT A SHEPHERD

> And still there are fields where the laborers are few ...
> and still straying sheep to be led.
> —Albert Orsborn

It is not a coincidence that a lowly shepherd was anointed king of Israel. As Samuel sought to recognize the future king, the Lord directed him not to look at the outward appearance, "for God sees not as man sees ... but the Lord looks at the heart." (1 Samuel 16:7) The Salvation Army's poet-laureate, General Albert Orsborn encapsulated the inward touch of the Holy Spirit on a servant-leader's heart with these words:

> The Savior of men came to seek and to save
>   The souls who were lost to the good;
> His Spirit was moved for the world which He loved
> With the boundless compassion of God ...
>
> O Savior of men, touch my spirit again,
>   And grant that Thy servant may be
> Intense every day, as I labor and pray,
>   Both instant and constant for Thee.

Albert Orsborn, the Poet-General

What is God looking for in a leader?
Certainly, a Salvationist leader must claim to know Christ. As the songwriter Ruth Tracy has written, "Only as I truly know Thee can I make Thee truly known." Albert Orsborn concludes another song with this potent step-by-step progression, "First to know Thee, then to serve Thee, then to see Thee as Thou art." Jesus says, "He calls his own sheep by name and leads them out ... He goes ahead of them, and the sheep follow him because they know his voice." (John 10:3b-4, *NASB*) Jesus goes before us as we lead. His voice directs our paths. I am grateful that, day by day, that still small voice reveals to me my next steps.

With a heart of compassion
Jesus, the Good Shepherd, even today, "sees the multitudes. He feels compassion for them, because they are distressed and downcast like sheep without a shepherd." (Matthew 9:36, *NASB*) He reminds His disciples to see with a heart of compassion like His own. "The harvest is plentiful, but the workers are few. Therefore beseech the Lord of the harvest to send out workers into His harvest." (Matthew 9:37-38, *NAS*) **Herein lie the deep roots of Salvation Army music-making,** from the Booths to the present day, whether at Regent Hall or in Soweto. **Effective leaders direct their "heart to God and hand to man."**

Martin Luther had a friend who pledged to uphold Luther in his battle for the Reformation. One night this fellow monk experienced a disturbing dream in which he saw a vast field of corn. He witnessed one solitary man in a field, desperately trying to reap the harvest, an impossible and heartbreaking task. When he caught a glimpse of the reaper's face, he realized it was his friend Luther. The monk promptly left the pious solitude of the monastery and went down into the world to labor in the harvest.[13] Yes, every leader is strengthened by those who sow in prayer or support ministries with their gifts, but **the Lord needs workers readied for a waiting harvest.**

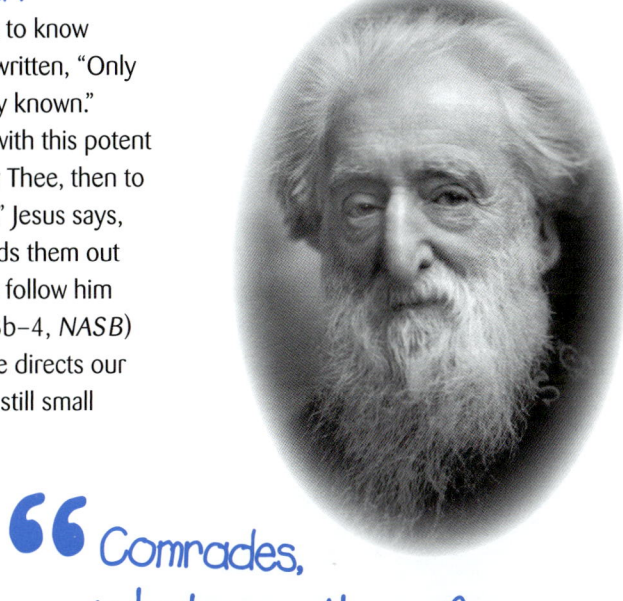

> "Comrades, whatever other gifts you have, if you are to succeed, you must have hearts, and hearts that can feel."
> —William Booth

Our love language

What does this have to do with Salvation Army music and arts? We arguably have some of the finest resources in the church. We can boast of fine ensembles, composers, arrangers, and conductors. We are entrusted with generous funding from an admiring public permitting the purchase of instruments and even subsidies for music instruction. Like a block of clay before a sculptor, these vast resources mean very little, unless "worked." Here is a concern. Beautiful young people pass through our gyms, after-school programs, and Sunday schools, yet we neglect to shape their young voices for use in corporate worship. Some music would be better assimilated coupled with a dancer's reflective interpretation. In some band rooms, instruments and music lay dormant, a veritable "valley of dry bones."

Commissioner Samuel Logan Brengle wrote in an article entitled "The Future of The Salvation Army:"

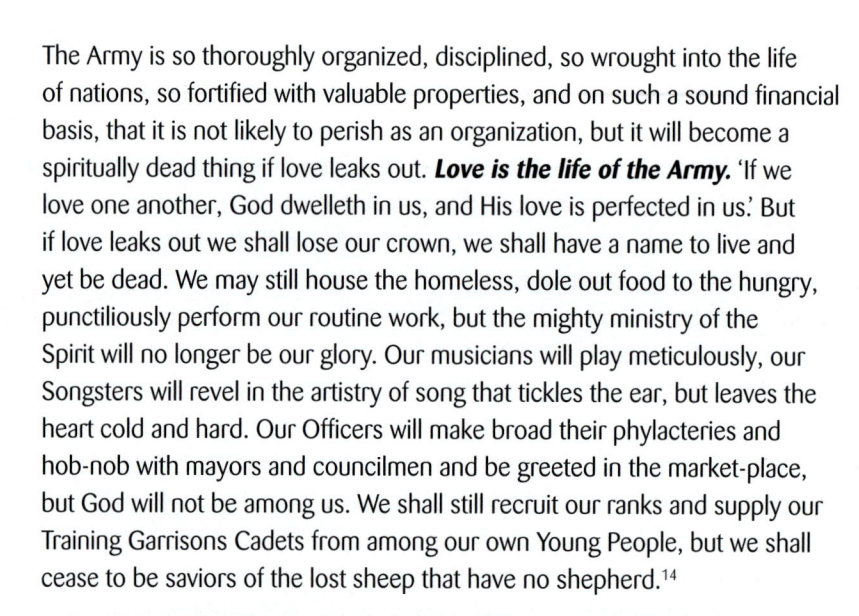

> The Army is so thoroughly organized, disciplined, so wrought into the life of nations, so fortified with valuable properties, and on such a sound financial basis, that it is not likely to perish as an organization, but it will become a spiritually dead thing if love leaks out. **Love is the life of the Army.** 'If we love one another, God dwelleth in us, and His love is perfected in us.' But if love leaks out we shall lose our crown, we shall have a name to live and yet be dead. We may still house the homeless, dole out food to the hungry, punctiliously perform our routine work, but the mighty ministry of the Spirit will no longer be our glory. Our musicians will play meticulously, our Songsters will revel in the artistry of song that tickles the ear, but leaves the heart cold and hard. Our Officers will make broad their phylacteries and hob-nob with mayors and councilmen and be greeted in the market-place, but God will not be among us. We shall still recruit our ranks and supply our Training Garrisons Cadets from among our own Young People, but we shall cease to be saviors of the lost sheep that have no shepherd.[14]

Commissioner Samuel Logan Brengle, Ambassador of Holiness

It will take more than a trace of chromosome to preserve our Salvation Army DNA and move forward into the future. Jesus said, "Whoever believes in me, as the Scripture has said, streams of living water will flow from within him." (John 7:38) Early Army music-making, married with dramatic conversions, joined other signs and wonders in a mighty outpouring of the Holy Spirit. The love language of music flowed freely out of these initial impulses of passion and still reaches down to us today.

Let the beat go on! …

On a visit to record The Salvation Army's work in Zimbabwe, photographer Doug MacLellan took this photograph of a boy from the Howard High School. Against a backdrop of hardship, famine, and danger of life in Zimbabwe, the photo captures the innocence of a wide-eyed youngster faithfully beating his hand-drum, holding on to a hope that things will get better.

"Who shall separate us from the love of Christ?" asks the apostle Paul, "Shall trouble or hardship or persecution or famine or nakedness or danger or sword? … No, in all these things we are more than conquerors through him who loved us." (Romans 8:35,37) The Bible passage and this wonderfully evocative photograph provoked Kevin Sims to pen these verses—a cry for hope … Listen, as the beat goes on! …

PRELUDE | THE LOVE LANGUAGE OF MUSIC

The Beat Goes On

Slowly, slowly, build the beat,
Clap your hands, move your feet,
Bang the drum and make it strong,
Feel the rhythm of the song.

Quickly, quickly, spread the word,
Good news means souls are stirred.
Sing of joy that can be found –
Take this message, pass it round.

Softly, softly, like a breeze,
Fear is spreading like disease.
Keep it back with faith and hope,
Cleansing doubt like holy soap!

Louder, louder, tell it out,
Spread the message, give a shout.
God's love is the song we sing,
Love that conquers anything!

—Kevin Sims[15]

Part One
MUSIC MINISTERS

CHAPTER ONE

FROM MINSTRELS TO MINISTERS
Daring to Draw Near

Your procession has come into view, O God, the procession of my God and King into the sanctuary. In front are the singers, after them the musicians; with them are the maidens playing tambourines. Praise God in the great congregation ...
—Psalm 68:24–26

SCENE 1

Imagine receiving a request to share your musical gifts at the home of a distinguished community leader. This individual has given much in service and gifts to your organization. On the appointed day, and equipped with the necessary music, you arrive at the imposing entrance to this estate. You are ushered in by a gracious butler with the utmost dignity and led directly to a splendid instrument. Without comment, you commence playing. Your best efforts at music-making fill the air but seem not to be received over the clamor of lively conversation and hearty laughter. After you complete your well thought-out program, you pack up. On the way home you come to an alarming realization: **You never met or spoke with the host!**

In **Chapter One**, we explore:
- ways to cultivate a community of musician-worshipers through corporate devotions, small groups and one-on-one mentoring.
- the role of Salvationist musicians and artists in worship, evangelism, and concert settings.
- giving attention to the lifeline of Sunday worship and getting it right with our musical offerings, including practical ideas to enhance worship and communication.

SCENE 2

Now imagine the same request, the same distinguished host, and the same imposing entrance. This time, you get caught up in a lively conversation as the host himself personally greets you. He allows time for you to share your heart. When you eventually get to playing, he seems to listen as though he knows you. His presence seems to embrace you, and you are strangely warmed. You draw nearer and nearer to his spirit, as he seems to draw closer to you. **You desire never to leave his house!**

Minstrels … ?

In Scene 1 the minstrel, although well prepared, somehow misses speaking with the host. Scene 2 illustrates the musician as minister, whose first intent is to draw near to God and minister to *His* heart.[1] How many of us as church musicians find ourselves on the way home from a service or concert with a nagging dissatisfaction? Somehow we didn't get to converse with the King. We didn't even see or greet Him!

Interestingly, the terms **minstrel** (*menestral*) and **minister** (*ministre*) come from the same root word—a servant. Minstrels were a class of medieval entertainers who sang, recited, and accompanied themselves on an instrument, like the harp. A revival of the minstrelsy emerged in early 19th-century America with bands of public performers who sang songs and told jokes.[2] Much of today's popular music derives from this minstrel tradition.[3] **The intention of minstrels was simply to give a fine performance to please their audiences.**

… or Ministers?

The title minister evolved as more akin to a public servant, as in government and diplomatic officials. The meaning, as extended to Protestant clergy over the centuries, effectively limited the label minister in the same way that the title **priest** (*pontifex*, Latin for bridge-builder) or **presbyter** (*elder*) became exclusive to Anglican, Catholic, or Eastern Orthodox clergy. But it was not God's intention to limit the term minister to clergy. Through Christ, the new and living way, access to God has become the privilege of every believer. Peter attests to the priesthood of believers when he writes, "Present yourselves as building stones for the construction of a sanctuary vibrant with life, in which you'll serve as holy priests offering Christ-approved lives up to God." (1 Peter 2:5, *The Message*) **The minister-priest offers gifts to minister to the Lord.**

Chapter 1 | FROM MINSTRELS TO MINISTERS

COME NEAR TO ME

The true nature of holy worship is powerfully illustrated in Ezekiel 44, following an epoch during which kings, foreigners, and even priests flagrantly violated the Temple code. The eastern gate was the route of the return of the Lord's glory to the Temple. God commanded that it now be kept shut so that no access by mere humans could defile its holiness. Royalty could eat their portion of the sacrificial meals, but with a symbolic limited access through the vestibule, rather than the secure gate doors. The Temple would be in the Lord's control, not the king's. Foreigners believed in a plurality of gods and made the rounds to worship in temples where they were welcomed. Only Yahweh would now be worshiped in the Lord's Temple.[4] To those priests who had violated the Temple with ministry to idols, God says, "They shall not come near Me as a priest to Me, nor come near any of My holy things, nor into the most holy place … but the priests, the Levites, the sons of Zadok, who kept charge of my sanctuary when the children of Israel went astray from Me, they shall come near to Me to minister to Me …" (Ezekiel 44:13,15, *ASB*)

Earlier in the same book, Ezekiel illustrates the distinction between a minstrel and a minister when speaking of God. The prophet says, "Indeed, to them you are nothing more than one who sings love songs with a beautiful voice and plays an instrument well, for they hear your words but do not put them into practice." (Ezekiel 33:32) Ministry is music *plus* "something more," as Catherine Marshall wrote. Eugene Peterson paraphrases, "God helping you: Take your everyday, ordinary life—your sleeping, eating, going-to-work, and walking-around life— and place it before God as an offering. Embracing what God does for you is the best thing you can do for him." (Romans 12:1, *The Message*) Jazz artist Charlie Parker echoes the heartfelt sentiment of many leaders when he says, "If you don't live it, it won't come out of your horn."[5]

> "Come near to Me to minister to Me."

DARING TO DRAW NEAR

Richard Foster writes passionately: "Today the heart of God is an open wound of love. He aches over our distance and preoccupation. He mourns that we do not draw near to Him. He grieves that we have forgotten Him. He weeps over our obsession with muchness and manyness. He longs for our presence."[6]

The writer of the book of Hebrews puts it this way: *"Let us draw near to God with a sincere heart in the full assurance of faith, having our hearts sprinkled to cleanse us from a guilty conscience and having our bodies washed with pure water. Let us hold unswervingly to the hope we profess, for He who promised is faithful. And let us consider how we may spur one another on toward love and good deeds. Let us not give up meeting together, as some are in the habit of doing, but let us encourage one another."* – Hebrews 10:22–25

Ministry *to* the Lord must take precedence over all other work, which although good in itself can rear its head as a subtle form of idolatry.

Richard Foster, in *Celebration of Discipline*, warns that, "Service flows out of worship … Activity is the enemy of adoration … One grave temptation we

"Let us draw near to God." —Hebrews 10:22–25

The Beat Goes On

29

all face is to run around answering calls to service without ministering to the Lord Himself."[7] If properly focused, our arts offerings enhance the worshiping community in three ways:

> 1. **The closer we come to God, the closer we come to each other.**
> 2. **There is a holy expectancy nurtured in meeting together to praise God.**
> 3. **Being a part of the act of worship builds the faith community.**

Before we can minister musically as a group, we must find ways to cultivate our community of worshipers who desire to follow God's command for ministers to "Come near to Me." (Ezekiel 44:15, *ASB*)

Corporate devotions

One avenue is through corporate devotions—a pause in an otherwise busy day, which unifies the group. This needs to be more than perfunctory Bible reading. The Word of God is living and active and should have an immediacy and relevance for your group. Prayerfully selecting a series or devotional book over a "hit-or-miss" approach helps give ongoing focus to this time of sharing, as it builds community.

We can also worship in the rehearsal properly by making sure that our ensemble members have a personal understanding of what they are playing or singing. Conductors sometimes elect for devotions to look more deeply at the text and Scripture associated with music in the current repertoire. Sometimes a shared testimony can provide devotional inspiration, which is another way of building our team—from the inside out.

Divide and conquer (Small Groups)

For our present tactile generation, breaking into small groups increases accountability. It also allows shy members, who would rarely contribute in a full-group discussion, a chance to share their hearts. Small groups encourage a sense of belonging. Most often, small groups work best when a leader introduces the topic to the full group, then gives some follow-up questions to the small group leaders. Breaking into small groups widens the network of leaders preparing for discussion and increases participation in prayer times.

One-on-one mentoring (Prayer Partners)

To deepen the spiritual accountability within your ensemble, small groups can be strategically designed out of two or three sets of mentoring partners. This means matching an older, more mature mentor with a younger person of the same gender as prayer partners. Another option is peer-to-peer partnering, in which matching partners of the same age and sex permits increased openness and accountability. Prayer partners are asked to commit to:

- pray for their partner once a day.
- be in touch once a week.
- spend time together once a month.

www.music.saconnects.org

? 1 BAR REST

In Hebrews 10:24 we read, "Consider how we may spur one another on toward love and good deeds."

1. Prayerfully consider the best possibilities for establishing a strong devotional thrust to your rehearsal time.

2. What topics or material might work?

3. Who in your group might best take responsibility for overseeing devotions?

FROM SPECTATOR TO PARTICIPANT

The Kierkegaard paradigm—A theatrical metaphor

The wise sage Søren Kierkegaard pictures worship as an "unfolding drama." He asks...

In a worship service:

>Who are the actors?
>Who is the prompter?
>And who is the audience?

The common response is:

>The pastors and musicians are *the actors.*
>The prompter is *God.*
>And the congregation is *the audience.*

In *The New Worship,* Barry Liesch imaginatively transfers Kierkegaard's theatrical metaphor to the unfolding drama of a football game. The worship leaders become the players, God is the coach, and the congregation is the audience in the stands watching it all play out.[8]

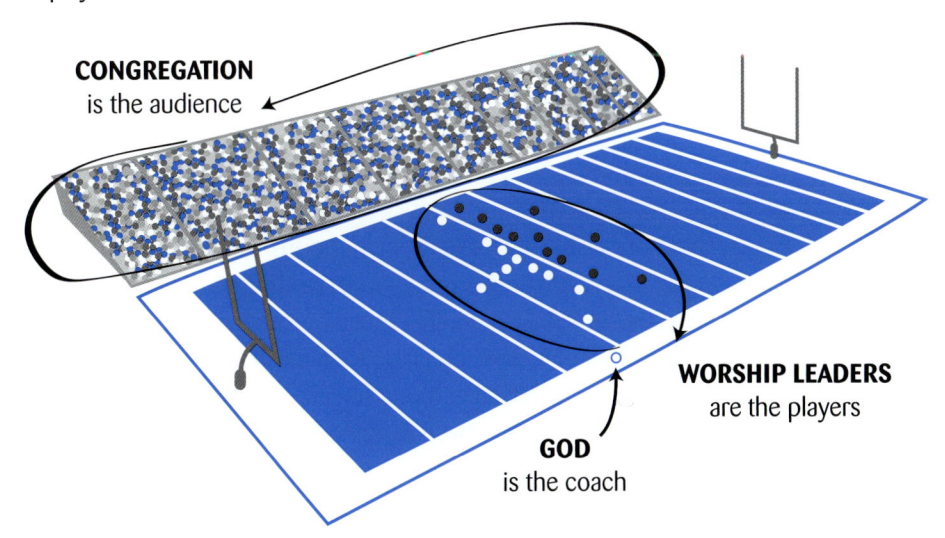

CONGREGATION is the audience

WORSHIP LEADERS are the players

GOD is the coach

However, Kierkegaard challenges us by suggesting that this is how we should function:

The pastor is the prompter.
All of the participants in worship and
the congregation are the actors.
They perform for Almighty God—*the Audience of One.*

In Kierkegaard's words, "God himself is present ... [and] is the critical theatergoer, who looks on to see how the lines are spoken and how they are listened to ... The listener is the actor, who in all truth acts before God."[9] Using Liesch's illustration, the worship leaders (coaches) then prompt the congregation (players) to "perform" worship for God (the audience).

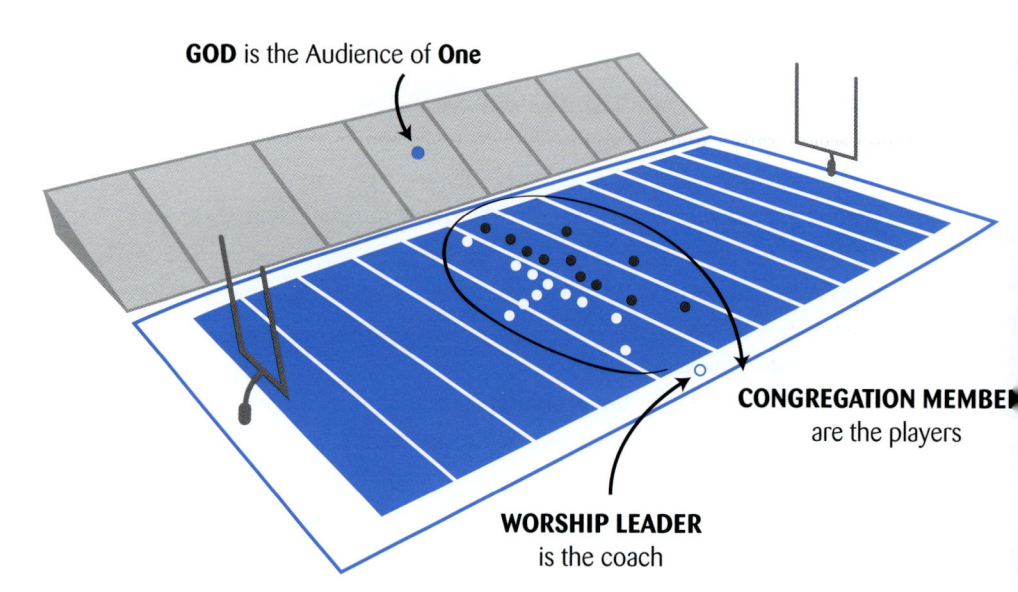

GOD is the Audience of **One**

CONGREGATION MEMBERS
are the players

WORSHIP LEADER
is the coach

If congregations understand that worship is not a spectator sport—that is, something done for them—they can become active player-participants in the journey. This perspective turns the tables on the speaker or musicians as performers becoming the focus of the service, while passive hearers act as the ones who evaluate the performance. ("I really liked the sermon this morning.") We worship for the Audience of One. In subsequent chapters (Chapter Four—The Corps Leadership Team, Chapter Five—The Song Leader, and Chapters Eighteen and Nineteen—The Worship Leader) we will explore how the worship leader-prompter remains an active worshiper, but also an audience in the sense of worship as an interaction with God that reveals Himself to us and we respond to Him.[10]

Pew potatoes?

If we accept Kierkegaard's premise, then Salvationist musicians and artists must ask **how to transition listeners from spectators to participants.** This is a formidable challenge as we "live in a culture that breeds spectators. The average American watches over five hours of television daily, living much of their lives vicariously through characters that flit across a screen."[11] As couch potatoes, we pore over sports events, reality shows, and television news beamed incessantly into our living rooms or onto the screens of our handheld devices. How easily churchgoers assume a **pew potato** posture in church, challenging worship leaders "to entertain, even bless me."[12] But God is not another character who flits across our spiritual screens. God longs for a relationship *with* us. Tommy Coombes, the worship leader from *Maranatha! Music* stresses, "God's highest desire is to fellowship with us. As pastors and worship leaders, our job is to enable that, to make participants out of spectators." According to Sally Morgenthaler, our intention then is "to help people pour out what God pours in." She adds, "Spectator worship has always been and will always be an oxymoron."

On the flip side, Kierkegaard's metaphor dispels the worship leader's performance, either as a musician or preacher, and downplays congregational evaluation, even approval. Worship leaders, while prompting the service, are joined with the congregation as active worshipers. Approval seeking and personal recognition take a backseat. Rather, what is essential is The Audience of One revealing Himself and how we, the congregation and worship leaders, respond to Him. The focus is rightly placed on the devotional intent of the service, rather than on an individual.[13] Philip Yancey writes, "Tensions and anxieties flame within me the moment I forget I am living my life for the one-man audience of Christ and slip into living my life to assert myself in a competitive world. Previously, my main motivation in life was to do a painting of myself, filled with bright colors and profound insights, so that all who looked upon it would be impressed. Now, however, I find that my role is to be a mirror, to brightly reflect the image of God through me. Or perhaps the metaphor of stained glass would serve better, for, after all, God will illumine through my personality and body."[14]

Worship, evangelism, and concerts

A spectator can be someone who "sits and soaks in" our worship service, the casual observer passing an open-air meeting, or the intrigued concertgoer. Is it possible to make the transformation from a spectator to one who is fully participating in worship to the Audience of One? As a point of reference, Salvationist musicians and artists offer up gifts in three broad arenas:

SUNDAY WORSHIP

PURPOSE	Focus on worship of the Almighty and draw others into His kingdom.
GOAL	For each worshiper to be a full participant to the Audience of One.
DIFFICULTIES	Keeping the attention off our offerings and focused on the Audience of One, while giving the Holy Spirit leadership and free reign.

STREET EVANGELISM

PURPOSE	Draw attention and get a listening ear in order to present the Gospel.
GOAL	Attract spectators.
DIFFICULTIES	How do we keep folks' attention? And how do we get out of the way to allow the Holy Spirit to draw listeners in?

CONCERTS

PURPOSE — Bring people into a listening experience which reflects something of God.

GOAL — What are our intentions? Are concerts to be evangelism and excite the spectator toward participation? Or should we try to go further and bring listeners into a worship experience?

DIFFICULTIES — How do we keep folks' attention? How do we best present the Gospel and how much? Do we give the Holy Spirit breathing room within our programming? A good test is whether people happily come back to our concerts.

1 BAR REST

1. What was the most exciting concert or worship service you ever attended? What made it appealing for you? What components of the programming and content made it work for you?

2. What was the worst concert or worship service that you have experienced? What made it unappealing?

3. What forms of evangelism, using music and arts, have you experienced? Was there a response? Did you feel a connection? Why or why not?

Open air meeting in Atlantic City, 1927.

MUSIC FOR EVANGELISM

The Salvation Army has been a militant expression of the evangelical church since its inception. Salvation Army music-making has rightly been a vital part of that evangelistic thrust. Consider this description of Salvation Army outreach in New York, circa 1895:

> Vaudeville was not the only popular attraction that the Army added to its arsenal. Its parades became more spectacular, with ever more elaborate floats and costumed battalions. Similarly, its evangelical street workers invented ever more dramatic ploys to attract spectators. Loud bands remained the first line of attack, but Salvationists also circulated handbills advertising staged 'trials' of the devil, 'John Barleycorn,' and even Robert Ingersoll, the most famous atheist of the day. Army officers preached from coffins, held marathon hymn-singing contests, and appeared as 'specialty' acts … Officers had to devise marketing strategies that borrowed from but did not fully partake of the consumerist ethos.[15]

This statement is consistent with Salvation Army ideals for evangelism. Attract attention and a listening ear in order to share the Gospel succinctly. **The goal is to draw in spectators and move them toward participation** through the presentation of the Gospel message. These Army pioneers were not afraid to engage their contemporary culture. As William Booth once said, "The man must blow his horn and shut his eyes, and believe while he plays that he is blowing salvation into somebody."

Above: Billie Parkins, principal cornetist of the New York Staff Band, accompanies a song at Kensico, 1931.
Below: Joe the Turk playing saxophone at an open air.

Montclair Citadel (New Jersey) Songsters, Christmas 2008

So how does a concert work?

While open-air ministry has waned, Salvation Army musicians continue to concertize. Our stated purpose is: "the glorification of God and the salvation of souls."[16] Concerts include music with a message, prayer, and a Bible reading, but may lack the imaginative, evangelistic zeal of our spiritual forefathers.

Should our concerts be designed to move spectators to become participants in worship? Consider rock concerts and the level of participation down front. A large ovation and dance response spurs the band on. What about the rich interaction between preacher and parishioners in livelier worship services? What is our participatory intent with sacred concerts? Do we aim toward what some label a "worship experience?" In all of this, how do we best re-present Christ? We must constantly ask these questions as we prepare our musical offerings.

Hearts touching hearts

The answer rests less with the technique and expression of the presentation than with the intent of the heart. All the striving for high-level execution, technical support, and intentional communication, while important, must be girded with God's holy presence. By sharing a sense of heartfelt worship in testimony and song, the minister-musicians can bring an authenticity to concerts that genuinely touches listeners. Ministering to the Audience of One doesn't just happen. We work to enable each member to experience "the power of the resurrection of Jesus Christ," be it through small groups or one-on-one mentoring.

While participatory worship may seem unnatural to our couch-potato society, it is the very mystery of God reaching out to humans with His love that proves attractive. *Our music making should attract spectators, but more importantly it should also move them toward participation in a worship experience.* Rather than concertgoers sitting back and watching a sacred performance, we pray that their hearts connect with the heart of the Creator. True worship facilitates a divine encounter.

? 1 BAR REST

Envision a worship service or important performance. What is happening within your group? Where is their focus? How is the congregation/audience responding? Where are you in this picture?

THE MUSIC MINISTER'S TOOLBOX

Getting it Right with our Music Offerings

In light of what Sally Morgenthaler calls "worship evangelism," music leaders must be sensitive to the needs of the multiple generations within our congregation, our audience, and our group when considering repertoire.

Good repertoire selection is culturally relevant or consciously takes the audience out of their cultural box.

Knowing our audience or congregation is as important as knowing our singers. Standard repertoire, from classics to spirituals to hymns, can prove appealing to churched *and* unchurched because it moves the musicians and listeners away from their familiar culture and music. For example, some popular contemporary Christian music can sound exactly like that of the world, whereas the unchurched may be more convinced in their faith if the music is a fresh experience. Conversely, a Latin or swing item may attract more spectators than a Salvation Army "club" offering. Folks may think, "Wow, they play my style of music at church." This works both ways.

Good repertoire selection serves the service.

Too often musical selections can interrupt, rather than enhance, the flow of meetings with a *highbrow* selection or something the band favors. A misguided choice of music may not only intrude on the flow and spirit of a meeting, but may preempt what might have been a precious moment in worship. Aim to genuinely serve the service with an appropriate item that blends into the flow of the service. Pieces programmed to impress place the focus on the performers. Musical offerings are not offerings unless they focus upward to God and outward to others.

Good repertoire selection involves honing down a program to a measured proportion.

In Acts 20, Luke tells the story of Eutychus who "was sinking into a deep sleep as Paul talked on and on." Eutychus subsequently falls out of a third story window and is picked up dead. Paul wraps his arms around him and says, "Don't be alarmed, he's alive!" Luke records that Paul then went upstairs, broke bread, and continued talking until daylight. Army concerts and meetings are too often over-programmed and fall within what is sometimes known as the Eutychus syndrome. Remember that "less is more."

Church musicians today, especially with an ever-increasing cultural media overload, need to carefully consider the pace and length of our presentations. This may mean giving up playing or singing that latest lengthy opus. To encourage return encounters, leave the audience wanting more. Excising favored "little darlin's"[17] can be a difficult but necessary exercise to keep a program in balance. On the other hand, sometimes players need to be coerced into sacrificing a bit with a piece that really functions well within a service. A good test is to ask whether a non-musician enjoyed a selection, or if children would thrill to sit through your programs.[18]

> **Too many pieces of music finish too long after the end.**
> —Igor Stravinsky

"Yeah, the band always plays this one when the bigwigs come to visit … Jolly good show it is!"

In maintaining flow in programming, beware of dead space or—what is more likely—too much talking between items. Much music speaks for itself and does not require introduction. On the other hand, choose to help the listener make important text associations by printing or projecting words, visual images, or related Scripture.

Good repertoire selection is about educating players and congregation.
Think about the musical and spiritual aspirations for your group. In planning a season's repertoire, consider these questions:

- Where are we now and where have we been with our current repertoire?
- What pieces or styles of music have been well received by this audience or corps?
- Is our Sunday morning programming functioning well within the service?
- Which pieces do we know well but could give up?
- What pieces should we continue with or come back to after a time?
- What new items will enhance our programming?
- What genre or styles have we avoided?
- What repertoire will connect an evangelistic message with an audience?
- What is the program missing? An opener? A great closing sequence? A solo item? A devotional invitation item? What encore? What congregational involvement? Humor—when and what? Explain to your groups some of these stretching decisions, particularly how items fit into the big picture.
- Ask yourself, "Will my groups grow into or grow out of these choices?" There is merit in playing an easier piece exceptionally well where the expressive freedom can be achieved, especially if it is music of substance.
- Choose songs just for the group's edification, not necessarily to be performed, as warm-ups, for devotional significance or a musical challenge.

In *An Hour on Sunday*, Nancy Beach poses four questions related to selecting Sunday service music:

1. Does this piece move us?
2. Is it theologically sound and biblically true?
3. Does it have artistic integrity? Avoid the preachy, simplistic, manipulative, fairy tale ending which misrepresents life as it really is.
4. Is it tasteful? Humor that draws from a low denominator with innuendo or crude language is just not appropriate in church. Be similarly discerning with costuming, dance moves, and video clips.

Good repertoire selection is an ongoing process.
What are you listening to? Work to listen outside your box. Take inventory of your group's listening and that of your congregation. Attend concerts and other worship services. Consider why a memorable concert really worked for you. Ask why a service didn't flow. Discipline yourself to review music constantly and organize a system to have ideas on file for future use. File by occasion, church holiday, or type of ensemble.

1 BAR REST

Be creative in designing a concert for your corps ensembles. Note the length of items and total duration of the program. Be prepared to give a rationale for how the program flows.

IDEAS TO ENHANCE WORSHIP AND COMMUNICATION

From intimate simplicity to soaring descants

- Have the children or teens render a simple prayer chorus, like *Teach Me How to Love Thee* or *Be Still* as the call to worship. The congregation is hard pressed to converse when children share their simple message.

- Allow the congregation to sing unaccompanied. While some songs work best with piano or band, and others better with guitar, commence with a solitary instrumentalist to provoke intimacy, and then let the voices continue unaccompanied. Be tasteful and appropriate.

- Vary the instrumental forces for song accompaniment, selections, and offertory. Create an aura of majesty by uniting musical forces. This can include creating opportunities to join the children's voices with the adults by exchanging verses, or having the treble voices join on the refrain with a soaring descant. Some hymns have magnificent refrains that can be taught to the children and thus make them active participants in worship. (For an example of a simple descant refrain, see p. 149 in Chapter Seven on singing company leadership. For ideas about how to create a descant from an alto or tenor part sung an octave higher, see pp. 279–283 in the section on re-voicing hymns in Chapter Thirteen.)

- Engage the participation of your young singers in the service by teaching them the doxology or the sung benediction, including a three-part "amen."

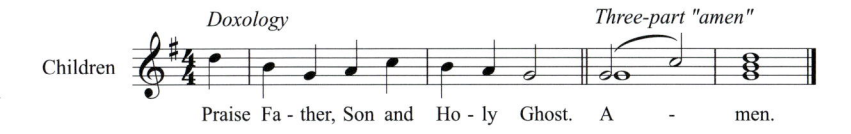

Children: Praise Fa-ther, Son and Ho-ly Ghost. A — men.

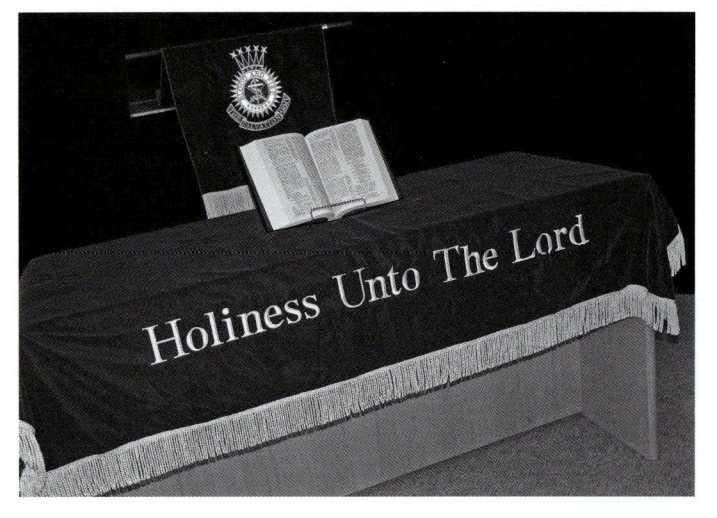

Meeting elements

- Take the offering from the front or rear, requiring worshipers to move to the offering plate. Occasionally sing a hymn or chorus during the offering or recycle a chorus from earlier in the service.

- Create opportunities for the worship team, band, songsters and kids groups to sit among the congregation. Close physical proximity encourages interaction. Some bands configure seating off the platform in with the congregation. The objective is to represent Christ as one body.

- Encourage families to worship together. Others can "adopt" young people without caregivers in church, nurturing a spirit of belonging. This helps the young people learn how to sit in church.

- Use a seventh-inning stretch. "Say good morning to someone you may not have met before or you have not seen in a while." This builds body life.

The spoken word

- Use Scripture or hymn texts as the basis for spoken prayer, call to worship, or benediction.

- Interactive responsive readings bring the Scripture alive. For instance, from Psalm 24:

  Speaker: *"Who is the King of Glory?"*
  Congregation: *"The Lord strong and mighty"*

  Or from Psalm 136:

  Speaker: *"Give thanks to the Lord, for he is good."*
  Congregation: *"His love endures forever."*

- Many hymn texts function well as spoken introductions, prayers, or call's to worship.

- Use a dramatized Bible passage for Scripture reading as prelude to the sermon or call to worship.

- Ask a dancer to interpret through movement a Scripture passage as it is read.

- Set the tone for a songster or band selection with a dialogue using Scripture and/or lines from the song being shared. Project the lyrics or related Scripture during the musical selection to aid in understanding of the text and emotion of the music.

www.music.saconnects.org

Congregational song

- Connect generations of worshipers by using traditional or seasonal songs for congregational singing. The Christmas season in particular affords opportunities to sing classical fare, even in different languages. This ennobles the worship.

- A concert of prayer is a journey in prayer rendered in song. Begin with adoration *upward*. "Now let us praise the Lord for His greatness, with thanks in our hearts." Then move *inward*. "Now let us pray for personal forgiveness before our Sovereign God and for a real sense of direction in our lives and the lives of our families." Lastly, move *outward*. "Bring to the Lord your concerns for our own families, our corps family, co-workers, and outreach." Encourage worshipers to use the altar or simply pray at their seats. Allow a freedom in the Spirit.

- Using an upbeat congregational song, open the meeting for brief testimonies between verses focused on a subject such as, "I am thankful for..."

- When introducing new songs or choruses, use the keyboard or track the first week. The next week ask a soloist or the band to render the tune. Following that, have the songsters introduce and lead it. Repeat the chorus in coming weeks.

- Vary the accompaniment between verses by using the band, piano, organ, and/or worship team. Within each ensemble, exchange colors, for instance, between the *women's* and *men's voices* or between the *brights* (cornets and trombones) and *mellows* (horns, baritones, euphoniums and basses). Change key or vary voicings and harmonizations. (More on this in the **Piano Worship** and **Worship Leading** chapters.)

- Having reviewed a new song or chorus in rehearsal, songsters are able to gird up the singing from their seats in the congregation or as church choirs have for generations, from the platform.

The Beat Goes On

MUSIC MINISTRY RESOURCES

BOOKS ON MINISTERING IN WORSHIP
An Hour on Sunday, Nancy Beach (Zondervan)
Desiring Repetition: Søren Kierkegaard's Metaphor of the Theater in dialogue with Contemporary Worship Leader Models, Andrew Thompson, www.sorenkierkegaard.nl/artikelen/Engels/099.%20desiringrepetition.pdf
From Memory to Imagination: Reforming the Church's Music, C. Randall Bradley (Eerdmans)
Jubilate! Church Music in the Evangelical Tradition, Donald Hustad (Hope)
Making Sunday Special, Ken Mains (Word)
Mastering Worship, Jack Hayford, John Killinger and Howard Stevenson (Multnomah)
Music and Ministry–A Biblical Counterpoint, Calvin Johansson (Hendrickson)
Performer as Priest and Prophet, Judith Rock and Norman Mealy (Harper and Row)
Profiles of Worship, Meeting Plans for Ten-Week Series on Worship (The Salvation Army, USA Central)
Reinventing Sunday, Brad Berglund (Judson Press)
The Ministry of Music–A Complete Handbook for the Music Leader in the Local Church, Kenneth Osbeck (Kregel Publications)
The Christian, the Arts and Truth–Regaining the Vision of Greatness, Frank Gaebelein (Multnomah)
The New Worship–Straight Talk on Music and the Church, Barry Liesch (Baker Books)
The Sacred in Music, Albert Blackwell (Westminster John Knox Press)
The Worship Sourcebook with Companion CD, (CRC Publications)
Times of Refreshing, Tom Kraeuter (Emerald Books)
Whatever Happened to Worship? A.W. Tozer (Christian Publications)
Worship Is a Verb–Eight Profiles for Transforming Worship, Robert Webber (Hendrickson)
Worship Evangelism: Inviting Unbelievers into the Presence of God, Sally Morgenthaler (Zondervan)

RECOMMENDED DEVOTIONAL SERIES
Can You Hear Me? Brad Jersak (Freshwind Press)
From Mission Tourists to Global Citizens, Tim Dearborn (InterVarsity Press)
Hand Me Another Brick, Chuck Swindoll (Thomas Nelson)
Slaying the Giants in Your Life, David Jeremiah (Thomas Nelson)
The Heart of the Artist, Rory Noland (Zondervan)
The Musician's Core (published by The Salvation Army, USA Central). Divides the core principles of **The Heart of the Artist** (Rory Noland) over a 40-week study especially designed for small groups within Salvation Army music and arts ensembles.
The Prayer of Jabez, Bruce Wilkinson (Multnomah)

From Spectator to Participant
Moving from the Couch to the Chapel

Crowds don't disbelieve in God, but they disqualify themselves from strenuous, personal participation ... How can people who are conditioned to a life of distraction and indulgence be moved to live at their best, to be artists of the everyday, to plunge into life and not loiter on the fringes?
—*Eugene Peterson*[19]

More on this in Chapter Two straight ahead ...

CHAPTER TWO

SUNDAY MORNING
A Lifeline to the Church

Enter into His gates with thanksgiving, and into His courts with praise; be thankful unto Him, and bless His name. —Psalm 100:4 *(KJV)*

A CALL TO WORSHIP

A visitor, it is said, walked into the quietness of a Quaker meeting, turned to someone nearby, and inquired, "When does the service begin?" The answer came back, "As soon as the meeting is over." Far more than a clever play on words, this response illustrates how our service should emanate out from the meeting hour on Sunday. Salvationists "worship and proclaim the living God, by daily living which demonstrates all that we profess with our lips."[1]

"A lot is at stake on Sunday mornings," says Nancy Beach in her engaging book *An Hour on Sunday.* Some opt for a sleep-in, the Sunday paper, watching a ballgame, or supporting their child's sporting event. A few are undecided on whether to go to service that day while others rush to church, just making it. She notes that it is a big challenge to get a visitor to come back.[2] In many places the members of the music sections are among the most faithful because of their week-to-week responsibilities in the worship service.

While our culture may show signs of apathy and even disdain for church, there are also signs that people are engaged in a profound search for spirituality. Whether that seeking is a byproduct of economic uncertainty or the hard knocks of life, our society shows a genuine hunger for truth, for hope, for inner peace, and genuine community. We must act on a belief that Sunday mornings at our local corps can be a gateway to God's dramatic work in the hearts and lives of people.

Chapter Two aims to assist current and emerging music leaders, and their corps officers, in making Sunday morning worship vital and vibrant. We ask:

- **What word, what song?** How is the uniqueness of the church community reflected in the service order and choice of songs for Sunday worship?
- **What plan?** What worship elements will intentionally connect to our present congregation?
- **What offering?** How do we assure that our music is an offering?
- **Who makes this happen?** How can corps officers partner with the ministry team to make the Sunday service a true worship experience?
- **How to make this work?** How can music leaders best manage their allotted rehearsal time to meet the weekly demands of Sunday worship and more?

...and on the 7th day, thou shalt turn on the lights, check the heat, projector and sound system, do the pick-ups, be sure the bulletin and powerpoint ready, pray with the singing leaders, preach, greet folks, teach Sunday School, counsel folks, take folks home, shut off the lights, get something to eat ... and, oh, yes, REST!

Heart to God, Hand to Man

In Chapter One we pointed out the danger of activity becoming the enemy of adoration. "Service flows out of worship," cautions Richard Foster.³ The Salvation Army is well known for extending its "hand to man." A healthy corps will care for the poor, visit the infirmed, and minister to youth and elderly with weekly programs. Nancy Beach contends that all these good works necessarily reach back to Sunday worship.

Our old slogan rightly commences with "heart to God." Commissioner Robert Street reminds us, "Christ says 'Come to Me' before He says 'Go into the world.' We find the springs of our spiritual life in our turning to God in private moments of prayer and devotion, as well as in our worship together."⁴ The Sunday meeting is what unifies the congregation's mission. It is what propels the people to want to serve God during the week. And it draws them back the following Sunday to be restored and invigorated to face another week. The meeting defines what matters to a corps and its leaders. In short, the Sunday meeting is a *"lifeline to the church's life."* ⁵

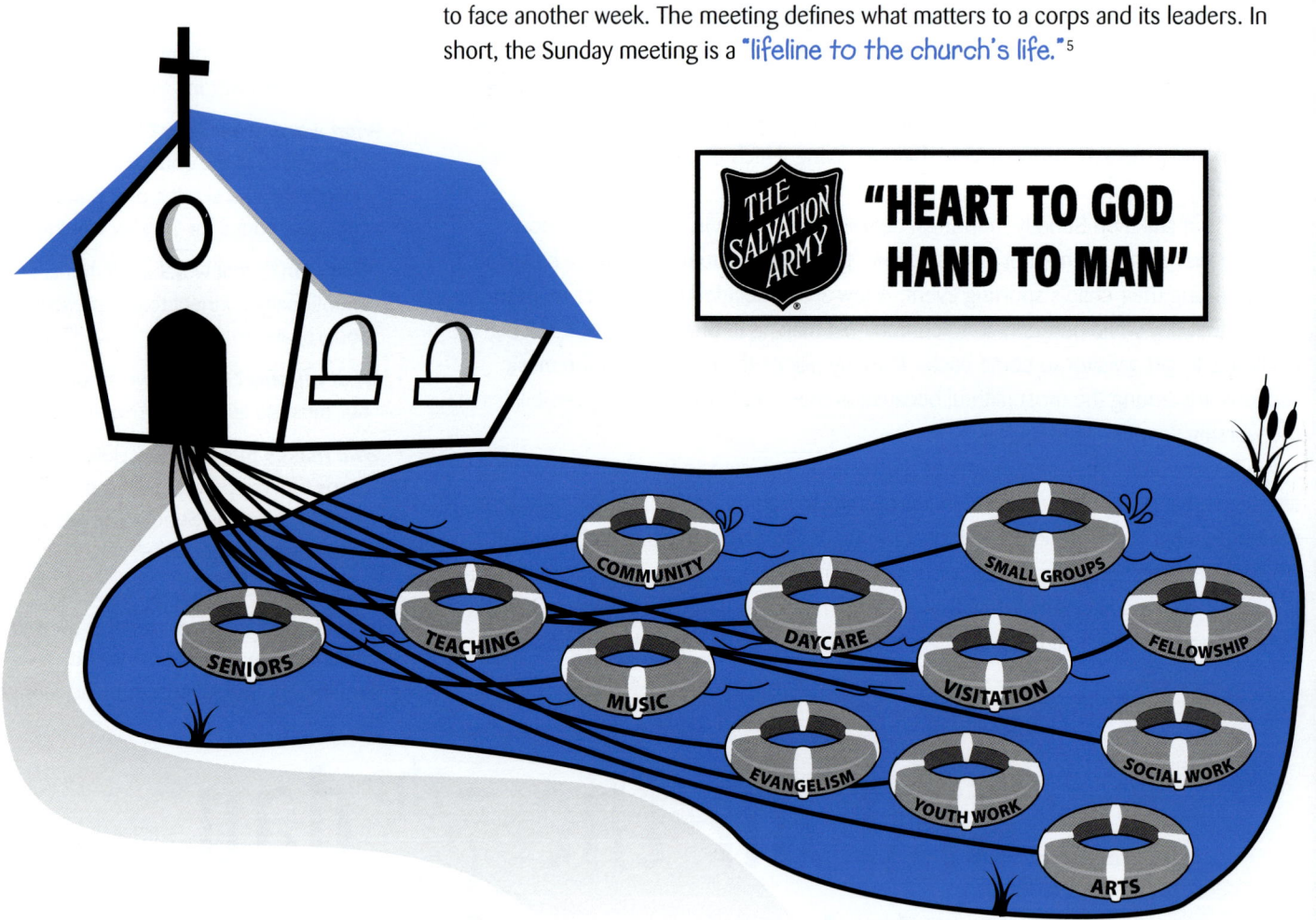

Richard Foster speaks for many of us when he says, "Many times we may not 'feel' like worship. Perhaps you have had so many disappointing experiences in the past that you think it is hardly worth it. There is such a low sense of the power of God. Few people are adequately prepared." Then Foster resolutely advises, "But you need to go anyway. You need to offer a sacrifice of worship. You need to be *with* the people of God."⁶ Isaac Pennington says that when people are gathered for genuine worship, "They are like a heap of fresh and burning coals warming one another as a great strength and freshness and vigor of life flows into all."⁷

Deep calls to deep

So how do we draw people toward the warm glow of Sunday morning worship? There are "attractions" that can kindle such a fire:

1. If we purchase tickets to a movie, we do so expecting to be touched by the emotion of that film. Singing in particular can be a medium for the expression of emotion, reaching to an inner place.

2. Prayer is countercultural. In a world of ever-present ringtones, tapping keystrokes, background music, and noise, finding a place of real stillness leaves even the skeptic with a sense of wonder and awe. "Tis to the quiet heart He loves to come," states one Salvation Army songwriter.[8]

3. Art and beauty draw us closer to God. C. S. Lewis called these "drippings of grace," which can awaken a thirst for God. Countless pairs of ear buds and blaring speakers attest to the draw of music on our daily lives. When we peer into a piece of music, it is like a mirror that provides a glimpse deep into our souls.

4. The stories of changed lives, testimonies to dramatic transformation, touch our own story. An intangible is unearthed. We recognize Christ in each other and affirm there is something more we want in our lives. In true worship we are changed, as we take our first baby steps in faith, confession, asking for forgiveness, or praying for a loved one. A changed life is infectious.

5. We can plan and rehearse with all the right techniques and methods, yet the moment of revelation and measure of worship is Spirit touching spirit, our spirits ignited and warmed by divine fire.

Let's consider ways to craft services with the potential for God to do His mighty work in the hearts of our worshiping community. As Nancy Beach reminds us, "Our goal is for God to anoint our work, resulting in what we call transcendent moments."[9]

WHAT WORD, WHAT SONG?

As corps officers and music leaders, we can limit the dynamism of the hour on Sunday when we fall back on prescribed blueprints from our own history. "Tradition is the living faith of the dead. Traditionalism is the dead faith of the living," states church historian Jaroslav Pelikan. How easy it is to succumb to a pattern of the "same old, same old," mirroring the choices and actions of our predecessors. A simple first step is to ask which traditions are still vibrant and retain value. This could be the family altar time, the pastoral prayer, or the singing of hymns that link us to former generations.

In our humanness, we are apt to replicate what we grew up with. Or we try to live in the afterglow of a mountaintop experience we personally long to savor. Our congregation was not present at either of these places; therefore it is not their experience. It is far more beneficial to prayerfully ask the Spirit what music, what word, what prayer will touch our people today. I am fond of the analogy of ministry as "a generous flood of life-giving river," suggesting vibrant refreshment, power, and even positive ions![10]

> " A simple first step is to ask which traditions are still vibrant and retain value. "

"Hmm ... What song will touch our people today?"

What do we see? Whose vision? Where do we start?

What we offer the fellowship of believers must come from taking careful stock of the ever-changing landscape of our community. While tradition and history have value, be sure to keep worship fresh by living in the moment, reflective of where your people are now. In many churches, whole services are designed around a specific people or culture, with some young (contemporary services), older (classic, traditional), or a blend of generations (blended, mosaic).

The Holy Spirit's work is not confined to one style of worship. In fact, as Hillsong songwriter Darlene Zschech says, an *old song*, shared in a moment of adoration, becomes a *new song*.[11] The Salvation Army affirmation statement on worship says, "We sing the ancient song of creation to its Creator, we sing the new song of the redeemed to their Redeemer, we hear proclaimed the word of redemption, the call to mission and the promise of life in the Spirit."[12]

What music?

Just speaking about church music is loaded emotionally. To add cultural adaptation to the discussion intensifies an already arduous quest. For instance, some find it difficult to recognize that Salvation Army music-making in their neighborhood, in this day and age, may not rest in the exclusive realm of a brass band. And yet, I have worked in an inner-city corps for years and have been consistently surprised by the level of appreciation for even a beginner's band playing simple hymn tunes, something that seems far removed from that neighborhood's musical preferences.

One can hardly imagine a silent Salvation Army, devoid of its free-flowing music-making. For an officer to discover with his or her ministry team what this sounds like is an "Army essential." Where there are no capable live musicians, this may mean using a CD of a brass band playing hymn tunes or an iWorship DVD track as folks enter the chapel or to accompany congregational singing. Aspire to some kind of live music-making by establishing an after-school music school, the specifics of which we consider in the next chapter. Where there are already musicians, the officer and team of music leaders choose to respect what is already happening, hopefully well-represented in a weekly commitment to rehearsal and Sunday meetings. Officers should pose three essential questions to their music leaders: "What is the mission/purpose of your group?" "What can I do to help you?" and "How can I belong?"

New song?

The church has proven over generations that there is great value in structure, even ritual. Yet there are times when we should ask if the order of service template has grown tired, or at best, predictable. Is it time to revisit the Song Book or venture into more contemporary songs? Forbearance is essential with bridging classic and contemporary song. There is a time for the bedrock songs of the church that carry the doctrinal heritage of our faith. On the other hand, one of the ways that God speaks to His people, at this moment, is through *new song*. It is a theme repeated over and over in the Psalms.

The music used in a corps will often reflect either the preferred musical style of its music leaders and corps officer, or, better yet, the preferred music style of the people of the corps. What might work best would be the preferred music styles of all, since preference is so personal. It is of vital importance for the music leaders and officers to identify the musical languages that most successfully communicate with their people.[13]

What we offer the fellowship of believers must come from taking careful stock of the ever-changing landscape of our community.

Sharing the vision

Often, a veteran music leader struggles to see the potential for widening the reach of even historically mainline ensembles like the songsters and band on Sunday mornings. The leader may need help in catching that vision. Someone, possibly the officer, can share ways to ease the musical section into a fresh avenue of expression. The goal is for the congregation, following the guidance of the Holy Spirit, to become the sole proprietor of our song.

In my long service as bandmaster, there were two occasions when my concept of Salvation Army banding was sorely tested and stretched. In both cases, our paramount concern in making adjustments to our music-making was to maintain the vitality of our congregational song, which benefited our Sunday mornings as a worshiping body.

Throwing the baby out with the bathwater!

The first occasion followed attendance by our officers at a church growth workshop. The relevance of the corps band and songsters was brought into question. This conversation, with my strong feelings to the contrary, fortunately didn't get past the leadership circle. Later, I learned that the church growth advocates were not aware of the number of Salvation Army corps with resilient, longstanding "homogeneous groups" called corps bands. In many places, corps bands were the sole support for congregational singing.

The officer, himself trained as a Salvationist musician, was delighted when, as bandmaster, I opted to reach toward the musical style that was being advocated, with hopes of reaching a wider audience. We began to use the then-new *Hallelujah Choruses* with our still-intact corps band. Looking back, it may seem odd that the first praise and worship choruses sung at our corps were without the aid of a guitarist or even an adequate drummer.

Within a decade, we had not only an outstanding corps band but a genuinely effective praise team. Some Sundays the corps band traded off leadership of the congregational singing with the praise team. Joint efforts proved anointed, particularly on "high holy days," when both groups and congregation united as one exultant voice.

A change of scenery

Those banner days were short-lived. Within a span of just a year and a half, thirty-five soldiers moved on, mostly due to relocation for school and vocation. This included a number of key musicians. The corps band was severely handicapped, and not even one guitarist could be found to lead worship choruses, although we had two fine drummers! We could sense that the praise team was sorely missed, and thankfully, the corps officer was not ready to give up on live music-making.

Despite our losses, we determined to again create anointed moments of transcendence in music. We moved the ensemble down next to the piano in the congregation, and I led the singing and band selections from the piano with the ensemble in a supporting role. Again I was indebted to the *Hallelujah Choruses* series, which offered a nice mix of Salvation Army songs, hymns, and new worship choruses for piano with the option of adding brass and rhythm players. (See Chapter Fourteen for details on practical Salvation Army brass publications, including the *Hallelujah Choruses*). The physical placement of all the meeting participants off the platform was certainly a plus, as it brought us closer together, facing in the same direction, as one voice.

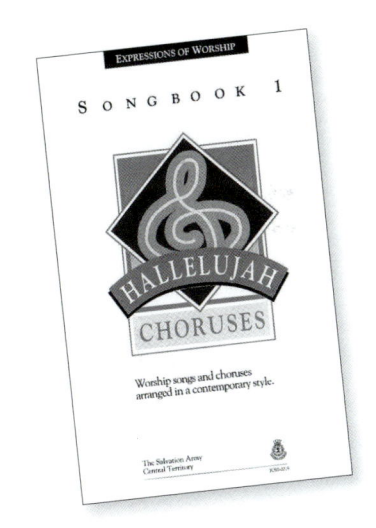

In one instance, adapting to the available conditions at hand brought a congregation suffering loss closer together as a family. In both cases, the congregation benefited from *new song*, bringing a vibrant freshness and relevance some thought we lacked to our weekly worship. In this way, the music served the service.

Not getting detoured?

Blaise Pascal once wrote to a friend, "I have made this letter longer than usual because I lack the time to make it short." In an accelerating, sound byte-oriented society, too much talk earns a switch-off. Few of us fare well at extemporizing. In addition to sermons, testimonies, announcements, and prayer, introductions to musical offerings can also become long-winded. Each element requires forethought so that the path of the worship service is not detoured or slowed. With the advent of projected media, there are a number of ways to reduce rambling chatter.

LORD, I THINK HE'S HAVING TROUBLE FINISHING THIS SERMON…

Canadian Salvationist Kim Garreffa cautions worship leaders to limit their *sermonizing* by respecting the time allotted to them. "If the Spirit is moving and people come to the mercy seat at worship time, that is different. But my officer and I always work together, and I allow him to dictate how much the worship time will be extended." Kim adds, "I am, first and foremost, a servant to the congregation, to my worship team, and to my officer."

A nugget every Sunday

"Our goal is to avoid a smattering of scattered mountaintop experiences," says Nancy Beach. "We aim to see people in our services challenged, convicted, and changed with an increasing regularity." She teaches that a good reference point for worship planning is to *recall when our soul has been either overwhelmed or quieted by music or art in the church.*[14] This is a good conversation for corps officers to have with their music leaders. Many times after a service, I discover that the moment of transcendence was not in a point of a sermon but from a line of a song or a Scripture passage that seems to burn within me. A touching presentation in song or a challenge in testimony can act as a catalyst for anointed moments. Salvation Army worshipers yearn for more of what Fanny Crosby called "a foretaste of glory divine."

Spirit touching spirit, UNintentionally

A sermon based on James' and John's request to sit on either side of Jesus in Glory led to such a moment for me. The "God-Man sent to earth" squelched their arrogance and brought the conversation back down to earth, as Jesus defined greatness as being a servant of all. (Mark 10:43) The enigma for the disciples, and for us listening in, is the premise that learning to serve is the standard for greatness in God's economy. I heard the familiar mantra: "No work is below us … It is earthy, and even gritty, to befriend the forsaken."

> "Can you recall when your soul has been either overwhelmed or quieted by music or art in the church?"

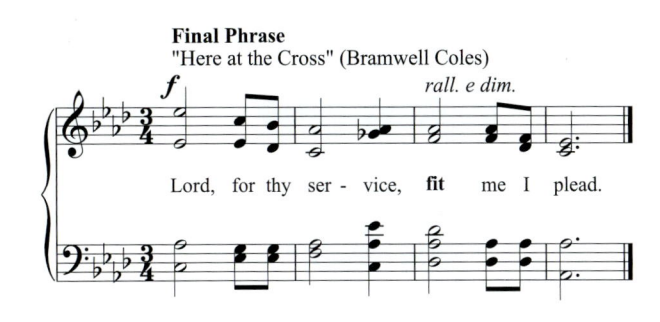

The speaker then quoted familiar lines of Bramwell Coles at a rapid fire pace, almost as an afterthought: "How can I better serve Thee, Lord? or Thou who hast done so much for me" ... until a three-letter word in the final phrase of the chorus stunned me. "Lord, for Thy service, *fit* me I plead." Much like the disciples, I usually elected to grandstand and self-promote in the name of my faith. I knew in my heart that I was a far cry from ministering with a towel; I was unwilling in my heart to get my hands dirty, much less reach out to the unlovely.

Whenever I had previously considered this passage, I looked for ways to "pay penance" by forcing my sights downward toward the disenfranchised. On this Sunday morning I reversed course and chose to aspire upward to this brand of greatness, wondering how God could "fit" me for His service. Like many, I had wallowed in the words of servant models like Mother Teresa and St. Francis. Yet I had never come close to that dangerous place of vulnerability. On that Sunday morning, one little word became for me a transcendent "nugget."

In response to those who may say that they are not being spiritually fed, some officers maintain that on any given Sunday, there will be such a nugget that speaks directly and personally to the heart. Some are intentionally planted by the worship planner and others in response to the Holy Spirit. God is there, anxious to meet with every member of a congregation. It is the responsibility of each congregant to "enter into His gates with thanksgiving," (Psalm 100:4) expectant and seeking nourishment. As songwriter Richard Blanchard put it, "Bread of heaven, feed me till I want no more."

Spirit touching spirit, INtentionally

A powerful example of creating intentional moments of transcendence is what some call "cardboard testimonies." Before a worship gathering, individuals are each given a cardboard box which has been broken open to a flat surface. On one side, each person uses a large marker to prayerfully record a "giant" that has plagued their spiritual walk. On the reverse, a corresponding spiritual transformation is noted in large letters:

Giiant	Flipside
Went through the motions	God moves me
Depression was my friend	God ended that friendship
Lying in religion	Living in relationship
Took a wrong path	Now I follow Jesus

> "Every Sunday, there will be one nugget which speaks directly and personally to the heart."

Later in the meeting, with only an underscore of soft music, the testimonies are unveiled one at a time. First the side with the confession is held up, and then the flipside with the statement of redemption. The succinct yet powerful accumulation of testimonies creates an openness of penitence and consecration within the congregation. Those observing reflect on where they may stand with their own "giants" and may feel compelled to pray for those who daringly shared their confessions. A vital encounter takes place when our spirits recognize Christ moving in another. It follows naturally that we become more like Christ, making His light shine in us even brighter, which continues the cycle. This is just one more reason to "not forsake our own assembling together." (Hebrews 10:25, *NASB*)

WHAT PLAN?

Mining for gold, with INtentionality
In order to create these possibilities, effective worship planners try to envision how the worshipers will respond to all aspects of the worship service:

... by varying topical themes
Nancy Beach teaches that a balance is required between topics that are *vertical,* about God and His nature, and those dealing with human relationships, which we call *horizontal.* After a series of weeks of one or the other, it may be time to shift the focus. Holidays, of course, suggest meeting topics, and we can also draw a rhythm from the seasons. September and January are good times to discuss new beginnings; topics related to fresh-start resolutions, such as time management, physical fitness, finances, and spiritual disciplines.[15]

... by targeting your audience
Targeting the make-up of your Sunday congregation, considering their needs, worries, and issues, makes it easier to connect with them in worship services. For the newest arrivals or the unchurched, drama, contemporary music, and multimedia presentations are familiar and prove an effective entry point. To determine if your service is reaching the unchurched, ask yourself what would be attractive and compelling enough for the parents of your child's dance, music, or athletic teams to want to return to your corps again.

... by catering to diverse musical tastes
Several generations ago, Marshall McLuhan taught us that the packaging affects the message. As he said, "the medium is the message." This principle is played out every day in our media with the branding of everything from fast food to corporations and political candidates. If there are radio stations for nearly every conceivable musical preference, then what music we choose for worship goes beyond which church holiday we may be observing. It says something about our brand of church.

Some music in church culture speaks deeply to the generation of my four young adult daughters but earns limited airplay from their parents. The same is true for my parents' generation. They are understandably confused by the appeal of a rock and roll band—once deemed the devil's music—singing songs about Jesus. From the seventies on, the music of pop culture has infiltrated the church. Via the information highway, it has rapidly become a global language.

Among the older generations, there are those who quietly rebel against what Thomas Begler calls the *juvenilization* of the church, which requires all generations sharing a worship space to sing the preferred songs of adolescents.[16] Unfortunately this juvenilization has trickled down into today's congregations, which are sorely void of holiness teaching and preaching, and its foremost participatory proponent, holiness hymnody. Into this vacuum, we pour our "young" worship songs, stalling a great deal of maturation into spiritual adulthood.[17] The well-intentioned focus to meet kids where they are brands youth culture as the most accepted culture, which unobtrusively "exalts young people as the spiritual gold standard of authenticity and passion."[18]

Fortunately there are church musicians, including Salvationists in praise bands, who seek to remedy this imbalance by cherishing the richness and depth of our sung theology. Knowing several generations are in the room with diverse tastes and passions, these song leaders try to touch the different generations with different styles. Sometimes

Should all generations have to sing the preferred songs of adolescents?

we pray that some folks can adjust a bit out of their culture while we stretch a bit out of ours. Some mainline churches have responded to this diversity of tastes by becoming like a movie multiplex, offering different style services which cater to different target audiences at different times.

... by ministering to the children
Excusing the young ones to junior church or including a children's five is a hybrid of this mentality. The family sits together for much of the adult service and then the children receive age-appropriate spiritual instruction. If your congregation includes young couples, a well-managed nursery is a must. Parents are not going to come to church to watch their children. They can do that more easily at home.

What's the plan?

A former boss of mine was fond of saying "failing to plan is planning to fail." There is a lowest common denominator afloat which permits "anything for Jesus" in our offerings. This requires little, if any, forethought. Habitually the bar is set so low that, "even if only one person is reached, we did not labor in vain." We might understand the good intent of this oft-maligned prayer, but the subtext reads, "Why should anyone listen? We're not at all prepared." We tend to forget the depth of God's holiness, and our unworthiness, when we approach God with a careless, even cavalier familiarity.[19]

LACK OF PLANNING ON YOUR PART DOES NOT CONSTITUTE AN EMERGENCY ON MY PART, ESPECIALLY ON SUNDAYS!

We must aim higher, so that every person present experiences the life-changing beauty and power of God's presence. In The Salvation Army we believe in the priesthood of all believers, meaning that a child can hear from God as profoundly as the adult morning speaker. As a military metaphor, this might be called total mobilization.

Ephesians 4:15 admonishes us to speak the truth in love. First we need to decide who we are trying to reach. As stated in Chapter One, one goal is to transform "spectators into participants." Different arenas and thereby different audiences, be it an open-air, worship service, or a concert, call for different approaches. Too often any intentionality is confined to the safety of our fine-tuned box (pun intended) with our "club offerings." For bandsmen this can be a well-worn march book or a shortlist of Sallie devotional favorites, both having questionable relevance to an uninformed listener. Praise band leaders can just as easily fall into the comfort of a Top Five list.

A planned service is not less spiritual than one that seems to unfold spontaneously. Experience and time spent in prayer and the Word aid the subconscious germination of ideas for worship through the Holy Spirit. It is a balancing act to know when to make a dramatic change in direction, but a circus performer wouldn't dare get on that tightrope in front of a crowd without hours of preparation and coaching. Even in my worship experiences in Africa, what gives the impression of being spontaneous is born out of years of repetition and prayer. The songs are familiar and the movements even standardized, allowing for a freedom of joyous expression in the Spirit.

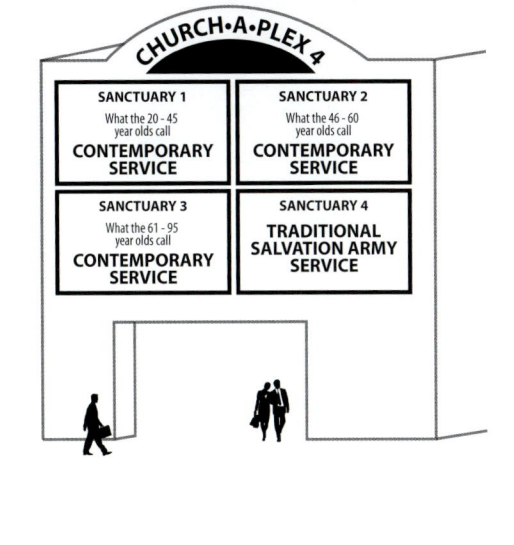

This echoes the **generational resonance,** as Major JoAnn Shade calls it, of using a classic hymn that we can picture our grandparents singing. All the more reason that we should nurture our collective memory of these treasures in song! A few years back, a visit to a Lutheran Christmas Eve service sung in German uncannily linked Herr Burgmayer to his ancestors in Bavaria.

The overall target length of the service, and particularly the flow of the meeting, is of vital importance. The entire worship team strives to be on the same page in regard to the content, intentionality, and length of each respective meeting element. Various models of worship design are outlined in Appendix 2.1. The influences of Revivalism, Methodism, the Quakers, and Pentecostalism have marked Salvation Army worship. Elements of church liturgy and the lectionary bring richness to the worship experience. Other worship leaders may prefer a free-and-easy approach, with lots of inspirational singing and a strong appeal following a Bible message.

"You don't observe communion?"

"Why do you wear those uniforms?"

Salvation Army worship

In a presentation entitled "Worship—The Jewel on the Crest," Colonel Richard Munn identifies eight features unique to Salvation Army worship:

SIMPLE BUILDINGS ... where the poor are comfortable.

PORTABLE HOLINESS ... worship in gyms, outdoors, and social service centers.

HERITAGE OF BRASS BANDS ... a uniquely unifying component.

LATIN AMERICAN AND AFRICAN PENTECOSTALISM ... an increasing presence.

PAGEANTRY ... ceremonies, flags, crest, drums, enrollments, and more.

THE PRIESTHOOD OF THE BELIEVERS ... cherished, if not implemented.

We called ourselves a **"CHURCH"** three or four decades ago ... and then, reluctantly.

RELIGIOUS-CHARITABLE nomenclature.[20]

We should not assume that the unchurched, the newcomer, young people, or even longstanding stalwart soldiers comprehend or embrace the richness of our often exuberant style of worship and outreach. If the Sunday service is a **lifeline to the church's life,** then it defines what matters to a corps and its leaders. Colonel Munn reminds us that our unique altar furnishings, sacramental position, and military metaphor all emanate from the Salvationists' concept of God. This continues to evolve over our history into the Army's working theology of worship, as Munn outlines:

THE SALVATION MEETING
The God who saves ... Our call to the mercy seat

THE HOLINESS MEETING
The God who is holy ... Our holiness table

THE PARISHIONERS
The God who has a special care for the poor ... Our special calling

THE ARMY
The God who is militantly opposed to evil ... Our quasi-military structure

THE SACRAMENT OF THE ORDINARY
The God who is everywhere present ... Our sacramental theology

THE HUSBAND AND WIFE TEAM OF OFFICERS
The God who is egalitarian ... Our female preachers and leaders

THE ONE ARMY IN MORE THAN 125 COUNTRIES
The God of the whole world ... Our internationalism[21]

Meeting with God
Another essential hallmark of Salvation Army worship has been a freedom in worship, in response to the promptings of the Holy Spirit. We can allow for freshness in our order of service. For example, should the use of the mercy seat be limited to after the sermon or should it be open all the time? The meeting leader learns to read the room and act as a conduit for response and reflection. One might pause, awaiting God's direction to move forward. While projected images aid focus in worship, they needn't restrict us from using an unplanned song, creating a "God moment" in response to the Spirit. We can feed the words, call out a chorus number, or have the projectionist catch up to the chorus on the fly. What is essential is to guard these holy times by not allowing any *business* of church—announcements and unnecessary chatter—to infringe on the experience of the Holy. We hold our gifts loosely, even daring to deviate from the tech sheet and remain consistent with our ministry mission. Everything says, "It is not about me or my group, but focused on meeting with God, here today, in this place, at this very moment in time."

> "It is not about me or my group, but focused on meeting with God, here today, in this place, at this very moment in time."

Play *skillfully* for your community of faith
The Psalmist exclaims, "Sing to Him a new song; play *skillfully,* and shout for joy!" (Psalm 33:3) It is a call to musical excellence, yes, but is about more than getting every note in the right place. *It is a summons for leaders to become "experts in the styles of music which work best for their community of faith,"* some of which are far removed from those with which they may have grown up. We must seek to *"become fluent in our faith community's primary musical languages,"* working continually to become better and better.[22] David understood this when he said, "I will not offer burnt offerings to the Lord my God which cost me nothing." (2 Samuel 24:24, *NASB*)

"To play skillfully is a summons for leaders to become experts in the styles of music which work best for their community of faith" Dave Williamson.

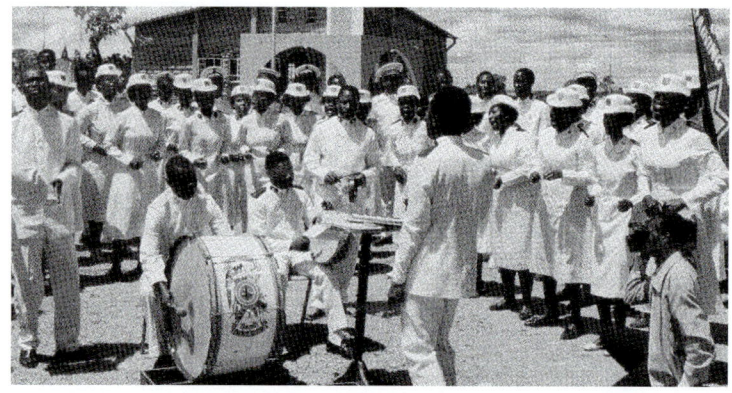

Nairobi Central Corps Songsters present their vibrant songs, in expressive African style.

In this light, there are a number of challenges with playing skillfully in Salvation Army culture. For one, in this day of a preponderance of recordings and instantaneous communication, a bandmaster in Africa can hear an offering by the International Staff Band based in England within minutes of an actual performance. Today's media increasingly allows Christians from all corners of the globe to celebrate with the very same praise songs. In a positive sense, we embrace the multiculturalism of One Army when Westerners attempt to assimilate into our music-making cultural elements such as the drumming and dance of Africa or the brass sections in salsa worship bands in South America.

Considering the ever-burgeoning musical sophistication of Army music-making, a natural tendency is to try and emulate the Sunday morning offerings used in a city like London in an American suburb like Levittown, Pennsylvania, my hometown. It is possible that the concept of playing skillfully can become about the music leader's elevating the people into a learned preferred style. More often, it is meeting the people where they can freely celebrate the Giver, not the gift. The old song reminds us, "Tis a gift to be simple." Years ago, Erik Leidzén acknowledged this when he declared that his Salvation Army offerings were written for "the little old lady in the third row."

In Chapter Fourteen, we substantiate that a Salvation Army brass band is remarkably effective in a variety of styles. In the past several generations, bands have learned to pepper our meetings and concerts with rock, country, jazz, and Latin stylings. If our ministry goals are connection and communication, using idioms that our congregations understand can help members feel natural speaking their musical language in praise and worship to God.

Other expressions?

We can also ask if we have added other art forms, such as dance, timbrels or drama, to our toolbox, perhaps in combination with established songsters, band, or praise band. Bringing in special guests, musicians, or artists can lift the expectations of a Sunday morning. Do we effectively use children, who can bring their own spontaneity to any occasion? There are, of course, traditions that transcend generations. *Silent Night* sung by candlelight to close a Christmas Eve service unites worshipers across generations, even centuries. But perhaps the other 90 percent of a Christmas service can be out of the mold. The church should be the first place searching for freshness. In order to do this, worship planners rub shoulders with worshipers, listening, searching, and noticing what inspires them. It takes courage to take a risk, step out, and permit an idea to break new ground, but sometimes we need that new song.[23]

2 BARS REST

1. Recall times when your soul has been overwhelmed or quieted by music or art in the church. What were the circumstances, and to what effect?

2. Consider specific ways that your services can be honed down or permitted the freedom to change course.

3. Are you fully utilizing the mercy seat? Discuss with music leaders/pianists signals or approaches to be taken when there is a response at the mercy seat.

4. Do you agree that on any given Sunday, there can be nuggets, such as a phrase of a song or Scripture portion, that can touch each individual congregant uniquely?

5. How easy is it to follow what is happening in your worship service? How much would the language you use be understood by non-Christians?

6. What do you think are the primary musical languages of your corps? What can you do to enrich your musical vocabulary to embrace the place where your congregation will feel a freedom in worship?

WHAT OFFERING?

Working with artsy types

Unfortunate negative stereotypes are associated with church artists, and Salvationist musicians are not exempt. The mainstream media would have us believe that artsy types are temperamental, difficult, moody, and deaf to criticism. They are characterized as stuck in a flighty, undisciplined lifestyle, which permits sketchy punctuality and meeting attendance. As one pastor quipped, "I just leave those artsy types alone."[24]

However, an honest appraisal would acknowledge that most artists within the Church have hard-working servant's hearts. In order to master their craft, they follow a disciplined regimen. And most are never late! Some years ago, for the jacket of an album that spotlighted up-and-coming soloists titled *We Are an Offering*, I wrote:

> The act of offering one's musical gift encompasses days, weeks, even years of forethought and preparation. Each day begins with warm-ups to develop a pleasing quality of sound and the ability to get around the instrument. It can be a lonely life in a spare practice room. Armed with only an instrument and a few simple accoutrements—a stand, pencil, and music—the performer, day in and day out, sacrificially gives much to hone his skill to eventually share his gifts for public offering.[25]

The corps officer will wisely acknowledge and respect worship leaders. In The Salvation Army, this includes song leaders, bandmasters, timbrel, dance, and drama leaders.

Salvationist worship leader, Mark Hood.

These local leaders are people of purpose who sacrifice time and energy in hopes of connecting with the congregation. "Church music is a functional art which must be judged by how well it serves God and the church in a particular cultural context." [26]

Salvationist songwriter Mark Hood rightly points out that "generations of Salvation Army kids grow up looking for validation and self-worth from how well they play or what group they play in, or in what chair they sit ... We tend to glamorize musicians in the church and elevate them to higher status levels. The problem is that we musicians begin to find our own sense of significance in what we do for Jesus, instead of who we ARE in Jesus."[27] We fully intend for music and arts in our corps to be a functioning ministry from week to week in Sunday worship. But artist-leaders, because of their training, can easily slip into a minstrel mindset, where the focus falls to the praise of people.

Eugene Peterson counsels artists and church leaders alike:

> A life of excellence comes from a life of faith, from being far more interested in God than self ... As a pastor, I encourage others to live at their best and provide guidance in doing it. But how do I do this without inadvertently inciting pride and arrogance? How do I stimulate an appetite for excellence without feeding at the same time a selfish determination to elbow anyone aside who gets in the way? ... The difficult pastoral art is to encourage people to grow in excellence and to live selflessly, at one and the same time to lose the self and find the self.

Peterson continues, "It is paradoxical, but not impossible."[28] The difference from the real cutthroat art world is the grace that can be extended. The pastor allows the musician-minister to maintain artistic integrity, assuming that they will strive to be the best they can be on a given Sunday, judiciously using the gifts and personnel available to that leader. The rest is left to the Spirit.[29]

Sharing the limelight

It can be difficult for up-front performer types, like teachers, worship leaders, and most involved in the arts to share the limelight. By nature, perfectionists will never find anyone up to their ability, so they focus on doing things themselves. They thereby resist empowering others. The ministry team should not allow a few *performers* to undermine the corps' ability to reach its arms out and involve the wider church body in offering their gifts.[30] The sum of the whole will always be greater than the sum of the parts. This takes measured restraint, and a willingness to share the "stage."

In Chapter One we introduced Kierkegaard's theatrical metaphor in which the congregation performs for God, the Audience of One, while the worship leaders are directors. This illustration is helpful in getting the focus off the "Entertain me ... Bless me with a song ... Inspire me with your sermon" mentality of what can sometimes seem like *pew potato* congregations. But it proves troubling for church musicians whose lifelong pursuit has been the applause of their audience. Kennan Birch turns the metaphor in a way that clarifies the all-important interactive relationship of the artist in the church to the Master Artist:

> The Artist has given me a ticket to the concert of life. His all-consuming music touches every part of me. Everything I see, hear, touch, taste, smell or even comprehend is part of the music of the Artist. May I never forget that I am the audience, and not the Artist; that I am the receiver, and not the Giver ... May I never choose to ignore the music of the Artist or attribute the music to me and happenstance, for therein would lie my greatest offense ... May my life not be known for the things I have done, but for the music I hear, the praise I express, and for encouraging others to listen to the music ... But the greatest experience lies not simply in enjoying the music and applauding the Artist. It is found when I lay down my life and become an instrument in the hands of the Artist, and He begins to play His music through me. That is where I find meaning and purpose, and a heart that becomes fully alive.[31]

> "We need torchbearers who not only play notes, but reach through those notations to the music those penned notes try to capture. For me every time I play is a personal conversation ... a prayer ... between me and God ... the giver of the gift. How privileged we are."
> —Cornet soloist Terry Camsey[32]

Ever since Jubal was dubbed "the father of all those who play the harp and flute" (Genesis 4:21), or the Holy Spirit first equipped the artisan Bezalel to craft the Tabernacle furniture (Exodus 31:1-5), artists have viewed the world *positively*, with sincere sensitivity, out of a big heart. In *Windows of the Soul*, Ken Gire commends all those who offer their artistic gifts when he writes, "We learn from the artist, from those who work in paint or words, or musical notes, from those who have eyes that see and ears that hear and hearts that feel deeply and passionately about all that is sacred and dear to God."[33] It may sound obvious, but the music leader needs to know that the corps officer sincerely *wants* the music to work on Sunday morning. As a pastor, choose to cherish and place your benediction on the lives and ministry of your artist-musicians.

Pastor Reuben Welch speaks as though he has just been welcomed into a new appointment when he says,

> I myself am on my own journey. I don't come out of a vacuum. I'm in the process of my own pilgrimage. And I know that you don't come out of a vacuum either—that you are on your journey. And what I believe with all my heart is that in the grace and mercy of God, our providential meeting together can be God's time for some new and fresh thing.[34]

Corps officers must embrace, and even celebrate their leaders. And yes, leaders can do the same for their corps officers. The Apostle Paul reminded fellow believers, *"Be devoted to one another in brotherly love. Honor one another above yourselves. Never be lacking in zeal, but keep your spiritual fervor, serving the Lord. Be joyful in hope, patient in affliction, and faithful in prayer."* (Romans 12:10-12) With hopeful hearts, corps officers and locals venture forward. *"Consecrate yourselves, for tomorrow the Lord will do amazing things among you."* (Joshua 3:5)

? 2 BARS REST

1. What are ways that corps officers can support their musicians and artists in becoming the best music ministers they can be?

2. How can we be sure that the artistic endeavors of our corps are anointed by the Holy Spirit?

3. How does one savor something he or she has done artistically that God has blessed, without being prideful about it?

4. What do you and the leaders around you consider to be your spiritual gifts? Is there opportunity for those around you to exercise their gifts as God intended? How can we confirm one another's gifts to benefit the church body as a whole?

5. How can you unveil and utilize the gifts of those who have never contributed to a Sunday morning service?

WHO MAKES THIS HAPPEN? Ministry as a Partnership

A worship *team*

Picture yourself as the bandmaster, songster or worship leader when an officer comes into a new appointment. I recall an officer sincerely inquiring how our worship committee worked. (It must have been working very well!) I grin now to think that he was humbly suggesting he would like to be a part of that process. Yes, yes, yes! Most music leaders are happy to play through possible tunes, be asked for suggestions on theme-related songs, or look for appropriate music to steer a meeting in a certain direction.

The effective meeting planner bears in mind that music groups require preparation time, particularly an opportunity to rehearse the tunes for Sunday. It is safer to ask the meeting pianist before a meeting if they know a chorus than to have her try to sort out the best key while the corps officer transitions into a prayer meeting. An email reminder from the meeting planner asking for any suggestions or clarifications can put the supporting cast on the same page, relieving a great deal of Sunday morning *performance pressure*.

Who can we depend on?

There is wisdom in the officers learning something about the personalities and possibilities around them. Observe and respect each individual's make-up. There will be those who copiously highlight their specific responsibilities, are hard-pressed to move ahead or alter a plan, and most of all, dislike last-minute requests. Others live in the moment and may struggle to see the bigger picture. Some music leaders find it difficult to function without a theme.

In terms of service intent, most music leaders wish for more than a few tune numbers left on the conductor's stand. Also disconcerting is passing off the major points and supporting Scripture to the tech person just before the service. Especially in the first year of a new appointment, the corps officer needs to discover how the music sections best function leading up to Sunday morning. Conversely, the musicians learn what they can expect from their new corps officer. *Men and women of integrity know how to extend grace to one another, agreeing to do their best in the situation with what they have.*

Evaluate the following elements of worship by placing an "X" on the continuums below which you feel best describes your worship service:

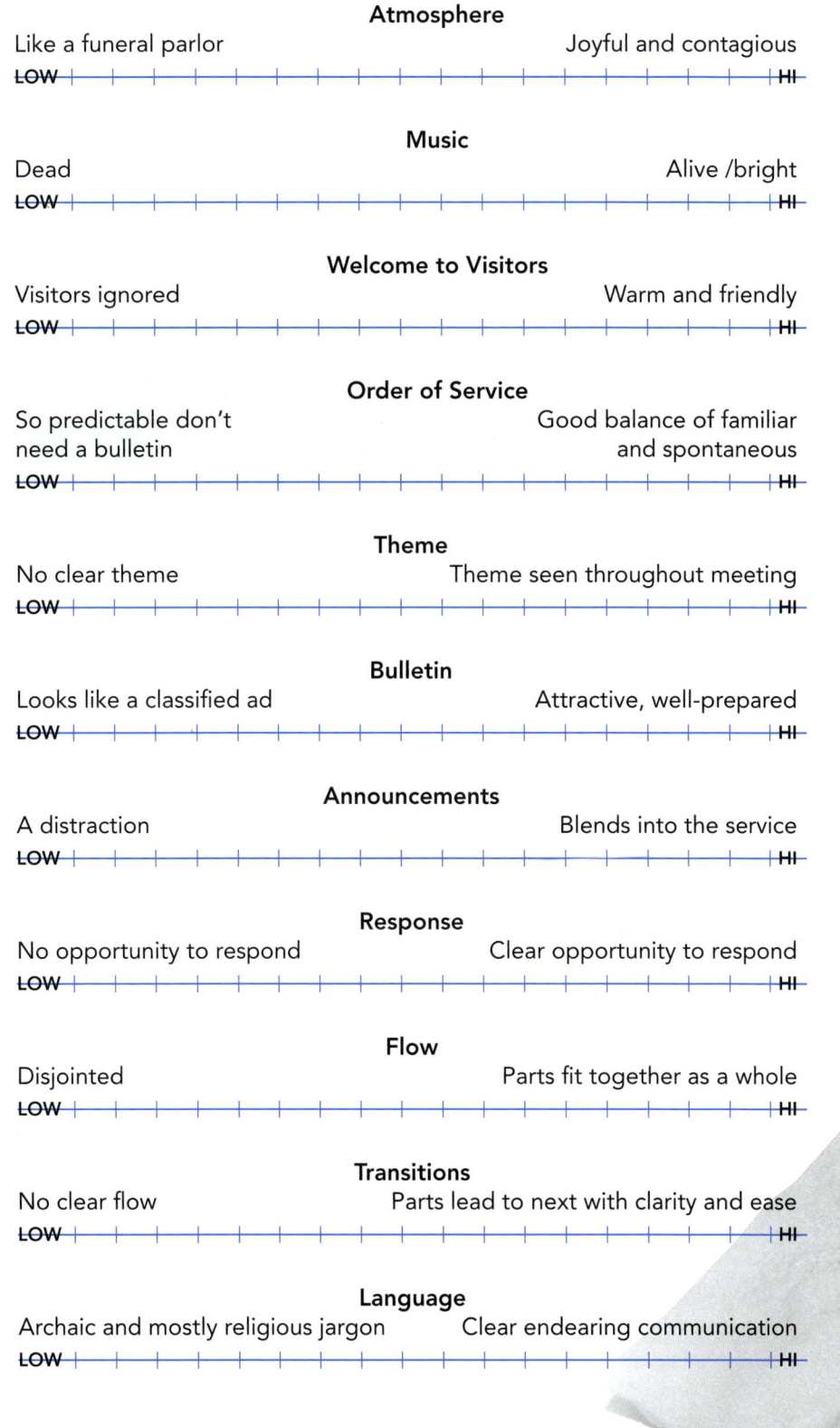

Atmosphere
Like a funeral parlor — Joyful and contagious
LOW |———————————————| HI

Music
Dead — Alive /bright
LOW |———————————————| HI

Welcome to Visitors
Visitors ignored — Warm and friendly
LOW |———————————————| HI

Order of Service
So predictable don't need a bulletin — Good balance of familiar and spontaneous
LOW |———————————————| HI

Theme
No clear theme — Theme seen throughout meeting
LOW |———————————————| HI

Bulletin
Looks like a classified ad — Attractive, well-prepared
LOW |———————————————| HI

Announcements
A distraction — Blends into the service
LOW |———————————————| HI

Response
No opportunity to respond — Clear opportunity to respond
LOW |———————————————| HI

Flow
Disjointed — Parts fit together as a whole
LOW |———————————————| HI

Transitions
No clear flow — Parts lead to next with clarity and ease
LOW |———————————————| HI

Language
Archaic and mostly religious jargon — Clear endearing communication
LOW |———————————————| HI

The Beat Goes On

Collaborating as a worship committee.

The Worship Committee

The writer of Proverbs states, "Plans fail for lack of counsel, but with many advisers they succeed" (Proverbs 15:22). One way for the officer to encourage an exchange of worship planning ideas is by scheduling periodic worship planning sessions that cover the essential components of a six- to eight-week series of Sundays. It speeds the process for the officer to have settled on a theme or topics for the series of services beforehand. The members of the worship committee (music and arts leaders, as well as the pastoral team) can then brainstorm to facilitate a creative process.

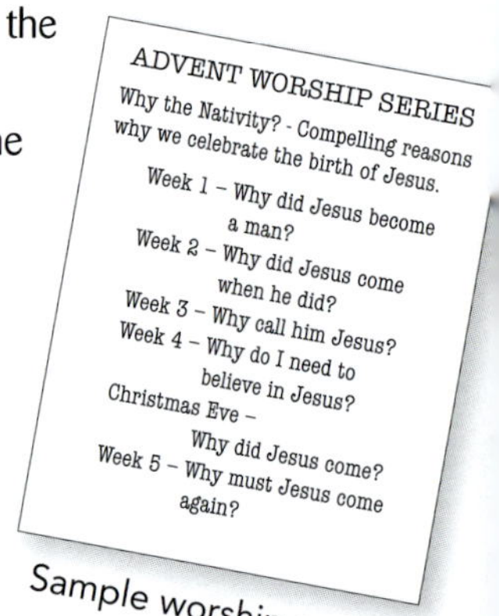

During the imaginative phase, any negative judging of ideas is discouraged. Any and all input can be stepping stones toward a crystallization of a concept. Occasionally a fresh idea *will* synthesize (the one you wish you had thought of!). Once an approach is agreed upon, assignments for either an individual or a group are made to give the meeting practical legs. They sit with it, sing through it, pray through it, and hone in on an effective order of meeting components. On Sunday, they set a *huddle* time before the service for the *cast* to go over any last-minute reminders and to pray.

ADVENT WORSHIP SERIES
Why the Nativity? - Compelling reasons why we celebrate the birth of Jesus.
Week 1 – Why did Jesus become a man?
Week 2 – Why did Jesus come when he did?
Week 3 – Why call him Jesus?
Week 4 – Why do I need to believe in Jesus?
Christmas Eve –
Why did Jesus come?
Week 5 – Why must Jesus come again?

Sample worship series

Pre-meeting prayer huddle.

"sanctified amazement" (*term of endearment*) \'san(k) - tə - fɪd ə - 'maz - mənt\ in light-hearted church lingo, the happy result of the Holy Spirit unifying various components of a worship service (the choice of Scripture, sermon topic, songs, or special music) thematically without the worship leaders having consciously planned or communicated the same.

Beyond "sanctified amazement"

The order of service for many corps remains virtually unchanged from week-to-week, requiring only a mere typographical alteration of the date, sermon, and song titles to the Sunday bulletin. In other places, there is hardly a plan, possibly a list of components, or occasionally the worship leaders stand in "sanctified amazement" when the Holy Spirit miraculously brings things together. As Peggy Thomas says, "We can be more intentional. The Holy Spirit can actually move two weeks *before* a worship service."[35] One way to give the service focus and direction is to center all the worship components around a theme or series of topics which reinforces a word, Scripture text, or holiday observance such as Advent, Palm Sunday, or Mother's Day.

The God who speaks/The people who respond

With a little imagination, worship planners can disturb the "boilerplate" template—or lack of one! They can do this by varying the order of service and by recognizing the need for *the worship experience to become a dialogue between the God who speaks and we, the people who take the means and time in the service to respond.* This is in line with our discussion in the previous chapter of a God who longs for a relationship with us. In Robert Schaper's words, "Worship is the expression of a relationship in which God the Father **reveals** himself and his love in Christ, and by his Holy Spirit administers grace, to which we **respond** in faith, gratitude, and obedience."[36]

God's presence is **revealed** (shown in gray) and challenges us in worship through:

- **The Gathering:** Prelude music, call to worship, songs, prayers of the people, greeting one another, doxology, testimonies of praise, musical selections, dance and drama, interpretive prayer, song, and Scripture.
- **The Word:** Scripture, sermon, prayers to illuminate the Scripture, video clips that comment on the Word, a solo or drama that reflects a text or story.

God's people **respond** (shown in blue) in worship through:

- **Response:** Times of reflection, congregational singing (vertical and horizontal—discussed further in Chapter Eighteen, p. 382), intercessory and spontaneous prayers, testimonies, and invitation to salvation or discipleship.
- **The Sending:** Congregational song/chorus, challenge/charge, benediction, announcements, postlude.[37]

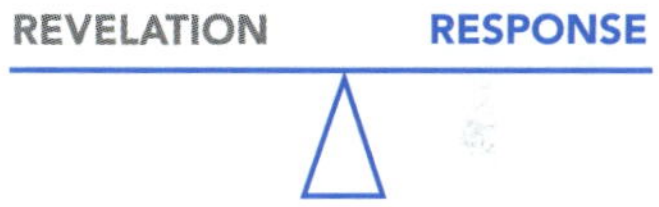

Balancing revelation and response

Looking at what might be considered the template of a standard Salvation Army meeting,[38] we see a comparatively small amount of time given to the **worshipers' response (Response and Sending)** to **God's revelation** (Gathering and Word).

Praise Band (3 songs)	Gathering
Announcements/Offering	Sending/Response
Welcome/Call to Worship	Gathering
Prayer	Gathering
Song	?
Scripture	Word
Drama/Solo/Testimony	Gathering/Word/Response
Songsters/Band Selection	?
Sermon	Word
Invitation/Song	Response
Benediction	Sending

In this model (other than the announcements and offering time and the possible inclusion of a testimony) the opportunity for worshipers to respond to the challenge and revelation of *God's Word* follows the sermon almost exclusively. And that is if the officer chooses to make an appeal or use a sending-out song. The abundance of *Gathering* elements reflects the *pew potato* posture (see Chapter One, pp. 32–33) of many churchgoers who wait for worship leaders "to entertain, even bless me."

As worship leaders, we then spend an inordinate amount of energy bringing our congregants "into" worship, or as is sometimes heard, "preparing them to meet with God." This imbalance sharply contrasts with the vibrant expressions of our evangelical movement. From its inception it was response-driven, not only deliberating with extended altar calls, but allowing manifold opportunities for singing and testimony in *response* to the moving of the Holy Spirit.

A FOURFOLD PATTERN FOR WORSHIP

The Gathering — The Word — Response — The Sending
REVELATION — RESPONSE

BALANCING

REVELATION | RESPONSE

More than an "hour on Sunday?"

Our "spectator clocks" have been conditioned by television to go off at the hour mark … The exception is if we are given the opportunity to interact, where we lose track of time … If those we lead in worship have a sense of being rushed or pushed in their process of personal interaction with God, they shut down and revert to being spectators. But if they have a sense of being nurtured into worship … they will likely let down their defenses and allow God to work … It takes time to do business with God.

—Sally Morgenthaler

Changin' it up (a little at a time)

The following meeting outline seeks to balance multiple opportunities for response over the course of the meeting. It does break a few taboos. For instance, the praise band offers just one song at the start, but this allows the praise band to help facilitate a response as part of the appeal and sending out following the sermon.

Praise Band (1 song)	**Gathering**
Call to Worship	**Gathering**
Drama	**Word**
Response Song	**Word/Response**
Solo	**Response**
Prayer	**Response**
Songsters/Band Selection	*****
Sermon	**Word**
3 Songs	**Response**
Announcements/Offering	**Sending/Response**
Benediction	**Sending**
Benediction Song	**Sending**

*Peggy Thomas suggests that the music and arts sections can with some imagination (while seeking to appeal to multiple senses—sight, sound, touch, etc.) fulfill or support any of the components of an effective worship service, including the sermon, Scripture, prayer, and invitation.

With fifty-two Sundays in a year, it is easy for ideas to get old quickly and the order of service to look quite identical from week to week.[39] Being consistent in our preparation week in and week out can be challenging. Despite the obstacles, I have observed and experienced marvelous partnerships between corps officers and their musician-artists. These happy confluences resulted from hours of dreaming, prayer, dialogue, planning, and rehearsal.

I have also experienced Sundays where communication, imagination, and forethought were severely lacking. Officers can avoid this by sharing their best intentions for a meeting, particularly in regard to message content. A brief conversation or communication can enlighten others on the worship committee. Suggestions can then be made to enhance worship. Mutuality develops as the musicians become versatile enough to anticipate the officers' stream of thinking. In exchange, growing expectation and trust are garnered among the officers, the ministry team, and the congregation.

THE REHEARSAL LEADER'S TOOLBOX—Working the Plan

Seasonal rehearsal planning

Repertoire selection is key! Having just the right musical offerings for each Sunday is an on-going challenge. If an ensemble or worship team embraces a selection because of its depth or appropriateness to an occasion, the music leader's work in rehearsal is eased. Selecting music well in advance makes the rehearsal leader's job in the weekly practices less stressful. Many music and worship leaders divide the rehearsal year into two terms: September through December and then January through May. Four considerations aid effective repertoire selection over a term:

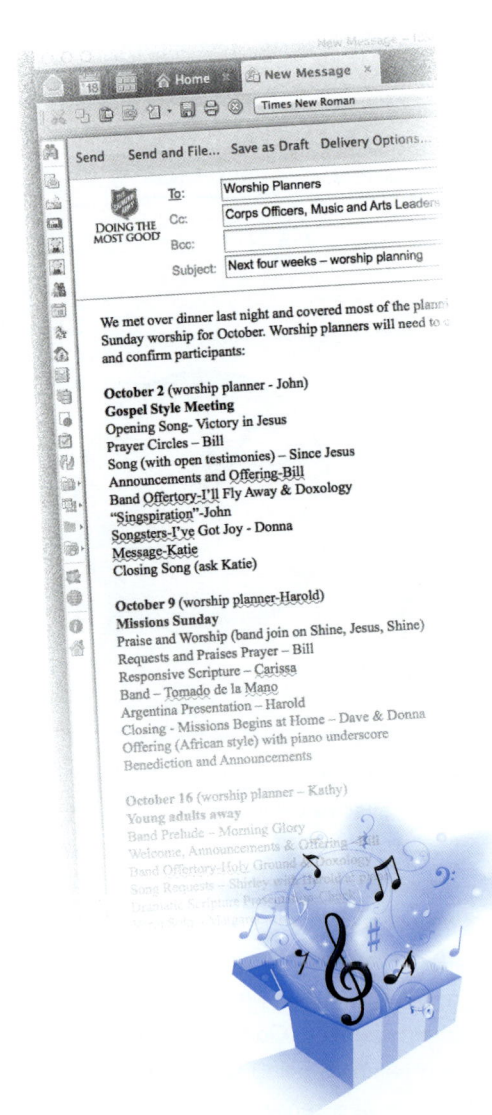

1. The "church" calendar
The worship team can first identify the Sundays for which holidays will be observed. These include: Thanksgiving, Advent, Christmas, Lent, Palm Sunday, Easter, Mother's Day, Father's Day, and Memorial Day.

2. Salvation Army observances
Next the team identifies Salvation Army program-related Sundays. Examples are: Rally Day, Harvest Festival, Music Sunday, World Services Ingathering, women's or men's emphasis, or Corps Cadet/Junior Soldier Sundays where the youth plan and carry out most of the meeting.

3. Sermon series
The officer-speaker can help by providing themes for an upcoming sermon series and other isolated Sundays. The music leaders can then begin to look for pieces best suited for those Sundays. Together they can bring ideas to the periodic worship committee meeting to carve out a six-to-eight week plan for upcoming worship services.

4. Special meetings or upcoming concerts
The corps officers and worship team are wise to take into account any other events or concerts your groups may be working toward, and in what season. It is a good discipline to work from a theme and stick to it.

Salvation Army/Holiday Observances

September 10	Sunday School Promotion
October 7	Homecoming
October 2	Senior Soldier Day of Renewal
November 4	Corps Cadet Sunday
November 18	Thanksgiving Sunday / Junior Soldier Enrollment
December	Advent Series

Weekly Corps Band Spring Schedule

2/20	Spiritual Medley as singalong
2/27	Just As I Am/There is a Redeemer
3/6	Breathe/Turn Your Eyes Upon Jesus
3/13	Lord Make Calvary (Pendel Brass away)
3/20	(Corps Retreat) Jason – Give Me Jesus solo, Gospel John (for fun) and Here At the Cross
3/25	(Tenebrae) What Wondrous Love (with video) When I Survey
3/27	(Easter)He is Risen/He is Lord Closing song – Thine is the Glory

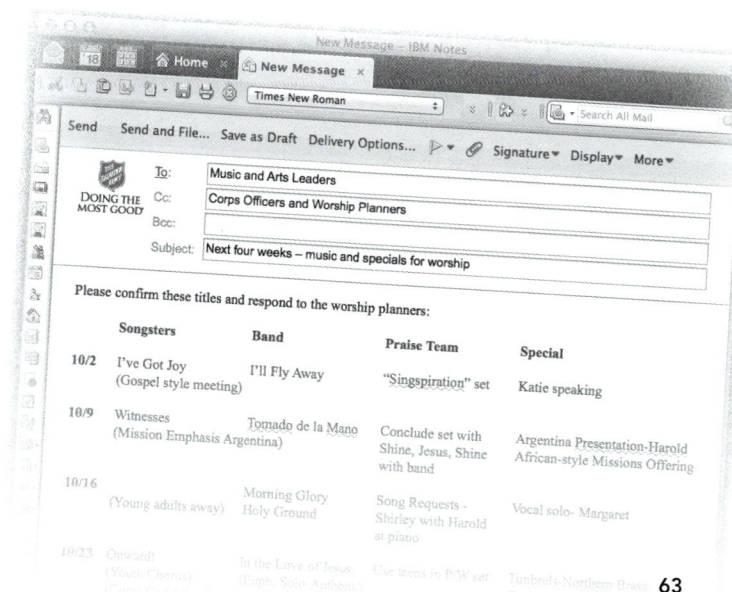

Failing to plan is planning to fail

Chances are very high that you'll see this little title again in this book! I wonder where that is? Umm maybe back on page 51 of this chapter?

Once the list of selections for Sunday worship and other performances for a term has been established, the next step is for the music leaders to map out realistic rehearsal objectives over a period of weeks. This means honestly assessing the group's ability to absorb the projected list and carefully calculating the rehearsal time available. **Plan two or three weeks rehearsal time per selection for adults, and four to six weeks for children.**

There is nothing wrong with choosing simpler music with quick rehearsal turnover or repeating songs to balance the time needed for more difficult selections. On the other hand, you may have to abandon or put off some more challenging works because there just isn't enough rehearsal time available to be ready when needed. Hold in reserve a few easy, backup pieces for Sunday absences related to divisional/territorial events or holidays. Senior sections are given a little breathing room when youth music sections take responsibility for the music for meetings on a periodic basis.

Break down the plan into weekly doses

Once music and worship leaders have settled on the repertoire for a term, they begin to envision a corresponding plan of attack for rehearsals over the long term. One well-known bandmaster rehearses items in four-week cycles. **He lays out a four-week grid to completely prepare his next concert over four rehearsals.**[40]

It is impossible to cover a full program every rehearsal, so he may slot a march or solo accompaniment for weeks two and four. A devotional selection may be slotted for weeks one and two and used on the Sunday following. The major works should be rehearsed every week, but perhaps covering just isolated sections in detail. Carefully come up with a strategy over the long term.

The final week before a performance (in this case, the Week 4 Rehearsal) limits the time for "nitty-gritty" work, giving more attention to a run-through of the program.

FOUR-WEEK REHEARSAL PLAN GRID

The bold numbers [**6**] are a possible rehearsal order with an estimated time allotment [**10′**] for each piece.
The bold highlighted titles [***Morning Glory***] must be performance-ready for that coming Sunday worship or concert.

REPERTOIRE for upcoming 4 weeks	WEEK 1 REHEARSAL ready for October 2	WEEK 2 REHEARSAL ready for October 9	WEEK 3 REHEARSAL ready for October 16	WEEK 4 REHEARSAL ready for October 23
Morning Glory	**6** *Morning Glory* 10′ (back half)	**7** *Morning Glory* 10′ (front half)	**2 *Morning Glory*** 10′ (finish for Sunday)	
I'll Fly Away	**2** *I'll Fly Away* 10′ (finish, play down)			**6** *I'll Fly Away* 10′ (review for concert)
Tomado de la Mano	**4** *Tomado* 15′ (transitions from back)	**3 *Tomado de la Mano*** 10′ (finish)		**8** *Tomado de la Mano* 10′ (review)
Holy Ground		**1** *Holy Ground* 10′ (overview, work transitions)	**3 *Holy Ground*** 10′ (finish)	
St. Clements Variations	**7** *St. Clements* 10′ (final section)	**6** *St. Clements* 15′ (front two variations)	**4** *St. Clements* 15′ (work back half, review opening)	**3 *St. Clements*** 15′ (play down, review trouble-spots)
The King	**3** *The King* 15′ (overview)	**2** *The King* 10′ (by section)	**8** *The King* 10′ (details, spot check)	**4** *The King* (review) 10′
In the Love of Jesus (Euph. Solo)			**6** *In the Love* 10′ (euph. solo overview)	**2** *In the Love* 8′ (finish)
Northern Brass		*Northern Brass* 10′ (overview)	**7** *Northern Brass* 10′ (work from back)	***Northern Brass*** 12′ (finish, rehearse with timbrels)
Song Accompaniments	**1** *Victory in Jesus* (2+1) *Since Jesus* (2+1) *Closing Song* _____ 10′	**4** *Shine, Jesus, Shine* 5′ (with praise team)	**1** *Closing Song* _____ 5′	**1** *Closing Song* _____ 5′
Devotions/ Announcements	**5** Chapter 2a (John) 20′	**5** Chapter 2b (Katie) 20′	**5** Chapter 3a (Dave) 20′	**5** Chapter 3b (Emma) 20′

A plan of attack

Next, music leaders hone in on a **plan for the weekly rehearsal**. Factors such as anticipated absence or lateness, the time it takes a group to become focused, and the deadlines for that week weigh heavily on the rehearsal order. Estimate the time and rehearsal placement best suited to work through each piece. The pace of the rehearsal should vary in style and tempo to keep interest high.

Music sections, be it worship band, brass band, or songsters, are well advised to commence and conclude rehearsals with moderately demanding pieces. Rehearse the most challenging music in the early to middle of the rehearsal when musicians are likely to be most receptive and attentive. Aim to get things absolutely correct early on, including the piece's style. Allowing compromises with dynamics, phrasing, articulation, expression, (or wrong notes!) are difficult to unlearn. Pace is crucial. For instance, an extended amount of work on a series of slow devotional songs will tire the singer's voices quickly. Here is one possible rhythm for an adult rehearsal:

1. Old material/Warm-ups—Gathering time/Just get going! (bright)

2. New material—Go easy on the detail (devotional)

3. Current material—Hard, nitty-gritty work (polish)*

4. New material—Just read, get overview (keep relaxed)

5. Old material—Spot-check transitions or selected trouble spots and then sing or play Sunday's songs on the platform, creating a confident finish.*

*Some groups include devotions, prayer, and announcements as a break about two-thirds through rehearsal. Others prefer it at the conclusion.

2 BARS REST

1. Consider ways that seasonal or term planning can benefit your week-to-week rehearsal regimen. Look for ways to more efficiently manage the rehearsal time available, yet be properly prepared for Sunday worship or a concert.

2. Plan an evening's rehearsal of current repertoire at your corps. Stick to the time constraints you currently have. Carefully craft the rehearsal sequence and strategies to maximize effectiveness.

Worship – A Jewel on the Crest?[41]

Over half a century ago, A.W. Tozer famously described worship as "the missing jewel of the evangelical church." The remainder of Tozer's statement is less familiar, but well worth considering as Salvationists: "We're organized; we work; we have our agendas. We have almost everything, but there's one thing that the churches, even the gospel churches, do not have: that is the ability to worship. We are not cultivating the art of worship. It's the one shining gem that is lost to the modern church, and I believe we ought to search for this until we find it."⁴²

As Salvationists, we should not be pulling out of the parking lot on Sunday wondering if we have met with God. Something significant can happen each Sunday if we worship in spirit and in truth, reach out to our people with intentionality, and seek moments of transcendence. Worship is not only the ultimate purpose for which we were created, it must be the vital lifeline to all that we do as a movement. Yes, "the service begins as soon as the meeting is over." As one benediction has it, "Go in peace and *serve* the Lord."

Is the search for the missing jewel still on in The Salvation Army today? That's a question worth asking each and every Sunday.

? 2 BARS REST

1. In Psalm 69:9, David wrote, "Zeal for your house consumes me." Ask yourself, "How is my zeal for God's church? Is my passion for the Bride of Christ increasing or waning from Sunday to Sunday?"

2. Are you intentional in your worship planning? Do you have a worship committee that regularly looks at the effectiveness and flow of the worship service? How can we best communicate with each other to keep everybody on the same page?

3. Have your worship services remained fresh and vibrant? Is there a vehicle for a free flow of ideas? How could the exchange of ideas be improved? Survey the sample worship planning models and meeting plans found in Appendix 2.1. Glean ideas that may benefit your corps' Sunday worship.

WORSHIP DESIGN RESOURCES

Alternative Worship: *Resources from and for the Emerging Church*, Johnny Baker et. al. (Baker Book House). Includes resource CD.

Designing Worship Teams: *Discovering and Birthing the Drama of Twenty-First Century Worship*, Cathy Townley (Abingdon Press)

God's Singers—The Worship-Leading Choir, Dave Williamson (in:ciite media), available in leader's or singer's versions.

Emerging Worship: *Creating Worship Gatherings for New Generations*, Dan Kimball (Zondervan)

Five Keys to Engaging Worship, John Chisum (Engage Press)

In His Presence: *Appreciating Your Worship Tradition*, Robert Schaper (Thomas Nelson)

Praying Twice: *The Music and Words of Congregational Song*, Brian Wren (Westminster/John Knox Press)

The Worship Architect: *A Blueprint for Designing Culturally Relevant and Biblically Faithful Services*, Constance Cherry (Baker)

The Worship Workshop: *Creative Ways to Design Worship Together*, Marcia McFee, (Abington Press)

Taking Flight with Creativity: *Worship Design Teams that Work*, Len Wilson and Jason Moore (Abingdon Press)

The Words We Sing, Nan Corbitt Allen (Beacon Hill Press)

TOOLS FOR WORSHIP

Hallelujah Choruses CD/DVD congregational accompaniment tracks.
  For more information, see The Salvation Army Brass Band Publications listing at the conclusion of Chapter Fourteen.
Hymn Tune CDs—The Chicago Staff Band and Norridge Citadel bands have recorded 218 melodies from the *Salvation Army Tune Book* onto 12 CDs for congregational use.
Salvation Army Song Book, including comprehensive thematic, metric, and Scripture references, as well as word and tune searches and applications. (The Salvation Army)
Salvation Army Tune Book, in miniature 1st cornet tune book or piano version. (The Salvation Army)
The Worship Sourcebook, John Witvliet and Emily Brink, eds. (Baker Book House)

Sunday morning worship, Oruro, Bolivia.

The Music Man

Hey Dorothy!

Sup Harry B!

There's lots more we could say about Sunday worship.

No worries man.

What should we do?

Readers will get the down-low about enabling music in worship in other chapters.

Awesome sauce! =D

Peace out H Burger!

The Beat Goes On

CHAPTER THREE

HAND ME DOWN *MY* SILVER TRUMPET
Making Things Happen at Your Corps

By God's mighty power at work within us, we are able to do far more than we would ever dare to ask or even dream of—infinitely beyond our highest prayers, desires, thoughts and hopes. (Ephesians 3:20, Living Bible)

THE NEW SONG GROWS UP IN THE SHADE OF THE OLD!

The year is 1524. The place is the home of Martin Luther, the great Protestant Reformer. Two eminent musicians of the time, Conrad Rupff and Johann Walther, were Luther's house guests for three weeks. The German biographer Kostlin depicts the trio at work:

> While Walther and Rupff sat at the table, bending over music sheets with pen in hand, Father Luther walked up and down the room, trying on the fife [a type of flute] the tunes that poured from his memory and his imagination to ally themselves with the poems he had discovered, until he had made the verse-melody rhythmically finished, well-rounded, strong and compactly whole.

In **Chapter Three**, we:
- discover "hammering techniques" to help dream, and design a music and arts school for *your* corps.
- survey models of music and arts schools.
- consider essential steps for starting and growing a music and arts program at *your* corps.
- examine four magnets that draw participants into a program, and essential steps for maintaining rehearsal and classroom discipline.

Luther's manuscript of "A Mighty Fortress is Our God"

LUTHER AND THE PEOPLE'S SONG

In the history of Protestant church music, this was an historic moment! The Reformation had opened the floodgates to the use of one's native tongue in Scripture, and now song! Within five years, Luther had brought the world's first musical press to Wittenberg. Soon the first vernacular mass and congregational hymn-book was available to German worshipers, an outward expression of the priesthood of *all* believers.

Luther, no less a musician than a theologian, did not stop there. He required every parish to have a cantor [song/choir leader], organist, choir school, and body of trained singers and instrumentalists. As a result of Luther's visionary church music education scheme, Germany became the most musically educated nation in Europe, spawning the later glories of Bach, Haydn, Mozart, Beethoven, and Brahms.[1]

> "Secular music, do you say, belongs to the devil? Does it? Well, if it did I would plunder him for it, for he has no right to a single note... Every note, strain, and harmony is divine, and belong to us."
>
> —William Booth

Booth robs the devil of his best tunes[2]

To bring this into Salvation Army context, most of us are familiar with the Founder's attraction to popularist melodies, which were prudently appropriated from the music hall, minstrel troupes, sentimental ballads, and American civil war or gospel songs.[3] Known by a large portion of the audience, they could be sung, in the Founder's words "right off, without any loss of time."[4] Like Luther, the Founder placed great value on corporate singing, especially as the familiar tunes married to sacred texts gained a ready entrance "for the sentiments which we want to convey to their hearts."[5]

As did Luther, the visionary Booth looked beyond the moment. As early as 1880, Booth advocated for a mass movement of musical engagement, interestingly not confined to brass instruments, nor to males:

> "We do here express our desire that as many of our officers and soldiers generally, *male and female*, as have the ability for so doing, *shall learn to play on some instrument*. This includes violins, bass viols, concertinas, cornets, or any brass instrument, drums, or anything else that will make a pleasant sound for the Lord."[6]

Within a decade of the Founder's "order," Richard Slater, head of the newly formed Musical Department, was checking proofs for instrumental tutors for the cornet, euphonium and bombardon (Eb Bass). The completed series included manuals for clarinet, concertina, autoharp, piano, drums and fifes, soprano cornet, tenor horn, baritone [horn], Bb trombone, bass trombone, and drums.[7] From these roots, The Salvation Army's ongoing music education initiative was birthed. By Booth's seventy-fifth birthday in 1904, there were as many as 17,000 Salvationist bandsmen worldwide.[8] Within Slater's lifetime, by 1927 the 1,000th Salvation Army brass band was celebrated in Great Britain.[9] Today, hundreds of thousands participate in Salvation Army music-making in over 125 countries.

Richard Slater with Fred Fry and Henry Hill, the Salvation Army's first music department.

To the next generation and beyond!

It is our good fortune today that we follow in this legacy of church music education. While Luther was referring to styles of music, he did not "permit the old wood to be cut down, recognizing the new song must grow up in the shade of the old." May we today, with the urgency and vision of these church reformers, also learn how to refashion the old, and even invent something new. In so doing, the beat goes on!

MOSES AND THE HANDMADE TRUMPETS

This pattern of refashioning the old to provoke effective means in the moment has a long history. In Numbers 10:1–2 we read that the Lord instructed Moses, "Make two silver trumpets for yourself; you shall make them of hammered work; you shall use them for calling the congregation and for directing the movement of the camps." *(NKJV)* God's instructions are purposeful and personal. He tells Moses that the trumpets would summon the people together, for worship and battle, or tell the people when to pull themselves together and get ready to move again. Secondly, Moses is not to hire someone to make these trumpets. He is not to rent, borrow, or use a ready-made trumpet. The Lord's command is for Moses to hammer out the two trumpets himself. A guild of priestly musicians would learn to blow them until they clearly sounded out the required message. (Numbers 10:8)

There are "trumpets" for sale everywhere. Model after-school programs, groundbreaking curriculum, or exemplary choral and instrumental ensembles have been forged and hammered out by others. They are readily available from conferences, catalogs, Christian bookstores, or other churches. We are tempted to copy and paste them into our own corps music ministry program but each of us must hammer out our own trumpet. You are called to clearly signal your people to come together and prepare them to become music ministers. Take from this chapter some "hammering" techniques. Listen, watch, and learn. Don't just buy into someone else's ready-made plan. Why? Because it won't fit. Dream. Then take your dreams to God. Let God reshape the dream to make it His plan.[10]

3 BARS REST

Consider dreams you have for your corps, The Salvation Army, or yourself. Believe that one person can make things happen, then picture an avenue of ministry the Lord has placed on your heart. Begin to articulate and share this vision. Go ahead and dream. Dream your biggest dreams. Ephesians 3:20 says that when you dream big, you can be sure that God's dreams are even bigger!

> "God called you to a life of purpose far beyond what you think yourself capable of living, and promised you adequate strength to fulfill your destiny."
> —Eugene Peterson

SALLIE SALVOS

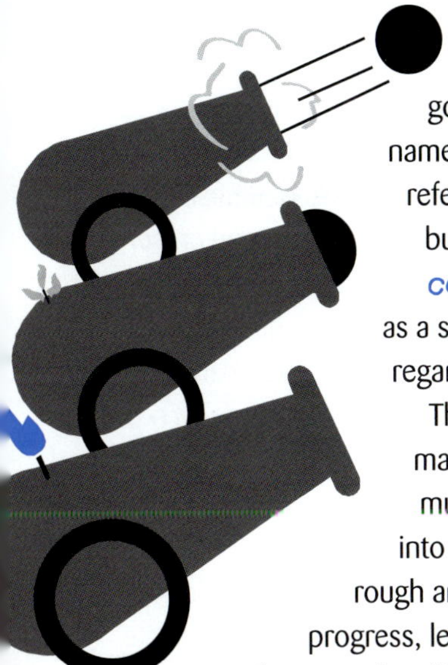

The Salvation Army's mission is "to preach the gospel of Jesus Christ and meet human needs in His name without discrimination." The term discrimination refers not only to race, gender, and economic status, but also to age. Jesus himself said, "Let the children come to me." Plato wrote that it is our responsibility as a society to allow children to develop their talents, regardless of the class to which they are born.

The Salvation Army in this postmodern age offers manifold opportunities for using art, drama, dance, and music to attract youth and incorporate their efforts into worship of their Creator. When the going gets a little rough and we wonder if our young students are making any progress, let's keep in mind that the S's on our tunics can stand for more than "Saved to Serve." From the earliest days, soldiers in Booth's Army understood that they were "engaged in a terrific battle against sin, and were expected to do their share of fighting in the salvation war. Music came to be seen as an appropriate weapon in such warfare."[11] In the United Kingdom and Down Under, Salvationists are sometimes colloquially called "Salvos." This label suits Salvationists well in its original meaning as "a simultaneous discharge of guns."[12] We engage the enemy on a number of fronts with these seven salvos that use Salvation Army music and arts to positively impact the lives of young people today.

1. Social work in our corps halls

Involvement in youth music and arts ensembles at The Salvation Army is a social work in that it allows opportunities for young people to be exposed to the Gospel through personal interaction and song content. This is particularly true of verses based on Scripture texts. Think of a song you learned as a child, the words of which you probably can still remember today. Luther, Wesley, and Booth seized every opportunity to pass on doctrinal truths through song.

We also provide a structured focus to the lives of many young people. The fruits of learned skills—disciplined daily practice, teamwork, development of reading skills, and intentional mentoring—yield life-long results.

2. Superior music education

The Salvation Army offers quality music and arts instruction in many corps, even as many schools are defaulting in music and arts education. The Salvation Army offers not only instrumental and vocal instruction, but often also timbrel, mime, drama, and dance experiences. This is coupled with Christian education, such as Junior Soldier or Corps Cadet classes. Many fine, well-known churches do not give their young people this blended opportunity and we do it without charge!

Our instrumental music resources, in particular, are respected worldwide. This is yet another reason why we should not apologize or have an inferiority complex about our youth and music programming. School music directors love "Sallie-trained" musicians.

3. Sacrifice of praise

Performing in youth music and arts ensembles gives young people a weekly obligation to offer a sacrifice of praise in worship. In our Salvationist military jargon, we call this being "on duty." Young people are busy preparing and presenting their gifts in worship, bringing expectation and expression to their worship experience. To this end, we need to encourage leaders to use our young singers, timbrelists, dancers, and instrumentalists as active participants in weekly worship. The challenge with young people is to move the focus away from a performance mentality toward a call to minister to the Lord Himself and then to others.

4. Sharing with family

When we include children in the worship service, we create opportunities to invite and reach family members. In some corps, the child is not permitted to perform a solo without a family member present. In addition to our goal of exposing the child's family to the presentation of the Gospel, the family sees the child's progress and the Army's influence on his or her life. Parents will then be more apt to encourage home practice and seek out other Army ministries for themselves.

Building parental interaction and trust is paramount. Sharing a report on a child's progress builds bridges. Persuade parents to come when their child is on duty. According to George Barna, many churches enroll children in their programs and may

Three generations of banding together: Robert, John, and Zachary Doctor, members of the Pasadena Tabernacle Band.

not even seek to make contact with the family. A majority of churchgoing parents lack the spiritual inclination or sense of urgency to set the bar any higher than enabling their children to get to church activities. The irony is that "four out of five parents (85 per cent) believe they have the primary responsibility for the moral and spiritual development of their children, yet more than two out of three of them abdicate this responsibility to the church."[13] Nurture an ongoing dialogue and partnership with parents. As one director of children's ministry put it, "Our goal is to become the greatest friend and best support a parent has ever had."[14]

To secure our investment with young people, target parental involvement. Parents can be asked to help with fund-raisers, distribute flyers, check uniforms, prepare snacks, and more. Follow-up home visits will delight your young students and begin to build trust with caregivers. Once or twice a year, hold a corps junior music recital for which each student is required to prepare a solo. Invite a guest soloist as a model. Choose a great song or dance item to present the Gospel clearly. Be sure folks leave understanding why The Salvation Army seeks to train children in ministry.

5. Special opportunities

Salvationist musicians and artists have many opportunities for extending their experience and sphere of friends, including regional and divisional music days, music camps, conservatories, competitions, territorial arts and music camps, and regional music schools. These initiate and perpetuate music and arts ministry. *Divisional ensembles work best under the premise that young people are consistent in their service to their corps.* The Salvation Army also offers more and more leadership training opportunities that aim to strengthen local corps ministry. (This will be discussed more fully in Chapter Four.)

Pendel Singers: *Face to Face* recording, 1998.

6. Standards and seasons

There are occasions where we fail in getting our young people to a level of competence so that as teens they are not embarrassed by their lack of skill. *Many secretly desire to sing well enough to eventually function commendably in the songsters or worship team.* Look for opportunities to work on the singer's skills together.

Major Jim Farrell grew up in a boy's home for orphans in New York City, and knew what it was like to feel alone. "What saved me growing up were the frequent visits by The Salvation Army to the boy's home," Farrell said. "More specifically, it was the fact that The Salvation Army taught me how to play a horn and eventually that became my ticket out of trouble."

Take time to teach the basics of tone matching, vocal production, and music reading while children are young. Eliminate the fear of flying!

Mistakes, even rebellious behavior, happen. Seasons of unsatisfactory involvement, attitude, and faith-walk on the part of some developing artists are unfortunately inevitable. Leaders learn to tread carefully while waiting out the heartache. *Sometimes tough love is required.* Most important, be readily available to talk things out.

7. Structure, love, and prayer

Kids need structure and discipline. Do not cancel rehearsals. Be there for them. Make a conscious decision not to accept second best. It is a compromise of your love standard.

Be patient and work step by step.
This is the very act of discipleship!

Love the children through your consistent work at the corps. Set *short-term* week-to-week goals with practice sheets. Ask weekly how practice went. Record and praise progress. Re-teach the difficult concepts and answer children's questions. Follow through on *long-term* seasonal goals with persistent method bookwork, recital solos, evaluations, and scholarship incentives.

We cannot underestimate the power of praying for every child in our sphere of influence. *Pray* for every kid. *Pray* often. *Pray* specifically.

3 BARS REST

Reflect on the seven Sallie Salvos listed above as you consider the Apostle Paul's counsel to the Corinthians written nearly two thousand years ago:

Remember: A stingy planter gets a stingy crop; a lavish planter gets a lavish crop. I want each of you to take plenty of time to think it over, and make up your own mind what you will give. That will protect you against sob stories and arm-twisting. God loves it when the giver delights in the giving.

God can pour on the blessings in astonishing ways so that you're ready for anything and everything, more than just ready to do what needs to be done...This most generous God who gives seed to the farmer that becomes bread for your meals is more than extravagant with you. He gives you something you can then give away, which grows into full-formed lives, robust in God, wealthy in every way, so that you can be generous in every way, producing with us great praise to God.

Carrying out this social relief work involves far more than helping meet the bare needs of poor Christians. It also produces abundant and bountiful thanksgivings to God. This relief offering is a prod to live at your very best, showing your gratitude to God by being openly obedient to the plain meaning of the Message of Christ.

—2 Corinthians 9:6-8, 10-12, *The Message*

JOEY'S ADVENTURE IN SOUND

Joey heard the music through the window. He heard young voices and various instruments start, stop, and repeat bits over and over. Some of it didn't sound that terrific. He paused and listened for a while. How he wished he could get into that building without being noticed and just watch. He ventured around to the front of the building and peered through the front door. The outside door opened, but he found himself confronted with a second security door. He pushed the button next to the door, with no response. The lights were out in the nearby office. He wondered how these kids got in.

Just then a uniformed gentleman walked by the glass door and popped the door open, apparently reasoning that Joey was late to the youth band rehearsal. "How we doin' today?" he said, not waiting for an answer. "You better get moving. You're pretty late for band practice." Joey headed toward the room where the sound was coming from and peeked through the window in the door. In a semicircle of chairs sat a mixture of boys and girls, some tall, some short, some really young and some teens, all holding instruments. When the leader stopped, Joey found it odd that some peered at the leader, while others engaged in chatter, and even a bit of laughter. All of a sudden, one girl leaped up from her seat and headed toward the door. Joey had been discovered.

3 BARS REST

Where do new students come from in your corps situation? Is the community and corps community aware of your program? What obstacles exist to new children or adults joining your groups? How do you lose members? Ask yourself honestly what keeps the kids coming week to week. Is everyone included? What exceptions are made for those with special needs or the "overcommitted," often the most gifted? How successful are the kids at achieving personal progress?

MUSIC AND ARTS SCHOOL MODELS

Let's look at some models of successful Salvation Army corps music and arts programs, to glean aspects that will help hammer out a structure best suited to *your* corps.

Model #1 Community-based

Neighborhood children are recruited annually to the community-based music and dance school through word of mouth in the neighborhood, a simple flyer, and the annual rally day. A successful recital can go a long way in recruitment. Among the tables at the Saturday afternoon rally day is a music table, where young people are invited to try instruments, view a performance video, and meet the music staff. Children who are already participating in after-school music can help at your table by encouraging the visitors to give the program a try.

A typical afternoon of music instruction includes a rotation of theory, sightsinging, and percussion for rhythmic reading, as well as opportunities in brass, percussion, voice, piano, and guitar. Students progress from the beginner's group (Band C) to intermediate (Band B) and advanced groups (Band A). Refer to Chapter Six, p. 141 and Chapter Eight, pp. 169–170 for more on graded models. Following a supper break, there can be opportunities for Christian education, such as junior soldiers and corps cadets, before the senior songster and band rehearsals. Two recitals a year and periodic Sunday performance requirements bridge parents and students into the corps worship and fellowship.

Model #2 Link to after-school program

Music and dance is offered to the weekday after-school population one or two afternoons a week as a part of the structured curriculum. A foundational rotation in small groups covers music theory, sight-singing, piano and brass lessons, finishing with ensemble rehearsals. The program runs from an hour and a half to two hours twice a week. Funding linked to the after-school program allows for the hiring of young Salvationists to teach, creating a link to the congregation at large. The after-school brass concentration is purposely positioned on the same afternoon as the corps music rehearsals.

Model #3 Traditional flavor

Youth music and arts rehearsals are held as soon as possible after school. Following a supper break, senior rehearsals take place. The evening of choice seems to be Wednesday—halfway between Sundays. This gives the worship planners a little breathing room, as Tuesday can come so quickly. Some rehearsals happen on Thursdays and Fridays, although the latter never in football country! Doing youth music rehearsals on Friday evenings separately from the senior rehearsal night allows more time to work with the children, as it is not a school night. This could easily then segue into youth group. The negative of Fridays is that in a corps, there are typically numerous weekend events, which may preclude the attendance of instructors and use of the van. Many corps run a Bible study, craft class, women's, or men's club simultaneously with rehearsals to make it more of a family night.

Model #4 Jumpstart regional music schools

Several corps join together on a regular basis and share music instructors for a season or two. This approach can be effective in areas with corps at close proximity. There is the difficulty of performing on Sunday morning as ensembles, although the region may already have a monthly Sunday afternoon or evening praise meeting. Create opportunities to celebrate student progress. The goal is to widen the teaching base after a season or two and eventually allow the corps to run its own music program. A new corps plant can benefit from a similar plan by having young people participate in the music program of an established corps (sometimes already meeting in the same facility) until their own local leaders can be developed.

Model #5 Sunday commuters

To facilitate youth music instruction in a "commuter" corps, where families are unlikely to make another long commute to the corps, a fellowship luncheon follows Sunday morning worship. A tightly structured youth band and choir program follows, including instruction in timbrels, computer-assisted theory, singing company, gym time, and Bible study. Parents assist in leadership of the program or are engaged in small group Bible studies. Families are on their way home by 3:00. On the first Sunday of the month, called Celebration Sunday, all the youth music groups participate in a 45-minute Sunday school program, which draws other children and parents who do not normally attend Sunday school. A variant on this plan has the youth music and arts program on Saturday mornings.

Chapter 3 | HAND ME DOWN *MY* SILVER TRUMPET

Model #6 The yuppie model

With both parents working through the afternoon, youngsters cannot get to the corps until after supper. Interested band locals offer youth music instruction during the songster rehearsal time. In this way families arrive together and spouses not involved in the senior band rehearsal can get their children home at a decent hour. The youth band—a step up from the beginner band—plays for Sunday school opening weekly with the singing company contributing periodically.

Model #7 All that jazz

Opportunities in ballet, tap, and jazz are offered on an afternoon into early evening, separate from music instruction. Classes are organized by age and ability. Dance soloists and groups are frequent contributors to Sunday worship. A choreodrama team (a form of story-telling that mixes mime, sacred dance, and drama) meets on Sunday afternoons just before the evening service.

Model #8 Kroc Centers and beyond

Music and dance is offered *every* weekday afternoon and evening, as well as all day Saturday over the fall and spring semesters. A summer session offers instruction during the mornings as well. Most students receive weekly lessons, but some receive instruction following the highly successful *El Sistema* model. This has the same instrumental students in sectionals and full ensemble rehearsals for two hours every weekday afternoon. Opportunities for private lessons, solo, and group performance are foundational. Building this kind of music school permits qualified teachers to build their own studios and a corresponding fee structure with scholarship options. Teachers need to strongly support the mission of the center and The Salvation Army.

Model #9 Private lesson studios

In exchange for teaching other youngsters, teens and young adults are given a weekly private lesson by top-rate teachers. Some of these lessons are subsidized 50% to allow the highest quality instruction for these teens. This initiative aids the music school organizer in covering students on the corps rehearsal day and allows these apprentice teachers continued personal development. Teacher training workshops held the first week of September and January equip these young instructors to be more effective as teachers as they progress on their instruments.

Apprentice is mentored

Apprentice becomes the mentor

3 BARS REST

Consider which specific attributes of these models might be most beneficial in your corps setting.

The Beat Goes On

PREPARATION IS EVERYTHING!

Let's consider **ten steps** to starting and growing a music or arts program at your corps.

Step 1. Strengths and dreams. Begin by listing the positive attributes of your corps' music program. If no program is in place yet, look at the individual possibilities, such as a pool of young people or possible leaders. Next, note ways that your corps might capitalize on these strengths in terms of music and arts. Make a list of short and long-term goals. Some might piggyback off corps strengths. For example, a choir can be created with youngsters who are already in a latchkey program, then they can be bridged into the corps.

Step 2. Meet with corps leaders to strategize how and when specific activities can happen. Explore interfacing of scheduling with other corps activities such as after-school programs or Christian education opportunities, like Corps Cadets or Junior Soldiers. Carefully assemble the leadership team. Involve willing hands with even nominal skills, including teens still developing in your program. Also look at contacts at local colleges and universities. Remember to do the necessary background checks as required by Salvation Army procedures. Establish entrance and practice policy with the use of forms for instrument use, any fees, or contracts for attendance and practice. Sample forms are included in the Appendix 3.1.

Strengths	Challenges
Corps location easy to attract children	Getting enough leaders to corps by 4:00
Great group of teens who could be trained as leader-helpers	Teens desiring private instruction need to get to Corps Cadets also
Sunday morning congregation very accepting of solos, singing company and beginner/youth band contributions	Getting children and teens to Sunday School and church (early, on time and in uniform!)
Good supply of instruments, method books, stands and music	Limited rehearsal and lesson locations because of after-school program
Food supplies and kitchen staff in place from after-school program	Most can only commit to one afternoon/evening a week

Many corps fine tune the music school timetable and associated teaching assignments with planning meetings held the first week of September and the first week of January, prior to the return to activities. We suggest limiting new enrollment to the beginning of October and February only, so that the schedule is only adjusted for newcomers twice in a season. This focuses the instruction in the month of September and January on the returning students, before the influx of new students necessitates amendments to the timetable.[15]

Chapter 3 | HAND ME DOWN *MY* SILVER TRUMPET

TUESDAY CORPS ACTIVITIES

4:00	Music Classes and Lessons
6:15	Supper Fellowship (for those remaining)
6:45	Women's Craft Time, Children's Hour, Junior Soldiers, Senior Songsters
7:45	Devotions (young people go home after devotions)
8:00	Senior Band (homework time for those remaining)

Step 3. Organize the program time period. Some after-school music programs require all participants to attend basic skills rotation classes, such as theory, sight-singing, and chorus. Some programs allow an additional option such as piano, drums, dance, or guitar, in addition to a principal brass instrument or singing. Your schedule should reflect your priorities and available help.

TUESDAY MUSIC SCHOOL

4:00	Basic Skills Rotations (20 minutes each)/ Theory, Sightsinging, Private Lessons
5:00	Youth Band Practice/ Beginner Private and Group Lessons
5:40	Singing Company/ Private Lessons for Teens
6:15	Supper Fellowship
6:45	Senior Music Activities begin/ Junior Soldier Classes

Step 4. Set a timetable to get things in place: instruments, stands and method books ready, start date, invitation letters, performance goals, leadership planning, and training meetings.

Step 5. Establish a pattern of making necessary adjustments in scheduling as students and groups make progress. Move on from mistakes. Develop a parental support team to help with supper, the library, uniforms, and classroom discipline.

Step 6. Clarify responsibilities for members in a team code of ethics. Establish few but clear rules. (More on this follows at the end of this chapter.) Give teachers a specific schedule, list of students, and job responsibilities. Help them keep the students' short- and long-term goals in the forefront to establish consistent week-to-week progress. For instance, short-term goals might be to complete a page a week in the method book and begin a new solo. Long-term achievements might be to finish a level and perform that solo by the end of the year.

READINESS TIMETABLE

Two months before	Schedule rally day to recruit new students
One month before	Fall planning meeting Announce and post start date Contact returning students Recruit and train support staff
Two weeks before	Ready stands and instruments Locate method books and junior band music Set start and cut-off date for new students
One week before	Give out teaching assignments Emphasize practice expectations
One hour before	Room set-up/Equipment readied
Start date	Get feedback from staff
Week following	Fine tune schedule Follow-up calls to missing students and parents

INDIVIDUAL TEACHER'S SCHEDULE

For Priscilla

4:00	Beginner Voice in Lower Hall
5:00	Beginner Lessons and Beginner Band (last 10 minutes) in Lower Hall
5:40	Singing Company in Chapel
6:15	Dismiss for Supper (store music in Band Room)

BIG, BIG NEWS!!

Your child is singing this coming Sunday at 11:00 a.m.

(DO NOT forget uniform)

You are welcome to invite family and bring your camera.

It will be a proud moment!

Step 7. Communicate, communicate, communicate! Greet parents at the door and give updates on their child's progress. Send home notes about upcoming recitals and special Sundays. Weekly announcements should be kept brief and to the point. Phone reminders to parents before events may be necessary, as well as inquiries after absence.

Step 8. Develop team thinking. Work for maximum cooperation within the team. Accentuate the positive. Spot problems and develop the best team solution.

Step 9. Recognition. Post student progress on charts in a hallway or music room. Award certificates and prizes for method book and level completion. Thank leaders publicly at recitals or with a special outing.

Step 10. Pray for each student, leader, worship service, and performance. Pray for faith to carry on with a consistent focus and vision.

The Beat Goes On

? 3 BARS REST

1. Consider ways to accomplish steps 1, 2, and 3 in your corps situation.

2. Take time to work through a set of goals, schedule, and action timetable for your corps music program.

THE YOUTH LEADER'S TOOLBOX

You get more with a kind word ... and consistency

Whether large corporation or sports franchise, no successful organization operates without expectations and boundaries. Young people are drawn and kept in our music and arts programs through four magnets.[16]

1. The magnet of success
Kids are drawn to quality. Begin with just two young people if that's all you have, but make sure their performances are something that will make the performers, you, and their caregivers proud.

2. The magnet of standards
If kids sense a high standard being set and kept, they will be drawn to it. In so doing we give them a taste of spiritual integrity. Judiciously choose music that will not come off as silly or embarrassing. Give them something good. Do not lower your standards in deference to their numbers or skills. Kids appreciate being challenged and drawn up to music outside their own world.

3. The magnet of friendship
Young people want to relate to each other and earn the respect of their instructors. Reach out and touch with your interest and listening ear. Others will see the closeness and want to be a part of the "family."

4. The magnet of consistency
Make it your goal not to cancel or come unprepared. Start and end on time. Consistency is essential to young people growing up in uncertain environments.

? 3 BARS REST

Take time to consider what the standards for participation in your Salvation Army music groups should be. Do your participants understand and embrace the mission of The Salvation Army? What is the meeting and rehearsal attendance policy? What are the musical standards? What is the uniform to be worn? How can a newcomer or outsider join your groups? What other standards should be included?

Classroom discipline

An essential safeguard is to never leave young people in teaching areas, entrances, or hallways unattended. Whenever possible instruct in groups of two or more with good visibility. Very often, an instructor needs to ask lots of "why" questions to define and then positively confront a behavior. Let's look at how some of these challenges can be remedied in a classroom setting.

Child is not CLEAR on what is expected
Be sure the class location, assigned seating, getting of folders, instruments, and class routine become familiar, common ground. Use attention-getting warm-ups, such as echo clapping—using different parts of the body, ending with finger claps that are quiet. Give specific directions. "Go home and practice" is not enough. Give a specific assignment and suggested amount of time for practicing each day. Keep your instructions simple and clear.

Child is testing AUTHORITY
Children and teens find security in knowing that a competent, confident adult is in charge. They need to know who is in charge. In modifying behavior, re-emphasize cooperation and teamwork. Deliberately separate students who are acting up by moving closer to the offender while continuing the lesson. Sometimes direct eye contact coupled with silence, while you wait, can do the trick. On other occasions it may work to act flabbergasted at unsatisfactory actions or, conversely, to ignore a behavior.

Child has different RULES at home or school
Point out that there are different expectations for different places. People behave differently in a courtroom than at a ballgame. Be specific yet positive in corrections. Keep your cool. Condemn the behavior, not the person. Have an adult assistant nearby to give attention to the problem child, allowing the director to maintain control of the rehearsal with the remainder of the group.

Child's INTEREST is not there
Be flexible and sensitive in planning. Do not be afraid to go to plan B when something is not working. Allow the group to assist in setting goals. Be consistent with a few but firm house rules.

Child NEEDS more activity
Plan shifts in pace, mood, and activity. Avoid delays. Keep moving. Vocal groups should sing more than the conductor talks. Give special jobs to more active students. Thoroughly prepare your music and have a plan. (Young people know if you don't have one.) Start and end on time. Successfully perform often. Few things motivate like a good deadline.

Child longs for a GREETING and rewards
Allow time to greet the children and let them tell you about their day. A bad day at school or home can work its way out with reactionary behavior. Pray for your students by name. Praise often. Positive reinforcement can foster productive behavior. Use incentives and prizes to reward progress, attendance and good behavior. Build memories.

> "You can look at a tender shoot on a vine and anticipate the harvest. In the same way, love those who are not yet good!"
> —Guigo I, *Meditations*

> "People don't CARE how much you know until they know how much you CARE."
> —Theodore Roosevelt

Even when you want to let things go, or you really cannot ascertain what to do with a certain behavior, remember to maintain a disciplined teaching environment because children need to know that you CARE for them as people.

3 BARS REST

Take time to formulate (1) routines, (2) rules, and (3) room set-up for your corps youth music program. Pledge to be consistent from week to week with this regimen.

YOUTH MUSIC LEADER'S RESOURCES

Children's Music Ministry, Connie Fortunato (David C. Cook)
Directing the Children's Choir, Shirley W. McRae (Schirmer)
El Sistema USA, http://elsistemausa.org
Every Child Can Succeed: Making the Most of Your Child's Learning Style, Cythias Tobias (Focus on the Family)
Sticky Teams: Keeping Your Leadership Team and Staff on the Same Page, Larry Osborne (Zondervan)
The Chorister, bi-monthly periodical for children's choir leaders. (Choristers Guild)
Transforming Children Into Spiritual Champions, George Barna (Gospel Light)

THE DREAM-MAKER'S PRAYER

Now glory be to God who
(by His mighty power at work within us)
is able to **do** far more than we would
ever **dare** to ask or even **dream** if!

    Infinitely **beyond** our highest prayers,
    highest desires,
    our highest thoughts,
    or our highest hopes. Amen!
    (paraphrase of Ephesians 3:20)

Children's outing with Joe the Turk

CHAPTER FOUR

WORKERS TOGETHER
The Corps Leadership Team

Be shepherds of God's flock that is under your care, serving as overseers—not because you must, but because you are willing, as God wants you to be ... eager to serve, not lording it over those entrusted to you, but being examples to the flock. —1 Peter 5:2–3

IN THE VALLEY OF DRY BONES

"Harold, I need you to come over to my corps this afternoon," the newly arrived officer declared over the phone, "I have something I want to show you." Feeling somewhat intimidated by the tone of his voice, I wasted little time and motored over to the nearby building. As I entered the chapel, I noticed that behind the podium, the usually spare platform furnishings had been replaced by folding chairs arranged in the semblance of a band formation. Brass instruments rested on each chair, some propped up and others randomly scattered among the chairs. Curved bell horns and baritones, trombones awkwardly leaning on chairs, plus tubas, cornets, and even a few headless drums gave an arresting impression that the instruments were being held and played. On closer inspection, it was clear that most of the instruments were dated and tarnished from neglect. I guessed correctly that the officer had emptied the instrument closet of its entire inventory to create this ghost of a band. With intense urgency, he uttered words I have not forgotten: "This is the valley of dry bones. We need to breathe life into these horns."

Present and emerging music leaders, alongside their corps officers, can intentionally foster a Spirit-filled, working relationship. In **Chapter Four**, we ask:

- How can the corps officer engage the congregation, using the musicians and artists, with a unified purpose and direction?
- How does the corps officer assure the "present future" of the corps by identifying and empowering leaders from a young age?
- How can we engage succeeding generations within the corps?
- How can we retain and engage our "present future" in leadership roles within the corps?

> **present future** (*term*) \'pre-zent 'fyü-cher\ In this chapter we use the term "present future" to help shift our perception of the "present" as making sense only in light of the past, to more correctly looking at our "present" in light of the future. In Reggie McNeal's words, "We think we are headed toward the future. The truth is, the future is headed toward us."[1]

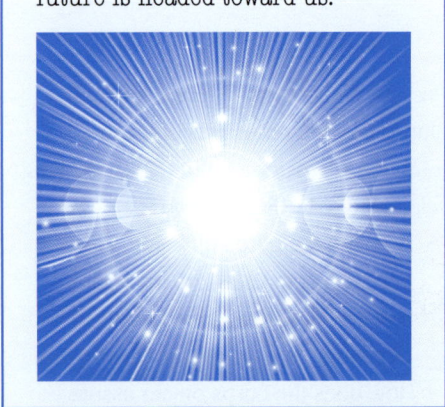

As we conversed, he disclosed that the instruments had been staged on Saturday and he had used those same words with his Sunday congregation. One can almost picture a Disneyesque cartoon scene with the wind howling, first from a distance, then making its way down the aisles. As the rising torrent swirls around the platform, one by one, the unattended instruments are lifted up as though being played. The first sputtering utterances evolve into a disturbing cacophony of blaring brass which, by some strange pervading force, climaxes into a grand martial theme. A living, breathing band is born, or more correctly, reborn.

Those instruments remained on the platform for weeks, a reminder of that officer's bold vision. He foresaw kids practicing on that platform every afternoon, and playing on Sundays inside and outside that building. He would be able to emphasize the disciplines of practice, teamwork, personal hygiene, uniform wearing, and showing up on time for rehearsals with instrument and the proper books in tow. He anticipated the manifold benefits afforded to his Salvationist musicians at regional, divisional, and territorial events. He desired for them to have the opportunity to spend several weeks away from that blighted neighborhood at summer camp. His vision extended to the possibility of touring the world.

Salvation Army music does not rest in the exclusive realm of the brass band. Such a "dry bones" vision might be played out for a praise band, choir, dance, timbrel, or drama group. This officer taught me much about engaging folks in pursuit of a vision, praying and working it into a reality of live music-making within the corps setting.

PEOPLE OF PURPOSE

The day soldiers stop bringing you their problems is the day you have stopped leading them. They have either lost confidence that you can help them or concluded that you do not care. Either case is a failure of leadership. —Colin Powell

Early Salvation Army music-making was conditionally permitted by the Founder, though William Booth did fear that it could become music for music's sake, as he had known in the churches of his day.[2] "Playing an instrument gave the soldier a feeling of belonging, of fulfilling a role in the great salvation crusade: the alto horn or valve trombone was his badge of merit, visible proof to the world that he was no longer a poor and lonely drudge, but a bandsman in The Salvation Army, a person of consequence at last."[3] Many hearts were *captured* by hearing a Salvation Army band on the march, in the open air, or in the Army hall. Consistent with linking people and purpose, popular tunes were "shamelessly expropriated" into lines of religious verse, "allowing any audience to sing along without feeling awkward or self-conscious."[4]

The first recorded "capture of a profane ditty from the music hall" occurred during the visit of General William Booth to Worcester, England, in February 1882 when

"Sailor" Fielder sang "Bless His name, He sets me free!" This was a set of religious words by William Baugh, previously printed in the Christmas 1881 issue of the *War Cry*, written to a well-known barroom tune, "Champagne Charlie Is My Name." (Obviously present-day copyright restrictions preclude this kind of piracy today!) When some of Booth's most staunch supporters protested these transformations of popular tunes, Booth enticed them to attend a demonstration at Clapton Congress Hall in May 1882. The audience repeated over and over again some of these newly dressed-up choruses to the enthusiastic accompaniment of hand clapping (said to be introduced as an aid to singing for the first time) and the waving of handkerchiefs. In *The History of The Salvation Army, Volume II*, Robert Sandall records that the donors "backed their approval with munificent donations towards the purchase of the National Training Barracks."

Today, The Salvation Army continues to link the music of the populace into church culture through music adapted from pop, Gospel, Latin, and rock idioms. Over one hundred thirty years later, one can hear the words of *Jesus Loves Me*, sung to the Flintstones theme music, echoing through our Sunday Schools. Our principal target audience remains the disenfranchised, particularly those without means, but our ministry extends to all economic levels.

The corps officer's role

The intersection of the corps officer and Salvation Army music ministry has evolved over the years. Early Salvation Army officers were itinerant evangelists who might remain in a corps appointment for a mere six months, then move on. The corps would carry on, sometimes without an officer, which vested continuing "ownership" by the congregation. It was the soldier's work to meet new folks, through open-air meetings or in their daily routine, and bring them along to services.

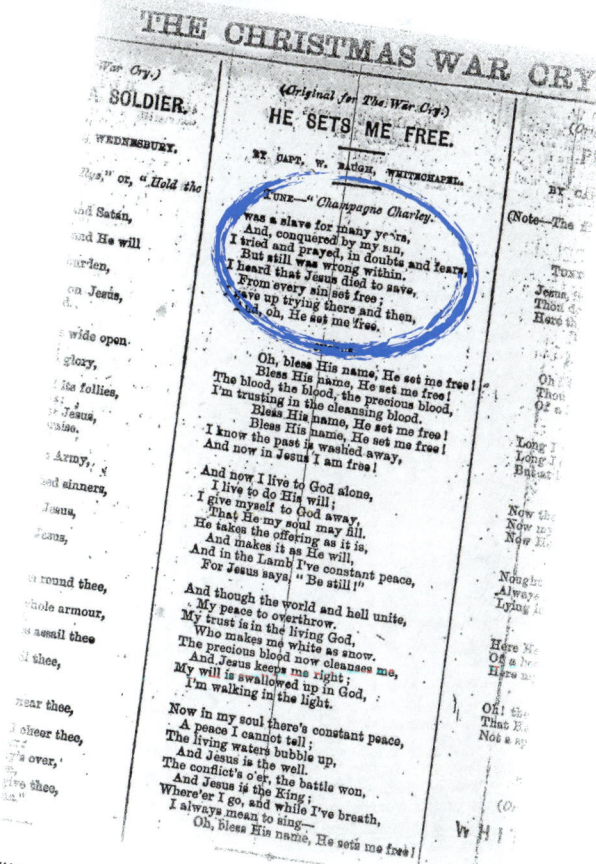

"He Sets Me Free" lyrics, first published in the Christmas *War Cry*, 1881

One of the tools for enticing and holding new member-soldiers has been involvement in Salvation Army music and arts programs. Today's corps officer has an opportunity to partner with musicians and artists as a means of equipping and empowering the corps for outreach, worship, and discipleship.

4 BARS REST

1. What visions do you have for music and arts in your corps? What are some of the faith-steps you can take to breathe life into those dreams?

2. How can we intentionally make a way for musicians and artists to be included in the salvation war and prevent our music and arts sections from becoming exclusive to insiders?

> "Everything rises and falls on leadership."
>
> –John Maxwell

BETTER YOUNG THAN NEVER

We often counsel the young that leaders need their energy and idealism, and that they can benefit from the attention and wisdom of their elders. But too often the old guard does not allow an emerging influencer to sit at the table and become part of the conversation.

The kids' table

Do you recollect being required to sit at a table separated from the adult's table at large family gatherings? Your noisy, pint-sized company included cousins close in age and younger siblings. Happily banished to the kids' table, lively conversation would be peppered with occasional outbursts of laughter. In marked contrast, at first there would be hardly a peep around the adult table, except for the clink of fine silver against china as famished diners remained fixed, heads-down on the task at hand. Minding your manners mattered little at the kids' table. You had a kid-sized portion served on a small plate while the adults gorged themselves with mountains of food piled high on fine china.

THE ONGOING SAGA OF THE ADULT TABLE

Meanwhile back at the corps one can imagine the ensuing conversation around the adult table: "Leave us alone," say the elders at the leadership table. "Allow us to enjoy our meal. Remain at the kids' table while we pass our favorite recipes back and forth around our own table." Unfortunately, without youthful influence, the adults don't say much about the menu so it remains pretty much the same.

Over weeks, months and even years, the team of leaders carries on with their "meals." Sometimes they reshuffle the seating arrangement around the table and even include an occasional visitor. The suggestion of bringing any new, youthful members to the adult table is often met with skepticism.

One day while absorbed in the ritual of their meal, it suddenly dawns on the select few at the leadership table that the once-animated kids' table has gone eerily quiet. "Do you hear anything from the kitchen table?" they ask while sipping their tea. "Where did the young voices go?" With an uncanny prophetic voice, one mutters under her breath, "Maybe they slipped outside?"

A veteran diner expresses his deep regrets at missing their quiet exit while taking a second helping. "Quiet exit, my foot!" another exclaims. "How could you miss their exit? They bolted out of here a long time ago! Who would want to still be eating at the kids' table after all these years?"

No one dared speak, for everyone around the table had failed to see the vital need to bring fresh, youthful influence into the loop. Even the most patient youngster will only wait so long for their turn to move up to the adult table. Now the old guard yearned for the noisy, disruptive, and messy kids who brought life and vitality to the **present future** of the gathering. In the aftermath of the meal, **the kids' table sat undisturbed, an empty nest**. The team of leaders had been caught napping.

It is no secret that if we don't give our young people **entrée to the table** and offer them opportunities to share ideas and conversation the overwhelming tendency is for the kids to **fly the coop.** Dawson McAllister, a national youth ministry specialist, says "90% of kids active in high school youth groups do not go to church by the time they are sophomores in college. One third of these will never return.

Too often, we leave our emerging leaders knocking their knees against the kids' table. Our attitude needs to be: **Better young than never!**

The leaders of tomorrow, today

We can vigorously train, nurture, and encourage our young people into leadership roles. Even at a young age, one can spot those who exhibit an inclination toward leadership. Others surprise us and emerge as leaders, and even become our officers as they mature. Delaying succession of the young is one of the devil's most effective tactics. Teens have affected history from revivals to revolutions. Consider the amazing saga of Eliza Shirley who commenced the work of The Salvation Army in America at just seventeen years of age.

The Salvation Army pours a lot of energy and resources into our young people with events, initiatives, conferences, and hours of travel. This large-scale investment often grants us a term of nurture in The Salvation Army, even if it is brief. Those who mentor young people learn to understand that the relationship with you, and particularly with

Eliza Shirley introduced The Salvation Army to Philadelphia at age seventeen.

Jesus, is what really matters. One must ask if we can do better at retaining successive generations to worship and service in The Salvation Army. We must consider ways to more effectively come alongside our young people.

Forever too young

Paul emboldens the incessantly tethered young when he commands Timothy, "Don't let anyone look down on you because you are young, but set an example for the believers in speech, in life, in love, in faith and in purity." (1 Timothy 4:12) The word Paul uses for young is *neotetos*, meaning of military age. Surprisingly, this period lasted up to age forty. William Barclay tells us that at the time of the writing of this letter, Paul might have known Timothy for fifteen years. This might have made Timothy more an adult than a youth at possibly thirty years of age. So why does Paul say, "Let no man despise thy youth"? (1Timothy 4:12, *KJV*) Perhaps it is because age is always relative. To the newly arrived freshman in high school, the seniors loom large and seem so much older. Three years later, as these freshmen approach graduation, the perception is strangely inverted. The incoming freshmen seem to have shrunk and appear comparatively small and young.[5]

In the same way, in our corps, the generation that follows will always seem young to the one before. We have a tendency to allow our Timothys to remain stranded in the fountain of youth, as if they will forever be young. Yet all teens long for increased independence, earned when leaders and parents entrust them with a duty, which in most cases, they can handle. Like Paul, we must expect our Timothys to discharge their responsibility with a measure of maturity. But too often, our present postmodern culture dismisses youth from any accountability, or taking of blame when things go awry. Unfortunately our culture has bought into a Peter Pan mentality of adolescence in which one never has to grow up. Adults, struggling to maintain an impression of youthfulness themselves, inadvertently send a message to teens that they can act like kids forever. But who honestly wants to replay their middle school years or continue to act on the misguided impulses of youth? **The supporting cast, from corps officers to music leaders, needs to release the frozen, youthful picture we hold of our students.**

Silence the critics

Teens may present themselves as invincible and expert, but what they fear most is a condescending put-down. Wounds run deep and can persist for years, a reason many consider accepting any leadership role too risky. Criticism of leadership, at any age, is never far away. Paul assures us that even the harshest criticism is quieted by exemplary conduct: "Teach believers with your life: by word, by demeanor, by love, by faith, by integrity." (1 Timothy 4:12, *The Message*) Actions speak louder than words and can quiet the harshest critics! Even if gifted from an early age, a musician's tone or a dancer's footwork takes a backseat to standout integrity. Paul speaks of Timothy's sincere faith, acknowledging the powerful thread that runs from his grandmother Lois through his mother Eunice, which Paul says, "now lives in you also." (2 Timothy 1:5) We know that Timothy traveled with Paul and also experienced hardships alongside stalwarts of the early church, like Barnabas and Silas. Who are the exemplars for our modern-day Timothys to model themselves after today? **The supporting cast, from corps officers to music leaders, must model standout integrity in leadership for the next generation.**

Authority over seniority

From the earliest age, we are taught to respect those who are, as the song says, "older and wiser, teaching me what to do."[6] Paul breaks the mold, stating that a young person like Timothy can stand in authority, not based on seniority but on an exemplary life. The leader cares for others, no matter what they do to him, choosing not to harbor grudges. As a youngster in Scouts, I was challenged to live a life of integrity and follow well as a prerequisite to leadership. **The supporting cast, from corps officer to music leaders, notices exemplary membership and responds positively when that person is called to lead.**

Who are the examples for our modern day Timothys to model themselves after today?

Loyalty, even in adversity

As leaders, we compromise the future when we set the bar low rather than challenging our youth to live even more godly lives than our present generation. William Barclay asks, "What use is Christianity unless it can prove that it produces the best men and women, living their lives according to the standards of Jesus Christ?"

This impetus is set in motion by modeling a purity of mind and heart that seeks after the will of God. Paul reminds young leaders like Timothy that his authority is in agreement with the elders and the Holy Spirit: "That special gift of ministry you were given when the leaders of the church laid hands on you and prayed—keep that dusted off and in use." (1 Timothy 4:14, *The Message*) God does not manifest gifts just for individuals but also to affirm the work of the Holy Spirit within the body of Christ. Paul cheerleads enthusiastically, **"Cultivate these things. Immerse yourself in them. The people will all see you mature right before their eyes!"** (1 Timothy 4:15, *The Message*)

Children learn what they live

From the earliest age, young people know. During the service, in the lobby, in the parking lot, in the van, in the classroom, or sitting at a fellowship meal, kids are all eyes and ears. They know if you know their name. They know if you believe in them. They know when you are cutting corners with your interest and time. They just know! Paul's charge to Timothy leaves little room for a careless, condescending view of the youth within our sphere of influence.

Years ago, the detrimental effect of negative role models played out dramatically right before our eyes. One of our teens from songsters was positively beaming about a relationship she was in. We were puzzled by this. From our perspective, all we observed was constant fighting and flare-ups between the two of them. Unfortunately, having grown up in a home filled with contention, she aspired to mirror what she had lived with all her life. In the constant flare-ups, this young lady thought she had arrived at adulthood.[7] Children do learn what they live![8]

Choose to accentuate what is right: "Thank you for being such a big help today. Did you see how happy it made folks?" By choosing where our attention goes, where we go, what we purchase, and with whom we travel, we subliminally attempt to empower

The Beat Goes On

ourselves.⁹ These choices reveal what we seek in ourselves and betray the values to which we aspire. What more important calling is there than to direct young people's hearts and minds toward the true, noble, right, pure, lovely, admirable and praiseworthy? (cf. Philippians 4:8) We instruct with our very lives!

Every child matters

A baby dedication is such a happy occasion! We are asked to pray for the child and for the parents as they are charged to raise up the child in the ways of the Lord. Bedazzled by the charm of the baby and the absolutely glowing parents, we approvingly nod yes. **But a well-meaning pledge can easily become mere lip service.** We must ask ourselves: Is it too much to see Joey or Susie as the future bandmaster, singing company leader, or corps officer? Outside the immediate family, who will prove faithful in prayer and guidance to secure the child's rightful place in the Body of Christ?

Lt. Colonel June Rader used to say that children are unknowingly drawn to the spirit of Jesus in their teachers. Remember that children are watching. They are impressionable and absorb so much, even at the youngest ages. It is exhilarating to watch language, memory, and personality develop in our children and grandchildren. Leaders of the Catholic Church have been widely quoted as saying, "Give us a child until he is seven years old and we'll have him for life."¹⁰

Who's really teaching our kids?

When we ask an immature teen to be responsible for junior church and hand them a supply of videos and games, we undervalue our future. Studies indicate that our best opportunity to present the Gospel is to elementary age children.¹¹ Corps officers can support making the kids' table as attractive as possible, staffing it with the most capable teachers for that age group. First things first. Our young people need to hear and comprehend the Gospel story.

Corps officers can help ensure that the youth pastor and music teachers do not get sidetracked into an intense period of instruction with hardly a reference to the One we are preparing to worship. Be sure the Word is taught to your musicians through devotions or by relating Scripture to songs. Encourage leaders to conclude rehearsal in a prayer circle with a sung benediction.

Heading off to junior church

We must intentionally invest in our young people from an early age if they are to walk into the future with Jesus.

Although group lessons and rehearsals are important, one-on-one lessons offer opportunities to identify gifts and leadership potential in youngsters. Students will recall an instructor's funny expressions and mannerisms, but more importantly glean much from their example and belief in them. As your rapport develops, they will test, but ultimately see, your reliance on divine guidance. Permit interruptions in lessons to discuss life challenges at home or school. Your best advice: Learn to trust God and He will direct your path. Together, corps officers and leaders can help keep the children's emerging gifts focused on the Giver.

Win them one by one

Corps officers and leaders can help young people discern their strengths and weaknesses. If students struggle to find practice time, help them specifically identify the time and place and what they will practice each day. Together, leaders can make a concerted effort to aid this youngster in developing self-discipline. As discussed in Chapter Three, many of our young Salvationists go home to an environment of uncertainty and inconsistency. *By your words and actions, make certain these precious children of God know they are not standing alone.* Share your pride, not only in their hard work, but in the good choices they are making!

4 BARS REST

1. What was it like to sit at the adult table for the first time? How would you rate your corps' openness to including the young in your conversations? How can we make room for youth at the leadership table now?

2. Who are the "officer-heroes" who modeled leadership in your life? What attracted you to their influence?

3. What criteria determine leadership placement in your setting? Is it gifts, education, experience, musicianship, natural leadership, or something else?

4. What steps can your corps take to allow young people to be heard, trained, utilized, and empowered?

ADULTS AT THE KIDS' TABLE

> *The Holy Spirit displays God's power through each of us as a means of helping the entire church ... Those parts of the body that seem weaker are indispensable, and the parts that we think are less honorable we treat with special honor.* —1 Corinthians 12:7, *TLB*, and 12:22-23, *NIV*

How adult leaders can support the music program

There was a time when corps officers were out virtually every evening of the week facilitating corps programs. To make things more manageable, some loaded a full gamut of corps activities into one long afternoon and evening. Others chose to compartmentalize the ministry load, entrusting program leadership to local officers, leaving the officer absent from the evening devoted to music.

But even officers not musically inclined can take in a portion of the weekly music rehearsals. Their presence shows interest and encourages those who give their time. The officers can encourage and reach out to the musicians and artists, feel the pulse of the musical and spiritual preparation, and glean ideas to benefit worship planning. Beyond delivering a list of tunes or the order of service for Sunday, actually giving lessons, conducting a group, or helping to drive the kids home, corps officers can uphold a music leadership team with their presence and availability.

"As a corps officer I would try and attend as many corps band rehearsals as possible. Oftentimes the music the band would be working on would lead to an inspiring thought or concept as it related to Sunday preparation."
—Commissioner Steven Hedgren[12]

I want to be a bridge
Though I'm not strong
I want to be a bridge
So wide, so long
That over me from doubt
To faith may pass
The lad in search of God,
The seeking lass.

Put steel into my faith,
And concrete too,
That men may travel
Over me
To you!

—John Gowans
From O Lord, Not More Verse!

Intentional bridging

Nine bridges for corps officers and adult leaders to interact with their youngsters are offered here. For adult leaders, it may prove as simple as taking a few minutes to sit at the kids' table!

BRIDGE #1

My corps, my community

I always admired one corps officer who weekly, at the time music activities were to begin, left his office and did not respond to calls. It meant a lot that he gave his full attention to the young people and caregivers moving through the corps building. This intentional interaction was consistent with his weekly Thursday afternoon walk through the neighborhood, when he would visit with folks who sat on their porches, greet shop owners, and talk with kids playing on the streets. His presence linked our corps to the community, and the music and dance program became a bridge to our neighborhood.

BRIDGE #2

Spiritual formation

I recall visiting a corps where everyone paused during the supper meal as the leader told a story and shared a brief spiritual application. Another took the boys and girls for half an hour and invested in their spiritual lives. Junior soldier preparation classes and corps cadets can be integrated into the schedule with music activities. One corps officer stayed and contributed to devotions held between senior songster and band rehearsals for both groups.

BRIDGE #3

Time-in at the kids' table

Time-in is an intentional one-on-one interaction that says to the child, "I know your name. I have an interest in your progress and who you are." When supper is included in the music night's schedule, some leaders make it a point to mix with different kids every week, then greet parents as they come to pick up their children. Bridges are built to Sunday morning and other ministries in the corps. The leaders remind the young people that we expect to see them on Sunday.

BRIDGE #4

The one-minute manager

An officer who is not musically inclined can observe the lessons or rehearsals in progress. One officer came quite regularly for the first half of band rehearsal, just to capture the tenor of things. (Honestly, I think everyone did behave better with him there.) He would often be spotted leafing through the songbook or a pew Bible, exploring ideas while we rehearsed. It seemed that a phrase or a song would spark an idea for his sermon. The connection was not lost on our musicians.

BRIDGE #5

Lead by example

Once I was hosting a renowned band from overseas. The driver of the truck carrying their instruments got lost. As the host, I was embarrassed because the group had planned on a quick set-up to allow time for a much-needed rest before dinner. Over an hour later, the equipment truck arrived and, to my surprise, the first person to start unloading was this famous bandmaster. From that day on, I began to notice folks *who led by example, who did not ask anything more from their members than from themselves.* In this way, we can show our youngsters what kind of leader we want them to be.

When we spot a natural leader, the adult leader should encourage this inclination. For instance, take the emerging leader to teacher training workshops. Once there, don't just sit in the lobby and wait. Go to the actual training session and find out what is being taught. This enables a conversation over lunch, or on the ride home, about how you could apply the lessons learned together back at the corps.

BRIDGE #6

The open door

Although phones, e-mail, and texting expedite communication, getting to the heart of matters requires open-door communication. Nabi Saleh, the founder of a highly successful Australian coffee franchise, gives this advice: "We aren't in the coffee business, serving people. We're in the people business, serving coffee." *Salvationists are in the people business.* Too often conversations with local officers gravitate to corps-related business and rarely touch on family, work, school, and life in general. A caring officer-pastor comes down to the corps on Monday nights to play basketball or prays with other women on Friday mornings. Time over a breakfast or lunch allows the officer to get to know the struggles and triumphs of leadership team members.

BRIDGE #7

Backing up the frontline

Many officers come alongside their leaders by making behind-the-scenes calls and visits. They validate the musicians' week-to-week hard work during the announcements by encouraging the congregation to come out for the recital or stay for Sunday school to hear and encourage the young musicians. *A nod of approval can go a long way.* These officers keep their eyes and ears open for opportunities to fund equipment purchases and expand the teaching staff.

BRIDGE #8

Divide and conquer

It is physically impossible for the corps officers or music leaders to give each fledgling youngster the time needed to nurture them in utilizing their gifts in the church. Yet a majority of members of our congregations feel their gifts are not utilized.[13] Herein lies a tremendous challenge—and an opportunity.

Our culture today has a way of discouraging real face-to-face relationships, but this need is in the heart of every man, woman, and child, placed there by God Himself. One colloquialism says, "No one cares how much you know, until they know how much you care."[14] We can strengthen our togetherness as a music section or a church by incorporating effective, relationship-building experiences into our already established rehearsal and Sunday time frames. Providing opportunity for mentoring and prayer partnerships proves a vital link in moving minstrels to ministers and reversing an alarming exodus of teens.

If we start growing our children's leadership potential from a young age, we will raise the odds that they will feel empowered and remain as Salvationist leaders. Some may even become officer-leaders themselves. An equally desperate need is to nurture leaders dedicated to the local corps who remain steadfast to their corps, despite the revolving door of the officer farewell cycle. Widely admired corps music ensembles generally have been nurtured by long-standing leadership who "gut it out" in the crucible of service from season to season. We should embrace and hang onto these saints!

BRIDGE #9

Building up the temple

All these possibilities and more are temple-building exercises. Corps officers and music leaders with their fledgling eagles echo the interactions of the Levite musician-priests with their offspring as they busied themselves within the Temple courts. (More on this in Chapter Eight.) The conversations, transporting kids, moving equipment, helping put folders together, and last-minute calls all serve as models for the day when they will teach, lead, or mentor others.

Do we send that message? *Only if we model it ourselves.* Be interactive. Love the children and teens with your attention. Sometimes I really look forward to giving a lesson to relish the ways that my students are growing in the wisdom and ways of the Lord. They hardly see it, but they are already bearing a mantle of leadership, being readied to soar higher than this aging eagle ever flew.

An even playing field—a little less entitlement, please

First and foremost, deep within our Salvation Army DNA is the missionary zeal to reach out wider and farther to the lost and disenfranchised. It mirrors these challenging words of Jesus:

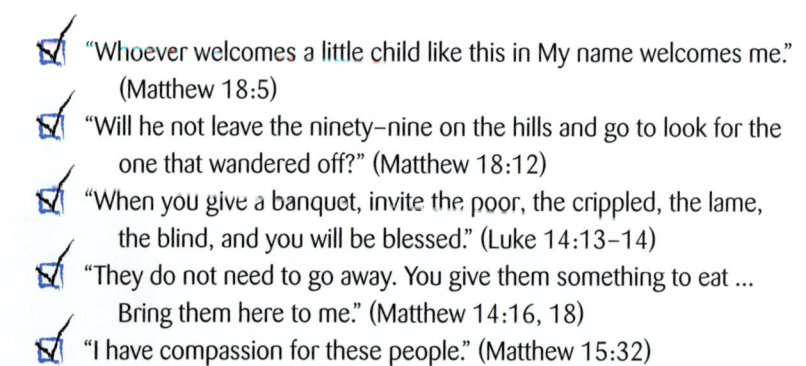

- ☑ "Whoever welcomes a little child like this in My name welcomes me." (Matthew 18:5)
- ☑ "Will he not leave the ninety-nine on the hills and go to look for the one that wandered off?" (Matthew 18:12)
- ☑ "When you give a banquet, invite the poor, the crippled, the lame, the blind, and you will be blessed." (Luke 14:13-14)
- ☑ "They do not need to go away. You give them something to eat ... Bring them here to me." (Matthew 14:16, 18)
- ☑ "I have compassion for these people." (Matthew 15:32)

These admonitions of Jesus are a far cry from the favored treatment we, as well-meaning parents, sometimes afford our offspring. Church growth experts taught us a generation ago that adult commitments to the church peak during the child-rearing years. As parents, we tried not to give our kids preference over kids from the community. Even though our family traveled as a music ministry, for example, we would rarely put those items on display at our home corps. We did our best not to place our kids in favored seats in ensembles or give them solos. But frankly, because they put in the work and were faithfully there every week, this probably wasn't the perception. (Please forgive my blind side on this!)

My own daughters, from infancy into their teen years, went on visitation ministries with us in the corps neighborhood. It was not always safe, but they learned to love their friends enough to track them down when they missed Sunday school or church. The corps sponsored some of these kids to travel with our girls on overseas mission trips. We shared heartbreak when one of our corps kids failed, after years of lessons and hours together in rehearsals. On the other hand, championship trophies for singing and many miles of travel created memories, which were celebrated by all.

The Burgmayer Family, 1995

Today some of our young people remain in The Salvation Army as officers and local officers. As they begin their own journey as parents, we pray that they will happily recall the beat of the bass drum they followed back to the corps in "time for Sunday school." *Mission calls us out of our houses, out of our comfort zones and routines and calls us to "move into the neighborhood."* Our corps kids experienced this on the streets of Philadelphia. Parents and kids were rescued. Frederick Buechner describes it this way, "The place God calls you is the place where your deep gladness and the world's deep hunger meet."

The Barney Family, 2014

> Some want to live within the sound
> Of church and chapel bell;
> I want to run a rescue shop,
> Within a yard of hell.
> —C.T. Studd [15]

The Beat Goes On

COME AND DINE AT THE ADULT TABLE (WELL, MAYBE?)

Withholding entrée into the dining room of influence is less about preventing the same mistakes we made, than disavowing any emerging influence to interrupt your meal. —John Maxwell

THE KIDS' MEAL

Allow me to share another kid-sized scenario. As a child, do you recall waiting after the evening service for what seemed like an eternity? Dad was stuck in a meeting that was supposed to last just half an hour, so you hung out with your friends, scurrying around the adults who were happily preoccupied in polite formalities. An occasional outburst earned you a glare and a whispered reprimand. Mom grabbed your hand, but as she became more enraptured in her conversation, you happily sprang free and returned to your friends. No one was surprised that the meeting went beyond late. You watched as Mom and Dad shut off the lights. To subdue your obvious hunger, you were treated to a kids' meal on the way home! Surprise! It is not your first kids' meal and neither will it be your last. You do wonder, though, when you will ever graduate to the adult menu. You think, the kids' menu is getting old fast!

Having searched my own memory, I cannot recall moving from the kids' meal to the adult menu. I do, however, remember the first time I was permitted to sit at the adult table and share in mature conversation. Curious eyes peered at me from around the table as I uttered a sheepishly delivered response. I left the table acutely aware of my youth but yearning to contribute better next time. I secretly rejoiced in my heart, knowing my parents, aunts, and uncles would welcome me back.

"Ironically, most churches are started by young eagles," states Larry Osborne in his book *Sticky Teams*. "But soon after getting their nest built, nicely appointed, and fully furnished, they start to marginalize the next batch of eagles, asking them to sit at the *kids' table* and wait for their turn at middle-aged leadership."[16] Osborne asserts that when a church stops growing, evangelizing, and making a mark in its community, it comes down to what he calls the "twenty-year death cycle." If the young eagles that began that church's generation are still holding the strongest influence twenty years later, chances are high that the church is graying and culturally out of touch—bent on preserving the heritage of its past, rather than projecting into the future.[17]

Back to the table

Paul tells the church at Ephesus, "It was he [Christ] who gave some to be apostles, some to be prophets, some to be evangelists, and some to be pastors and teachers, to prepare God's people for works of service, so that the body of Christ may be built up ..." (Ephesians 4:11–12) This calls off the pastoral one-leader show! The call is for Christian leaders to lead by equipping the entire body of Christ. Peter seconds this Spirit-ordained partnership when he charges: "Each one should use whatever gift he has received to serve others, faithfully administering God's grace in its various forms." (1 Peter 4:10) Repeat, the one-leader show is off! Neither is 5% of the church supposed to do 95% of the work! If young people become bored with church and leave, it is probably because they did not find a place nor a role. Corps officers, as pastors, are to be in the business of equipping those around them. The business community calls it,

Alone we can do so little; TOGETHER we can do so much.
—Helen Keller

COLLABORATION

"hiring for growth." We choose to give particular attention to the young eagles, anticipating a fresh harvest with anointed, trained eagles waiting in the wings and ready to soar!

Throw your nets on the other side!

How do we keep the young eagles at the kids' table from bolting out the back door? How do we know what the next generation needs? A vast majority of church-going youth will stop attending church before finishing college. Within a decade, nearly a third may return.[18] If you still have college students in your fold, you deserve congratulations. Mark Dowds contends that you must have "thrown your net on the other side," referring to Jesus' famous command to the fisherman who had caught no fish even though they had fished through the night.[19] To reach and keep any generation, things in the church may need to change and move in another direction.

Change, a threatening opportunity

The Chinese epigram for crisis (c) is really made up of two characters: *threatening* and *opportunity*, or more exactly, crucial point.[20] In speaking of change, Eugene Peterson states, "You would think that of all places, all communities, it would be the church where we would most welcome the creativity and freshness and adventure of new things, but instead that's the very place we are most threatened." Our seven last words become: "We've never done it that way before."[21]

When championing a change, stay within the boundaries of trust. There is a tendency to shock or bully folks to kick-start and emphasize a new direction. True creativity enhances community rather than disrupts it! Remember, more binds us as a body than divides us. Move ahead with dignity, maintaining the rigor, discipline, and hard work that made the enterprise work from its inception. Affirm the up-and-comers and encourage them to extend their creativity and intuition with fresh steps. Folks can only take so much newness without feeling manipulated. Truth be told, we treasure our formative years, especially our music, because it touches our roots and emotions. It is safer to mix the old with the new, remaining sensitive to the congregational response.

Speaking of the current young adult generation, Dowds insists,

> They are entrepreneurial, meaning they want to be their own boss ... These young people do not want to **work** for William and Catherine Booth, they want to **be** William and Catherine Booth. These new radicals want to discover why the Booths started The Salvation Army in order to re-interpret this in the world they live in ... They are asking questions and poking around to discover what the true heart of The Salvation Army really is. They are finding this process difficult due to the differing answers they receive on their journey. Unfortunately they are hearing prescribed methodologies more than prescribed hearts. They meet people who want to teach them their techniques, instead of those who are able to lead them to a place where God will touch their passions. Imagine trying to pass Saul's armor onto the little boy David. How easily we neglect the heart!
>
> We need to lead this generation to the feet of Jesus, like Mary, or encourage them to have a listening heart, like Solomon. We can inspire them with the stories of God's faithfulness to His people, like that of Moses and Joshua, but we need to release them from the pressure of how it always has been done. They are asking to see the true heart of our Movement. Administering an organization that makes a difference in the lives of the

危 A time of danger

机 A time of opportunity

> To serve **the present age,**
> My calling to fulfill,
> O may it all my powers engage,
> To do my Master's will!
> —Charles Wesley

oppressed of our society is not enough. This generation requires deep links to people who will bring them to the hopeless and homeless.[22]

But what must change?

God continues to stir hearts into faithful service and leadership in their local corps. Peter Farthing, an Australian Salvationist writing in *The Officer* magazine, believes the Holy Spirit is moving in the church the world over. Where the Spirit is moving, leaders are called to action, aiding the renewal of God's Church for *today's* world. **We can speak (and even sing) of a glorious past, but we need to ask where the streams of living water are leading us in our present age.** Farthing sees a paradigm shift, spearheaded by the Holy Spirit, from a **program-centered corps** to a **ministry-driven model,** which immensely affects leadership style.[23]

For "the greatest generation," which lived through World War II, a major theme of church-goers was devotion to God expressed through service. The upholding of standards became closely linked to Christian life. Quasi-military jargon included phrases like "being on duty" for a service or event. A committed Salvationist would "get involved, wear uniform, join a section of the corps, and become busy at the corps," performing all these activities like a badge of honor.[24] The greatest generation used a **program model,** where the corps had a full schedule of activities in which members were expected to participate. In this model, the leadership determines the program and the lay people are recruited to work it. All of this is carefully resourced, regulated, and monitored by headquarters. The program and events easily become *what we do.*

Farthing seems well-acquainted with the older generation's highly held values. **Yet he admires the younger generation's desire for spiritual authenticity.** He loves that these Salvationists value worship, Bible study, prayer, and the embracing of the spiritual gifts. An outpouring of new fight songs, to new upbeat tunes, are manifestations of a willingness of the young to engage in spiritual warfare, befitting a *salvation army.* Farthing discerns that "this younger generation tends not to think of themselves in terms of getting involved and doing their duty, but rather of using their gifts and finding fulfilling service." Meeting content and attendance is less formalized and results in a bent toward contemporary music gleaned from other churches. To some this embodies a regrettable loss of Salvation Army culture. To others, bridging across denominational lines is a much-needed reprieve from an insular Army culture.

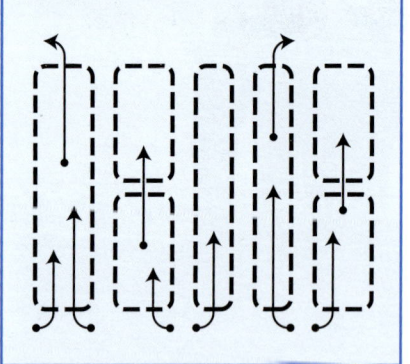

The consequence of this paradigm shift from a **program-centered corps** to a **ministry-driven model** moves the initiative for new ministries onto soldiers and officers alike. People are trained and released for service on the basis of their gifts and spiritual maturity. The empowerment of strong lay leadership, alongside oft-transitioning officers, more effectively penetrates the local community. This tends to reduce an emphasis on who holds what position and permits an increased diversity in leadership. A climate of control is eased to allow one of trust. Many have not caught onto this yet!

Bill Hull, a church consultant, warns, "unless more accept this change, the spiritual power will be diffused and absorbed by old unworkable structures ... and the enthusiasm of the people will wane."[25]

This present generation is not opposed to preserving our Salvation Army DNA; they are able to look back while keeping one eye on current culture. These young people are rightly asking how to connect with God and reach people. Maintaining Army music solely for Army music's sake is a dangerous

---

program-centered model
Leadership determines a full schedule of activities and lay people are recruited to work it.

ministry-driven model
People are trained and released for service on the basis of their gifts and spiritual maturity.

road. Many of this generation recognize that passion in the Spirit comes first, then the program. For those entering the circle of leadership, this is an invaluable perspective.

No doubt, we must invest deeply to take our young eagles to the level of understanding that truly empowers them. Occasionally, there are emerging leaders who can fill in the blanks before we speak or explain something without being prompted. But usually, it takes far more than a weekend conference or a foray through an informative text. Season by season, week by week, even hour by hour, we attempt to drip principles into the people around us. We may not realize our influence, but far better to start young, than never!

> *Maintaining Army music for Army music's sake is a dangerous road … This generation recognizes that passion in the Spirit comes first, then the program.*

Breathing life into the valley of dry bones

The officer who called me into his chapel to view his valley of dry bones readily admitted that he could hardly carry a tune in a bucket. He was determined to give his young people every opportunity that could be afforded them as Salvation Army musicians. He brought in model musicians and hired a corps pianist-teacher. In time these kids won awards. The battered instruments that they started on were replaced with shiny new horns. Some of the young people even took their music-making overseas. The corps has endured dramatic transitions in leadership and location, but there is still a small but faithful brass band in that inner-city corps today. Some question its cultural relevance. Yet it is the band, along with other sister music groups, that weekly carries forth an essential component of Army heritage and culture by, in the Founder's words, "organizing the singing."

Chances are the music program that you grew up in was intentionally seeded and nurtured with the "blood, sweat, and tears" of a faithful leader long since forgotten. There are programs that have proven amazingly successful in the past, but, if pressed, you might admit they have outlived their usefulness. It would be better if they had existed only for a time. Perhaps it is time for a praise team, a drum corps, a Gospel choir, or some other company of musician-artists at your corps. The goal should be to have live musicians effectively minister to your particular congregation from Sunday to Sunday at this present time and beyond.

I have to confess that on my initial visit to that valley of dry bones, all I saw was a mishmash of instruments. "How can these bones possibly live in this place under these conditions?" I wondered. My sentiments echoed those of the house of Israel, "Our bones are dried up, our hope is gone, there's nothing left of us." (Ezekiel 37:11, *The Message*) In response to this mentality of decline, Andrew Vertigan, a British Salvationist asks, "Is it possible that as Christians we have allowed the enemy to shape our thinking that nothing good can come from these bones?"[26] Boldly, he declares, **"If what you see seems more dead than alive, perhaps you need to get on your knees and pray for the Spirit to breathe life into it."**[27] Would that we, like the prophet of old, might witness, "the glory of the Lord" again filling the temple. (Ezekiel 43:5)

Now years later, when I visit various corps, especially those with a legacy of music-making, I sometimes imagine folks entering through the platform door, carrying

The Beat Goes On

instruments and engaged in lively conversation while others are already warming-up. I can almost hear the live band accompanying hearty singing with folks clapping along, perhaps effectively enhanced by a rhythm section and fine voices. Although a wisp of air helps produce the sound coming out of the speakers that play today's recorded tracks, few things compare with the vibrancy of breath producing sound in a company of live instrumentalists. Rather than preside over a graveyard, we can follow the pattern of the prophet: *So I prophesied, just as he commanded me. The breath entered them and they came alive! They stood up on their feet, a huge army!* (Ezekiel 37:10, *The Message*)

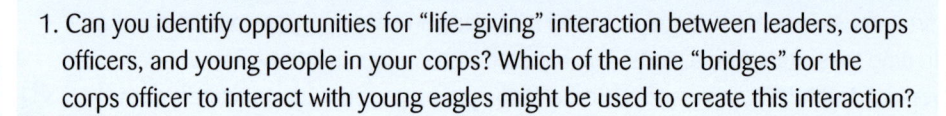

4 BARS REST

1. Can you identify opportunities for "life-giving" interaction between leaders, corps officers, and young people in your corps? Which of the nine "bridges" for the corps officer to interact with young eagles might be used to create this interaction?

2. Do you picture your corps as program-centered or more ministry-driven? How so? What changes might be more in line with the vision of the corps?

3. What practices can help the music leaders, corps pianist, and/or worship leader, know the "mind of the pastor," and serve to unify the body-life of the corps?

CORPS DYNAMICS RESOURCES

Ancient-Future Faith: *Rethinking Evangelicalism for a Postmodern World*, Robert E. Webber (Baker Book House)

For the Beauty of the Church: *Casting a Vision for the Arts*, David Taylor, ed. (Baker Books)

Sacred Space: *Creating Multisensory Worship Experiences for Youth Ministry*, Dan Kimball and Lilly Lewin. With CD. (Zondervan)

The Emerging Church, Dan Kimball et. al. (Zondervan)

The Great Emergence, *How Christianity is Changing and Why*, Phyllis Tickle (Baker Books)

The New Reformation: *Returning the Ministry to the People of God*, Greg Ogden (Zondervan)

The Present Future—*Six Tough Questions for the Church*, Reggie McNeal (InterVarsity Press)

The Younger Evangelicals: *Facing the Challenge of the New World*, Robert E. Webber (Baker Book House)

Thriving as an Artist in the Church: *Hope and Help for You and Your Ministry Team*, Rory Noland (Zondervan)

Velvet Elvis: *Repainting the Christian Faith*, Rob Bell (Zondervan)

Worship Evangelism: *Inviting Unbelievers into the Presence of God*, Sally Morgenthaler (Zondervan)

"You don't have to do big things, but the little things you are doing in your corner of influence must be done with great conviction, great wisdom and great love."
—Ruth Krehbiel Jacobs
Founder, Choristers Guild

CHAPTER FIVE

THEN SINGS MY SOUL!
The Song Leader

Let us take the common songs of our own people as they sing them at harvest, at village festivals, for use in our churches. Men can as well praise God in one tune as the other, and it is a pity such pretty songs as these should be kept any longer from the service of their Master. —Martin Luther

Dear Sun Day Song,

I have recently been thrust into the role of song leader at my corps. We have a band and an okay pianist and, like many congregations, a variety of folks, young and old. Most really don't get it, if you know what I mean. What can I do to upgrade the congregational singing in my corps?

Lost in His service,
Got Song?

In **Chapter Five**, we learn how to:
- locate the words and music for Sunday worship, including how to copy "right," make text readable, and use the metrical index.
- look at a script for song leading.
- find new songs and effective congregational song accompaniments.
- practice beat patterns for three basic time signatures.
- start a song with a downbeat or "pick-up," or how to end a song with a cut-off.

THE SALVATION ARMY
FOUNDED IN 1865 BY WILLIAM AND CATHERINE BOOTH

BRIGADIER SUN DAY SONG
11:00 SOUL BOULEVARD
SALVATION TOWN, S.A.

Dear Ms. Song,

There are some essential steps in choosing the "proper" song. First, be sure to select songs en route to the corps or, even better, while the band is playing the prelude. The frenetic flapping of pages in full view of the congregation is a helpful distraction. Next, choose the tune by making up a number, or by muttering, "Let's try tune number …?" This keeps the pianist and bandmaster on their toes with their fingers apprehensively leafing through the tune book.

If you dare to give some forethought to tune selection, by all means choose a new tune to refresh old, unfamiliar words. In your excitement for this new marriage of words and text, be sure that the tune requires repeating the final line two and a half times. For example, "O Master, Let Me Walk with Thee" gets an unexpected lift enjoined with the lively "And Above the Rest" tune. When you run out of words, just default to the original "this note shall swell" chorus, which no one knows anymore.

Most of our congregations represent a fair cross–section of intellect and taste. (Do not confuse the two!) Play it safe and always pick a song at the lowest common denominator. A wise comrade once said, "The shallower the song, the deeper the blessing." Speaking of blessing, if you are blessed to have a praise band, pick a song of Isaac Watts' vintage and fully frustrate the guitarists with a chord change on every beat. And remember that repeating a mantra of the same few words over and over really piques the interest of the "greatest" generation!

Now as to leading the song properly, keep the bandmaster off balance by pretending to end your introductory comments, and then suddenly starting up with another idea.

Got Song? — Page 2

Just as he brings his arm down for the band to start, pretend not to notice that indeed one player did observe his aborted downbeat, during which the bandmaster has virtually dislocated his shoulder trying to stop the near debacle. On the other hand (pun intended), it may be simpler to just start the verse without ever looking his way or signaling your intentions.

For real dramatic effect, create longer and longer pauses to throw off your musicians. "He lives..., He lives…., He lives………" (You know the drill, right?) The more surprises the better, especially if you get the congregation to try to clap along. While you're at this, look disparagingly at any suggestion of exuberance, movement, or joy.

I know you've been told otherwise, but tempo does not matter a bit! Give devotional songs a lift by singing them at a good clip, and many happy songs deserve a slow and thoughtful rendition. In fact, why not vary the tempo dramatically from verse to verse? Encourage lengthy testimonies between verses of songs, but be sure everyone has to remain standing in order to hear better.

Always sing your improvised alto or baritone part directly into the mike. Even better, amaze your congregation by arbitrarily switching parts, and octave, at will. This effect works particularly well when fed through the hallway, nursery, and exterior speakers without the supporting congregation. It gives the neighborhood your best impression.

Surprise! Speaking of solos, out of the blue, way after everyone has forgotten, suddenly blurt out, "Let's sing that chorus again." You may end up starting that one yourself and flying solo, but better to be "moved by the Spirit." Finally, if anything doesn't go quite right, take a cue from the standup soloist and glare at your piano player. I mean glare.[1]

Lost in endless song,

Sun Day Song

P.S. What a wonderful coincidence that we share the same last name!

WE NEED A SONG LEADER

Song leaders have partnered in ministry with preachers over generations. Famous collaborations include Charles and John Wesley, Ira Sankey with Dwight L. Moody, Homer Rodeheaver with Billy Sunday, and George Beverly Shea with Billy Graham. The song leader stands and faces the people, singing with heart and voice, giving an aural and visual image of how each congregant should participate. A true song leader draws all worshipers into the moment.

In the Hebrew tradition, the song leader, or cantor, is known as *Ba'al Tefillah*, marvelously defined as *the master of prayer*. Rabbi Abraham Heschel tells us, "The mission of the cantor is to lead in prayer.... He must identify himself with the congregation. His task is to represent as well as inspire a community.... The music is not an end in itself but a means of religious experience. Its function is to help us to live through a moment of confrontation with the presence of God: to expose ourselves to him in praise, in self-scrutiny and in hope."[2]

Contrary to the satirical letter exchange with Ms. Song, the song leader should discover which songs their congregation really respond to, and why. The song leader continually collects songs and enlarges the congregation's repertoire. The song leader knows the songbook and embraces the full narrative of a song. The song leader learns the tunes and discovers what a tune will sound like with a new text, and vice versa. Reminiscent of the song leader partnerships of former generations, the song leader is acutely aware of the mood that is set by a tune married to a text. Importantly, the song leader does not choose just a charming lyric, but also learns to select complementary music that ultimately "serves the service."[3]

A generation ago Alice Parker commented, "For too long we have relied on the organ [in The Salvation Army, the band], choir, keyboard and the hymnal to 'make it easy' for the congregation to sing."[4] In this era of projected lyrics, amplified instruments, and sophisticated arrangements, congregations seem to be saying, "The music will continue whether we sing or not." The result in many places is lethargic, passive congregational singing. Out of respect for the service, worshipers stand and seem to be listening, but many do not sing.

Relying on instruments, whether plugged or unplugged, discounts the reality that the only instrument that copes with words is the human voice. Song is after all music *and words*, which requires a song leader! Take a cue from the itinerant revival teams of old. Few things bind a congregation together like vibrant song. Nurture a partnership with your congregation, and like the cantors of old proclaim, "How good it is to sing praises to our God, how pleasant and fitting to praise Him!" (Psalm 147:1) Lead on!

PREACHER

John Wesley (1703–1791)

Dwight L. Moody (1837–1899)

Billy Sunday (1862–1935)

Billy Graham (1918–)

SONG LEADER

Charles Wesley (1707–1786)

Ira Sankey (1840–1908)

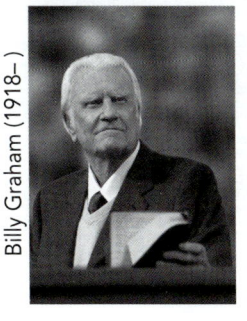

Homer Rodeheaver (1880–1955)

George Beverly Shea (1909–2013)

5 BARS REST

1. The opening question–and–answer letter exchange emphasizes how *not* to conduct oneself as a meeting leader. Reread the response letter, and then suggest ways to correct some of the answers to benefit the congregation and supporting musicians.

2. Reflect on the congregational singing in your corps. If the participation in song seems passive, do you think it is a matter of songs that are unfamiliar or difficult to learn? Is the instrumental support too loud, so that folks hesitate to sing since they cannot hear themselves? Or could it simply be a lack of effective song leadership?

OUR TREASURY OF SALVATION ARMY SONG

Salvation Army song, like The Salvation Army itself, was birthed in the open-air. In *Sing the Happy Song,* Brindley Boon recounts the first recorded evidence of Christian Mission music-making, from William Booth's 1865 diary: "We formed a procession and sang down the Whitechapel Road to the Room. We had an efficient band of singers, and as we passed along the spacious and crowded thoroughfare singing 'We're bound for the land of the pure and the holy,' the people ran from every side." Boon astutely observes an entirely unrehearsed blueprint for Salvation Army singing with the use of this song: **the testimony**–"We're bound for the land..." and **the appeal**–"Say will you go to the Eden above?" Several editions have commenced with the Founder's Song–"O Boundless Salvation." But William Booth placed this song–"To the Eden Above"–first in many early publications, including his "Revival Songs" and The Salvation Army "Penny Song Book."[5]

W. T. Stead, writing in 1895, marveled at the early Salvation Army's outpouring of song: "This latest birth … owes at least as much of its astonishing success to its hymns as to its disciples. No religious denomination or organization of any kind has done so much to develop verse-writing. Every week *The War Cry* is filled with new hymns … They have long since passed the fresh and sweet simplicity of war songs like: 'The devil and me, we can't agree, I hate him, and he hates me.'" Stead commends enthusiastically a song like "Blessed Lord, in Thee Is Refuge" from the pen of the Founder's son, Herbert Booth, which remains in our song book today.[6]

In the nineteenth century, Brooklyn-based Henry Ward Beecher was one of the most famous preachers of his day. In speaking of Railton and the Hallelujah Lassies' invasion of New York, he was quoted to say, "That these people will sing their way round the world in spite of us is already being

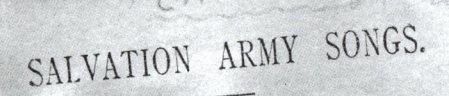

www.music.saconnects.org

fulfilled, for on sea and on land their *songs* have been heard all round the globe."[7] Typical of the practice of adapting religious words to "profane ditties of the music hall," Railton apparently was fond of singing the words, "O, how I love Jesus" to a popular air, "So early in the morning."[8]

For Salvationists, "less churchy" Salvation Army songs, even militant airs, quickly took the place of the revival hymns of the day.[9] Brindley Boon credits the Fry Family, also the Army's first bandsmen, with collecting the new words and music: "When a new song was heard the words would be swiftly taken down while the melody was recorded."[10] Apparently, Ernest and Bert Fry were able shorthand scribes while elder brother Fred was a tonic *sol–fa* expert who transcribed the tunes. Some of the Army's best songs by Herbert Booth and Richard Slater date from the first songster brigade, founded in 1883 in Clapton, England, as the Salvation Songsters.[11]

One practical and economic innovation for disseminating new songs was *The Salvation Soldier's Song Book* (1885). Paper-covered, with 251 tunes for congregational use, it sold for just a penny.[12] The rich outpouring of Salvation Army song dates back to the Booths—William, Herbert, and Evangeline—and has continued in later years with songs by Albert Orsborn, Catherine Baird, and John Gowans. The latest edition of the *Salvation Army Song Book* is the sixth major collection of songs, dating back to 1878.

Response and revelation

Evangelical Christians treasure two books—the Bible and their songbook. Martin Luther "gave the German people in their own language the Bible and the hymnbook, so that God might speak *directly* to them in His Word, and that they might *directly* answer Him in their songs."[13] Congregational singing permits a united *response* to the gospel.

The Pilgrim forefathers journeyed to church carrying two books, the then-new King James Bible and the Bay Psalm Book, the very first book of any kind printed in the American colonies. Both were used as a basis for family and private devotions.[14] In the same way, Salvationists daily underline and meditate on songs and passages in their handy one-volume edition of *The Song Book of The Salvation Army* combined with the *New Testament and Psalms*.

Many song texts, bathed in Scripture, summon us to response, yet also carry divine revelation. General Albert Orsborn may have put it best when he wrote in the Foreword to the 1953 edition: *"The upward reaching of the soul, the downward reach of the love of God, the incense of devotion, the canticles of praise, are all here."* Our songbook serves as both a devotional treasury of sacred poetry, particularly espousing the Salvation Army's strong holiness doctrine, and a highly functional expression of our evangelical thrust. In the words of the Army's Founder William Booth, *"We sing of salvation and aim to save souls by singing as well as by proclaiming the gospel of the grace of God."*

King James Bible title page, 1611

Bay Psalm Book, title page, 1640

In the preface to an early songbook, William Booth also wrote:

> *Let us persevere in our singing…How thoughtlessly many sing familiar words. Yet here is a great treasury of truth if you will but search into its riches. Be determined that by God's grace you will never sing what you do not really mean and that you will be fit to sing all you find here.*
>
> *Sing to make the world hear! The highest value of our singing after all has not been the mere gladness we have felt because of our own salvation, but the joy of pouring out the praises of our God to those who have not known Him, or of arousing them by our singing to new thoughts and a new life.*
>
> *Sing till your whole soul is lifted up to God, and then sing till you lift the eyes of those who know not God to Him who is the fountain of our joy. I cannot imagine that in Heaven itself we can cease to remember and repeat to each other the strains our souls have reveled in most here below. Till then, let us all sing!*

— William Booth

623

Nottingham, 256; Randolph, 257; Consecration Hymn, 246 (combine two verses); All for Thee, 241 (combine three verses); Hendon, 249 (repeat last line of verse)
Romans 12:1, 2   7.7.7.7.

TAKE my life and let it be
Consecrated, Lord, to thee;
Take my moments and my days,
Let them flow in ceaseless praise.

2 Take my hands and let them move
At the impulse of thy love;
Take my feet and let them be
Swift and beautiful for thee.

3 Take my voice and let me sing
Always, only for my King;
Take my lips and let them be
Filled with messages from thee.

4 Take my silver and my gold,
Not a mite would I withhold;
Take my intellect and use
Every power as thou shalt choose.

5 Take my will and make it thine,
It shall be no longer mine;
Take my heart, it is thine own,
It shall be thy royal throne.

6 Take my love; my Lord, I pour
At thy feet its treasure-store;
Take myself and I will be
Ever, only, all for thee.

Frances Ridley Havergal (1836-1879)

The Salvation Army Song Book and Tune Book

The continued Salvation Army use of a "words only" songbook, supported by separate piano and band tune books, creates a number of challenges for the meeting planner, leader, congregation, and supporting musicians. **Since there are separate volumes for the words and music, there is a songbook-number and a separate tune book-number to deal with.** As not all lyrics are printed in the piano book,[15] the pianist and/or bandmaster must look up the words, to be assured that the tune chosen is the best and to be aware of how many verses are indicated. The song leader can help by indicating which verses will be sung, or in the case where a verse is read, by cueing all that "we will now sing the final verse."

Some songs in the *Piano Tune Book* include lyrics, particularly in irregular meter familiar to the set of words indicated.

605 A Mighty Fortress

MARTIN LUTHER (1483-1546)

A might-y for-tress is our God, A bul-wark nev-er fail-ing;
Did we in our own strength con-fide, Our striv-ing would be los-ing;
And though this world, with de-mons filled, Should threat-en to un-do us;
That word a-bove all earth-ly powers, No thanks to them a-bid-eth;

Some tunes in the *Piano Tune Book* appear without lyrics, principally those in regular meter, allowing for multiple options of text.

Song book and tune book numbers used in this chapter are from the 2015 edition.

831 **Slane**

Irish traditional melody

THE EVOLUTION OF HYMNS, GOSPEL SONGS, AND WORSHIP CHORUSES

It helps first to have some understanding of song structure, which dates back several hundred years. In ***hymns***, verse words were conceived to allow the possibility of repeating the same music, but with fresh words for each verse. So a hymn like *Come Thou Fount of Every Blessing* has three verses of words utilizing the same hymn tune melody. Some hymns conclude each verse **(V)** with a brief refrain **(R)**, as in *For the Beauty of the Earth*, where each verse concludes with the same words and music: "Father, unto Thee we raise/This our sacrifice of praise."

Today's praise and worship songs follow in the tradition of the ***gospel song***, where a more extended refrain, which became known as the *chorus*, follows each verse. If we call the verses **(V)** and the chorus **(C)**, then a song of three verses with their unvarying choruses would be summarized as having **VCVCVC** form. A good example is Fanny Crosby's *Blessed Assurance* with its chorus, *"This is my story, / this is my song, / Praising my Savior all the day long."* In the evangelical tradition, the song leaders would choose to repeat the final chorus, bringing the *singspiration* to a rousing conclusion.

A HYMN A WEEK?
"Most contemporary choruses can't replace the solid theology and lyrical beauty of time-tested hymns. To paraphrase St. Bernard of Clairvaux, 'what language could we borrow to thank our Dearest Friend' without the treasury of hymn texts?"
–Greg Asimakoupoulos

HYMNS = Verses (VVV)

830 Glory to the Lamb, 327; Nettleton, 374
1 Samuel 7:12 8.7.8.7. Troch.

Verse 1: COME, thou Fount of every blessing,
Tune my heart to sing thy grace,
Streams of mercy, never ceasing,
Call for songs of loudest praise.

Verse 2: O to grace how great a debtor
Daily I'm constrained to be!
Let that grace, Lord, like a fetter,
Bind my wandering heart to thee.

Verse 3: Prone to wander, Lord, I feel it,
Prone to leave the God I love;
Here's my heart, Lord, take and seal it,
Seal it for thy courts above.
Robert Robinson (1735-1790)

HYMNS = Verses with Refrains (VRVRVR)

14 England's Lane, 277; Wells, 286; Dix, 276
Hebrews 13:15 7.7.7.7.7.7.

Verse 1: FOR the beauty of the earth,
For the beauty of the skies,
For the love which from our birth
Over and around us lies,
Refrain: *Father, unto thee we raise*
This our sacrifice of praise.

Verse 2: For the beauty of each hour
Of the day and of the night,
Hill and vale and tree and flower,
Sun and moon and stars of light,
Refrain: *Father, unto thee we raise*
This our sacrifice of praise.

Verse 3: For the joy of human love,
Brother, sister, parent, child,
Friends of earth, and friends above,
For all gentle thoughts and mild,
Refrain: *Father, unto thee we raise*
This our sacrifice of praise.
Folliott Sandford Pierpoint (1835-1917)

GOSPEL SONG = Verses + Choruses (VCVCVC)

455 Blessed Assurance, 577
Hebrews 10:22 Irregular

Verse 1: BLESSED assurance, Jesus is mine;
O what a foretaste of glory divine!
Heir of salvation, purchase of God,
Born of his Spirit, washed in his blood.
Chorus: *This is my story, this is my song,*
Praising my Savior all the day long.

Verse 2: Perfect submission, perfect delight,
Visions of rapture burst on my sight;
Angels descending, bring from above
Echoes of mercy, whispers of love.
Chorus: *This is my story, this is my song,*
Praising my Savior all the day long.

Verse 3: Perfect submission, all is at rest;
I, in my Savior, am happy and blest.
Watching and waiting, looking above,
Filled with his goodness, lost in his love.
Chorus: *This is my story, this is my song,*
Praising my Savior all the day long.
Fanny Crosby (1820-1915)

PRAISE + WORSHIP CHORUS with Bridge (VCVCBCC)

114 Here I am to Worship, 653
John 8:12 Irregular

Verse 1: LIGHT of the world, you stepped down…
Chorus: *Here I am to worship…*
Verse 2: King of all days, Oh so highly…
Chorus: *Here I am to worship…*
Bridge: I'll never know how much it cost…
Chorus: *Here I am to worship…(usually repeated)*
Words and Music by Tim Hughes
© Copyright 2003 Thankyou Music

Pop songwriters discovered that after two verses/choruses, a melodic departure was required to keep interest. One possibility was to change key, which we will consider in the Piano Chapter Seventeen. Alternately, songwriters began to conceive a little bridge passage, which we label as **(B)**. The bridge usually utilizes contrasting material that builds to a satisfactory return back to the verse **(V)**/chorus **(C)**. The full song form then becomes **VCVCBVC**. A version that moves from the bridge directly back to a final chorus would be summed up as **VCVCBC**. This verse/chorus, verse/chorus, bridge, final chorus structure is the norm for many of today's ***praise and worship songs***.

FINDING AND PROJECTING THE RIGHT WORDS

The "words only" congregational Song Book is divided into a number of primary sections with subtitles under each. The songs in each section are set out in alphabetical order. These subsections are designed to aid the meeting leader in selecting thematically related songs. To aid meeting planning, thematic and Scripture reference searches, in addition to metrical, title/first line and tune-to-song indexes are available as applications for the most recent Song Book. A "See also:" listing concludes each section for related songs which may appear in other sections of the Song Book.

CONTENTS

THE ETERNAL GOD
  God the Father
    Holy, Loving, Creator and Ruler

  God the Son
    The Name of Jesus
    The Advent and Birth of Jesus
    The Life and Teaching of Jesus
    The Suffering and Death of Jesus
    The Resurrection and Ascension of Jesus
    The Power and Glory of Jesus

  God the Holy Spirit
    The Person of the Holy Spirit
    The Indwelling of the Holy Spirit
    The Work of the Holy Spirit

OUR RESPONSE TO GOD
  Worship
    Meeting Together
    Praise and Adoration

  Salvation
    Invitation and Challenge
    Forgiveness
    Repentance, Faith and Regeneration
    Eternal Hope

  Holiness
    Devotion
    Discipleship
    Wholeness
    Means of Grace
      Prayer
      Scriptures
      The Church

  Life and service
    Testimony
    Worldwide Witness
    Warfare
    Stewardship
    Justice
    Reconciliation

  Dedication of Children
  Enrollment of Soldiers

BENEDICTIONS

SCRIPTURE INDEX

1 SAMUEL
3:9 — 775

1 KINGS
8:12–53 — 822

2 KINGS
6:15–17 — 486

1 CHRONICLES
16:30 — 52
22:13 — 814
22:15 — 998
29:13 — 45, 508
29:15 — 27

2 CHRONICLES
15:12–15 — 882
32:7 — 814

NEHEMIAH
1:7 — 630
9:5 — 391, 982

ESTHER
4:14 — 814

JOB
19:25 — 223, 224, 229
35:10 — 663
38:6–7 — 100

THEMATIC INDEX

God – Creation
54; 77; 320; 346; 463; 664

God – Faithfulness
19; 21; 22; 25; 26; 40

God – Glory
225; 261; 270; 277; 383

God – Grace and Mercy
52; 453; 455; 754; 793; 830

God – Love
91; 207; 241; 302; 342; 377; 385; 395; 490; 524; 536; 605; 621; 631; 810; 823

God – Majesty and Power
6; 376; 479; 745; 760

God – Mercy
383; 460; 748; 943

God – Presence
85; 342; 363; 573; 605; 611; 715; 822

God – Protection, Care and Guidance
16; 28; 353; 372; 549; 651; 745; 794

Chapter 5 | THEN SINGS MY SOUL!

INDEX TO THE SONGS	
God's love is as high as the heavens	24
God's love is as wide as creation	24
God's love is wonderful	25
God's love to me is wonderful	25
God's love, God's love	*24*
Goodness and mercy all my life	62
Great Father of Glory, pure Father of light	37
Great is Thy faithfulness	*26*
Great is Thy faithfulness, O God my Father	**26**
Guide me, O Thou great Jehovah	27

In looking for a particular song, first lines of ALL verses and choruses in the Song Book are included in the index. **First verses are indicated in bold type**, other verses in Roman type, and *choruses in italics*. The most recent Song Book does not have a separate section for stand-alone choruses but integrates these topically into the main body of songs.

When announcing a song, it is the practice of many song leaders to give both the song number and the page number. "Let us turn to song number 254, found on page 83 in the Song Book." This helps acclimate the newcomer to the Song Book. As the song leader outlines the first verse words, all are assured that they have the correct song.

83		GOD THE SON
254	Our God reigns, 793 *Isaiah 52:7-10*	Irregular

HOW lovely on the mountains are the f
  of him
Who brings good news. c
Proclaiming peace
  of happin
Our c

Making projected or printed text readable

For many people the eyes are a gateway to the heart and mind. In the same way that a heard wrong note or word can distract worshipers, so a poor visual presentation of the all-important lyrical content can diminish the worship experience.[16] As a leader, work with your media people to make handouts and slides as clear and attractive as possible. Here are some artistic and legal guidelines that govern the reproduction of song lyrics.

Stick to the poetry

Avoid squeezing (or justifying) lyrics just to make them fit. Rather spread out the lyrics, maintaining the line-by-line poetic scheme. Commence each phrase flush left on a new line, which is far easier to read than lines centered. Avoid what literary folks call **widows** and **orphans**, loosely described as a single word, line (or article) left alone on a succeeding line or page. These prove awkward to read. Re-size or split the phrase as two phrases to avoid a solitary word on a line by itself.

orphan (*term*) \ˈȯr - fən \ first line of a paragraph that gets cut off and stranded at the bottom of a paragraph as in the one you are reading right now. One might say the *orphan* is abandoned early in life, near the "birth" of the paragraph.

widow (*term*) \ˈwi - dō\ A single line of text should never reside by itself without the rest of its paragraph family. The first or last line of a paragraph sometimes gets separated from its paragraph family and stranded on a line by itself in another column, or sometimes on the next page. One might say the widow is abandoned late after the elderly paragraph husband dies on the previous page, leaving the widow to carry on by herself.[17]

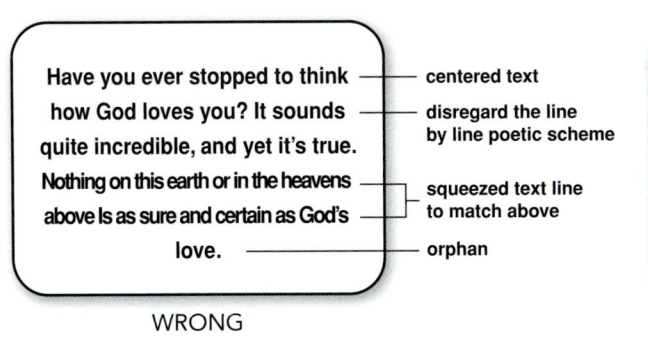

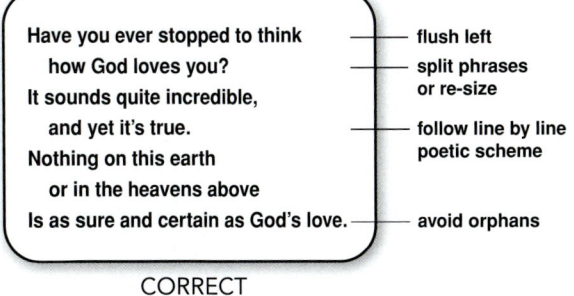

WRONG

Have you ever stopped to think — centered text
how God loves you? It sounds — disregard the line
quite incredible, and yet it's true. by line poetic scheme
Nothing on this earth or in the heavens — squeezed text line
above Is as sure and certain as God's to match above
love. — orphan

CORRECT

Have you ever stopped to think — flush left
  how God loves you?
It sounds quite incredible, — split phrases
  and yet it's true. or re-size
Nothing on this earth — follow line by line
  or in the heavens above poetic scheme
Is as sure and certain as God's love. — avoid orphans

The Beat Goes On

Big and BOLD

Type size needs to be large enough, using a readable font style. For projected text this is probably no smaller than 24 points. Do not use ALL CAPS, which is hard to read. Avoid *serif fonts* on dark backgrounds. These are the ones with flourishes and "tails" on each letter like Times, Goudy, American Typewriter, and **Rockwell**. The serifs tend to look faded after one duplication. Effective *sans serif* fonts are Arial, Avant Garde, Helvetica, and Tahoma. The background color needs to be dark if the type is to be light and vice versa. White type on yellow, or orange on red will not be legible.

TEXT LEGIBLE WITH MUTED BACKGROUND

SANS SERIF FONT

SERIF FONT

**** AVOID THESE!!! ****

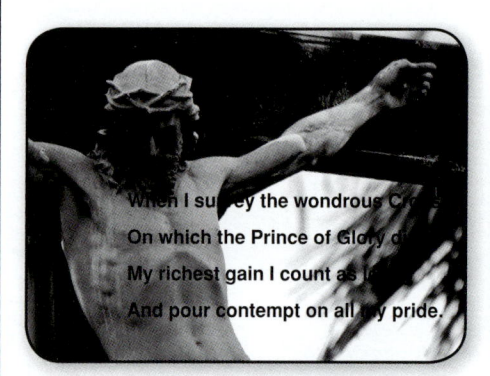

TEXT ILLEGIBLE WITH DARK BACKGROUND

TEXT TOO SMALL

SERIF FONTS WITH DARK BACKGROUND

The devil can be in the details

Use spell check, but also proofread your work. Few things distract worshipers like a misspelled word, especially if it changes the meaning of the phrase. The names of the writers of the words and music should appear in small font after the final verse with a notice of copyright ownership and your church CCLI license number. This actually cues both the singers and the tech operator that this is the final slide of a song. Use a blank, **black** slide as the first and last slide.

Come and warship!
Blessed insurance
Amazing face
Swing low, sweet clarinet

On Jordan's story banks I stare
And cash a wishful eye
To Canada's far and hippy land
I am down for the promised land.

PERHAPS GOD DOESN'T KNOW ABOUT AUTOCORRECT?

www.music.saconnects.org

Copy right?

Most churches today subscribe to a church copyright licensing organization. In the U.S. and Canada, the sliding (by congregation size) annual fee for CCLI (Christian Copyright Licensing International) allows reproduction rights on certain copyrights, focusing particularly on congregational usage. Each of The Salvation Army United States territories and the Canada and Bermuda Territory pays CCLI a reduced bulk rate to cover each ministry unit. Some territories underwrite this annual fee. The copyright licensing organization pays the royalties due the copyright owners based on a survey of the songs used over a sample quarter every two years.

The copyright license allows you to copy a song (or retype the words) as a congregational insert or projected slide. Filing a single copy of your playlist and bulletin each week facilitates the bi-annual, quarterly reporting to CCLI. In other countries, similar church copyright licensing services are used, such as CopyCare in the United Kingdom.

For your musicians, this **does not** mean that you can purchase a single copy of a songbook and make photocopies. If you have purchased enough copies of various songbooks for each member of your team, you may photocopy pages from these for easy access on Sundays. A number of online services grant access to worship song lyrics, sound samples, and downloads of lead sheets, chord sheets, and SATB hymn sheets. Songs beyond copyright, such as the older hymns and Gospel songs, are known as public domain (PD) songs and may be duplicated, if not copyrighted as an arrangement. No copyright notice (dated 1922 or before) will be indicated under these songs.[18]

A CCLI license **does** permit someone who does not read music to create a chord chart of a song from a published/purchased collection or hymnal and duplicate it. (Refer to Chapter Eighteen, p. 385 for a full description of a chord chart.) The same is true for a lyric sheet with chords made by sorting out a song "by ear." Use of these songs should be reported. Rather than a copyright ©, the copyright protection for recordings appears as a P in a circle ℗ which stands for Pressing. Therefore the CCLI license **does not** permit duplication of practice recordings for your musicians from a rehearsal or a single purchased copy of a copyrighted song.[19]

The Church Copyright License Annual Fee - U.S. (2013)

Category	Church Size	Annual Fee
AH	1 - 24	
A	25 - 99	$55
B	100 - 199	$116
C	200 - 499	$196
		$261

PROPER COPYRIGHT NOTICE

Great is Thy Faithfulness
Thomas Chisholm/William Runyan
© 1923. Renewal 1951 Hope Publishing Co.

When I Survey the Wondrous Cross
Isaac Watts/Lowell Mason
Public Domain

Face to Face, Pendel Singers,
℗ The Salvation Army - Philadelphia

O, How I Love Jesus
Frederick Whitfield/Traditional American Melody
Public Domain

```
G        Bm/D         G
O,   how  I   love  Je - sus,

D7                G/D    Am/D
O,   how  I   love  Je - sus,

G        Bm/D       G      Em   G7/D
O,   how  I   love  Je  -  sus,

     Am       G/D   D7    G
Be - cause  He  first  loved  me!
```

CHORD CHART

FINDING THE RIGHT TUNE

Above the song text in the Song Book appears a large bold song number, a related Scripture reference, and at least one suggested tune name and number. About 690 of the songs and choruses in the present Song Book have only one recommended tune. For instance, Song 1, *A Mighty Fortress is Our God*, lists *Ein' feste Burg*, number 605, as the sole suitable tune. Many songs and choruses work only with their established melody. Many of these happily appear in the *Piano Tune Book* with text.[20]

For most of the songs that have a number of hymn tune options, the lyrics are not included in the *Piano Tune Book*. The most recent *Salvation Army Song Book* has 348 songs with two tune possibilities, and the remaining forty-three tunes with three to five tune options.[21] Listing tune options is important as an established lyric may be used in different parts of the world to a different tune. For instance, in the United States, song 52, *O Worship the King*, is often sung to *Hanover* (TB 479), while in the

1 Ein' feste Burg, 605
Psalm 46:1   Irregular

A MIGHTY fortress is our God,
A bulwark never failing.
Our helper he

52 Hanover, 479; Houghton, 480;
Laudate Dominum, 481
Psalm 104   10.10.11.11.
O WORSHIP the King, all glorious ab-
O gratefully sing his pow-
Our shield and

> **89** Grimsby, 75; Richmond, 107; Azmon, 59
> Revelation 5:11 C.M.
>
> O FOR a thousand tongues to sing
> My great Redeemer's praise,
> The glories of...

> **2** St. Francis, 43
> Psalm 96 L.M.
>
> ALL creatures of our God and King
> Lift up your voice and with...
> Alleluia! Alle...

Long Meter

Hursley
I dare to be different (requires Chorus)
I love Him better every day
I'll serve my Lord alone
It was on the cross
Lambton Green
Llangollen

8.7.8.7.8.7. Trochaic

At thy feet I bow adoring
Austria (repeat last two lines)
Bithynia
Blessed Lord
Bread of Heaven
Come and worship
Cwm Rhondda
Guide me, great Jehovah
Happy People
Helmsley
Living Waters

United Kingdom *Laudate Dominum* (TB 481) is used. *O for a Thousand Tongues* (Song 89) is familiar in the United States to the tune of *Azmon* (TB 59), while *Richmond* (107) or *Grimsby* (75) is utilized elsewhere. In general practice, the more familiar tune is indicated first, but this can sometimes be the preferred British choice.

Song 2, *All Creatures of Our God and King* lists only one tune, *St. Francis* (TB 43). However, also indicated are the initials L.M. (for Long Meter), which are the metrical dimensions of each verse of this song. This allows the meeting leader to consult the metrical index to substitute a tune with a similar meter. As a matter of convention, we use SASB as an abbreviation for the "words-only" *Salvation Army Song Book*. SATB refers to the *Salvation Army Tune Book*, where the tune book numbers are found. Sometimes we drop the SA and use simply SB for Song Book and TB for Tune Book.

The Metrical Index

Meter, as applied to poetry, considers the number of lines in a verse (or stanza), the number of syllables in a line, and the unique arrangement of syllables in relation to stress (or accentuation). Often verses are formed of pairs of lines. In the case of *Praise, My Soul* (SASB 55), we have six lines or three pairs of lines. There is an alternation of eight and seven syllables for each line within those pairs. Note that for line five, it is necessary to repeat, *"Praise Him"* [indicated in brackets] to fulfill the meter. In your introduction of the song, alert the congregation to implied "repeated" phrases.

> **55** Praise my soul, 406; Triumph, 408
> Psalm 103 8.7.8.7.8.7. Troch.
>
> 8 syllables — PRAISE, my soul, the king of Heaven,
> 7 syllables — To His feet Thy tribute bring;
>
> 8 syllables — Ransomed, healed, restored, forgiven,
> 7 syllables — Who like Thee His praise should sing?
>
> 8 syllables — Praise Him! [Praise Him! Praise Him! Praise Him!]
> 7 syllables — Praise the everlasting king.

Within each line, the strong syllable (in **bold**) is consistently followed by a weak one. This meter is called *trochaic*.

> 8 syllables — **PRAISE** my **soul**, the **king** of **Hea**-ven,
> 7 syllables — **To** His **feet** Thy **tri**-bute **bring**;

Thus in the Metrical Index at the back of the Song Book, *Praise My Soul* (SATB 406) is listed as **8.7.8.7.8.7. Trochaic**. Referring to that category in the index, one can see a listing of tunes that could alternatively be used with the words to *Praise My Soul* (SASB 55). A good safeguard is to check that all verses are compatible with syllables and accents. Use a piano or 1st cornet tune book for this. A tune should sensibly and sensitively reflect the words of the song. The tune *At Thy Feet I Bow Adoring* (SATB 393), while listed in this metrical category, might seem a little saccharine for this uplifting text.

Note that even though the number and lines may agree, the stresses may not. For instance, 8.7.8.7.8.7. Trochaic has a strong-to-weak stress pattern, while 8.7.8.7.8.7.

Iambic has the opposite weak-to-strong pattern. Some meters are so frequently encountered that they have become better known by a label rather than by numbers.

These are the first six categories noted in the Metrical Index. All of them are *Iambic* (following the weak-to-**strong** pattern) in character:

Long Meter (abbreviated L.M)	Four lines of eight syllables (8.8.8.8.)
Double Long Meter (D.L.M)	Eight lines of eight syllables (8.8.8.8. Double)
Common Meter (C.M.)	Four lines (8.6.8.6.)
Double Common Meter (D.C.M.)	Eight lines (Common meter repeated)
Short Meter (S.M.)	Four lines (6.6.8.6.)
Double Short Meter (D.S.M.)	Eight lines (Short meter repeated)

In the Metrical Index, all other meters are indicated by the number of syllables by line. In some cases, the differences in stress are also recognized. For example, the accents of song 609, My **all** is **on** the **al**-tar, which is 7.6.7.6. Iambic (note the weak-to-**strong** stress), differ from those of song 178, **Je**-sus **keep** me **near** the **cross**, which is 7.6.7.6. Trochaic (**strong**-to-weak).²²

To summarize this in the simplest terms, it is essential that the song leader (and song writer!) understand that the strong poetic syllable must fall on a strong musical accent. In this way, there is a correlation with the "barring" of the music. Consider two examples: "We're a /**band** that shall **con**–quer the /**foe**." Note how the words fall on the **strong** march-like first and third beats and are correctly matched by the music. The second example demonstrates an "unhappy marriage" of music and words where the natural text accents fall improperly with the music.

Meter categories that are consistent in their stress pattern are simply known by their syllable numbers. For instance, 6.5.6.5. is always *trochaic*. An asterisk (*) indicates that the tune can be used for that meter by making small adjustments, such as tying two notes under one syllable, repeating lines or using the verse and chorus together. No metrical alternative is indicated above a song text for hymns like *A Mighty Fortress,* which either have a unique metrical footprint or simply would not be considered with an alternative melody.

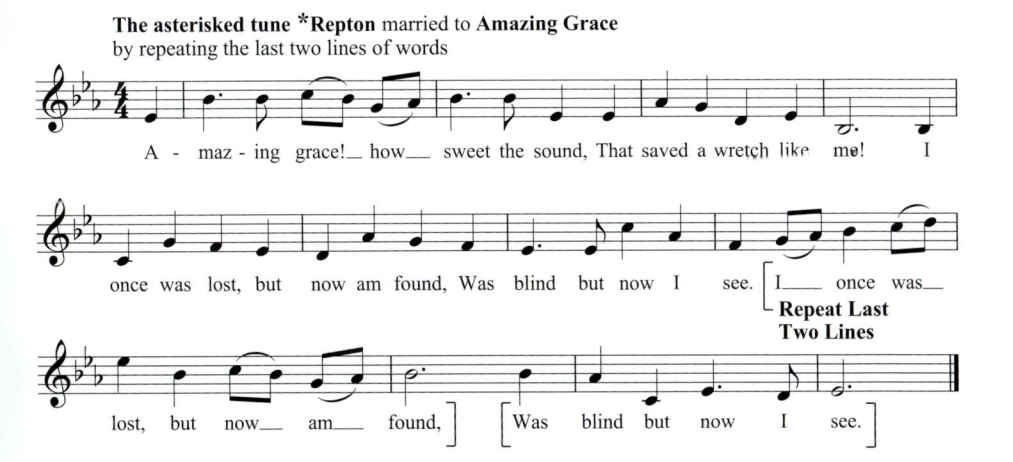

The two-fold intent of all this is succinctly summarized by the Founder in the foreword to an early edition of *The Salvation Army Song Book,* "Sing till your whole soul is lifted up to God, and then sing till you lift the eyes of those who know not God to him who is the fountain of all our joy." May it be so as you minister from week to week in song!

? 5 BARS REST

1. Leaf through the *Salvation Army Song Book* and identify a hymn, a hymn with a refrain, a gospel song, and a chorus (with and without a bridge.)

2. Select a hymn, song, or chorus and properly prepare a handout of the text suitable for a bulletin and/or a slide to be projected. Choose font type and size carefully, avoid widows and orphans, check spelling, and include proper songwriter/copyright identification.

3. Identify possible tunes that can be used with *All Hail the Power* (SB 73), *Jesus, Keep Me Near the Cross* (SB 178), and *Come, Thou Fount* (SB 830). Using the Tune Book, sing through these tune options to check for any lines that would need to be repeated.

4. Refer to the metrical index to consider a "fresh" tune option for *My Jesus, I Love Thee* (SB 878-11.11.11.11.) or *Jesus Shall Reign* (SB 258-Long Meter).

BEFORE INTRODUCING A SONG

Check the words with the tune

Be sure you review all verses of the song and, using a first cornet or piano tune book, check that the selected tune works. As mentioned in the survey of the Metrical Index, our Salvation Army "words-only" songbook includes some song texts that require repetition of selected phrases, for which only one or two lines might be indicated. Be sure to alert the congregation to the repeated lyrics. For example, song 391, *Stand Up and Bless the Lord,* is printed with a one-line refrain in italics:

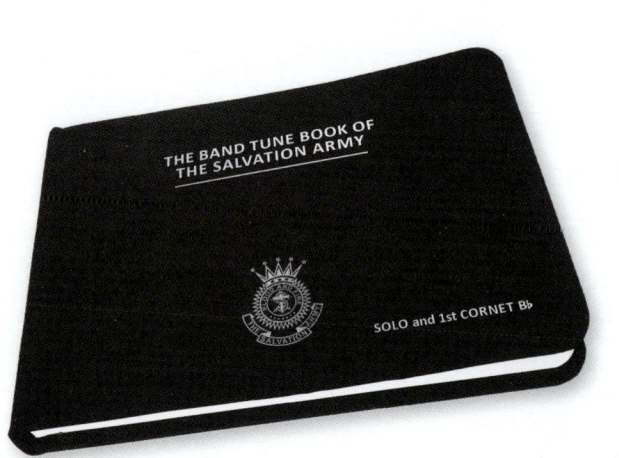

Refrain | *Praise ye the Lord, hallelujah!*

This refrain used with the suggested tune *Falcon Street* (TB 149) dictates the following text usage:

Refrain | *Praise ye the Lord, hallelujah!*
Praise ye the Lord, hallelujah!
Hallelujah, hallelujah,
Hallelujah! Praise ye the Lord!

This is where reference to a Piano Tune Book with both the words and music or a quick consult around the piano can help sort things out.

Double-check the projected text or song sheets

Notwithstanding all the safeguards suggested for creating slides of lyrics for Sunday worship, check the slides beforehand to be sure of how many verses are "in the computer." The song leader may opt for selected verses, for instance, verses 1, 2, and 5.

Sometimes it is wise to specify the hymnal being used. Often the text found in the *Salvation Army Song Book* differs from that found in some online hymn services in exact wording/translation and verse order. *Crown Him with Many Crowns* is one such example.

To outline or not?

After ascertaining the number of verses, decide how you might present the song. The practice of outlining verses dates to a time when there were no songbooks and served to aid those with limited reading skills. The outlining gives the congregation more time to "inhale" the words and their meaning, especially songs with rich devotional substance. Taking a break after a few verses and reciting a verse allows the bandsmen a rest and time to absorb a portion of the text. If projecting the lyrics, you will still want to use your songbook (or a printed version of the slides) at the podium, in case the slides don't come up properly. It is helpful to have in front of you the entire song for quick reference, to be certain of what text should be coming up when.

Be absolutely sure how the song starts

We will consider later in this section how to start songs that begin on the downbeat or commence with a pick-up. Be settled on the correct tempo. Note that sometimes the verses have a terrific number of words, and so are traditionally sung slower than the chorus. *God's Soldier* (SASB 954) is an example. A brighter tempo is assumed for each chorus, so the bandmaster or pianist will look for your "hand of guidance" going into and coming out of the chorus. If you wish to repeat the chorus, give a "C" signal with your cupped hand to your instrumentalists. Commissioner Samuel Brengle was known to slow the tempo down so that people could absorb the words more fully.

Before you approach the podium, establish if there will be an introduction by the band and/or piano. Introductions are marked with a bracket in the latest SA tune book, *Magnify*, or *Scripture-Based Songs* collections. Many of the *Hallelujah Choruses* have introductions, and sometime interludes, that you can absorb by referring to the demonstration tracks.

> **USE HYMN STORIES**
> Add poignancy and interest to a song introduction by making a quick search into the when and why of older songs and hymns. Joseph Scriven lost his fiancé to a drowning just prior to his wedding and penned *What a Friend We Have in Jesus*. Martin Rickart was performing as many as 50 funerals a day because of famine following the Thirty Years' War, yet he could declare *Now Thank We All Our God*.

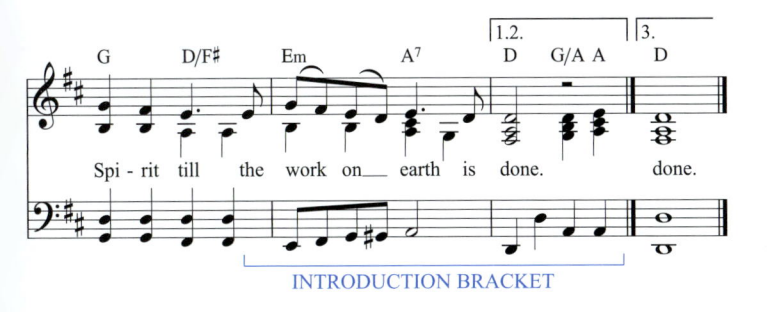

INTRODUCTION BRACKET

A SCRIPT FOR SONG LEADING

GREET THE CONGREGATION
With your eyes up and using a warm, projected voice, greet the congregation, *"Good morning."* (Some congregations will respond, *"Good morning."*) You continue, *"We welcome you to…(brief greeting)."*

ANNOUNCE SONG NUMBER, PAGE NUMBER, AND TITLE LINE
"Please turn in your Song Book to song number 85, found on page 32, 'Jesus, the very thought of Thee.'" Keep your head up and reach out with your eyes (as you have located the page beforehand) to encourage folks to locate the song.

ANNOUNCE SONG

RELATE THE SONG TO THAT DAY'S THEME
Use Scripture or highlight a meaningful phrase. Quick research in a concordance, hymn storybook, or *Companion to the Songbook* can yield a meaningful introductory comment. *"The writer of this song, Bernard of Clairvaux, was a much revered monk who lived in the Middle Ages. Day by day he would faithfully kneel in contemplation and his soul would be filled with a 'sweetness'* (word emphasized) *that would transcend the dark and difficult time in which he lived."*

YOU MAY WISH TO OUTLINE THE FIRST VERSE
"Jesus, the very thought of Thee … " and then announce the verses to be sung. *"I invite you to stand (or remain seated), as we sing verses 1 and 2."*

LIFT YOUR RIGHT HAND
This signals to the bandmaster or pianist that you are ready to start. Some meeting leaders will then say, *"We will have an introduction from the band"* (agreed upon beforehand) or *"We will be led by the band with an introduction."* (In this case, the bandmaster takes the lead of the song, turning and facing the congregation with songbook in hand.)

GIVE A START BEAT AT THE CONCLUSION OF THE INTRODUCTION
Alternatively, if there is to be no introduction, the musicians may look to the song leader for a starting beat to commence together. (Remember that the musicians are looking for this gesture before each verse.)

Use **your voice** to lead the song, singing into the microphone. Appropriate body language should reflect the message of the song. Make eye contact, keeping your head out of the songbook as much as possible, especially between verses. This encourages the congregation to sing heartily.

DOWNBEAT

AS YOU CONCLUDE A VERSE, RAISE YOUR RIGHT ARM
This signals that *"we are going to the next verse without a break."* If you place your hand down and back, the musicians can see that *"we are preparing to stop at the conclusion of this verse."*

Because singing more than two consecutive verses proves tiresome for congregation and band, the song leader will often ask the congregation to join in reading verse 3, *"O hope of every contrite heart!..."*

UPBEAT

SIGNAL TO BAND, WILL STOP

UNDERSCORE A MEANINGFUL PHRASE
The song leader may wish to make a comment before or after a verse to reiterate the sequence or story to the words. Reflecting on verse 3, one might add, *"Jesus is our joy, He is our hope…How good it is to seek Him today."*

TO CONTINUE, USE THE SAME ROUTINE
"Let us continue by singing the final two verses." Your arm goes up and the musicians begin right on the verse with your starting beat. Some song leaders will cut the congregation off on the final chord and ask the congregation to remain standing for prayer.

Following the amen, gesture the congregation to be seated, with a simple, *"You may be seated."* Take note of the program and be careful not to ask the congregation to sit if they will have to get up again soon.

A song presented in the middle of the service is sometimes introduced *"as an opportunity to share your testimony."* Avoid any jokes, "grading" of the singing, or any hint of embarrassing anyone, even when the accompaniment may not be perfect or as planned. Keep everything focused on the message of the song.

YOU MAY BE SEATED

PRINT THE SONG
There is great value in seeing the whole song printed in the bulletin, songbook, or on a song sheet. The printed words allow the worshiper to reflect back on the poetry of previous verses and the story of the song, even after the song has been sung. There may also be a few in your congregation who are visually challenged, for whom a large print songbook may be necessary. On the other hand, a projected image literally keeps *"everyone on the same page,"* focused forward and up.

FOOD, GLORIOUS FOOD

Sing a new song (occasionally!)
The temptation to limit your song choices to the "Top Five" weekly favorites can be likened to eating breakfast for three meals a day. Even if you *love* breakfast, that can become boring! Paul counsels us not to deprive ourselves of a sumptuous, well-balanced diet of "psalms, hymns, and spiritual songs." (Colossians 3:16) Why are we hesitant to sing new songs or to revive old ones? If truth be told, the real reason is it takes practice to learn to play *and* sing a new song! And, of course, the supporting musicians and the congregation get comfortable with a routine. The freshness of a "new song" regrettably is lost on familiarity.

Breakfast three times a day?

Breakfast   Lunch   Dinner

Sundays before
In Sunday's worship, all the subliminal tactics that work with the band for "selling" a theme chorus or hymn of the month are fair game. A number of Sundays before you introduce the new chorus, play it through the sound system or use it as prelude or postlude as folks enter and exit the sanctuary. Utilize it as an offertory, underscore, or segue before another part of the service. After a time, introduce the words by having it rendered as a vocal solo with synchronized projected text. All this means the song is not really new when you "introduce" it to your congregation.

Back in the day … can still work today!
In the days of *free and easy* chorus sings, sometimes known as *singspiration,* the song

The Beat Goes On

leader would enthusiastically announce that she was going to teach a new chorus. She might have previewed the chorus before the meeting with the pianist (or not!). The song leader would simply sing the song through once by herself with sketchy accompaniment. Then she would slow things down and outline the words with the music continuing in the background. Sometimes she might repeat the words and music line by line. She would then ask the congregation to try the whole chorus. As the words were not available in print or projected, the song leader would continue to speak the words, as the congregation tried the chorus again. The outlining of words would subside as singers and instrumentalists around her became more familiar with the song.

"Feeding" the words

The idea of *feeding* words in song, just preceding the next line, is common practice in present day gospel music and is a useful technique for a song leader to cue a supporting choir and congregation. While in the process of introducing the song, have your *prepared* singers stick to the melody in unison. Of course, today we can project lyrics nearly on the fly, so feeding of words is not as essential. It is interesting how handicapped worship feels today when the projector goes down. Yet how many choruses were learned by rote before we had projectors!

If the song is in verse-chorus form, you might teach the chorus first, which often is catchier. Then introduce a verse. Be sure to remain positive and encouraging. "I think we've got it. Let's try it one more time from the verse." Even if there are more verses, one may be enough for the first week. Be sure to segue to something familiar after your new song. Never open a set with a new song. Folks need to warm up and focus. It is also ill advised to bring two new songs to the table at one sitting. This is akin to trying two new main courses at one meal!

Congregational song accompaniments

Many hymnals make suggestions of medleys, usually based on a theme which the keyboardist can follow in sequence. Check with your bandmaster on a specific song or hymn for which there may be a special arrangement suitable for congregational singing. Be sure that all parties agree—leader, projected slides, keyboardist or band—on what the sequence of verses will be.

The Salvation Army in Chicago produces the *Hallelujah Choruses* series, which balances the latest SA and other praise chorus offerings, arrangements of time-honored classic hymns, and some selections from the rich heritage of Salvation Army song. The arrangements allow multiple options, such as the use of praise band with SAB voices, with or without a small instrumental contingent. *Hallelujah Choruses* arrangements can also be effectively rendered with just brass band/ensemble or, in most cases, by combining these various components. Suggestions for the "layering" of the various ensembles are given in the score. A demonstration/accompaniment track and visuals make this series useful to corps with limited resources and allows the song leader to become familiar with the roadmap.

Similarly, The Salvation Army UK Territory has produced a collection of praise choruses called *Magnify*, arranged for keyboard and/or band. This same Salvation Army publisher has also produced highly useful sets and a favorites book of *Scripture-Based Songs* for band use. The minimum instrumentation required for these collections is covered in Chapter Fourteen on pp. 308-309.

Chapter 5 | THEN SINGS MY SOUL!

THE SONG LEADER'S TOOLBOX

Everybody can learn simple beat patterns

When the conductor makes an up-and-down motion, he or she is said to be *beating time*. One down-and-up arm motion represents one *beat*, or making the analogy with your heartbeat, one *pulse*. A *tempo* designates how fast the beats are going. A metronome marking of 80 beats per minute is considered a moderate (*moderato*) tempo. 120 bpm (or two beats per second) would be considered a fast (*allegro*) tempo and 60 bpm (one beat per second) is slow (*adagio*).

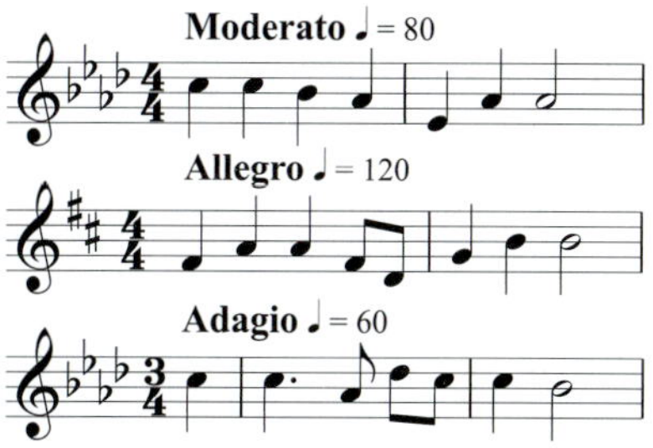

Beats are most commonly grouped into a recurring rhythm of four (**1**-2-3-4, **1**-2-3-4), three (**1**-2-3, **1**-2-3), or two (**1**-2, **1**-2) beats per measure. Two bar lines delineate a *measure* (or bar). At the beginning of the music, just after the clef sign, a *time signature* will be indicated. A measure of four beats is said to be in 4/4 time, while 3/4 time has three beats and 2/4 just two beats.

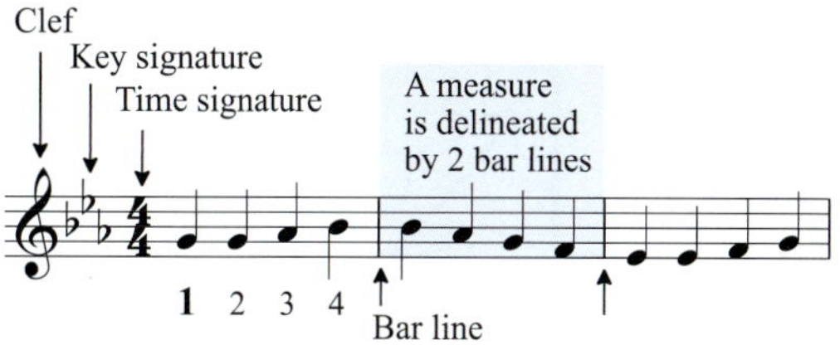

The "Invitation" PREPARATORY BEAT and DOWNBEAT

DOWNBEAT with Emphasis on One

Sing the verse of *Jesus Loves Me* (SASB 807) and feel how four beats fit into each of the eight measures. As you sing, you should feel how beat 1 is stronger and more emphasized.

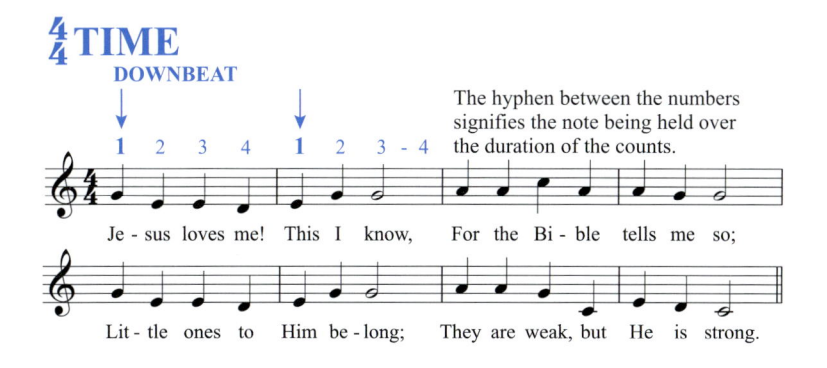

Reference the Chapter Five online folder for **audio accompaniments to the four song-leading examples** in this section.

The strongest beat in a bar is what we call the DOWNBEAT. Beat 1 is logically called the downbeat, because that is what the conductor does, he/she brings the beat down.

THE **DOWNBEAT** GESTURE

The "Invitation" PREPARATORY BEAT

In order to bring the beat down, you must start beating one count earlier. You can liken this to taking a breath on the beat before you begin to actually vocalize or sound a note on a brass instrument. A good preparatory beat is a summons or invitation that begins from a still position, which Max Rudolf calls Attention (Att).²³ The sequence starts still at Attention, then Up Slant (the prep beat), and Down (the downbeat).

Good news! Because the downbeat is conducted as beat 1 down, this same preparatory beat pattern will work on songs that start on the downbeat in 4/4, 3/4, and 2/4 time: Attention, then up slant, and down (1). It is this motion that the bandmaster, pianist, and your congregation are looking for to commence each verse of a song when the song starts on the downbeat (beat 1) of the measure.

The Beat Goes On

"The How Do I Stop This Train" CUT-OFF

Now more good news! On the last note of a song, bring your hand back to the still attention position and then do the same prep motion to a downbeat, up slant, and down (1). Stop at that down moment to make a simple *cut-off.*

THE 4, 3, and 2 BEAT PATTERNS

4/4 BEAT PATTERN

In order to complete the 4/4 pattern, go left (beat 2), and across right (beat 3) and then up on a slant (beat 4), ready for another downbeat (beat 1). That's all there is to beating 4/4 time: Down (1) – Left (2) – Right (3) – Up (4). Then start over! Note from the diagram that beats 2 and 4 Slant up and Left. The downbeat (1) will be clear if it is the lowest and strongest beat. Now sing the verse to *Jesus Loves Me* again, beating 4/4 time as you do it.

Chances are that most songs you will lead with a congregation will have four beats to the measure. 4/4 time is so common that it is sometimes called *common time,* and the 4/4 is replaced with a "C" as the time signature.

Common (C) time signature = 4/4 time

3/4 BEAT PATTERN

If, however, you encounter a song that feels like a waltz (**1**-2-3, **1**-2-3), then the song is in 3/4 time (sometimes known as *triple meter*). Logically, it uses a *triangle pattern.* The downbeat (1) is the same, down, *but beat 2 goes to the right* (or out, since you are using your right hand), then the slant up for beat 3, ready to begin the 3/4 pattern again. Lots of folks are so used to beat 2 in 4/4 going to the left, that they have to concentrate to remember to take beat 2 in 3/4 time to the right: 3/4 time = Down (1) – Right (2) – Up Slant (3). Sing *Praise to the Lord, the Almighty* (SASB 56) while beating 3/4 time. Be sure the downbeat (1) is the strongest and lowest beat. Beat 2 to the right should be more of a slant up right.

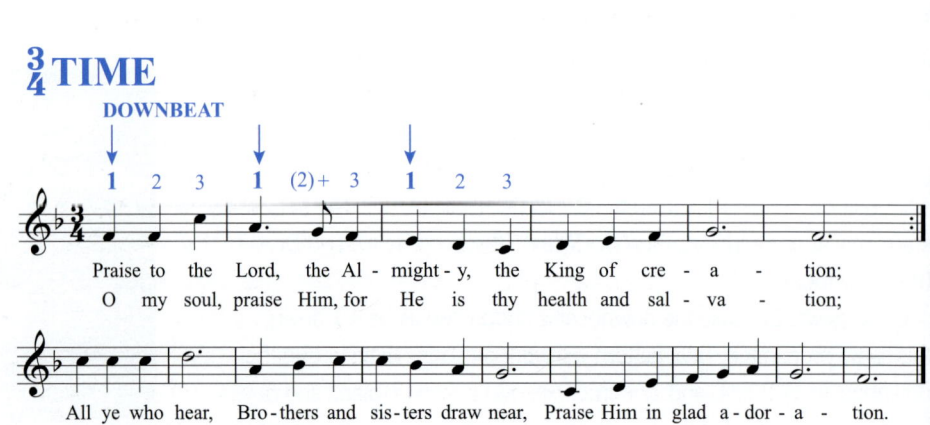

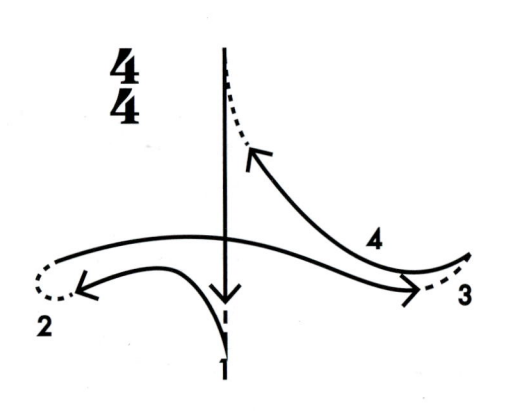

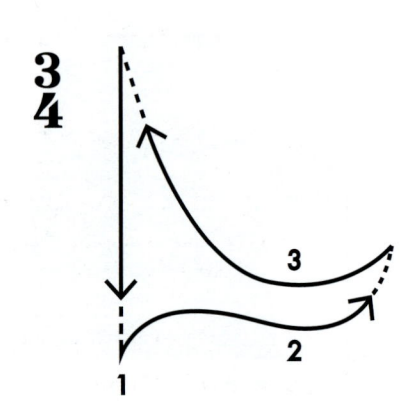

3/4 TIME

Praise to the Lord, the Al-might-y, the King of cre-a-tion;
O my soul, praise Him, for He is thy health and sal-va-tion;
All ye who hear, Bro-thers and sis-ters draw near, Praise Him in glad a-dor-a-tion.

2/4 BEAT PATTERN

To beat in 2/4 time (**1**-2, **1**-2, sometimes known as *duple time*), we simply employ a Down (1) – Up (2) motion. The downbeat (1) should be strong and then beat 2 weak. We sometimes call this a *downstairs–upstairs pattern*, where we imagine touching the bottom step and then the top stair.

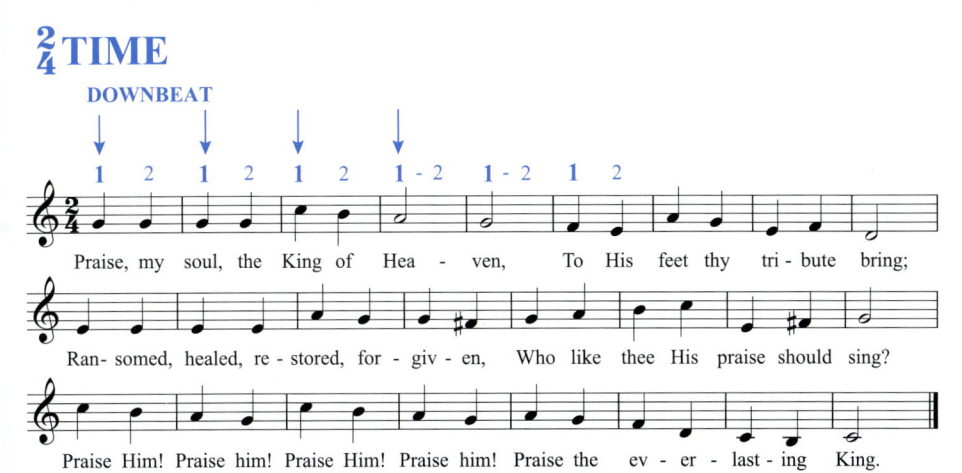

2/4 TIME

DOWNBEAT

1 2   1 2   1 2   1 - 2   1 - 2   1 2

Praise, my soul, the King of Hea- ven, To His feet thy tri- bute bring;
Ran- somed, healed, re- stored, for- giv- en, Who like thee His praise should sing?
Praise Him! Praise him! Praise Him! Praise him! Praise the ev- er- last- ing King.

5 BARS REST

Congratulations! You've learned how to conduct 4/4, 3/4, and 2/4 patterns and how to make an invitation preparatory pick-up and a cut-off.

1. To recap, the **preparatory beat** precedes exactly one beat before a song's first note. The size, speed, and intensity of that prep beat establish the dynamic, tempo, and style of the song. A light, quick motion signals a moderately soft, but fast tempo, while an unhurried, yet muscular motion signals a loud, slow pace. The song leader's right hand still–ATTENTION–moment signals to the band or pianist that we will begin. The conductor follows your prep "invitation" and all the forces begin together. Practice a series of preparatory beats, emphatically counting along, with the emphasis on **1**. (4–**1**, or 3–**1**, 2–**1**)

2. Practice beating the **4/4, 3/4,** and **2/4 patterns,** sometimes counting along (**1**-2-3-4, **1**-2-3-4), sometimes singing as you conduct. It can be fun to do this in a group, following each other's leadership using a Christmas carol book, such as *Carolers' Favorites* (CF). Note that the three carols selected in 3/4 time begin with a pickup note to the downbeat. In order to start, the song leader needs to show a preparatory beat (with a breath) on beat two, moving to the starting note pickup on beat three. (More on beat patterns, pickups, and fermatas can be found in the Conducting Chapters Twenty and Twenty-One, *Conducting Fundamentals*.) Once you've sung through the carol, make a cut-off for the end of each verse and begin the next verse with a clear preparatory beat.

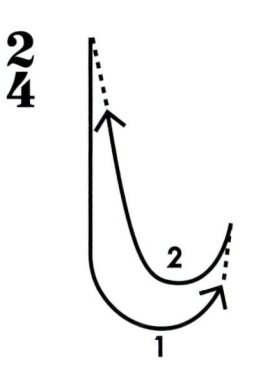

Hear ye, hear ye, even if you are left-handed, we always, always conduct the beat patterns with our Right Hand - always, always!

Hint: Keep your right arm generally in front of your torso, rather than swinging out of the "batter's box" for beats 2, 3, or 4

Accompaniment tracks for these **Christmas carols** are accessible in the Chapter Five online folder.

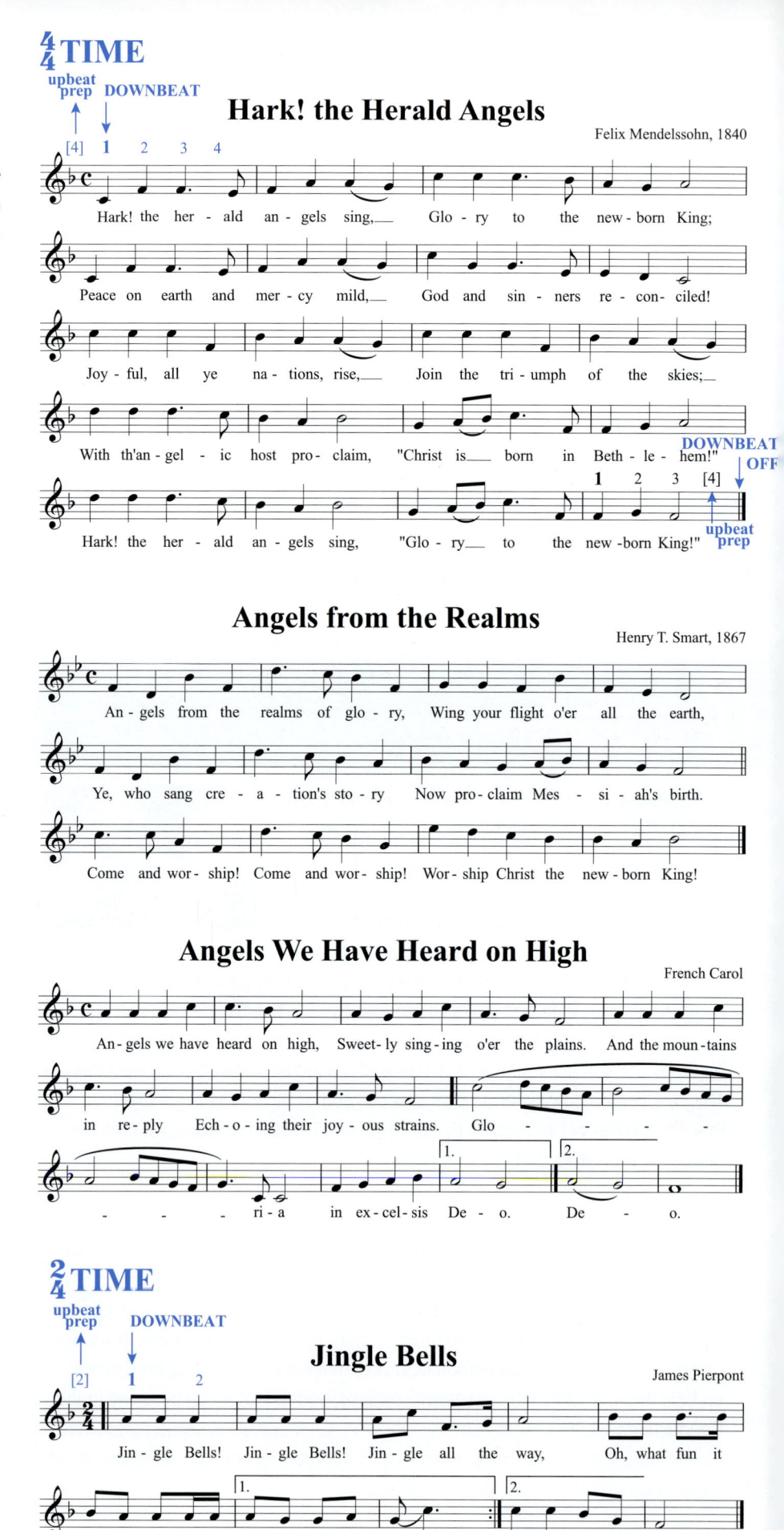

Hark! the Herald Angels
Felix Mendelssohn, 1840

Hark! the her-ald an-gels sing, Glo-ry to the new-born King;
Peace on earth and mer-cy mild, God and sin-ners re-con-ciled!
Joy-ful, all ye na-tions, rise, Join the tri-umph of the skies;
With th'an-gel-ic host pro-claim, "Christ is born in Beth-le-hem!"
Hark! the her-ald an-gels sing, "Glo-ry to the new-born King!"

Angels from the Realms
Henry T. Smart, 1867

An-gels from the realms of glo-ry, Wing your flight o'er all the earth,
Ye, who sang cre-a-tion's sto-ry Now pro-claim Mes-si-ah's birth.
Come and wor-ship! Come and wor-ship! Wor-ship Christ the new-born King!

Angels We Have Heard on High
French Carol

An-gels we have heard on high, Sweet-ly sing-ing o'er the plains. And the moun-tains in re-ply Ech-o-ing their joy-ous strains. Glo - - - ri - a in ex-cel-sis De - o. De - o.

Jingle Bells
James Pierpont

Jin-gle Bells! Jin-gle Bells! Jin-gle all the way, Oh, what fun it is to ride In a one-horse o-pen sleigh. one-horse o-pen sleigh!

Joy to the World!

George F. Handel, 1742

Joy to the world! the Lord is come; Let earth re-ceive her King; Let ev-'ry heart pre-pare Him room, And heav'n and na-ture sing, And heav'n and na-ture sing, And heav'n and heav'n and na-ture sing.

Deck the Halls

Welsh Traditional

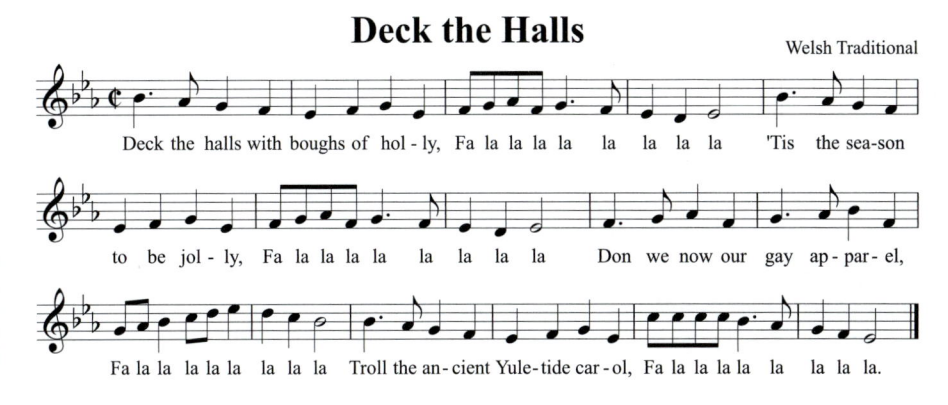

Deck the halls with boughs of hol-ly, Fa la la la la la la la la 'Tis the sea-son to be jol-ly, Fa la la la la la la la la Don we now our gay ap-par-el, Fa la la la la la la la la Troll the an-cient Yule-tide car-ol, Fa la la la la la la la la.

3/4 TIME

2nd beat prep | 3rd beat pickup | DOWNBEAT
[2] 3 | 1 2 3

Away in a Manger

Attr. James R. Murray, 1887

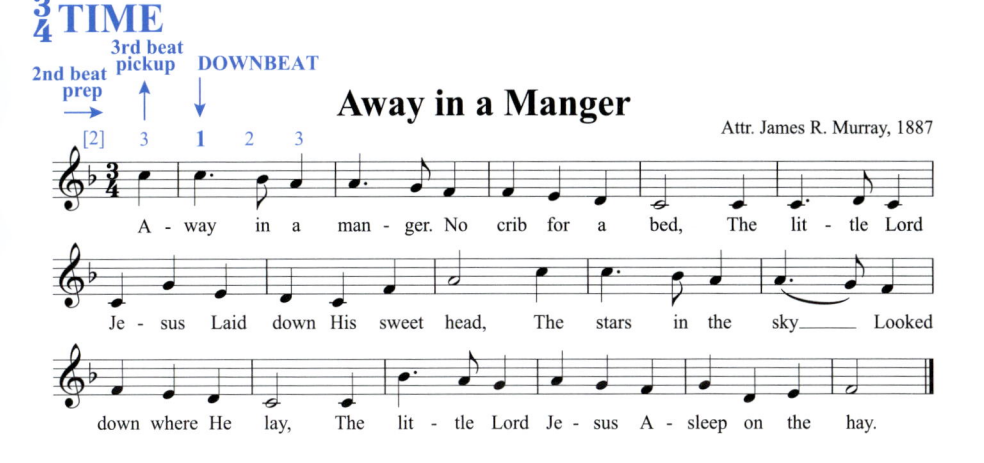

A-way in a man-ger. No crib for a bed, The lit-tle Lord Je-sus Laid down His sweet head, The stars in the sky Looked down where He lay, The lit-tle Lord Je-sus A-sleep on the hay.

The First Noel

English Traditional

The first No-el the an-gels did say Was to cer-tain poor shep-herds in field as they lay; In fields where they lay, keep-ing their sheep On a cold win-ter's night that was so deep. No-el, No-el, No-el, No-el, Born is the King of Is-ra-el.

The Beat Goes On

O Christmas Tree

German Folk Melody

O Christmas tree, O Christmas tree! Thou tree most fair and lovely! O lovely! The sight of thee at Christmastide Spreads hope and gladness far and wide. O Christmas tree, O Christmas tree! Thou tree most fair and lovely.

> Every spiritual awakening has produced songs that have fueled the movement's fire.
> —Greg Asimakoupoulos

SONG LEADER RESOURCES

In addition to many fine worship leader resources listed for Chapters Eighteen and Nineteen, the following articles and books will prove helpful to the song leader. Applications to locate Salvation Army songs by word or Scripture search, metrical index, music-to-words index, alphabetical, and first line listing are also available.

Cantos de Alabanza y Adoración/*Songs of Praise and Adoration*, Bilingual Hymnal/ Spanish and English side-by-side (Editorial Mundo Hispano)
Concordance to the Songbook, William Metcalf (Campfield Press)
Jubilate! *Church Music in the Evangelical Tradition*, Donald Hustad (Hope)
Mastering Worship–Chapter Four, "Keys to Congregational Singing," Howard Stevenson (Multnomah)
Melodious Accord, Alice Parker (Liturgy Training Publications)
Praying Twice: *The Music and Words of Congregational Song*, Brian Wren (Westminster/John Knox Press)
Salvation Army Song Book (words only) Also available in large print version
Salvation Army Piano Tune Book in two volumes—Volume 1 (music only, without lyrics) and Volume 2 (irregular meter songs, words with music)
Salvation Army Tune Book (1st cornet)
Songs of Salvation—ARC Songbook (Salvation Army, Des Plaines, IL), 200 songs in music and words with easy piano format, including chord and capo symbols.
The Words We Sing, Nan Corbitt Allen (Beacon Hill Press)
The Worship Sourcebook (Baker Books) Useful for calls to worship and linking Scripture.
Old Salvation Army Songs available online.
Other church hymnals and online song and chorus resources are also available.

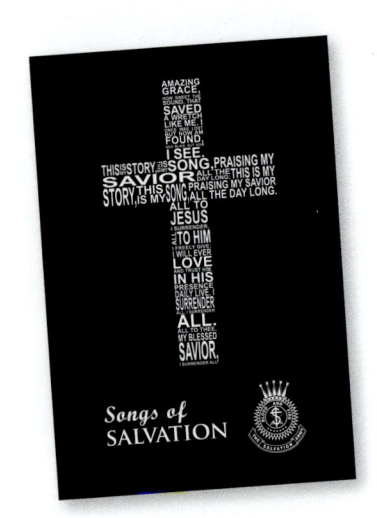

> So much more on congregational singing found in the Worship Leader Chapters Eighteen and Nineteen. Also valuable tips for corps pianists in Chapters Sixteen and Seventeen.

HYMN STORY COLLECTIONS

101 Hymn Stories, Kenneth Osbeck, (Kregel Publications)
Abide With Me—*The World of Victorian Hymns*, Ian Bradley (GIA)
Companion to the Songbook, Gordon Taylor (Campfield Press)
Great Songs of Faith—*365 Devotions based on Popular Hymns*, William and Randy Peterson (Tyndale)
Hymns That Live, Frank Colquhoun (InterVarsity)
Sing It Again, J. Irving Erickson (Covenant)
Sing the Happy Song! *A History of Salvation Army Vocal Music*, Brindley Boon (Salvationist Publishing and Supplies)
Songs in the Night, Henry Gariepy (Eerdmans)
The Gospel in Hymns, Albert Edward Bailey (Scribners)

Part Two
YOUTH MUSIC MINISTRY

CHAPTER SIX

LET THE CHILDREN SING!
Training Young Singers Through Small Group Instruction

"From the mouths of children and infants come songs of praise to You."
—Psalm 8:2a, *ERV*

FROM THE MOUTHS OF CHILDREN...

Few things stir the heart like a child singing. It may be the most underrated of God's secret weapons. Put a child up to sing and, except for the occasional blinking camera flash, all conversation and movement ceases. Innocence steals our attention. It is as though the children have been given a direct pipeline to the Father.

"Except ye become as a little child..." the Master said. Who are these children? They are the girl who is too obese for her young age and the overactive boy who just cannot sit still. They are the subjects of abuse or disenfranchised parents. One young child failed an exam today because it is impossible to be home, let alone to study. Another is secretly ashamed because she can barely read or write. Some know their voices aren't quite right. One boy knows it because those around him give off subtle signals when he struggles to find his pitch. A girl knows it because she is "placed" between singers or even asked to mouth the words. Without some remedial work, these young people will lose the freedom to worship freely in song. Perhaps 50 years of congregational singing will be hampered, held back and hidden, if they sing at all.

The Psalmist wrote: "From the mouths of children and infants come songs of praise to You." How do we make this ring true for all the children who enter our doors? How do we trade a child's embarrassment, inhibition, and withdrawal—born out of the airwaves of our noisy culture—into a lifetime of worshipful song? The Master also said, "Suffer the little children to come unto Me and forbid them not." (Mark 10:14, KJV) What if we spent a few minutes each week "singing" personally with a precious little one? Chances are it wouldn't be just about singing. "What did happen in math class today? Oh, you didn't have lunch. Let's get something to eat."

In **Chapter Six**, we learn how to teach children to:

- experience and replicate unison pitch.
- experience high, low, and middle pitches.
- recognize and sing stepwise pitches.
- use their voices properly, through warm-up preparations (including physical movements) that reinforce the boot camp basics—projection, posture, range extension, mouth formation, breath control, and diction.
- read stepwise melodies.

VOICE
with BEGINNER singers

time-in (*term*) \'tɪm - 'in\ is a one-on-one session intentionally aimed at getting a student caught up to the group with a particular skill.

Hints for helping untuned singers

Many adults in our worship services today are hesitant, even embarrassed, to join in congregational singing because they have been labeled "tone-deaf" or unable to "carry a tune." It is crucial that our children be engaged in tone matching at a young age in order to allow all of our worshipers to sing from Sunday to Sunday with all their hearts. Pitch issues are best dealt with at a young age. Therefore, we must choose not to relegate what we will call the "untuned" singer to a back row seat to mouth the words.

Carrying a tune requires *the ability to hear individual pitches, produce one's own pitches in imitation*, and *then ascertain whether those pitches are accurate*. Tone matching, or more specifically "experiencing a unison," is an important prerequisite to imitating melodies. It may require some "time-in"—just you and the child away from the group. Consider some of these techniques:

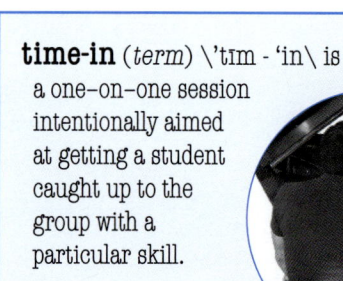

Goal #1

EXPERIENCE UNISON PITCH

From the first infant years, begin matching the pitch the youngster sings or coos. Do this anywhere—in the car, while giving a bath, or at bedtime. Identification with the experience of unison is an important benchmark. Avoid the keyboard. The human voice is far more effective.

Exposure to pitched material

Listening to beautiful tone will birth beautiful tone … and the earlier the better. Play recordings of lovely singing to your child while you are traveling or at bedtime. Much music in the mainstream media carries little real pitch content and poor quality of sound. Have the child listen to music with a full spectrum of performed pitches and rich tone colors from an early age.

Inability to concentrate

The children who come to you may be either hyperactive or sluggish because of improper nourishment, lack of rest, or lack of attention. Before or after rehearsal, hear your youngsters out. And keep in mind that hunger, dehydration, social problems, allergies, poor eyesight, or hearing loss can cause behavioral issues. You might want to provide a healthful snack, remembering that sweets are not the best idea. Before you get to work, take as little as 10 seconds to require hands and mouths to be still. This can assist youngsters in "shutting down" enough to focus on the task at hand.

Fear of failure

The last thing a child or teen wants is to look or sound awkward in front of his or her peers. Fear of failure can manifest itself in hesitant shyness or noisy obnoxiousness. Make improving pitch accuracy a team effort. Discreetly pitch-match in every rehearsal. Singing next to or behind the student's ear, rather than face-to-face, yields the best results.[1] Be strategic in seating children with weaker voices between or in front of children with stronger voices. Praise even the slightest improvement.

Tone deafness

Singers who appear to have a very limited range are often labeled tone-deaf. Begin by matching the accessible pitches the student offers. Be sure the student is using good posture and is in her "singing channel," rather than in speaking, whispering, or shouting mode, while she "sings." Use a target posted on a board or pad to show the student visually if their pitch is too high or too low. Challenge your singers to center the pitch on the bull's-eye. The goal is to extend the range both up and down, using the experience of unison.

Goal #2 — EXPERIENCE HIGH, LOW, AND MIDDLE

Early on, legendary children's choir conductor Helen Kemp likes to ask the choristers to switch through their voice channels. (Yes, gesture that we are switching the TV channels with a remote.) Have them repeat after you, using the appropriate volume and color in the voice:

"I speak like this."
(speak in a normal voice)

"I whisper like this."
(whisper)

"I YELL LIKE THIS!"
(yell)

"I sing like this."[2]
(demonstrate in a "head" voice)

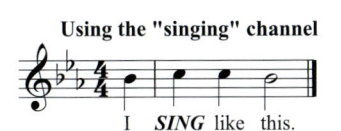

Yoo-hoo!

Next ask the children to imitate your "yoo-hoo" or "cuckoo" based on the descending *"so-mi"* intervals. It can help to draw two bull's-eyes and have children point to the center of each as they sing with you. If the pitch is off, adjust the child's finger to show where they are, either high or low, and challenge them to hit the note right on the target.

High, low, and middle

On Sesame Street the characters occasionally sing, "high, low, and middle." Ask children to sing and simultaneously position their hands to approximate the high, low, and eventually middle pitches. The range you choose to use depends on the age of the child. If a child "skies" into a stratospheric screech, suggest pulling down a helium balloon into the middle range, as he or she may not have physically experienced this range before. Singing with them, slide from their pitch to the desired one. Sirens and squiggles (quick oscillations up and down) with accompanying hand gestures can encourage their voices into their proper register.

For a 6-year-old: B-3 for low, F#-4 for middle, and C# or D-5 for high (seven to eight semitones maximum between the pitches).

For a 12-year old: A-3 for low, G-4 for middle, and F-5 for high (ten to eleven semitones between pitches).[3]

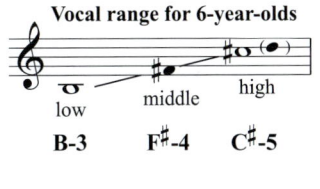

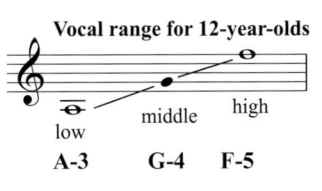

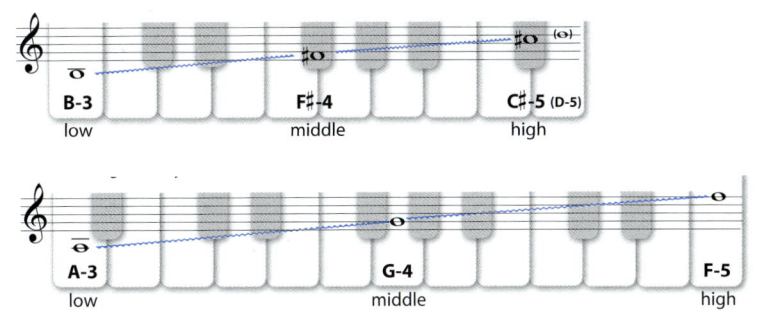

Vocal range for 6-year-olds
low B-3, middle F#-4, high C#-5

Vocal range for 12-year-olds
low A-3, middle G-4, high F-5

The Beat Goes On

Boys can sing higher than girls!

Boys, mistakenly imitating male singers, often have never experienced their upper register. Ask the boys to pretend they are holding a fishing rod and reel with their left hand. As they turn the reel with their right hand, have them imitate the fish coming up to the rod. The fast motion of the right hand turning in circles at the level of the lower ribs seems to help engage the breath and speed up the airflow needed for higher singing. A challenge for the boys to sing higher than the girls often works.

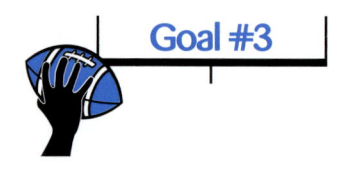

Goal #3: RECOGNIZE AND SING STEPWISE PITCHES

Having already taught how to accurately repeat tones, our third goal at the beginning stages with young voices is to get them to **recognize and sing stepwise pitches**. Pitches move in three ways:

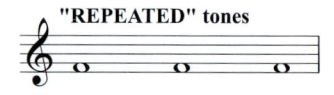

1. **"Repeated"** tones reiterate an initial pitch. Notes that are on the *same* line or space sound the *same*, in fact, they have the *same* sound.

2. Other pitches move up and down by **"step."** Notes that move by step are placed ascending or descending, alternating between lines and spaces on the staff. A helpful analogy is using every step when climbing or descending stairs.

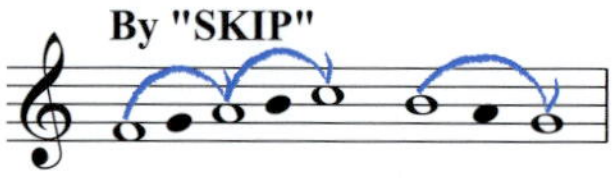

3. Another series of pitches may include **"skips,"** with a distance greater than a step between the notes. This is akin to skipping steps as you ascend or descend a staircase.

It is imperative that we use the gateways of learning—eyes, ears, and touch—to get this aural concept across.

The big staff

If you are outside, use sidewalk chalk to make a staff big enough to walk on. If inside, use masking tape to make a staff on the floor. Include a treble clef with your artwork.

Notes that look the same . . .

Begin by singing two identical notes in succession (for instance, F–F). Ask children to put one foot **in the space** and the opposite foot on the same space. Do the same for the next line (G–G), by asking then to put their foot **on top of the line**. This kinesthetically reinforces the concept of "repeated notes." The expression we can use is, "Notes that are on the *same* line or space sound the *same*. In fact, they have the *same* name."

Next we are going to physically experience musical steps on the staff. So introduce the first (lowest) space name as F and sing it as F, as children place their feet along that space. Next move to the second line up, singing it as G and so on. Be absolutely clear when you ask the student to put his or her foot on or point to the actual line. The expression "on the line" must be clarified to mean on top of the line, which actually extends into the space above and below. If the child can see through the middle of the note and see a space—Ah-ha, then it's a space note. If one sees a line in the middle—*voila*, then it is a line note.

Chapter 6 | LET THE CHILDREN SING!

Stepwise pitches

Next, introduce pitches that move by step. Direct students to put their left feet on the first space as *do* and then right hands on the second line as *re*. Be sure to sing the *solfege* names as you do this. At this point restrict your teaching to notes going up or down by step. You can play a game of musical twister with your group by asking the students to put their left hands on *re*, right feet on *mi*, right feet on *fa*, and so forth, up and down by step.

> **solfeggio** (*term*) \säl-'fej-ē-ō\ or more commonly called *solfege* (pronounced säl-fezh). With children we intentionally start with the more accessible *solfeggio* syllable names, rather than letter names. The major scale contains the following syllables as we ascend up the scale: *do* (pronounced doh), *re* (ray), *mi* (mee), *fa* (fah), *so* (soh), *la* (lah), *ti* (tee), and finishing with an octave higher *do*. See Goal #5 on p. 136 for a fuller explanation of *solfeggio*.

The major scale in SOLFEGE syllables

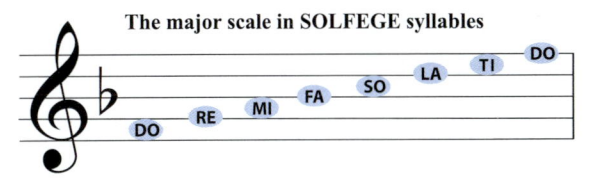

Notes on a large board

Move from the staff on the floor to a large staff drawn on a board which shows pitches going up and down by step. Use just three notes to start, going up and down from the first space and first line (*do–re–mi–re–do*). Have the children point to the notes as you sing. Then have the children sing along with you. Encourage them by letting them know that they are really "reading" music!

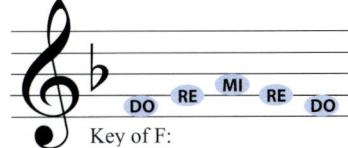

Key of F:

Holding actual music

When you move to actual music, require students to use their fingers to follow the notes. At first the instructor should sing along. Later have the group sing while you listen. Eventually each student should sing a few notes or phrases alone. At this stage, go for success by using a simple melody or easy exercises from a beginning solfeggio book.

Stepwise solfege exercise
do do re re mi   mi mi re re do

Solfege a hymn tune
do do re mi re mi fa mi re mi
mi mi mi re do   re mi re do

6 BARS REST

1. Inventory how you and your individual students learn best. Is it by hearing, doing, or seeing? Consider how you might best use the gateways of learning in these beginning stages.

2. A number of techniques to help students hear and match pitch have been introduced. An important first step is to get to know each individual's voice. Consider how to include tone-matching in your group warm-ups. Also take note of students who may need special attention and carve out time-in to train them individually to match pitch, especially while they are young.

What's the score?
See **What's the Score?**
Chapter Ten, pp. 205–208 for steps to reading music notation.

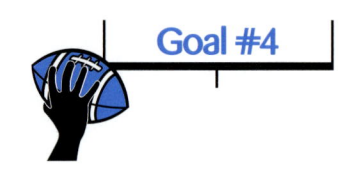

Goal #4 — ESTABLISH THE BASICS with INTERMEDIATE vocal group

The sound of children's voices has great appeal the world over. Nurturing a beautiful sound requires a consistent regimen, one that the singing company leader consciously embeds in warm-ups, teaching, and rehearsal. Legendary coach Vince Lombardi was infamous for hammering away at basics. He would hold up a football and dramatically announce, "Gentlemen, this is a football." This analogy mirrors Priscilla Burgmayer's weekly Boot Camp Basic Training, outlined below, which in the end will generate beautiful sound from your choir.

Projection

It is important to establish that good voice projection is not about shouting or any combination of "voices," but must be singing. (Remember to use our "singing" channel.) Work on this through unison singing, emphasizing good vowel sounds. Pick a spot or clock across the room to aim for. Extending the arm out toward the target as the youngsters commence the sound helps give the feeling of the sound going out. At times, the leader should stand back from the group and encourage the group to fill the room with their voices.

Posture

Just as there is a posture required of a baseball player at the plate, a swimmer ready to commence a race, or a basketball player ready to hit a jump-shot, so there is a proper posture for singing. Singing is best achieved standing. Here is a posture checklist from the head down to the feet:

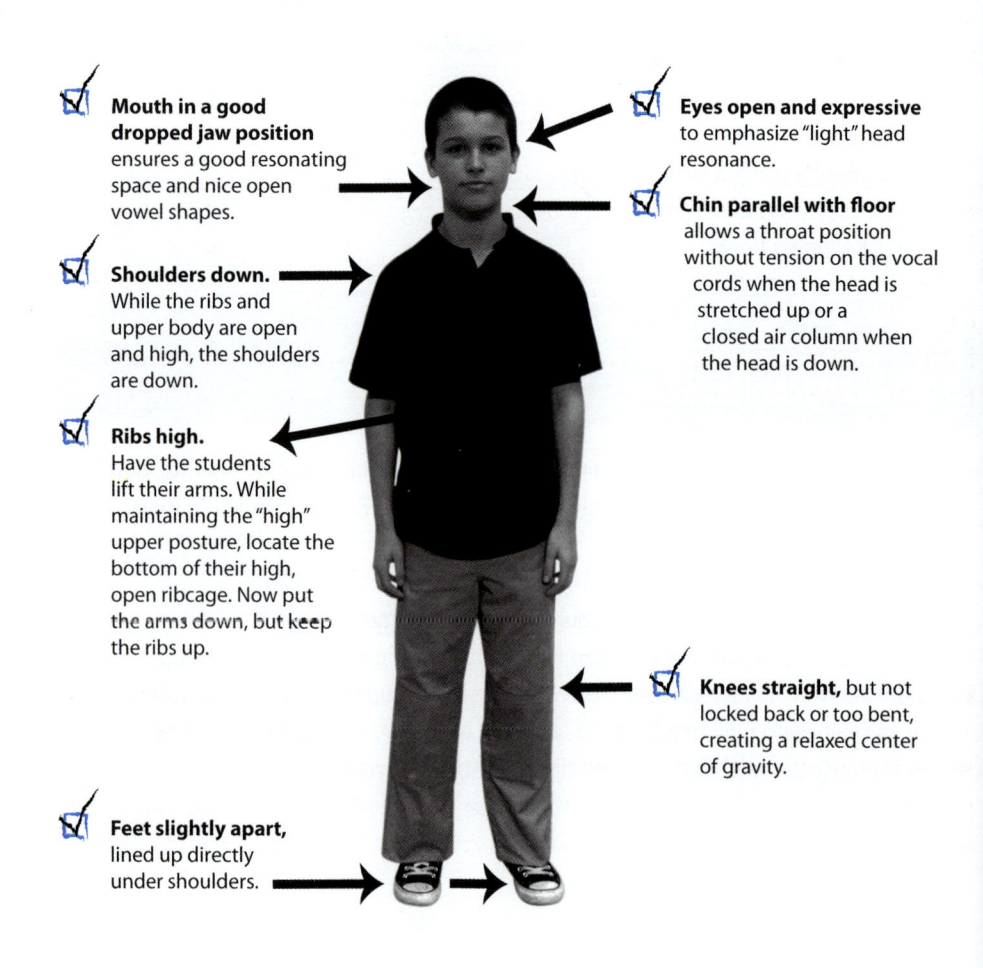

- ☑ **Mouth in a good dropped jaw position** ensures a good resonating space and nice open vowel shapes.

- ☑ **Shoulders down.** While the ribs and upper body are open and high, the shoulders are down.

- ☑ **Ribs high.** Have the students lift their arms. While maintaining the "high" upper posture, locate the bottom of their high, open ribcage. Now put the arms down, but keep the ribs up.

- ☑ **Feet slightly apart,** lined up directly under shoulders.

- ☑ **Eyes open and expressive** to emphasize "light" head resonance.

- ☑ **Chin parallel with floor** allows a throat position without tension on the vocal cords when the head is stretched up or a closed air column when the head is down.

- ☑ **Knees straight,** but not locked back or too bent, creating a relaxed center of gravity.

Fun warm-ups

Helen Kemp, a leading American exponent of children's choirs, has developed a treasure trove of warm-ups and props to reinforce proper posture and placement of the voice. Warm-ups help extend range into the head voice. Relax to finish in the lower register.

Posture "rap" and breathing test

This warm-up reminds the singers of the steps (from the feet up to the head) of a proper singing posture, concluding with a fun contest to see who can count-sing the longest. Instruct the singers to sit when they run out of air. Remind the singers to keep their shoulders down and take a quick, deep and quiet breath, learning to exhale only enough air to sing through the counts. Keep tabs on the counts from week to week, and congratulate the group as they extend their record best.

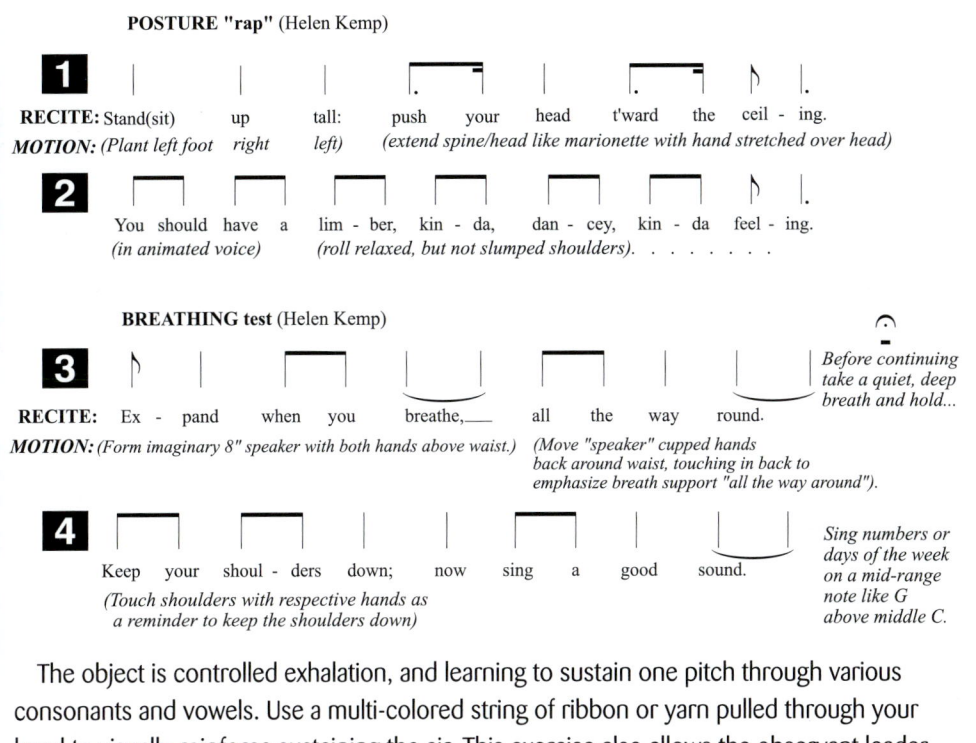

POSTURE "rap" (Helen Kemp)

1
RECITE: Stand(sit) up tall: push your head t'ward the ceil - ing.
MOTION: (Plant left foot right left) (extend spine/head like marionette with hand stretched over head)

2
You should have a lim - ber, kin - da, dan - cey, kin - da feel - ing.
(in animated voice) (roll relaxed, but not slumped shoulders).

BREATHING test (Helen Kemp)

3
RECITE: Ex - pand when you breathe, all the way round.
Before continuing take a quiet, deep breath and hold...
MOTION: (Form imaginary 8" speaker with both hands above waist.) (Move "speaker" cupped hands back around waist, touching in back to emphasize breath support "all the way around").

4
Keep your shoul - ders down; now sing a good sound.
(Touch shoulders with respective hands as a reminder to keep the shoulders down)
Sing numbers or days of the week on a mid-range note like G above middle C.

The object is controlled exhalation, and learning to sustain one pitch through various consonants and vowels. Use a multi-colored string of ribbon or yarn pulled through your hand to visually reinforce sustaining the air. This exercise also allows the observant leader to identify the singers who have difficulty singing a unison pitch in tune with other voices.[4]

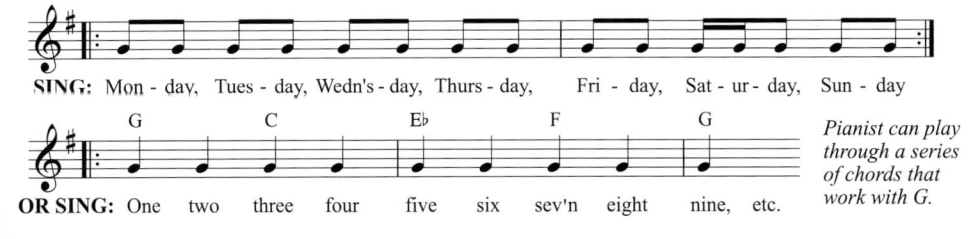

SING: Mon - day, Tues - day, Wedn's - day, Thurs - day, Fri - day, Sat - ur - day, Sun - day
G   C   Eb   F   G
OR SING: One two three four five six sev'n eight nine, etc.

Pianist can play through a series of chords that work with G.

Echo clapping

This "greeting" warm-up establishes focus and builds rhythmic unity. Ask the children to echo simple rhythmic patterns, even guessing the names clapped. Activate listening and eye-hand skills by varying patterns with clapping, knee slaps (also known as patchen), finger snaps, and quiet finger taps (on the ball of the hand).

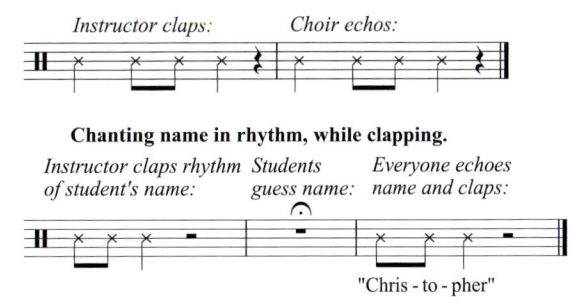

Instructor claps: *Choir echos:*

Chanting name in rhythm, while clapping.
Instructor claps rhythm of student's name: *Students guess name:* *Everyone echoes name and claps:*

"Chris - to - pher"

The Beat Goes On

Breath support (for breathiness)

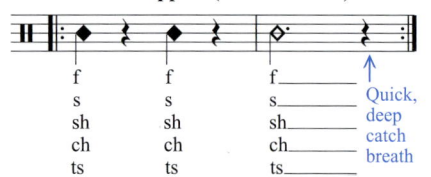

f f f
s s s
sh sh sh
ch ch ch
ts ts ts

Quick, deep catch breath

Activate the breath
Think of posture as tall and buoyant, with chest and shoulders quiet. Use a little diaphragm bounce and a gentle impulse from below the waistline. Teach the young singers how to take a quick, deep "catch breath." A fun follow-up is to try using the rhythms of a three-part round, like *Row, Row, Row Your Boat*, with each group using different breath consonants (*f, s, sh, ch,* or *ts*) or lip trill buzzes (*Brrr, Zzzz, Vvv*).

Flat tire hiss

Flat tire hiss (for breath control)

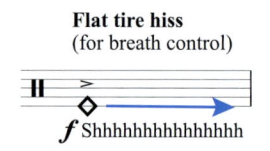

f Shhhhhhhhhhhhhhh

Allow the children to tense their two hands held together with squeezed thumbs on top to simulate the tension of air escaping from a large truck tire. After taking and holding a deep and quiet breath, commence on signal with an explosive *"Sh"* sound, which the singers should try to sustain as long as possible. This awakens and connects the air stream to the diaphragmatic support and develops breath control.

Who are you? (for resonance)
Oliver Owl, rudely awakened, looks down and sings:
G   Ab   A
WHO are you? WHO are you? WHO etc.

Owl at the window
Use a hand gesture (or puppet) to suggest the owl coming to a window, inquiring in song, "Who are you?" Start this *"do-so-do"* warm-up in a medium register and ascend by half-steps, eventually switching to a neutral *"ah"* syllable for the higher notes. The object is to maintain a *legato* line and sustain pitch accurately.

Over on the top tones[5]
The head register is best developed by training the upper medium-high voice *downward*. This exercise from Helen Kemp purposely works best when the singing, head-register channel is not abruptly dropped into the chest-register speaking or yelling channel. To avoid weak, whispery tones from G down to middle C, encourage the children to carry the quality of the head voice downward, assuring a bright, light, clear, forward, and thereby resonant sound.

* The symbol (arrow up and over) seeks to convey the idea of approaching high notes with the energy emanating up and over the top like a Ferris wheel

Over the top tones (Helen Kemp)
Use up-and-over Ferris wheel motion
[Up by semitones]
O-ver on the top tones, light and clear the low-er tones

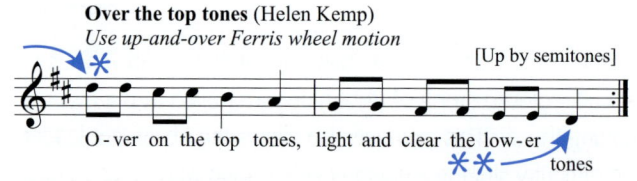

** The other arrow (down and up) is a visual reminder to support the lower notes that often tend to slip downward and out of tune.

Sighs for relaxation

Sighs (for relaxation)

Sighs with a long *glissando* descent also encourage the placement of the voice in the head register (not familiar to many young singers), then moving down into lower registers. It is also a good way to relax out of stretching, warm-up exercises. Encourage a wide-open relaxed throat and use a sweeping arm motion to emphasize the up-and-over energy. Don't be afraid to allow the voices to grovel in their lowest range for a moment. If you ascend again, the exercise easily morphs into imitating the sound of a roller coaster ride.

FUN DICTION CHANT:

Chester Cheetah chewed a chunk of cheap and chunky cheddar cheese.

—Valerie Mack

Diction chants
Use tongue twisters like "Unique New York" and bits of Dr. Seuss's *Fox and Sox* to warm-up the articulators (chanting *"Lips, teeth, tip of the tongue"*). Save valuable rehearsal time by securing the difficult diction in the warm-up. (*"We will listen to the Spirit speaking, and the Spirit of the Lord obey."*) Be sure the words are easily understood. Singing in a foreign language benefits vowel formation.

Imagery with props

Use assorted props hidden in a goody bag to create anticipation, fun, and relaxation in the rehearsal. These can aid in tone-matching, vocal technique, and range extension.

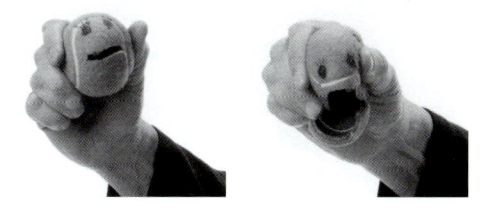

- To demonstrate mouth formations, slit the side of a tennis ball to create a mouth. Draw eyes and nose on it and name it! Another tennis ball can have a very small slit to represent the barely open mouth and another over-slit or torn down at the sides to represent unacceptable yelling.

- A thick rubber band stretched vertically serves as a visual reminder of the sensation of a north-south head voice orientation. Ask the children to sing "*Jesus Loves Me*" using an east-west orientation, which produces a wide childish-sounding "ee" sound. Then have them sing the same chorus with a north-south mouth orientation. Strumming different pitches on a rubber band can also be a fun way for students to visualize how the vocal cords work.

- Use a puppet to demonstrate a proper dropped jaw. A unicorn puppet works particularly well to indicate proper projection of the head voice.

- A beanbag can be thrown to illustrate trajectory and aiming the voice.

- A target like a clock at the back of the room can become the object on which to focus projection.

- Picture cards (see children's choir resource list) help students mimic a variety of pitch sounds to develop familiarity with the sensation of the head voice.

- A slinky can demonstrate a bouncing pulse and energy.

- A ball of yarn or string of colorful ribbons can be a visual aid in developing long, deep breathing. Sing through the days of the week several times on a single pitch as the youngsters watch the varied colors and lengths pass through your hand—and mysteriously out of your goody bag.

Use props to access "gateways of learning" in vocal training

? 6 BARS REST

Which of the "Boot Camp Basic Training" elements should you emphasize more in your rehearsals? Make note of which exercises or props would aid your group in covering all areas of their basic training:

- Projection
- Posture
- Range extension
- Diction
- Mouth formation
- Breath control

Monday...
Tuesday...
Wednesday...
Thursday...

Goal #5 — READ STEPWISE MELODIES

What is *solfeggio*?

Music is often called the universal language and the nearly universal language for reading music is known as *solfeggio*, which uses syllables to identify tones. Most folks are surprised to learn that some form of *solfeggio* has been around for a millennium. Over half of English-speaking Salvation Army songsters, particularly those in Africa and India, do not read music notation, as bandsmen do, but rely on *solfege* syllables to learn a new song's pitches and rhythms.

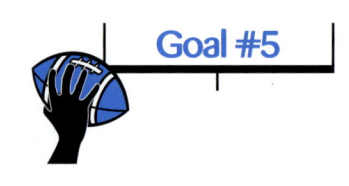

ABOUT TONIC SOL-FA

In 1841 Reverend John Curwen received a commission from a conference of Sunday school teachers to discover and promote the simplest way of teaching music for use in Sunday school singing. Curwen adapted a method of sol-fa notation developed by Sarah Glover of Norwich, England (1785-1867) which utilized the first letter (in lower case) of each of the solfege tones (*do, re, m, fa, so, la, ti*), and a rhythmic notation system which utilized bar lines, half bar lines and semicolons prefixing strong beats, medium beats and weak beats respectively in each measure. For marking the subdivisions of beats Curwen used a full stop for half divisions and a comma for quarter divisions. For continuation of a tone from one beat to the next he employed a dash. As he originally conceived it, Curwen aimed to develop music literacy in three successive phases: firstly reading from sol-fa notation, secondly reading from staff notation in conjunction with sol-fa notation below, and thirdly reading from staff notation alone.

Sarah Glover's Tonic Sol-Fa Ladder

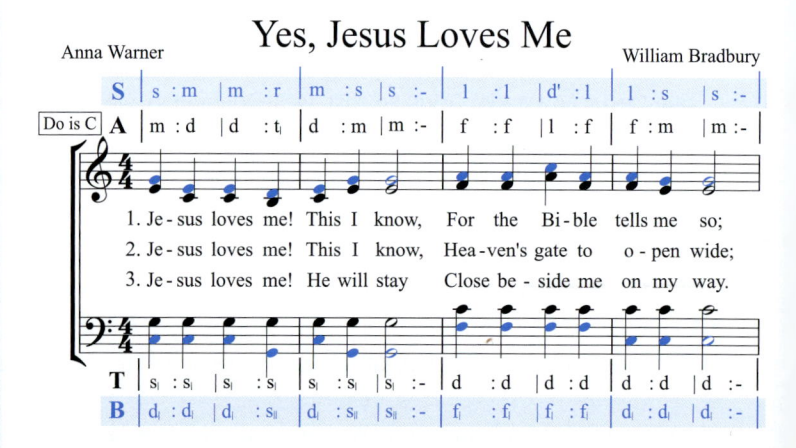

Yes, Jesus Loves Me
Anna Warner — William Bradbury

1. Jesus loves me! This I know, For the Bible tells me so;
2. Jesus loves me! This I know, Heaven's gate to open wide;
3. Jesus loves me! He will stay Close beside me on my way.

In *solfeggio*, degrees of the scale have designated syllable names rather than letter names. The major scale contains the following syllables as we ascend up the scale: do (pronounced doh), re (ray), mi (mee), fa (fah), so or sol (both pronounced soh), la (lah), ti (tee), and finishing with an octave-higher do. Many in the West are familiar with *solfege* scale names through the "Do Re Mi" song from *The Sound of Music*. In some parts of the world, the seventh step of the scale is sometimes sung as si (see), rather than as ti (tee). There are two methods of applying the syllables to the scale degrees:

Fixed-do

One is known as fixed-do, where the syllable do is always the note C, re is D, etc. In many parts of the world fixed-do, rather than letter names, is used to identify pitches for instrumentalists and singers alike.

Fixed "do" solfeggio
The note C is always "do"
do re mi fa so la ti do'

Movable-do

In the *movable-do* system, sometimes known as tonic sol-fa, the do can be moved to any scale position according to the key signature. This example shows F as do in the key of F, and G as do in the key of G. Compare this movable-do version in the key of G to the same melody in G, utilizing fixed-do syllables.

The application of *solfeggio* is best reinforced by using the Curwen hand signs or by adjusting your hand by levels to help indicate the pitches going up or down. Pointing to syllables on a solfege tree is useful in group settings. To practice the hand signs, the chorus "God is So Good" is an excellent example based on the lower five scale tones (*do-re-mi-fa-so*). "Alleluia" uses the four upper scale tones (*so-la-ti-do*). Some music software programs allow you to indicate the solfege syllables under or within each note.

Moveable "do" solfeggio
New "do" for each key

Melody in F: do do do re mi so mi
Same melody in G: do do do re mi so mi

In fixed "do"

Melody in C: do do do re mi so mi
Same melody in C: so so so la ti re ti

Chapter 6 | LET THE CHILDREN SING!

CURWEN HAND SIGNS

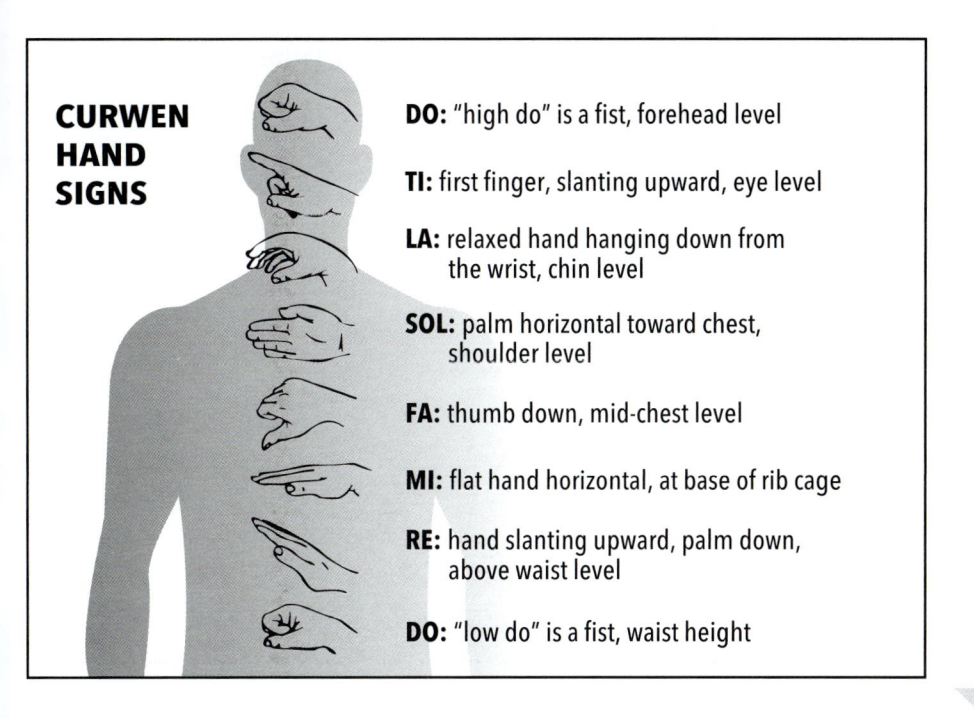

DO: "high do" is a fist, forehead level

TI: first finger, slanting upward, eye level

LA: relaxed hand hanging down from the wrist, chin level

SOL: palm horizontal toward chest, shoulder level

FA: thumb down, mid-chest level

MI: flat hand horizontal, at base of rib cage

RE: hand slanting upward, palm down, above waist level

DO: "low do" is a fist, waist height

SOLFEGE TREE
Chromatic Scale
(each ↗ represents a half step)

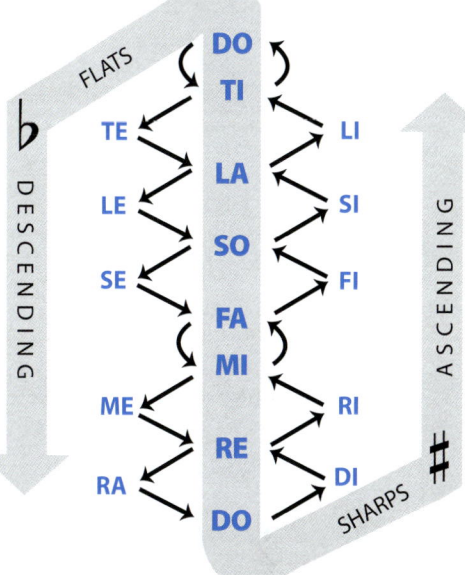

FLATS — DESCENDING
DO TI
TE — LI
LA
LE — SI
SO
SE — FI
FA
MI
ME — RI
RE
RA — DI
DO
SHARPS — ASCENDING

God is So Good
in solfege with Curwen hand signs

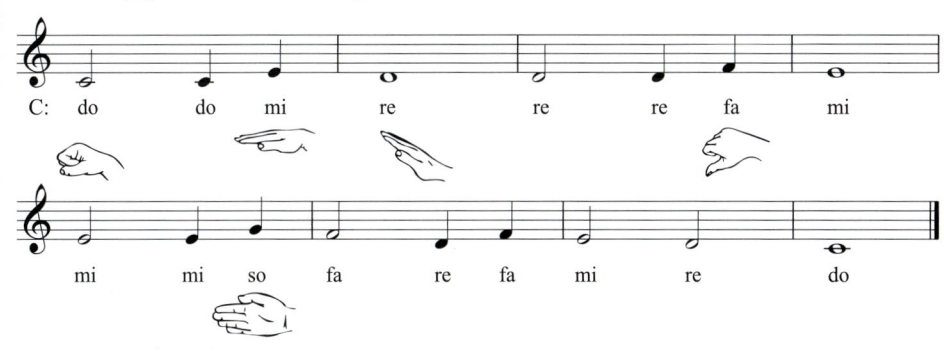

C: do do mi re re re fa mi
mi mi so fa re fa mi re do

Alleluia
in solfege with Curwen hand signs

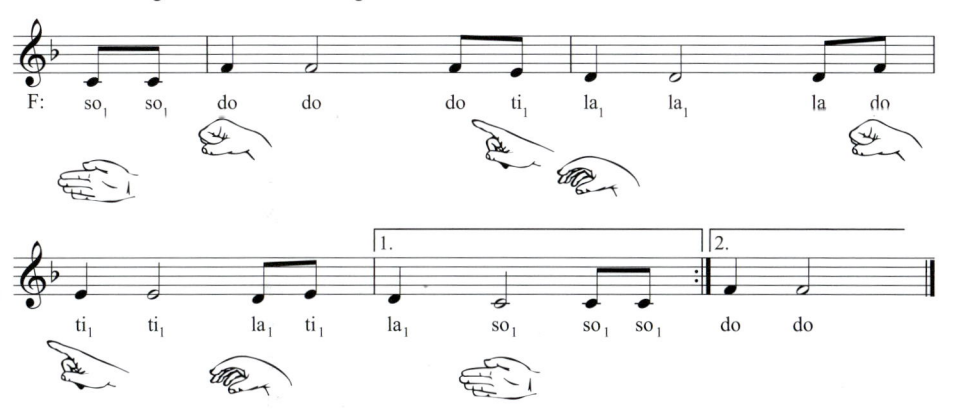

F: so₁ so₁ do do do ti₁ la₁ la₁ la do

ti₁ ti₁ la₁ ti₁ la₁ so₁ so₁ so₁ do do

The subscript (so₁) indicates notes lower than do.

The Beat Goes On

FINDING "DO" in **flat** keys

find *the next to the last* flat (♭)

and that names **"do"**

do is E♭

If the key signature indicates *flats* (♭), locate **the next to the last flat** (one in from the right), which identifies the name of the major key and its "do."

do is F | do is C

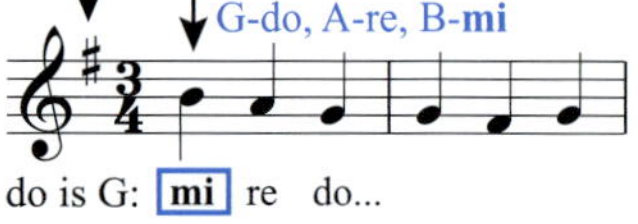

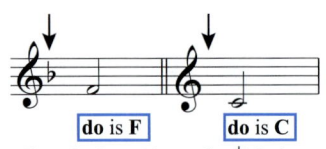

Since the *key with one flat* (♭) lacks a penultimate flat before it, we have to memorize that as in *the key of F*. The *key of C* lacks *any flats and sharps*.

ORDER OF FLATS

Battle
Ends
And
Down
Goes
Charles
Father

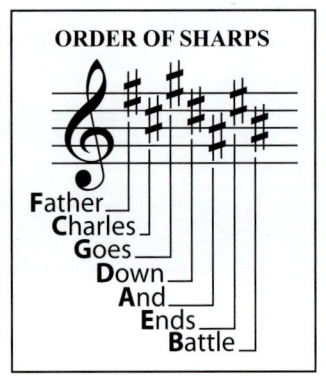

ORDER OF SHARPS

Father
Charles
Goes
Down
And
Ends
Battle

FINDING "DO" in **sharp** keys

find *the last* sharp (♯)

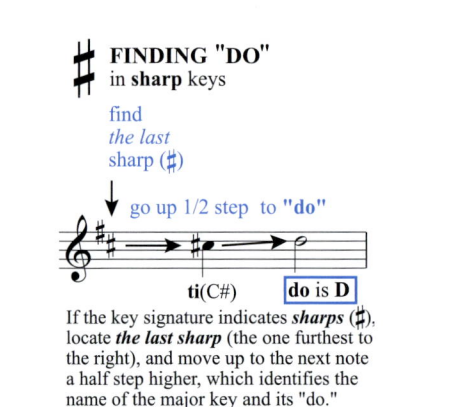

go up 1/2 step to **"do"**

ti(C♯) do is D

If the key signature indicates *sharps* (♯), locate **the last sharp** (the one furthest to the right), and move up to the next note a half step higher, which identifies the name of the major key and its "do."

If you see flats, this is what you need to know   Call the last one *"fa"* to find *"mi" "re" "do."*
do do do   re   re   re   mi   mi   mi   mi   fa   so so so so   fa   fa   fa   mi   re   do

When you see a sharp,   call the last one "ti,"   Go up to "do"   and that's the key!
do   re   mi fa   so   so   so   la   la   ti   ti   do   do   do   do   do   ti   do

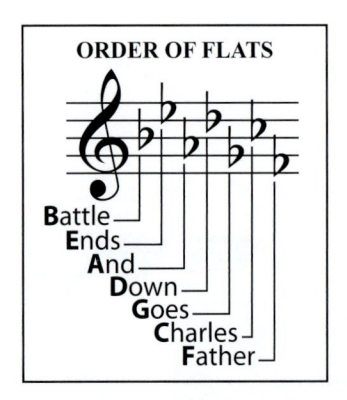

FINDING THE FIRST NOTE in **solfege**

Determine "do" from the key signature: F♯→G

Based on "do," determine the solfege scale degree of the first note: G-do, A-re, B-**mi**

do is G: **mi** re do...

See Appendix 6.1 for an **Interval Reference Chart**

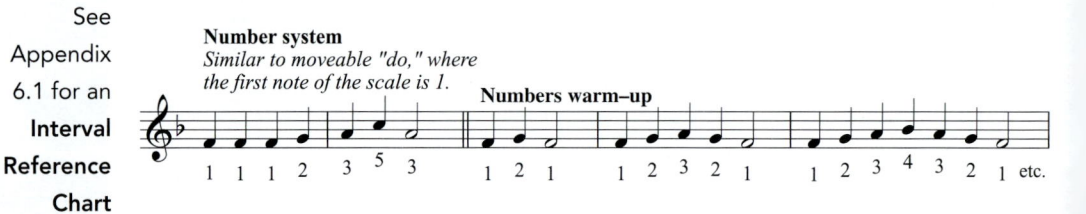

Number system

Others apply the principle of numbering each scale tone to the degrees of the scale. For example in the key of F, F would be 1, G is 2, A is 3, and so forth. An easily accessible warm-up employs adding a number, ascending and descending, like so: 1…1-2-1…1-2-3-2-1…1-2-3-4-3-2-1…etc. The concept of intervals transfers easily with the number system. Going from 1 to 5 constitutes a fifth, and the students already know how to count and sing up and down to the fifth. It links familiar song phrases with ascending and descending intervals.[6] The drawback with numbers is when you add accidentals.

Number system
Similar to moveable "do," where the first note of the scale is 1.

Numbers warm-up

1 1 1 2 3 5 3   1 2 1   1 2 3 2 1   1 2 3 4 3 2 1 etc.

Letter system

Instrumentalists in places like the United States and United Kingdom use the letter names to name notes and learn to apply a fingering or position to that letter name. Therefore it can be useful for the letter names to be reinforced in chorus and basically avoid confusion by sticking to one system of naming notes. However, it should be noted that youngsters move easily between these languages of music.

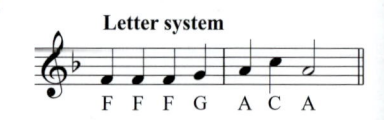

Letter system

F F F G A C A

Rhythmic syllables

Just as there are different approaches for reading pitch, there are several different systems for reading rhythm that are taught today. Zoltan Kodaly, a Hungarian music educator, devised a system involving rhythmic syllables, which is accessible to the youngest singers.

An American variant may be familiar which retains the use of *ta* for quarter notes and *ti* for eighths, but changes the original *ti-ri-ti-ri*, used in the Hungarian system for sixteenths, to *tic-ka-tic-ka* for subdivision of the beat. More recent adaptations of rhythmic syllables include the Gordon method (*du-de, du-ta-de-ta*), and the *ta-ka-di-mi* system. Both of these systems maintain a principal syllable (*du* or *ta* respectively) on the pulse beats.

Another method subdivides the measure with a combination number and syllable counting of beats, a method most often used in theory books.

See Appendix 6.2 for a summary of various **Rhythmic Syllable Systems.**

Rhythmic syllable options

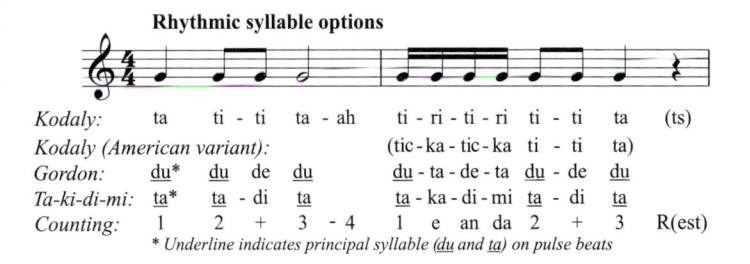

Kodaly:	ta	ti - ti	ta - ah	ti - ri - ti - ri	ti - ti	ta	(ts)
Kodaly (American variant):				(tic - ka - tic - ka	ti - ti	ta)
Gordon:	du*	du de du		du - ta - de - ta	du - de	du
Ta-ki-di-mi:	ta*	ta - di ta		ta - ka - di - mi	ta - di	ta
Counting:	1	2 + 3 - 4		1 e an da 2	+	3	R(est)

* Underline indicates principal syllable (<u>du</u> and <u>ta</u>) on pulse beats

The rhythmic syllables chart in Appendix 6.2 indicates a full summary of these options. There is some value in finding out which system is used in your local schools and adopting that rhythmic syllable system for consistency. Experience has shown that mishaps with rhythm are quite often as much of a stumbling block with music reading as is locating pitches. Teach your youngsters a way to work out absolutely correct rhythmic values.

Incorporating sight-singing in every rehearsal

There are many ways to incorporate sight-reading of music into your weekly routine. Use numbers, solfege scales, or intervals in your warm-ups:

The following "umbrella" diagram by Janeal Krehbiel drawn on the board helps students remember and visualize these intervals through warm-ups, utilizing either numbers or solfege syllables.[7]

Interval UMBRELLA warmup (Janeal Krehbiel)

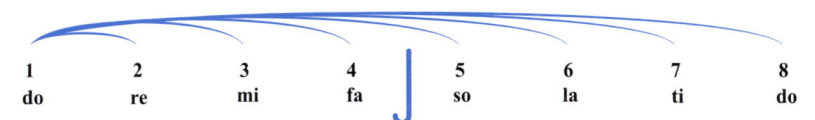

1	2	3	4	5	6	7	8
do	re	mi	fa	so	la	ti	do

This next exercise builds confidence with identifying ascending and descending intervals. After doing this exercise, ask students for isolated intervals by calling out a number from 2 to 7. To increase interest, divide the choir in half. Start one half with the ascending intervals, and the other half with the descending intervals. Then switch parts.[8]

Interval FOCUS warmup (Jim Hudson)

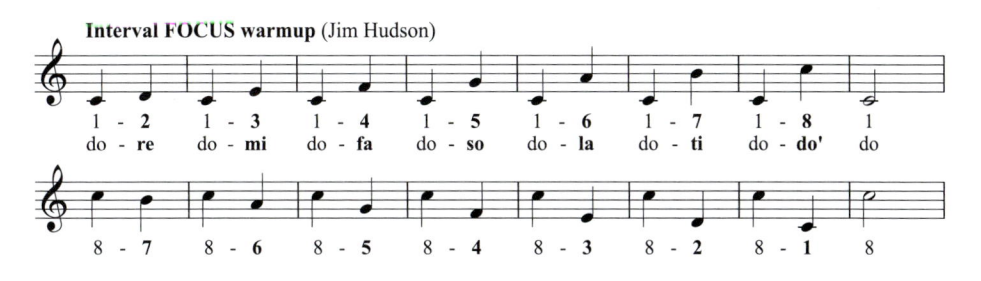

1 - 2	1 - 3	1 - 4	1 - 5	1 - 6	1 - 7	1 - 8	1
do - re	do - mi	do - fa	do - so	do - la	do - ti	do - do'	do
8 - 7	8 - 6	8 - 5	8 - 4	8 - 3	8 - 2	8 - 1	8

Use either numbers or solfege syllables for these incrementally-increasing scale patterns. Change keys as needed to suit your ensemble. As a stretch, sing in rounds, with different groups entering every two beats.[9]

Interval STEP warmup (Nancy Allen)

Use numbers: 1 1 2 1 1 2 3 2 1 1 2 3 4 3 2 1 1 2 3 4 5 4 3 2 1 1 2
Or solfege: do do re do do re mi re do d* r m f m r d d r m f s f m r d d r

3 4 5 6 5 4 3 2 1 1 2 3 4 5 6 7 6 5 4 3 2 1 etc.
m f s l s f m r d d r m f s l t l s f m r d etc.

* "do" may be abbreviated "d," "re" as "r," etc.

First steps at music reading

Use the board to isolate problem spots, pointing to notes slowly while the children sing along. Use an easy sight–singing book or hymnal, and find passages that are readable in easy keys like F or C. Aim for success by earmarking a section that you know most of the children can read. If using *solfege*, ask, "Who can tell us what the first note is in solfege?" Then, "What about the next three notes?" Give the starting note and have the kids sing the first few notes with the *solfege*, without the aid of the piano.

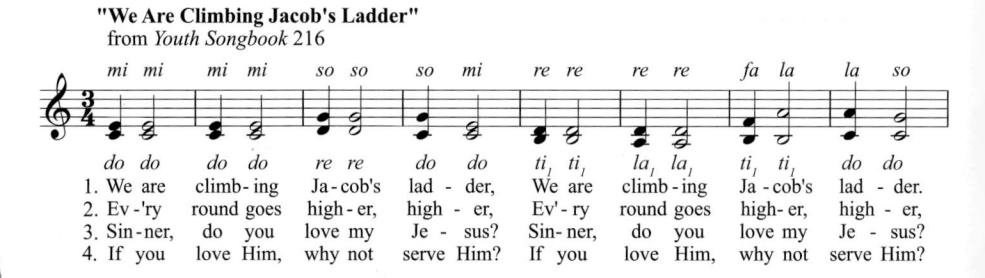

"We Are Climbing Jacob's Ladder"
from *Youth Songbook* 216

mi mi mi mi so so so mi re re re re fa la la so
do do do do re re do do ti₁ ti₁ la₁ la₁ ti₁ ti₁ do do

1. We are climb-ing Ja-cob's lad - der,
2. Ev-'ry round goes high-er, high-er,
3. Sin-ner, do you love my Je-sus?
4. If you love Him, why not serve Him?

We are climb-ing high-er, high-er, Ev'-ry round goes high-er, high-er,
Sin-ner, do you love my Je - sus? If you love Him, why not serve Him?

Each term choose one piece specifically to be read by your choristers.[10] Some conductors will transpose the written notation for the choir into the key of C, alter rhythmic values, or ignore the key signature to make it simpler to read. (The accompanist plays in the original key.) You may want to isolate the rhythm with Kodaly rhythmic syllables or counting for clarity, and then add the words.

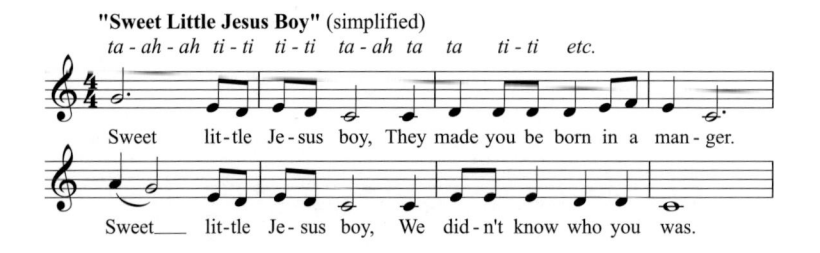

"O Come Little Children"
Original key/time signature

Transposed version for children to read, with augmented rhythm values

O come lit - tle child-ren, O come one and all, to

"Sweet Little Jesus Boy" (simplified)
ta - ah - ah ti - ti ti - ti ta - ah ta ta ti - ti etc.

Sweet lit-tle Je-sus boy, They made you be born in a man - ger.
Sweet___ lit-tle Je-sus boy, We did-n't know who you was.

Encourage and encourage as they take these first important steps in reading music. Even as you move on in your rehearsal with rote learning, have the students hold the music on the proper page. Students will begin to recognize passages they can read.

One wise sage teaches that youngsters come back to a program, not necessarily because it is fun or they make friends, but because they learn something new. This gives your students a sense of worth.

Sight-singing small groups

Sight-singing is more easily grasped in small groups, where individual attention and accountability are magnified. Below are three options to teach sight-singing, sometimes combined with other group instruction, in corps settings where a few additional helpers can be recruited. A sequence of voice levels appears in Appendix 6.3. Sight-singing method books are listed in the Children's Vocal Resources section that concludes this chapter. Other schedule models have been considered in Chapter Three, pp. 75-77.

Option A – Groups by level

Create a period of 20 minutes where everyone is sight-singing in small groups. Divide into three or four levels by ability, not age:

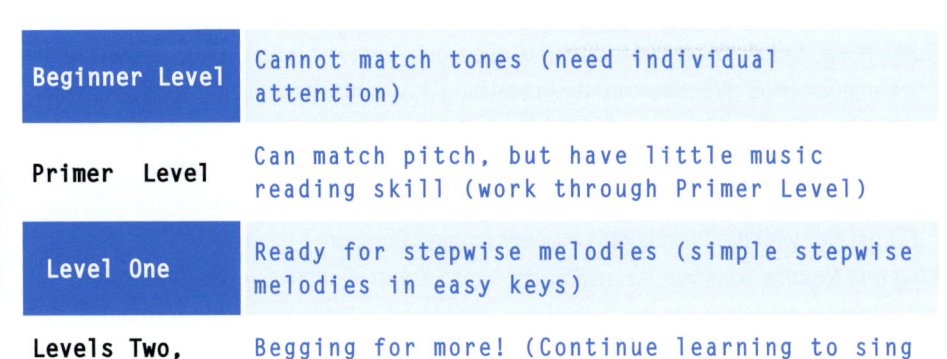

Beginner Level	Cannot match tones (need individual attention)
Primer Level	Can match pitch, but have little music reading skill (work through Primer Level)
Level One	Ready for stepwise melodies (simple stepwise melodies in easy keys)
Levels Two, Three & Four	Begging for more! (Continue learning to sing in other keys, intervals, and accidentals)

Option B – Voice group rotations

Create an hour-and-a-half rotation of various level voice groups with brass groups and dance and/or percussion classes. Each class should be 30 minutes long, including moving between classes:

PERIOD I	Beginner Voice	Advanced Brass	Timbrels/Dance/Percussion II
PERIOD II	Intermediate Voice	Beginner Brass	Timbrels/Dance/Percussion III
PERIOD III	Advanced Voice	Intermediate Brass	Timbrels/Dance/Percussion I

See Appendix 6.3 for a **Sequence of Voice Levels** a six-level M.A.P. Voice Curriculum.

Option C – Fundamentals rotations

Begin youth music program with a 45- to 60-minute rotation of fundamentals: theory, sight-singing, and percussion (for rhythm reading) for all students. Then move on to lessons and group rehearsals:

PERIOD I	Beginner Percussion	Intermediate Brass	Advanced Theory
PERIOD II	Intermediate Percussion	Beginner Brass	Intermediate Theory
PERIOD III	Advanced Percussion	Advanced Brass	Beginner Theory

6 BARS REST

1. How did you learn to read vocal music? Was it by letter names, solfege syllables, numbers, or a combination? Which do you think will work best with your young singers?

2. What pieces or melodies can you think of that are simple enough for intermediate singing groups to read? Remember to choose a key that requires head voice. Look for lyrics that are meaningful and memorable.

CHILDREN'S VOCAL RESOURCES

TRAINING CHILDREN'S VOICES

Body, Mind, Spirit, Voice, Helen Kemp (Concordia). Video of Helen Kemp demonstrating techniques choir directors can use in assisting boys with changing voices, youngsters with intonation problems, hesitant singers, and more.

Let the Children Sing! (Pendel Music Department, Philadelphia, PA). A video demonstration to train young singers through small group instruction by Priscilla Burgmayer with the Philadelphia Pioneer Singing Company.

Sing and Rejoice–Guiding Young Singers, Helen Kemp (Concordia). Video of Helen Kemp demonstrating successful techniques for both classroom and performance.

Teaching Kids to Sing, Kenneth H. Phillips (Schirmer). Book and DVD. Exercises for kids available on laminated notecards.

16 Graded Vocal Solos for High and Low Voice with Piano Accompaniment (Salvation Army USA East). Accompaniment and demonstration CD included.

PITCH READING METHODS

Melodia–A Course in Sight-Singing Solfeggio, Samuel W. Cole and Leo R. Lewis (Oliver Ditson Company). Available online from www.masterworkspress.com, including group photocopying rights. A time-honored comprehensive sight-singing book for youth and adults, available as **Book I** (stepwise singing), **Book II** (more keys), or **Books I–IV** (complete).

Finale and Sibelius music software packages that include alpha and visual solfege features allow the instructor to custom design sight-singing sheets.

Sound Concept Flash Cards–Preparing the Young Voice for Singing, Judy Carl Thompson with illustrations by Judith A. Burkholder (GIA Publications G–3870). Full color flash cards with suggested sounds noted on the reverse.

Steps to Harmony, Nicholas Palmer (Masterworks Press). Available online from www.masterworkspress.com. Progressive sight-singing method book in three parts (SSA). Bass clef companion books available. This series is available in four levels.

Takadimi System of Rhythm Solfege. For an excellent guide to using Takadimi in the elementary classroom, see Micheal Houlahan and Philip Tacka, **Kodály Today**– A Cognitive Approach to Elementary Music Education (Oxford University Press) or visit www.takadimi.net.

The Everything Singing Book, Bettina Sheppard (F. & W. Media, Inc.). Voice technique text includes practice CD.

See Chapter Twelve Songster Leader Resources for additional aids to warm–up, diction, and voice development.

Chapter 6 | LET THE CHILDREN SING!

The Sight Singer, Audrey Snyder (Warner Bros). Available in two or three mixed or treble voice editions.
Twenty-Four Progressive Vocalises, op. 85, vol. 395, Heinrich Panofka (G. Schirmer, Inc.).
Visual Solfege, Russell Nelson (OOP, Kjos).
The Wieneke Method, Philip and Valore Wieneke (Wieneke Music Publishing). Sight-singing method for church musicians in three levels, with solfege syllables and numbers indicated under the notes.

For a video demonstration of many of the principles outlined in Chapter Six, see Appendix 6.4 *Let the Children Sing! – Getting Started.*

Adjutant C. Emil Nelson leading YP Songster Brigade, 1936

"no, No, NO . . . Don't stop now!"
(says a wee little voice inside your voice box)
"HURRY . . . there's more stupendous tips for kids in Chapter Seven just ahead, and further along in Chapters Twelve & Thirteen on songsters . . . .
HURRY!"

The Beat Goes On

CHAPTER SEVEN

THE RIGHT SONG FOR YOUR KIDS!
Bit By Bit, Putting It Together

Whatever their path, young musicians under an encouraging director enjoy the experience of being part of something bigger than themselves, of learning how to harmonize with and benefit from the efforts of others. —Jane Kise, *LifeKeys*

THE HALCYON DAYS OF SINGING COMPANY

Nick Simmons-Smith, the Music and Creative Arts Education Secretary for The Salvation Army in the USA South, has a deep appreciation for the role of the singing company in corps life. In fact, aside from later piano studies, he says, *"it was the most important musical education experience of my youth."*

I first joined the Chelmsford Singing Company at age 6½. I remember the thrill of attending my first rehearsal and attempting to follow the music. Our singing company rehearsed every week on Tuesday night for 75 minutes. We always used music, and were taught how to anticipate intervals by the placement of notes on the staff. I was learning the trombone in the YP Band "learners" and that gave me some grounding in elementary music theory, but the practice of singing—listening to intervals, making a good sound that balanced with the ensemble, and matching pitch—was vital to my musical development. Our singing company numbered 30 strong, and for periods included 29 girls and one boy—that boy being lucky me! *The Chelmsford Singing Company sang every single Sunday and most Sundays we sang three times, meaning three different songs!*

One of my memories is how the singing company was set up. We had three rows—basically ordered by age. There was great pride in being promoted to the second row! The back row consisted of older junior soldiers and young senior soldiers. You could be a junior soldier until you were 18, but could become a senior soldier at age 14. This engendered a culture of "passing it on." The older girls would also be attending senior songster practice, but that four-year period where you could have dual-membership was also invaluable to the younger members of the group. Those in the back rows were our role models, and provided positive examples of good singing, behavior, and leadership. There is no doubt we sounded good, since we had maturing voices in the back row, and to my mind success bred success.

In **Chapter Seven,** we learn how to:
- intentionally choose unison and simple two-part songs to suit your singing company for performance, and/or to encourage music reading.
- build confidence in holding a part, in some measure, by use of strategic seating.
- make sure your well-rehearsed details jell on Sunday morning or at other performances.
- approach a new song for children.
- strategically learn a song over a six-week period.

Nick Simmons-Smith, age 7, on the occasion of his enrollment as a YP band member.

The amount of rehearsal time, the approach of our leader as a music educator, the substantial exposure to new music, and the regular performance opportunities were the major reasons for our success. It is interesting to note that when my peer group now gathers for an event, we are quick to recall these halcyon days of the Chelmsford Singing Company. What I have found amazing is how many singing company songs we are able to sing from memory! This is a fine testament to the teaching we received in our singing company days, but also to the spiritual truths contained in those songs that we have held onto.[1]

Beyond beginners

In a later chapter on youth band leadership, we will consider ways to get beyond the ongoing cycle of beginner instrumentalists, too few of whom progress enough to enjoy and function well in bands. Counteracting attrition requires guided structure and ongoing consistency of instruction. Students (especially self-conscious teens) are not going to risk remaining in an environment where they can't perform with confidence.

The challenge may be even more acute for the choral instructor, as there are fewer barriers to protect a singer's space. Instrumentalists have their instruments, music stands and a conductor between them and the listener. The singer's own instrument is not only uniquely theirs, but seems so much more exposed. Where memorization of words and music is assumed, a protective barrier is removed. Add to that the vulnerability of the body and facial language inherent in communicating as a singer. Singers, young and old, can rightfully feel very unguarded!

Teaching a full singing company

The goals covered in the previous chapter on pitch-matching, recognizing, reading, and singing stepwise melodies are essential first steps. They may be best achieved in small groups or with individual attention. We continue the learning sequence of children's voice instruction in this chapter with Goals #6 and #7, looking at ways to further young singers' ability within the context of the full singing company rehearsal. Of paramount importance is the choice of songs to both extend the young musician's facility, as well as increase confidence and enjoyment in their choral experience. We can plan to reinforce here the boot camp basics—projection, posture, range extension, mouth formation, breath control, and diction—through our intentional repertoire choices and careful forethought.

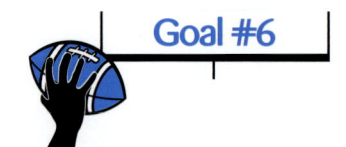

Goal #6 — DEVELOP UNISON AND SIMPLE TWO-PART SINGING

Just the right songs

The most vital preparation for a season or term is to find songs that really fit the group you are working with at that moment. Helen Kemp suggests six parameters in choosing music for children's voices:

1. **Text.** What thoughts will be planted in young hearts and minds? Is it theologically strong?

2. **Melody.** Does it embrace and enhance the text? How are the phrases shaped?
3. **Vocal range.** Is it appropriate for the age group?
4. **Personality.** Does the piece make your choristers want to sing it?
5. **Accompaniment.** Does it support and add beauty to the choral sound? Can my accompanist play it?
6. **Good investment.** Is the piece worthy of inclusion in the permanent library?[2]

Ideal child's range

Search for unison songs with ranges high enough to require the use of "head–voice–mix" voice.[3] An ideal range for elementary age children is from D above middle C to the D an octave higher.

Select two pieces each semester for students to sight-read entirely. Choose some songs for the group to just read through. Other pieces will be taught by rote. For holidays such as Christmas, or special observances such as Junior Soldier Day of Renewal, choose music appropriate to those occasions. Look for memorable, beautiful-sounding words that are meaningful to make the greatest impact on your children. Scripture-based songs are valuable as well. As Nick Simmons-Smith attested, years later your grown singing company members will recall whole verses of a favorite song from childhood!

Begin by teaching the rhythm, using Kodaly syllables with younger children or traditional counting with middle school age and older. Then add the pitches and finally the words.

O Come to My Heart, Lord Jesus
(Refrain from *Caroler's Favorites* #35)

Young child:	ta	ta	ti - ti	ta	ta	ta - ah	ta	ti - ti	ta	ti - ti	ta	ta	ta - ah - ah
Middle school:	4	1	2 an	3	4	1 - 2	3	4 an	1	2 an	3	4	1 - 2 - 3
then add Pitches in rhythm:	so	so	mi fa	so	do'	do'		ti	la la	so	do re	mi	re	do
Words:	O	come	to my	heart,	Lord	Je - sus!		There	is room	in	my heart	for		Thee.

Superscript do¹ describes the high do, an octave above do.

Work without the piano or accompaniment track, adding the accompaniment later. Be strategic and plan ahead for difficult passages with unfamiliar intervals, rhythms, and accidentals. Sing *a cappella,* without accompaniment, as much as possible to build the student's ear and sound. Locate some canons or rounds to introduce independent two-part singing. Many sight-singing books include simple two-part duet sections. Rotate the children between parts so that all children develop their vocal ranges and are reading. Too often, only the good readers get allocated to harmony parts. Avoid labeling the parts as soprano and alto. Instead, call them simply parts 1 and 2, assuming that both are of equal importance. (See *Win Them One by One,* later in this chapter, as an example of a song with two *equal* parts.)

INTRODUCE MORE ADVANCED CONCEPTS

Part singing!

Once choir members are reading stepwise pitches and simple intervals well, and can hold a simple part, we can expand their musicianship. They are ready to learn new intervals, accidentals, major and minor keys, as well as approach the concept of *modulation,* or change of key. We can stretch the youngsters with an understanding of more mature lyrics, expanding their range, and by teaching them to project a round, full sound. We can now work on vowels, consonants, and tone colors in warm-ups and rehearsal to achieve clearer diction.

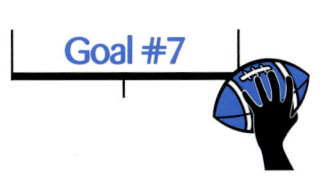

Goal #7

See **Diction Helps**, Chapter Twelve, pp. 258–262.

For a video demonstration introducing part-singing, see Appendix 7.1 **Let the Children Sing! – The Intermediate Group.**

They are now ready to sing with more personal expression. They will begin to develop their own individual tonal quality, which will contribute to the group's choral sound. As the reading improves, move on to songs that employ simple parallel harmonies in thirds or sixths.

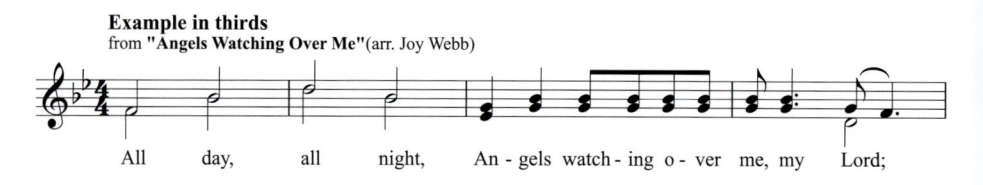

Example in thirds
from "Angels Watching Over Me" (arr. Joy Webb)

All day, all night, An-gels watch-ing o-ver me, my Lord;

See Chapter Sixteen, **Keyboard Basics**, pp. 344–345 for an explanation of I–IV–V harmonies.

Next try part-singing based on simple I–IV–V chord harmonies. Using Joy Webb's *Kum Ba Yah* three-part harmony, first ask the entire ensemble to sing through each part. This alleviates the fear of singing in harmony. It also helps them become aware of what the other parts are doing.

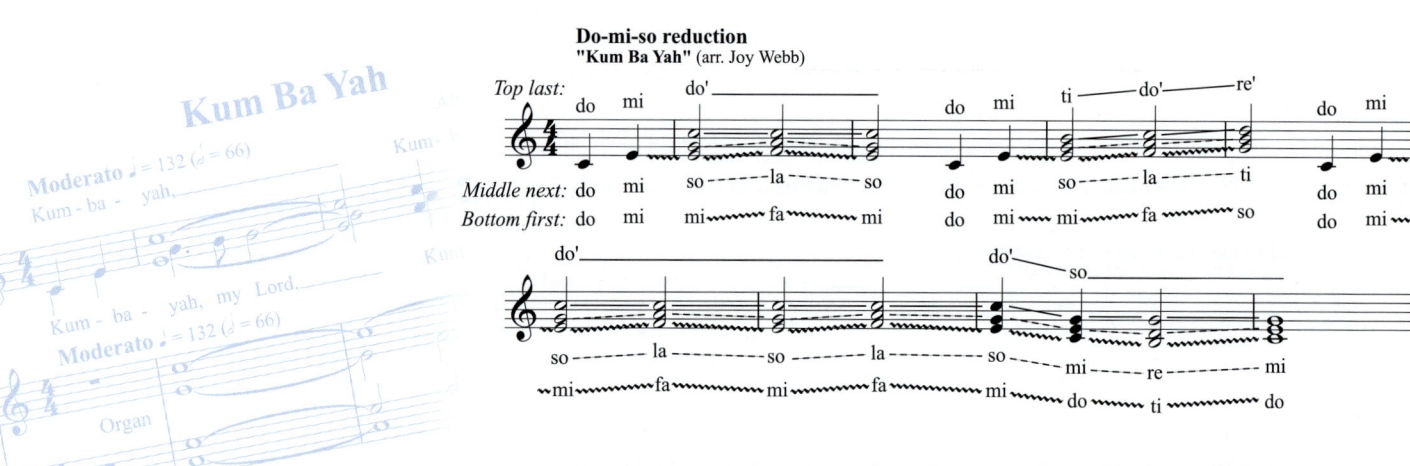

Do-mi-so reduction
"Kum Ba Yah" (arr. Joy Webb)

Top last: do mi do' do mi ti do' re' do mi
Middle next: do mi so—la—so do mi so—la—ti do mi
Bottom first: do mi mi—fa—mi do mi—mi—fa—so do mi

do' do' so
so—la—so—la—so—mi—re—mi
mi—fa—mi—fa—mi—do—ti—do

Once everyone has sung every part, then divide into part groups. The three sections can be physically spread apart for rehearsal. First ask the middles to sing their part alone, as it is the most difficult to hear. Have it become "their" tune. Next rehearse the bottom part, then couple it with the middle part. Once children hear the melody part, it is hard for them to hear anything else, so rehearse the melody part last.

"Kum Ba Yah" (performance version)

Tops & Bottoms: Kum-ba-yah,_____ Kum-ba-yah._____ Kum-ba-

Middles: Kum-ba-yah, my Lord,_____ Kum-ba-yah._____ Kum-ba-

Seating formations

Placement in the choir formation should be fairly consistent from week to week as an aid to developing teamwork and rehearsal discipline. There will be occasions when shifting one or two voices may aid the overall sound and learning curve of your group.

- **Strong, tuneful singers** are best placed strategically in the center and rear of sections.
- **Wiggly singers** are best placed either in the middle front, where they are directly in your line of vision, or between well-behaved singers.

- **Tonally challenged singers** are placed to the sides and back, although a room's acoustic may counteract your intent to hide them.
- **Quiet voices** should be next to loud ones, but insist on a balance.
- **A strong teen or adult singer** can assist with learning the harmony parts.
- **Adult or teen helpers** should sit between or behind children who have behavior concerns.

Caught in the act of worship

Continue to value unison singing. A simple chorus like *Thank you, Lord, for saving my soul* sung in unison by children's voices can provide a quieting call to worship. Choose a back-of-the-room "Jesus spot" target for youngsters to focus on as they sing to God. Give opportunities for solo singing to develop poise and individual progress. Carefully select songs or brief solos within pieces that can strengthen an individual's weaknesses and build on their strengths. For church holidays teach a hymn descant that the children can sing from their seats over the refrain, elevating the majesty of the moment.

Conducting a singing company or youth chorus requires much more than beating time. There is great value in a group's memorization of words to enable them to communicate through their performances. Ask the children to identify their favorite phrase of a song and tell the group why. Teach them to learn to read the faces of the congregation and to ask themselves, "Who needs these words today?" Let the children contribute in a meaningful way in worship. Keep God as the source of the ministry. Pray specifically for pieces. Pray for each child. Pray together in word and song.

The Beat Goes On

Dear Parents and Caregivers,

Your child will be performing next Wednesday, March 10 at 6:30 p.m. at The Salvation Army. Uniform black skirts or pants and white top are required. All children are asked to be at the corps by 4:30 p.m. for rehearsal. A supper will be provided for participants.

Please invite family and friends!

See you then.

Before a performance

Send a note to parents reminding them that the group will be performing. Include date, time, and instructions about required uniform for their children. Be specific, simple, and clear with details. Encourage parents to bring family and friends.

A brief rehearsal just before the performance will bring your well-rehearsed details to the fore and help the group focus for performance. The group should sit together in their regular assigned order to make the transition to the platform a quiet and efficient one. Practice getting into place at the rehearsal before the performance, so that this is familiar. Do not begin the piece until you have the children's total concentration, with every singer standing still and eyes focused on you. Tactfully encourage enthusiastic parents not to wave, shoot photos, or call out names before or during the performance.

7 BARS REST

1. Consider how you might further your group's development by:
   - Extending reading skills.
   - Learning to project sound more fully with unison singing.
   - Moving from canons to *do-mi-sol* harmonies.
   - Giving advanced students solo work.

2. What are ways you can see your children being used as a meaningful part of worship?

3. How do you pray for this ministry, particularly for your students and helpers?

THE SINGING COMPANY LEADER'S TOOLBOX

Approaching a New Children's Song

Many factors contribute to successful performances over the span of a season. Design a week-to-week routine and stick to it. Be specific about your rehearsal goals. Consistency of approach and preparation helps your members respond. Prepare warm-ups to wake up the body and voice and move the mind into rehearsal mode. Sight-sing something accessible at every rehearsal. Move into new material, then onto a song in progress with some hard detail work. Review a familiar song as a reward and finish with the song for the coming week's performance.

It is good practice to complete a song's preparation two weeks ahead of the performance. Familiarity breeds comfort and allows communication. A consistent performance standard engenders better and better performances. Resist accepting second best.

The following two sets of strategic teaching plans illustrate these concepts. The first song, *Win Them One by One,* is strophic. This means there are a number of verses followed by a chorus presented without variance in the music and parts. A song like this can be accomplished in just a few weeks. In contrast, *They Should Know!* contains varied verses with formidable rhythmic and pitch challenges. It will require careful planning to be learned in six weeks.

Stephen Sondheim's clever lyric, "Bit by bit, putting it together" sums up the week-by-week process of children's choir leadership. I am indebted to my wife, Priscilla, who

Chapter 7 | THE RIGHT SONG FOR YOUR KIDS!

I have watched from my less vulnerable seat at the piano. She has lived and breathed much of what is contained in this chapter. Every week she strategized anew to bring the children closer to a spirit of worship through their song.

There is more on **Rehearsal Planning** in Chapter Twenty-Three.

Win Them One By One

Win Them One by One is a delightful song by C. Austin Miles, originally copyrighted in 1915. This adaptation for children's voices is from *Children's Praise,* The Salvation Army, USA South, 2010. It updates the language in the verses, but retains the catchy chorus with a stylistically appropriate march accompaniment. Young and old will quickly grasp the meaning of the song to "bring the one next to you" and "we'll win them one by one." This winsome song (pun intended) proves a real "toe-tapper" for listeners and singers alike.

Depending on the concentrated rehearsal time your singing company has, the leader may wish to address the words to the chorus parts in week one, then add the pitches in week two, including the ending. In weeks three and four, introduce the verses and work the transitions between verse and chorus. This piece can serve as a catalyst for your children to bring in new children. Set an example yourself by seeking to welcome new people into the fellowship.

Divide and conquer

A quick look at the overall song reveals two verses using basically quarter note rhythms. The main melody takes in a range of just a sixth. In the key of F, the range rests comfortably from the first space F (*do*) to the fourth line D (*la*). [Reference score A] It is recommended that everyone learn the verses at first, but to save on memorization and feature more children, choose soloists to exchange phrases or verses. [B]

The verse includes two accidentals, which require chromatic syllables. [C] If F is *do*, then F# is sung a half step higher and in solfege, called *"di"* (pronounced dee). If Bb is called *fa*, then B natural is rendered as *"fi"* (pronounced fee) and sounds a half step higher. You may wish to note these syllables on the vocal copies for

The Beat Goes On

151

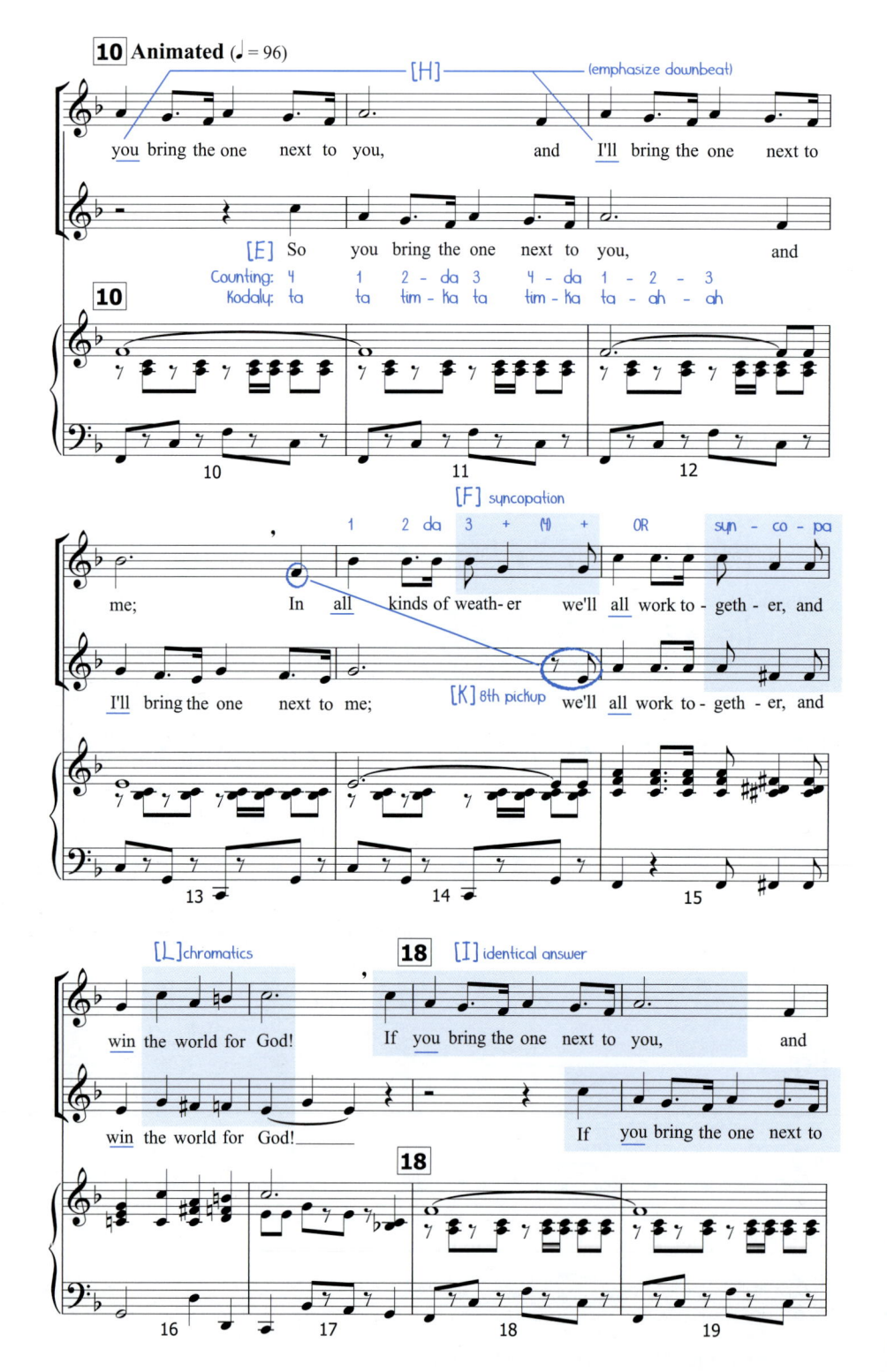

reference. To eliminate guesswork with pitches, isolate the bracketed *"re-di-re"* and *"mi-mi-fi-fi-sol"* passages and make sure these pitches are absolutely correct from the beginning. Once youngsters learn wrong notes, the habit rarely can be broken.

Have the children circle the breath marks. [D] Do breathing exercises in warm-ups so they will be confident singing through these four-bar phrases on one breath. Reward them with encouragement when they accomplish this.

First the chorus words in rhythm

A great deal of the charm lies in the animated chorus (m. 10 ff.) with its answering Group 2 part, march-like dotted rhythms and syncopation. The choir should be divided fairly equally, placing some of the better high voices in Group 1 to achieve a bright, confident ending. First establish the dotted rhythm between the quarters by echoing (So__ you__bring the one__next to you___), using Kodaly syllables (ta---tim-ka-ta---tim-ka-ta-ya-ya) or counting (1----2--dah 3---4-dah 1-2-3). [E]

Once the first four bars of the chorus are secure (mm.10-13, in two parts), introduce syncopation as a shift in the pattern of emphasis. At mm. 14-15, the syncopation occurs off of beat three. [F]

A third rhythmic figure in the chorus to be reconciled is the repetitions of "win them," commencing at measure 24. [G] These are syncopated off of beats one and three. Teach the second part, still chanting in rhythm, "win them, one by one," at the same time. Note that the final "win them" at m. 26 has both parts with the same words lined up rhythmically.

Once these various rhythms are secure, word-chant both parts all the way through the chorus. In good march style, emphasize the pickup into the downbeat of each phrase (If you bring…and I'll bring). **[H]** The accompanist can play the piano part as the choir chants to heighten the steady march pulse.

Now to the chorus pitches

Similar to the verses, the range in the Group 1 part is limited from F to D (or *do* to *la*). The Group 2 part adds an E (*ti*) below the F. Note that the first answering figure (m. 18, like m. 10, "you bring the one next to you") is identical, **[I]** while the second one (m. 21, like m. 13, "you bring the one next to you") answers a step lower. **[J]**

At measure 14, where the first syncopation is introduced, the pickup on the word "we'll" is not a quarter as before, but an eighth, which lines up with Group 1. **[K]** Work out the chromatic quarters at m. 16 slowly, with many repetitions. **[L]** After all, the word "rehearsal" means literally to re-hear. The Ds and Cs in the Group 1 part should sound nice and bright. **[M]**

Note that "We'll win them" at m. 24 starts in unison and moves to the harmony on the syncopation. Those who know the original will realize how the phrase has been extrapolated by repeats. **[N]**

On the repeat of the chorus, ask one or two Group 1 singers to go up to the high F (*sol* to *do'*) on the concluding bars. **[O]**

Verse and chorus in sequence

Learning how to alternate between the slower, more *cantabile* tempo of the verses and the animated march feel of the two-part chorus includes negotiating the long pickup to the chorus. How long you opt to hold it can be a bit of a tease. The introduction of just one bar and the repeat back after the first chorus will need some attention. Be sure to have a conversation with your youngsters about sharing with friends, neighbors, and family "one by one."

A reference audio recording of **Win Them One by One** is accessible in the Chapter Seven online folder.

The full score to **They Should Know!** is printed on pp. 159–162 of this chapter.

A SIX-WEEK REHEARSAL PLAN: THEY SHOULD KNOW!

Here is a suggested plan to teach *They Should Know!* in six rehearsal weeks. This song, with words by John Gowans and music by Ivor Bosanko, appears in *New Songs for Young People,* March 1985, SA, London. A reference audio recording is in the Chapter Seven online folder.

WEEK ONE

1. Warm-up, using the interval of the sixth (from middle C up to A).

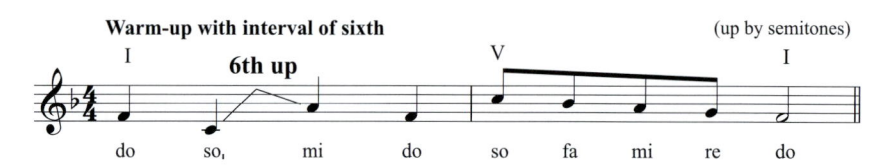

   Warm-up with interval of sixth (up by semitones)

   I — 6th up — V — I

   do so, mi do so fa mi re do

2. Away from the music, troubleshoot the tricky rhythms at measures 11–12. Clap or slap knees for the rests (sometimes called *patchen*) to get the rhythm secure. GO rest, rest/THEY rest, rest/SHOULD KNOW rest/ IT SURE-LY MUST SHOW **[Reference score A, commencing on p. 159]**

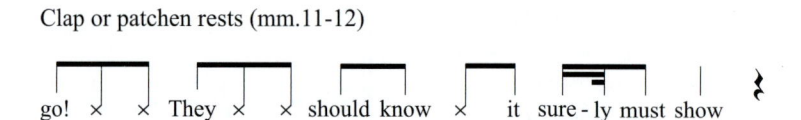

   Clap or patchen rests (mm.11-12)

   go! x x They x x should know x it sure-ly must show

3. Go back to the beginning of verse one and introduce the words in rhythm. Be careful of the syncopated rhythms in mm. 3–4 and mm. 7–8. Put lots of emphasis on beat one to give each phrase some bounce. **[B]** Underline downbeat words as a reminder: If <u>you</u>, If <u>all</u>, Then <u>folk</u>. Do the same, using the second verse words in the correct rhythm.

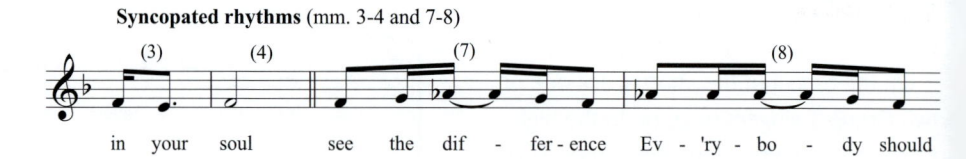

   Syncopated rhythms (mm. 3-4 and 7-8)

   (3) (4) (7) (8)

   in your soul see the dif - fer - ence Ev - 'ry - bo - dy should

4. Add the pitches. Use your hand to visually reinforce the level of the pitches. The *sol,-mi* sixth interval we used in the warm-up begins the first three phrases. Note the different pickup on "Your feet." **[C]** Get these phrases secure by going slowly at first and stopping at "feet" if necessary to reinforce this difference.

5. Phrase four **[D]** – "Your feet…" brings us back to GO rest, rest/THEY rest, rest/SHOULD KNOW rest/ IT SURE-LY MUST SHOW. **[A]** Review this, then go from the beginning a few times singing verse 1 up to measure 12 with the accompaniment. Go on to your next song.

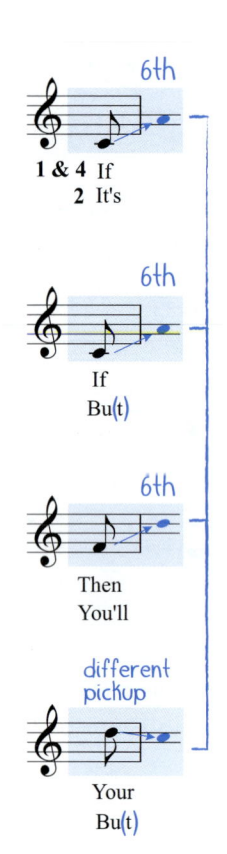

1 & 4 If — 6th
2 It's

If — 6th
Bu(t)

Then — 6th
You'll

different pickup
Your
Bu(t)

WEEK TWO

1. Use the four pickup notes isolated in sequence from [E] as a warm-up, with the first verse pickup words. This initiates the process of memorizing the first words of each phrase of the first verse words.

Verse 1 warm-up (up by semitones)

I — IV — I

If you... If all... Then folk... Your feet...

2. Review verse one from the beginning. Remind the children of the words, but always in the correct rhythm. Do not forget to strive for the bouncy downbeats. [F] Also begin to work on articulation. For instance: Your fee**t** with a crisp "t," (m.9) getting the "t" on the end of mus**t** (m. 12) or the "d" on shoul**d** (m.11). Repeat the *patchen* on GO rest, rest/THEY rest, rest/SHOULD KNOW rest/ IT SURE-LY MUST SHOW. [A] They will remember this if you make it physically active.

3. Introduce the new material starting at m. 13. Be prepared to split the group in two. The low voices sing first, "And on your face…" with stems down. The high voices answer following the stems going up with "There's no more pouting." Both groups finish together, with "You have got God's sunshine in your soul!" Drill this slowly with the *crescendo,* sensing the climax to the music. [G]

4. Teach the coda at m. 29. [H] Maintain the same two groupings. Note the dynamic contrast. Always teach the harmony part first. Lastly, go back to the beginning and try the complete first verse with the first ending and the final verse, noted as verse four, which is a repeat of the verse one words, going into the coda. Go on to your next song.

WEEK THREE

1. After your greeting, warm-up and tone-match something related to the new piece you will begin that night. Also reiterate the *sol,-mi* pickup interval to *They Should Know,* now reinforcing the verse two pickup words, then work on other pieces.

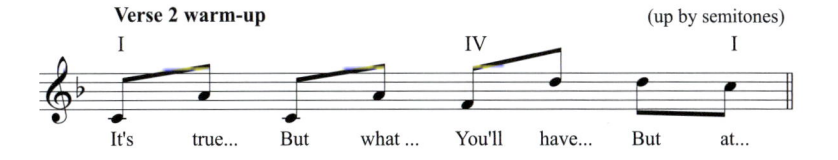

Verse 2 warm-up (up by semitones)

I — IV — I

It's true... But what ... You'll have... But at...

2. Begin work on *They Should Know* by reviewing the *patchen* GO rest, rest/ THEY rest, rest, SHOULD KNOW rest/ IT SURE-LY MUST SHOW. [A] Next review the second verse words for this phrase using the same *patchen* technique. [I] PRAYER! rest, rest/IF rest, rest/YOU DO! rest/ YOU'LL SURE-LY GET THROUGH!

3. Since the remainder of the second verse melody is the same as verse one, finish out the verse. Drill both versions several times, continuing all the way to the end of the verse ("sunshine in your soul!").

FIRST VERSE: GO! rest, rest/THEY…sunshine in your soul.
SECOND VERSE: PRAYER! rest, rest/IF……..sunshine in your soul.

4. Begin learning the words to verse two, but slowly. Since you already taught the four pickups in the warm-up and the melody is the same as in verse one, learning the verse two words should go quickly. Once this is mastered, review the first verse words from memory, then sing through both verses, using copies for the second verse only. If time allows, also review verse four going into the coda learned last week. Conclude with review songs.

WEEK FOUR

1. After greeting, warm-up and tone-match material related to a new piece. Then repeat the second verse pickup warm-up from Week Three. Segue to work on another piece.

Verse Two Diction Details

I(t's) true tha(t) you…
　wat(ch) an(d) pray,
Bu(t) wha(t) you have…
　ta(k)e away.
Bu(t) a(t) the time…
　ca-(t)as-tro-phe, (pr)ove…

2. Begin today's work on *They Should Know* by drilling the second verse words with an aim toward memorizing all of verse two. **The leader must know the words from memory before the rehearsal!** Have a list of diction trouble-spots ready before rehearsal and work through these one by one. One approach is to simply ask the group to echo selected words with the exaggerated diction you model. Remind the young people to feel the emphasis on the first downbeat of each phrase.

Learning verse two words with simple motions:

　It's true that you will have to watch (motion to eye) and pray (praying hands).
　But what you have (shake head and hand) no one can take away.
　You'll have your share (hands up to guard one side of head)
　　of life's calamity,

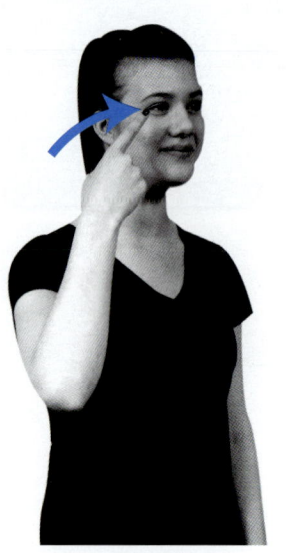

…to watch 　　　…and pray 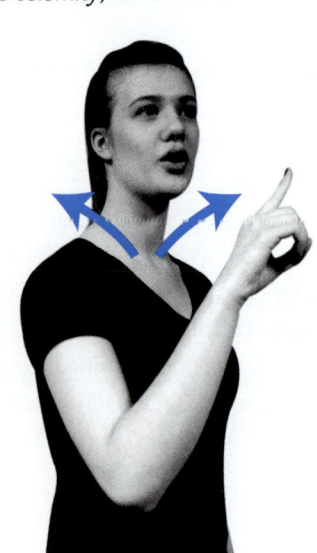　　　…no one can take away 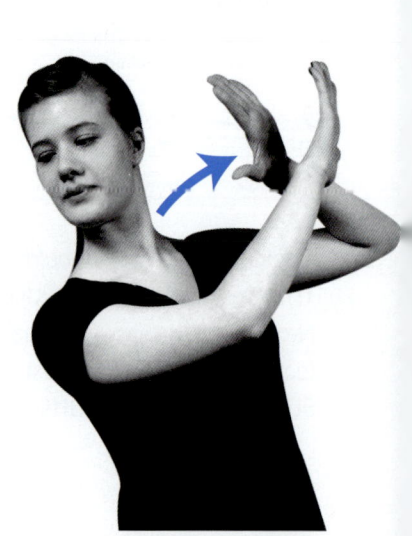　　　…share of life's calamity

Chapter 7 | THE RIGHT SONG FOR YOUR KIDS!

No one's free (both hands open and move out from waist) from all care,
But at the time of your catastrophe (bigger motion with hands up to guard one side of head)
Prove (first finger resolutely point up) *the answer is prayer!...*

3. Review verses one and two several times, including a refresher on how to get to the coda from verse one, labeled as verse four (back at m.3). Require good posture. The leader must give clear indications of pickup entrances and cut-offs, as well as articulation. This is covered in more detail in Chapters Twenty and Twenty-One on conducting. Most importantly, give off excitement and energy. Finally, encourage, encourage, encourage, "That's great. Give yourselves a hand. We just have one verse left to learn next week." Segue to other songs.

WEEK FIVE

1. The transitional third verse melody, although similar with its syncopations on beats three and four, maintains a descending fifth interval between beats two and three of measures 19, 21, 23. [J] Note that earlier at bar 7, the interval returned down a sixth to the F [K], while in bar 9 it is a fifth. [L] To reinforce these descending fifths, warm-up with a modulatory (ascending by half steps) exercise.

(up by semitones)
5th down

1 2 3 4 5 1
do re mi fa so do

2. The words to verse three (mm. 19-28) are not easy and neither are the corresponding chromatic shifts. Begin learning the third verse pitches in rhythm using a "doot" syllable first, proceeding two bars at a time. (See [M] mm. 19-20, then 21-22, 23-24, and 25-26)

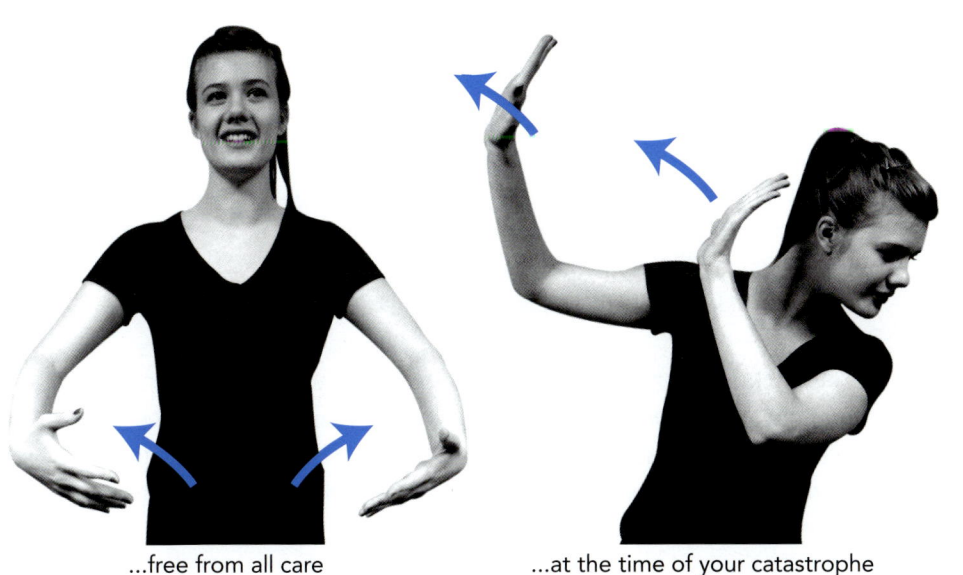

...free from all care　　　...at the time of your catastrophe　　　...prove the answer is prayer!

The Beat Goes On　　　157

Grading dynamics by progressively adding voices

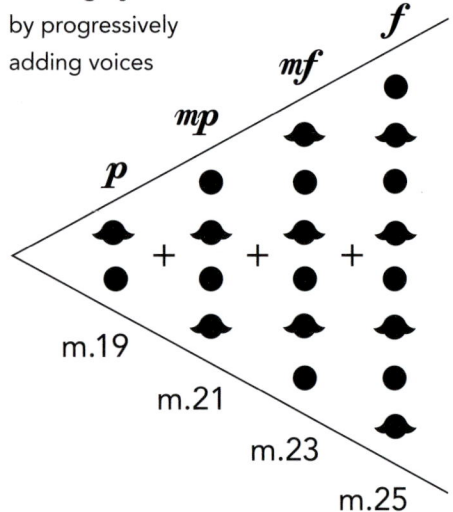

p *mp* *mf* *f*

m.19
m.21
m.23
m.25

3. Begin to link the phrases, still using "doot," with the half step modulations up between mm. 20–21 and 22–23. [N]

4. Considering the difficulty of the words and the graded dynamics called for, the following plan may ease the learning curve with this section as we incorporate the words:

   - At m. 19, use only your two most reliable voices (who also memorize well) to begin the third verse (*If the grey clouds...*)
   - At m. 21, add two to four more voices on the next phrase at m. 21 (*If dark despairing...*)
   - At m. 23, add four to six more voices (*The inner sunshine...*)
   - At m. 25, add the weakest voices (*You have your own supply...*)
   - Finally, everyone sings *"GO rest, rest/THEY rest, rest..."* which they already know.

   In this way you have orchestrated the required dynamics, created an assortment of vocal colors, and also overcome a stumbling block for memorization. Position these groupings in your formation so you can cue them easily, with good eye contact. Children are naturally inquisitive, so they will hear each other's parts just by listening.

5. Give good attention to the *fermata* on "show" to be held at *fortissimo* with a round "O" sound. [O] Be sure all eyes are on you. Allow a slight break before the D.C. accompaniment begins. (D.C., for *da capo*, means "return to the beginning.") Save the diphthong final short "I" sound for the cutoff.

WEEK SIX

1. Use a chromatic, modulatory warm-up as you move into rehearsal. Work on other pieces, then return to *They Should Know*. Work to reinforce the third verse words with good diction and dynamics. For memorization's sake, start by chanting the words in rhythm and then adding pitches.

2. Our last challenge is to begin with verse three at m. 19 and teach the return to verse four (*da capo*) following the fermata. Drill verses three and four without copies several times going into the *coda*, so that the ending is secure.

3. Get into standing formation and go from start to finish with accompaniment. This assumes that you, the conductor, are thoroughly familiar with the road map. Do not stop! We learn much from what we may miss. If you or the youngsters forget something, keep going until the shape of the entire piece from start to finish is familiar. Be certain that you give clear signals and cues, especially at the beginning of each verse and line.

4. Finally, challenge the choir to sing the piece all the way through accompanied, but without your leadership. This assures memorization of the piece and causes the choristers to get more information from the accompaniment. Stand at the back of the room and at the conclusion, applaud enthusiastically!

THEY SHOULD KNOW!

John Gowans
Ivor Bosanko

Bright and rhythmic ♩ = 100

UNISON

1 & 4 If you have go(t | G)od's sun-shine in your soul,
2 It's true that you will have to watch an(d) pray,

If all your life is un-der His con-trol,
Bu(t) wha(t you) have no one can take a-way. (ta-kah)

Then fol(k) should sure-ly see the dif-fer-ence, Ev-'ry-bo-dy should know! Your
You'll have your share of life's ca-la-mi-ty, No one(s) free from all care, Bu(t)

[B] underline indicates strong emphasis
[F] bouncy downbeats
[K] down 6th
round "o"
[C] different pickup
[E]

©1985 Salvationist Publishing, used with permission
New Songs for Young People - March, 1985

[D] phrase four
[L]
down 5th
fee(t) shoul(d (d)ance to ev - 'ry mel - o - dy, Ev - 'ry - where that you
at the time of your ca - tas - tro - phe Prove the an - swer is
2 d's
flip "r"
9
10
[A] x = clap or patchen
TWO PARTS
go! x x They x x shoul(d) know! It sure - ly mus(t) show!
2nd verse patchen
[I] prayer! x x If x x you do, You'll sure - ly ge(t) through!
LOW An(d)
11
12
[G] two parts to unison
last time to CODA
becoming louder
HIGH
to unison
There's no more pou(t) - ing, no more pin - ing
on your face i(t) shoul(d) be shin - ing now.
LOW If
mp cresc.
13
14
UNISON
1.
D.
you have go(t) God's sun - shine in your soul!
(4 beats)
15
16

Chapter 7 | THE RIGHT SONG FOR YOUR KIDS!

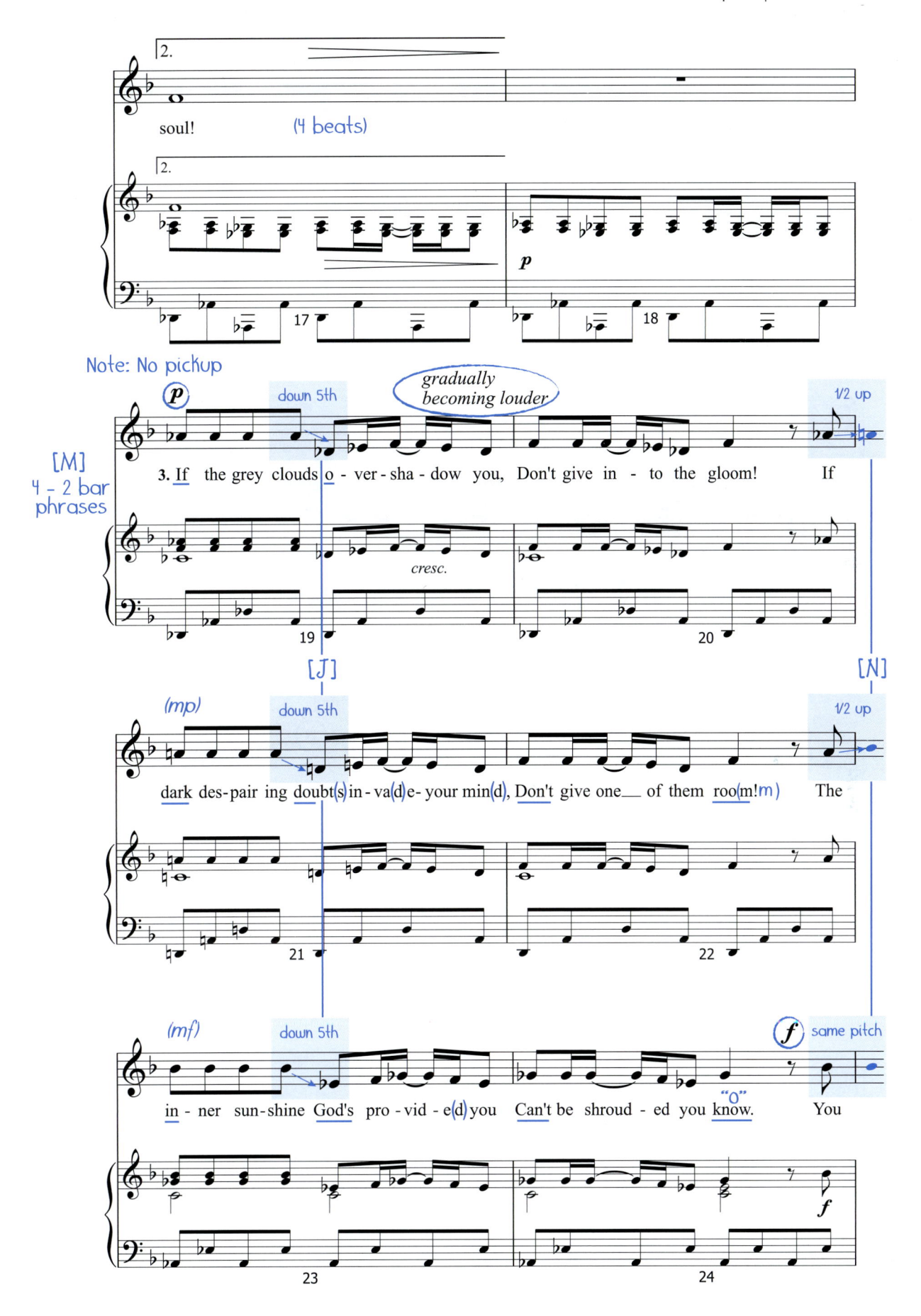

The Beat Goes On

different down 4th
have your own sup - ply in - side of you Ev - 'ry - where that you
25
26
[O]
D.C.
ff
go! They should know! It sure - ly must show!
"O"
27
28
[H]
CODA
UNISON
note contrasting dynamics
you have got God's sun - shine in your soul, sun - shine in your
29
30
TWO PARTS
soul, sun - shine in your soul!
ō
oo
31
32
33

7 BARS REST

1. Try these group singing company activities, which use both the eye and ear gates to encourage music reading:

   - **Musical fingers**—Ask each child to follow the *printed music* with his/her finger, while the pianist plays the singer's *melodic line* until someone calls out, "Stop!" Ask on what word we stopped. By repeating the process (and stopping at other random spots), the singers will hear (and follow) the melody over and over.

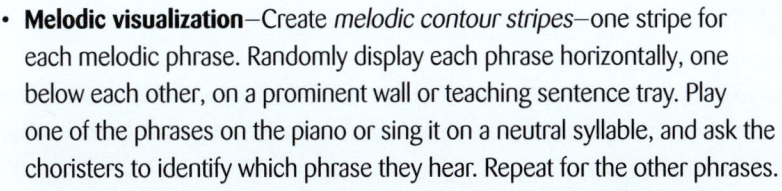

   - **Melodic visualization**—Create *melodic contour stripes*—one stripe for each melodic phrase. Randomly display each phrase horizontally, one below each other, on a prominent wall or teaching sentence tray. Play one of the phrases on the piano or sing it on a neutral syllable, and ask the choristers to identify which phrase they hear. Repeat for the other phrases.
     To conclude, play the song from the beginning and have the singers put the phrases in the correct order, top to bottom. If you leave a space below each phrase, you can then continue teaching the song with the corresponding lyrics added below each phrase. Later, to aid memorization, you can begin to remove the music and/or lyric stripes one by one.

   - **Color-coded phrases**—An alternative has each *melodic phrase stripe color-coded,* phrase 1 as blue, phrase 2 as green, etc. The exception to the color-coding would be if phrase 1 and 3 are the same melodic contour, then they should have the same identifying color dot or stripe.
     Assign groups of singers to each respective color group, teaching the phrases color by color, having only each color group sing their phrase at the proper time. The other singers are assimilating the musical contour of the phrases, while watching the music (and listening) to the other groups.[4]

2. Devise a plan to complete a song over several weeks. Refer to the two songs above or the sample "plans of attack" in Chapters Twelve and Thirteen on songster leadership, and Chapter Twenty-Three on rehearsal strategy.

3. Commit to memory (and share with your choristers) the *Choristers' Prayer:*

   > *Bless, O Lord, us thy servants*
   > *who minister in the temple.*
   > *Grant that what we sing with our lips,*
   > *we may believe in our hearts.*
   > *And what we believe in our hearts*
   > *we may show forth in our lives.*
   > *Through Jesus Christ our Lord.*
   > *Amen.*[5]

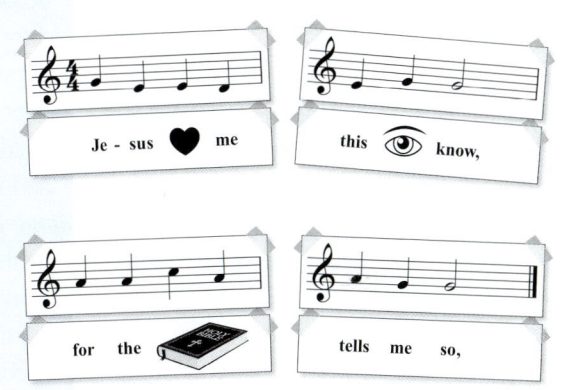

SINGING COMPANY LEADER'S RESOURCES

SALVATION ARMY PUBLICATIONS FOR CHILDREN

Children's Praise is a series of children's songs designed for Salvation Army singing companies and young soloists, with keyboard accompaniment, published by The Salvation Army, USA South. A choral demonstration-accompaniment recording is available. *Children's Praise* is available online at no cost, including the sheet music in PDF format, demonstration/accompaniment tracks, and projectable words.

Sing to the Lord Children's Voice Series replaced *New Songs for Young People* in 1993. This 32-page volume is released annually by Salvationist Publishing and Supplies, UK, and includes songs for singing companies that are useful for all worship situations. An accompaniment/demonstration of parts CD is also available for each issue. Available through Salvation Army Supplies and Purchasing departments or as a standing order subscription (see Appendix 14.3).

Songs of Joy, Joy Webb (Salvationist Publishing and Supplies) is a collection of simple children's songs and arrangements including *Kum Ba Yah, Angels Watching Over Me,* and the *Caribbean Lord's Prayer.*

Singing Company Album is a collection of arrangements for children's chorus published by the Western Territory USA. This album was published in years that the Western Territory held its singing company competition. Years 1991, 1997, 1999, and 2001 are available through Salvation Army Supplies and Purchasing departments with piano accompaniment tracks.

Psalms, Hymns and Spiritual Songs (The Salvation Army, USA East) is a collection of contemporary one and two-part choral settings suitable for adult chorus, youth chorus, men's or women's vocal ensembles, and children's chorus. This series has been created to meet the needs of conductors and vocal ensembles that require unison and occasional two-part arrangements with limited voice ranges and easy to medium difficulty level piano accompaniments.

Songs of Praise (The Salvation Army, NHQ) is a collection of 254 songs with words and music featuring well known hymns, spirituals, Gospel songs and more recent contemporary Christian songs. Each song is published with SATB harmonization with full text, allowing for part singing, if desired, as well as piano accompaniment. It was originally titled *Youth Songbook.*

REHEARSAL PREPARATION

Beyond the Downbeat, Sandra Willetts (Abingdon Press). Although designed for adult choir leaders, this user-friendly book includes many principles of diction, seating formations, etc. applicable to children's choirs.

Children's Choral Guide, Priscilla Burgmayer (The Salvation Army). Helps for rehearsal preparation and rehearsals, including vocal warm-ups for children. Available through the Pendel Music Department. Also published in back of each issue of *Children's Praise* (The Salvation Army, USA South) since Volume 10.

Children Sing His Praise—*A Handbook for Children's Choir Directors*, edited by Donald Rotermund (Concordia). Includes valuable teaching from Helen Kemp.

The Chorister, Bi-monthly periodical for children's choir leaders (Choristers Guild).

Directing the Children's Choir, Shirley W. McRae (Schirmer).

We Will Sing! *Choral Music Experience for Classroom Choirs,* Doreen Rao (Boosey & Hawkes).

If you cannot teach me to fly, teach me to sing.
—J.M. Barrie, author of *Peter Pan*

CHAPTER EIGHT

ALL HAIL TO DANIEL'S BAND!
Building an Instrumental Program from the Bottom Up

Building up the temple, building up the temple,
Building up the temple of the Lord.
Oh, sister, won't you help me?
Brother, won't you help me?
Building up the temple of the Lord.
(Sunday school chorus)

JIMMY GETS JUNIOR BAND

Music can be instrumental in corps growth! (Pun intended.) Jimmy lived a few blocks from The Salvation Army. His desperate mother came to the Army for assistance. The officer wisely took note of the address of mom and her three children and on his weekly afternoon stroll through the neighborhood, dropped by and checked on things. Soon the officer began to work with Jimmy's mom, not only providing food and carfare, but also helping her budget to pay her bills on time.

An invitation was extended to the children to attend The Salvation Army's after-school boys' and girls' programming, Sunday school, and the youth music program. The corps had a small but faithful ensemble for a band. Jimmy and his two sisters took special delight in watching how the end-chair cornet player turned red in the face when playing high notes. Soon Jimmy and his siblings were learning to play instruments. They received weekly private lessons, studied theory, and learned to sight-sing. This prepared them for the singing company, as well as the junior band, which played every week in Sunday school. Regional music schools, summer music camp, and conservatory provided incentives for them to work their way up through the youth band to the divisional band. Today mom and all three offspring are active Salvationists! These children were the first in their family to have such a strong experience with music. Chances are they will pass their love of music on to their own children.

In **Chapter Eight**, we learn:
- how to use short- and long-term incentives to build a corps instrumental music program.
- about resources and methods to equip an effective youth band.

FROM GENERATION TO GENERATION

Passing musical expertise onto another generation dates back to David's grand organizational scheme for establishing the Temple in Jerusalem. "One generation will commend your works to another," declared David in Psalm 145:4. Imagine with me the ongoing sounds of instruction as the chronicler gives us a tantalizingly brief view into the multigenerational ministry of music around the Temple courts: "All these were under the direction of their fathers for the music of the temple of the Lord, with cymbals, lyres and harps, for the ministry at the house of God. Asaph, Jeduthun, and Heman were under the supervision of the king. Along with their relatives—*all of them trained and skilled in music for the Lord*—they numbered 288." (1 Chronicles 25:6-7) When the chronicler tells us, "Young and old alike, teacher as well as student, cast lots for their duties" (I Chron. 25:8), we see the integration of several generations into a mammoth effort to provide the ongoing music for the Temple worship.[1]

Three generations of banding together: Robert, John, and Zachary Doctor, members of the Pasadena Tabernacle Band

One of the strengths of Salvation Army banding is the opportunity for several generations, even within a family, to share in the joy of music making. According to David's plan, the Levitical Temple musicians understood that it was the responsibility of their family to carry on the duties of the previous generation. We know from the story of Samuel that children at a young age became part of the bustle of religious duties within the Temple. No doubt there was a sense of high calling even in the most menial tasks but particularly in training the next generation of instrumentalists. I imagine a time-honored scheme to test and improve competence, with rehearsals to pass on the established traditions in song.

Doesn't this sound like a Salvation Army youth band program? The teacher sits next to the student giving necessary correction ("Remember the accidentals carry through the measure, Jimmy"), armed with a dose of assuring encouragement. ("That's it, you've got it!")

The Ultimate Challenge

In an article called "Beginning Brass—The Ultimate Challenge," former Chicago Staff Bandmaster William Himes gives us a glimpse into the first day of lessons. Unfortunately, in Army circles, this all-too-familiar scene lies a fair distance from David's noble vision of training the next generation of musician-priests:

> We can have a room full of wide-eyed, excited youngsters, ready to discover the mysterious concoction of valves, slides and plumbing of brass instruments, but what is our response to this initial outburst of enthusiasm?
>
> We recruit leaders who are inexperienced and untrained, and then we do not give them any preparation or budget. They will be lucky if we have identified a suitable day and rehearsal time in the corps schedule, along with a room with reasonable lighting and instructional space.
>
> Scrounging though our inventory, we reluctantly part with only the most aged of instruments, usually in battered condition, missing corks and springs, with equally bashed-up cases.
>
> As for the excited neophyte players assembled, we save the best for last: the challenge of starting brass sounds on grungy, ill-fitting mouthpieces, often more decrepit than their corresponding instruments.[2]

The Temple music revived!

Bill Himes asks, "Is it any wonder that our beginning instrumental programs can be short-lived experiments in corps programming?" For those familiar with the narrative in Chronicles, not long after the David–Solomon Temple era, things went sour—and fast. There was little sign of the Temple priests, maintenance staff, gatekeepers, or the musicians and singers.

Enter a new monarch: Hezekiah. At just 25 years of age, he ordered the Temple doors to be repaired and the priests to consecrate themselves and the Temple as David had prescribed. Is it too much to suggest that the roots of the Temple musician-priests ran generationally wide and deep? The musically trained remnant, like a deep-rooted tree, apparently weathered the howling storms of conflict, conquest, and idol-worship. The songs of Zion may have been hushed, but they were not silenced. At Hezekiah's urgent command, "The Levites stood ready with David's instruments, and the priests with their trumpets." (2 Chronicles 29:26) **Talk about dusting off old horns with grungy mouthpieces!** These instruments were more than 250 years old![3] "The whole assembly bowed in worship, while the singers sang and the trumpeters played...so the service of the temple of the Lord was re-established. Hezekiah and all the people rejoiced... because it was done so quickly." (2 Chronicles 29:28, 35-36)

> "One generation will commend your works to another."
> —Psalm 145:4

In many corps, vintage photos bespeak a splendid legacy of what a corps band or songsters used to be in the "good old days," when there were two meetings on Sunday and a march to an open-air. The junior band played each week for the Sunday school opening and once a month for meetings. In the words of one admiring professional musician, "Salvation Army junior bands have a lot to answer for, being a breeding ground for dozens of symphonic principal trumpet players."[4] Yet over time, the culture of many of our corps has changed. The band and songsters may not be the sole musical support for congregational worship and may be looked upon as a mere vestige of bygone days. But as the Founder discovered, instrumental music organizes the singing, and few things bring a congregation together like hearty singing.

Bedford Corps (UK) Young People's Band

WHAT, ME? THE YOUTH BAND LEADER?

From generation to generation

Have you noticed that successful youth band leaders really enjoy kids and those youngsters are drawn to the leaders? Teaching learners or leading a youth band takes a special kind of person. There seems to be an unspoken understanding that such leaders see more in their kids than the kids see in themselves.

Wise leaders elect to surround themselves with people who share their vision, who are willing to stay the course week in and week out with a "stick-to-it-ness" reminiscent of Hezekiah. Success stories, like the one about Jimmy, are the product of godly living reflected in reverent service. Our students begin to "see Jesus." In turn, these young musicians turn toward God and acknowledge His claim on their lives. They may not fully understand why or what is going on, but they see something of purpose on rehearsal nights and Sundays. It is, as we discussed in Chapter Three, a "social work" within our citadel walls. We accept the God-given responsibility to care for His precious children and encourage them to praise Him with music. What a privilege to follow in the steps of generations before us, not unlike the Levite clans who carried forth the sounds of salvation!

Live long and prosper (even if working with kids!)

The chronicle of Hezekiah closes with these words of commendation. "In everything that Hezekiah undertook in the service of God's temple and in obedience to the law and the commands, he sought his God and worked wholeheartedly. And so he prospered." (2 Chronicles 31:21) Are the "temple courts" of your corps quiet? Has the band room become a dusty museum rather than a hive of activity? Swing wide the door of the band room—and your heart—and consecrate yourself to this noble service! Kids *are* still drawn to shiny brass instruments! Remember the thrill of holding your first instrument. Recall that first solo or your first rehearsal in a real band. We all start somewhere. Someone chooses to share an important part of his or her life with the next generation of learners. That someone could be you!

Kids are still drawn to shiny brass instruments!

> **"What a privilege to follow in the footsteps of other generations."**
> —Psalm 145:4
> (author's paraphrase)

8 BARS REST

1. Consider how you began your own journey as an instrumentalist. Who were your mentors? How were you taught? Was it effective? What were your first banding experiences? Did you enjoy them, and learn something each time? What would you do differently?

2. "We cannot afford to skip another generation," some say. Is there a nucleus of interest in teaching learners and supporting a youth band? Can you see yourself involved as a teacher or leader? What part of your corps musical history might be resuscitated in the present? Find out what's in that bandroom!

3. Who are the "pied-piper" types within your sphere who seem to inspire and connect with kids? Are there potential leaders who will prove consistent and firm? Do others share your vision for integrating music within The Salvation Army? Are there corps members or musicians from area schools with specific musical gifts who would be willing to teach or give inspirational clinics, concerts, or master classes?

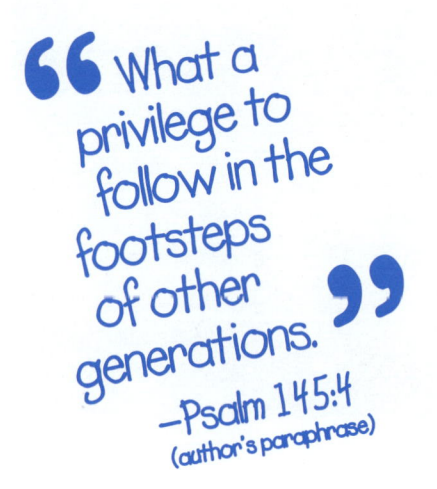

DRIP, DRIP, DRIP!

Week by week with short-term goals and long-term incentives

The probing yet patient teacher, asks the student, "How do you put a hole in a stone?" The student offers a variety of answers, most of which suggest some sort of drilling. The wise and venerable master counsels his student, "Drops wear down the stone not only by strength but constant falling ... therefore, we are taught to work tirelessly, to allow no day to pass without a line written." The master teacher was Johann Fux who lived from 1660 to 1741. The "drip-drip-drip" dialogue is found in his famous treatise on musical counterpoint, which "tutored" the likes of Mozart, Haydn, Beethoven, and Brahms.[5]

Fux's wise counsel reminds us that learning takes place best in small doses on a consistent basis. In our era of instant gratification, we are prone to leave our housework or studying for the last minute, yet we still hope for success. Human nature seems prone to operate under deadlines, yet numerous studies indicate that strategizing the use of our time maximizes results. What follows are suggestions of a necessary mix of short-term (week to week) and long-term (seasonal) goals to bring about the consistent progress of developing instrumentalists. *The overriding principle is to create opportunities for young people to progress in their music-making through daily practice.*

DAY TO DAY PRACTICE

Drops wear down the stone not only by strength but constant falling ... therefore, we are taught to work tirelessly, to allow no day to pass without a line written.

—Johann Fux (1725)

Short-term goals

Private or small-group session
Consistently give attainable work for a one-week period. For instance, ask the student to finish one page from the method book and a new scale. Be specific and record expectations in a student log book. Some teachers circle the number or put a due date on each exercise in the method book and/or use assignment sheets. For younger students, ask them to color in a part of a picture each time they practice. After lessons, record the week's progress on a chart in the band room or adjacent hallway.

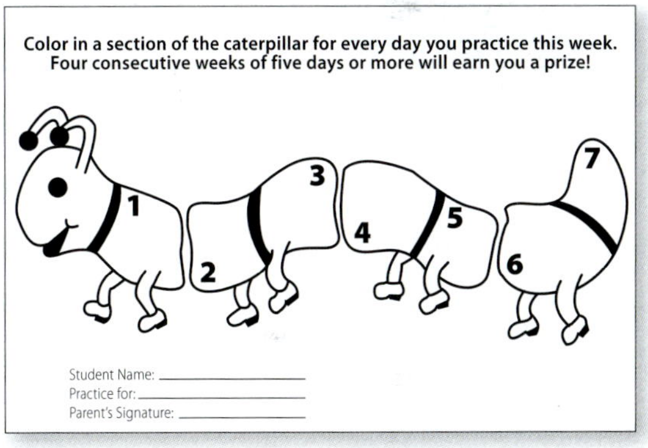

To encourage students to practice the whole page, not just the songs or lines they like, Bill Quick, a highly successful public school music teacher, suggests creating a P.A.W. Club (Page-A-Week Club). Have on hand a supply of small paw stickers. Students earn a P.A.W. Club sticker every week they complete a whole page in their lesson book. Use one sticker on the page completed, one at the end of the line in the student log book or assignment sheet, and one on the chart in the band room.

Sometimes it is preferable to work in pairs or threes. Peer pressure pushes students along. This session can be 20-30 minutes, depending on the age of the students.

Long-term incentives

Method book
Set realistic goals with each student to complete a level or book by the end of the season. In the Music Arts Proficiency (M.A.P.) Curriculum, level completion includes requirements for method bookwork, scale or drum rudiments, solo work, theory, ensemble, and sight-reading. (M.A.P. Brass Guidelines are found in Appendix 8.1.) Admission to the Divisional Prep Band requires Primer Level completion; Youth Band, Level II completion; while Level IV completion qualifies musicians for the Divisional Band.

In a corps setting we can establish long-term incentives for individual players to move up through a three-tiered structure within the junior band program. The C Band

"I'm going to make it into the B band by Christmas!"

HEAR YE! Don't miss our winter recital! Every child will be performing a solo and you will want to be there to cheer them on!

We aim to be a "player" in the artistic, social, and spiritual formation of each individual young person.

is made up of new learners, definitely at the beginning stages. The B Band, even if just a few members, has reached intermediate Level II. The A Band members have completed at least Level III competency and work on more advanced pieces as an ensemble. Completion of Level III is a suggested minimum requirement for admittance to a corps senior band. This permits a level of competence to play from most of The Salvation Army Band Tune Book. It is music to the youth bandleader's ears to hear a youngster say, "I'm going to make it into the B Band by Christmas."

Solo work

Students should know at the beginning of the season that they will perform at least three different solos. They will play for the winter and spring recital, plus something for Sunday school opening and/or the private evaluation solo.

The instructor should guide the student in the solo selections. Too often students "undershoot" for fear of not getting the piece done in time, or they simply procrastinate. Other students "overshoot," and the success factor is lost to nerves and lack of preparedness. The method books contain appropriate solos. Thanks to the USA Southern Territory's American Instrumental Ensemble Series (AIES) we have an ever-increasing number of practical solos for young players. Other recommended solo collections for brass and snare drum are included in the resources list at the conclusion of Chapter Nine.

Scholarships

Many corps subsidize fees for divisional music camps, conservatories, or similar territorial camps. These scholarships can be used as incentives for participation and attendance. Soldiers, corps, or senior bands may wish to sponsor a child, allowing opportunity for the student to "earn" his or her way to camp through significant musical progress.

8 BARS REST

Inventory short-and long-term goals that your young people might strive for this season. Think of a motivational way to put this before them.

THE TRUMPET SHALL SOUND!

Building a beginner instrumental program

One aim of this chapter is to share insight into nurturing young people's ongoing learning through the use of short- and long-term goals. Another is to equip teachers to start new learners in the instrumental medium. It is imperative for you, the leader, to be convinced that this is an essential ministry. We aim to be a "player" in the artistic, social, and spiritual formation of each individual young person. It is well documented that improvement in reading and math skills follows effective music instruction. Performing develops self-esteem and presentation skills. Consistency in practice and attendance builds self-discipline. Weekly exposure to a caring mentor fosters humility and accountability. The long-range goal is to move students through the beginner, intermediate, and youth bands into the senior band. These ensembles perform often in Sunday school, worship, and outreach. Because of this, we cultivate a ministry team with strong bonds of fellowship.

Recruit and assess students

In this postmodern culture, music and arts allow a hands-on activity that is attractive as outreach. We can recruit from the neighborhood, rally day, local schools, community center, and other corps outreach programs, including Sunday school and girls' and boys' programs. In doing so, we hope to bridge these young people into corps membership.

Readiness for participation in instrumental programs depends upon each student's physical and intellectual maturity. It is recommended that beginning brass students be at least eight years of age—third grade and up. Before that age, begin with piano, violin, or simple percussion instruments,[6] where second teeth are not an issue. Guitar is not recommended for elementary age children; their hands are too small. A ukulele can work as a pre-instrument in the same manner that recorders are used in elementary classrooms.

Choosing a brass instrument

In choosing the correct brass instrument for each student, consider teeth formation, lip size, and physical stature. Some advocate starting all new learners on cornet, then switching later. But sometimes an already-developing physique may suggest a larger instrument. Some brass instructors simply separate the Bb instruments (all in treble clef) from the Eb instruments. Others advocate a high-pitched group on cornet and a low-pitched one on trombone or baritone (commencing with bass clef, to be compatible with school literature). As the child grows, a switch can be made from baritone to tuba. If braces will be a factor in the foreseeable future, then recommend an instrument with a larger mouthpiece, which puts less pressure directly over the braces.

Allow students to voice their preferences, but only allow switches at the beginning of a term. Often a student started on cornet will experience physical difficulty with playing high or low. Experimenting with a larger instrument may better suit a student's embouchure and make it easier to produce an improved sound over a wider range. Salvationist instructors ought not to shy away from teaching trombone, although often, smaller elementary age children cannot reach sixth position. You may also make an instrument choice to fill a need in your existing ensemble.

Even at beginning stages, avoid the temptation to mechanically work through exercises at the expense of allowing the student to make a satisfying sound. Students require a good sound model to emulate. This can be in the form of a recording, as required in the Suzuki method,[8] and/or a good player sitting next to them. *The best arbiter of instrument placement is the sound the student is producing.* A pinched or hard, forced sound suggests moving to a bigger instrument. A student with a "starved breath" sound might consider moving to a smaller bore instrument, where more breath resistance would improve the tone.

Who should play drums?

If asked, far more students than you can ever handle will sign up for drums. In the same way that we strategically place students on brass instruments, candidates for the percussion class need to be judiciously assessed and selected. You will spin your wheels without significant progress if a child exhibits limited wrist mobility, is extremely double-jointed, or lacks the basic muscle development or coordination to keep a steady beat.[9] A simple test is to ask the student to play a C scale on a keyboard percussion instrument using alternate sticking. This allows you to determine if the student can hold the sticks, keep from folding in, maintain a steady beat, and coordinate hand-to-hand motion.

"Which instrument should I play?"

embouchure (*term*) \'äm - bu - shur\ describes the mouth, lip, chin, and cheek muscles, tensed and shaped in a cooperative manner, so that when blown through, set an air column into vibration when the lips are placed upon the mouthpiece of a brass instrument.[7]

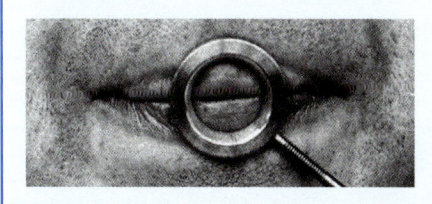

More on holding drumsticks properly, and beginning percussion instruction in Chapter Nine, pp. 191–194.

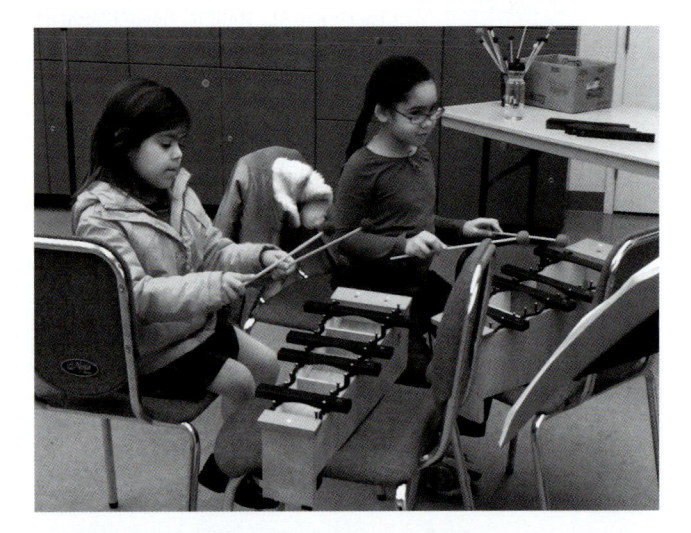

When percussionists "fold in" while playing with a matched grip, they change the angle of their hands, so that the back of the hand is no longer level and the thumbnails do not face each other. One or both hands is angled away from the drum. "Folding in" changes where the stick hits the drum, resulting in a different sound being produced by each hand.

For younger students, rhythm/motion singing games are a good place to develop a sense of pulse. If students start too early on snare drum, they often lack the basic muscle development to hold their hand position without folding in, play from the arm without bending the wrists correctly, lose the "V" needed for a matching sound when switching hands, or use too much arm motion. There is something to be said for the programs that do not offer a percussion major or class, principally because they don't have a capable instructor. Some curricula, like the El Sistema model, require all students to receive weekly rhythmic training. This greatly benefits their music reading skills. In time, those with a natural inclination toward percussion emerge.

Admission policy for new students

In Chapter Three (p. 78), we recommended limiting admission of new students to the beginning of October and January. This allows a month in September to settle your schedule and take time to review with returning students. This also establishes just two occasions where one needs to rethink the overall music school schedule to accommodate new students. By placing newcomers on waiting lists, you can anticipate changes in schedule. If students have had some instruction at school or elsewhere, it is recommended that an entrance evaluation for correct placement be given on their instruments and in sight-singing and theory. Ability, rather than age, determines placement. This may mean that a teen begins in a class with a grade school student, but hypothetically will move through the level requirements quickly and catch up to peers.

See Chapter Nine, **The Brass and Drum Instructors Toolbox,** for tips on starting and giving lessons to beginning instrumentalists.

Ready equipment and music

Well in advance of your start date, be sure the brass and percussion instruments are in *good working order*. Too often, hand-me-down instruments from the senior band are barely playable, even by seasoned players. Some repairs, like split valve corks, stuck slides, valves, or trombone slides needing attention, can be taken care of in-house. Leaks and the like may require a trip to the repair shop. Inspect the instruments well in advance to allow time for repair. Quality medium-depth mouthpieces are also essential. (Bach cornet 5C or trombone 12 mouthpieces are good student choices.) A shallow antique mouthpiece will create an explosive production, which is difficult for young players to control. Use name tags or masking tape to label each case

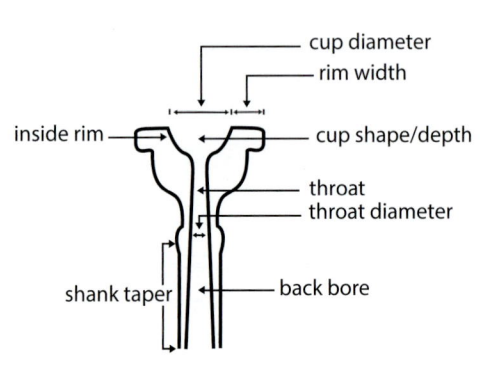

	Size/Shape	Effect
Cup	Large	more volume and control
	Small	less fatigue
	Deep	darker tone color (timbre)
	Shallow	brighter tone color (timbre)
Rim	Wide	more endurance
	Narrow	more flexibility and range
	Sharp	more precision of attack and brilliance
	Round	improved comfort
Throat	Small	more resistance, endurance, and brilliance
	Large	more blowing freedom, volume, and tone

and instrument with student's names. Also prepare the lease/loan instrument agreement for the caregiver's signature. (See Appendix 8.2 for a sample.)

There always seems to be a need for more instruments. Your corps may need to lease or purchase horns or junior percussion kits (JPKs).[10] Some corps run radio or newspaper ads appealing for used instruments. Some search online while others apply for grants through local foundations. Be sure to purchase method books and theory books in plenty of time through your divisional music director or local store. Some well-tested method and supplemental books are included in the resource list at the end of this chapter.

Avoid the makeshift propping up of music against the inside of a horn case or on the chapel pew, which inhibits posture and the embouchure. Check to be sure you have a sufficient number of functioning music stands, as well as folders prepared for your ensembles, labeled with name and part.

Junior Percussion Kit (JPK)

Scheduling

In Chapter Three we looked at various models for setting priorities and scheduling for after-school music and arts programs. In this chapter we began by emphasizing the importance of consistency of instruction from week to week. *Allow 30 minutes, once a week, for private instrumental or small-group instruction.* Secondly, allow an additional 20–30 minutes each week, depending on age and attention span, for theory and/or sight-singing.

If small group instruction is necessary, teach the Eb and Bb instruments separately to start. Even with beginners, allow a portion of time to begin playing together as a band. The playing together of simple unison exercises from a method book can begin to build a sense of ensemble and camaraderie. As students progress, schedule an intermediate/junior band period.

Locate instructors

Do not go at this alone. Look for folks who have some musical skill, knowledge of band instruments, and technique. Look for team players who are willing to share in the leader's vision. They should be willing to invest, be consistent, and love children. To develop a program, the teacher needs desire, patience, compassion, and foresight. Sometimes volunteers from a nearby corps can help, or the corps can afford to employ a local schoolteacher, college student, or community band member. Also, gather other support staff to cook supper, greet students at the door, help with uniforms, discipline, and set-up.

Expectations for students

Initially ask students to practice their weekly assignments for 10 minutes a day, five days a week. Once they get their instruments out, 10 minutes will multiply to 20, even 30 minutes a day, but the key for students is to get that instrument out every day.

	M	T	W	TH	F
E♭/ A♭ Scales	✓	✓	✓	✓	✓
Arbans p. 26	✓	✓		✓	✓
Solo work: "At Peace with My God"			✓	✓	✓
Clarke p. 2	✓	✓	✓	✓	✓

BRASS LESSON 1A

Date: 7/14/15

1) Check practice sheets, homework
2) Long tones, longest note contest
3) Scales C, introduce F (B♭!), #66 ex.
4) Method Book __pg 16__
   __B♭! #64 & 65__
   __Bingo #63__
   __Review slurs__
5) Solo work __start Sawmill Creek p.20__
6) Homework __F scale, Sawmill m.3-16, Bingo #63__
7) Upcoming performances, info __Recital on Aug. 30th__
8) Prayer requests & prayer
   __Jane's Grandmom__
   __Joe's brother's broken arm__
   __Our C.O.'s vacation__

Additional **Home Practice Suggestions** are included in Appendix 8.4.

BIG, BIG NEWS!!!!

Dear Parents,
 Don't miss seeing your child perform a solo on his/her instrument this coming Sunday at 9:30am during our Sunday School Opening.

Bring the whole family! It'll be a proud moment!

The use of practice sheets or a log book aids this process. Many method books have a practice log in the front of the book. In situations where the instrument cannot safely go home with the child, present opportunities to practice at the corps after school through a sign-out sheet in the corps office. The student must also be consistent in attendance at classes, Sunday school, and worship, while maintaining a good attitude. Some music schools insist that a contract be signed by students and their parents at the commencement of a season. (See sample contract in Appendix 8.3.) The student should perform in proper uniform on a regular basis in corps recitals, solo contests, and with the junior band.

Some corps require a parent or caregiver to be in attendance when the student presents a solo. This affords The Salvation Army an opportunity to interact with the parents and allows parents to witness their child's progress. Students who fulfill these expectations may then earn scholarships to music camp, enjoy rewards, or participate in special musical outings.

Expectations for teachers

If the instructor is the last one to arrive, it can be said that the students "own the room." Aim to be early enough to set up and give yourself a few minutes' break before heading into a lesson. This puts you in charge of the rehearsal room and allows you a moment to pray over the room. Music to be rehearsed that day can be quietly playing in the background as students arrive. Greet the students at the door, giving them an opportunity to chat and transition from their day at school.

Give lesson assignments in writing each week.

Ask parents to initial practice sheets periodically. Use positive peer pressure and weekly prizes to motivate work. To stimulate steady development, post progress charts. Reward good behavior as well as lessons completed. The instructor can expect students to be enthusiastic at first, but interest may taper off. Look for fresh ways to keep interest high from week to week. Encourage, encourage, encourage with positive remarks!

Maintain regular parental contact by sending notices home, meeting parents at the door, and giving progress reports. An occasional home visit, with an invitation to attend services, can go a long way. Be sure to keep good attendance records. After one or two absences, make contact with the student's home. Your class roster should include name, address, email address, phone, and caregiver's name. Note the best time to call and caregiver's name. Consider using a database or application to keep teaching records, contact information, and personalized form letters. Once each season, invite caregivers to sit with their children in an open rehearsal on stage. Parents can participate by following the part and vocalizing, or playing along. This permits a better glimpse of what it is like to be a band member.

8 BARS REST

Put together an initial to-do list for getting your corps instrumental program off the ground in the coming season. Refer to the steps listed above.

THE YOUTH BAND REHEARSAL

The ensemble experience

Just a few generations ago, today's time-consuming diversions of television, video games, cell phones, computers, and social media did not exist. Despite dramatic shifts of culture since the heyday of bands, few in and out of our movement would want to see The Salvation Army without its unique form of banding. While many churches are cultivating instrumental music, our movement's music-making is seen as a role model for the highest quality literature and performance.

"What is missing in many places," remarks an experienced Canadian Salvationist musician, "are junior bands." It really is that simple. *Year in and year out we give individual or small group lessons without making bands.* Participating in an ensemble teaches teamwork and responsibility and raises the level of accountability of each player musically and in terms of attendance. Aim to play together every week. At the early stages this may be a brief 10-minute period, where your band reviews together a song from their method book. Perform often, preferably every week in Sunday school. There is nothing like a good deadline. Encourage the congregation to cheer on a completed exercise from a method book. Some kids may want to write lyrics to a method book exercise that expresses a testimony or worship of God. Nurture Salvationism through devotions (see Chapter One, pp. 27-30), prayer, and developing a sense of duty and responsibility, including uniform-wearing. A good junior band will grow into a good senior band.

Standing in the middle of a group of beginning instrumentalists is perilous business. Achieving a reliable performance on a Sunday morning, several days after rehearsal, without the habitually misplaced mouthpiece, sticky valves, or missing music takes a special brand of perseverance coupled with patience. The paramount challenge is to get a diverse assembly of young players to act and breathe together. Teamwork requires the instrumentalists to receive and respond to instruction from a leader, and equally complement and respect those around them in the ensemble. What more valuable life skills could benefit a young person's development?

Oh yes, I will remember to bring my horn and music on Sunday!

The youth band rehearsal

To make this happen, the youth band leader should have the band set up, with music and stands in place. This allows students to move in an orderly fashion into their assigned seats. There are challenges with this, as youngsters come from different locations or directly from school. Note that musical ability may not be the final arbiter of seating, but a prudent plan separates two players who tend to chat or cause trouble with one another. It is good to have another teen or adult sitting in to help the newest beginners (pointing in the music, etc.) and to help troubleshoot around you. Cell phones are off and out of sight, including those of the instructors. Bill Quick has just two simple rules for his rehearsals: "What we do, we do together" and "Only one person talks at a time."

Rehearsal Rules

Rule #1: What we do, we do together.

Rule #2: Only one person talks at a time.

Be consistent in the way you begin rehearsal, using easy scales on long tones, for instance, perhaps in a round based on thirds. Posting the rehearsal order helps the students prepare mentally as they put their music in order. It also speeds the transitions between pieces and sends a message that you are prepared and ready to work.

Round in Half Notes
- Choose a scale in the key of your first piece
- Start with all parts in unison, and then
- Assign sections to start two notes apart in a round

Appendix 8.5 lists all major and minor scale sheets, correlated by number to permit the simultaneous rehearsal of instrumentalists reading treble clef in Bb and Eb pitch, or bass clef. Although you may have provided a scale sheet like this in the folder, avoid reference to it. Rather, encourage listening around and building teamwork right from the start of rehearsal. Use the scale of the key of your first piece to establish the necessary accidentals in students' minds, fingers, and ears.

Have the percussionists play a simple beat cadence to help keep time. Remind the players to sit on the edge of their chairs, take a deep breath, and watch the leader for the start, ending, and correct tempo. A logical next step divides the band into groups, rendering the scale with staggered entrances as a round. One can also instruct the students to subdivide the long tone into eighths (quavers) to warm up the tongue and unify rhythmic pulse. When the first group of players reaches the end of their scale, they should hold the note for as long as possible until all the instruments are united on the last pitch. This encourages the students to listen for tuning.

Round in Eighths

...continue back down

The Tuning Note

Bb instruments play:

Eb instruments play:

C concert pitch instruments play:

The tune-up

Ask a reliable low brass player to sound a concert Bb (C for the Bb instuments and G for the Ebs). Ask everyone to first sing that pitch, in their octave, as you go from section to section and tune. By singing the pitch, each player is listening "inside" before sounding the note. It is never too early to ask if *the pitch sounds a little high (or sharp)* and explain that we must *make the horn longer by pulling the slide out. If the note sounds low (flat)* to the tuning note being sung, *then the horn needs to be made shorter, and so we push the tuning slide in.*
Have student helpers aid the others with their tuning slide.

To test the tuning and continue to warm up, play through a familiar hymn tune from one of the listing of first band books at the conclusion of this chapter. Be expressive but clear with the tempo and dynamics to encourage everyone to follow the conductor. This differentiates the experience from the sectional/small group lesson, during which someone may have been beating time. Make sure all parts are made to feel important by listening for balance or bringing out moving parts. Instruct players to start by bringing their horns up and breathing together. Conclude with horns up until the leader brings his or her hands down.

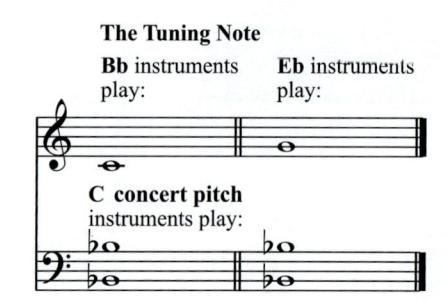

PUSH IN b

PULL OUT #

THE NEW PIECE

When moving on to new pieces, it is essential that the youth band leader carefully chooses a piece that is challenging yet accessible to the full ensemble. It takes time to locate easy graded music that sounds great and is also enjoyable for the players. Play to your group's strengths. For instance, you may have two good drummers and an outstanding tuba player, so something that uses the drums with a bass line will help your band sound good. On the other hand, do not pick a piece that requires drums if you don't have any. On occasion it may be necessary to write a simplified part for the new learners who may lack the range or technical skills to cover the part.

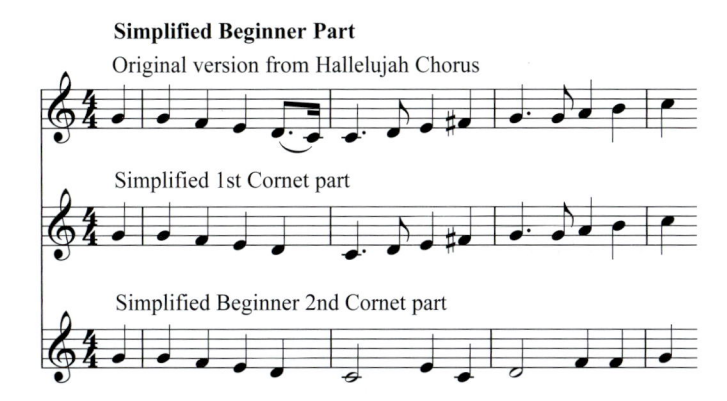

LEARNING TO TROUBLESHOOT

Some elements of band leadership and guidance on developing rehearsal strategies introduced here are covered more fully in Chapter Eleven, *From Score Reading to Score Study,* and Chapter Fifteen, *Score Study to Rehearsal Strategy.* As we look at Major Hollie Ruthberg's easy setting of **This Little Light of Mine**, four distinguishing factors will help troubleshoot the most challenging bits. Rather than struggling to play the piece straight through, be proactive and address the trouble spots first. Then the piece will come together more successfully. This arrangement suits a group that has a few 1st Cornet players musically a little ahead of the rest of the ensemble. A reference recording is in the Chapter Eight online folder.

See Chapter Ten, **What's the Score?** to get started with score-reading.

Troubleshoot #1: Bbs and Ebs

Although we are in the key of C for the Bb instruments and in G (one sharp) for the Eb instruments, there are a few other flatted notes that may not be familiar (Bb, fingered 1, and Eb, fingered 2 & 3). Before we begin to play this piece, we can ask the band to play a B, then explain that it can be lowered or flatted to Bb by using the first valve. Do likewise with the Eb. After the players have tried this, ask them to circle and count how many Bbs and Ebs they have on their parts, so that they have located them. **[Reference A] (*This Little Light of Mine* score on the next two pages.)**

Give special attention to these measures as the flatted note is not repeated and does not move up by step, but rather moves up by a skip. Note that the second ending in Cornet II and Horn II combines both of the earlier measures with the accidentals. **[B]** (The conductor need not discuss the F# with the Eb instruments, as the arranger has cleverly avoided any F# despite the key signature indicating one sharp.)

The Beat Goes On

THIS LITTLE LIGHT OF MINE

Spiritual
arr. Hollie Ruthberg

Troubleshoot #2: The basic rhythms

A quick glance across the score reveals the use of whole notes (known in the United Kingdom and elsewhere as semibreves), half notes (minims) and quarter notes (crotchets). Only the Cornet I and Percussion parts use eighths (quavers) and they are repeated on the same pitch. [C] Most of the quarter notes are marked *staccato* with a dot above or below the head of the note, meaning the note will be played detached or short. [D] Other quarter notes appear in pairs under an arching slur line, which connects one note to another without a break. Teach the rhythmic pattern of the first two bars of parts II, III, and IV right from the start. [E] Give special attention to the Cornet II and Horn II parts moving from the whole note to the two staccato quarters, followed by two slurred quarter notes. [F] Once learned, these rhythmic patterns repeat in two-bar phrases.

Troubleshoot #3: Cornet I versus the other parts

The arrangement is in four parts. Building from the bottom up, we need at least one player on either the Eb or Bb Bass IV part. This can be a tuba or euphonium player. Horn, trombone, or baritone will suffice on part III while we need a horn or cornet on part II and at least one cornet on the Cornet I part. These four parts are synonymous with the Soprano/Alto/Tenor/Bass (SATB) voicing of choral music. [G] A quick glance across the score will reveal that Cornet I is playing the melody against a contrasting chordal backdrop by the other three parts. This suggests that the three lower parts be worked out together, first rhythmically (including the *staccato* articulations), then with the pitches. The Cornet I rhythmic pattern is consistent over two bars [H], answered by the snare drum in the alternate bars. [I] Note in m. 10, that the Cornet I is asked to play an Eb, as a kind of altered blues note, fingered 2&3. [J]

Troubleshoot #4: First and second endings [K]

The concept of first and second endings and the necessary repeat back to the beginning will need to be reviewed. Note the *crescendo* for the entire band in the second ending [L] and the three accented notes in the rhythmically unified conclusion. [M]

Chapter 8 | ALL HAIL TO DANIEL'S BAND!

From 38 Sunday School Choruses for Young Bands
© 2016 The Salvation Army USA East

Teachable moments

To summarize all of your focused work, it is important to play through the whole arrangement without stopping. To build the band's confidence, create teachable moments as you move on to more familiar pieces and music for Sunday. Be strategic with the pace of your rehearsal. Vary the pace by moving from slow pieces to fast and challenging to easy. Encourage, encourage, and encourage. Ask questions and more questions to test the student's knowledge and to spot-check how they are doing. Sometimes, demonstrating the wrong way to play something, then asking how to correct it, helps teach the "better" way.

Kids know when you are prepared, so work out some "method to your madness" before the rehearsal. Be proactive and break down challenging trouble spots into accessible steps. With young people, it is vital to keep moving. When you stop, the next instruction needs to be readily on the tip of your tongue. Keep all sections engaged by not lingering too long with one section. Knowing your group's abilities, you can gauge their limits, but continue to challenge them. Choose never to settle for second best. **Something learned or accomplished each rehearsal is what brings kids back for more.**

For more on **Making the Rehearsal Work**, see Chapter Twenty-Three.

Thank you for teaching me

After a closing prayer, I ask the band members what we accomplished this rehearsal. Then I ask, "And how do we close rehearsal?" In the Asian tradition, they respond in unison, "Thank you for teaching me." The instructor reminds them that someone has made an effort on their behalf and has taught them something new today by responding with, "Thank you for learning." A foundational bond of mutual trust and respect is strengthened from week to week. Leading a junior band may be risky business, requiring ongoing preparation, enthusiasm, and great patience. But it is a noble social work, bringing the next generation of Salvationists into the fold, and so... *The Beat Goes On!*

Student: "Thank you for teaching me."
Teacher: "Thank you for learning."

THE YOUTH BAND LEADER'S SURVIVAL KIT[11]

For the Band
Mouthpiece puller
Extra mouthpieces
Petroleum jelly or light grease for slides
Trombone slide oil
Valve oil
Alcohol swabs (to clean mouthpieces)
Hand sanitizer (for those sharing mallets)
Extra set of method books
Extra music parts
Snake
Set of small screwdrivers
Extra corks
Rubber bands (for emergency repairs)
Pliers/wrench (to tighten music stands)
Supply of pencils

For the Percussionists
Drum key
Pairs of drum sticks and brushes
One general bass drum mallet and a matched pair for rolling
Timpani and cymbal mallets
Triangle clip, cord, and beaters
Pitch-pipes
Extra snare

For the Conductor
Metronome/tuner (available as apps)
Baton
Pocket musical dictionary
Markers, chalk
Staff paper
Roster and calendar (software)

BEGINNER BRASS AND YOUTH BAND REPERTOIRE

FIRST BAND BOOKS*

American Instrumental Ensemble Series (AIES) is a graded series that offers practical, playable arrangements for small brass ensembles to brass bands with complete instrumentation. There are four new pieces for each level (*I-IV*) published annually. *Grade I* pieces target beginning ensembles. Rhythms are kept extremely simple. Articulation and dynamic changes are minimal. The maximum length is 50 measures. Pitch ranges have been limited primarily to an octave. *Grade II* pieces introduce eighth notes and ranges are extended, with accidentals being more common. The maximum length is expanded to 60 measures. *Grade III* pieces included dotted rhythms and more keys. *Grade IV* pieces require a wider range of notes and keys.

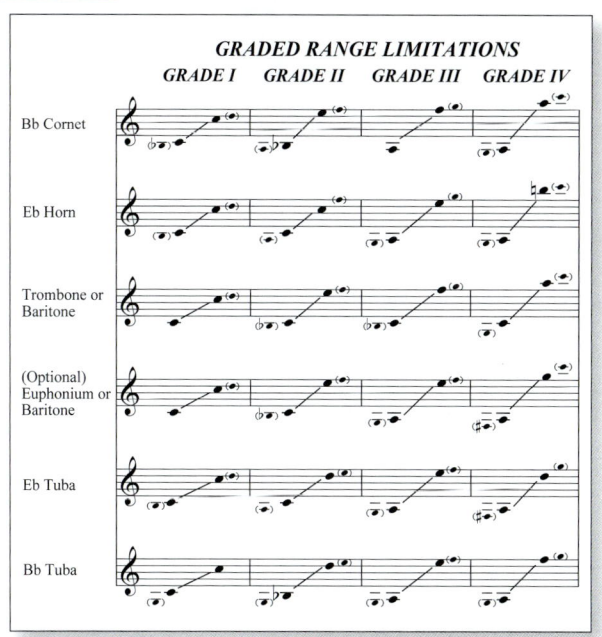

Basic Brass, Winds & Percussion (BB) by Thomas Scheibner is a three-part series of 35 hymn tunes for beginning instrumentalists. All three parts, for either Bb, Eb, or C, appear in the same book. (*Grades II to III*)

Brass Music for Young Bands (B) by leading composers and arrangers in a progressively graded format. Instrumentation is standard four-part arranging with an optional fifth euphonium and percussion part. (*Grades I to III*)

Cactus Series by Ralph Pearce. *Grade ½* series of selections available directly from Ralph Pearce. Some 2nd Cornet parts have just two or three notes. Some titles available are: *Seek Ye First, Beethoven Themes, Deck the Halls, Mighty God, March Saints, We Give Thanks.* Large print makes it accessible to even the youngest musicians.

First Book of Hymn Tunes (HT) provides a wide range of sacred and holiday music that is playable by the least experienced instrumentalist. These 30 tunes are arranged in progressive order of difficulty with the new concepts for each tune noted at the bottom of the score page. All music in this publication will sound complete with only three parts. The pieces may also be played in two parts and are printed in book form as duets: Parts 1&2 Bb; 1&2 Eb; 1&3 Bb; 1&3 Eb. Optional percussion, including C-part, is also available. (*Grades I to III*)

From the Beginning (FB) by David Catherwood. A graded series of band/ensemble music. Contents include: *Kum Bah Yah, When the Saints, As the Deer, Father We Love You, This Is the Day, Easy Classics,* Christmas arrangements, plus many others! Instrumental parts for: 1st Cornet, 2nd Cornet, Horn, Baritone/Trombone, Euphonium, Bass Eb. All parts use only notes of C scale plus F sharp and B flat. 2nd Cornet mainly C-G. Books are available at www.opus3music.com.

*All of these beginner brass and youth band collections, except the materials from Ralph Pearce and David Catherwood, are available from Salvation Army Supplies and Purchasing departments.

Hollie Ruthberg's Sunday School Choruses for Young Bands (SSC)
38 simple arrangements useful for Sunday school opening in four-part format, including a section of beginner exercises. (Grades ½ to II)

First Things First (FTF) Volumes 1&2, provides 16 elementary pieces for a four-part ensemble at an early stage of development, including titles like *Deep and Wide, God is Good, I Love You, Lord, My God is So Big,* and *Jesus Loves Me*. (Grades I to III)

MUSIC FOR COMBINED BEGINNER AND SENIOR BANDS

Young Artist Series. William Himes has written a number of pieces that feature beginners with the senior band. Pieces like *Muffins Rhapsody* and *Classics in Brass* are available from the Central Territory Music Department online. Ralph Pearce and Harold Burgmayer have also written a number of pieces in a similar format, useful in corps and musicamp settings, available directly from these arrangers.

DEVOTIONAL SERIES FOR YOUTH

Children, Can You Hear Me, Brad Jersak (Fresh Wind Press)
Experiencing God–Youth Edition, Henry Blackaby and Claude King (Lifeway)
Lord, Teach Me to Pray for Kids, Kay Arthur and Janna Arndt (Harvest House)
Prayer from *Pulse* series, Darrell Pearson (Gospel Light)
Secrets of the Vine for Kids, Bruce Wilkinson (Thomas Nelson)
Teachings of Jesus from *Pulse* series, Tim Baker (Gospel Light)
Ten Challenges of A World Changer, Ron Luce (Thomas Nelson)
The Bondage Breaker–Youth Edition, Neil T. Anderson and Dave Park (Harvest House)
The Power of a Praying Kid, Stormie Omartian (Harvest House)
Youth Alpha, Nicky Gumbel (Alpha North America)

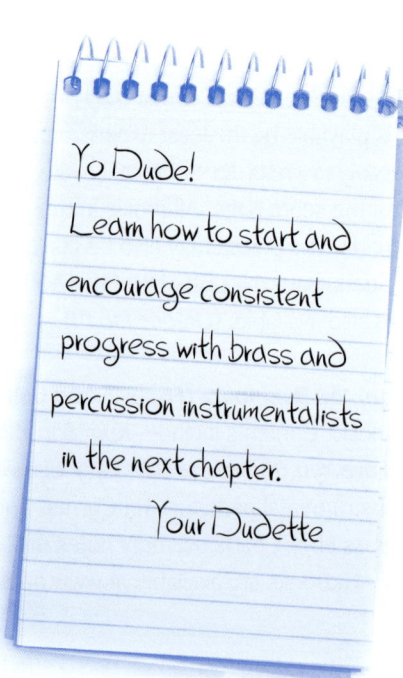

Yo Dude!
Learn how to start and encourage consistent progress with brass and percussion instrumentalists in the next chapter.
Your Dudette

CHAPTER NINE

GOD'S SPECIAL INSTRUMENTS
The Brass and Drum Instructor's Toolbox

It is the supreme art of the teacher to awaken joy in creative expression and knowledge. —Albert Einstein

TWO LESSONS AHEAD

Jose is a camp staff member who, at the start of each summer, tries to beg out of teaching a MusicMakers class. We endeavor to expose our seven- and eight-year olds to a rotation of twenty minute doses of various musical disciplines, such as piano, theory, brass, rhythm, and sight-singing. Jose does not consider himself drawn to kids. Rather than be a camp counselor, he enjoys facilitating camp programs with starting fires, making deliveries, and providing for others. He never set out to study music, yet each year during our music camp week, Jose agrees to interact with the youngest campers for two periods a day.

After the initial polite decline, Jose usually comes back to us, saying he will help, but that he needs the method book to practice. Each year he studies from the very beginning of the method book and takes himself *just two lessons ahead* of where these neophyte players will go. He is dependable and conscientious with the children and they respond with delight to his instruction, proving to be one of our most effective and consistent instructors.

In **Chapter Nine**, we learn how to:
- start beginner instrumentalists.
- effectively give a brass lesson, including specific trombone pointers.
- take advancing instrumentalists further.
- establish routines for percussionists.

WHO ME, TEACH?

The gift of teaching is among the motivational spiritual gifts listed in Romans 12:6-8. The Greek word used here for a person who teaches is *didasko* which means, simply, "to teach or give instruction."[1] The effective teacher constantly seeks ways to get across an essential practice or principle. Prepared teachers unfold the basics in a logical and understandable manner. This requires the self-discipline of preparation, self-control in the student's presence, and, like my young friend Jose, private study.

Many times the most talented musicians are not the best teachers for beginners. Often they have not had to struggle or re-learn material, simultaneously giving careful consideration to how their students will really "get" the concepts. In every generation of Salvation Army music-making, there have been those, perhaps less gifted, who apply themselves faithfully to staying a *marginal "two lessons ahead"* of their students. This is how hundreds of young musicians get their start and many recall with thanks the humble efforts of their first music teacher.

The Beat Goes On

3 cheers for teachers who... TEACH SKILLS FOR MAKING A LIVING!

Furthermore, as Salvationist instructors, many of us want to extend a hand of direction into our student's lives, helping them get past what can be formidable societal obstacles that effectively threaten their futures. At the risk of "preaching to the choir," studies show a student's involvement in music education lowers drop-out rates and translates into higher academic achievement, regardless of socioeconomic status. Any argument for better test scores is an argument for musical training. Students' abstract reasoning skills improve more through hands-on music than computer instruction. Similarly, arts education improves math skills in proportion to the student's investment in the arts, even after a mere six months.[5]

3 cheers for teachers who... TEACH LIFE SKILLS!

Specialists in music education tell us that within the realm of music-making our students are exposed to life skills including time management, problem solving, decision making, critical thinking, citizenship, creativity, innovation, social skills, building community, communication, and affirming other cultures. In particular, there is the student's discipline of being accountable to oneself for personal practice, assessment, and progress. In return, students acquire a sense of self-worth, become aware of their own personal values, abilities, weaknesses, and goals, and develop sensibilities to contribute positively to the whole.[4]

3 cheers for teachers who... TOUCH LIVES!

Within our Salvation Army musical heritage, and reaching even as far back as the intergenerational instruction of the Levite Temple musicians, is a belief in the intrinsic power of music, but further, in the truth that is the bedrock of our music-making—"God in you, God in me, Making us all we can be."[2] We choose to teach as a touchstone in young people's lives. In the teacher's consistency and correction, the student perceives that, "There is importance in working to develop the gift God has placed within me, to His glory."[3]

Music students across all socioeconomic levels are more cooperative, self-confident, and better able to express themselves than other students. This is all the more reason for The Salvation Army to invest time and resources into music-making with our young people. It is a social work, marvelously linked to our worship, well worth pursuing. Yet another reason to cheer our teachers on! *Three cheers for our teachers who, week in and week out, are God's special instruments in the lives of our young people!*

GETTING STARTED ON A BRASS INSTRUMENT

Assembling the instrument[6]
Open the case right side up.

With the mouthpiece in the right hand, place it into the leadpipe on your horn. Gently turn the mouthpiece to the right, but not too tightly. (Trombone assembly and holding is explained on p. 187.) Caution students against "popping" the mouthpiece with the hand.

Posture
To teach correct posture for playing, start by standing with shoulders down, not slumped, and relaxed, while keeping the chest cavity open and high to allow for maximum air. (Refer to the breathing section in Chapter Six on pp. 132–133.)

From the student's standing position, the instructor can gently position the chair behind the student's knees, instructing the student to slowly sit at the edge of the chair, while maintaining good posture from the waist up. We can describe this as "standing from the waist up." The student's back remains straight with head erect, not touching the back of the chair.

Do not allow the players to compromise strong posture when they bring the instrument up to their lips. *"Bring the instrument to you, not your body to the instrument."*

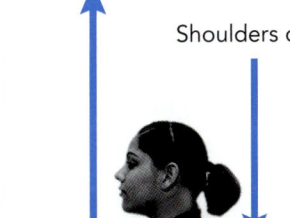

Chest open and high

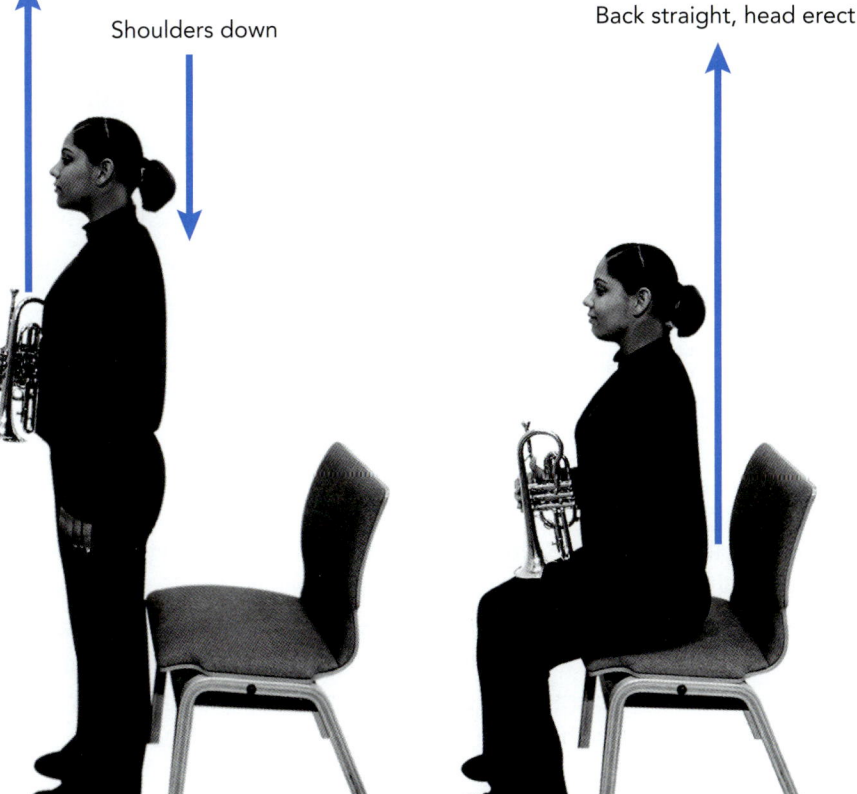

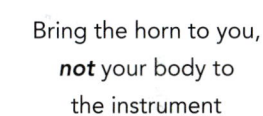

Shoulders down

Back straight, head erect

Bring the horn to you, *not* your body to the instrument

The Beat Goes On

See Appendix 9.1 for a
Brass Treble Clef Fingering Chart

Holding the horn

Cornets are held in the left hand with the fingers around the valve casing. If the first valve has a saddle or trigger, the left thumb is positioned to operate it. As the student grows, the fourth finger may be used in the third-valve trigger. Hold the instrument firmly, but without tension. Emphasize that the left hand is the holding mechanism, not the right hand operating the valves. Place the right thumb under the leadpipe between the first and second valves. Now place the tips of the first three fingers on the valve caps. The fingers should be curved and relaxed. For smaller hands, placing the right little finger on the pinky ring may not be possible.

Horn, baritone, euphonium, and **tuba** players can steady the instrument at an angle, but upright, with their left hand wrapped around the tubing of the horn. Place the tips of the right hand fingers on the valve tops.

With **all valved brass instruments,** keep the right wrist straight and both elbows away from the body.

Embouchure

Embouchure is defined on p. 171 of Chapter Eight

To approximate the correct way to form the mouth to play a brass instrument, ask the beginning student to form the mouth as if blowing up a balloon. The lips are rolled in slightly, just a little over the teeth.

The "corners" of the lips should be held against the teeth in a slightly contracted position, not a long line. Eric Dina likes to ask his students what Mom and Dad's favorite cookie is? HMMM brings the corners back.

What kind of cookie?
HMMMmmmm..............

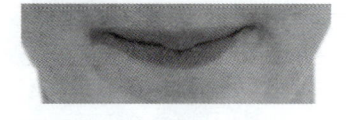

Cheeks should be held in, not puffed out.
Chin should be flattened, not bunched or too relaxed.
Jaw should be slightly pushed forward.

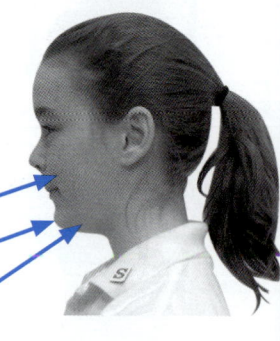

Blowing air

After forming the embouchure properly, have students place the fingers of their hand about six inches in front of their faces, or about the same distance from a lit candle.

DO NOT let the shoulders rise as your student takes a deep, quiet breath supported by the diaphragm (the muscle below the ribs which controls the air flow from the lungs). Renowned trumpeter Phil Smith teaches that a deep exhalation of air will feel "warm and moist," close to body temperature, as opposed to a "cool, not as moist" shallow breath.

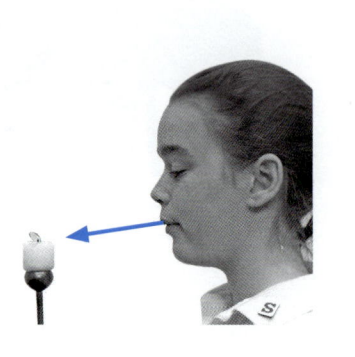

Ask the student to create a steady air stream, perhaps over a count of eight. The air should hit the hand or maintain a steady candle flame. If the air is hitting below the hand, have the student slightly push out the jaw. Remind the students not to puff their cheeks.

Chapter 9 | GOD'S SPECIAL INSTRUMENTS

Making the "BUZZ"

- Take a deep breath.
- Form the embouchure described above.
- Blow out a controlled, steady stream of air.

Buzzzzzzz

- Attempt to produce a buzzing sound with the lips. If this does not happen at first, try again. Do not let the student get discouraged. Most of the time, a student can create some type of buzzing sound within a few minutes.

- If a buzz cannot be made with just the lips, have the student attempt to blow into the mouthpiece removed from the horn. It is preferable to work without the mouthpiece at first because the correct way to produce a sound on a brass instrument is to blow air, rather than to rely on mouthpiece pressure.

The mouthpiece

Holding the small end, or shank, of the mouthpiece, place the cup of the mouthpiece at the center of the lips. Not only should the mouthpiece be centered from left to right, but it is best centered from top to bottom.

Exceptions abound with this "centering" premise, sometimes because of illnesses like Bell's palsy, where a side or corner of the muscles around the mouth may have been weakened. The goal is to have the airstream from the buzz go directly down the hole of the mouthpiece, so check the flow of the air created by the buzz.

Achieve a full, open, round sound on the mouthpiece, without stuttering, before putting the mouthpiece on the instrument.

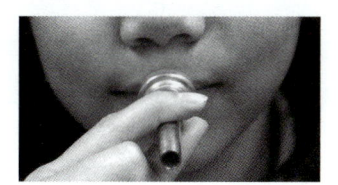

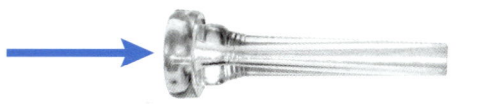

TROMBONE POINTERS[1]

Assembling the trombone

Open the case right side up and be sure the slide is locked before removing the instrument from the case.

Hold the bell section in the left hand. Point the bell toward the floor holding the receiver to the right.

Hold the slide section by the braces in the right hand with the "U" of the slide section down. Put the longer side of the slide section into the bell receiver.

Make a "V" angle between the two sections. The exact angle is determined by the size of your hand.

Tighten the lock that holds the two sections together. Put the mouthpiece into the mouthpiece receiver with your right hand. Drop the mouthpiece in lightly and give it a gentle turn to the right. Never lean on the mouthpiece, push, or bang it into the receiver.

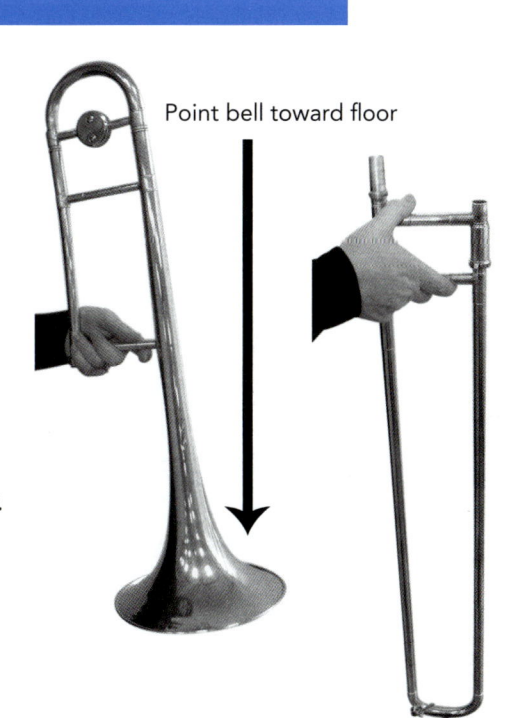

Point bell toward floor

See Appendix 9.2 for **Trombone Position Charts** in treble and bass clefs.

The Beat Goes On

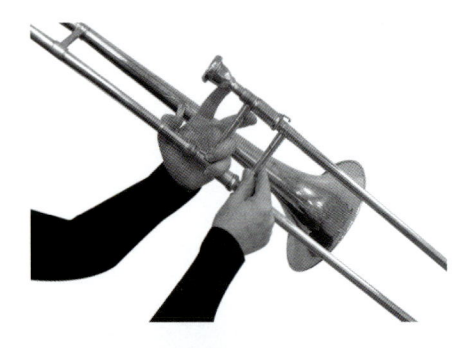

Lubricating the slide

Rest the tip of the bottom of the slide on the floor.

Unlock the slide and lift the inner slide.

Place five or six drops of slide oil on each inner slide at the bottom where the slide is slightly thicker.

To evenly spread the oil, move the outer slide up and down easily over the inner slide.

Holding the trombone

Sit up straight on the edge of chair or stand erect. (See previous posture notes.)

Place the left thumb around the bell brace. Place the other fingers of the left hand around the first slide brace and the left index finger on or near the mouthpiece.

With the right hand, hold the bottom of the slide brace with the thumb, index, and middle finger. Keep the right wrist flexible and the elbows away from the body.

Trombonists are encouraged to hold the trombone up, almost perpendicular to the floor so that the bell is pointed straight out in front of the player. The weight of the instrument should be supported by the left hand, rather than putting too much weight on the slide. Music stands should be raised to assist with this erect posture and playing position. Do not allow the bell to be played directly into the stand. Since trombonists in the brass band usually sit to the conductor's right, they should play slightly to the left of the stand, so that they always keep the conductor in clear view over the top of the stand.

TWELVE TIPS FOR GIVING A BEGINNER BRASS LESSON[8]

Buzzzzzzz

For fun buzzing exercises, see Appendix 9.3—**What's the Buzz About Buzzing?**

1. **Start by buzzing** a tune or rhythm pattern gleaned from the lesson material. This establishes the embouchure and improves endurance. Most importantly, the buzzing "wakes up" the ear, the air, and the brain.

2. **Follow this step-by-step sequence** when approaching a new song or exercise:
   - Clap and count the rhythm (1-2 3-4/1-2-3-4).
   - Speak note names in rhythm (E___ D___/C_____).
   - Sing note names in rhythm.
   - Sing note names in rhythm *while* performing fingerings on the instrument—E(1/2)___ D(1/3)___/C(open)_____).
   - *Occasionally* the teacher may demonstrate before the student plays the exercise.
   - Student plays through with teacher. ("Now let's try it together.")
   - Student plays through without teacher. ("Now you try it on your own.")

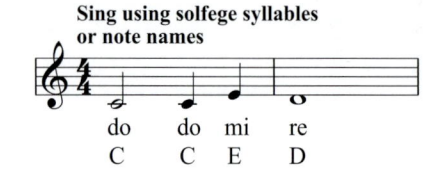

3. **Alternate playing with rhythm exercises or singing**
   - Rhythm exercises can utilize clapping, stomping, mouthpiece buzzing, rhythm sticks. Allow students to learn to count passages or identify demonstrated rhythms.
   - Sing through an exercise using solfege syllables or note names.
   - Occasionally it can be beneficial for the teacher to **demonstrate a passage** and allow the student to evaluate your performance. Ask questions like: "Were my half notes (minims) longer or shorter than my quarter notes (crotchets)?" "How many slurs did I play?" "In which measure did I play *staccato*?"

4. **Don't be afraid to linger on one exercise.** Reinforcement is important. Often students are anxious to pass a page of exercises without really "making music." Extra time on an exercise gives the student a chance to develop confidence and musicality.

5. **Don't be afraid to move on.** You can always go back later or skip to the next section of exercises. Keep things fresh and interesting to challenge the student. If a student has a mental block with an exercise, move on and come back to it later.

6. **Have your instrument handy!** Most students can imitate a sound or technique better than they can produce it from verbal instruction alone. Try to sense the most effective balance between demonstration and instruction.

7. **Teach students *how* to practice** by isolating and working through tough spots in the music together. Ask students what the objective of an exercise is and work to achieve that. Circle the trouble spot and instruct students to practice ONLY what is inside the circle.

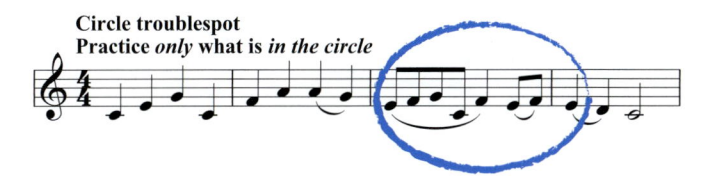

8. **Be patient and consistent.** If a student is having a problem with something, don't give up on it quickly. Discover another approach. Students sometimes need more time to work things out.

9. **Use the correct "address."** The "*note* is what is wrong," not "*you* are wrong." Many people unknowingly closely associate themselves with their art. Substitute use of the "we" pronoun for the more threatening "you." Give sensitive instruction and verbal evaluation. Be aware of the lasting effects of words, facial expressions, tone of voice, and your attitude toward them. Give praise where it is due and always, always encourage.

10. **Ask questions** throughout the lesson. The more involved a student is, the more he or she will remember.

11. **"On time is late,"** or so the expression goes. Be early and prepared. Students know when you have a plan or objective. If you care about the lesson, they will too.

12. **End the lesson with something students can play well** so that they walk away feeling satisfied!

TO INFINITY AND BEYOND

Helps for advancing brass players
Warm up, always!
- Long tones, in easy registers with gentle dynamic contrasts, prepare the lips for playing. Some players buzz in the mouthpiece before moving to long tones. Pedal tones require proper breath control and develop intonation, overtones, and the upper register.

> **pedal tones** (*term*) \'pe - dəl tōns\ artificial tones produced below the normal range of a brass instrument (a written low F#) that can relax and strengthen the embouchure.

- Lip slurs build facial strength. Rely on the air and the tongue to do the work. At a slower rate, use an "ah"–"ee" exchange within the mouth to bridge between slurred notes. (Use ah-ee for ascending slurs and the reverse, ee-ah, for descending slurs.)

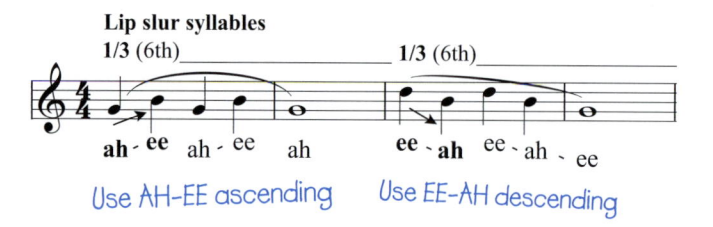

Lip slur syllables

ah-ee ah-ee ah   ee-ah ee-ah ee

Use AH-EE ascending   Use EE-AH descending

Refer to Appendix 9.4 for **Major and Minor Scales**

- Practice scales daily to develop range, facility, and motor memory. Remain relaxed by playing these slowly and softly. Range is best extended by going up and over notes. Do not keep trying to hit a high note if it is missed. Keep going.

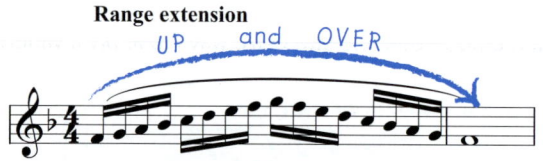

Range extension

UP and OVER

- Articulation exercises warm up the tongue and lips.

Articulation exercise

- To allow time to rejuvenate blood flow, rest between exercises.

Breathing
- To achieve a relaxed breath, inhale deeply with a low breath, feel the breath, and see the chest and abdomen expand.
- Open and relax the throat and chest, as if yawning, especially during the transition from inhaling to exhaling.
- Exhale with power from the abdominal muscles, not from the shoulders and throat. The sound of the latter is apparent, often labeled as "singing from your throat."
- Adopt exercises to strengthen breathing skills. For instance, inhale over four seconds, hold for four seconds without tension, blow all air out for four seconds, hold for four seconds. Repeat and expand the length of time.

Full Breath   Shallow Breath

Resonance (creating more space for the sound to vibrate)
- When playing, keep the inside of the mouth open in an "ah" or "oh" shape. Keep space between the upper and lower teeth.
- The tongue should be low in the mouth, especially in the lower register.
- To allow maximum air flow when supporting the instrument, keep the upper body upright and hold arms away from the rib cage.

High register
- Use lots of breath support. A "big breath in" decreases the tension of the lip muscles. Flexibility and lip slur exercises strengthen the facial muscles to accomplish upper-register notes, but depend on the correct amount of air.

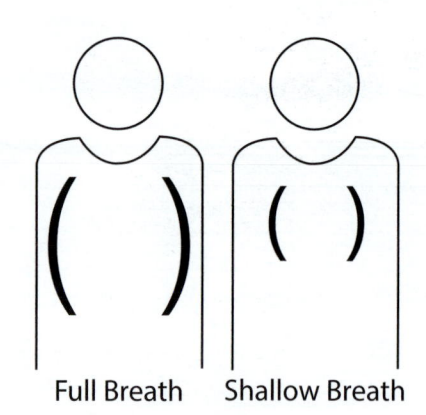

- The pressure of the mouthpiece on a student's lips should not be so hard as to leave an indent that is visible after playing awhile. Strive for a "perfect seal," not dependent on mouthpiece pressure, permitting the air and the tongue to do the work.

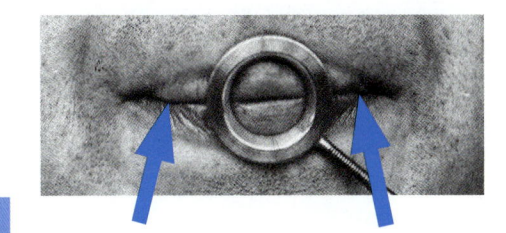

9 BARS REST

1. On your own, practice the steps to starting a beginner brass player. Proceed slowly to gain a complete understanding of the mechanics of each step. There is value in discovering how to blow through the instrument improperly, then learning how not to make these sounds, so as to quickly remedy students' errors when they come up.

2. Utilize a variety of "gateways to learning" – seeing, hearing, or touching – to aid students' learning curve on their instruments. Choose upcoming pages in a current student method book and strategize ways to apply a variety of approaches (note names, counting, syllables, fingering, singing, demonstration, or questions) to the next lesson. Keep a mental inventory of which techniques work best with which students.

3. Apply some of the "Helps for Advancing Brass Players" to your own warm-up and practice regimen, so you can demonstrate these effectively.

GETTING STARTED ON THE SNARE DRUM[9]

The matched grip

The matched grip is used for most percussion instruments:

- Position the snare drum slightly below the waist, which enables the performer to play with the arms hanging naturally with no muscle tension. The forearms should be angled slightly down.
- Stand six to eight inches away from the drum so that the tips of the drumsticks are positioned over the correct playing area (slightly off center toward the side of the drum away from the performer).
- Grip the sticks between the ball of the thumb and the second joint of the first finger at a balance point about 3/4 back from the stick tip. Curve all the fingers around the stick in a natural, relaxed way.
- The thumb should be flat, on the side of the stick. The first finger should be curved and relaxed.
- The back of the hand should be up and level with the back of the stick across the padded part of the hand.
- The arms should hang naturally, with the wrists straight, creating an extension of the arm so that the sticks form an inverted "V" over the correct playing area. For softer playing, the tips of the sticks strike over the snare bed, closer to the edge of the drum.
- The wrists should bend up to initiate the stroke. Do not let the wrists drop or turn.

More on grips

Appendix 9.5 gives a more complete description of the snare drum hand position for both hands of the *matched grip* and the right hand of the *traditional grip.* The alternative traditional grip is still used by some school marching bands and jazz drummers and is presented in the Appendix 9.6. Also, for the proper grip of timpani mallets, we use a hand-shaking illustration to teach the *modified French grip with the thumbs up for timpani,* rather than the *German grip with the back of the hand up,* as used for the snare drum grip. With mallet percussion, *the matched grip is modified by curving the index finger* more to compensate for the thinner stick and sliding the hand back on the mallet to balance the mallet head.

Traditional grip  — French grip for timpani  — German grip for mallets

ESTABLISHING A SNARE DRUM ROUTINE

Each practice and lesson session should follow a routine that works as a warm-up and review, as well as a sequential way to expand the drummer's vocabulary of rudiments and rhythms. Use a metronome or beat time to maintain a steady tempo. Remember that, "the prime function of a drummer is to keep time!" In each lesson or practice session include:

- ☑ Warm-ups based on the lesson to follow.
- ☑ A playing review of the rudiments learned to date.
- ☑ Introduction and/or practice of new rudiments following the six-level sequence.
- ☑ Practice or performance for the teacher of the last assigned lesson in the lesson book.
- ☑ Explanation of the next lesson, highlighting new material.
- ☑ Sight reading. In lessons it is helpful if sight reading is in the form of a duet to be played by the student and teacher.

For a complete six-level sequence of **Snare Drum Rudiments**, see Appendix 9.7

More specifics about the snare drum lesson routine follow. Correlate these with the six-level sequence outlined in Appendix 9.7, which includes recommended method books as well as a progressive sequence of all the rudiments.

Snare drum basics

Assume proper body position and physical set-up, including placement of the music stand. The best area for a good, full sound is halfway between the edge and the center of the drum, over the snare bed. The edge, over the drum shell, is good for soft playing and special effects. For a deader, more rudimental sound, move the sticks toward the center. Use proper stick position.

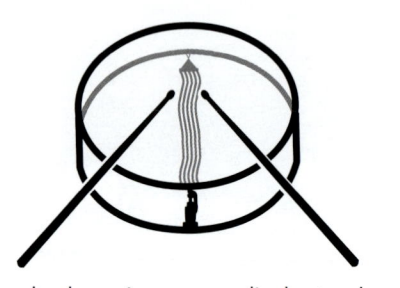

Snare bed running perpendicular to player

GOOD stick position

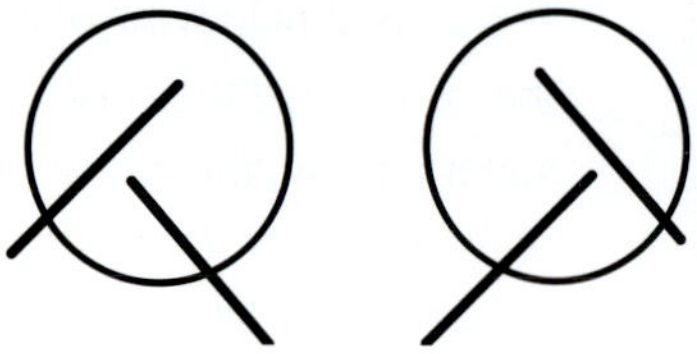

BAD stick positions

Identify basic drum strokes:
- **UP STROKE** starts low and ends high to change from soft to loud.
- **DOWN STROKE** starts high and ends low to change from loud to soft.
- **FULL STROKE** starts and ends high, for loud playing.
- **TAP** starts and ends low, used for most playing.

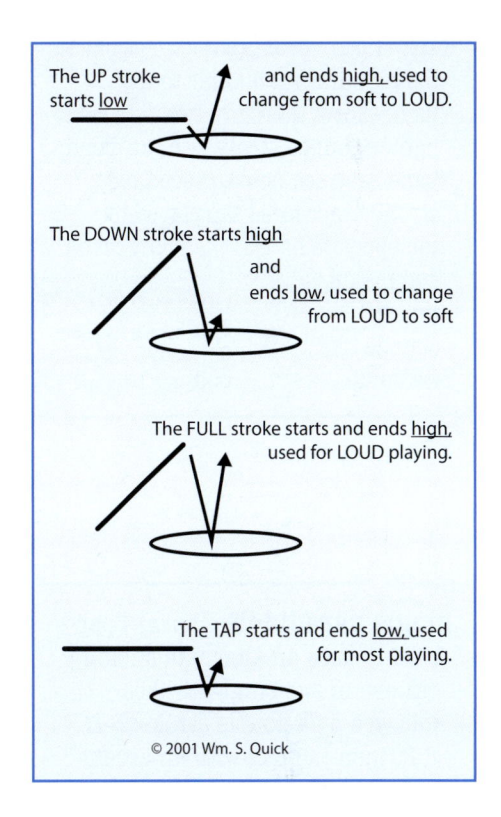

Rudiments

Rolls are best practiced open (slow) to closed (fast) to open (slow). It is important to slow down if tension is felt in the hands. Always stay relaxed when playing:

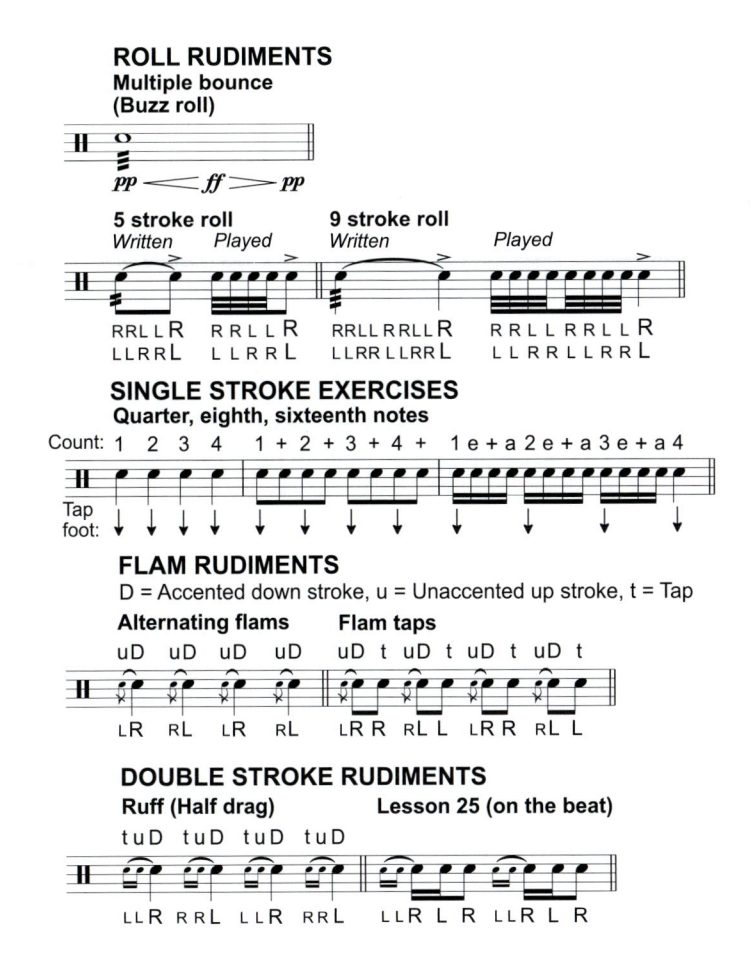

ROLL RUDIMENTS
Multiple bounce (Buzz roll)

5 stroke roll — Written / Played
RRLL R   RRLL R
LLRR L   LLRR L

9 stroke roll — Written / Played
RRLLRRLL R   RRLL RRLL R
LLRRLLRR L   LLRR LLRR L

SINGLE STROKE EXERCISES
Quarter, eighth, sixteenth notes
Count: 1 2 3 4   1 + 2 + 3 + 4 +   1 e + a 2 e + a 3 e + a 4
Tap foot: ↓ ↓ ↓ ↓   ↓   ↓   ↓   ↓   ↓   ↓   ↓   ↓

FLAM RUDIMENTS
D = Accented down stroke, u = Unaccented up stroke, t = Tap

Alternating flams
uD uD uD uD
LR RL LR RL

Flam taps
uD t uD t uD t uD t
LR R RL L LR R RL L

DOUBLE STROKE RUDIMENTS

Ruff (Half drag)
tuD tuD tuD tuD
LLR RRL LLR RRL

Lesson 25 (on the beat)
LLR L LLR L LLR L LLR L

The UP stroke starts low and ends high, used to change from soft to LOUD.

The DOWN stroke starts high and ends low, used to change from LOUD to soft.

The FULL stroke starts and ends high, used for LOUD playing.

The TAP starts and ends low, used for most playing.

© 2001 Wm. S. Quick

---

flam (*term*) \'flam\ a combination of a single, quiet grace note stroke and a single, louder primary note. The primary note is played in rhythm, with the grace note, lighter in weight, preceding it. Think of the syllable "lam," which is one syllable. "Flam" still sounds as one syllable, but it's slightly longer. This is a good way to conceptualize a correct-sounding flam.

uD
LR

Practice same-hand flams first, using a tap and a full stroke. Once mastered, alternate hands. Alternating flams are played with an up stroke and down stroke. Same-hand flams are used in orchestral playing for consistency of sound, while alternate flams are most often used in traditional rudimental playing and are the standard required rudiment.

Basic snare drum warm-up exercises

Single stroke warm-ups:
- Series of right-hand taps at steady tempo and then slow to fast: **RRRRRRR** etc.
- Series of left-hand taps at steady tempo and then slow to fast: **LLLLLLL** etc.
- Alternate series: **RRRR/LLLL** etc. (work for equal quality of sound between hands).

The Beat Goes On

ruff (*term*) \'ref\ (sometimes called the half drag) is similar to the flam, except there are two detached lighter bounce strokes on the same hand as grace notes, preceding a stronger accented tap played by the opposite hand. Like many drum rudiments, the ruff sounds like its name.

tuD tuD tuD
LLR RRL LLR

- Hourglass warm-up (repeat bottom to top to bottom without duplicating patterns, eventually add flams and ruffs to the beginning of each grouping).

Example: 4-3-2-1-2-3-4
RRRR/LLLL
RRR/LLL
RR/LL
R/L
RR/LL
RRR/LLL
RRRR/LLLL

- Alternate several single strokes per hand with bounce strokes.
- **1+2: RLLRLL** and **LRRLRR** and **2+1: RRLRRL** and **LLRLLR**

With single-stroke exercises, most passages are played with alternate sticking. A right-hand lead helps make the sound more consistent. Controlled double-bounce strokes or paradiddles may be substituted for speed.

Rhythmic reading

Most band instrumental books have corresponding percussion method books, so that drummers can play with an ensemble right away. Standard percussion parts use the percussion clef on a five-line stave. Common practice places the bass drum on the bottom space, cymbals in the next space up, snare drum in the next. The top spaces and lines are reserved for triangle, tambourine, woodblock, and other auxiliary percussion. Separate books are available that also introduce beginners to timpani and bells.

Percussion Notation
— auxiliary percussion
— snare drum
— cymbals
— bass drum

single paradiddle (*term*) \'par-ə-did-l\ uses an alternate sticking pattern of two single strokes followed by a double stroke: R-L-R-R, then L-R-L-L, with an accent on the first of each group of four.

D u t t D u t t
R L R R L R L L

Paradiddle sounds like its name.

See Appendix 14.1 for **Technique Tips for Concert Percussion**.

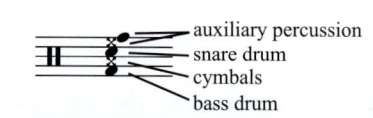

? 9 BARS REST

Work through the drum rudiments for yourself, found in Appendix 9.7, to become familiar enough with the sequence of the rudiments and strokes to teach them effectively. This hands-on knowledge will enable the youth band conductor to effectively include the percussion section in band rehearsals.

BRASS AND PERCUSSION INSTRUCTION

BOOKS ON INSTRUMENTAL INSTRUCTION

All Together! *Teaching Music in Groups* (ABRSM Publishing)
Instrumental Music Education, Evan Feldman (Routledge)
Mommy, Can We Practice Now? Marie Parkinson, (Ability Development)
  Illustrations and ideas to encourage daily practice.
The Creative Director, *Alternative Rehearsal Techniques*, Edward S. Lisk (Meredith Music)
The Inner Game of Music, Barry Green (Anchor Press)

Refer to Orff, Suzuki, and Kodaly methods, particularly for early childhood pre-instrument training

BRASS METHOD BOOKS

Arban's Complete Conservatory Method (Carl Fischer) for intermediate and advanced levels (after completion of *Tradition of Excellence* 2). Best used in combination with the *Arban's Companion* (see Appendix 9.8) which sequentially organizes the Arban's book into 24 lessons.

Quickstart (SA, USA South) is a band method book that covers the same material as Book 1 of a standard band method book. *Quickstart* is designed specifically for Salvation Army bands, as it is coordinated with the *First Book of Hymn Tunes* and *Basic Brass, Winds & Percussion* three-part books. *Quickstart* is designed for a class made up of Bb instrumentalists, although an "E-flat Options" supplement is available.

Tradition of Excellence (Kjos) for beginner and intermediate students (formerly *Standard of Excellence*) is available in a standard or enhanced version. The enhanced version includes software that allows a student's playing to be evaluated and recorded by the computer, with feedback given for areas which need improvement. A conductor's score with teacher's notes is available. *Tradition of Excellence* is available for all brass band treble-clef instruments (Eb horn, Bb trombone treble clef, etc, with the exception of Eb tuba in treble clef), plus percussion and winds.

See Appendix 9.9 for a **Guide for Teaching and Rehearsing in Spanish-Speaking Cultures**.

ADVANCED BRASS METHOD BOOKS

Clarke Technical Studies and **Clarke Characteristic Studies** (Carl Fischer)
Daily Drills & Technical Studies for Trumpet, Max Schlossburg (M. Baron)
My First Clarke For the Developing Trumpet Student, Sean O'Loughlin (Carl Fischer)
Saint-Jacome Grand Method (Carl Fischer)
The Allen Vizzutti Trumpet Method (Alfred)–Book 1 (Technical Studies), *Book 2* (Harmonic Studies), *Book 3* (Melodic Studies)
36 Etudes Transcendantes for Trumpet, Cornet or Flugelhorn, Theo Charlier

MORE ADVANCED FOR HORN AND BARITONE:
Sixty Selected Studies for French Horn, C. Kopprasch (Carl Fischer)

MORE ADVANCED FOR TROMBONE:
Melodious Etudes for Trombone–Books I,II,III, Joannes Rochut (Carl Fischer)
Sixty Studies for Trombone, C. Kopprasch (Carl Fischer)

MORE ADVANCED FOR EUPHONIUM:
Advanced Concert Studies and New Concert Studies, Steven Meade (De Haske Publications)

MORE ADVANCED FOR TUBA:
70 Studies for BBb Tuba, Vladislav Blazhevich (Robert King)
43 Bel Canto Studies for Tuba (or Bass Trombone), Marco Bordogni (Robert King)

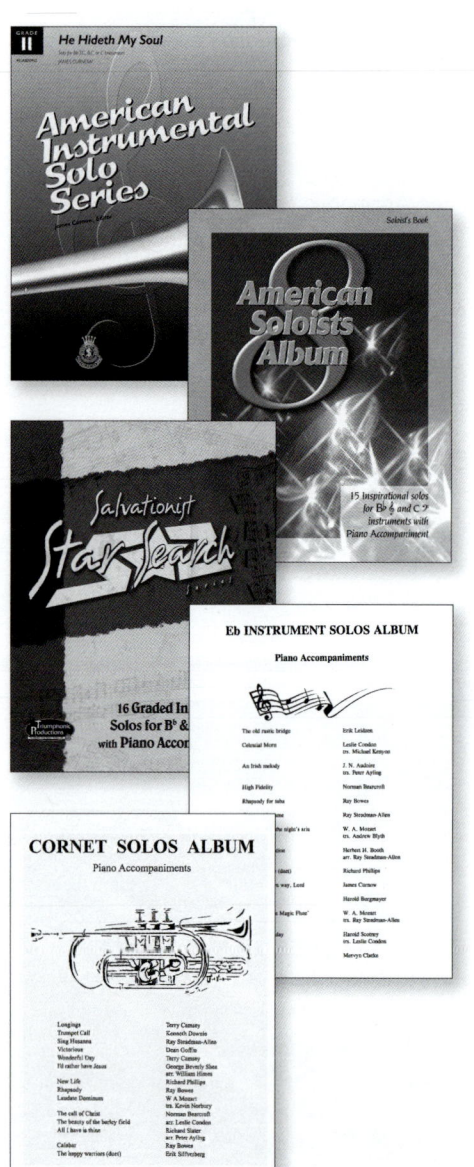

Salvation Army brass solo collections

American Instrumental Solo Series (Salvation Army, Atlanta) Four graded solos (one each for Levels 1-4) are published each year for use with piano or AIES accompaniment.

American Soloist Albums 1-8 (Salvation Army, New York) are collections of brass solos at a variety of levels, including a Trio album (No. 2) and a Christmas album (No. 7). CD accompaniment and performance recordings are available for some of these collections.

Star Search Brass Solos (Salvation Army, New York) includes sixteen solos, four solos each at Levels 1 through 4, with piano or CD accompaniments for either Bb or Eb instruments.

The Salvation Army Instrumental Albums (Salvation Army, London) are brass instrument-specific collections with piano accompaniment of classic and more recent Salvation Army solos. Examples include: *Cornet Solo Albums, Nos. 10, 11, 24, 29, Euphonium Album, No. 2, Trombone Album, No. 30,* and *Eb Instrument Album, No. 14*.[10]

PERCUSSION

SNARE DRUM METHOD BOOKS

Fundamentals of Rhythm for the Drummer, Joe Maroni (Mel Bay) for *Levels Primer, I & II*

Here's the Drum, *Volumes I & II*, Emile Sholle (Brook) for *Levels III & IV*

Portraits in Rhythm, Anthony Cirone (Belwin-Mills) for *Level V*

SUPPLEMENTAL PERCUSSION BOOKS

Breeze–Easy Method I Drums, John Kinyon (Warner Bros.)

Breeze–Easy Percussion Ensembles, Saul Feldstein (Warner Bros.)

Musical Studies for the Intermediate Snare Drummer, Garwood Whaley (Joel Rothman)

Rhythmsicles, Malletsicles, and more for a variety of percussion ensembles (Row–Loff Productions)

Southern Special, William Schinstine (Southern Music)

Studying Rhythm, Anne Carothers Hall (Prentice Hall)

Snare drum solo collections
For Levels Primer to II:
Contest Solos for the Young Snare Drummer, Murray Houliff (Kendor)
More Contest Solos for the Young Snare Drummer, Murray Houliff (Kendor)
Snare Drum: The Competition Collection, Thomas A. Brown (Belwin-Mills)
Winning Snare Drum Solos for the Beginner, Thomas A. Brown (Kendor)

For Level III:
Contest Solos for the Intermediate Snare Drummer, Murray Houliff (Kendor)
More Contest Solos for the Intermediate Snare Drummer, Murray Houliff (Kendor)
The Solo Snare Drummer, Volume 1, Pratt, Schinstine & Moore (Permus Publications)

For Levels IV and V:
Advanced Solos for Snare Drum, John Beck (Kendor Music) for Levels IV & V
The New Pratt Book, Contest Solos for Snare Drum, John S. Pratt (Permus Publications)

MALLET PERCUSSION BOOKS
Breeze Easy Trumpet, Book 1, John Kinyon (Alfred) recommended starter book for mallet percussion using the flat-side "band keys." Roll from half notes and larger.
Fundamental Method for Mallets, Books 1 & 2 (Alfred)
Learn To Play Oboe, Book 1, James McBeth (Alfred) recommended second book working in concert pitch keys

Mallet solo collections
Mallet Percussion Solo Collections for elementary to intermediate levels
Classic Festival Solos, Volumes 1 & 2, J. Lamb, ed. (M. & W. Burnett)
Mallet Percussion: The Competition Collection, Thomas Brown (Alfred)

TIMPANI METHOD BOOKS
Concepts for Timpani, John Beck (Carl Fischer)
Fundamental Method for Timpani, Mitchell Peters (Alfred)
Fundamental Studies for Timpani, Garwood Whaley (Joel Rothman)
Modern Method for Tympani, Saul Goodman (Mills Music)
Musical Studies for the Intermediate Timpanist, Garwood Whaley (Joel Rothman)
Primary Handbook for Timpani, Garwood Whaley (Meredith Music)

Timpani solo collections: easy to advanced levels
Timp Hits, Thomas Brown (Kendor)
10 Intermediate Timpani Solos, John Beck (Kendor)
Fundamental Solos for Timpani, Mitchell Peters (Alfred)
The Developing Solo Timpanist, William J. Schinstine (Southern Music)

Dear Longing for More,
Didn't get enough? Youth band leaders can benefit their young players by spending time in the Bandmaster Chapters 14 & 15.
Musically speaking,
Downbeat Harry

Part Three
ADULT MUSIC MINISTRY

CHAPTER TEN

WHAT'S THE SCORE?
How to 'Hear' a Vocal or Brass Score

The ability to read scores accurately and fluently is the obvious first step to understanding what a composer has written and how he wishes it to sound.
—Eric Leinsdorf, orchestral conductor

SCORES OF MEANINGS!

I don't know about you, but I enjoy exploring the stories behind words, known as their etymology. A derivative root and a bit of historical context can bring a word alive. Some words can have **scores** of meanings! (wordplay intended) How did a system of parallel staffs arranged one above another become known, more than 300 years ago, as a **musical score?** Of the multiple definitions available from Mr. Webster, speculate with me on a few explanations:

The first known use of the word **score** occurred in medieval England in the 14th century, as the word **scor**, derived from the Norse word **skor**, which meant **to notch or tally**.[1] They apparently counted large numbers of sheep with a notch in a stick for each 20 of their precious flock. Lincoln famously commenced his Gettysburg address with the phrase, "Four*score* and seven years ago."

Based on this root meaning I mused that perhaps the word score was used for music because there were **twenty staves on a page**. But alas, the answer is *no*. Musicologists tell us that for generations (as early as the 13th century), staves were stacked *only* in pairs.[2] It also proves a wee bit troubling that the counting of scores later made its way into games (first used for cards in 1742), indebtedness, sports, and even revenge.[3]

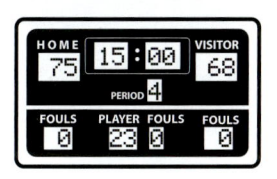

Around 1400, the verb "to score" emerged, meaning to cut (which also gave us another sheep word, shear). A plausible musical explanation, as in **"to score a line"** (like a scratch or incision) made me wonder if the musical term score evolved out of traditional music engraving, where staff lines were created by dragging a five-pronged scoring tool across a zinc or pewter plate. The first recorded use of the word score in a musical sense, however, was apparently in 1701, and derived from the practice of **"connecting related staves by scores of lines,"** bringing us happily full circle.[4]

In Chapter Ten we:

- give you tools to be able to read and thereby hear a vocal or brass score.
- consider seven steps to learning a new song, and ways to approach a new band score.

www.musicprintinghistory.org

> **score** (*term*) \'skȯ(ə)r\ the score shows the conductor, in musical notation, all of the parts of an ensemble (band, choir, etc.) with a separate stave for each part. Simultaneously sounded notes are aligned vertically.[6]

> **octavo** (*term*) \ahk-'tah-vō\ Most often, choral scores are printed on octavo size paper, roughly 14" x 10" sheets, folded in half to a 7" width in a stapled book format. Octavo literally means "cut eight from a sheet," so the octavo evolved as a printer's standard, but also proved a convenient size for singers to hold.

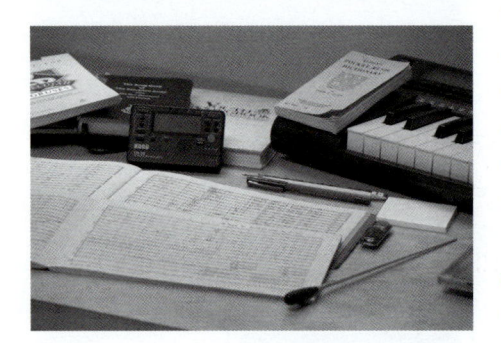

For those new to reading music notation, right now would be a good time to review the steps to sightsinging set out in the Singing Company Chapter Six.

Before the advent of scores, musicians used partbooks.

Scores today

Instrumental scores allow the conductor to view all the instrumental parts, with each part on separate staves in vertical alignment. Separate instrumental parts are then provided for each performer. In contrast, vocalists sing from a complete score of all the voice parts, and can view the accompaniment indicated below in piano score.

Learning to realize what a score sounds like requires musical imagination, intuition, memory, emotions, and especially what is sometimes referred to as *"the inner ear, the ability to imagine and hear music in our mind."* How many of us wake with an alluring melody looping through our imagination? Sitting in a movie theater, we intuitively sense, through the soundtrack, when trouble or romance looms. And how many of us associate a certain song with a landmark event in our lives? From birth to our waning years, we are ambushed with music. Daily, if unconsciously, we develop an ear and memory for music.

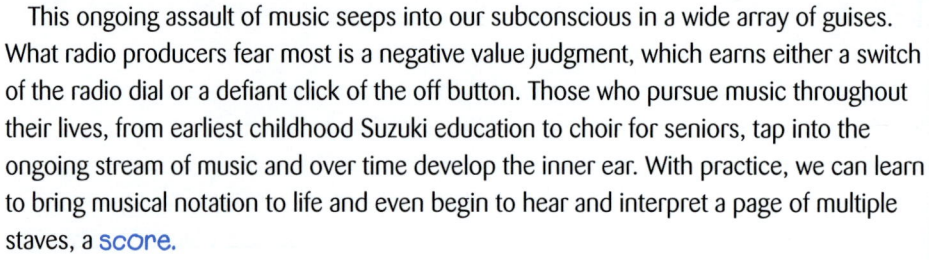

This ongoing assault of music seeps into our subconscious in a wide array of guises. What radio producers fear most is a negative value judgment, which earns either a switch of the radio dial or a defiant click of the off button. Those who pursue music throughout their lives, from earliest childhood Suzuki education to choir for seniors, tap into the ongoing stream of music and over time develop the inner ear. With practice, we can learn to bring musical notation to life and even begin to hear and interpret a page of multiple staves, a *score.*

Aids to score reading

Consider these helpful aids for ensemble leaders, most of which are available as applications on today's hand-held electronic devices. For Salvation Army purposes, we recommend ready access to:

- a Song Book and Bible for quick reference to texts
- a metronome to identify correct tempos
- a pocket-sized musical terms dictionary to look up words (many in *Italian*) governing expression
- a keyboard as an aid to hearing and learning the score
- a device to play recordings that will help form a concept of the "ideal" sound and performance
- and, oh yes, you have the option of using a baton!

Instrumentalists and vocalists who aspire to be conductors naturally benefit from learning to sight-read music, learning which helps them anticipate and imagine sounds on the printed page with more fluidity. The course we will explore encourages the bandmaster or songster leader to become an avid reader of musical scores. Like most things musical, score reading is a skill developed over years of practice, in and out of the rehearsal room.

Chapter 10 | WHAT'S THE SCORE?

HOW CAN WE 'HEAR' A SCORE?

THE 'IMAGINED' SOUND[6]

When attempting to read a score, begin by hearing an imagined sound. At first, you may be able to distinguish *melodic* or *rhythmic* patterns. As scores are generally arranged from the bass voice up, read from the bottom up, learning to assimilate a sense of the *harmonic* layering. Depend on your memory bank of sound samples to simulate in your inner ear the colors of the different instruments described on paper. With repeated readings, you can gradually form an aural picture of the music, and imagine the sound of the score scrolling before you.

THE 'IDEAL' SOUND

During this process of discovering the sound of the score, apply the sound of a model ensemble you know from your listening. As the aural picture crystallizes, assume the highest standards of performance of the notes before you and rely on the memory of that ideal sound in your playback of the score.

THE 'REAL' SOUND

A harsh reality can set in when your live ensemble attempts to replicate the notes of the score in rehearsal. The conductor "hears" the real sound of the ensemble in front of her, while keeping her imagined score in mind and aspiring for that ideal sound in her memory. Score reading while conducting involves hearing on these three levels virtually simultaneously.

WHY DO WE READ?

"Reading maketh a full man," wrote Francis Bacon. Just as every successful writer is a compulsive reader, it is impossible to become a musician without listening to music. For conductors and composers, listening to music with a score in hand is an unequivocal first step. It expands our musical vocabulary and teaches us through our eye- and ear-gates how the voices and instruments work in combination. A musical score, like a good book, has its own voice. It is alive and can carry us to distant times and places. Singers observe full vocal scores, but the novice instrumental conductor makes a sizeable leap from a single-line instrumental part to reading multi-layered score pages.

Hear ye, hear ye, Conducting begins with score study, Not a baton!

A STACK OF SCORES

When I first became a bandmaster, I kept a stack of scores on my bedside table. These scores, many that my band would never play, became my bedtime reading. I was an eclectic reader, not limiting myself solely to Salvation Army publications. My young heart yearned to blend the sounds of our culture with my Salvation Army experience. (This was before I had consciously worked at acquiring melodic or harmonic listening skills.) I looked for the principal themes, trying to imagine what the accompaniment sounded like, guessing how the key and meter transitions worked. Sometimes my imaginings proved incorrect, and I had to learn quickly, on the spot in rehearsal, how the music really sounded. At other times, the music was wildly better than I imagined.

All that night-by-night thumbing through scores increased my score-reading dexterity. Over time, my batting average in hearing more of what appeared on the score improved. There are

The Beat Goes On

> Just as the reading of books helps form our taste, conductors learn to make value judgments, looking for clarity of intent (**the message**), represented in logical thought and structure (**the music**).

still times when I get it wrong. But through repeated readings, both in and out of rehearsal, with and without a recording, I work to assimilate those phrases and harmonies into my musical vocabulary. There is a certain investigative thrill in reversing the composer's process and discovering why a passage is striking or how a profoundly simple phrase really works.

If we can discover how a composer put the music together, we have more clues about how to interpret it correctly. (More on this in the Songster Leader, Bandmaster, and Conducting chapters.) We also learn to discern quickly which pieces will or will not work with our ensembles.

HOW DID YOU LEARN TO READ?

There are parallels between learning to read a language and learning to read music. *A whole array of sounds and images precedes most recognition of letter or note representations in print.* As a father of four daughters, I spent countless bedtime hours reading stories to my girls. At first they could not read the letters that formed words, but they were receiving and processing the aural and associated pictorial information. Later they would recognize the letter and word impressions in print from what was stored in their memory banks. Like many children, they habitually asked for the story to be repeated. Unwittingly, our girls were assimilating the sounds of words and phrases, which in time seeded their reading skills. An elderly man once inquired of me if I read to my girls. His question revealed the great value he placed on literacy, and his personal regrets as a father for not taking full advantage of those precious moments of connection with his offspring.

Feeding the ears

We applied the same logic to learning music. After the lights went out, each girl had her own playlist of classical music that wound its way into her imagination. (For obvious, sleepy-time reasons, boisterous brass band and orchestra recordings were reserved for long car rides!) Our girls began playing instruments in the Suzuki school of training, initially developing basic technical competence on their instruments before being taught to read music.

When we did introduce notation, use of a simple grab-bag of popsicle sticks for rhythm coupled with magnetic note-heads aided the recognition of already familiar aural concepts. (See pp. 136-141 in the Singing Company Chapter Six for more ideas on ways to introduce children to music reading at a young age.) We also taught our girls music theory in the car on long trips, mostly through an exchange of *solfege* syllables,

Chapter 10 | WHAT'S THE SCORE?

relying on the inner ear, rarely resorting to a writing implement. (More on that in the Postlude.) The point is, our memories can be programmed to access and recognize the sounds around us, even from our youngest years. While peering at a printed score, we seek to recognize what we see and hear by referring to a lifetime of memories in sound.

Seventy-six trombones and the 'think system'

In *The Music Man,* the fast-talking con man "Professor" Harold Hill promises the townsfolk that he can teach the town's children to play in a magnificent marching band. Hill has the beginning musicians ostensibly learning to play by always thinking and singing the *Minuet in G.* The plot thickens, of course, when after weeks an actual tone has yet to be produced out of any of the youngster's sparkling new instruments. Even if there is limited plausibility that beginning instrumentalists can learn to play this way, the Music Man may have been on to something with his "think system" as it relates to conductors.

A walk through the woods

Score reading is like walking down a path through the woods with an alert, concentrated mind and an observant, perceptive attitude. Each time you do it, you discover something new in the environment. If you do it three, four, or five times every day, eventually you will get to know the path and its environment so well that you will be able to walk through it with your eyes closed, yet see, hear, and smell the surroundings.[7] Let's try a score-reading exercise where we first attempt to imagine what we see on the score, and then, using our inner ear, imagine what we hear.

UNRAVELING 'THE MYSTERY OF THE FIVE LINES'

Score–Reading Exercises #1 and #2

What do you SEE? What do you HEAR?

Allow me to re-imagine how I began to read scores. As an introductory exercise to score reading, let's use the first few measures of Bill Himes' setting of *Nothing But Thy Blood*. This is based on a well-loved melody by Donna Peterson, with words by Richard Slater, the father of Salvation Army music.[8] As musical detectives, we commence our investigation asking what we see. Scanning the score, we look for visual clues of movement in the score. Then, with our inner ears, we ask what these visual clues might sound like. **The probing musical detective begins his inquiry...**

SCENE 1: THE FIVE LINES CASE BEGINS...WITH OUR EYES

Clue #1: Can you SEE any rhythmic movement?
Our initial impression with this score is to follow the **rhythmic** movement of the four parts across the page, not necessarily in strict tempo. It is helpful to assume that the rhythms are vertically aligned at regular intervals to reflect the forward movement of the music in time from left to right. For instance, four eighth-notes take the same measured left-to-right space as a simultaneously sounded held half-note. We can visually see, and thereby aurally surmise, what parts move together. For instance, the Horn II and Bass IV land on the third beat together [Reference score A, next page] while the Trombone II and Euphonium work in tandem [B].

The Beat Goes On

Looking for...
RHYTHMIC MOVEMENT

Excerpted from *Hallelujah Choruses*, No. 98, mm. 1-2, arr. Wm. Himes
This arrangement Copyright © 2000 The Salvation Army, Des Plaines, IL

Clue #2: Can you SEE pitch profiles?

On the next reading, we imagine the **pitches** applied to the rhythmic shifts we previously identified. In this brief example, the pitches generally descend down the scale by step at varying rhythmic intervals. This step-wise motion is reflected in the musical notation, with the higher-sounding pitches moving visually down from line-to-space, and space-to-line, rather than skipping a line or space. At this stage, we are not concerned about hearing the exact starting pitches for each part, but rather seeing the visual profile and pace of the gradual descent by scale steps. [C]

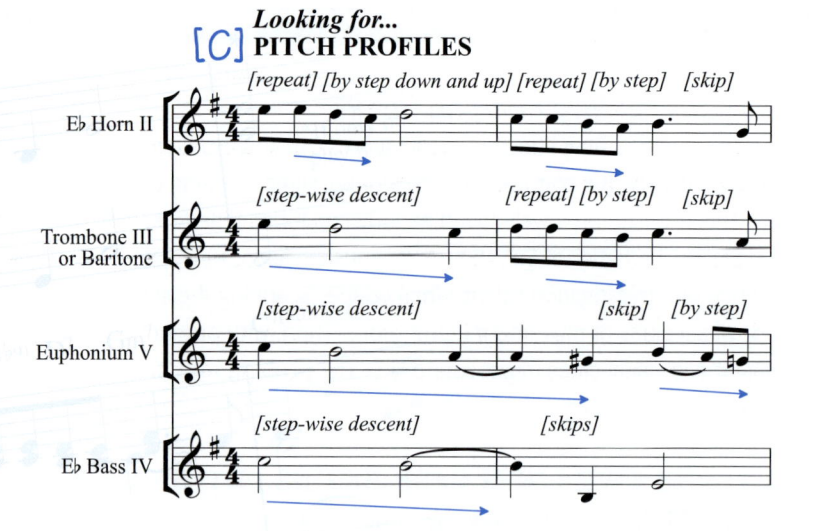

Looking for...
PITCH PROFILES

SCENE 2: THE FIVE LINES CASE CONTINUES...WITH OUR EARS

Clue #1: Can you HEAR any of the harmonic combinations?

Next we look for easily identifiable **harmonic** combinations and try to imagine how they sound, this time becoming more precise about starting pitches. The Trombone III and Euphonium V parts have already been identified as moving down in parallel motion. We first hear the Euphonium part pitches (C-B-A or, in *solfeggio*, *do-ti-la*), and then add tones a third higher, imagining the Trombone playing (E-D-C or, *mi-re-do*) in the same rhythm over it, in what we call

Chapter 10 | WHAT'S THE SCORE?

parallel thirds. [D] For the purposes of these score-reading exercises, we will read the solfege syllables as they appear in the transposed band keys.

In the same bar, we also hear the simple melodic pattern of the Horn II part (E-E-D-C-D or, *mi-mi-re-do-re*) lining up together on the third beat with the half notes moving down in the Eb Tuba IV part (from C to B, or *do* to *ti*). [E]

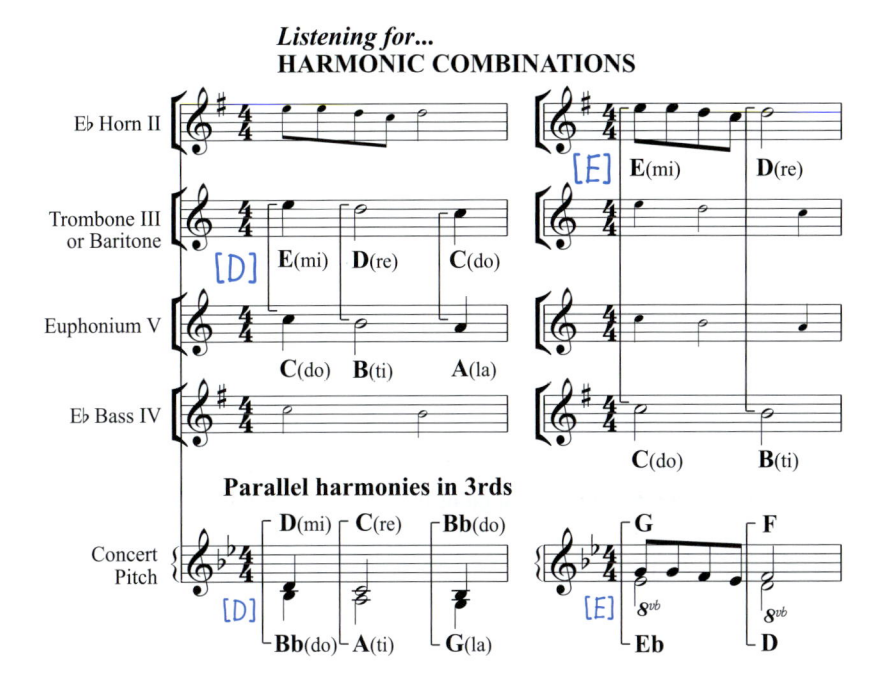

Listening for...
HARMONIC COMBINATIONS

Parallel harmonies in 3rds

Clue #2: Can you *HEAR* the color, dynamics, and expression?

Continuing this additive step-by-step process, if we haven't already done it, we specifically apply the **colors** of the horn, trombone, euphonium, and tuba to the correct instrumental lines, individually and then in combination. Proper instrumental color is highly dependent on **dynamics** and **expression.** In this case, we imagine the entire ensemble playing at a quiet, *piano* dynamic, using a warm, *legato* (smooth, connected) approach. [F]

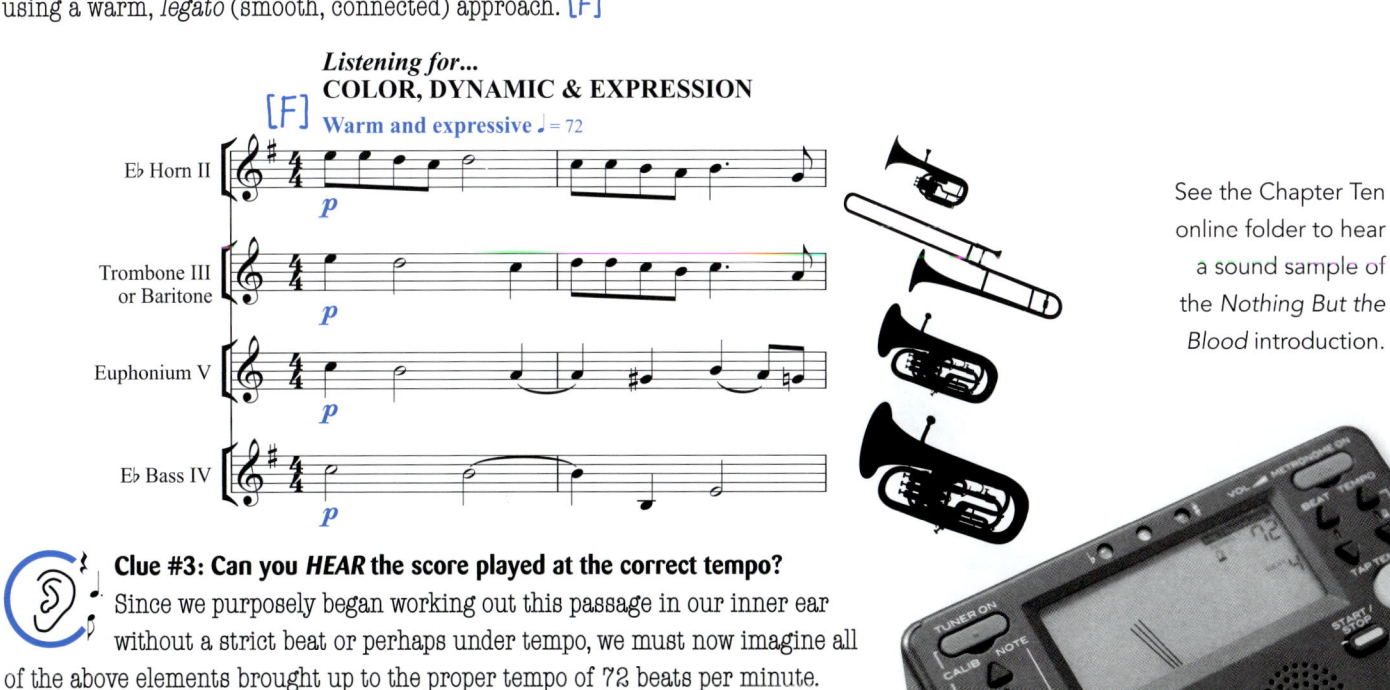

Listening for...
COLOR, DYNAMIC & EXPRESSION

[F] Warm and expressive ♩ = 72

See the Chapter Ten online folder to hear a sound sample of the *Nothing But the Blood* introduction.

Clue #3: Can you *HEAR* the score played at the correct tempo?

Since we purposely began working out this passage in our inner ear without a strict beat or perhaps under tempo, we must now imagine all of the above elements brought up to the proper tempo of 72 beats per minute.

The Beat Goes On

Score–Reading Exercise #3

UNRAVELING 'THE MYSTERY OF THE FIVE LINES'

Applying colors to what you see and hear

The composer's act of coloring a score by choosing instrumental or vocal colors is akin to the painterly application of colors and depth to an artist's pencil sketch. The composer can avail himself of an extensive palette of sound colors, ranging from the bright cornet or soaring descant of a boy soprano to the rumble of the lowest timpani or deep resonance of a second bass singer. It is important for the conductor to be able to recognize, recall, and apply instrumental or vocal colors in the imagination.

Consider how quickly we can recognize another person's speaking voice by its sound, without actually seeing the person. So it is with voice parts, instruments, choirs, and ensembles. It is an exercise in hearing. Our investigation into a score branches out as we consider steps to access our inner ear by what we call internalizing the sound.[9]
The probing musical detective continues his inquiry...

SCENE 3: THERE'S MORE TO THE FIVE LINES CASE... IN OUR INNER EAR

What is your favorite color?

How about your favorite instrument?

What is your least favorite color?

Your least favorite instrument color?

In **THIS** book, I am only allowed to paint with **BLACK** & **BLUE** on white!

Can you HEAR any vocal colors?
Clue #1: Choose a familiar song or chorus and sing it aloud to yourself.

Clue #2: Next hear/imagine yourself singing this song played back in your inner ear, without making any sound.

Clue #3: Now take the same aural memory of this melody and apply a different instrument to the tune, like a piano, cornet, or a bass guitar, playing only that melody.

Clue #4: Painters are trained to love ALL the colors available to them by disciplining themselves to work with their least favorite colors. The same can be true for musicians, who are generally most familiar with their own voice or instrumental part. Conductors, too, can expand their score-reading palette. If you are a soprano, alter the octave and imagine yourself as a bass. If you are a tenor, imagine yourself singing with the color of an alto. If you are an adult, imagine children's voices performing or singing this song.

The colors of a vocal score

In this brief exercise, we have called up from our own aural computer memory banks some of the timbres needed to internalize the color and sound of a *vocal score*. When first attempting to read a score, novice conductors tend to follow the trail of the principal melody or stay in familiar terrain, only seeking out their own vocal or instrumental parts. Obviously we need to canvass the score for further clues to solve the mystery of the five lines.

With experience we can learn to read and even scan the full musical score without stopping, in the same manner that we would read a book. A seasoned score reader identifies the voices of the principal characters and unearths from the musical clues how the essential story of the music unfolds.

WHAT'S THE VOCAL SCORE?

Seven steps to learning a new song

In rehearsal, the conductor's goal is to bring the real sound of the ensemble closer to the imagined sounds gleaned from our score reading. Let's discover some steps toward score reading, looking first at how to read and assimilate a vocal score. Because the majority of Salvation Army band pieces are essentially arrangements of songs, both instrumental and vocal leaders benefit from learning this process.

The following seven steps are designed for you as a leader to absorb the contents of a song, so that you, in turn, can teach it. Whether working with adults or youth, keep in mind that vocal music uses five essential elements:

1. WORDS 2. PITCH 3. RHYTHM
4. DYNAMICS 5. EXPRESSION

As we teach a song, a wise game plan isolates the learning to just one or two of those areas at a time. Teenagers think they can do five things at a time: Chat online, practice, eat, watch TV, and do their homework. Parents and teachers agree that this kind of multi-tasking is counterproductive and needs to be limited to one or possibly two of these activities. *With choral reading, it is far better to isolate step-by-step learning to just one or two of the areas (words, pitch, rhythm, dynamics or expression) at a time.* Let's look at the third verse of *Come Home*,[11] based on words by Will Thompson, set to a fresh melody by Chris Mallett:

> **timbre** (*term*) \'tamh - br\ is the quality of tone distinctive of a particular singing voice or musical instrument given by its overtones and resonance, by which the ear recognizes and identifies that sound.[10]

Step #1

Read the words **ALOUD**.

> **O for the wonderful love
> he has promised,
> Promised for you and for me!
> Though we have sinned,
> he has mercy and pardon,
> Pardon for you and for me!**

What do the words say? Ask how you as the leader will be able to convey that message. As you read, don't get trapped by rhymes and "sing-song." Try to convey the meaning by use of inflection and phrasing. *Reading aloud helps you hear the sound of the words and flow of the phrases.*

Now read the verse again with inflections and phrasing that reveal the meaning you sense in the text. Notice the unusual back-to-back repetition of the words "promised" and "pardon." (Hint: Repeated words in sequence should not sound the same.)

Identify the essential verbs that should receive emphasis *(for instance, "has promised, have sinned")*. Where are the nicest-sounding words *("wonderful love")*? Identify the difficult-sounding words and decide how best to render them *(like the "v" and "s" sounds in "have sinned")*.

The Beat Goes On

Step #2

TAP or **CLAP** the rhythm of the melody.

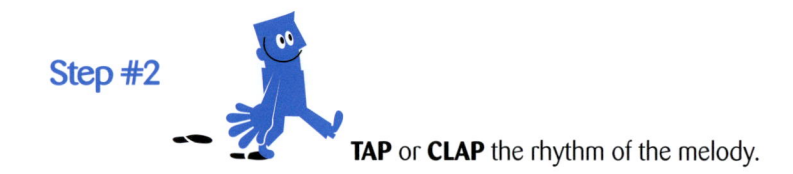

For the basics on **Counting and use of Rhythmic Syllables**, see Chapter Six, pp. 138-139 and Appendix 6.2.

Most songs are based on just a few rhythmic patterns. *Work through the rhythms enough so that you can accurately reproduce the rhythmic patterns of the melody.* Get a mental image of how these patterns sound and then tap or clap them. If there are harmony parts with different rhythm, do the same for those patterns.

```
ta  ti - ti  ta  ti - ti              ta - ah - ah  [rest]
1    2   +   3    4   +               1  -  2 - 3   [off]
```

Step #3

Read the words **ALOUD** again in the **CORRECT RHYTHM**.

Combine your mental images of the word and melodic rhythms into one composite sound pattern. Take note of the phrases that do not flow easily and will require special attention in rehearsal. When combining the words with the rhythm, some added emphasis is felt on beat one of each bar, as if beat one is propelling the rest of the measure. Put another way, we press down on beat <u>one</u> (indicated by <u>underlines</u>) and then release on beats two, three, and four.

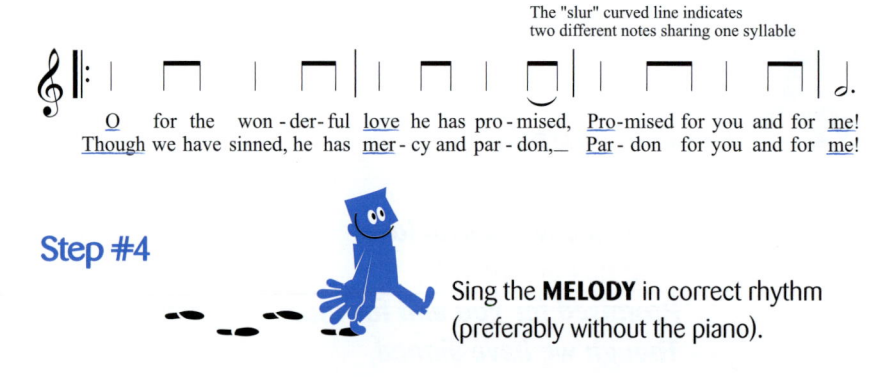

The "slur" curved line indicates two different notes sharing one syllable

<u>O</u>   for the   won - der - для   <u>love</u>   he has pro - mised,   <u>Pro</u> - mised   for you and for   <u>me</u>!
<u>Though</u>   we have   sinned,   he has   <u>mer</u> - cy and par - don,   <u>Par</u> - don   for you and for   <u>me</u>!

Step #4

Sing the **MELODY** in correct rhythm (preferably without the piano).

Reading the pitch notation, sing the melody, combining the melody and correct rhythm on a neutral syllable. Introduce the actual text, dynamics, and expression as you repeat the music. If you are unfamiliar with reading pitch notation, ask someone to play the melody line alone in strict rhythm and tempo while you listen with the music in front of you. An audio track can substitute if you can hear the vocal lines clearly, but *do not sing along at first*. After allowing your inner ear some repetitions of the melody line, begin to sing along, using the words and rhythms you have already tapped out and spoken. As you are learning the melody line, take note of difficult phrases that will require more teaching time or a special strategy with your ensemble.

Women / Men

La la la la la la la la la la la la___ la la la la la la la___

Next sing the **HARMONY** part.

Your careful study reveals that while the rhythm between the parts for the women and men are nearly identical, the pitches are different. *It usually is best to teach the harmony part first*, so that it becomes the "melody" for that section. Sing through the men's part on a neutral syllable like "la." Make note to move exactly on beat three in the fourth bar.

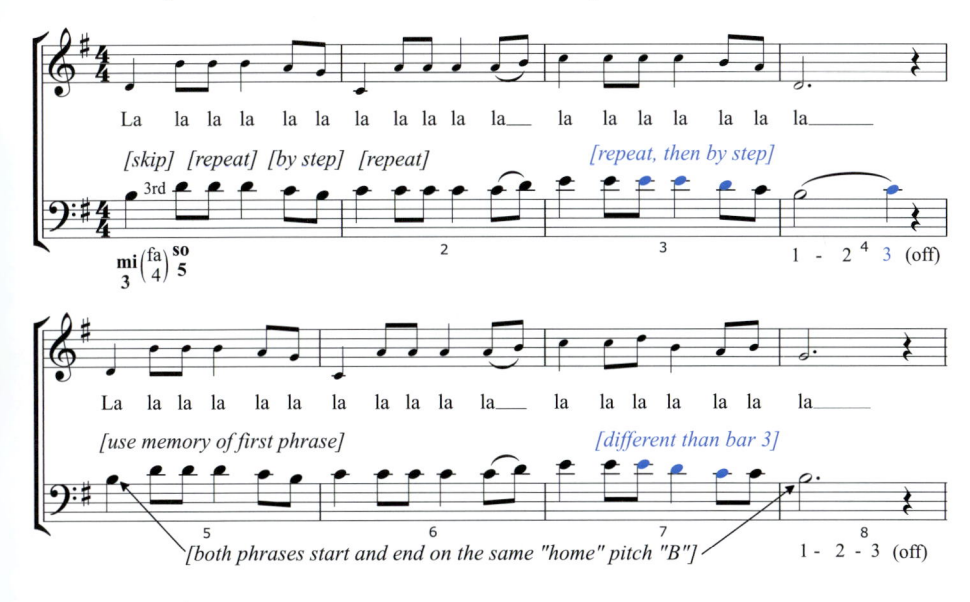

Then move to the **MELODY** part.

Now sing the women's part, using a neutral syllable. The women should learn to feel how the initial low note in the bar propels the melody through the measure. The low note will require more air to sound. The opening sixth interval can be learned by counting up six steps or by using a *do–la* interval.

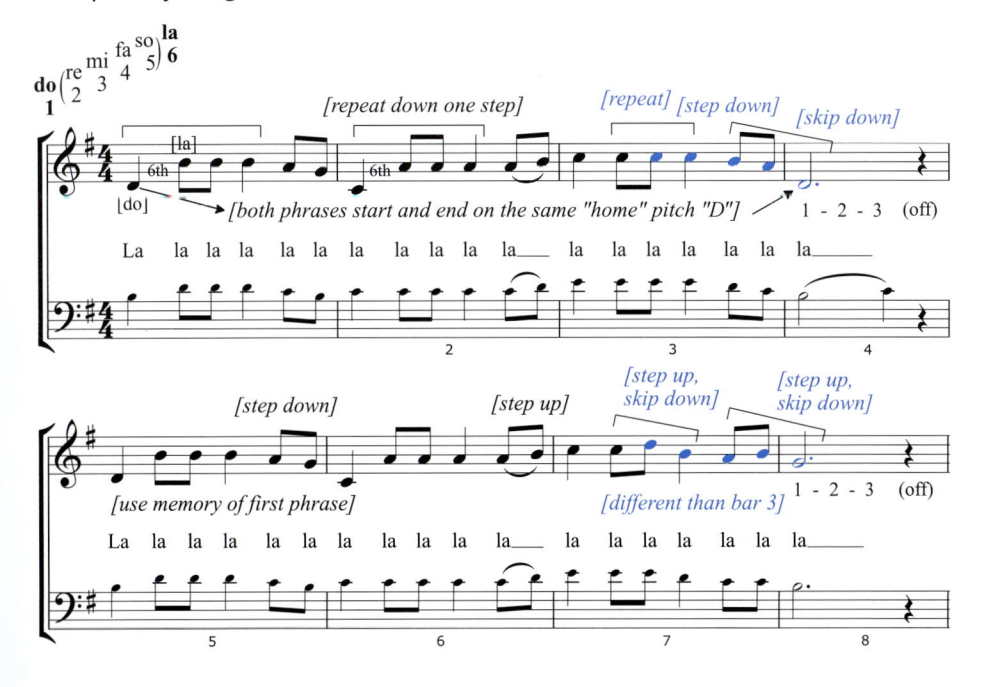

The Beat Goes On

Sing with the **PHRASING.**

Note that although the melody might be rendered in two four-bar phrases, the repeated words—"promised" and "pardon"—suggest an additional breath between them. Now sing with the phrasing indicated.

The "phrase" curved line indicates the distance to carry the breath through a phrase

Rather than showing phrase lines, conductors or singers will use a breath mark (comma or check)

3. O for the won-der-ful love he has pro-mised, Pro-mised for you and for me!

Though we have sinned, he has mer-cy and par-don,— Par-don for you and for me!

Step #5

Have the accompaniment played while you **LISTEN**.

Mentally fit your images of the melody, words, and rhythm to the accompaniment. *Notice how the accompaniment works or contrasts with the melody.* A demo track has been provided with just the piano accompaniment. Listen to *Come Home* (verse 3)— piano accompaniment only to compare the piano accompaniment with the voice parts.

In this case, the voice parts are clearly a part of the right hand of the piano part with a lilting broken chording, known as *arpeggiation*, in the left hand.

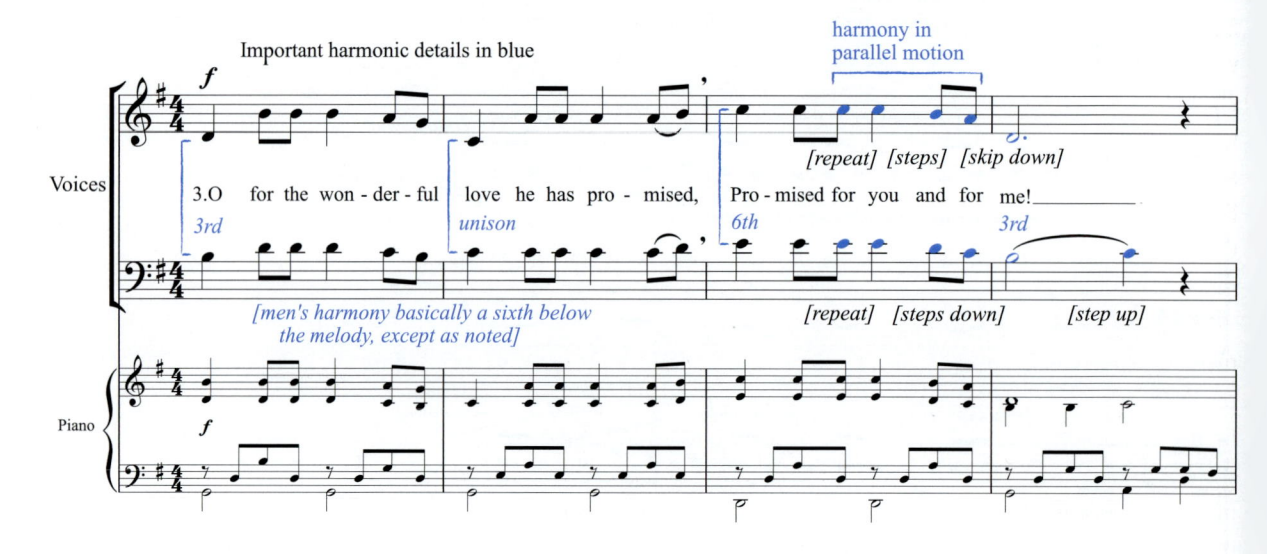

Important harmonic details in blue

harmony in parallel motion

[repeat] [steps] [skip down]

Voices

3. O for the won-der-ful love he has pro-mised, Pro-mised for you and for me!

3rd unison 6th 3rd

[men's harmony basically a sixth below the melody, except as noted]

[repeat] [steps down] [step up]

Piano

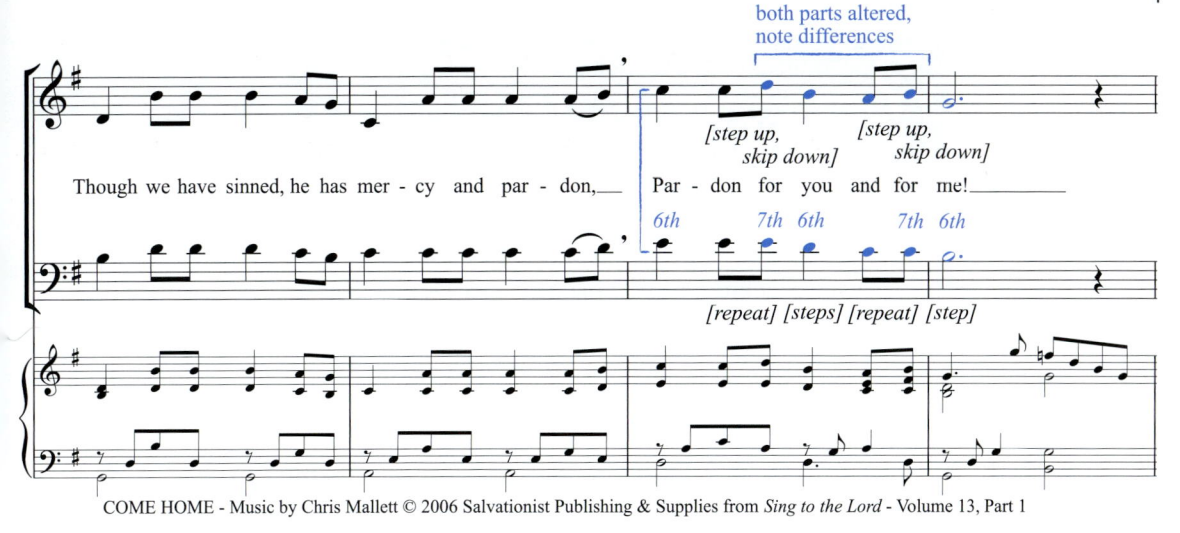

COME HOME - Music by Chris Mallett © 2006 Salvationist Publishing & Supplies from *Sing to the Lord* - Volume 13, Part 1

Step #6

SING the melody with the complete accompaniment.

Take the lead. *Do not wait for the accompaniment to sing the melody for you,* or even lead you to the next pitch or rhythm. The contour and rhythm of the melody are already in your memory bank. Get used to the accompaniment. How many times have you seen young soloists get up and attempt a solo having not heard the accompaniment part? It usually is not how the soloist imagined it, and his troubled face shows it!

If you are privy to a split-track accompaniment, use the *accompaniment only* side. Work to differentiate the melody from what you expect the accompaniment to do.

Step #7

MEMORIZE!

Some find it helpful to write out the lyrics by hand as an aid to memorization. Others work section by section, identify key words for each line of the song, or use motions as an aid to memorization. You can probably accomplish a verse in the car on the way to work, or even a whole song on a longer journey. Accumulate confidence in singing the song from memory by repeating the song with and without accompaniment many times. For audio files, see *Come Home* (verse 3)—demonstration and accompaniment versions. Go back to the music quickly to identify the things you missed, before testing your memory again.

Build on your experiences working with the essential components—words and their meaning, the rhythms, the melody line, and the relation of the melody to the accompaniment. As you learn the notes and rhythms, consider how to appropriately render the melody line with expression. The clearer the image of the entire song becomes in your mind, the more you can concentrate on conveying its meaning and develop a plan for teaching it to your ensemble. Later in this chapter, we will give attention to bringing elements of our score study into the rehearsal planning process.

Helps for memorization are considered in The Songster Leader Chapter Thirteen, pp. 267–269, and in the final Conducting Chapter Twenty-Three, pp. 520–523.

Retrace your STEPS often!

10 BARS REST

Applying the 'Steps to Learning a Song'
Choose two songs that are unfamiliar to you, but that you might consider using with your songster brigade in the future. Practice learning those songs following the seven steps outlined above. Do not move on to the next step until each element is correct:

> **STEP 1**: Words
> **STEP 2**: Rhythm
> **STEP 3**: Words combined with the rhythm
> **STEP 4**: Melody in correct rhythm
> **STEP 5**: Absorbing the accompaniment
> **STEP 6**: Singing with the accompaniment
> **STEP 7**: Memorize

Begin to capture the meaning of the song, by using the words and dynamics to bring the appropriate expression to the song.

Score–Reading Exercise #4

UNRAVELING 'THE MYSTERY OF THE FIVE LINES'

What's the band score?

In Score-Reading Exercise #3 above, we introduced a technique of internalizing the sound of the voices and piano by accessing the inner ear and the aural library of sound colors stored in our memory banks. In Score-Reading Exercise #4 below, we expand the number of musical lines we are listening to at one time and also extend the range of colors to include brass instruments.[12] The source material for this unraveling of clues will be Erik Leidzén's classic brass arrangement of *What A Friend,* published in the American Band Journal No. 55. Once again we are drawing from an aural catalog of familiar instrumental timbres. Here the probing musical detective asks,
"Can I *HEAR* the instrumental colors?"

See Chapter Six—Singing Company, pp. 136–139 for help with reading musical notation.

SCENE 4: MORE CLUES TO *THE FIVE LINES CASE*... USING OUR INNER EAR

Clue #1: *HEAR* a phrase
To begin to hear a band score with our inner ear, we first identify a musical phrase that is recognizable to us in the score. We attempt to hear it without the aid of a recording, an instrument, or our voice. We'll start with the melody in the 1st Cornet part.

We follow the melodic profile of Bars 1 and 2: First we recognize repeated pitches, starting relatively high, then up by step, then a series of descending steps and skips. En route, there is another repeated tone (the last note of bar 1 into the first of bar 2). To know how long to hold each tone, we examine the rhythmic profile, noticing that the first and seventh notes get held longer than the others.

Bars 3 and 4 have an identical rhythmic profile, but this time the melody follows a more jagged, melodic ascent, using a series of skips, which occasionally reference each other, finally falling by step.

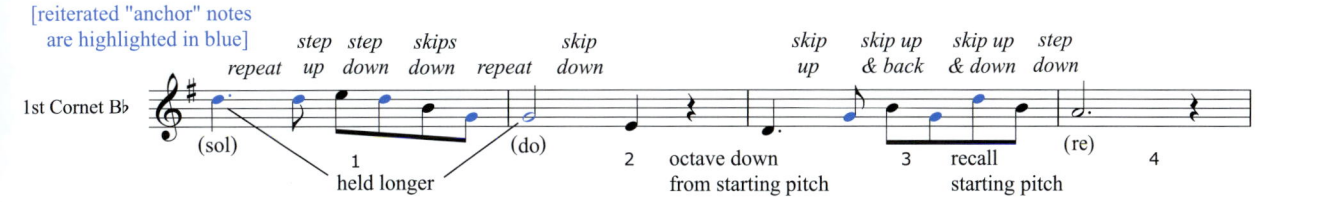

Clue #2: APPLY instrumental timbres

Similar to what we did in the vocal score-reading exercise, next we apply an instrumental timbre, such as a cornet or trombone, to the musical line we are reading. In our imaginations, we arbitrarily vary the instrumental timbres being applied to that same melody, from cornets and horns, to trombones and tubas, regardless of what instrument part line we are reading. With the score excerpt above, we can imagine the melody line played by a solo cornetist, and then a full cornet section.

Clue #3: HEAR a second phrase

Next we locate a second independent line that happens simultaneously with the first phrase. This could be the Euphonium part, which complements the 1st cornet part. To initially aid our hearing of both parts, we think through the first line while, at the same time, we play the new second line on the piano. Another option is to try singing out loud the new second line, while simultaneously thinking the internalized first line.

In the opening of *What A Friend* there is a contrasting line in the Euphonium part. Since the euphonium has a rest on the initial downbeat, we listen for the 1st cornet starting note, and then skip down a third to commence the euphonium descending scale. The euphonium then "mirrors" the 1st Cornet part, ascending by steps and skips, and then in bar 2 harmonizes a third under the 1st Cornet tune.

The euphonium in bar 3 again rests on the downbeat before ascending with the same profile of notes as the 1st Cornet melody, but at a more rapid pace. Bar 4 has the euphonium answering the bar 3 melody, but again allowing a breath on the downbeat.

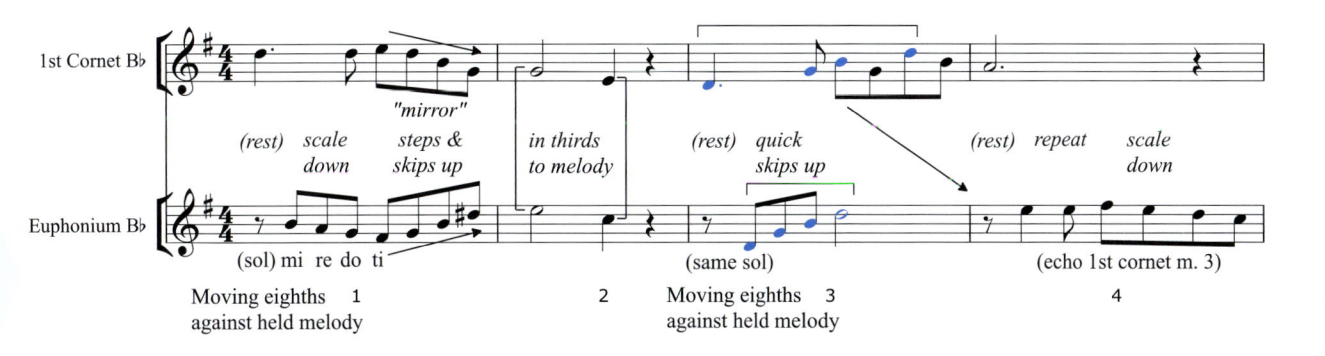

The Beat Goes On

Clue #4: HEAR both lines

After developing an aural picture of the interaction between phrase 1 and phrase 2, we attempt to hear the two lines together without an aural crutch. We try this exercise with other phrases in various combinations, in this case, attempting to hear the bass line under the principal melody or countermelody.

Begin by developing an aural picture of the interaction of the lines between the 1st Cornet and Euphonium parts, applying the color of these prominent parts, individually and in tandem. Next attempt to hear the Bass part, as it supports the 1st Cornet melody and/or the Euphonium countermelody.

Clue #5: APPLY expression, dynamics, and tempo

As the internalized lines become familiar, we apply the notated musical elements of expression, dynamics, and correct tempo to our evolving aural picture of the music. [Reference the full score on the next page]

Clue #6: APPLY harmonies

At this point it can be fairly easy to hear the harmonic supporting voices that may be notated a third or sixth below or above the melody line already learned. We work to hear a good balance between the lines, giving the principal melody prominence.

Clue #7: APPLY style

Finally, we experiment in our imaginations with various *tempi*, dynamics, and attacks. We draw out the contrasting character between a theme (for instance, in the first cornet part) and its simultaneously sounding countermelody (many times, in the euphonium), by rendering one with a slightly more detached articulation, while the melody is played with a smoothly connected airstream.

Chapter 10 | WHAT'S THE SCORE?

Gospel Song – WHAT A FRIEND

C. C. CONVERSE
Arr. ERIK LEIDZEN

Moderato sostenuto

[Score excerpt for 1st Cornet B♭, 2nd Cornet B♭, 1st Horn E♭, 2nd Horn E♭, 1st Trombone B♭, 2nd Trombone B♭, Euphonium B♭, Bass E♭, Bass B♭, and Basic Harmony, with annotations:]

- CNTS. in 3rds
- CNT. 2 8va TRB. 1
- HNS. double CNTS.
- answer
- HN. & EUPH. in 3rds
- HN. 1 8va to EUPH.
- HN/TRB. in 3rds
- TRB. 8vb CNT. 2
- answer
- TRB. in 3rds
- EUPH. 8vb to HN. in 3rds with CNT. 1
- Arpeggio carried up to CNT. 2
- Sustained bass foundation

See Chapter Fourteen for more on brass transpositions and making a score reduction

American Band Journal No. 55 © The Salvation Army- New York

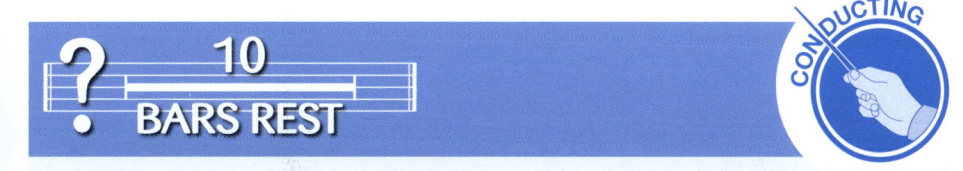

10 BARS REST

Conducting variations in score-reading

1. Conduct a section of music in silence, attempting to hear as much as you can. Start by using a slow tempo. On occasion, interrupt the silence by singing out loud a part from the score precisely in rhythm and tempo, while still conducting. This could be a passage that you might want to accentuate to emphasize its importance.

10 BARS REST *continued*

2. As a hands-on conducting exercise, conduct one part or rhythm, while learning a simultaneously-sounding part, accompaniment, or rhythm. Then conduct one of these parts while you imagine the other. After that, reverse the process.

Two part listening exercise
"I'm in His Hands" (Phil Laeger/Stanley Ditmer)

Slowly and tenderly (♩ = 66)

Ladies: I'm in his hands, I'm in his hands; What-ev-er the fu-ture holds I'm in his hands, The days I can-not see Have all been planned for me; His way is best, you see;

Men: I'm in his hands, I'm in his hands; What-e'er the fu-ture holds I'm in his hands, The days I can not see Have all been planned for me; His way is best, you see; I'm in his hands.

© 2006 The Salvation Army
USA Eastern Territory

Score–Reading Exercises #5 and #6

UNRAVELING 'THE MYSTERY OF THE FIVE LINES'

Coloring the score

To aid the transition to reading a full band score, which we will develop more fully in the next chapter, several score pages from the Trio section of the march *God's Children* (TS 825) by William Himes are reprinted with permission for the purpose of your personal study in the Score Reading Exercises #5 & #6 ahead on pp. 220-221. The probing musical detective inquires, **"Can I *SEE* the instrumental color combinations?**

SCENE 5: THE CASE OF COLORING *OUTSIDE* 'THE FIVE LINES'...WITH OUR EYES

Clue #1: *CANVASS* the score—Trio section of *God's Children* in living color.
Using a half-dozen crayons, highlighters, or markers, spend a few minutes covering these score pages with color. Before commencing your artwork, make some decisions as to what each line or voice actually contributes to the music, and group them with appropriate colors. For instance, you may elect to isolate the melody, countermelody, accompaniment, rhythmic elements, bass line, etc., each with their own coloration. Let yourself go and do not hesitate to color all of the notated bars, not just starts and stops.[13]

Clue #2: *FOLLOW* the trail.
Once your coloring is complete, take time to examine what your color scheme reveals about the roadmap of this portion of the march.

Clue #3: *SUBSTANTIATE* the trail.
Next, follow the score, while listening to the recording of the *Trio to God's Children*, which commences at Letter D. Consider if the recorded real sound matches that of your imagined or ideal sound.

Scoping out the score

After satisfactorily completing the coloring exercise, begin to "scope out" the Trio section of *God's Children,* from letter D to the end. Do not refer to a recording or keyboard. You want to stimulate real score-reading by exercising your inner ear, figuratively converting the "living color" into "living sound." Just concentrate on realizing the music. The probing musical detective begins this further inquiry by asking,
"Can I *SEE* and *SUBSEQUENTLY* hear the instrumental color combinations?"

SCENE 6: GETTING *INSIDE* 'THE FIVE LINES'... WITH OUR EYES AND EARS

Clue #1: *GLOSS* over the details
Read through the score several successive times *without stopping,* possibly at a slower tempo to start.

+

Clue #2: *UNCOVER* the aural memory banks
For now, do your best to identify the instrument parts and their individual and combined timbres from your own aural memory banks. For a detailed explanation of the instruments of the brass band, take a look at pages 290-293 of the Bandmaster Chapter Fourteen.

SCORE-READING RESOURCES

How to Read a Score, Gordon Jacob (Boosey and Hawkes)
MLR Instrumental Score Reading, Richard Grunow and James Froseth (GIA)
Preparatory Exercises in Score Reading, R. O. Morris and Howard Ferguson (Oxford)
The Conductor's Score, Elizabeth Green and Nicolai Malko (Prentice-Hall)
The Mind's Ear: Exercises for Improving the Musical Imagination of Performers, Listeners and Composers, Bruce Adolphe (MMB Music)

More clues to score study just ahead in Chapter Eleven

TRIO TO GOD'S CHILDREN

I am a child of God

Chapter 10 | WHAT'S THE SCORE?

The Beat Goes On

221

CHAPTER ELEVEN

FROM SCORE READING TO SCORE STUDY
Marking a Vocal or Brass Score

Study the full score with hands behind the back ... Learn the music and afterwards impose the music on the arms and not the arms on the music.
—Margaret Hillis, choral conductor

THE INVESTIGATION UNEARTHS MORE!

In the six "detective" score-reading scenes in the previous chapter, we've learned how score study is a step-by-step, *additive* learning process. As we read the score, we turn up more and more musical clues to weigh against what we already hear. In the process, we color the unfolding clues with sound timbres from our memory bank. Leaving no stone unturned, we learn more and more about the real musical story by replaying it with added expression, dynamics, *tempi*, and accompanying harmonies.

A band or chorus leader can accumulate a wealth of aural information about a musical passage by repeated readings of a score, and yet, upon further study, discover something new and fresh not noticed before. In some ways, these discoveries are like collective clues. The private investigator turns up one clue, which leads to another, and yet another, ad infinitum. Ultimately, an accumulation of musical discoveries serves to illuminate a larger picture of the piece, and with deliberation, leads us to *unravel even more mysteries embedded in the five lines of each stave.* Such is the marvelous trail of score study. We open a score and wonder what we will discover in our ongoing search for the music!

A Tapestry of Layers

Just as we separated the elements of a song earlier in the previous chapter, so it can be beneficial with a band score to search for clues in what we will call the "layers" of a score. Unlike the layers of an onion, which envelop each succeeding layer, these layers are analogous to a tapestry in which each thread is interwoven, and thereby interrelated, with other threads. To illustrate our discussion of layers in a band piece, refer to the full score version of *God's Children* on pages 227–230 of this chapter.

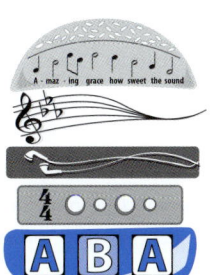

The Structural Layer: The Form

All forms of art have a structure or architecture that we discern as its shape. On our initial readings, we intuitively look for the basic sections of the piece that define an overall design. Transitions, key, and style changes serve to articulate the basic sections of a piece. For instance, after a brief introduction, a march opens with a lively *march strain.* This is usually followed by a contrasting, more lyrical section or bass melody. The original march strain returns before we modulate (change key) for the second half of the march called the *trio.* The trio theme is usually first presented by a slimmed-down trio grouping of instruments, thus its name. A *break strain,* which often refers to introductory music from the first half of the march, builds toward the concluding full-blown repeat of the trio theme. These broad sections are shown across the top of the *God's Children* score in blue boxes. [A]

In Chapter Eleven we:
- identify the structural, rhythmic, melodic, harmonic and textual "layers" of a score.
- learn how to mark the song or score to aid the "hearing" and the clear interpretation of the score.

The Beat Goes On

A simple diagram of the form of the march:

INTRO	A section	B section	A section
	march strain	contrasting, bass melody	march strain, altered
TRIO INTRO	Trio melody	Break strain	Trio melody
w/key change	slimmed down	refer to earlier material	full-blown

For **Glossary of Salvation Army Musical Forms** see Appendix 11.1.

With experience, we recognize the form of pieces more rapidly. From our band experience, we probably are familiar with the structure of a march, prelude, selection, meditation, sets of variations, etc. Emerging conductors can intuitively apply their knowledge of these forms to establish a sense of flow and direction. From a rehearsal point of view, the most work usually goes into successfully navigating transitions between the major sections of the piece.

The Rhythmic Layer: Meter and Motifs

Unlike visual art, music functions over time. Musicians borrow the term *meter* from the poets to encompass the basic pulse, placement of accents, and/or the rhythm of a phrase. The most common meters in music are those of 4, 3, and 2, but even within these three we learn to emphasize the downbeat more than the other beats. The choice of meter and establishment of the corresponding *tempi* are vital to correct interpretation of music.

There often arises the question of the right *tempo* for a piece of music. Despite the composer's tempo indications, there can be great discrepancies in tempo between two performances, based on the conductor's personal preference and the technical ability of the musicians. *God's Children* is marked **Allegro** (♩ = 120). **[B]**

As we begin to study a score, we see that basic rhythmic patterns, or what we sometimes call *motifs,* unify the music. This rhythmic "galop" motif has become associated with various Western shows and commercials.

"William Tell Galop" rhythm

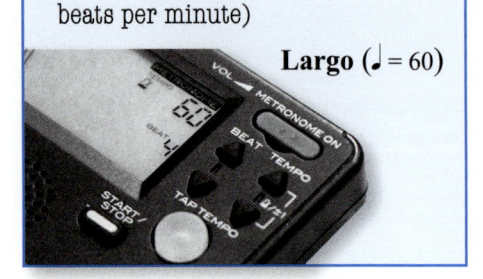

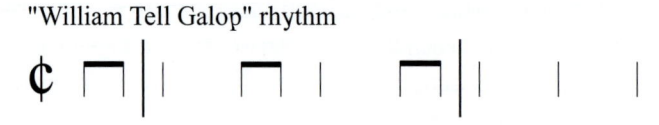

Opera composer Gioacchino Rossini (1792–1868) could never have imagined that the primary rhythmic gesture from the concluding movement of his *Overture to William Tell* would be permanently usurped by producers of Western films. This rhythmic pattern propels the music. Most pieces use just two or three rhythmic ideas to form the music. The conductor needs to identify these concepts. Much rehearsal time can be saved by rehearsing isolated examples of the basic rhythmic motifs and then assuming that players will carry this knowledge to music with a similar rhythmic profile. Unusual rhythms, such as syncopation, may need extra attention.

The basic rhythmic motif to *God's Children* is a quarter note followed by a dotted eighth and sixteenth, then four eighths. This motif is found on virtually every page of the march. *(This is marked in the score as* **[C]** *at the first measure).*

[C] motif — Allegro ♩ = 120

---

tempo (*term*) \'tem - pō\ the rate of speed of a musical piece or passage indicated by one of a **series of directions** (such as *largo*, meaning slow; *andante*, walking speed; or *allegro*, fast), or by a **metronome indication** (♩=60, equivalent to a rate of 60 beats per minute)

Largo (♩ = 60)

WHOA! THIS IS *WAY* TOO FAST!

The Melodic Layer: Themes and Countermelodies

We usually mark the main *theme* of a section with an asterisk or bracket to signify that this melody needs to be in the forefront. [D] (Note the 1st cornet part at Letter A marked with an asterisk.*) As we imagine the melody in our inner ear, we begin to shape the phrases and feel where the line is going. We identify its ebb and flow and consider the color of sound and attack required, as well as related dynamics and breathing.

Often the composer creates a *countermelody* that answers or responds to the main theme. (See the euphonium part at Letter A marked as [E], *played 2nd time only*.) First we sing through the countermelody in our inner ear, independently experiencing its shape and line. Then we begin to hear how these two melodies interact together. They often contrast in style.

syncopation (*term*) \sin - kə - 'pā - shən\ temporary displacement of the natural metrical pulse or accent in the music.[1] The opening bar of the chorus *I Am a Child of God* uses syncopation.

THEME/COUNTERMELODY
God's Children (William Himes)

The Harmonic Layer: Keys and Accidentals

Musicians refer to melodies and countermelodies as linear or *horizontal*, while the harmonies act as their *vertical* support system. A melody suggests a harmonic treatment, which is usually based in what we call a *tonality* or *key*. The conductor should know his major and minor key signatures and subsequently be able to identify the basic key scheme of a piece. Note that brass players' fingering or position errors most often have to do with not correctly observing the key signature. Like most marches, *God's Children* is built on a two-key scheme. (Noted as [F] in the score at the beginning and letter D.)

key (*term*) \'kē\ a central tone (or tonality) to which other tones (represented in that key's scale) support and tend toward.

Key of D

	A section	B section	A section
INTRO (G major) Start in tonic (I), home key	march strain	contrasting, bass melody	march strain, altered
TRIO INTRO (C major) subdominant (IV) key	Trio melody slimmed down	Break strain refer to earlier material	Trio melody full-blown

For more on key signatures, see Chapter Six, p. 138 and **Circle of Fifths**—Piano Chapter Seventeen, p. 365.

See harmonic rhythm—
Letter B, *God's Children*, measures 15–26, pp. 227–228

Guide to Tuning Tendencies—
Bandmaster Chapter Fourteen, p. 300

A recording of the march—*God's Children* (William Himes) is available in the Chapter Eleven online folder.

The conductor looks to see how the tonality or key works in support of the melody and countermelody. A study of the foundational bass line and the accompanying rhythm and figuration can give insight into the "heartbeat" of the piece. The pace at which the harmonies change is known as harmonic rhythm. Sometimes this can be at the rate of one chord per measure, as found in most of letter A of *God's Children* or, as in letter B, at a more rapid pace [G], as the composer moves away from the primary key [H].

Accidentals are the flat (♭), sharp (♯) and natural (♮) signs that alter pitches by a half step up or down. (For a full definition, see Bandmaster Chapter Fifteen, p. 4.) These are important for conductors to note, as a "moving away" from a key area is signaled by accidentals. Accidentals require extra concentration from players to use correct fingerings/positions and make adjustments in tuning. A good example in *God's Children* of such a trouble spot is the first and second endings of letter B *(marked as [I] in the score)* where players will need to be reminded that once indicated, an accidental affects the same note throughout that bar. The usual instruction is to say that accidentals "carry through" the measure.

The Text Layer: Phrasing and Meaning

In Chapter Ten, we became acquainted with the songster piece *Come Home*. We suggested that study of the meaning and sound of the lyrics was a good starting place with vocal music because melodies and harmonies are usually birthed from the text. Through this process, the conductor considers how the text sounds when sung and looks carefully at diction, breathing, and color of sound.

Because much of Salvation Army instrumental music is based on songs that have associated text, it is highly beneficial for the instrumental conductor to become familiar with those corresponding texts. This aids the conductor in expressing the line, dynamics, and phrasing of these melodies. Most Salvation Army scores refer to a source songbook or publication number, so the text can be readily accessed. The words to the chorus "I am a Child of God" (not from our songbook) are noted on the score at letter D [J]. It would be inappropriate to suggest a breath be taken in the middle of the second bar of D in *God's Children*, which would be in the middle of the word "hallelujah" if the song were sung. Familiarity with the text places the correct breath after the third beat of D4 (after the word "Amen," which completes the phrase).

D TRIO MELODY
"I am a child of God"

[J] Text: I am a child of God, hal-le-lu-jah, I am a child of God, a-men. I have washed my robes in the cleans-ing foun-tain, I am a child of God.

After becoming familiar with the text, the conductor should next ask how the arranger has elected to convey the meaning and character of the text through the other elements of the music, particularly the harmonies and rhythm. In *God's Children*, the composer uses a sprightly march accompaniment to express the joy and assurance of the text. A slow dirge would certainly not be appropriate.

Chapter 11 | FROM SCORE READING TO SCORE STUDY

March – GOD'S CHILDREN

WILLIAM HIMES

[A] Introduction
[B] Allegro ♩ = 120 (tempo)
[C] motif
A SECTION march strain
[D] * melody
[E] 2nd time only — countermelody
[F] in G major (I)
(key identified in Bb pitch)

B SECTION contrasting melody

(in Bb pitch) [F] in C major (IV) [G] am D⁷♭⁹ G^maj7 em

Copyright © 1978 Salvationist Publishing & Supplies Ltd.

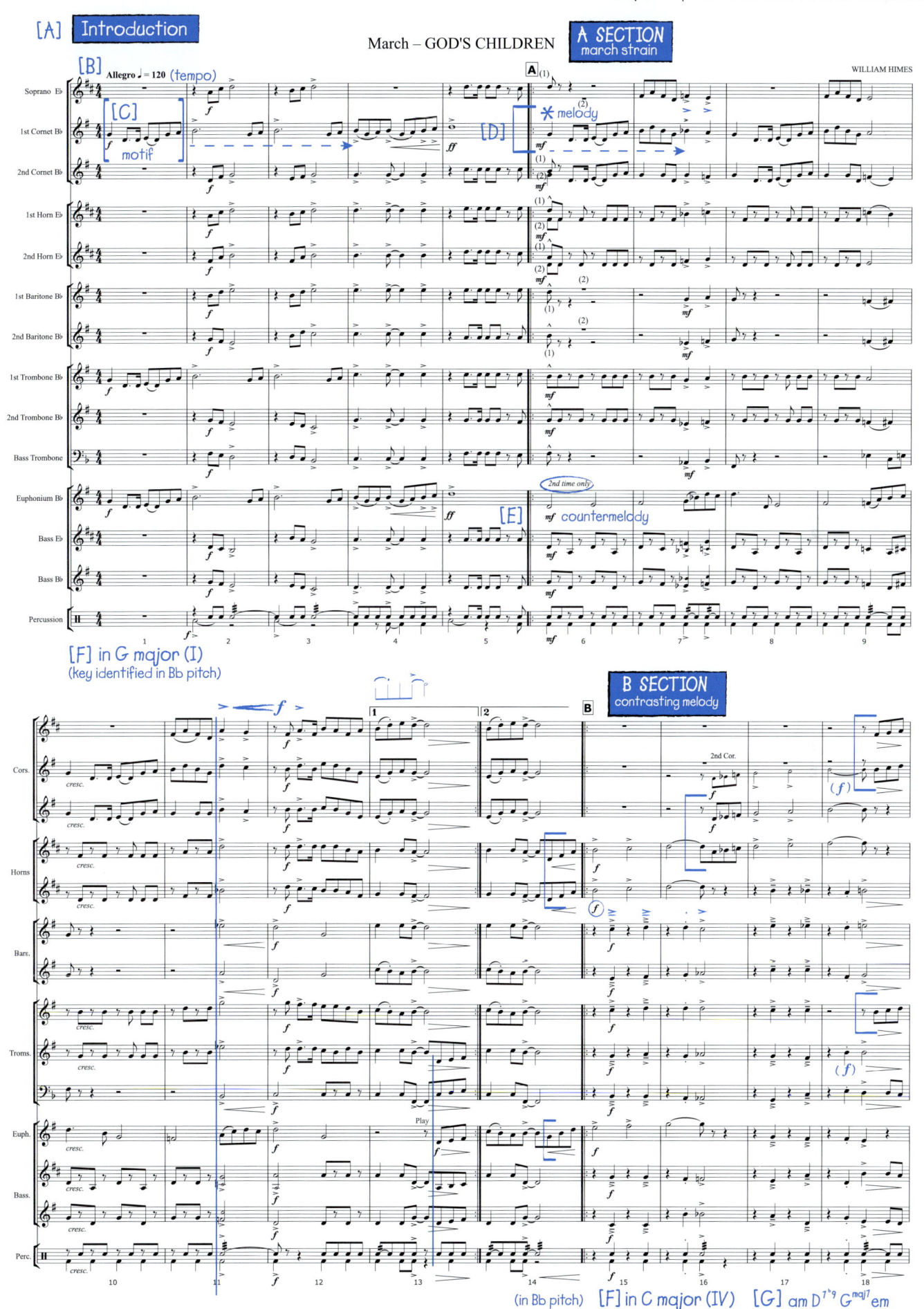

The Beat Goes On

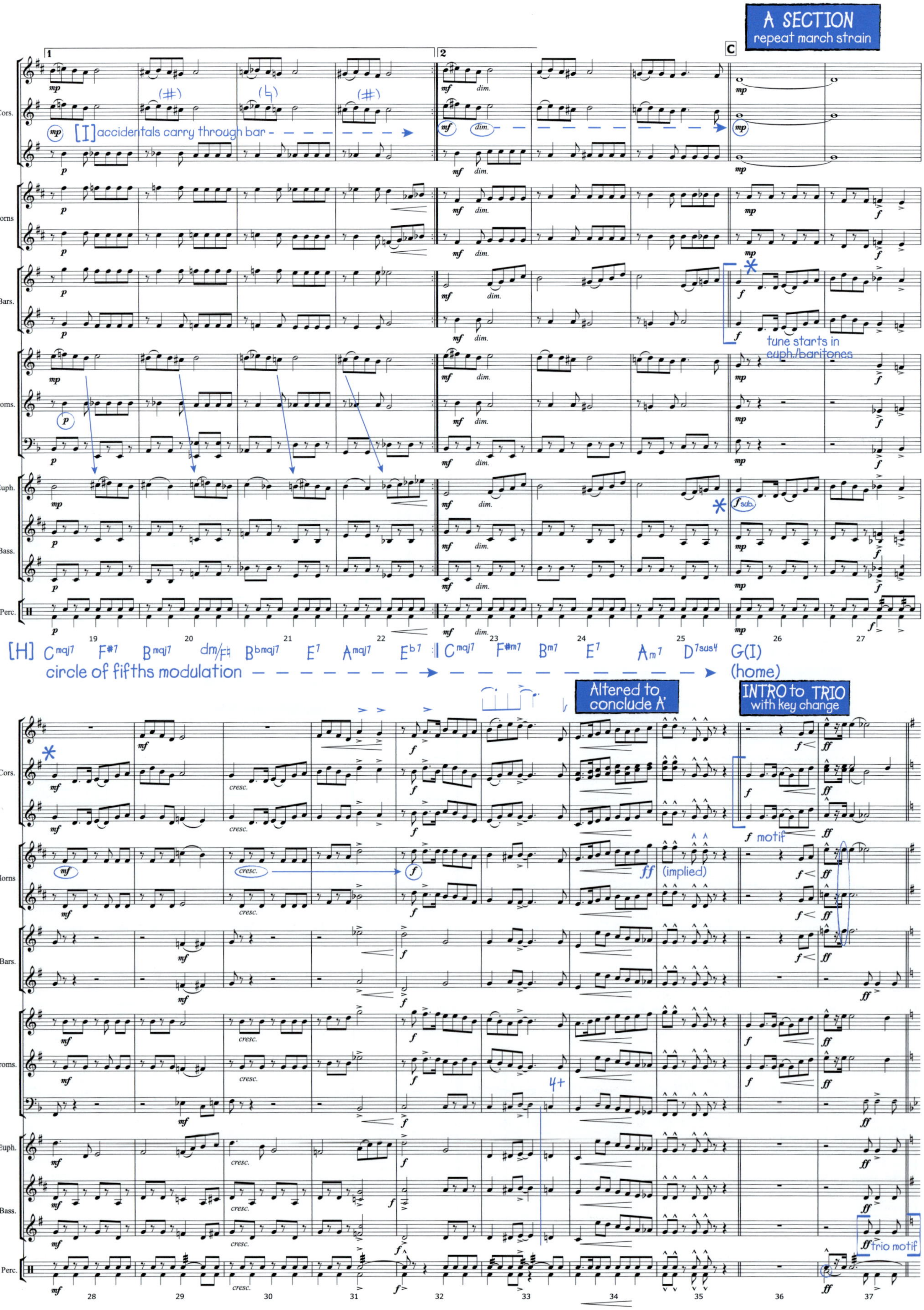
A SECTION
repeat march strain
C
Cors.
Horns
Bars.
Troms.
Euph.
Bass.
Perc.
[I] accidentals carry through bar
tune starts in euph./baritones
[H] Cmaj7 F#7 Bmaj7 dm/F♮ B♭maj7 E7 Amaj7 E♭7 | Cmaj7 F#m7 Bm7 E7 Am7 D7sus4 G(I)
circle of fifths modulation
(home)
Altered to conclude A'
INTRO to TRIO
with key change
motif
(implied)
trio motif

Chapter 11 | FROM SCORE READING TO SCORE STUDY

The Beat Goes On

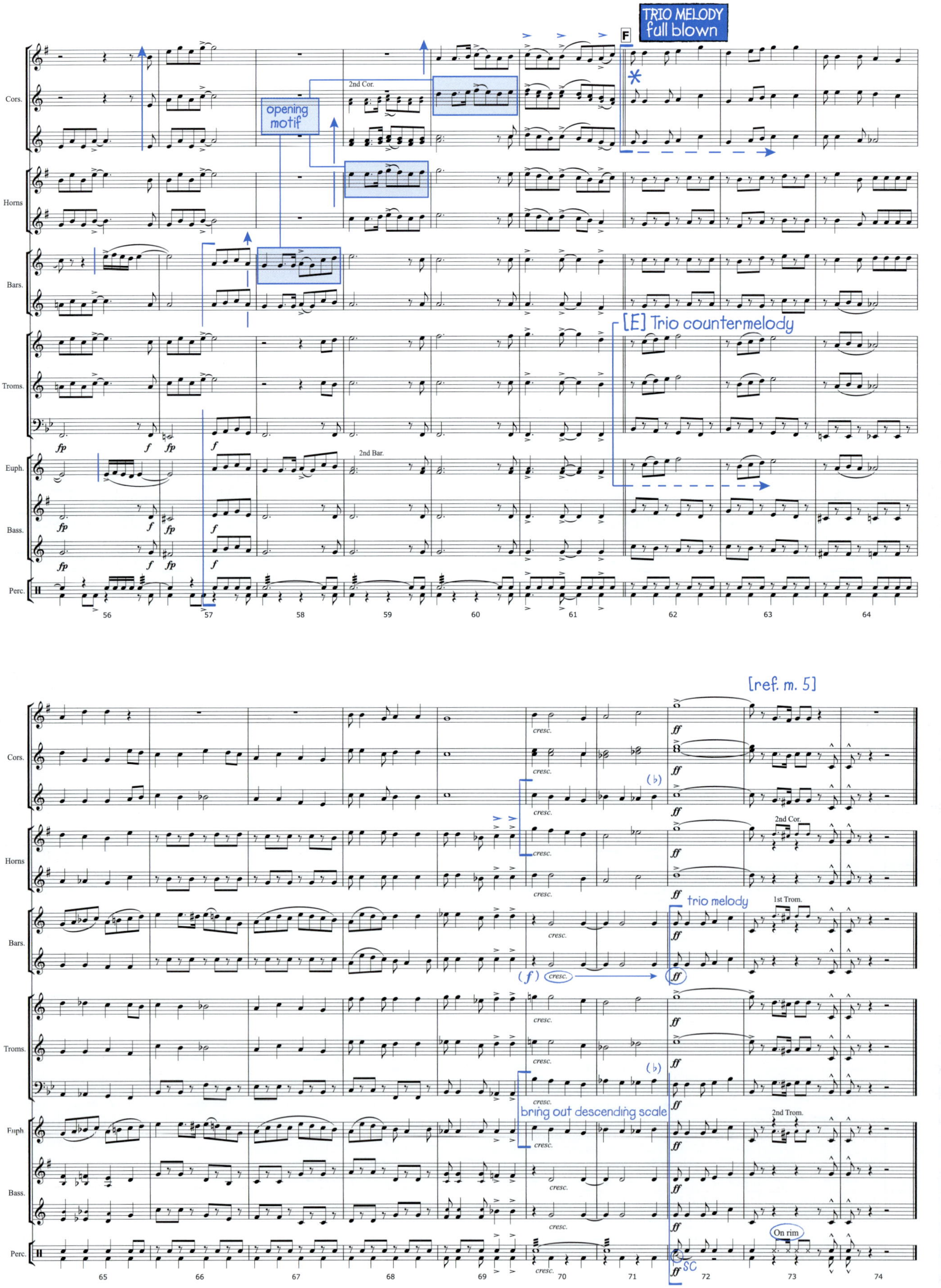
TRIO MELODY full blown
F
Cors.
Horns
Bars.
Troms.
Euph.
Bass.
Perc.
2nd Cor.
opening motif
2nd Bar.
[E] Trio countermelody
56
57
58
59
60
61
62
63
64
[ref. m. 5]
cresc.
ff
2nd Cor.
trio melody
1st Trom.
(f)
bring out descending scale
2nd Trom.
On rim
SC
65
66
67
68
69
70
71
72
73
74

11 BARS REST

1. Play through the march *God's Children* with the score, solely using your inner ear. Be a detective and discover more and more clues to how the composer/arranger shaped the structural, rhythmic, melodic, harmonic, and textual layers to make a convincing whole.

2. Locate two brass pieces that are unfamiliar to you, but hold some future possibility with your ensemble. Begin to score-read these pieces, looking for clues and searching through the layers to reveal the music essence and practical viability.

MARKS ON A SCORE

Moving from Score Reading to Score Study

While engrossed in a cliff-hanger book, we can hardly wait to turn the page, let alone take time to make a note in the margin or underline a passage. The practice of highlighting, marking, or taking notes is usually reserved for instructional books, designed for us to stop, reflect, and take something more from our reading. As school students, we quickly learn that in order to recall important historical or scientific premises, we must re-visit information, and often!

Today, it is unfortunate that a word like *study* conjures up unpleasant memories of scurrying through voluminous amounts of pages in order to pass an exam. The word *study* in its original meaning suggested pausing to contemplate, giving careful and extended consideration and attention to a subject. Musicians even use the term *study* (in French, *étude*) for an exercise designed to practice a point of technique. In order to acquire the skill, an *étude* requires time-consuming attention given to meaningful repetition, embodied in penciled reminders of articulations, dynamics, and phrasing.

Enough re-reading already!

We speak in the Songster Leader Chapter Thirteen of taking our singers past the point of *re-reading* their parts over and over again until they really begin to know and own the essence of a piece of music. Then they require only a peripheral glance at the printed page. The happy result is increased listening and a better sound because faces are out of copies and eyes are engaged on their leader.

For this to happen, leaders of bands, singing companies, songsters, or worship bands must themselves have gone beyond the re-reading stage to the stage of careful, attentive study. As the famous German conductor Hans von Bülow said, "You must have the score in your head and not your head in the score."[3]

One valuable tool for score study is the judicious marking of entrances and essential events in the music. One would never underline every line of a book, such as we did earlier in Score-Reading Exercise #5. But a few (and I emphasize, few) selected highlights can help the conductor maximize attention on what the ensemble is doing, rather than habitually re-reading the score.

"You must have the score in your head and not your head in the score."

The Beat Goes On

Peter Boonshaft describes it this way,

> *A score is like a prompter on an opera stage. When a singer forgets a line the prompter says one word, just enough to refresh the singer's memory. The prompter does not read the entire line. We all know a score should be used as cue cards for rehearsal, not as a script to be read.*[4]

"Always remember that markings made in the score are primarily for the purpose of learning the score."[5]
—Elizabeth Green

Moving on to score study

In the initial stages of score reading, seek to unravel the "big picture" score layers, using sticky notes or an erasable pencil in the score margin. As you home in on the details, don't mark the obvious entrances or, for instance, a full top-to-bottom lineup of dynamics. Use simple symbols, many of which you can personalize for your own quick reference.

As you enter into a rehearsal or a performance, these markings can help in anticipating what is required of you, particularly with cueing entrances and changes in dynamics, expression, and tempo. The markings also aid in your absorbing the score almost well enough to do it by memory. But even more importantly, they suggest time-saving devices, teachable moments, and analogies that engage and give ownership of the music to our ensembles.

My own method of score marking has evolved over the years, and may vary from a few marks to reference notes, according to the difficulty of the piece. I offer below a vocabulary of basic shorthand for effectively marking scores. Remember that there is a "marked" difference (wordplay intended) between markings made on a score that help you follow the score, as opposed to those made for the purpose of learning the score. Your musicians, even the learners, can easily distinguish one from the other. The musical results (and learning curve) prove proportional to the depth of your understanding of the piece. (More on this in Listen and Respond Chapter Twenty-Three.)

Brackets or asterisks

- **An asterisk or bracket at an entrance** indicates that an instrumental part is taking the melody, solo line, or principal theme. Some conductors include the initials for the voice or instrumental part(s) over the bracket.

    Brass instruments shorthand: CNT (cornet) HN (horn) TRB (trombone) BAR (baritone) EUPH (Euphonium) TBA (Tuba)

    Brass parts shorthand: SC (solo cornet), 1C (1st cornet), 2C (2nd cornet), FL (flugel), SH (solo horn) TRB1 (1st trombone), 2B (2nd baritone), E (euphonium), Eb (Eb tuba), Bb (Bb tuba)

    Singers voice parts shorthand: S (soprano), A (alto), T (tenor), B (bass), S2 (soprano 2), T2 (tenor 2)

    Percussion shorthand: SD (snare drum), BD (bass drum), CC (clash cymbals), SC (suspended cymbal), Xyl. (xylophone) Gl. (glockenspiel), Tri. (triangle), TT (tam-tam), HH (hi-hat), Tamb. (tambourine)

- **A vertical bracket** is used to highlight the entrance of a section of the ensemble. The pairing of brackets identifies parts in unisons or octaves, or parts having a similar harmonic or rhythmic profile. [A]

- **A vertical slash** at the end of a phrase is placed at the exact cut-off of the note to indicate that a cue is needed to give a uniform conclusion to the note. [B] This mark is critical to use with concluding hard syllables in vocal music, with an indication of the desired consonant sound above the vertical slash/line.

- **Save valuable rehearsal time** by bracketing the measure numbers of passages that are either repeated or stylistically equivalent [mm. 1-2 = mm. 5-6 and 13-14]. [C] Later indications would vary along the lines of [13-14 = 1-2 and 5-6].

Gospel Song – WHAT A FRIEND

C. C. CONVERSE
Arr. ERIK LEIDZEN

American Band Journal No. 55 © The Salvation Army- New York

Circles, underlines, or highlights

- Conductors **circle or highlight important dynamics or expression** to bring these to their attention. Some enlarge these across the top or middle of the score. Others use red for *forte* or blue for *piano,* or they use different shapes (for instance, a square around *mf,* triangle around *mp* and circle around *pp*). [D]

- **Underline or highlight instructions** for the use of mutes, flutter-tongue, tremolo fingerings, or the abbreviation of a percussion instrument being used. [E]

- **Highlight important tempo or expression changes,** like *Andante* or *dolce.* Note translations of musical expression terms (often in *Italian*) above these terms. [F]

- **Using various shorthand,** vocalists will underline or call out the primary vowels or consonants to be sounded or articulated, including reminders to form round vowels, neutralize or flip r's, etc. (See Chapter Twelve, pp. 258–262 for more on singer's diction.)

Overstriking

- Conductors choose to **reiterate selected** *crescendo* **or** *diminuendo* **hairpins** above or over the printed markings as a way of highlighting their importance. [G]

- **Convert the** *cresc.* **or** *dim.* **abbreviation** to an overstrike of an actual *crescendo* or *diminuendo* hairpin so you can easily see the duration. Indicate the start, peak and finish dynamics for easy reference. [H]

- **Extend an arrow** across long stretches of sustained dynamics to indicate the exact length of either maintaining a dynamic, [I] or the space permitted to complete a *crescendo* or *diminuendo* to a new dynamic. Include counts to measure the climax, or a smooth *diminuendo*. (See example in Chapter Thirteen, p. 268.)

- **Extend a slanted arrow** to show either a *ritard* in tempo or an *accelerando*. [J] Include the start and finish *tempi*. Add counts to help measure a smooth ascent or descent in *tempo*.

- **Note any stylistically appropriate articulation** desired that may not be indicated in the score, like *staccato, accents,* or daylight space between notes. [K]

- **Breath marks** (sometimes shown as checks) and/or **phrase lines** indicate the shape of phrases and the proper place to breathe. [L] Extend an arrow or dotted line to signal carrying the breath across a phrase.

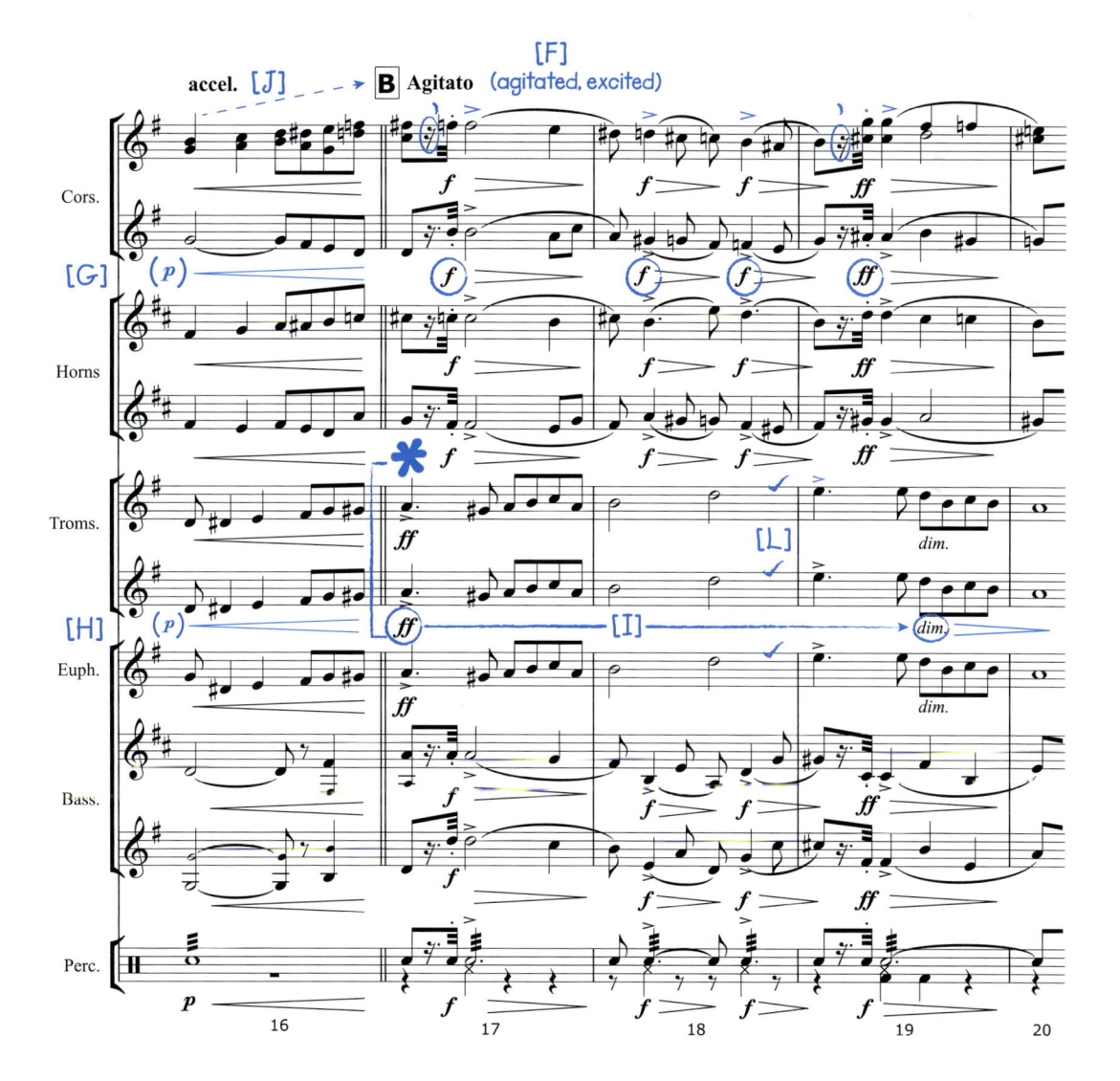

See the Chapter Eleven online folder to view and listen to the full score of *What A Friend* (Erik Leidzén).

Added cues or notes

- At points of dramatic changes in tempo, note in the top margin the old tempo in parentheses, then a slash at the point of the tempo shift, followed by the new tempo indication. [M]

DRAMATIC CHANGE IN TEMPO
Shout Salvation - Mov't. I (Robert Redhead)

- A similar technique can be helpful when the tempo increases to a point where the conductor actually moves from four beats to two per measure (show ♩ = 152 and then 𝅗𝅥 = 76) anticipating a meter change. [N]

SHIFT IN METER PATTERN
Shout Salvation - Mov't. III (Robert Redhead)

- Add notes or cues at page turns [O] or repeats (Ex: back to letter A on page 9) to help negotiate page turns. [P]

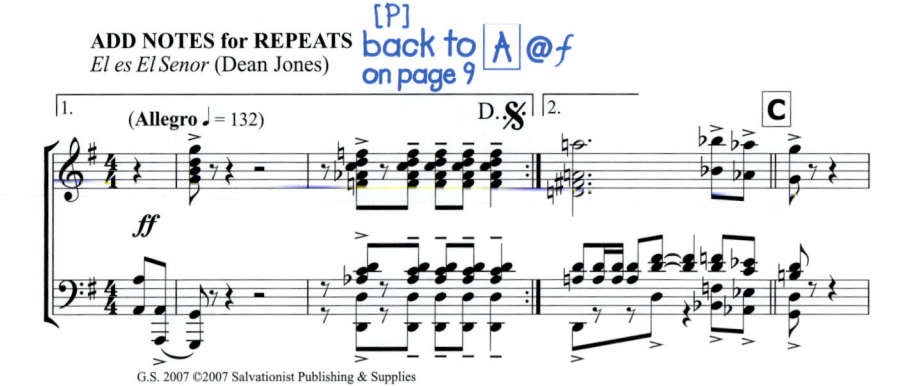

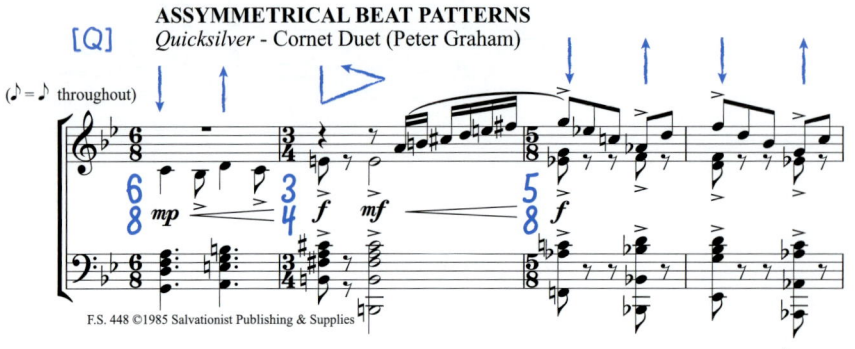

CUE PAGE TURNS
Shout Salvation - Mov't. I (Robert Redhead)

ADD NOTES for REPEATS
El es El Senor (Dean Jones)

- Add a beat pattern symbol or breakdown of beat patterns across the middle or top of the score. [Q]

ASSYMMETRICAL BEAT PATTERNS
Quicksilver - Cornet Duet (Peter Graham)

A MARKED VOCAL SCORE
All for Thee - MS 1976
FRANCES RIDLEY HAVERGAL

All for Thee

PAUL KELLNER

(Sheet music: Andante moderato ♩ = 84, mp)

1. Take my life and let it be Con-se-cra-ted, Lord, to Thee;
4. Take my sil-ver and my gold, Not a mite would I with-hold;

Take my mo-ments and my days, Let them flow in cease-less praise.
Take my in-tel-lect, and use Ev-ry pow'r as Thou shalt choose.

ALL VOICES: HARMONY

2. Take my hands, and let them move At the im-pulse of Thy love; Take my feet, and
5. Take my will, and make it Thine, I(t) shall be no long-er mine; Take my heart, it

let them be Swift and beau-ti-ful for Thee. 3. Take my voice, and let me sing
is Thine own, I(t) shall be Thy roy-al throne. 6. Take my love; my Lord, I pour

Al-ways, on-ly for my King; Take my lips, and let them be
At Thy feet its trea-sure-store; Take my-self and I will be

Filled with mes-sa-ges from Thee. All for Thee, All for Thee.
Ev-er, on-ly, all for Thee.

D.C. rall. e dim.

Copyright © 1976 Salvationist Publishing

See the Chapter Eleven online folder for an audio recording of *All For Thee*.

Score markings by Beatrice Holz, reprinted with permission. International Phonetic Alphabet (IPA) vowel symbols have been used, found in brackets: [a] - bright *ah*, [ɛ] - open *eh*, [ə] - a schwa, as in *about*, [ɔ] - open *oh*, like *aw*, [ʌ] - short *uh* sound, as in *cup*, [u] - pure *oo*. See Appendix 12.2 for more on the International Phonetic Alphabet (IPA). The superscript "r" in m.2 (v.4) and m. 24 (v. 5) indicate that the "r" is not sounded, and the vowel should only be minimally "influenced" by the "r," but primarily be held as a vowel.

SEVEN STEPS AND MARKING A NEW SONG

Seven Steps to Learning a Song, using Chris Mallett's song *Come Home*, were introduced in Chapter Ten, pp. 209-213.

Let's revisit the third verse of Chris Mallett's song *Come Home,* following the seven steps to learning a song, and consider how leaders might mark their vocal scores in preparation for rehearsal. A properly marked score helps anticipate rehearsal and conducting requirements.

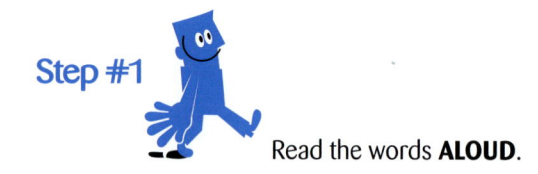

Step #1

Read the words **ALOUD**.

Marking words in your vocal score gives on-the-spot reminders of your best intentions to allow the text to speak clearly. There are opportunities for beautiful vowel color, as well as diction pitfalls, that we mark as a ready reference in rehearsal and performance. Refer to these marked examples:

☑ The tall "O" markings at bar 1 and 5 help us realize a rounded, open "O" sound to begin each phrase.

☑ A slash on the "r" indicates the use of an "ah" vowel, rather than the abrasive "r" sound in the words, like "won-der-ful." (bar 1)

Chapter 11 | FROM SCORE READING TO SCORE STUDY

☑ A small squiggled line (bar 2) acts as a reminder that we want a brief flipped "r" in the word "promised" to make the "r" audible.

☑ The double "o" with the line over it serves as a reminder to enjoy the pure "oo" sound. (bar 3)

☑ Underline the "d" in "sinned" (bar 5) as a reminder to enunciate the "d" before commencing the "h" of "He."

Steps #2 & #3

TAP or **CLAP** the rhythm of the melody. Read the words **ALOUD** again in the **CORRECT RHYTHM.**

☑ The basic rhythmic pattern is:
Long ____, short–short, Long ____, short–short.
Add a bit of a rhythmic lilt by giving emphasis to beats one and three, suggested by the underlined numbers **1** and **3** (bar 1).

☑ This basic rhythmic pattern is repeated over three bars before the phrase ending with a dotted half note. The counting "Me–2–3–Off" is noted in bars 4 and 8 to place the release at the start of beat four.

Step #4

Sing the **MELODY** in correct rhythm (preferably without the piano).

☑ Looking first at the men's harmony part, notice that their line moves *by step* over a range limited to *just four notes* with the exception of an *initial skip of a third*.

☑ The highlighted differences in pitch in the men's part in bars 3–4 versus bars 7–8 will have to be rehearsed. Remember the word "rehearse" means "re-hear," so don't be afraid to repeat these bars to lock in the differences.

☑ Looking next at the women's part melody, begin by learning the two *sixth* intervals in bars 1 and 2. The interval of the sixth can be correctly identified by counting up six from the "D" (**1**–2–3–4–5–**6**) or by singing from *do* to *la* in *solfege* (**do**–re–mi–fa-sol–**la**). Memory of the beginning of the first phrase should easily secure the identical initial notes of the second.

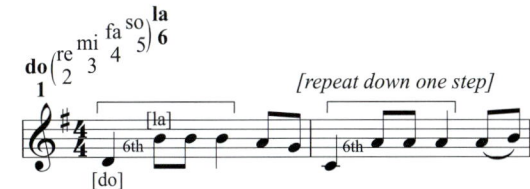

☑ Commencing on beat 4 of mm. 1 and 5 of the women's part, there is a sequence of four notes (A-G-C-A) that may prove tricky as a melodic sequence, and perhaps should be taught as an isolated group. Since this note grouping begins and ends on the note "A," the line extended from the "A" on the fourth beat to the "A" on beat two in the next bar, helps reinforce aural recollection of the first "A" (bars 5-6).

The Beat Goes On

239

- ☑ As with the men's part, with the women's part, compare and plan to rehearse the *differences* in bars 3–4 and bars 7–8.

- ☑ A *tenuto* line is indicated under the initial low note in bars 1 and 5 to suggest that emphasis be given to this initial low note (requiring more air to sound), which helps propel the melody through the phrase.

- ☑ Although the melody might be rendered in two four-bar phrases, the repeated words "promised" and "pardon" suggest an added breath mark between them (bars 2–3 and bars 6–7).

The demonstration and accompaniment audio files for *Come Home* are found in the Chapter Ten online folder.

Steps #5 & #6

Have the accompaniment played while you **LISTEN. SING** the melody with the complete accompaniment.

- ☑ As mentioned earlier, the voice parts are clearly a part of the right hand of the piano part with a lilting broken chord *arpeggiation* in the left hand.

- ☑ Link the initial piano note in bar 1 to the men's entrance, as it is actually the men's harmony note, but sounding an octave higher.

Step #7

MEMORIZE!

- ☑ Focus on the first words of each line as a means of remembering the remainder of the line. For example, *"O for the wonderful … carries on into "love he has promised." and "Though we have sinned ... leads to … he has mercy..."* The repeat of *"promised"* and *"pardon"* also aids the memorization, both times finishing with *"… for you and for me."*

- ☑ Memorize also as a conductor, with the breaths in the exact place. Actually sing the ends of phrases as "Me-2-3-off." If conductors are going to ask their groups to memorize songs, it follows that a well-prepared songster leader has studied enough to sing *all* parts almost from memory.

Don't forget to retrace your STEPS often.

11 BARS REST

Three more score-reading exercises

Imagining an isolated part: When studying scores, follow the trail of an isolated part, adding proper phrasing and other interpretative dimensions. Mark the part as though you were the instrumentalist or singer in that section of the ensemble. Consciously put yourself in an unfamiliar role. For instance, become a bass singer if you are a female, a trombonist if you play a cornet. Pretend you are the accompanist or one of the percussionists. Internally imagine yourself playing or singing that part all the way through, including counting rests (which conductors rarely have to do).

Listening, African style: In a reverse exercise, listen to a recording and attempt to follow, imagine, and visualize an isolated part all the way through a piece. Some African Salvationists listen exclusively to their parts and then try to replay them from memory.

Making score study as natural as reading a book: Read and study all kinds of vocal or brass scores. Try to identify the structural, rhythmic, melodic, harmonic, and text layers. Consider where markings would aid you as a conductor in the translation of the imaginary score into an accurate and pleasing reality.

SCORE STUDY RESOURCES

An Invitation to Band Arranging, Erik Leidzén (Presser)
Colour and Texture in the Brass Band, Ray Steadman-Allen (Salvationist Publishing)
Composers on Composing for Band, *Volumes 1 & 2* (GIA)
Guide to Score Study for the Wind Band, Frank Battisti and Robert Garafalo (Meredith Music)
On Becoming a Conductor, Frank Battisti (Meredith Music)
Precision Conducting, Timothy Sharp (Roger Dean)
Teaching Music with Passion, Peter Boonshaft (Meredith Music)
The Study of Orchestration, Samuel Adler (Norton)

```
Hey Harold,
I guess it's a good idea to read & mark scores,
but when do I get to conduct 4 real?
Itching2Go

Dear Itching2Go
Don't miss more VIP tips on score study for
leaders in Chaps 13-15. We did introduce beat
patterns at the end of Chap 5. We finally conduct
4 real in Chaps 20-22. C U there!
Harold
```

CHAPTER TWELVE

AWAKE MY VOICE AND SING!
The Songster Leader

Make us see our little company as a member of the great Christian Church on earth, and help us willingly and gladly to join our singing, be it feeble or good, to the song of the Church. —Dietrich Bonhoeffer, *Life Together*

MOMENT BY MOMENT

Physics teaches us that when a solitary voice joins another voice at the same pitch, the frequency of sound waves per second increases twofold. We need not empirically confirm this; we have experienced it! When we blend our voice with the one next to us there is a mystical connection, *spirit to spirit*. The physical sensation of sound creates a spiritual union. In music, two voices may sound simultaneously, each one expressing itself to the fullest. Yet at the same time the singers listen and respond to one another. Robert Shaw once wrote, "You can't see the voice, you can't touch it, you frequently have to depend on someone else even to hear it."[1] The exchange with voices around us, while inherently intangible, evolves into a tangible shared experience. Such is the essence of the choral art.

We would be hard-pressed to believe that William Booth, the Founder of The Salvation Army and a songwriter himself, did not comprehend the natural beauty of uniting voices in song. Booth, like Wesley, placed great value on the subliminal absorption of doctrinal truths through the singing of words. However, in an address to the fledging Christian Mission, Booth poured scorn on "buying a musical machine and getting some half-taught schoolgirl or ungodly musician to play it," and on "selecting a few people, converted or unconverted… to lead the congregation just because they happen accidentally to have melodious voices." He famously quipped: "I have found choirs to be possessed of three devils…the quarreling devil, the dressing devil and the courting devil."[2]

Through the combination of some unfortunate experiences with choirs and the Founder's "mistaken idea that voices singing in combination could not make the words to be heard distinctly," for a considerable time Booth limited singing to solos and congregational song. With due attention to enunciation, the Fry Family, the "Singing, Speaking and Praying Brigades" organized by Herbert Booth, and then the blending of Salvation Army words with national airs by delegates to the International Congress of 1886, paved the way for the establishment of songster brigades.[3]

Corporate song has fascinated choristers, composers, conductors, and listeners over millennia and, in the end, Booth heartily embraced its unifying power. The words of Salvationist pioneer William Pearson capture this conviction: "We will sing…till the world is full of joy…We will sing and shout till the Master comes." Singing is the language of children and angels alike. As Longfellow put it:

> God sent His singers upon the earth
> With songs of sadness and of mirth,
> That *they might touch the hearts of men,*
> And bring them back to Heaven again.[4]

In **Chapter Twelve**, we:

- learn how to link hearts and voices through an effective songster rehearsal.
- examine warm-up strategies and diction considerations.
- consider the impact of praise choruses and Gospel music on the worshiping songster brigade.

Singing, Speaking and Praying Brigade (1886)
Includes Richard Slater (holding violin), B/M Fred Fry (upper right), and 21 year old future General, Miss Eva Booth (to the right of the woman holding the infant)

When just right, the experience goes beyond a linking of hearts and voices. The singular, yet concerted effort to articulate words, pitches, rhythm, expression, and meaning marks the *moment*. Even in an age of ever-present technology, the music really only exists in that moment. The work of the singer is to be fully engaged in that moment. The work of the choral conductor is to create those *moments* of transcendence and connection.

THE WORSHIPING CHOIR

Choirs have been leading worship for a least a millennium! From the flanked rows of cathedral choristers to the massed vocal forces of revival crusades to the simplest village chapel choir, voices in chorus have led and introduced "new song." The birthing of Salvation Army songster brigades was deferred in part because the Founder was not interested in "music for music's sake," as he had observed it in many church choirs. Richard Slater, known as the father of Salvation Army music, strove for an inclusiveness that allowed every Salvationist the opportunity to make a contribution and particularly that the music was always to be "for the glory of God." In the words of Colonels Gwen and Robert Redhead, this became a hallmark of the Army's "free-giving of service for the Lord."[5]

Looking back in church history, as the liturgical mass was established, it was the supporting choir that guided the congregation through the Mass's variegated landscape. Protestant reformers strove to bring the Word in song onto the lips of the people, and choirs led the new hymn and psalm settings. Composers began to create music to bridge elements of the service. A varied stream of choral offerings from responses, motets, and anthems became moments of reflection for the congregation. These offerings aspired to great beauty, an artistry offered to the glory of God. In The Salvation Army, the choir anthem became known as the songster message or songster selection and was consistently positioned before the sermon.

In the past century, a huge music publishing industry has advanced the stand-alone choir anthem. For church holidays, the choir might transform the entire service into music, for which the cantatas of Bach and the oratorios of Handel are the formidable precedents. Whether it was with a Sunday songster selection or an Easter cantata, choirs traversed toward a performance mode, which meant that we were not far from the Founder's genuine concern that Army music-making would become "music for music's sake." Not unlike some Salvation Army bands, some songster brigades began to adopt a "take-it-or-leave-it" approach to their songster message. A cartoon in a Christian magazine some years ago showed announcement boards fronting two churches set next to each other. The first read, "We care about you." The second read, "Yes, but we've got better music." How many of us have frequented a church or corps solely for the quality of the music? The beautiful architecture, acoustics, warm fellowship, or the speaking are a bonus, but it is far better to focus on where the real ministry is taking place.

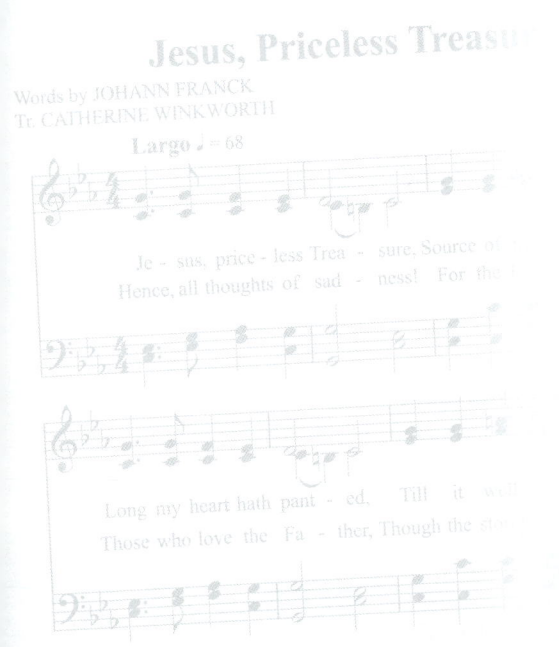

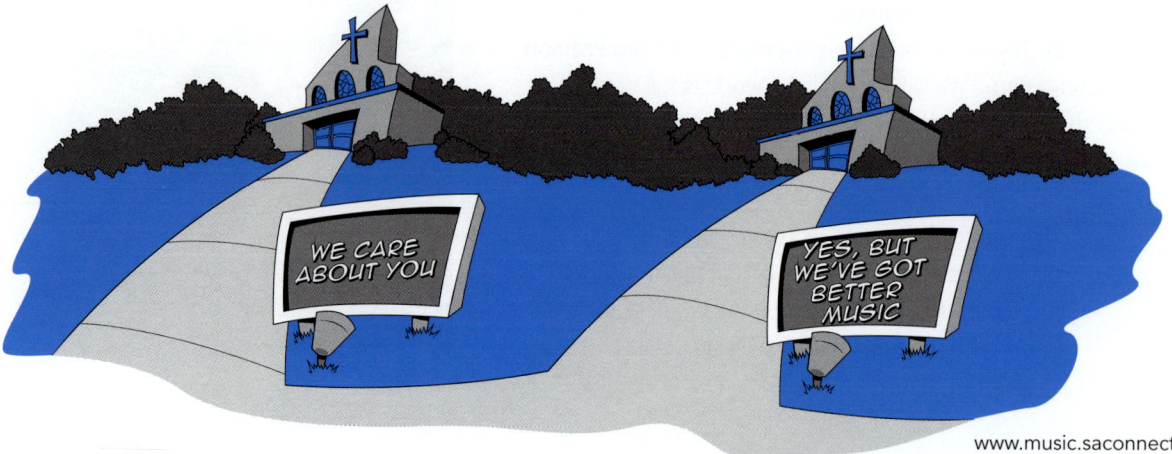

The impact of praise choruses

With the first seedlings of pop-based worship choruses, church choirs that had long ago relinquished leadership of congregational song ironically greeted this "new song" with suspicion, or in some cases, even angst. Many predicted that the existence of publishers and the choirs who consumed their materials would wane. As demand would have it, publishers who couldn't beat them, joined them. They began to publish more pop-driven arrangements, especially choral settings of the new genre "worship choruses." The occasional quote of an established hymn crossed the developing cultural divide and sanctioned the piece approvingly as "blended worship." In a dramatic about-face, many sacred publishers began to release spectacular hymn *concertato* settings (in which the florid backing tracks proved handy). They allowed the choir, organ, and/or accompaniment track to engage the congregation in four verses of a "classic" hymn. At nearly the same time, Salvation Army songster brigades were relieved of the earlier restrictions on their use of "outside" sacred publications.

The impact of Gospel choirs

Another important strand in the transformation of church choirs and songster brigades sprang from the black Gospel tradition. It was surprising in the early nineties to enter an Army hall in Scandinavia and see the platform strewn with microphones and a supporting cast of keyboard, bass guitar, and drum kit ready to accompany. Two or three singers would wrap themselves around a microphone, allowing a remix with reverberant effects. Rather than the choir sound emanating from the platform, the sound mix was consciously dispersed throughout the worship space.

The Reverend Martin Luther King, Jr. often noted that, eleven o'clock on Sunday morning is the most racially segregated hour of the week in America. Certainly a hallmark of the black church tradition resides in its joy of singing. With hardly a reference to the African-American hymnal resting in the pew, a hymn, essentially learned through extensive repetitions, erupts spontaneously, along with its characteristic clapping and movement. One observes a unique battery of signals from the song leader and pianist. A jazz-based array of chord substitutions and syncopated rhythms give Gospel music its instantly recognizable color.

No doubt one line of tension is the freedom in Gospel offerings from the tyranny of the page. Many well-known Gospel songwriters hardly read music, and train their choirs in parts by rote. Those used to clutching a piece of music find assimilating and moving to the Gospel-style music difficult, if not uncomfortable. Reynolds Chapman suggests that these songs are important because they are the "annals of the black church." Encapsulated within each song is "the story of God's faithfulness to the black church" which touches the history of that culture and the individual's own journey and travail.[6] When things are right, there is a uniting surge toward a climax, which can seem to outsiders at least one repetition too many! The song peaks when the congregation seems to be mystically linked to the song of their ancestors. Dietrich Bonhoeffer, who frequented churches in Harlem, describes this experience in *Life Together*: "It is not you that sings, it is the Church that is singing, and you, as a member of the church, may share in its song ... Thus all singing together ... serves to widen our spiritual horizon." A Salvationist might describe it, in the Founder's words, as "touching the wave."

Even in places where reconciliation may not seem apparent, Gospel music transcends cultural barriers. Today, hardly a chapel or sanctuary is without a *djembe*, which has a deep historical connection to African hand drumming. Its insistent pulsing is an audible emblem of the worship song in our day, mirroring the beat of the bass drum associated with marches and open airs in former generations.

The worshiping choir in action

Cross-pollinating the accessible contemporary offerings of the worship band with the freedom of song rooted in black church tradition has aroused many choir directors to again engage congregations in song. Sidestepping the performance agenda revives the notion of God's people—choir and congregation—coming into His holy presence. Shifting the onus of song leadership over to the choir also takes the attention off a solitary worship leader. The inherent temptation to evaluate that individual's approach, choices, or musicality can distract us from centering our worship. The worship-leading choir reflects the congregation, with its multiple expressions and emotions filtered through the sentiment of the song.

In response to these trends, some songster leaders opt to sing exclusively arrangements of contemporary worship music. In some ways, the engagement with the congregation is through familiarity. In concert settings, these choirs pursue a process of pre-engagement, where a greeting, humor, heartfelt testimonies, and interviews break down barriers. Through their stories, the audience begins to see songster members as real people with stories like their own. A songster brigade should constantly be asking how and what to communicate.

One Australian Salvationist advocate of the worshiping choir, Eastern Territorial Songster Leader Gavin Whitehouse, speaks of having the songsters expand on what has transpired in the praise and worship segment.[7] This means the songster leader is making choices of worship songs to engage the congregation and consciously meet them where they are. Fans of American football can liken this to the running back seeing a momentary crease in the blocking in front of him and seizing the opening. The songster leader attentively looks for openings for God to work in the songsters and congregation alike.

Another view, identified in Chapter One as worship evangelism (p.37), looks at our increasingly multicultural society in which music and language the world over is accessible nearly instantaneously "24/7." Exposure through the media to other cultures and traditions colors our worldview and, ultimately, our faith-view. The musical backdrop to television advertising today can run the gamut from Gregorian chant to swing to snippets of Mozart. In our digital age, audiences are conditioned to switch channels or to tune out at will. The momentary sound bite is the cultural inclination. The only chance for in-depth listening seems to require judicious use of multimedia. Considering all these accessible distractions, training a choir to present the widest possible range of styles should easily expand the chances of making an audience connection. Different combinations of voices, soloists, and introductions help maintain a thriving energy between these offerings. We can dither about the devil having all the best tunes or our taking them back, but for centuries, music of all kinds has called us to worship.

Chapter 12 | AWAKE MY VOICE AND SING!

Major Len Ballantine describes a "worship-leading choir as a people-present ministry which is intentional, rooted in a calling to make music ministry—real ministry. We are not watching a choreographed musical event ... We are participating in a worship experience. We are not spectators, but witnesses to a human connection—a warm and personable face to match the face of Jesus being lifted in song."[8] Eugene Peterson paraphrases the biblical directive this way: "Allow the Word of Christ to have the run of the house. Give it plenty of room in your hearts as you sing your hearts out to God." (Colossians 3:15–16, *The Message*)

12 BARS REST

1. Do you (or your songsters) feel your personal music-making enhances or takes away from the quality of weekly worship?

2. Do you (or your songsters) feel a performance pressure? Does this performance factor tend to detract from the quality of worship?

3. Do you feel that some of your music-making is more entertainment than the stuff that enhances worship?

4. Do your concerts or worship services feel authentic or are you "playing at church"? What steps can move the songsters toward transcendence in worship?

5. For practical vocal technique tips which will aid the Worshiping Choir, see pp. 415-419 in Chapter Nineteen on Worship Band leadership.

LINKING HEARTS AND VOICES

The effective songster rehearsal

A songster leader who prepares well can approach a rehearsal confident that his or her group will not only be ready for Sunday but will also grow together and enjoy the experience. Pray for the group's unity and focus, the message of the songs, each member, your rehearsal objectives, upcoming Sundays and performances, and particularly for the quietness of God's spirit to permeate each moment together.

Prep time

Give two hours of your prep time to each hour of rehearsal. Take time to make a game plan. Prioritize and then measure, by estimating rehearsal time required, the extent to which your objectives can be accomplished. As the leader, you should memorize text, music, repeats, and overall form. Create visuals to aid the choir's learning curve. Share your plan with your accompanist. Most passages are best introduced by your modeled pitches and rehearsed *a cappella*. The piano, with its inherent percussiveness and intonation inconsistencies, is not always helpful to singers. If using accompaniment tracks, employ them sparingly during rehearsal. When the group is ready to rehearse with the track, be sure each track is easily cued and ready.

The Beat Goes On

Dear Marvelous Singers,

Great connection on Sunday!

For this week, ladies are asked to memorize verse one and men on verse two. All voices, please, on verse three.

It may help to first learn the rhymed pairs that end each line:

- *Lord rhymes with reward,*
- *require with inspire,*
- *command with hand,*
- *and foe with go.*

Luv,
Harold

Have objectives
Raise the expectations for your songster brigade by stating your objectives and affirming progress step by step. Periodically, explain where the group is heading, sharing the long-range picture, especially with large-scale works or a big concert on the horizon. Always give a brief bit of homework; for instance, "Please memorize the words to the chorus." This can be accomplished by the songsters en route to rehearsal and reinforced by an email reminder of the text.

Folders ready
When the songsters enter the room, folders should be ready. Too much time is lost when the occasional octavo does not make it into the folder. If you do not have mailboxes that can be used for each songster, give out the stack of new music with names noted, so it is easy to identify anyone who did not get the new titles at the end of rehearsal. If significant musical cuts or departures with text and diction will be made, then list these on a separate handout, and provide pencils to mark their copies accordingly. This "luv note" might include aids to memorization or warm-up preparations based on trouble spots within the music.

Honor the singer's time
All of this readiness signals your intention to honor songsters' time and speed the learning curve. Insist on punctuality. ("On time is late.") Begin and conclude on time. It is a matter of mutual respect and focus to insure that chatter does not waste time. If the conductor values the songsters' time, in exchange the songsters will put more value on that time, thereby improving the overall experience. Keep the business in the background by emailing announcements or writing them on the board in the rehearsal room.

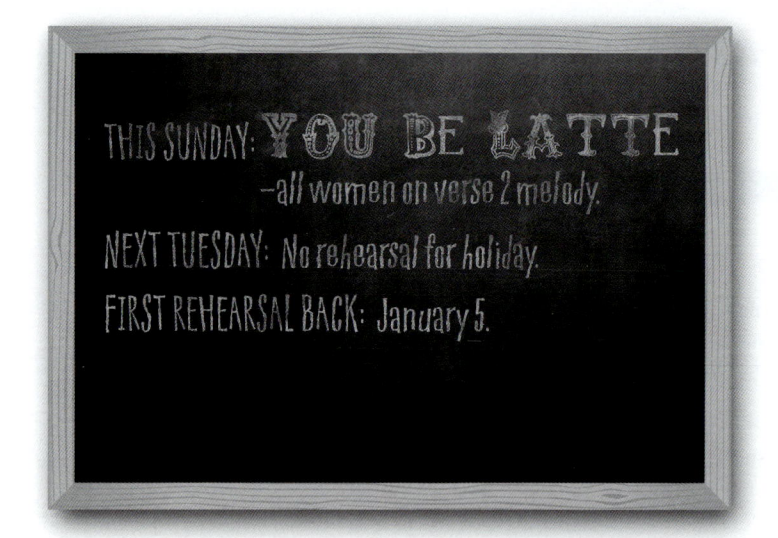

THIS SUNDAY: YOU BE LATTE
—all women on verse 2 melody.
NEXT TUESDAY: No rehearsal for holiday.
FIRST REHEARSAL BACK: January 5.

Prepare the room
If possible, rehearse in a workable, pleasant surrounding with minimal distractions. Flexible seating allows a group to face into each other and see and hear better. Be sure the room temperature, ventilation, lighting, and acoustics are optimal. An overheated room makes for a sluggish rehearsal. Avoid carpets where possible, as they absorb the reverberation. The conductor should dress for success. Wear something comfortable, yet dignified, to convey your authority. Bright colors convey an upbeat energy. Your choristers will copy your posture, breathing, and expression. While most of the rehearsal will take place standing, make opportunities to stretch, sit, and move about.

Make music
In rehearsal, it is helpful for the conductor to vocalize starting pitches or demonstrate passages. Once in flight, don't sing along. Instead, listen to the actual sound of the songster brigade. Roam the room as you listen. As discussed in Chapter Twenty-Three on rehearsal preparation, begin and end rehearsal with familiar repertoire. The goal is to make music in rehearsal, so for tough spots, it is more productive to learn notes in a sectional. Knotty spots may require a "strive-and-come-back-later" strategy. Too much time with an isolated passage or section of the brigade can detour the trajectory of your rehearsal.

Don't talk, sing!

Remember that songsters are volunteers. Keep a firm rein on your tongue. Avoid pontifications. Choristers learn more by doing than by hearing explanations. Keep moving, avoid tangents, yet be precise. *Give no more than two instructions at a time.* Having your music and words memorized ahead of time allows you to keep consistent eye-to-eye contact with your singers. Encourage teamwork and give attention to all sections of the songster brigade. An audio or video recording of your rehearsal will reveal if you are talking too much or too fast. The playback allows you to observe the effectiveness of your teaching techniques, your demeanor, and the pace of the rehearsal.

Be flexible

It takes preparation and skill to maximize time in rehearsal by getting the pace right. A fine balance exists between setting good patterns of learning and sticking to your plan, while also keeping everyone interested and engaged. Occasionally, mood, the pace of learning, or external circumstances can dictate a change in direction. With experience, the conductor learns to confidently deviate from the plan and redeem the time, often for the better.[9]

Songster Leader Gavin Whitehouse in rehearsal.

12 BARS REST

1. Evaluate the effectiveness of a recent choir rehearsal you led. Catalog for yourself the moments or techniques used in the rehearsal that really worked, as well as those that may have failed. Assess the pace and overall results.

2. Sketch a rehearsal plan for an impending concert list. Strategize carefully to create flow, variety, and an effective pace.

Lots more on **rehearsal planning** in Chapter Twenty-Three

IT'S ALL IN THE WARM-UP! (Well, almost all)

A fine choral performance can be the result of wise repertoire selection, skillful rehearsal management, and the giftedness of the ensemble. Many times, however, the path to a successful, communicative performance is established in the vocal warm-up. To aid listening and attention to the conductor, warm-ups are learned by rote and sung from memory.[10]

International Staff Songster Leader Dorothy Nancekievill in action.

Relax in the voice

Life is full of anxieties. Members of volunteer ensembles are coming from various stresses of work, home, and school. Choral conductors seek to alleviate these stresses, at least for the time of rehearsal, through the enjoyable release of singing. A proper vocal warm-up gives a physical start to the rehearsals and helps establish focus. Singing is not always understood to be a physical activity. We wouldn't consider entering into a strenuous athletic match without stretching. Reaches, stretching, shoulder rubs, and head and shoulder rolls to preface singing help relax the body. Establish a warm-up routine that allows the individual to lose themselves in their singing instrument before diving into repertoire. The inclusion of physical gestures and movement in the warm-up sequence help the singers to relax in the voice as they move from "just" singing toward "beautiful sound."[11]

The Beat Goes On

Listening around

Many characteristics of quality group singing are dependent on learning to listen "chorally" to one's own voice and the voices of those around us. Singers who do not blend tend to hear only themselves, while timid voices tend to lose themselves in the surrounding sound. Placement of sections and sitting more in the round, rather than in rows, encourages listening. There are various schools of thought ranging from using quartet groups in mixed formations to sections across a row. The warm-up is an excellent place to establish the balance between "personal space" and the "corporate objective." To develop listening partnerships, rehearse in the formations in which you will perform.

CHOIR FORMATIONS
to promote balance and
• LISTENING AROUND •

SSSSAAAATTTTBBBB — Promotes easy cueing by section and equal access for all parts to the audience.

SSSSTTTTBBBBAAAA — Placing the men between the sopranos and altos promotes stronger intonation and helps the inexperienced altos hold their part.

SSssaaAAttTTbbBB — Voices that tend to dominate (soprano I, alto II, tenor I and bass II) are in the back and voices that need enhancement (soprano II, alto I, tenor II and bass I) are placed in the front.

BBBBSSSSAAAATTTT — Men's voices tend to be louder than women's. By putting men behind the women, the overall sound will be more homogenized. Soprano and bass are still in close proximity to aid intonation.

SSSSBBBBTTTTAAAA — Weakest section front and center.

Lots more on **"listening around"** in Chapter Twenty-Three, pp. 505–508.

Think, breathe, sing

Proper posture and breathing are best managed in the warm-up. From this starting point we can reinforce posture throughout the rehearsal. When not standing for rehearsal, singers should sit close to the front of the chair, with either one or both legs flat on the floor in front of them. The other leg can be back, under the chair. Remember that holding music tends to drag the head down. Encourage singers with folders to keep their chins level, in line with the conductor as well as their music. Given opportunity, singers will choose to slouch, which hampers proper breath support. Insufficient "fuel" for singing—that is, a lack of air—yields a strained, breathy sound. Proper breathing permits a free, resonant tone.

THINK
Imagine the music

BREATHE
Quiet and deep

SING
Controlled air stream

Chapter 12 | AWAKE MY VOICE AND SING!

Good singing posture STANDING

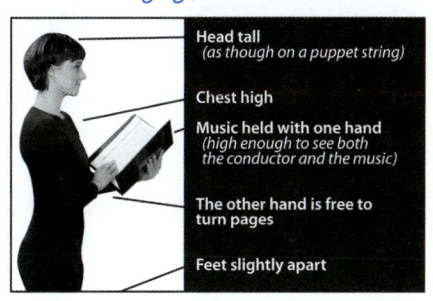

- Head tall (as though on a puppet string)
- Chest high
- Music held with one hand (high enough to see both the conductor and the music)
- The other hand is free to turn pages
- Feet slightly apart

Good singing posture SITTING

- Sit tall, away from the back of the chair
- Never rest elbows on knees while singing
- Feet flat on floor, one slightly in front of the other

The direct correlation of the conductor's own body backdrop, posture, and breath to the resultant choral sound is considered in Chapter Twenty, pp. 439–441.

We train our singers to THINK, (that is, to get an aural picture of what they will sing), BREATHE (quiet and deep), and then SING (with a controlled air stream). Too often we mix up the sequence, or worse, skip a step. The pipe in front of the throat is the trachea, also called the windpipe. A quiet breath encourages a relaxed, low larynx. Aim for the sensation of all sounds feeling spacious, high and forward. A harsh, edgy sound usually emanates from not singing "on the breath." This means that the sounding of the pitch within the vocal cords, the resonance around it, and the air stream are not integrated.

Commence most warm-ups in the upper part of a comfortable mid-range and move upward by half step. Use descending patterns, intentionally bringing the quality of tone of the head-voice mix down. (Refer to footnote 3 of Chapter Seven for an explanation of the head-voice mix.) Starting at a lower pitch and moving upward usually results in forcing a less desirable chest-voice tone. Singers can feel a proper head mix vibration by placing the heel of the hand on their forehead.

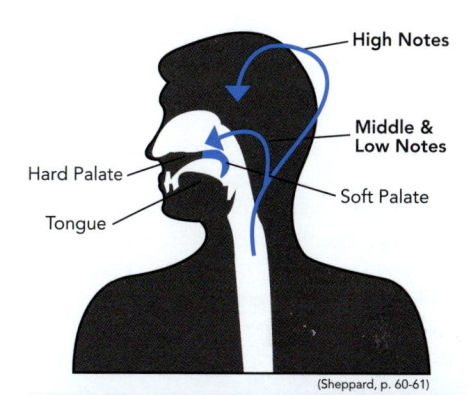

(Sheppard, p. 60-61)

IMAGES TO MAINTAIN VERTICAL THROAT POSITION

HIGH NOTES:
Picture the sound traveling in the shape of a question mark around the back and top of your head.

MIDDLE AND LOW NOTES:
Picture the sound traveling across the roof of your mouth rather than out of your mouth.

ROSES:
Imagine inhaling the scent of roses to lift the soft palate to an appropriate height according to pitch.

APPLE:
Imagine that you are biting into an apple to lift the upper jaw.

Unify vowels

The very heart of great choral sound and blend is *consistent vowel production*. Preliminary work on vowels saves valuable rehearsal time later. With an "oo" vowel, the tip of the tongue touches the back of the bottom teeth and feels forward in the mouth. The lips form a slightly rounded "oo" shape and the sound should feel high and forward. The conductor is encouraged to adapt a hand gesture to reinforce the shape, sound, and blend desired for each vowel.[12]

The "ee" vowel proves more troublesome, as it can sound spread and strident. To avoid a pinched, child-like sounding vocal color, we suggest the imagery of a north-south facial orientation, rather than a wide east-west smile. Physically the "ee' vowel forms a forward arch in the tongue, with the tip of the tongue still touching the back of the bottom teeth. We can avoid the spread east-west sound by encouraging the choir to

"OO" Jaw relaxed and down with lips out and loose. Form a pure "oo" with a tiny "oh" on the lips.

"OO" Warm-up Hand Motion: Fingers and thumb pull an imaginary "oo" straight out from lips.

Good north-south "EE" formed with an "ee" inside and an "oo" on the lips, thinking vertically.

"EE" Warm-up Hand Motion: Pinch two fingers and thumb and pull the sound smoothly up, out of top of the head.

Spread east-west "ee" (not good for choral singing).

The Beat Goes On

"AH" Think "aw" with a relaxed, dropped jaw to avoid spreading the vowel.

"OH" Form a pure round "o" on the lips.

"EH" Think a vertical "eh" sound, like "red." [13]

"AH" Warm-up Hand Motion: Cup both hands in front of the face, one on top of another, forming a circular space between. Maintain the position of the top cupped hand, dropping the other slowly as the "ah" vowel is formed. An alternative is to place the lower hand at the base of the sternum, and lift the top hand to maintain a lifted soft palate.

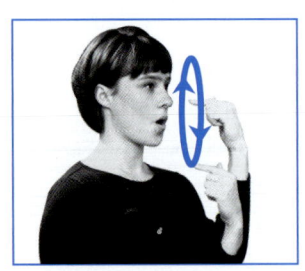

"OH" Warm-up Hand Motion: Finger makes circular motion around lips.

"EH" Warm-up Hand Motion: Start with both open hands parallel to face and together motion away and down from face.

wrap their lips around the sound and actually form an "oo" behind the "ee" vowel. The conductor uses a vertical gesture to encourage a unified head sound "ee" vowel.

Proper head sound placement of the "oo" and "ee" vowels should be carried on with the other vowels. Use of hand gestures during the warm-up can reinforce the best shape and sound for each vowel. When these vowels surface later in the rehearsal, your physical reminder will suffice to reclaim the vowel color you want. Sometimes it is necessary to gently advise trained solo singers to modify their vowel formations to blend into the choral context. A fuller discussion on choral diction, including specifics on consonants and vowel modification, follows in this chapter.

Tune the "fa" and "ti"

In the melodic context, the natural half-steps of the major scale—steps 3 to 4 (*mi* to *fa*) and steps 7 to 8 (*ti* to *do*) tend to be sung "small" in ascending passages and conversely, "large" in descending ones. When descending, advise all singers, but especially the altos and basses, not to *crescendo* when descending and to keep the intervals small.

Scale work and canons in the warm-up will improve linear intonation, but hearing the half-steps within a harmonic context proves even more beneficial. These objectives are best accomplished with minimal support of the piano, pausing occasionally to ask singers to recover the starting pitch, which builds aural memory.

More on **scales** and **use of *solfeggio* syllables** in Chapter Six, pp. 136–138.

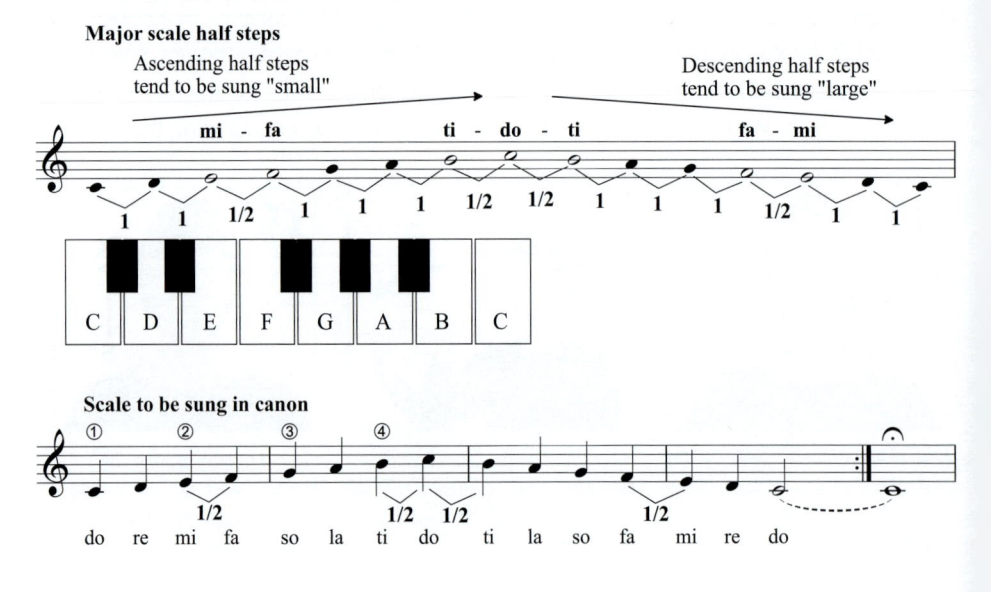

Tuning natural half steps in harmonic context
(mi to fa, ti to do)

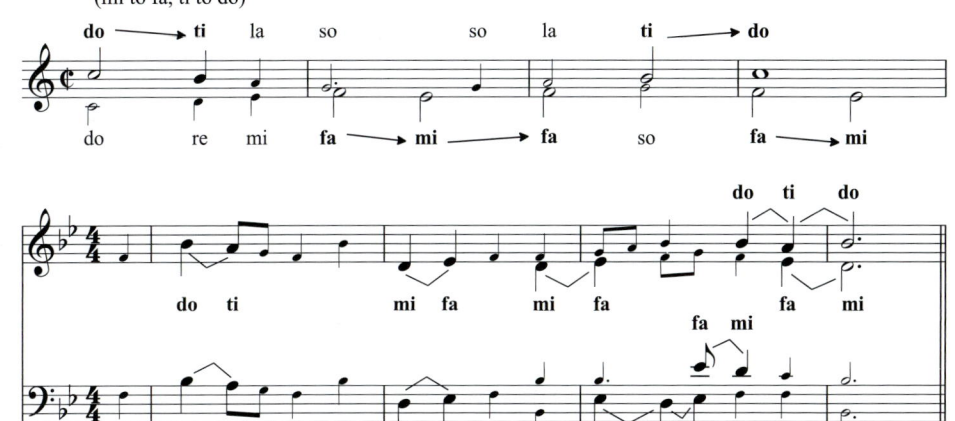

Connect stylistically

Near the conclusion of the warm-up segment, use a "preparation," as some call it, which logically presents the correct style or feel for a song. This can also occur midstream in rehearsal when you want to change styles. A pop warm-up would not best precede work on a classical piece. In your rehearsal preparation, look for warm-ups *within* the pieces you are teaching. This is especially effective in troubleshooting tough passages. References to color imagery aid the choir in utilizing the appropriate vocal color for that style of music. Traditionally the color spectrum ran from Renaissance white, with little vibrato, gradually warming up through yellow, orange, and finally the rich lush Romantic red, with its thick, wide vibrato. Another approach simply asks for a sparkling blue and warm orange vocal color. If you desire a brighter vowel color, suggest using a cool breath, and for the darker, a warm breath.

"Preparation" warm-ups based on repertoire

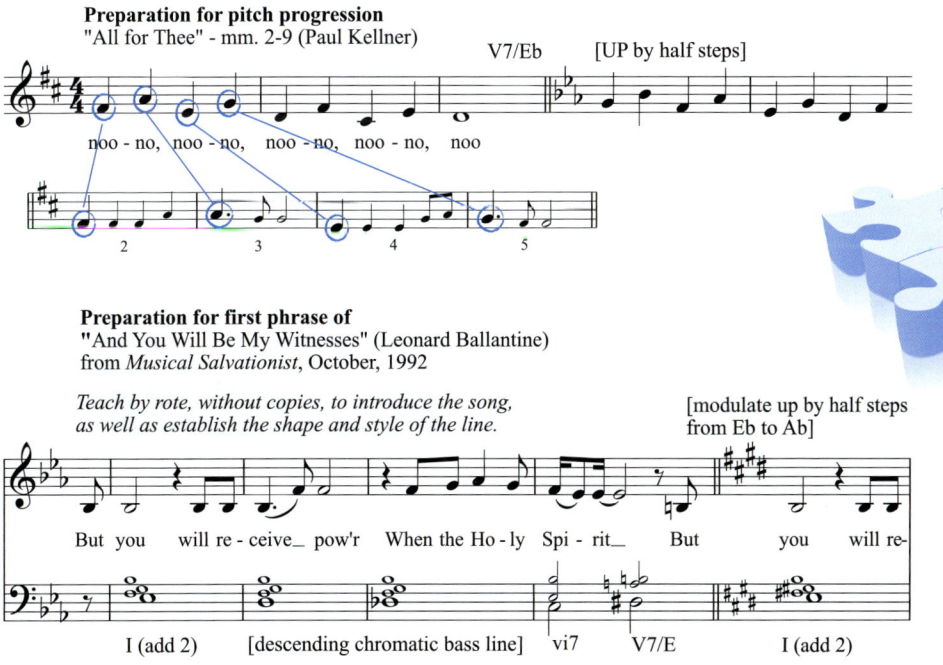

Preparation for pitch progression
"All for Thee" - mm. 2-9 (Paul Kellner)

Reference **marked score copy** of *All for Thee* in Chapter Eleven, p. 237.

Preparation for first phrase of
"And You Will Be My Witnesses" (Leonard Ballantine)
from *Musical Salvationist*, October, 1992

Teach by rote, without copies, to introduce the song, as well as establish the shape and style of the line.

Preparation using the "Consolation" melody from
"How Sweet the Name" (James Curnow)
from *Sing to the Lord*, vol. 3, part 1, 1996, SP&S

Cycle through essential vowel sounds by phrase. This familiarizes singers with the shape of the line and phrasing in minor mode, while unifying vowels.

Oo_____ Ee_____ Ah_____ Oh_____ Oo_____
[modulate by half step to F# minor]

Preparation of chromatic scale steps, ascending and descending
for "In the Love of Jesus" (William Hammond)
from *Gems for Songsters,* pp. 22-23, SP&S

*Begin with females ascending and males descending and then switch.
Then ask sopranos and tenors to sing the top part and the altos and basses the bottom.*

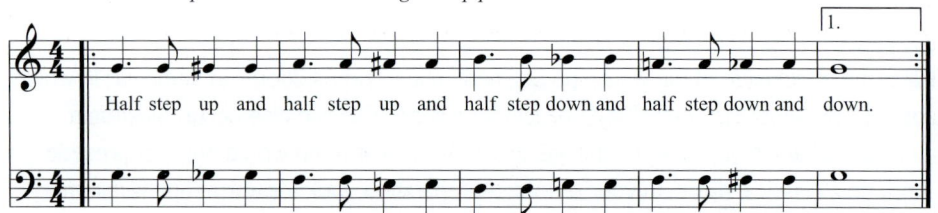

Half step up and half step up and half step down and half step down and down.

Half step down and half step down and half step up and half step up and up.

In unison, modulate down

Move starting pitch down by half steps to Eb, to the "In the Love of Jesus" chorus

"In the Love of Jesus" chorus

Half step down — Half step up and — In the love of Je-sus there is

Half step down — Half step down and

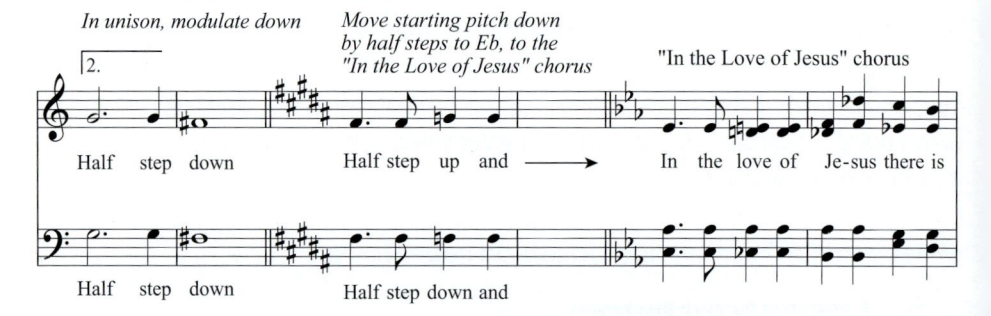

A NINE-STEP CHORAL WARM-UP

This sample warm-up sequence, organized with the help of William Rollins, brings a brigade together and establishes physical and vocal readiness.

Step 1. Stretch and relax the body.
Stand and stretch the arms high above the head. Gently roll head and then shoulders. Give each other a shoulder and back rub.

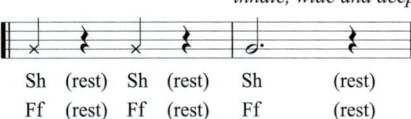

Step 2. Activate the breath and diaphragm.
Activate the core muscles in the abdomen-diaphragm by chanting a series of repeated consonants. Utilize a good quick, but deep catch breath linking each series. Give reminders on taking in and holding a deep, quiet breath, while keeping the shoulders down, before reciting:

On each catch breath, inhale, wide and deep

Sh (rest) Sh (rest) Sh (rest)
Ff (rest) Ff (rest) Ff (rest)

Sing numbers or days of week on a mid-range note like G above middle C. (The pianist can play through a series of chords which work with G.)[14]

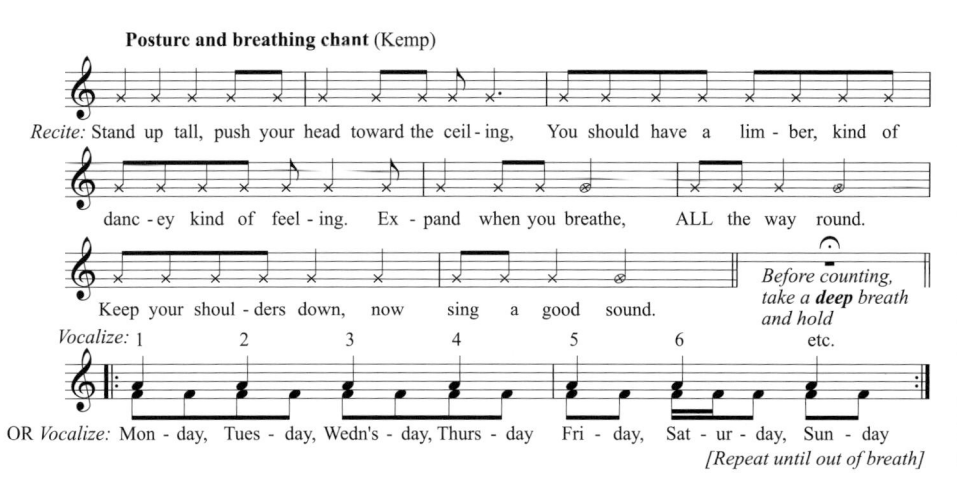

Posture and breathing chant (Kemp)

Recite: Stand up tall, push your head toward the ceil-ing, You should have a lim-ber, kind of danc-ey kind of feel-ing. Ex-pand when you breathe, ALL the way round. Keep your shoul-ders down, now sing a good sound. *Before counting, take a **deep** breath and hold*

Vocalize: 1 2 3 4 5 6 etc.

OR *Vocalize:* Mon-day, Tues-day, Wedn's-day, Thurs-day Fri-day, Sat-ur-day, Sun-day
[Repeat until out of breath]

Step 3. Warm up the resonators.
Bend forward at the waist with arms dangling down. Hum a mid-range note (perhaps an Eb above middle C) at a soft enough volume to enable each singer to hear themselves and those around them. In a *hum,* the sound can come only through the nose, which means it automatically travels up to the resonating spaces in the facial mask. Humming is nature's way of achieving the head-sound mix automatically.[15] The exception is a lip-based "M" sound. Avoiding a "buzzy" hum requires teeth to be slightly apart and lips lightly together. Another way to warm up the resonators uses a simple *staccato* pattern on the syllable *mum.*

Hum to warm up resonators (Willetts)

Hum: Mum, mum, mum, mum, mum

Step 4. Form the vowels in unison or harmony.
Using the same rhythmic pattern, substitute the vowel sounds –mee-meh-mah-moh-moo. Remind singers to create lots of space in the mouth with a dropped jaw, indicated by a cave formed in front of the ear. Use hand gestures to emphasize the correct shapes of the vowels. (See pp. 251-252.) A variation of this warm-up places each section in a comfortable voice range in four-part harmony. Aim for unified vowel color across the brigade.

Form vowels in unison
Commence each vowel with lots of 'mm" sound.
Vocalize: *Can substitute Nee, Neh...* V7
*Mee, meh, mah, moh, moo [Up by semitones]

Form vowels in harmony
Again use lots of 'mm" sound.
Vocalize: V7 * Alternate Zee or Nee
*Mee, meh, mah, moh, moo Mee, meh, mah, etc.

Step 5. Form up vowels in sequence.
There are lots of fun ways to learn to smoothly connect vowels while expanding range and agility.

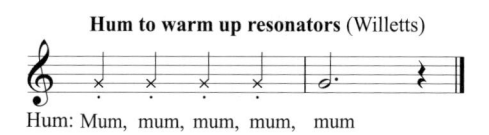

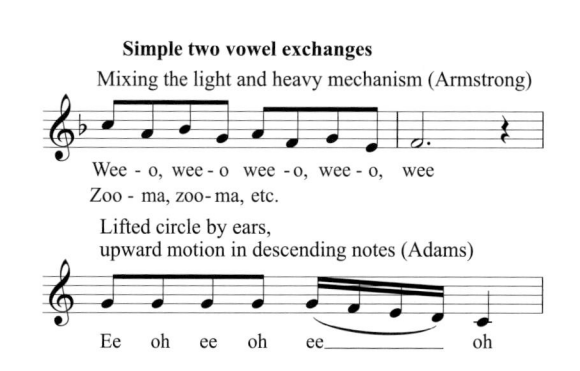

Simple two vowel exchanges
Mixing the light and heavy mechanism (Armstrong)

Wee - o, wee - o wee - o, wee - o, wee
Zoo - ma, zoo - ma, etc.

Lifted circle by ears,
upward motion in descending notes (Adams)

Ee oh ee oh ee oh

Bumblebee

Bum - ble bee,___ bum - ble - bee,___ bum - ble - bee___ bum - ble - bee.
Bum - ble bee,___ bum - ble - bee,___ bum - ble, bee,___ bum - ble - bee.

Step 6. Activate the articulators.

On a single pitch, speak or intone one of these phrases several times.

Chant:
Lips, teeth, tip of the tongue

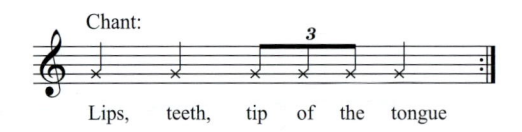

[Up by semitones] 
Pa - pa, pa - pa picked a pot of peas, of peas   Pa - pa, pa - pa picked a

Ferris wheel motion

Step 7. Extend the range.

Commence fairly low and move up by half steps with each repetition. Use a "Ferris wheel" hand motion to help singers sense the energy of sound going up and over the high tones. As we ascend, a small, pressed and airy sound will lack freedom and vocal color because of a lack of space. Remind singers to keep the throat open and maximize their sense of vertical space by making all sounds "spacious, high and forward."[16] Rest the palm of your hand on the forehead to check for the vibration of sound when properly placed high and forward.

Work well past the range required in the current repertoire. As the choir approaches the upper register, switch from the text to a neutral "ah" vowel. After stretching into the upper register, relax the voice by extending down to a lower extreme. Also remind the singers not to crescendo when descending to keep the sound light.

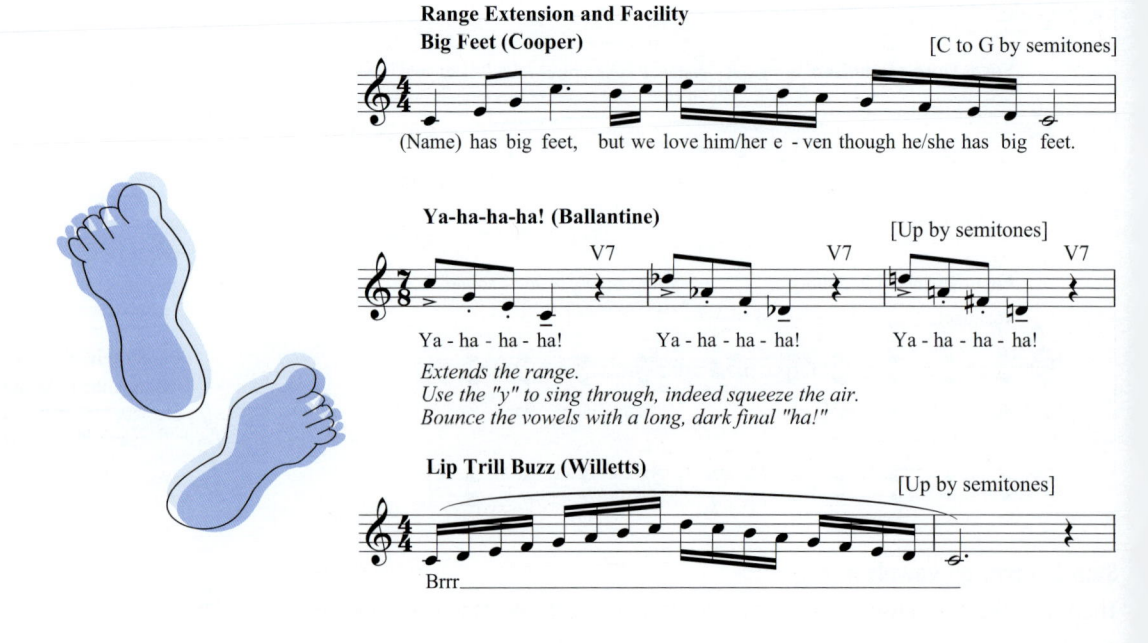

Palm on forehead

Range Extension and Facility
Big Feet (Cooper)   [C to G by semitones]

(Name) has big feet, but we love him/her e - ven though he/she has big feet.

Ya-ha-ha-ha! (Ballantine)   [Up by semitones]
   V7   V7   V7
Ya - ha - ha - ha!   Ya - ha - ha - ha!   Ya - ha - ha - ha!

Extends the range.
Use the "y" to sing through, indeed squeeze the air.
Bounce the vowels with a long, dark final "ha!"

Lip Trill Buzz (Willetts)   [Up by semitones]

Brrr___

Señora (Ballantine)

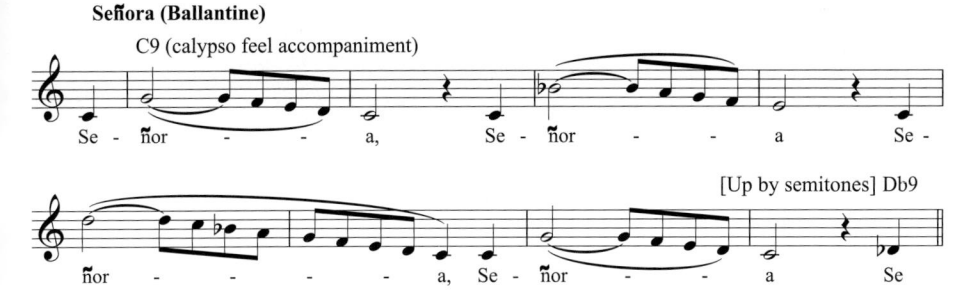

C9 (calypso feel accompaniment)

Se - ñor - a, Se - ñor - a Se -

[Up by semitones] Db9

ñor - a, Se - ñor - a Se

See Appendix 17.1 for more **Choral Warm-Up Piano Accompaniments**, including a sample of the "Señora" warm-up accompaniment.

Step 8. Tune half steps.

Below are two examples to aid tuning. In the first, sing a chromatic passage slowly, listening carefully to secure each half–step shift. Be careful that descending half steps do not become incrementally too large. A second exercise starts with a tone in octaves between the women and men. Signal for individual sections (soprano, alto, tenor and bass) to move up and down by half or whole steps, while the other section(s) maintain their pitch and subsequently move likewise. Allow the harmonies to arbitrarily shift tonally or fall into a tone cluster, that is, a strongly dissonant group of tones lying very close to each other (like d-d#-e-f or e-f-g-a). The intention is not a logical harmonic sequence, but rather, that each singer concentrates on making precise half step maneuvers. To build pitch memory, periodically stop and ask for the initial octave pitch.

Chromatic mirror warm-ups (Trinkley)
In two parts, women and men, full notes
In four parts, add soprano and tenor cued notes

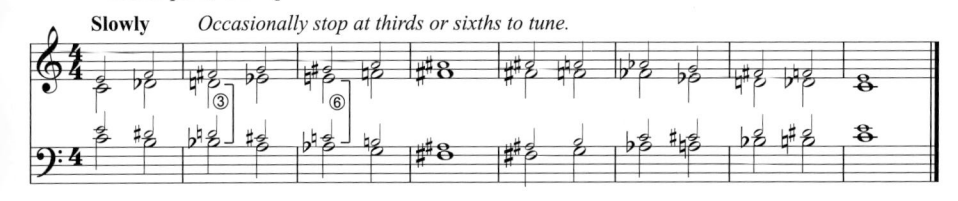

Slowly *Occasionally stop at thirds or sixths to tune.*

Chromatic tuning and pitch memory

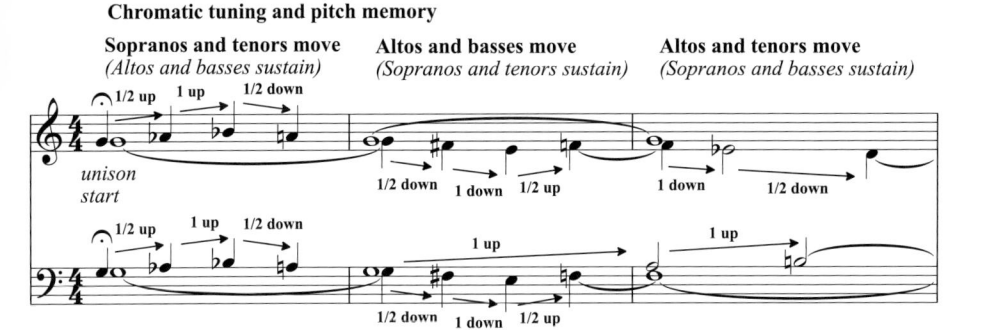

Sopranos and tenors move
(Altos and basses sustain)

Altos and basses move
(Sopranos and tenors sustain)

Altos and tenors move
(Sopranos and basses sustain)

Execute these **tuning exercises** on a variety of vowels.

All parts move independently

All parts move together

Women down Men up

recall first pitch

The **principles of tuning** are considered in detail in the Bandmaster Chapter Fourteen, pp. 298-303.

Step 9. Sing.

Sing something familiar to bridge into your rehearsal. Relax with a few sighs before sitting down and proceeding with the rehearsal.

12 BARS REST

1. Organize a warm-up sequence that will benefit your songsters at this time.

2. Conceive some preparation warm-ups that will aid in the introduction of new selections or help conquer trouble spots in current repertoire.

DICTION HELPS[17]

ē = mee
ā = meh
ah = mah
ō = moh
oō = moo

Pure vowels

The key to beautiful vocal sound is Pure Vowels. Possibly 95% of the sounds of singing are vowels! Strive for a full, resonant sound that you can feel and hear as you sing. Start from a yawn or descending sigh to open and relax the voice "mechanism." Strive to move smoothly from one vowel to the next. Maintain pitch as vowels change from light to dark. Al-le-lu-ia is pronounced ah-leh (not lay-ee)-loo-yah.

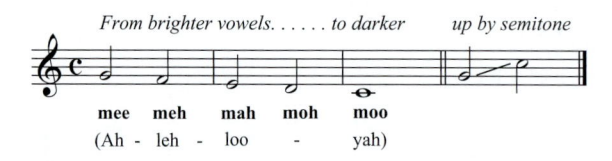

From brighter vowels...... to darker   up by semitone

mee   meh   mah   moh   moo
(Ah - leh - loo - yah)

Subordinate vowels

Develop a smooth flow of color from Pure Vowels to Subordinate Vowels. At first, choose a Pure Vowel (shown in boxes) and alternate between it and a neighboring Subordinate Vowel. Make each vowel distinct. Eventually learn the full spectrum of vowels from bright to dark.

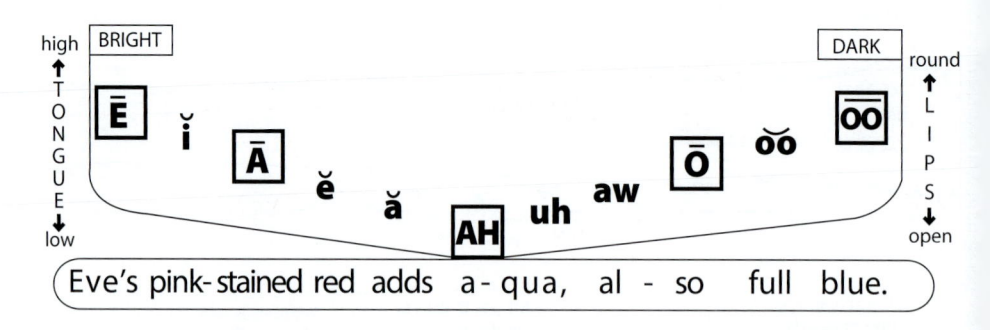

high — TONGUE — low   BRIGHT   Ē ĭ Ā ĕ ă AH uh aw Ō oŏ OO   DARK   round — LIPS — open

Eve's pink-stained red adds a-qua, al-so full blue.

For helpful symbols for **vowel pronunciation** see the International Phonetic Alphabet (IPA) found in Appendix 12.1.

Mixed or blended vowels

With Mixed or Blended Vowels, such as diphthongs, the highlighted sustained primary vowel should be firmly sounded. Do not permit it to "creep" into the vanishing vowel, which should be sounded distinctly and quickly.

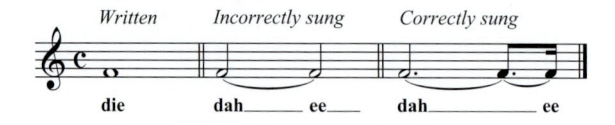

Written   Incorrectly sung   Correctly sung

die   dah_____ ee_____   dah_____ ee

To aid the singers in remembering this in the course of a piece, recommend that the primary vowel can be written in caps over the text:

Primary Vowel	EH	AH	O	AH	AH	AW	AH
Actual Text	May	I	go	buy	my	toy	now?
Pronunciation	mEH_ee	AH_ee	gOH_oo	bAH_ee	mAH_ee	tAW_ee	nAH_oo

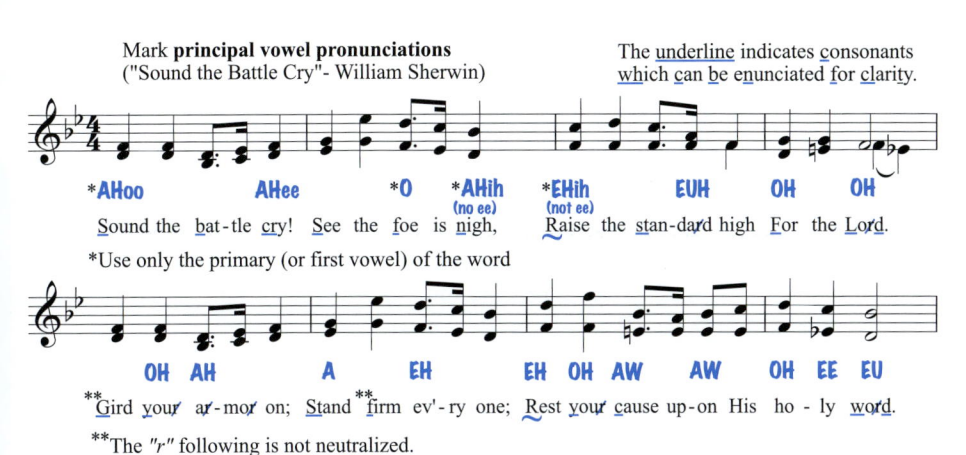

Mark **principal vowel pronunciations**
("Sound the Battle Cry"- William Sherwin)

The <u>underline</u> indicates <u>c</u>onsonants which <u>c</u>an <u>b</u>e <u>e</u>nunciated for <u>c</u>larity.

*AHoo AHee *O *AHih (no ee) *EHih (not ee) EUH OH OH
<u>S</u>ound the <u>b</u>at-tle <u>c</u>ry! <u>S</u>ee the <u>f</u>oe is <u>n</u>igh, <u>R</u>aise the <u>s</u>tan-da<u>r</u>d high <u>F</u>or the Lo<u>r</u>d.

*Use only the primary (or first vowel) of the word

OH AH A EH EH OH AW AW OH EE EU
**<u>G</u>ird your a<u>r</u>-mo<u>r</u> on; <u>S</u>tand **<u>f</u>irm ev'-ry one; <u>R</u>est you<u>r</u> <u>c</u>ause up-on His ho-ly wo<u>r</u>d.

**The "r" following is not neutralized.

TO "R" OR NOT TO "R," THAT IS THE QUESTION

RULE 1: Neutralize (not sound) the "R" before a consonant

such as, hea<u>r</u>t becomes *haht*
or at the end of the word, eve<u>r</u> becomes *ehvah*.

The vowel is colored by the "R," yet is not sounded. Regional dialects can sometimes confuse the actual vowel sound you want. When neutralizing the "R," heart is *haht*, not *hot*, dark is *dahk*, not *dock*, and part is sung as *paht*, not *pot*. Do not sound the "R" in Lord. Use *Lawd*.

RULE 2: Neutralize (not sound) the "R" before any pause or breath

such as, when life is *ovah*,
rather than ove<u>r</u>...[pause]

Replace what would be a harsh concluding "R" sound with a more pleasing tone at the conclusion of the word *before* the breath.

hea*r*t

eve*r*

ove*r*

a*R*ise

*r*est

so*rr*ow

When in Maine, we enjoy LOBSTAH & CHOWDAH!

> ### RULE 3: Sound or flip an "R" before vowels
>
> such as, "a-Rise"
>
> The choice of whether to sound an American "R" or to use a flipped "R" depends on the style of the music and the range of the pitch being sung.
>
> #### Use a traditional "R"
>
> - before a vowel when sung by most American choral ensembles in folk or contemporary styles
>
> #### Flip the "R"
>
> The flipped "R" is also sometimes referred to as a "tongue tap" since the tongue touches the upper gum ridge just once. Those who cannot flip the "R" can substitute a D.
>
> - with more formal music
> - on occasion *between* vowels
> - on the topmost pitches of one's range where the flipped "R" is easier to intone.
>
> #### With a doubled "R," only one "R" is sounded
>
> The second "R" is sounded at the beginning of the *next* vowel.
>
> - never rest, would be sung *neh-vuh rest*
> - sor-row, when printed under separate notes, would be sung *sah-roh*

VARIOUS TREATMENTS OF THE LETTER "R"

Singers Mark	O	AH	EH	O	AH	AH	OO
Actual Text	No	never	dearest	for	Thou	art	poor
Pronunciation	nO_	⚡	sound r	⚡		ah_t	pOO_r

2. O perfect redemption, the purchase of blood!
   — *neutralize, before consonant*
   — *sound or flip first consonant of word, before vowel*
   — *neutralize, before consonant*

   To every believer the promise of God;
   — *sound or flip, between two vowel sounds*
   — *neutralize, before consonant*
   — *sound or flip, before vowel*

   The vilest offender who truly believes,
   — *neutralize, before consonant*
   — *sound, before vowel*

   That moment from Jesus a pardon receives.
   — *sound or flip, before vowel*
   — *neutralize, before consonant*
   — *first consonant of word, before vowel*

   ...And give him the glory; great things he hath done!
   — *sound or flip, between two vowel sounds*
   — *sound or flip, before vowel*

CONSONANTS

While vowels create color and define pitch, consonants create articulation and thereby define rhythm. In Robert Shaw's words, "The vowels give our singing beauty; the consonants give it drama." The conductor uses a slower release with voiced consonants to encourage the singers to sustain the inherent pitch resonance. A quicker gesture is used with the unvoiced consonants, which are shorter as they cannot sustain tone.

Voiced and unvoiced consonant partners

The consonant sounds of b, d, j, and the soft g sound on the lips, as in "George," carry fragmentary pitch, allowing an opportunity for a brief pitched sound. Consider the difference between the "b" and "p" sounds in the word *pebble*, where the "p" is quick and more explosive. Because the "b" carries the resonance, the end of the word requires an added *"uh"* to make the consonant intelligible. Sob becomes *sobuh*, beg, *beguh*, and feed, *feeduh*. Avoid the temptation to make the closing "d" a hard "t" sound as *God-uh* becomes *got* (although this is sometimes effective on loud, high chords.)

The closing "b" can easily slip to a "p," so that *rib-uh* becomes *rip* and *David-uh* begets *Davit*. A quick, precise, correct enunciation of the "ch" sound avoids confusion: *choose* can sound like *shoes*, or *much* become *mush!* A "ch" sound you don't want is: Oh, *donchu*, which sounds like a mix between a "j" sound and a sneeze. "Oh, don't you" requires a "t" with a sliver of break before the differentiated "u" sound: *doooonnt yoo*.

Another voiced consonant combination is the "th" sound, which allows a small, pressurized opening of tone. "As with gladness" requires the "th" voiced sound, otherwise *faith* becomes *face* and *breathes* morphs to *breeze*. The "t" must be articulated, as in *soft-ly*. otherwise we get *softly*. The "t," since it is short, is often merged with the next vowel, *migh-tbe* for might be or *se___tfree* for set free, or *grea___tsoul* for great soul.

A quick, hard "c" sound used with k, c, q (and sometimes ch) can bring life and vigor to your choir's quiver. In contrast, the soft "g" is not as cutting and can be voiced as in *guide* or *guilt*. Ask for an "n" sound before a hard "g" or hard "d" consonant to aid pitch placement, as in *nglide* or *ndie*. The "z" sounds (x, zh, sometimes s) allow voicing, as opposed to an extended or early "s" which *isssss* an unpleassssing *hisssss*. Be precise in placing quick "s" or "sh" sounds.

The "w" which commences words is preceded by an "oo" sound, so *wise* is pronounced *oo-ise*, or *awake* is *a-oo-wake*. There is no "oo" with the "wh" but a gentle blowing, almost forming a whistle sound. A breathy kind of air projects the start of "h" words, like *happy*, *heaven*, and *hope*.

The voiced "v" sound requires a vibrant buzzing of the lips which depends on sufficient air, but in the same way we blow air to form an "f" sound: "With a voice of singing"…as opposed to "send the fire." For clarity, the "v" must be sounded, otherwise "we offer up our lives" can sound like "lies." There are occasions where the "v" should be vibrated early as in *divv-ine* or *devv-otion*. There are two anomalies with the "v" sound: The oft-used contraction *heav'n* pushes the "v" to the very edge of the word, *hea___vn* and "I love you" is best rendered *I loview*.

A number of voiced consonants lack corresponding unvoiced partners, but carry great sustainable pitch, like "l, m, n, ng." One can vocalize on these consonants: name (*nnamme*), someday (*sommday*), amen (*ah-mmenn*).

VOICED CONSONANTS	UNVOICED PARTNERS*
b (bib)	**p** (pep)
d (dad)	**t** (toot)
j or **g** (judge)	**ch** (church)
	*uses corresponding tongue/lip placement
th (the)	**t** (toot)
	th (thinketh)
g (George)	**k** (c, q, ch) cook, quick, choir
	hard g (gag)
z (pizazz)	**s** (song)
x (as z –xerox)	**sh** (shush)
zh (pleasure)	
s (as z –is)	
w (wow)	**wh** (when)
	h (heehaw)
v (valve)	**f** (fife)
m, n, ng (mom, nun, ring)	
y (you)	
r (rings)	
l (lull)	

OTHER SUGGESTIONS ON DICTION

Daniel Sitteth

Words with either a *u* or *ew* spelling, like *duty, dew, new, lute, suit, tune* and *enthuse*, use a glide we associate with the letter *y* preceded by the *oo* vowel, resulting in the same sound as the word *you* after the consonants *d, n, l, s, t* and *th*. As a memory aid, Madeline Marshall cleverly distributes these consonants into the two words: DaNieL SiTteTH.[18]

The flipped "L"

Similar to the flipped "R" considered above, the "L" consonant also needs to be *flipped* in combination with other consonants, otherwise the word *blood* comes across as *bud*.

To link or not to link

Linking words together is an important element to the *connectedness* that characterizes beautiful *legato* singing. A key to this is "working to intensify the voiced consonants."[19] There are times, however, when words linked together can be audibly mistaken for another combination. If the concluding consonant of the first word *big* is linked to the second word *eyes*, then the second word can seem like *guys*. "And He walks with me" can, for instance, sound like *"Andy walks with me"* or "Gladly the cross I bear" sounds like *"Glad Lee, the cross-eyed bear."*[20] Similarly, two words in succession that end in the same vowel sound, like *the evening* (not *theevening*) or "so old," (not *sold*) require separation to be understood as intended.[21]

Use the dictionary

Sandra Willetts reminds singers in doubt to look up correct pronunciations. For instance, *beside* and *deliver* are phonetically indicated in the dictionary as *bih-side* and *dih-liver*, rather than *dee-liver* or *dah-liver*. Willetts muses that "if you sing "*dee-lever* (with the wide *ee*)," you are talking about major surgery! She also points out that sometimes there are words that we *say* differently than we *sing*. We say, *ee-vul*, yet we sing *ee-vihl*. While the first is what is indicated in the dictionary, Willetts advocates using the first when the note value for the second syllable is short, yet explains the second sung version as a way to brighten the vowel to an "*ih*" which is far more satisfactory to vocalize.[22]

12 BARS REST

Work through the vowels and then consonants of a new song. Develop a shorthand for yourself that clearly reinforces your best intentions by underscoring consonants to be emphasized or flipped, and those to be negated. Mark the shaped sounds of primary vowels and the exact beat location of closing consonants.

For more on **Marking Vocal Scores with Phonetics** in the Score Study Chapter Eleven, pp. 237–240.

GLAD LEE THE CROSS-EYED BEAR

CHORAL TRAINING RESOURCES

WARM-UP and VOICE TRAINING COLLECTIONS

Daily Workout for a Beautiful Voice, Charlotte Adams (Santa Barbara Music)
Evoking Sound—*The Choral Warm-Up*, text and rehearsal cards, James Jordan (GIA)
Group Vocal Technique, James Jordan (Hinshaw)
Group Vocal Technique—*The Vocalise Cards,* Frauke Haasemann (Hinshaw)
Making More Sense of How to Sing—*Multisensory Techniques for Voice Lessons and Choir Rehearsals*, Alan Gumm (Meredith Music)
Successful Warm-Ups, Nancy Telfer (Kjos)
The Choral Warm-Up Collection, Sally Abrecht, ed. (Alfred)
The Complete Choral Warm-Up, Russell Robinson and Jay Althouse (Alfred)
The Everything Singing Book, Bettina Shepherd (Adams Media)
Working with Male Voices, Video with Jerry Blackstone (Santa Barbara Music)

MUSIC NOTATION

Steps to Harmony, Nicholas Palmer (Masterworks Press). Available online from www.masterworkspress.com. Progressive sight-singing method book (four levels) which can be sung in unison, 2-part, or 3-part. Both treble and bass clef books are available.
Successful Sight-Singing, Books I and II, Nancy Telfer (Kjos Music)
The Choral Reader, Maurice Gardner (Staff Music) for treble voices
The Sight-Singer, Volumes I and II, Audrey Snyder (Warner Bros.) available for two and three part mixed voices or unison/two part treble voices.
Tone Syllables, Fred Waring (Shawnee Press)
Youth Song Book (*Songs of Praise*) of The Salvation Army (SA, Alexandria, VA)

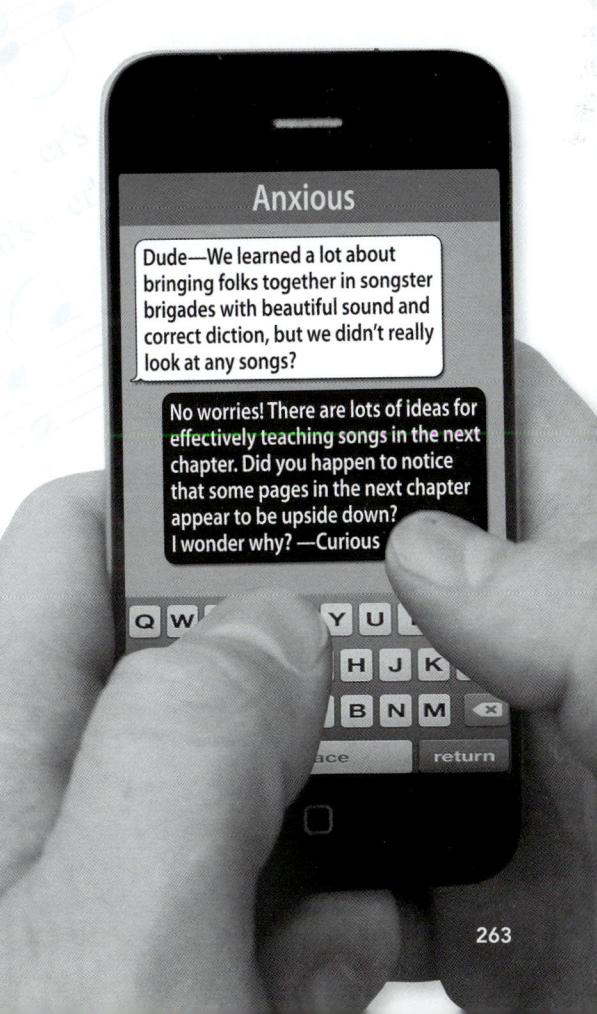

CHAPTER THIRTEEN

THE EFFECTIVE SONGSTER REHEARSAL
The Songster Leader's Toolbox

The only way of "mastering" one's material is to abandon the whole concept of mastery and to cooperate with it in love: Whosoever will be a lord of life, let that one be its servant...The business of the creator is not to escape from his material medium or to bully it, but to serve it; but to serve it he must love it.
—Dorothy Sayers, *The Mind of the Maker*

CAROL'S SECRET
A Choral Fantasy of Words

In keeping with the meaning of her name, Carol's "joyful song" strategies caused her songsters to never miss a practice—or a beat. Carol reveals that her defining moment came a few years back when she decided that for too long the songster members had the upper hand in beguiling conductors. According to this report, Carol's namesake cheerful disposition, coupled with a high-pitched disregard for choral training, has effectively arrested her trebling and gained her a basses for control over her alto zealous constituents. Carol's secret apparently is an ancient treatise eloquently entitled *Thah Sad But Oars Guyed 2 Coral Kon Duck* (loosely translated from a pre-solfege dialect as *The Saboteur's Guide to Choral Conduct*). We reprint portions of it here just as it appears in the original manuscript. In music terms, it is, auspiciously, inverted so that common-time choristers cannot dee-sigh-fur its age-old secrets. The *Living Verb* translation is indicated in *italics*:

In **Chapter Thirteen**, we:
- study techniques for building a beautiful choral sound.
- look at rehearsal strategies for effectively teaching a song.
- think about ways to re-voice a hymn for your songster brigade.

The Saboteur's Guide to Choral Conduct

THE ART OF THE START

1. **Doppio movimento** (Double time)—Even though it is often said that on time is late, always choose to arrive fashionably late, permitting the songsters to admire where you store your folder, stand, pencil, water, and glasses. Naturally in *double time*, your sharp songsters will be flat sure that these are "accidentally" more difficult to locate.

   WISDOM OF THE AGES: *Choral conductors are well prepared and arrive in plenty of time to greet their choristers, starting and ending on time.*

"*You can flip the page now...*"

"*...Oh, that's much better.*"

KINDLY CORRECTION

2. Battuta incrementale (*Beating time incrementally*)—Remind the choir that they are behind the beat. If they say they can't see your beat, as many commonly claim, make your actual downbeat descend incrementally *faster* to help them catch up.

Wisdom of the Ages: Choral conducting is far more than beating time. The choral conductor devises rehearsal strategies to engender a unity of rhythm, diction, and blend within the choir.

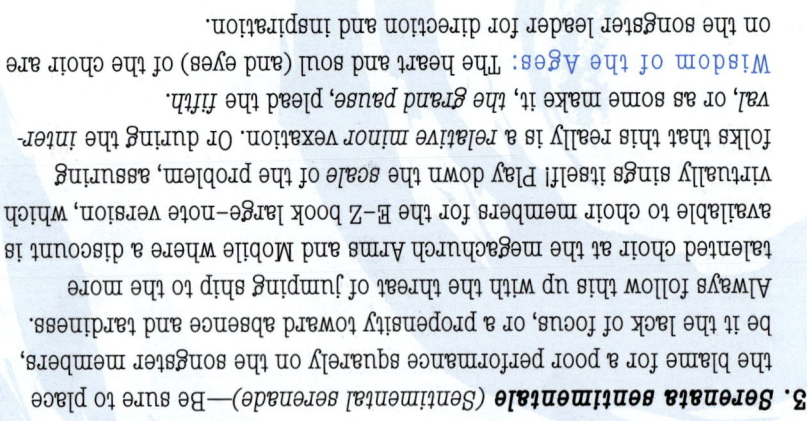

3. Serenata sentimentale (*Sentimental serenade*)—Be sure to place the blame for a poor performance squarely on the songster members, be it the lack of focus, or a propensity toward absence and tardiness. Always follow this up with the threat of jumping ship to the more talented choir at the megachurch at the Arms and Mobile where a discount is available to choir members for the E-Z book large-note version, which virtually sings itself! Play down the scale of the problem, assuring folks that this really is a *relative minor vexation*. Or during the interval, or as some make it, the *grand pause*, plead the fifth.

Wisdom of the Ages: The heart and soul (and eyes) of the choir are on the songster leader for direction and inspiration.

THE MINOR MERITS OF MARKING AND MEMORIZATION

4. Ben marcato (*Well marked*)—Don't remove that *pencil* from your ear! It gives the appearance that you are hard at work. Also, be absolutely sure your songsters never ever mark their music, in ink especially, or even in pencil. The marring of the copies with useless breath marks and helpful pronunciation insults the reach of our well-oiled memories.

Wisdom of the Ages: A sure sign of retention of details, which can make or break a performance, is each chorister ready for a rehearsal with music and pencil in hand.

5. Impromptu impetuoso (*Impetuous improvisation*)—A stupendous landmark ten-measure survey indicates that conductors should never conduct or ask their choir to sing from memory, as the audience will think that you can't read music.

Wisdom of the Ages: Getting the chorister's eyes out of the music as soon as possible increases dramatically the learning (and listening) curve and the visual impression of the choir.

266

www.music.saconnects.org

Chapter 13 | THE EFFECTIVE SONGSTER REHEARSAL

BUILDING BEAUTIFUL SOUND

Group rehearsal techniques

Leadership of a songster brigade is daunting business. One can possess a significant amount of musical skill, yet it is the leader's ongoing challenge to prove effective in rehearsal with the singers in their given situation. The telltale sign of a fine songster brigade is its *sound*. Some weaknesses and traits may appear to be immutable, but with diligent forethought, a leader can nurture the vocal ensemble into an effective worship-leading body, with its own distinct, winsome personality and tone.

A number of the group rehearsal techniques discussed in this section follow logically on the presentation of warm-up and diction helps found in the previous chapter. Also, some of the active warm-ups and imagery with props found in Chapter Six, pp. 132–135 can be adapted for teens and adults. Appendix 13.1 *Fixes for Choir* includes other practical rehearsal remedies.

The intent is to bring the rehearsal alive by incorporating counting and physical gestures, which in turn will secure improved clarity and quality of vocal tone. The wise songster leader looks for opportunities to "divide and conquer," as choral music is the convergence of three primary elements—*pitch, rhythm, and text*. Isolating one or two of these speeds the learning process. Empowering section leaders to make sure their respective section knows these elements can accelerate the process toward real music-making.

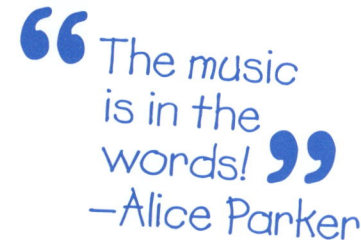

> "The music is in the words!"
> —Alice Parker

Absorbing text

Speak the text aloud and pause to consider how it sounds. Weigh the important syllables and where they peak and valley. It is never too early to ask which are the singer's favorite phrases and why. This builds ownership in the song.

George Bernard Shaw once famously called the English and Americans two peoples separated by a common language. Adapt a heightened, exaggerated speech, imitating a British accent for clarity of diction. Encourage the choir to feel the spaciousness of words.

Set short term, weekly goals for memorization. Type out the lyrics to aid the process. Create simple, appropriate gestures for the key words or phrases that mirror the meaning and direction of the line. Teach the gesture with the text chanted. Remove the text and simply do the gestures alone as the choir images the text in time. Then ask the choir to sing the text, while you continue to make the simple motions. This is a great aid to memorization and gives the conductor a physical vocabulary to "feed" words and phrasing. Assure the choir that they will not have to perform with these motions, but their remembrance of these movements will aid in the quality of performance. More tips on memorization are found in Chapter Twenty-Three, pp. 520–523.

"Everything I SPEAK..."

Create motions to aid memorization and sense of line
"Known to You" (David Catherwood) - mm. 19-23

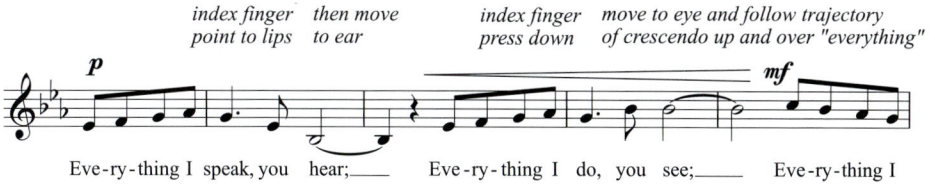

index finger point to lips / then move to ear / index finger press down / move to eye and follow trajectory of crescendo up and over "everything"

"...you HEAR."

Another possibility is to sing the text on a stationary chord or tone cluster, but in correct rhythm, remembering that speaking a text is quite different from singing one.

The Beat Goes On

Vowels and **consonants** are considered in detail in Chapter Twelve, pp. 258–262.

The principles of **count-singing** are applied to instrumental ensembles in Chapter Fourteen, p. 294.

For more on **exploring dynamics** see Chapter Twenty-Two, pp. 492–496 and Chapter Twenty Three, pp. 517–519.

Diction clarity
Eliminate all consonants and sing using only vowels. This clarifies the quickness required for the vowel changes.

As an aid to memorization, move the tempo up gradually to an extreme, pushing the limits of clarity and diction. Then return to the correct tempo, hopefully with improved enunciation and sparkle.

Count-singing
Choose not to apply text until the pitches and rhythm (and even phrasing and dynamics) are anchored via rhythmic count-singing. Some conductors use a modified "tee" for beat three. (Shaw uses "One-an-Two-an-Tee-an-Four-an.") Count-singing helps singers feel the underlying pulse and the counting aids with the exact placement of consonants.

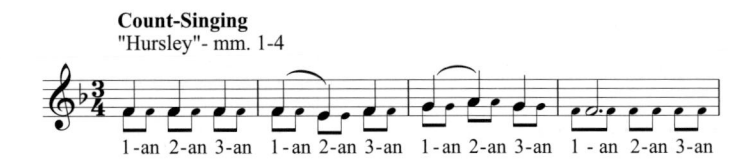

Count-Singing
"Hursley"- mm. 1-4

1-an 2-an 3-an   1-an 2-an 3-an   1-an 2-an 3-an   1-an 2-an 3-an

While continuing to sing, emphasize strong beats with some natural movements like walking, stomps, leg pats, swinging arms, and clapping. The goal is to internalize the pulse and make the words and corresponding rhythmic energy second nature.

Count-dynamics
Count-dynamics asks singers to count a *crescendo* getting louder with the numbers and reversing the numbers for *diminuendos*. This is particularly effective with a *crescendo* or *diminuendo* requested over a long stretch, as the numbers help gauge the *crescendo* not to move too quickly to the "shout" and the *diminuendo* is measured by the numbers to not "sag" too quickly, creating an even descent. Then ask two sections to sing the passage, applying these learned dynamics, while the other sections continue count-dynamics. Switch roles and then have everyone sing, while you remind folks of counts at important junctures.

Count-Dynamics
"How Beautiful Upon the Mountains" (James Curnow) - mm. 13-19

Heads up

Dorothy Nancekievill likes to remind her choristers that, "When heads go down, we lose tempo." Many singers re-read notes, even after they know them. Begin to memorize almost at once. Blend and pitch will improve.

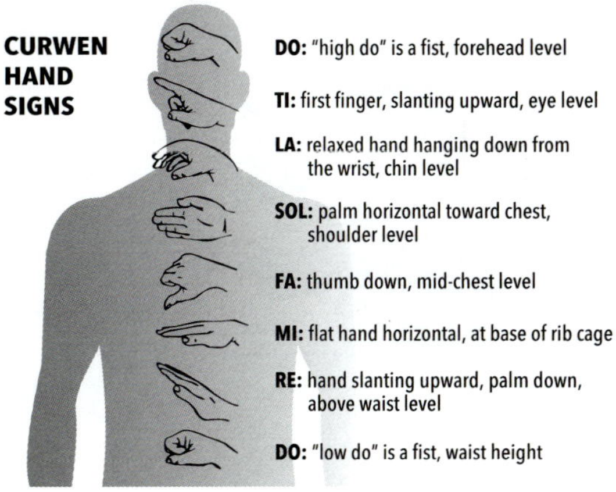

Establishing pitch

– *Before teaching the* RHYTHM:
  Utilize *solfege* with hand signals for trouble spots in the warm-up preparation.
– *Before teaching* PITCHES:
  Introduce the *solfege* of a difficult passage with hand signals or by pointing on a *solfege* tree. (See Chapter Six, p. 136) This works best when you do not let on what piece you are exposing them to, as you are building aural memory and retention. Once the pitches seem secure, than move to the printed copy.
– *Before applying the* TEXT :
  Establish phrasing and shape of the musical line by vocalizing on neutral syllables. The peaks and valleys of the earlier text reading should now be mirrored in the ebb and flow of the note phrases. Depending on the style of the song, neutral pitched consonants, like *zoo, zum, zah,* encourage fluidity of line. Vary the syllables or the voices will tire.

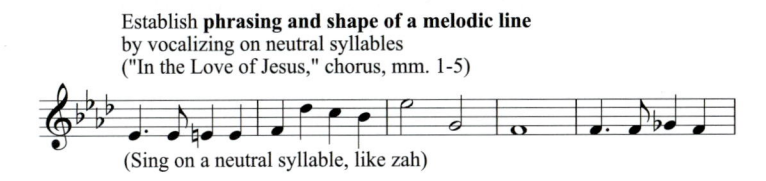

Establish **phrasing and shape of a melodic line** by vocalizing on neutral syllables ("In the Love of Jesus," chorus, mm. 1-5)
(Sing on a neutral syllable, like zah)

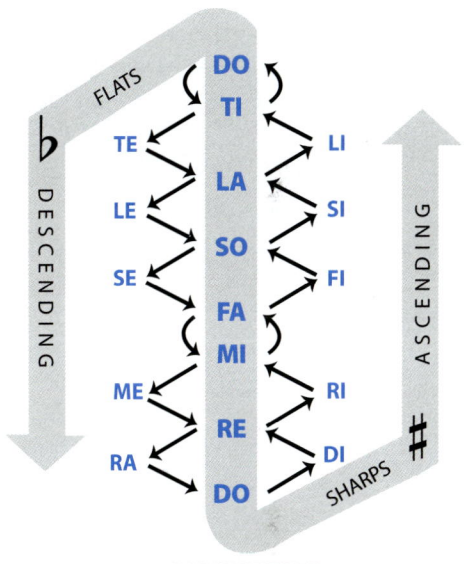

CURWEN HAND SIGNS

- **DO:** "high do" is a fist, forehead level
- **TI:** first finger, slanting upward, eye level
- **LA:** relaxed hand hanging down from the wrist, chin level
- **SOL:** palm horizontal toward chest, shoulder level
- **FA:** thumb down, mid-chest level
- **MI:** flat hand horizontal, at base of rib cage
- **RE:** hand slanting upward, palm down, above waist level
- **DO:** "low do" is a fist, waist height

Staccato Syllables

Choose a passage and instruct the choir to articulate only the starts of pitches using *staccato* "doot" syllables. The notated rhythm is maintained, but longer values have a short start, leaving the remainder of the note value silent. This exercise aids the correct rhythmic placement of dotted rhythms and moving inner parts. Not only is the pulse internalized but limiting the wiggle room with pitch disavows approximate pitch or "scooping." Be aware that undue weight on a consonant or a misconstrued vowel sound can inhibit accurate pitch.

Full value version with words
"In the Love of Jesus" (William Hammond) chorus, mm. 9-12

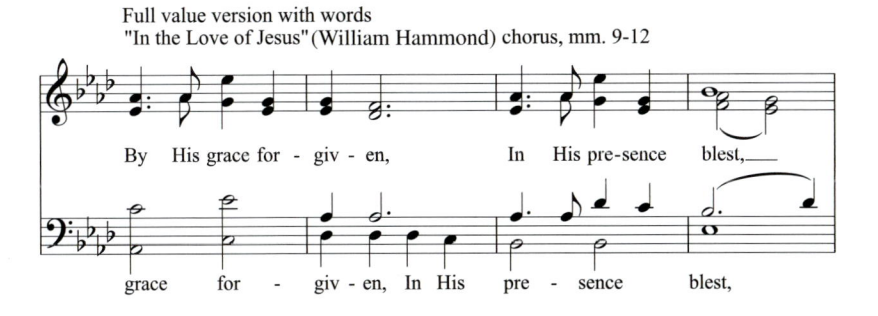

By His grace for - giv - en, In His pre - sence blest,
grace for - giv - en, In His pre - sence blest,

Version using **staccato syllables**
"In the Love of Jesus" chorus, mm. 9-12

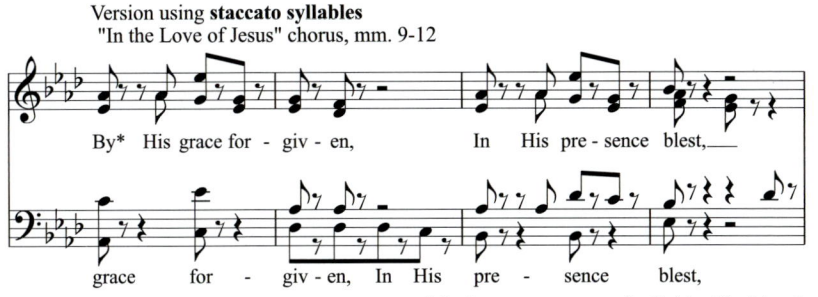

By* His grace for - giv - en, In His pre - sence blest,
grace for - giv - en, In His pre - sence blest,

*Option to use a neutral syllable, like "doot"

SOLFEGE TREE
Chromatic Scale
(each ↗ represents a half step)

FLATS — DESCENDING: DO, TE, LE, SE, ME, RA, DO
Center: DO, TI, LA, SO, FA, MI, RE, DO
SHARPS — ASCENDING: LI, SI, FI, RI, DI

The principle of **staccato syllables** may also effectively be applied to **slurred passages**. See Chapter Fourteen, p. 295.

Ferris wheel motion

Up-and-over range extension

The "up-and-over" motion utilized in the warm-up for range extension can be applied to high passages in repertoire. (See Chapter Twelve, pp. 256-257) At first disregard the lyrics and use an open neutral vowel, like "oh" or "ah." The energy of the ascending hand carries up and over the high tone. The analogy of the Ferris wheel suggests that there needs to be an increase in the speed of the air just before a leap or high note. Use the same motion for sighs, which should always start high and descend. If employing "roller coaster" siren *glissandos*, remind folks to maintain a vertical spaciousness in the back of their mouth.

Tuning Up!

Vowels must be unified to sing in tune. Insecure notes and imprecise rhythms often contribute to weak intonation.

FLATNESS

Sensitize singers to exact intervals, particularly half steps. With descending intervals, think small. Think high as a note is repeated or goes low. Be sure to carry the air to the end of a long phrase.

SHARPNESS

Reverse of flatness. Widen intervals as you ascend, but as you go higher, think lower with your breath support.

Singing too loud, too soft, or in wrong voice register (for instance, when pop singers use chest voice exclusively) can unravel pitch and blend.

NOT ALL NOTES... ARE CREATED EQUAL
Lots more on **tuning** in the Bandmaster Chapter Fourteen, pp. 298–303.

Aural aura

Some sounds and pitches in different registers are just not *heard* easily or are even a part of some singers' listening vocabularies. Similarly, certain meters are not easily *felt*. Today's listeners assimilate few songs in minor keys or waltz tempos because they are rarely heard over the pop airwaves. If you anticipate that the aural content, such as a waltz in three, is unfamiliar, consider "dropping back ten yards and punting." Conjure up aural or physical ways to bring these anomalies into the *ears* of your choir.

Warm-up preparation using waltz tempo (Armstrong)
Two arm circles, up on toes [Up by semitones]
I love to sing, I love to sing, I love

Warm-up preparation using a minor triad (Artz)
(up by half steps) 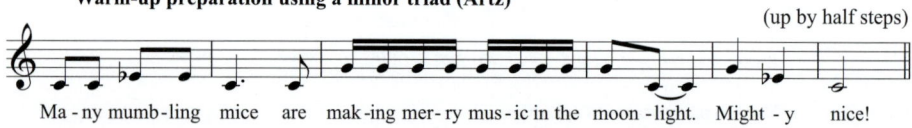
Ma-ny mum-bling mice are mak-ing mer-ry mu-sic in the moon-light. Might-y nice!

Active listening

Ask singers to listen with their inner ear without actually singing and to try to identify a harmonic part within a texture. Applying the inherent logic of "moveable *do*" solfege, for instance, singing "*la* to *la*" for the minor scale, can breed familiarity with the feeling of more unfamiliar minor tonality.

More on cultivating strong **listening** habits in Chapter Twenty-Three.

Use "LA to LA" to sing the relative minor scale
relative Eb Major scale
(and back up)

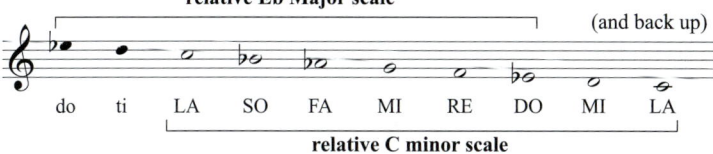

do ti LA SO FA MI RE DO MI LA
relative C minor scale

Unless they mark, they will not remember
Encourage songsters to mark breathing, specific articulation (particularly in regard to the length of notes), dynamics, and diction concerns. Train your singers to mark as you work together, particularly the exact beat of breath or consonant placements. Suggested markings are recommended in Chapter Eleven on Score Study (pp. 233-237) and are utilized in a song studied later in this chapter.

SETTING A SPIRITUAL STANDARD

Intentionality
Overall, have a purpose for every warm-up, isolated interval drill, range-stretching exercise, and coloring of the tone relating to the style and demands of each piece. Work together on tone, diction, and dynamics while encouraging listening and increased familiarity. This develops confidence, which spawns ownership. The brigade knows when they have gone beyond the notes to making music and giving their best to the Lord.

Formations and focus
Rehearse the piece in different formations: by sections, in quartets, a close huddle (so everyone hears), to spread far apart (where everyone has to stretch their ears to hear more). Choose a focal point. Testimony songs are sung eyeball-to-eyeball to someone in the congregation. Paeans of praise call for uplifted eyes. Heads down during prayer solos suggests prayer, while random raised hands signal praise and blessing. Stepping out into the congregation exchanges individual boldness for group strength and draws the congregation in—a ministry in sound.

Strategies for **choir formation** were introduced in Chapter Twelve, p. 250.

Music of the heart
Select a soloist, not necessarily on the premise that she/he has the superior delivery, but because her/his heart can best reach within the song. Occasionally ask the soloist to share in rehearsal what he or she feels in offering this testimony in song. Allow openness. Exposing our hearts permits rehearsals to become sacred. Having exchanged ideas, singers will find that certain phrases well up with deep conviction and touch the audience. From the first reading of a piece, intentionally aim for this kind of ownership— a fragrant offering unto the Most High!

Vocal Soloist Jude Gotrich

13 BARS REST

1. Review selections in your current songster folder for ways to apply some of these rehearsal techniques. Begin with small doses, but avoid being gimmicky. Honor your singers by looking for creative ways to speed the learning curve, achieve great sound, and make the rehearsal "performance" vibrant and memorable.

More on effective **rehearsal strategies** in Chapter Twenty-Three.

2. Be a sponge! Observe rehearsals, attend conferences, purchase recordings, or sit under someone who is effective in achieving great sound with their choir. Bring back to your songster brigade much more than new repertoire.

FROM VOCAL SCORE TO REHEARSAL PREPARATION

A STRATEGY FOR "ONLY THIS I ASK"

Vocal conductors are always looking for pieces that are a good fit for their group. Previewing a piece from a recording on the way to work without music in front of you will not give you enough information to make an informed decision. Take a good look at the music, preferably at the piano, to consider whether the piece sits within the strengths and limitations of your group.

Following an initial reading, concentrate on the voice parts, identify the major sections/layers of the piece, and mark each section, considering possible rehearsal strategies. Learn the road map. Become absolutely familiar with repeats and how the piece begins and ends. Give special attention to difficult rhythms, pitches, key changes, and transitions. Study how the accompaniment works with the voices and read through the text to mark breathing and diction cues. Use warm-ups to teach tricky phrases and rhythms before the songster brigade even looks at the printed copy.

As an example, let's take a look at "Only This I Ask," a song by Australian Salvationist Graeme Press found in *Psalms, Hymns and Spiritual Songs*, Book I—No. 3.[1]

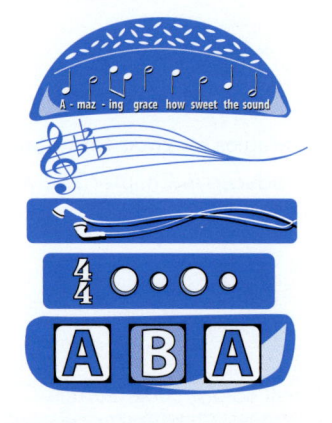

Layers

A quick look at our layers reveals *structurally* a refrain preceding two verses, followed by a final refrain with a brief coda. *Rhythmically,* there are some consistent syncopation and rhythm patterns. *Melodically,* the tune is mostly stepwise within the range of a seventh, with a few melodic drops in pitch of a fourth and a fifth (mm. 9-10). The introductory piano lines are nicely reiterated over the vocal ending (mm. 58-59). There is a very logical and pleasing *harmonic* progression to the piece, with a modulation from G to Ab up a half step for the final refrain and coda. A second voice part is occasionally suggested in cued notes. The *text* is adapted from Psalm 27.

Layers, as it relates to score study, were introduced in Chapter Eleven, pp. 223–226.

Usefulness

The piece works well as a prelude to prayer or worship. The refrain is easily accessible for congregation involvement with projected text. For the conductor, "Only This I Ask" gives opportunity to work with simple syncopation in a pleasant and accessible psalm setting with occasional part-singing.

PITCH

RHYTHM

TEXT

LOOKING FOR THE TROUBLE!

Reflecting on our layers analysis so far, we remind ourselves that there are *three major elements to our singing—pitch, rhythm, and text*. Often it is advantageous to the learning process to eliminate one or two elements and secure the more difficult element first.

Refrain first

In the case of "Only This I Ask," the rhythm should probably be worked through first combined with the text. This allows an opportunity to establish a bouncy style and place

Chapter 13 | THE EFFECTIVE SONGSTER REHEARSAL

ROADMAP | Refrain 1 | Verse 1 | Refrain 2 | Verse 2 | Concluding Refrain w/Coda
Key of G: | | | | | Key of Ab:

ONLY THIS I ASK

Graeme Press
Adapted from Psalm 27

Graeme Press (ASCAP)

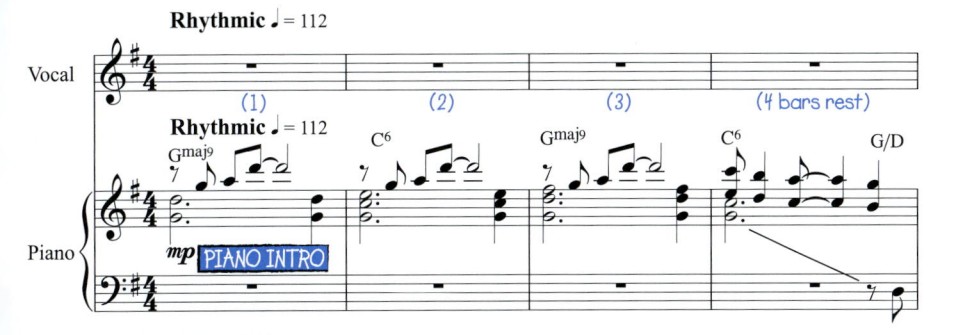

Australian Salvationist composer Graeme Press

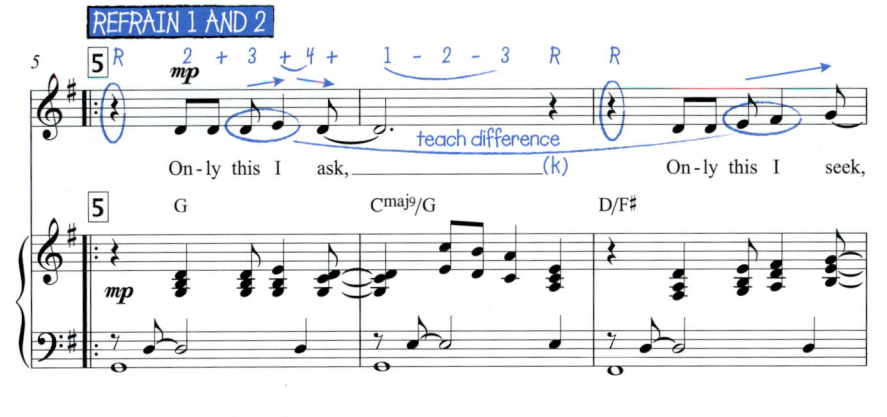

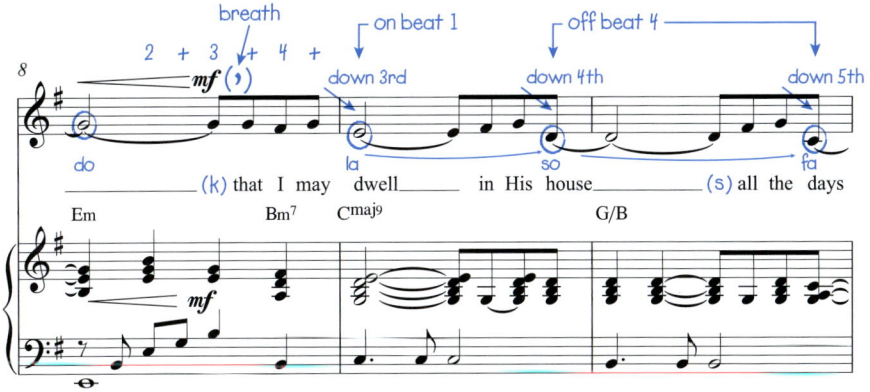

Copyright © 1996 The Salvation Army USA East

the articulating consonants in their proper place. For instance, the "k" on "ask" will go just before beat four of m. 6. Notice that most new words work *off* of beat 3. For instance, "Only this I seek (– 2 – 3) that I may dwell (– 2 – 3) in His house (– 2 – 3) all the days..." Be sure to complete the syllable with the closing consonant, beginning with the vowel *on* the third beat: "(s)ee<u>k</u>, (d)we<u>ll</u>, (h)ou<u>se</u>, (d)ay<u>s</u>." Take note that "dwell" is the only word commencing on the beat in this phrase. To assist the singer in feeling the pulse, the leader may wish to clap or count out loud to help clarify the syncopation. Most songsters will need to breathe after "seek" in bars 8 and 16 in order to *not* breathe in the midst of the phrase that follows.

A reference recording of *Only This I Ask* is accessible in the Chapter Thirteen online folder.

See Appendix 13.2 for **Rehearsal Plans for Songster Leaders** – Emphasizing Elementary Music-Reading.

The Beat Goes On

273

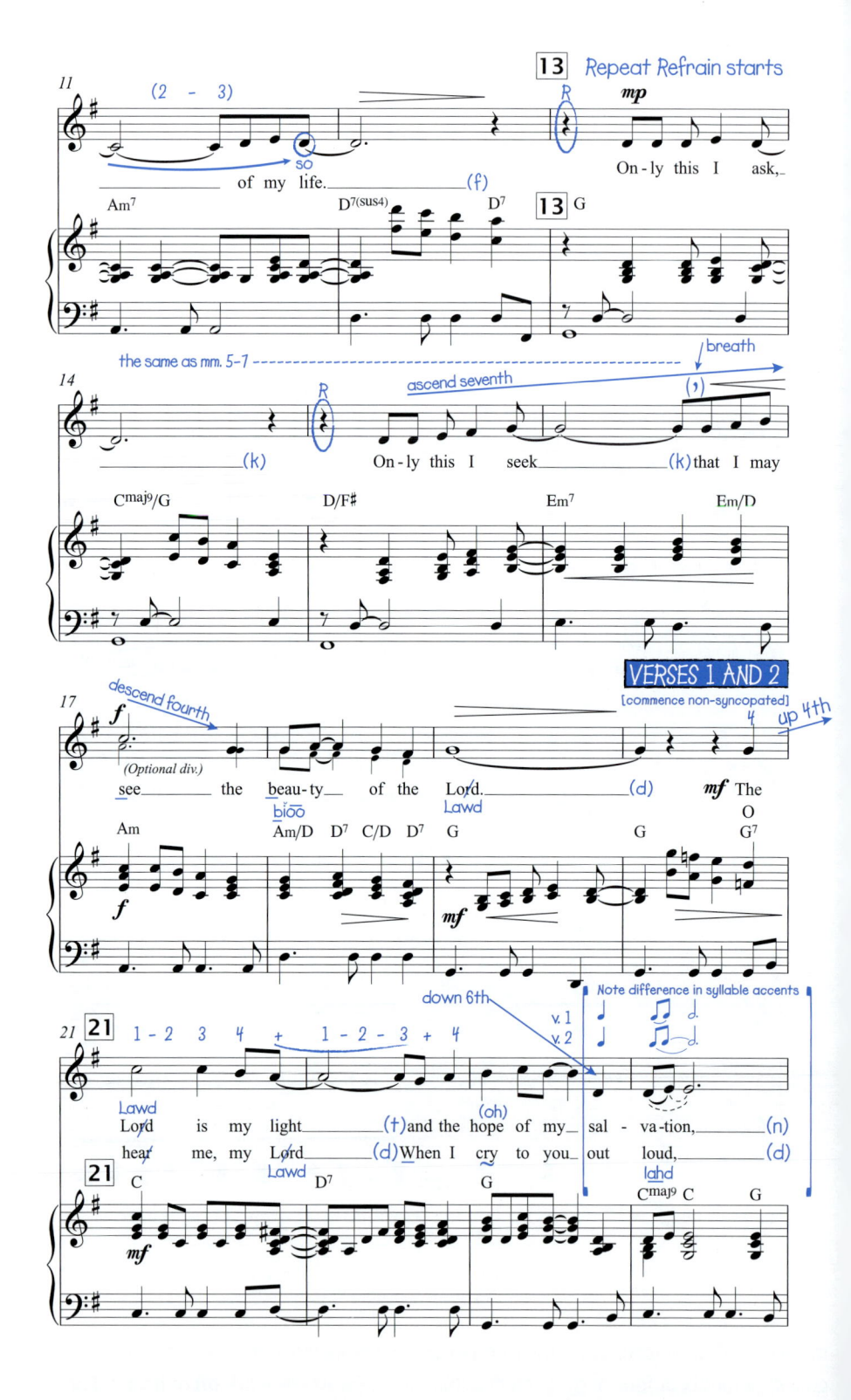

Apply the pitches once the rhythm and text are secure. Teach carefully the subtle step-wise differences between mm. 5 and 7, as well the descending intervals of mm. 8–10.

Verses Next

Moving on to the two verses (m. 21), again begin with the rhythm and text first. Start slowly in addressing some of the tenuous text concerns, such as negating the "r" in words like "Lord (lawd), hear (he/eh), your (yoh), answer (an-seuh) or fear (fe/eh)."

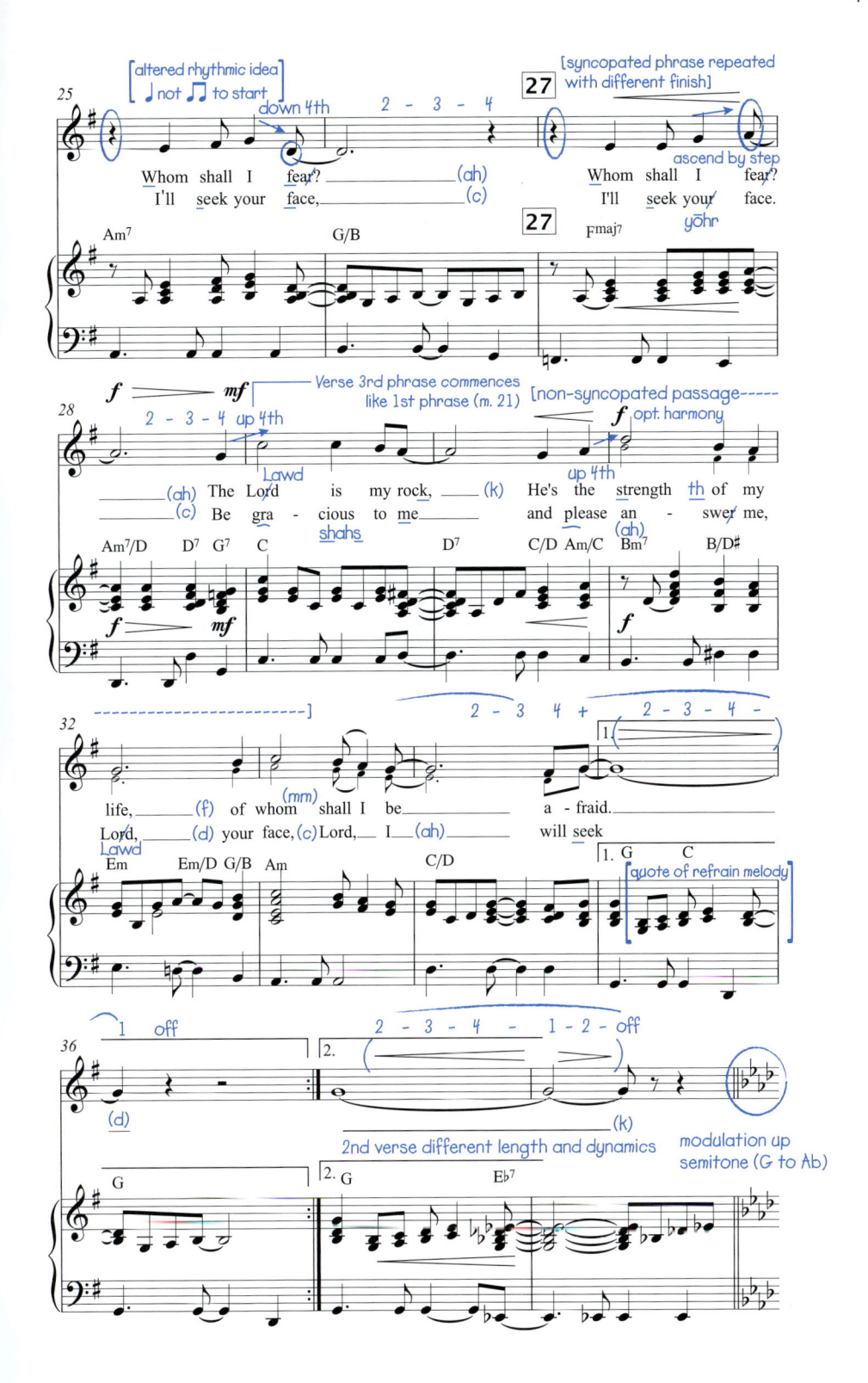

Other consonants can be emphasized for dramatic effect, like "<u>c</u>ry, <u>s</u>trength, <u>p</u>lease, <u>f</u>ace, <u>g</u>racious." As is sometimes the case with contemporary songs, accent and syllable structure are not consistent from verse to verse. One such spot is the end of the first phrase of the verse (mm. 23-24) with the words, "hope of my salvation/cry to you out loud." A little extra drill will be necessary in securing the differences. Emphasize that the concluding measures to the verses (mm. 31 ff.) start non–syncopated and then become syncopated again.

Concluding Refrain

To conclude, allow the singers to enjoy the added refrain in the new key at m. 39. Next learn the ending in parts. Men may double the soprano while the altos render the harmony. Notice that the text is slightly altered from "beauty of the Lord" to "beauty of you Lord" at mm. 52 and 58. Be sure to underscore the differences between the final phrase of the refrain (mm. 50–53) and the extended version that creates the coda from m. 54 on. To add meaning to the rehearsal or performance, take opportunity to read portions from Psalm 27, perhaps with piano backing.

Chapter 13 | THE EFFECTIVE SONGSTER REHEARSAL

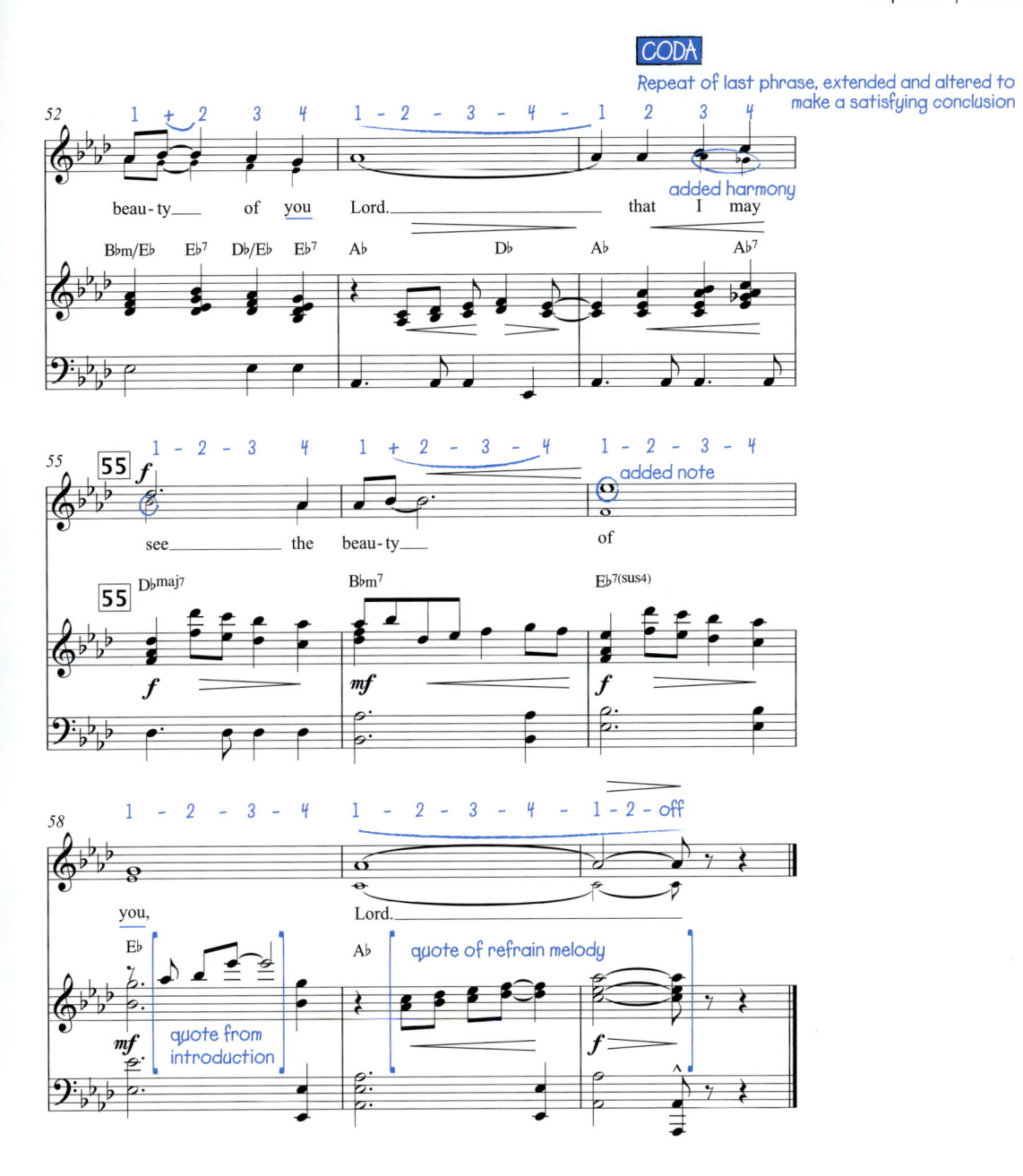

IT'S JUST A HYMN!

Hymn-tune playing in brass band circles is understood to be paramount in building roundness of sound through control of the air stream, which regulates dynamics and balance. Perhaps it is because hymns are sung as congregational songs that there is a tendency to devalue hymn-singing in a choir setting. "It's just a hymn," some will quip.

In the 130-plus year history of Salvation Army songster music, the great majority of pieces were strophic settings—multiple verses set to the same tune. Occasionally the printed copy would instruct the men to sing on verse two, for instance, but it became common practice for the songster leader to "arrange" the piece. He or she might ask the women to sing the melody on verse one; men only on the second; a soloist with the choir humming the harmony behind; and to conclude, all voices on their parts on verse four. This practice not only created a variety of color over the long haul of the four verses, but also saved precious rehearsal time by limiting the amount of text each section had to digest. While The Salvation Army is still publishing some strophic settings, where all the stanzas are set to the same music, our tendency is to rely on more developed, "through-composed" arrangements available from a host of publishers. The **logic** (a verse-by-verse setting, to enhance the text) and **inspiration** (which builds to a marvelous conclusion) is highly valued. What we may be missing, however, is what the brass band prizes about hymn-tune playing—the simplicity, training, and flexibility.

Typical **strophic setting** with verses assigned
("I'm A Soldier," Continental Air, arr. Erik Silfverberg)

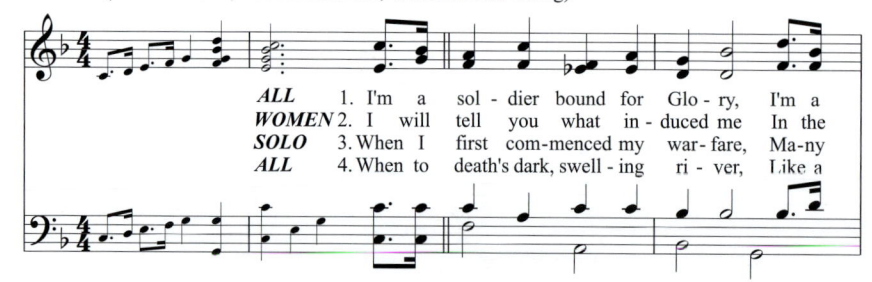

ALL	1. I'm a soldier bound for Glory, I'm a
WOMEN	2. I will tell you what induced me In the
SOLO	3. When I first commenced my warfare, Many
ALL	4. When to death's dark, swelling river, Like a

The simplicity of working with a few stanzas of music on one page of music in a standardized four-part harmony is easily apparent. Training opportunities—with sound, color, balance, and dynamic range—mirror those of the brass band, but it is the flexibility afforded the songster leader to handcraft an arrangement of verses designed for his or her brigade that makes working with strophic settings so valuable. Ownership is built into the process. Although you may have a preconceived plan, a rhetorical question like, "Let's try just the men in parts on verse two," shares the responsibility for the final outcome of the piece with the songsters. Together, you "discover" your own arrangement.

Key and tessitura

Flexibility in changing key is another tremendous advantage, especially when freed from the key of the notated accompaniment or track through *a cappella* singing. There are occasions when pieces are best transposed to a different key to improve the overall color and effect of the music, often proving to "sit" better with the voices. The prevailing compass of a passage is said to describe a song's *tessitura*, the area where the majority of the notes lie within the comfortable range of a singer. If the majority of the notes rest in the upper part of the singer's range, the song is said to be placed in the singer's high tessitura, and utilizing primarily a head tone, should sound bright and clear. On the other hand, moving voices into a lower tessitura, using chest voice, can create a warmer color, perhaps reflective of the text.

As singers blend from chest voice into the head voice, there is a change in vocal sensation commonly identified as "singing on the break," which varies according to the individual's range. The technical term is *passaggio*, which literally means "passage to the next register." Singers describe the feeling of the break as a narrowing. Bettina Sheppard likens it to moving through the narrow neck of the hourglass as the bridge between the chest and head voice.[2] Melodies in certain keys sound uncomfortably strained or pushed if they move back and forth over the break. The overall vocal color will improve if the melody is strategically shifted to a key that doesn't cross the break with frequency. A summary of voice ranges and tessitura appears in Appendix 13.3.

Like many wind instruments in the orchestra, singers have a variety of colors available to them, depending on where the range placement of the melody or voice part sits. Tenors and sopranos tend to sound brilliant in their upper registers, while

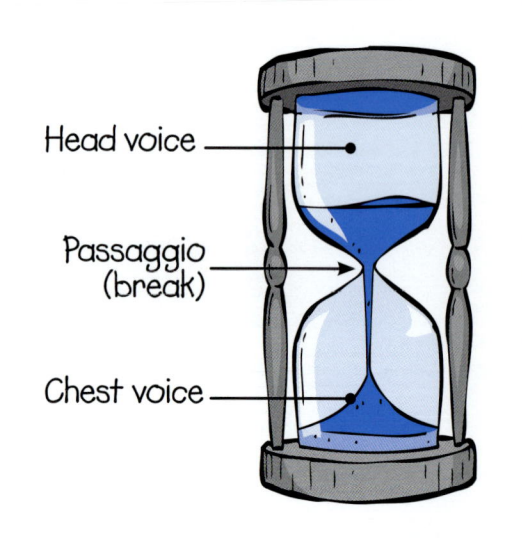

> "The flexibility afforded the songster leader to *handcraft* an arrangement of verses designed for *his* or *her* brigade makes working with strophic settings so valuable."

Head voice
Passaggio (break)
Chest voice

altos and basses should avoid high-end tessitura, favoring their lush mid-to-low registers. To maximize the sound of each section, as much as possible choose a key that places each singer in his or her best-sounding tessitura. Avoid extended singing in the low and high extremes, or around the break, as this tires singers quickly.

"This is My Father's World" (arr. Burgmayer)

HIGH TESSITURA (Bright)
Most voices fairly high in their range

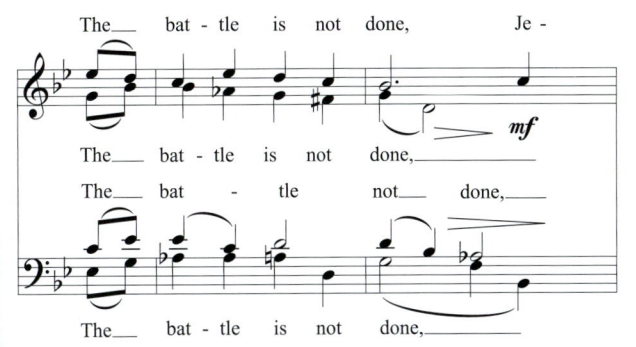

MID-RANGE TESSITURA (Warmer color)
All parts in a comfortable register

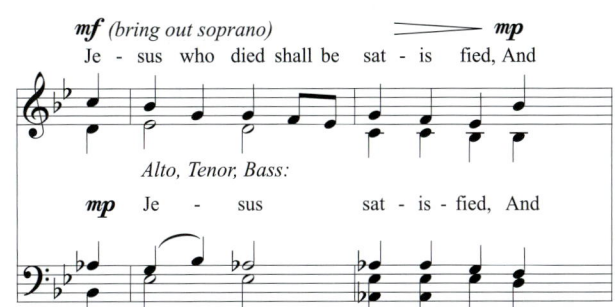

LOW TESSITURA (Lush)
All voices at low extreme of their range

WAYS TO RE-VOICE HYMNS FOR BRIGADES

We will assume that the songster leader can make choices to color verses with varying voice groups and soloists. Another approach is to *re-voice an SATB setting*, choosing not to alter any of the harmonies indicated. We can reassign parts and octaves to create varieties of colors in combination. Depending on the setting, key, and harmonization you choose to work from, some voicings will work better than others. Check the ranges of parts, especially when the voices are moved an octave higher. Obviously your choristers will need a pencil to indicate where they are singing on each verse. Here are some examples of re-voicings based on an SATB refrain found in *The Youth Songbook*.[3]

REFRAIN - For the Beauty of the Earth
Conrad Kocher - Youth Songbook No.6

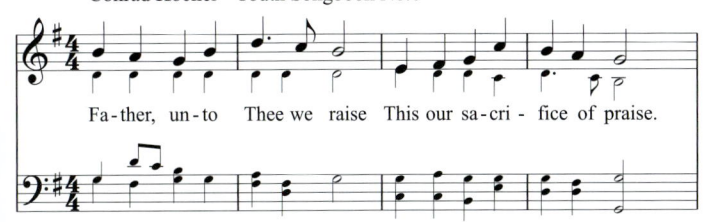

BRILLIANT MIXED VOICINGS

1. SATB Brilliant (sung with or without accompaniment)

SOPRANO sing alto part an octave higher (be sure range is reasonable)
ALTO (or ALL OTHER VOICES) sing soprano melody

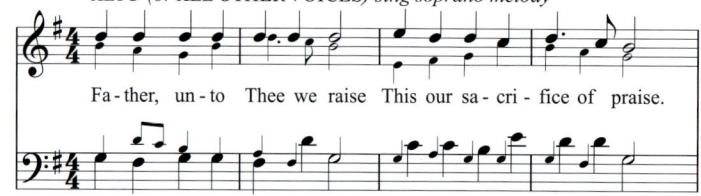

Fa - ther, un - to Thee we raise This our sa - cri - fice of praise.

TENOR and BASS sing tenor and bass parts
(option to shift bass octave up, ad lib. for added brilliance)

2. UNISON VOICES Brilliant
Vary accompaniment and harmonizations behind the vocal lines

Fa - ther, un - to Thee we raise This our sa - cri - fice of praise.

MEN SINGING THE MELODY

3. TWO PART Mixed Voices
Play accompaniment in four parts as notated

WOMEN sing alto part

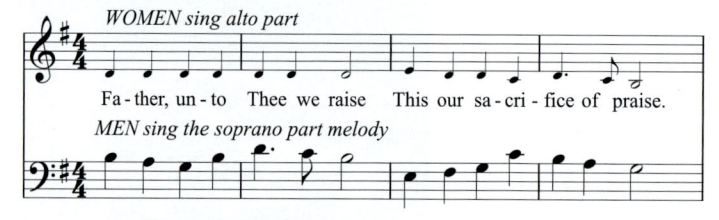

Fa - ther, un - to Thee we raise This our sa - cri - fice of praise.

MEN sing the soprano part melody

4. SAB (Men with melody)
Play accompaniment in four parts as notated
SOPRANO sing alto part
ALTO sing tenor part (in octave, as written)

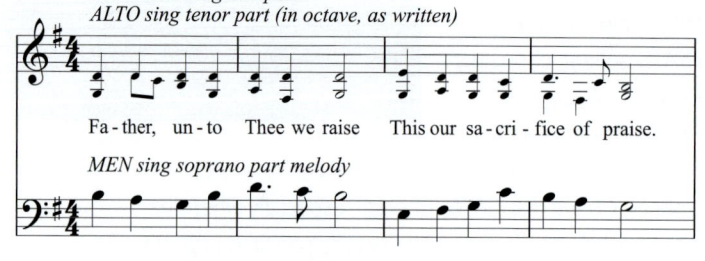

Fa - ther, un - to Thee we raise This our sa - cri - fice of praise.

MEN sing soprano part melody

5. MELODY with SOPRANO DESCANT
Excellent for refrain or final verse
Play accompaniment in four parts as notated, double bass octave

WOMEN sing alto part an octave higher (check range)

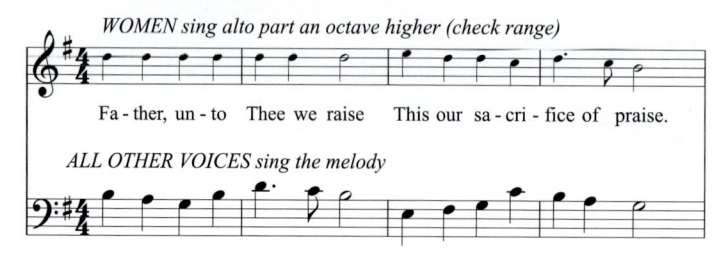

Fa - ther, un - to Thee we raise This our sa - cri - fice of praise.

ALL OTHER VOICES sing the melody

Chapter 13 | THE EFFECTIVE SONGSTER REHEARSAL

6. SATB Early Church Voicing

SOPRANO sing tenor part an octave higher
ALTO sing alto part

Fa - ther, un - to Thee we raise   This our sa - cri - fice of praise.

TENOR sing soprano melody

BASS sing bass part

MEN OR WOMEN ALONE

7. TTBB - Traditional Male Voicing (unaccompanied)

TENOR 1 sing alto part (in octave as written)
TENOR 2 sing tenor part (in octave as written)

Fa - ther, un - to Thee we raise   This our sa - cri - fice of praise.

BASS 1 sing soprano melody an octave low

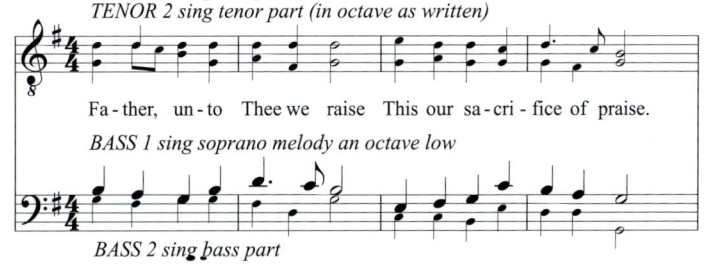

BASS 2 sing bass part

8. SSA Three Part Ladies (Do not play bass part)

SOPRANO 1 sing soprano melody, SOPRANO 2 sing alto part

Fa - ther, un - to Thee we raise   This our sa - cri - fice of praise.

ALTO sing tenor part (in octave as written)

VOICING EXCHANGES

9. ALTERNATE GROUPINGS by phrase (call and response)

SOLOIST (or Quartet in parts)   *ALL VOICES (in parts)*

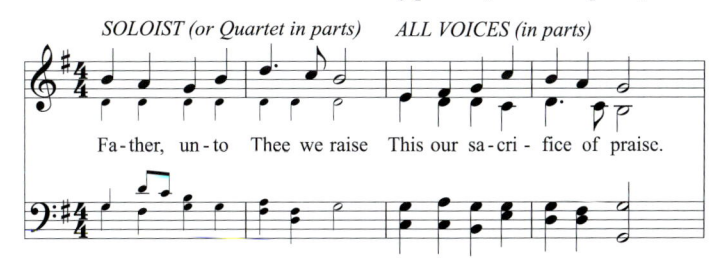

Fa - ther, un - to Thee we raise   This our sa - cri - fice of praise.

10. SSA/TTBB
Alternate phrases (or stanza) between female/treble and male voices
with the melody line exclusively (accompanied) or in parts (unaccompanied)

SSA voicing, like 5.   *TTBB voicing, like 6.*

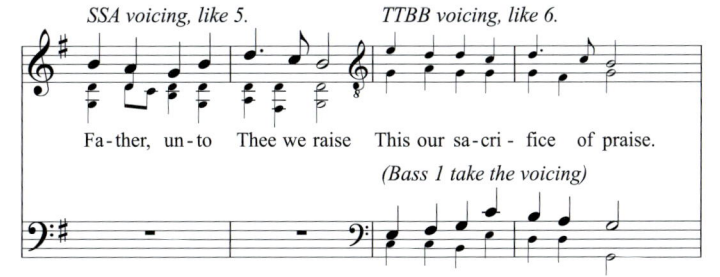

Fa - ther, un - to Thee we raise   This our sa - cri - fice   of praise.

(Bass 1 take the voicing)

The Beat Goes On

FOR THE BEAUTY OF THE EARTH

A re-voiced arrangement

Here is an example of an arrangement and working plan to re-voice "For the Beauty of the Earth" as harmonized in *The Youth Songbook/Songs of Praise*, No. 6. The words are by Folliott S. Pierpoint and the music by Conrad Kocher. The piece proves suitable as a call to worship for spring, harvest, or general use. The concluding refrain allows for congregational involvement. The goal is to create a colorful praise anthem with occasional four-part singing.

For the Beauty of the Earth

FOLLIOTT S. PIERPONT — CONRAD KOCHER

Moderato ♩ = 84

VERSES:
- V. 1 ALL VOICES in unison
- V. 2 LADIES or CHILDREN in two parts
- V. 3 MEN in unison on melody or parts
  - T1 - alto
  - T2 - tenor
  - B1 - soprano melody
  - B2 - bass
- V. 4 ALL VOICES on melody except a few sopranos (or trebles) singing the alto part as a DESCANT an octave high (piano play right hand up an octave and add octave to bass line.)

REFRAIN:
ALL VOICES in parts on all verses (Repeat Refrain after Verse 4)

Verses:
1. For the beauty of the earth, For the beauty of the skies,
2. For the beauty of each hour Of the day and of the night,
3. For the joy of human love, Brother, sister, parent, child,
4. For each perfect gift of thine To our race so freely given,

For the love which from our birth Over and around us lies,
Hill and vale and tree and flower, Sun and moon and stars of light,
Friends on earth, and friends above, For all gentle thoughts and mild,
Graces human and divine, Flow'rs of earth and buds of heav'n,

Refrain: Father, unto Thee we raise This our sacrifice of praise.

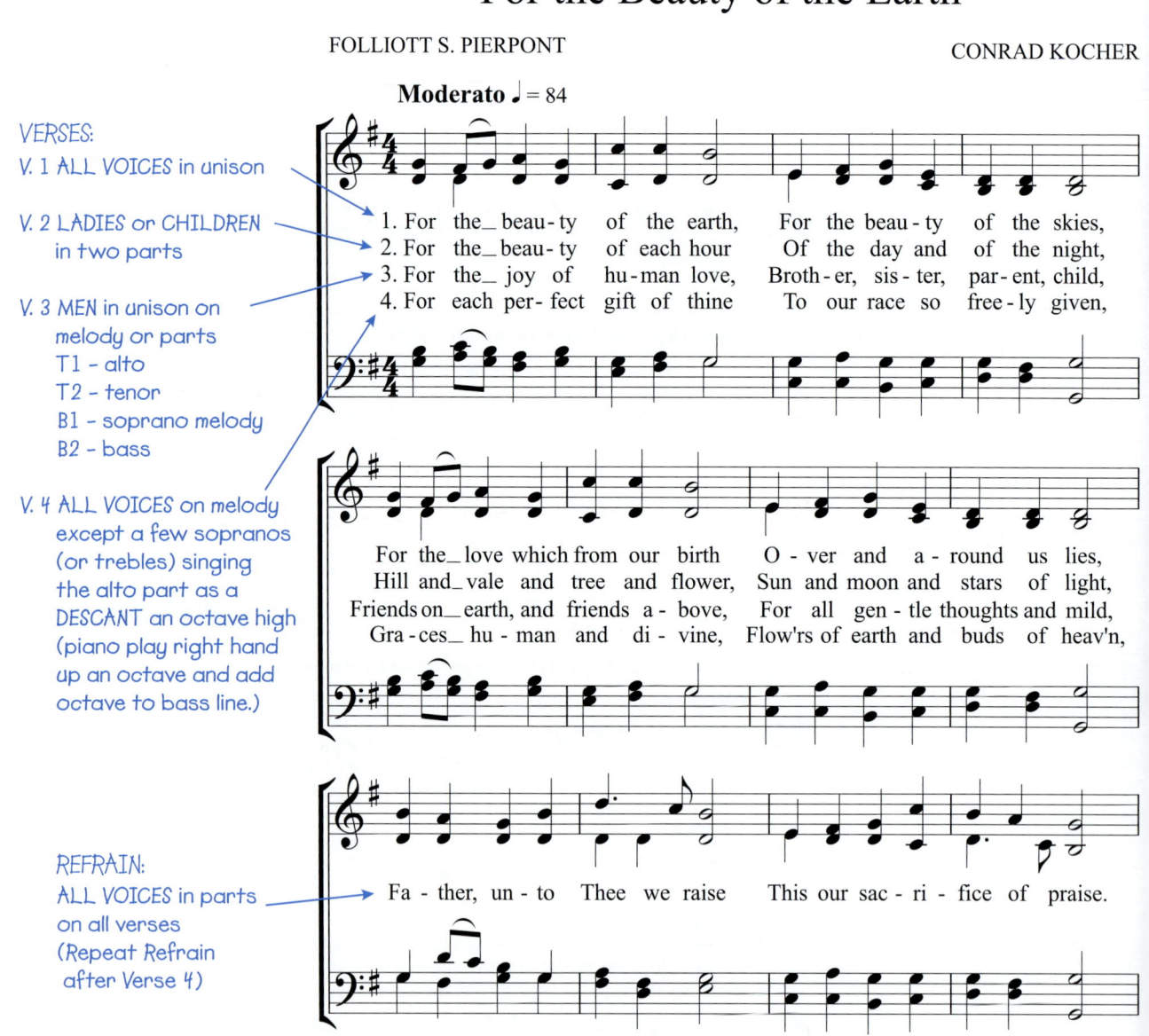

Reprinted with permission from the Youth Songbook
(Salvation Army - USA EAST)

The plan

In preparing this hymn as an anthem, the songster leader will notice that only eight measures of music need to be learned, as the first four bars are repeated. To further simplify matters, it is recommended that the full four-part harmony be taught *only* for the concluding four-bar refrain ("Father unto Thee we raise/This our sacrifice of praise"). Teach this first, working from the bass up. (Notice how simple the alto part is.) Then work back through the verses, being creative with different voicings but using the already-learned harmony for the refrain each time. For instance:

Verse 1. For the first presentation, use all voices in unison on melody.

Verse 2. Women or children only, perhaps in two parts (soprano and alto). The treble voices reflect the second verse "natural beauty" lyrics.

Verse 3. The male voices are appropriate for the "people" lyric. Men's voices, either in unison on melody or in parts. (If you have the readers, this arrangement works particularly well in four-part male voicing: Tenors I sing alto, in octave as written; Tenors II sing tenor; Basses I sing melody, an octave down, and Basses II sing bass.)

Verse 4. Make a triumphant finish with all voices in unison, except for a few sopranos or children singing the alto an octave higher as a descant. The alto/descant line continues through the refrain to make a brilliant ending. Repeat the refrain on verse 4 with a *rallentando* (continuing the alto descant) to create a brilliant ending.

This song may be presented *a cappella* or accompanied as notated in *The Youth Songbook*. Since the "ah" in Father is repeated with each refrain, the notes could be learned first on "ah," working for a full round sound and maintaining four-bar phrasing. In adding text, the singers should keep that nice round "ah" sound in mind. Remember to negate the "r" on words like *over* (o-vah), *father* (fah-thah), *our*, and *hour* (both of the latter emphasizing the "ah" sound).

13 BARS REST

1. More Rehearsal Plans for Songster Leaders and copies of the respective pieces, without conductor's markings, are available in Appendix 13.2. Choose a vocal score to study and mark. Prepare it strategically for a series of rehearsals.

2. Re-voice a hymn or SATB setting to suit your songster brigade.

---

a cappella (*term*)
\äk - ə - 'pel - ə\
In *Italian*, literally, "in the chapel," meaning as the choir traditionally sang in chapel, without any instrumental accompaniment.

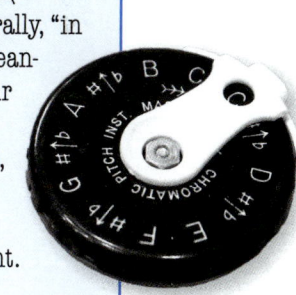

THERE IS MUSIC EVERYWHERE!

SALVATION ARMY CHORAL PUBLICATIONS

Almost from its inception, The Salvation Army has been publishing songs. *We are a singing Army;* it is estimated that more than 10,000 vocal works have been published to date. Today Salvation Army publications for teen and adult voices may be considered in two groupings: *Choral Series* and *Songbooks.* A listing of *Children's Choral Series* are noted at the conclusion of Chapter Seven. A number of these songs may be applicable for adults and some adult material may prove useful for children. Many of these publications are available through a subscription plan administered by each territory. Through this plan, music will be sent directly to your corps upon release, with one annual billing. Most come with accompaniment, rehearsal, and demonstration tracks.

CHORAL SERIES

Gems for Songsters 1-8 (Salvation Army, London) features collections of favorite vocal pieces in a hardback book format.

Psalms, Hymns and Spiritual Songs (Salvation Army, New York) is a collection of contemporary one-and two-part choral settings for vocal groups of various ages. Demonstration/accompaniment tracks are available.

Sing Praise (Salvation Army, Atlanta) is a periodic collection of SAB arrangements for teen and adult choirs. Demonstration/accompaniment tracks are available. As of 2015, *Sing Praise* is released as a single book with demonstration and accompaniment CD, with reprintable PDF files for ease of copying.

Sing to the Lord Mixed Voices Series (Salvation Army, London) replaced the century-old *Musical Salvationist* in January 1994. Each issue contains eight to twelve songs scored for SATB voices with piano accompaniment. *Sing to the Lord* is published three times annually.

SONGBOOKS and SONG COLLECTIONS

Carolers' Favorites (Salvation Army, New York) and **New Christmas Praise** (Salvation Army, London) are particularly useful for songster brigades at Christmas.

The Hallelujah Choruses (Salvation Army, Chicago, IL) publishes vocal parts in SAB format with piano accompaniment or to partner with a live rhythm section. The Salvation Army in Atlanta released two volumes of a **Contemporary Songbook**, also in SAB format, to be used with rhythm section accompaniment. Backing tracks are available for both the *Hallelujah Choruses* and the *Contemporary Songbook*.

Songs of Praise, formerly *The Youth Songbook*, (Salvation Army, Alexandria, VA) is a collection of 254 congregational songs with the words and music presented together in SATB format.

SONGSTER LEADERSHIP RESOURCES

Beyond the Downbeat, Sandra Willetts (Abingdon Press)
Choral Director's Rehearsal and Performance Guide, Lewis Gordon (Parker)
Choral Music—Technique and Artistry, Charles Heffernan (Prentice Hall)
Diction: Italian, Latin, French, German, John Moriarty (Schirmer)
Enhancing Musicality Through Movement DVD, Rodney Eichenberger (Santa Barbara)
Have We Had This Conversation? John Yarrington (Schott/Bradshaw)
The Perfect Blend Book and DVD, Timothy Seelig (Shawnee Press)
Ready, Set, Sing DVD, Jefferson Johnson (Santa Barbara); includes vowel hand signs
The Choral Director's Cookbook, (Meredith Music)
The Singer's Manual of English Diction, Madeline Marshall (Schirmer)
Upbeat Downbeat: *Basic Conducting Patterns and Techniques,* Sandra Willetts (Abingdon Press)

Dear Singing Enthusiast,
I recommend taking a look at Chapter Nineteen for more "contemporary" tips to help singers in worshiping choirs and praise bands... Good practical stuff!
A Friend of Singers

CHAPTER FOURTEEN

STRIKE UP THE BAND!
The Bandmaster's Rehearsal and Sunday Preparation

If the trumpet does not sound a clear call, who will get ready for the battle?
—I Corinthians 14:8

BOOTH AND THE BIRTH OF THE SALVATION ARMY BAND

William Booth's first recorded use of brass instrumentalists is found in correspondence from 1877: "The last Sabbath we had a little novelty which apparently worked well. Among the converts are two members of a brass band—one who plays cornet, and to utilize him at once Brother Russell put him with his cornet in the front rank of the procession…**He certainly improved the singing and brought crowds all along the march.** Then Booth adds, "Wondering curiously what we should do next."[1]

About a year later, when a mob took to singing popular songs to drown the voices of the Salvationists, the Fry Family band—father and three sons—were persuaded to bring their brass instruments to open-air meetings. Robert Sandall records, **"Their concerted playing quickly put an end to the interruption."** Again we witness the brass suppressing the opposing crowd and organizing the singing. Proceeding with caution, Booth agreed to add bands to the arsenal of ways The Salvation Army would **attract people and organize the singing.** He did so only after a trial set of meetings utilizing the Fry band. Interestingly enough, one officer "was at first shocked by the idea of a brass band taking part in religious meetings, but soon…reported that the 'Hallelujah brass band' was doing good service."[2] **And so the corps band was born.**

Booth later declared, "People seem to think I have said, 'I will have an Army and captains, and **bands of music,'** but these things were not in my mind." The Founder and those early-day bandsmen could hardly have imagined the international escalation of Army music-making, prophetically echoed by William Pearson in his words of 1882:

With a thousand bands and a thousand drums
We will praise the Lord in bright happy homes[3]

The march king, John Philip Sousa, once wrote, "How close to God beautiful music brings us, does it not? If you want to know one of the very good reasons why the world

In **Chapter Fourteen**, we:
- examine the beginnings of The Salvation Army corps band and its practicalities for week-to-week ministry today.
- study thoroughly the instrumentation of the brass band, including percussion.
- consider ways to train the band within the weekly rehearsal, giving practical suggestions for improving rhythm, sound, tuning, and blend.
- survey available Salvation Army publications for brass ensembles, ranging from a simple quartet to a full General Series brass band.

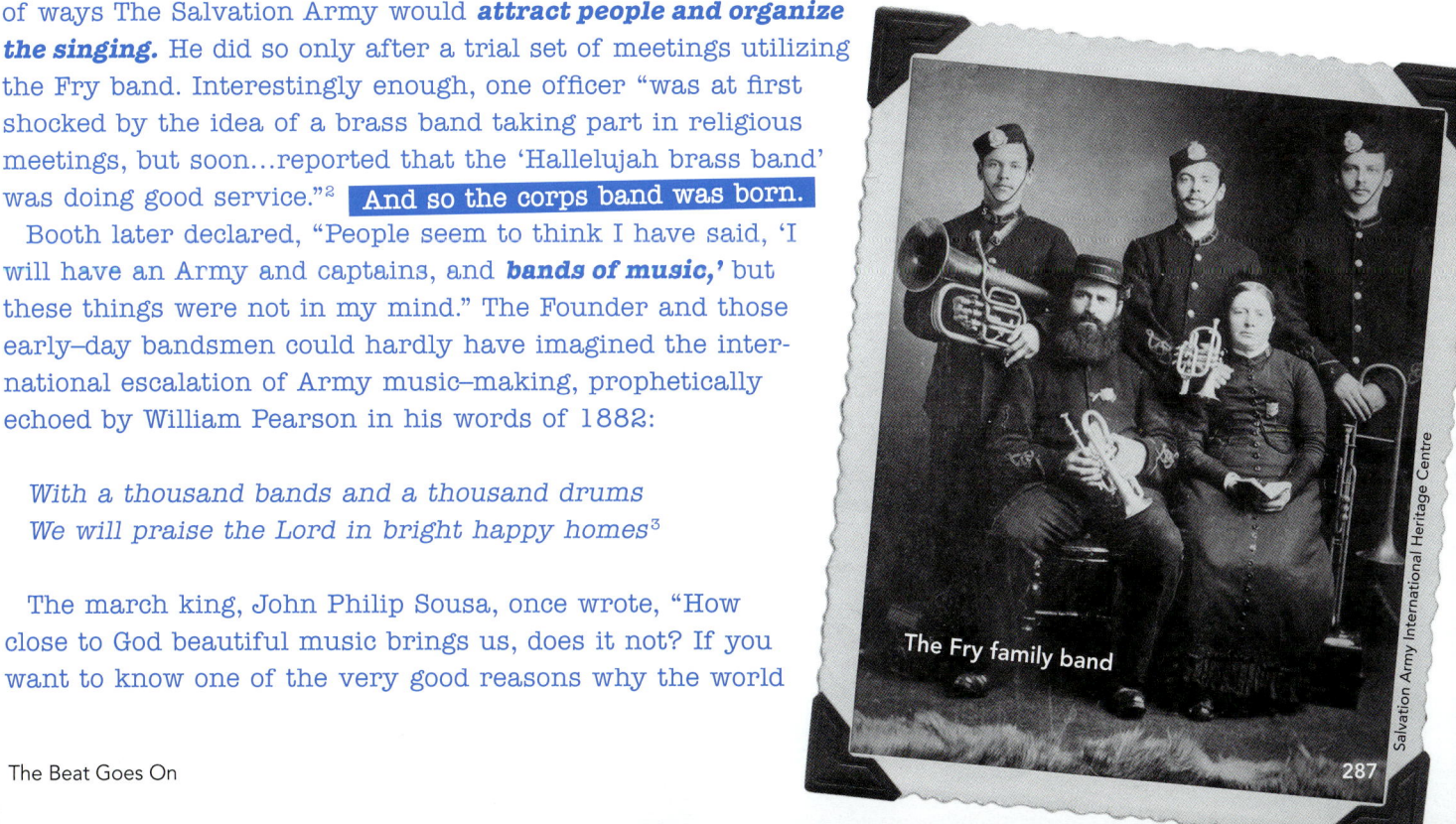

The Fry family band

"needs bands, just ask one of the Salvation Army warriors who for years have marched, carrying the message of the Cross, through the back alleys of life. Let me tell of the armies of men who have been turned toward a better life by first hearing the sounds of a Salvation Army band. The next time you hear a Salvation Army band, no matter how humble, take off your hat."[4]

Earlier chapters contain a great deal of material related to the bandmaster's role:

- Chapters One and Two consider appropriate repertoire selection and worship planning.
- Chapter Three touches on establishing order and discipline in a rehearsal setting.
- Chapter Four examines the role of the corps officer in encouraging music in the corps.
- Chapter Five surveys the songbook, and introduces the basic beat patterns for song-leading.
- In Chapters Eight and Nine, we discover ways that the youth band practice creates opportunities for developing listening and teamwork within an ensemble. We also explore rehearsal techniques to proactively troubleshoot and claim teachable moments.
- Chapters Ten and Eleven examines how to "hear" and mark a vocal or brass score by breaking it down into its component "layers."
- Chapters Twelve and Thirteen focus on creating active choral rehearsal practices and creating a rhythm in rehearsal planning. Many of these techniques also prove successful in the band rehearsal.

THE BRASS BAND TODAY—DYNAMO OR DINOSAUR?

Writing over a century after the birthing of the first corps bands in The Salvation Army, Bill Himes defended its usefulness, even in today's media-driven culture:

Bandmaster William Himes, OF

In the first place, *a brass band is flexible.* Whether in parade or festival, prison or cathedral, outside or indoors, the brass band can function more efficiently and effectively than any other instrumental combination. Having taught high school band, I know that weather can render woodwinds ineffective or inoperative, but brass instruments can function in wide temperature extremes that leave their woodwind and string cousins in the dust (or snow)!

A brass band is versatile. Those who think its music is out of touch with contemporary Christian music have not been paying attention to the style and sound of our brass publications in the last few years. The Army in America is leading the way in production of quality brass music, often effectively playable with as few as four, which swings, rocks, and sets toes (and hopefully hearts) a-tapping with gospel tunes known in and out of our Movement.

Have you ever heard a symphony orchestra play a march? It sounds pretty lame, doesn't it? Have you heard a jazz band play a hymn tune? It just doesn't make it! Have you heard a concert band try to swing or rock? Not convincingly, I bet. Yet from "Star Lake" to "Treasures from Tchaikovsky" to "Deep Harmony," a brass band can play in all of these idioms and do so convincingly! In fact, it has taken me many years to reach the conclusion that no other musical combination can match its adaptability and versatility.

A brass band is acoustical. In this age of electronic music, with its synthesizers, drum machines, sequencers, recorded tape tracks, and megawatt amplifiers, it is refreshing to hear music produced by a group of committed Christian musicians that is pure, natural, and unamplified!

My final point is at least as important as all the others combined: **A band is practical.** The wonder of the brass band is that it is, technically speaking, a model of simplicity. From cornet to tuba, only one set of fingerings and a working knowledge of treble clef are required. With this minimum working knowledge, participants can play, teach, and conduct brass ensembles with surprising proficiency. No one who conducts a concert band or orchestra can make that claim.

With their versatility, flexibility, and practicality, it would be a tragedy to abandon our brass bands at this point. Let's not throw the baby out with the bathwater. Given the fact that the largest churches in our community are developing instrumental programs at an unprecedented rate, it would be an unfortunate irony to lose one of our greatest assets.[5]

14 BARS REST

1. Take an objective look at the makeup of your corps band. What are some of the strengths of your group? What are the challenges? When is your band at its best?

2. How do you approach a new season with your corps band? Do you plan for the whole season: Fall and then Spring? Seasonal (Advent, Lent, etc.)? Four to six weeks, or week-to-week? How do you become acquainted with new repertoire or ideas?

3. How do you choose the appropriate selection for a Sunday? Do you work from a sermon series in consultation with your corps officer-pastor? Are you part of a worship committee? Do you have input into the layout of the worship service? Do you look through the latest publications or do you work from the church calendar?

4. Do you rehearse the song accompaniments for Sunday services? Is there a system whereby tune book or other chorus arrangement numbers are available to you in time for review in that week's rehearsal? Do they become a part of the warm-up or are they rehearsed elsewhere?

For more on **Sunday and seasonal worship planning**, see Sunday Worship Chapter Two and Conducting Chapter Twenty-Three.

5. Is there an order to your weekly rehearsal? Are there strategies you use to ensure that Sunday's music is ready? How do you keep interest consistent from week to week?

6. How is the band nurtured and prepared for worship spiritually from week to week?

7. What is your corps band's Sunday morning routine? When do you meet? Do you use a board or share a handout listing that day's order of pieces and instructions? When do you make announcements and pray?

8. Do you ever trade off or partner with the corps pianist, organist, or praise band? How is this coordinated?

9. How do you as the bandmaster remain faithful musically and consistent spiritually from week to week over the course of a season? Do you have a support system? How do you receive feedback?

10. What are your greatest joys in being a corps bandmaster?

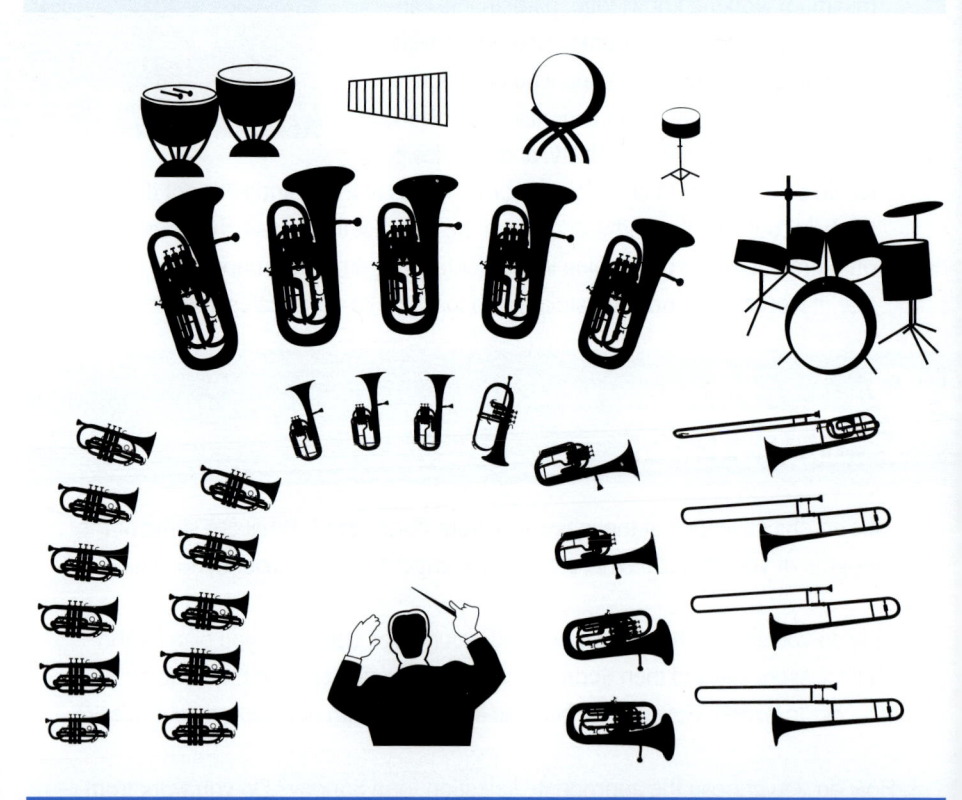

Band Today:
Prel: Lord Reign in Me
    (HC 177)
Song: All Hail the Power
    (HC 141 with praise band)
Song: Great Is Thy Faithfulness
    (TB 983 - 4 bar intro,
    v. 2 piano only)
Selection: Tis So Sweet (A 1-
Song: It Is Well
    (TB 695 - 3+2

---

transposing notation (*term*)
\trans - ˈpōzing nō - ˈtā - shən\
The majority of brass band instrumentations require "transposed" parts, which are not written in its actual pitch to compensate for instruments whose fundamental pitch is Bb or Eb, rather than C, as with the piano.

THE INSTRUMENTS OF THE BRASS BAND

Just as songster leaders are encouraged to "know thy singers," so bandmasters need to know their players and their instruments. Time spent tutoring students on brass band instruments, including trombone and percussion, proves valuable later when one is guiding an ensemble from the middle of a band. There is a basic consistency to the transposing notation for brass band instrumentalists, as all players, with the exception of the bass trombonist, use treble clef fingerings or positions. Historically, it is said that this uniformity of clefs and fingering allowed cornet players to easily switch to low brass instruments. These transpositions (meaning literally changing the note position on the staff), particularly for the Bb and Eb instruments, remain uniform even in today's modern wind band with the clarinet and sax families.

Bb Cornet and Flugelhorn

The soprano voice of the brass band is the cornet, which has a mellower counterpart in the flugelhorn. To match the piano playing middle C, the Bb cornet or flugelhorn will play a written D, using the treble clef. The transposition is **one whole step up** from the pitch of the piano or what is commonly known as "concert pitch."

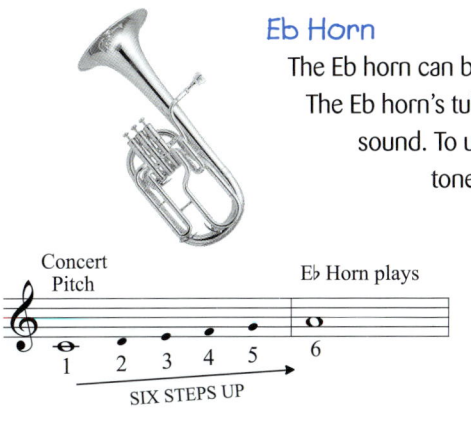

Eb Horn

The Eb horn can be likened to the alto voice of the brass family. The Eb horn's tubing is in the shape of a cone, giving it a mellow sound. To understand how the shape of the tubing effects tone color, contrast the sound of the cylindrical, and therefore brighter-sounding orchestral trumpet and the conical cornet or horn. However, I hesitate to call the Eb horn an alto horn, as it is labeled a tenor horn outside the U.S. The Eb horn is notated **up a major sixth** from the concert pitch desired.

For a detailed explanation of the **brass band instrument transpositions**, see Chapter Fifteen, pp. 322–328.

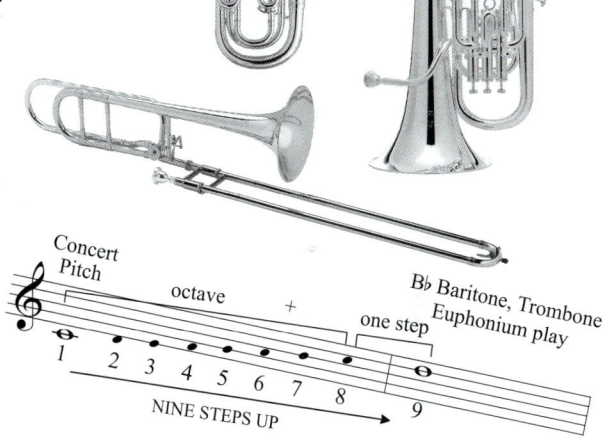

Bb Baritone, Bb Trombone, and Bb Euphonium

In brass band tradition, the tenor voicing falls to the baritone, trombone, and euphonium players who read parts notated in treble clef, but actually sound an octave and a step lower than notated. The piano middle C is written as a fourth line treble clef D, a transposition **up a major 9th or an octave plus one step**. The trombone and the baritone have a smaller bore than the euphonium (The bore is the size of the opening as the instrument flares out.) The trombone is a cylindrical or bright instrument, while the euphonium with its larger conical bore creates a warmer sonority. It is sometimes described as the cello of the brass band.

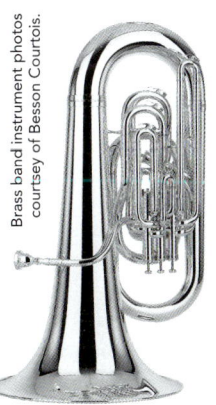

Eb and Bb Bass Tubas

The bass voice of the brass band is the tuba, also called bass. These parts are also written in treble clef, keeping the fingering uniform from the top of the band down. The C below middle C on the piano (the bass clef second space C) is notated as a second space A in treble clef for the smaller Eb Bass—a transposition of **an octave and a major sixth**. The C below that on the piano (two ledger lines under the bass clef staff) is notated for Bb tuba as a D just under the staff in treble clef. This transposition is based on the Bb **one-step higher** shift as for the cornet, but noted **two octaves higher**.

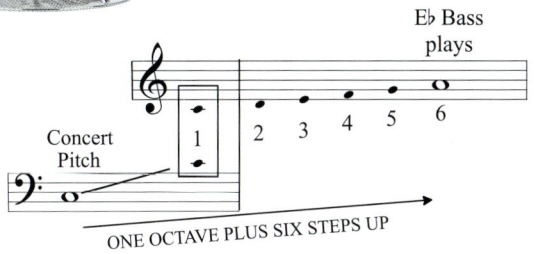

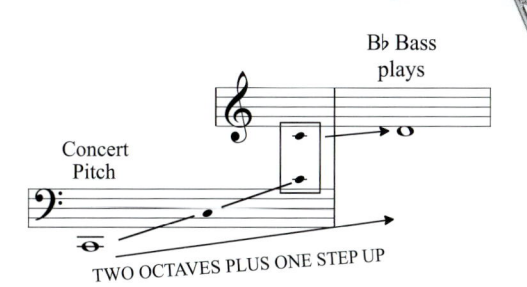

Brass band instrument photos courtesy of Besson Courtois.

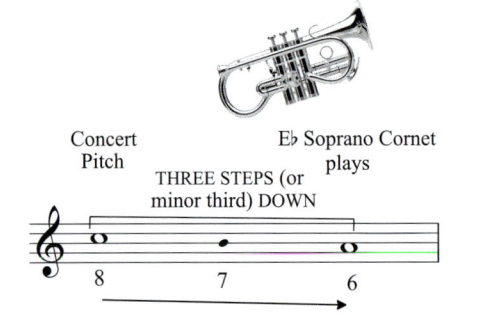

Eb Soprano Cornet

Current brass band practice allows for one Eb soprano cornet. This instrument is smaller than the Bb cornet and therefore the highest voice available to a brass band composer. A third space treble clef C on the piano is notated as a second space A in treble clef of the Eb soprano cornet—a transposition of a **minor 3rd down**.

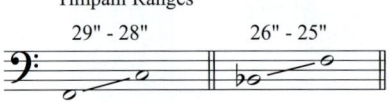

Bass Trombone and Timpani

In the brass band, the only instruments using bass clef in "concert pitch" are the bass trombone and timpani. **No transposition is necessary**, as the actual sound matches the written notes. A standard pair of timpani will cover the range of an octave from F to F. Changes in pitch are manipulated with foot pedals.

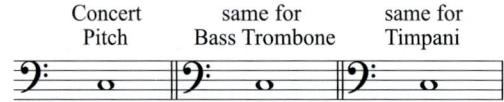

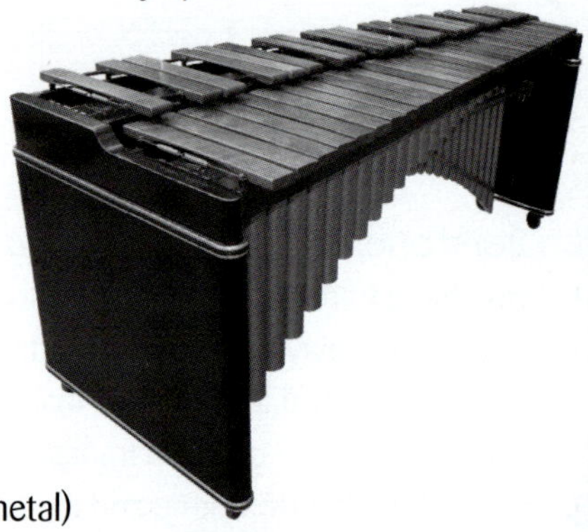

Mallet Percussion

Parts for mallet percussion are notated in concert pitch in treble clef usually as Percussion 1. The actual sound of a glockenspiel part will sound two octaves higher than written. The xylophone and chimes part will sound one octave higher, while the vibraphone will sound as written. Arrangers will suggest a preferred choice of mallets (soft, yarn, hard, or metal) which greatly affect the color and dynamic desired.

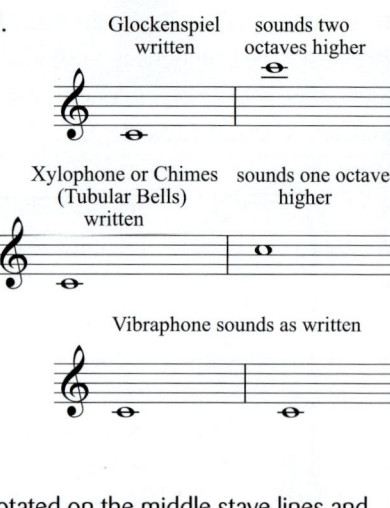

Other Percussion

Standard percussion parts use the percussion clef on a five-line stave, often labeled as Percussion 2. Common practice places the bass drum on the bottom space, cymbals in the second space up, snare drum in the third. The top spaces and lines are reserved for triangle, tambourine, and other auxiliary percussion. **Parts notated for drum set** will use the top space or line for notation of the high-hat or ride cymbal, with the bass and snare drum in their normal positions. **Tom-tom fills** are usually notated on the middle stave lines and spaces descending by pitch from highest to lowest finishing with the bass drum.

See Appendix 14.1 for **Technique Tips for Concert Percussion**.

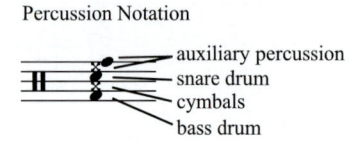

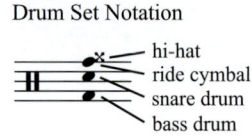

www.music.saconnects.org

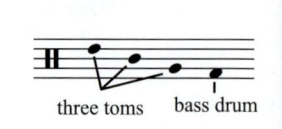

Key Transpositions

In the brass band we need only be concerned about the correct key for the Bb, Eb, and C instruments. It is helpful for the brass band conductor to understand that the transposition of keys mirrors those of the note transpositions explained above. The sharps and flats, or absence of the same, at the beginning of each staff indicates the tonal center or main note of a composition, known as its **key**. For a *major key using sharps, the keynote is one tone above the last sharp in the signature*. For *flats, the key is on the pitch of the next-to-the-last flat in the signature*. The **concert key** is the name for the home key for instruments like the piano, flute, or violin, which do not require compensating transposition. They are sometimes said to be in C pitch.

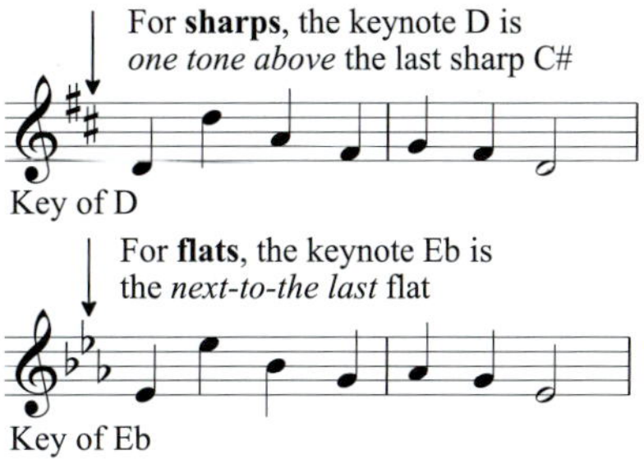

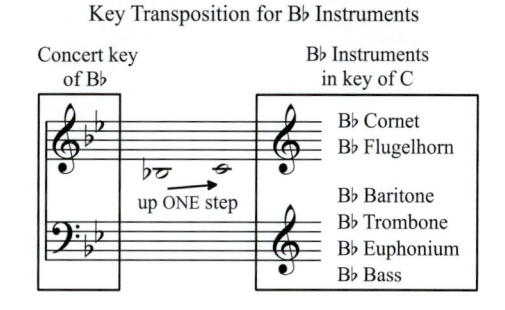

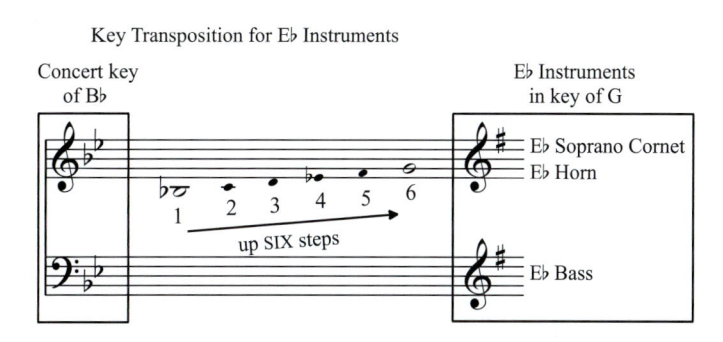

Bb pitch—In the concert key of Bb, which has two flats, the Bb instruments (cornet, baritone, trombone, euphonium, and Bb tuba) will have a key signature of no flats and sharps; that is, C. This mirrors the Bb cornet transposition that is found by going *up one whole step* from *the concert key*.

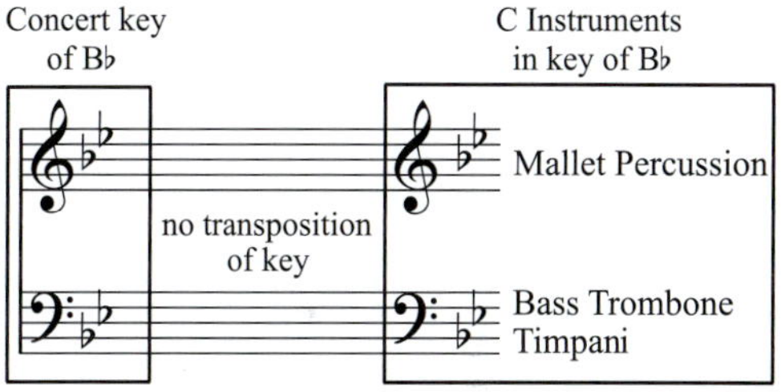

Eb pitch—Similarly, in the concert key of Bb, the Eb horn, Eb soprano, and Eb tuba will transpose the key of Bb *up a major sixth* to G. Therefore, these Eb instruments will have a key signature of one sharp.

C pitch—The concert pitch instruments—bass trombone, mallet percussion, and timpani—will be in Bb with a key signature of two flats.

BAND TRAINING

No Uncertain Sound Revisited

Many times the personal musical development of band members slows considerably upon acceptance into a senior or divisional band. As teens mature, the short- and long-term goals of a youngster's private and group lessons are soon consumed by work, school, and family obligations. After students graduate from high school, Salvation Army banding on rehearsal night and Sunday may become the sole opportunity to play during a typical week. The once-faithful junior band members who were playing every day find themselves barely getting onto the corps platform on time. Some band members practice or at least warm-up daily, but except for those who aspire to teach or perform music, they are the minority.

Because of this, both players and bandmaster need to permit within the weekly rehearsal not only teachable moments (referred to in Chapter Eight, p. 180), but also what is known as **band training**. While there may exist an ongoing tension between performance and mission, the bandmaster should strive to improve the sound and effect of the corps band as a matter of stewardship. This parallels the essential spiritual shepherding

Eric Ball conducting at Star Lake Musicamp.

pulse (*noun*) \'pəls\ The word used for the regular throbbing of blood through the arteries is applied to music where it becomes "to feel the beat or pulse." Conductors also use the term for a subdivision of beats, for instance, feeling the pulse of a series of paired eighths undergirding a notated bar of four quarter notes.

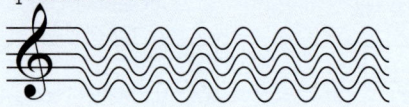

crescendo (*adj*) \'krə - shen - dō\
diminuendo (*adj*) \'də - min - yə - wə - dō\ (or *decrescendo*) are the standard terms for increasing or decreasing loudness. They are abbreviated as *cresc.* and *dim.* (*decresc.*), or indicated by the < and > signs.

considered in Chapter One. With the varied experiences, skill sets, and attention spans found within a corps band, the bandmaster assumes multiple roles. In addition to serving as conductor, he or she must be part leader, teacher, trainer, mentor, even psychologist. If the band is to improve, the bandmaster discreetly finds opportunities to instill essential banding concepts into the weekly rehearsal. The essence of most of the band training tips cited here comes from a series, *No Uncertain Sound*, by Eric Ball. Published in the sixties in The Salvation Army's now extinct *Musician* magazine, its time-honored wisdom transcends its own generation.

Inner rhythm and pulse

"From our heartbeats to the cycles of days, nights, months, and years, all of life pulsates with rhythm!" (Eric Ball). Music, with its innate rhythm, is an expression of life. Even in slow, sustained music we can instill a feeling for the pulse. Take a hymn tune and ask the players to subdivide all longer values into eighth (quaver) pulses. Then ask half the band to play the values as notated, while the other half continues the eighth pulses. Midstream, reverse the roles and later, bring all parts back to the notated long values, still maintaining the feeling of the eighth pulses.

Subdivide hymn tune into eighths (quaver) pulses

This pulsing exercise is also useful when trying to grade *crescendos* and *diminuendos*. For example, mentally count up or down the pulses to make an evenly graduated *crescendo* or *diminuendo* over two bars. The count-singing, staccato syllables, and count-dynamics exercises introduced in Chapter Thirteen can also bring rhythmic vitality to the band's performance.

Count-Singing crescendos and diminuendos

Inner rhythm and pulse extends to the feeling of the beats across a bar. Instruct your players, particularly the tubas, to feel the STRONG-weak-medium-weak inner rhythm of 4/4 time; the STRONG-weak-weak of 3/4 time and the STRONG-weak in measures of 2/4.

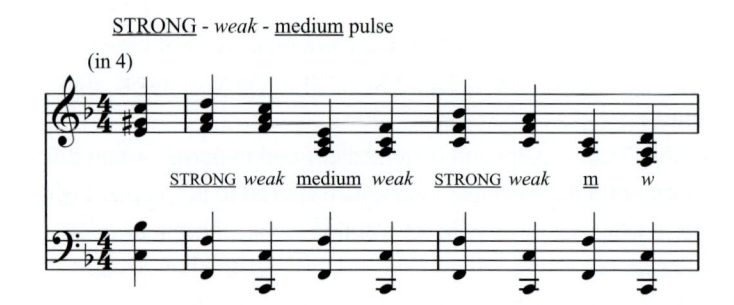

STRONG - weak - medium pulse (in 4)
STRONG weak medium weak STRONG weak m w

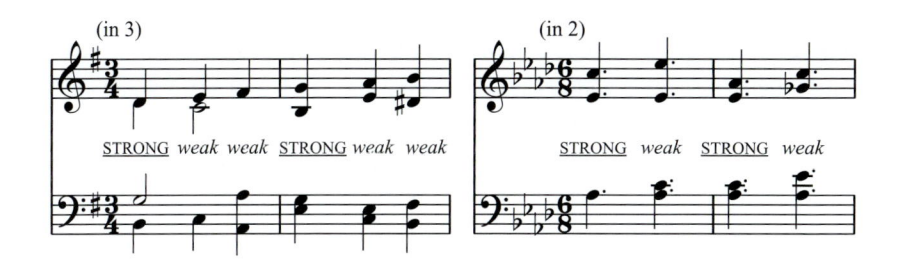

> **preparatory beat** (term) \'pri - par - ə - tōr - ē bēt\ A general rule that the conductor will give an extra beat, strictly in time, before the music actually begins. For instance, to begin a piece on the first count of a 4/4 bar, the conductor will indicate a preparatory beat one count earlier, on beat four.
> (For more on the preparatory beat, see Chapters Twenty and Twenty-One.)

Attack, sustain, release

A musical tone is composed of three elements—an attack, the tone sustained, and then its release. Absolute precision and unanimity across the ensemble as the norm can be nurtured by choosing a closing chord from a hymn tune. Instruct the band to take a deep, wide breath and, following the indication of your preparatory beat, attack the note firmly, hold it evenly, then release it cleanly. Concentrate solely on this task, compelling the players to listen "together." Ask how this "feels" on the breath and with the tongue.

It can be revealing to alternate the chords between the *brights* (cornets and trombones) and *mellows* (horns, baritones euphoniums and tubas), or the upper end of the band (cornets and horns) and the lower brass. Careful listening aims to unify the approach right through the band. For example, ask the low brass to articulate as precisely as the cornets. Vary the dynamic of the chord from *piano* to *forte*. Use a clear preliminary upbeat for both the attack and the release.

As chords do not exist musically in isolation, choose a tune that is homophonic. This means the chords change together with the melody without any passing tones. The hymn tune "St. Anne" is a good example. Ask the band to play each chord with a precise attack and release, allowing a brief separation of "daylight" between each chord.

Vary the weight of the dynamics. Even at piano, maintain the energy and precision. Next ask the band to narrow the gaps between the chords and draw the notes together into phrases. Even at slow tempos, the action of the tongue, valves, or slide remains quick.

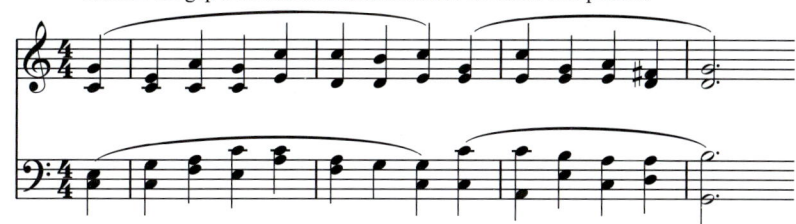

Slurs

In a similar manner, request the players to take the slurs off slurred passages and articulate them first with daylight space between each note. Remind them to feel both the pulse and a precise start and release. There should be an increased sense of precision and pulse when you put the slurs back on.

The Beat Goes On

Groupings of four are a microcosm of the 4/4 bar with a STRONG-weak-medium-weak inner rhythm. A triplet sounds as STRONG-weak-weak and a paired duple as STRONG-weak. The "weak" finish to these groupings reinforces the rule of thumb that when notes are slurred, take some length off the last of the slur. This creates some daylight for clarity's sake and shapes the close of the slurred figure.

Groupings of 4
STRONG - weak - medium - weak

S - w - m - w

Groupings of 3
STRONG - weak - weak

S - w - w S - w - w S - w - w S

> **tempo** (*noun*) \'tem - pō\ The rate of speed of a composition or section of a piece, as indicated by either a metronome mark ($\quarternote = 60$), meaning 60 beats per minute or one beat per second, or expressive inscriptions like **Adagio** (slow) or **Allegro** (fast), which permit considerable latitude in the choice of tempo.

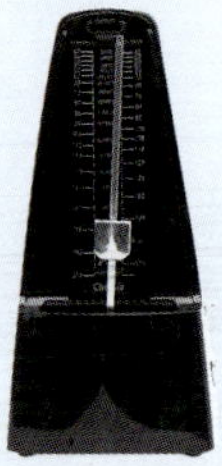

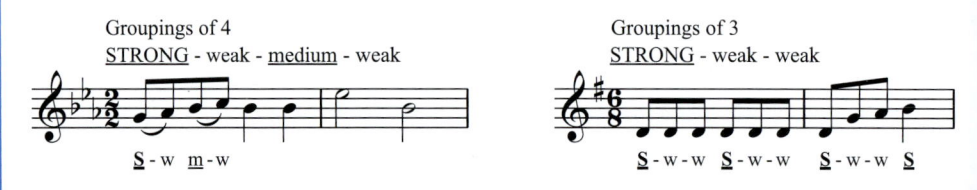

The overall goal is for the band to experience the attack, sustain, and release rhythmically in any style or *tempo* of music. Insist on a steady accompaniment pulse (sometimes tap the beat, rather than conduct) to troubleshoot sixteenth (semiquaver) passages from dragging or the descending eighth (quaver) ones from rushing. Make every player an active listener, feeling the rhythmic pulse from within.

Inner ear and sound

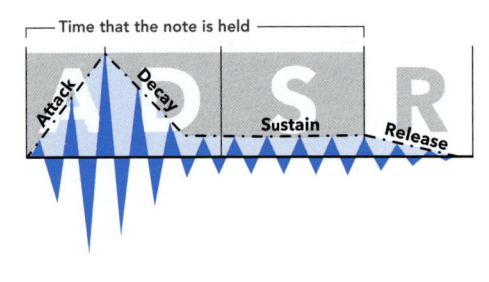

In today's studio technology, it is possible to sample an ideal tone and replicate it in different ranges throughout the spectrum of the band. In fact, this is the basic premise behind the "creation" of synthesized music. The attack, decay, sustain, and release (ADSR) for an instrumental color is analyzed and reproduced through digital signals and, *voila*, we are supposed to believe that we are hearing a saxophone. This Stepford Wives approach to music making disavows the infinite variations of instrumental tone color, which, when blended together, create the unique sound of an ensemble. Each band will have its own unique sound. **Bandmasters may have in their inner ear an idealized composite tone for their band, but are held accountable for the reality of a wide inequality of sound production in front of them.** Band members need to be reminded that, unlike the piano, tone on a brass instrument doesn't just happen. It is something created in the "inner ear." It begins with an image of an ideal sound, perhaps from a recording, and exhibits an innate beauty or power that one aspires to emulate.

Many bandmasters concentrate their focused band training for quality of sound through hymn tune playing. This is not difficult to fit into your allotted time because hymn tunes need to be rehearsed for Sunday worship. Play the hymn tunes at a *mezzo forte* or *forte* level, with the goal being roundness of sound. Encourage players to build a library of recordings of exemplary tone. Train the players to stagger the breath within their section where necessary to keep the line and the tone rich and flowing, especially in the bass line.

See Chapter Twenty-Three for more on bringing out the essential lines and achieving balance across the ensemble.

Balance

Balance within the harmonic framework is critical. The intensity and depth of sound is dependent on secondary parts sounding as strong as the leaders, and the bass voice being the strongest (see Acoustic Pyramid on next page). In a hypothetical "pyramid" strategy maximizing resonance, there are three 2nd horns, two 1st horns, and one solo horn to create a balanced chord. Due to the tuba's invaluable low-end overtones, bass players are often asked to play above the indicated dynamic to give the band a resonant, rich tone. Render the hymn tune with different color combinations. For instance, use the brights alone, working for a balance within the sections themselves. Then bring the entire ensemble together more sensitized to "listening" outside and within their section. Having raised the level of accountability and interaction, especially within the secondary and lower parts, the total band sound improves.

As players advance, they learn to intuitively subordinate their part for another or alternatively, to bring out the melody or a moving part. Having spent time in the score, the bandmaster will explain the relative importance of each section, be it the accompaniment, countermelody, or the melody. Naturally we never want to lose the principal theme in the balance, but there are also the moments when a descending bass line should be brought out to signal an impending modulation or transition. Even though the melody will be kept in the forefront, the accompaniment must be balanced within itself. It takes secure rhythm and pitch balance to negotiate swift color shifts between sections. The analogy of the first group passing off to the second, who receive it expectantly, encourages active listening. The interplay encourages the players' understanding of the surrounding musical context. Everyone is responsible for the balance, overall sound color, and relative dynamic levels.

ACOUSTIC "PYRAMID"

- **S**OPRANO VOICES — 1st Cornet, Bells, Triangle, Cymbal — *p* — 25%
- **A**LTO VOICES — 2nd Cornet, 1st Horn — *mp* — 50%
- **T**ENOR VOICES — 2nd Horn, Baritone, Trombone, Tom-Toms — *mf* — 75%
- **B**ASS VOICES — Euphonium, Bass Trombone, Basses, Timpani, Bass Drum — *f* — 100%

relative rate of cresc./decresc.

Dynamics

An essential component of a chord's color rests in its relative dynamic level. One simple technique, useful midstream in rehearsal, is to ask the entire band to take the dynamic down one notch. Emphasize that the goal is a uniform, balanced dynamic across the ensemble. You might identify the dynamic just played as *mezzo forte* and state that we need the ensemble as a whole to be at a *mezzo piano* level. Next ask the band to take the dynamic down even another notch to *piano* without losing the quality or precision of sound. When every player concentrates on this task, it is surprising the controlled soft dynamics that can be achieved. Remind the band members to remember the color of the desired dynamic for when the band returns to that spot.

One sign of a controlled sound is to be able to play a lively march quietly, while maintaining its characteristic rhythmic impulse and clarity. When the music tends to lose control, the first thing to go will be the quiet dynamic. Eric Ball suggests that quiet drama can be maintained at *pianissimo*. He likens it to the contrast between an out-of-control shout to an intense hiss, or someone shouting "I love you" in a large noisy crowd, as opposed to a lover's mouthing, barely above a whisper, "I love you." Few things are as dramatically powerful as effective soft playing. As a safeguard though, when a soloist or section is being asked to make a difficult or high entry, better to ask for a dynamic higher to avoid timid or split tones.

pp p mp mf f ff f mf mp p pp

Maintaining quality of sound

One of the most demanding things to accomplish in music is a well-graded *diminuendo*. There can be a tendency to slope too quickly to a soft dynamic, sometimes described as an exponential, rather than a linear *diminuendo*. In the process, the tone deteriorates and intonation is affected. Further, some players may *diminuendo* more quickly than others, disrupting the balance within a chord by exposing certain instruments while masking others.

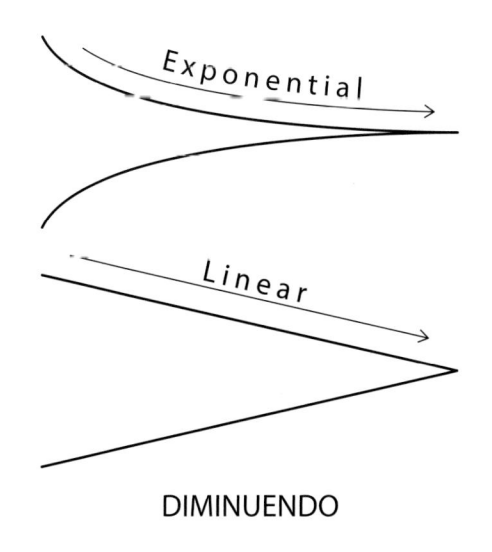

DIMINUENDO — Exponential / Linear

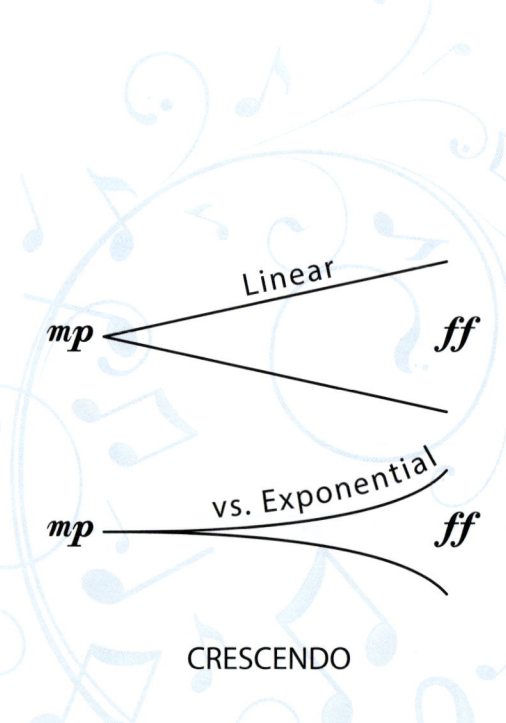

Remind players that they create the tone and that each player must still strive to fill the horn with air, even at soft dynamics. As an exercise, attempt a section of a quick march at a *pianissimo* level. Suggest to bandsmen that they intently listen around and resist the temptation to starve the tone. The bandmaster should step back and roam the hall to hear what the listener will hear. From that vantage point, the bandmaster becomes the final arbiter of the dynamics. To achieve the all-important balance even at a soft dynamic, the cornets and trombones reduce their volume, while horns and tubas are asked for a little more sound.

Another formidable challenge is increasing the weight of sound as the ensemble crescendos towards a full-throated *fortissimo*. Aspire for an enrichment of tone, rather than a loudening. Instruct the band to think of their tone as a circulating sphere touching the inside edges of the instrument, rather than a sound blown straight through the horn. Some bandmasters actually prefer the explosive effect of an exponential *crescendo* over an evenly graded linear one.

Whatever the choice, it is essential for the band to have been trained to move through benchmarks unified in sound level and balance. As the band approaches the *fortissimo*, Eric Ball contends two things happen. First the cornets and trombones will outweigh the others and the round tone (described by the sound "O") will thin out to a piercing sound (described as the sound "EE"). Second, he says many believe the cornet-trombone group has a wider dynamic range than the saxhorn mellows. This means the bright instruments can play **both** louder **and** softer. Try to reconcile this disparity by rehearsing a *crescendo* alternating between the two choirs, and then mixing them. Work to retain the quality and balance of tone as it becomes louder, retaining the round "O" sound.

NOT ALL NOTES ARE CREATED EQUAL

Tuning brass instruments

All notes are NOT created equal. Exacting acoustical studies prove that the spacing between the tones of a scale is never precisely a whole or half step. Some notes within a scale have a natural tendency to sound sharp, while others slightly flat. The varying deviance of notes within a scale, and subsequently between keys, gives a melody its unique character and value. To illustrate this apparent inexactitude, consider a synthesizer producing pitches at strict equal intervals. We sense something artificial, rightly judging the resultant music as "canned." While instruments like the piano are tuned with "equal" spacing between the 12 notes of the chromatic scale, the acoustical tendencies between any two notes are never equal. It is essential to realize that **each pitch played on a brass instrument is variable dependent on the key, the unfolding organic melody line, and its corresponding harmonic support.**

The diagram on the next page illustrates the mechanics by which brass instruments negotiate half steps. It is essential to any discussion on intonation to grasp that **the mechanism is imperfect, approximating half steps with certain tendencies.** Most brass instruments are designed to play fairly well in tune with open or limited valves (or on trombone, with the first few positions). This is why we usually tune to open-valve or first-position tones. With the addition of multiple valves (or going further down the slide of the trombone), there is a pitch differential, which increases over each half step incrementally, yet at varying rates. The same Pythagoras we associate with geometry identified this acoustical phenomenon many centuries ago. Even today the widening gap between pitches is known as the Pythagorean comma. The "comma" explains why the valve combinations of 1/3 and 1/2/3 or sixth and seventh position on the trombone, sound sharp, having the "largest" half steps.[6]

As a point of reference, let's examine how the valve or slide on a brass instrument alters pitch, essentially by unfolding half-steps:

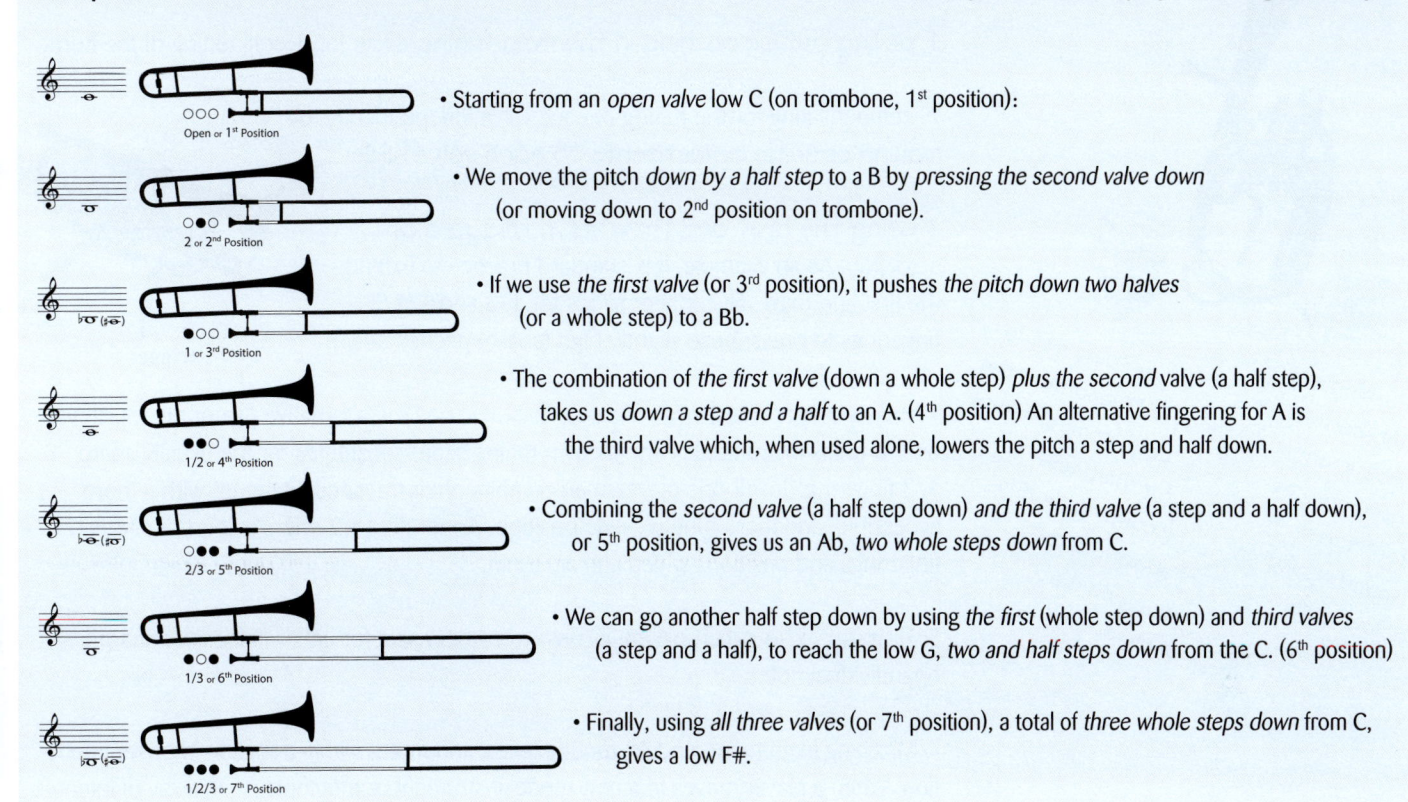

- Starting from an *open valve* low C (on trombone, 1st position):
  Open or 1st Position

- We move the pitch *down by a half step* to a B by *pressing the second valve down* (or moving down to 2nd position on trombone).
  2 or 2nd Position

- If we use *the first valve* (or 3rd position), it pushes *the pitch down two halves* (or a whole step) to a Bb.
  1 or 3rd Position

- The combination of *the first valve* (down a whole step) *plus the second* valve (a half step), takes us *down a step and a half* to an A. (4th position) An alternative fingering for A is the third valve which, when used alone, lowers the pitch a step and half down.
  1/2 or 4th Position

- Combining the *second valve* (a half step down) *and the third valve* (a step and a half down), or 5th position, gives us an Ab, *two whole steps down* from C.
  2/3 or 5th Position

- We can go another half step down by using *the first* (whole step down) and *third valves* (a step and a half), to reach the low G, *two and half steps down* from the C. (6th position)
  1/3 or 6th Position

- Finally, using *all three valves* (or 7th position), a total of *three whole steps down* from C, gives a low F#.
  1/2/3 or 7th Position

The tuning note

In the Youth Band Rehearsal section of Chapter Eight (p. 176), we advocated for an ensemble using a tuning note, as well as warming up on hymn tunes to work on tuning within the harmonic context. Allow for a general tuning on open valve/first position tones, after warming up at the commencement of rehearsals. In band situations, **a concert Bb is usually used as the tuning note, meaning C for the Bb instruments and G for the Eb ones,** as the open-valve/first-position notes are the easiest to tune on the instrument. Many conductors rely on digital tuners, which graphically show the variance, whether **FLAT**, meaning *under pitch*, or **SHARP**, meaning *above pitch*.

Some conductors tune to the Bb of the fixed-pitch instruments, like the piano or mallet instruments. Just as an orchestra would tune after an intermission, use a general tuning note after a rehearsal break. The ambient temperature affects pitch, so an instrument left on a chair likely has cooled and will sound *flat*, while an instrument resting in a warm environment tends to pitch *sharp*. Returning to the instrument, the player learns to compensate gradually as the instrument either warms or cools. If possible, use a tuning note before filing out of the band room on Sunday mornings.

Brass band tuning notes
Open valves/1st position

Bb Instruments in treble clef
Eb Instruments in treble clef
C Low Brass Instruments in bass clef

Ways to tune your instrument

While a general tuning can be helpful in aligning instrumentalists to a home pitch, the concept of tuning encompasses all 12 notes of the scale. To this end, players require training to familiarize themselves with the variability and challenges of tuning "within" their own instrument. The trombone slide, the violin string, and the human voice have physical mechanisms that permit easy adjustments to pitch. But when playing valved or keyed instruments, players must learn to counteract these natural tendencies of variability.

Individual pitches can be adjusted in several ways:

1. pulling out or pushing in the main tuning slide for overall tuning of the horn.

2. compensating for the tuning of each valve independently, by making specific adjustments to each valve slide.

3. using the first and third valve triggers or saddles. As an example, it is standard practice to extend the first and third valve trigger slides for 1/3 and 1/2/3 fingerings to press these slightly high (sharp) pitches down.

4. using alternate fingerings or positions. The alternative use of the fourth valve on low brass instruments (with its own tuning slide) substitutes for the usually sharp 1/3 fingering. Trombone players can combine their transposing trigger with a more accessible, and more tuneful, slide position. Appendix 14.2 offers a chart of alternate fingerings and positions which can aid tuning.

5. "lipping" the pitch up or down to compensate for either flatness or sharpness on individual notes.

Matching instrument models, mouthpieces, and mutes within a section improve intonation. When a player moves to a new model instrument or mouthpiece, an array of intonation adjustments need to be learned. Tuning adjustments also have to be made for mutes, as inserting a mute usually makes the instrument sound sharp, especially in the low register. Therefore when inserting a mute, the player should pull the main tuning slide out perhaps a ¼" and replace the slide to its original position when removing the mute. Trombone players who are actively listening, tune by making slight adjustments to slide position.

In view of the variance in the "half steps" and subsequent tuning between valves and slide positions, Dr. Ronald Holz has provided this helpful guide to general pitch tendencies of treble clef reading brass instruments. Note that tuning is affected by the valves used and the octave register of each note.

Guide to tuning tendencies
Treble clef reading brass band instruments

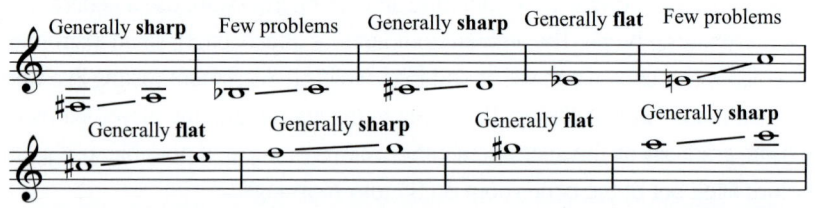

Portions of an instrument's range are described as in the high, low, and middle register.

Pushing a slide **IN** shortens the instrument and compensates for flatness (sounding slightly below pitch).

Extending a slide **OUT** lengthens the horn, compensating for sharpness (sounding slightly above pitch) by bringing the pitch down.

tonality (term) \'tō - na - lə - tē\ refers to key, the result of relating a series of notes and chords to a focal point, which becomes the tonal center, or **tonic**, of a musical composition.

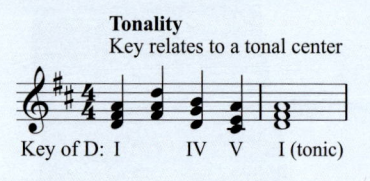

Tonality
Key relates to a tonal center

Key of D: I   IV   V   I (tonic)

SCALES REQUIRE TUNING

Playing scales and playing in tune are inseparable! It is generally understood that daily scale practice equips players to gain facility in a variety of keys. What is less often considered is that each scale across the chromatic spectrum provides it's own unique tuning issues within its own tonality. Scale work in all keys gives players a feeling for the nuances and discrepancies across particular keys. One constantly asks, "Which notes do I have to adjust when playing in this key?"

"Centering" pitch

Scales should be played slowly to help players center each tone, by adjusting as needed. (Recall the visualization of this concept using a bull's-eye target in the Singing Company Chapter Six, p. 129) A properly centered tone gives the richest resonance on any given note. *Players know when they hit the mark, as the centered tone speaks with ease and a feeling of rightness.*

Instruments vary greatly in the amount the notes need to be adjusted up or down with a given fingering or position. Adjacent notes in a scale often respond in dissimilar ways. For example, within a scale, the third step sounds sharp toward the fourth of the scale, and the leading tone leans up toward tonic.[7] Remember that the intonation within brass instruments is more favorable in the flat keys.

A second line G♯ (the third tone in the E scale or the leading tone in A) may require a slight triggering of the third valve out to compensate for the natural sharpness within those scales. Its enharmonic equivalent, a second-space A♭ (the fourth tone of the E♭ scale or the root of the A♭ scale), while fingered the same, will sound nearly in tune without an adjustment. *Practicing scales helps solidify these conventions that counteract the intonation inconsistencies across the horn.*

In approaching high notes, emphasize the supported air and energy applied in the upward motion of the ferris wheel, thinking *"up and over."* With low notes, one often needs to think *"down and under"* to compensate for any flattening of pitch. Slowing a passage of wide intervals aids tuning. Use the analogy of hitting the exact center of a target for each note.

enharmonic tones (*term*) \'en-här-'mä-nik tōns\ are different "spellings" of the same tone, for example, G♯ and A♭, used when changing from one key to another.

Enharmonic spelling of the same tone

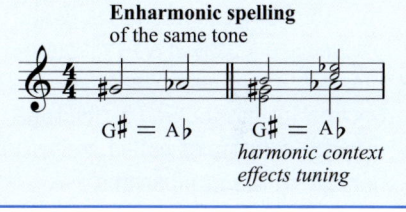

G♯ = A♭   G♯ = A♭

harmonic context effects tuning

Scales in thirds

As an ensemble, there is further benefit in playing scales in a round two notes apart, which creates stacked thirds. (Refer to The Youth Band Rehearsal section in Chapter Eight on p. 176.) *In addition to tuning the pitches within the scale line itself, the scale-based rounds help ground that tonality and its tuning idiosyncrasies.*

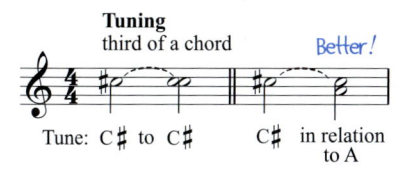

For instance, when in A major, it is far better to tune a C♯ against its fundamental pitch A, forcing one to tune the third of the chord (normally sharp), rather than tuning directly C♯ to C♯.

Rehearsal time given to scales in thirds is a useful preparatory exercise when a section of a piece may move into remote keys beyond the familiar, more easily tuned "educational" keys like F, B♭ and E♭. In-tune playing is the result of the pitches of a melodic line being part and parcel of a given key tonality and its harmonic support. When returning to general repertoire, remind the band members to apply the pitch adjustments made within the scale to notes in the related key.

Tuning third of a chord   *Better!*

Tune: C♯ to C♯   C♯ in relation to A

Scales in rounds
Tuning thirds and triads

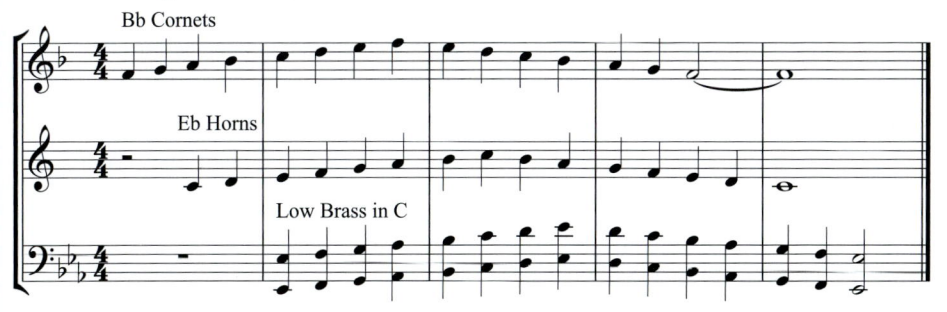

Bb Cornets

Eb Horns

Low Brass in C

The Beat Goes On

As a helpful aid, Appendix 8.5 lists all major and minor scales, correlated by number to permit the simultaneous rehearsal of instrumentalists reading treble clef in Bb and Eb pitch, or C parts in bass clef, as in this example:

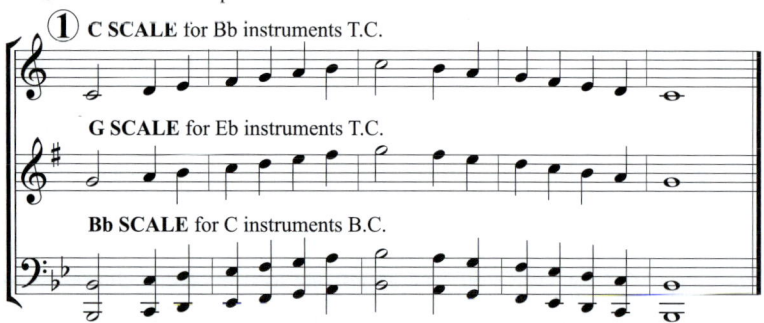

Bb concert scale in various transpositions

① C SCALE for Bb instruments T.C.

G SCALE for Eb instruments T.C.

Bb SCALE for C instruments B.C.

Blend affects intonation

In *The Creative Director,* Edward Lisk claims that balance and blend precede accurate intonation.[8] Lisk trains his players to lose their identity in the section by constantly asking if they hear themselves. (The goal is *not* to!) Two steps precede spot-on intonation within a band: achieving good tone quality and blending into a section.

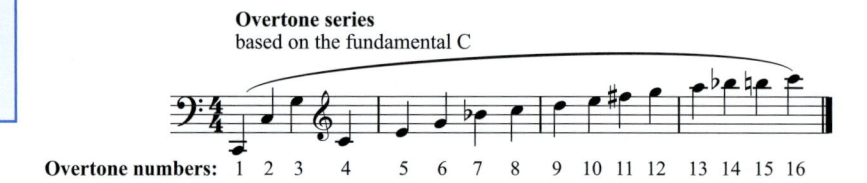

Overtone series based on the fundamental C

Overtone numbers: 1 2 3 4 5 6 7 8 9 10 11 12 13 14 15 16

overtone series (*term*) \ˈō - ver - tōn sir - ēz\ Acoustically all pitches are a part of a fundamental that contains many overtones. Spot-on intonation and a rich tone quality (sometimes called *sonority*) depend on the number and strength of the overtones sounding within a pitch.

TONE QUALITY
Required to TUNE

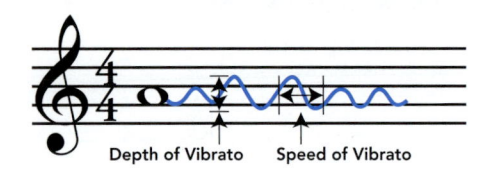

Depth of Vibrato   Speed of Vibrato

1. The bandmaster must require proper posture and breathing to compensate for poor tone quality. Unfortunately the player with poor tone quality will be heard. Both the blend and intonation of the section are jeopardized without correction. Poor articulation, breath control, and fatigue also prevent pitch from remaining centered. Also affecting the quality of sound in a section is the use of *vibrato*. This is a minute fluctuation of pitch, which serves to heighten the expressive range of a musical line. In Chapter Twelve (p. 253), we referred to color imagery running the gamut from Renaissance white with little vibrato, gradually warming up through yellow, orange, and finally the rich lush Romantic red, with its thick, wide vibrato. Agreement needs to be made within a band as to the amount of vibrato to be used by an ensemble, similarly dependent on the style of a piece. Vibrato, as a varied fluctuation of pitch, affects intonation and quality of tone, ranging from nearly none to what might be called a wobble. Recent Army repertoire calls for less vibrato than that of several generations back.

BLEND
Required to TUNE

2. The bandmaster must require all players to produce a tone that blends into the section. Studies have shown that one player will interpret a loud neighboring player as sounding flat and those around will adjust downwards. In fact, the pitch may have been accurate, but too loud, thereby making the lead player now sound sharp because the players around have adjusted down.[9] The preferred, and more tuneful, solution is to stress improving dynamic balance within each section of the band. Rather than asking the protruding voice to do less, it is more effective to counter this by requiring the surrounding players to raise their dynamic level.

If after these two steps, players can still hear themselves, then they are playing out of tune. Playing with poor tone quality is somewhat synonymous with singer's intonation being affected by poorly shaped vowels, as discussed in the Songster Leader Chapters on pages 258 and 270. This counteracts both spot-on intonation and a pleasing blend. The exception to this blend rule permits instrumental soloists to adjust themselves slightly sharp to "stand out" in contrast to the accompanying ensemble, who should keep their pitch low.[10]

Every note thoughtfully placed

Not all notes are created equal, but we can work together to help our players match pitch. The bandmaster should emphasize ongoing "active listening." The underlying hallmark of a great band is the listening that goes on between players, sections, and the leader. When working on precision or dynamics, the tuning will improve as the group listens within itself.

Controlling the dynamic range of an instrument prevents the tendency of flattening when trying to get soft and sharpening when getting louder. The responsibility of tuning constantly rests with the players, but can be watchfully mentored by the bandmaster. With experience, players tackle the peculiarities of tuning on their instruments, learning to center their pitch. Correct intonation does not just happen. Every note should be thoughtfully placed, listening to those around within the context of the section and across the band.

WORKING OTHER ANGLES

Rehearse beyond necessity

To give the impression of ease, the effective bandmaster chooses to rehearse beyond necessity. For example, with a technical passage, many conductors will drill a detail slowly at first, eventually bringing the repetitions of the figuration up to the tempo desired. Just as singers rehearse words at a hyper tempo to improve enunciation, players should go beyond the metronome marking required to extend their dexterity, motor memory, and confidence.

Piggybacking off this principle, when there is a passage requiring great sustaining power, like a *fortissimo* conclusion, purposely rehearse it slowly, insisting on the same intensity dynamically. (Usually there is just a bit more players can give!) Subsequently segue back to the slower proper tempo, where there should now be a reserve, as well as added confidence and control. Rehearse high passages well past the required note pattern, assuring upper range facility.

The words tell all

It is far easier to demonstrate a line's shape, phrasing, and dynamics with singing rather than with explanation. Referring to the related text helps bring the players closer to the composer's intended emotion. Talk about the words. Ask how the band members feel about the music. Inquire as to what they hear in the music. All of this brings ownership to the music-making. On the flip side, pressing bandsmen to sing their part will save the chops, aid listening to other parts, and can be especially helpful when working out difficult rhythms.

Reference text
"The Present Age" (FS 342 - Leslie Condon)
Appassionata (♩ = 56)

I'll fol-low Thee___ of life the gi-ver,___ I'll fol-low Thee___ de-ny Thee___ [never?]

Bringing out the melody

Whether working vocally or playing, during rehearsal ask sections to stand when they think they have the melody. This aids the player's awareness of their place in the picture, be it in the foreground, middle, or background. Players may not be aware that they have the principal melody. Conversely, they are made physically aware of when to back off and be supportive, silly grins and all!

Divide and Conquer

Some bandmasters choose to divide and conquer by having half the section play only an accented eighth (quaver) when encountering heavily accented *sforzando* (*sfz*) or *forte-piano* (*fp*) figures. They would not sustain the piano tone, but re-enter at the impending crescendo. This effect amplifies the dynamic contrast. If there is a series of *forte-piano* (*fp*) notes, those players would similarly play only the accents, helping to unify the coloration of the line of bell-tones. An equivalent dovetailing can bring clarity and unity to a passage of running sixteenths.

sforzando (*term*) \ sfórt - 'sän - dō\ An Italian word meaning literally with a *forced sound*, so played with a strong accent. Abbr. (*sfz*)

forte-piano (*term*) \ fór - tā - pē - 'a - nō\ An Italian word meaning to commence the note loudly, but immediately render the remainder of the note at a soft dynamic. Abbr. (*fp*)

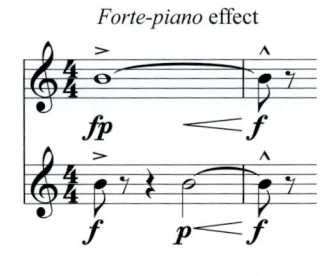

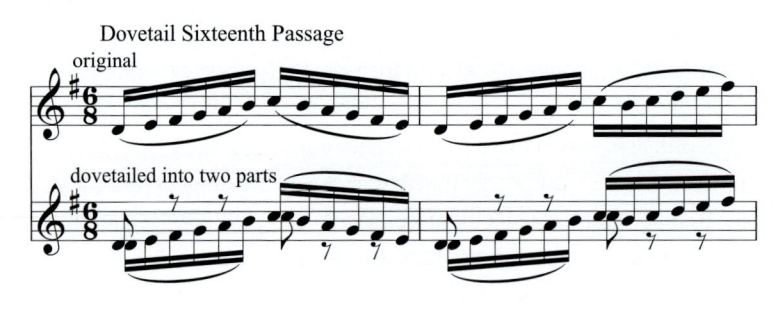

You Cannot Run Before You Walk

Bear in mind that the bandmaster should work from week to week on the group's deficiencies, while creatively capitalizing on its strengths. This premise runs from the moment of repertoire selection into the rehearsal time given to band training. Learn to strike a manageable balance. You cannot run before you walk! Moving too quickly to matters of interpretation, when the basic notes and balance are far from within grasp, garners frustration. *Learn your band's pace and learning curve. Gauge the band's limitations carefully.*

Chapter 14 | STRIKE UP THE BAND!

DAN RATHER INTERVIEWS STOKOWSKI

At age 94, Leopold Stokowski, the legendary conductor of the Disney film *Fantasia*, gave a televised interview on the news show *60 Minutes*. Suddenly, during the lively exchange, the roles reversed and Stokowski inquired if the interviewer Dan Rather had ever played a musical instrument. Mr. Rather responded that he had played clarinet in his youth. Stokowski then pressed him to estimate on a percentage scale how much effort Rather had given to his clarinet. Mr. Rather responded with some confidence that perhaps he had given a 90% effort. With a quiet, yet direct glare, Stokowski countered that as the conductor, he required 110%. A 90% effort from any of his players was never enough.

Following an excruciatingly awkward silence, Stokowski proceeded to inquire of Dan Rather why he should remain any longer for the interview. One observer noted, "He scared me when he jumped out of his chair." The camera followed the hunched-over Stokowski with his telltale long white hair as he ushered himself off the set, leaving the bow-tied Dan Rather abandoned with an embarrassed grin across his face.[11]

The buck stops where?
As a bandmaster, you learn to give much more than you hope to receive, many times sacrificing your own musical preferences and ideas. Nonetheless, while studying a score, work out strategies to achieve unanimity of attack and style. You are hearing mentally the kind of approach and dynamics you wish the band to achieve. At the first reading, the stark reality can be frighteningly dissimilar to what you imagined. You are tempted to ask how seriously to take the words of another stern taskmaster, Gustav Mahler, who famously lamented, "There are no bad orchestras, only bad conductors." The challenge to make the band sound good, even great, is placed squarely on the bandmaster's shoulders. In this we may understand the wisdom of Eric Ball when he says, *"The music of the running stream is caused by the obstacles it encounters." And so ... the beat goes on!*

More on learning to better **"listen and respond"** to your ensemble in Chapter Twenty-Three.

The Beat Goes On

14 BARS REST

Application of Band Training Techniques

1. Identify sections in your current band repertoire where count-singing, staccato syllables, count-dynamics (see Chapter Thirteen, pp. 268–269) might clarify the rhythmic vitality of your band's presentation.

2. Are there pieces that could benefit from experimenting with daylight chords to increase the uniformity of the ensemble's attack and release?

3. Locate a slurred passage to work into strict rhythm, by slowing the tempo, taking the slurs off, and emphasizing the groupings. Consider a strategy to establish a unified accompaniment and then combine accompaniment and the slurred florid passage.

4. Identify a piece that engenders the best sound from your band. (This is not necessarily the band's favorite piece.) Analyze why the arrangement suits the makeup of your group. Look for another piece that works similarly and might prove equally successful.

5. Now consider a piece in your repertoire that seems to make for a more tenuous performance. Consider what adjustments in strategy can be made to improve the aural picture.

6. What steps can you make with your band to increase its dynamic range? Locate sections to work on creating quiet drama, perhaps a long *diminuendo* or *crescendo* measured assuredly. Practice a chord a half step higher or develop some reserve with a robust closing passage.

7. Take time to inventory tuning issues. Consider non-threatening strategies to train the band members to tune on an ongoing basis.

8. Are there passages where you need to rehearse beyond the essentials? Worthy goals might be to increase agility, range, or sustaining power.

9. What pieces would benefit from a survey of the related text? Are there opportunities within the rehearsal context for players to sing their parts or stand if a section has the melody?

10. Be honest and consider pieces that should be put aside until the band has matured further. What pieces represent success or an attainable, meaningful challenge?

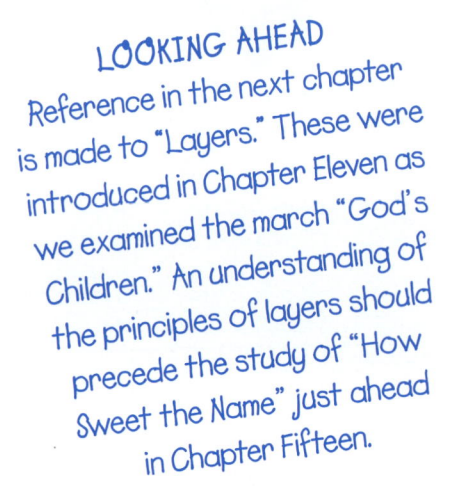

LOOKING AHEAD

Reference in the next chapter is made to "Layers." These were introduced in Chapter Eleven as we examined the march "God's Children." An understanding of the principles of layers should precede the study of "How Sweet the Name" just ahead in Chapter Fifteen.

SALVATION ARMY BRASS PUBLICATIONS

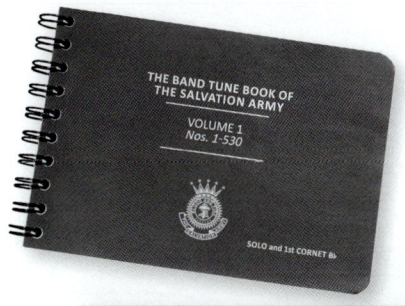

The Salvation Army Band Tune Books (SATB) are designed to allow as few as four players to satisfactorily cover the essential SATB four parts.

SOPRANO (I)	Solo and 1st Cornet
ALTO (II)	2nd Cornet or Solo and 1st Horn
TENOR (III)	2nd Horn or Baritone
BASS (IV)	Eb or Bb Bass

The tune book is available for a full General Series instrumentation, but be sure to satisfactorily cover the essential four parts. Soprano cornet, flugelhorn, 1st, 2nd, and bass trombone, and percussion are optional parts that enhance and color the hymn tune arrangements. There is only one baritone part, which follows strictly the tenor voice III of the hymn tune harmonization. The euphonium V part (also optional) includes the melody line, cued to allow the euphonium to take the melody to give the cornets a break on selected verses. **Christmas Praise (CP)**, published in London in two books, follows this tune book format, with a compatible keyboard/vocal book.

Part books are available for all corresponding F parts (II and III for French horns) and all C parts, which include part I in octaves and part II in C, both allowing for possible use with flutes, oboes, and violins, at the conductor's discretion. Parts III, IV and V are also available notated in bass clef. The two keyboard volumes, which include chord and capo symbols, allows the organ, piano, or rhythm instruments to trade off verses or play along with the band. Refer to Chapter Seventeen on Piano Worship for more details.

The **American Instrumental Ensemble Series (AIES)**, published in Atlanta, is a graded series (Grades 1 to 4) using a four-part scheme with the added option of euphonium (V) and two percussion parts. For more detail, see Chapter Eight, p. 181.

> PART I–1st Cornet
> PART II–2nd Cornet or 1st Horn
> PART III–2nd Horn or Baritone/Trombone
> PART IV–Eb or Bb Bass
> PART V–Euphonium (optional, cued when important or has melody)
> Percussion 1 and 2 (optional)

The **Unity Series (US)**, published in London, employs a comparable distribution of an essential four parts (I-IV), but the euphonium is an essential fifth part (V). Also, the 1st cornet (I) part may have occasional two-part divisi parts that require another 1st cornet player.

The **Brass Ensemble Series (BES)** and **Brass Music for Young Bands (BMYB)**, both published in New York, utilize a similar four- and-five part scheme. The **New York Sextet Series (SJ)** is designed for six parts: two cornets, horn, trombone, euphonium, and tuba with no percussion. **Caroler's Favorites (CF)**, also published in New York, is designed in four parts with optional euphonium fifth part, along with a compatible keyboard/vocal book.

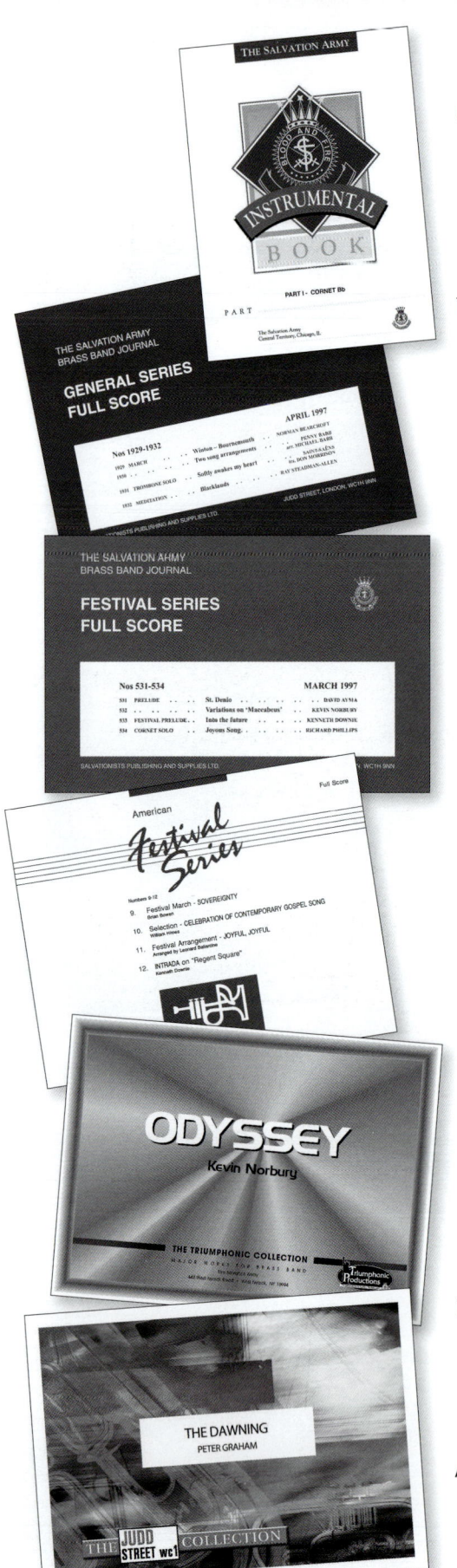

Hallelujah Choruses (HC), published in Chicago, also uses a five-part format (as in the Unity Series) with the option of including or layering rhythm section instruments and vocalists. To allow for bright and mellow color options, some of the inner parts (II, III and V) will note a preference for second horn versus the baritone, or trombone only, without the baritone, by cross-cueing.

The Salvation Army brass band has evolved over the past 100-plus years into the standard instrumentation used for **General and Festival Series (GS or FS)**, published in London, and listed here in score order. An **American Festival Series (AFS)**, is published in Chicago using the same instrumentation. The most difficult festival pieces are published under the titles **Triumphonic Series** (New York) and The **Judd Street Collection** (London). Note the minimum number of players required for each series and a suggested full complement:

GENERAL SERIES

Instrumentation	Minimum Number of Players per Part	Full Complement
Eb Soprano Cornet	1	1
Solo Bb Cornets	3	4 or 5
1st Bb Cornets	1	2
2nd Bb Cornets	1	2
Bb Flugelhorn	1	1
Solo Eb Horn	1	1 or 2
1st Eb Horn	1	1
2nd Eb Horn	1	1
1st Bb Baritone	1	1
2nd Bb Baritone	1	1
1st Bb Trombone	1	1 or 2
2nd Bb Trombone	1	1
Bass Trombone	1	1
Solo Euphonium	1	2
Eb Bass Tuba	1 or 2	2 or 3
Bb Bass Tuba	1	2
Percussion	1	2 or 3
17 Total Parts	**19 to 20 players minimum**	**26 to 31 full complement**

Triumph Series (TS), published in London, is designed for fewer players and parts with any essential soprano and trombone parts being cued as a safeguard. The essential parts, indicated with an asterisk* below are: 1st Cornet, 2nd Cornet or 1st horn, 1st Baritone, Euphonium, and one Bass.[12] A continuous bass line is indicated in both bass parts.

Also adhering to the Triumph Series format, **Scripture Based Songs (SBS)**, also published in London, is a series of arrangements of recent congregational songs and choruses, published in sets of 12 songs, without a supporting keyboard volume.

TRIUMPH SERIES

Instrumentation	Minimum Number of Players per Part	Full Complement
Eb Soprano Cornet	1 (optional)	1
1st Bb Cornet*	2 (divisi, varies)	3 to 5
2nd Bb Cornet*	1	3 (includes flugelhorn)
1st Eb Horn*	1	2
2nd Eb Horn	1	2
1st Bb Baritone*	1	1
2nd Bb Baritone	1	1
1st Bb Trombone	1	1
2nd Bb Trombone	1	1
Bass Trombone	1 (optional)	1
Solo Euphonium*	1	2
Eb Bass Tuba*	1 (either bass part)	2
Bb Bass Tuba*	1 (essential)	2
Percussion	1 (optional)	2
14 Total Parts *Essential parts	**11 to 15** players minimum	**24 to 26** full complement

The **American Band Journal (ABJ)**, published in New York, was designed by Erik Leidzén to allow for two contrasting quartets of *brights* (cornets and trombones) and *mellows* (horns, baritones, euphoniums, and tubas) within the ensemble. 1st Bb Cornet is permitted divisi passages, thus requiring a minimum of three cornet players with ABJ scoring. Soprano, Flugelhorn, one Baritone part, Bass Trombone, and Percussion are available as optional additional parts. The numbers indicated in parentheses are the minimum number of players needed on each part:

AMERICAN BAND JOURNAL

NINE ESSENTIAL PARTS		OPTIONAL PARTS
BRIGHTS (5 min. players)	**MELLOWS** (4 min. players)	
1st Bb Cornets (2)*		Eb Soprano Cornet, optional (1)
2nd Bb Cornets (1)		Bb Flugelhorn, optional (1)
	1st Eb Horn (1)	
	2nd Eb Horn (1)	
		Bb Baritone, optional (1)
1st Bb Trombone (1)		
2nd Bb Trombone (1)		Bass Trombone, optional (1)
	Solo Euphonium (1)	
	Eb Bass Tuba (1) or	Either bass part essential
	Bb Bass Tuba (1)	
		Percussion, optional (2)
Minimum of 9 players required		**16 to 24 players** full complement

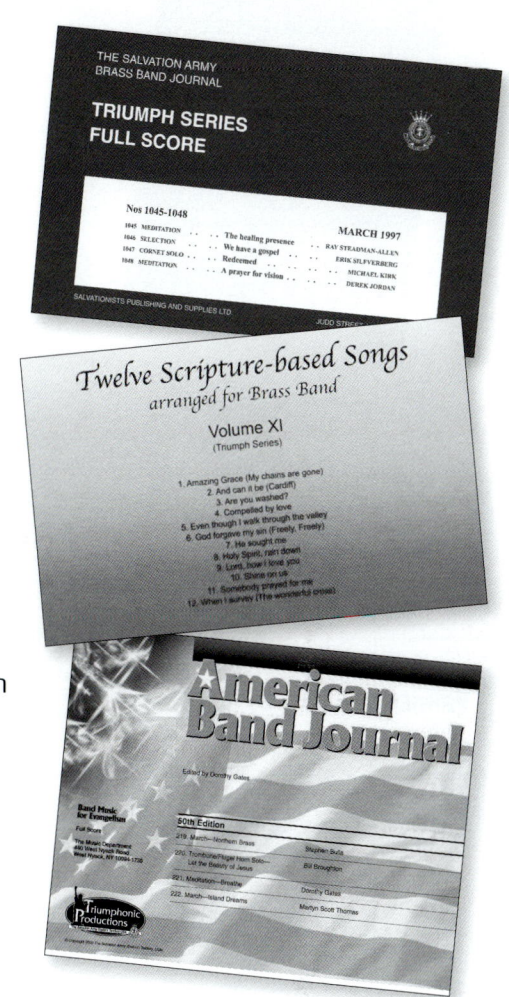

*(1st Cornet uses two part divisi, so use two 1st Cornets for every one 2nd Cornet)

The **Brass Level Guidelines** chart gives an overview of the relative difficulty of these and other Salvation Army brass publications by what educators call grade level. (Not to be confused with school grades.) Included is the suggested range, key, rhythmic, and correlated school band level required for each level. Corresponding range guidelines were previously outlined in Chapter Eight on p. 181. A survey of the first 500 tunes in the 1987 1st Cornet Salvation Army tune book reveals possibly 28 tunes which either because of range, key, or rhythm can be considered of Grade 2 difficulty. This suggests that for a band to function effectively in support of congregational singing, players need to achieve a minimum Grade 3 expertise.

For a comprehensive index of Salvation Army published brass ensemble and band music notated by grade level, consult the **Instrumental Music Index of Salvation Army Band Publications**. This has been compiled by William Himes and is available on CD or online from the Central Territory Music Department. In the United States, any of the above brass publications can be placed on a **standing order subscription** through your respective territorial music department. This can be renewed or altered annually.

BRASS LEVEL GUIDELINES

	RANGE	KEYS*/ SCALES	RHYTHM	ENSEMBLE SUPPLEMENT **
LEVEL PRIMER OR ½		C (F)	4/4	Quickstart - very easy First Book of Hymn Tunes – very easy Sunday School Choruses – very easy First Things First – very easy
LEVEL ONE		F, G, B♭	3/4 2/4 on same pitch	American Instrumental Ensemble Series – Grade I Brass Music for Young Bands - easy First Book of Hymn Tunes - easy First Things First - easy Basic Brass, Winds, & Percussion - easy
LEVEL TWO		E♭, D	no dotted rhythms	American Instrumental Ensemble Series – Grade II Unity Series - medium easy Brass Music for Young Bands - medium easy Basic Brass, Winds, & Percussion - medium easy
LEVEL THREE		A♭, A	Half Time	Salvation Army Tune Book – easy American Band Journal – early intermediate Triumph Series – early intermediate Unity Series – early intermediate American Instrumental Ensemble Series – Grade III Hallelujah Choruses - medium easy
LEVEL FOUR		Chromatic Scale – all major keys	6/8 9/8 12/8	Salvation Army Tune Book – more difficult Triumph Series – intermediate American Band Journal – intermediate American Instrumental Ensemble Series – Grade IV Hallelujah Choruses - intermediate
LEVEL FIVE		Minor keys	compound meters	American Band Journal – upper intermediate General and Festival Series - difficult

*Keys are indicated in B♭ pitch (C-F equals B♭-E♭ in concert pitch)

For a comprehensive index of SA published brass ensemble and band music notated **by grade level, consult the *Instrumental Music Index of Salvation Army Band Publications*, compiled by William Himes and available from the US Central Territory.

Instrumental Series Difficulty Levels

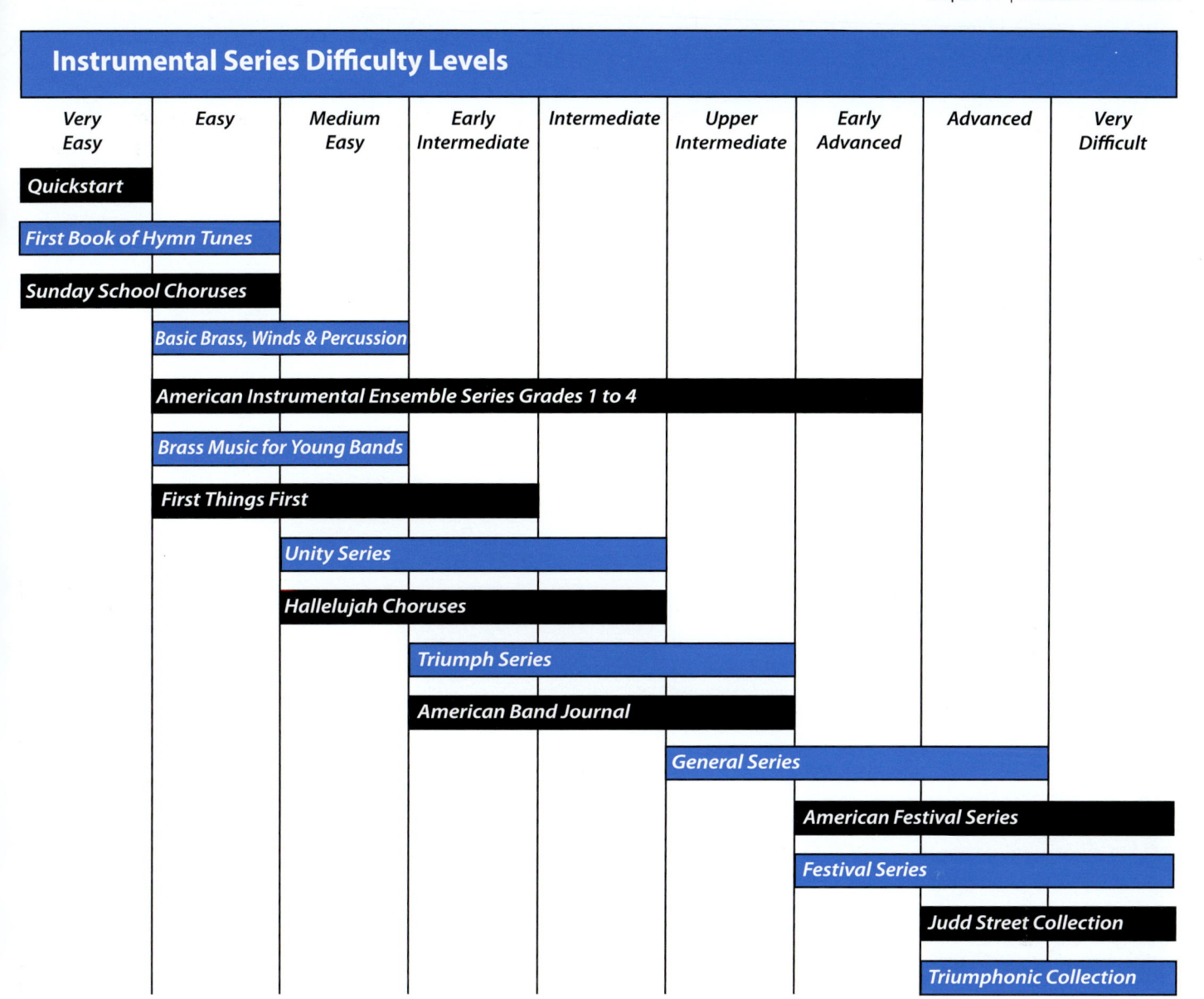

Very Easy	Easy	Medium Easy	Early Intermediate	Intermediate	Upper Intermediate	Early Advanced	Advanced	Very Difficult
Quickstart								
First Book of Hymn Tunes								
Sunday School Choruses								
	Basic Brass, Winds & Percussion							
	American Instrumental Ensemble Series Grades 1 to 4							
	Brass Music for Young Bands							
	First Things First							
		Unity Series						
		Hallelujah Choruses						
			Triumph Series					
			American Band Journal					
					General Series			
						American Festival Series		
						Festival Series		
							Judd Street Collection	
							Triumphonic Collection	

A subscription allows for publications that fit your ensemble in terms of instrumentation or grade level to be automatically sent to you at the time of release. You will receive a single billing for all these music publications once a year. (A sample subscription form can be found in Appendix 14.3.)

THE BANDMASTER'S RESOURCES

A Practical Guide to Instrumentation for the Brass Band, Edrich Siebert (Studio Music)

Brass Bands of The Salvation Army, *Volumes One and Two*, Ronald W. Holz (Streets Publishing)

"No Uncertain Sound" series of articles by Eric Ball, *The Musician*.

Play the Music Play, Brindley Boon (SP&S)

Salvation Army Band Music Index: American, Canadian and UK/IHQ Publications, 1884 to Present, Fred Cleighton (Canada: SA THQ Music Dept.)

samusicindex.com—searchable for titles of Salvation Army publications

The Ultimate Index—Salvation Army song reference book

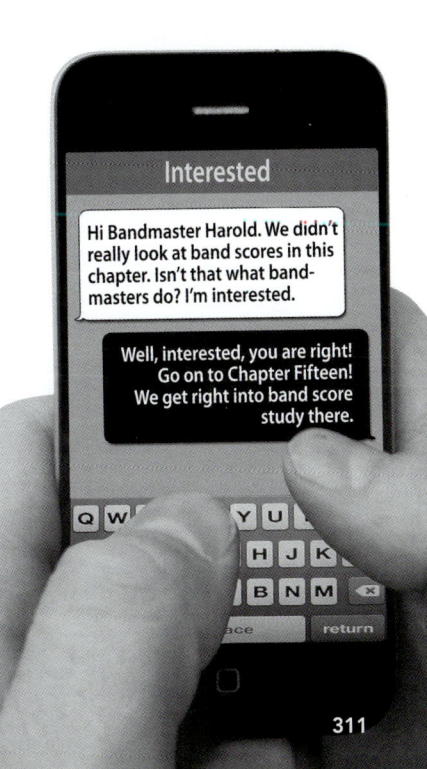

CHAPTER FIFTEEN

SCORE STUDY TO REHEARSAL STRATEGY
The Bandmaster's Toolbox

*Chenaniah, leader of the Levites in music,
should direct the music, for he understood it.*
—I Chronicles 15:22[1]

FROM SONGSTER ANTHEM TO BRASS TRANSCRIPTION

In the Salvation Army there are many arrangements of hymn tunes, generally with several verses set to reflect the associated text. The score we will study here was originally a choral setting based on the hymn tune *French*, but entitled *How Sweet the Name*.[2] We have reprinted the original choral version, arranged by Ronald Tremain, and the subsequent brass version set for brass band by Donald Osgood.[3] The Osgood arrangement of *How Sweet the Name* unfortunately cannot be effectively rendered by a smaller corps band. A full minimum General Series complement is required (see Chapter Fourteen, p. 308 about scoring for GS), with the possible exclusion of second cornet, second horn, second baritone, second and bass trombone. But even these parts have small passages that are not doubled or cued. The bass part can be covered by either Bb or Eb Bass, but the use of both parts ideally helps achieve the sound of the organ pedal octaves. Before working through the "layers," listen to the entire hymn setting, first in its original choral version and then in one for brass. Reference recordings of *How Sweet the Name (Songster and Brass Band Versions)* are available in the Chapter Fifteen online folder.

In **Chapter Fifteen**, we will:

- look further at ways to translate brass score study into rehearsal strategies by analyzing a piece for its inherent structural, rhythmic, melodic, harmonic, and text "layers."
- make a piano reduction from a brass band score, a valuable exercise to getting inside a score's form, instrumentation, and harmonic language.

The Beat Goes On

How Sweet the Name of Jesus Sounds

Original Choral/Organ (music only version)

Tune: *French*
Arr. Ronald Tremain

©1947 Salvationist Publishing and Supplies

STRUCTURAL LAYER

Let's make a careful comparison of this vocal score on page 314, with the *How Sweet the Name* brass score which commences on page 318. The arranger differentiates the multi-verse structure of the original choral version through contrasting instrumental groups.

Introduction: Verse 1 – MELLOWS
In the choral original, all voices sing the *French* tune in unison with a chordal organ accompaniment. The brass version (beginning on p. 318) features the mellows (horns, baritones, euphoniums, and tubas) with occasional descending color by the brights (cornets and trombones). Note that the section entrances are bracketed. An asterisk indicates that the flugelhorn, solo horn, and euphonium (doubled an octave below), have the hymn melody.

Letter A: Verse 2 – BRIGHTS
In the choral original, the men sing the tune accompanied by the women in three parts. The brass version (reference p. 319) features the brights (cornets and trombones), with the euphonium doubling the bass trombone to help bring out the hymn melody (marked with an asterisk.) The conductor brackets the entrance of the cornets and trombones, as well as the ascending color by the mellows used to cover the ends of phrase. Notice the proper placement of the breath in upper parts provided by the arranger.

Letter B: Verse 3 – CHAMBER MUSIC
At letter B (p. 320) the brass arranger elects to have the brights take up the first verse chorale melody and harmonization with occasional color added by the mellows. A rich lower octave "pedal" is added by the BBb tuba, which is cued in Eb tuba in the absence of the bass trombone or Bb bass. An asterisk draws attention to the solo cornet pickup to B where the melody lies. For the second phrase, the melody is briefly moved down the octave (note the asterisks in the baritones and first trombone) and concludes with a more intimate *one-on-a-part* reduction in forces, with the melody in the soprano and solo cornets. The horns and baritones intersperse connecting phrases, which varies the overall color of the lines.

Letter C: Verse 4 – ORGAN PIPES
In the choral original, most voices sing the tune in unison, accompanied by larger organ accompaniment with an added soprano *descant* melody. The arranger of the brass version (p. 321) provides a fuller new harmonization at letter C that includes octave doublings to simulate the octave doubling of organ pipes. The melody, marked with an asterisk, is found in first and second cornet, flugel, and first horn, with the euphonium doubling an octave below. The descant line in soprano and solo cornet, and the concluding entrances for trombones and percussion, add to the dramatic conclusion. The arranger has judiciously indicated *tenuto* quarters preceded by a breath mark at bar 28. A breath for the entire ensemble is implied before the fourth beat of measure 30.

RHYTHMIC LAYER

The *French* hymn tune consists of two phrases of four bars with a one-beat pickup to each phrase. There is a consistent quarter-note pulse in the hymn line, except at the end of the phrase, which feels like a fermata although written out for three beats. Occasionally the arranger uses moving eighth notes in the accompaniment to build interest. The final verse is marked *molto largamente* (meaning "very broadly") for dramatic effect.

---

cued notes (*nouns*) \'kyüd nōts\
appear smaller, and are indicated in parts to be played in the absence of an essential voice (such as the Eb bass cued notes at letter B of *How Sweet the Name* to be played in the absence of the Bb bass).

descant (*noun*) \'de - skant\
a somewhat florid melody sung by a few trebles or sopranos, which soars above the hymn.

tenuto (*noun*) \'te - nü - tü\
a line under or over a notehead calls for a held, sustained full value.

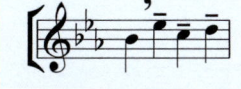

The Beat Goes On

MELODIC LAYER

The melodic line of the tune "French" is mostly stepwise and very much centered around *do* and *sol*. The range encompasses an octave. The second phrase descends from the high *do* and has one deviation with an accidental turn (in bar six with the G natural.)

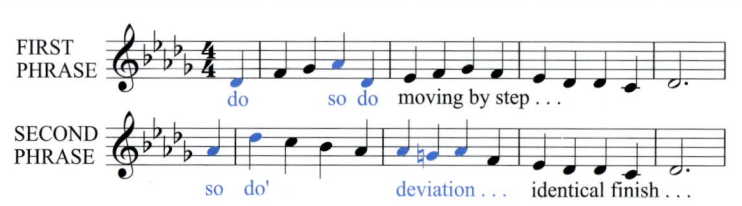

FIRST PHRASE — do   so do   moving by step...

SECOND PHRASE — so   do'   deviation...   identical finish...

There are lovely *counterpoints* in the soprano voice of the verse two and three versions. For these verses, the conductor would anticipate bringing out the melody, not allowing it to be overshadowed by the higher voices. Breathing follows the four bar phrase.

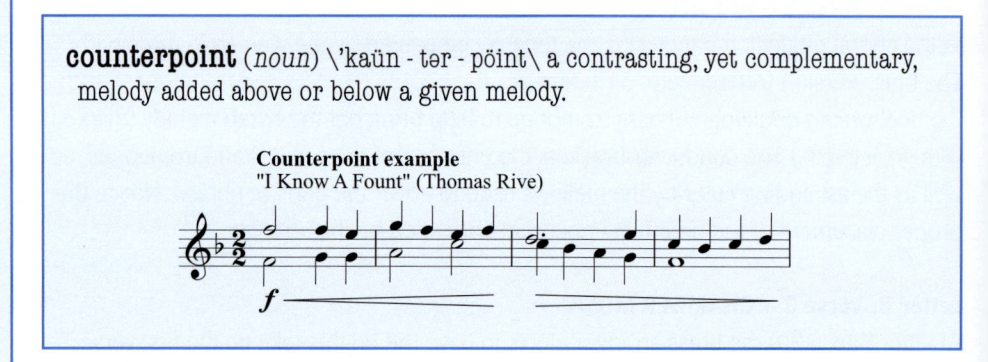

counterpoint (*noun*) \'kaün - tər - pöint\ a contrasting, yet complementary, melody added above or below a given melody.

Counterpoint example
"I Know A Fount" (Thomas Rive)

accidentals (*noun*) \'ak - sə - den -təl\ signs used in musical notation to indicate chromatic (by half step) alterations or to cancel them. A sharp sign (♯) raises the pitch by a half step. A sharp (♯) in front of an F alters an F up a half step to an F♯. A flat sign (♭) lowers the pitch by a half step. A flat (♭) in front of a B alters a B down a half step to B♭. The natural sign (♮) cancels flats or sharps either indicated in the key signature or earlier in a bar. Accidentals apply to the note before which they appear, as well as all the notes of the same pitch within the same measure.

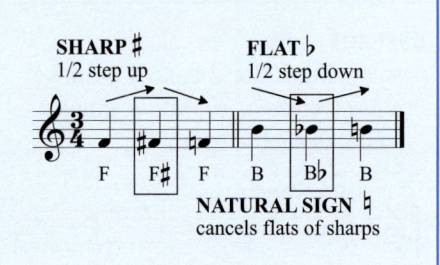

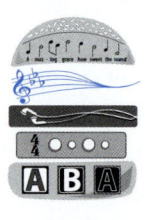

SHARP ♯ 1/2 step up   FLAT ♭ 1/2 step down
F F♯ F   B B♭ B
NATURAL SIGN ♮ cancels flats of sharps

HARMONIC LAYER

The arranger has given us three harmonizations, all in the same key of D♭ concert. Each harmonization reflects the solidly diatonic stepwise melody. Note in the band transcription at letter B the careful re-voicing of verse three based on the first harmonization, but now exchanging the tune between instrumental parts. The one-on-a-part ensemble just before letter C adds to the drama of the final verse with the soprano descant and the addition of octave voicings to simulate the octave doublings of organ pipes.

TEXT LAYER

The text for *How Sweet the Name* can be found in the *Salvation Army Song Book*. The author, John Newton, also wrote the words to *Amazing Grace*. Verses 1, 3, 4, and 5 probably best line up with this four–verse band arrangement. Some conductors will copy the words into the score to have them readily available. Further research into the text reveals it is based on Song of Solomon 1:3b: "Your name is like perfume poured out." To Newton, healing, soothing, and calming effects are found in the name of Jesus. Other names applied to God, such as rock, shield, and hiding place, pepper succeeding verses. The final organ pipes verse echoes the poet looking toward heavenly praise, yet straining to adequately exalt the Name until his last earthly "fleeting breath."

The repeated use of recordings in the early stages of score study can limit the conductor from forming his own vision of the correct tempo, style, dynamics, and expression. After isolating the details of each layer, it is good practice to "play through" the entire piece in your mind's eye, allowing the details to enhance your overall vision of the piece.

FROM LAYERS TO REHEARSAL TACTICS

After a piece has been analyzed and marked, we are ready to prepare the score for rehearsal purposes. Somewhere in the process of analyzing the piece, rehearsal tactics begin to suggest themselves. These can be listed by the main sections of the piece or more often at the transitions of key and tempo. Returning to the arrangement of *How Sweet the Name–French*, the following is a listing by section of rehearsal concerns:

Introduction: Verse 1 – MELLOWS
- Aim for a clean balanced start with the mellows (horns, baritones, euphoniums, and tubas), securing the four-bar phrase of the hymn melody. [Reference score A] Even though the solo horn part gets quite high, the mellows remain dynamically at *mezzo-forte*.
- A careful entrance of the "descending color" by the one-on-a-part brights (cornets and trombones) includes a slight swell in the dynamics. [B]

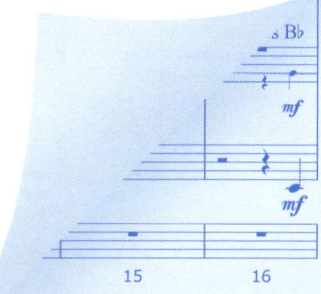

Letter A: Verse 2 – BRIGHTS
- Secure a relatively softer (*mezzo piano*) entrance of the blended brights (cornets and trombones). [C] Bring out the euphonium doubling the bass trombone carrying the hymn melody. [D]
- The "ascending" color by the mellows is used to cover the end of the phrase of the brights breathing after beat 1 in m.12. Work for a uniform *crescendo* to *mezzo forte* through m. 12. [E]

Letter B: Verse 3 – CHAMBER MUSIC
- The principal concern of letter B is the movement of the melody between instruments and octaves. [F] Note the swelling of dynamics *only* in the occasional color added by the mellows.
- The more intimate one-on-a-part reduction in forces [G; mm. 22-24] brings the dynamic down before the large sounds of letter C.

Letter C: Verse 4 – ORGAN PIPES
- Secure a full *forte* pickup to letter C with broad lines in all parts. [H] The melody, found in first and second cornet, flugel, and first horn, with the euphonium doubling the lower octave, should be brought out. The soprano and solo cornet *descant* line need not be pushed, as it will speak for itself in a high register. [I]
- The *tenuto* entrance by the trombones supplemented by the percussion sets up the two-bar *crescendo* to *fortissimo*. [J] A prolonged third beat followed by a breath in m. 30 will need to be indicated. In the concluding two bars, avoid the tendency to overblow.

Barring any major note or rhythmic mishaps, the conductor will probably be able to rehearse this piece within the confines of these concerns. Because of the instrumentation scheme used by this arranger, it may prove fruitful to contrast work on the Introduction (mellows at *mezzo forte* with descending bright color with a swell) against Letter A (the brights at reduced dynamic of *mezzo piano* with ascending color in the mellows with a uniform *crescendo* for the full ensemble.) Then work back and forth between the *mixed chamber* music of Letter B with its reduced dynamics and the *broad organ* sounds of Letter C. Remember the word rehearsal is derived from "re-hear." In the process of the repetition, the eight concerns noted above would be addressed. The point is that your analysis of the score and the list of anticipated problems have advanced a logical rehearsal plan.

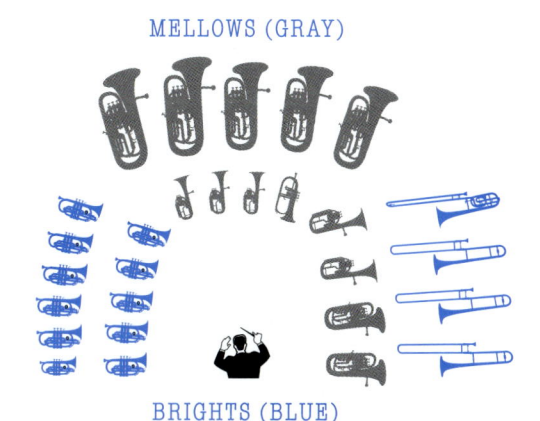

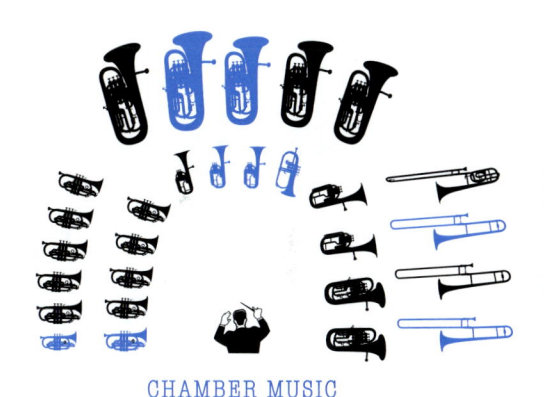

How Sweet the Name
(French)

Ronald Tremain
Arr. Donald Osgood

Introduction Verse 1 - MELLOWS

©1960 Salvationist Publishing and Supplies

Letter A Verse 2 - BRIGHTS

Letter B Verse 3 - CHAMBER MUSIC

Letter C Verse 4 - ORGAN PIPES
Poco largamente ♩ = 66
molto largamente
Sops.
Vocal
Altos, Tenors & Basses
cresc.
C
Molto largamente ♩ = 60
ben tenuto
Org.
cont. 8ves
[I]
Descant
Tutti
Melody
Cors.
[H]
Horns
Bars.
[J]
Troms.
Euph.
Bass.
Perc.
S.D.
L.C.
B.D.
25
26
27
28
29
30
31

15 BARS REST

1. Choose another brass score to analyze for layers to study, mark, and prepare rehearsal strategies.

2. *Timeout with a little help from my friends!* In a group setting, choose a four- or five-part brass ensemble piece to allow the parts to be rendered live, ideally from copies of the score. The ensemble should first play through the whole piece, next identify the major sections/layers of the piece, and then work through marking each section, considering possible rehearsal strategies. Use a simple street march or a selection linking three different songs.

FROM BAND SCORE TO PIANO REDUCTION

The hands-on/pencil-to-paper exercise of making a piano reduction from a full band score is an invaluable aid to improving a conductor's score-reading, particularly by becoming more familiar with the instruments and their related transpositions. We will work step-by step through Erik Silfverberg's Hymn Tune Arrangement—*Stella* Triumph Series (TS) 651 or Favorite Triumph Series (FTS) No. 3–28.[4] An audio recording of *Stella* (Erik Silfverberg) is available in the Chapter Fifteen online folder. Note that his very "safe" scoring of *Stella* allows for the possibility of playing this piece with just the 1st and 2nd cornet parts (1st cornet playing only the top divisi), both horn parts, euphonium and a bass part. The baritone and trombone parts, while enriching the color of the arrangement, are satisfactorily doubled in the essential parts noted above. Another alternative is 1st baritone in lieu of 2nd horn.

The Transposed Score

Along the left margin of the score's initial page, instruments are named in full, and their sections are grouped by end brackets. Generally speaking, most scores line up sections from the highest-pitched (cornets) at the top to the lowest (basses) at the bottom, with percussion included below the basses. Many times the actual part designations and in what transposition each part is notated is not indicated. On this Triumph Series score, we have superimposed the transposition required from the notated pitch to that of the piano, called concert pitch (or one based in C).

This summary of transpositions bears out what was discussed previously in Chapter Fourteen. In the brass band we need only concern ourselves with transposition of instruments in Bb, Eb, and C, with care given to the correct octave in the low brass. We also considered how the instruments are transposed from concert pitch to what appears in the score and actual parts. Now we will *reverse* the process, reducing the full transposed band score to a two-stave piano version.

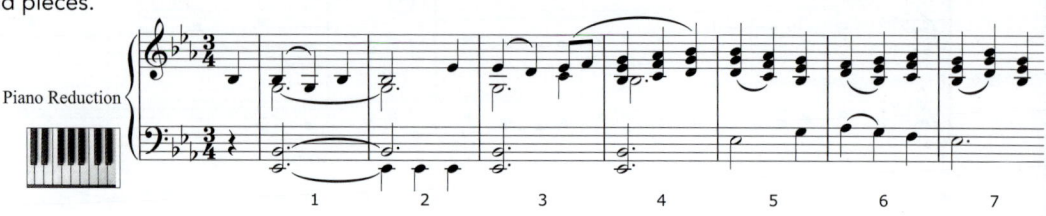

---

piano reduction (*term*) \pe - 'an - o ri - ' dek - shen\ Composers and arrangers generally sketch musical works in **short score**, that is using just two or three staves to outline the basic melodic, harmonic and rhythmic elements of a piece. The short score is then referenced to assign specific instruments to the melodies and harmonies in what we call an **orchestration**. As work on the **full score** proceeds, elements of expression and dynamics are added.

Reversing this process, known as making a **piano reduction**, condenses or simplifies an existing musical score into two staves, playable on the piano by one person. Reducing a large score to its melodic, harmonic and rhythmic essentials greatly aids musical analysis and score study.

See Chapter Twenty-Three, pp. 518–519, to view **piano reductions** of excerpts from several well known Salvation Army band pieces.

Chapter 15 | SCORE STUDY TO REHEARSAL STRATEGY

From notated pitch to concert pitch

Hymn Tune Arrangement – Stella

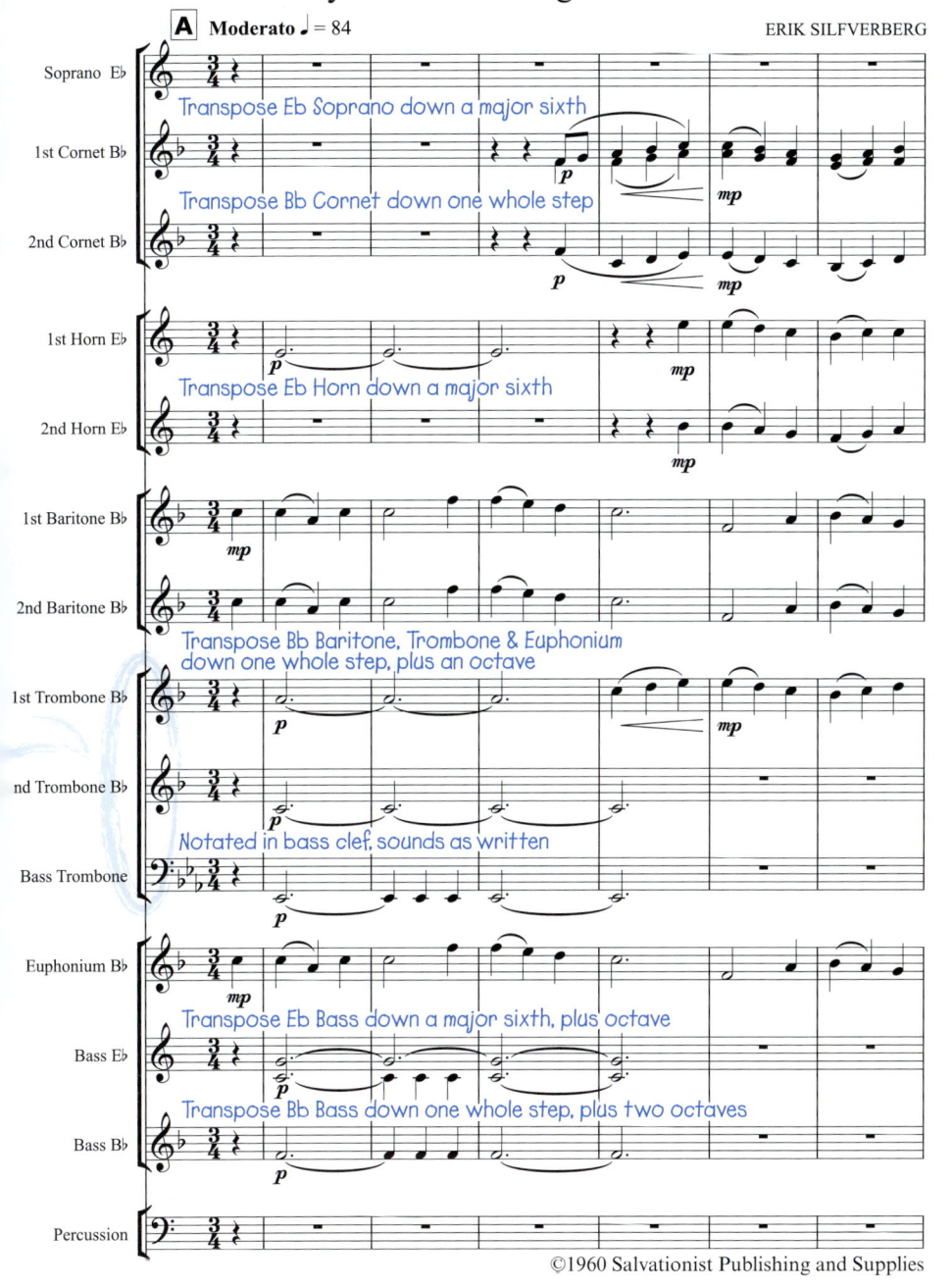

ERIK SILFVERBERG

Moderato ♩ = 84

Transpose Eb Soprano down a major sixth

Transpose Bb Cornet down one whole step

Transpose Eb Horn down a major sixth

Transpose Bb Baritone, Trombone & Euphonium down one whole step, plus an octave

Notated in bass clef, sounds as written

Transpose Eb Bass down a major sixth, plus octave

Transpose Bb Bass down one whole step, plus two octaves

©1960 Salvationist Publishing and Supplies

The Bb pitched instruments

The *Stella* score has the Bb instruments (cornet, baritone, trombone, euphonium, and Bb tuba) in the band key of F, which has one flat (Concert Eb). To compensate for the Bb instruments being manufactured a step lower (Bb) than concert pitch (C), the notated instrumental part appears transposed a whole step up. To make the piano reduction in concert pitch, we reverse this and **move the key down one step** to the key of Eb, which has three flats. In the same way, the transposition of the notes of the Bb instrument parts are **moved down by one whole step** to the piano C pitch.

Bandmaster Erik Silfverberg

Bb Cornet
Bb Baritone
Bb Trombone
Bb Euphonium
Bb Bass

Bb Instruments Transposition to Concert Pitch Key Signature

ONE STEP DOWN

Key of F → Key of Eb

Brass band instrument photos courtesy of Besson Courtois.

The Beat Goes On

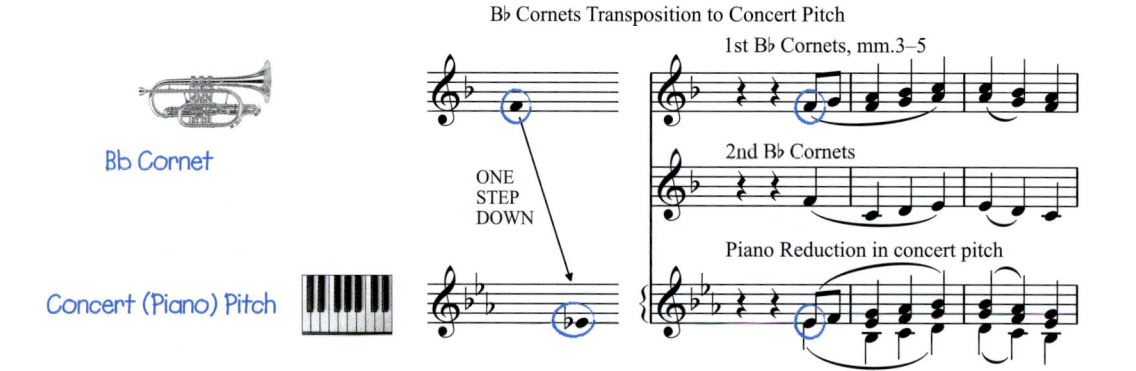

Bb Cornet

Concert (Piano) Pitch

Bb Cornets Transposition to Concert Pitch

ONE STEP DOWN

1st Bb Cornets, mm.3–5

2nd Bb Cornets

Piano Reduction in concert pitch

With the use of the treble clef in all parts, except the bass trombone, *an additional octave displacement* below must be considered for the baritone, trombone, and euphonium and *an additional two octaves* for the Bb bass (sometimes known as the BBb tuba for that reason).

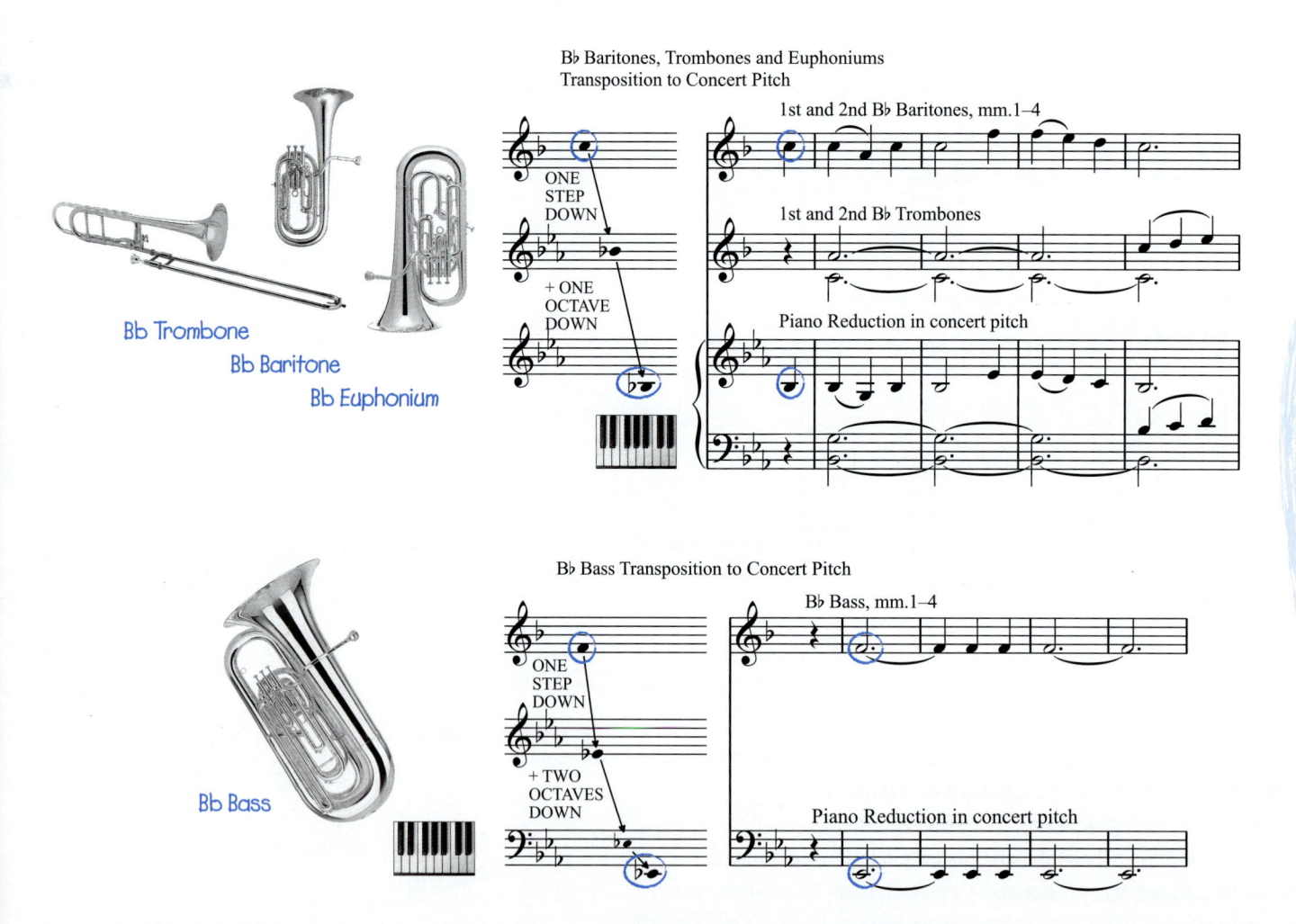

Bb Trombone
Bb Baritone
Bb Euphonium

Bb Baritones, Trombones and Euphoniums Transposition to Concert Pitch

ONE STEP DOWN

+ ONE OCTAVE DOWN

1st and 2nd Bb Baritones, mm.1–4

1st and 2nd Bb Trombones

Piano Reduction in concert pitch

Bb Bass

Bb Bass Transposition to Concert Pitch

ONE STEP DOWN

+ TWO OCTAVES DOWN

Bb Bass, mm.1–4

Piano Reduction in concert pitch

A good example of this *octave compensation* is found comparing the notated pitches in the 2nd cornet and 1st trombone parts in bars 5–7, both *sounding the same concert pitch*, found here.

The E♭ pitched instruments

As the standard brass band evolved, the instruments which bridged range-wise between the B♭ transposing instruments were placed in E♭ pitch, which is *down a fourth* from B♭. Therefore the key for the E♭ instruments (E♭ horn, E♭ soprano, and E♭ tuba) will be *down a fourth* from F, which is the key of C, with no flats and sharps.

The **key transpositions** for brass instruments was introduced in the previous Chapter Fourteen, p. 7.

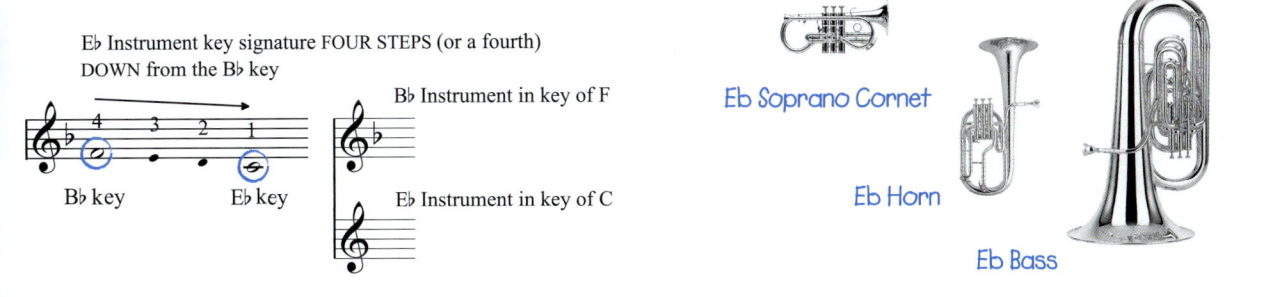

E♭ Soprano Cornet

E♭ Horn

E♭ Bass

To compensate for this fourth relationship on the printed part, the transposed E♭ horn parts appear a *perfect fifth higher* from the B♭ cornets.

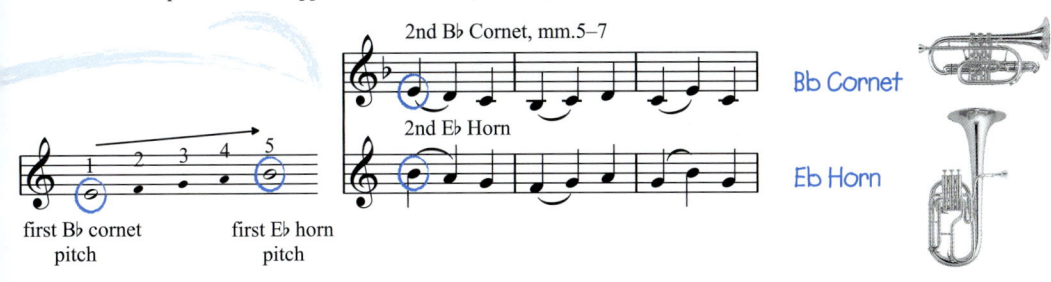

B♭ Cornet

E♭ Horn

With the B♭ baritone, trombone, and euphonium parts being notated in treble clef, which is one step, plus an octave above their C piano pitch, the E♭ horn parts will appear transposed to be a perfect fourth below these B♭ counterparts.

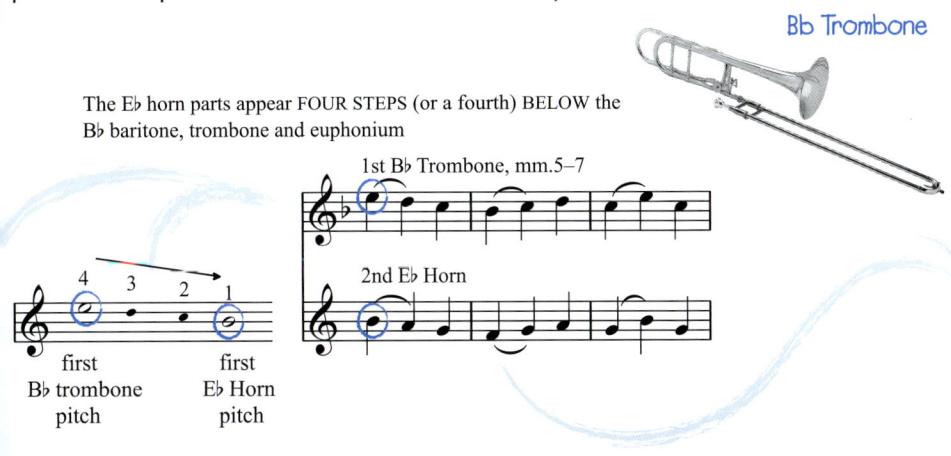

B♭ Trombone

Compare B♭ cornet to E♭ horn to B♭ trombone transpositions

Compare the 2nd horn part in measures 5-7 to the same bars in the 2nd cornet and 1st Trombone example considered above. *All three parts are playing the same concert pitches.*

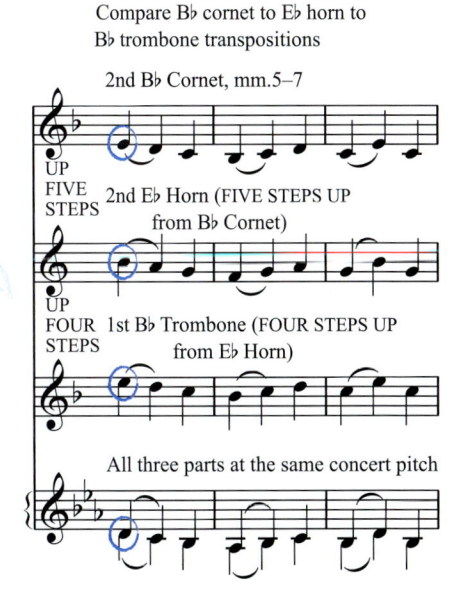

The Eb Bass is the smaller of the two tubas, so to achieve the same concert pitch as the Bb Bass, it is notated *a fourth below* the Bb Bass. Compare the written pitches of the Eb Bass part with that of the Bb bass at letter B. In actual fact, the Eb bass pitch is notated a *major sixth, plus an octave,* above concert pitch.

Compare the written pitches of the Eb and Bb Basses. The Eb Bass is notated FOUR STEPS (or a fourth) BELOW the Bb Bass.

Eb Bass, mm.17–20 (Letter B)

Bb Bass

first Bb Bass pitch   first Eb Bass pitch

Bb Bass

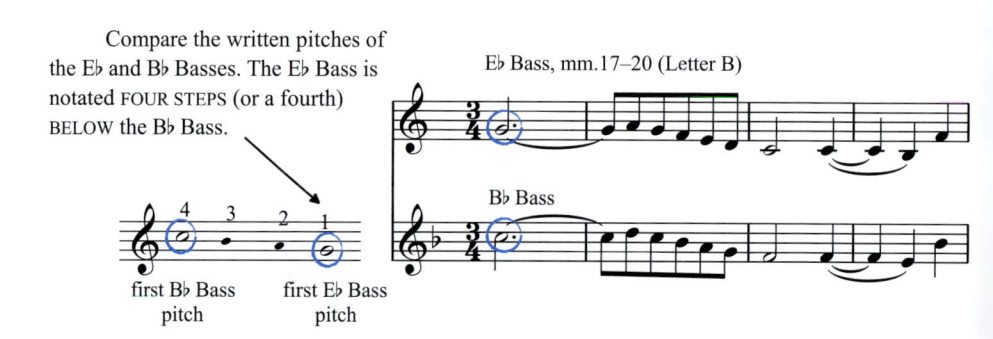

Reading in bass clef

While the Eb Bass in the brass band is always written in treble clef, one can *mentally apply the bass clef* and the necessary change of key (Eb Bass in C, go down a major sixth to Eb concert) and realize that the written notation represents the actual concert pitch.

Eb Bass

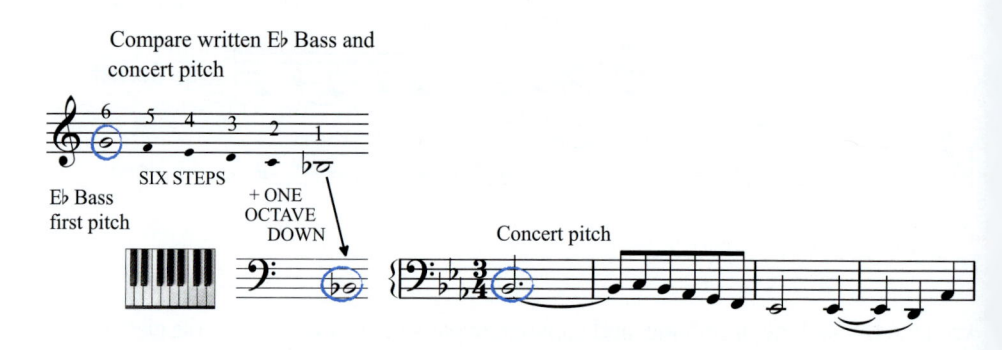

Compare written Eb Bass and concert pitch

Eb Bass first pitch   SIX STEPS   + ONE OCTAVE DOWN   Concert pitch

This is a handy shortcut for tuba players who may only read bass clef. Apply bass clef to the Eb bass part-notated pitches, with the key and any accidentals *down a major sixth.* Compare the bass trombone C-concert pitches at letter F in *Stella* to the Eb Bass as notated. They match visually with the exception of the last beat of bar 3, where the bass trombone has a concert A♮. Thinking up a major sixth requires a sharp (♯) on the F in the bass tuba part. Another way for the player to check is to notice the half step down in the Eb bass part from the G to the F♯, which in comparable concert pitch would have Bb move down a half step to A♮.

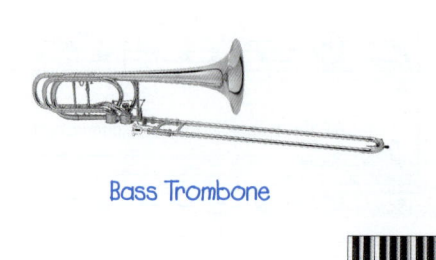

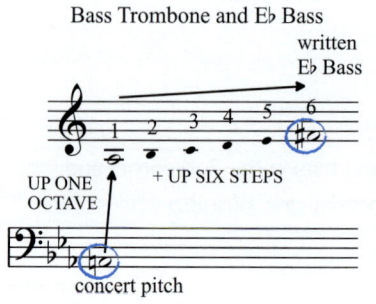

Bass Trombone

Compare concert pitch Bass Trombone and Eb Bass

written Eb Bass

UP ONE OCTAVE   + UP SIX STEPS

concert pitch

Eb Bass, mm.64–67 (Letter F)

G to F♯ (½ step down)

Bass Trombone in concert pitch

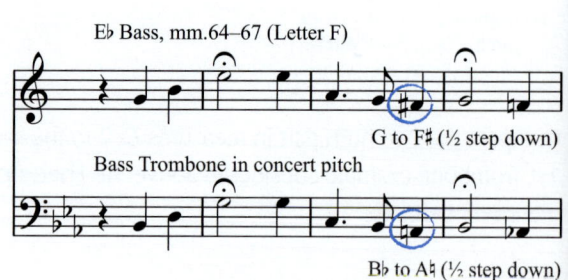

Bb to A♮ (½ step down)

Another bass clef shortcut

The relationship between reading bass clef and the Eb treble clef transposition can also be exploited both for the purposes of easy transposition to and from a piano reduction and for Eb horn players reading from piano bass clef lines. If we look again at the 2nd horn part at measures 5-6 of letter A as notated, we commence on a treble clef-notated third line B. If we *apply the bass clef* to that third line note, we would call it a D. The concert D an octave higher would match the notated treble clef B in the horn part, so with relative ease this transposition is made by simply *copying the part in the bass clef, but an octave higher.* If a horn player were reading the tenor line from a hymnal, they could *visually apply the treble clef,* but playing down the octave. Similar to the Eb Bass, the key and any accidentals are transposed down a major sixth.

By applying the bass clef (and correct key signature) to the Eb Horn part, one can read the actual concert pitch, sounding up one octave

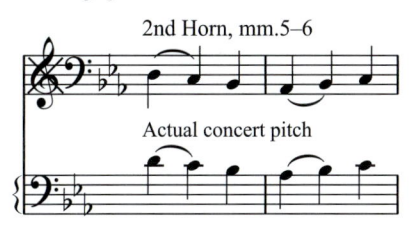

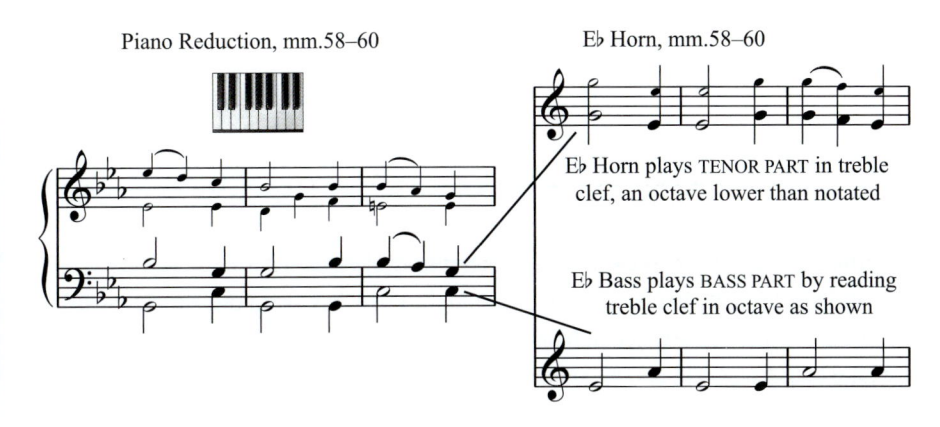

Eb Horn plays TENOR PART in treble clef, an octave lower than notated

Eb Bass plays BASS PART by reading treble clef in octave as shown

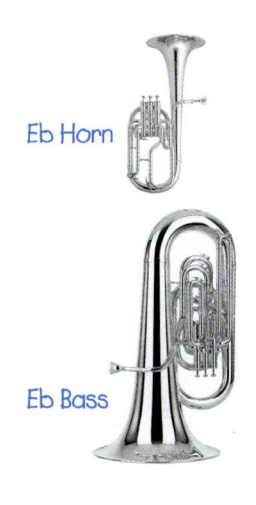

The Eb soprano cornet will often double a line or play an octave above. When at the same pitch, the Eb Soprano is notated a *fourth below* the cornet in Bb. When being asked to play an octave above, the Eb Soprano is *notated a fifth above* the Bb cornet. Letter B in *Stella* shows four bars where the part combines both functions.

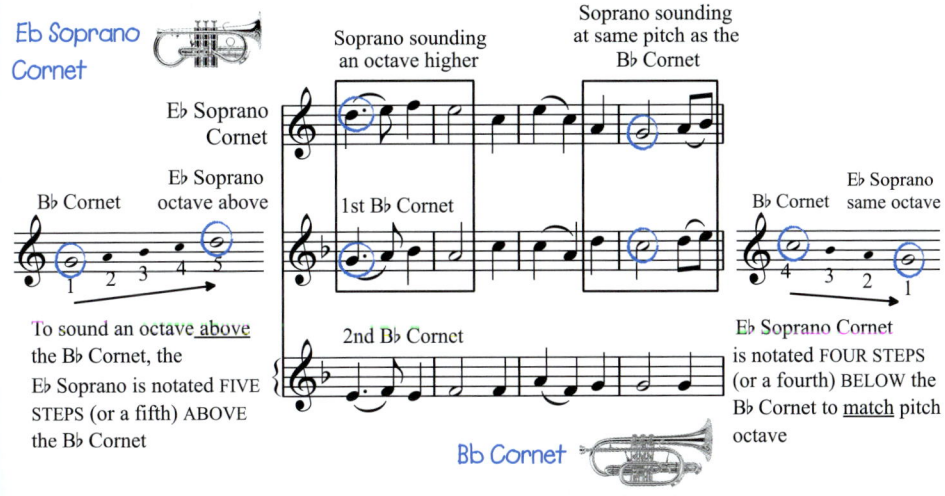

To sound an octave above the Bb Cornet, the Eb Soprano is notated FIVE STEPS (or a fifth) ABOVE the Bb Cornet

Eb Soprano Cornet is notated FOUR STEPS (or a fourth) BELOW the Bb Cornet to match pitch octave

Transposition Summary – Brass Band to Piano

When making a piano reduction, all *Bb parts* require the key and pitches to move *down by one whole step* to concert C pitch:

- Bb baritone, trombone, and euphonium (since notated in treble clef) require *one whole step, plus an octave down.*
- The Bb bass will *sound one whole step, plus two octaves* below the treble clef notation.

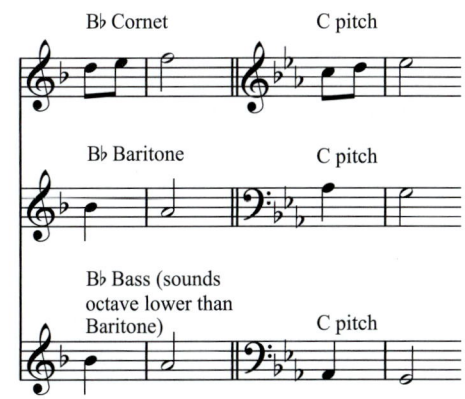

The Beat Goes On

Eb parts require a key and pitch *shift down a major sixth:*
- Eb horn parts will appear on the score *a fifth higher* than the Bb cornets and *a fourth lower* than the Bb baritone, trombone, and euphonium.
- The Eb soprano cornet is notated *a fourth below* the cornet in Bb. When being asked to play an octave above, the Eb Soprano is *a fifth above* the Bb cornet.

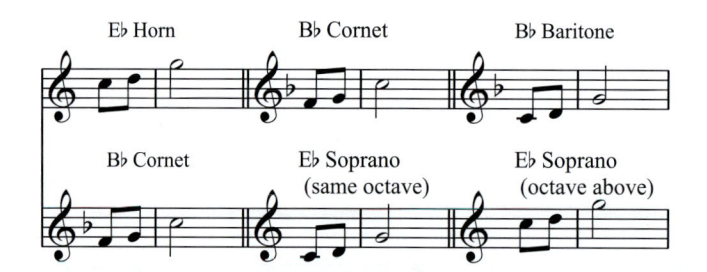

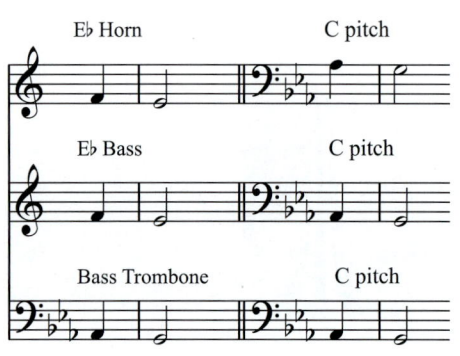

Bass clef "copying" shortcuts:
- Eb horn parts *may be copied an octave higher* in bass clef, applying a new key signature a major sixth down and checking any accidentals similarly.
- The Eb bass part *may be copied in bass clef* retaining the same lines and spaces. Like the horns, one must apply a new key signature a major sixth down and check any accidentals similarly.
- The bass trombone part is notated at concert pitch and *may simply be copied as is in bass clef.* This is a good way to check the Eb bass transposition.

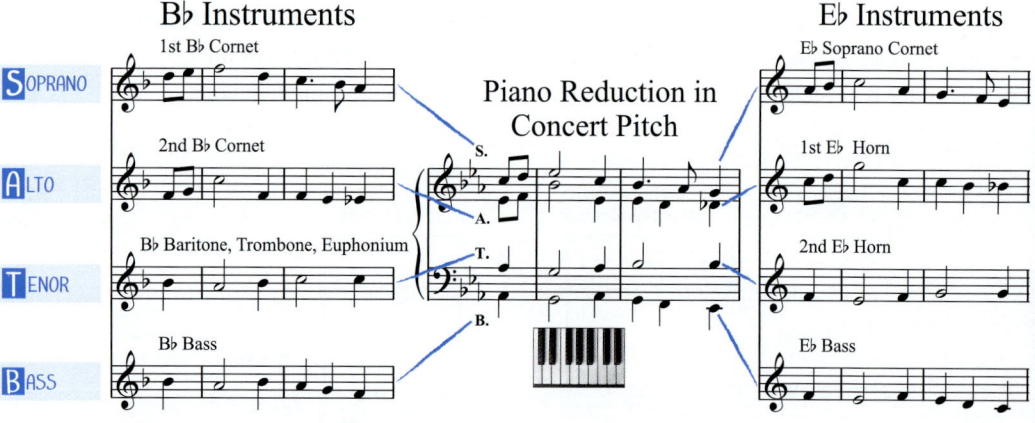

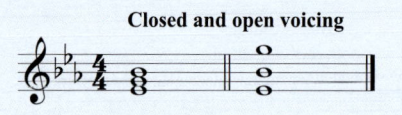

STELLA BY PIANO REDUCTION

Letter A

The arranger's acute initiation into balance and color will become apparent as we work through this piano reduction. The "solo" pick-up entrance by the baritones and euphoniums introduces the *Stella* melody [Reference *Stella* score A]. The opening note C, transposed one step and an octave down, becomes a Bb just below middle C on the piano. Even though it is low, show this in the right hand treble clef part. A simple open-voiced chord rests under the melody. Only three notes are required in the piano reduction. The bass fifths are doubled by the 2nd and bass trombone. Remember that the piano reduction must work "under the hands," so the top note is best shown in the right hand alto voice. This concert G is doubled in 1st trombone and 1st horn. The cornets

closed and open voicing

(*term*) \ When chord tones are stacked as close as possible, the chord is described as being in closed position. When in open voicing, the same chord tones are used, but more widely dispersed vertically.

Closed and open voicing

Hymn Tune Arrangement – Stella

ERIK SILFVERBERG

©1960 Salvationist Publishing and Supplies

The ties which sustain chords across barlines (i.e. in basses and trombones, mm. 3–4, 9–10) are not indicated so that the chord will sound at each bar when rendered at the piano.

enter on the last beat of bar 3 and follow a triadic line that is doubled by 1st trombone and horns, while the *Stella* melody continues in the baritones and euphoniums. [B] As a piano transcription, it is probably simplest to transpose the cornet triad down a step to concert pitch in the right hand and keep the continuing Stella melody independent in the left hand.

> **triad** (*term*) \ a chord of three tones, consisting of a root tone with its third and fifth above.
>
> F triad — root, third, fifth

At bars 9–12, the opening low brass chord is replaced by coloration in three parts in the cornets over a sustained bass *pedal point*. The *Stella* melody is now indicated in the lower right hand part. [C, on p. 329]

pedal point (*term*) \ a long-held note, often in the bass, sounding against changing harmonies. (The term evolved from an organ pedal tone held down with one's foot, while playing changing chords with the hands above)

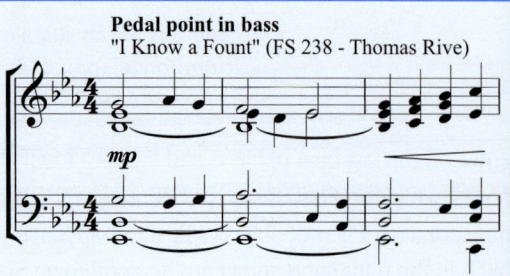

Pedal point in bass
"I Know a Fount" (FS 238 - Thomas Rive)

Bars 13–16 retain the horn and 1st trombone doubling of bars 5–8, so one need only transpose the cornet notes into the right hand and the melody in the bass in the left. [D, on p. 330] Some ties are taken off the bass notes so that they will sound in the piano version.

Letter B
Two significant color changes take place approaching letter B. As the melody is passed to the 1st cornet and soprano, the baritone/euphoniums take up a descending scale figure. As a piano reduction, letter B begins with a three-part voicing in the right hand, passing the scale to the left hand. [E, on p. 330]

The first *tutti* of the piece at B5 includes satisfying octave doublings of the melody (soprano and euphonium) and alto voice (2nd baritone and 2nd trombone). In the piano reduction, ignore the Bb bass cue allowing the bass line to ascend to emphasize the tuba modulation into letter C. [F, m. 22 on p. 331]

Letter C
The arranger Erik Silfverberg consciously chooses to modulate to give the horns the *Stella* melody with a mellow accompaniment (baritones, euphoniums, and basses) for the second verse The key signature for the Bb instruments is two flats, or Bb, which transposed for the piano is Ab, or four flats. The Eb instruments are in one

flat. F is the sixth note of the A♭ scale, and this key signature is confirmed by the four flats indicated in the bass trombone part. [G, m. 25 on p. 331]

In this section (Letter C) we can utilize the bass clef "copying" shortcuts with the E♭ horns and E♭ bass. Simply copy the E♭ bass part (with stems down) into the bass clef left-hand stave. The euphonium notes are added above as a tenor part (stems up). The F at letter C in the euphonium part is a bass clef third space E♭ in concert pitch. At letter C, apply the bass clef to the 1st horn's first treble clef written C, which gives us a concert pitch E♭. Transferring up the octave, we begin the tune with an E♭ on the first line in the treble clef right hand. As an alto part, the 2nd horn first note will be an Ab. The 1st baritone doubles the 2nd horn until the last beat of C4 where all the horns take the melody and the baritones carry on with the alto voice. [G on p. 331]

Letter D and Letter E

After a cadence (m. 36), a florid ascending bass line in octaves ramps up to a full *tutti* which signals modulation back to the original key of Eb concert. The simplest piano rendering of this section has the bass line in octaves with the other three notes in the right hand. [H, m. 36 on p. 332] A dramatic reduction of color reduces the scoring to a light three-part texture, which is marked *pianissimo*. [I, Letter E on p. 333] Transpose the two cornet parts down a step. Note the soprano does add the octave above at E5 and the

2nd cornet and 1st horn double the bottom 1st cornet. The euphonium notes can be notated in the left hand bass clef part. Again think down one step, but transfer this to bass clef, so the pickup E is a ledger line bass clef D just above middle C.

Other instruments join at E8. [J, on p. 334] Notice the octave doublings in the basses. The doubled melody found in 1st trombone may or may not be included in the piano version between the two hands.

Letter F

Letter F retains the same *tutti* character with the soprano alternating between doubling the melody and the alto voice an octave above. [K]

15 BARS REST

Follow similar steps as with *Stella*, to make a piano reduction of *What A Friend* (Erik Leidzén) found in the Appendix 15.1. Making transcriptions is a time honored exercise in score study, which reveals much about the form, instrumentation and harmonic language of a piece.

SCORE PREPARATION RESOURCES

Guide to Score Study for the Wind Band Conductor, Frank Battisti and Robert Garofalo (Meredith Music)
The Brass Band Conductor, Denis Wright (Duckworth)
The Creative Director, Edward S. Lisk (Meredith Music Publications)
The Song Book of The Salvation Army (SA- London)
The Technique of Orchestration, 4th Edition, Kent Kennan and Donald Grantham, (Prentice-Hall)

Two of the Salvation Army's "march kings," Erik Leidzén and Bramwell Coles seen on the final weekend of Star Lake Musicamp 1948. The score is the manuscript of Leidzén's *Meditation on Richmond*, which was the first item published (in January, 1950 Festival Series) as Leidzén was "on his way back" into Salvation Army service.

Don't STOP now! ... the beat goes on!

There is a lot of important information about playing the piano, leading worship bands and conducting in Chapters Sixteen, Seventeen, Eighteen, Nineteen, Twenty, Twenty-One, Twenty-Two, and Twenty-Three...

Part Four
WORSHIP LEADERSHIP

CHAPTER SIXTEEN

PLAY ME A SONG, YOU'RE THE PIANO-MAN
Keyboard Basics

Few 19th-century churches would consider using a piano for its services—the piano was a secular instrument, and not suitable for sacred purposes! —Donald Hustad, *Jubilate*

This chapter is the first of two about the piano. One of the challenges in presenting these chapters on facilitating keyboard instruction is the widening gap between those keyboardists who "play by ear" (or loosely follow chord changes on a lead sheet) and those who "require the printed page." Pianists at either end of the spectrum (and many in between) will benefit from working through both chapters. Much of this is best accomplished *at a keyboard*.

Chapter Sixteen is designed for the aspiring pianist or piano instructor looking to gain facility at the keyboard *with or without notated music.* We consider:

- a basic acquaintance with the piano keyboard
- correct development of technique through scales and cadences
- learning to "play by ear" through a practical "hands-on-the-piano" study of basic triads, progressions, inversions, secondary, and dominant seventh chords

GETTING ACQUAINTED WITH THE PIANO

Study of the piano is a "hands-on" general musicianship course. Not only is one learning to play an instrument valuable to worship, but many pianists also eventually offer their skills as leaders, accompanists, and teachers. A pianist acquires a good sound on the piano by using proper hand positions and fingerings and, above all else, playing music with lyrical motion. But it's not just about learning to play piano. The keyboard has been the backbone for the music of weekly worship for centuries; so **the ideal outcome of Salvation Army piano instruction is to nurture meeting pianists who can sight-read hymn tunes and also play choruses by ear or follow chord changes.**

Finding middle C
Notice that the black keys on a piano are in sets of twos and threes. Locate all the sets of two black keys. C is the white key to the left of the two black keys. On a traditional acoustic piano you will find seven of the C's. Middle C is the fourth C from the bottom and top, basically in the middle of the piano. In the beginning, middle C will be played by either the left or right thumb.

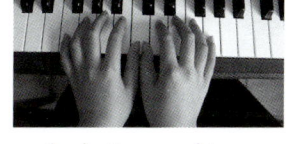

Body position
Sit with back straight in a relaxed position, using only the forward half of the bench. Place the bench far enough from the piano to allow freedom of both arms. When your hands are on the keys, the forearms should be parallel to the keyboard, with the wrist straight, not bent up or down. Adjust the bench height accordingly. The edge of the knees should be two inches or less under the piano.

Hand positions
The hand position should be the same as when the arm is relaxed at your side, with the normal curve of the fingers. In the beginning, each finger is assigned a number, running from each thumb as #1, through each pinky as #5.

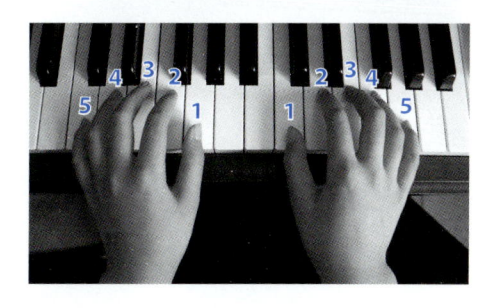

The Beat Goes On

Striking the keys

Fingers should be relaxed, but curved, so that when playing they resemble the legs of a walking crab. After depressing a key, release and continue to rest the finger lightly on top of the key until the next stroke.

Remember to keep the first joint (knuckle) of every finger, except the thumbs, always curved. Keep the thumb relaxed so that it strikes the key with the soft pad at the outside of the nail. With passage work, the thumb acts as a hinge and is the key to moving swiftly up and down the keyboard. Avoid any tension in the arms.

Using the sustain pedal

The sustain pedal is the one on the far right of the piano pedals. It allows notes to ring after a key has been depressed. Release the pedal when striking the next note and press down immediately. This is known as the "up–down" technique. Instruction as to when to use the sustain pedal is indicated by a bracket underneath the piano staff. When this pedal bracket appears in the music, the pedal is usually released and depressed again at a change of chords. Use of the sustain pedal should not be introduced too early. Wait until the student's feet can reach the floor. Timely pedal changes facilitate clarity from chord to chord, rather than a muddy overlapping of chords.

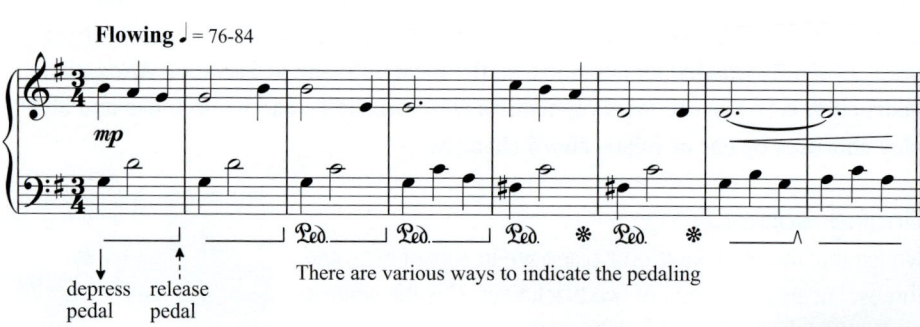

↓ depress pedal
↑ release pedal

There are various ways to indicate the pedaling

Touch

To achieve a pleasing, smooth, and connected *(legato)* sound, the end of one note should be the beginning of the next, as keys played consecutively are depressed and raised simultaneously.

For a brilliant sound, the finger should meet the key with the tip of the finger. To play *staccato* (separated), strike and release the key quickly. For *marcato* (heavily accented), strike the key heavily. When attempting either of these styles, use a stiff wrist. Be sure that the entire hand, fingers, and wrist follow through the striking of a key.

Chapter 16 | PLAY ME A SONG, YOU'RE THE PIANO-MAN

Scale playing

"The Metronome is Your Best Friend"

Practicing scales needs to be a part of the pianist's daily routine. Scale playing develops correct hand position, as well as accuracy and strength in one's sound. When practicing scales:

- ☑ Always use the correct fingering. (For a complete listing of scales for piano, see Appendix 16.1).
- ☑ Use a metronome (available as a phone application) to retain a constant *tempo*.
- ☑ Practice one hand at a time at first.
- ☑ Then try hands together.
- ☑ With hands together, remain at a slow speed until accuracy and correct hand position with hands together are attained.
- ☑ Increase the speed of the metronome slowly to make progress.

motor memory (*term*) \'mōt - ər 'mem - ə - rē \ The ability to recall previously executed movements.

Daily scale practice cannot be emphasized enough, as it is central to gaining a rich piano tone, acquiring facility with different keys, and developing motor memory. Working in strict rhythm develops a pianist's own inner metronome as well as finger-control. With increased facility comes increased freedom.

C scale, two hands, one octave, ascending and descending, with proper fingering

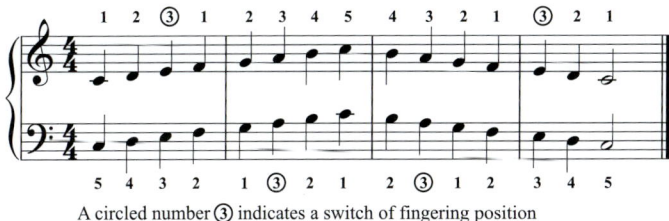

A circled number ③ indicates a switch of fingering position

Left Hand   Right Hand

On-the-job training

Children who enjoy music, like to sing, demonstrate tunefulness, and keep a steady rhythm can be identified as future pianists. We seek to link these young people to qualified piano instructors who work well with children. Some locations have an "Operation: Piano-Player" program which helps subsidize lessons. When pianists are ready to play their first piano piece, use them as a prelude to the morning worship or during the Sunday school opening. Most any piece—not necessarily a hymn—from the method book will do. Make sure young pianists have an opportunity to perform in a season-finale recital. Encourage them to attend music camp or conservatory, where they will receive more intense daily instruction and have opportunities to perform keyboard solos.[1]

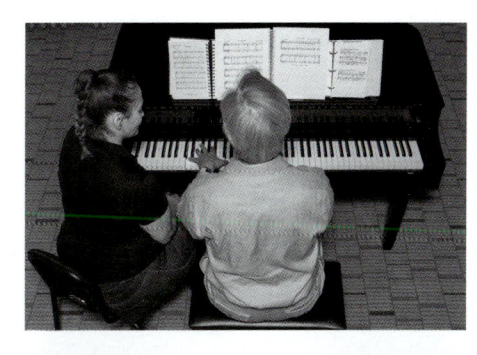

Piano mentor

As the pianists develop, arrange for the students to be on the Sunday morning schedule for preludes and offertories. Begin to use the *Simplified Piano Tune Book* as part of the weekly lessons, so they become acquainted with accessible arrangements for accompanying congregational singing. When specific hymn tunes are ready, make an effort to program these tunes in worship with the student playing along. These can be a "four-hands" duet or rendered using two keyboards. The piano students can also play along with the youth band,[2] or with someone on another keyboard or guitar during the Sunday school opening.

In the service

As students advance, schedule them to play with the instructor for the whole of the service. (Be sure to practice all the congregational songs, the prelude, offertory, and transitions in advance.) Assure them that you have everything covered, and they can drop out when they feel overwhelmed or sense a big mistake coming on. Whisper to them during the service (even when playing) to let them know what is coming up. Your instructions might go like this: "Ready? 1 – 2 – ready – play … Again, slower this time … Softer … Be ready to repeat … Just the chorus this time … Last time." After the service, discuss how things went and choose one or two things to work on for next time, hopefully just a few weeks down the road, to keep the experience fresh.

? 16 BARS REST

1. Double-check that you and your students use proper body and hand positions at the piano. Work to develop a fluid, full piano touch through daily scale practice by always maintaining correct fingerings and relying on the metronome to keep a measured tempo. Refer to Appendix 16.1 for scale fingerings.

2. Identify and engage developing pianists to mentor with on-the-job training at the piano during worship services or Sunday school opening.

CHORDING AND PLAYING BY EAR

In this "hands-on" section, the instructor (or ambitious student) is given a crash course in **chording** at the piano. Building from basic scales and arpeggios, parallel harmonies in thirds and sixths are introduced. Next we learn to identify major, minor, and diminished triads found in scales built on triads. We begin to play melodies and related I–IV–V harmonies by ear. For the advancing student, further instruction into inversions and secondary triads encourages smooth voice-leading. Finally, the dominant seventh chord is introduced. This sequence is best experienced at a keyboard, combining the theoretical concepts with essential aural and visual recognition.

Demonstrations of the piano examples may be found in the Chapter Sixteen online folder.

First steps—Finding your way around the piano

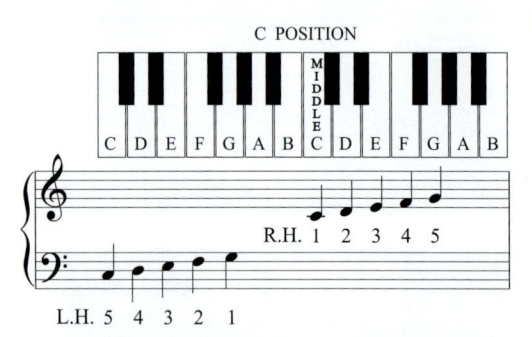

In the previous section, we asked the student to find the black and white keys, noting that the black keys sometimes appear in sets of three, alternated with sets of twos. We located C as the note on the white key just to the left of the two black keys. We asked the student to find all the Cs on the piano. Now we introduce D as the next white key up to the right, then E, then F, and finally G. We show the student how to play C–D–E–F–G using their five right hand fingers, commencing with the thumb as 1 on C, D–2, E–3, etc. Next we introduce C to G using the left hand, commencing with the pinky–5 up through the thumb–1.

Another step is to have the students enjoy playing C to G and back down in several octaves. They can even try playing them in contrary motion at the same time or two octaves apart with both hands. Have the student reinforce the note names by singing them as they play in the middle C register.

Next, move into a beginner method book. Many of these indicate both the fingering and notes. What is important is for the students to differentiate: **(1) notes that stay at** the same level, look and sound the same, (2) notes that go up on the staff, sound higher and (3) notes that go lower on the staff, sound lower. In time the note names will come, but music reading begins in the recognition of visual positioning on the staff.

Scales

Earlier in this chapter, we emphasized the importance of the pianist developing finger strength and a resultant, consistent touch through daily scale practice. Finger exercises, like scales, should coincide with the keys being encountered in songs or the method book.

Begin with the C scale (see music on page 341), ascending and then descending over one octave, starting with the right hand, fingering as so:

1-2-3, 1-2-3-4-5-4-3-2-1, 3-2-1

Next learn the left hand independently:

5-4-3-2-1, 3-2-1-2-3, 1-2-3-4-5

Then begin to work both hands together, slowly at first and then increasing the speed. Again reinforce the note names by asking the student to sing along as they ascend and descend the scales.

An enjoyable variant is to begin with both thumbs on middle C and practice the scale with the hands ascending and descending in contrary motion:

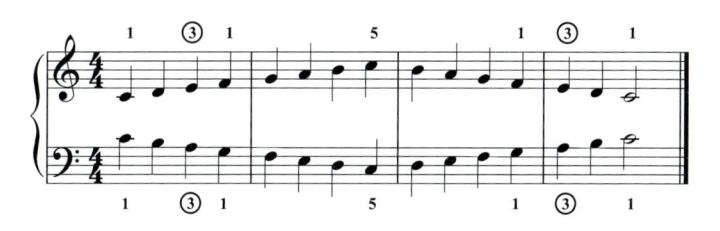

Cadences

At the conclusion of executing a scale, it is common practice to play a series of chords known as a **I–IV–V–I** cadence. The I chord in the key of C is C–E–G, IV is F–A–C and V is G–B–D and then back to I, which is C–E–G. Notice that the note order from bottom to top is sometimes altered to permit the I–IV–V–I cadence to work *without* moving the hand position. Like the rendering of scales, always use the correct fingering when playing cadences, so that they can become second nature.

Playing simple cadences is a vital first step for learning to play piano by ear. Many songs, in virtually any style of music from classic to folk to pop, rely on just these three chords—**I**, **IV** and **V**. Incorporating cadences (in a number of keys) into your daily regimen develops aural and motor memory, so that one learns to play these chord sequences almost without thinking.

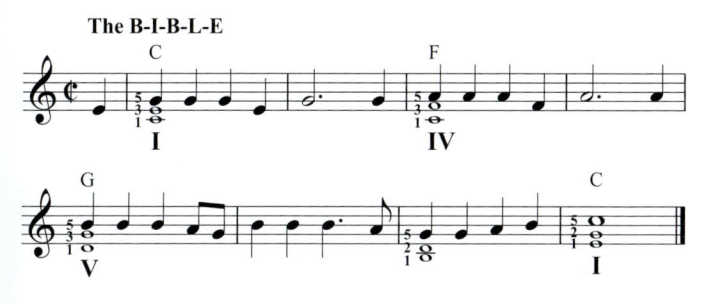

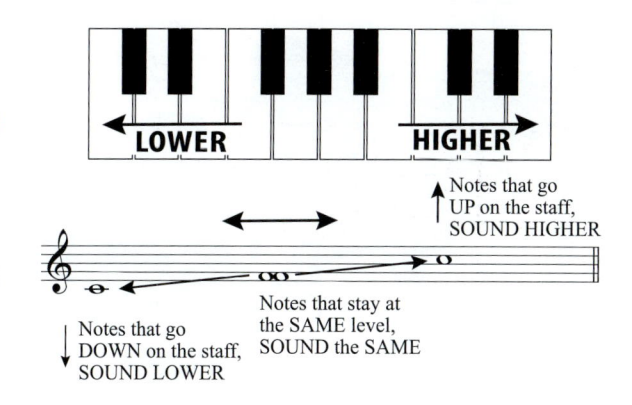

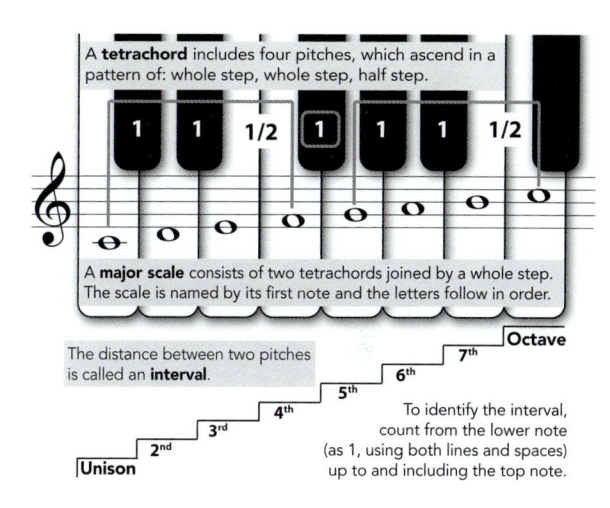

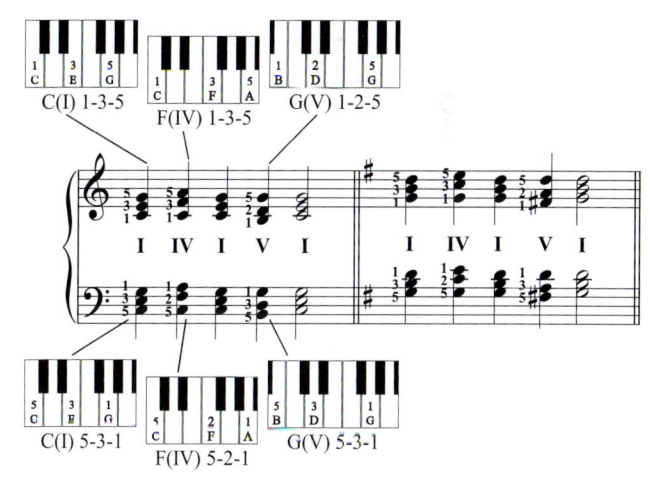

I–IV–V chords are explained further, later in this chapter, on p. 347. For a complete reference of **I–IV–V–I** cadences, see the scale sheets in Appendix 16.1

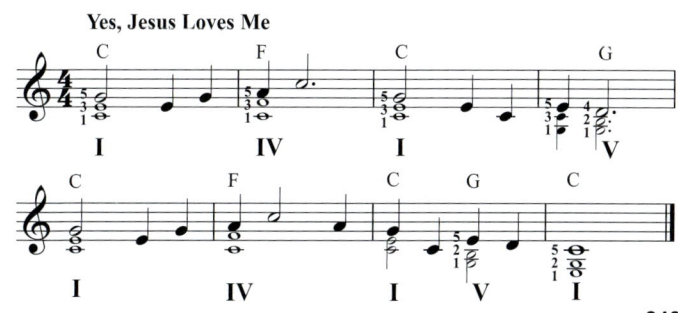

The B-I-B-L-E

Yes, Jesus Loves Me

The Beat Goes On

Playing by EAR

There are a number of approaches one can take to introduce playing choruses by ear:

- **Give a good starting note and the first few notes of a melody and have the student try to figure out the remainder of a tune they already know.** It may benefit them to notate the melody. You may wish to play simple chords underneath with your left hand to supplement their execution of the melody, planting the seeds of the chording they could try to add next.

Give first few notes of melody
Instructor complete corresponding left hand chords

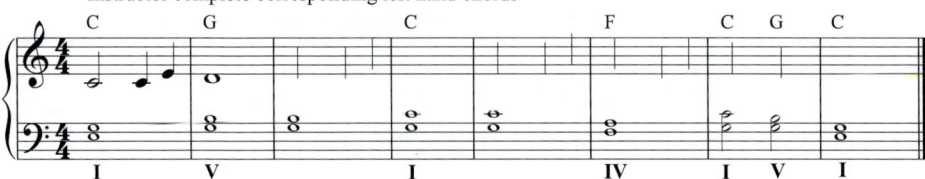

chord (term) \'kȯerd\ the sounding together of three or more tones producing what we call harmony.

- 3 or more notes — CHORD
- R-3-5 — TRIAD
- 2 note — INTERVAL
- 3rd note — IMPLIED

- Later have them **identify the chord that could go with the first measure of the tune. Have them search for the next chord, and so forth.** They can begin by using the **I–IV–V–I** chords they have already learned with their scales to accompany in the left hand. Eventually, have the student transition from *block chords,* where all the tones of the chord are sounded simultaneously to *broken chords,* where the notes of the chord are sounded in succession.

Student sings melody, while working out the left hand chords

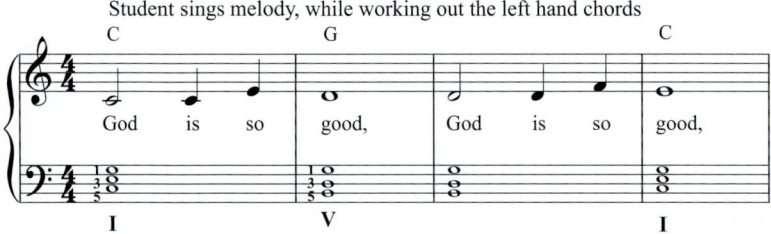

God is so good, God is so good,

Transition left hand block chords to broken chords
Then try to sing the melody with broken chords

God is so good, He's so good to me.

- Many times a chorus can be effectively accompanied without playing the melody. A third approach is to simply **ask the student pianist to sing a chorus along with a variation of the familiar I–IV–V–I cadence.**

Play simple chords while singing the chorus line

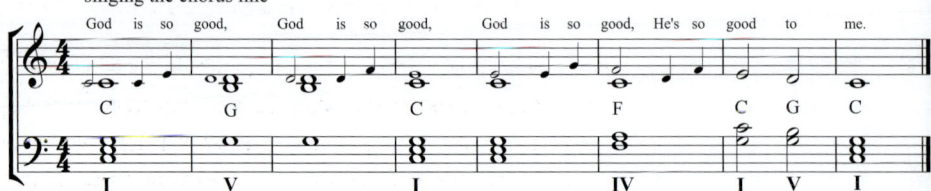

God is so good, God is so good, God is so good, He's so good to me.

344

www.music.saconnects.org

- With time, it is important to **do this exercise in different keys,** as choruses need to be played in their best key for congregational singing. At first, ask your student to learn the same chorus in the keys of C, F and G.

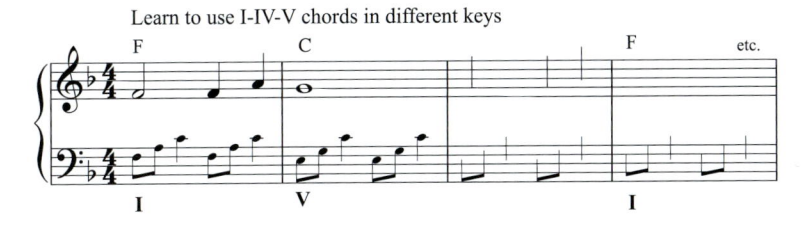

Learn to use I–IV–V chords in different keys

16 BARS REST

1. An effective ear-training exercise to differentiate **I–IV–V** chords is to sing the scale numbers (or solfege) of each triad as you play them in different keys, as follows:

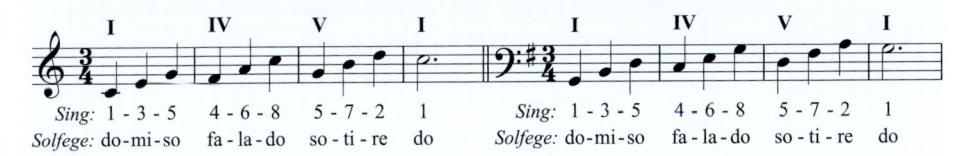

   Sing: 1 - 3 - 5   4 - 6 - 8   5 - 7 - 2   1   Sing: 1 - 3 - 5   4 - 6 - 8   5 - 7 - 2   1
   Solfege: do-mi-so   fa-la-do   so-ti-re   do   Solfege: do-mi-so   fa-la-do   so-ti-re   do

   Solfege syllables are explained on pp. 136–137 of Singing Company Chapter Six.

2. Continue to work to play by ear at the keyboard by discovering choruses and songs that are based on **I–IV–V** chords. Try to play them in different keys or play the chords and sing along. Some possibilities include "God is so Good," "Jesus Loves Me," and "Alleluia."

SCALES EXPAND INTO TRIADS

In a very elementary explanation, a scale consists of seven different tones—one for each letter of the musical alphabet (A through G), plus a repeat of the first tone at the octave to complete the scale. The C major scale falls on the white keys from C to C.

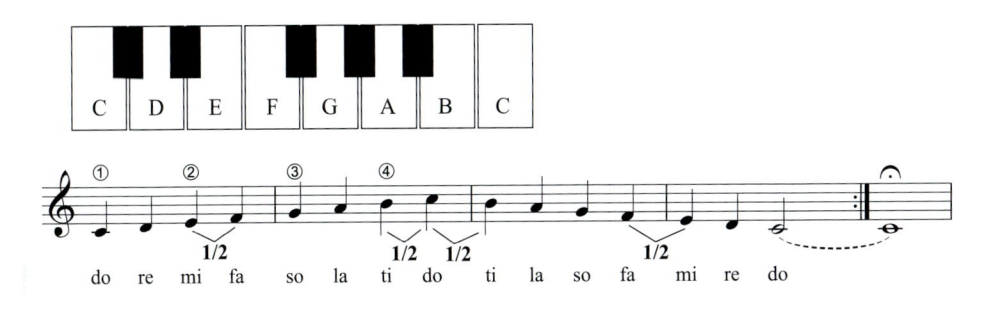

do   re   mi   fa   so   la   ti   do   ti   la   so   fa   mi   re   do

The Beat Goes On

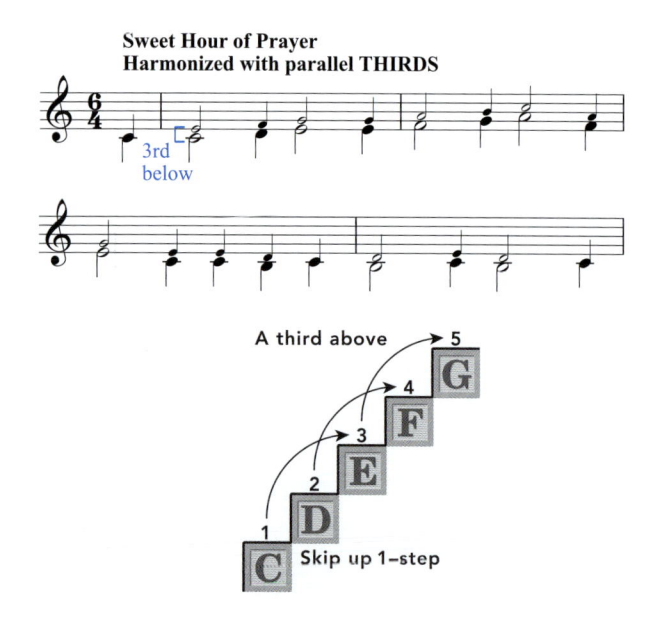

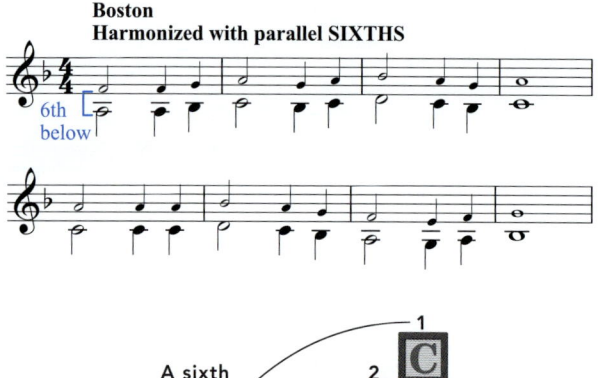

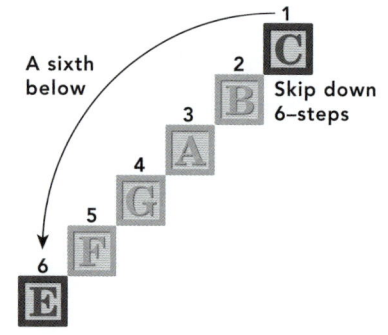

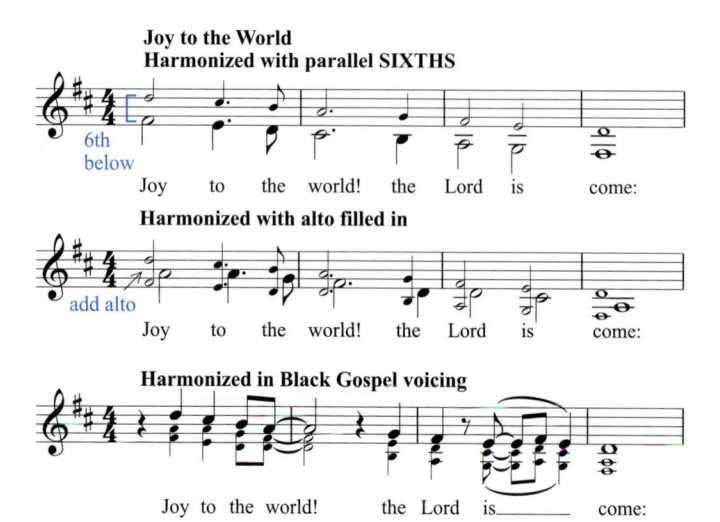

A third above

To introduce simple harmonization one can harmonize the scale by adding a note a third above. (C is 1, D is the second note up, and E is the third.) It is like skipping one step as you ascend stairs. One foot is on the lower step C and the other on E. The same holds true for the other steps of the C scale as you ascend (D and F, E and G, etc.) For instance, have the left hand start on C (below middle C), while the right hand starts on the E above middle C.

Practice playing the scale with added thirds, either above or below, going up and down. If one tries this in another key, then the flats or sharps indicated in the key signature are observed in the scale and the harmonized thirds.

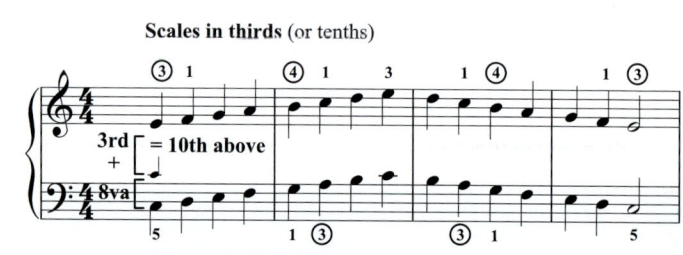

By transferring the left hand down an octave, we create a scale in tenths

A sixth below

Another **simple harmonic device is to reverse the voicing, playing the scale accompanied by the tone a sixth below**. In this case, the right hand starts on middle C, while the left hand starts six steps below on E.

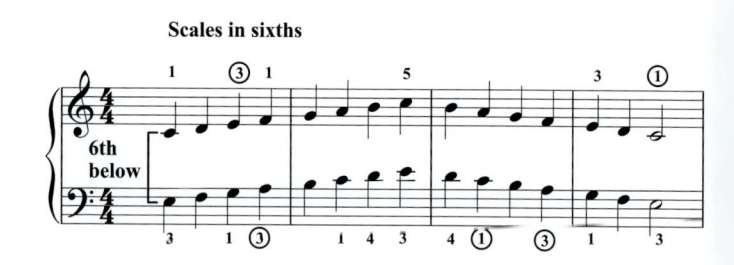

When combined this way, voices are said to be in parallel motion, as found in parts of the familiar carol "Joy to the World."

In Baroque practice, **chords with parallel fifths and octaves are not found appealing harmonically, with the exception of parallel chords with the third of the triad in the bass**. By using the "sixth below" note as the bass tone, the left hand descends or ascends by scale steps playing the third of the chord, with the right hand playing the root and the fifth. This harmonic treatment (with the third of the chord a sixth below the melody note) is familiar today, particularly in the choir parts of Gospel-style arrangements.

A triad as stacked thirds

If you take the first, third and fifth notes of the C scale (C-E-G) and stack them, you get what is known as a triad. Notice that we skip a step moving from the third tone (E) up to the fifth tone (G).

If we return to our C scale ascending in thirds (see opposite page), we can add another tone on top of each note, which is called the fifth. **Remember to skip from the third tone of the scale up to the fifth.** By alternating root, third, and fifth (that is, skipping over the second and the fourth), the notes of the triad are either **all on a line or all in a space.**

triad *(term)* \ a chord of three tones, consisting of a root tone with its third and fifth above.

fifth
third
root
F triad

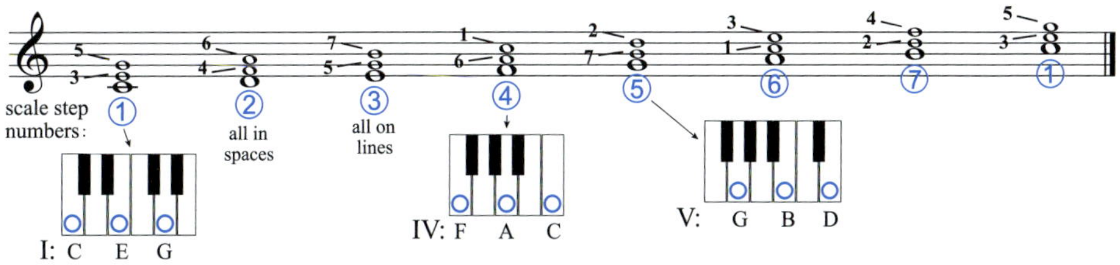

scale step numbers:
all in spaces
all on lines
I: C E G
IV: F A C
V: G B D

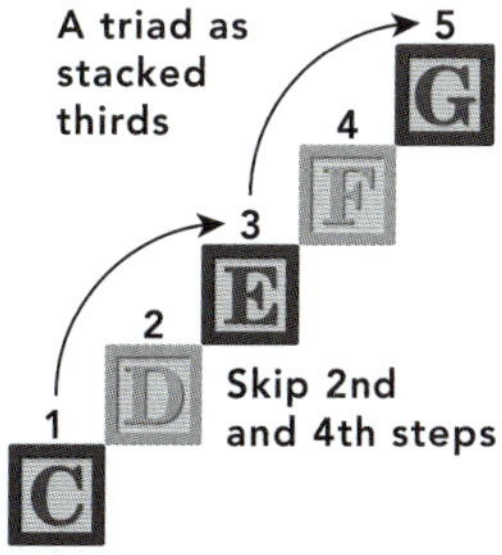

A triad as stacked thirds
Skip 2nd and 4th steps

Notice below that the triad for each step of the scale has a name (tonic, supertonic, mediant, subdominant, etc.) that relates to each scale degree (I–ii–iii–IV, etc.). Some music theorists use lowercase numerals and letters for the minor chords, while others use all capital Roman numerals. A lowercase "m" (for minor) is indicated after letter names. As you play up the scale, become familiar with the difference between the brighter major chords and the more somber minor and diminished ones. The arrow (⌒) indicates the triad to which the first triad, by virtue of its position in the scale, is tonally drawn. We sometimes call this "tonal magnetism."

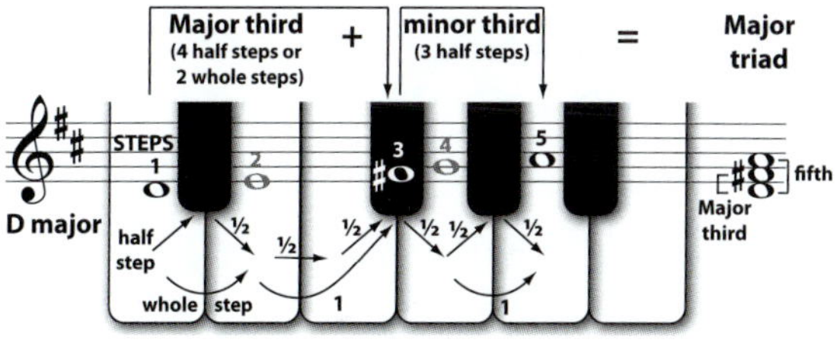

Major third (4 half steps or 2 whole steps)
+
minor third (3 half steps)
=
Major triad
STEPS
D major
half step
whole step
fifth
Major third

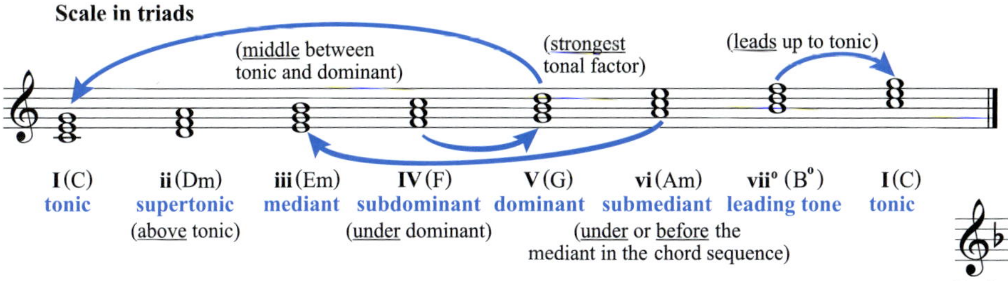

Scale in triads
(middle between tonic and dominant)
(strongest tonal factor)
(leads up to tonic)
I (C) tonic
ii (Dm) supertonic (above tonic)
iii (Em) mediant
IV (F) subdominant (under dominant)
V (G) dominant
vi (Am) submediant (under or before the mediant in the chord sequence)
vii° (B°) leading tone
I (C) tonic

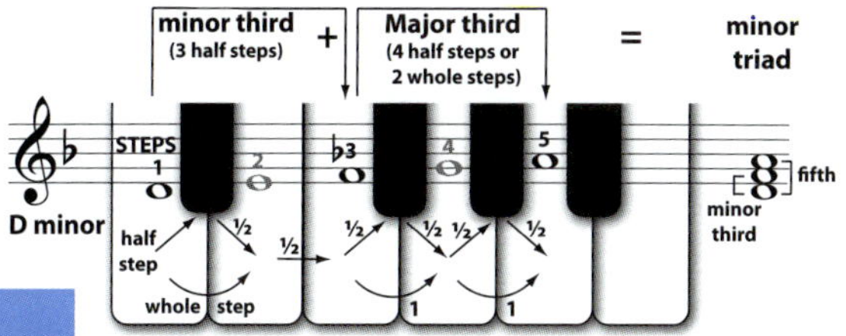

minor third (3 half steps)
+
Major third (4 half steps or 2 whole steps)
=
minor triad
STEPS
D minor
half step
whole step
fifth
minor third

16 BARS REST

1. Choose other keys to construct scales in thirds and sixths (or try to render "Joy to the World" in several keys in the same manner as the example above).

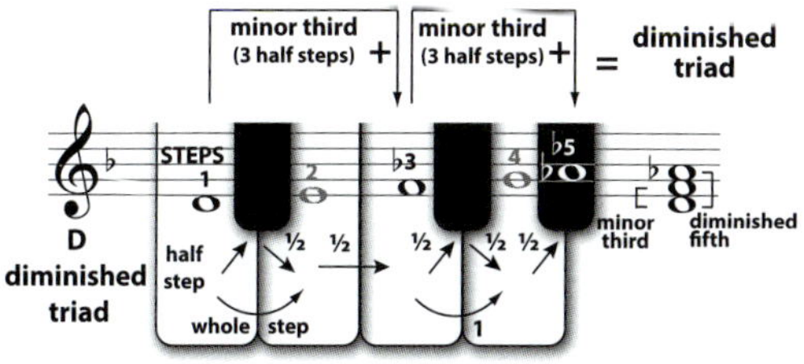

minor third (3 half steps)
+
minor third (3 half steps)
+
=
diminished triad
STEPS
D diminished triad
half step
whole step
minor third
diminished fifth

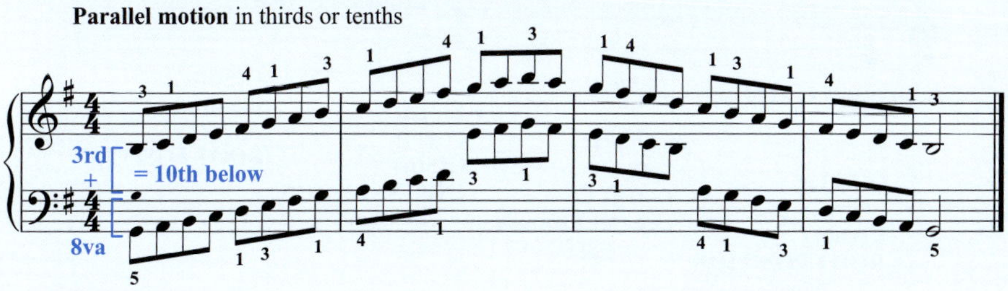

Parallel motion in thirds or tenths
3rd + 8va = 10th below

Parallel motion in sixths

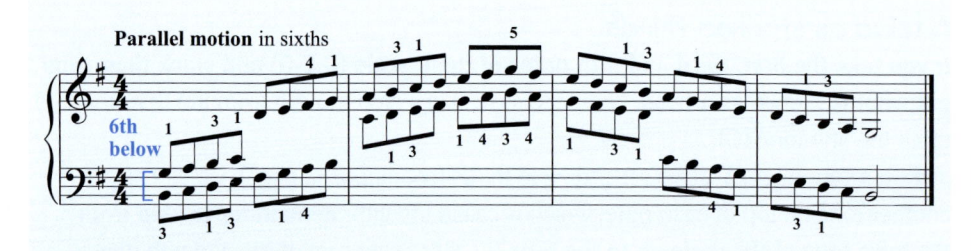

2. Practice playing triads going up and down various scales, singing the chord name or number as you go along.

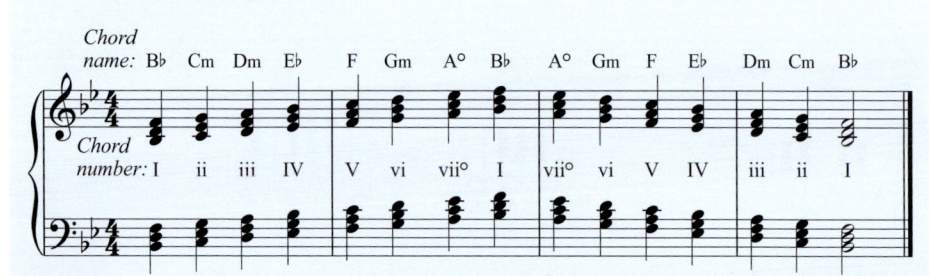

3. Another good ear-training exercise is to sing the root position chord bass note, using the chord name or number. For instance, one might sing C–F–C–G–C or I–IV–I–V–I, while playing the chord progressions.

CHORDS CAN BE INVERTED

Bye, bye to boring block chords

So far, we have dealt with triads exclusively in what we call root position, using the scale steps (1, 2, 3, etc.) as the bottom note of the triad. The root is the lowest note of the three notes in the triad with the others stacked on top. A series of chords, all in root position, are commonly called *block chords*. We can move the relative octave of any note in a triad either up or down to *invert* the triad. **If the lowest note in the new inverted triad is the third, then the triad is said to be in** *1st inversion*. **If the bottom note is the fifth of the triad, then it is in** *2nd inversion*.

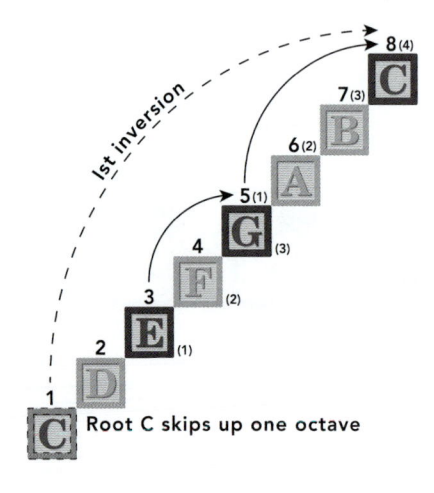

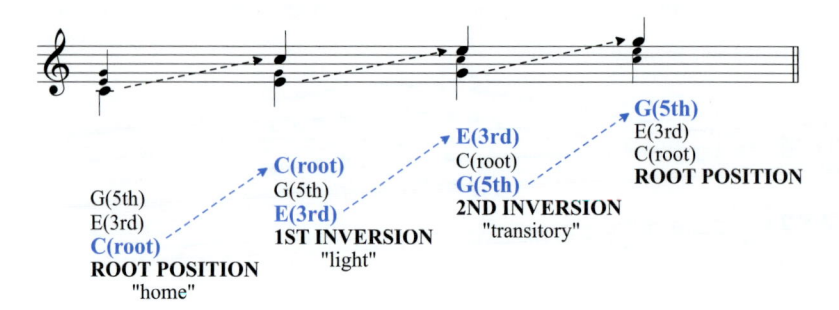

G(5th)   C(root)   E(3rd)   G(5th)
E(3rd)   G(5th)   C(root)   E(3rd)
C(root) E(3rd)   G(5th)   C(root)
ROOT POSITION   1ST INVERSION   2ND INVERSION   ROOT POSITION
"home"   "light"   "transitory"

348   www.music.saconnects.org

Dead weight

Practicing triads and chords with the proper fingering helps develop motor memory, so that one begins to play and hear these inversions intuitively. Further, this exercise gives the teacher an opportunity to introduce the concept of using "dead weight" to get power out of the chords, and to relax the arms while playing. Basically when you practice playing solid triads, throw your arm up in the air and allow it to drop into the chord, using dead weight only. Don't force it. No muscle should be used in the drop, so that the weight of the arm itself creates the power. You may find you're not always accurate hitting the chords this way, but the accuracy will develop over time. This technique may also be applied to scale-playing, in that the first note of the scale should be a dead-weight drop. With subsequent notes, only the fingers do the work, without any arm tension.[3]

When playing through the inversions from root position, to 1st inversion, 2nd inversion, and in reverse, listen for the distinctive harmonic implications and color of each inversion. For instance, the 1st inversion triad suggests "lightness" with the third in the bass; the 2nd inversion has a transitory feeling with the fifth in the bass, while the root position triad carries a settled finality.

16 BARS REST

1. Practice playing inversions of individual triads ascending and descending, using a "dead-weight" approach and listening to and identifying the different inversions. Proper fingering is shown in Appendix 16.2.

2. Practice playing triads ascending with the right hand up the major scale. Next do the same in first inversion, and then in second inversion. Try a few different scales to get familiar with using chords in different keys. The song "Lean on Me" is one popular example using parallel chords.

3. "Joy to the World" incorporates the left hand playing the lowest note of the 1st inversion (the third of the triad) and the top upper notes (the root and the fifth) in the right. Try harmonizing other melodies using similar parallel motion with the third in left hand. Here are two examples:

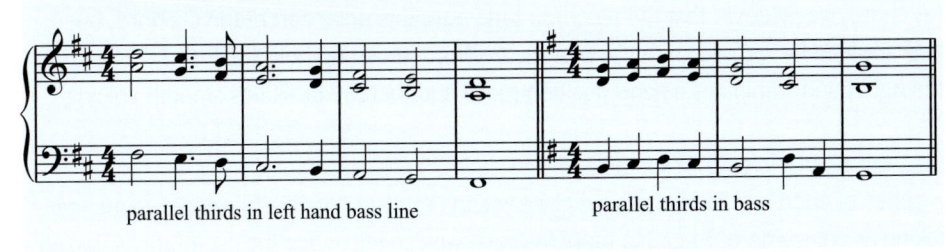

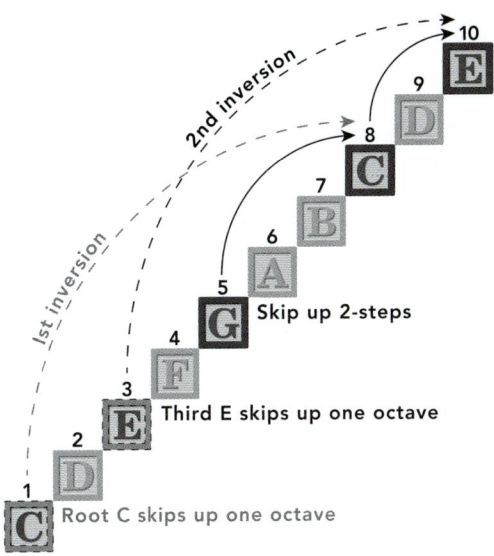

parallel thirds in left hand bass line

parallel thirds in bass

INVERSIONS HELP US "VOICE-LEAD"

Contrary motion

It is advantageous for a keyboardist to learn to voice-lead, rather than play block chords always in root position, which can require numerous shifts of hand position. Learning to play a series of chords utilizing inversions and common tones helps eliminate movement of hand position. Effective voice-leading increases facility and eliminates the jarring effect between chord changes caused by leaps in the voice lines. To take things a step further, it is common practice to attempt to have the bass notes descend if the right hand chords ascend and vice versa. This is an important component of voice-leading known as creating **contrary motion** between the voices.

Common tones

Creating smooth transitions between chord changes is dependent on what we call **voice-leading.** Consider each tone of the triad as a separate voice, for example, the soprano, alto, and tenor voice. First, choose to use an inversion that maintains a common tone between the two chords. Note in the example that middle C is common between the C (I) and F (IV) chords. Therefore, it is easiest to allow the C to be the bottom note of the F (IV) chord, by placing the F chord in second inversion.

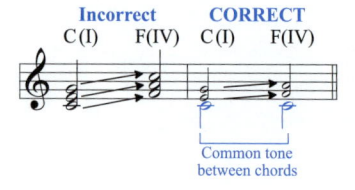

To complete the progression between the C and F chord, with the C as the common tone bottom voice, the E of the C chord moves up by half step to the F of the F chord, and the G of the C chord moves up to the A of the F chord.

Voice-lead by step

Presuming that the common tone between chords is an easily repeated pitch, the next most accessible intervals for singers are the whole and half steps, especially those within the home key's scale, thus the term, "voice-leading." The goal is to avoid forcing either hand to switch position. For example, the most fluid way to play the progression of chords from C to A(minor) to F requires some chords to be inverted, keeping C as the common tone, and all other voices moving up or down by a whole or half step.

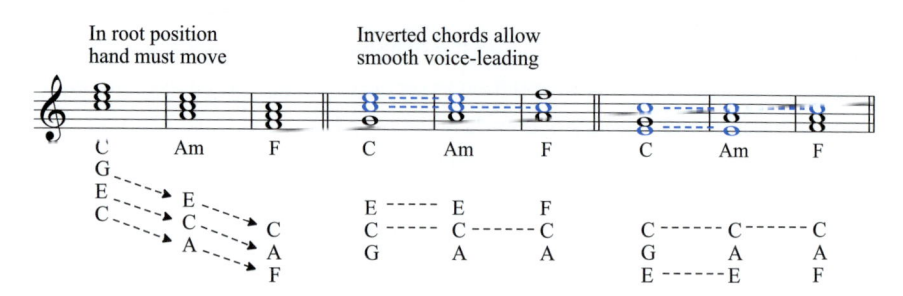

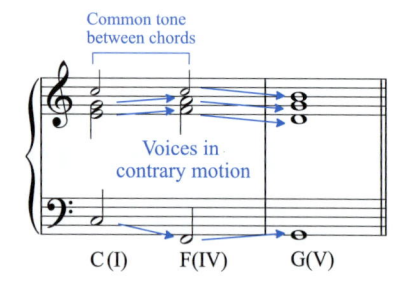

As shown to the left, if we try to move from the C chord (I) to F (IV) and then to the G (V) chord, we discover that the common tone note C is not a part of the G chord, but can logically lead by step down to the B of the G chord. Inverting both the F and G chords in the right hand eliminates a hand position move and thereby facilitates smooth voicing.

Use of secondary chords

A series of chords is known as a **progression,** implying that the harmonic sequence is taking us somewhere. To create more interest, we can introduce the use of triads, based on the **ii** and **vi** step tones of the scale. The **I–IV–V major triads**, that we previously considered, exclusively use tones within the respective key signature. The resultant tones

---

contrary motion (*term*) \'kän-trer-ē 'mō-shən\ parts moving in the opposite direction; one part rises as the other falls.

voice-leading (*term*) \'vöis-lēd-ing\ The essence of efficient voice-leading is striving to find the shortest distance (and any common tones) between notes in the two chords, which keeps the chord progressions smooth and uncomplicated.

in the same key of the **ii** and **vi** *minor triads* include a *minor third*, which is a half step lower than the third of the major triad with the same root and fifth.

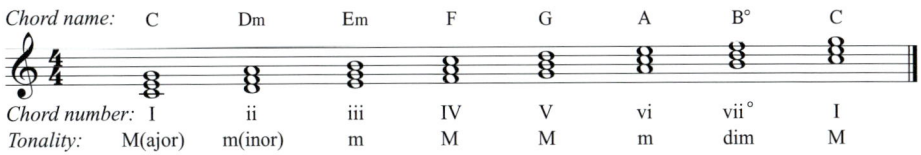

Chord name: C Dm Em F G A B° C
Chord number: I ii iii IV V vi vii° I
Tonality: M(ajor) m(inor) m M M m dim M

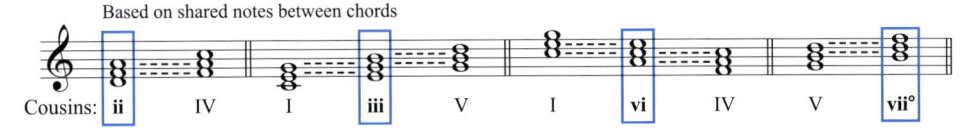

Possible substitute **SECONDARY CHORDS**
Based on shared notes between chords

Cousins: ii IV I iii V I vi IV V vii°

The ii, iii, vi, vii° chords can add significant flavor to the chord palette.

We can branch out and add poignancy to more reflective music, by exploring the use of alternative minor and diminished chords in place of the plainer sounding major chords. Some minor chords substitute well for what can be characterized as their "cousins" in major. For instance, use **ii** in place of **IV**, **iii** in place of **I** or **V**, and **vi** instead of **I**. Each of these chords shares two of its three notes with at least one major "cousin."

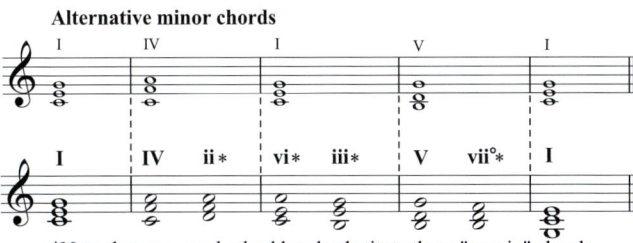

Alternative minor chords

I IV I V I

I IV ii* vi* iii* V vii°* I

*Note that you can *both* add and substitute these "cousin" chords

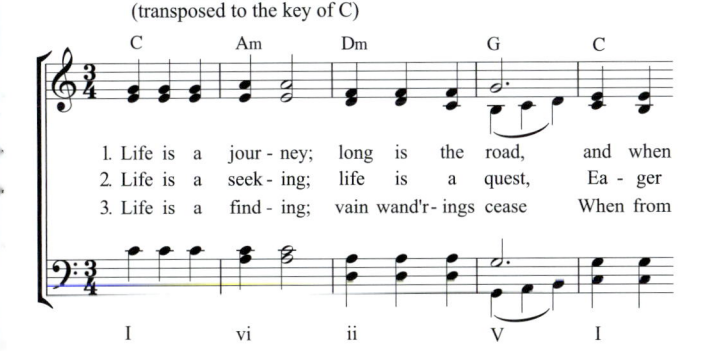

"The Well is Deep" arr. Norman Bearcroft
(transposed to the key of C)

C Am Dm G C

1. Life is a jour-ney; long is the road, and when
2. Life is a seek-ing; life is a quest, Ea-ger
3. Life is a find-ing; vain wand'r-ings cease When from

I vi ii V I

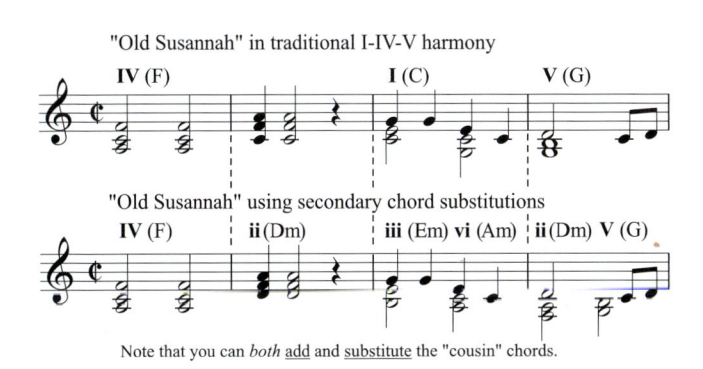

"Old Susannah" in traditional I-IV-V harmony

IV (F) I (C) V (G)

"Old Susannah" using secondary chord substitutions

IV (F) ii (Dm) iii (Em) vi (Am) ii (Dm) V (G)

Note that you can *both* add and substitute the "cousin" chords.

One familiar progression using secondary minor chords is **I–vi–ii–V–I**, or using the chord names in the key of C, these chords would be C–Am–Dm–G–C. Consider the effective variance of harmonic coloring by the inclusion of alternative minor chords in this example:

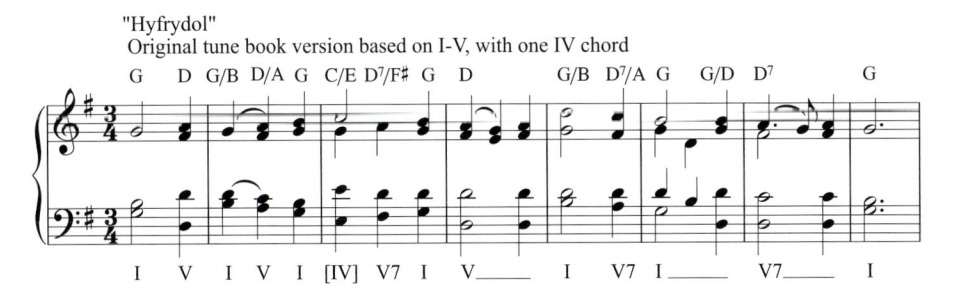

"Hyfrydol"
Original tune book version based on I-V, with one IV chord

G D G/B D/A G C/E D7/F# G D G/B D7/A G G/D D7 G

I V I V I [IV] V7 I V___ I V7 I___ V7___ I

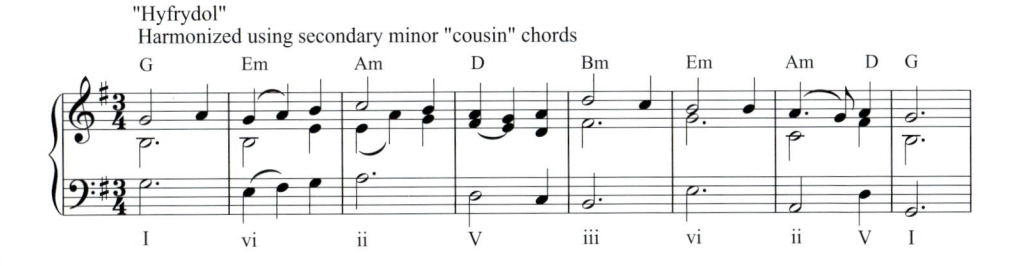

"Hyfrydol"
Harmonized using secondary minor "cousin" chords

G Em Am D Bm Em Am D G

I vi ii V iii vi ii V I

There is also tremendous value in exploring these same chord progressions, but in first inversion, and then second. Listen carefully to discover the inherent color of each of these triads in their inversions. Notice that in some cases, inverting the first triad shifts the common tone to another voice, dictating inversion of the next triad as well.

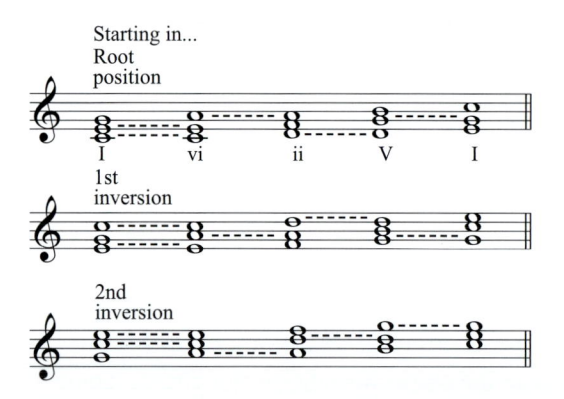

When practicing chord progressions, use good "up-down" pedal technique as introduced on p. 340 of this chapter.

16 BARS REST

1. Practice playing progressions in a variety of keys using voice-leading principles; for example, **I–IV–ii–V–I** or **I–vi–IV–ii–V–I**. It may be easier to first sort out the right hand voice-leading and then add the bass notes, striving for contrary motion. Sing the chord name or number as you play to help develop your ear. Here are two examples:

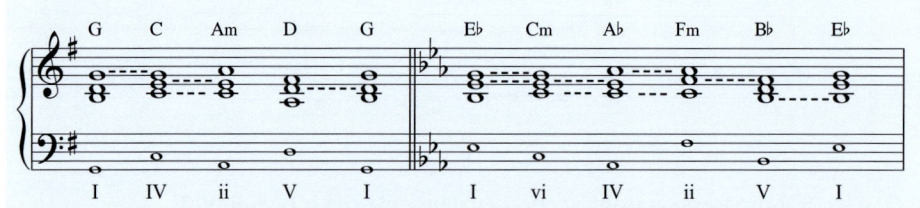

2. Try to figure out the basic progression to a familiar chorus in different keys. Avoid using block chords exclusively in root position by keeping the notes "under the hands" with smooth voice-leading that makes use of inversions.

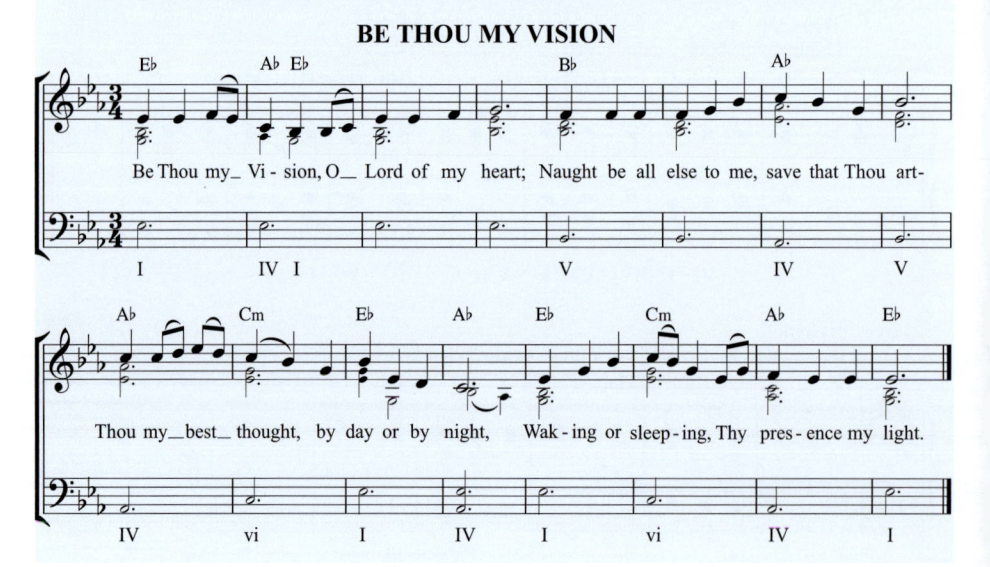

BE THOU MY VISION

Be Thou my Vi-sion, O Lord of my heart; Naught be all else to me, save that Thou art—
Thou my best thought, by day or by night, Wak-ing or sleep-ing, Thy pres-ence my light.

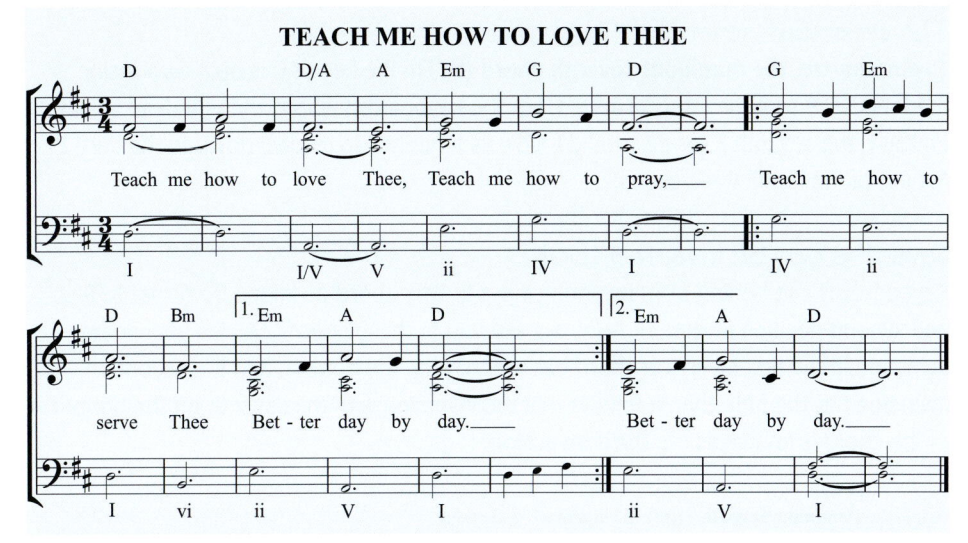

TEACH ME HOW TO LOVE THEE

THE DOMINANT SEVENTH (V7) CHORD

We should not leave this introductory overview of keyboard practice without considering the most important driving force in Western music: **the harmonic progression from the dominant seventh (V7) chord resolving to the tonic (I) chord.**

The dominant (V) chord

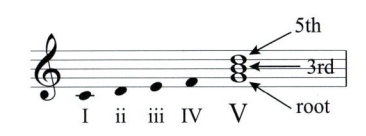

In any key, **the dominant chord is built on the fifth step of the scale**, thus the convention of using the Roman numeral **V**. In the key of C, the root of the dominant chord is G, the fifth note of the scale in our "home" key of C. Using the principle of stacked thirds we've learned, the dominant chord tones then are G (the root), B (the third), and D (the fifth). Remember, we use only notes in the key of the tonic (**I**), which, in this case, is the key of C. We move on the staff either from line-to-line, or space-to-space.

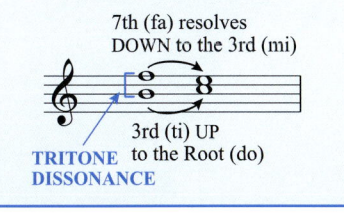

Adding the seventh

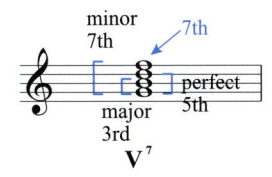

Adding an interval of a third above the G-B-D triad in the key of C gives us the seventh F. The pull from the dominant (**V**) to the tonic (**I**) chord is even stronger with the addition of the seventh, because the seventh creates an unresolved dissonance between the third and the seventh of the V chord that wants to move the harmony toward its tonic home.

Tendency tones

There is a tendency in music for *active tones* to resolve to *repose tones.* Examples using solfege syllables include: *re to do; fa to mi; la to so; ti to do;* and *so to do.* As a useful aural reminder, I like to utilize a simple little tune with solfege syllables to describe the "tonal magnetism" which dictates the resolution of the dominant seventh chord (**V7**) to its tonic (**I**) home. That is, the bass note *so* wants to resolve up to *do, ti* up to *do,* and *re* down to *do.* The seventh of the V chord, in this case, the F (or *fa*), resolves down to the E (*mi*) which is the major third of the I chord, giving the satisfying sense of arriving home.

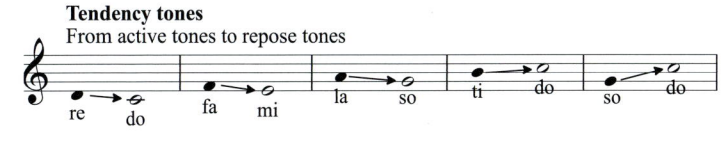

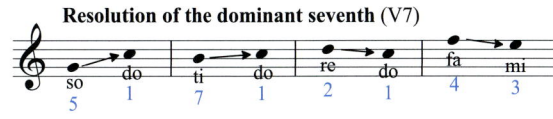

In the words of theorist Ed Roseman, the **dominant chord (V)** suffers from a form of "musical homesickness, being restless, tense and expectant—a wound-up spring. It is just dying to get back home to the tonic (**I**) chord."[4]

tritone (*term*) \'trī - tōn\
a musical interval consisting of three whole steps (for instance, B up to F, or C to F#). The tritone dissonance in the dominant seventh (V7) chord between the fourth (*fa*) and seventh (*ti*) scale degrees are separated respectively from the third (*mi*) and root (*do*) degrees of the tonic (I) triad by only a half step, which explains the "tonal magnetism" in the resolution of the dominant seventh (V7) to the tonic (I) chord.

Resolution of dominant seventh
[so resolves to do, re to do, ti to so, fa to mi]

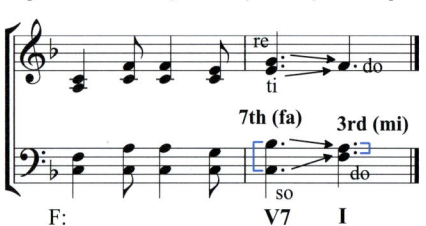

The dominant seventh (V7) chord

To summarize, the dominant seventh chord (V7) in the key of C is built on a major triad (G–B–D) with the F (or *fa*) added. For the keyboardist who is trying to lead voices logically, the seventh F (or *fa*) should follow its tendency to resolve down to the third E (or *mi*) of the home tonic chord.

Sevenths can be inverted too!

Keyboardists can benefit from exploring ways to vary chord positions from root to first and second position inversion. Adding a seventh to these chords creates yet another inversion. If the first inversion chord has the third on the bottom, and the second inversion has the fifth, then it follows that the inversion with the seventh on the bottom of the chord is known as the **third inversion.**

Dominant Seventh - Broken chords and inversions

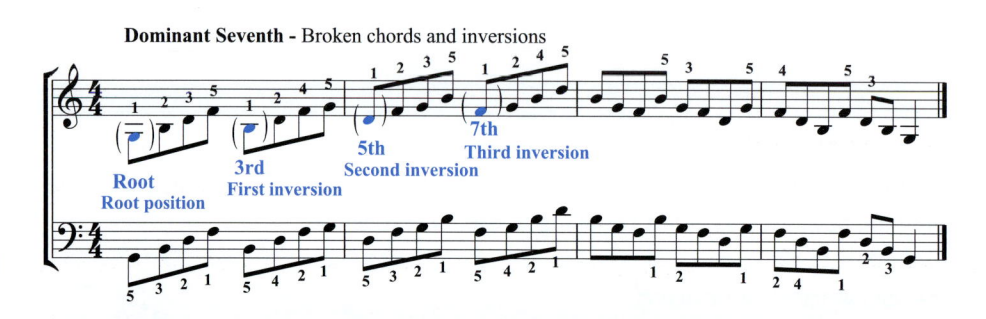

Other seventh chords are introduced in Chapter Seventeen (p. 367) and more discussion on seventh chords follows in the Chapter Nineteen Worship Band Leader Toolbox (pp. 408–409).

16 BARS REST

Diminished chords are defined on p. 368 of Chapter Seventeen.

1. Experiment at the keyboard with all the triads within various major scales. Learn to identify their tonality—whether major or minor.

2. Add the V7 to the regimen of practicing the I-IV-V7-I cadences in different keys. Reference Appendix 16.3.

C MAJOR CADENCES in three positions

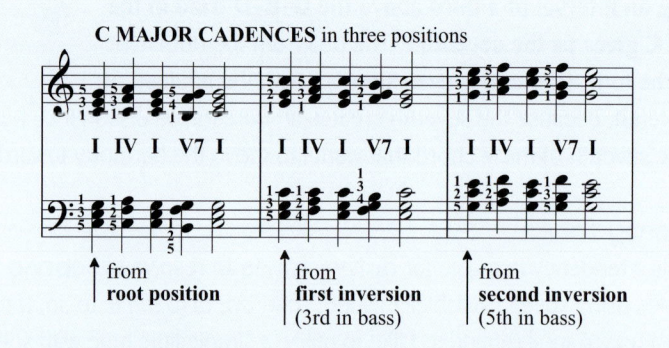

from **root position**

from **first inversion** (3rd in bass)

from **second inversion** (5th in bass)

3. Practice playing inversions of V7 chords ascending and descending. Reference Appendix 16.4.

4. Fingers itching for more? Want to learn to play from a lead sheet? Go to Appendix 16.5 for instruction in **How to Play from a Lead Sheet** at the piano. Also, Appendix 16.6 outlines a six level piano cirriculum.

PIANO INSTRUCTION RESOURCES

PIANO METHOD BOOKS
Basic Piano for Adults, Helene Robinson (Wadsworth)
Bastien Piano Series (Kjos) Graded series in levels – Primer, plus Levels One–Four
John Thompson's Easiest Piano Course
John Thompson's Modern Course 1–4
Suzuki Piano School 1–4 (Suzuki Method International)

PIANO BY EAR INSTRUCTIONAL RESOURCES
The Basic Book of Scales, Chords, Arpeggios & Cadences (Alfred)
Chords for Kids (Flame Tree Publishing)
   Index of fingering of all chords on accessible keyboard diagrams.
Improvising & Arranging on the Keyboard, James Oestereich & Earl Pennington
   (Prentice-Hall)
Chorus books with chord symbols
Fake books of jazz standards
Computer-assisted keyboard instruction

PIANO TECHNIQUE BOOKS
The Art of Finger Dexterity, Czerny (Schirmer)
The Basic Book of Scales, Chords, Arpeggios & Cadences (Alfred)
Hanon – The Virtuoso Pianist (Schirmer)
Junior Hanon, Hanon/Small (Alfred)
The School of Mechanism, Duvernoy (Schirmer)
The School of Velocity, Czerny (Schirmer)
Short School of Velocity, Kohler (Schirmer)
Technical Studies, Pischna (Schirmer)

CLASSIC SOLO PIANO WORKS
Complete Lyric Pieces, Grieg (Dover)
Complete Preludes & Etudes, Chopin (Dover)
Eighteen Short Preludes, J. S. Bach (Alfred)
Inventions and Sinfoni, J. S. Bach (Peters)
Selected Works for Piano, Mozart (Dover)
Sonata Album, in two books (Schirmer)
Sonatina Album, Clementi, Kuhlau and others (Presser)

> Dear Pianist,
> To consider piano stylings for worship services, go on to Chapter Seventeen!
> Harold

CHAPTER SEVENTEEN

KEYBOARD WORSHIP
The Meeting Pianist

Playing the piano for worship is a ministry in itself and requires me to enter into each phase of the worship time, into each phrase of the sung material, and into each place where discontinuity threatens to distract the worshiper off course. —Leonard Ballantine

A WORSHIP PIANIST

Bram Rader succinctly sums up the role of a worship pianist when he writes, "As a Christ–centered Salvationist musician, I find it a great responsibility and privilege to share my musical gifts whenever and wherever I can, whether as a congregational accompanist at the corps or as a piano soloist at a high profile musical event. I pray always that God will be glorified, not only through my musical excellence, but also through my public demeanor and the attitudes of my mind and heart with others. Jesus Christ came to share His love and I pray that, with the active presence of the Holy Spirit in my life, I will do the same."[1]

In **Chapter Seventeen**, we consider the pianist in a worship setting, mostly from the vantage point of reading and interpreting music from the printed page. We examine techniques to:

- enhance the flow of worship with introductions and transitions, including giving support to prayer times
- "reinterpret" what appears on the printed page of the piano tune book or hymnal with harmonic enhancement and modulation
- help the pianist become a valued accompanist for soloists and vocal ensembles

PIANO WORSHIP

Playing the piano for a meeting or service requires much more than being ready with a few congregational songs. With experience, an intuition develops that melds the purpose and direction for the service with our best musical intentions. Effectively linking the various elements of the service from the keyboard is a matter of preparation (looking ahead at the order of service) and a discerning spontaneity (a response to worship in the moment). Just as the keyboardist learns to play some things by ear—that is, to sense where the harmony is going—so the worship pianist begins to gauge where a meeting is heading and intuitively "directs, adds to and enhances the flow of the service."[2]

Effectively rendered **prelude music** creates an air of expectancy for the impending worship. Songs chosen may follow that day's theme, seamlessly leading up to the first words of welcome from the podium or the call to worship. Many hymnals today suggest medleys based on themes.

Introductions to **congregational songs** set the tune melody, mood, and tempo, and establish the starting key in the congregant's ear. It is a "wake-up" call to singing! Some song leaders are happy to have the pianist playing the tune as they introduce the song. Be careful to select a starting point for your introduction that does not replicate the first phrase of the song, or the song leader may inadvertently start prematurely. The introduction should elicit an unmistakable sense of the tune and give a clear signal as to when to start singing.

The Beat Goes On

In some worship settings, the pianist provides the introduction and the band joins the congregation. This eliminates the difficulty of the band navigating an effective introduction. When the band is using the Salvation Army tune books, the pianist plays from *The Salvation Army Piano Tune Book*. Sometimes a bracketed key signature will be found in the left hand corner above the first score. This indicates the piano "concert pitch" key that correlates with the band tune books. For example, a bracketed [Db] indicates that the pianist must play the hymn in Db (or five flats), rather than as notated in D (two sharps). In most cases, this is a matter of reading the same notes but using flats rather than sharps. Accidentals are adjusted accordingly down a half step. A "natural" is read as a "flat" and a "sharp" as a "natural."

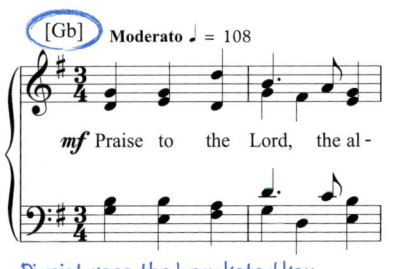

Pianist uses the bracketed key when playing with the band.

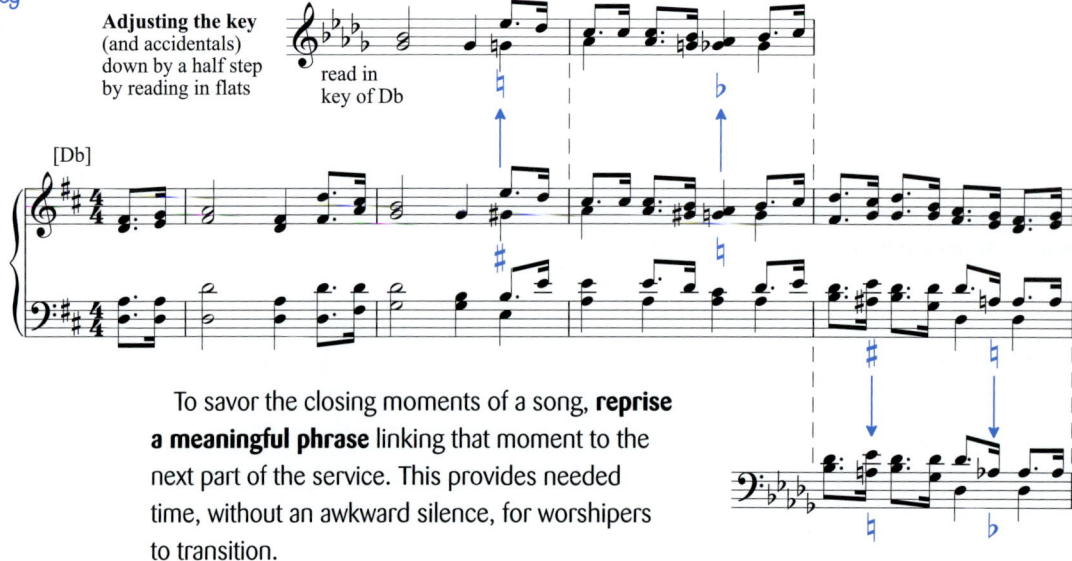

Adjusting the key (and accidentals) down by a half step by reading in flats

read in key of Db

To savor the closing moments of a song, **reprise a meaningful phrase** linking that moment to the next part of the service. This provides needed time, without an awkward silence, for worshipers to transition.

Reprise a meaningful phrase

The art of piano PRAYing[3]

Following the conclusion of the sermon, there are times when a simple piano **underscore** helps make the transition into a time of prayer and response. The speaker may provide the pianist with one or two possible choruses, or may suggest the pianist take the lead. It is wise to ask the speaker's preference prior to the meeting. Initially, the pianist can sensitively commence at a slower tempo than the chorus is sung, as prayer meetings sometimes need the time. As you sense the leader's readiness to sing, bring the chorus back into tempo. Choruses are integrated with the songs and hymns in the most recent Song Book, so notated versions with chord symbols are available for reference.

Underscore for prayer

Should the meeting leader require more time and therefore, more music, have a few appropriate songs or choruses (and their most singable key) identified ahead of time. It can be effective to cease the music midway through the prayer, drawing all the attention to the prayer and then creating a brief musical segue out of the prayer after the "amen."

Be sensitive. Don't assume that the meeting leader will always want a piano underscore to prayer, as it can prove a distraction.

Segue out of prayer

During the sermon, a song or chorus will often come to the pianist's mind that can be located prior to approaching the keyboard. Listen for the Spirit's leading, which gives confidence to your piano ministry. If the piano is near an altar, the pianist needs to minimize the volume to allow the interaction of those at the altar. Prayer accompaniment requires some variety. For instance, when replaying a chorus after it has been sung, render it differently than while singing, but not so much that your "noodling" is noticed. For some people, the music and associated words of a chorus can distract them from prayer. Judiciously reduce things to a few chordal essentials with no recognizable melody.[4]

Avoid the "music box effect" of playing the harmonization a few octaves higher than the normal range. This tinkling effect can draw attention away from the prayer time to the music. What actually works better is playing the chorus an octave lower, in the male voice range, using the sparest support to avoid murky harmonies. Keep track of where you are in the harmonic progression of the chorus, being able to quickly expedite a preparatory phrase which crescendos in sound, moves into the normal singing tempo, and signals an intuitive reentry of the congregation.[5] As a prayer meeting subsides, recap a chorus to allow folks to settle in before transitioning to the closing song or benediction.

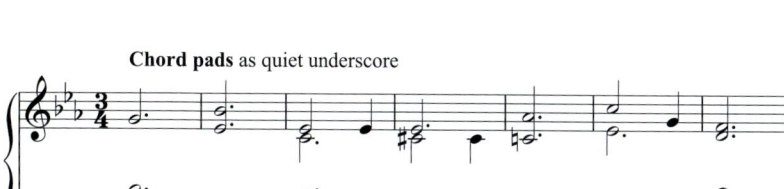

Simplified transition

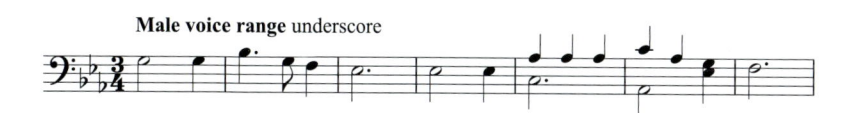

Chord pads as quiet underscore

Male voice range underscore

It is helpful to have readily accessible any liturgical elements that are repeated from week to week such as the **doxology** or **choral benediction**. These often follow immediately after a congregational song. The same can be useful for a theme chorus or seasonal staple, like the use of "O Come, Immanuel" with Advent readings. Many corps pianists will reprise an uplifting version of a verse of the closing hymn as a "sending out" **postlude** following the spoken or sung benediction.

17 BARS REST

1. Using a piano tune book, adapt a hymn as a prelude "call to worship" by creating repeats of a meaningful section or phrase, concluding in a logical manner that sets up the first words to be spoken in the worship itself.

2. Practice congregational songs, using a "wake-up call" introduction. (These are marked in the new tune book.) Vary the volume, voicing and texture of each verse

The Beat Goes On

to reflect the related text. Create a brief reprise that permits "breathing room" in the worship and aids in providing a seamless transition. Also practice transforming the song into an uplifting "sending-out" postlude.

3. Improvise on a prayer chorus (in its most singable key), first as a simple underscore, without direct reference to the melody line. Practice providing a transition to a fuller version of the chorus suitable for congregational singing. Reprise a final phrase as a concluding "settling in."

4. Prepare any weekly "liturgical" elements for ready reference, such as the doxology, choral benediction, or seasonal theme chorus.

HANDS ON! Elaborating on the Piano Tune Book

Now don't go away, especially if you are one who prefers to have music in front of you! Many songs and hymns as presented in the piano tune book were not arranged with the piano in mind, but for SATB voices, instrumentation, or the organ. The melody is always in the right hand upper voice and the basic chordal approach works well for the organ with its added octaves creating a larger sonic picture.

This next section explores ways for the pianist to elaborate on what is presented in the hymnal or piano tune book and is best worked through playing the examples at the keyboard. The worship pianist is ever on the lookout for opportunities to create the proper mood. Subtle nuances can move the drama of the music. Altering registers, playing a thicker texture, adding a flourish, and extending or repeating a phrase can help communicate the meaning of the words and enhance the shared journey in worship.

Simple arpeggiation or broken chords

Arpeggiate the block chords based on the chords in the hymnal voicing:

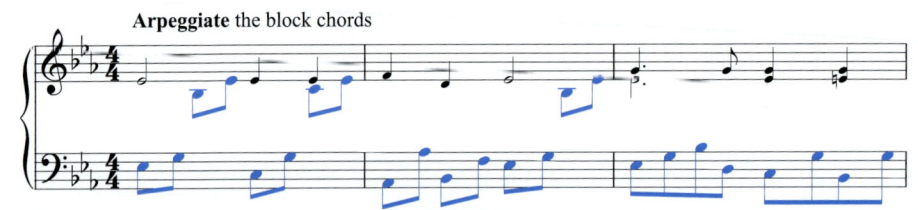

Play the soprano and bass voices first and then create a broken texture with the alto and tenor notes played as eighths (quavers) between the beats:

---

arpeggio (*term*) \'är - 'pe - jē -ō\ harp-like; that is, the playing of a chord with its notes sounded in succession rather than simultaneously as in a **block chord**. An arpeggio is sometimes called a **broken chord**.

Block chords   **Arpeggio** (broken) chords

Demonstrations of these *"at-the-piano" examples* may be found in the Chapter Seventeen online folder.

Play the melody with the right hand while the left hand fills in the remaining beats:

Melody in right hand, left hand **arpeggiate harmony**

Original left hand harmonization indicated with cues

Elaboration

Chords of long duration allow time for repeated chord soundings an octave higher or in ascending or descending inversions:

Chord soundings
shown in cued notes

Embellish and connect longer notes in a bass line or other voice by connecting notes by step or via arpeggios. Try adding passing notes to the inner voices or bass line of the existing hymn arrangement. Scales can be added, ending on a melody tone or bass note. Often this is best accomplished by ignoring the notated tenor part:

Embellish and connect longer notes by step or via arpeggios

(Linking arpeggio)   (Add arpeggio)

(Ignore original tenor part, using three voices)
(Add passing tones to bass line by step)
(Add arpeggio to bass)   (Scale tones added)

(Add arpeggio connecting inner voice to the melody)   (Inner voice descending by step)   (Moving inner voice)

(Added passing tone)   (Maintain ascending scale)

(Embellish bass line with passing tone scale tones)   (Alter bass line with chromatic scale tones)

Len Ballantine suggests the suspension is "a modern version of the plagal or church cadence, **IV-I**, providing a decidedly 'Amen' feel to the music…Suspended tones are useful in creating interest and musical tension in manipulating the flow of the music."[6] Basically a tone is suspended over a nonrelated chord, creating a musical tension

The Beat Goes On

passing tones (*term*) \'pa - sing 'tōns\ A melodic skip may be filled with passing tones, which fill in the intervening steps with tones that may be foreign to the momentary harmony.

between the suspended tone and that chord begging for the now-dissonant suspended tone to be resolved within that chord. A pianist can create a pleasing tension by introducing a 4 to 3 suspension where only the third of a chord is notated. Similarly, one can delay the finality of resolution to the root of a chord with a 2 to 1 suspension.

Organ octaves (or doubling at the octave)

Traditional hymn writing works well for the organ because the organ sounds additional octaves, creating a wider aural spectrum than the notated four-part harmony. One way to replicate organ octaves is to play the soprano, alto, and tenor voices in the right hand an octave higher and play the bass line in octaves in the left hand. **Organ octaves** work best to create dignity, majesty, and fullness to congregational singing, especially on a climactic concluding verse.

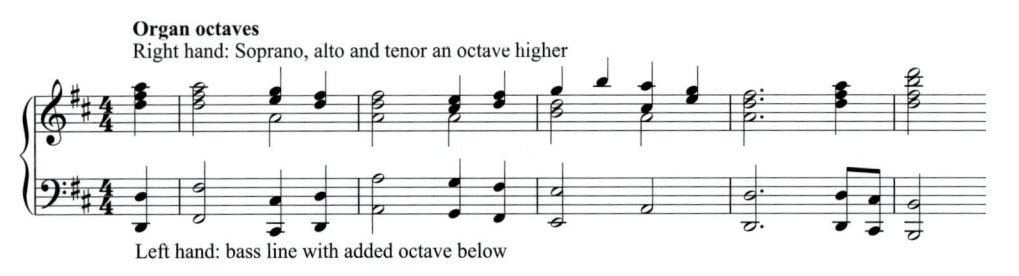

Accompaniment style

Another approach utilizes the left hand by playing the bass note in octaves on the downbeat and on succeeding beats playing the chord above. The right hand plays a series of chords, in what we call **chordal style**, an octave higher. The time signature affects the left-hand chords. For instance, in 4/4 time, play a left-hand bass octave on beats 1 and 4 and chords on beats 2 and 3, or beats 1 and 3 with the chords in between on beats 2 and 4. In 6/8 or 6/4 time, the bass note octaves work best on beats 1 and 4 with chords in between on beats 2 and/or 3, and 5 and/or 6, respectively.

In your daily listening, take note of the salient features of accompaniments in different styles of music. Compare, for instance, a march with its strong regulated pulse to the syncopation of much Latin or Caribbean music. Whether it is Celtic, Jewish, Gospel,

Chapter 17 | KEYBOARD WORSHIP

Country, Ballad, or Rock Music, each style has a foundational accompaniment scheme that helps us identify a culture's musical footprint. Learning to assimilate different styles can enrich the pianist's available palette.

As an exercise, Canadian Salvationist Kim Garreffa suggests playing "I Have Decided to Follow Jesus" first as an upbeat Sunday school chorus. Next, render it in Gospel style, then reflectively, as it is often used in prayer meetings. Finally, build to a robust, resolute version. The mood is transformed by the approach to the accompaniment. Explore different style accompaniments, but as a Salvationist pianist, sensitively yield to the restraints of the song's text and the mood of the service at that moment.

"I Have Decided to Follow Jesus" (for Sunday School)

"I Have Decided to Follow Jesus" (Gospel style)

"I Have Decided to Follow Jesus" (Prayer Meeting)

"I Have Decided to Follow Jesus" (Climactic Finish)

THE CIRCLE OF FIFTHS AND YOU!

Chord choices can be altered to create interest, especially on repeats. But the pianist should never divert to a sudden use of jazz, pop, or Gospel formulas that will distract congregational singing. Pleasing chord choices can be derived by looking at the chord options for a melody tone. For instance, the chord options available for the chord tone G in the key of C are a C chord, where G is the fifth; E minor, with G as the third; and the G chord, with G as the root. One choice can generally be eliminated immediately because of harmonic context. In this case, the G chord determines the key decisively in preceding the finality of the C chord, while the passing E minor chord pulls from one stable chord to another.

Chord choices for the melody tone "G"

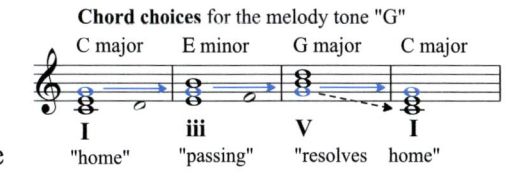

C major	E minor	G major	C major
I	iii	V	I
"home"	"passing"	"resolves"	"home"

The Beat Goes On

"Kum Bah Yah" basic triadic harmony

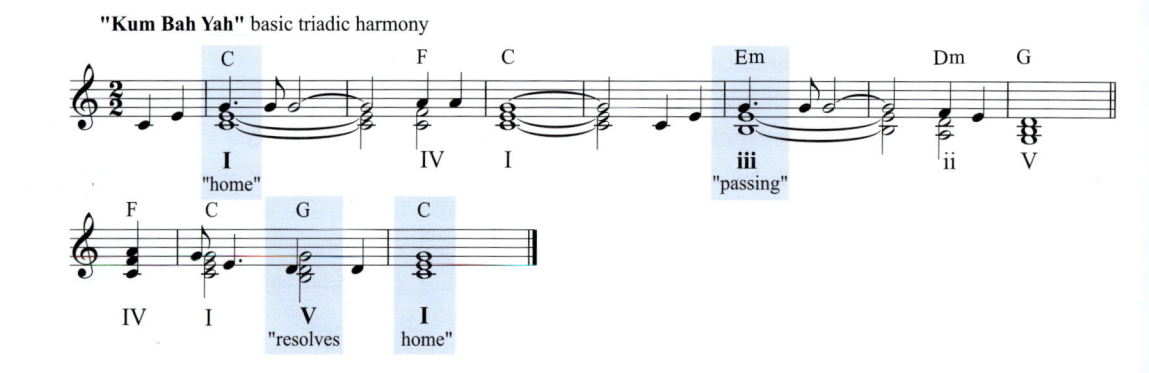

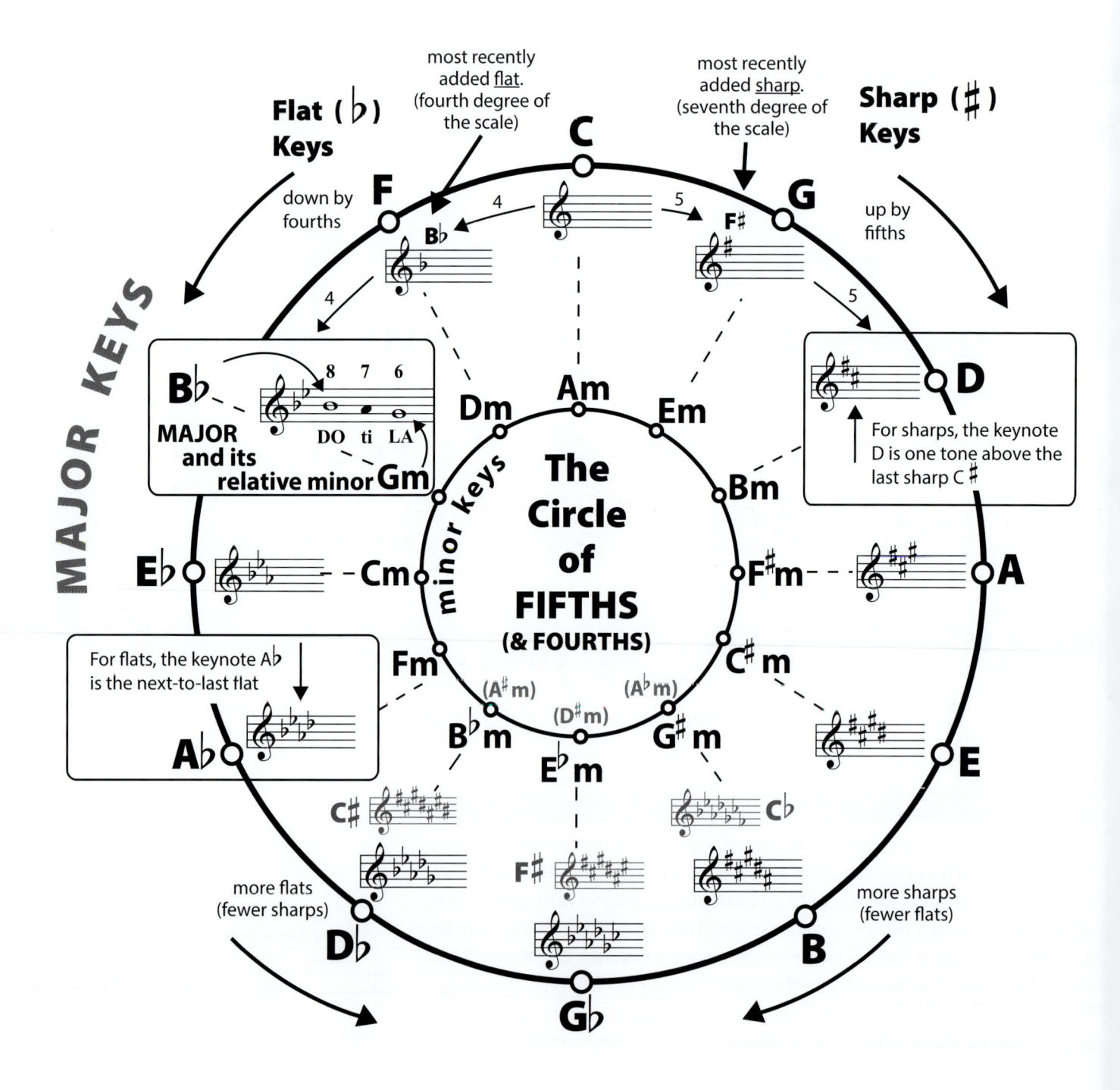

C	F	C	Em	Dm	G
I "home"	IV	I	iii "passing"	ii	V

F	C	G	C
IV	I	V "resolves"	I "home"

The Circle of FIFTHS (& FOURTHS)

Flat (♭) Keys — down by fourths — **MAJOR KEYS** — up by fifths — **Sharp (♯) Keys**

most recently added flat. (fourth degree of the scale)

most recently added sharp. (seventh degree of the scale)

Major keys (outer): C, F, B♭, E♭, A♭, D♭, G♭, B, E, A, D, G

Minor keys (inner): Am, Dm, Gm, Cm, Fm, B♭m, (D♯m), (A♯m)/(A♭m), E♭m, G♯m, C♯m, F♯m, Bm, Em

B♭ MAJOR and its relative minor Gm — 8 7 6 — DO ti LA

For flats, the keynote A♭ is the next-to-last flat

For sharps, the keynote D is one tone above the last sharp C♯

more flats (fewer sharps)

more sharps (fewer flats)

364

www.music.saconnects.org

The Circle of Fifths (and Fourths)

The circle of fifths illustrates graphically that each root is a **perfect fifth** (the fifth tone of the scale) **above** the preceding root as you move clockwise (more sharps or less flats). If you move counterclockwise around the circle (more flats or less sharps), each root is a **perfect fifth below** the preceding root. Perhaps a more inclusive designation would be the Circle of Fifths and Fourths, since a circle reaches infinitely in **both** directions. Moving clockwise each root is also a fourth below, or in a counterclockwise motion, each root is a perfect fourth above.

The Circle of Fifths marvelously describes relationships of keys and chords.
The closer the keys are to each other on the circle, the more notes they have in common, the more closely related they are musically, and the more likely they are to be found close together in a musical phrase or piece. In comparing the notes of the C and G scales, we discover that the key of G shares six of its seven notes with its immediate neighbor, the key of C, making it easy to transition from one to another because they share so many notes.

Keys on opposite sides of the Circle (like C versus F#)
will have very few notes in common (just B and E#/F), and for this reason, the C chord sounds abrupt next to the F# chord.

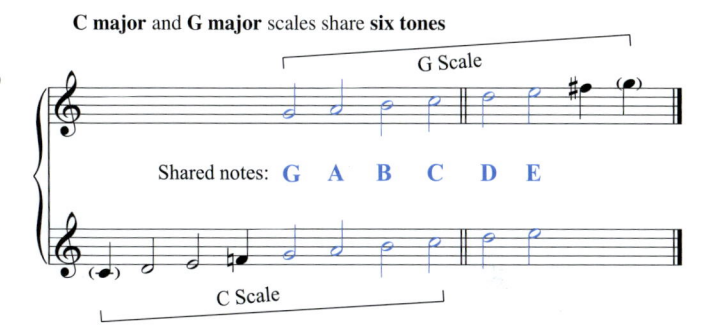

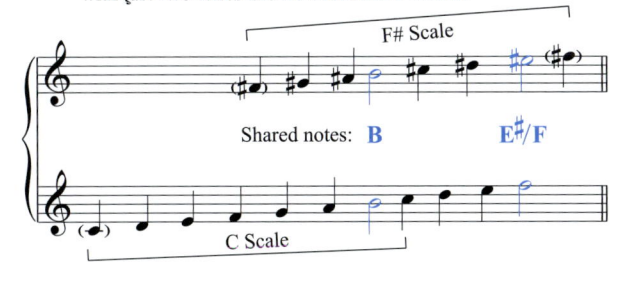

Compare this with the progression of chords next to each other, like the key of C next to its neighbor the key of F, with the common tone C between the two triads. The "neighborly" progression C–F–C sounds quite natural in comparison with that of the "distant" C–F#–C.

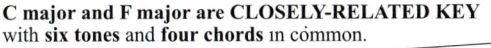

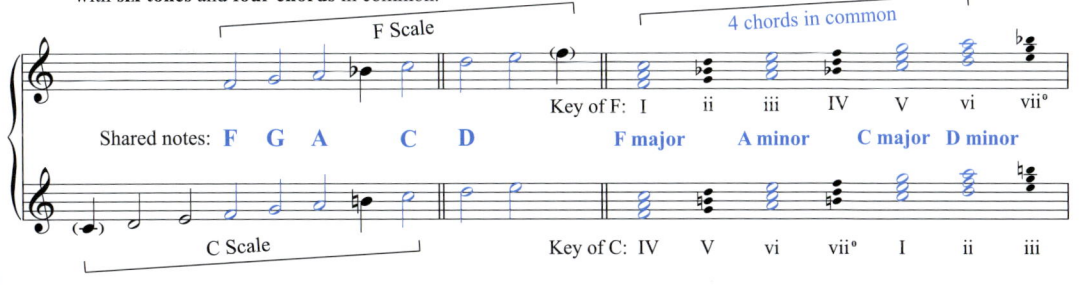

Mr. Rogers encouraged children for years, opening his program by singing, *"Won't you be my neighbor?"*

Won't you be my neighbor?
We learned in Chapter Sixteen (p. 347) that in traditional harmonic practice, Roman numerals identify the scale tone the chord is based on, that is "I" for the triad built on the first step of the scale, "ii" for the second, etc. Note that uppercase Roman numerals are used for major triads, while lowercase for the minor ones.

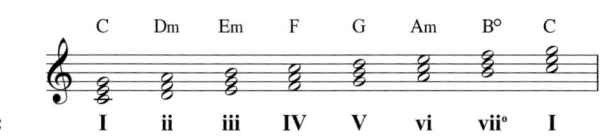

I chord flanked by **IV** and **V** on the circle

Relative minor chords clustered on inner circle

The relationship between the **V** and **I** chords is the strongest in any key, followed by the **IV** chord. These three chords (**I–IV–V**) provide the harmonic basis for a myriad of songs, from classics to rock, including numerous hymns and choruses. The Circle of Fifths takes this "neighborly" tendency a step further when one realizes that any **I** chord is surrounded on either side of the Circle by its companion **IV** and **V** chords. The same applies to the minor chords found on the inner circle, and if both circles are applied together, six of the seven diatonic chords in the key of C are clustered around C at 12:00 on the circle: C, dm, em, F, G, and am.[7]

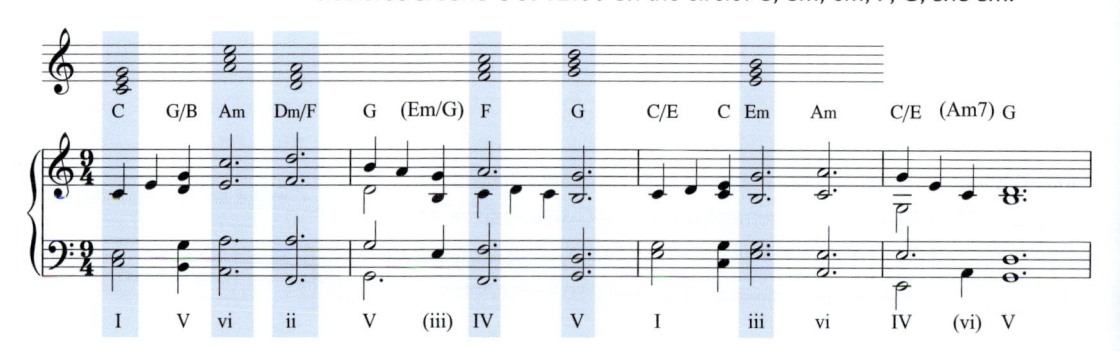

APPLYING THE CIRCLE OF FIFTHS AT THE KEYBOARD

Under the hands

So how can we practically translate the harmonic correlations of the Circle of Fifths into the pianist's hands? Close proximity on the Circle suggests more shared notes and ease of connecting chord to chord. Our first step is to do everything we can to maintain common tones between chords to keep the chords "under the hands," as we call it. Avoiding the shifting of hand positions helps make the progression between chords sound smooth and connected.

I–IV–V–I Cadence

Practice of the standard cadential formula (**I–IV–V–I**), in all major and minor keys, gives the pianist what Len Ballantine calls "a tactile sense of home base." (The piano scale sheets found in Appendix 16.1 conclude with cadences in all keys.) The Circle teaches us that the **IV** and **V** chords needed in any specific key flank the **I** chord. Its related minor **vi** chord on the inner circle is flanked by **ii** and **iii**. All these chords are built on the first six steps of that scale and, because of their proximity, sound natural next to each other because they share notes in common.

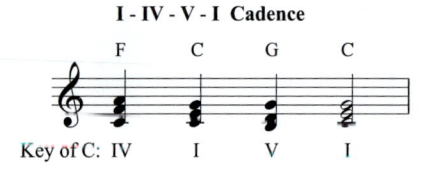

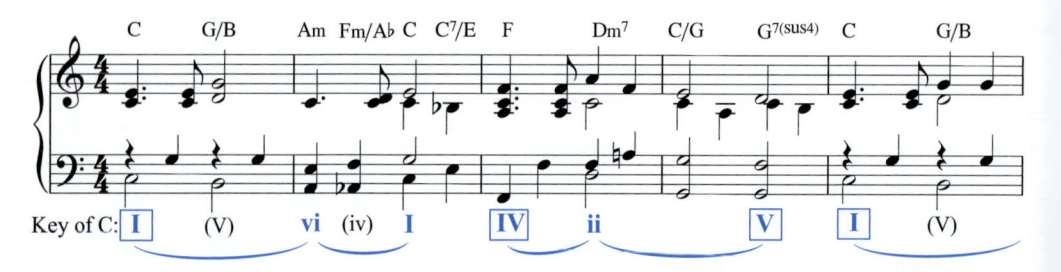

Minor cousins

In Chapter Sixteen (pp. 350–351) we suggest that secondary minor chords substitute well for what can be characterized as their cousins in major. Experiment with using **ii** in place of **IV**, **iii** in place of **I** or **V**, and **vi** instead of **I**. Note that these chords share two of their three notes with at least one major cousin. There are occasions when the reverse, reverting from a minor chord back to a major chord, can engender a sense of finality.

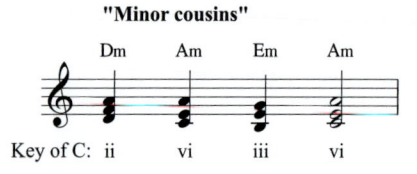

Chapter 17 | KEYBOARD WORSHIP

Traditional harmonization of "Fairest Lord Jesus"

Key of Eb: I (I) ii V I vi VI ii V I I IV I V V7 I

Altered harmonization using "minor cousins"

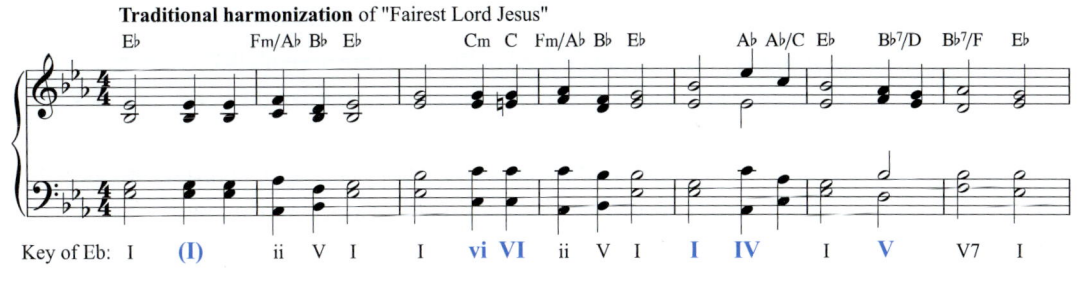

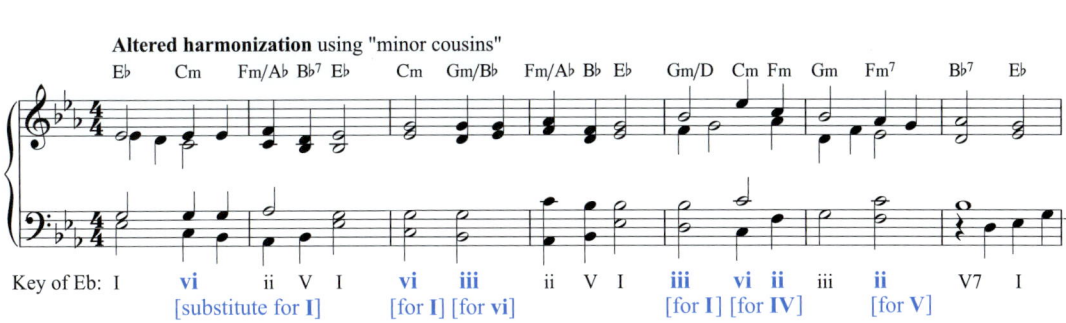

Key of Eb: I vi ii V I vi iii ii V I iii vi ii iii ii V7 I
 [substitute for I]   [for I] [for vi]   [for I] [for IV]   [for V]

Added sevenths

As is common musical practice, we identify each major scale step by Roman numerals, using caps for major chords (**I**, **IV**, **V**) and lower case for the minor and diminished ones (**ii**, **iii**, **vi** and **vii°**). If we stack one more tone (using only notes that are contained within a selected key) on top of the root-third-fifth triads of our major scale tones, we create **four types of seventh chords:**

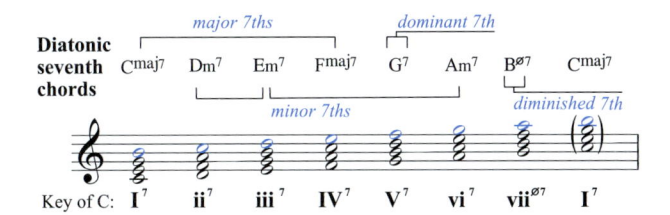

Diatonic seventh chords: Cmaj7 Dm7 Em7 Fmaj7 G7 Am7 Bø7 Cmaj7
— major 7ths — | — dominant 7th —
— minor 7ths — | — diminished 7th —

Key of C: I7 ii7 iii7 IV7 V7 vi7 viiø7 I7

Major sevenths — Cmaj7, Fmaj7 — major 7th, major 3rd — I7, IV7

Minor sevenths — Dm7, Em7, Am7 — minor 7th, minor 3rd — ii7, iii7, vi7

Dominant seventh — G7 — minor 7th, major 3rd — V7

For scale steps I and IV, the seventh note found within the scale above the root is known as the major seventh (M7). **Major seventh chords** (a major triad plus a major seventh) occur with **I** and **IV** chords. For instance in the key of C, the Cmaj7 chord would use the tones C-E-G, with the seventh B natural and the Fmaj7 chord would use the tones F-A-C-E.

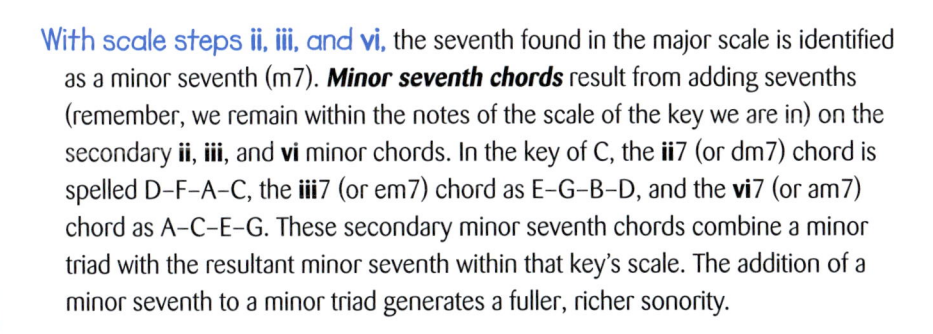

With scale steps ii, iii, and vi, the seventh found in the major scale is identified as a minor seventh (m7). **Minor seventh chords** result from adding sevenths (remember, we remain within the notes of the scale of the key we are in) on the secondary **ii**, **iii**, and **vi** minor chords. In the key of C, the **ii**7 (or dm7) chord is spelled D-F-A-C, the **iii**7 (or em7) chord as E-G-B-D, and the **vi**7 (or am7) chord as A-C-E-G. These secondary minor seventh chords combine a minor triad with the resultant minor seventh within that key's scale. The addition of a minor seventh to a minor triad generates a fuller, richer sonority.

For scale step V, a dominant seventh chord results. At the conclusion of Chapter Sixteen, we introduced the **dominant seventh chord** (pp. 353-354). In the key of C, the dominant seventh (**V7**) is built on a major triad (G-B-D) with the F (or *fa*) added. This seventh of the G7 chord is a minor seventh built over a major triad, creating a different sonority than the minor seventh over the minor triad (the minor

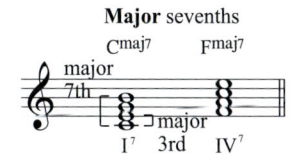

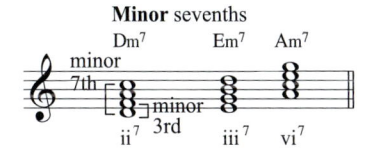

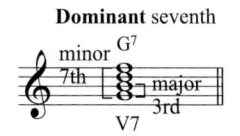

The Beat Goes On

seventh chord). The seventh F (or *fa*) of the dominant seventh (**V7**) chord has a strong tendency to resolve to E (or *mi*), which is the third of the home tonic (**I**) key.

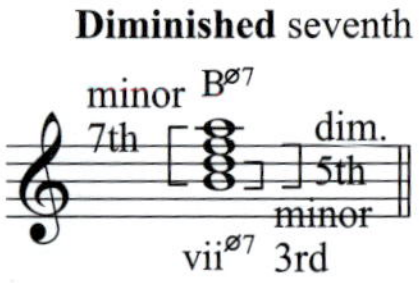

For scale step **vii**, a **diminished seventh chord** is the result of building on the root of the seventh tone of the major scale, which yields a minor third, a flatted fifth (known as a diminished fifth), and a minor seventh.

Diminished seventh

17 BARS REST

1. Sitting at the keyboard, peruse the piano tune book or a hymnal for ways to incorporate arpeggios, elaboration of chords, passing and suspended tones, octave doublings, and chord substitutions using the Circle of Fifths.

2. Next take scale triads in various keys and add sevenths. Learn to differentiate their unique seventh qualities: M7 (major 7th), m7 (minor 7th), V7 (dominant 7th), or dim7 (diminished 7th).

3. Following the **I–vi–ii–V–I** pattern we looked at near the conclusion of Chapter Sixteen, use this progression in various keys, but now add sevenths to create a different sonority. Link the chords by sustaining connective common tones, and aim to keep the other intervals by step as much as possible.

    Good "under the hands" voice-leading using seventh chords

4. Look for opportunities to substitute a major or minor seventh chord where a chord substitution makes the melody tone a seventh. This technique works well in parallel motion, creating a pleasing harmonic diversion.

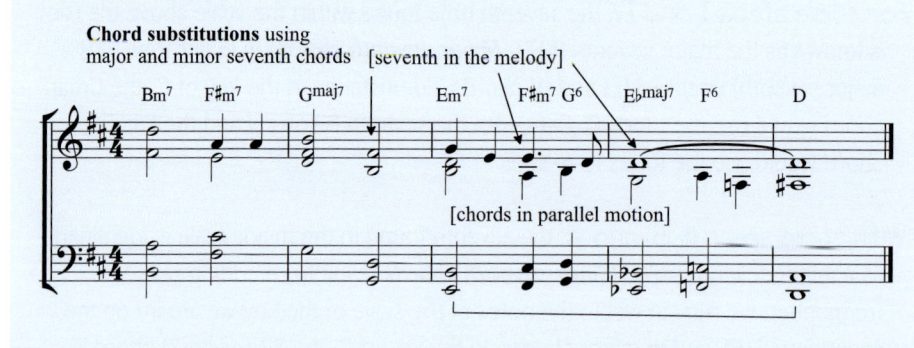

    Chord substitutions using major and minor seventh chords [seventh in the melody]
    [chords in parallel motion]

More on **seventh chords** in the Worship Leader's Toolbox Chapter Nineteen, pp. 408–409.

key (*term*) \'kē\ a central tone (or tonal center) to which other tones (represented in that key's scale) support and tend toward.

♭ **FINDING "DO"** in **flat** keys

find *the next to the last* flat (♭)

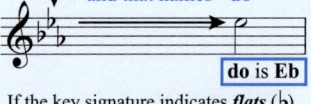

and that names "do"

do is E♭

If the key signature indicates *flats* (♭), locate **the next to the last flat** (one in from the right), which identifies the name of the major key and its "do."

do is F   **do is C**

Since the *key with one flat* (♭) lacks a penultimate flat before it, we have to memorize that as in *the key of F*. The *key of C lacks any flats and sharps*.

♯ **FINDING "DO"** in **sharp** keys

find *the last* sharp (♯)

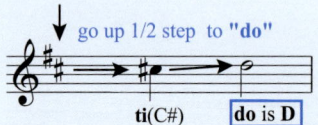

go up 1/2 step to "do"

ti(C♯)   **do is D**

If the key signature indicates *sharps* (♯), locate **the last sharp** (the one furthest to the right), and move up to the next note a half step higher, which identifies the name of the major key and its "do."

MODULATION

More musical magic with numbers

With the emergence of praise and worship segments, some forethought and practice should be given to creating seamless transitions that not only link tunes without an awkward silence but also aid flow from song to song. Often the succeeding song in a set is sung in a different key, requiring a transitional segue in order to move to a new key. *Modulation is the process of moving to another key so that it seems inevitable and smooth, while creating interest and freshness.*

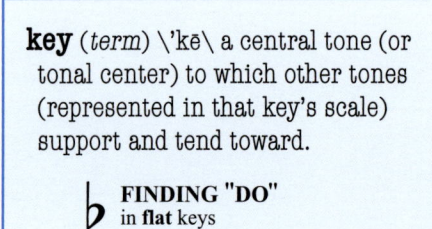

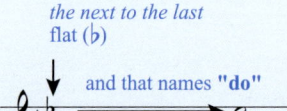

Chapter 17 | KEYBOARD WORSHIP

What follows are some practical steps for making key changes at the piano. The function of the dominant seventh (built on the fifth tone of the scale, using its root, major third, fifth, and minor seventh) is key to modulation as it exerts its gravitational pull towards a new home key center.[8] The modulation chart, found in Appendix 18.1 provides a useful reference to enhance these instructions.

Modulating from C to G major

Altering the F to F# "pulls" toward the new "do" of G

Old key of C: I (II7) (V)

The neighborly circle of fifths and fourths strikes again!

Modulating a fourth up does not require a transition chord. For instance, if song 1 is in C, you can simply start the next song in F. The pitch C acts as a linking common tone bridge between the two keys. To solidify the key change in the singer's ear, you can opt to insert a V or V7 chord (C or C7) just prior to the commencement of song 2 in the key of F.

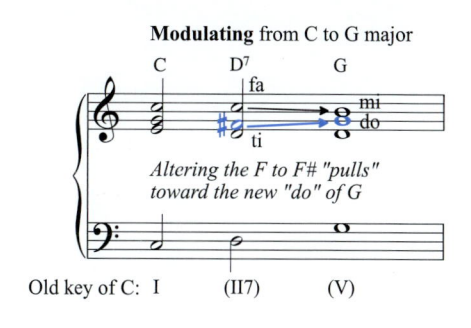

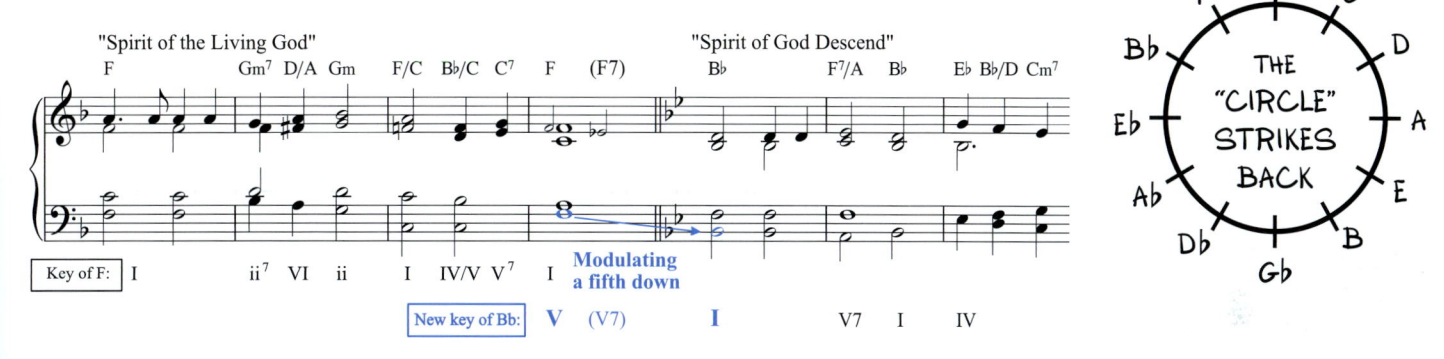

"Spirit of the Living God"   "Spirit of God Descend"

Key of F: I   ii7 VI ii   I IV/V V7   I
Modulating a fifth down
New key of Bb: V (V7)   I   V7 I IV

THE "CIRCLE" STRIKES BACK

Descending to ascend (by half or whole steps)

A descending bass line with a lowered seventh can land you quickly on the V7 (dominant seventh) chord, then you can easily move **to keys either a half or whole step higher**.

[Db] Modulate UP by HALF STEP to [D]

Db Db/Cb A7   D

Key of Db: V7 → I
New Key of D: V7 → I

A half-step lift

Modulation can also be used to uplift a final verse **up a half step**. This is easily achieved by reading a song that was in flats (Gb) in the next sharp key (G). In either case, any accidentals outside of the key signature need to be adjusted accordingly. (Going up a half step, *flats* become *natural*, *naturals* become *sharp*.) To set up the new key, a **pivot** to the new half-step-higher key is created by changing the final old-key tonic (I) chord to the dominant seventh of the new higher key. Learn to hear the gravitational pull of the dominant seventh, especially the seventh of the V7 to the third of the I chord. This modulation works best when the root is the melody tone of the last chord.

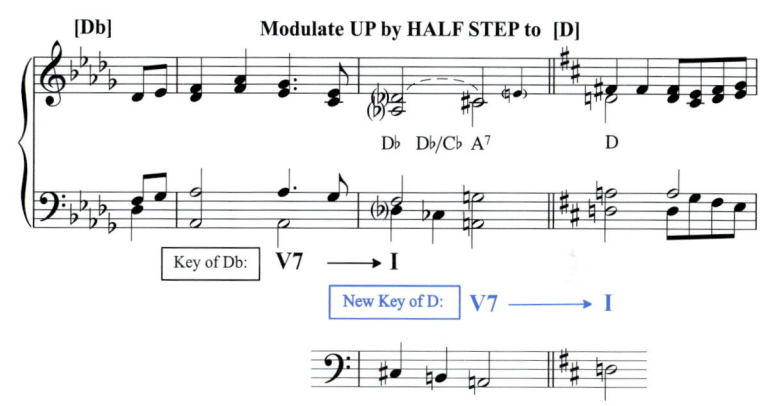

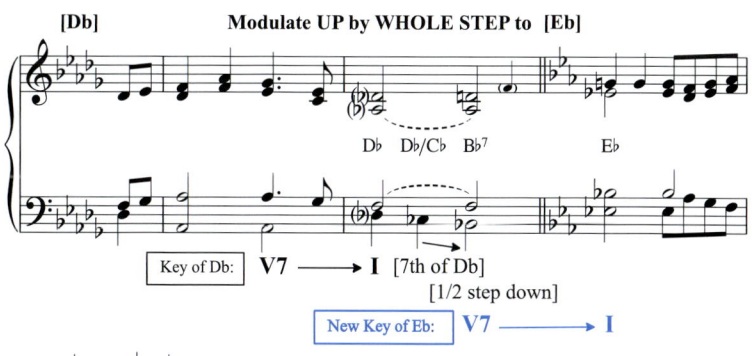

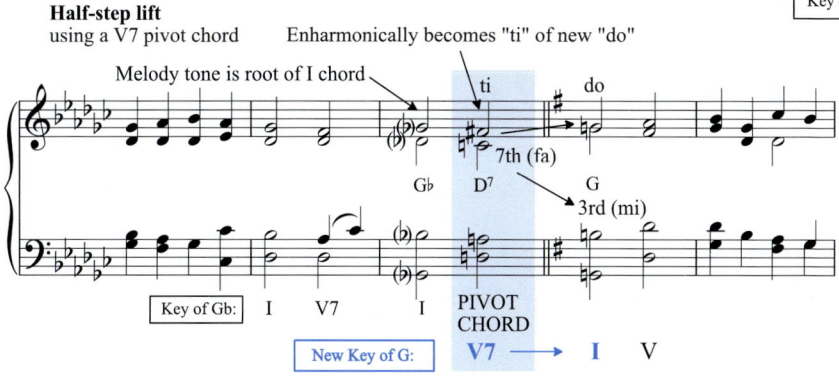

[Db] Modulate UP by WHOLE STEP to [Eb]

Db Db/Cb Bb7   Eb

Key of Db: V7 → I [7th of Db]
[1/2 step down]
New Key of Eb: V7 → I

Half-step lift
using a V7 pivot chord   Enharmonically becomes "ti" of new "do"
Melody tone is root of I chord
ti do
Gb D7 G
7th (fa)
3rd (mi)

Key of Gb: I V7 I   PIVOT CHORD
New Key of G: V7 → I V

The Beat Goes On

pivot chord (term)
\'pi - vət 'kawrd\
acts as a doorway or pivot into a new key. Sometimes this is a chord common to both the old and new keys, or simply a single chord, like the V7 that conveniently contains a common and leading tone to the new key.

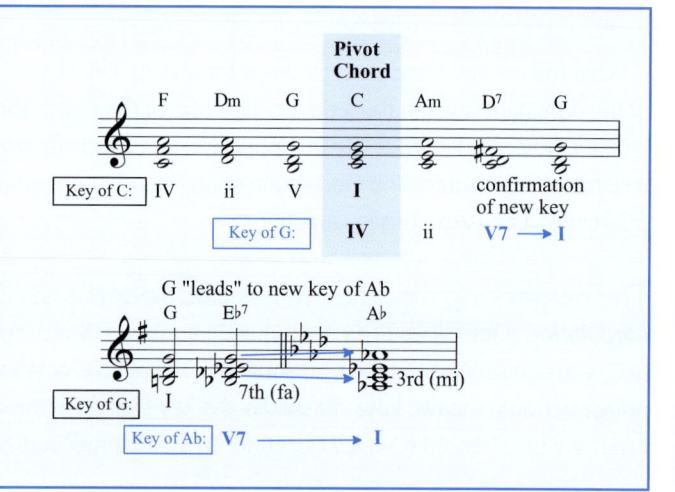

More on **slash notation** in the Worship Leader's Toolbox Chapter Nineteen, p. 409.

More numbers – IV/V

Slash notation used between two chord symbols indicates a chord played over a single bass note. In the key of C, **F/G** would indicate an F chord (F–A–C) played over a single bass note G in the left hand. What is commonly known as **IV** over **V** (**IV/V**) is a popular way to pivot into a more remote key. Using the key of C again as a starting point, the Bb chord with a C in the bass will lead into the key of F. The modulation can be reinforced with a V7 chord (C7) after the IV/V (Bb/C) to make the key change sound more complete.

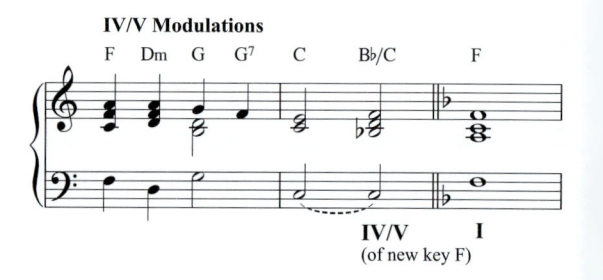

Mediant (by thirds) modulations

The third step of the scale, known as the **mediant**, is halfway between the tonic (**I**) and the dominant (**V**). Mediant (**iii** or **III**) is the name given to the interval distance of a major or minor third above or below a tonic. With a major scale, the mediant interval is a major third; for instance, in G, up two whole steps to B natural. The g minor scale has two flats and the minor third is a half step lower than the major third, making the mediant tone a Bb.

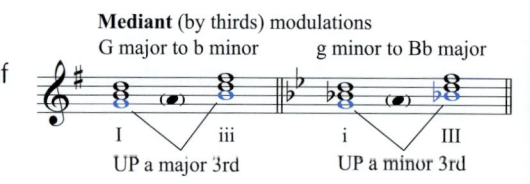

Mediant modulations help cover wider interval distances smoothly. In many cases, a simple shift between the mediant relationship chords is all that is necessary without pivot chords. There are four possible scenarios, utilizing both major and minor thirds and going either up or down:

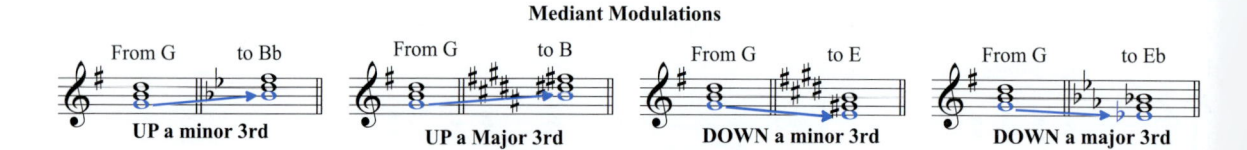

Two to Five to One

Cadences using Roman numerals were introduced in the Keyboard Basics Chapter Sixteen, p. 343–347.

Previously we learned how the triad (root–third–fifth) built on each step of the scale is identified by a Roman numeral. One fail-safe way to modulate smoothly and instantly from one major key to ANY other major key utilizes the triads built on the scale tones

2, 5, and 1, specifically using the sequence of chords **ii7**–**V7**–**I**. Notice that the roots of these three chords are neighbors and follow the pattern of the Circle of Fifths. The note D is down five steps to G, and then five more steps down to C.

ii7 "Don't look back."⁹ So from your present tonic (I) chord (for example, Ab), go to the ii7 of the key to which you want to modulate. That is, if you want to move to the key of C, then the second step of the C scale is D. The triad built on D in the key of C would be a minor triad made up of the notes D-F-A. The added minor seventh C completes the dm7 or ii7 chord. The added minor seventh C helps "pull" the ii7 toward the dominant (V) of our new key C. That is, the C resolves by half step down to the B natural of the G7 chord.

V7 Next move from the ii7 to the dominant seventh (V7) of the new key of C. In contrast to the minor seventh (m7) chord, the dominant seventh is made up of a major triad built on the fifth step of the scale (G-B-D) with an added minor seventh F.

I We successfully modulate to the key of C by moving to the tonic chord (I) of C (using the notes C-E-G). Listen particularly for the magnetic pull of the root G of the V7 to the root of the C chord (I) and the seventh F of the V7 to the third E of the C chord, confirming this modulation.

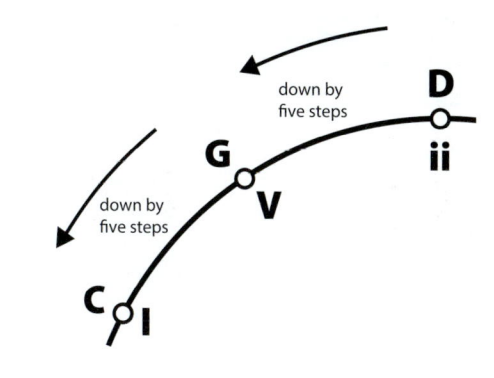

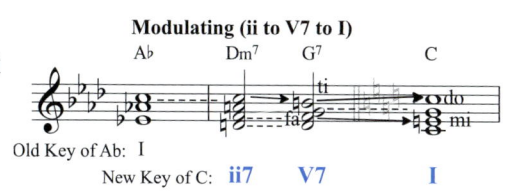

17 BARS REST

1. At the keyboard, practice modulating from verse to verse, moving up by a half or whole step. Some possible approaches include using a descending bass line with a lowered seventh, or creating a pivot by changing the final initial-key tonic (I) chord to the dominant seventh (V7) of the new higher key.

2. Practice ways to link a variety of songs or hymns by creating smooth transitional modulations. Utilize **IV/V** chords or the **ii7** to **V7** to **I** progression.

3. Improvise on a hymn, moving in and out of at least three keys, utilizing mediant modulations to shift key by thirds even from phrase to phrase. Obviously this exercise is not suited to congregational singing, but can be useful when extemporizing on a hymn phrase or transitioning to a new key.

More about **chords** in Chapter Nineteen.

LESS IS MORE!

Accompanying soloists and songsters

A good accompanist is said to be "the most important member of the choir" (Dorothy Nancekievill), "a treasure" (David Walker), even "a pearl of great price" (Shirley McRae). An accompanist can make or break a rehearsal, as a piano can be an aid, or a distraction to a soloist or songster brigade. With experience, an accompanist senses when playing is interfering or, more importantly, when the vocalist or brigade needs to be propped up.

Less pitches

Playing through a piece or banging out the melody is counterproductive. Allow your soloist or songster brigade to sing independently, without the piano as a crutch. With choirs, it is preferable for the singers to imitate sung pitches rather than played ones. Male conductors will want to sing in a clear light *falsetto* in the correct octave when working with treble voices. The accompanist should simply provide the first few notes or chords before the entrance, get them started, and stop playing. This is difficult, as you want to "feed" the notes to aid the learning curve, but actually, the opposite is more beneficial. The presence of played pitches makes the singers more dependent on the piano.

For many young ears, matching pitch is far more attainable with another voice than with a keyboard. Even if notated in the accompaniment, avoid duplicating the melody line to allow choirs, and especially soloists, freedom in rendering their vocal lines. It is difficult for a pianist to match human pitch and also the voice's attack, release, and nuance. Choose instead to provide minimal harmonic support (the chord changes can come in handy here), keeping a steady tempo, while giving a sense of musical direction. This means you are making decisions constantly on *what to leave out* of the accompaniment. *Less is more!* Sometimes simply using the alto or tenor voice as a countermelody can steer you away from duplicating the melody pitches.

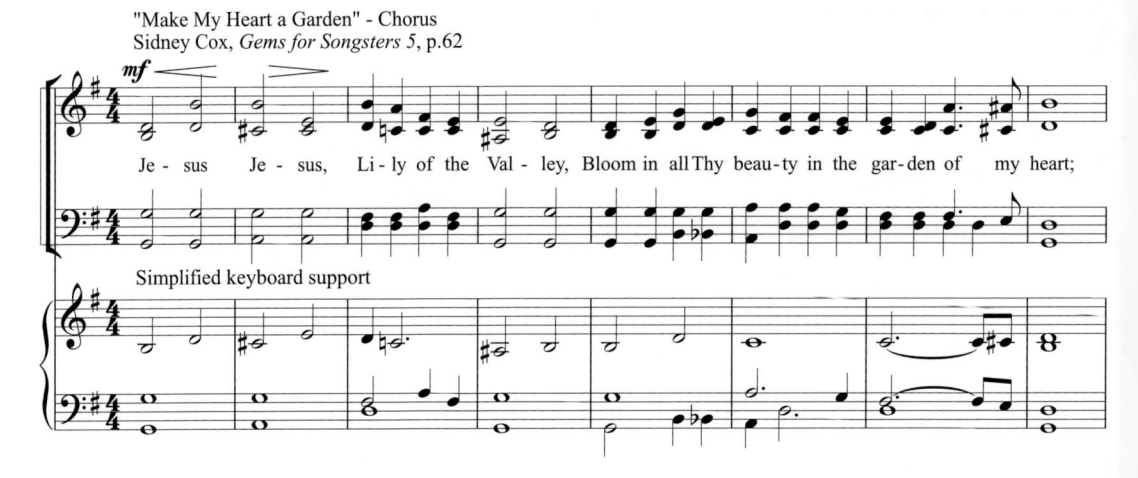

"Make My Heart a Garden" - Chorus
Sidney Cox, *Gems for Songsters 5*, p.62

The accompanist in a songster setting is always actively listening to the singers to determine the feeling of the line and the desired dynamics. The accompanist's role is to provide clean, crisp rhythmic support while keeping an eye on the conductor. With children, harmonic function is the last component developed in a child's awareness of musical elements, so avoid lush, heavy keyboard harmonies or orchestral tracks. A thick accompaniment often confuses the proper performance of vocal parts. As part of the learning process, the leader may, on occasions ask the accompanist to support a harmony part, for instance, asking for the alto part with spare bass support. Some conductors also advocate playing the actual pitches plus the octave above to aid hearing tones in the lower register. For high-register tones, play the actual pitches plus the octave below to give acoustic support.

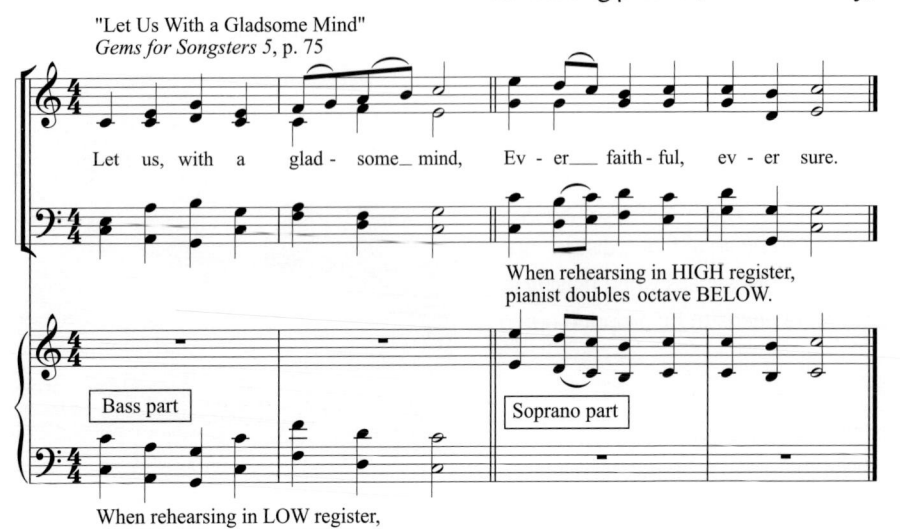

"Let Us With a Gladsome Mind"
Gems for Songsters 5, p. 75

Less volume

Many conductors err on the side of asking for more piano or backing track to push the choir's relative volume level. First and foremost, songster brigades, soloists, and congregations must be able to hear their own voices. If you want a singing company to sing out more, reduce the volume. If the piano is too loud behind a soloist, the singer is relegated to using a more forced sound. When the piano and/or worship band is too loud, congregations choose *not* to sing.

The soft pedal can be a valuable aid. *Less really is more!* A harsh, percussive piano attack will conflict with your singer's best nuances. Play musically with a gentle touch to achieve a transparent texture. One way to sound more professional is to voice an important countermelody (not the singer's melody) at a full volume with the accompanying notes a degree below. This gives the effect of a full piano sound without masking the lines the singers are seeking to project.

"The Well is Deep" Norman Bearcroft
Musical Salvationist, April 1981, p. 29

And I, be-liev-ing, find in-deed That Christ is the Wa-ter of Life.

Pianist play countermelody at full volume
Accompaniment a degree softer

The sound of a piano or speaker facing directly towards your voices tends to overwhelm their voices. Avoid this. Also be sure the piano is tuned on a regular basis. Extreme temperature and humidity shifts adversely affect the tuning and action of a piano. A dehumidifier device installed in the piano can aid in keeping the instrument tuned and prevent the wood of the inner workings from permanently cracking.

More helpful hints

It is courteous for an accompanist to be given new repertoire before the music's initial rehearsal. Although effective accompanists learn the "mind of their conductor" over time, it accelerates the choir's learning process for the conductor to give them advance notice of *tempi*, dynamics, modification of voice parts, cuts, and anticipated problem spots. Such information can be shared before or after rehearsal or communicated by email. Duplicating your rehearsal plan gives the accompanist a good perspective on what the trajectory and goals are for the rehearsal. A heads-up of specific warm-ups that address problem spots allows the accompanist to reduce the learning curve by transitioning without delay to starting pitches and by providing upbeat accompaniments.

See Appendix 17.1 for more **Choral Warm-Up Piano Accompaniments**.

Warm-up modulation sequence to keys one half-step higher

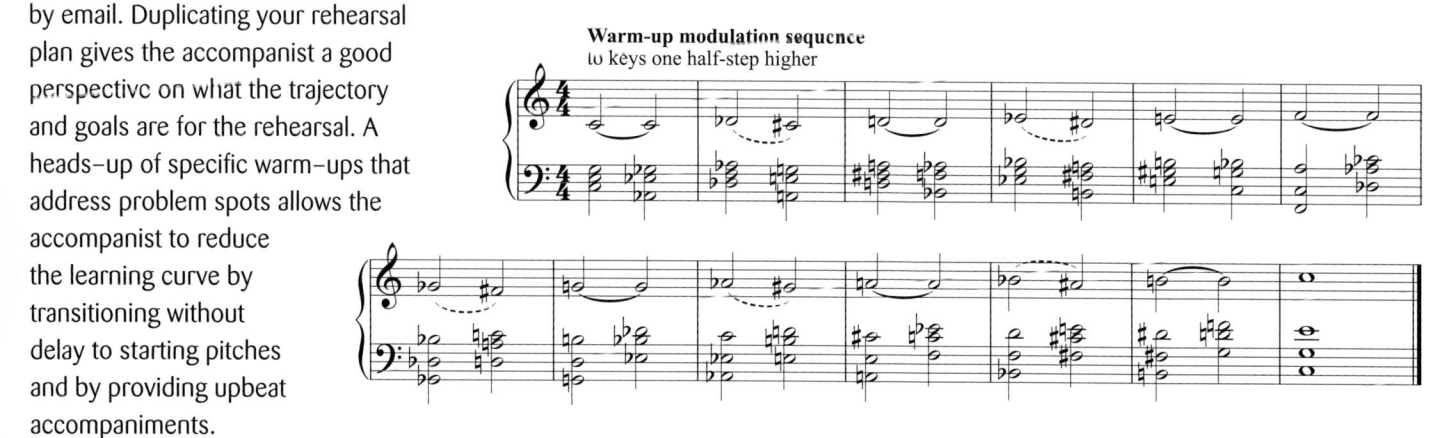

TODAY'S REHEARSAL:

1. WARM-UP
   Me-May-Ma-Mo-Moo (start in C)
   Ah-Ee (from Bb)
   (From Just Like John)
   Ya da-ba-da-ba dot
   (m. 1-2, from C)
   Amazing love...(mm. 93-96, p.4, from A)

2. IN THIS QUIET MOMENT
   m. 45 p cresc. to 51 ff
   m. 35 mp decresc. to 40 p
   check altos 41-44
   m. 31 mp cresc. to 35 sub. mp
   sing from 31 to end

3. JUST LIKE JOHN
   E in two parts (men 1st)
   F men (basses 1st)
   D ladies to E, then F
   Back to beginning
   Teach B, try 2 pages

4. MOURNING INTO DANCING
   Learn 48-55 (Your anger lasts)
   Teach Wo-o-o, m. 64 (sop. db. men)
   Work out 65 to end,
   Back to 40, try to end a few times

Thanks, Lorena

On occasion, children's choir conductors will provide their choristers with vocal parts in C or F to allow them to "read" the musical notation more easily. The accompanist may be asked to play in the original notated key that sits best for their voices or to transpose to a better key. (Many published pieces are written too low for children, while many songs in our Song Book feel too high!) Here again, advance notice helps the accompanist work this out prior to rehearsal, perhaps by using shorthand chord symbols to confirm the transposition.

Simplified Notation for Singers
"I Am Praying" Leonard Ballantine
Original in E, Transposed to F

[Musical notation: so re so do fa mi re do — "I am praying blessed Saviour, to be more and more like thee"]

If you are the conductor *and* you absolutely must accompany a choir yourself from the piano, or as many organists do from the organ, find ways to get away from the keyboard. Roam the room to hear what the group's balance and projection is really like. Obviously being able to stand in front of the choir and maintain eye contact is of great benefit.

"Day of Victory" Ivor Bosanko
Original in Eb, Transposed to C

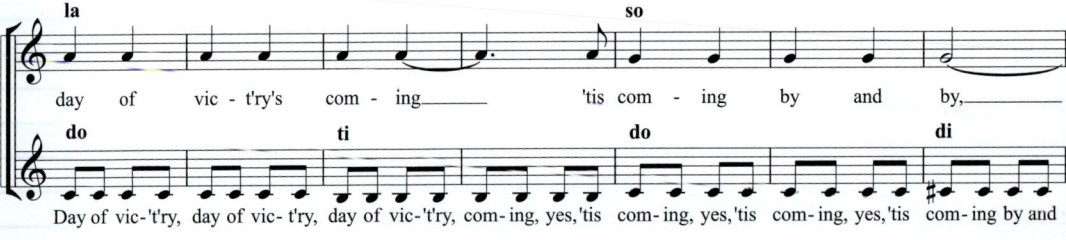

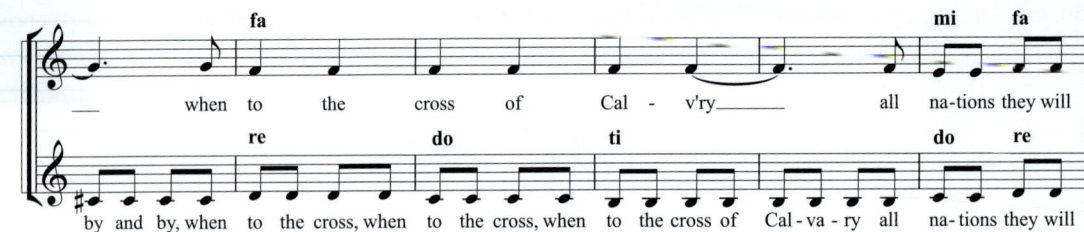

[Musical notation: "For the day of vic't'ry's coming by and by! The day of vic't'ry's coming, yes, 'tis coming by and by! Day of vic't'ry's coming, 'tis coming by and by, Day of vic-t'ry, day of vic-t'ry, day of vic-t'ry, coming, yes, 'tis coming, yes, 'tis coming, yes, 'tis coming by and by, when to the cross of Cal-v'ry all nations they will"]

DEAR PIANIST, MAKE SURE YOU TAKE A GOOD LOOK AT THE WORSHIP LEADERS' CHAPTERS 16

17 BARS REST

1. Practice playing chords chromatically ascending and descending in support of warm-ups. Refer to Appendix 17.1.

2. Practice thinning out accompaniments by avoiding the melody tones and creating new textures.

3. Try transposing a chorus or song up a step. Transpose notes by step or by recognizing chord changes.

MEETING PIANIST RESOURCES

PIANO OFFERTORY COLLECTIONS

Encore! (Salvation Army, USA West), graded arrangements (Levels 1 to 4) for solo piano of Salvation Army and church songs.
Musical Offerings (Salvation Army, New York), available in several volumes, at various grade levels.
Well-Tempered Praise/Well Tempered Christmas, Mark Hayes (GlorySound)

SONGBOOKS and SONG COLLECTIONS

Carolers' Favorites (Salvation Army, New York) and **Christmas Praise** (Salvation Army, United Kingdom), *the latter* is available in two volumes, one with traditional carols and the other with newer carols. Both of these collections correlate with brass parts and include the words with the music, useful for songsters and carol sings.

The Hallelujah Choruses (Salvation Army, Des Plaines, IL), piano versions available in two Keyboard Instrumental Books (HC 1-100 & HC 101-200). These collections are designed for SAB vocal parts with piano, including chord changes below. There is also a smaller volume available for each ten-song issue in lead sheet format (words, including Spanish translation, and melody, with chord symbols provided above the melody.) Parts are available for rhythm section and 3-part brass section.

Magnify (Salvation Army, United Kingdom), collection of praise songs and choruses in accessible piano settings that correlate with brass band parts. Introductions and chord symbols included.

Salvation Army Piano Tune Book (Salvation Army, United Kingdom), The latest piano tune book includes a bracket for introductions, as well as chord symbols for all songs and choruses. **Volume 1** contains 530 tunes with definable meters, allowing interchangeability of texts with tunes, thereby appearing *with music only*, with the exception of about 20 songs where the words are required to appear with the music because of copyright. **Volume 2** contains 420 irregular meter tunes, *with the words included*, plus 7 national songs and anthems without words.

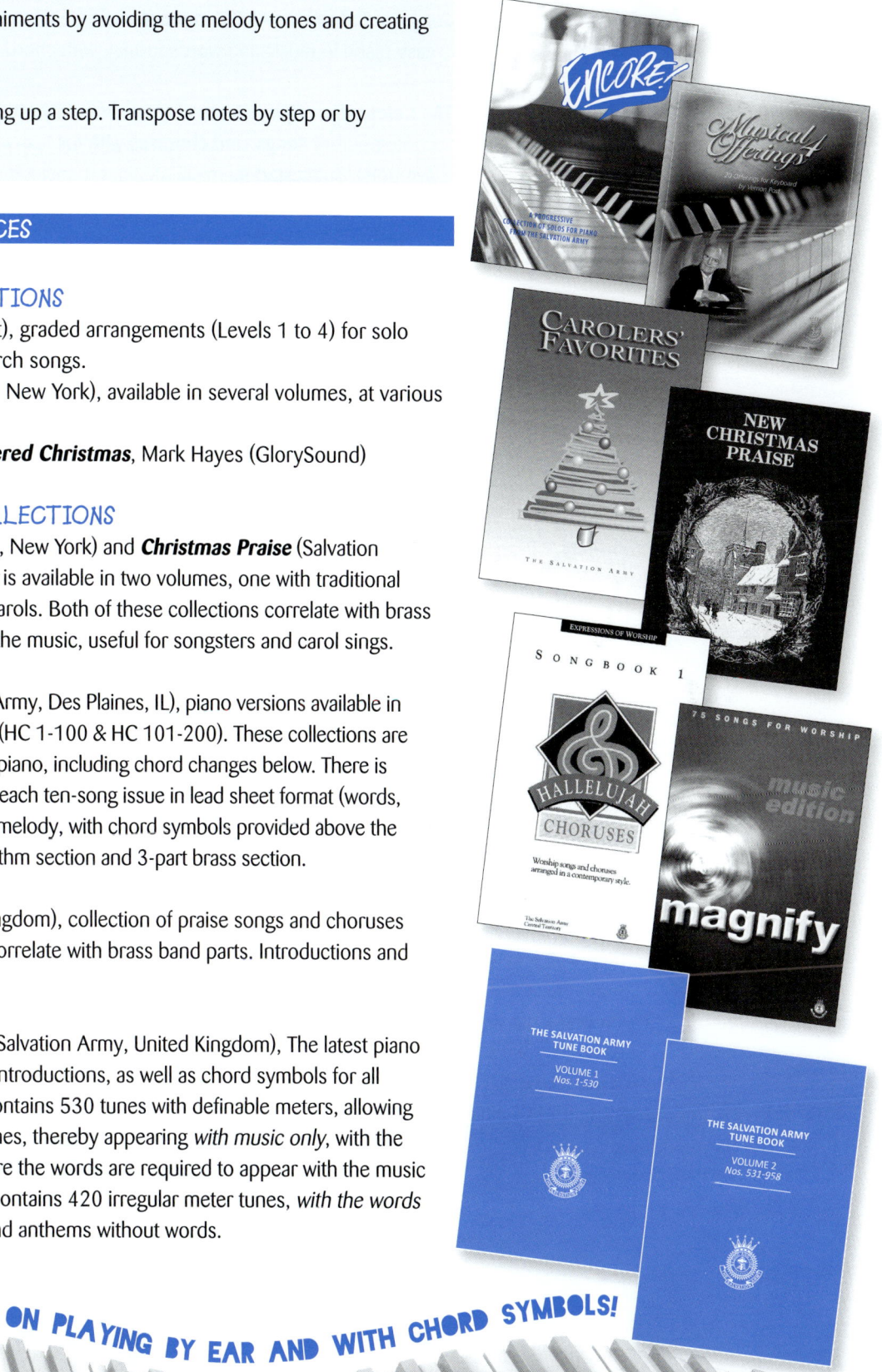

AND 17 FOR MORE TIPS ON PLAYING BY EAR AND WITH CHORD SYMBOLS!

The Beat Goes On

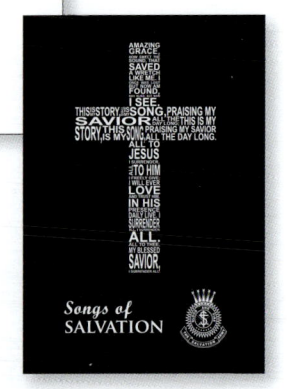

Songs of Fellowship (Kingsway Music), uses a hymnal format, with chord symbols in two volumes, includes traditional hymns and contemporary songs.

Songs of Praise, formerly *Youth Songbook* (Salvation Army, Alexandria, VA). 254 songs and hymns published in hymnal format with all verses included with the music.

Songs of Salvation—ARC Songbook (Salvation Army, Des Plaines, IL) 200 songs with easy piano in music and words format, with chord and capo symbols.

The Celebration Hymnal (Word Music/Integrity Music) includes hymns, contemporary songs, and choruses with full text with the music (without chord symbols). Suggested thematic medleys, concluding verse arrangements, and transitions are provided.

PLAYING IT *RIGHT*?

"You haven't got it *right!*" says the exasperated piano teacher. Junior is holding his hands the way he's been told. His fingering is exceptional. He has memorized the piece perfectly. He has hit all the proper notes with deadly accuracy, but his heart's not in it, only his fingers. What he's playing is a sort of music, but nothing that will start voices singing or feet tapping. He has succeeded in boring everybody to death, including himself.

Jesus said to his disciples, "Unless your righteousness exceeds that of the scribes and Pharisees, you will never enter the kingdom of heaven." —Matthew 5:20, *RSV*. The scribes and Pharisees were playing by the Book. They didn't slip up on a single do or don't. But they were getting it all wrong.

Righteousness is getting it all *right*. If you play it the way it's supposed to be played, there shouldn't be a still foot in the house.
—Frederick Buechner,
Wishful Thinking

CHAPTER EIGHTEEN

MORE THAN A SONG
Leading the Worship Team

You thrill me, Lord, with all You have done for me!
I sing for joy because of what You have done.
   —Psalm 92:4 *(NLT)*

FLOW, RIVER, FLOW

Imagine the concluding scene of an epic movie spectacular set in the ancient city of Jerusalem. Underneath the city runs a network of channels, known as the waters of Siloam, that supplies water to the city. In a splendid vision, Ezekiel pictures this water emanating from within God's house—the high and holy Temple (47:1–9). Its torrent flows east, and as he is led in measured intervals, the waters rise to Ezekiel's ankles, to his knees, to his waist, until he is taken up and can no longer walk in the rushing current.

But there's more! The camera follows the river as it gushes out into the arid, waterless Jordan Valley to the east. The water brings life to everything along its path, including the salty abyss of the Dead Sea. What were once lifeless waters miraculously appear fresh. In the Hebrew, they "are healed." The dramatic scenario closes with a voice exuberantly proclaiming, "It will come about that every living creature which swarms in every place where the river goes, *will live*" (Ezekiel 47:9a, *NAS, emphasis added*).[1]

In **Chapter Eighteen**, we learn how to:
- design a playlist
- prepare the music and "layer" arrangements
- create seamless transitions
- prepare effective praise band rehearsals

> "The leader must keep his toes at the edge of the river, ever attentive to the direction that the water is flowing."
>
> —Bob Sorge

The psalmist prophetically alluded to these life-giving waters when he wrote, "There is a river whose streams make glad the city of God" (Psalm 46:4). It is a timeless analogy, this ever-flowing river of God, in the Holy Spirit, that washes over our souls with cleansing and refreshment. When Jesus spoke of the Spirit, He said, "If anyone is thirsty, let him come to Me and drink. He who believes in Me, as the Scripture said, 'From his innermost being will flow rivers of living water' " (John 7:37–38, NAS). The Sunday-to-Sunday goal of the worship team leader is to find and follow that river. Salvation Army poet laureate Albert Orsborn may have summed it up best when he wrote:

> Light, life and love are in
>   that healing fountain,
> All I require to cleanse me
>   and restore…
> From a hill I know,
> Healing waters flow;
> O rise, Immanuel's tide,
> And my soul overflow!

ANOTHER SUNDAY . . . ON OUR TOES

In Chapter One we began by contrasting the minstrel-performer with the minister-priest. The first minstrel scene gives the impression that God—the host—was unavailable. But God, in fact, is omnipresent and always available. For some of us, it takes time to learn to embrace this ready access to the Holy Spirit. It is the posture of artist-musicians that makes the difference, as they leave themselves open to a connection to the eternal. Like Moses, we choose not to move without a sense of God's presence (Exodus 33:15).

Following the river

As in our story about Ezekiel, the Scriptures eloquently picture the presence of the Holy Spirit as a river of living water flowing from the throne of God (Revelation 22:1–2). Bob Sorge suggests that the worship leader's responsibility is twofold. First, "the leader must keep his toes at the edge of the river, ever attentive to the direction that the water is flowing." On occasion the Holy Spirit may gently chide us, saying, "This song is great, but it is not the direction I am going this morning." The leader needs to be ever listening, while remaining humble, discerning, and flexible.

While…staying tuned into the congregation

At the same time, Sorge reminds us, the worship leader needs to be tuned in to the congregation. If they are not following your lead, then you must ask what you can do to help them move in the direction you sense the Spirit is going. More often than not, this is not done by stirring up the singing, but rather a quieting in prayer, until you sense the congregation has been ushered into the flow of the river. Prayer before rehearsals and services helps keep the leader in tune with the Spirit's direction. Be prepared for occasional surprises from the Holy Spirit, who likes to keep us on our toes.

Chapter 18 | MORE THAN A SONG

WHEELS WITHIN WHEELS?

Let's use our cinematic imaginations again and flash back to an earlier vision of Ezekiel (1:15–21). From a distance, we see a creature with what appears to be a high-rimmed wheel full of eyes around it. As the camera closes in, there are actually a pair of wheels, seemingly interconnected to the other, each on a different axis. We discover that one wheel intersects the other at right angles, yet is linked and miraculously led by astounding-looking creatures.

With the wheels ready to go in any direction, in an instant these creatures rise to fly in concert, and are they fast! The spirit of these living creatures seems to control this odd assemblage of wheels. With the camera surveying the vast scene, a voice declares, "Wherever the spirit would go, they would go, and the wheels would rise along with them, because the spirit of the living creatures was in the wheels" (Ezekiel 1:20).

One Quarterback

Learning to follow the promptings of the real worship leader—the Holy Spirit—does not dismiss or diminish the importance of having a lead worshiper. All the jokes about how committees do not function with real lucidity apply here. There are occasions when a song emanates from the pianist, the podium, or even from within the congregation. But on the whole, worship teams function best under one person—*someone gifted in helping us travel together.* This lead worshiper is seeking the Spirit for a sense of direction. This is where another Sunday begins, with the leader in prayer during the week in advance. This can be a "full-time job" as the Spirit may speak at anytime as we "work away at this ministry" (Philippians 3:3, *The Message*).

PRAYING A PLAYLIST

Preparation of the heart

Someone once remarked to the pilot of a record-setting supersonic jet, "You must take the most frightful risks." His immediate response was, "The one thing to be quite sure of in my job is to see to it that I *never* take *any* risks!" This sound judgment can be amply applied to the high-risk calling of worship-leading. Let's look at ways to reduce the margin of error on Sunday mornings and yet allow a free flow of expression within the worshiping body.

Philippians 3:3 reminds us that we "worship by the Spirit." Eugene Peterson paraphrases it this way: "The *real* believers are the ones that the Spirit of God leads to work away at this ministry, filling the air with Christ's praise as we do it." Paul goes even further when he says, "We couldn't carry this off by our own efforts, and we know it" (Philippians 3:4). This knowledge can be a tremendous release to the lead worshiper. We are reminded that we cannot *make* worship happen in our own strength, no matter how terrific our plan, credentials, experience, or practice. Matt Redman says, "The Holy Spirit will always take us deeper."

> We cannot *make* worship happen in our own strength, no matter how terrific our plan, credentials, experience or practice.

The Beat Goes On

On the other hand, accepting a position of dependence raises the risk level! We are forced to listen with regularity to the faintest whisper of His voice. Ken Gire likens it to a dance, as we follow the Spirit's lead, step by step, and for which we may not know the ending.[2] Such "weakness and dependence," Oswald Chambers once said, "will always be an occasion for the Spirit of God to manifest His power."

Beyond the Top Five

We are hard pressed to imagine the Holy Spirit as the real worship leader if we routinely string together songs limited to a Top Five list. Even more inadequate is an "in the Spirit" mode, which somehow commends a lack of forethought. Scripture instructs us that everything in worship should be done in "a fitting and orderly way" (1 Cor. 14:40). Your officer-pastor can be found daily seeking something in his or her devotions to bring to the people. He may opt to work from the lectionary, which demands time in various Scriptures, studying passages that may be unfamiliar ground. She may seek to center her thoughts on a theme, season, or book of the Bible. All of these avenues bring depth, structure, and beauty to the worship experience. In tandem with the Spirit, the worship leader can piggyback off these initiatives.

CREATING THE PLAYLIST

In a practical sense, the goal for the worship band rehearsal is to have a Holy Spirit-crafted playlist ready that is Holy Spirit-crafted for that Sunday. Let's consider some steps to make this happen. Since the bandmaster or songster leader would have similiar questions, request that the meeting planner send out an email of the suggested program outline early in the week. This will give you an opportunity to fill in your titles and even make suggestions to improve the flow of the meeting:

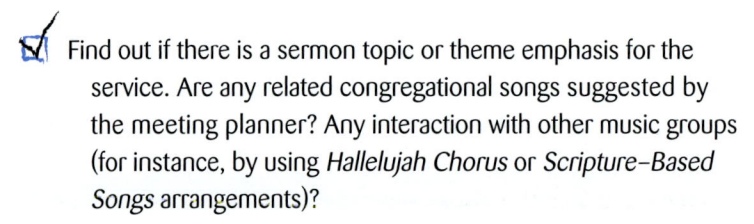

- ☑ Find out if there is a sermon topic or theme emphasis for the service. Are any related congregational songs suggested by the meeting planner? Any interaction with other music groups (for instance, by using *Hallelujah Chorus* or *Scripture-Based Songs* arrangements)?

- ☑ Find out where your musical offerings are being slotted and the time allotted. To aim for the seamless transitions we considered in the Keyboard Worship Chapter Seventeen (pp. 357-358), take note of what comes before and after each item.

- ☑ Ascertain what personnel are available for that Sunday. Confirm rehearsal and sound check times.

- ☑ Schedule a block of time, well in advance of your worship team rehearsal, to:
  1. choose songs
  2. locate the required music and/or charts
  3. decide how to "arrange" the songs
  4. lay out a rehearsal plan

In Chapter Twenty-Three we will talk about strategically thinking through a series of weeks at one sitting, especially relating to a sermon series or a season, such as Advent

---

WORSHIP'S TOP FIVE
PROVEN TO WORK EVERY SUNDAY

1. "Forever First"
2. "Perpetually Next"
3. "Works Every Time"
4. "Invariably Touching"
5. "Always the Closer"

> Musicians are more like the old-fashioned jukebox in a restaurant—all the songs contained therein are likely similar in style and function... We need to think outside ourselves to the church community.
>
> —C. Randall Bradley

or Lent. Once in the cycle, it doesn't hurt to prepare something extra, or get a week ahead in your preparation, especially in a region where inclement weather can cause the cancellation of rehearsals.

Three test questions[3]

"What songs will help us enter into a spirit of worship?"

There are several schools of thought on creating a worship package or set. The primary question is, "What songs will help us enter into a spirit of worship?" Folks, both young and old, can be quick to pass judgment on our choice of songs, as the writer of this letter demonstrates:

> "I am no music scholar, but I feel I know appropriate church music when I hear it. Last Sunday's new hymn—if you call it that—sounded like a sentimental love ballad one would expect to hear crooned in a bar. If you insist on exposing us to rubbish like this—in God's house—don't be surprised if many of the faithful look for a new place to worship. The hymns we grew up with are all we need." From a letter written in 1863 regarding a new hymn called "Just As I Am."[4]

There are times when the congregation can be wooed into a contemplative mood by music played at a slow or medium tempo, and soft or moderate volume. At the other extreme, a higher decibel level and faster tempos can jumpstart an up-tempo celebratory mood. A strong topical emphasis calls for a more reflective approach that focuses on the power of strong lyrics.

When grouping songs, it is common to use several in the same tempo and then carefully transition to another mode. Avoid alternating between fast and slow songs, which tends to feel choppy. Shun too many slow songs in a row or overdoing cute songs. Begin in familiar territory, even in a low key as voices "wake up." Rarely commence your set with a new song. If you do, introduce an accessible section, like the chorus, and then cycle back to the verses, connected by the now-familiar chorus.

"What do we want folks to think about today?"

The jumpstart entrance into worship often primarily touches our *right-brained* emotions. John 4 teaches us that we must "worship in spirit and in truth," requiring a reaching across to the thought process on the *left side* of our brain. A second approach follows a central theme, by asking, "What do we want folks to think about today?" This could relate to the meeting theme, but as Dave Williamson says, "That can be overkill. God is so much more diverse, and the needed expression of the people broader, than theming the entire service allows."[5] Even after consulting with the speaker of the day, a thematically related songlist may not emerge, but perhaps there is one song that can be identified to close your set that can act as a springboard for the message.[6]

THEME: God's Guidance and Care
1. *Come, Thou Fount*
2. *In His Time*
3. *The Power of Your Love*

THEME: Hunger for God
1. *Be Thou My Vision*
2. *Open Our Eyes*
3. *As The Deer*

THE TEMPLE COURTS

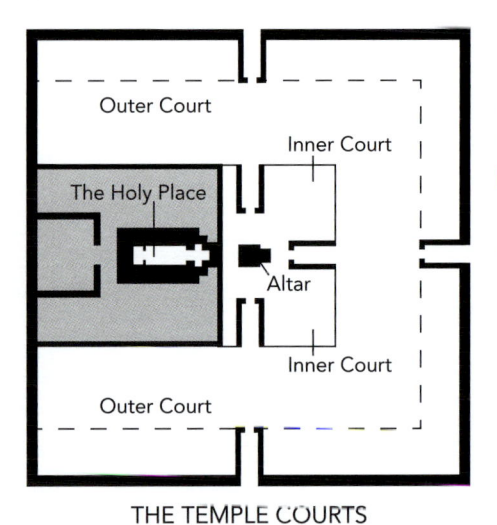

At other times, the worship leader can be guided by the Holy Spirit to songs that follow a logical thought process, often moving from the Outer Court (singing about God) into the Inner Court (responding to God's presence) or even the most intimate Holy Place (songs about what God has done). As we see in this example from Dave Williamson, choosing to transition to the chorus first, rather than the verse, can open up possibilities:

> *"The ending lyric of "Days of Elijah" is "out of Zion's hill salvation comes." Ask yourself, "What thought that opens the next song builds on that ending thought?" You come up with "Mighty to Save," chorus first, which begins by saying, "Savior, you can move the mountain/My God is mighty to save …" Then from the last lines of "Mighty" which go, "You rose and conquered the grave, Jesus conquered the grave"… we decide to move further into the inner court with "Your grace is enough," which begins by saying, "Great is Your faithfulness, O God… so remember Your children … Your grace is enough."…To conclude, we want to move into a song that goes deeper, yet still relates in some cognitive way. We choose "Shout to the Lord," which begins, "My Jesus, my Savior, Lord there is none like You."*[7]

Songset	Tempo	Worship Progression
1. *Days of Elijah*	uptempo	outer court
2. *Mighty to Save*	moderate tempo	outer, but ends inner court
3. *Your Grace is Enough*	uptempo	inner court
4. *Shout to the Lord*	power ballad	inner court, Holy of Holies

"Who are we singing to?"

A third approach asks, "Who are we singing to?" Hymns really were conceived as *sung prayers,* which explains the concluding intoned "Amen." Prayers sung *up* to God are regarded as **vertical** worship. One group of vertical hymns thanks and adores God as the Almighty. Hymns like *Holy, Holy, Holy, A Mighty Fortress,* and *Lord, I Lift Your Name on High* fit this category. Other hymns or songs are addressed *to* God, but they are asking God to do something like, *Teach Me How to Love Thee,* or *Change My Heart, O God.* Songs that encourage or admonish others (or ourselves) are identified as **horizontal**, because rather than declaring something *up to* God, they state something *about* God *out* to the people. It is common to sing two vertical uplifting songs and then one to encourage others to respond to God.

This "set" begins with adoration (sung vertically to God), asks God for something (sung vertically to God) and closes by encouraging others (sung horizontally to the people).

From Vertical to Horizontal	Who singing to?
1. *Lord, I Lift Your Name*	adoration to God ↑
2. *Change My Heart, Oh God*	petition God ↑
3. *Soon and Very Soon*	sung to people →

VERTICAL — SUNG TO (OR ABOUT) GOD

HORIZONTAL — SUNG TO ENCOURAGE OTHERS (OR OURSELVES)

A similar approach follows the ACTS acronym (Adoration, Confession, Thanksgiving, Supplication). It commences with vertical adoration, moves to a song of confession, followed by a song of encouragement and thanks, and closes with a song asking God to do something on behalf of others.

ACTS
1. *Holy, Holy, Holy* (adoration)
2. *Create in Me a Clean Heart* (confession)
3. *Give Thanks* (thanksgiving)
4. *Shine, Jesus Shine* (supplication)

Message
God is majestic and powerful
Jesus forgives me, even when I fail
I praise God for what He has done in my life
Prayer to enlarge the body of Christ

The flow of a worship song set often downshifts from a brisk tempo through a moderate song, closing with a slow, meditative offering. To move the worshiper's attention away from what can become routine, the opposite may also prove effective, where a quiet start unfolds toward a climactic portrait of the unfathomable depth of God's love.

From Quiet to Climax
1. *His Eye is On the Sparrow*
2. *God Will Make a Way*
3. *'Tis So Sweet to Trust in Jesus*
4. *Oh for a Thousand Tongues*

Subliminal Message
God watches over His children
God can be trusted, even when life hurts
God can bring good out of bad
God is big and powerful

Aids for song selection

While some meeting themes suggest numerous song options, other themes prove difficult in locating just the right song. To aid song selection, some song leaders create their own computer databases with quick access to lists of songs sorted by theme, key, tempo, Scripture reference, and even service placement (opening song, reflection, closing song, offertory, prayer, and the like).

A subscription to a song service also permits various theme, Scripture, key, and/or word searches. The most recent *Salvation Army Piano Tune Book* includes chord symbols (with capo), as well as associated song texts to a majority of the songs. Our songbook includes alphabetical, topical, Scripture, metrical and word search indexes, which are also available as a computer searchable format for handy research.

The worship leader should constantly search for fresh contemporary music. This listening should be eclectic and go beyond the current popularity of a top five list of choruses, which can become stale offerings because of what Bob Sorge calls overfamiliarity or overkill.[8] Look at choruses by Salvationists or local writers. Search the internet or take suggestions from members of your congregation and worship team. It can be helpful to ask the congregation what their favorites are. We serve the service and our congregation when we put our own personal taste aside, and choose songs that foster a connection with the congregation on any given Sunday.

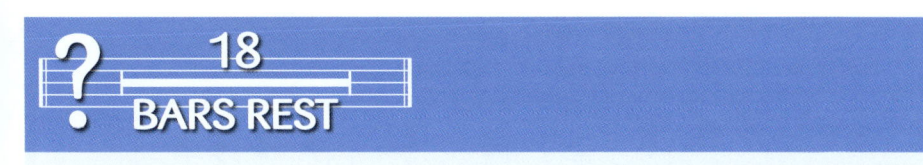

SCRIPTURE INDEX

1 SAMUEL 3:9	775
1 KINGS 8:12-53	822
2 KINGS 19:15	134

THEMATIC INDEX

God – Grace and Mercy 44
55, 453, 509, 699   593

God – Love
32, 207, 241, 342, 357,
439, 490, 601, 615, 634

God – Majesty and Power
6, 376, 573

Become friends with Scripture, topical, and word search indexes in the Salvation Army Song Book and other hymnals to aid in devising worship playlists.

capo (*term*) \'kā - pō\ A device which locks across a fret of the guitar, stopping all strings at the desired fret, thereby raising the pitch by a number of half steps without requiring a change in fingering by the player. Capo 2(C) means the capo is placed on the second fret, and the guitarist plays the alternative (usually more accessible) chords indicated in parentheses. (More on capo in Chapter Nineteen–p. 413).

Capo 2(C) (C)   (F)   (G)
         D D/F#   G   A
         Moderato ♩ = 76

18 | BARS REST

1. Think about how you currently choose songs for Sunday worship. Are you in a rut, reusing the same old top five list? Are you able to link your song list to

18 BARS REST *continued*

meeting or sermon content? Reflecting on the story that opened this chapter, do you ever experience "the river"?

2. Do you ever receive prompts from the Holy Spirit prior to Sunday, or in the moment during worship? Or does your mind wander, causing you to miss the "flow of the Spirit"?

3. Survey the worship songs that you have been using against the three test questions. How do you think you could fine-tune your selections and their strategic placement to better serve the service?

LOCATING THE MUSIC AND WORDS

Music and words in print form exist in most churches in hymnals or song collections. Many of these compilations include chord symbols with capo, including the latest *Salvation Army Piano Tune Book*. More recent popular songs and choruses are published in songbook collections. Choral publishers produce arrangements of praise choruses and hymn settings designed for congregational use with praise team, choir, and supporting instrumental resources.

Use of printed music saves time, especially in getting singers to agree on what alto and baritone notes are to be sung. Reference to a printed page also can quickly settle matters of correct rhythm and note values. If a printed copy has been purchased for each member of your team, you may elect to copy the song being used. It is highly recommended to enlarge it to fill the entire page. (Refer to Chapter Five, p. 111, regarding

Peering into the computer monitor, the meeting planner exclaims, "I just know the RIGHT SONG is in here somewhere!"

Bless His Holy Name

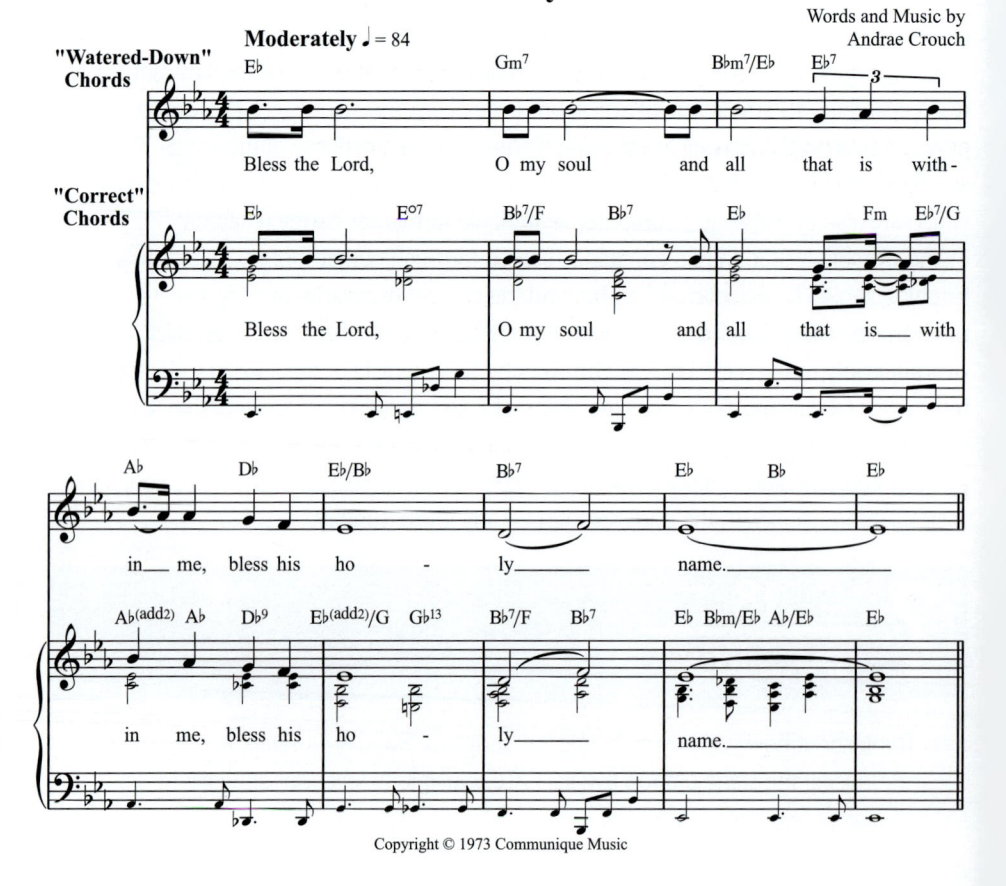

Words and Music by Andrae Crouch

Bless His Holy Name is rendered, first with the "watered-down" chords, and then the "correct" chords in the Chapter Eighteen online folder.

Copyright © 1973 Communique Music

Chord charts

An unhappy task before my weekly junior band rehearsal used to be picking up what was left behind from Sunday service; photocopied pages of lyrics with minimal chord symbols that had seemingly blown off the stands onto the stage floor. In some places, these chord chart sheets now seem to be ubiquitous because they are easily accessed on-line. In this format, chord symbols are indicated where the chords change above the typed lyrics. In Chapter Nineteen, we will consider ways to elaborate on these simplified chords.

One recommendation is to put the chord chart pages in three ring binders, perhaps in plastic covers. Titles can be arranged alphabetically with dividers. Pages can be pulled for the rehearsal or Sunday but then returned to their proper place to be used again in the future. Another option is for the leader to collect the song parts, by title, into a single clear plastic sleeve. Catalog the sets of sleeves alphabetically. Each week before rehearsal or the sound check, the worship leader pulls the pages of chord charts needed from the sleeved sets and puts them in the worship band's binders in the order required. More and more folks are moving these pages into their electronic devices and, with the swipe of their fingers, move on to the next tune.

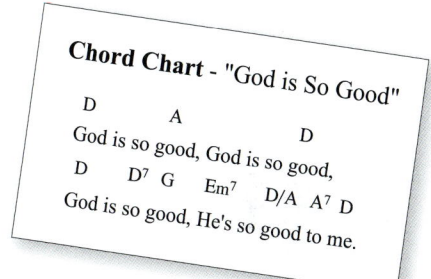

Lead sheets

Like words-only songbooks and projected lyrics, approximations of tunes abound. A more beneficial solution is the use of lead sheets. These combine a single staff melody line with lyrics and letter chord symbols placed directly above the note where the chord should change, thus the designation by jazz and commercial artists as "chord changes." Chord placement over the exact notation of the melody, as found in most contemporary collections and hymnals, is certainly more secure than the printed-out chord charts where the chords are approximated above the words.

Players will best equip themselves by learning to read the notes and rhythm of the melody and also securing knowledge of how to construct the corresponding chords. In situations where the guitar is the lead instrument for worship, you may wish to refer to websites which have downloadable songs in lead sheet format. These are produced with guitar players in mind. The chords have been simplified without compromising the harmonic integrity of the hymn, yet are updated enough to sound contemporary.

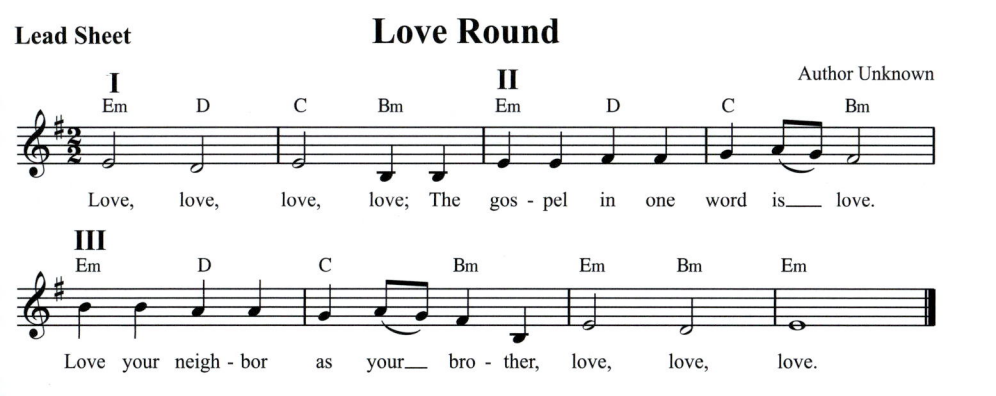

Choral octavos designed for congregational use, occasionally include a bulletin-size insert with a single line melody with the lyrics printed on the back cover of the octavo, with permission to reprint in the church bulletin. This practice has long been used in the Anglican Church for congregational responses. Photocopying for congregational use is covered under your CCLI license, so delight your congregation with a notated version of a new chorus. More folks can follow a musical line than you may imagine.

> The publisher hereby grants permission to reprint the material within the box for congregational participation provided that a sufficient quantity of copies of the entire anthem has been purchased for the musicians. The music is to be reproduced with the title and all credits including the copyright notice.

We Are An Offering
Words and Music by Dwight Liles

We lift our voic-es,___ We lift our hands, we lift our lives___ up to you, we are an of-fer-ing;___ Lord, use our voic-es,___ Lord, use our hands, Lord, use our lives_ they are yours, we are an of-fer-ing.___ We are an of-fer-ing.___

Copyright © 1984 Bug and Bear Music
Reproduced by Permission of the Publisher

Words only

The Salvation Army follows in the tradition of some denominations that print *words only* songbooks. With the exceptions of some incidental music-and-words collections, Salvationists are accustomed to sorting out the tune by ear with just the words in front of them. The advantage of holding a book over a projected lyric is being able to follow the flow of the lyric, which often follows a story or line of doctrinal truth. Sharing a book with the person singing next to you can help folks feel more a part of the community of worshipers. Large print editions are helpful for those with vision weakness.

The projected image, on the other hand, aids singing by focusing the congregation's attention out of the copy upward and provides the freedom to clap or lift hands in worship. In many cases there is easy access to song lyrics via the internet. For corps with limited resources, many publishers now include the tracks and visuals, including lyrics already cued, and prepared in a visually appealing digital format.

ARRANGING THE PLAYLIST

Earlier we considered three test questions in approaching our playlists. How we decide to arrange the songs in our song-set can emphasize the best of each of these possibilities:

Test Question #1:
"What songs can help us enter into a spirit of worship?" Establish a mood or atmosphere.

---

254 Our God reigns, 793
Isaiah 52:7-10   Irregular

HOW lovely on the mountains are the feet
  of him
Who brings good news, good news,
Proclaiming peace, announcing news
  of happiness,
Our God reigns, our God reigns.

*Our God reigns, our God reigns,
Our God reigns, our God reigns.*

©1974 New Jerusalem Music

Test Question #2:
"What do we want folks to think about today?" Emphasize the lyrical content.

Test Question #3:
"Who are we singing to?" Balance vertical—to God—worship with the horizontal—to the people.

Layering
To have all your forces "full out" on all verses of a hymn or song will not only discourage the congregation from participating, but will negate the opportunity to set a mood as you journey through the *story* of the words. As a fundamental principle, verses should not exceed 85% volume, with the chorus or refrain sung at near 100%.[9] In today's contemporary music recording scene, the producer sitting next to the engineer often assumes the role of arranger, without manuscript paper, by giving arranging suggestions from the sound booth. The producer may make suggestions as to song layout and reinforce the shape of that layout by creating "layers" after the fact in the cutting room as a track is edited.

Recording layers in the studio
The term layers being used in the context of a worship team is not to be confused with the layers we used for analysis in the Score Study, Bandmaster, and Songster Leader Chapters. In the case of the worship band using a click track, the drum track is considered the first layer, then the bass, then usually the guitar, keyboard, and finally, the voices and horns. Recordings are often made through this process of overdubbing one track layer over another.

An alternate method has each instrumentalist and vocalist in separate booths or rooms. This prevents any bleed between the recorded track layers, giving the engineer an independently recorded track layer for each musician. The group can then record all parts at the same time through the use of headphones or monitors, giving the arranger-producer and the mixing engineer the option to highlight, reduce, or eliminate certain vocal or instrumental layers in the final mix.

Build verse by verse
When presenting a hymn with four verses, a way of avoiding monotony is to mix and match your vocalists, varying the voices by verse. One approach would be to commence with a soloist to gently introduce the hymn in a quiet mood. For verse two, invite the congregation to join, with perhaps a male and female duet leading. Verse three can build a little with all men singing the melody with the congregation, and harmony from the women of the team. The final full-out verse has the praise team singers in four part harmony and the congregation continuing on the melody. This well thought-out progression, if fully rehearsed, would bring dynamics and vitality to what could have been a flat sing through a worthy hymn.

Painting the lyrics
Not all hymns or gospel songs build verse by verse to climactic conclusion. Take some clues from your careful review of the text. For example, the third verse of *How Great Thou Art* ("And when I think that God, His Son not sparing…") suggests a quieter, even slower tempo than the first two verses. As one leads into verse four ("When Christ shall come…") the *tempo* picks up slightly in the first half, but when

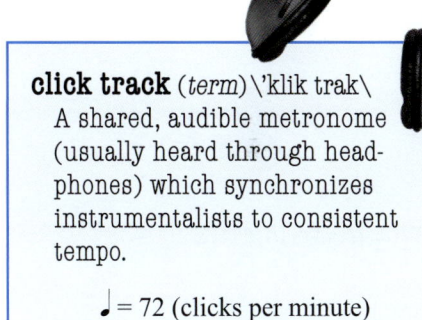

---

click track (*term*) \'klik trak\
A shared, audible metronome (usually heard through headphones) which synchronizes instrumentalists to consistent tempo.

♩ = 72 (clicks per minute)

The Voices in Layers

Verse 1: Male soloist

Verse 2: Male/Female duet
Invite congregation to join

Verse 3: Men and congregation melody
Ladies in harmony

Verse 4: Voices in 4 parts
Congregation on melody

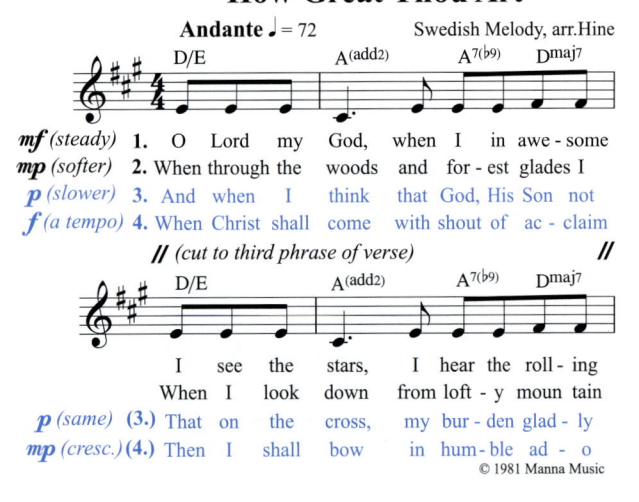

How Great Thou Art

Andante ♩ = 72   Swedish Melody, arr. Hine

mf (steady) 1. O Lord my God, when I in awe-some
mp (softer) 2. When through the woods and for-est glades I
p (slower) 3. And when I think that God, His Son not
f (a tempo) 4. When Christ shall come with shout of ac-claim

// (cut to third phrase of verse) //

I see the stars, I hear the roll-ing
When I look down from loft-y moun-tain
p (same) (3.) That on the cross, my bur-den glad-ly
mp (cresc.) (4.) Then I shall bow in hum-ble ad-o

© 1981 Manna Music

See the Chapter Eighteen online folder to hear these two examples in minor mode.

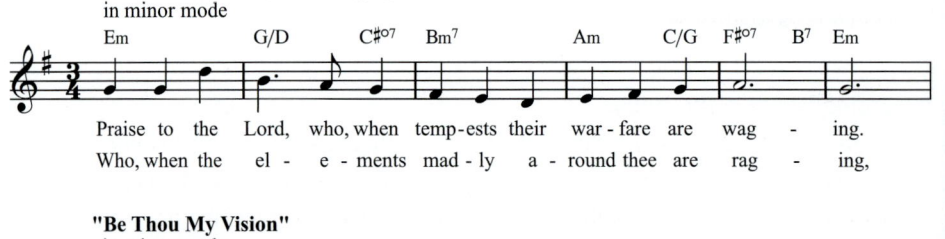

The Instruments in Layers

Verse 1: Keys only, half note chords

Verse 2: ADD bass guitar, soft drums

Verse 3: ADD guitars, drums shift to kick pattern

Verse 4: Keys fill out with broken chords and wider octaves. Drums add cymbals

---

we hit the line "Then I shall bow in humble adoration" the music should regress to the quieter, more reverent tone. Then during the last line a drum or cymbal roll builds to the triumphant final refrain. *O Boundless Salvation* is similar, where after the bold opening verse, subsequent verses, like verse two, are more somber ("My sins they are many…").

Shifts to minor mode

Another way to create texture and interest in the journey of a hymn text is to shift harmonically to the minor mode while maintaining the original melody. Chords of the relative minor work well on the third verse of *Praise to the Lord, the Almighty* to reflect "tempests of … warfare … raging." The relative minor also works well on selected verses of *Be Thou My Vision*. In Chapter Seventeen (p. 369), we discussed ennobling a final verse by modulating up a key while slowing to a stately tempo.[10]

"Praise to the Lord, the Almighty"
in minor mode

Praise to the Lord, who, when temp-ests their war-fare are wag - ing.
Who, when the el - e - ments mad-ly a - round thee are rag - ing,

"Be Thou My Vision"
in minor mode

Be Thou my wis-dom, and Thou my true Word; I ev-er with Thee and thou with me,

Layering in the band

We can apply the same principles of **layering to the supporting instrumentalists** in the worship band to create interest, just as an arranger would with an ensemble. The introductory bars and verse one can be presented as simple block chords from the keyboard. As we transition into verse two, the bass and drums join softly. Drums assume a fuller role, as guitars enter for verse three and then a more active keyboard (or even full band) is added for the final climactic verse.

Listening for your part

Stories are told of African Salvationist musicians who travel miles to hear a performance. They often listen differently than a Western Salvationist does. They tune in intentionally on their part, hoping to reproduce it from memory when they get home! In a similar manner, we can train ourselves as leaders and players to listen and watch for the subtle, but effective ways that professional players nuance their music. When listening to an orchestra, ask: How much and what percussion is there on the first verse? When do the back-up vocals come in? Ask how the verses are differentiated from one another. Importantly, consider how the orchestra dictates the emotional tone of the offering.[11] Listening outside our musical comfort zone will spawn many lessons. Consider looking into African styles like Highlife from Ghana or Township Jazz from South Africa to add rhythmic excitement to arrangements. Latino/Cuban rhythms are foundational to modern popular music and well worth the study.[12]

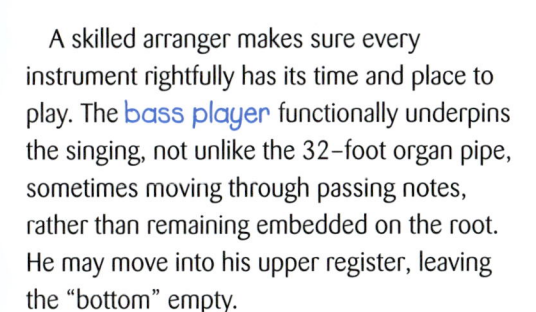

Chapter 18 | MORE THAN A SONG

Every player matters

A skilled arranger makes sure every instrument rightfully has its time and place to play. The bass player functionally underpins the singing, not unlike the 32-foot organ pipe, sometimes moving through passing notes, rather than remaining embedded on the root. He may move into his upper register, leaving the "bottom" empty. Drummers sometimes circle on the cymbals or with brushes, play exclusively on the high-hat, resort to cymbal rolls, or judiciously use the rim. Guitarists can vary strums or pick simple lines. Many of the concepts previously considered in elaborating on the Piano Tune Book (see Chapter Seventeen, pp. 360-363) can be useful to the keyboard player, such as reducing chords to the very minimum or varying inversions, registers, and arpeggiation. All instrumentalists can benefit from a reminder that an ensemble's clarity and conciseness are usually products of fewer notes and yes, less volume. Less really is more!

INSTRUMENTAL TECHNIQUES to help vary arrangements from verse to verse[13]

Guitar
1. Finger pick
2. Soft strum with thumb
3. Strum softly with pick, add strokes
4. Full strum

Drums
1. Simple kick with light rim shot
2. Alternate kick with hi-hat
3. Kick, sub snare, hi-hat
4. Same, add rolls and crash cymbals

Keys
1. Sustain chords half to full measure
2. Move chords to different inversions
3. Broken chords on quarter/eighth notes

Bass
1. Stay on root
2. Add passing tones
3. Patterns in high register

The Beat Goes On

riff (*term*) \'rif\ In jazz or rock, a short melodic motive often repeated over changing harmonies. It may be presented as accompaniment or as melody, or sometimes in call-and-response fashion.

Opus One Riff Lines
Moderately, with a beat ♩ = 120

Opus One (Sy Oliver & Sid Garris)
© 1946 Embassy Music

Coloring the music

Worship leader Steve Kranz likens shaping a musical space to painting a canvas. A painter would never paint every color on every inch of a canvas, resulting in an indiscernible mess. Constant playing at full throttle forces the congregation to switch off. Convince the worship team that taking a rest doesn't make their role less important, but rather, their re-entry highlights their importance.[14] If there are two guitarists, one should play higher on the neck so as not to infringe on the musical space of the other. If a song is guitar-driven, then the keyboardist takes a backseat. Conversely, if a piece is piano-based, then the guitarist should be less rhythmic and limit her offerings to lead or fill riffs.

CREATING SEAMLESS TRANSITIONS

The well-known brass band composer, Eric Ball, often said that the most difficult bits of music to create were the transitions between songs in a selection. He further suggested that a well-written transition plays itself while one not so well conceived will require much rehearsal. As the church moves toward a more production-minded worship experience, creating exceptional, even seamless transitions, is a no less formidable challenge. The alternatives are the near silent dead-spots, while the congregation watches for what seems like an eternity as the worship band shuffles through their pages. Abrupt, choppy changes in tempo and volume, complete with the unintentional choreography of lively head-bobbing and arm-waving, can leave a congregation with a sense of whiplash. Music theorists teach us that the most effective key change or modulation is imperceptible. So it is with transitions between songs. A few simple principles can apply.[15]

Style, key, and theme in tempo

It should be fairly easy to negotiate between a pair of same-tempo tunes sung back to back, especially without a key change. To make a quick transition, the song leader can talk over/introduce the next song as the first song concludes (and the corresponding visual slide comes up at the same time). The seam will be less apparent if the songs are thematically linked, for instance, *How Great Is Our God* transitioning into *How Great Thou Art*. You do yourself a favor when you can link two songs in the same time signature and tempo, such as *Great is the Lord* and *He is Exalted,* both in 6/8 time.

Hear demonstrations of these transitions in the Chapter Eighteen online folder.

Link **"How Great is Our God"** (Tomlin) with **"How Great Thou Art"** (Hine)

Copyright © 2004 worshiptogether.com songs, Six Steps Music, Alletrope Music.
Leader (voiceover): *"Then sings my soul"*
Copyright © 1953, Renewed 1981 Manna Music

Link **"Great is the Lord"** (Smith) with **"He is Exalted"** (Paris)

Leader (voiceover): *"Let's sing, He is exalted"*
Copyright © 1982 Meadowgreen Music
Copyright © 1985 StraightWay Music and Mountain Spring Music

Sometimes lyrics of songs fit the theme so well that mixing meter is unavoidable. Working transitions from 4/4 time to 3/4 and back requires careful forethought. A switch to triple meter songs (in 3/4 and 6/8) often causes the music to lose energy, but can aid the transition to a slower song. Remember that people are reluctant to clap to waltz rhythms. Another option is to convert the 3/4 to 4/4 time. *Be Thou My Vision*, originally in 3/4 time, is often rendered in 4/4 utilizing an altered dotted rhythm:

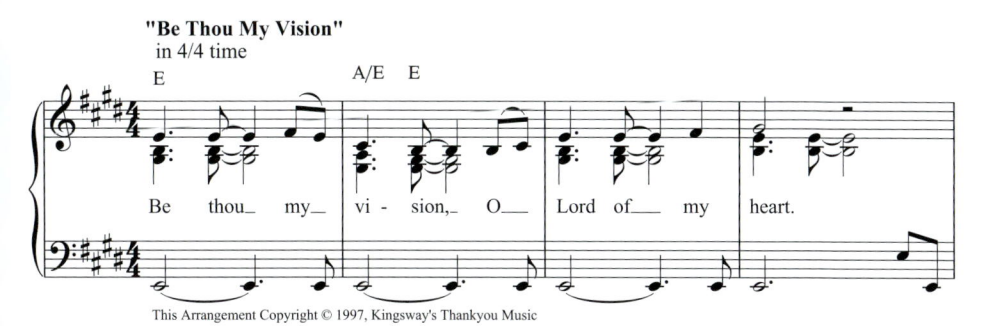

"Be Thou My Vision" in 4/4 time

This Arrangement Copyright © 1997, Kingsway's Thankyou Music

Modulation

To keep interest, it is advantageous to change key—what musicians call modulation—after two songs. The move toward a new key (with your transition talk-over) makes the changeover to a new song apparent. Some principles of modulation were introduced in Chapter Seventeen (pp. 368–371), with quick reference modulation guides found in the Appendix 18.1. Here is a chord chart example of a modulatory transition moving out of *We'll Understand It Better By and By* (in the key of G) into *When We All Get To Heaven* (in C). Notice how as the modulation measures take place, the worship leader ceases to sing, but rather gives the congregation introductory cues about the song to follow.

The other option that can create interest is to modulate up a half or whole step for the final verse of a song and set up the transition to the key for the next song. On-the-spot modulation is mostly a matter of practice. The leader can, however, ensure success by marking the new transposed chord symbols right on the music sheets prior to rehearsal. There are several ways to modulate:

- **ALPHABETICALLY**—One can modulate by *moving up by half step:* a D chord becomes an Eb, Eb becomes E, E becomes F, and G becomes Ab. Or *moving up by whole step:* C becomes D, or F becomes G. Observing the natural half steps, where the black keys are missing, to make a whole step modulation: Bb becomes C, and E becomes F#.

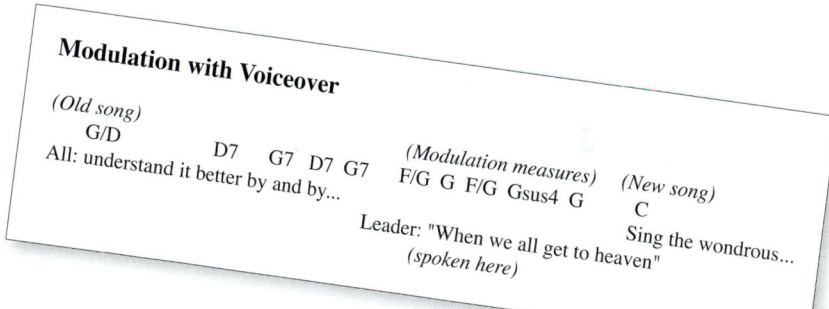

Modulating by HALF steps

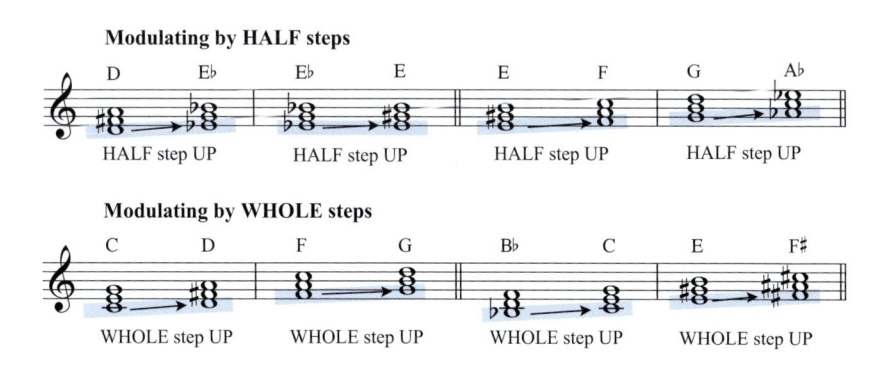

D → Eb | Eb → E | E → F | G → Ab
HALF step UP | HALF step UP | HALF step UP | HALF step UP

Modulating by WHOLE steps

C → D | F → G | Bb → C | E → F#
WHOLE step UP | WHOLE step UP | WHOLE step UP | WHOLE step UP

Modulation with Voiceover

(Old song)
G/D
All: understand it better by and by...   D7   G7   D7   G7   (Modulation measures)   (New song)
F/G G F/G Gsus4 G   C
Leader: "When we all get to heaven"   Sing the wondrous...
(spoken here)

CAUTION

The worship leader needs to recognize the limitations of the musicians in that some may struggle to play in more difficult keys (guitarists). For example, flat keys are difficult for less experienced guitarists. Not all will be able to modulate without written-out chords/parts.

- **NUMERICALLY**—For instance, the C, dm, F, and G chords in the key of C are based on the scale tones I, ii, IV, and V (the lowercase Roman numerals indicate a minor chord). The I, ii, IV, and V chords transposed *up one whole step* into the key of D, would be D, Em, G, and A.

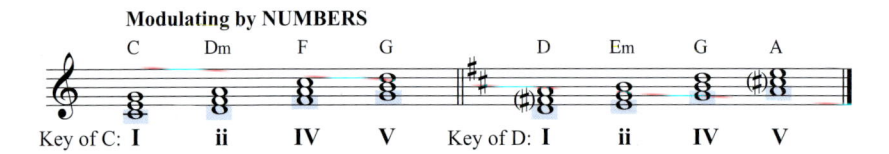

Modulating by NUMBERS

| Key of C: | I | ii | IV | V | Key of D: | I | ii | IV | V |

- **ELECTRONICALLY**—Many keyboards have transpose functions, which move the key *up or down by half steps* (1 takes the piano pitch up by one half step; 2 up a whole step; –1 down a half step, –3 down three half steps). In the next chapter (pp. 413), we will learn how the guitarist capo performs a similar chord-transposing function.

LOUD and *Fast* to Soft and S l o w

Sudden changes in volume and tempo are more difficult for the congregation to negotiate. When moving from an up-tempo, celebratory tune into a slow, reflective song, you can talk your way gradually from a loud, quick demonstrative voice down to a hushed, more settled tone. Your instrumentalists hopefully are in sync with your transition, both in tempo and dynamics. This settling down will be more apparent if you ask the standing congregation to sit. Many worship leaders will initiate applause for the Lord, especially after a bright song. The gradual *diminuendo* in the applause can help downshift your *segue* to a slower, softer offering. Sometimes an instrumental tag can be very effective to initiate the transition or conclude a set.

Soft and S l o w to LOUD and *Fast*

Naturally, the reverse effect, moving in stages from soft and slow to loud and fast can be realized in a similar fashion. Some song leaders end a softer tune with spoken prayer, and gradually bring the enthusiasm in their voices up as the music swells behind them. When moving into a quick tempo, a call for clapping helps build energy. Clapping at too quick a clip (from 132 bpm and faster) generally will not sustain itself, as folks won't clap for too long. Some think the limit is four minutes.[16] In the same vein, avoid treating the congregation like popcorn by starting and stopping, clapping or getting up and down, and up and down again. There is great value in allowing your congregation space for reflective contemplation with only a quiet musical backdrop or no music at all. Use members of your team to share a testimony or a Scripture verse with only the sparest of instrumental underscore.

18 BARS REST

1. Create several worship-set playlists, considering flow, content, and emotion. Design and practice seamless transitions through effective key and tempo changes.

2. Schematically layer some of the songs selected above, being sure your "arrangement" is appropriate and practical.

> "Music entices us to participate, and music is winsome and welcoming. When we sing with others, we are vulnerable, and vulnerability creates trust."
>
> —C. Randall Bradley

THE WORSHIP LEADER'S REHEARSAL PREP

Like many conductors and teachers, most worship team leaders intuitively pattern their rehearsals after the groups and leaders they themselves played or sang under. Not surprisingly, they often fall back on the same playlists they grew up with. This is not always a matter of the proverbial "how we always do it" syndrome. Suddenly thrust into leadership, the newly drafted quarterback has never had to ask how this team is going to be ready for Sunday's game. It is not just "another Sunday." Each Sunday has its unique challenges and the weekly rehearsal is the sole opportunity to prepare the team logistically, musically and spiritually. Having worked this far on your game plan, you now have:

- ☑ designed a playlist and reviewed it with the pastor/meeting planner
- ☑ prepared the copies
- ☑ settled on the "arrangements" and transitions for each song in the set

Now you, like a coach, need to have a strategy to communicate and rehearse all of your best intentions for Sunday morning.[17]

A "prepared" playlist

First and foremost, **pray** for each member of the team, for yourself in leadership, and for a clear vision of what needs to be done in this rehearsal. Bob Sorge defines worship leading as "taking your private cry and making it public."[18] The "hireling" who is just doing a job (as described in John 10:13), does not abandon his heart to God before the people. Your team members and congregation will respond to authenticity and vulnerability, but it all begins with prayer.

Prepare the playlist chart and organize it for all to see!
The successful rehearsal is about making music with a minimum of talk. The playlist should indicate for all of your musicians the introductions, the song and verse order, transitions, and concluding tags. An alternative is to indicate this information directly on the chord sheets or music. An example of a shorthand roadmap might be:

- **I** for introduction
- **V1** verse and number
- **C** chorus
- **B** bridge
- **T** closing tag

I V1 C V2 C B C C T

Marks save time
If there are key changes, notate the modulation segue and the new chord changes above the original chords. This will save valuable rehearsal time. Clearly describe your vocal and instrumental layers by verse for each song, noting which team member(s) will transition between songs with Scripture or prayer. Encourage members to mark their own cues during rehearsal. Indicate the call time for the sound check and specifically when in the service the group comes on.

Arrangement Layers
"How Great is Our God"

	VOCALS	BAND
Intro	Tony lead-in	Keys only (G)
V1	Tony solo	Add bass
C1	Add ladies on melody	Add light drums
V2	Ladies melody	Add guitar
C2	All voices in harmony	Build out
	[Modulate to A: G G/F Esus E]	
B	Voices in harmony (A)	Full band
C3(2X)	Reprise chorus	1x band tacet

All Things Are Possible
Key – C/D

Words and Music by **Darlene Zschech**
© 1997 Wondrous Worship

Verse 1
```
C2              Am7
   Almighty God    my Redeemer
C2              Am7
   My hiding place    my safe refuge
F2         G           Am   G
   No other name like Je - sus
F2              G
   No power can stand against You
```

Verse 2
```
C2              Am7
   My feet are plant - ed on this rock
C2              Am7        G
   And I will not   be shak - en
```

INTRO – |C |Am7 |C |Am7 (2X)
V1
V2
CH
INTRO (1X)
V2
CH
BRIDGE
CH (2X)
END – last line of BRIDGE

Set high expectations
The prepared playlist will help facilitate a productive rehearsal. Beyond saving valuable minutes of rehearsal, the prepared playlist and music placed on the stands set a high expectation for Sunday. Each team member sees the work that has to be accomplished within the prescribed rehearsal window. This prepared playlist is also of infinite value to the sound person to mark up as his or her tech sheet. Avoid asking the soundperson to "fly blind." Instead give him or her opportunity to better anticipate the layers of the arrangements or moments of transition. Remember that the sound engineer and media person are an integral part of the worship team. They should be engaged, as much as the singers and players, in all aspects of the preparation of the playlist for Sunday worship.[19]

Know your stuff!
One maxim has a leader spending two hours in preparation to every hour of actual rehearsal. This sounds like a lot, but time given to ongoing preparation as you approach rehearsal adds up quickly. Here are the steps taken by the worship leader before rehearsal:

- ☑ Prayerfully choose the appropriate music for the service.
- ☑ Locate the music, words, and chords.
- ☑ Work out transitions and mark accordingly.
- ☑ Write out any additional vocal and instrumental parts.

Once this preparation has taken place, the real "study" begins.
The same point we made in Chapter Eleven (From Score Reading to Score Study, pp. 231–232) of folks re-reading scores over and over, and never getting to score study, applies here. As a well-prepared music director, play through any transitions and modulations, knowing them so well that you can teach them succinctly. Be intentional on what will happen between verses, between songs, at key changes, and who will speak between songs. Establish tempos for yourself that are not so slow that the tempo drags, and yet not so fast that the congregation can't fit in the lyrics.

Looking for the "trouble"
In your study, make note of any tricky spots or vocal harmonies where you can anticipate rhythmic or pitch problems. Spend time with the lyrics, identifying any pronunciation that you may need to clarify. Mark understandable phonetics on the vocal copies before rehearsal to avoid time-consuming discussion. Plan to rehearse these potential problem areas before running the song. Get close to the meaning of the words. 1 Corinthians 14:15 *(KJV)* instructs us to "sing with the spirit, but with the understanding also." Often a line or two from the lyrics can form the basis for a devotional reflection, taking your group deeper into the songs.

> "Sing with the spirit, but with the understanding also."
> —1 Corinthians 14:15

Chapter 18 | MORE THAN A SONG

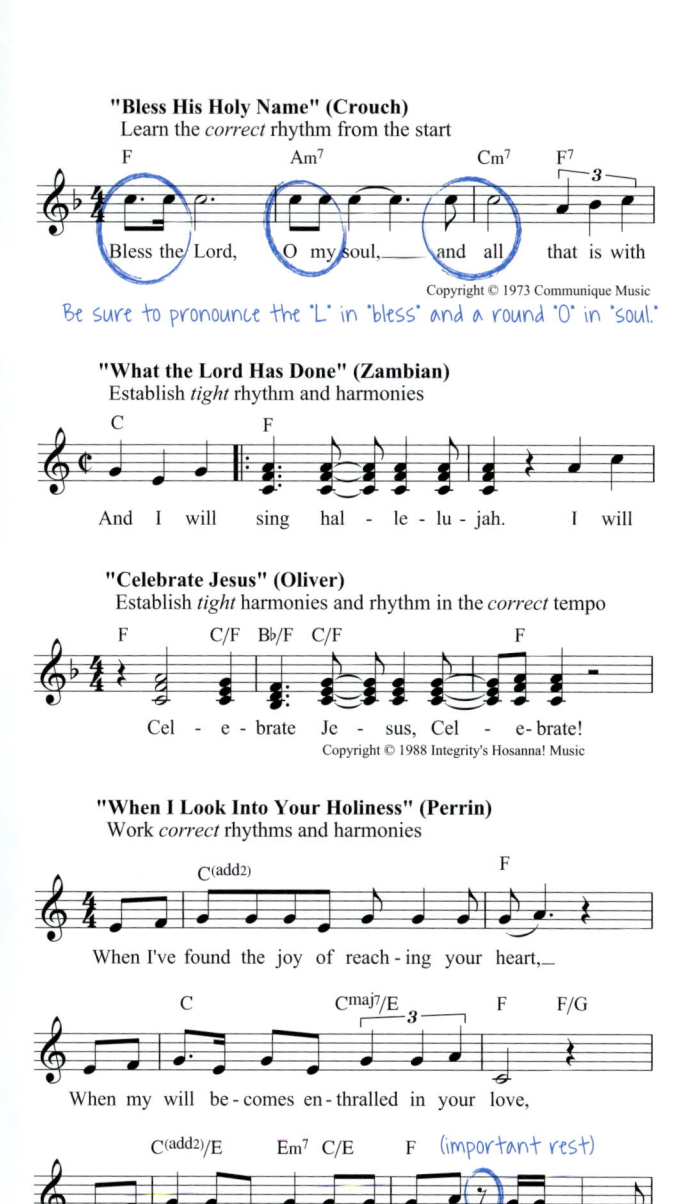

"Bless His Holy Name" (Crouch)
Learn the *correct* rhythm from the start

Be sure to pronounce the "L" in "bless" and a round "O" in "soul."

"What the Lord Has Done" (Zambian)
Establish *tight* rhythm and harmonies

"Celebrate Jesus" (Oliver)
Establish *tight* harmonies and rhythm in the *correct* tempo

"When I Look Into Your Holiness" (Perrin)
Work *correct* rhythms and harmonies

(important rest)

"Nothing But Thy Blood" (Peterson)
Learn the *correct* pitches and harmonies

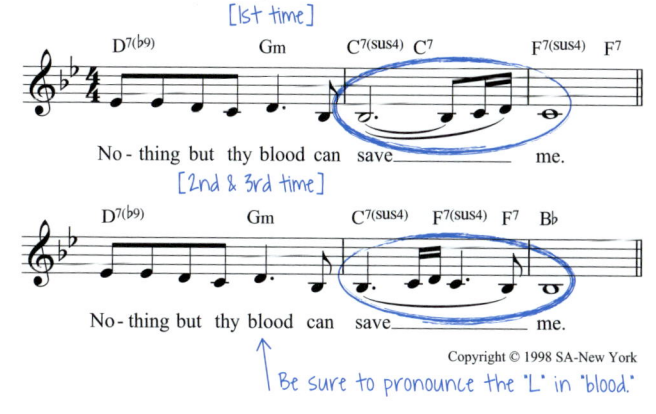

[1st time]
[2nd & 3rd time]

Be sure to pronounce the "L" in "blood."

"Soldier's Hymn" (Laeger)
Work out *correct* counting

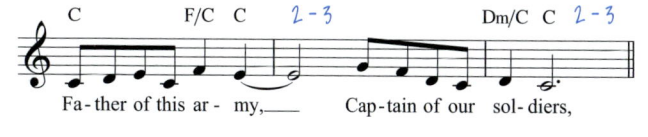

2-3   2-3
(later) 2-3-4   (same)

"I'm In His Hands" (Laeger)
Work out *correct* counting

1 2 - 1 2 + 1 R R 2 + 1 2

Testing the flow

A wise worship leader will play through the full set to confirm the transitions and balance of flow between the songs while timing the package as a whole. Be sure the set starts and links to the next portion of the service appropriately. For instance, one would bring the music down for the pastoral prayer or end on the upside to segue to a congregational greeting. Adjustments are more easily made to the playlist before rehearsal than when in the spotlight of rehearsal (sometimes lightheartedly known as "the heat of the battle").

Remember on Sunday to limit your talking and leave the sermonizing for the speaker of the day. An overextended "worship set" disrupts the flow of a meeting by stealing from the speaker's time. Conversely, if the Holy Spirit is moving, an altar response may call for the worship leader to extend the time in singing. In Africa, the speaker simply approaches the podium, pauses a moment and then motions down with his hands and the singing subsides. Respect for the officer as head and authority should never be violated. Learn to look and give each other cues so as to always be working together sensitively.

TESTING THE TIMING
Opening and closing worship sets

Timing	Element
10 min.	Musical prelude (band)
1 min.	Spoken call to worship
3 min.	Up-tempo gathering song
4 min.	Transition to adoration song
1 min.	Spoken call to confession (with underscore)
3 min.	Assurance of pardon song
	Bring down for testimony...

{ =12 } braces the middle five rows

...Be ready following sermon with

6 min.	Response choruses
2 min.	Sending out song
	Postlude walking music

{ =8 } braces the 6 and 2 min rows

Your Rehearsal Plan—An Arch

On the rehearsal day, the leader will arrive and set up early to allow time to greet members, and do a mini-sound check on the system, instruments, and lights. Readiness with marked copies, physical setup, and welcoming enthusiasm will set the stage for a productive rehearsal.[20]

                    Review song
        Try new tune   **Water break**
    Next hard work song   **Devotions & prayer**
  Then medium difficult tune   **Talk through transitions**
Open with familiar easy song   **Run Sunday's set/Benediction**

Short yardage

Avoid starting by rehearsing the playlist in order. Go for "short yardage" by opening rehearsal with something easy or familiar that requires little explanation or rehearsal. Folks may have rushed through traffic after a full day at school or work and need an easy entry into music-making. Moving on to a more difficult tune, be proactive with explaining or "checking" any trouble or transitions before playing down the tune. Some worship team leaders create teachable moments from within the playlist, allowing time for ongoing music education, such as instruction in music-reading.

The "hard work"

The "hard work," or newest song, should come either third or fourth, when folks are warmed up and concentration is highest. Work the nitty-gritty notes here and then try some new material or gradually review more accessible songs. Great gospel singers value singing with an acoustic piano or guitar unplugged, as we say, to build confidence in tuning, blend, and part learning.

Walk through Sunday

Before a break, allow time for prayer and devotions. During the break, remind vocalists to hydrate, drinking room temperature water while avoiding sweet, carbonated drinks! After the break, talk and "walk" through the transitions for this Sunday's set, then run Sunday's list from top to bottom without stopping. Finish with any schedule reminders. Leave the music in order for Sunday. Give a sincere thank you and close with a benediction. Some groups personalize the conclusion of rehearsal with a sung benediction or prayer chorus used solely for rehearsals.

18 BARS REST

1. Evaluate the congregational response to a playlist from a recent Sunday. Consider which songs went over well (sung with gusto) and which didn't (stopped singing or confused). Ask yourself which songs bear repeating. If a song didn't go so well this time, consider trying it again with another approach. Importantly, ask if there was a genuine connection with the congregation.

2. Next, evaluate the same set from the perspective of the worship band. Consider how the set flowed, using the criteria discussed above. Were the transitions smooth within the set, as well as coming on and going off the stage? Make note of any musical or technical improvements that could be made.

3. Take some time to actively listen "outside the box" to live performances, on the radio selections, online options, or recordings. Listen for individual instrumental techniques, as well as ways that arrangements have been layered.

4. *Did someone say practice?* Set aside time for you, the leader, to practice making seamless transitions and smooth modulations in a variety of keys.

WORSHIP TEAM RESOURCES

HELPS FOR WORSHIP TEAM LEADERS

Exploring Worship – *A Practical Guide to Praise & Worship*, Bob Sorge (Oasis House)
Extravagant Worship, Darlene Zschech (Bethany House)
Five Keys to Engaging Worship, John Chisum (Engage Press)
God's Singers, Dave Williamson (in:cite media)
The Complete Worship Leader, Kevin Navarro (Baker Book House)
The Heart of Worship Files, Matt Redman, ed. (Regal Books)
The Praise and Worship Team Instant Tune–Up, Douglas and Tami Flather (Zondervan)
The Unquenchable Worshipper: *Coming Back to the Heart of Worship*, Matt Redman (Regal Books)
The Worshiping Artist: *Equipping You and Your Ministry Team to Lead Others in Worship*, Rory Noland (Zondervan)
To Know You More: *Cultivating the Heart of the Worship Leader*, Andy Park (Intervarsity Press)
Worship Matters, Bob Kauflin (Crossway Books)
Worship Team Handbook, Alison Siewert, ed. (Intervarsity Press)

RESOURCES FOR CONGREGATIONAL PRAISE AND WORSHIP

Cantos de Alabanza y Adoración/*Songs of Praise and Adoration*, Bilingual Hymnal/ Spanish and English side-by-side (Editorial Mundo Hispano)
Praise Hymns and Choruses (Maranatha! Music)
Songs of Fellowship, Volumes 1 & 2 (Kingsway Press)
The Celebration Hymnal (Word and Integrity Music)

COMBINING RHYTHM SECTION WITH BRASS ENSEMBLE/BAND

Hallelujah Choruses (The Salvation Army USA Central Territory), available for rhythm section with punch brass (three parts) or brass ensemble/band in five part format.
Magnify– *75 Songs of Worship* (SA–London), Piano book with chords. Brass band in Triumph Series scoring.
The Salvation Army Piano Tune Book (SA–London) Two volume piano book with chords (and capo). *Volume II* includes lyrics. Brass band in SATB voicing with optional parts.

Dear Friends,
OK, so we've got a playlist and a rehearsal plan. It's time to go beyond the lead sheets, mikes, and cables, and worship the Lord with our music...in Chapter Nineteen, just ahead...

The Beat Goes On

CHAPTER NINETEEN

THE HOLY HASSLE OF ANOTHER SUNDAY
The Worship Leader's Toolbox

A new song is *put into* our mouths…We sing, yet not we, but the Eternal sings *in us*…
It is the Eternal Song of the Other, who sings *in us,* who sings *unto us,* and
through us into the world. —Thomas Kelly

WORSHIP…ANOTHER SUNDAY?

Can you recall a Sunday when there hasn't been some kind of difficulty? It could be the feedback of a misdirected microphone, the disturbing hum from stage amps, the miscued images on the screen, the vocals drowned out by instrumentals, or the all too often "I can't hear myself" sound mix. The result is a lackluster connection with the worshiping body and the Spirit. Not much mystery here, or even a sense of God's presence.

"We bring a sacrifice of praise…"

It is unfortunate that a worship band leader is said to be "leading" the people in worship. Is this not an inconvenient, even erroneous, label? As the musical set commences, the worship leader walks a veritable tightrope, balancing the mindsets of the corps officer, the musicians around him, and the congregation. Who bargained for a ministry with such high risks? Some are eagerly expectant, others focused elsewhere. It is a tenuous, if not unnerving, position to be in. Yet it is also one of high privilege.

In **Chapter Nineteen**, we learn how to:
- best position the worship team
- do an efficient sound check
- make adjustments on stage
- read and identify chord symbols
- chord on the guitar, including the use of the capo
- sing effective harmonies
- satisfactorily add to or subtract from chords

"We approach the throne of grace" with deep longing. In our heart of hearts we ask, "Lord, what are You looking for from Your people this morning?"

"You alone are my heart's desire, and I long to worship Thee."

Yet it is *another Sunday*. Beyond those blank stares, what can we do to help our brothers and sisters connect with the presence of God? Some heads are bowed. Some eyes meander. Can we be the catalyst to bring people together? "Spirit, blow the gentle breeze of Your strong wind upon us, now, this morning." (A mike squeal spoils the moment.)

Through another lens, though, you begin to sense the longing of the lonely and abandoned. You hear the song of a child of God yearning to be freed of a heavy load. You sense an aching search for answers. Is this just a feeling?

"Can you feel the mountains tremble?"

Risky business, this worship leading. Minstrel or minister? Performer or worshiper? You glance back at your instrumentalists as though motioning to say "Come with me."

"Swing wide ye heavenly gates…"

And then, in time, perhaps when we least expect it, we become aware of God's blessed presence. We feel His touch. Like the two men on the Emmaus Road, our hearts are strangely warmed for we have met with Jesus.

19 BARS REST

1. Recall a worship service that made a great impact on your life. What made it work for you?

2. Now recall the worst worship service you ever experienced. What things went wrong for you? What were the obstacles? How might they have been overcome?

3. Which of the author's thoughts in the account above can you identify with?

Chapter 19 | THE HOLY HASSLE OF ANOTHER SUNDAY

LOCATION, LOCATION, LOCATION!

Positioning the worship band
Traditionally church stages were designed to accommodate a choir, accompanying piano or organ and, of course, the pulpit area. In many Salvation Army corps, a platform space for the brass band has been afforded behind the pulpit. As worship bands have become part of mainstream churches, accommodating enough space with good visual sightlines for participants and congregants can prove to be a challenge.

Brass band and worship band share the stage
If the corps has a brass band, one approach is to place the worship band, including the drum kit, to one side of the platform, for example, behind the second cornet section. This way the drum set can be used by both bands. There is a visual advantage as the worship band is up on the stage, but if the screen drops down at the back of the stage, the worship band may require a video monitor tilted up on the floor or a courtesy screen projected on the rear wall.

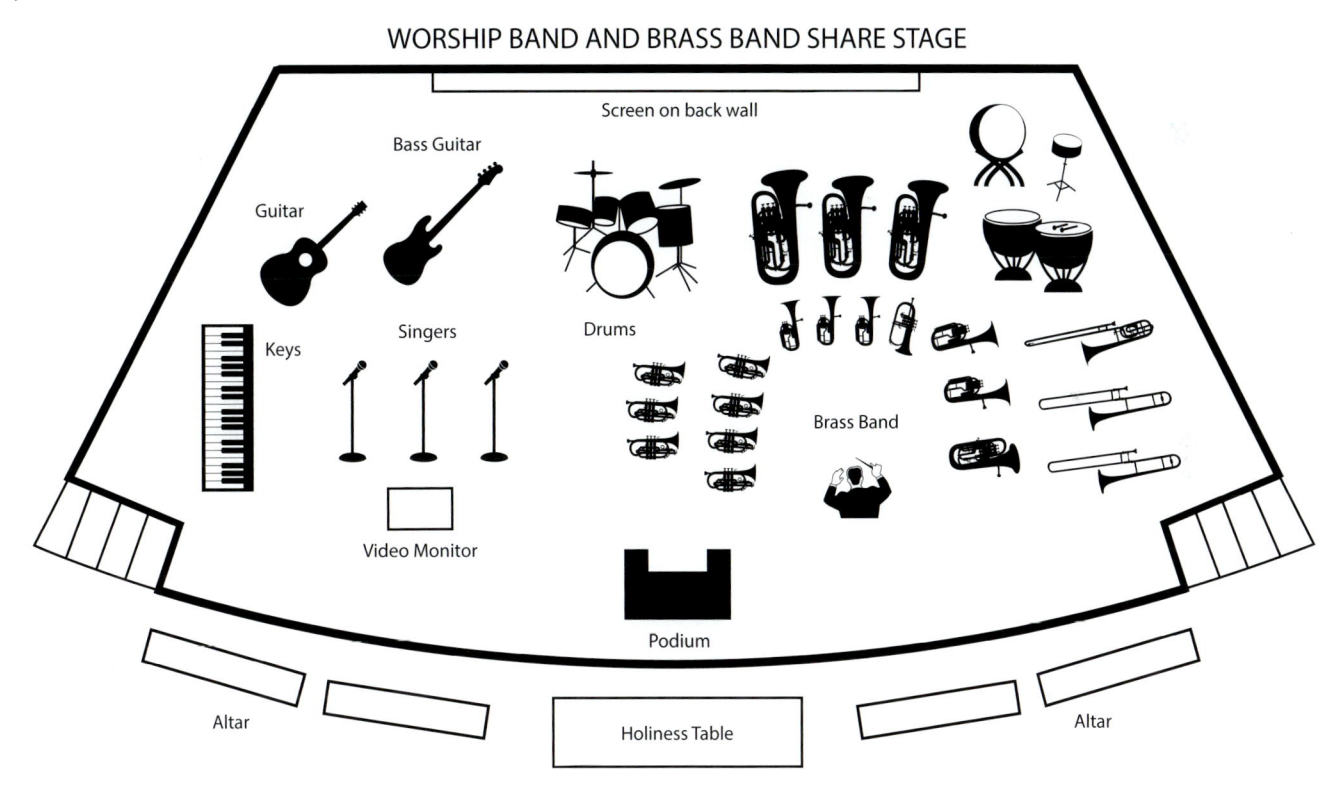

WORSHIP BAND AND BRASS BAND SHARE STAGE

Diagram showing stage layout with: Screen on back wall, Guitar, Bass Guitar, Keys, Singers, Drums, Brass Band, Video Monitor, Podium, Altar (left and right), Holiness Table.

Worship band around piano on floor (Illustrated on next page)
An alternative follows on the tradition of placing the piano and organ on opposite sides of the room at the front of the hall. If the keyboard player prefers an acoustic piano, then the worship band encircles itself around the keyboard, with singers in front of the keyboard and instrumentalists behind. Since all the worship band members stand, except perhaps the keyboard player, the visibility for both congregation and band can function well. The drawbacks are that space around the piano may be at a premium, the singer's microphones may sit in the "hotspot" for feedback just in front and down from the speaker cluster, and a courtesy monitor may be required because of screen placement behind, on the platform. This option also brings the hubbub of papers, instruments, stands, and cables nearer to the congregation and the altar area.

The Beat Goes On

WORSHIP BAND ENCIRCLE ACOUSTIC PIANO

Edge of Platform

Bass Guitar — Guitar — Drums — Acoustic Piano — Singers — Monitors — Podium — Holiness Table — Altar — Organ

---

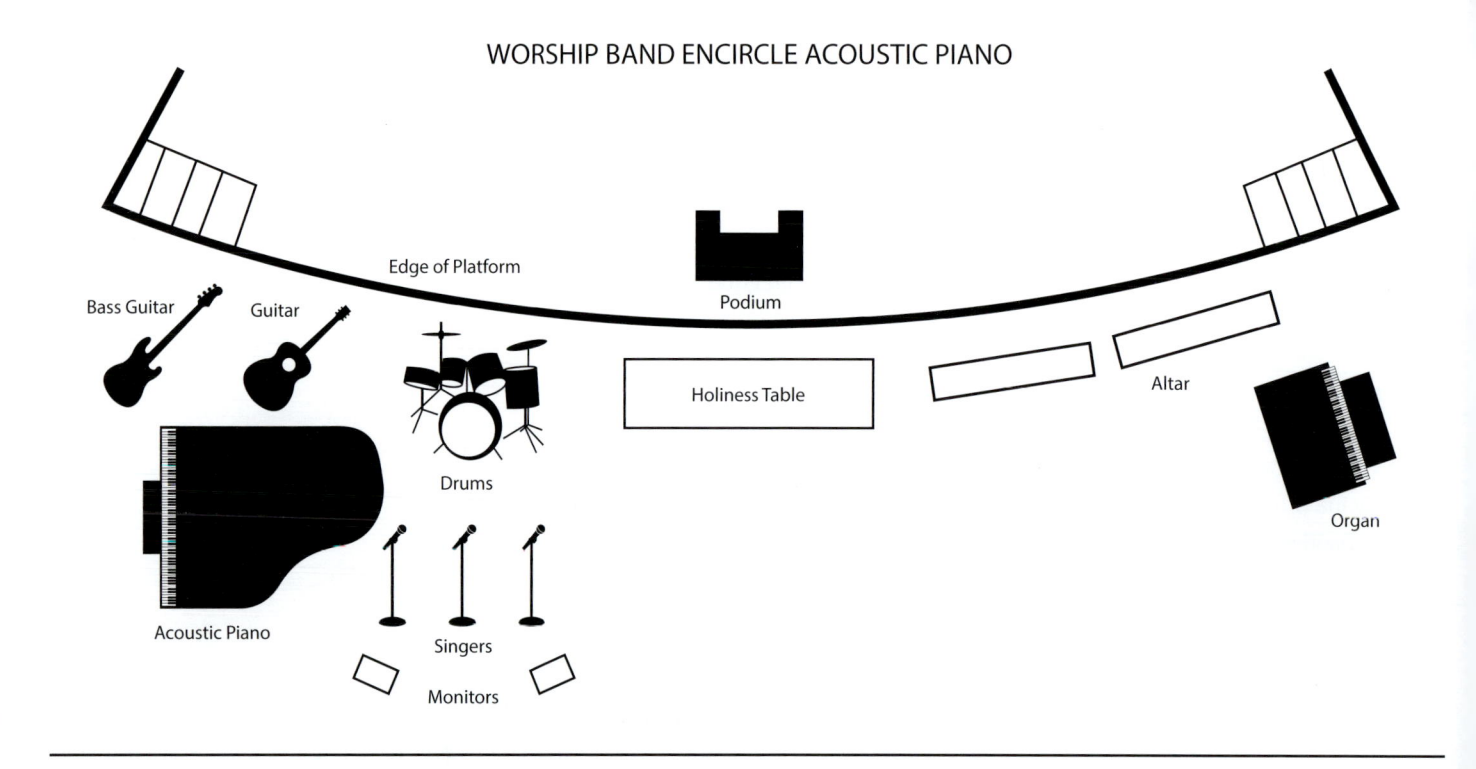

Worship band on platform

If the worship band has the platform to itself, screen placement can become a challenge. Many new churches opt to use two side screens angled in toward the congregation. This permits increased visibility for congregation, worship team, and speaker. Learning to subtly peek around the back or to the side to check if a slide comes up properly can become a fine art! Screens hung in front of the entire stage magnify this problem, requiring visual monitors.

The great majority of us have to work things out in less than ideal conditions. Worship bands should aspire to have the intense eyeball-to-eyeball communication of a string quartet, while connecting eyeball-to-eyeball with the congregation—and smiling, of course! The chief requirement for positioning your worship band is **sightlines**.

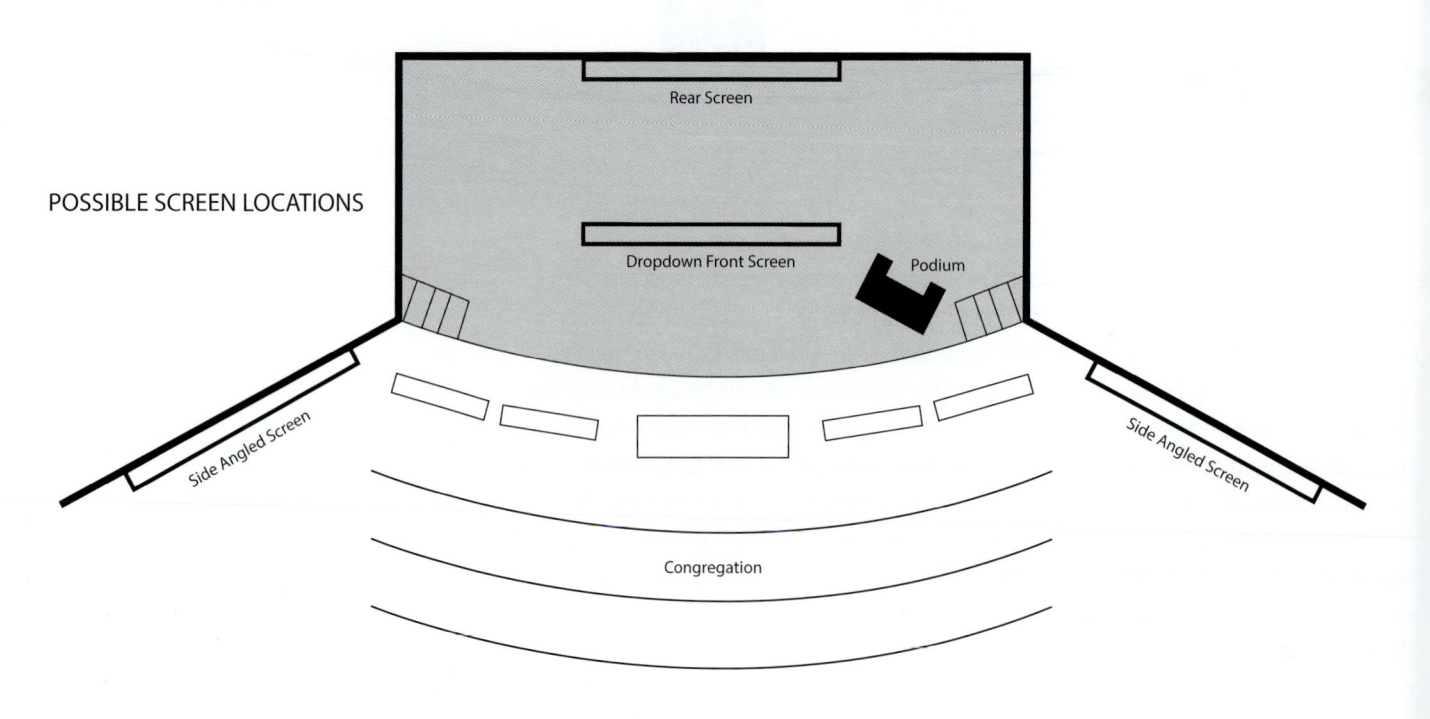

POSSIBLE SCREEN LOCATIONS

Rear Screen — Dropdown Front Screen — Podium — Side Angled Screen — Side Angled Screen — Congregation

Chapter 19 | THE HOLY HASSLE OF ANOTHER SUNDAY

Everyone can see each other (and the congregation)

You will rarely see a rock band set up in a straight line across the stage. Although all the musicians should be able to see the crowd, the leader at the keyboard is usually neatly set next to the drum set, meaning it is only those to his left and right who can see his cues. **It is better to create a curve left and right back to the leader to give all the musicians and singers sightlines to the congregation.**

STRAIGHT-LINE SET-UP

Guitar   Bass Guitar   Drums   Keys   Soprano Alto Tenor
                                 Monitors

Advantages:
- Bassist and drummer close to one another
- Acoustical advantage with singers close together

Disadvantages:
- Instrumentalists cannot see singers
- Singers cannot see leader or eyes of instrumentalists

CURVED OR INVERTED V SET-UP

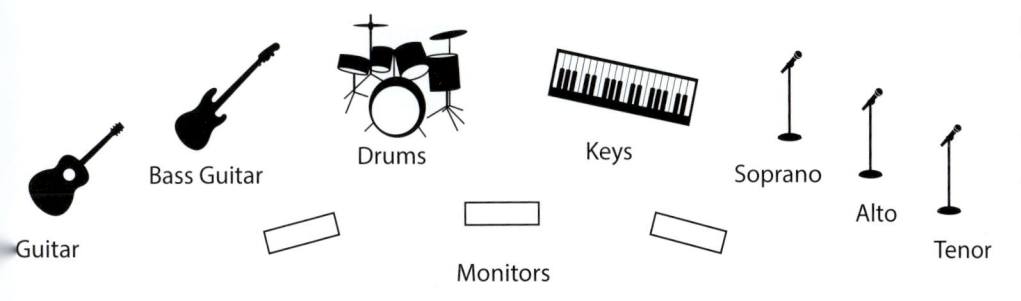

Guitar   Bass Guitar   Drums   Keys   Soprano   Alto   Tenor
                         Monitors

Advantages:
- Everyone can see leader (and give signals to team members)
- Everyone can see each other
- BONUS—The congregation can see everybody and everyone in the band can see the congregation

Everyone can see the leader (and his cues)

Whether set back on one side of the platform behind the brass band or clustered in front of the hall around the piano, both setups have the advantage of the musicians being able to hear one another, with singers in front, backed by the band. If the singers are looking out, they have no sightlines with the band, and particularly the leader if he is at the keyboard.

A compromise is to put the keyboard leader out to the side in line with the singers, angled out slightly to face the congregation, but allowing a sightline to all members of the worship team.

Digital keyboards take less space than acoustic grands and if the keyboard-leader stands, rather than sits, the sightlines are improved for the worship band and congregation alike. Most bass players prefer to stand to the right of the drums next to the ride cymbal, with their amp behind the drum stool. This helps lock in tempo. Sometimes they set up behind the pianist to read over his or her shoulder. In all cases, to avoid missing any visual cues, the sound technician needs to be able to see everyone.

Bass player to the right of ride cymbal with bass amp behind *drummer*

Keyboard player in line with singers' sightlines to *all members* of worship band

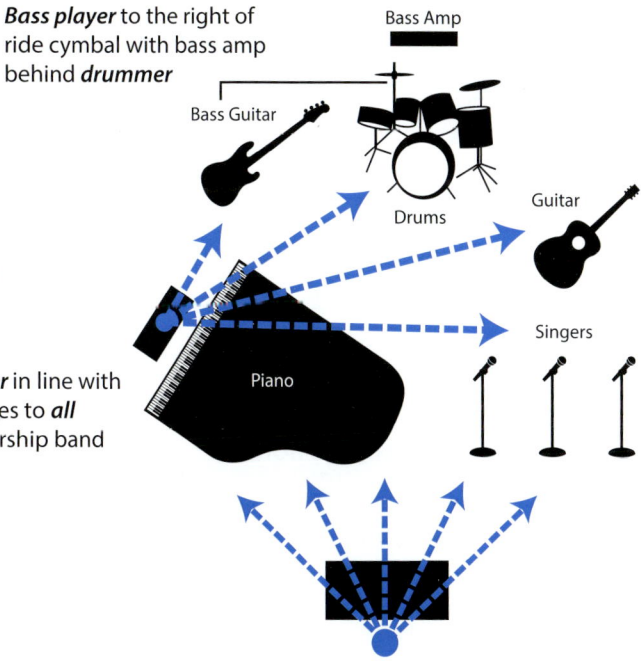

Soundman able to see *everyone*

The Beat Goes On

403

monitor speakers (*term*) \'mä - nə - tər 'spē - kərs\ sometimes known as stage monitors or foldback, are loudspeakers (typically on the floor in wedge-shaped cabinets) facing the stage performers during live or studio performances. The monitor sound is amplified by a power amp and may be produced on the same mixing console as the main (or house) mix for the audience, which emanates from **house speakers** facing the audience. The separate monitor mix is kept devoid of any effects or reverberation being added to the house mix to help the performers stay in tune and in sync. Use of **"in-ear" monitors** eliminates the often excessive amount of monitor mix emanating from the stage.

MONITOR MIX

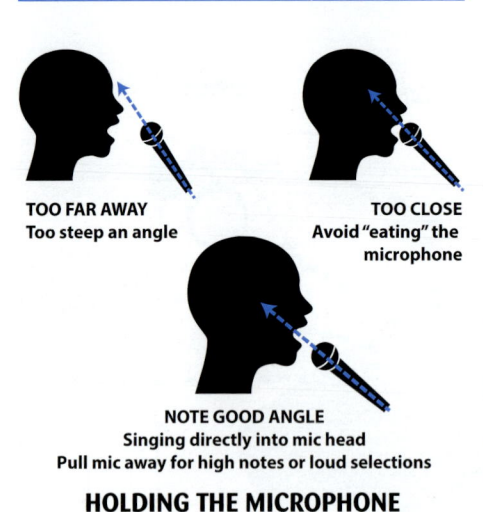

TOO FAR AWAY
Too steep an angle

TOO CLOSE
Avoid "eating" the microphone

NOTE GOOD ANGLE
Singing directly into mic head
Pull mic away for high notes or loud selections

HOLDING THE MICROPHONE

SOUND, SOUND, SOUND!

The effective sound check

An old-fashioned stereo mix would clearly emanate from two very directional speakers, and one could distinguish sound left from right. The basic premise of today's contemporary sound reinforcement, however, has sound radiating throughout the room. The goal is to have great sound in all corners of the room, including for the musicians on the platform. A prideful sound person can blare decibels, but if congregants cannot hear themselves singing, **they will cease to sing!** Herein lies the difference between mastering a concert and facilitating sound for worship: Everyone is asking, "Can I hear myself?" Ironic, isn't it? A room full of sound with multiple voices singing *to* God, but many ask, "Can I hear *myself*?"

We are going to assume that over time your worship band and the sound person have settled on a stage set-up. Setting levels is best worked through on a rehearsal night with a quick check on Sunday morning. An efficient sound check begins with an understanding that there will be no talking or warming up as the engineer goes through the following steps, speaking through the monitor system from a microphone at his or her console.[1]

Step 1: House speakers down and off/Monitor speakers up
Be sure first that the vocalists and then the instrumentalists can hear themselves in their monitors. Keep the house speakers off to isolate the monitors for the stage musicians so that you won't advertise your sound check to the entire building. The monitor mix will be fine-tuned as you go along. This step is to make sure that there is sound emanating from all monitors.

Step 2: Individual singers at the mics
Have the vocalists, one by one, sing into their microphone at a similar dynamic level and from the location where they will be for the worship service. Ask if they can hear themselves in the monitor. Be sure the singer is positioned properly on the mike (as though holding an ice cream cone).

Step 3: All singers singing together
Have the vocalists render an *a cappella* passage. Make sure they can each hear clearly. Most of the time vocal intonation issues in a sound mix can be attributed to not being able to hear oneself and the other singers.

Step 4: Instrumentalists individually
Have individual instrumentalists play a phrase. Players are looking to hear themselves either in the monitors (at the keyboard) or from their own amplifiers (for instance, bass and guitar players). Remind members to not play or tune while others complete the sound check.[2]

SINGERS' MIX

Step 5: All instrumentalists together
Have the worship leader count off a spot where everyone plays. Listen for a balance between the members of the band. One player should not overpower another. Everyone should be able to hear themselves in the mix. Typically the keyboardist and drummer can hear the bass and guitar from their amps. The keyboardist needs to hear himself in the keyboard monitor. Drummers can positively affect the balance by using hot rods, wire, and plastic brushes, as well as sticks, to give more subtle effects and not drown out the band or congregation. If a stage or room is acoustically quite live, or if the drum set is next to a hard surface wall, then a drum shield or booth should be considered to contain the sound.

Step 6: Now bring all players and singers together
Use a section of a song that reaches a full dynamic to be sure of the blend in the monitors. Vocalists will need to hear the piano, in particular, in their monitor mix. Once these levels are established, have the sound person ease the house speakers up and set this level and balance. We cannot emphasize enough that a worship band that has been set too loud discourages congregational singing. One rationale for the increased use of in-ear monitors[3] is the reduction of on-stage sound emanating from the instrumentalists, which can negatively overwhelm the vocals, and most importantly, the worshiping congregation. The difficulty is entrusting the sound engineer with mixing in just enough of the essential elements, yet still allowing the vocalists and musicians to hear the congregation.

A "balancing" act

- ☑ **The musicians on stage** need to remember that what they are hearing on stage and what the engineer hears is completely different.

- ☑ **The vocalists and band** need to learn to trust the engineer to control the various elements of sound.

- ☑ **The engineer** needs to remember that the worship team is there to provide accompaniment to congregational singing. If the monitor mix is "hot" from the stage, or the house speakers are so high that you can't hear the congregation singing, then the band is too loud.[4]

SING, SING, SING

Making adjustments on stage
Fix the mix
Once a performance begins, sound levels can go askew. If musicians want the person controlling sound to adjust their volume, they should look directly toward the engineer. He "looks" for the sound technician (sometimes with a hand gesture toward his monitor or by motioning up or down). Both instrumentalists and vocalists need to be as discreet

The view from the sound booth.

as possible with these signals so as to not distract from the worship. This means the engineer, especially on an opening tune, needs to watch the band carefully.

By visually scanning the musicians, a good engineer can tell when things are not right on stage. If he senses a problem or gets a prompt from one of the musicians, the engineer can patch into the monitor mix via headphones to figure out what is *not* happening. The actual house mix that the congregation is getting is entrusted to the hands (and ears) of the engineer, who is strategically placed out in the room (not in an isolated sound booth.)

Unless a practice is dedicated solely to lyrics, the sound engineer should be present at all worship team rehearsals. The frenetic pace of Sunday mornings permits only a quick sound check. Set-up and levels are best accomplished during the weekly rehearsals. This is also an opportunity for the sound person to get to know the flow of the playlist and the adjustments to make between different songs.

Signals and cues

Like instrumentalists in ensembles or singers in choirs, team members will look for signals or cues from their "conductor." The song leader should learn to conduct pauses and changes in tempo, as well as a few other hand gestures to signal a repeated line, addition, or subtraction of instruments [A]. Direction is needed to start and end songs, especially at transitions. Often the leader will establish a new tempo or style from her instrument and then nod to bring the singers in.

Many worship leaders borrow from the gospel tradition and anticipate the next verse or repeated line by speaking or singing over the last note of a verse or chorus. This engenders energy and excitement, but also serves as a verbal reminder to the media person and the team as to what should come up next. In a practical way, even if the media person doesn't quite get the next cue on time, the congregation has already been fed the words.[5]

Heads-up

For times when a change of course may be necessary, a gospel choir circular motion [B] can mean, "We are going to repeat back to a verse." A cupped hand "C" [C] is a standard signal for repeating the chorus. A closed fist [D] conveys that "we will wrap it up soon." Just as a conductor pauses and gives a preparation before his cutoff, the leader turns toward the band, lifts his head, guitar or arm, pauses [E], and then brings down for a clear cutoff [F]. All of these gestures need to be understood by the tech crew as well, assuring that the corresponding visual images and text come up correctly.

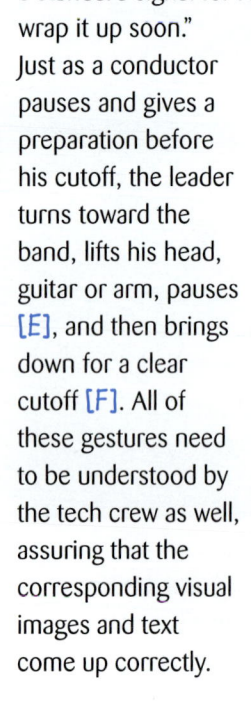

See Chapter Five—The Song Leader, pp. 109–111, for a helpful discussion on projected images.

Shifting gears

Before the advent of projected words and the addition of soundboards to our chapels, an "unplugged" song leader could veer off-script and invoke the assistance of a pianist, without being deemed inconsiderate or unprofessional. Many of today's congregations have become accustomed to respond to what comes up on the screen. The worship leader needs to have the freedom to **skip to the next song** on the pre-planned playlist. The media person will discreetly shift ahead a few slides. When *adding a song*, a simple introduction can give the media person and the musicians time to locate the lyrics and music.

Disclosing possible **additional chorus titles** beforehand to the musicians and tech folks helps facilitate the freedom to move in the Spirit. This flexibility is not unlike the interaction between a preacher and prayer meeting pianist. There are times when chorus ideas that ideally encapsulate what God is saying to His people on that day may come to a preacher or worship leader in the moment, either from a Scripture text or a point in a sermon.

19 BARS REST

Create time for your worship team to watch themselves on video replay from a recent service. (You can even bring popcorn!) Another possibility is to record the mix that is going through the board and play it back. As the leader, review this playback before it is shown to the group. This creates an opportunity to not only hear the notes, but to discuss the visual cues and body language. The group may need to review the recording two or three times to observe everything that is going on. It is equally important to take the opportunity to affirm the positive aspects of what you see or hear. Watch carefully that eyes are not wandering, but rather reaching out to the congregation, up and out of the music.

CHORDS, CHORDS, AND MORE CHORDS!

The worship team's harmonic toolbox

A sampling of a series of chords is usually enough for us to decipher the style of a piece. Perhaps too often, it becomes a turn-off for a listener or worshiper. How does this work? A series of chords suggests harmonic principles (I hesitate to call them rules), which we intuitively absorb over the years through our listening. These harmonic tendencies have successfully traversed centuries of music history, even up to today. We take for granted the system of major and minor keys, use of the circle of fifths, or nuances, such as suspensions, which bring tension and release to the musical commentary.

For many worship band musicians, these "tendencies" in harmony are absorbed through listening and playing, rather than through exercises in music theory or harmonic practice. *For those on the worship team who will select playlists and arrange the sequence of instrumentation, there is great value in becoming students of chords and how they define the style of an arrangement.*

Expanding your vocabulary of chords grants your worship team greater creative license and a wider stylistic sweep. This section augments the worship team's harmonic toolbox

DETOUR ➡

Readers who are primarily interested in effectively singing vocals may skip past the discussion of chord symbols (pp. 407–411), and chording on guitar (pp. 412–414), and move on to the **"HOW TO SING HARMONIES"** section (pp. 415–419).

The Beat Goes On

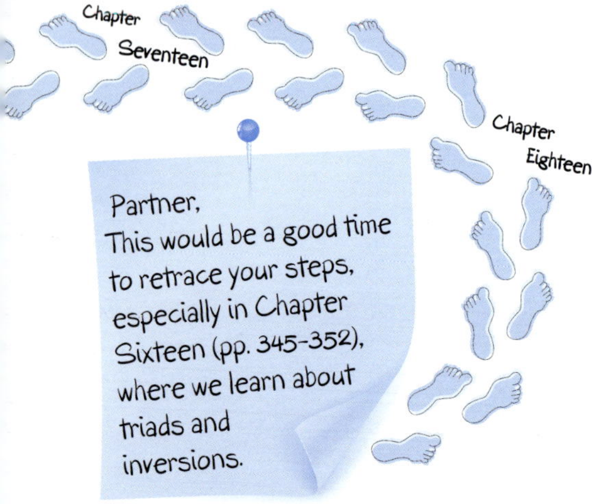

Partner,
This would be a good time to retrace your steps, especially in Chapter Sixteen (pp. 345-352), where we learn about triads and inversions.

by summarizing four broad categories related to the use and practice of chords in today's contemporary Christian music:[6]

- Basic principles of reading and hearing "chord changes"
- Chording on the guitar
- Knowing how and when to add (+) or subtract (-) to "plain Jane" chords
- Learning how to sing characteristic harmonies in three styles: gospel, rock, and contemporary worship

The "how-to" of chord symbols

The basic principles of triads, chords, their inversions, substitutions, and modulation are considered in Chapters Sixteen and Seventeen. We have reserved an explanation of the shorthand of chord changes for this section, as it is the universally understood language for guitar, bass, and keyboard players alike.[7]

Chord types 101

CHORD TYPE	SHORTHAND	INTERVAL STEP			STACKED THIRDS	SAMPLE IN "C"
Major	none* or M	1	3	5	major, minor	C - E - G
minor	m	1	♭3	5	minor, major	C - E♭ - G
diminished	° or dim	1	♭3	♭5	minor, minor	C - E♭ - G♭
augmented	+ or aug	1	3	♯5	major, major	C - E - G♯
suspended	4, sus or sus4	1	4	5	P4, major 2	C - F - G

*A chord noted in CAPITAL letters is assumed to be major unless otherwise indicated. For instance, D = D major, or B♭ = B♭ major, but Dm = D minor, or B♭° = B♭ diminished.

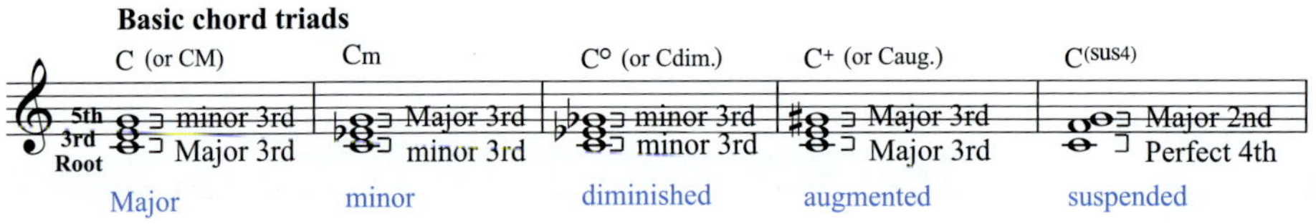

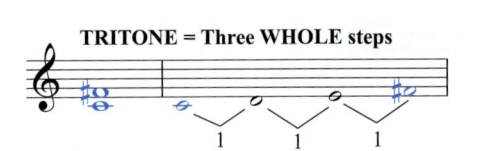

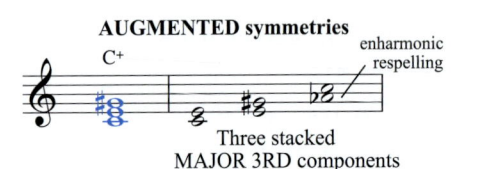

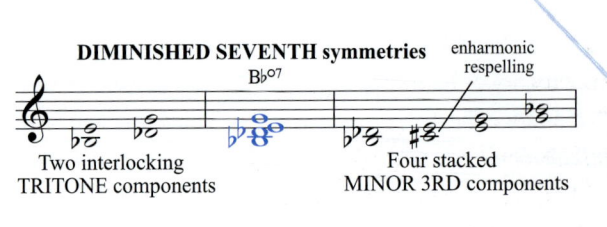

Basic chord triads

TRITONE = Three WHOLE steps

AUGMENTED symmetries
C+
Three stacked MAJOR 3RD components
enharmonic respelling

DIMINISHED SEVENTH symmetries
B♭°7
Two interlocking TRITONE components
Four stacked MINOR 3RD components
enharmonic respelling

Chords with sevenths

In Chapter Seventeen—The Meeting Pianist's Toolbox, pp. 367-368, we considered four chords **with the seventh added**, perhaps best understood from the music notation below the reference chart on the next page. When we examine the seventh chords built on the steps of a major scale, we find the **I** and **IV** to be major seventh chords; the ii, iii and vi to be minor sevenths; the **V** to be a dominant seventh; and the vii to be diminished seventh, thus the Roman numerals indications under the chord type.

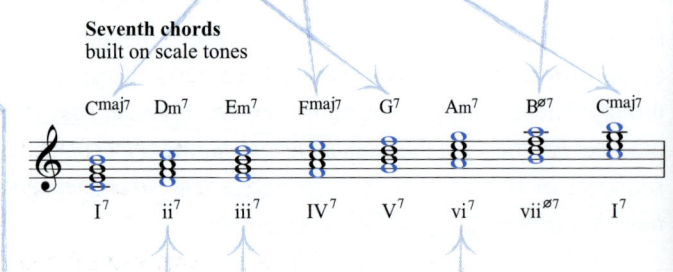

Seventh chords built on scale tones

Cmaj7 Dm7 Em7 Fmaj7 G7 Am7 Bø7 Cmaj7

I7   ii7   iii7   IV7   V7   vi7   viiø7   I7

SEVENTH CHORD	SHORT-HAND	STEPS	TRIAD + SEVENTH	SAMPLE IN "C"
Major seventh I7 IV7	maj7 (or △7)	1 3 5 7	major triad + major 7th	C - E - G - B
Dominant seventh V7	V7	1 3 5 ♭7	major triad + minor 7th	C - E - G - B♭
Minor seventh ii7, iii7, vi7	m7	1 ♭3 5 ♭7	minor triad + minor 7th	C - E♭ - G - B♭
Half-diminished seventh viiø7	m7♭5 (or Ø7)	1 ♭3 ♭5 ♭7	diminished triad (minor 3rd + flat 5th) + minor 7th	C - E♭ - G♭ - B♭
Diminished seventh vii°7	°7	1 ♭3 ♭5 ♭♭7	diminished triad (minor 3rd + flat 5th) + diminished 7th (or double flat 7th)	C - E♭ - G♭ - B♭♭

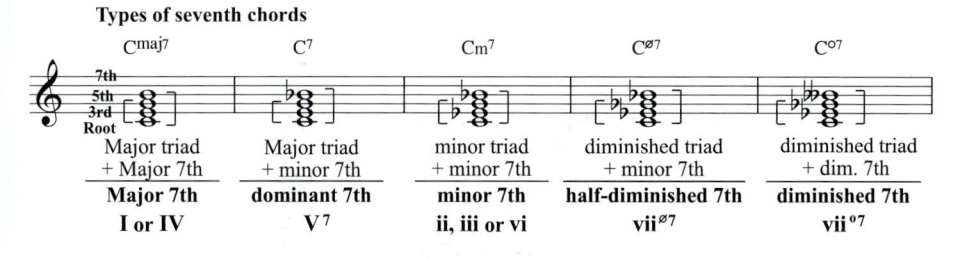

Types of seventh chords

- C^maj7 — Major triad + Major 7th — **Major 7th** — I or IV
- C7 — Major triad + minor 7th — **dominant 7th** — V7
- Cm7 — minor triad + minor 7th — **minor 7th** — ii, iii or vi
- Cø7 — diminished triad + minor 7th — **half-diminished 7th** — viiø7
- C°7 — diminished triad + dim. 7th — **diminished 7th** — vii°7

Inversions and slash notation

In Chapter Sixteen we also examined the **inversion of triads**, taking the bottom note of the triad and placing it above the others, which creates musical interest (see "Bye, Bye to Boring Block Chords," pp. 348–352). **In chord symbol notation, this process is much simplified as the note to be played as the bottom bass note is designated under or beside the chord** (C/E). Bass guitar players and keyboardists should be made well aware of this so that both are playing the same bass note, creating a musically satisfying inversion (C7/E). In some cases, the bass note might not be a chord tone found in the basic triad. Examples include Cm/F or the useful chord to modulate to the key of F: B♭/C.

Slash notation (chord/bass note)
C/E   C/G   C7/E   C/F   B♭/C

Beyond sevenths

Some songs will stack **an additional chord tone** beyond sevenths, which technically are labeled 9th, 11th, and 13th chords. Note that most additions to basic chords involve the dominant 7th chord: C7(9), C7(♭9). No third would be included in the C7(sus4). A C maj9 includes the major 7th. An add 9 chord would be a C major triad with added 9, no seventh. Playing through these extension chords, your ear will guide you through these conventions.

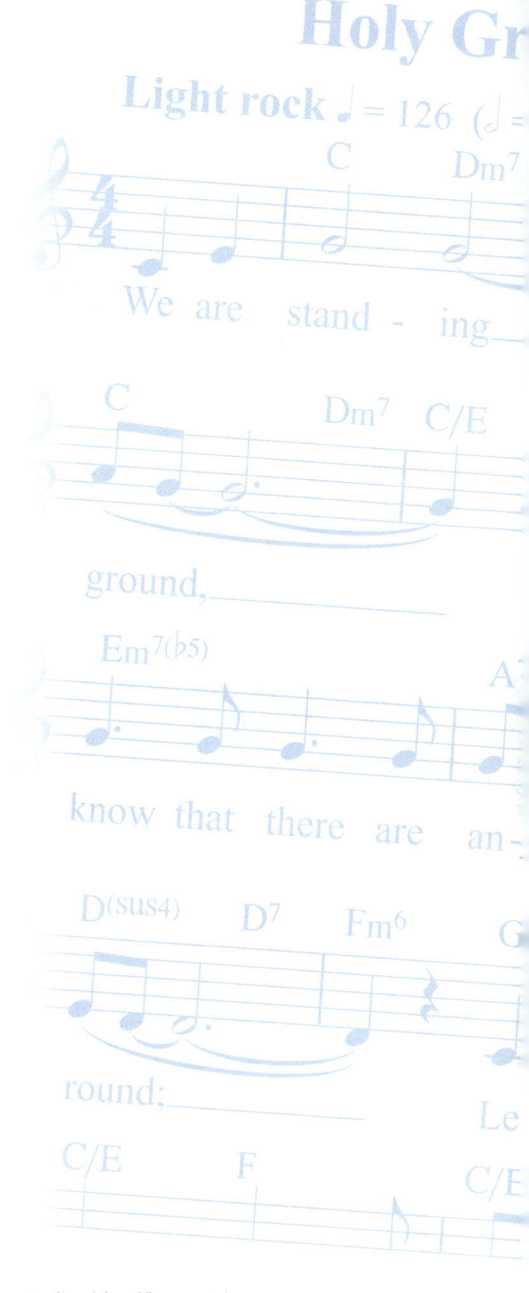

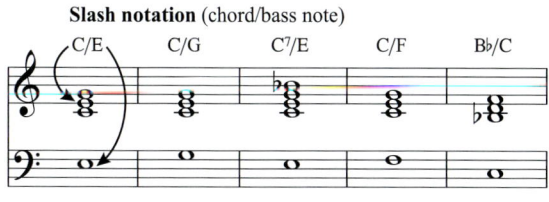

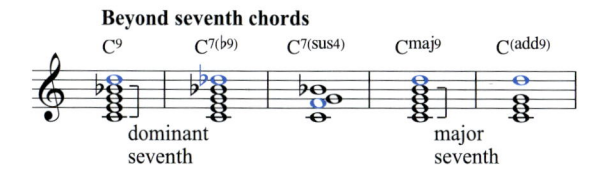

Beyond seventh chords
C9 — C7(♭9) — C7(sus4) — Cmaj9 — C(add9)
dominant seventh   major seventh

Chord tones "color" the style

In contemporary worship music today, the most prevalent chords are probably the **added 9th** (sometimes known as sus2 or sus9), **the minor 7th**, and **IV/V chords** [A]. The **major 7th chord** [B] suggests a jazz or 70s feel. For most upbeat worship music, a few simple **open fifth "power chords"** [C] permeate. In contrast, a slower piece allows time for more subtle, complex progressions of chords away from their tonal center, many times following the **familiar circle of fifths** pattern [D]. When the worship music is influenced by an ethnic expression, the proper chord choice is legislated by that style of music. For instance, minor keys characterize Hebrew-influenced songs, such as *King of Kings* [E] or *Jehovah-Jireh*. The Celtic trend favors open chording and pentatonic scales, in songs such as *Jesus Be the Center* and *In Christ Alone* [F]. The Caribbean sound is based in major keys and full triads, as found in *What the Lord has Done* or *Teach Me to Dance* [G].

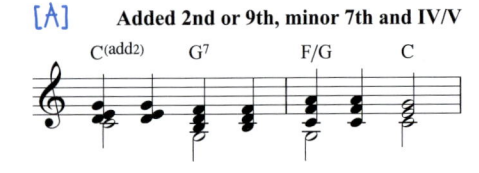

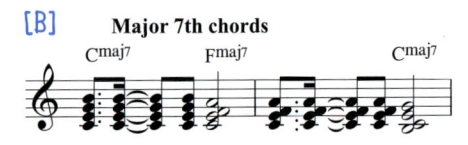

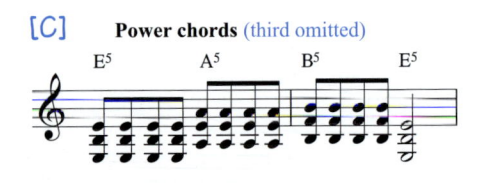

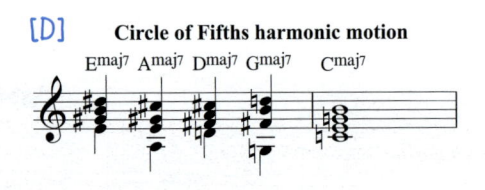

Did you say practice?

Like the church organist or pianist who learns to sight-read and elaborate on hymns based on the hymnal guide, one cannot emphasize enough the practicing of a series of chord changes (and in a variety of keys!). Irving Berlin had a transposing piano made for him, so he could write his songs mostly playing on the black keys in the key of Gb or F#. In today's pop scene, apparently Stevie Wonder favors Eb minor, while his bass player detunes a half step, playing in the "sharp" key of E minor.[8]

One of the problems with key choice is that most guitarists like the sharp-side keys of G, D, A, E, and even B, much to the keyboardist's dismay. Meanwhile many pianists favor the flat-side keys of Eb, Ab, and Db, which guitarists avoid. The guitarist preference for sharp keys rests partly in the use of less fingering per chord, but primarily because the open strings have the best ring, with an E major chord being the strongest sounding chord a guitarist can play.[9] Rather than transposing via a keyboard, transpose function key, or a guitar capo, how much more useful for keyboardists and guitarists to discipline themselves to "walk their hands—and ears" into less familiar keys!

Practice chord sequences in many keys. A good way to practice is using a pop song fake book, which will have an extensive range of chords and keys. Presumably you'll have some idea of how the songs are supposed to sound [H]. Also shuffle "flash cards" and practice chord changes in different sequences.

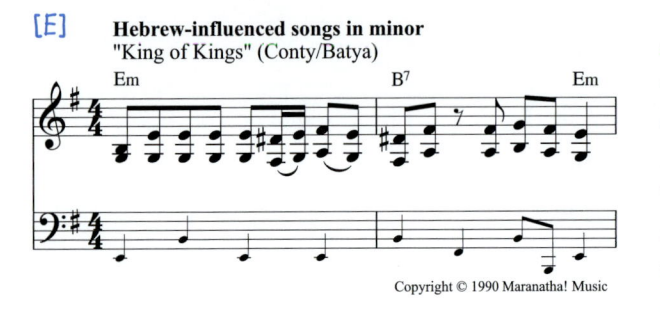

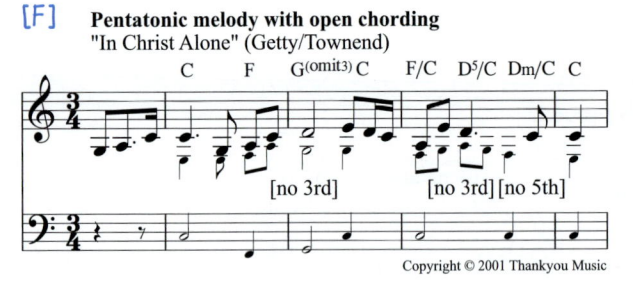

These examples of **piano stylings** are demonstrated in the Chapter Nineteen online folder.

[H] **Fake book pop standards**
"Somewhere over the Rainbow" (Harburg/Arlen)

| Eb | Cm | Gm | Eb7 | Ab | Abmaj7 Ab7 | Gm7 Eb Gm7 E° |

Some - where   o - ver the rain - bow   way   up   high,

Copyright Renewal © 1966 Metro-Goldwyn-Mayer and Leo Feist

Hearing the color of chords

As you practice chords, become familiar with their individual color and their "best behavior." Major chords are said to be "happy and heroic," while minor chords "sad and lonely." Diminished (to make smaller) chords spell "suspense," while augmented (to increase the fifth) chords are more "dreamy." Both are unstable and need to go somewhere.

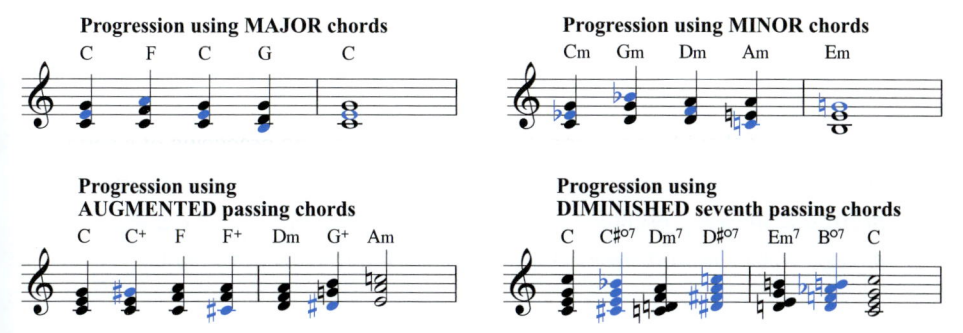

Progression using MAJOR chords
C F C G C

Progression using MINOR chords
Cm Gm Dm Am Em

Progression using AUGMENTED passing chords
C C+ F F+ Dm G+ Am

Progression using DIMINISHED seventh passing chords
C C#°7 Dm7 D#°7 Em7 B°7 C

Likewise, suspended chords are pulling to a more stable chord. Listen for the chord progression that brings a sense of finality. Usually the sus number gives you a clue (sus9 resolves to 8, sus4 to 3 and sus2 to 1).

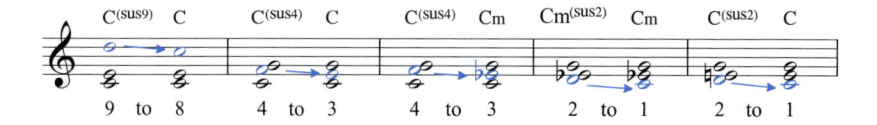

C(sus9) C   C(sus4) C   C(sus4) Cm   Cm(sus2) Cm   C(sus2) C
9 to 8   4 to 3   4 to 3   2 to 1   2 to 1

The major seventh has a much brighter glow than its dominant seventh (V7) cousin, which has a strong tendency to resolve to the tonic home chord (I) or alternatively turnabout to the minor vi chord. The minor seventh (ii7) often acts as a suitable substitution for IV.

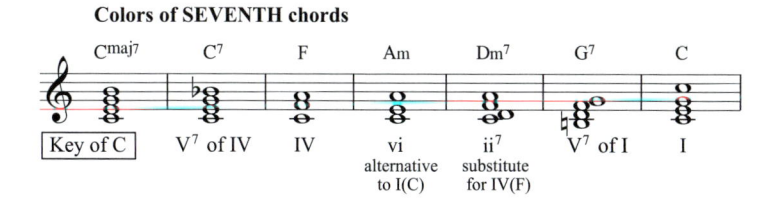

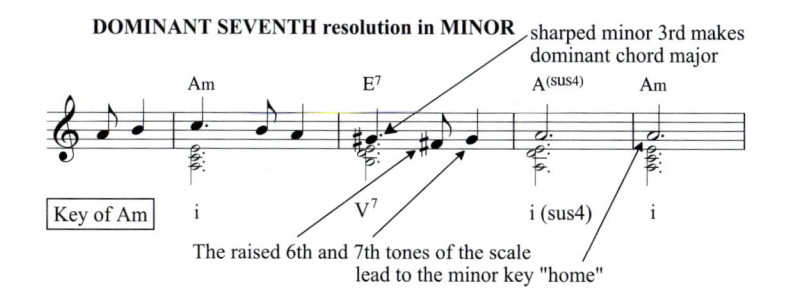

Colors of SEVENTH chords

Cmaj7	C7	F	Am	Dm7	G7	C
Key of C	V7 of IV	IV	vi alternative to I(C)	ii7 substitute for IV(F)	V7 of I	I

DOMINANT SEVENTH resolution in MINOR

sharped minor 3rd makes dominant chord major

Am E7 A(sus4) Am

Key of Am: i   V7   i (sus4)   i

The raised 6th and 7th tones of the scale lead to the minor key "home"

For keyboard players looking for more instruction on **playing chords**, refer to Chapter Sixteen - Keyboard Basics. See Appendix 16.5 for instruction on **How To Play from a Lead Sheet.**

CHORDING ON GUITAR

Basic guitar chords

Most songbooks and hymnals that indicate chord symbols stick to an elementary set of chords. They are all played below the fourth fret of the guitar, and most don't require more than three fingers.[10]

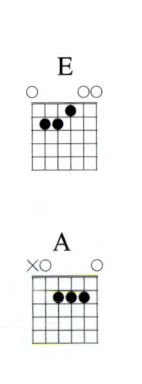

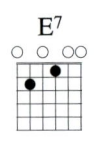

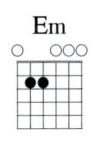

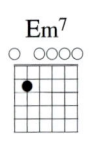

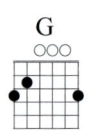

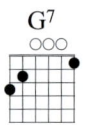

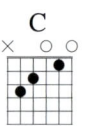

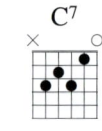

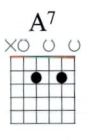

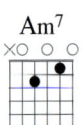

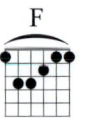

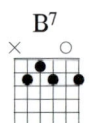

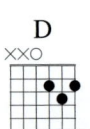

E   E⁷   Em   Em⁷   G   G⁷   C   C⁷

A   A⁷   Am   Am⁷   F   F⁷   B⁷   Bm

D   D⁷   Dm

Strings and frets:

The guitar chord boxes show the guitar fretboard in an upright position. The **horizontal lines** represent the **frets**. The **vertical lines** represent the **guitar strings**, which are from lowest/thickest (left) to highest/thinnest (right).

E-A-D-G-B-E
Elephants And Donkeys Grow Big Ears

Another way to view the six strings is from the floor going up, that is:

E-B-G-D-A-E
Every Boy Gets Dessert After Eating

Dots, numbers, Os and Xs, plus the nut:

The **dots** (or in some cases, **numbers**) indicate **where to place your fingers.** An **O** at the top of the chord chart indicates a **string that is played open** (meaning, no left-hand finger pressing on that string). The **X** above the chord chart indicates a **string that should not be played.**

Guitar fingering

STRINGS & FRETS

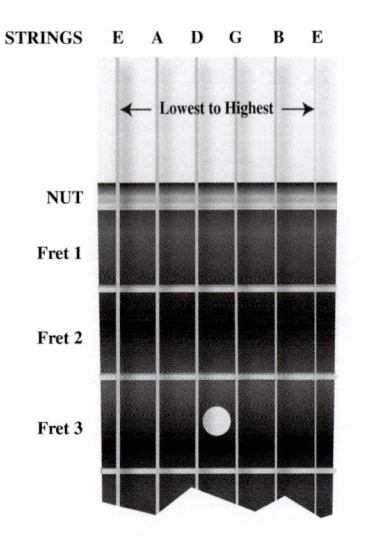

STRINGS: E A D G B E
← Lowest to Highest →
NUT
Fret 1
Fret 2
Fret 3

OPEN STRINGS O'S & X'S

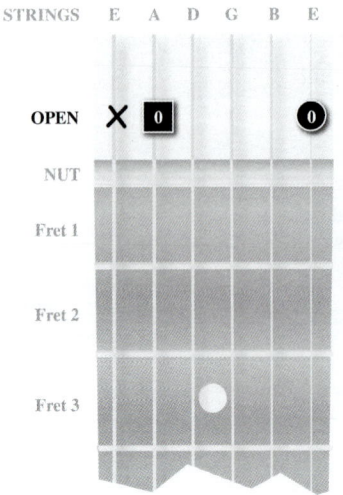

STRINGS: E A D G B E
OPEN: X 0   0
NUT
Fret 1
Fret 2
Fret 3

An **O** at the top of the chord chart indicates a string that is played open (meaning, no left-hand finger pressing on that string).

The **X** above the chord chart indicates a string that should not be played.

BAR & CIRCLE NUMBERS

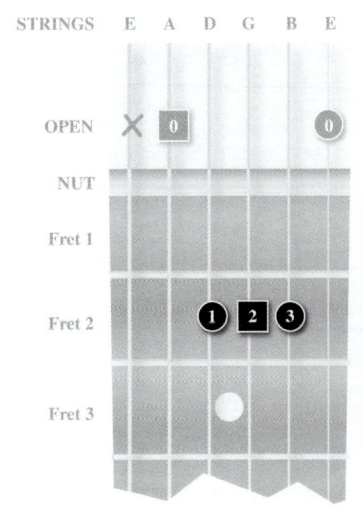

STRINGS: E A D G B E
OPEN: X   0
NUT
Fret 1
Fret 2: ① ② ③
Fret 3

The **circled** and **squared** dots show the notes to be played, with the numbers relating to the fingers that should fret the notes. Square notes indicate the "root" note. The index finger is finger 1, and the rest of the fingers follow in numerical order.

Chapter 19 | THE HOLY HASSLE OF ANOTHER SUNDAY

Fret numbers, bars, and circle numbers
Where the chord is to be played farther down the neck, the fret number is shown to the left of the diagram. Where a bar appears between notes the specified finger should hold down the notes across the strings shown. The circled numbers show the notes to be played, with the numbers relating to the fingers that should fret the notes.[11]

Bar chords
Bar chords get their name because you use the index finger to hold down all six strings at once, thus preventing or "barring" each of the strings from sounding any lower notes. Bar chords are ideal for power chords, which were created in rock music to accommodate a much less muddied effect with guitar distortion.[12] The advantage of learning bar chords is that once you know eight of them, you can use them in any key![13]

Bar chord

> **power chord** (*term*) \'pau - ər - 'kord\ A combination of tones using the bass note of the chord and the fifth (C-G), leaving out the third found in conventional chords (C-E-G) Sometimes the bass note is doubled an octave above (C4-G4-C5). With the advent of distortion and effects for electric guitars, normal open chords sounded fuzzy and complicated, while the truncated power chord sounded full, without the middle note of the triad. The guitarist needs only use the bottom two strings to play a power chord, which is easier than facilitating the whole hand to play a conventional chord.

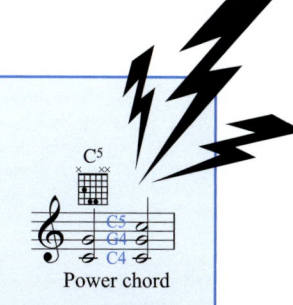

Power chord

Use of the Capo
Another alternative that guitarists have at their disposal is the use of a capo. (Interestingly, capo is pronounced cape-po in the US and cap-po in the UK.) The capo is a device which locks across a fret of the guitar, stopping all strings at the desired fret, thereby raising the pitch by a number of half steps without requiring a change in fingering by the player. The "pincher" type capo locks across a fret of your guitar quickly and can be installed with one hand. It can be placed on the head of your guitar until you need to make the quick transition. You should be able to hold a chord with your left hand and reach around with your right hand to grab and install the capo.

The capo instruction can be found in the left-hand corner of the song or chord sheet, and is especially useful for "unfriendly" guitar keys (mostly, the flats). **Capo 3(C)**, for example, means place the capo at the third fret and play the simple chords in the parentheses. Like Irving Berlin's famous transposing piano, you are "playing" your guitar in C, but it is actually sounding in Eb. Capo chording is generally limited to ten chords: C, D, Dm, E, Em, F, G, A, Am, and B7.[14]

See Appendix 19.1 for MAP Guitar curriculum (six levels). Also valuable for young learners is the MAP Ukulele curriculum (Beginner Levels Primer and One only).

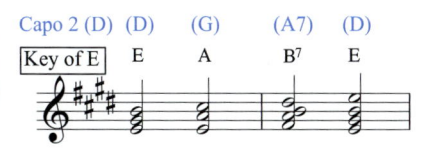

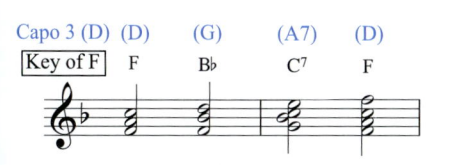

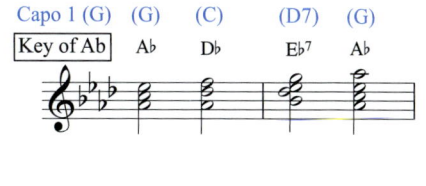

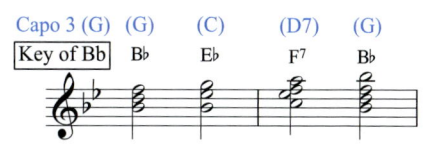

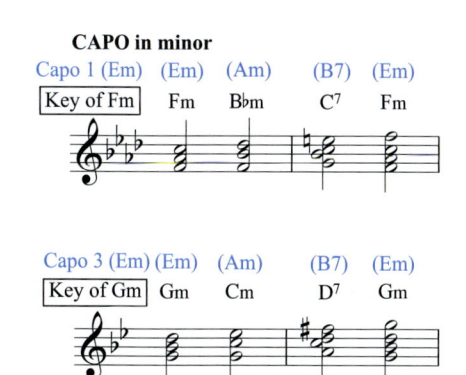

Power chord

Capo

Use of the CAPO
Capo 1 (D) (D) (G) (A7) (D)
Key of Eb Eb Ab Bb7 Eb

Place the capo on the first fret.
You play in D and the guitar sounds in Eb.

Capo 2 (D) (D) (G) (A7) (D)
Key of E E A B7 E

Capo 1 (G) (G) (C) (D7) (G)
Key of Ab Ab Db Eb7 Ab

CAPO in minor
Capo 1 (Em) (Em) (Am) (B7) (Em)
Key of Fm Fm Bbm C7 Fm

Capo 3 (D) (D) (G) (A7) (D)
Key of F F Bb C7 F

Capo 3 (G) (G) (C) (D7) (G)
Key of Bb Bb Eb F7 Bb

Capo 3 (Em) (Em) (Am) (B7) (Em)
Key of Gm Gm Cm D7 Gm

The Beat Goes On

Inversion and sus chords[15]

Inversion chords are chords in which the bass note is different from the root of the chord. **The chord is to the left of the slash and the bass note is on the right.** In the example below, Eb/Db means an Eb chord (Eb-G-Bb) is played over a Db bass tone.

In a *sus4 chord*, the major 3rd is being replaced by the 4th. *Without the 3rd,* the chord is neither a major or minor, but rather *"suspends" the listener until it is resolved, usually to the same chord with its 3rd.* The **sus2 chord** also substitutes the 2nd for the 3rd, and often can stand on its own, without a resolution to its neighborly 3rd, thereby working well as a substitution for major chords.

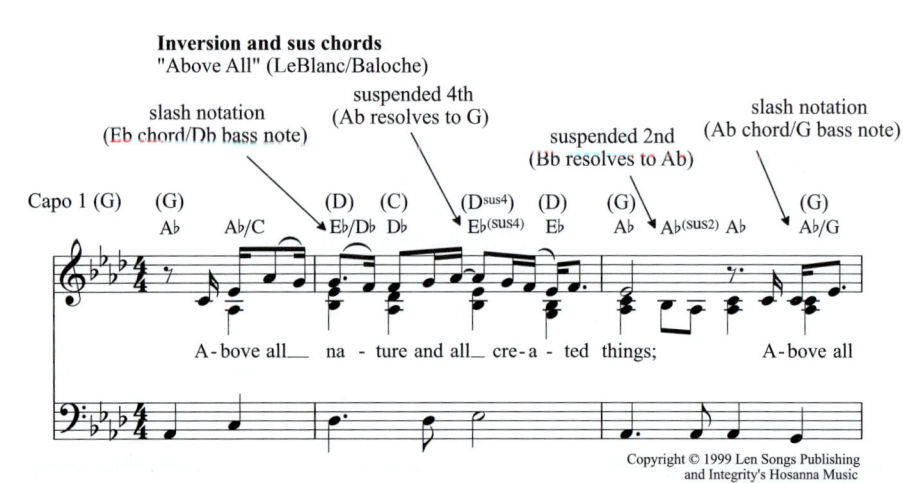

Inversion and sus chords
"Above All" (LeBlanc/Baloche)

Copyright © 1999 Len Songs Publishing and Integrity's Hosanna Music

19 BARS REST

Chording on Guitar

1. Before you bring any new chords into worship, be sure you can play them cleanly, perfectly, without thinking, and without hesitation (something my piano teacher called "without stuttering"). To accomplish this, make a stack of flash cards with a chord name on each card. Shuffle them and then spread the first few out and play through them in an absolutely steady rhythm using a metronome or drum machine. (Much can be said about a rhythm player who cannot keep time.)

2. When learning any musical skill, there is no substitute for developing motor memory by beginning your drill slowly, and then incrementally increasing the tempo. Do this for basic and bar chords, as well as with chords using the capo.

www.music.saconnects.org

HOW TO SING HARMONIES

Selecting singers for the worship team
Not all singers, even the best ones, should necessarily be on the platform leading worship. There is a place for the encouraging energy of quality, enthusiastic singing emanating from all quarters of the room. Further, being a vocalist on the worship team is not the place to commence your solo-singing career. You are part of a team. Last, and this is often difficult to grasp, the leader needs to select singers with a quick ear and memory, who can take the lead with singing, but also who can **harmonize in the background.**

For some worship leaders, this is the primary criterion for whether a singer is brought on a worship team. All the components that pertain to exemplary songster membership pertain to worship team singers. These include: preparedness, promptness, voice warmed-up, and good attention to diction, breath support, pitch, blend, and vocal production.

Harmonizing by ear
The piano chapters addressed pianists who function either with **or** without music. In the same manner, this toolbox section is designed to acquaint vocalists who read music, and those who don't, with **how to harmonize in a variety of pop styles**. Traditional SATB choral music is based on time-honored harmonic principles of voice-leading (also discussed in Chapter Sixteen, pp. 350). One important hallmark of the traditional voice-leading is avoiding parallel fifths and octaves through the use of contrary or oblique motion. Students of harmony have for centuries endured an onslaught of red pencil marks correcting these harmonic "errors."

Voices in parallel motion
Under the influence of a variety of cultural expressions around the turn of the 20th century, impressionist composers like Debussy and Ravel assimilated a now-familiar harmonic language, capitalizing on the once-banned **parallel motion**. The harmonies of 50s doo-wop groups, or 40s vocal groups such as the Andrew Sisters and The Mills Brothers were based primarily on triads moving in parallel motion. And these were preceded by the spirituals and songs based on the pentatonic (five-note/black notes on the piano) scale harmonies heard in African-American churches. Nashville arranger Dave Williamson explains it this way: **"The three voices start and remain bunched together in three-part harmony, moving in the same direction as the melody."**[16]

Demonstrations of these **vocal stylings** may be found in the Chapter Nineteen online folder.

Parallel, oblique and contrary motion
"Joyful, Joyful, We Adore Thee"

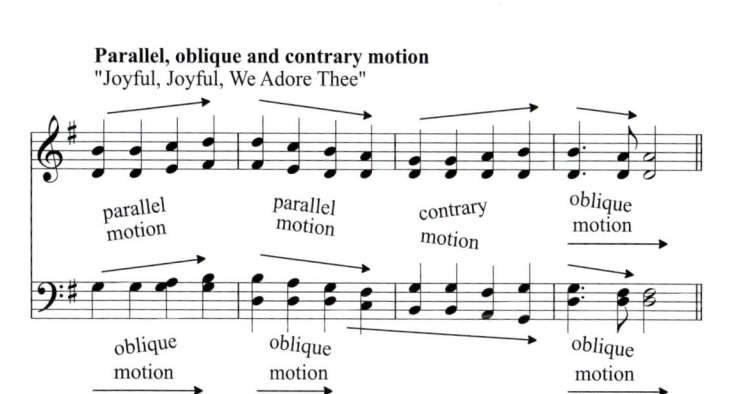

Voices in parallel motion
"Boogie Woogie Bugle Boy" as sung by The Andrews Sisters
He was a fa-mous trum-pet man out Chi-ca-go-way___ He

Music and Words by Don Raye and Hughie Prince
Copyright © 1943 Universal-MCA Music Publishing

African-American Spiritual
"Wade in the Water"
Em   Em/D   Cmaj7   Em/B   Am9   Am9/G   F#m7(b5)   B7(#5)
Wade in the wa-ter, wade in the wa-ter chil-dren,
[Voices in parallel motion]

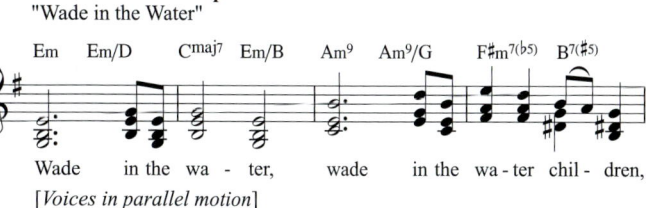

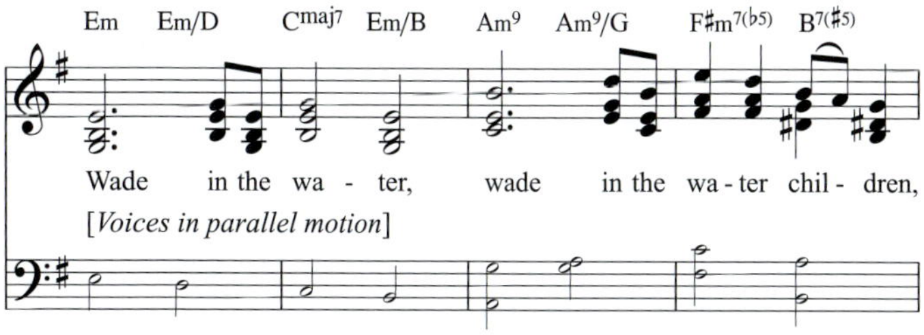

In a broad generalization, most black gospel and country music groups use three-part parallel chords. Rock music uses just one harmony note, often sung by a female, roughly in parallel motion over the male voice melody. To demonstrate this, we will show three ways to harmonize an elementary chord sequence, and then consider vocal harmonization in the gospel, rock, and contemporary worship styles using: **Four-part Traditional I-V-I Harmony**; **Three-part Gospel Harmony**; and **Two-part Rock Harmony**.

VASA (Sweden) Gospel Choir

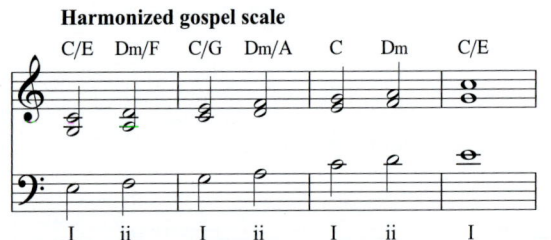

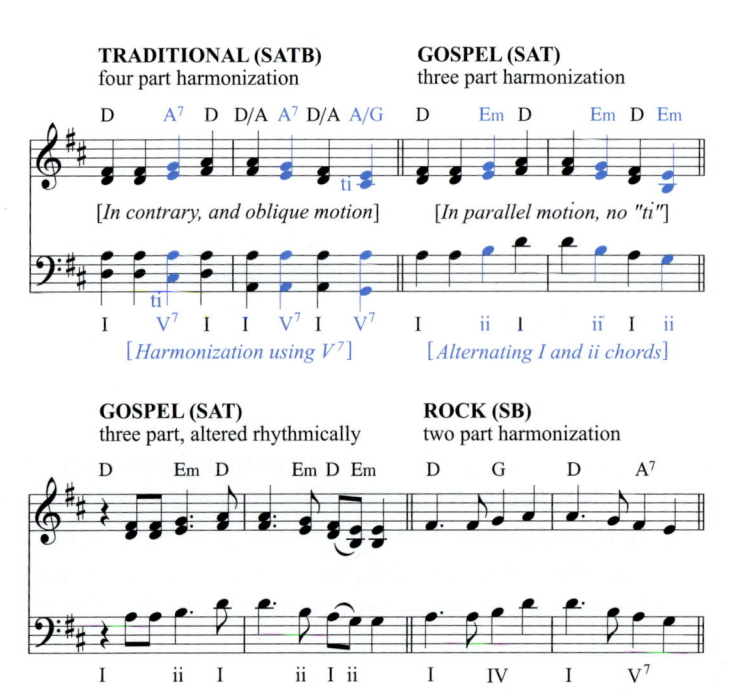

Gospel harmony

The scale that generates the characteristic gospel sound uses just six notes with the starting tone repeated at the octave. This means bypassing the seventh tone *(ti)* of our traditional major scale. The harmonization of this "Gospel Scale" also avoids any chords that use the seventh tone *(ti)* of the scale.

Gospel (and some country) artists intuitively assimilate this principle by ear. The Gospel Scale, always less the seventh, drives what we hear as gospel harmonies. To clarify, we contrast the traditional **V** chord harmonization, with the usual "gospel" substitution using the **ii** chord, which is the result of the elimination of the scale tone *"ti."* (Note that *"ti"* is the third of what would have been a **V** chord.) Thereby a basic gospel harmonization becomes as simple as an alternation between just two chords—the **I** and **ii** chords.

The soprano carries the melody in gospel music, accompanied in mostly parallel motion by altos just underneath them, again based on the scale, less *"ti"*. Under that are the men, mostly in a tenor/baritone range. I hesitate to call the male part a baritone part, because it usually falls in the male upper register. Any semblance of a traditional bass part has been eliminated in contemporary gospel music. If basses are used at all, they double the soprano melody down the octave.

Rock harmony

Songs in the rock idiom use a simple, no-frills diatonic (no added chromatics) melody, coupled with a streamlined set of chords. Note that *"ti"* is back. In contrast to gospel sounds, the typical rock vocal harmony is just two-part (with an occasional three-part passage). Harmonies at thirds and sixths are familiar in traditional music, and even classic pop. Thirds are occasionally employed, but ***rock harmonies for vocalists are based on open-voiced chords***, like open fifths. Arrangers in the rock style will often think in three–part harmony of the chord, and then delete the middle part to create the characteristic open rock sounds. The power chords that guitarists use in rock music are also open–voiced chords, usually based on two notes—the root and the fifth.

Traditional vocalization (SAB)

E
C♯m
A
E
Wak - ing___ or sleep - ing,___ thy___ pre - sence___ my light.

Rock open voicing (male harmony)

E5
C♯5
A5
E5
Wak - ing___ or sleep - ing,___ thy___ pre - sence___ my light.

Male lead rock version (female harmony)

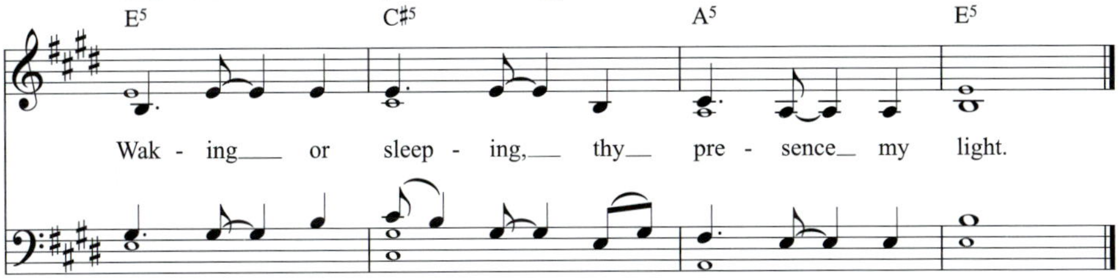
E5
C♯5
A5
E5
Wak - ing___ or sleep - ing,___ thy___ pre - sence___ my light.

Contemporary worship harmony

In contemporary worship, styling elements of parallelism are amalgamated with both open and traditional SATB voicing, while combining the influence of gospel, rock, and traditional choir harmonies. Therefore, ***the practice of voices moving in parallel motion may be interwoven with voices following the well-worn tenets of traditional SATB voice–leading***. Reflecting this eclectic mix of styles, basses can both have the traditional bass part that they long for, or sometimes may be asked to sing the lead melody down an octave, in gospel tradition. It is important that the sung bass part be in agreement with what the keyboard or bass guitarist is playing.

Contemporary worship choir (with optional bass)

E E/D♯ E/D C♯m Amaj7 F♯m7 F♯m/A A A(sus2) E
Wak - ing or___ sleep - ing,___ thy___ pre - sence my light.

Beyond harmonies: *Other stylistic considerations for singers*

The effective singer seeks to assimilate the influences, differences, and similarities of gospel, rock, and contemporary worship vocal stylings. In many ways, this can be a lifelong pursuit, not unlike the instrumentalist attempting to easily crisscross between the classics and jazz.

While it is an essential element, the music's harmonic language is only one portion of its stylistic footprint. Any attempt at a composite summary of the salient stylistic characteristics for singers must also include such interrelated things as vocal approach, technique, pronunciation, and rhythm. It is hard to imagine a gospel singer without a wide vibrato, a rock singer singing strictly on-the-beat, or a contemporary worship singer extending a long phrase. All three of these examples defy the characteristic sound of that style, and thereby would not ring true. The singer and worship team leader will benefit from listening for, and embracing, each of the elements included in the chart below and illustrated in the corresponding musical examples.

ELEMENTS of VOCAL STYLE

	GOSPEL	ROCK	GOSPEL + ROCK= CONTEMPORARY WORSHIP
HARMONY	• Three-part SAB (no *ti*) • Harmonies built of thirds and fourths (I-ii in place of I-V) • Occasional chromatic shifts • Bell tone pyramids	Two-part high male lead, low female harmony in simple open 5ths or occasional three-part SAB voicing	Occasional four-part SATB traditional voicings, or SAT voices in Gospel voicing, with a conventional bass line
PRONUNCIATION	Urban Southern USA	Conversational (Sing as you speak)	Conversational
VIBRATO	As much as a full step up and down	Very little vibrato	Some vibrato
TEXT PHRASING	Occasional split text or staccato phrasing	Shorter–held notes	Why so many breaths? Shortened phrases
RHYTHM	• Syncopation, a little behind the beat, never rushed • Occasional anticipation, where the note arrives before you expect it	• Altered rhythms rock syncopation, sung behind the beat • Delayed resolution (conversational phrasing)	Rhythmic groove
EFFECTS	Scoops, slides, rapid crescendo effects	Licks, elaborations Dancing around notes	High key puts men in upper register and ladies in low, often singing melody at same unison pitch
SOUND QUALITY	Energy and attack	Energetic, young, bright	Bright

Chapter 19 | THE HOLY HASSLE OF ANOTHER SUNDAY

GOSPEL vocalization (Three-part SAT)

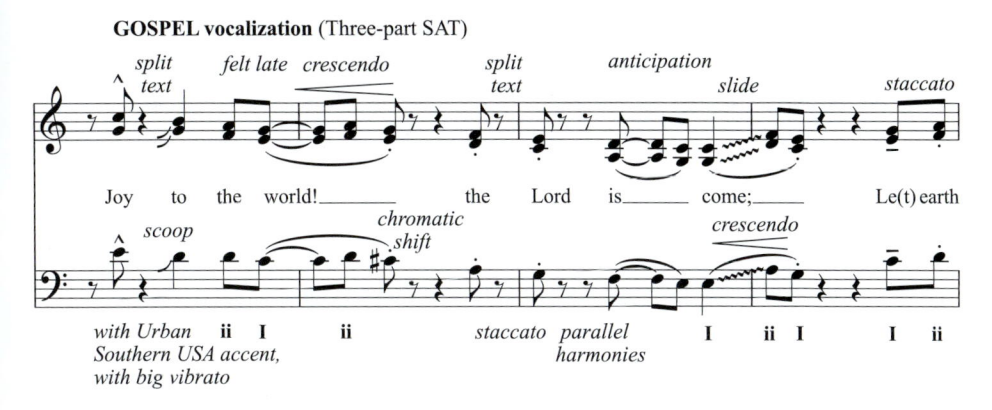

[Musical notation with annotations: split text, felt late, crescendo, split text, anticipation, slide, staccato; lyrics: "Joy to the world! the Lord is come; Le(t) earth"; scoop, chromatic shift, crescendo; with Urban Southern USA accent, with big vibrato; ii I ii staccato parallel harmonies I ii I I ii]

ROCK vocalization (Two-part SB)

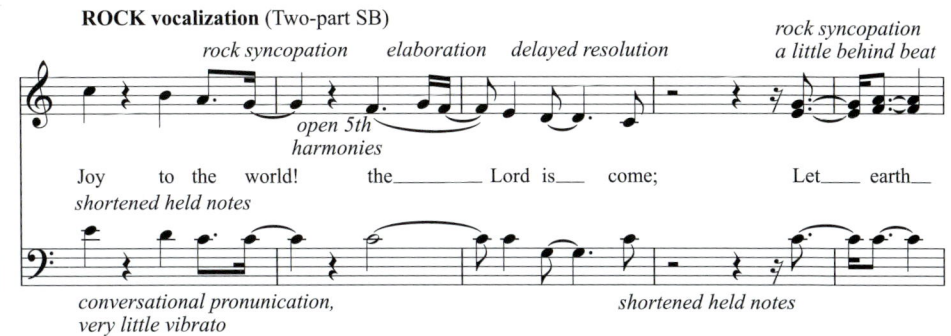

[Musical notation with annotations: rock syncopation, elaboration, delayed resolution, rock syncopation a little behind beat; lyrics: "Joy to the world! the Lord is come; Let earth"; shortened held notes; open 5th harmonies; conversational pronunciation, very little vibrato; shortened held notes]

WORSHIP vocalization (Four part SAT + B)

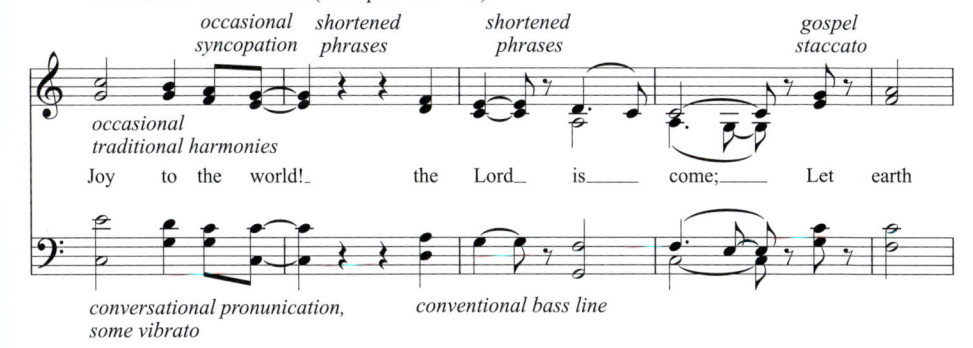

[Musical notation with annotations: occasional syncopation, shortened phrases, shortened phrases, gospel staccato; occasional traditional harmonies; lyrics: "Joy to the world! the Lord is come; Let earth"; conversational pronunciation, some vibrato; conventional bass line]

19 BARS REST

Beyond Garage Band Vocals

1. Vocalize random melodies while playing through a series of chord changes or looped sequence. This process helps the singer begin to imagine pitches that function well within the harmonic framework.

2. Just as instrumentalists play along with recordings to "lift" chord changes and riffs, so singers can learn much by "singing along" with the best singers. Don't forget to try and work out vocal harmonies as well.

The Beat Goes On

3. Much can be gleaned by singing in all kinds of choirs. The essential elements of posture, breathing, vocal technique, blend, and note-reading all help to equip singers.

4. Find a willing partner(s) and practice harmonizing melodies *a cappella* using parallel motion gospel, rock, or contemporary worship styles. Be sure to use any elements, such as vocal approach, vibrato, phrasing, pronunciation, effects, or sound quality, to make the performance stylistically convincing.

KNOWING WHEN TO SUBTRACT "−" FROM OR ADD "+" TO CHORDS

Keyboardists and/or guitarists can stylistically enrich the sounds of the chords they play by the strategic addition and subtraction of notes or combinations of notes. In this further survey of chord types, we consider added chord types that can work in conjunction with "plain Jane" chords. In other cases, they cannot coexist without a disturbing clash. For instance, a guitarist can play a G chord, while the keyboard player can play the richer sounding G major 7th chord. What often will not work is a guitarist using a Gsus4 chord, while the keyboardist plays a "plain Jane" G chord, as the sus4 tone clashes with the 3rd of the G chord.[17]

A word of caution in regard to chord and lead sheets: these chord symbols can be too simplified or inaccurate. Trust your ear on this. Sometimes you will want to change, add, or delete notes from chords. Make sure you come to these decisions before rehearsal, so that you can alert the other players with a minimum of discussion.[18]

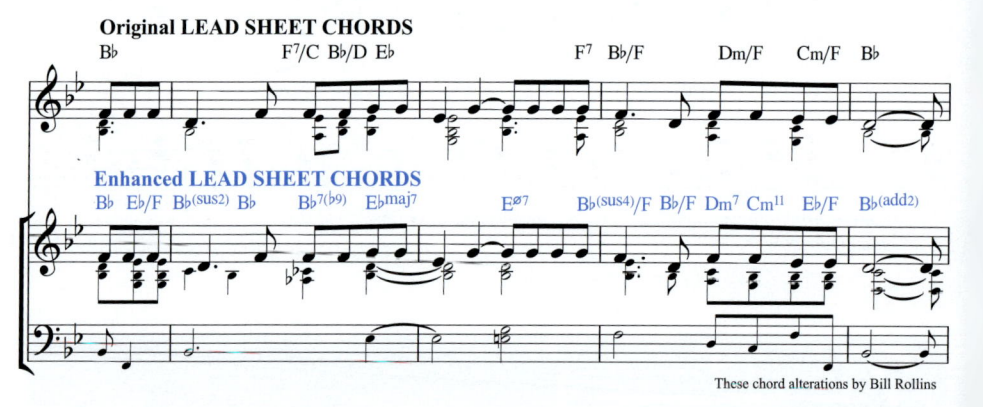

These chord alterations by Bill Rollins

Add to enhance chords

Simple additions to chords can help make the overall sound richer and stylistically more appropriate. This is particularly true in black gospel music where the vocalists use fairly simple harmonies, surrounded by jazz chords featuring added or altered tones. When chords do not fit well under the hands, try changing the inversion, by moving the bottom note of the chord to the top.

ADDING "+" to *MAJOR* chords

Most chord substitutions will sound fine when played on top of the simplified chords shown in fake books or printed chord charts. If you amp up a plain G chord by **adding a 2nd, 6th, or major 7th**, you should probably do it consistently throughout the song. Most additional notes can be tolerated on top of the plain chords. For instance, the guitarist can play a G chord while the keyboardist plays that G major 7 or dominant 7th chord.

Chapter 19 | THE HOLY HASSLE OF ANOTHER SUNDAY

Basic major chord	G	(G, B, D)	solid statement
+ major 2nd	G2	(G, A, B, D)	sounds richer, okay with G
+ major 6th	G6	(G, B, D, E)	country, show tunes
+ major 7th	Gmaj7	(G, B, D, F#)	more jazzy, smooth

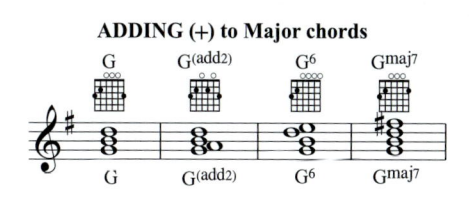

ADDING (+) to Major chords

ADDING " + " to MINOR chords

Written minor chord	Gm	(G, B♭, D)	bland
+ minor 2nd	Gm2	(G, A, B♭, D)	mysterious, for ballads
+ minor 7th	Gm7	(G, B♭, D, F)	country, older show tunes

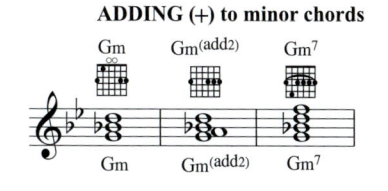

ADDING (+) to minor chords

ADDING " + " beyond SEVENTHS

Continuing to stack thirds allows us to **expand 7th chords to various 9th and 11th chords**. With these chords the keyboardist should play the root in the left hand and the other notes (the 3rd, 5th, 7th and 9th) will then fit under the right hand. Remember that the major 9 chord (Cma9) includes a major seventh. The minor 9 (Cm9) and 9th (C9) chords include a minor seventh.

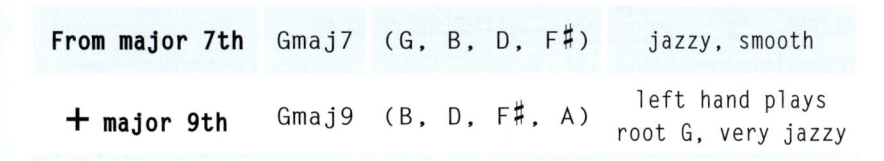

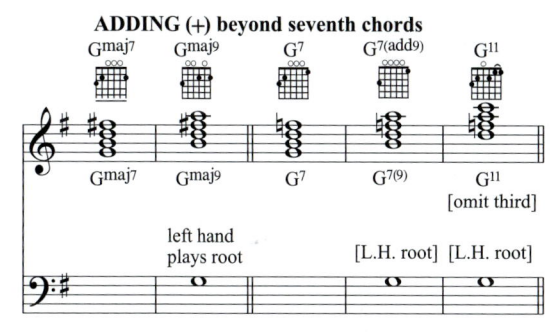

ADDING (+) beyond seventh chords

From major 7th	Gmaj7	(G, B, D, F#)	jazzy, smooth
+ major 9th	Gmaj9	(B, D, F#, A)	left hand plays root G, very jazzy
From dominant 7th	G7	(G, B, D, F)	okay, country
+ minor 9th	G9	(B, D, F, A)	LH plays root G, sounds richer
+ minor 11th	G11	(D, F, A, C)	LH plays root G, chord glows

When to SUBTRACT " − " the FIFTH

The Cm9 or C9 chord played by a keyboardist can coexist with a guitarist playing a Cm or C major chord. However, **the fifth of a major or minor 9th chord is often dropped**. Similarly with the funky C7#9 chord, we **omit the fifth**, so we play a major third on the bottom of the right hand, a flat seventh next and a minor third above that, with the C in the left hand bass.

SUBTRACT (−) the fifth

Minor chord	Gm	(G, B♭, D)	bland, okay with Gm9
+ minor 9th	Gm9	(B♭, *omit* D, F, A)	LH plays root G, smooth

The Beat Goes On

(continued...)

SUBTRACT (–) the fifth

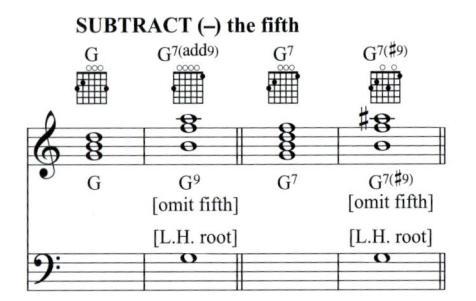

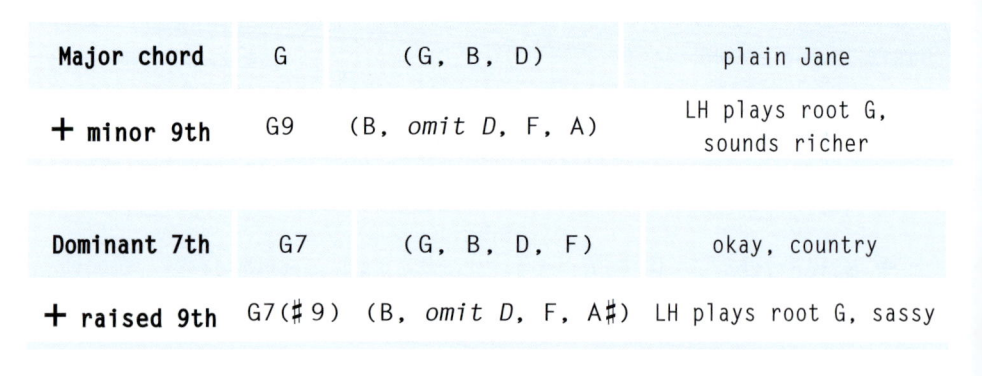

G   G7(add9)   G7   G7(#9)

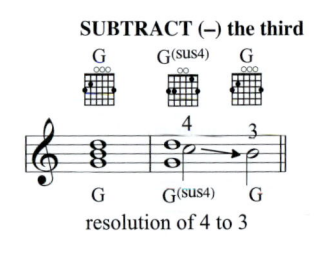

G   G9   G7   G7(#9)
[omit fifth]   [omit fifth]
[L.H. root]   [L.H. root]

Major chord	G	(G, B, D)	plain Jane
+ minor 9th	G9	(B, omit D, F, A)	LH plays root G, sounds richer

Dominant 7th	G7	(G, B, D, F)	okay, country
+ raised 9th	G7(#9)	(B, omit D, F, A#)	LH plays root G, sassy

When to SUBTRACT "–" the THIRD

Sus chords (sus2, sus4 or sus9) are best matched with a chord **without a third** to avoid an unpleasing clash. Hopefully your singers will hear these alterations and, if they are harmonizing, adjust accordingly.

SUBTRACT (–) the third

G   G(sus4)   G

G   G(sus4)   G
resolution of 4 to 3

Basic chord	Gm	(G, B♭, D)	plain Jane
Alter to sus4	Gsus4	(G, C, D)	must resolve 4 to 3

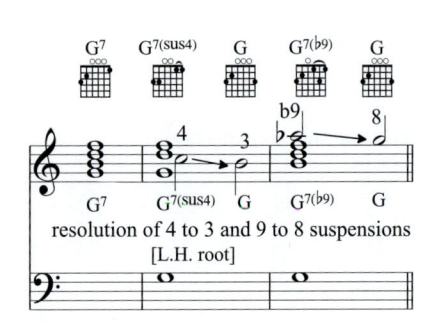

Based on V7	G7	(G, B, D, F)	okay, country
+ sus4	G7(sus4)	(D, F, G, C)	LH root G, resolves to G7
+ ♭9	G7(♭9)	(B, D, F, A♭)	resolves to G7

G7   G7(sus4)   G   G7(♭9)   G

G7   G7(sus4)   G   G7(♭9)   G
resolution of 4 to 3 and 9 to 8 suspensions
[L.H. root]

When to ALTER "+" or "–" FIFTHS and NINTHS

Altered fifths and ninths are rarely used in worship music, but are more familiar to gospel stylings, based on **alterations of both the fifth and the ninth** to the dominant seventh (V7) chord. Gospel singers perform straightforward triadic harmonies against these colorful altered chords.

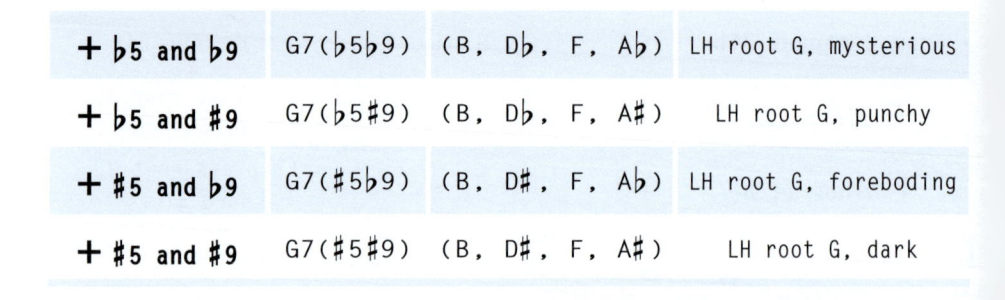

ALTER (+ or –) the fifths and ninths

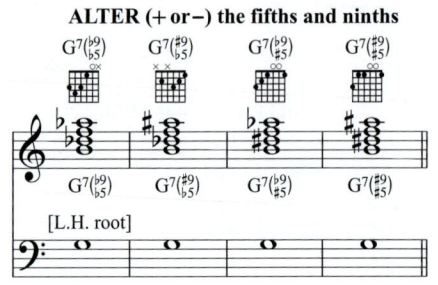

G7(♭9/♭5)   G7(#9/♭5)   G7(♭9/#5)   G7(#9/#5)

G7(♭9/♭5)   G7(#9/♭5)   G7(♭9/#5)   G7(#9/#5)
[L.H. root]

+ ♭5 and ♭9	G7(♭5♭9)	(B, D♭, F, A♭)	LH root G, mysterious
+ ♭5 and #9	G7(♭5#9)	(B, D♭, F, A#)	LH root G, punchy
+ #5 and ♭9	G7(#5♭9)	(B, D#, F, A♭)	LH root G, foreboding
+ #5 and #9	G7(#5#9)	(B, D#, F, A#)	LH root G, dark

GOSPEL VOICING - Vocal *Triads* over *Altered Fifths* and *Ninths*

VOICES: F   (G) F   Fm   Em E♭m Dm
Lyrics: Man   What a man.   I wan-na know.

BAND: E7(#9/♭5)   A7(#9/#5)   B7(#9/♭5)   Fm7   C7(#9) B7(#9) B♭7(#9) A7(#9/#5)

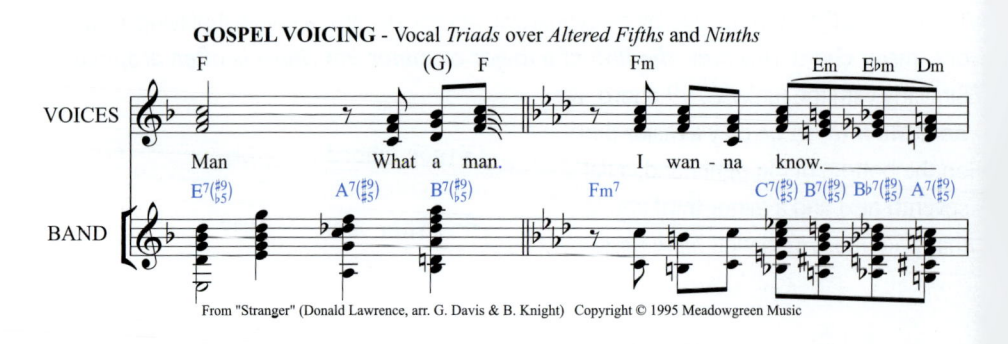

From "Stranger" (Donald Lawrence, arr. G. Davis & B. Knight) Copyright © 1995 Meadowgreen Music

19 BARS REST

Beyond Plain Jane Chords

1. Practice expanding major and minor chords with the addition of the **2nd**, **6th**, or **7th tones**. (For example, D can be expanded to D2, D6, D7, or Dmaj7, while Dm to Dm2, Dm6 or Dm7.) Learn to identify each chord's characteristic color in your listening and daily practice.

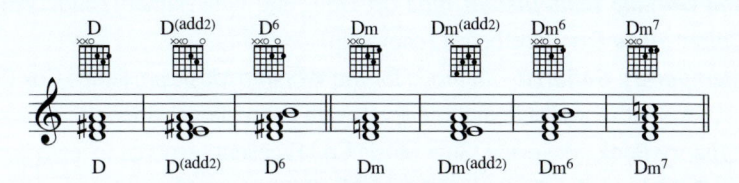

2. Practice expanding seventh chords in major and minor keys to various **9ths** and **11th chords**, with or without **flatted** or **sharped alterations**. Remember that as a matter of practicality, there are occasions when the fifth is dropped, or the root played by the bass or in the left hand. (Examples include D9, Dm9, Dmaj9, D11, D7♯9.)

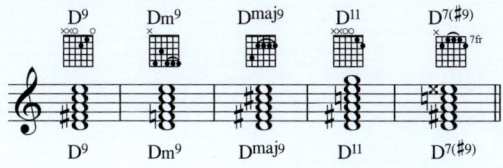

3. Practice properly resolving **sus** or **altered chords** in a variety of keys. (For example, Dsus4 resolves to D, D7sus4 to D7, D7♭9 to D7.) Become familiar with the pull of these suspended resolutions, realizing that they cannot coexist with chords that include resolved 3rds, so the timing of these chord substitutions must be communicated to all the band members.

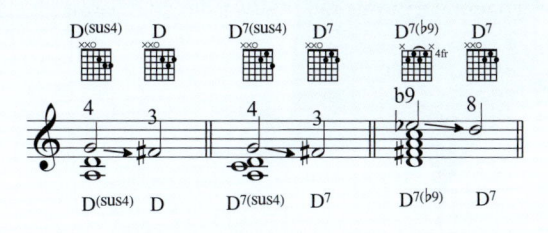

MORE WORSHIP TEAM RESOURCES

AUDIO AND MEDIA

Audio, Video, and Media in the Ministry, Floyd Richmond (Thomas Nelson)

Digital Storytellers: *The Art of Communicating the Gospel in Worship*, Len Wilson (Abingdon Press) with DVD

For the Sake of the Gospel: *A Media Ministry Primer*, Kent V. Wilson (Augsburg Fortress) with DVD

House of Worship Sound Reinforcement, Jamie Rio and Chris Buono (Webber Institute)

The Wired Church 2.0, Len Wilson (Abingdon Press)

The Beat Goes On

The Worship Media Handbook, Jeff McIntosh (Church Motion Graphics)
Video Ministry: *Using Media in Worship without Going Hollywood*, Constance Stella (Abingdon Press) with DVD

INSTRUMENTAL AND VOCAL HELPS

Beyond Salsa Piano: *The Cuban Timba Piano Revolution: Volumes 1 and 2*, Kevin Moore (www.timba.com) Supplemental audio tracks available

God's Singers–*The Worship-Leading Choir*, Dave Williamson (in:ciite media), available in leaders or singers version

Praise and Worship Team Instant Tune-Up, Doug and Tami Flather (Zondervan)

Praise Guitar Made Easy (Fretboard Fellowship)

The Contemporary Guitarist–*Methods for the Worship Musician*, James Cox (Salvation Army—USA South), available in three levels with instructional videos

The Jazz Theory Book, M. Levine (Sher Music Co.) Excellent resource to learn jazz harmony

The Salsa Guidebook for Piano and Ensemble, R. Manleon (Sher Music)

Whoa! God showed up BIG-TIME! The people really worshiped!

Looking ahead...
PART FIVE: THE CONDUCTOR'S TOOLBOX

www.music.saconnects.org

Part Five
THE CONDUCTOR'S TOOLBOX

CHAPTER TWENTY

WHERE'S THE BEAT?
Conducting Fundamentals

At the most fundamental level the conductor's job is ... to provide a rhythmic frame of reference (through his beat) and a visual representation of the music's content (through the expression in his beat). —Gunther Schuller[1]

WHY YOU WORRY? ... JUST DO THIS!
Riccardo Muti instructs a policeman on the simplicity of conducting

In **Chapter Twenty**, we address the fundamental mechanics of conducting, considering:
- beat gesture
- the 4, 3, 2 and 6 patterns
- body language

Upon receiving a prestigious lifetime achievement award, world–famous Italian conductor Riccardo Muti responded with a humorous but delightful tale. It recounted a casual conversation with a policeman on the simplicity of conducting:

"My teacher of conducting was Antonino Votto, first assistant to Toscanini, during the Golden Age of the great opera house La Scala. When asked how to do this or how to do that, he always said [uttered with a charming Italian accent]: **"Why YOU worry? You don't have to play, just do THIS** [Muti calmly lifts his arm and forms a simple downbeat, and confidently adds] **and something WILL happen."**

Muti elegantly continues, with an air of delight, "A few weeks ago I had a conversation with a policeman who was speaking about how difficult life is today, you know, with the financial crisis, and he said, 'You know, I have 1,200 euros per month and I have several children.' So I said to him, 'Don't worry. If you want to change your life—and I want to help you because you are such a nice guy—you come to my house and in three minutes I will teach you how to conduct the *Unfinished Symphony* of Schubert.'" [Audience laughter subsides, as Muti continues his charming tale]

"The policeman, of course, asks, 'What is **THAT** (referring to the *Unfinished*)?' And Muti, emphatically responded, **'THAT** [emphasis on 'that'] is *not* important. You can earn, in one evening, more than you earn in a year.' Naturally the policeman asked, 'How is that?' And I said: 'You know, the first movement is in three. That means [Muti begins to beat in three, as he counts out loud] one, and don't forget to move the arm to the right part of yourself [Muti flings his arm to the right on two, and continues] two, and then three.'"

Theme from Movement I
Schubert "Unfinished" Symphony
Allegro moderato

The Beat Goes On

427

Opening Theme from Movement I
Schubert "Unfinished" Symphony
Allegro moderato

FIRST MOVEMENT

With an air of propriety, Maestro Muti assures the policeman, "And so you will see if you do **THIS**, they will start." [Muti begins to sing the opening to Schubert's 'Unfinished,' while pretending to cajole and prod the policeman on] "Keep going ... Don't stop ... keep going!" Then the Maestro's singing stops, and he instructs the policeman, "Then when the orchestra stops, that means that the first movement is over."

Becoming somewhat emotional, and tongue-tied, Muti continues, "Then in that moment what you do ... in that moment the public you know, sometimes we hear some delicate cough in the intervals in the pause. So the music ends *pianissimo* for the first movement. When you stop ... In that moment you try to look very inspired. [Muti lifts his head] Don't look at the orchestra because then you can meet some eyes that are looking at you in a very strange way. [Scattered chuckles] So just look in the sky, you know [Muti looks up] and sometimes the audience is very affected by this. [Repeating the sober head lift] And the audience thinks: 'Oh, he is dreaming about ... you know, the music ... '"

Theme from Movement II
Schubert "Unfinished" Symphony
Andante con moto

SECOND MOVEMENT

Muti turns his head, as though suddenly startled and utters, "And you look, and when you see that the players have readied their instruments [Muti begins to lift his hands like holding a violin] then you set your hands [He then abandons the violin for a downbeat gesture] and do exactly what you did before." He reminds the neophyte conductor with a right hand downbeat gesture, "Don't forget to move out on the second beat." Muti adds with confidence, "And so, you know, it will be!" The Maestro begins to sing the opening to the second movement, as he utters, knowingly, "It starts the second movement, you know, of the symphony."

But then he advises the policeman, "Fortunately there's only two movements, so when **THEY** stop, **YOU** stop." There is a momentary pause without motion, and then Muti begins to turn, instructing, "So then you turn ... you take your applause ... and **THEN** [enthusiastic emphasis on **THEN**] you take the check, you see." To which, Muti adds in the sweetest broken English, "This is what is about conducting."

JUST LEARNING TO CONDUCT

Momentarily assuming a professorial role, Muti reflects on what he has said and consults the memory of a conversation with another conducting mentor: "Vittorio Gui said to me when he was 90 years old and I was just 27 years, 'Muti, what a pity to be near to death just now that I was learning how to conduct.' He meant not to beat time, but to get from the souls of the musicians the music, the feelings." Muti continues, by reiterating, "The feelings, **NOT** the notes. The notes are the concrete expressions of the feelings. And that is something that makes conducting the most difficult profession in the world. Because we have an idea that is to be expressed through the arms and then has to go through the instruments, that are played by the fingers or the mouth of players, and goes out to the public." With a sigh, he mutters, "And that is a long way." [Muti lifts his arms, as though to conduct] "To beat time is very easy, anybody can do that." Muti motions loosely

> "He meant not to beat time, but to get from the souls of the musicians the music, the feelings." Muti continues, by reiterating, "The feelings, not the notes."

with his arms, and repeats simply, "Anybody." But then adds, "To make music is very, very difficult."

Speaking now to the audience, Maestro Muti reflects on where exactly he is on *HIS* journey as a conductor, "Now everybody is thinking in this room, *'What YOU think? What is YOUR position?'* [Muti pauses to close] I think that I am in the middle of the road. And I'm sure that I will never get to the other part of the river, because behind the notes lies the infinite. That means God, and we are very small in front of God."[2]

HANDLING TRAFFIC OR MAKING MUSIC?

What does traffic have to do with making music?

As novice conductors we are like the inquiring policeman, dreaming of grand gestures eliciting marvelous music-making. Instead, we may feel trapped as though directing traffic at a busy intersection. Yes, we are musicians in a volunteer army, but Johnny is distracted, while looking at his phone. Suzy doesn't even have her horn up. Maybe she's lost. Sid on drums still hasn't found his part, and Carolyn has managed to play a B natural instead of a B flat for the third time! How does one imagine, no less hear, the music at such a busy intersection?

Some say there are only two kinds of conductors: those who **handle traffic** and those who **make music**.[3] Certainly the first affects the other: if you can't handle traffic, how can you make music? No wonder a well-trained singer can be terrified to lead a group. Giving clear "traffic signals" tests the coordination of some, while many lack the confidence and facility with beat patterns or score-reading.

As you work through Chapters Twenty through Twenty-Three, assess for yourself areas where you might need work as a conductor. It might be beat patterns, baton technique, score-reading, expressive gesture, or maintaining a focused rehearsal. As Maestro Muti attested, conducting carries with it a lifetime learning curve, ideally driven by a desire to inspire musician-ministers to do their best to make music together.

Maestro as teacher

The Italian title *maestro* has evolved over generations as a prefix to the name of eminent conductors as a sign of utmost respect for their musical knowledge. How easily the root meaning of *maestro*, which is "to teach," slips out of our vision.[4] As a bandmaster I am known as the "maestro de banda" in Hispanic settings, with its more literal translation "teacher of the band," which far better suits a volunteer army of musician-ministers. Removing the mantle of "master" connotes a cooperative, mutually respectful classroom, where the conductor-teacher's best intentions (and good-will) engage every player or singer.

In the Salvation Army context, the result is an ensemble that reaches beyond the "busy intersection" of the proper production of notes, or even the nuances of the music. This allows the breath of the Holy Spirit (the ultimate maestro-teacher) to touch the music, capturing a blessing and allowing the ensemble to become the voice of God. These moments of transcendence—intersecting body, mind and spirit—are what make Salvation Army music-making unique.

Unfinished, WHY?

The title page of the "Unfinished" Symphony was dated October 22, 1822. Six months later Schubert received a Diploma of Honor, and gave the two movements as a token of gratitude. A piano sketch of a Scherzo (and the first nine bars scored) survive, but no Finale, though Schubert lived for another six years.

Take a few moments to review the **4, 3 and 2 patterns** introduced in Chapter Five (pp. 119–121) before heading into this busy intersection of Beat Patterns!

20 BARS REST

1. Some picture themselves easily as conductors. Others cannot. A well-trained singer or instrumentalist can be terrified to lead a group, even though he or she has the knowledge and skill. Some folks struggle with coordination. Others have never taken the time to learn how to beat basic patterns or improve their music-reading skills. How comfortable are you with leading a music group?
2. Is a rehearsal simply a class in which the conductor teaches the performers how to play the music?
3. How do you know what makes good conducting technique? What do you think you'll need to work on as a conductor? (An honest appraisal will help you know where to focus the development of your skills.)
4. How do you "practice" conducting?

"The Man in the Mirror"
Note that nearly all diagrams and photos of conducting gestures in Chapters Twenty are shown reversed left–right, as though the conductor is following his/her pattern in a mirror. This allows the student to trace the patterns from their vantage point, looking out on an imaginary ensemble.

THE BEAT PATTERNS

The *LEGATO, STACCATO,* and *MARCATO* gestures

The fundamental 4, 3, and 2 patterns were introduced in Chapter Five. In this section, we will expand our time-beating skills to reflect *legato*, *staccato*, or *marcato* articulation.[5] Since the conductor's gesture is intended to represent music, it is recommended that you sing along as you learn the beat patterns. This helps you internalize how each component of the beat functions, both musically and with an increasing awareness of the kinesthetic "muscle sense" required for expressive conducting.[6] Audio files of the music examples in this chapter are available for practice in the Chapter Twenty online folder.

legato (*term*) \le - ʼgä - tō\
A passage marked *legato* or indicated by a slur line calls for the sound to smoothly connect from one note to another without a break. For wind players, this calls for no tonguing articulation of successive notes.

staccato (*term*) \stä - ʼkä - tō\
The opposite of *legato*, a passage marked *staccato* (abbreviated, *stacc.*) or indicated by small dots under or over the notes, calls for notes of shortened, detached duration, clearly separating one note from another. A light accent is implied.

marcato (*term*) \mär - ʼkä - tō\
A passage marked *marcato*, or specified by an arrow-shaped accent (>), a tent-shaped *martellato* (∧) literally meaning, "hammering" or *sforzando* (*sfz*) sign, meaning "forced sound," calls for varying degrees of a marked, emphatic heavy accent.

The LEGATO pattern is smooth, rounded, and connected, emphasizing the horizontal plane, while limiting the beat pattern of vertical motion. Imagine standing in a pool, running your open hands with palms down lightly across water that is nearly chest high.[7] To intensify the *legato*, the loop or curve of the rebound is increased.

Use LEGATO Pattern

Break Thou the Bread of Life

mp Andante ♩ = 84

Break Thou the bread of life, O Lord, to me.

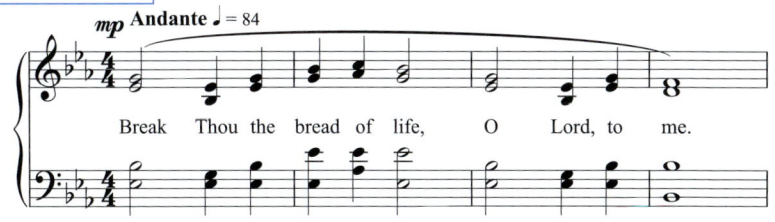

The STACCATO pattern is light, with quick, limited angular rebounds from beat to beat. Imagine flicking a number of insects off a countertop. The separation and lightness required of *staccato* music comes from a wrist action (combined to a small degree with the forearm) that springs or snaps on each beat.

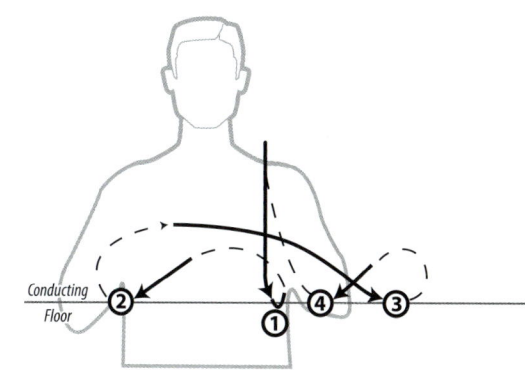

Use STACCATO Pattern

In My Heart There Rings a Melody

mf Allegro ♩ = 104

In my heart there rings a mel-o-dy, There rings a mel-o-dy with

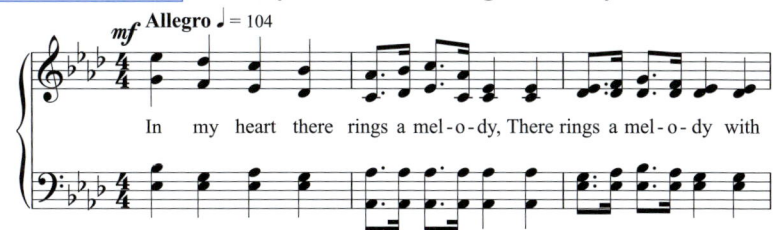

In contrast, a MARCATO pattern requires a low center of gravity (felt like lifting a heavy box) because of the implied "weight" of the music. Bring the pattern down and away with deep, angular, yet abrupt motions as though boxing. There is little wrist action, as the wrist and arm become unified.

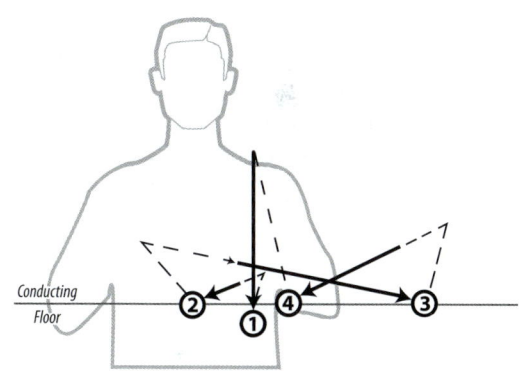

Use MARCATO Pattern

Sound the Battle Cry!

f Allegro ♩ = 104

Rouse, then, sold-iers, ral-ly round the ban-ner! Read-y, stead-y,

THE FOUR BASIC BEAT PATTERNS

Work to become thoroughly familiar with the four fundamental beat patterns of 4, 3, 2, and 6. Remember that when your hand drops downward, your arm remains parallel to the floor, this being the line of the beat-point. With practice, modifications will be made to the beat patterns to account for different tempos and characteristics. For instance, we use shorter loops for faster tempos, or more angular turns for *marcato* music.

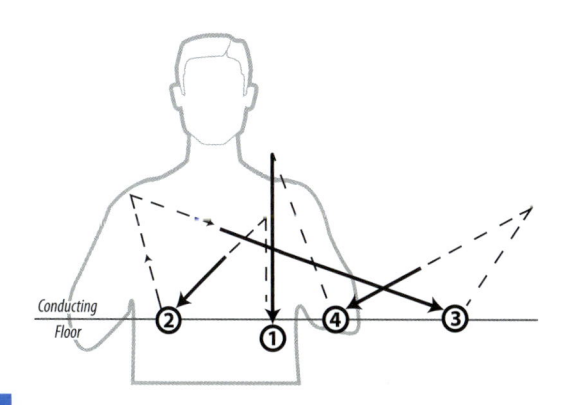

About the conducting patterns—the beat stroke is shown solid (→) and the reflex rebound is shown dashed (- - -). The desired point of the beat is indicated with circled numbers (②).

The Beat Goes On

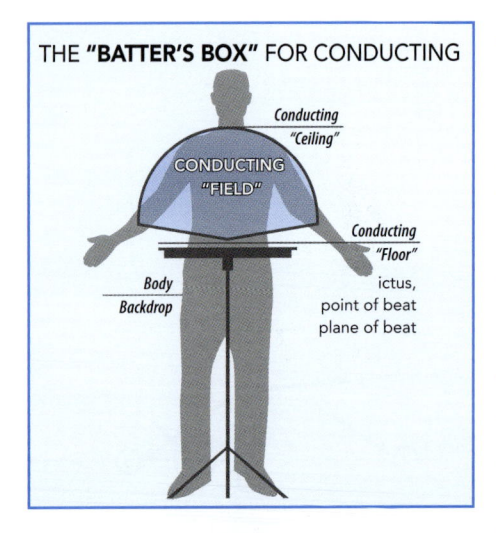

THE "BATTER'S BOX" FOR CONDUCTING

Conducting "Ceiling"
CONDUCTING "FIELD"
Conducting "Floor"
Body Backdrop
ictus, point of beat plane of beat

The batter's box

The "batter's box" for beat patterns, as we like to call it, reaches across the shoulders (which we will call "the ceiling"), as wide as the arms stretched out at a 45° angle and down to the waist (with the stand set just below that). The bottom **horizontal plane** (called "the floor") is the plane of the beat and runs parallel to the floor at about the base of the sternum, encompassing the area from side to side in front of the torso. The beat must not extend below your stand at waist height, because it will not be seen by ensemble members.[8]

Where's the beat?

The right arm/hand positioning extends out from **floor** to **ceiling** at a comfortable distance (roughly, a foot) on a vertical plane directly in front of the right shoulder. The place where these **horizontal and vertical planes** intersect is the point where the beat pulse is felt.[9]

THE FOUR PATTERN for 4/4, 4/2, and 12/8 in 4

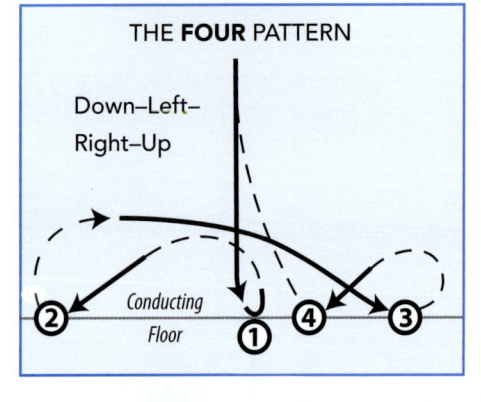

BEAT ONE Down
Descend vertically from "the ceiling" of the batter's box and vertical plane of the backdrop to the floor point of BEAT ONE, marking the downbeat as the strongest beat. Rebound to the conductor's left, with the palm facing down.

BEAT TWO Left
Tap BEAT TWO at the level of the conducting floor, and rebound up and across the body, once again keeping the palm down.

BEAT THREE Right
Tap BEAT THREE on the conductor's right. The large motion across the body from the conductor's left shoulder to the extreme right conducting floor makes BEAT THREE appears to be the second strongest beat in the FOUR PATTERN.

BEAT FOUR Up
Swing the motion up and in, before tapping BEAT FOUR at a mid-point level, making it the weakest beat to the eye.

The rebound for BEAT FOUR ascends up in a continuous line from the point of BEAT FOUR to "the ceiling" of your pattern forming another preparation before descending to create another BEAT ONE.

THE FOUR PATTERN
Down–Left–Right–Up
Conducting Floor

| BEAT ONE | BEAT TWO | BEAT THREE | BEAT FOUR |

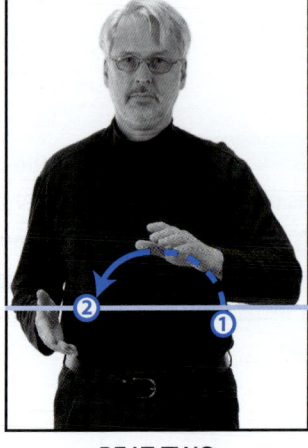

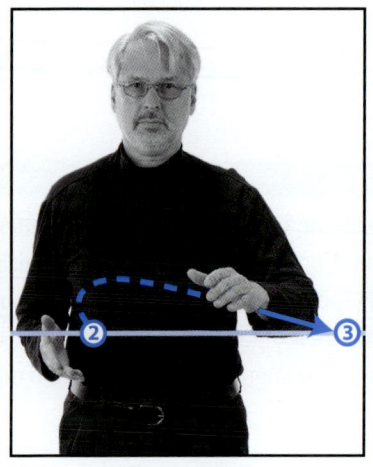

Chapter 20 | WHERE'S THE BEAT?

CAUTION FOUR PATTERN

The FOUR PATTERN can easily become imbalanced, creating confusion as to beat placement. Student conductors often conduct the FOUR PATTERN as an upward spiral, creating a series of beats with BEAT THREE just above ONE, and BEAT FOUR above that. This imbalanced pattern is caused by a stiff elbow, which doesn't allow the arm to swing far enough to the right to touch the right side floor (and include that side of the ensemble!)

BEAT THREE in 4/4 time is necessarily larger than BEATS TWO and FOUR, because BEAT THREE moves across the body. **[A]** Beat TWO and THREE should be an equal distance left and right from the vertical axis. **[B]**

An imbalance happens when the motion from BEAT TWO to BEAT THREE goes too far (and strong) to the extreme right, implying a crescendo you may not want. **[C]**

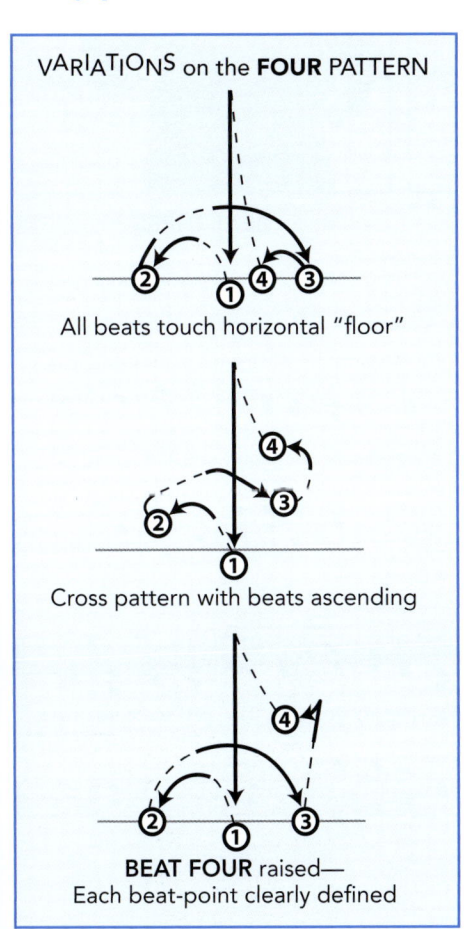

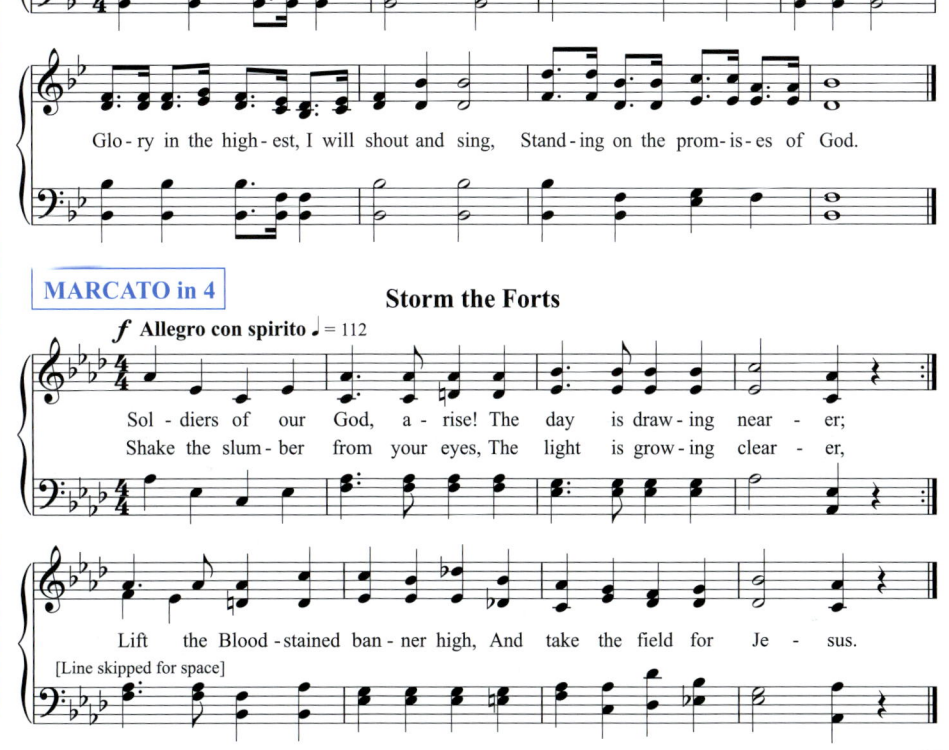

**** DO THESE!!! ****   AVOID THIS!!!

[A]   [B]   [C]

VERTICAL PLANE

BEAT THREE too far implies a crescendo

VARIATIONS on the FOUR PATTERN

All beats touch horizontal "floor"

Cross pattern with beats ascending

BEAT FOUR raised—
Each beat-point clearly defined

LEGATO in 4   When I Survey the Wondrous Cross

mf Andante ♩ = 84

When I sur-vey the won-drous cross On which the Prince of
My rich-est gain I count but loss,

glo-ry died And pour con-tempt on all my pride.

STACCATO in 4   Standing on the Promises

mp Allegro ♩ = 104

Stand-ing on the pro-mis-es of Christ my King! Thro' e-ter-nal a-ges let His prais-es ring;

Glo-ry in the high-est, I will shout and sing, Stand-ing on the prom-is-es of God.

MARCATO in 4   Storm the Forts

f Allegro con spirito ♩ = 112

Sol-diers of our God, a-rise! The day is draw-ing near-er;
Shake the slum-ber from your eyes, The light is grow-ing clear-er,

Lift the Blood-stained ban-ner high, And take the field for Je-sus.
[Line skipped for space]

The Beat Goes On

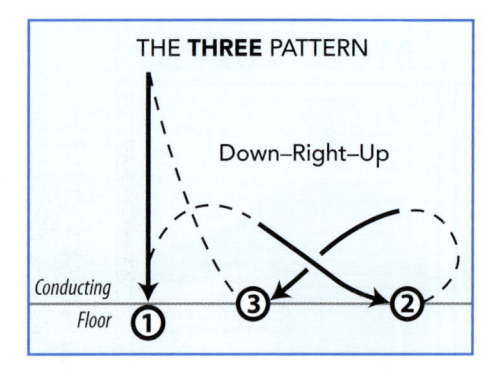

THE THREE PATTERN

Down–Right–Up

THE THREE PATTERN for 3/4, 3/2, and 9/8 in 3

BEAT ONE down
Use an identical downbeat preparation as the Four Pattern, moving from the "conducting ceiling" and direct center to the point of BEAT ONE.

Downbeat rebound to the right to the BEAT TWO point with the palm facing down.

BEAT TWO right
Tap BEAT TWO, which actually touches the "conducting floor," making it the second strongest beat. (Notice that this is the same point as BEAT THREE in the FOUR PATTERN.)

BEAT THREE up
Swing the motion up and in, before tapping BEAT THREE at a mid-point level, making it the weakest beat to the eye. (This is a similar spot to BEAT FOUR in the FOUR PATTERN.)

The rebound for BEAT THREE ascends up in a continuous line from the point of BEAT THREE to the ceiling of your pattern, forming another preparation before descending to create another BEAT ONE.

BEAT ONE  **BEAT TWO**  **BEAT THREE**

LEGATO in 3

Be Thou My Vision

mp **Moderato** ♩ = 96

Be thou my Vi-sion, O Lord of my heart; Naught be all else to me, save that Thou art,

Thou my best thought, by day or by night, Wak-ing or sleep-ing, Thy pre-sence my light.

STACCATO in 3

He Giveth More Grace

mf Moderato ♩ = 96

He giveth more grace as our burdens grow greater, He
added afflictions he added his mercy, To
sendeth more strength as our labors increase, To
multiplied trials he multiplies peace.

MARCATO in 3

Come Thou Almighty King

Moderato ♩ = 92

Come Thou almighty King, Help us Thy name to sing, Help us to praise;
Father, all glorious, O'er all victorious, Come and reign over us, Ancient of Days.

"Don't forget to keep your beat patterns within the batter's box."

CAUTION: THREE PATTERN

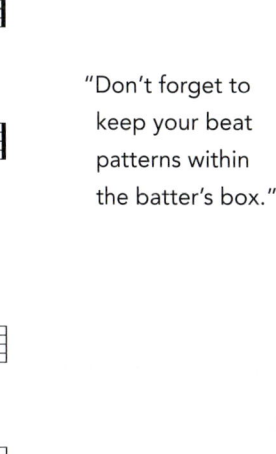

We often teach the THREE PATTERN as a right triangle, however some conductors place BEAT THREE on a plane midway between BEATS ONE and TWO, so that it is clear that BEAT ONE is the downbeat.

Be sure to extend BEAT TWO far enough to the right and not "sky" up with BEAT THREE. Work to have all beats touch the horizontal plane floor.

Take care not to go too far up for BEAT THREE in 3/4 time, which overextends your pattern and implies a crescendo.

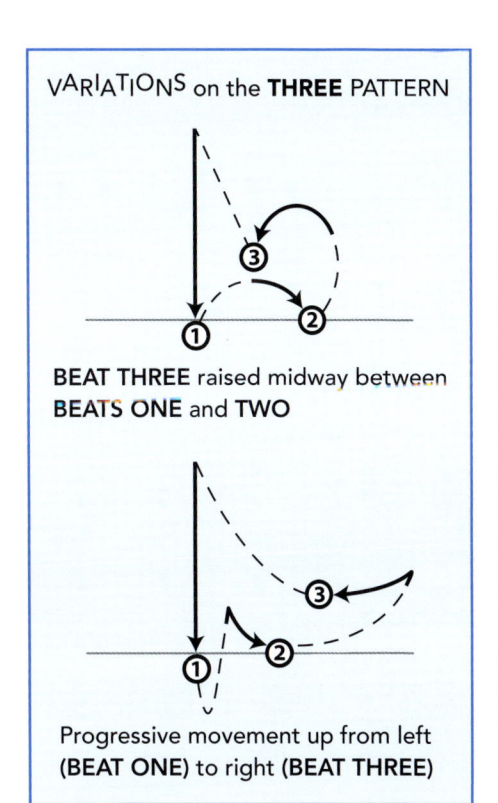

VARIATIONS on the THREE PATTERN

BEAT THREE raised midway between **BEATS ONE** and **TWO**

Progressive movement up from left (BEAT ONE) to right (BEAT THREE)

** AVOID THIS!!! **

Overextending BEAT THREE

The Beat Goes On

THE TWO PATTERN Downstairs/Upstairs

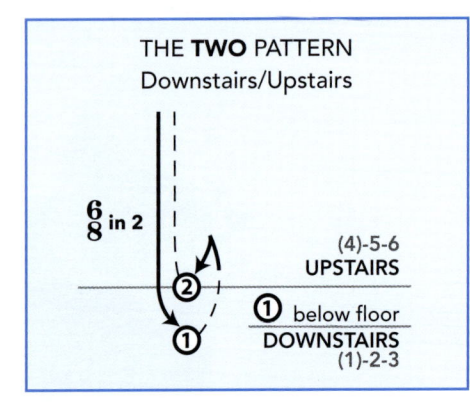

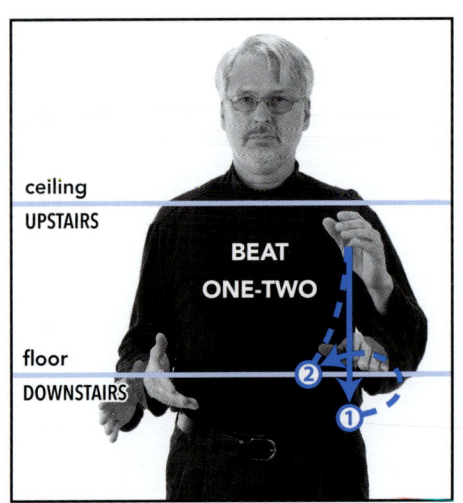

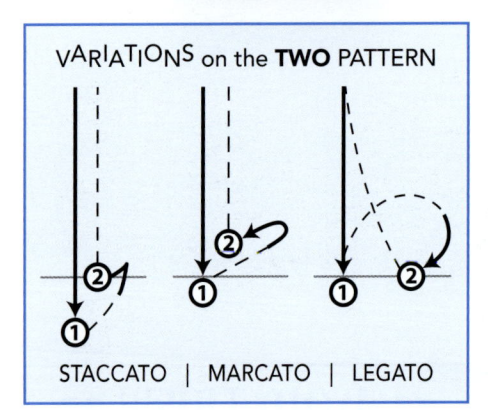

6/8 in 2
- ① below floor DOWNSTAIRS (1)-2-3
- ② (4)-5-6 UPSTAIRS

ceiling UPSTAIRS
BEAT ONE-TWO
floor DOWNSTAIRS

VARIATIONS on the TWO PATTERN
STACCATO | MARCATO | LEGATO

compound time (term) \'käm-paùnd-tĭm\ A meter that includes a triple subdivision within the beat. For example, in 6/8 time, the bar is divided into two dotted quarters, each comprised of three eighths.

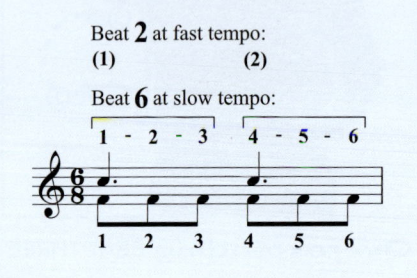

Beat **2** at fast tempo:
(1)   (2)

Beat **6** at slow tempo:
1 - 2 - 3   4 - 5 - 6

THE TWO PATTERN for 2/4, 2/2, alla breve, cut time, and 6/8 in 2

BEAT ONE down
Use an identical downbeat preparation as the THREE PATTERN, moving from the "conducting ceiling" along the vertical plane and direct center, but this time to a point slightly below the horizontal floor, marking BEAT ONE. This downstairs exception aids beat clarity. Rebound nearly vertically a little out to the right, making a slim "U" or "V" shape, depending on the articulation.

BEAT TWO up
Tap the horizontal floor for BEAT TWO, making it the weaker beat, appearing higher than BEAT ONE. The rebound for BEAT TWO ascends up in a continuous line from the point of BEAT TWO to the "conducting ceiling" of your pattern, forming another "preparation" before descending to create another BEAT ONE. The staccato TWO PATTERN uses a snap wrist with very little rebound. The marcato TWO is angular. Make a deep "V" on the rebound with BEAT ONE on the conducting floor, not below.

CAUTION TWO PATTERN Sometimes beginner conductors reverse the rebound of BEAT ONE, moving it to the left, rather than the right. Be careful not to rebound too high after BEAT ONE, or BEAT TWO will look like another BEAT ONE. Sometimes we differentiate each beat's height placement by calling them **downstairs** (for DOWNBEAT ONE) and **upstairs** (for UPBEAT TWO).

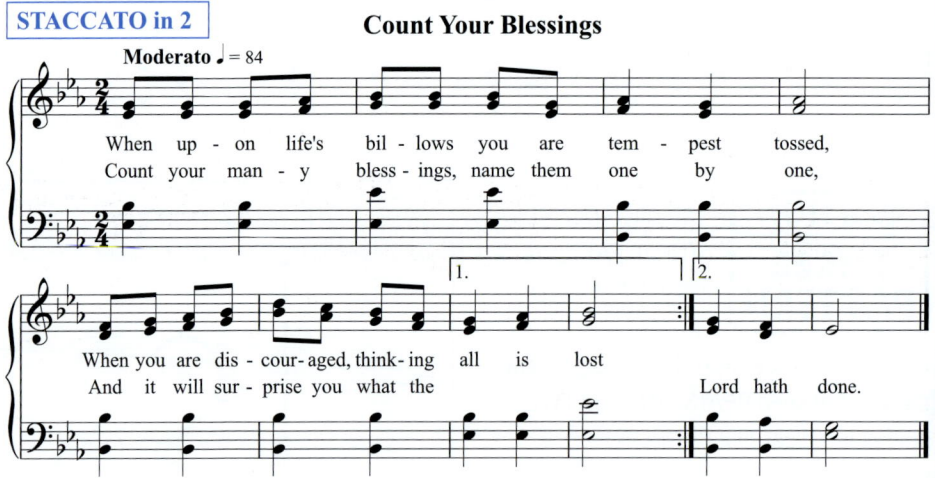

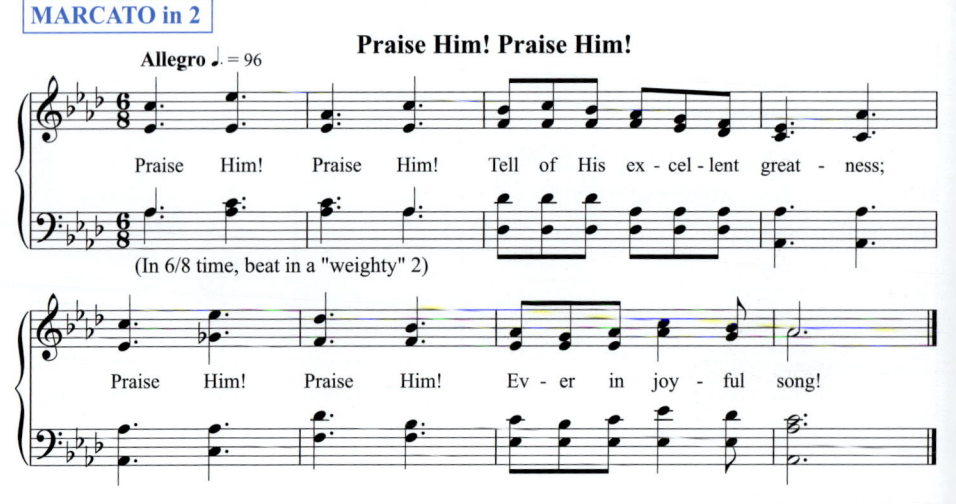

STACCATO in 2
Count Your Blessings
Moderato ♩ = 84

When up-on life's bil-lows you are tem-pest tossed,
Count your man-y bless-ings, name them one by one,
When you are dis-cour-aged, think-ing all is lost
And it will sur-prise you what the Lord hath done.

MARCATO in 2
Praise Him! Praise Him!
Allegro ♩. = 96

Praise Him! Praise Him! Tell of His ex-cel-lent great-ness;
(In 6/8 time, beat in a "weighty" 2)
Praise Him! Praise Him! Ev-er in joy-ful song!

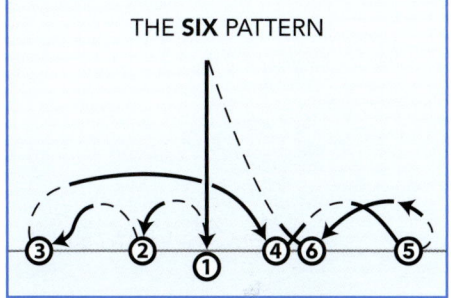

Chapter 20 | WHERE'S THE BEAT?

LEGATO in 2

Moderato ♩ = 92

Praise, My Soul

Praise, my soul, the King of Heav-en, To His feet thy tri-bute bring;
Ran-somed, healed, re-stored, for-giv-en, Who like thee His praise should sing?
Praise him! praise him! Praise him, praise him! Praise the ev-er-last-ing King.

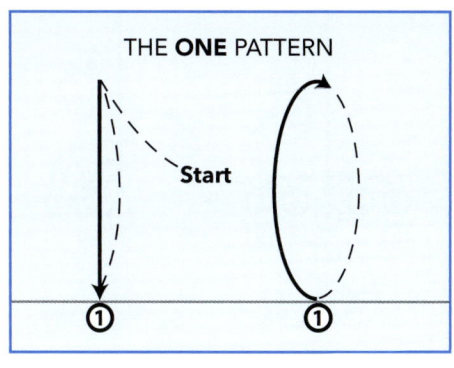

THE ONE PATTERN

Start

THE SIX PATTERN

THE SIX PATTERN for 6/8, 6/4 compound time

The standard SIX–BEAT PATTERN is organized musically as two accented beats (BEATS ONE and FOUR) with two secondary unaccented pulses between them (BEATS TWO–THREE and FIVE–SIX).

The most common SIX PATTERN (known as German Style), uses BEATS ONE, TWO, and THREE to the conductor's left, and then BEATS FOUR, FIVE, and SIX to the right giving each beat its own readily identifiable placement.

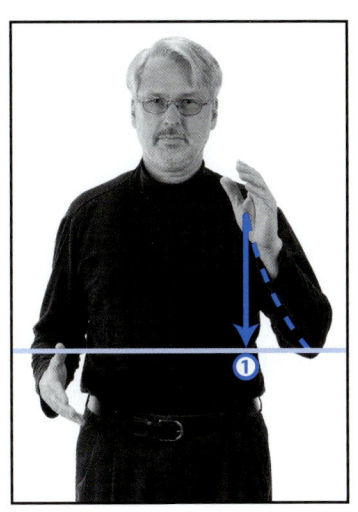

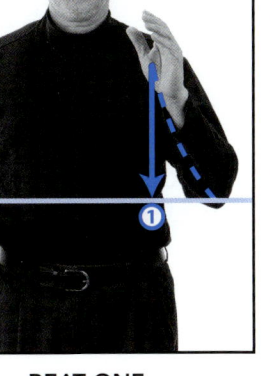

BEAT ONE 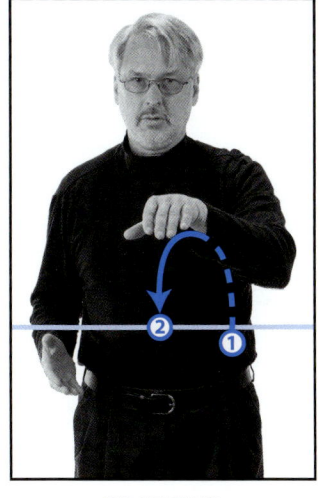 **BEAT TWO** 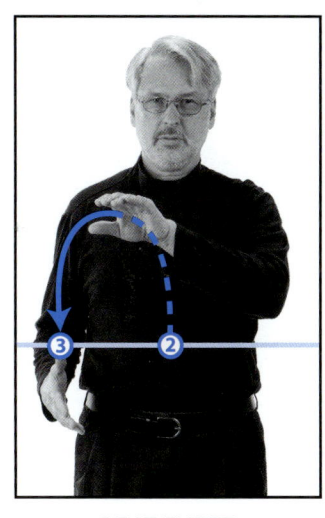 **BEAT THREE**

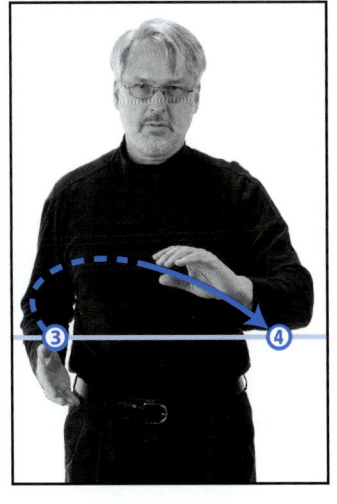

BEAT FOUR 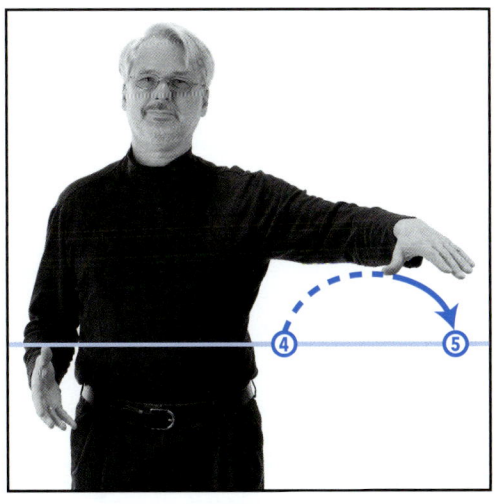 **BEAT FIVE** 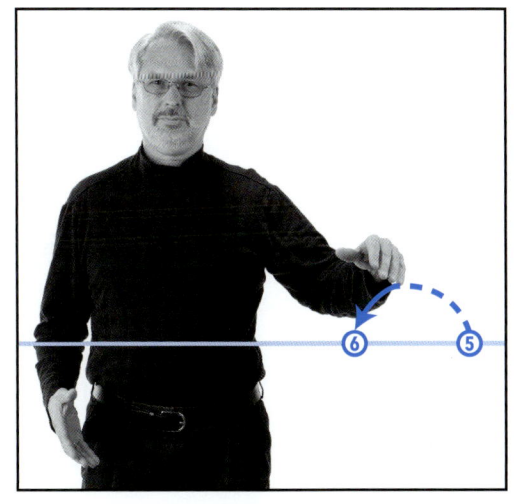 **BEAT SIX**

The Beat Goes On

437

VARIATIONS on the SIX PATTERN

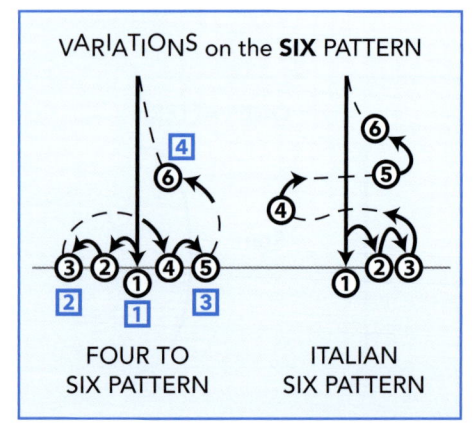

FOUR TO SIX PATTERN

ITALIAN SIX PATTERN

In essence, the SIX PATTERN is an extension of the FOUR PATTERN, adding one beat on each side of the primary beats, with each beat equally placed along the horizontal "floor."

An alternative Italian Style SIX PATTERN follows a downstairs (1–2–3)/upstairs (4–5–6) pattern, which is essentially a subdivided 2, which means the first and fourth counts are considerably more marked than the other beats.

LEGATO in 6

Jesus Keep Me Near the Cross

Andante con moto ♪ = 100, *mp*

Jesus, keep me near the Cross; There's a precious fountain, Free to all, a healing stream, Flows from Cal-v'ry's mountain, Flows from Cal-v'ry's mountain.

f *dim.*

In the Cross, in the Cross Be my glory ever

VERSE in 6, CHORUS in 2

Trusting As the Moments Fly

Andante ♪ = 104, *mp*

Simply trusting ev-'ry day, Trusting through a storm-y way, Even when my faith is small,

mf *Piu mosso* ♩. = 52

Trusting Jesus, that is all. Trusting as the moments fly, Trusting as the

cresc. *f*

days go by, Trusting him what-e'er be-fall, trusting Jesus, that is all.

CAUTION SIX PATTERN

In the standard German style SIX PATTERN, the rebound of BEAT THREE crosses over the vertical axis to BEAT FOUR. That fourth beat-point must appear to the conductor's right beyond the vertical axis, so as not to be mistaken for BEAT ONE.

Some conductors will use a pair of "triangle" THREE patterns for SIX, which proves confusing to the ensemble as BEATS ONE, TWO, and THREE appear identical to BEATS FOUR, FIVE, and SIX.

20 BARS REST

1. Practice the basic beat patterns (4, 3, 2, and 6) at different tempos, and with varying styles of articulation: *legato*, *staccato*, and *marcato*. Use a mirror or video camera to see if your beat patterns are clear.

2. Beat time, while you and your friends sing familiar songs. Ask your partners if they can see the bottom of your beat clearly, especially beat one. Look for faults in your patterns and correct them.[10]

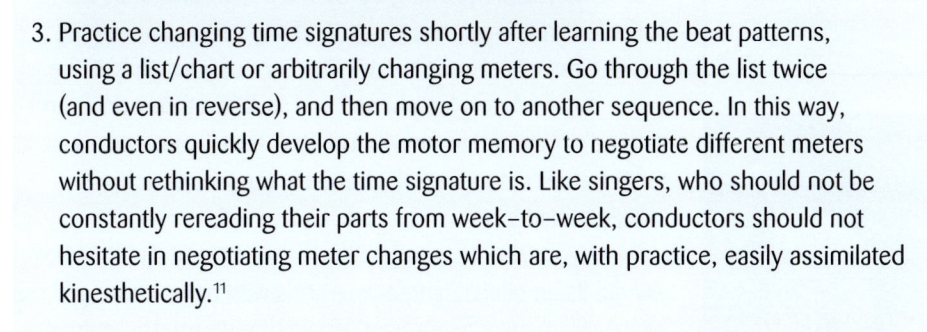

3. Practice changing time signatures shortly after learning the beat patterns, using a list/chart or arbitrarily changing meters. Go through the list twice (and even in reverse), and then move on to another sequence. In this way, conductors quickly develop the motor memory to negotiate different meters without rethinking what the time signature is. Like singers, who should not be constantly rereading their parts from week-to-week, conductors should not hesitate in negotiating meter changes which are, with practice, easily assimilated kinesthetically.[11]

4	3	2	6	3	2
3	6	4	2	4	3
2	4	3	4	6	4
6	2	4	3	2	6

THE CONDUCTING LANGUAGE

Body language is a major factor in communication. Conducting is essentially the art of making visual preparation for sounds to come.[12] Beat patterns, not unlike spoken instructions, serve to guide players and singers. The conductor's overall posture and movement in the arms, hands, breath, body backdrop, lower body, head, and facial expression can speak louder than what the baton is saying. The goal is to bring all of these elements into agreement with the intention of your beat pattern.

Body backdrop

Posture affects the music. The conductor, particularly in front of singers and wind players, will want to model a body posture that encourages the essential breathing apparatus. James Jordan asserts, "The most important skill a choral conductor must develop is the ability to open the body so that breath can fall into it."[13] Feet should be

The Beat Goes On

slightly apart (just inside your shoulder width) with the weight of the body distributed equally between the balls of the feet and the heels, with knees relaxed, allowing for a little spring. Some conductors place one foot slightly in front, as some singers do. This more aggressive position conveys a strong sense of leadership and control.[14]

A shorter stature conductor may benefit from using a podium, not so much for his or her own line of vision, but so all ensemble members can see the conductor's full arm movement without straining. Avoid a high podium that forces instrumentalists to look up at a steep angle. The bottom of the beat is what counts. Another option has the conductor standing farther back from the ensemble, permitting the conductor a wider angle of vision and improved hearing. Place the stand at a slight angle facing you rather than a nearly flat position, which forces the conductor's head and eyes down. A stand placed too high obscures the conductor's gesture.

**** AVOID THESE!!! ****

Music stand too high  | Bending forward  | Leaning back

Posture carries the sound

Conductors must avoid stooping, or bending forward (which gives the perception of begging for notes), or conversely, leaning back. The natural tendency of the head is to be pulled backward and downward.[15] To reverse this tendency think of extending your spine to release the neck muscles forward and up, enabling your head to float in balance at the top of the spine.

Imagine you are growing down into the ground while being pulled up and away from the ground, on a string running up through the top of your head.[16] The core of your body is the spine. To promote a lengthened and widened torso, envision the line of your spine running up the internal center of your torso (rather than a line which merely touches your back shoulder blades).

Posture carries the sound. Shorten your body and the choir will dip flat in pitch. Tighten your arms with bad posture and the pitch will sharpen. In contrast, lengthen your trunk and there will be an added vibrancy to your ensemble's sound.

The breath

To facilitate breathing, allow the shoulders and lower back to widen out to the sides. The chest cavity sternum (breastbone) is held high to encourage deep, wide breathing, while the shoulders are down in a relaxed, normal position. If the leader's shoulders creep up, the singers and players will do the same, creating unwanted tension. The quality of sound of an ensemble (and especially the vocal color of a choir) is directly affected by the breath of the conductor, which in turn, affects the rhythmic vitality of the music.[17]

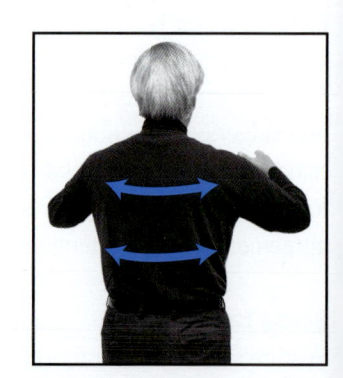

Extended spine

To facilitate breathing, allow shoulders and lower back to WIDEN out to sides.

Chapter 20 | WHERE'S THE BEAT?

The face and eyes

Thorough familiarity with the score permits you to hold your head erect, out of the score, facing the players as much as possible. Avoid mannerisms, like scratching your ear, brushing your hand through your hair, and the like. Since much nonverbal communication takes place from eye to eye, the conductor's countenance becomes a strong dramatic focus. Strive for a chamber music interaction with the eyes and breath-supporting cue preparations, entrances, and releases. Guard against reacting negatively with the face; make sure all facial gestures complement your other body language.

Embracing the sound

Leave an open, central channel of communication within the "embrace" of the arms. Crossing a beat pattern up into the face area blocks essential facial information, so it is best to keep arms around their right and left axis, which extends out from the shoulders.[18] Conductors of singers most often use both hands, presenting a balanced, aligned picture, with arms outstretched and slightly curved up and in, as though holding the sound. The curve of the arms is followed through with the wrists and hands, with the hands inside the line of the elbows.[19]

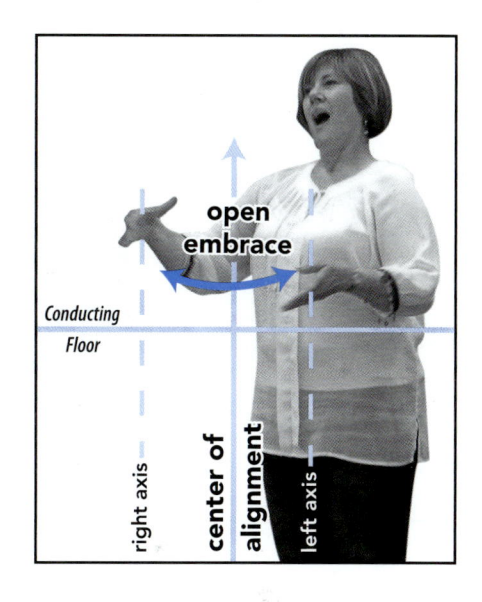

Touching the sound

The fingers are slightly rounded with a relaxed space between them. The shape of the hands can directly influence the color of a sound being produced by your ensemble. With choirs, a flat, clenched hand will result in a thin, edgy sound, while a rounded hand shape can more naturally mirror a desired vowel sound.[20] The sound exists directly in front of the conductor. The hands should not reach for the sound, but figuratively be in a position to "touch" the sound.[21]

Ensembles are accustomed to the right hand traditionally giving the beat, while the left hand supports with interpretive gestures. This does not suggest that the arms function separately from one another. It suggests instead that conductors develop the ability to coordinate all the functions between the arms, hands, fingers, head, face, and body into a unified picture. In baseball, a left-handed pitcher is known as a southpaw, a term coined in 1885 in a ballpark in Chicago, so situated that the pitcher's left arm was toward the south (south + paw). Those leaders who are left-handed must learn to present the beat with their right hand. As a result, they usually have the advantage when adding left-hand expression.[22]

Vowel diction is addressed in Songster Chapter Twelve, pp. 258–259.

The Beat Goes On

441

20 BARS REST

MUSCLE "RELEASE" EXERCISES

Breath is the core of all conducting gesture, establishing tempo, color, and style of the music. These exercises help facilitate muscle release, especially from the torso, allowing a free, "body-open" breath:

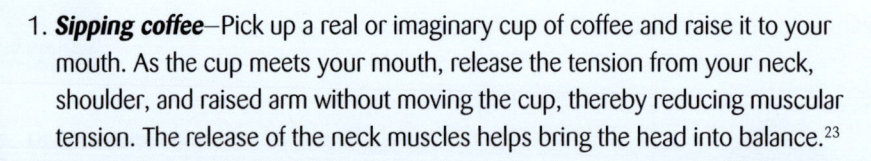

1. **Sipping coffee**—Pick up a real or imaginary cup of coffee and raise it to your mouth. As the cup meets your mouth, release the tension from your neck, shoulder, and raised arm without moving the cup, thereby reducing muscular tension. The release of the neck muscles helps bring the head into balance.[23]

2. **A weightless book bag**—Stand and pick up a book bag with one hand. Place it back on the floor and pick it up a second time, being sensitive to the sensation in your arms and upper body. Pick up the book bag a third time, but this time use only a minimum of muscular effort. The exercise helps you avoid the overexertion of muscles, which we call holding or locking. When beating time, you should not be feeling your arms, elbows, or shoulders, but should focus on a gesture centered on the preparation breath.[24]

3. **Lugging grocery bags**—Consider how you would carry two grocery bags filled with heavy canned goods (without a shopping cart) from the store to your car. Support the weight of the bags from underneath while encircling the circumference of the bags to be sure they don't fall. This exercise simulates an anticipatory posture, which holds the sound of the ensemble.[25]

DEEP BREATHING EXERCISES

In James Jordan's words, "Your [the conductor's] breath mechanism is the genesis of all music making ... The breath initiates the motion of the hands."[26] These exercises sensitize the conductor to the sensation of air dropping into the body:

1. **Starting the lawnmower**—Pretend you are starting a lawnmower. Place one leg in front of the other and grasp the pull cord. As you rapidly pull the cord toward you as though to start the mower, inhale rapidly and fill your lungs with as much air as possible. Immediately exhale the air with a forceful *sshhhhhhh*. Repeat several times. This exercise allows you to experience large amounts of air coming into the body, while at the same time allowing the muscles around the ribs to open for the breath to enter the body.[27]

2. **Surprise!**—Standing in your preparation posture, place your hands flat on your body below your navel. Imagine that someone suddenly surprises you from behind, startling you. Your mouth opens and air falls into your body and drops to the level within your body where your hands rest. If the muscles around the lower torso are unrestricted then you should feel a "ball of air" low in your body. The goal is to get the air to drop as low as the pelvis. This deep breathing signals to your ensemble to open their bodies to "breathe now."[28]

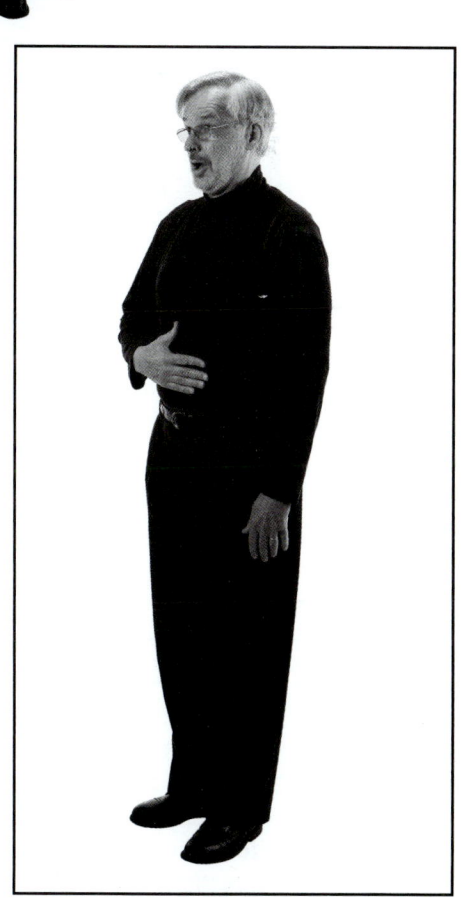

THE BEAT GESTURE

The concept of a conductor beating time has evolved over several centuries. Even those who do not read music intuitively associate the leader's vertical downbeats with the start of each vertical bar line on the page—an essential first step to ensemble music-reading. As a natural downward gesture of emphasis, the first beat of a bar must be clearly distinguishable from the other beats. Any inclination towards a sideward motion obscures the essential downward force of gravity.

THE DOWNBEAT GESTURE

Soldiers march to beats (Hep–2–3–4).

Dancers move to counts (5–6–7–8).

Camera-ready
In Chapter Twenty-Three, we will discuss ways to convince players and singers to "watch" the conductor. Be mindful that players and singers are primarily focused on the music on their stands or in their hands, so conductors get a mere peripheral glance much of the time. Therefore the leader's objective is to make everything as clear as possible for the performers, even at a glance at any moment. In the television industry, this is known as "camera-ready."

When they lose their place in the music, ensemble members rely on the downbeat being dependably clear so that they can recover their place or count. This principle negates the use of extraneous, fussy movements, like nudges, hitches, or motions between beats, which often happen too late and lead to a slowing of tempo. *Soldiers march to beats (Hep–2–3–4) and dancers move to counts (5–6–7–8).* Even when there are secondary accents or syncopation in the score, **give beats**, rather than rhythms. It is better to allow the musicians to put the notes between your beats.[29]

Oh no, a physics lesson!
An essential tenet of physics teaches us that **for every action there is an equal and opposite reaction**. When one throws a ball to the ground, the force of the downward throw **(the action)** gains momentum because of gravity. When the ball hits the ground (similar to the point of the downbeat), the ball reverses direction and bounces upward **(the reaction)**. The ascent of the ball is slower than its descent because it is moving against gravity. Therefore the ball does not return to the level from which it was dropped.[30]

Applied to conducting downbeats, the hand on a rebound **(1) never reaches the full height from which it dropped** (some suggest just half or a third the rebound), while **(2) the rebound or ascent will be slower than the descent**. Thereby, the conductor learns that the sensation of a correct rebound moves more slowly than the descent to the point of the beat.[31]

BEAT STROKE (action)

DROP HEIGHT (accelerates with gravity as ball drops)

REBOUND (reaction)

BOUNCE HEIGHT (gradually slowed by gravity)

---

ictus (*term*) \'ik - təss\ is derived from the Latin word for "stroke" and applied to music from its poetic meaning as "a recurring stress or beat in a rhythmic or metrical series of sounds."[32] In conducting, the word **ictus** refers to the part of the gesture that touches an imaginary plane marking the instant when the beat occurs. The **ictus** is the **point of the rebound**, and the **rebound** is the **flexible reaction to the ictus**.[33]

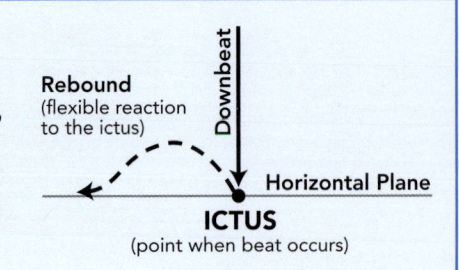

Rebound (flexible reaction to the ictus)

Downbeat

Horizontal Plane

ICTUS (point when beat occurs)

Chapter 20 | WHERE'S THE BEAT?

Prep, downbeat, and rebound

The three essential elements of the conductor's beat gesture were introduced in the concluding pp. 119–121 of the Song Leading Chapter Five:

The **DOWNBEAT** in THREE MOVEMENTS

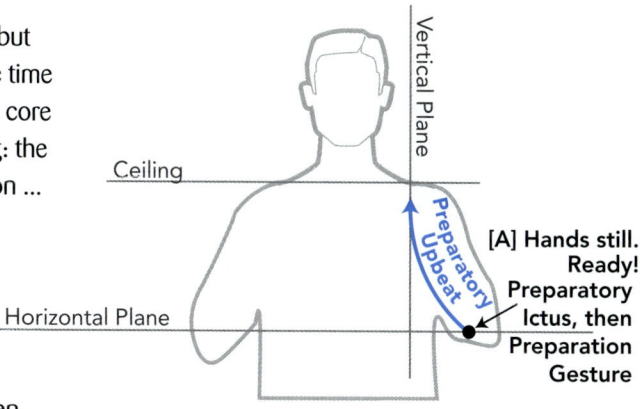

1. The preparatory upbeat signals not only the *tempo* and meter, but determines the character of the intended sound. It generally takes the time of exactly one beat of the time-beating gestures that follow. [A] At its core is the **breath**. In Leonard Bernstein's words, "It is exactly like breathing: the preparation is like an inhalation, and the music sounds like an exhalation ... so it is with music: we inhale on the upbeat and sing out a phrase of music, then inhale again and breathe out the next phrase."[34]

    Breathing with the preparatory gesture is essential to initial rhythmic precision. Drop your jaw sufficiently to convey the initial breath, and don't breathe through the nose.[35] The body needs to be open to receive the air before you breathe, and then receive it quietly. Remember to think of the air flowing into and out of your lungs, rather than pulling it in or pushing it out.

    James Jordan speaks of "feeling the roundness of your breath as they [your arms] embrace the sound."[36] It is during the preparatory gesture that the conductor is "imaging" the sound *before* it starts.

    [A] Hands still. Ready! Preparatory Ictus, then Preparation Gesture

    [A] PREPARATORY UPBEAT

2. The downbeat gesture itself is a motion directly down to the bottom point of the beat. [B] This "ictus" point marks where the desired sound is to occur and emphasizes the downbeat's importance. (Full definition on the previous page.) When you are not using a baton, the point of the beat exits through the tip of the middle finger.[37] One cannot underscore enough that the ictus point does not represent duration, but rather a moment in time, marking the beginning of a period in time. McElheran suggests the ictus point is like a starter's gun, with the next unit commencing at beat two, etc. (By extension, a half note's duration extends from the ictus point of beat one all the way to the precise moment that beat three commences.)[38]

    It is essential to put aside the notion of the ensemble being exactly "with" the conductor's downbeat. If the ensemble produces the sound simultaneously with the impulse of the ictus, the immediate effect would be a slowing of tempo. To be clear, the instant when the beat stops falling and begins to rise is "ideally" known as beat one. That is when the note begins its life.[39] We say ideally, as most instrumentalists and singers learn to delay the actual sound of the beat in agreement with the conductor. **In reality, the conductor moves forward with his gesture, not waiting for the sound to speak, and thereby is truly "directing" the ensemble, rather than "following" the sound.**

    [B] Downbeat Ictus (where note begins)

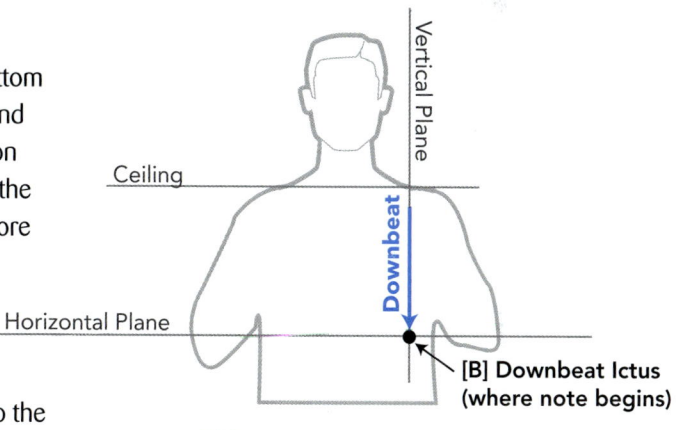

    [B] DOWNBEAT GESTURE

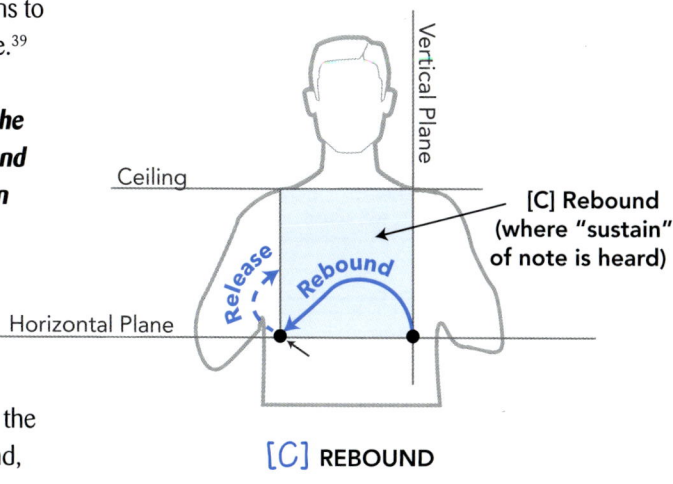

3. The rebound or bounce is the immediate reaction to the ictus point of the beat, which, to keep the downbeat uniformly recognizable, moves upwards, becoming the preparatory gesture for the next beat to come. [C] This is where the "sustain" of the note is heard, and the conductor is already interacting with this sound, ready to make adjustments to the next beat.

    [C] Rebound (where "sustain" of note is heard)

    [C] REBOUND

The Beat Goes On

445

The rebound closes with a *release*, based on the energy of the downward ictus. Bounce immediately and avoid any hesitation (or double hitch) by keeping the hands constantly moving. Your hand should only appear to stop at the very top of the beat, then only for an instant, similar to a ball thrown straight up in the air. If you pretend that your arm has weight, the beat will have a heftier character and appear to bounce better.

Exactly where is the beat?

Certain principles of conducting just make good sense!

- Here's one: In order to follow, performers must know what you are going to do before you do it.
- The part of that principle that will make you scratch your head says: To say that performers are to theoretically "follow" the conductor, implies being behind.
- Therefore, it follows that: Players and singers actually anticipate and perform with the conductor.

To prevent late-sounding downbeats, strive to have the right hand fall downward at a constant, even pace. If one accelerates the descent to the ictus, the downbeat will certainly sound *late*. [A] Paradoxically, a similar result follows if you gradually put the brakes on toward the bottom of the beat. Your performers will perceive a rapid fall at the beginning and expect it to continue in a steady pace. The result will be an unintended *early* entrance. [B] After a few rounds of premature starts, your musicians will become gun-shy and choose to play it safe. This will then be *later* than you desire. On the other hand, an ensemble may respond to a "hot stove beat," comprised of a slowing-as-you-descend downbeat, answered by a quick flare-up rebound, by playing *behind* the intended beat. [C]

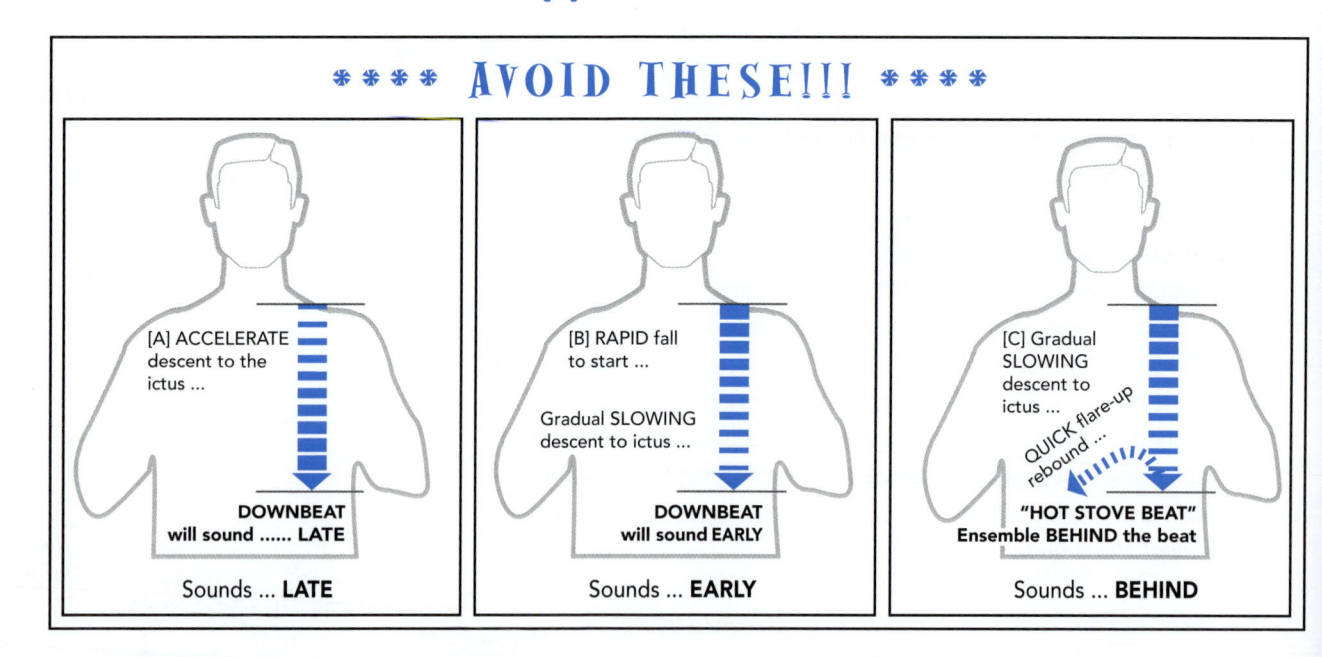

**** AVOID THESE!!! ****

[A] ACCELERATE descent to the ictus ...
DOWNBEAT will sound ...... LATE
Sounds ... LATE

[B] RAPID fall to start ...
Gradual SLOWING descent to ictus ...
DOWNBEAT will sound EARLY
Sounds ... EARLY

[C] Gradual SLOWING descent to ictus ...
QUICK flare-up rebound ...
"HOT STOVE BEAT" Ensemble BEHIND the beat
Sounds ... BEHIND

20 BARS REST

WHERE'S YOUR BEAT?

1. After many years of conducting young players, I discovered that I was "permitting" an extremely late beat. This is prevalent in the band fraternity and sometimes hard for the audience to watch. Practice in front of a mirror, or watch a video of your conducting to analyze the timed response to your beat. Slow your beat down to study the clarity and consistency of its path, pace, and timing.

2. Test whether the "level" of your beats is consistent by tapping a table, an ironing board or countertop at elbow height (representing the bounce level "floor" for most beats). Without looking down, go through all the beat patterns using the correct motions, being sure you tap the table. This "touching" also serves as a reminder to "bounce" or "spring" on each beat, rather than float, or stop moving. Become cognizant of when and where the hand is bouncing, while maintaining a steady tempo.[40]

CONDUCTING FUNDAMENTALS RESOURCES

Basic Techniques of Conducting, Kenneth Phillips (Oxford)
Conducting–A Hands–On Approach, Anthony Maiello (Alfred)
Conducting from the Inside Out, DVD, Allan McMurray (Santa Barbara)
Conducting Technique, Brock McElheran (Oxford)
Evoking Sound–Fundamentals of Choral Conducting and Rehearsing, James Jordan (GIA)
Evoking Sound, DVD, James Jordan with Heather Buchanan (GIA)
On Becoming a Conductor, Lessons and Meditations on the Art of Conducting, Frank Battisti (Meredith Music)
Precision Conducting, Timothy Sharp (Roger Dean)
The Modern Conductor, Elizabeth Green (Prentice Hall)
Upbeat Downbeat: Basic Conducting Patterns and Techniques, Sandra Willetts (Abingdon Press)

Okay, now that we've learned to handle traffic with some fundamentals of conducting, let's move on to the next intersection and consider whether it's safe to baton or not, and then learn how to start, stop and cue your moving vehicle. That is, your ensemble... Of course, the conductor exhibits great caution when standing at the intersection of players, singers and great music!

CHAPTER TWENTY-ONE

STICKS, STARTS AND STOPS
More Conducting Fundamentals

*The first beat in the bar goes down and the last beat goes up;
the rest is experience.* —Max Rudolph

FROM AURAL TO VISUAL— THE EVOLUTION OF CONDUCTING

Early church chant conducting emphasized horizontal motions as a means to allow the line to move forward. The leader's hand motions were used to show different groups of notes. The musical notation of the time did not show actual pitches, but rather various signs to represent those conducting gestures. The singers of the day memorized all their music, so the choirmaster needed only to consult the manuscript with the conducting notation to refresh their memory of the details.

Chapter Twenty-One considers more fundamental mechanics of conducting, including:
- baton use
- starts and entrance cues
- pauses and cutoffs

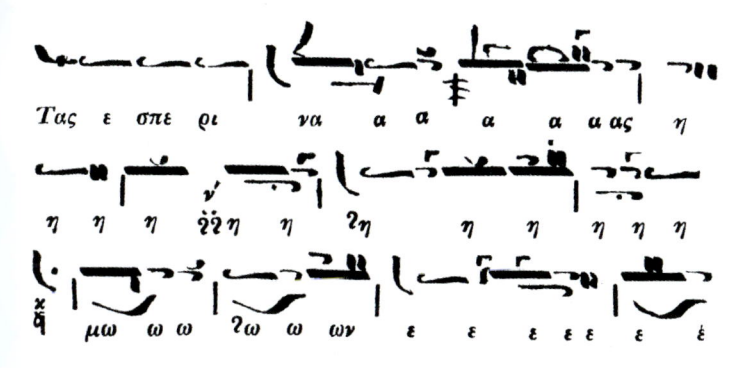

This went along just fine until Guido d'Arezzo invented the system of *solfeggio* (c. 1000). No late Medieval or Renaissance music textbook was complete without a drawing of the so-called "Guidonian hand." Pupils were taught to sing intervals as the teacher pointed with the index finger of his right hand to the different joints of his open left hand. Each one of the joints stood for one of the 20 notes of the system, but any other note, such as F# or Eb, was considered "outside the hand."[1]

A precursor of today's musical staff followed, which for the first time allowed singers to look at a page of music, and sing it without having learned the lines by heart. One of the singers gave the pulse (known as the tactus) with a simple "down–up" motion.

As ensembles grew in size in the Classical period, more direction than the continuo player or principal violinist or cellist was deemed necessary to indicate the spatial location between beats. With the advent of geometric "maps," or what we now call beat patterns, conducting inadvertently evolved from a mainly aural art to a visual one.[2]

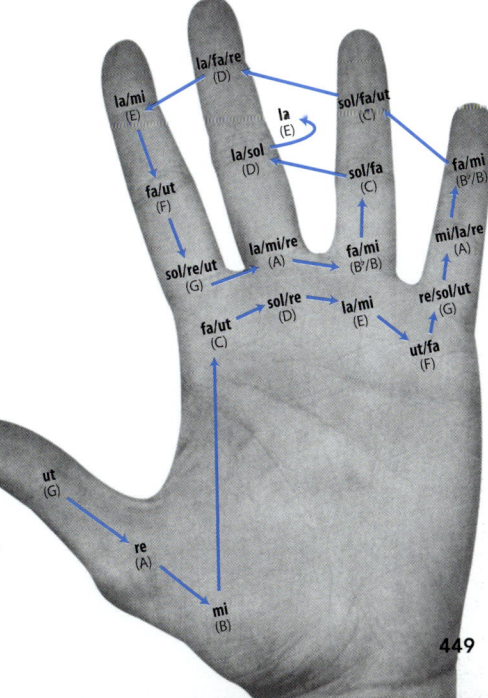

The Beat Goes On

TO BATON OR NOT TO BATON?

The earliest conducting was done with gestures of hands alone; then a few nods and signs from a keyboardist. From there it evolved into an audible beating, then a silent waving of a string player's bow. This resulted in the use of a baton and what Elizabeth Green calls, "patterned rhythmic designs."[3] Conducting with a baton has emerged today as a sophisticated, effective sign language, from which the slightest gesture of the tip of the stick can evoke a precise response from well-trained players. Perhaps difficult to believe, but Jean-Baptiste Lully (1632–87), a preeminent French ballet and opera composer, tragically died from injuries sustained to his foot while he was beating time on the floor with a cane.[4]

Myths about baton use

Let's begin by dispelling some myths about baton use:[5]

Myth #1: *A baton is always used with instrumental ensembles*, not with choruses. This assumption presumes that choruses never perform biting, incisive rhythms. On the other hand (pun intended), conductors often ask their instrumentalists to play smoothly, as though they are singers, and their success can benefit from the conductor's shaping of the hands and fingers, sans baton.

Myth #2: *A baton gives a more precise point to the beat.* The beat can be as easily "rounded" (lacking any point) or blurred, with or without a baton. The hand can be ever so precise and incisive, and additionally hide any nervous quiver, better than a baton.

Myth #3: *A baton can be better seen than the hand.* This depends on the backdrop, the colors the conductor is wearing (for instance, a white shirt versus a dark jacket, using a white baton) or lighting in the room (a white baton against a lit room, versus a darkened one), and the distance from the performers (which favors the hands over a skinny baton).

Myth #4: *A baton adds rigidity to the beat*, which detracts from the flowing quality required in *cantabile* passages. This is probably the main reason some conductors elect to put the baton down in slow sections. There are great *cantabile* conductors who give stunning, articulate performances without the benefit of a baton. The baton also reduces fatigue in a conductor's arm by shortening the distance the arm needs to travel. More intimate expression may suggest working without a baton, while for more precise clarity, one can discreetly pick up the baton in *tempo*.[6]

Baton...

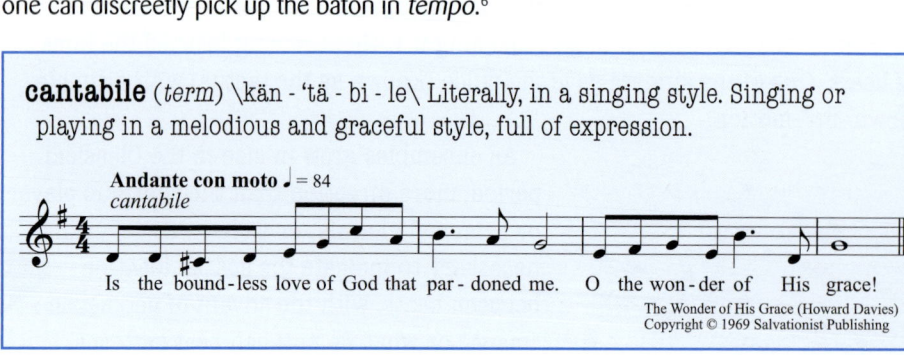

NO baton...

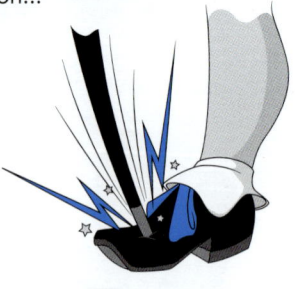

EXTREME baton...

---

cantabile (*term*) \kän - 'tä - bi - le\ Literally, in a singing style. Singing or playing in a melodious and graceful style, full of expression.

Andante con moto ♩ = 84
cantabile

Is the bound-less love of God that par-doned me. O the won-der of His grace!

The Wonder of His Grace (Howard Davies)
Copyright © 1969 Salvationist Publishing

Choosing a baton

The choice of a baton is a matter of personal preference centering on three criteria: the length of the baton, the type of handle, and the feel of the balance.

- The size and proximity to the ensemble, as well as the conductor's torso size, affects the **length of the baton** selected. Standard baton lengths (including the handle) are *10, 12, 14, and 16 inches*. The conductor maintains good arm positioning with the elbow up and extended. The baton, if positioned correctly and the correct length, will angle, from the hand along the vertical plane, slightly to the left. This positions the tip of the baton at the center of the body torso, along the line of buttons on a shirt or blouse.

- **Baton handles** are made of *rubber*, *cork*, or a *variety of woods in pear-shaped* and *tapered shapes*, or in *turned aluminum* with a cusp in the handle. The handle choice is affected by hand size and the desired grip, which allows for the subtle response action needed in conducting. A conductor may hold a large handle under the fingers with too much grip and at a baton angle too far left to compensate for the palm of a small hand. Conversely, small ball-like handles may encourage too much wrist action, as the conductor holds the baton primarily on the shaft, reducing the flexibility to vary articulation.

- A good baton is light in weight and **well-balanced**. A baton in motion must appear to float horizontally. The material of the shaft affects the overall weight of the baton. Options range from *wood* (some prone to snap or splinter), *graphite* (when hollowed out, the lightest), to *fiberglass* (the sturdiest and cheapest). Balance points may vary with batons. Typically one can balance the baton on one finger at the juncture between the shaft and the handle, or lay the baton across the upturned palm of the hand without it falling.

Holding the baton

The conducting gesture should be projected to the tip of the baton, facilitated by a slightly flexible wrist. We think of the baton as an extension of the arm, held mostly in a direct line to the forearm. The wrist, as the only link to the hand, should respond with ease to the movements of the arm, and the baton, in turn, to the hand and wrist.

The basic grip

With *the basic grip*, hold the baton as though shaking hands with someone, with the hand wrapped around the baton, and the butt end against the fleshy hollow near the base of the thumb.[7] The principal elements of Elizabeth Green's step-by-step description of the basic grip[8] are indicated below.

- Fundamentally, the stick is held between the tip of the thumb and the side of the index finger.
- The stick contacts the index finger between the middle joint of the finger and the nail.
- The thumb should bend outward slightly at the knuckle, which relieves muscular tension in the wrist and lower arm.
- An open space is thereby formed between the thumb and side of the first finger.

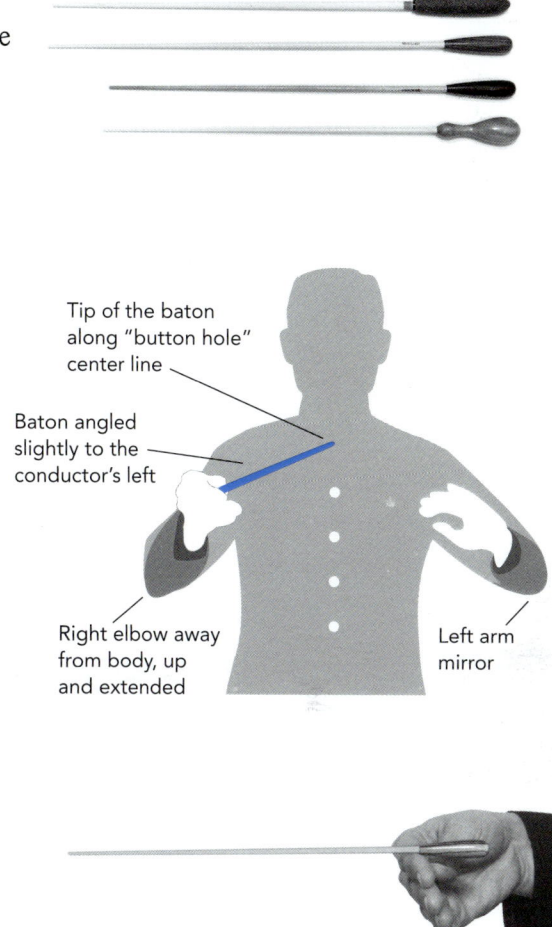

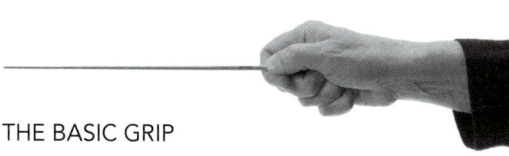

Tip of the baton along "button hole" center line

Baton angled slightly to the conductor's left

Right elbow away from body, up and extended

Left arm mirror

WELL-BALANCED

THE BASIC GRIP
Note correctly bent thumb for good control.

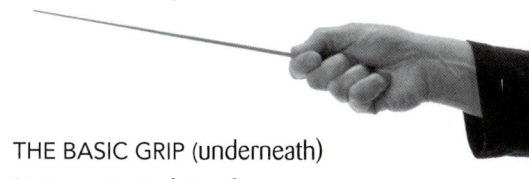

THE BASIC GRIP (underneath)
Note contact of ring finger.

- The ring finger lightly contacts the heel of the baton, creating a three-point grip, which is both flexible and secure: tip of thumb, side of first finger, and ball of the ring finger.
- When beating time, the palm of the hand should face the floor, permitting the hand to move freely up and down in the wrist joint.
- The tip of the baton should point forward, not leftward, in continuation of the line of the forearm through the hand.
- The tapping of each beat should be felt at the tip of the stick.

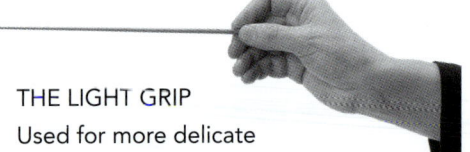

The light grip

For music of a lighter quality, *the light grip* may be preferred. A wider hollow is created between the thumb and middle finger by moving the contact with the baton on the second finger up, midway between the top knuckle and the tip of the finger. An alternative light grip replaces the second finger baton contact with the first finger. All of these grips are interchangeable, used interpretatively as the music demands. [9]

THE LIGHT GRIP
Used for more delicate musical passages.

Slips and fixes [10]

- Avoid pressing the index finger on the tip of the stick. This transfers "stiffness" to the other fingers, and inadvertently transfers the point of the beat indirectly to the wrist.

- Keep contact between the heel of the baton and the palm of the hand. If the butt of the baton "floats," attention is drawn to the now overly-flexible wrist and the tip of the baton hangs too freely, hampering precision.

- Avoid allowing the heel of the baton to slide under the base of the little finger, which forces the baton out of direct line with the forearm and causes it to point undesirably left and up.

- Neither should you permit the bottom of the baton to slip under the little finger, causing it to protrude beyond the palm of the hand. To remedy this, make a straight line from the elbow to the base joint of the middle finger and adjust the stick properly under the thumb.

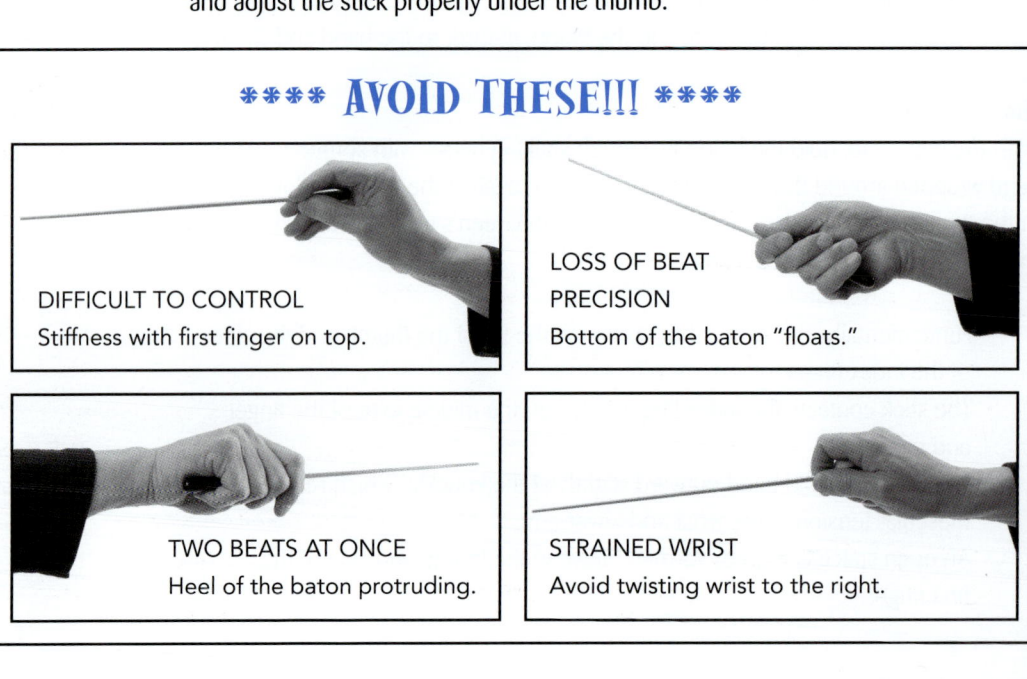

**** AVOID THESE!!! ****

DIFFICULT TO CONTROL
Stiffness with first finger on top.

LOSS OF BEAT PRECISION
Bottom of the baton "floats."

TWO BEATS AT ONCE
Heel of the baton protruding.

STRAINED WRIST
Avoid twisting wrist to the right.

Chapter 21 | STICKS, STARTS AND STOPS

[A] [B] [C] [D]

Note: These four images show the conductor from the ensemble's perspective.

Seeing the beat

Altering the level of the bounce or ictus point creates enough momentary uncertainty that players lose their security in anticipating the beat. Another difficulty is a matter of optics. Our eyes follow large movements in a two-dimensional manner, either sideways or up and down. A motion toward or away from a performer is perceived as a negligible difference. [A] If one points the baton directly at the players, they cannot see the baton. [B] Better to use a little angle. [C]

This optical principle extends to players or singers on the conductor's periphery—to the left and right—when beats are made to the side. Beats two and three in 4/4 meter, for instance, appear to be coming toward them. [D] These individuals can really only see the vertical beats with clarity, giving yet another reason for the leader to back up from the ensemble to allow an improved line of vision, even for beats that extend to the side.

21 BARS REST

Exercises to develop baton technique

1. Hold the baton correctly while reading or studying a book. This simple practice promotes a feeling of ease and familiarity with the baton, as though one has an unnoticed, added appendage.[11]

2. With a baton, practice swatting imaginary flies using plenty of wrist action, stopping short when the stick is horizontal and the forearm is parallel to the floor. If the end of the baton seems to vibrate, it probably is too long, so cut some of the baton off.[12]

3. First, without a baton, try to acquire the feeling of bouncing a ball by tapping with the tips of your fingers. Then repeat the same, but this time with a baton. Note that too much flexibility in the wrist is as bad as none at all, so keep the wrist action small.[13]

4. Attend different kinds of rehearsals and concerts and observe how well you can see the conductor's beat. Ask yourself if the ensemble is actually following the stick or the hand, and if the gestures are clear. If using a baton, consider how the baton captures the mood of the music more effectively than the hand, and vice versa.[14]

The Beat Goes On

STARTS AND ENTRANCE CUES

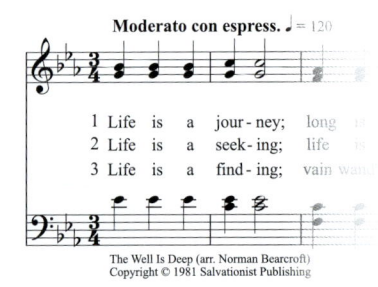

Moderato con espress. ♩ = 120

1 Life is a jour-ney; long
2 Life is a seek-ing; life
3 Life is a find-ing; vain

The Well Is Deep (arr. Norman Bearcroft)
Copyright © 1981 Salvationist Publishing

The PREPARATORY BEAT

The initial downbeat is the most important gesture in conducting. Within just one beat, as the conductor breathes with the ensemble, and descends to the bottom of the starting beat, the musicians learn the tempo, dynamic, mood, and exact moment at which to commence the piece. The principles of preparatory beats for entrance **on a full beat**, and for those **off the beat** also carry over into cueing entrances for a soloist, section, or the entire ensemble over the span of a piece.

Entrances on a full beat

When the entrance of a piece occurs "on" a note value of a full beat, the preparation for the entrance calls for a full beat preparation before that beat of entrance. In 4/4 time, if the music is to begin on BEAT ONE, then the preparation requires the point of BEAT FOUR and its rebound, leading into BEAT ONE. In 2/4 time, if the music begins on BEAT TWO, then the beat of preparation is BEAT ONE, including the preceding rebound.

To amplify what we explained in the previous chapter (p. 445): In order to bring the initial beat down, you must start beating one count earlier. Conductors liken this to taking a breath on the beat before you begin to actually vocalize or sound a note on a brass instrument. A good preparatory beat is a summons or invitation that begins from a still, ready position, which Max Rudolf calls **Attention (Att)**. The sequence starts still at **Attention**, then makes the **Prep Beat** (coupled with the breath), and then the **Initial Beat**. Use the appropriate articulation action (for instance, *legato*, *staccato*, or *marcato*), coupled with the corresponding breath to help actualize a **Prep Beat** that is: (1) anticipatory in character and mood, and (2) exactly one beat before the **Initial Beat**, thereby indicating the correct tempo.

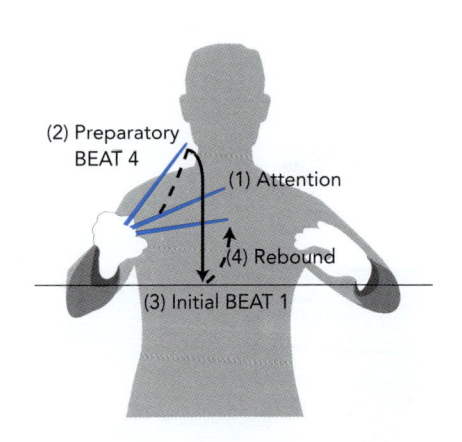

(2) Preparatory BEAT 4
(1) Attention
(4) Rebound
(3) Initial BEAT 1

ATTENTION    PREP BEAT    INITIAL DOWNBEAT

[A]   [B]   [C]

Preparing entrances

In order to prepare an entrance **the conductor must first determine on which beat the entrance occurs and picture the gesture back a beat.** The preparatory gesture is usually initiated by the right hand/arm turned toward the ensemble, section, or soloist a few beats in advance. The left hand can aid in signaling the character of the entrance, for instance, with the hand down for quieter entries, [A] or the hand open for more forceful statements, [B] eventually joining simultaneously with the right hand on the downbeat.

Both hands held with palms facing up toward the section or soloist can be a welcoming gesture before giving an entrance cue. [C] Prepare to cue an entrance within a piece at least two beats before. Face the instrumentalists and singers and anticipate visually with your eyes and face what you are trying to say with your hands. Remember two things: (1) Keep the bottom floor of your beat consistent, so players can anticipate exactly where you intend the beat to happen, and (2) Do not stop at the bottom of your beat; rather, remember to bounce.

Slow or fast gestures for singers

The color, attack, and release of the assortment of vowels and consonants available to singers (covered in Chapter Twelve, pp. 258–262) calls for a correspondingly varied prep beat, release, and rebound. **The gesture should mirror and encourage the inherent resonance of the starting and ending vowels and consonants.**

The vowel color should be reflected in the shape of the hand and fingers. Sing and conduct yourself using a sustained pitch on the different vowels. Notice the hand position you use.[15] Vowels use more open, slow release gestures to initiate and sustain the vowel's tone color (**O** come, **o** come). Consonants as articulators require a quick stroke gesture for *fast unvoiced consonants*, like **c**, **k**, **f**, **p**, **t**, **s**. (Silent nigh**t**, holy nigh**t**). The *slow resonant consonants*, like **l**, **m**, **n**, **ng**, some **th's**, **v**, **z**, call for a slow wrist rebound allowing time to sustain the resonance (Noe**l**, noe**l**).[16]

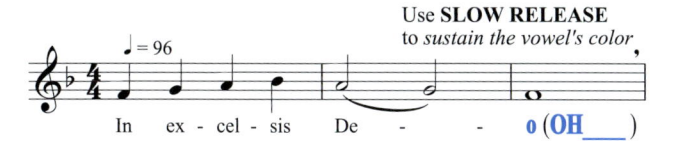

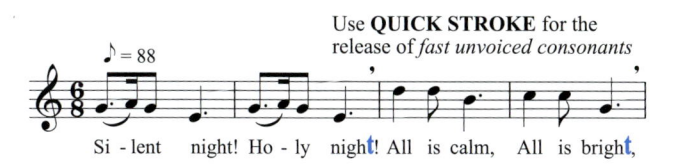

Remember to bounce, bounce, bounce

Use **SLOW RELEASE** to *sustain the vowel's color*
In ex - cel - sis De - - o (OH___)

Use **QUICK STROKE** for the release of *fast unvoiced consonants*
Si - lent night! Ho - ly night! All is calm, All is bright,

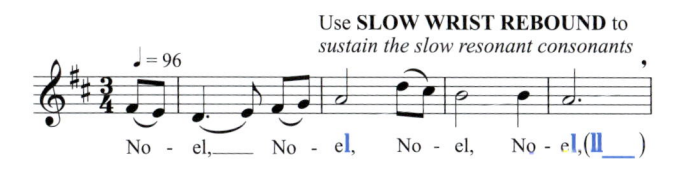

Use **SLOW WRIST REBOUND** to *sustain the slow resonant consonants*
No - el,___ No - el, No - el, No - el,(l___)

The **shaping of vowels** with the conductor's hands was introduced in Chapter Twenty, p. 441.

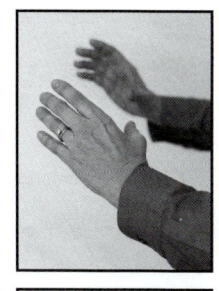

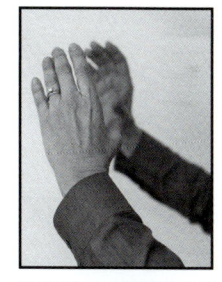

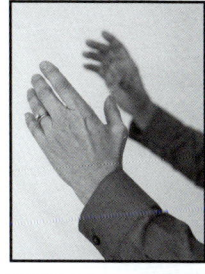

How do you get to Carnegie Hall? Practice, practice, practice ...

It is time well spent to work through the following selection of entrances, which commence on different beats in various meters. Vary the expression in the gesture (*legato, staccato, marcato,* etc.) as suggested by that particular song's character and tempo.

Entrances ON the BEAT

When the entrance of a piece occurs on a note value of a full beat, *a full beat preparation is required.*

ON THE DOWNBEAT

4/4: Upbeat prep on BEAT FOUR to downbeat on BEAT ONE

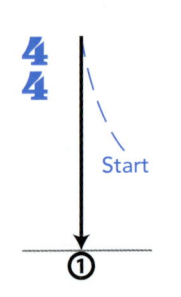

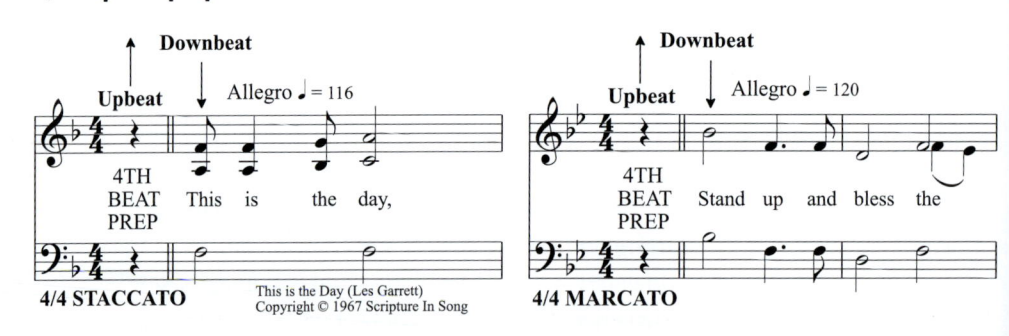

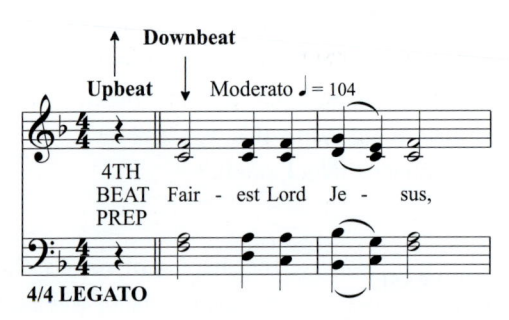

4/4 STACCATO — Allegro ♩ = 116 — 4TH BEAT PREP — "This is the day,"
This is the Day (Les Garrett) Copyright © 1967 Scripture In Song

4/4 MARCATO — Allegro ♩ = 120 — 4TH BEAT PREP — "Stand up and bless the"

4/4 LEGATO — Moderato ♩ = 104 — 4TH BEAT PREP — "Fair-est Lord Je-sus,"

3/4: Upbeat prep on BEAT THREE to downbeat on BEAT ONE

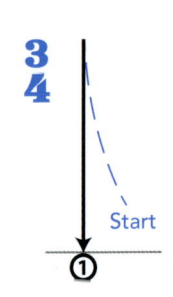

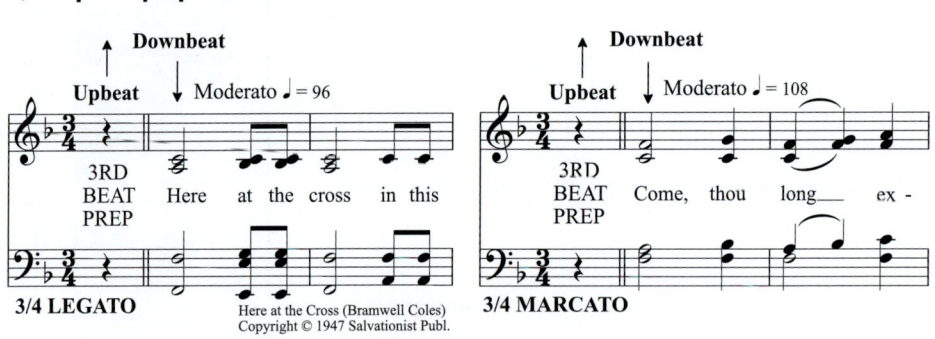

3/4 LEGATO — Moderato ♩ = 96 — 3RD BEAT PREP — "Here at the cross in this"
Here at the Cross (Bramwell Coles) Copyright © 1947 Salvationist Publ.

3/4 MARCATO — Moderato ♩ = 108 — 3RD BEAT PREP — "Come, thou long ex-"

2/2 (cut time): Upbeat prep on BEAT TWO to downbeat on BEAT ONE

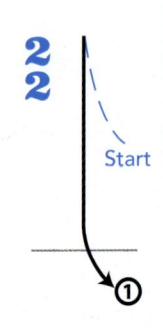

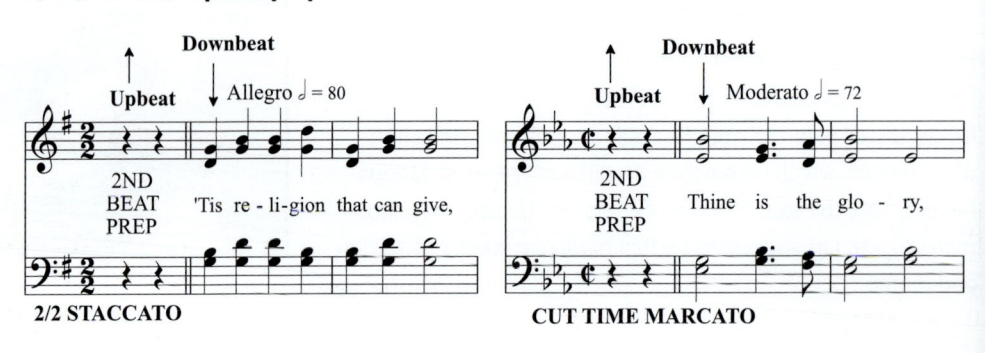

2/2 STACCATO — Allegro 𝅗𝅥 = 80 — 2ND BEAT PREP — "'Tis re-li-gion that can give,"

CUT TIME MARCATO — Moderato 𝅗𝅥 = 72 — 2ND BEAT PREP — "Thine is the glo-ry,"

ONE BEAT PICKUP

4/4: One beat prep on BEAT THREE to upbeat on BEAT FOUR

4/4 LEGATO
(Beat 4 pickup)
3RD BEAT PREP — When morn-ing gilds the skies,___ My

4/4 STACCATO
(Beat 4 pickup)
3RD BEAT PREP — God's love is won-der-ful, God's
God's Love is Wonderful (Sidney Cox)
Copyright © 1932 Salvationist Publ.

4/4 MARCATO
(Beat 4 pickup)
3RD BEAT PREP — All hail the pow'r of Je-sus' name! Let

3/4: One beat prep on BEAT TWO to upbeat on BEAT THREE

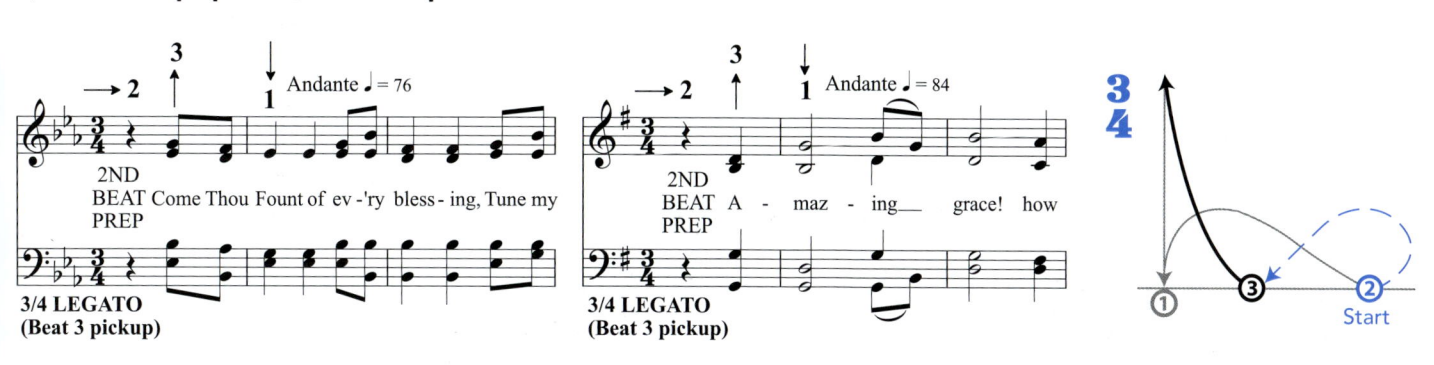

3/4 LEGATO
(Beat 3 pickup)
2ND BEAT PREP — Come Thou Fount of ev-'ry bless-ing, Tune my

3/4 LEGATO
(Beat 3 pickup)
2ND BEAT PREP — A - maz - ing___ grace! how

2/4 (or 2/2): One beat prep on BEAT ONE to upbeat on BEAT TWO

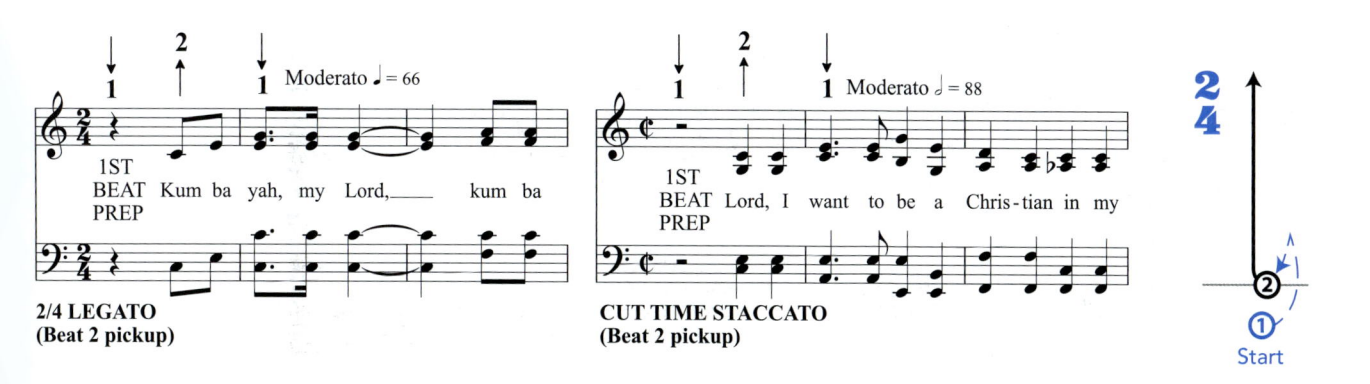

2/4 LEGATO
(Beat 2 pickup)
1ST BEAT PREP — Kum ba yah, my Lord,___ kum ba

CUT TIME STACCATO
(Beat 2 pickup)
1ST BEAT PREP — Lord, I want to be a Chris-tian in my

The Beat Goes On

ONE BEAT PICKUP (continued)
6/8: One beat prep on BEAT FIVE to upbeat on BEAT SIX

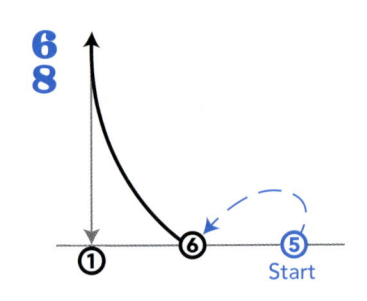

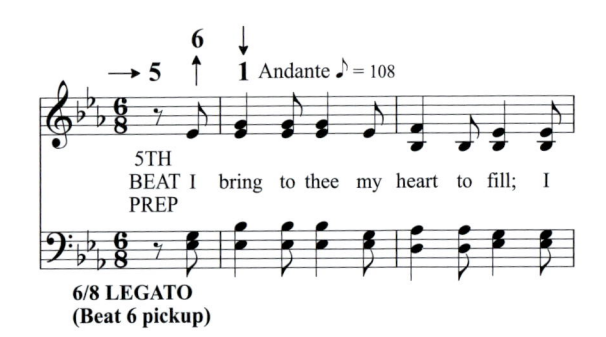

6/8 LEGATO (Beat 6 pickup) — Andante ♪ = 108
5TH BEAT PREP: "I bring to thee my heart to fill; I"

TWO BEAT PICKUP
4/4: One beat prep on BEAT TWO to set up BEAT THREE

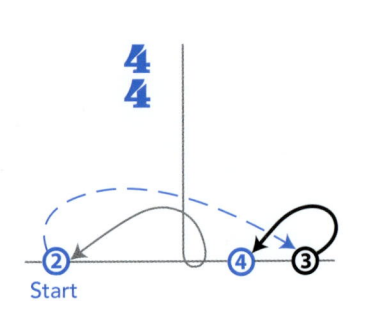

4/4 LEGATO (Beat 3 pickup) — With reverence ♩ = 72
2ND BEAT PREP: "It is well____ with my / It is well"

4/4 LEGATO (Beat 3 pickup) — Simply ♩ = 76
2ND BEAT PREP: "Here I am to wor-ship, Here I"

Here I Am to Worship (Tim Hughes)
Copyright © 2000 Thankyou Music

THREE BEAT PICKUP
4/4: One beat prep on BEAT ONE to set up BEAT TWO

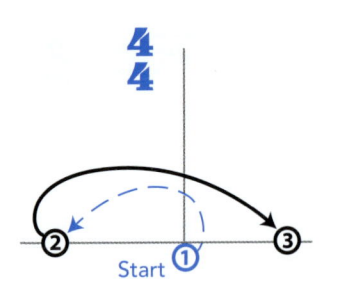

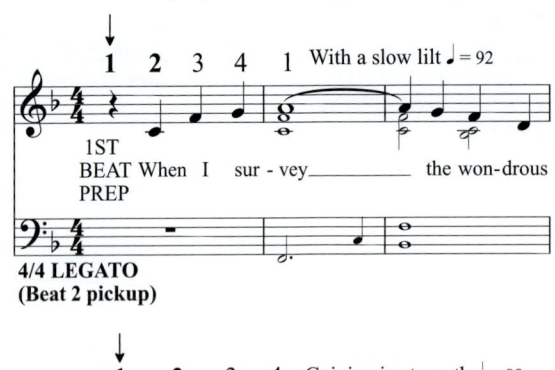

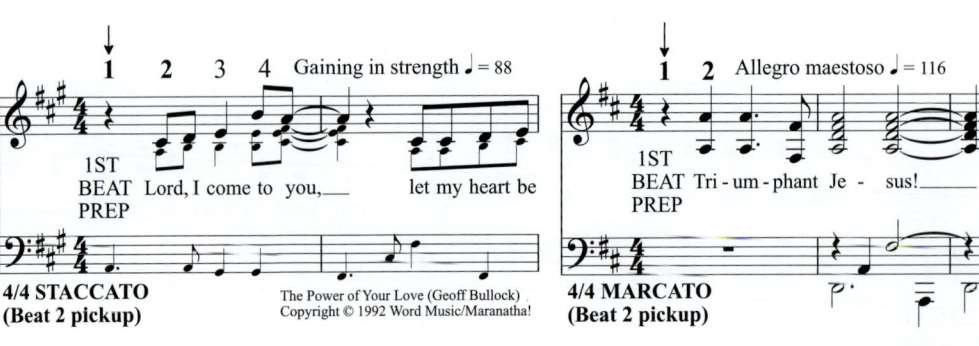

4/4 LEGATO (Beat 2 pickup) — With a slow lilt ♩ = 92
1ST BEAT PREP: "When I sur-vey____ the won-drous"

4/4 STACCATO (Beat 2 pickup) — Gaining in strength ♩ = 88
1ST BEAT PREP: "Lord, I come to you,____ let my heart be"

The Power of Your Love (Geoff Bullock)
Copyright © 1992 Word Music/Maranatha!

4/4 MARCATO (Beat 2 pickup) — Allegro maestoso ♩ = 116
1ST BEAT PREP: "Tri-um-phant Je-sus!"

Entrances ON the HALF BEAT

When an entrance begins on a half beat, the preparatory beat is reduced to the start of the beat on which the entrance half beat occurs. If the music begins on the second half of BEAT TWO in 3/4 time, then the preparation is merely a BEAT TWO gesture. For this type of offbeat entrance, the beat gesture is the sole preparation.[17]

Starting BETWEEN BEATS

3/4

HALF BEAT pickup on the "and" of BEAT TWO

Start here, motionless

HALF BEAT PICKUPS

4/4: Prep beat on BEAT THREE to prepare the "AND" of BEAT THREE

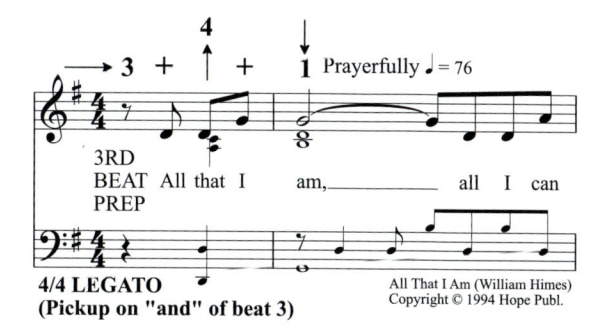

Prayerfully ♩ = 76

3RD BEAT PREP — All that I am, all I can

4/4 LEGATO
(Pickup on "and" of beat 3)

All That I Am (William Himes)
Copyright © 1994 Hope Publ.

4/4: Prep beat on BEAT TWO to prepare the "AND" of 2

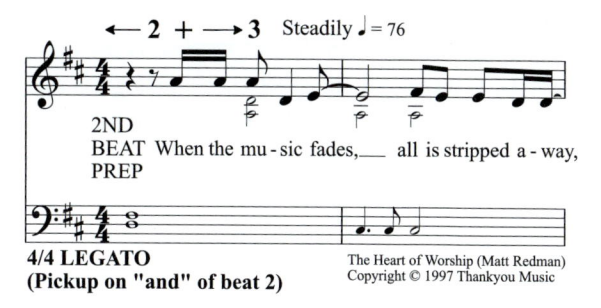

Steadily ♩ = 76

2ND BEAT PREP — When the mu-sic fades, all is stripped a-way,

4/4 LEGATO
(Pickup on "and" of beat 2)

The Heart of Worship (Matt Redman)
Copyright © 1997 Thankyou Music

3/4: Prep beat on BEAT TWO to prepare the "AND" of 2

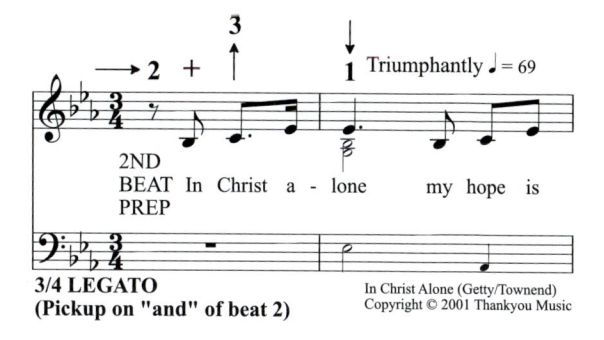

Triumphantly ♩ = 69

2ND BEAT PREP — In Christ a-lone my hope is

3/4 LEGATO
(Pickup on "and" of beat 2)

In Christ Alone (Getty/Townend)
Copyright © 2001 Thankyou Music

4/4: Prep beat on BEAT ONE to prepare the "AND" of 1

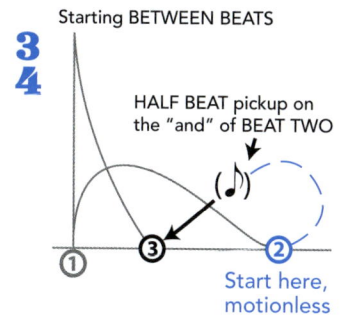

Steadily ♩ = 76

1ST BEAT PREP — I'm com-ing back to the heart of wor-ship

4/4 LEGATO
(Pickup on "and" of beat 1)

The Heart of Worship (Matt Redman)
Copyright © 1997 Thankyou Music

The Beat Goes On

2/2: Prep beat on BEAT ONE to prepare the "AND" of 1

2/2 LEGATO
(Pickup on "and" of beat 1)

How Much More (John Larsson)
Copyright © 1970 Salvationist Publ.

4/4: Prep beat on BEAT ONE to prepare the "AND" of 1

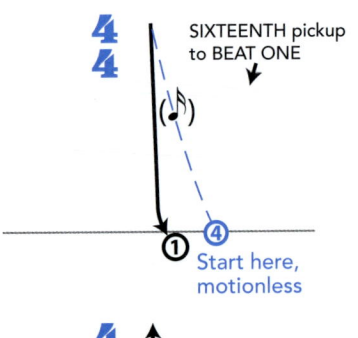

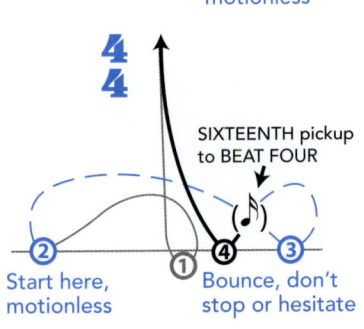

4/4 LEGATO
(Pickup on "and" of beat 1)

Wake Up, O Sleeper (Graham Kendrick)
Copyright © 1994 Make Way Music

Entrances on LESS THAN a HALF BEAT

When an entrance occurs that uses less than a half beat (For instance, a sixteenth pick-up to BEAT ONE) **then the preparation is the full beat that contains the pickup note**, similar to an on-the-beat entrance. The logic is that the full beat preparation gives enough information to determine the length of the note of entrance.[18] Because of the difficulty of executing certain starts, especially in fast tempo, conductors will sometimes give an extra count to secure precision, meaning a full beat PLUS the beat with the pickup.[19]

4/4: Prep beat on BEAT THREE to prepare sixteenth pickup to BEAT FOUR

4/4 STACCATO
(Pickup on "and" of beat 3)

12/8: Prep beat on BEAT THREE to prepare triplet pickup on BEAT FOUR

12/8 (Beat in 4) MARCATO
(Pickup on beat 4)

When the Glory (John Larsson)
Copyright © 1976 Salvationist Publ.

2/2: Quick prep beat on BEAT TWO to prepare eighth pickup to BEAT ONE

2/2 STACCATO
(Pickup on the "and" of beat 2)

His Loving Touch (Iva L. Samples)
Copyright © 1974 Salvationist Publ.

21 BARS REST

Fits and starts

1. First practice lots of songs that commence on BEAT ONE. Vary the tempo and effort action (for instance, *legato*, *staccato* or *marcato*) as suggested by the song.

2. Once confident with BEAT ONE starts, practice the other beat and pickup entrances and starts, thus varying the beat of preparation. Ask your partners if you have successfully conveyed the tempo, volume, and mood before you reach the bottom of the starting beat.

PAUSES AND CUT-OFFS

Final releases

The simple formula for the "Invitation" Preparatory Beat applies well to a final stop at the end of a piece or section: start still at **Attention**, then **Up Slant** (Preparation), and then **Down** (the Cutoff), returning to exactly where you started. Gestured by either hand, final stops are made by strongly tapping the point of the beat, coupled with a rebound that visually reflects the intensity and reverberation of the concluding tone.

Cutoff gestures

When the final note is a held chord, hold the sound in your hands until it is time to tap the closing beat. This gesture works best for a percussive or punctuated cutoff. A full-circle motion visually ties a knot in the space in front of the body backdrop, providing more time for a final chord of sustained character. As a rule, circular motions (like the tied knot) express *legato*, while angular motions (the up-down tapped beat) work better as a gesture for *non-legato*.[20] There are occasions when a closing chord is marked to fade to silence. A slowing, downward motion helps savor the moment.

PREP   TAP RELEASE

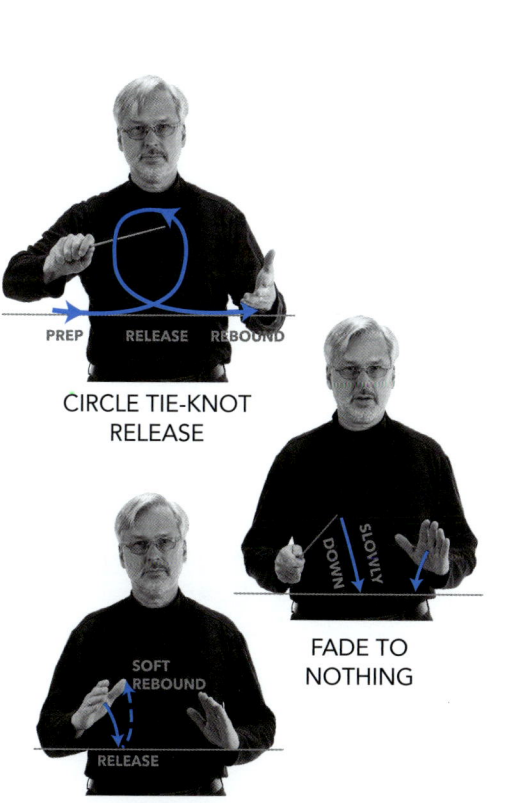

CIRCLE TIE-KNOT RELEASE

FADE TO NOTHING

SOFT REBOUND RELEASE

Cutoffs with singers

With singers, releasing the sound at the end of a piece is directly related to the consonant or vowel that ends the word. James Jordan describes the basic gesture for a release as a "cushioned up-down release." When the final sound is reached, the hand floats at the point where the ictus would normally appear. Prior to the ending of the sound, the hand moves gently upward, reflecting the quality of sound desired, dependent on dynamics and color. The singers release the sound when the leader's hand touches an imaginary soft rubber cushion and gently rebounds at its own speed upward.[21]

If the closing sound is a *vowel*, then no further gesture is needed to effect the release. If, however, a *consonant* closes the piece, then the fingertips and hand should reflect

> "The last note is not the end of the music."
> – Daniel Barenboim, pianist-conductor

CONDUCTING CONSONANT ARTICULATIONS		
STACCATO	LEGATO	MARCATO
F ⟷	F	B
S ⟷	S	D
K	L	G
P	M	
T	V ⟷	V
	Z ⟷	Z etc.

Refer to the **Diction Helps** on pages 258–262 in Chapter Twelve for more detail on the proper vocalization of vowels and consonants.

The following musical examples may be accessed in the Chapter Twenty online folder.

the inherent quality of that consonant articulation, whether *legato*, *staccato*, *marcato*, or a combination. Practice in a mirror saying various consonants, while acquiring the "feel" for them as conducted articulations.[22]

Phrasal stops

A gesture to close a phrase must be prepared and readied two beats in advance, commencing with a visual cue from the eyes, and moving into either the right or left hand. This beat tap is gentler than a final stop, representing a midstream stop or phrase ending. The tap is placed on the beat or half beat where it occurs.

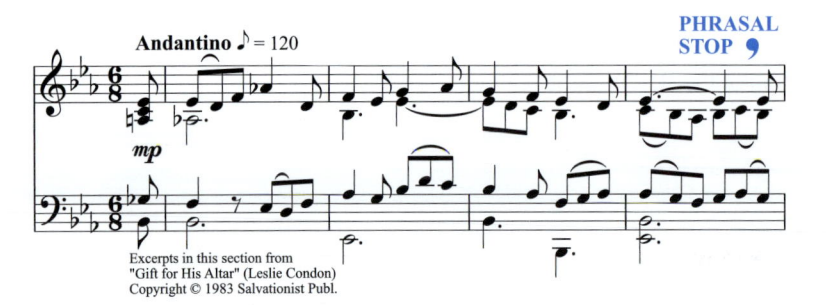

Excerpts in this section from
"Gift for His Altar" (Leslie Condon)
Copyright © 1983 Salvationist Publ.

Note that for singers, the breath is being taken in for the next phrase at the same moment as the closing consonant is being produced. Therefore, we need not conduct the consonant, but rather concentrate on a rhythmic breath. In reality, you, the conductor, begin your breath for the next phrase while the singers are finishing their phrase.[23]

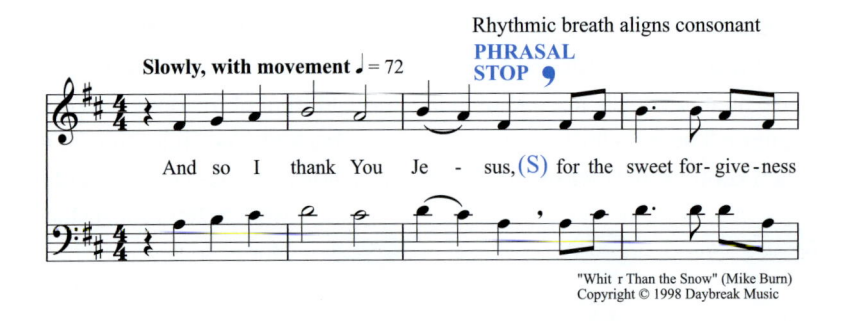

"Whiter Than the Snow" (Mike Burn)
Copyright © 1998 Daybreak Music

fermata (*term*) \fer-ˈmä-tə\
Sometimes called a pause or hold, the symbol ⁀ placed over a note or rest indicates that it is to be prolonged beyond its normal duration, usually with a suspension of the regular metrical pulse.[24]

Fermatas

When you come to a fermata, hold the hand relatively still, letting the note continue as long as you wish at the bottom of the beat. If the hold is long, the hands will have to move slightly (and slowly) out to maintain the quality of sound. There are three possibilities for what happens after the fermata hold,[25] ranging from no break in sound to a short rhythmic break or a long period of silence:

Chapter 21 | STICKS, STARTS AND STOPS

1. NO CUT AFTERWARDS: *If there is to be no silence or cutoff after the fermata, have the sound continue uninterrupted by moving smoothly into the next beat* (moving up and then over). The left hand should be held motionless and then mirror the right hand when it starts moving again. If a portion of the ensemble is to hold a chord across, while the other musicians play a pickup note, then hold the chord with the left hand, while the right hand gives the prep and beat for the pickup.[26]

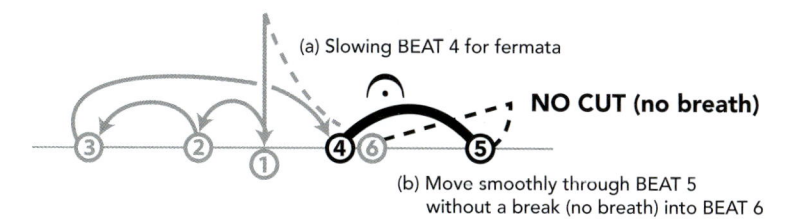

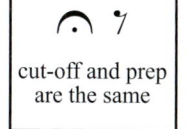

(a) Slowing BEAT 4 for fermata

NO CUT (no breath)

(b) Move smoothly through BEAT 5 without a break (no breath) into BEAT 6

FERMATA STOP #1   1 2 3 4̂ (5) 6

Prep
NO CUT
Hold, then move smoothly to next beat

2. SHORT CUT AFTERWARDS: *If there is to be a brief break (of about a beat), then repeat the beat on which the fermata occurred and continue.* The repeated downward beat acts as a cutoff and also as the prep for the next note. This is the most common fermata gesture. Note that the length of the silence is shown by how long you take between the cutoff and the next bounce. This length can vary, but musicians instinctively think rhythmically, marking the break as one beat or with a corresponding in-time breath. With a short duration break, avoid making a cutoff and a prep beat during the short period of silence, as this action will necessarily be hurried and prove confusing to the musicians.[27]

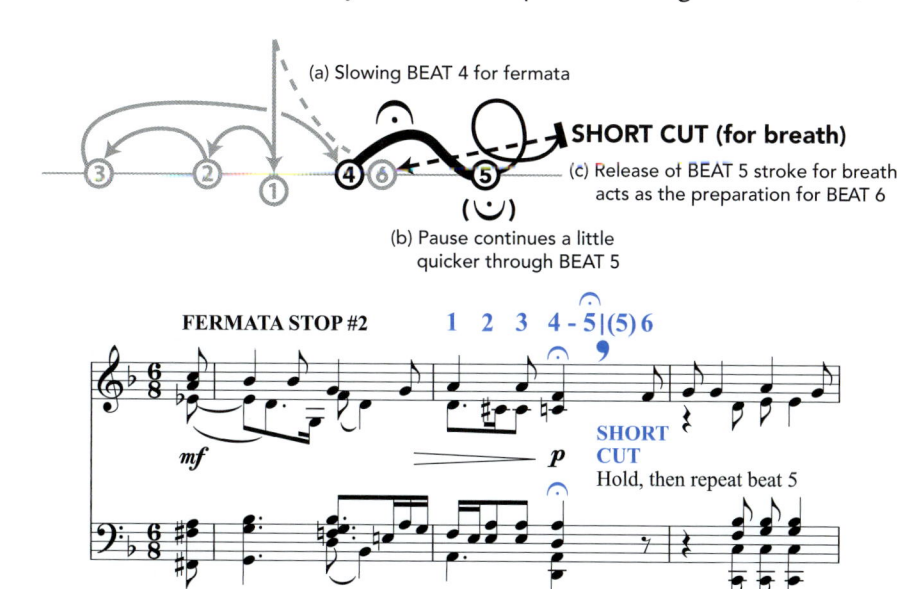

(a) Slowing BEAT 4 for fermata

SHORT CUT (for breath)

(c) Release of BEAT 5 stroke for breath acts as the preparation for BEAT 6

(b) Pause continues a little quicker through BEAT 5

FERMATA STOP #2   1 2 3 4 - 5|(5) 6

SHORT CUT
Hold, then repeat beat 5

The Beat Goes On

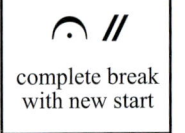

3. LONG CUT AFTERWARDS: *If there is to be a pause considerably longer than one beat, then give a cutoff*, hold still as long as desired, and then start the prep over, as though starting a piece. Be careful not to make the cutoff act also as the preliminary beat during the long silence, as the motion will prove too slow.[28]

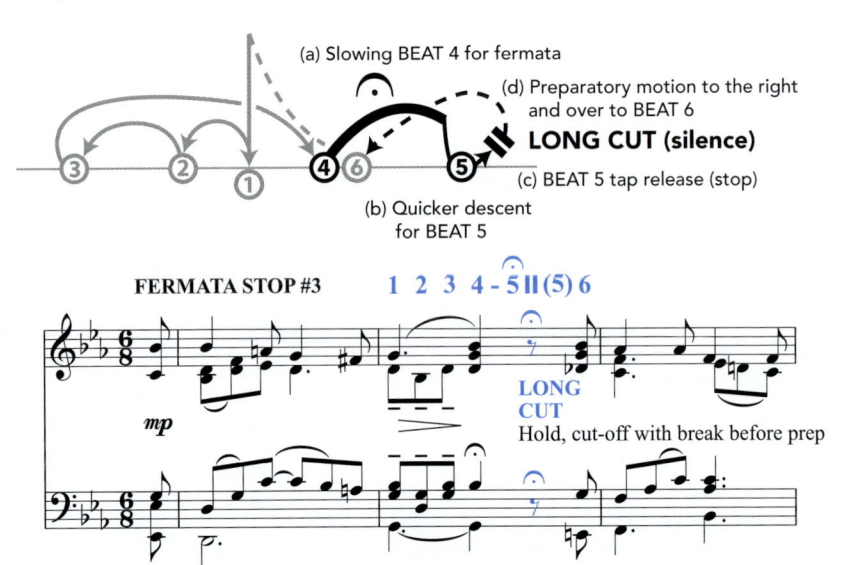

(a) Slowing BEAT 4 for fermata
(d) Preparatory motion to the right and over to BEAT 6
LONG CUT (silence)
(c) BEAT 5 tap release (stop)
(b) Quicker descent for BEAT 5

FERMATA STOP #3   1 2 3 4 - 5 ‖ (5) 6

LONG CUT
Hold, cut-off with break before prep

If there is a new tempo on the other side of the fermata, then the prep should be in the new tempo. Be careful of any cutoff transitions, making clarity the watchword. If you stop beating on a note of long value, the musicians will think you want to stop. Therefore, if a fermata is placed on a note of long duration, give all the necessary beats, holding on the final beat of that note.[29]

rit.   **F** a tempo ♪ = 120
BEAT THROUGH FERMATA   1 2 3 4 - 5 (5) 6

PREP in NEW TEMPO (and dynamic)

21 BARS REST

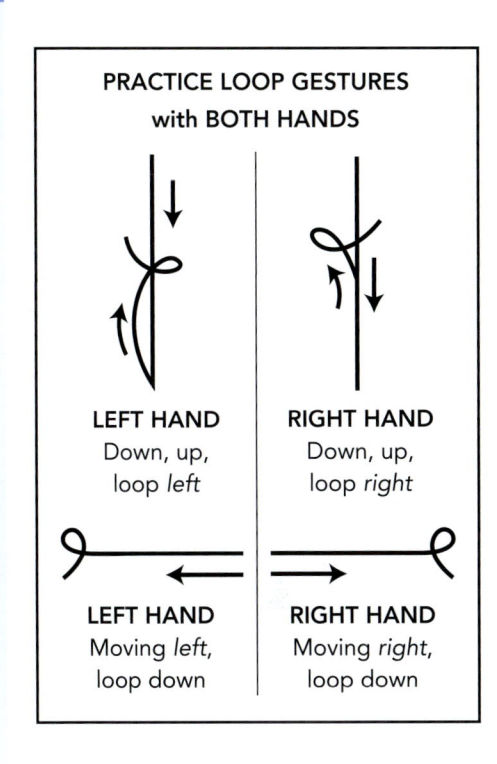

Odds and endings

1. Elizabeth Green recommends training the hands to uniformly execute various looping gestures useful for phrase endings and cutoffs. Exercise both hands separately and together.

2. Practice the three kinds of fermatas. Be critical of your cut-off transition for clarity and simplicity. The tendency is to be either ambiguous or overload the cut-off, with too little preliminary indication, or a motion that breaks the mood, and may even look like another downbeat.[30]

3. Practice endings and pauses on different beats in the bar in various meters.

4. Using a white board, and some friends, write a series of rhythms on the board and vary the application of fermata holds to different beats.[31]

PRACTICE LOOP GESTURES with BOTH HANDS

LEFT HAND
Down, up, loop *left*

RIGHT HAND
Down, up, loop *right*

LEFT HAND
Moving *left*, loop down

RIGHT HAND
Moving *right*, loop down

Hymn tune survey

5. Participants may take turns leading each other through hymn tunes, placing the hymn tune pages at podium height around a table facing each other. Everyone conducts and sings along, but one is selected to lead. The trainer gives the starting pitch and reminds the leaders of the meter, the prep beat, etc.

Conducting Fundamentals Resources are listed at the conclusion of Chapter Twenty.

6. If the participants have access to their instruments or additional players or singers, conductors can take turns conducting hymn tunes from *Songs of Praise* (formerly the *Youth Songbook*), *Songs of Salvation*, or the second volume of the most recent Salvation Army piano tune book (2015). These collections facilitate use of the piano/vocal book (which includes lyrics) as the score. Allow ten minutes per participant for this conducting exercise.

The most daunting task a novice driver faced in the days of stick-shift cars was having to pause on an incline, and then ease into gear to move ahead. For the conductor, getting a piece started and negotiating various intersections en route can prove to be a challenging part of "driving" an ensemble. There is much maneuvering to consider between the start and end of a journey. With experience the conductor learns to smoothly navigate the transitions. Now it is time to put your hand to the stick and shift into the next chapter on conducting ... Just ahead ...

CHAPTER TWENTY-TWO

GESTURE AND EXPRESSION
Expanding the Conductor's Toolbox

*The conductor listens, compares, evaluates and through the
use of gestures, communicates what he/she wants from players
in order to realize his/her imagined ideal.* —Frank Battisti

WHAT'S *IN* THE BEAT? The expressive conducting gesture reaches beyond the mere time-beating of patterns. The beat needs to project the characteristics of the music, with clarity of intent, the desired energy, and passion. As soon as the baton reaches an ictus beat-point, the conductor uses the remainder of the beat to indicate what is to happen on the next beat in terms of style, tempo, and dynamics. The speed, size, and consistency of the ictus beat-point, rebound, and release, moving from beat to beat, as well as the expressiveness in your face, eyes, and breath all help to realize your imagined ideal sound.

Conducting is not solely an outside-the-body expression. Gesture is, in fact, a reflection of your inner body attitude as initiated through the breath, and is capable of adjusting incrementally to each articulation.[1] Through your gestures, your imagined music *on the inside* finds an accurate expression *on the outside*. The intent of this chapter is to take your outward conducting mechanics further to enhance what you are sensing inwardly about the music, resulting in an increased freedom of expression.

The core principles of expressive conducting are succinctly summarized in the **FLRRT** acronym used by Jane Marshall:

In **Chapter Twenty-Two**, we expand the conductor's toolbox, considering:
- tempo
- the expressive beat gesture
- use of the left hand and cueing
- the art of phrasing

Focus—where the ensemble looks for visual clues as to the desired pulse and sound

Level—where the pulse is, and with what weight

Range—how big the pattern is, regulating the dynamics

Rebound—governs style, with its numerous variants, ranging from very short *staccato* to a long rebound *molto legato*

Tension—exhibited between the beats, appropriate to the style of music.

Remember three things:
1. **Keep your hands moving**. Stopping, particularly with singers, contradicts the activity of singing as an ongoing inhalation and exhalation process.

The Beat Goes On

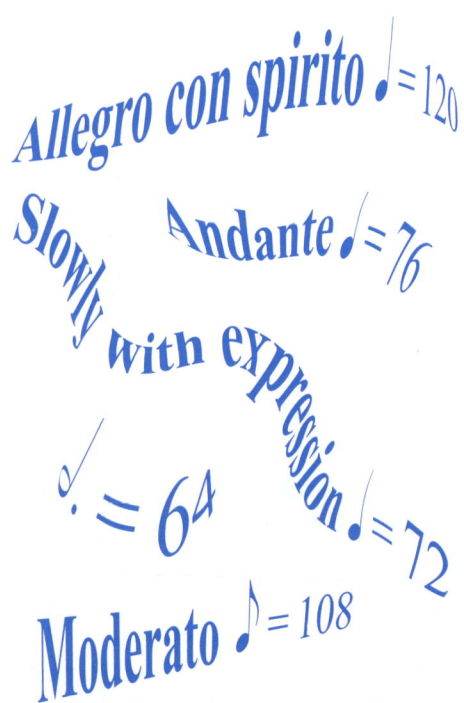

2. **Anticipate the sound of the music** by constantly keep an ideal tonal image before you, trying to realize this with the actual sound of the ensemble.
3. **Continually think along with the music**. A director's movements should never follow an ensemble, but rather always be slightly ahead of the ensemble in the giving of gestures and signals.[2]

TEMPO

Many players and listeners believe that the conductor's primary task is to set the correct tempo.[3] Music occurs in time. *Tempo* is the pulse governing the flow of that time. In many ways, tempo then controls the life of a piece.

Establishing the right tempo is a vital point of departure, somewhat analogous to what jazz musicians label "finding a groove."[4] A composer's first concern when entrusting a score to a conductor is an intrinsic grasp of the proper tempo.[5] Some contend that finding the right tempo is at least half the interpretation, or as Wagner famously asserted, ascertaining the correct tempo *was* the interpretation.[6]

Tempos tend to vary from day to day, rehearsal to performance, or even from generation to generation. Case in point: How many of today's marches are conceived to actually be marched to at a steady 112 beats per minute? Consistent with this trend, older marches are today routinely rendered at a quicker clip than was the norm used in our parents' or grandparents' day. Sousa is said to have conducted his *Stars and Stripes Forever* at about 120 beats per minute.[7] Today the norm is easily 12 beats faster.

Or consider Sidney Cox's chorus *Deep and Wide*. He intended it to be sung as a prayer chorus, at perhaps a moderately slow 76 beats per minute. Today we commonly find this chorus maligned in Sunday school openings at a brisk tempo, following the pattern of replacing the word "deep," and then the subsequent "wide" for the neutral syllable "hmm." This unfortunate practice, complete with lively hand motions, is perhaps memorable for kids but reduces the song's intended sense of wonder and awe when not rendered at the slower tempo.

Tempo, of necessity, must vary slightly depending on the acoustical environment. When performing in a highly reverberant venue, tempo is slowed so that the long recoil in sound does not become muddied. A dry acoustic (or a room full of bodies absorbing sound) may encourage a quicker clip. Recordings, less visual reinforcement, are generally taken a little faster than live performances. Avoid the tendency to drag slow tempos, or allow fast tempos to get away from you. "In the hands of a skilled conductor, the score seems to the listener to proceed in tempo, yet breathe as necessary to shape patterns. This subtle manipulation of tempo is a hallmark of artistry in any performer."[8]

What *tempo*?

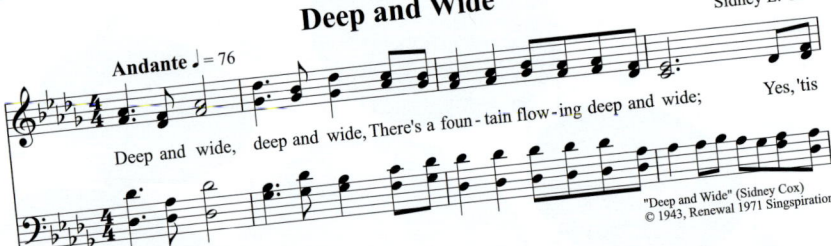

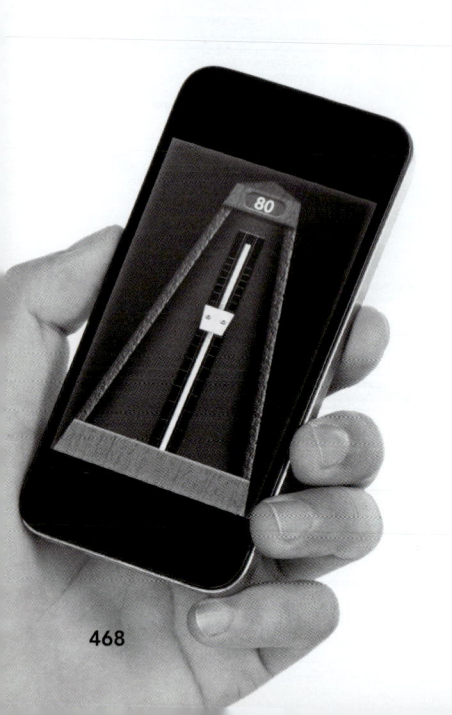

When first considering an unfamiliar score, the conductor endeavors to feel the music's innate pulse, acknowledging that a well-chosen tempo helps properly bring out a myriad of musical details, which otherwise might be unconvincing.[9] Leopold Mozart in his *Violinschule* (1756) advised that in settling on a tempo, the conductor should look for a characteristic, often recurring passage in the piece, one that might prove more enlightening than the beginning tempo. Time spent "living with the music" helps establish a playable or singable tempo, permitting a pleasing pacing of the unfolding phrases, judiciously gauged to help your ensemble sound its best.[10]

Identifying a characteristic phrase to help set tempo
Allegro con fuoco

Excerpt from Finale of Tchaikovsky's Fourth Symphony

As a facilitator, the conductor's job is to bring the music to life by conveying a feeling of the inner pulse while allowing proper rhythmic execution at a "correct," consistent tempo.[11] Most conductors agree that slow, serene music is possibly the most difficult to negotiate, requiring steady floating motions, delineated by a faint trace of bounce at the exact moment of beat impacts.[12] Elizabeth Green warns to avoid the temptation to settle at the tempo of your own heartbeat, as too often happens. The best tempo is not necessarily governed by the difficulty of the notation, but rather reflects the larger flow and interior motion of the piece. The conductor should give due consideration to the ability of their ensemble to play within a given tempo. Gauge the tempo for congregational singing according to each song.

FIXED TEMPO INDICATIONS[13]

*The numbers in parentheses indicate beats per minute

Largo (40–60*)	'lar–go	very slow and broad
Lento (50–60)	'len–toh	slowly
Adagio (55–65)	a–'dah–jio	slowly, with expression
Larghetto (60–70)	lar–'geht–toh	slightly faster than *largo*
Andante (70–84)	an–'dahn–teh	slowly, but with motion, literally "walking"
Andantino (84–100)	an–dahn–'tee–noh	diminutive; slightly faster than *andante*
Moderato (90–100)	mah–deh–'rah–toh	at a moderate pace
Allegretto (100–120)	al–leh–'gret–toh	slightly slower than *allegro*
Allegro (126–150)	al–'leh–groh	fast, lively
Vivace (140–160)	vee–vah–'chay	brisk, animated
Presto (156–180)	'pres–to	very fast
Prestissimo (180–208)	pres–'tis–see–moh	as fast as possible

CONDUCTOR'S NOTE:
In Chapter Twenty–Two, **all conducting diagrams continue as mirror images**, allowing the student conductor to "trace" the patterns. The photos, however, are as though viewing the conductor from the ensemble.

What size beat?

Tempo greatly affects the size of the conducting pattern, reflected for your musicians' understanding in the perception of weight in the conducting arm, and the flow of that arm from beat to beat. Obviously, if a piece accelerates, you are expected to beat faster (and the reverse), but a fast, large beat can make for an unclear transition. Conversely, a slow beat can have too few strokes, causing the music to atrophy.[14] In either case, the unhappy consequence is that players stop watching. To correct this, be aware that the size of a *forte* is influenced not only by volume, but also by tempo. Likewise, a slow, soft beat may require more movement.

S-T-E-A-D-Y as she goes

The importance of maintaining a steady tempo cannot be overemphasized, and the effort often requires corrective measures to bring the tempo back into sync. When performers are lagging, the natural inclination is to use a larger motion (to be noticed) and get control back (to where you want it). Yet the weightiness of the beats will slow tempo. **Enlarge the beat** to help hold back a rushing tempo, or indicate a slowing down. To increase tempo or to help performers catch up, **make the beat more concise**, using smaller, firmer beats.[15]

If tempo is uneven in a staccato passage, the sharpness of the beat should increase. In *legato* passages, adding a touch of *staccato* or *tenuto* to the beats can aid unsteady tempo. There are instances where responsibility lies with the conductor *not* to hurry or drag the tempo by choosing to use more or less beats than indicated in the time signature.

When to subdivide?

The term **subdivision** is used when the conductor changes the beat value to a smaller note value. For instance, a conductor might move from quarter-note beats, *subdividing* them into pairs of eighth-note beats.

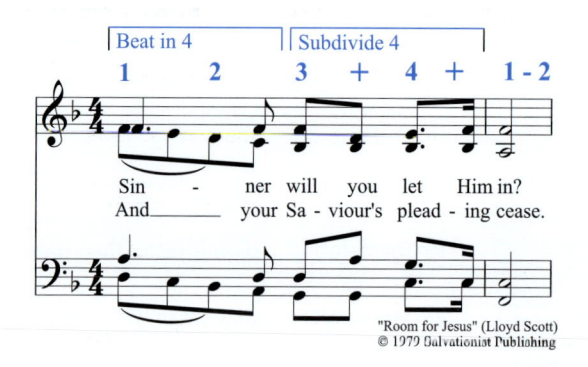

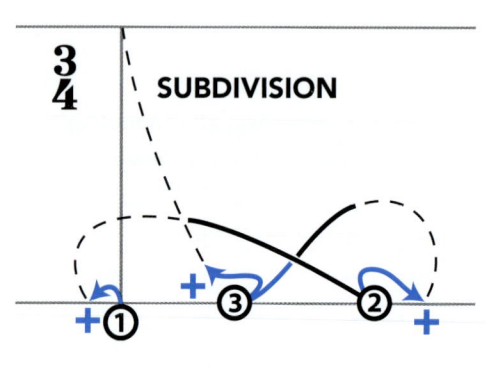

> "If a piece drags, use smaller beats.
>
> If a tempo rushes ahead, use larger beats."

"Room for Jesus" (Lloyd Scott)
© 1979 Salvationist Publishing

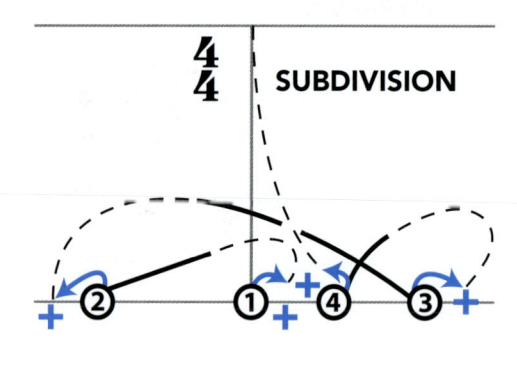

The rule of thumb with subdivisions is that the primary "on-the-beat" pulses remain within their prescribed beat pattern with large enough rebounds to stand out as the primary pulses. The less-emphasized secondary "and" pulses follow, **moving in the same direction that the primary beat was placed**. (In 4/4 time, BEAT TWO is to the conductor's left, so the subdivided "and" of BEAT TWO will loop farther out to the left and rebound across to the right for BEAT THREE, with the "and" of BEAT THREE farther out to the right.)

The sole exception to this rule is the DOWNBEAT because of its vertical descent. The DOWNBEAT subdivision should be placed in a direction opposing the next beat. In 3/4 time, BEAT TWO occurs on the conductor's right, so the "and" of BEAT ONE occurs to the left of the DOWNBEAT. The secondary pulses should be performed with reduced perception of weight in the arms, hands and wrist, keeping the emphasis clearly on the primary beats.

Chapter 22 | GESTURE AND EXPRESSION

The triple divisions

By extension, the beat patterns for compound meters like 6/8, 9/8 and 12/8 are based on the TWO-, THREE-, and FOUR-BEAT patterns respectively, but with two secondary subdivisions after each primary pulse, thus creating a triple division. Here again the primary beats (for instance, BEATS ONE, FOUR, and SEVEN in 9/8 time, which outline the basic THREE-BEAT pattern) receive more stress than the offshoot subdivisions.

Two secondary subdivisions follow each primary pulse

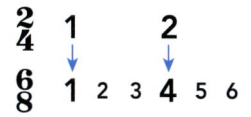

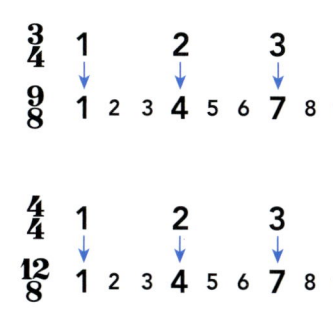

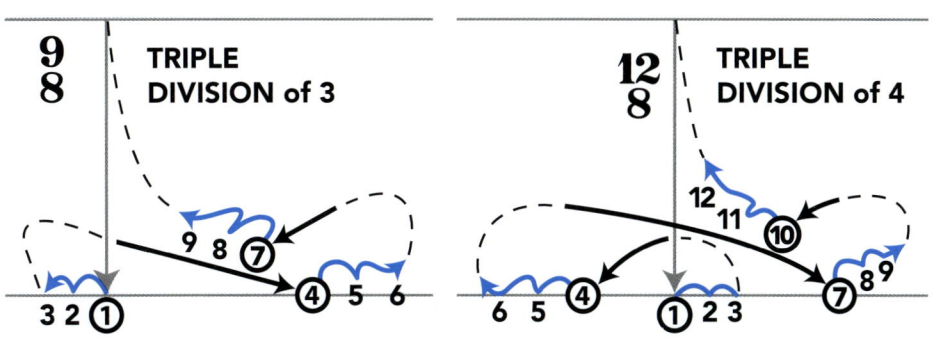

$\frac{2}{4}$ 1   2
$\frac{6}{8}$ 1 2 3   4 5 6

$\frac{3}{4}$ 1   2   3
$\frac{9}{8}$ 1 2 3   4 5 6   7 8 9

$\frac{4}{4}$ 1   2   3   4
$\frac{12}{8}$ 1 2 3   4 5 6   7 8 9   10 11 12

9/8 TRIPLE DIVISION of 3

12/8 TRIPLE DIVISION of 4

VARIATIONS IN TEMPO TERMS[16]

Italian Terms Worth Memorizing

accelerando (**accel.**)	aht–cheh–leh–'rahn–doh	gradually faster
allargando (**allarg.**)	ahl–lahr–'gahn–doh	broadening
meno mosso	'may–noh, 'moh–soh	less motion, slower (*meno* = less; *mosso* = moved, animated)
più mosso	pee–'ah, 'moh–soh	more motion, faster (*più* = more)
più allegro	pee–'ah, al–'leh–groh	more lively, faster
stringendo	strin–'jen–doh	hurrying; literally "squeezing"
rallentando (**rall.**)	rahl–len–'tahn–do	slowing down gradually, also indicated as *ritardando* (ree–tahr–'dahn–do) **ritard.**
ritenuto (**rit.**)	ree–teh–'noo–toh	held back, slowed down, usually a more sudden reduction in tempo than **ritard.** or **rall.**
a tempo	ah, 'tem–poh	in time; return to the original tempo
tempo primo	'tem–poh, 'pree–moh	first tempo
l'istesso tempo	lee–'steh–soh, 'tem–poh	same tempo (beat remains the same even though the meter changes)
rubato	roo–'bah–toh	disregarding of strict time; "stolen time;" what is taken from one note is given to another later
tenuto	teh–'noo–toh	holding a note to its full value, sometimes even longer

BEAT subDIVISION

"ONE"

BEAT 1 ⟶

"AND"

⟶ +

The Beat Goes On

ALTERING beat patterns

Experience teaches that it is usually easier to speed up after starting at a slower tempo than desired, than to curb an overly fast pace. In slow tempo, an altering of beat patterns may effectively prevent hurrying. For example, you might move from beating in 2 in 6/8 time to beating in 6, or elect to use a four-beat in 2/2 or cut-time. There are times when composers do not always think about the practical conducting side of things and a 2/2 is best negotiated in 4 or 6/8 in 2.[17] Inform your players to alter the meter indication on their parts to avoid confusion.

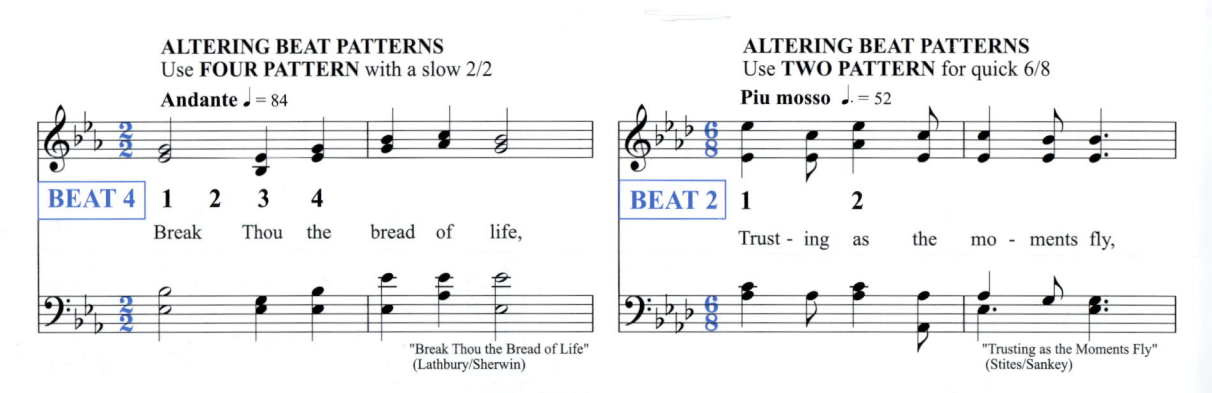

ALTERING BEAT PATTERNS
Use **FOUR PATTERN** with a slow 2/2

Andante ♩ = 84

BEAT 4 | 1 2 3 4

Break Thou the bread of life,

"Break Thou the Bread of Life"
(Lathbury/Sherwin)

ALTERING BEAT PATTERNS
Use **TWO PATTERN** for quick 6/8

Piu mosso ♩. = 52

BEAT 2 | 1 2

Trust-ing as the mo-ments fly,

"Trusting as the Moments Fly"
(Stites/Sankey)

The tempo is a-changin'

Another occasion to alter beat patterns is when tempo is changing. This can happen either incrementally, moving forward in tempo (switching from 4 into 2), or slowing out of tempo (gradually increasing beats from 3 into 9). In general, **a slowing of tempo** (*ritardando*) **requires larger gestures**, while an **increasing in tempo** (*accelerando*) **uses smaller gestures**.[18] By beating smaller rhythmic values, even the "less necessary" weak beats are played with more intensity.[19]

- **When a *ritardando* or *accelerando* is not temporary**, meaning it leads to a slower or faster section, it is often necessary to change the number of beats in a bar. Logically we gradually slow down in the first tempo, then gauge a point at which to increase the beats per measure; as an example, from two beats in a bar up to four. When gradually moving more quickly, there comes a point where we need to move, for instance, from three beats down to just one per bar. In both cases, to set up the new pulse in your mind, begin thinking subdivision of each beat about two full measures before starting to change tempo. To gradually slow down, provide more rounded beat-points and a more horizontal rebound, traveling away from the main beats more slowly. To gradually speed up, provide more angular, sharp beat-points with a more vertical rebound, moving away from the main beats more quickly.

SLOWING TEMPO

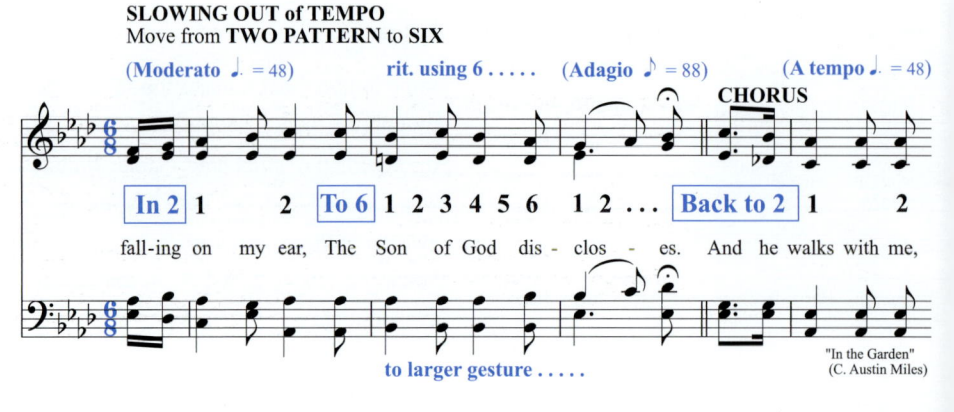

SLOWING OUT of TEMPO
Move from **TWO PATTERN** to **SIX**

(Moderato ♩. = 48)   rit. using 6 . . . . .   (Adagio ♪ = 88)   (A tempo ♩. = 48)

CHORUS

In 2 | 1 2 | To 6 | 1 2 3 4 5 6 | 1 2 . . . | Back to 2 | 1 2

fall-ing on my ear, The Son of God dis- clos- es. And he walks with me,

to larger gesture . . . . .

"In the Garden"
(C. Austin Miles)

Chapter 22 | GESTURE AND EXPRESSION

MOVING FORWARD in TEMPO
Move from **FOUR PATTERN** to **TWO**

(Moderato ♩ = 108)   accel. into 2 . . . . . Più mosso ♩ = 120
CHORUS

In 4 1 2 3 4 1.. Into 2 1 2

In all of life's ebb and flow. Je-sus, Je-sus, Je-sus,

to smaller gesture . . . . .

"He Keeps Me Singing"
(Luther Bridgers)

MOVING FORWARD

- In navigating a **transition in a new tempo on a DOWNBEAT**, it is beneficial to alter the last beat in the bar to the center of "the batter's box." Do not think of it as an upbeat, because it is here that a *rubato* beat can set up a new slow or fast tempo. The speed of the preparation from the ictus of the last beat in the bar to the ictus of the next first beat indicates the new pulse and type of beat.

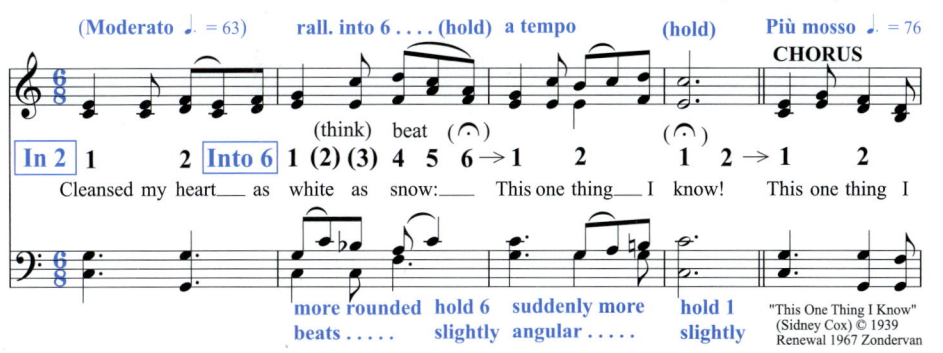

SLOWING DOWN TEMPO
Move from **TWO PATTERN** to **SIX** and back

SUDDEN NEW TEMPO
Prep in new tempo

(Moderato ♩. = 63)   rall. into 6 . . . . (hold) a tempo   (hold)   Più mosso ♩. = 76
(think) beat   CHORUS

In 2 1 2 Into 6 1 (2) (3) 4 5 6 →1 2   1 2 →1 2

Cleansed my heart as white as snow: This one thing I know! This one thing I

more rounded   hold 6   suddenly more   hold 1
beats . . . . . slightly   angular . . . . . slightly

"This One Thing I Know"
(Sidney Cox) © 1939
Renewal 1967 Zondervan

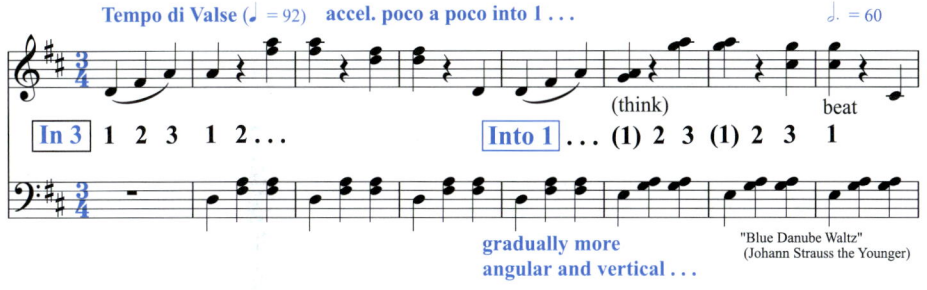

SPEEDING UP TEMPO
Move from **THREE PATTERN** to **ONE**

Tempo di Valse (♩ = 92)   accel. poco a poco into 1 . . .   ♩. = 60

In 3 1 2 3 1 2 . . .   Into 1 . . . (1) 2 3 (1) 2 3 1
                                                  (think)   beat

gradually more
angular and vertical . . .

"Blue Danube Waltz"
(Johann Strauss the Younger)

RETURN TO CENTER

- With **a sudden shift to a faster tempo**, control the rebound of the last beat of the slow tempo, returning to *center-front*. Stop momentarily to permit the slow tempo to complete itself. Then make a sudden, rhythmic preparatory beat upwards to set the new tempo.

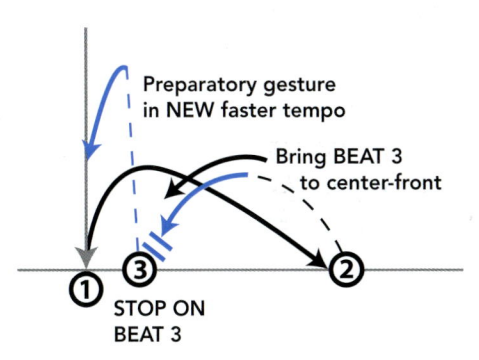

Preparatory gesture
in NEW faster tempo

Bring BEAT 3
to center-front

① STOP ON BEAT 3   ③   ②

SUDDEN SHIFT TO A FASTER TEMPO
Move from **THREE PATTERN** to **ONE**

Andantino (♩ = 92)   poco rall. (hold)   Allegro (♩. = 56)

In 3 3 1 2 3 1 2 . . .   1   To 1 1   1

Good ti-dings for Christ-mas and a hap-py New Year! We wish you a mer-ry Christ-mas, We

sudden prep
in new tempo

"We Wish You A Merry Christmas"
(Traditional English)

The Beat Goes On

- To give players a clear indication of the impending change when **gradually slowing the tempo**, add extra bounces in a subdivision before the actual slowdown to tempo. Subdivision can also highlight vital events or transition passages and tends to help hold the tempo slower.

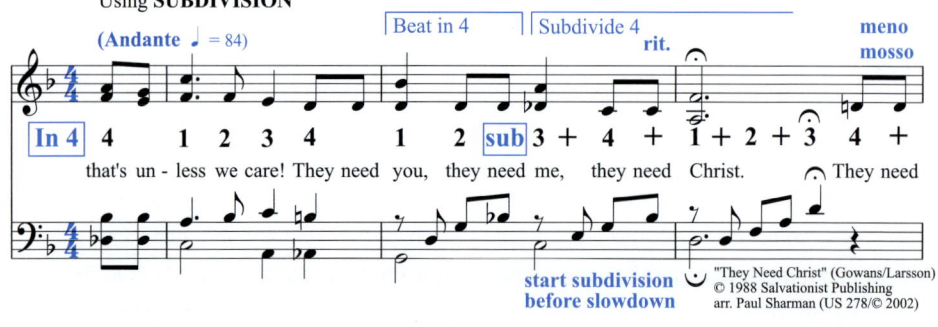

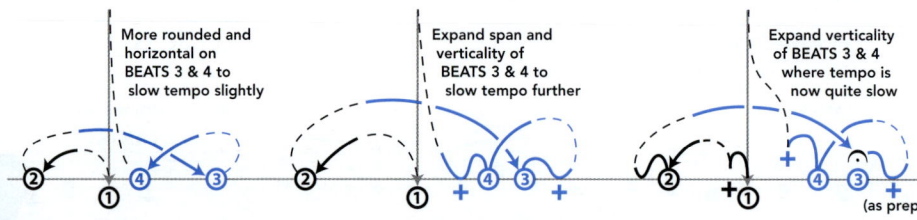

GRADUALLY SLOWING THE TEMPO
Using **SUBDIVISION**

"They Need Christ" (Gowans/Larsson)
© 1988 Salvationist Publishing
arr. Paul Sharman (US 278/© 2002)

start subdivision before slowdown

More rounded and horizontal on BEATS 3 & 4 to slow tempo slightly

Expand span and verticality of BEATS 3 & 4 to slow tempo further

Expand verticality of BEATS 3 & 4 where tempo is now quite slow

Downshifting

In days gone by, it was a rite of passage for novice auto drivers to develop enough skill with a stick shift to avoid stalling in a busy intersection. In order to reduce the car's speed as you approached the traffic light, it was necessary to gradually downshift to lower gears. A "merging" of beats that is moving smoothly, for example, from three beats in a measure into one, or from four beats down to two, is a sort of "downshifting" that helps facilitate a smooth transition into a faster tempo.[20]

When to subdivide or merge?

To determine when to subdivide or merge beats, always return to your imagined conception of the tempo and character of the section of music. For instance, when a SIX PATTERN is used, "My Bonnie Lies Over the Ocean" seems choppy, while "Drink to Me Only with Thine Eyes" takes on a more dignified air. Remember that there is a place where too many beats appear too fast, and are thereby ignored. A judicious use of beat-points helps prevent a dragging of tempo, while a more fluid motion, with fewer beats, allows the tempo to move more quickly.

WHEN TO MERGE?

WHEN TO SUBDIVIDE?

Use MORE beats in a bar:

1. to help solidify tempo

2. to facilitate certain accents or entrances

3. to keep a tempo slower

Use LESS beats in a bar:

1. to allow a more flowing motion, broader flow of the music

2. to give more time to bring out certain accents or entrances

3. to let a tempo move faster[21]

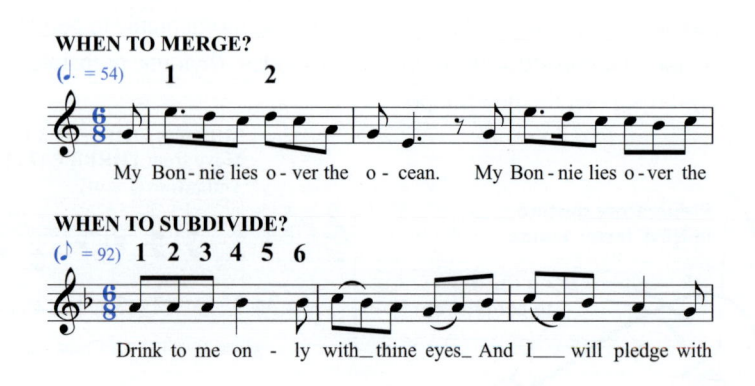

22 BARS REST

1. Recall times when you have felt in control of the tempo. What was the relationship of the size and speed of the beat to the tempo's correctness? Did the pulse hold steady, or did you have to take steps to hold back or increase tempo?

2. Practice subdivision of beats in a variety of meters (2/4, 3/4, 4/4), including the triple meter subdivisions (6/8, 9/8, and 12/8).

3. Practice transitioning to slower tempos, for example, moving from 2 into 6; 2 into 4; 3 into 9; or 4 into 12.

TRANSITIONING INTO SLOWER TEMPOS

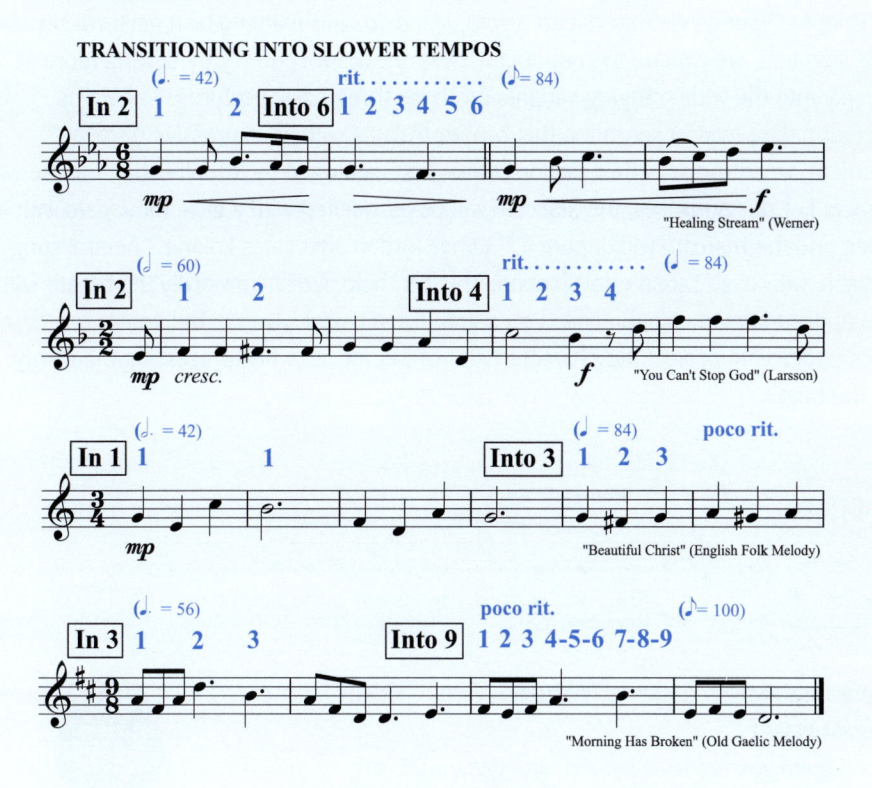

"Healing Stream" (Werner)

"You Can't Stop God" (Larsson)

"Beautiful Christ" (English Folk Melody)

"Morning Has Broken" (Old Gaelic Melody)

4. Practice transitioning into faster tempos, moving from 6 into 2; 4 into 2; 9 into 3; or 12 into 4.

TRANSITIONING INTO FASTER TEMPOS

"The Glory Song" (Gabriel)

"Just Where He Needs Me" (Grinsted)

IN CONTROL

The Beat Goes On

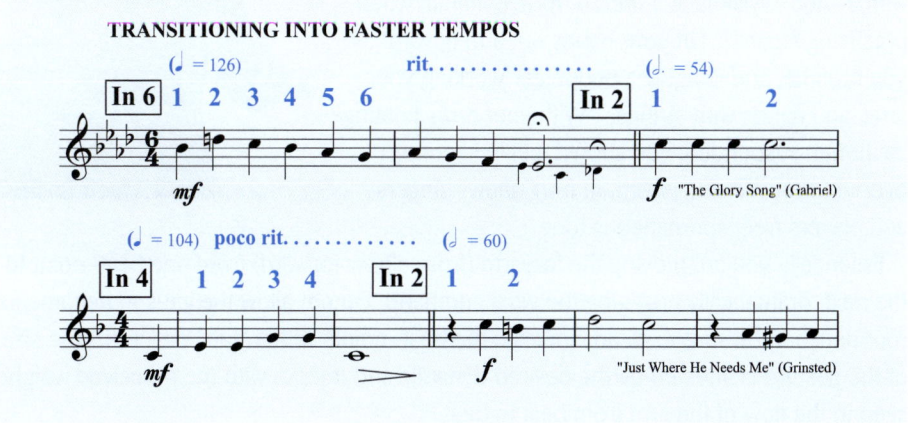

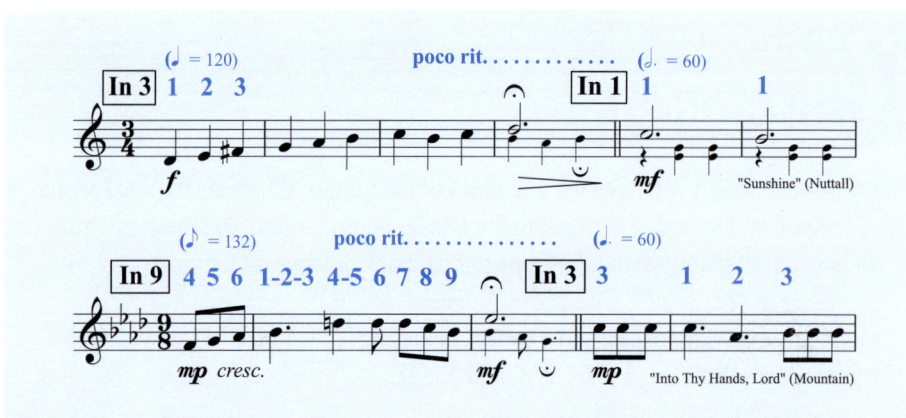

"Sunshine" (Nuttall)

"Into Thy Hands, Lord" (Mountain)

THE EXPRESSIVE BEAT GESTURE

In Chapter Twenty, we introduced *legato*, *staccato*, and *marcato* beat gestures. In this segment, we expand the conductor's expressive vocabulary by delving more deeply into the wide-ranging variants on those three basic gestures. To help us describe the physical sensation that best correlates with an expressive musical element, we introduce effort-action terms, first cataloged by Rudolf Laban for use with dance. For our purposes, the *staccato* will be associated with a flick, the *legato* with a float, and the *marcato* with a punch.[22] James Jordan advocates linking a neutral sung syllable with each Laban effort-action. This can help activate inwardly the breath with the appropriate articulation called for within the musical fabric.[23] The goal is for the beat patterns to project the characteristics of the music, while preserving the clarity of the beat.[24]

legato   cantabile
dolce
leggiero
espressivo   marcato
tenuto
staccato
agitato   sostenuto

SUSPENDED FLOAT MOTION

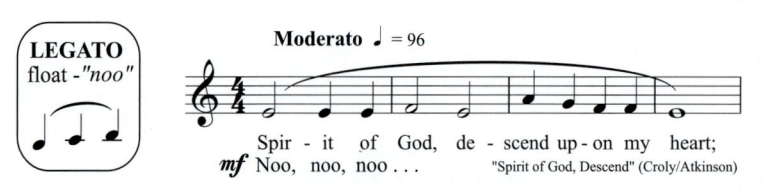

LEGATO float - *"noo"*

Moderato ♩ = 96

Spir - it of God, de - scend up - on my heart;
Noo, noo, noo . . .
"Spirit of God, Descend" (Croly/Atkinson)

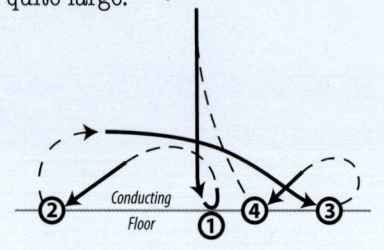

Legato, molto legato, tenuto

Legato FLOAT

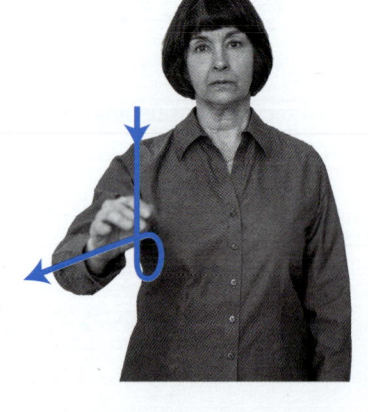

The **legato** gesture uses curved, arc-like motions to make smooth connections from beat to beat, seldom in straight lines. James Jordan advocates singing along with a "noo" syllable at a *mezzo-forte* dynamic when practicing *legato*.[26] Lift your hands out and upward as you breathe, and imagine a puppeteer working your arms and hands with strings.[27] With your arms floating as though suspended, you should feel little control over your movement, which, in turn, allows singers and players free, spontaneous tone.

Essentially you are moving the forearm (from elbow forward) from one beat-point to the next, dramatically engaging the wrist and hand. Do not allow the ictus to become too rounded, and be sure to clearly indicate the beat-points with a "tap" or "click." The size of the gesture is affected by the desired dynamic and tempo, with the perceived weight seen in the flow of the arm from beat to beat.[28]

expressive-*legato* beat (term) \li - 'gät - ō\ a curved, continuous motion, using a level of intensity in the forearm. The degree of intensity, as well as the shaping of the curves, varies with the emotional quality of the music. The size may be anywhere from fairly small to quite large.[25]

Chapter 22 | GESTURE AND EXPRESSION

CHARACTER TERMS[29]

Italian Terms Worth Memorizing

agitato	ah-jee-'tah-toh	agitated
animato	ah-nee-'mah-toh	animated
cantabile	kahn-'tah-be-leh	in a singing style
con brio	kon, 'bree-oh	with vigor
con bravura	kon, brah-'ver-ah	with boldness
con fuoco	kon, foo-'eh-koh	with fire
con tenerezza	kon, teh-neh-ret-'sah	with tenderness
dolce	'do-cheh	sweetly
espressivo	eh-spres-'see-voh	expressively
giocoso	jee-oh-'koh-so	humorously
legato	leh-'gah-toh	smoothly, connected
leggiero	led-'jeh-roh	light, nimble
pesante	peh-'sahn-teh	heavy
maestoso	mah-e-'sto-so	majestic
marcato	mar-'kah-toh	with marked rhythm
molto legato	'mol-toh, leh-'gah-toh	very connected
semplice	'sem-plee-cheh	simple, unaffected
sostenuto	so-steh-'noo-toh	sustained
staccato	stah-'kah-toh	short, detached
sotto voce	'sot-to, 'voh-cheh	subdued voice (literally "under the voice")
vivo	'vee-voh	lively

CONDUCTOR INDICATING THE BREATH

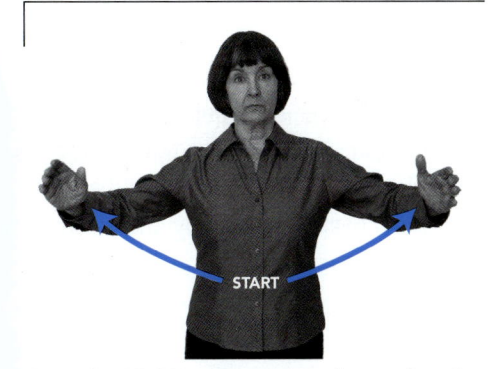

ANTICIPATION—Openness of arms, hands, and body signal readiness to accept air.

INHALATION—Hands and elbows angled down to summon a deep breath inhalation.

ARTICULATION—Rounded hands and arms, as though holding the sound, show the air readied to produce the sound.

The Beat Goes On

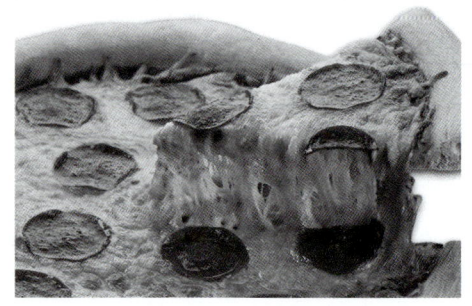

ELASTIC PULLING MOTION

MOLTO LEGATO
glide - "*nah*"

Maestoso ♩ = 69

Al - le - lu - ia!   Al - le - lu - ia!
ff Nah, nah, nah . . .   "All Creatures of our God and King" (St. Francis)

Molto legato GLIDE

There are many variants in expressive beat gesture. When the music calls for a **molto legato** gesture (perhaps in a *maestoso* section), create a pulling effort with the wrist and hand, as if the hand and arm are pulling on melted mozzarella cheese from a pizza. Allow the shoulder to be engaged in the *molto legato* gesture. The perceived weight to be applied to the music is reflected in the amount of resistance and the effort within the rebound effort.[30]

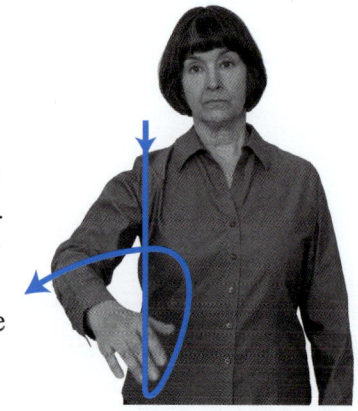

GENTLE PETTING MOTION

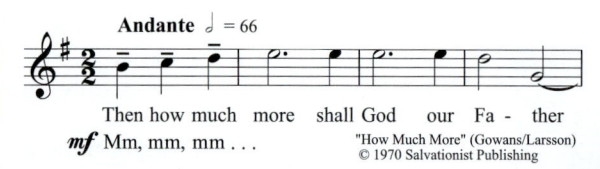

TENUTO
dab/press - "*mm*"

Andante ♩ = 66

Then how much more shall God our Fa - ther
mf Mm, mm, mm . . .   "How Much More" (Gowans/Larsson)
© 1970 Salvationist Publishing

Tenuto DAB/PRESS*

A **tenuto** is a type of "minihold," nearly melded to the next note, which necessitates stretching on the note on which it occurs. It is similar to a no-cut fermata (reference Chapter Twenty-One, p. 463). A *tenuto* glide gesture begins not before, but immediately *at* the beat-point where the *tenuto* emphasis begins.[31] It implies a heavier *legato* line, thereby maintaining the cohesion and connectivity of the *legato* gesture, yet with a subtle stop-motion on each count. This action can be likened to gently petting an animal at intervals.

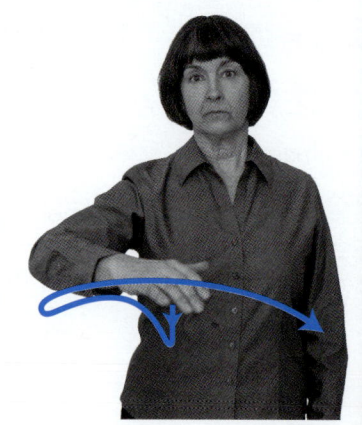

There is a slight drag on the *tenuto* beat accomplished by turning the hand at the wrist in the opposite direction from which the arm is moving.[32] For example, BEAT THREE in 4/4 would be indicated by the arm stretching to the right, with the hand/baton turned inward to the left. When the *tenuto* beat moves on, the hand/baton moves quickly to the right before moving inward for BEAT FOUR.

When using a baton with *tenuto*, we imagine the tip of the baton becoming heavy, so it drops below the level of the hand and wrist. The hand seems to pull upward or sideways after each beat-point. For example, if the baton is pointing downward, there needs to be a sensation of pulling upward while pulling downward on the tip of the stick at the same time, which creates intensity between beats.[33] In this way, the *tenuto* gesture also proves useful to hold back or maintain tempo.

*The terms used for movement imagery (float, glide, dab, press, flick, punch, slash) are derived from Laban dance effort-actions, applied to conducting. Hybrid combinations (like dab/press or punch/press) more closely simulate movements for *tenuto* and *marcato*.

Chapter 22 | GESTURE AND EXPRESSION

STACCATO tap-*"tee"*

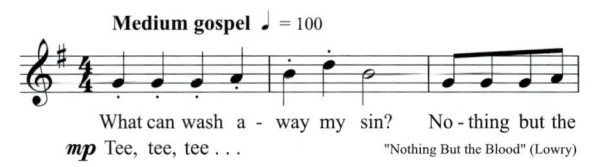

Medium gospel ♩ = 100

mp What can wash a-way my sin? No-thing but the Tee, tee, tee . . .
"Nothing But the Blood" (Lowry)

QUICK TAPPING MOTION

Staccato, light staccato

Staccato TAP

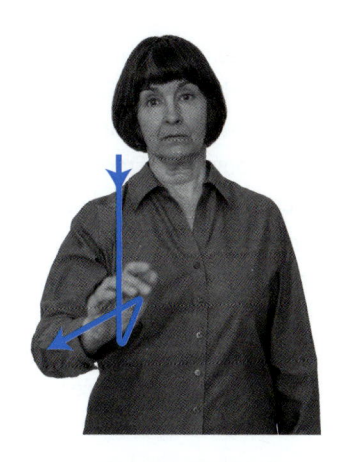

In the **staccato** gesture, the motion in the stick, hand, and arm is *stopped immediately after* the rebound. You can promote *staccato* motion by tapping imaginary drops of water from the tip of the stick. The tap is performed by the sudden motion of the hand in the wrist joint, ending in an abrupt stop at the end of the rebound, much like typing or tapping on a window. Pause, without motion, but only briefly, after each *staccato*.[35] Vocalize the syllable "tee" at *softer* dynamics when practicing *staccato*.[36]

full-staccato beat (term)
\stə - ˈkät - ō\ a quick, angular motion with a stop on each count. It is snappy and energetic, with a characteristic "bouncing" on the downbeat. The size may vary from small to large.[34]

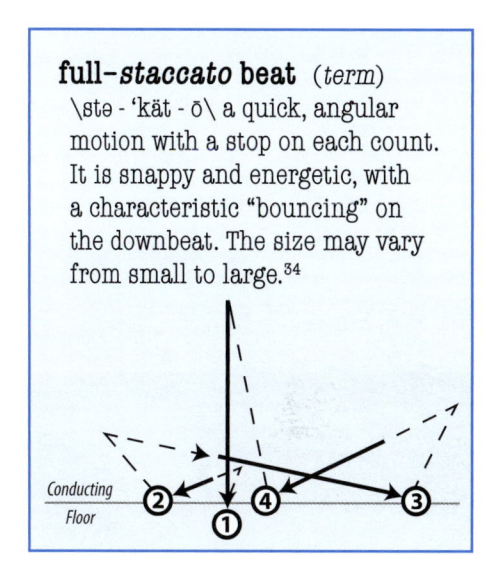

The aim is to hit crisply, with a small rebound at sharp angles, giving the appearance of not allowing the hand to stand still. Brock McElheran explains, "If someone lobs a ball gently against a wall, an observer can follow its path and anticipate exactly where it will strike; if a person stands motionless aiming a gun and suddenly pulls the trigger, the observer cannot possibly foretell the moment of the bullet's import."[37] So, we keep the hand moving, despite the necessary pint-sized *staccato* stops.[38] A reduced *staccato* gesture is useful to urge *tempo* forward.[39]

LIGHT STACCATO flick-*"dee"*

Tempo di marcia viva

p leggiero Dee, dee . . . *mf* > *p*
"Nutcracker March" (Tchaikovsky)

Light staccato FLICK

The **light staccato** gesture uses only the hand through the motion of the wrist.[40] It is a quick, minimal, straight motion with a stop on each count. James Jordan likens this quick motion of the hand to brushing debris off a desk or table, or snow off a windshield. The combination of lightness and the immediate movements from beat to beat gives the precision. To aid clarity, bring the forearm in and economize on the beat size, but keep the beat locations accurate and consistent. You can make players understand what kind of *staccato* you want by the beat alone.[41] Remember that all *staccato* gestures require a stop at the rebound. Generate crisp articulation by angles and quick movements.

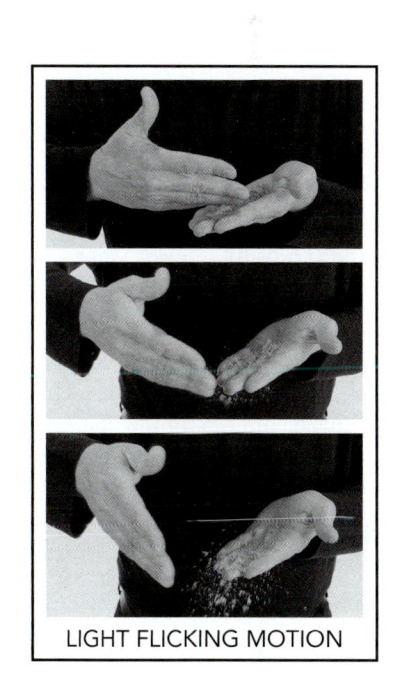

LIGHT FLICKING MOTION

The Beat Goes On

WEIGHTED PUNCHING MOTION

MARCATO
punch/press
-"dah"

Marziale ♩ = 112

f pesante Dah, dah, dah . . .   "March of the Three Kings" (Provencal Melody)

Marcato, accents

Marcato PUNCH/PRESS

Heavy, ponderous moments in the music require a *marcato* downward motion positioned at a lowered center of gravity. Your musicians need to perceive intensity in each beat, which we can liken to a punch motion. Use of the full arm emanating from the shoulder, not only increases the size of beat, but adds to the impression of increased weight. Vocalize a "dah" syllable at a *forte* dynamic when practicing *marcato*.[43] For a more energetic *marcato*, hit harder with a more angular turn on the beats.[44]

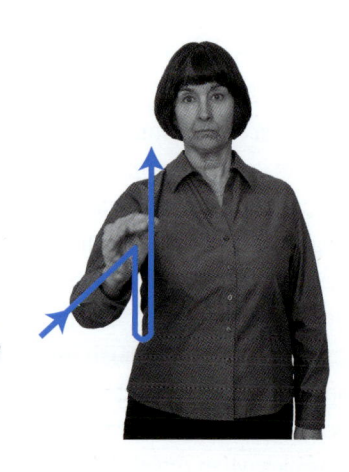

QUICK SLASHING MOTION

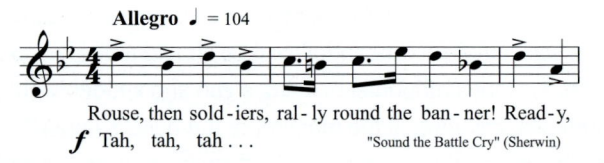

ACCENT
slash -"tah"

Allegro ♩ = 104

Rouse, then sold-iers, ral-ly round the ban-ner! Read-y,
f Tah, tah, tah . . .   "Sound the Battle Cry" (Sherwin)

Accents SLASH

Utilize the *marcato* motion for accents, but in microcosm. We can consider them as short volume changes. Prepare *accents* by the motion of the rebound that occurs immediately before they are to sound.[45] They call for a sharp, angled approach to the beat and an increased perception of weight by full use of arm and elbow. Choose not to bounce too high, which incorrectly implies a continuation of the loudness of the attack, rather than a diminishing in sound, as visually represented in the notated accent sign (>).

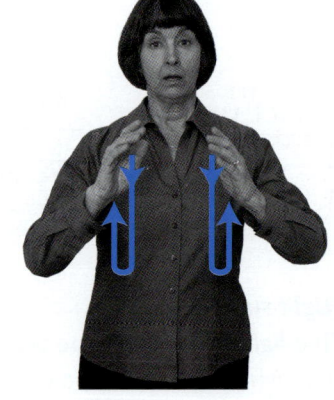

The left hand can help secure a unified attack by giving a strong, in-time preparation. Conductors sometimes try to get this result by hesitating just before the accent, which is often ineffective. At a *piano* dynamic, the leader makes a sharp motion toward the players, using the tip of the thumb and index finger together. At *forte*, the strong, downward motion extends to the hand or fist.

Shifting stylistically

When transitioning between the various articulations, remember that all rebound motions, whether for *legato*, *staccato*, *marcato*, or their variants, always continue in the same direction. That is, BEAT ONE always lifts upward. In the FOUR-pattern, BEAT TWO continues to the left before reversing direction. BEAT THREE continues to the right and the LAST BEAT moves upward to prepare for the next downbeat.

The possibility of anticipating any of the various articulations stylistically is activated not by the direction of the rebound, but rather by **the character and shape of the preceding**

marcato beat (*term*) \mär-'kät-ō\ a heavy motion with a stop on each count. It is forceful, sometimes aggressive in character, and medium to large in size. The gestures connecting the counts are slower than *staccato*, but may be either straight or curved, depending on the intensity of the music.[42]

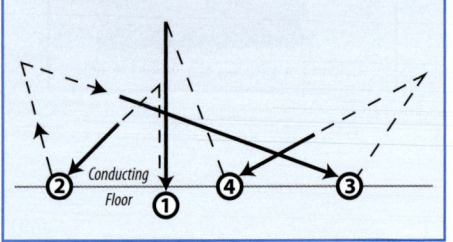

rebound. What BEAT THREE will sound like is shown from the ictus of BEAT TWO up to the ictus of BEAT THREE. For example, to facilitate a transition in beat character from *staccato* to *legato*, beat *staccato* as usual on the last *staccato* count [A], but instead of waiting on the STOP during that count [B], let the hand immediately continue in a *legato* motion to the next count.[46]

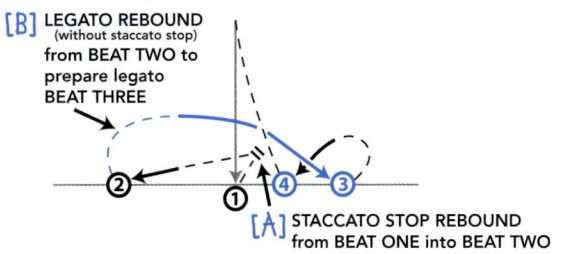

[B] LEGATO REBOUND (without staccato stop) from BEAT TWO to prepare legato BEAT THREE

[A] STACCATO STOP REBOUND from BEAT ONE into BEAT TWO

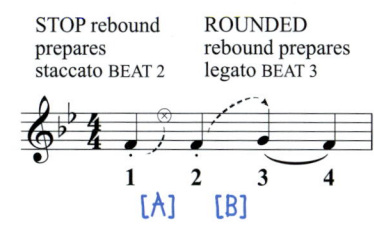

STOP rebound prepares staccato BEAT 2

ROUNDED rebound prepares legato BEAT 3

The **Gestural Contrasts** diagram,[47] viewed from left to right, moves from *light staccato* with its angular beats and light arm weight through a decreasing angularity and increasing arm weight–perception (*legato*) to the weightiest and more circular beat motions of *molto legato*, *tenuto*, and *fermata*. The variable synthesis of the angularity vs. circularity of the rebound, the size of the beat, and the perceived weight in the arm moving between the beats serve to characterize the desired articulation in the expressive beat gesture.

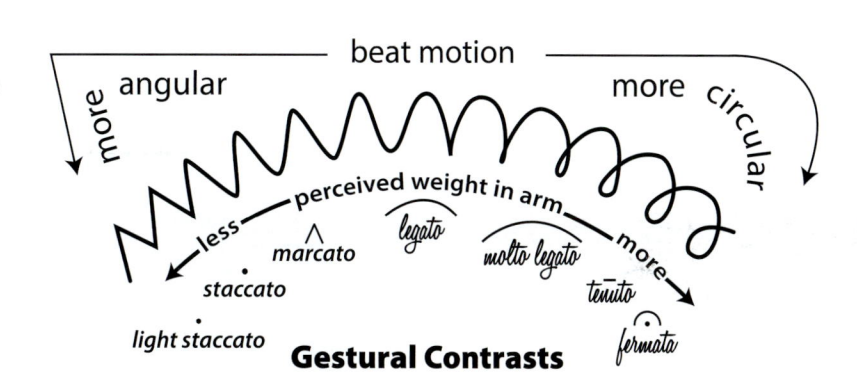

beat motion — more angular — more circular
less ← perceived weight in arm → more
light staccato · staccato · marcato · legato · molto legato · tenuto · fermata

Gestural Contrasts

? 22 BARS REST

1. Apply the following characteristics to beating various meters, using correspondingly appropriate dynamic levels: *legato*, *molto legato*, *tenuto*, *light staccato*, *staccato*, or *marcato*.

2. Sing an "oom-pah" pattern while beating time in various patterns, giving the beat on each "oom." Occasionally try to make a strong accent gesture on a "pah," using the right hand only, without subdividing or varying the tempo. This requires a sharp rebound on the previous beat.

ADDING ACCENTS on "PAHS"
Allegro con energia ♩ = 112
sharp rebound *before* accent
mp — *cresc.* — *mf*
"Praise" FS 163 (Wilfred Heaton)
© 1949 Salvationist Publishing

ACCENT
slash - "tah"

3. Practice preparing accents for various beats (in several meters).

ACCENTS on different beats
Allegro con energia ♩ = 112
mf — *cresc.* — *f*
"Praise" FS 163 (Wilfred Heaton)
© 1949 Salvationist Publishing

MARCATO
punch/press - "dah"

The Beat Goes On

STACCATO
tap - "tee"

MOLTO LEGATO
glide - "nah"

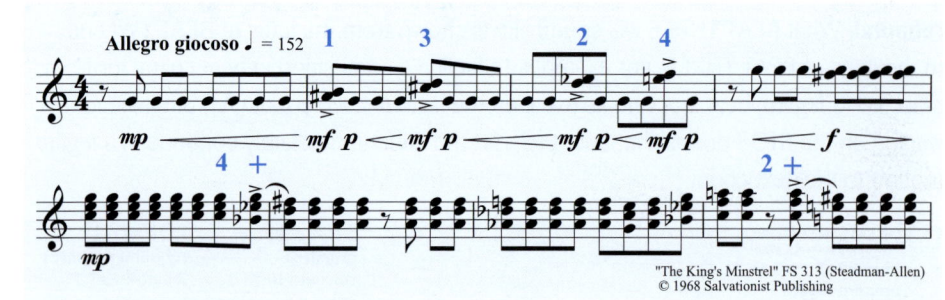

"The King's Minstrel" FS 313 (Steadman-Allen)
© 1968 Salvationist Publishing

"The Eternal Presence" FS 314 (Eric Ball)
© 1968 Salvationist Publishing

4. Conduct the following excerpt, varying the articulation characteristics from measure to measure. Be sure to indicate the change a beat ahead. Avoid bouncing too high with the accented tones. This incorrectly gives the impression of a continuation of loudness.

Indicate change a beat ahead 4 → 1

"Vesper Hymn" (Bortniansky)

5. Practice shifting between articulation characteristics, for instance, from *legato* to *molto legato*, from *tenuto* to *marcato*, or from *light staccato* to *staccato*. Do the reverse, shifting from *staccato* to *light staccato*, and so on, working back all the way to *legato*. This exercise simulates continual change in the character of the beat pattern with each new section or phrase of the music.[48]

PRACTICE altering ARTICULATION

Moderato ♩ = 84

1st time: legato . . . . molto legato . . . . tenuto . . . .
2nd time: staccato . . . . light staccato . . . . marcato . . . .

marcato . . . . light staccato . . . . staccato . . . .
tenuto . . . . molto legato . . . . legato . . . .

"Spanish Chant" (att. H. R. Bishop)

USE OF THE LEFT HAND

Common practice asserts that the right hand keeps **tempo**, leaving the left arm to enhance **expression**. In the instrumental realm, the left hand suggests phrasing, dynamics, shading, and articulation.[49] The right hand, properly trained, can effectively indicate the tempo, volume, character, and even phrasing cues when they fit into the beat pattern. One way to achieve this is to practice conducting with the left arm held behind the back.[50]

Choral conductors consciously mirror with the left hand to give their singers a balanced, aligned posture. The conductor should guard against a left hand extended out, "dancing" in time to the music. This can distract or block those on the conductor's left from seeing the right-hand beat gesture.[51] When not in use, allow the left hand to hang close to the body in a relaxed position, often at belt level, so as to not clutter up the landscape.

The left-hand duties extend beyond the scope of the right hand, and therefore must be trained for independence.[52] These duties include:

- ☑ indicating cues that do not fit into the beat pattern
- ☑ supplementing the right hand gesture to speed up or slow down
- ☑ reinforcing what the right hand is indicating, for instance, use the left hand to signal a sudden accent, dynamic change, climax, or important cue
- ☑ employing a gesture to indicate dynamics or encourage a richer sound
- ☑ adjusting balance
- ☑ facilitating page turns

From the inside out

While there is some interdependency between the arms, the conductor works to develop a unified coordination between the arms, hands, fingers, head, face, and body. Every aspect of the music must exist within the gestures, all in agreement with the right-hand beat function.[53]

By placing every dimension of a score under scrutiny, conductors discover a great deal within the music that is not indicated on the page. The conductor endeavors to enter the mind of the composer, exploring the spirit of a text and searching for the message of the music. It is a formidable task to interpret the score. Capitalizing on your accumulated musical experience, you will work from "the inside out" toward an accurate performance by utilizing outward gestures.

Elements of **score reading** and **score study** were introduced in Chapter Ten and Eleven and are explored further in the closing section of Chapter Twenty-Three.

International Staff Bandmaster
Stephen Cobb

22 BARS REST

To help initiate use of the left hand when conducting, try these four exercises:

1. First, turn on a recording or metronome, or sing. Maintain clear, flowing beat patterns, while exploring what you can do with your left hand.[54] Do things necessary to conducting, like reinforcing downbeats or even turning pages. Do *not* watch yourself in a mirror at this stage, so that you can concentrate on the feeling *inside* being manifested *outwardly*.

2. Next, while conducting different beat patterns, add some unrelated tasks, such as touching your nose or ear, or piling books. The object is to develop an automatic ongoing beat, *coupled with* independence in the left hand. With experience, the left hand will almost care for itself.

3. Using simulated performance, practice conducting using your *left hand only*. Do not give beat patterns, but rather concentrate solely on cueing and expressive gestures to be given by that hand.

4. In front of a mirror, conduct along with a familiar recording. Do not refer to a score. Watch how you use your left hand. Vary the beat on a whim, supplemented by left-hand action. Make sure the left-hand gestures improve the overall picture rather than detract from it. The most difficult use of both hands will be on the downbeat of a measure because the right hand will be coming down as the left hand is coming up. See that the rhythm of the right hand is not nudged by the left-hand motion.[55] When you are not using the left hand, return it to a position of complete relaxation at the belt buckle or side.

Cueing

Players and singers are looking for assurances from the leader through eye-to-eye contact and articulate cues. The conductor gives cues to set the mood, movement, and precise moment of the entrance. The cue is not a crutch. Players and singers still need to count rests. Even when trained to count every rest an effective cue improves the overall approach and character of entrances within an ensemble.[56]

Unfortunately, cueing a player who has lost his place usually produces a poor or late entrance. Aim for your musicians to be secure with their entrances through familiarity with the music, with or without a cue. To develop the ensemble's dependence on itself, there are times in rehearsal when the conductor should simply count off and not give cues. Choral conductors can test recall by occasionally not giving lyric cues in rehearsal.[57]

When to cue?[58]

- ☑ Important tutti entrances, when an entire section takes over the main melody or theme

- ☑ Solo passage or percussion moment, like a cymbal crash or timpani roll

- ☑ An exchange of rhythmic or melodic figures, sometimes called *motifs*, tossed from one instrument to another

- ☑ Tricky entrances, which may be difficult for performers. Your gestures aim to support high notes or give rhythmic assurance to an awkward entrance.

- ☑ After a long rest, where players have figuratively "gone to sleep"

- ☑ To control the moment, insuring a precise attack

- ☑ To give assurance or approval with a less significant cue. Second and third part players appreciate this because it raises their feeling of importance.

> **motif** (*term*) \mō - ˈtēf\ A short rhythmic and/or melodic idea that is sufficiently well defined to retain its identity when elaborated, transformed, or combined with other material. Thus the motif lends itself as a recognizable basic element from which a complex texture or even a whole composition is created.[59] Arguably the most familiar motif in music is the opening to Beethoven's *Fifth Symphony*. Beethoven uses both the descending third and the "short-short-short-long" rhythmic pattern to generate the entire first movement.

Cueing challenges

- ☑ Dispersing singers into a mixed formation—for instance, with singers in groups of quartets—maximizes tone, ensemble, and blend, but prevents a physical cue of sections. Cue as though the choir is in a familiar conventional arrangement, making motions of cues in front of you. Each section is still looking for a cue at the proper time and sees it easily. The cue actually aids the listener in hearing the entrance.

- ☑ With numerous entrances within close proximity, do not cue. Stick to the beat patterns. This can be coupled with an eye or head motion cue made without looking at the section or player.

Cueing effectively

Less is more! It is my experience that using less motion than I think I need aids clarity of gesture. Often your musicians can tell more about your intentions from your bodily expression than from fancy hand-waving. One way is by capitalizing on the use of your general facial expression, particularly your eyes. In quiet passages, use only the most subtle of movements—the eyes, a lift of eyebrows, or a nod of the head—so as to not disturb the mood. [A] The same applies when both hands are already occupied.[60] The face, combined with an open palm facing up or down, can effectively communicate a desired change in volume or power. [B]

Cueing planes

A cue using a baton is made in the manner of time-beating, but directed at the player or section to the conductor's right, center, or left. Cues are sometimes erroneously picked up by a section in front of or next to the one you intend to cue. To eliminate misinterpretation, cues to sections 6 and 7 should be on a higher plane to make clear that the cue is directed to people at the back of the ensemble. Cues to sections 2 and 3, in front of sections 1 and 4, are shown closer to the conductor's floor level. Cues to section 5 are shown logically slightly higher, at mid-level.[61]

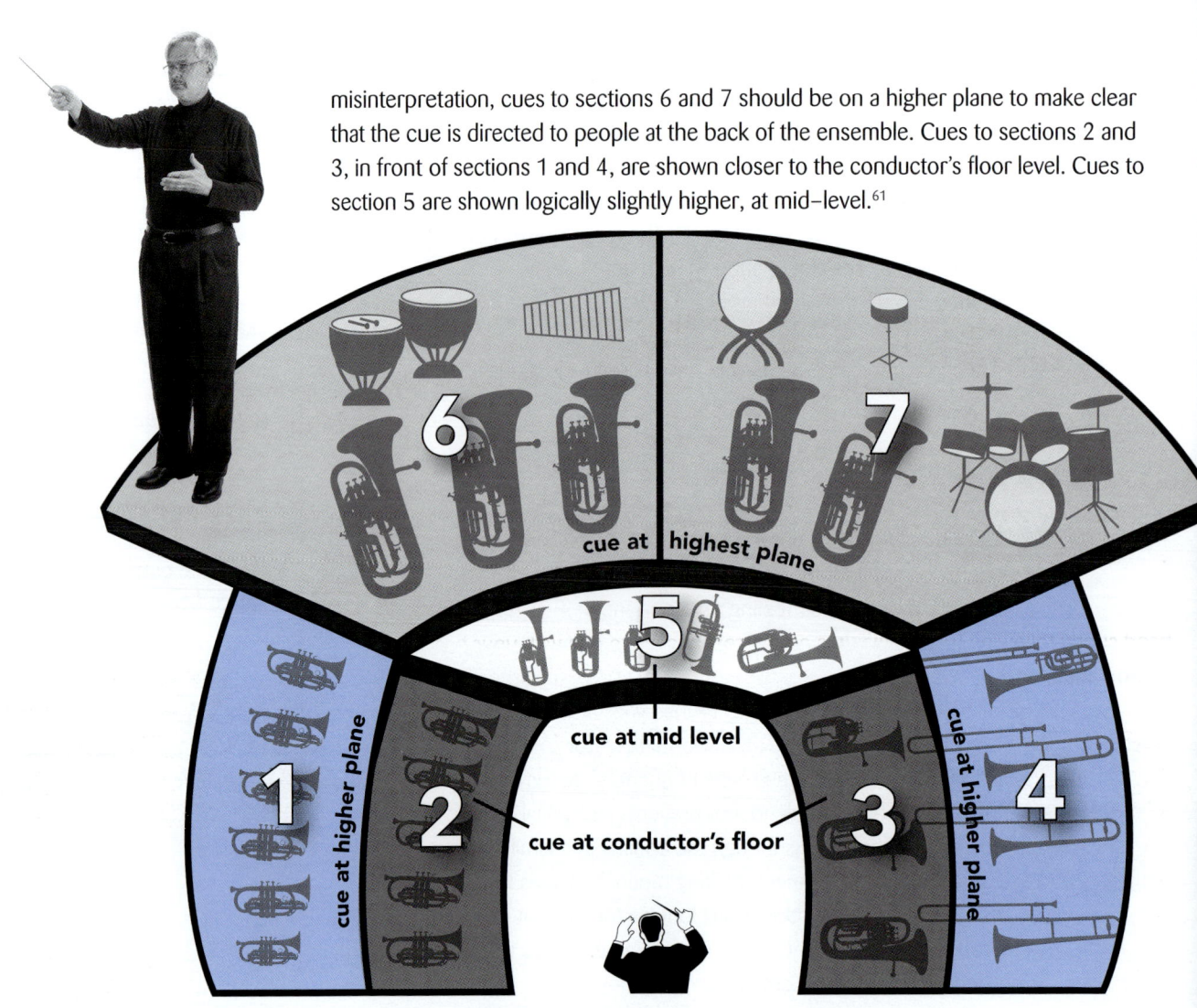

CUEING PLANES FOR INSTRUMENTAL

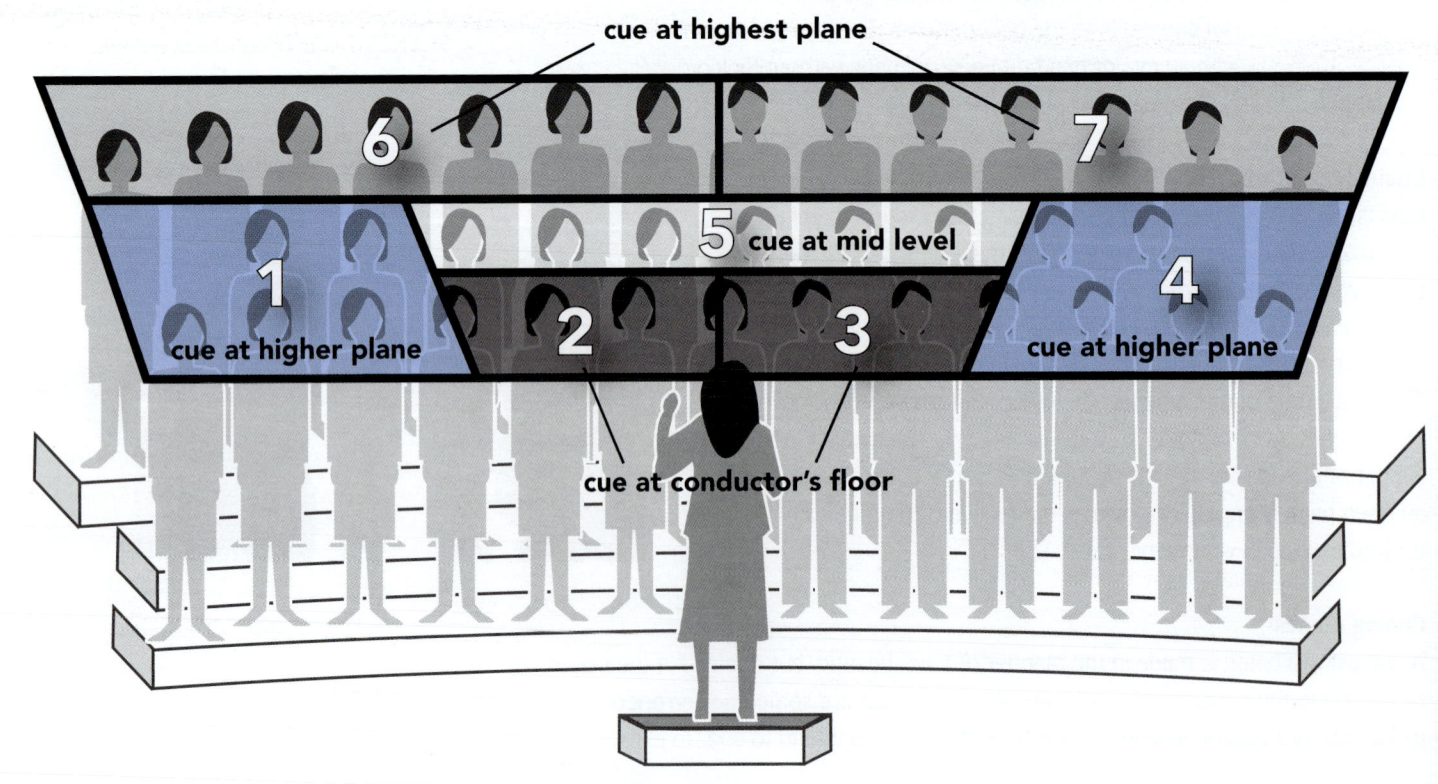

CUEING PLANES FOR CHOIRS

Chapter 22 | GESTURE AND EXPRESSION

The all-important eyes pave the way for an entrance, **so the eyes should move toward those being cued one beat in advance in slow music, or two beats in advance in quicker music**. Avoid crossing the arms, or leaning toward the performers when cueing.[62]

On the beat cues

When giving a left-hand cue, you can either give an indication on the beat-point, or render a preparatory gesture preceding the cue. When only the left hand is cueing, it should move out farther than the right hand/baton, which is beating time. If both hands are utilized, then both move outward toward the section or player. Strive to include interpretive qualities without causing a hitch or distraction in your beat pattern.

Left hand positions from left to right: Resting at side, resting at waist, extended for attention or mirroring, and further extended for cueing.

Sometimes a little more emphasis on a beat can be brought out by the accompanying rise and fall of your head or eyebrows, reinforced by the left hand subtly following this profile. It is counterproductive to cue with your head stuck in the score. Take a quick mental picture of the measures ahead. Look up and out through the cue, even if you momentarily lose your place in the score.

When cueing musicians on the left, you must turn the upper torso, head, left hand, and right hand in that direction while maintaining good body alignment. When turning the entire body, the traveling rule from basketball applies, which means you only move one foot at a time. So in motion toward the left, only the left foot moves, and vice versa.

This turning often proves necessary when cueing a section to the conductor's left on BEAT TWO in 3/4, or BEAT THREE in 4/4 time. In those instances, the movement is to your right, away from the section on your left. In the same way, a turn may be necessary with a cue to sections on your right because of the leftward motion of BEAT TWO in 4/4 time.

TURN for right hand BEAT-CUE to LEFT

TURN for right hand BEAT-CUE on RIGHT

BASKETBALL TRAVELING RULE

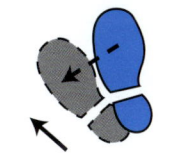

Motion to LEFT, only left foot moves

Motion to RIGHT, only right foot moves

The alternative gesture is to cue BEAT TWO (in 3/4), or BEAT THREE (in 4/4) with the left hand. Otherwise, simply use the right hand within the beat pattern for a cue on BEAT TWO in 4/4 time when cueing to the left. Be careful not to collide visually when the left hand moves to the right. In this case, a glance or a nod may be preferable, supported with a little more emphasis on the beat.[63]

Use left hand for BEAT-CUE on LEFT

OR right hand CROSS for BEAT-CUE on LEFT

* AVOID THIS! *

CROSSING hands

The Beat Goes On

ON THE BEAT CUES
"Canticle" mm. 15-30 (arr. Burgmayer)

See the Chapter Twenty-Two online folder to hear a number of these musical examples

SOP: He leads me in the right way, Though I walk through deep-est

ALTO: He leads in the right way for his name-sake, Though I walk,

dark-ness. For Thou, oh Lord, Thou art with me.

I will not be a-fraid, Lord. Thou, oh Lord, Thou art with me.

TEN: I will not be a-fraid, Lord. Oh Lord be with me.

BASS: I will not be a-fraid for

"CANTICLE" on-the-beat cues

LEFT HAND	BAR #	RIGHT HAND
LH indicate *mp*	15	RH give *legato* preparation
LH cue altos on BEAT 2	16	RH maintain 3 pattern
LH palm open for sustained sopranos	18	RH beat time with altos
LH cue alto downbeat	20	RH cue sopranos on BEAT 2
Reverse: LH cue altos on BEATS 2 & 3	21	RH cue sopranos on downbeat
LH cue tenor entrance	23	RH maintain 3 pattern
LH palm up holding soprano long tone	24	RH pick up tenor line
LH soprano release on BEAT 1	26	RH cue BEAT 3 soprano entrance
LH forward sweep for soprano *cresc.*	27	RH indicate breath and cue to alto
LH cue bass entrance	28	RH indicate breath after BEAT 3 in soprano alto

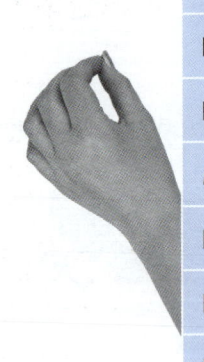

OFF-BEAT CUES and SYNCOPATION

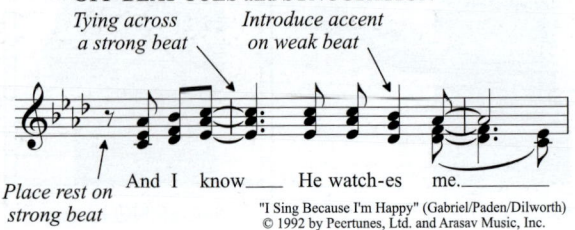

Tying across a strong beat →
Introduce accent on weak beat →
Place rest on strong beat ↑

And I know He watch-es me.

"I Sing Because I'm Happy" (Gabriel/Paden/Dilworth)
© 1992 by Peertunes, Ltd. and Arasav Music, Inc.

Off-beat cues, accents, syncopations

When the composer places an accent onto a normally weak beat, we call this **syncopation**. This can be the result of tying a note across a strong beat, introducing an accent on a weak beat, or placement of a rest on a strong beat, displacing the accent to an unexpected place.

Chapter 22 | GESTURE AND EXPRESSION

Conduct any off-beat cues, accents, or syncopations as though they were on the beat **before** the off-beat accent or syncopation, adding a bit more bounce than normally on the beat. Preserve the beat pattern. Do not attempt to conduct the off-beat accents. Rather allow the performer to syncopate around the steady pulse.

What has become known as the **gesture of syncopation** should be envisioned as an *accented* gesture. To help players and singers place an isolated syncopated entrance or accent properly, the conductor gives a strong beat stroke just prior to the off-beat syncopation as the preparation. Instead of continuing to beat time, the hand stops completely on the beat, before the beat that requires the after-beat response. The stopping of the hand brings attention to the rest and the ensuing syncopation. The hand remains still until the exact instant of the next beat following the syncopation, making an unprepared short, sharp gesture, *staccato* in nature. This pinpoints the instant of the next beat.[64] The size of the gesture of syncopation controls the dynamic.

> "Never beat syncopation. Keep the beat!"

THE GESTURE OF SYNCOPATION

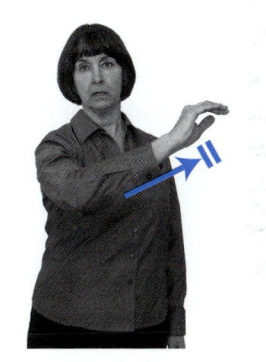

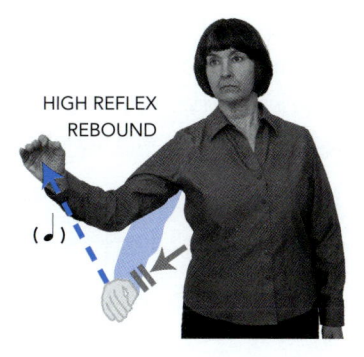

HIGH STOP on BEAT 2 — **STOP on BEAT 3 rest** — **MUSIC SOUNDS after BEAT 3**

For an accented entrance on the "and" of BEAT THREE, anticipate the cue with a preparation on BEAT TWO and a sharp stroke on BEAT THREE. Treat it as the entrance, but with a little more attack. We sometimes call this a "hot stove beat." In this case, we give BEAT THREE a red-hot touch, with a high bounce and stop, which indicates the syncopation.

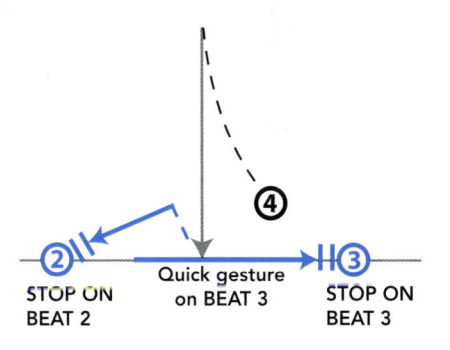

STOP ON BEAT 2 — Quick gesture on BEAT 3 — **STOP ON BEAT 3**

With a series of syncopated, off-beat accents, the conductor gives a quickened bounce **before** each syncopated note, as though reacting to a burn on your hand. The off-beat syncopation sounds while the hand and baton momentarily seem to pause.[65] It may take your musicians some rehearsal time to get acclimated to playing or singing syncopations between your beats, so allow rehearsal time for this.

GESTURE OF SYNCOPATION
Allegro giusto

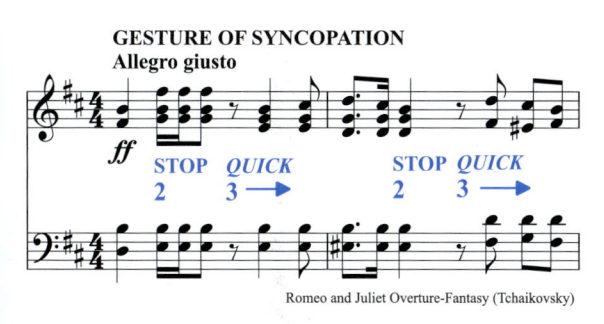

STOP QUICK STOP QUICK
  2   3   2   3

Romeo and Juliet Overture-Fantasy (Tchaikovsky)

SERIES OF SYNCOPATED OFF-BEATS
Strong strokes **ON** each beat

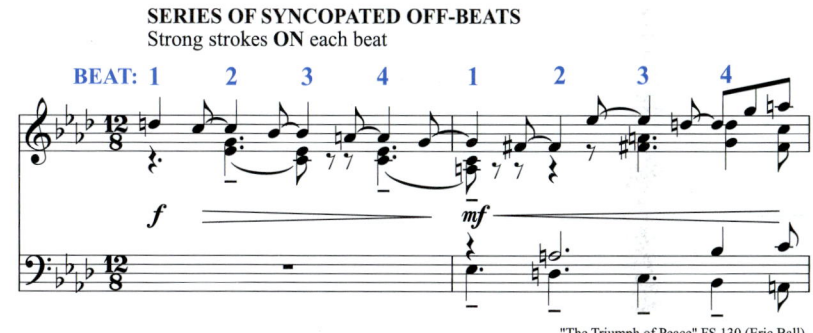

BEAT: 1 2 3 4 1 2 3 4

"The Triumph of Peace" FS 130 (Eric Ball)
© 1939 Salvationist Publishing

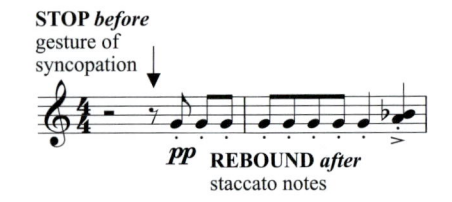

STOP *before* gesture of syncopation

pp **REBOUND** *after* staccato notes

Remember that the stop comes **before the beat with the gesture of syncopation**, and **after the rebound with staccato notes**.⁶⁶

22 BARS REST

Cueing exercises

1. A simple round is a good starting point to practice cueing. Give a clear preparation and start for each entrance, finishing note, or repeat.

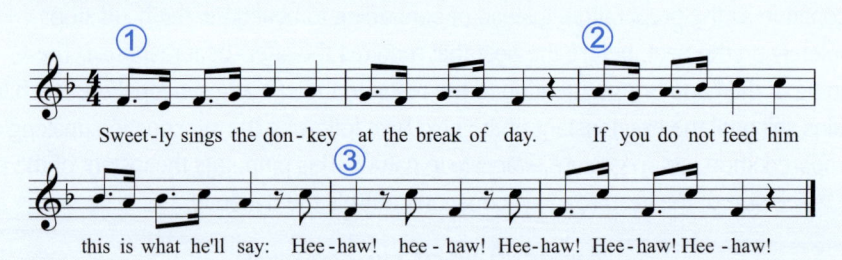

   ① Sweet-ly sings the don-key at the break of day. ② If you do not feed him
   ③ this is what he'll say: Hee-haw! hee-haw! Hee-haw! Hee-haw! Hee-haw!

2. While watching yourself in a mirror or while being videotaped, commence a beat pattern in the right hand. Bring the left hand into play by directing a cue or cutoff to an imaginary section, such as the sopranos or horns. To start, practice these cues on the beat. Begin with the left hand in a relaxed, belt position. One beat ahead, make an anticipatory up gesture that signals "ready." At the moment of the entrance, a decisive, downward motion signals "now." A variant of this exercise uses an imaginary ensemble set–off (or set ensemble without the players) where you mentally place starting cues, entrances, and cutoffs. Be prepared two beats before the needed moment of execution.

3. Ask a group to silently count to 10, giving only a few beats prep to establish the tempo. Instruct them that on 11 they are to shout "bang," without any facial or physical clues from you. The results usually prove ragged. Next repeat the counting, but on 10 look up and give an upbeat and then a vigorous downbeat on 11. The "bang" should line up better! This exercise is the closest thing to cueing a percussionist after umpteen bars rest for a solitary cymbal crash. Percussionists hesitate not because they're timid, but due to a need for assurance with their counting. Your eyes and preparation say "ready," and the subsequent cue says "now."⁶⁷

4. With the right hand conducting regular beat patterns, have the left hand cue entrances on a different beat in each bar.⁶⁸

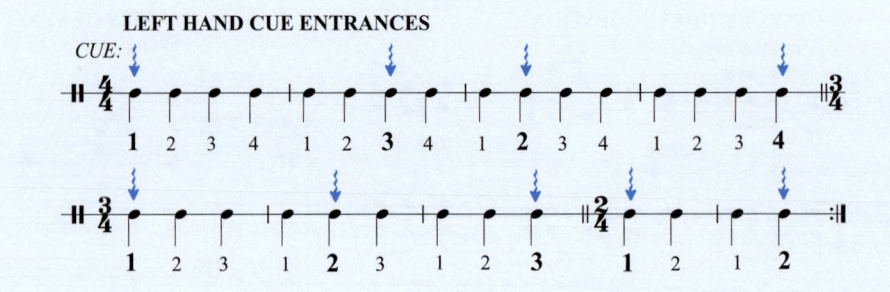

   LEFT HAND CUE ENTRANCES

5. In a similar manner, have the right hand conduct regular beat patterns, while the left hand cues cutoffs on a different beat in each bar.

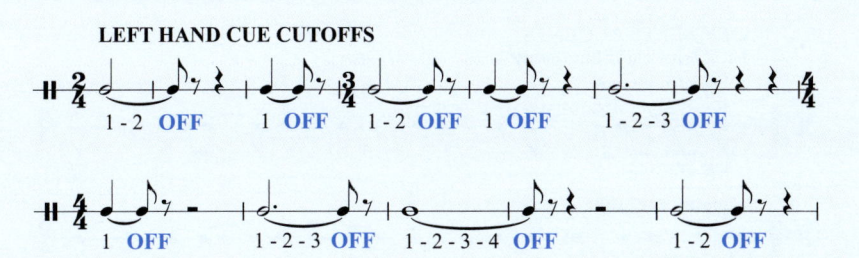

LEFT HAND CUE CUTOFFS

1 - 2   OFF   1   OFF   1 - 2   OFF   1   OFF   1 - 2 - 3   OFF

1   OFF   1 - 2 - 3   OFF   1 - 2 - 3 - 4   OFF   1 - 2   OFF

6. Practice conducting each meter pattern while singing syncopation against it. Always conduct beats, not the syncopation itself.

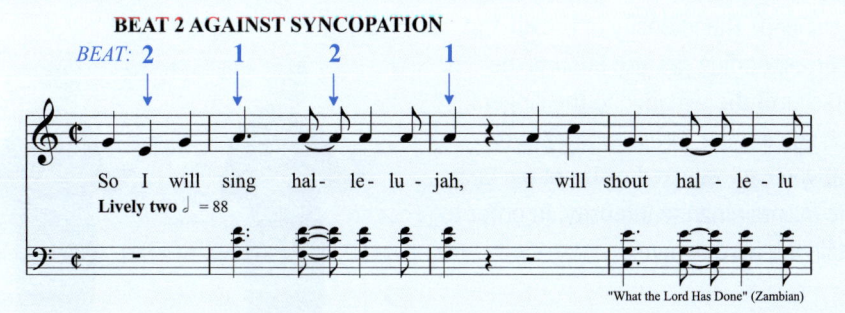

BEAT: 1 2 3 4 1 2 3 4

(WOMEN) Wi - der than the mind can re - a - lize,
Andante con espress. ♩ = 76

(MEN) His love is un - lim - it - ed and nev - er dies; Though we don't de -

"Everywhere" STTL (Larsson/Maycock)
© 2012 Salvationist Publishing

BEAT 3 AGAINST SYNCOPATION

BEAT: 1 2 3 1 2 3

Some - thing hap - pened, and now I know, He touched me and
Moderato ♩ = 96

"He Touched Me" (Gaither)
© 1963 William J. Gaither

BEAT 2 AGAINST SYNCOPATION

BEAT: 2 1 2 1

So I will sing hal - le - lu - jah, I will shout hal - le - lu
Lively two ♩ = 88

"What the Lord Has Done" (Zambian)

7. Maintain various beat patterns while negotiating page turns with the left hand. This is well worth the practice.

8. Practice accented off-beats as in these examples. Occasionally, a more dramatic gesture of syncopation may be required.

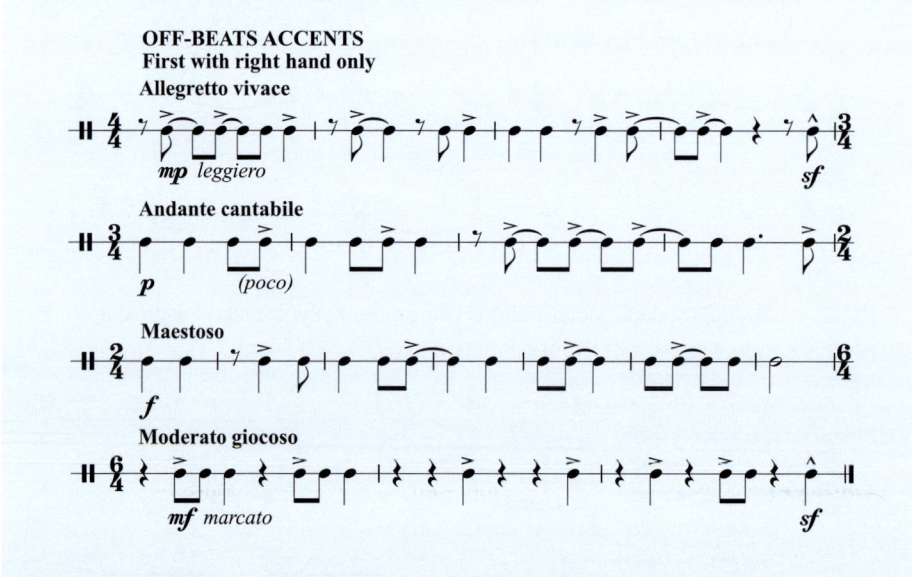

OFF-BEATS ACCENTS
First with right hand only
Allegretto vivace

mp leggiero ... *sf*

Andante cantabile

p (poco)

Maestoso

f

Moderato giocoso

mf marcato ... *sf*

EXPLORING DYNAMICS

In greater part than we realize, true instrumental colors called for by the composer are dependent on the *dynamics* designated in the score. Because it is far easier to play loud than soft, many bands seldom ever experience the quieter colors desired by the instrumentation. Similarly, with choirs, the magic of a *sotto voce* (in an undertone) passage is often lost to a less timid dynamic. In Battisti's words, "Dynamics are not added ornaments, but a vital part of a piece's construction."[69] Therefore it behooves you as a conductor to learn to exercise and demand a full range of dynamics. At the same time, be aware that relative differences in dynamics exist across various epochs and styles of music. A *forte* in an early Salvation Army march is not the same *forte* you want for a contemporary chorus arrangement.

BIG

Before considering cueing of dynamics, first explore the extremes of dynamics within your beat patterns. Start by making the beat as absurdly **large** as possible. Reduce the motion until it is controlled and not unseemly but still giving an impression of largeness. Especially with choirs, a large beat pattern does not necessarily produce a large sound. The intensity of breath and its corresponding gesture imparts the character of the dynamic to the singers.[70] Once you get the *fortissimo* (**ff**) you want, you can reduce the size of the beat while maintaining the intensity, in order to sustain the loud dynamic.

little

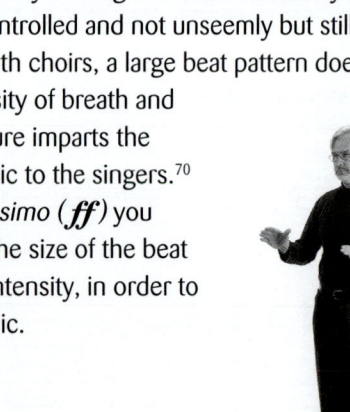

To explore a soft beat pattern, first beat as **tiny** as possible. Gradually enlarge the motion to a place where players and singers can clearly see the beat, even with quick glances at their music. Use of a baton allows a reduced hand motion, with only the tip of the baton making a slight motion.[71] If you mean to retain the color of a continuous soft dynamic like *piano* (*p*) or *pianissimo* (*pp*), be careful to keep the beat small. If you creep up bigger, the ensemble's dynamic will follow suit.

DYNAMIC TERMS[72]

Italian Terms Worth Memorizing

pianissimo (*pp*)	pee–ah–'ni–see–mo	very soft
piano (*p*)	pee–'ah–no	soft
mezzo piano (*mp*)	'met–so, pee–'ah–no	moderately soft
mezzo forte (*mf*)	'met–so, 'fohr–teh	moderately loud
forte (*f*)	'fohr–teh	loud
fortissimo (*ff*)	fohr–'tees–see–moh	very loud

Graded dynamics

Over time, the range of dynamics has expanded beyond the isolated *forte* and *piano* levels of 18th-century Classical music. Consequently the conductor learns how to modulate between a full range of dynamics, reflective of the score. Become equipped to do this by transitioning gradually from *fortissimo* (*ff*) to *pianissimo* (*pp*) and back again, using only the right hand (or both hands) conducting various beat patterns.

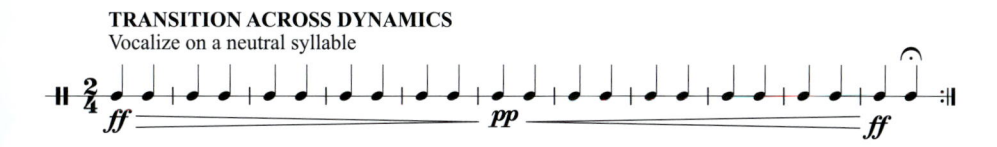

TRANSITION ACROSS DYNAMICS
Vocalize on a neutral syllable

Next, again only using the right-hand beat pattern, gradually mark for yourself a series of graded dynamics—from *fortissimo* (*ff*) to *forte* (*f*) to *mezzo forte* (*mf*) etc. down to *pianissimo* (*pp*) and then the reverse.

GRADED DYNAMIC LEVELS

Remember that as the conductor, you must show the performers what you want before they do it. **Anticipate, in your preparatory gesture, the dynamic range** you feel the score calls for at any given moment. Learn for yourself the size limits for your beat pattern at all dynamic levels. While you conduct, ask a friend to count out loud in continuous beats in any time signature. Show dynamic changes in your beats, and see if you can make him follow the volume changes you indicate.[73]

LEFT HAND INDICATING DYNAMICS

The Beat Goes On

BATON ARM   *p*   *mp*   *mf*   *f*

CHANGING DYNAMIC TERMS[74]

Italian Terms Worth Memorizing

crescendo (cresc.)	kreh–'shen–doh	becoming louder
decrescendo (decresc.)	day–kreh–'shen–doh	becoming softer
diminuendo (dim.)	dee–min–yoo–'en–doh	diminishing in volume
forte-piano (*fp*)	'fohr–teh – pee–'ah–no	loud attack, immediately soft
sforzando (*sfz*)	sfohr–'tsahn –toh	loudly accented
subito piano (sub. *p*)	soo–'bee–toh, pee–'ah–no	suddenly soft
subito forte (sub. *f*)	soo–'bee–toh, 'fohr–teh	suddenly loud

Gradual changes in dynamics

The intended expression within a phrase benefits from dynamics, which increase and decrease gradually, as opposed to strictly tiered dynamic levels. Right-hand gestures change in size to reflect the modulation in dynamics.[75] To indicate a **crescendo**, the palm of the left hand should be placed up and the arm lifted from the elbow to the desired level of *crescendo* by raising the arm and hands vertically.[76]

LEFT HAND CRESCENDO   *p* ——————————— *f*

Chapter 22 | GESTURE AND EXPRESSION

To indicate a **diminuendo**, turn the left hand gently to the side and then palm downward, descending back to the level of conducting floor. This movement is akin to pulling a vertical lever down using the left hand and arm.

f ──────────────────────── *p*   LEFT HAND DIMINUENDO

It is beneficial to practice *crescendo* and *diminuendo* (or *decrescendo*) in tandem. For example, while alternating meter gestures in the right hand, use the left hand to indicate four measures of *crescendo* followed by four measures of *decrescendo*. Allow the palm facing upward to "carry" the *crescendo*. Indicate the desired stretch of the *diminuendo* by turning the left hand to a downward position, returning back to the starting point. Vary the size of the time-beating gesture in the right hand to match the indications of dynamics in the left and vice versa. With experience, you will learn to avoid left-hand pauses and jerks induced by the rhythmic pulsing of the right-hand beats.[77]

PALM FACING OUT SIGNALS DIMINUENDO

PALM FACES UP CARRIES CRESCENDO

SUDDEN CHANGE OF DYNAMICS

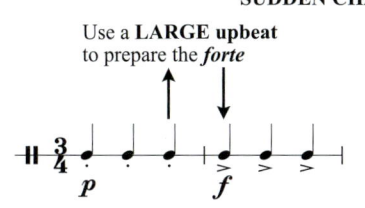

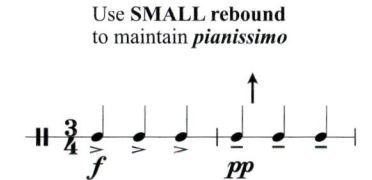

Use a **LARGE upbeat** to prepare the *forte*

Use **SMALL rebound** to maintain *pianissimo*

Sudden changes in dynamics

Moving either hand closer to the body connotes a softer dynamic, while moving away indicates more volume. A sudden retreat of the hands or arms signals a dramatic reduction in volume, while a gesture suddenly forward calls for an immediate increase in volume. Remember that you must show the performers what you want **before** they do it. For example, when indicating a sudden *forte* (*f*), give a large upbeat before the *forte* gesture. For a sudden *pianissimo* (*pp*), do not permit your beat to rebound high or the unhappy result will prove louder than desired.

Raising the left hand in a "stop" gesture helps indicate a sudden reduction in volume. We sometimes call this a "hot

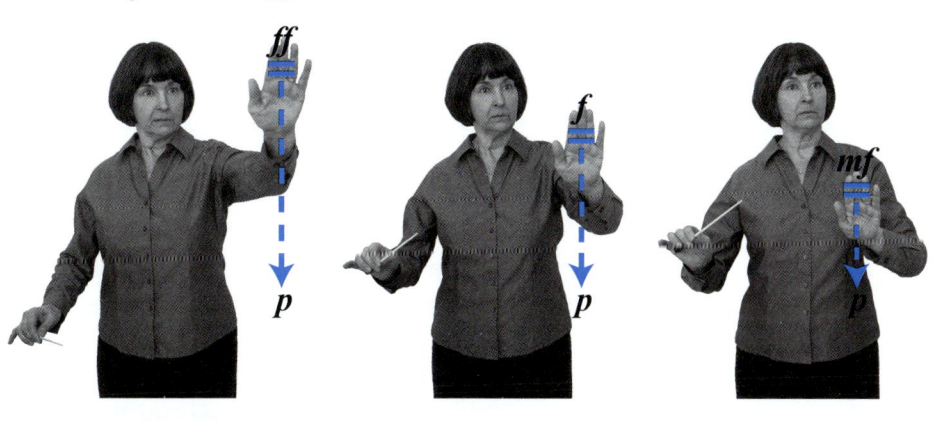

"HOT TOUCH" GESTURE
"Triumph of Peace" - Letter G

"The Triumph of Peace" FS 130 (Eric Ball)
© 1939 Salvationist Publishing

The Beat Goes On   495

touch," like the reaction to a hand touching a hot stove. It tells the ensemble there is an immediate decrease in volume, the magnitude of which must agree with the right hand beat pattern.

Left-hand complement
Sforzando (*sf*) attacks require a gesture that shows a suddenly loud volume, followed immediately by a soft gesture. An urgent, upward left palm suddenly facing the ensemble aids the *sforzando* gesture. Use the left hand in a supportive role to reinforce a *crescendo* or *diminuendo*. Emphasize a continuous *pianissimo* by making a pointed first finger "shhh" sign in front of the lips. Use a police officer's stop sign before a *subito* (or sudden) *pianissimo* (*pp*). When the left-hand palm is open and out, this indicates a big dynamic or supports a loud attack. In contrast, use of the left-hand palm down or out can indicate a desire to reduce the volume or suggest a gentle, softer approach to the sound.

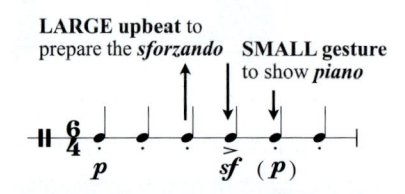

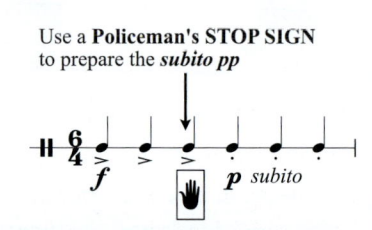

THE ART OF PHRASING

The art of conducting a phrase is not so much about the length of the line (for instance, when to breathe next), but about its *shape*. The proper distribution of energy as you approach and recede from a peak or high spot is fundamental. Sometimes the conductor may ask players or singers to use stagger breathing across a phrase or melodic fragment to carry the strength of the line.

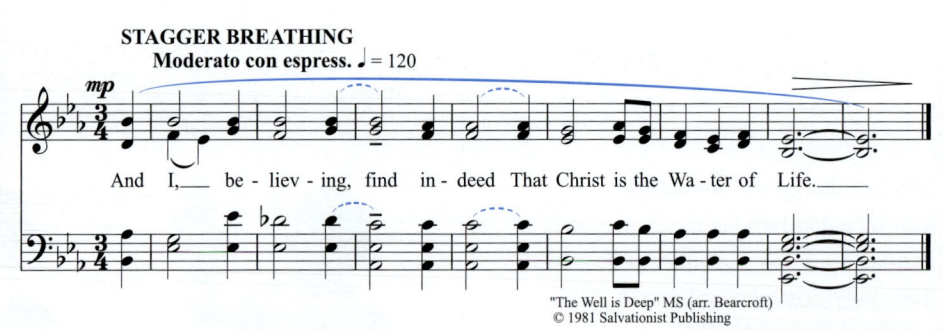

The beginning and ends of phrases
Longtime New York Staff Bandmaster Derek Smith used to teach that the end of the phrase should be tapered dynamically in order to disguise the breath. Although "methods of phrasing may vary, they have this in common: There is a decreased intensity at the end of a phrase, and a fresh motion at the beginning of the new one."[78] A slight break for the breath should be shown, yet with the rhythm remaining steady. If this is overdone, the sense of flow is disrupted.[79] Thus the performer is expected to shorten slightly the last note before the break for the breath. The conductor indicates this by stopping the hand in the middle of a flowing motion, which implies a breath or phrase mark.

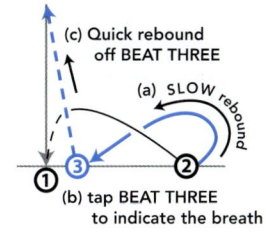

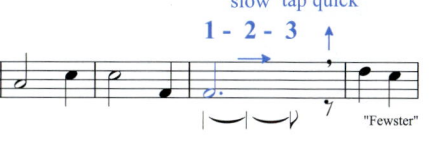

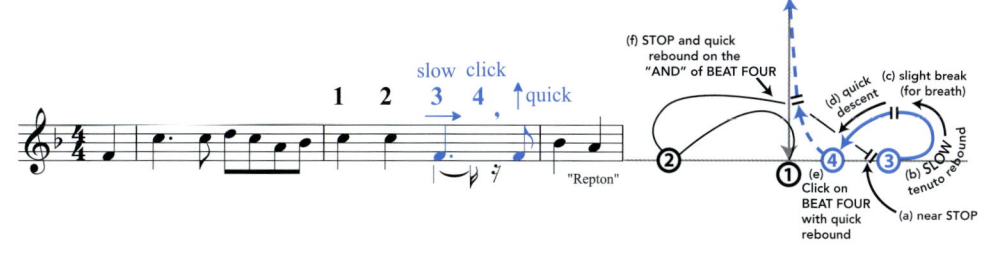

Chapter 22 | GESTURE AND EXPRESSION

Molding the musical line

There are a number of ways conductors can mold the musical line. In a way, it is like a dance, where the hands, arms, body, head, and eyes create shifting moods, from caressing a gentle melody to whipping the percussion section into furious motion. Varying the use of *legato*, *staccato*, and *tenuto* beats helps indicate the desired articulation. Subtle variations in beat, even from count to count, can express the inflections of the melody that are not indicated in the score, but rather implied. Changes in the size and intensity of the beat not only affect the dynamics, but also the phrasing.[80]

PLACE BREATH

INDICATE SHAPE OF PHRASE

The shaping of the phrases

The indications for the shapes of phrases are similar to those of *crescendo* and *diminuendo*, except that the phrasal gesture is more horizontal. A phrase shape may be indicated by the left hand, beginning at the center of the body and moving to the conductor's left in an upward, then downward arching line, like a rainbow, imitating the direction of the phrase. As the phrase tapers, so does the horizontal line that is moving from the center to the left. The tendency after a slow build-up can be to allow a downturn too quickly on the other side of a climax, rather than preserving the intensity in the decline.[81]

To indicate carrying over of the breath from note to note or the tying of a note, use a shorter gesture that outlines a semicircle. Begin in the center of body and arch up and out, descending to the center of the conducting plane.[82]

UPWARD ARCH SHAPES PHRASE

SHORT SEMICIRCLES CARRY OVER BREATH

Left-hand sustaining gestures

The left hand is a much-needed aid for indicating musical phrasing. A **horizontal sweep**, where the left arm is extended in front of the body with the hand open and thumb up (handshake style), indicates *legato* phrasing. The arm sweeps from right to left as if pulling through a heavy liquid. The gesture may be reversed from left to center.[83]

START SIDE SWEEP

SWEEP TO LEFT

EXTENDED SWEEP TO LEFT

The horizontal sweep from left to right: Middle position, sweep to left, and extended sweep.

The Beat Goes On

A **forward sweep** indicates continuous phrasing, unbroken by a breath, sometimes known as carrying or covering a phrase. The left arm is extended before the body with the hand open and the thumb up. For this gesture, the hand sweeps slowly forward and gives a little push at the point where the phrase is to be unbroken by the breath. Do not elevate the arm/hand, as this suggests a *crescendo*. Execute the forward sweep at the mid-level above the conducting floor, high enough to be easily seen.

The forward sweep from left to right: Left hand in center position, sweep to left, and extended sweep.

START FORWARD SWEEP

PUSH TO SWEEP THROUGH PHRASE

EXTENDED SWEEP TO LEFT

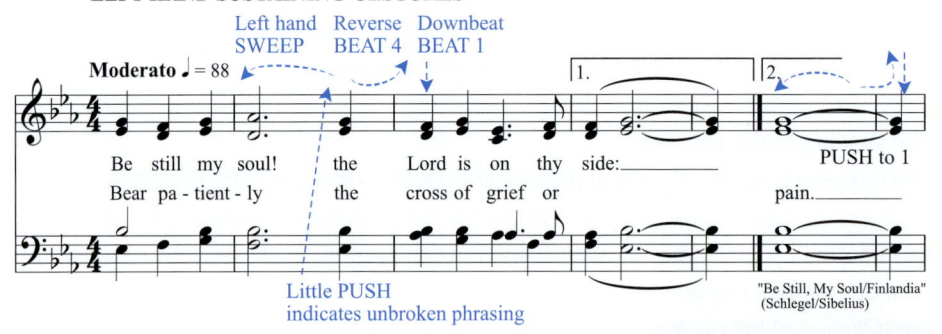

LEFT HAND SUSTAINING GESTURES

Left hand SWEEP — Reverse BEAT 4 — Downbeat BEAT 1

Moderato ♩ = 88

Be still my soul! the Lord is on thy side:___
Bear pa-tient-ly the cross of grief or pain.___

PUSH to 1

Little PUSH indicates unbroken phrasing

"Be Still, My Soul/Finlandia" (Schlegel/Sibelius)

Loving the music 
Conducting technique must serve your musical intentions. As a conductor, throw yourself into the task of drawing music from the performers, rather than merely going through a series of mechanical actions.[84] Strive for a natural combination of varied tempo, intensity, and articulation to bring out the nuance and expressiveness of the musical line as you imagine it. To highlight the nuances you want, sometimes it can help to slow, and then gradually elevate the tempo. But avoid straying too far from the composer's intentions. A performance should never sound mechanical or, for that matter, the same as the last time.[85] There is something to be said for loving the music so much that you lose yourself in it, bringing the music alive. And so, the beat goes on!

❓ 22 BARS REST

1. Conduct *crescendi* and *diminuendi* over one bar, then two, three, and more. Work to evenly negotiate the increase and decrease in volume while establishing the relative levels and size of the various dynamics. Do this in a variety of meters.

2. Conduct passages, varying the schemes for dynamics, as in this example:

LEFT HAND SUSTAINING GESTURES

Moderato ♩ = 84

"Spanish Chant" (Bishop)

① p ——————— f ——————— p
② p < f > p < f > p
③ f ——————— mp ——— mf
④ mf < > mp ——— f ——— p > pp
⑤ p ——— f ——— p < > p < mf

3. Conduct various lines with the right hand only. Clearly indicate the articulations while projecting the character and dynamics of the music.[86]

EXPRESSION IN GESTURE
Conduct the following using the *right hand only*, making the beat project the characteristics indicated.

Andante maestoso .... **rubato**

⑥ f ——— p < mf > p sf (p) < >

4. Practice with a friend (or a mirror), stopping beats slightly at the top to show the end of a phrase, without deviating from strict tempo.[87] Practice this in various time signatures.

5. With a group of friends, conduct some well-known songs or choruses. After some straightforward runs, change the dynamics, accents, phrasing, tempo, and character as much as possible without regard to the score markings. Ask for suggestions on what can be done better. Don't worry about starting and stopping. A simple "ready-sing" will do.[88]

6. The Conductor in the Mirror: Conduct in strict time to a recording of something familiar while watching yourself in the mirror. Use your ear and memory to conduct without a score. Make sure your beat is consistent yet reflects the changes in volume on the recording. Don't worry about missing things in the music. The important thing is to experience a lot of time-beating in different patterns, tempos, and volumes while watching your reflection in the mirror. Accurate score study can come later. Remember to show when changes are about to take place, rather than at the instant the music changes.[89]

7. In this chapter, we worked to expand the conductor's toolbox in establishing tempo, expressive character, use of the left hand, exploring dynamics, and the art of phrasing. Identify where you need to improve as a conductor and integrate the necessary adjustments of gesture into your weekly rehearsals.

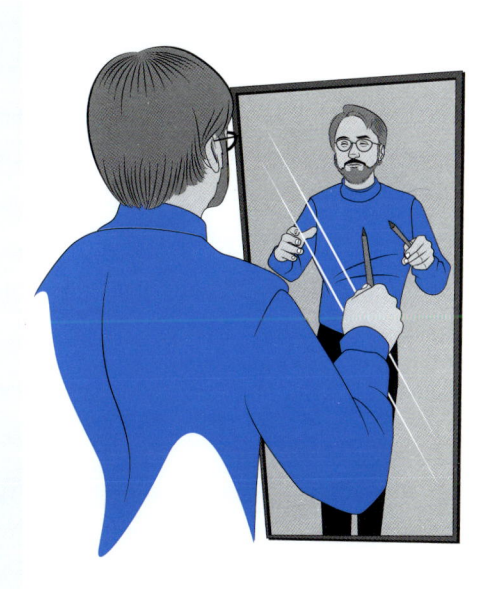

Conducting and Score Study Resources are found at the conclusion of Chapters Ten, Twenty, and Twenty-One.

CHAPTER TWENTY-THREE

LISTEN AND RESPOND
Making the Rehearsal Work

Notes, like words, are mere utterances of symbols, and within themselves are totally lacking and incapable of expression. It is the human response, not [the] mechanical [one] that creates the communication between the written symbol, the performer and the listener.
—William Revelli, legendary band director at the University of Michigan

Congratulations! You've made it to the final chapter on conducting! You can consider this a hidden track, a bonus chapter for those leaders seeking to be most effective in rehearsal. In Chapters Nine and Ten, we encouraged the practice of regularly reading scores. In the chapters on Singing Company (Six and Seven), Youth Band (Eight and Nine), Songster Leader (Twelve and Thirteen), and Bandmaster (Fourteen and Fifteen), we considered practical, specific approaches when standing in front of those ensembles. In the Song Leading Chapter (Five) and the preceding Conducting Chapters (Twenty, Twenty-One and Twenty-Two) we've looked at ways to technically and expressively communicate as a conductor. After covering so much territory, we can agree that there are lots of things to attend to while conducting. But the essential core of standing in front of any musical ensemble is learning how to *listen and respond*.

Do you recall that at the start of Chapter Twenty, Maestro Muti quoted his elderly mentor? After a lifetime of conducting, the mentor said that he was just learning how to conduct. Acquiring the skill to **listen** and absorb what your ensemble is giving you, and then to effectively **respond** in gesture and instruction is certainly not learned overnight. But diligence and a persistent passion to get *inside the music* will, in time, benefit your ensemble's rehearsal.

In **Chapter Twenty-Three**, we consider routines, listening, and mechanics necessary to an effective rehearsal, addressing:

- How do I get performers to watch me?
- How do I know when and how to stop?
- How can I get my ensemble inside the music?

A TALE OF TWO CONDUCTORS

During my years as an undergraduate architecture student, I sat under two rightfully revered Salvation Army bandmasters. I didn't realize for many years the sizable influence they had over my future as a trainer of instrumentalists and singers. One conductor, whom we will call Philip, appeared burly in front of us, bent over like a bear, with sweeping arms, yet giving indefatigable cues with his eyes and arms. The other leader, known here as Richard, stood upright, somewhat aloof, rarely glancing at us, as though staring at something at a distance. Philip anticipated cues, peering at a section bars in advance with a restless gaze; while Richard cued with a quick flick of his left hand, which could easily be missed.

With Philip, many of the standard repertoire pieces seemed stylistically branded on his memory. I appreciate now that I was forced to absorb the sentiment of another era. He repeated certain mantras over and over to bring out the shape of the line, dependent on adherence to its related text. With more recent music, he seemed to be learning the music with us, in real time. Richard pictured the music in piano reduction, and proved it by accompanying soloists from an open band score. This skill was complemented with a marvelous memory, as he rarely looked down at the score. He relished unraveling the mysteries of a new score, savoring the music for its own merit.

Having been a well-known soloist, Philip was definitely "training" his forces, always cajoling the music out of us. He didn't hesitate to isolate passages or players to force teamwork and stylistic consistency. Richard rarely drilled the music. Instead, he worked the overall shape of pieces, too often from the beginning of the piece or program, which meant he would run out of time to satisfactorily rehearse the piece's conclusion!

Temperamentally, Philip was fixed on drawing an emotional response from within the music. To our chagrin, Richard often displayed passion in a fairly direct manner at a player's ineptitude. Philip was shy and found it difficult to articulate his desires, giving an impression of sternness, yet he drew our respect from his personal discipline and passion for the music. Richard had a nearly unrivaled facility for work and an unflagging energy equal to the task. He used few, yet flamboyant expressions to describe the effect desired. Yet off the podium, he proved amiable, with a touch of wry sarcasm.

Philip strove for perfection in the details, conquering difficult passages by working a phrase incessantly until facility and balance were achieved. Therefore, he proved not as effective in short-term weekend or camp settings, where there is limited rehearsal time. Richard took the ensemble on an exciting, fast-paced ride which, although littered with shortcomings, seemed to carry exuberantly into an energetic performance.

LESSONS IN REHEARSAL ROUTINE

We may not realize it, but over time we unwittingly glean many of the expressions, gestures, techniques, even repertoire choices of those who have led us in the past. I can see now how the often-contrasting attributes of these two bandmasters were assimilated into my own band and songster leadership. Max Rudolph said, "The first beat in the bar goes down and the last beat goes up; the rest is experience."[1] Along the road of leadership there are very few genuine discoveries. Rather we learn and absorb in an indirect way from careful listening and observation, or more directly from our mistakes. What follows are tried and true lessons gleaned from my experience in the middle of an ensemble. I hope they will benefit your rehearsal routine.

Use the "correct address"

When a note mistake takes place, train yourself to make eye contact but without peering at the culprit (known to my players as "The Look"). Players and singers too easily feel that an attack on their artistry is personal. Bram Gregson suggests first addressing the *neighborhood* (the tuba section), then the *house* (the Eb tubas), and finally, if necessary, the *tenant* (Michael). By the time you get to the house, the players probably know who is making the mistake. When addressing the error, use the collective pronoun "we." This includes you with the others around you, rather than the personal finger-pointing "you."

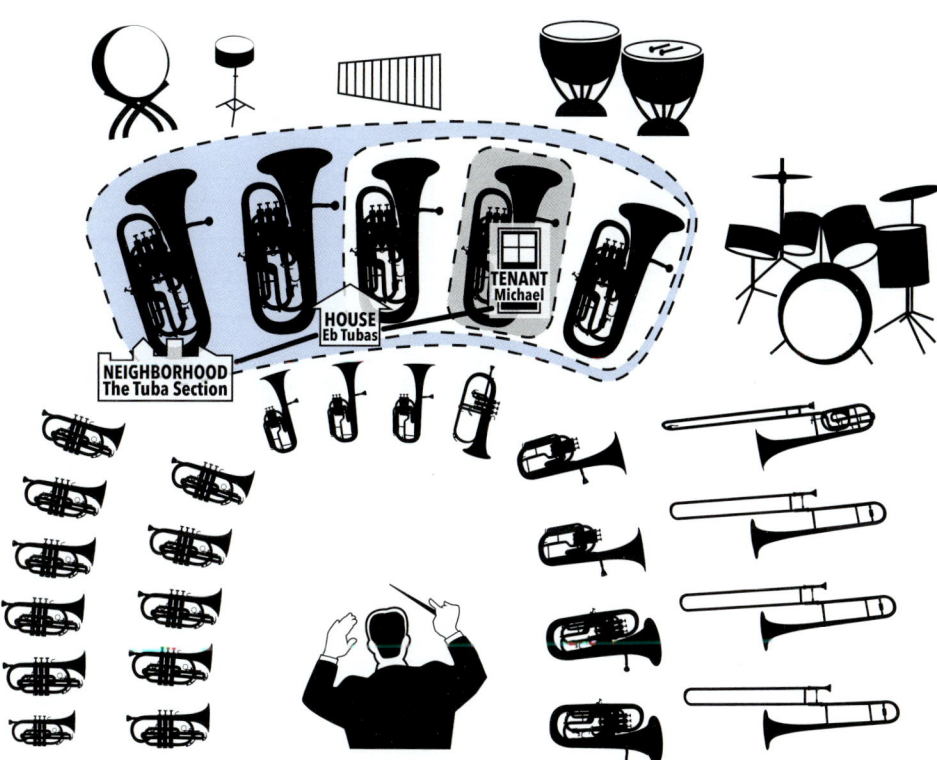

Give the instruction clearly (and just once!)

I have spent years training myself to enunciate and project my voice, attempting to communicate my intentions clearly and distinctly. Sometimes, when I am anxious to remedy errors and move forward, it is difficult to keep a slow enough pace that I don't skip words or concepts. My practice is to give an instruction only once. (If your musicians know that you will repeat the instruction, they unintentionally elect not to listen the first few times.) Be sure your percussionists at the back of the band or singers out on the perimeter are getting every word of what you are saying.

Make eye contact

Do not speak to the score on your stand. Eye contact is vital. Being naturally shy, I force my eyes up, even in general conversation, to make eye contact for cues. Some players never get out of their copies or are hiding in theirs. Others—the ones I love—have their eyes up, looking for the cue, as if to say, "Give it to me."

Discover your ensemble's unique sound

It may be the byproduct of easy access to recordings, but it is unfortunate that most ensembles today sound so alike! Style helps dictate the color of a piece, but as the leader, you should also search for your group's unique sound. Extend the pyramid principle to each section to achieve a round sound, with rich tone required from the second players, even more so than the upper parts. My score markings usually "follow the action," that is, the entrances and moving lines. There are times when a piece does not sound as I imagined. I then take what I learn from the band rehearsal home and reconfigure my aural picture of the styling and scope of the piece.

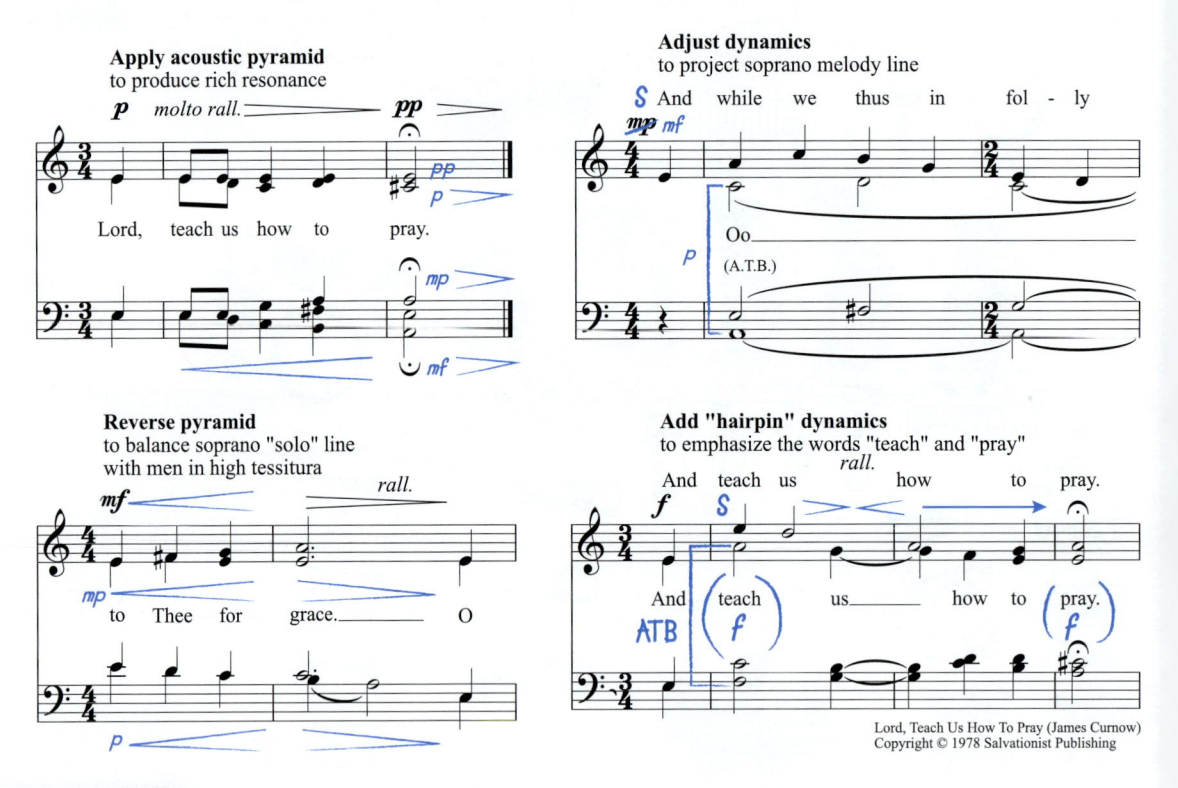

See Chapter Fourteen, page 296–297 for more on how applying the **pyramid principle** can improve your ensemble's balance. A recording of these excerpts of *Lord, Teach Us How to Pray* are found in the Chapter Twenty-Three online folder.

Lord, Teach Us How To Pray (James Curnow)
Copyright © 1978 Salvationist Publishing

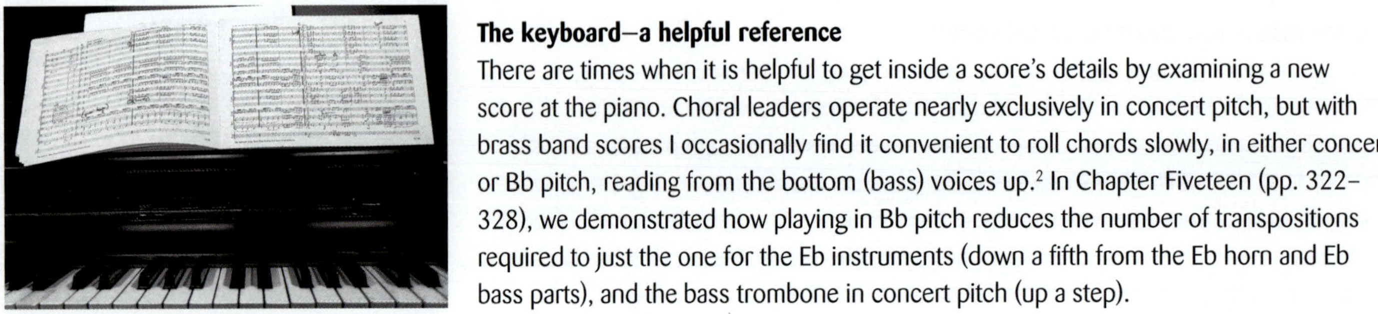

The keyboard—a helpful reference

There are times when it is helpful to get inside a score's details by examining a new score at the piano. Choral leaders operate nearly exclusively in concert pitch, but with brass band scores I occasionally find it convenient to roll chords slowly, in either concert or Bb pitch, reading from the bottom (bass) voices up.[2] In Chapter Fifteen (pp. 322–328), we demonstrated how playing in Bb pitch reduces the number of transpositions required to just the one for the Eb instruments (down a fifth from the Eb horn and Eb bass parts), and the bass trombone in concert pitch (up a step).

When to stop

Experience teaches when and how often to stop during rehearsals. Too many interruptions can frustrate players and their sense of the journey of the music. Some mistakes can be glossed over as players realize their errors without your correction. When a stop is necessary, the leader must quickly decide which instrumental section to rehearse, and how much. Working from the back of a piece allows an overlap of critical transitions between sections, while rehearsing from the front may give the ensemble a better handle on the narrative story line. Use the information in this chapter to explore ways to improve your ability to listen and respond, to aid the pace and effectiveness of rehearsals.

rehearse (verb) \re - 'hers\ means to **harrow again**, where an iron frame with spikes, drawn by a tractor or horse, plows to break up soil, cover seed or tear up weeds.[3] This root meaning of the term "**rehearse**" goes beyond the modern day meanings, like "to say again, repeat, train or make proficient," and gets closer to the true essence of a productive rehearsal.

23 BARS REST

1. Recall music mentors who have inspired you. What specific aspects of their teaching or conducting do you seem to emulate? What was it about those leaders and their approach that inspired you so much?

2. Observe rehearsals by other leaders and talk to the members and their respective conductors. Ask what makes them successful, or less so, bearing in mind the constraints of their allotted time. Glean lessons you can apply to your own situation.

3. Rehearse and perform under other conductors to remind yourself what it is like to sit under someone—and actually count rests!

LISTEN AND...RESPOND

Advice to young conductors: Be prepared. **Listen**. Conduct as frequently as possible. **Listen**. Try new ideas. **Listen**. Find a mentor. **Listen**. Watch yourself on video. **Listen**. Take risks. —Darren Dailey, conductor of Jacksonville Children's Choir

CAPPUCCINO AND THE FINE ART OF LISTENING

Over piping-hot cappuccinos, Maestros Animato and Placido engage in a lively exchange. They attempt to clarify for themselves the finer **distinctions between hearing as opposed to listening.** The parent will inquire, "Are you listening to me?" to which the offspring disparagingly responds, "I can hear you." Both know that the child has been otherwise preoccupied and has not been listening.

In conversation with Maestro Animato, his fellow conductor Placido astutely observes that the communication gap between conductor and ensemble can resemble those moments of disconnect between parent and child. They bemoan the fact that many conductors, and subsequently their ensembles, also lack a real depth of understanding about what they are hearing. We join the two maestros as they explore this tension.

Animato: Placido, do you think it is true that the ear only listens for what our minds direct it to hear?

Placido: Why yes, Animato, I really think so. In my experience, we hear what we listen for. So we have to remind ourselves over and over again to avoid distraction and stay focused on listening, both within ourselves imagining the score, as well as absorbing the response from the ensemble.[4]

Animato: Then, dear Placido, are you saying that what is meant to be heard in music must be heard within the leader before anyone else can hear it?[5]

Placido: Oh yes, indeed, Animato. And then it is critical to listen to what is actually getting back to us and ask, "Is what I am hearing what I want?"[6]

Animato: Yes, but sometimes I find it helps to listen for how the young people in my ensemble hear it, not necessarily listening for whether I get what I want.[7]

Placido: *(Placido pauses, contemplating Animato's point)* Oh Animato, that would make a valuable connection with the young musicians. *(Placido pauses again, and after some consideration, inquires)* Do you really do that? Can you listen for what they hear?

Animato: My dear Placido, I listen to my group and follow my instincts. In a way I relinquish my position as maestro. The sound becomes our teacher.[8] Does that make sense to you?

Placido: *(Placido gazes off, almost glazed over, not responding to Animato's inquiry)*

Animato: *(Seeking to break Placido's seeming distraction, Animato anxiously chides him)* Placido, do you hear me?... *(with a more robust tone)* Are you even listening?... Placido?... *(looking away from the table)* Your name says it all! *(Animato pauses with the realization that Placido is gripped by the playback in his mind of a passage of music. He has departed their conversation to listen to the music swirling around in his mind.)*

IS THAT PLACIDO DOMINGO?

animato (*rabiductor*)
\ah - nee - 'mah - toh\
lively, spirited, and full of vigor.

placido (*placiductor*)
\'plah - see - doh\
agreeable, pleasant, and calm.

www.music.saconnects.org

From the inside out...

You may recall from the introduction of Chapter Ten the threefold concept of hearing musical scores as an **"imagined" aural concept** of the piece heard through the playback in your mind's ear, as **an "ideal" sound**, embedded in your aural memory, yet tempered by **the actual "real" sound** in front of you as you conduct. It is no surprise that when beginning a new piece the real sound and the imagined or ideal ones are some distance apart.

As you, the conductor, work through the actual notes, the imagined and ideal sounds are hopefully brought into closer proximity. To make this happen, you need to conscientiously assimilate the composer's blueprint, genuinely attempting to re-create the musical ideas of the composer in your mind's ear and memory banks. Hints as to proper interpretation are facilitated by making comparisons between the markings on the score and an idealized vision as to style, approach, and length of notes in similar works.[9]

Living with the evidence

Frank Battisti wisely advises that the best time to listen to, or what we normally call "study a score," is when there is no pressure to learn it for a performance.[10] This is an excellent reason to regularly survey scores. When faced with an imminent performance deadline, the leader is diverted into strategizing how to teach the piece quickly, rather than taking time to draw out the intended aural scenario from an ensemble. The learning process requires repeated "harrowings," or readings, using one's own accumulated knowledge and artistry, before, during, and after rehearsal, to arrive at a convincing interpretation.

Back to looking for clues

We are all tempted to learn scores by blindly worshiping a recording, which in fact probably has flaws.[11] A better but more time-intensive practice is to compare performances, asking formatively **who** will comprehend this music. While listening, ask **what** you like about the sound or **why** an unexpected surprise catches your attention. Use your hands-on score study to expand your knowledge of harmony, counterpoint, and form, constantly inquiring into **how** the music is shaped. Ask **where** in historical context the music belongs, as proper instrumental or choral interpretation can sometimes prove more important to the performance than expert baton technique.[12]

The Beat Goes On

Learning from the Masters

To this end, I encourage emerging music leaders not to limit their listening and score-reading to Salvation Army choral or brass selections. I once had a student who enthusiastically absorbed the symphonies of Brahms, while another was smitten by the tone poems of Sibelius. Initially this *listening* was intended to hone their own orchestral playing. Yet by exposing themselves to music of stellar craft, they expanded their own artistic palette. Today, both are respected band and songster trainers who use their broad musical expertise to benefit others.

Listening outside your box

Dare I suggest that singers can learn from symphonic literature, pianists from opera, and band enthusiasts from listening to fine choirs? While listening and studying a less familiar musical genre, one begins to assimilate the right tempo, style, sound, ornament, or note length embodied in the stylistic and harmonic similarities of what we non-historians sometimes refer to as "what was in the air."[13]

> There are times to look back and take the tried and true way: "Stand by the ways and see and ask for the ancient paths, where the good way is, and walk in it."
> —Jeremiah 6:16, *NASB*

In the '60s, Salvationists began forming groups like The Joystrings, using the pop medium. In the '70s, Salvation Army bands started exploring jazz and rock idioms with pieces like *So Glad* (Himes) and *Daniel* (Gott). Today, much of our music crosses over into pop, Latin, and world music idioms, to which leaders should have more than a passing acquaintance.

With older Salvation Army literature, I challenge my students to try to place themselves in the environs and epoch of a piece's origin and try to imagine what it sounded like then. This admonition includes even recent generations, with the music of Leidzén, Condon, Ball, Steadman-Allen, and others before them. Too often we are guilty of applying a 21st-century finish coat to a fine piece of antique furniture. McElheran puts it well when comparing the Hudson Valley to the Rockies, suggesting both can be viewed as nearly flat. A well-experienced traveler knows the difference.[14]

Touching the wave

James Jordan makes the point that there is a place for analytical listening, wherein we constantly try to hear more and more in a score, simultaneously conditioning ourselves as conductors to anticipate trouble spots.[15] For those schooled in musical analysis, it can be difficult to set aside our critical or aesthetic tool kit, to allow the sounds to engulf us, and to simply *listen* to the music. When listening outside the box, avoid becoming sidetracked with value judgments of the music itself or a performance. Instead, remain open-minded as to what is inside the music. From this gateway, one can approach the inner core of meaning embedded within the music.

You may call it message, subtext or the inner place. It can be imagined when reading a score or heard when listening to a fine performance. Whatever you call it, it is a place music leaders want to visit in order to bring authenticity to the rendering of the music. The Founder's analogy of "touching the wave," from the song *O Boundless Salvation*, applies to this place. It is the experiential reference point that convincingly brings an authentic rendering of a piece to the rehearsal table. I happen to believe that our musicians, young and old, know when you've been there, and because they know, they trust us, their leaders, to take them on a journey to that special place.

The Founder's Song
"O Boundless Salvation"

The tide is now flow-ing, I'm touch-ing the wave,

? 23 BARS REST

1. Ponder the differences between hearing and listening. How can you remind yourself to listen, as Placido said in the dialogue, "over and over again"?

2. Consider ways to increase the amount you hear when conducting. One way is to practice listening to, or following part lines, both separately and together, as a section. Another approach is to audit other rehearsals with a reference score, locating errors or identifying things you might improve, while discovering techniques that worked well. Another valuable tack is to try to identify, without the aid of a score, how the varying sections of a piece unfold, revealing the underlying structure of the piece.

3. Referring back to Chapter Ten (What's the Score?, pp. 207–208), think about ways to associate different timbres with dynamic levels and quality of tone, and thereby broaden your aural imagination.

4. Think about your normal sphere of listening. Look for listening avenues away from your steady diet. Study a score with a period recording or style interpretation that is unfamiliar to you. When you hear something that is pleasing to your ears or an unexpected surprise, ask why. Read articles or watch shows about other arts and consider how to apply the principles presented to your musical craft.

> "Do not read to satisfy curiosity or to pass the time, but study such things as move your heart to devotion."
>
> —Thomas à Kempis, *The Imitation of Christ*

LISTEN AND... RESPOND

I don't make anything; I just try to listen and react.
—Frederick Fennel, renowned conductor of the Eastman Wind Ensemble

CONNECTING OVER A SECOND CUP

We eavesdrop again on the conversation between Animato and Placido. The focus of the discussion had centered on developing the conductor's inner **listening** skills. This essential practice aids the conductor in gaining a thorough knowledge of the score, which in turn shapes an informed, imagined interpretation.

Now the two maestros are passionately honing in on how the leader is to **respond** when comparing the ideal/imagined sounds with the reality of the rehearsal in progress. They ardently agree that conductors cannot make the music; they can only affect the way players perform it. So the conversation pursues this elusive intent of learning to *listen and...respond* to what is actually getting back to the leader.

Animato: Placido, here are the two big questions: "First, is what I am hearing what I want?"[16] Second, "Does it match my imagined reading of the score?"[17]

Placido: Yes, dear friend, it all comes down to those two points, doesn't it? The conductor's well–informed reading of a score will identify the essential errors. They are like alarms going off, aren't they? Sometimes startling, sometimes annoying, especially if they are repeated.

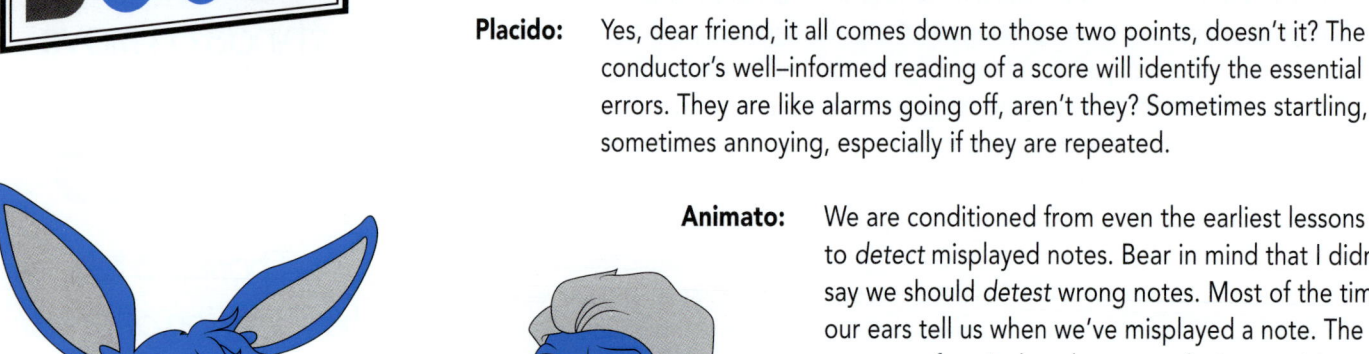

Animato: We are conditioned from even the earliest lessons to *detect* misplayed notes. Bear in mind that I didn't say we should *detest* wrong notes. Most of the time, our ears tell us when we've misplayed a note. The memory of a misplayed note results in a positive response, which says, "I'll not do that again."

Placido: We train our ensemble members to mark their parts to avoid the mishap the next time around.

Animato: I honestly believe that my players and singers want to make a connection with the music. Therefore I aim to make the less tangible aspects of music–making more tangible. For instance, a proper cue not only affirms the counting of an entrance, meaning they'll play with more assurance, but it draws the player's attention to what is surrounding the cue, like timing and balance.[18]

WHOA, PLACIDO IS REALLY GETTING ANIMATED!

Placido: *(in an anxious tone, losing his namesake composure momentarily)* Yes, but the process, my dear friend, doesn't stop there. The conductor listens to what is in front of him, sets it against his imagined picture of the music, and then has to take that comparison and *respond*.

Animato: I agree with you, my friend. It has been said that conductors cannot make music: they can only affect the way players perform it.[19] Pardon the conducting pun, but certainly we come up on the short end of the stick if our reference point is lacking. Sometimes we have insufficient knowledge of the score or are having trouble getting in touch with the music.[20]

Placido: Yes, and we have to bear in mind that we cannot hide the extent to which we listen and respond from our ensemble members. Just like youngsters who know if you can recall their name, our ensemble members know if you know where you are heading. The goal is to bring everybody on board, persuading every performer to come along on the journey.[21]

Animato: It takes time to develop genuine trust across our ensemble and that begins with digging as deep as possible into the story and mechanics of the music, listening to what your ensemble brings to the table, and responding with intelligence and enthusiasm. It is our responsibility as leader–teachers to facilitate a stimulating interaction with our ensemble.

Lessons in rehearsal mechanics

To be effective, the rehearsal leader learns to walk a few steps ahead of their ensemble, leading, yes, but also alertly anticipating and responding to any mishaps along the way. The leader studies the map, his score, as a reference to the peaks and valleys of the journey. Having walked these paths, the seasoned guide is familiar with the features, while a journey along "the road less traveled" requires a closer look at the map.

Well-trained ensembles assimilate these four functions of a rehearsal:

1. To become familiar with the music, working toward a flawless reading
2. To be in control of the various tempi and necessary related modifications around those tempi
3. To coordinate the elements of dynamics, rhythm, articulation, and phrasing
4. To assimilate the proper conception of style and spirit germane to the composition[22]

What follows is a trail of questions with viable responses to aid music leaders in efficiently navigating their way through a rehearsal. Touching on each of these four functions combines matters of timing, psychology, mechanics, and stick-to-itiveness. With apologies to the writer of Ecclesiastes, you will discover that there is a time to look and listen and a time to demand. There is a time to give instruction and a time to trust. There is a time to stop and a time to keep moving. Along the rehearsal path, there is a time for reference to words and the score, and a time to do without. Finally, there is a time to inquire, and a time to desist, allowing the music to suggest next steps on its own.

HOW DO I GET PERFORMERS TO WATCH ME?

The eyes have it! From the moment you begin your warm-up, where reading music is not required, all eyes need to be on you. It can help to assume that our young people, and even adults, do not understand the conducting language.[23] The leader's eyes lead the way, so endeavor to keep your eyes up and out, making eye contact.

What You See Is What You Get

The acronym WYSIWYG means "what you see is what you get," that is, what you see on your computer screen is exactly what will print in hard copy.[24] Applied to music-making, a similar expression might be (even if it sounds a bit backwards) **if you watch them, they will follow.** To bring everybody along we have to make it matter to every member. This means that we need to scan the entire ensemble and give everybody a cue at some time. This signals your positive reinforcement from eyeball to eyeball.[25]

Great rehearsal leaders and teachers get results because they are capable of working in small groups while maintaining an exceptional awareness of the larger group. When working with a section, we can listen with our ears to that section while keeping peripheral visual surveillance of everybody else.[26] Eye contact assures ensemble members that you expect them to remain engaged. You can help guide your ensemble better by evaluating the clarity and expression of your conducting gesture. A helpful way is to use Jane Marshall's FLRRT acronym.

> **F**ocus—where the ensemble looks for visual clues as to the desired pulse and sound
>
> **L**evel—where the pulse is, and with what weight
>
> **R**ange—how big the pattern is, regulating the dynamics
>
> **R**ebound—governs style, with its numerous variants, ranging from very short *staccato* to a long rebound *molto legato*
>
> **T**ension—exhibited between the beats, appropriate to the style of music

Absolutely correct?

I once heard a boy's choirmaster say to his group, "That's it. Thank you, that was *absolutely* correct." And as one might expect, I later heard, "We'll do that again, until it is *absolutely* correct."[27] The wordsmith in me rebelled inwardly against the redundancy of partnering the word "absolutely" with the word "correct." Isn't saying simply "correct" enough?

As I observed him working, though, I began to see the psychology behind the use of the word absolutely. Requiring players to stop instantly when you cease conducting or insisting on an absolutely correct initial attack goes beyond the time wasted on continued playing and needless chatter. By leaving absolutely no leeway, we give the ensemble a sense of security about where the box lies. **Insist on such things and they will watch** (rather than tooting well past your cutoff!)[28] Insistence on some absolutes increases your player's attentiveness to your best intentions embedded in your gestures.

In time your students believe you possess the knowledge necessary to help them reach their goals, and even take them beyond themselves.[29] The message is: *Together* we move forward. Like a coach working toward a playoff berth, few things are as exhilarating as taking your ensemble to a place they have never been. There are worship services, performances, recordings, or even rehearsals that they will never forget. It begins with instituting an absolutely correct box. Insist on it!

Establishing trust

To help improve an ensemble's acuity in observing your gesture, beat, and expression, you can play games to try to foil them. This can be as simple as tossing keys into the air, making the place where the keys land the ictus beat-point. Even if the exercise doesn't work particularly well, it allows an opportunity for some light-hearted levity. In so doing, your players and singers learn to watch more carefully.[30] Other examples include:

- Abruptly move tempo forward or back.
- Stop in the middle of a phrase, then suddenly continue where you left off.
- Start quickly, with little preparation, or even avoid any verbal preparation, and launch into a phrase.
- When you stop, leave your hands up in a ready position and repeat a passage immediately, uttering only a simple "and again." This diversion also promotes recall, disavowing use of the conductor's most hated three words, "Where are we?"

In a way you are playing a "trust game" with your ensemble, akin to asking them to fall backwards without looking. You, the teacher, **become their trusted guide**, the person who sets and raises the bar and brings the parts together.[31]

HOW DO I KNOW WHEN AND HOW TO STOP?

The less stopping the better because there is a great temptation for comments and chatter from kids and adults alike. Multiple stops also break the flow and line of the music we are trying to traverse. With new pieces, the ensemble needs to begin the process of sensing the overall shape of the piece. Leave the nitty-gritty detail work for a later rehearsal. Counter to conventional wisdom, I believe ensembles watch the conductor more when sight-reading because they are less familiar with the roadmap of the music.[32]

▶ Don't stop NOW!

Much time and effort can be wasted by stopping to repeat a full section over and over rather than isolating the few bars that are the stumbling block. Although becoming familiar with the surrounding context has value, learn to take a mental inventory of specific trouble spots to tackle later while covering sections.[33]

The other temptation is to use many words to describe a nonverbal process like music-making. **The ensemble should learn to rely on your facial and hand gestures.** We can refrain from stopping and repeating a passage if the leader is confident that the imperfections will be corrected without comment. At the instant of the mishap, avoid giving the proverbial "glare." Allow for an exchange of understanding glances or instruct your members to silently raise their hand to acknowledge their mistake without interrupting the rhythm of rehearsal.[34]

The Beat Goes On

Okay, we NEED to stop

While there is value to sight-reading large chunks of music, we want to avoid accumulated errors. These establish themselves as habits; consequently, the desired performance level is hampered early on. Naturally it is advisable to **stop when the style, approach, or general playing is incorrect**. Rather than figuratively plowing through sections, there is value in alternatively aiming for the highest possible level of performance in the first five minutes of rehearsal. You can do this by selecting an accessible sequence of measures typical of the piece and using it for in-depth rehearsal to set a valuable pattern for the piece or the entire rehearsal.[35]

How to stop

If you feel you must stop, know what you plan to say *before* you stop. Within your delayed response, unsolicited comments or humor can sidetrack the flow of rehearsal. Educate your ensemble to stop on your signal, meaning they observe the silence, awaiting your instruction. It is courteous for players and singers to interrupt the study of their part and momentarily look toward the conductor for an instruction, before returning attention to their copy to find the location in the music being discussed.[36]

Form your comments in understandable terms. **Give no more than two instructions per stop.** Often percussionists, singers, or other instrumentalists at the rear of the ensemble will say they did not hear the instruction. Speak loudly enough to be heard by the entire ensemble.

- **Where are we?** Announce distinctly and unmistakably where the music will be resumed: *"Let's begin two bars before Letter A."* Allow sufficient time to count bars, especially when letters, rather than rehearsal numbers, are used.[37] Choral leaders often give cues using an identifiable word, chord name, or pitch cue: *"Starting at Letter A on the word 'storm,' where we have unison A-flats."* Instrumental conductors will use a dynamic or expression term to confirm the entrance: *"Let's begin at Letter B, which is marked ff for everyone."*

- **Why repeat?** Avoid saying "once more" without explaining what is not right yet. Be sure the reason to repeat a passage is understood.[38] The ensemble may not be clear on what we are aiming for or what is actually wrong: *"We'll do that again, so that we can get the eighth notes lined up on beats three and four."*

- **How to repeat?** Give the instruction in the correct sequence. You can avoid having to repeat the corrective steps, by being sure everyone has the spot first.[39] Even with adults, you can say, *"Count with me, before letter F, 1-2-3-4 bars,"* so that they are counting with you. Then proceed to focus in on the specific problem at that spot in the music. *"Let's be sure that accidentals carry through the bar."*

- **Whom to rehearse?** When addressing a section or players, identify them as a group, not by their names. Then point out the passage in question.[40] If necessary to use names, maintain a friendlier tone by using first names, rank, or rank combined with names. I have found the practice of using solely last names degrading. *"Tenors and basses, let's try that entrance again two bars before Letter C."*

- **What to say, when?** The renowned conductor Pierre Monteux said, "When you [the leader] make a mistake, you must admit it, of course," but added with a twinkle, "You must not make mistakes too often."[41] Making music is quite personal, so harsh criticism or directly calling someone out is less effective than words of encouragement. The conductor seeks to nurture a sense of mutual respect with the ensemble by using positive words, even an occasional joke to relieve a tense moment. *"Okay, that's a good start. I am confident we can improve on that."*

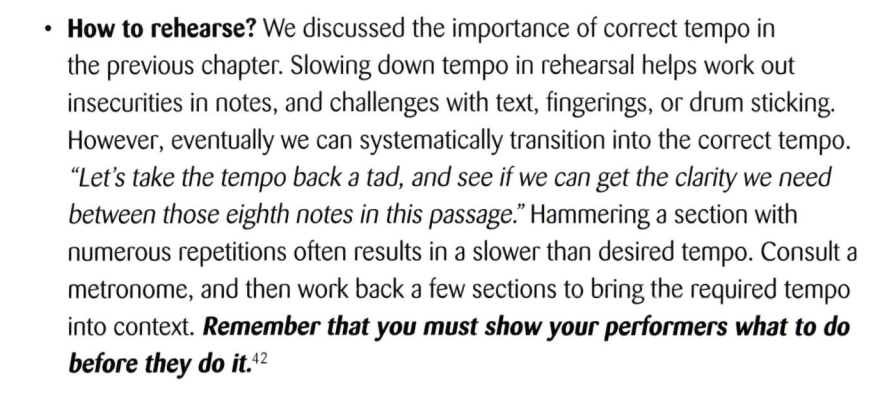

- **How to rehearse?** We discussed the importance of correct tempo in the previous chapter. Slowing down tempo in rehearsal helps work out insecurities in notes, and challenges with text, fingerings, or drum sticking. However, eventually we can systematically transition into the correct tempo. *"Let's take the tempo back a tad, and see if we can get the clarity we need between those eighth notes in this passage."* Hammering a section with numerous repetitions often results in a slower than desired tempo. Consult a metronome, and then work back a few sections to bring the required tempo into context. **Remember that you must show your performers what to do before they do it.**[42]

- **What's the limit?** Persist with a passage until the improvement is noticeable to all. Bring the ensemble members into the problem-solving process by asking if the passage in question is working better: *"That is definitely better, wouldn't you agree?"* There will be times when all parties will sense that they've reached their limit. In this case, suggest personal practice on that particular spot or in a sectional. *"We'll leave this section for now, but sopranos will need to take time to sort out the intervals and rhythm at Letter D."*

- **When to move on?** There is something to be said for keeping the interest of all sections of the ensemble engaged as uniformly as possible over the span of a rehearsal. With experience, leaders become cognizant of when to move on or run a complete reading from top-to-bottom in order to touch all elements of the program. *"We need to move on to make sure we have time to work on the ending."* Occasionally the initial moments of a performance will go really well, and I then find myself walking on a tightrope coming up to the conclusion, an unfortunate consequence of not wisely managing the available rehearsal time.

IS IT OKAY TO ALLOW QUESTIONS?[43]

Once, while I observed a colleague's rehearsal, a well-meaning singer voiced a question about something "back on page 3." Hoping to avoid a bump in the flow of his rehearsal, the leader skirted the question by quickly responding, "Right now, we are on page 10." In that moment, he could have blurted out, "You've got to be kidding me! Do you not realize how ill-timed this question is? Page 3? That was 10 minutes ago!" Knowing how skilled this choral trainer was, my third-person response might have been, "Be assured your leader has a plan to master this song, and since it may take several rehearsals, he won't possibly get to all the detail tonight."

"Back on page 3,...?"

"Isn't that F-sharp supposed to be natural?"

"Isn't the bass line slightly different there?"

"Where did you say to breathe?"

IS IT *STILL* OKAY TO ALLOW QUESTIONS?[43]

YES, at times inquiry can be helpful
There are great reasons for allowing questions from our ensemble members in rehearsal. For one, we want to encourage mutual learning, which may help us together find a better, more informed way. As a conductor, I know that I do not always hear the wrong notes or rhythms, but want them fixed before they become habit. There are occasions when the ensemble members are looking for clarity. And then there are teachable moments, which are best elicited by asking questions. However, the provocative inquiries usually come from the teacher, so that the students might discover various solutions for themselves.

NO, because we already know the answer
Unfortunately, though, there are some questions that solicit corrective measures aimed at the folks sitting around the one posing the question. We assume by the tone of the question that the questioner already knows the answer, and may be anxious to share some superior insight. Like the scene above, **the corrective underpinnings damage the overall morale of that moment in rehearsal.** Rather than becoming annoyed publicly, the leader is best to take this person aside privately, and explain that these kinds of interruptions are detrimental to the group's work-in-progress.

DEPENDS, maybe ask your section leader
There are also the not-paying-attention questions from the one who missed an instruction and poses a question such as, "Do you want the tenors to breathe here?" It is possible the leader has shown the breath and that the singer is seeking another solution. **This is a question that should be brought to the section leader** unobtrusively, who if need be can inquire of the conductor on behalf of the section, preferably on a break or after rehearsal.

I welcome questions, well-timed, of course, from my section leaders. They are the ones watching after the desired notes, rhythms, tempo, and articulation for their section. I value and expect their feedback after nearly every rehearsal because I know that I am not able to hear and sense everything that is happening in the midst of rehearsal. As Placido told us earlier in the first dialogue, "We hear what we listen for." At any moment in a rehearsal I may miss or bypass an error, because I am listening for a detail in another part of the ensemble.

NO, trust that your leader has a plan
One safeguard in regard to rehearsal questions is to **reveal the objectives ahead of, or at the start of rehearsal.** This permits your players or singers to understand the trajectory of that particular rehearsal. Today's rehearsal plan may require us to skip certain details. Assuming that we previously covered them, they will self-correct, or will be addressed on a future occasion. Another tactic is to give homework. This says to your ensemble, "Please come with these notes and rhythms prepared, so we can get beyond the notes and establish style and tone in our next rehearsal together." There is also value in talking through the why, wherefore, relative importance, and placement of your program choices.

"Well said, teacher! And no one dared to ask Him [Jesus] any more questions." —Luke 20:39-40, NIV

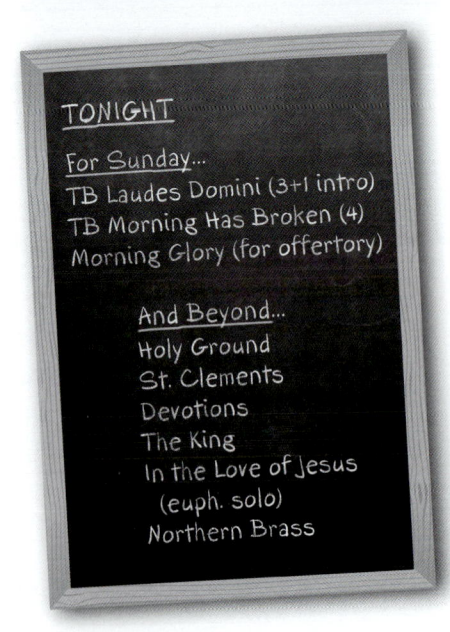

23 BARS REST

1. When you are in front of your ensemble, is what you hear what you want? Does it match your imagined reading of the score?

2. How well does your ensemble watch you? And how well are you watching your ensemble, so as to make eye contact?

3. Do you stop your ensemble too often, or too little? Evaluate yourself on giving verbal correction. Are you able to keep all sections engaged, yet still get concentrated work covered with specific sections?

4. Is there an understanding of the best time for questions, so as not to interrupt the flow of rehearsal? Do you use and appreciate input from your section leaders?

This conducting evaluation form is accessible full size in Appendix 23.1

HOW CAN I GET MY ENSEMBLE "INSIDE" THE MUSIC?

Let's remind ourselves that interpreting a score is a search for clues on a magical treasure hunt. (See Chapter Ten—What's the Score?) Beyond the right tempo, style, articulation, and expression, the leader seeks to effectively indicate a **core emotion** for the music. In rehearsal, leaders can communicate the inner sense of the music through their tone of voice, body language, facial expression, and enthusiasm.[44]

Geocaching, anyone?

Buried clues are found in the musical terms above and below the music. They are often in Italian, *giocoso* or *maestoso*, or sometimes in English, *graceful*. We ask our students to picture a place or dramatic scenario, or consider an analogy which helps link the music to the emotion of the piece. Sometimes an exaggerated gesture, like a sweeping arm, or a foot stomp can help bring understanding to the emotion of a dramatic climax.[45]

Most of these extroverted expressions would not be appropriate in public performance or worship. Reserve them for the rehearsal setting, when you are trying to **bring your musicians inside the piece**. Be advised that overconducting in rehearsal can spoil a performance. Less really is more! Yet there is some value in deliberately underconducting final rehearsals, allowing space to up-tick the emotion or tempo in performance.[46]

Coloring by dynamics

We spent some time in Chapter Twenty-two reconciling **the role of dynamics in correctly gauging the color** and expressiveness of a passage. (See pp. 492–496). We discover how to bring the correct emotion into the tone. At one extreme of the dynamic spectrum, we train our musicians to sing or play at a full volume, avoiding any forced sound or harshness of tone. At the other extreme, the individual may not be able to create a satisfactory *pianissimo*. Within a group, however, usually one can play or sing much softer than is possible solo. One risks losing the tone momentarily, but others around are there maintaining the sound.[47] In both the acoustical and emotional realms, we experience the sum of the parts as greater than the whole.

The Beat Goes On

When the desired color doesn't seem quite right, conductors sometimes opt to double or dovetail parts, for the same reasons that a wise music editor will offer cued options to cover a difficult, high, or exposed passage. Knowing your individual musicians' weaknesses and strengths, you may feel a need to add some strength or appropriate color to a vocal or instrumental line. Alterations in articulation or dynamics may also improve your aural vision without interfering with composer's conception. This is not rearranging but, in antique collector's language, retouching to restore the music to its rightful finish.[48]

Establishing dynamic levels

An experienced carpenter carries within his toolbox of repair experience, solutions that just make sense. By methodically establishing dynamic levels we honor our musicians' time, and bring facility, the proper color, and hue to the music.[49] Here are some techniques that the conductor can include in his or her toolbox to challenges with dynamics:

Sound files of these musical examples are available in the Chapter Twenty-Three online folder.

- **Dynamics in demanding passages**
  In practice, if a passage of some technical difficulty calls for a soft dynamic, drill it at a dynamic higher than written. As the passage becomes secure, then ask the ensemble to take the dynamics down a notch or two to the appropriate level.

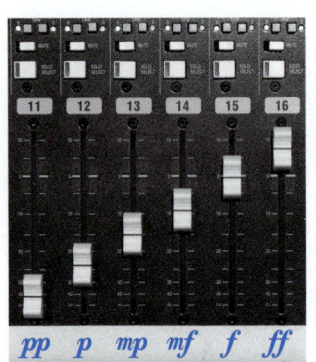

Rehearse at a higher dynamic and then reduce the dynamic by levels

"Sound Out the Proclamation" (Letter M)
Eric Ball © 1935 Salvationist Publishing

"Sound Out the Proclamation" (Letter O)
Eric Ball © 1935 Salvationist Publishing

www.music.saconnects.org

Chapter 23 | LISTEN AND RESPOND

- **Sudden dynamic shifts**

  If there is a transition that moves from loud to suddenly soft or vice versa, practice the correct dynamic on either side of the transition separately, then back to back, with a stop between. Allow time for the ensemble to absorb the required shift in dynamics. Once the shift is well-placed in the musician's aural memory, practice bridging the transition as written.

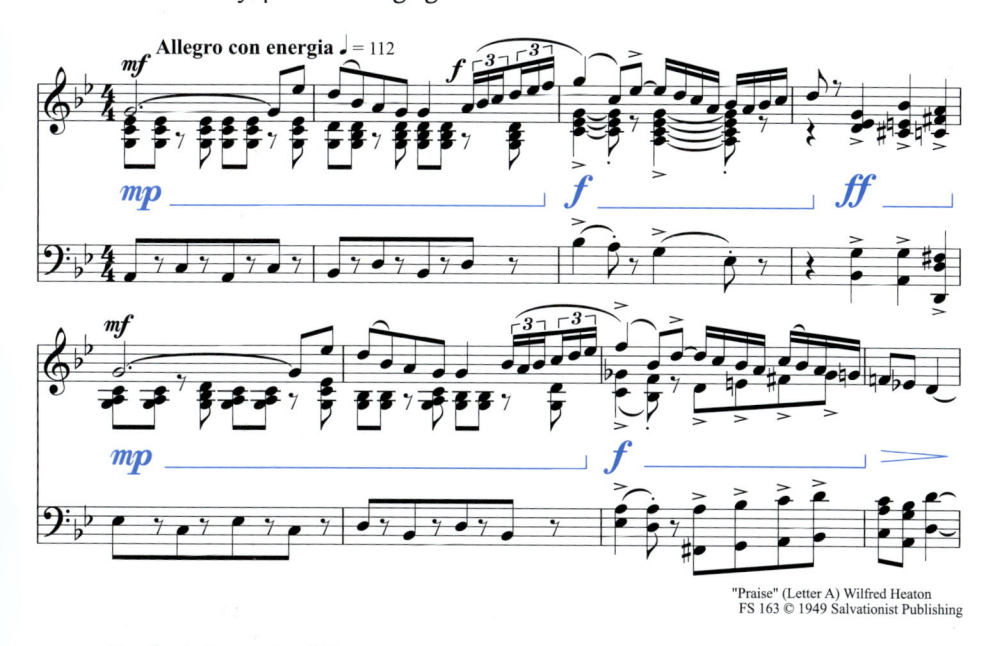

  "Praise" (Letter A) Wilfred Heaton
  FS 163 © 1949 Salvationist Publishing

- **Gradual dynamic shifts**

  A similar isolation technique can help gauge *crescendos* and *diminuendos*. Begin by achieving the softest and loudest points. Then gauge the gradual incline and decline between those established marker points.

  For more on **grading dynamics**, refer to the Count–Singing section in Chapter Thirteen, p. 268.

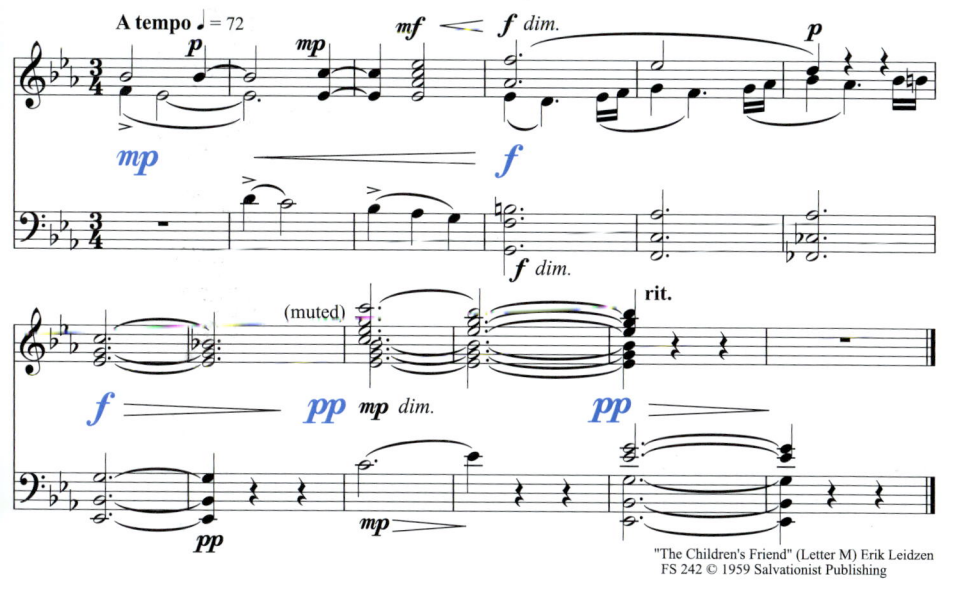

  Initially isolate softest and loudest peak dynamics

  "The Children's Friend" (Letter M) Erik Leidzen
  FS 242 © 1959 Salvationist Publishing

The Beat Goes On

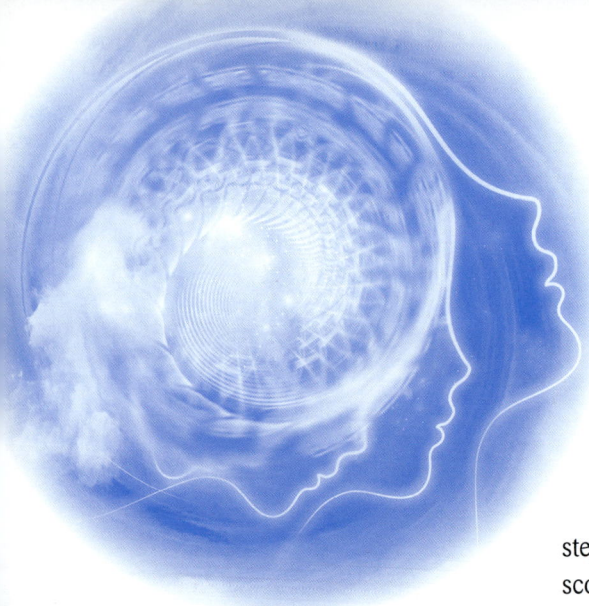

Why memorize?

"I am fearfully and wonderfully made," marveled the Psalmist (139:14). Humans are endowed with the uncanny instinct to link a mental concept of a desired music with the response of the skilled hands. As players or singers, we mentally listen for the sounds we want to come out of our instruments, and these sounds emanate from our instruments. Think about how easily we can recall songs from the radio! In the same way, music leaders can recall a desired sound, linked with an ideal realization of the music. Simultaneously, they bring it intuitively into the conductor's gesture. This miraculous integration of mental and physical facility is in great part a function of memory.

A fluid rehearsal is usually an informed one, in which thorough study has suggested steps to guide the ensemble through the roadmap of the piece. Even when using a score, there is tremendous value in memorizing difficult passages, combining mental and auditory repetitions with the requisite baton gestures, benefiting motor memory. The mind and the arm learn to move forward without reference to the printed page or audible sounds.[50]

Elect to conduct at least one piece from memory, but do so in rehearsal beforehand. With young singers, and even players, memorization is necessary to maintain attention and focus. To get started, simply move your stand away to the side, making it inconvenient for you to sneak a peek at your score. Embrace the increased connection between you and your ensemble members.

Conducting from memory in rehearsal can be more difficult than in performance as you have to make judgment calls on whether to stop.[51] Rather than having to recall rehearsal numbers, you can engage the ensemble in locating the spot by your description. If you need a quick reference to remedy inaccurate notes or rhythms, your score is just a step away.[52]

Removing the tyranny of the copy increases the freedom to keep your eyes on your players and singers. We are told that conductors hear their ensemble as much as 40% better because they are not re-reading and trying to imagine the music at the same time.[53] There are some of us who memorize quickly and can mount the podium without a score. Others struggle. They should memorize as much as possible, but then refer to the score as little as possible.[54]

There is also great advantage in being able to review the whole piece in your mind while walking, lying in bed, or driving. In the process of following the shape and journey of the piece, you can make mental notes of details that will need extra attention or pacing during the performance. One of my mantras is to not ask my ensemble to do something

It's not so much what you KNOW... It's what you NOTICE!

Chapter 23 | **LISTEN AND RESPOND**

I would not do myself. If I ask my singers to memorize a piece of music, I memorize the same portion myself. This facilitates the all-important eye contact. This equal footing builds rapport and increases the artistic thrill between you and the ensemble.

First, *MEMORIZE* WORDS, RHYTHMS and TUNE

[5] ALL VOICES in unison (opt. 8vb for Basses)

He's turned my mourn - ing in - to danc-ing_ a-gain, He's lift-ed_ my sor - rows

Sound files of these excerpts from *Mourning into Dancing* are accessible in the Chapter Twenty-Three online folder.

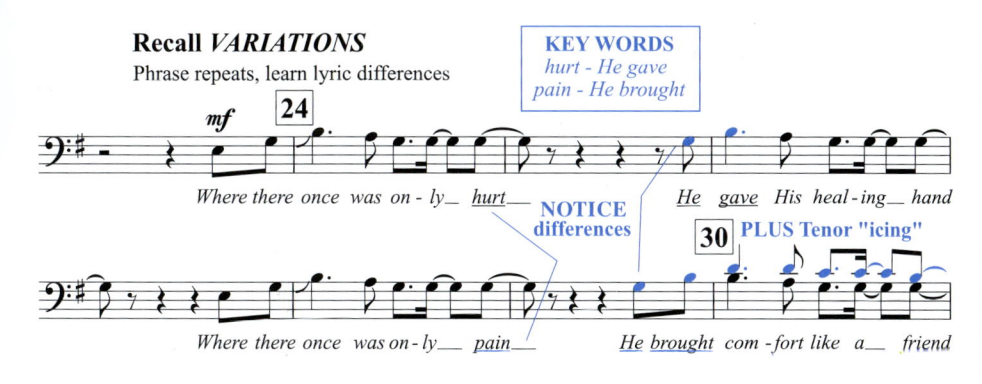

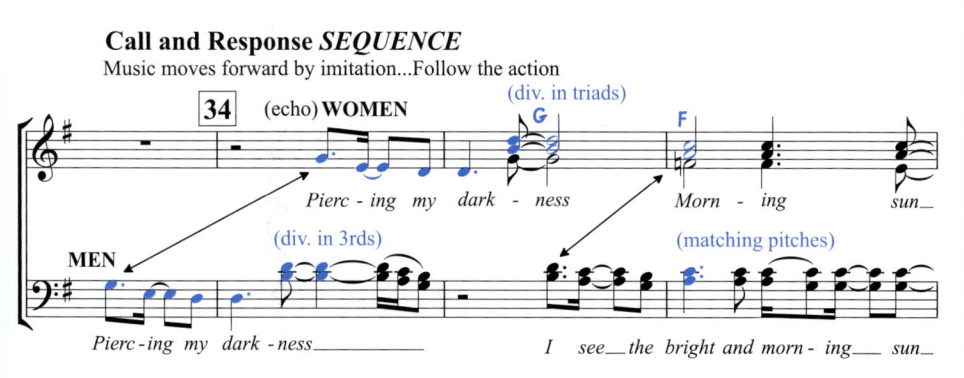

Next, *MEMORIZE* HARMONIES

[13] ALTOS basically a third below the melody

He's turned my mourn - ing in - to danc-ing_ a-gain, He's lift-ed_ my sor - rows

TENORS have their own memorable tune

He's turned my mourn - ing in - to danc-ing_ a-gain, He's lift-ed_ my sor - rows

BARITONES double soprano melody

He's turned my mourn - ing in - to danc-ing_ a-gain, He's lift-ed_ my sor - rows

BASS line in calypso style

He's turned my mourn - ing in - to danc-ing_ a-gain, He's lift-ed_ my sor - rows

"Mourning into Dancing" Tommy Walker
arr. Len Ballantine © 1992 Integrity's Praise! Music

Recall *VARIATIONS*
Phrase repeats, learn lyric differences

KEY WORDS
hurt - He gave
pain - He brought

mf [24]

Where there once was on - ly hurt **NOTICE differences** *He gave His heal-ing_ hand*

[30] PLUS Tenor "icing"

Where there once was on - ly_ pain_ He brought com - fort like a_ friend

Call and Response *SEQUENCE*
Music moves forward by imitation...Follow the action

[34] (echo) WOMEN (div. in triads)
G   F

*Pierc-ing my dark - ness   Morn - ing sun_*

MEN (div. in 3rds) (matching pitches)

*Pierc-ing my dark - ness_____   I see_ the bright and morn - ing_ sun_*

The Beat Goes On

521

Harmonic *RECALL*
Identify steps and solfege

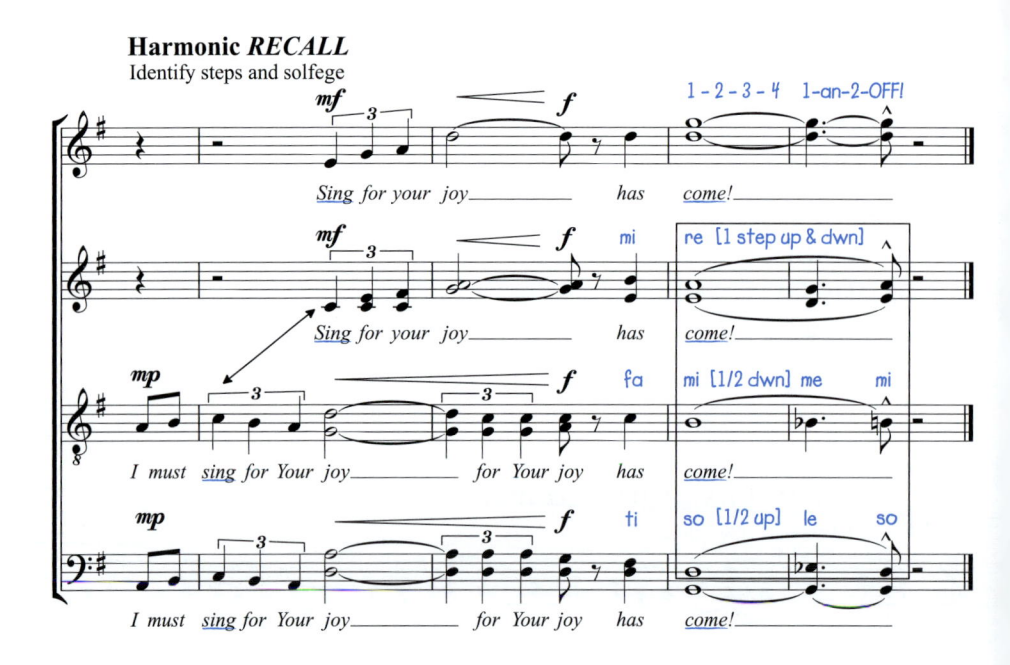

Sing for your joy___ has come!

re [1 step up & dwn]
mi

Sing for your joy___ has come!

fa mi [1/2 dwn] me mi

I must sing for Your joy___ for Your joy has come!

ti so [1/2 up] le so

I must sing for Your joy___ for Your joy has come!

> **" Practice DOES NOT make PERFECT.**
>
> **Practice makes PERMANENT. "**

Ways to memorize scores

Medical researchers tell us that "every repeated action makes a deeper and deeper impression on the brain center...until the action takes place as a matter of course, an instantaneous and uninhibited 'circuit' occurring in the brain."[55] To this end, the comment, "I can't memorize," is an illusion, as our "marvelously made" mind constantly builds memory. To memorize a passage of music therefore becomes an act of will in repeating the action (with sights and sounds), and wisely utilizing your best paths to remembering things. As it is said, "practice makes permanent."

Some conductors seem to visually photograph the pages, while others recollect the sounds aurally and then translate them into scrolling notation. Most of us memorize pieces by combining the aural memory (the big picture flow) with the visual (to recall details). Many folks respond intuitively to music by making beat gestures. Helpful muscle memory can be developed by beating along with your aural playback of a piece, trusting your ear to guide you, or conducting along with an actual recording–but not while driving![56]

- **Form follows function**
It can help to chart the major sections of the piece, calling attention to what Elizabeth Green calls "safety checks" at difficult transitions. This also benefits your rehearsal process.[57]

"Mourning into Dancing"
Tommy Walker, arr. Len Ballantine

♩=112 | 5 | 13
4/4 4 bar Intro (catcalls) | ‖: CHORUS 1* ALL unison — He's turned... | CHORUS 2* ALL harmony — He's turned...
*no "wo" 1st time

20 | 24 | 30
4 bar Interlude | ‖ VERSE MEN unison — Where there once... | LADIES parts MEN harmony | ALL unison — As it... :‖

40 | 48 | 52
‖ CHORUS ALL (wo) harmony — He's turned... | BRIDGE (LADIES ooh) MEN tune — Your anger... | ALL unison — But your favor...

56 | 1. | 2. 65
‖ CHORUS 1 ALL (wo) harmony — He's turned... | CHORUS 2 ALL (wo) harmony :‖ | ENDING LADIES___ MEN___ — I can't keep silent I must sing...

- **Picture geometries**
  With a series of fast cues, it can help to mark the margins of the score and then recall geometric reminders of the count outline. For instance, use triangles for three or up–down hash marks for two.[58]

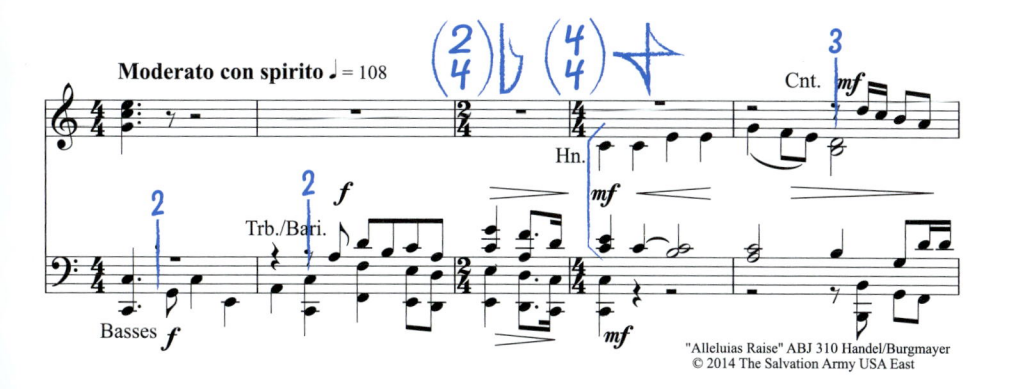

- **Counts**
  Subconscious counting is central to activities based on rhythmic pulse, like marching or dancing. When there is a relative stasis in the music, count the number of times a figuration or call and response passage repeats before changing direction. To secure entrances, know the exact bar counts of introductions and interludes, and subconsciously count along with your aural memory of the line.[59]

In the Score-Reading Chapter Eleven (pp. 233–241), we discussed ways to mark scores to aid **recall** of sections, text, and details.

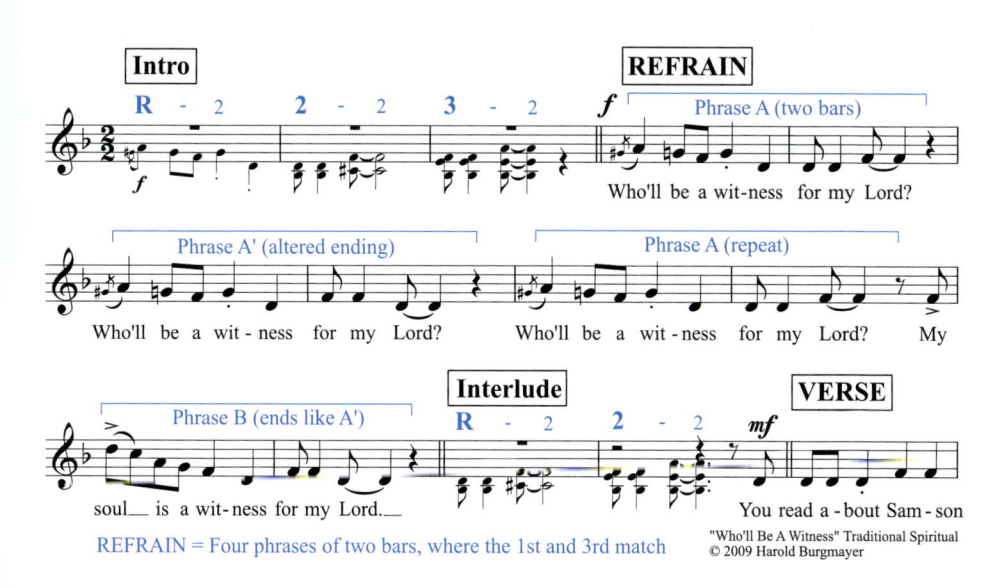

REFRAIN = Four phrases of two bars, where the 1st and 3rd match

1 and 2 and 3 and 4 and 1

The Beat Goes On

FROM SNAPSHOTS TO SLIDE SHOWS

Helpful hints and advice that enable leaders to successfully prepare their groups for weekly worship and other performances abound throughout this volume. I encourage you to re-visit some of those places.

- ☑ Chapter One speaks of making wise repertoire choices, giving due consideration to the rehearsal time required.

- ☑ In Chapter Two, we look at ways to strategize over a season or four- to-six-week term.

- ☑ In the Singing Company Chapters Six and Seven, Youth Band Chapters Eight and Nine, and Songster Leader Chapters Twelve and Thirteen, we consider short- and long-term plans for successfully rehearsing *Win Them One by One, They Should Know, This Little Light,* and *Only This I Ask.*

- ☑ Preparation as meeting pianist and accompanist, as well as a working knowledge of the Song Book, is considered in the Keyboard Worship Chapters Sixteen and Seventeen, and the Song Leading Chapter Five.

- ☑ The Bandmaster Chapters Fourteen and Fifteen, and Worship Leader Chapters Eighteen and Nineteen, delve into practical rehearsal strategies aimed at successful ministry Sunday to Sunday.

- ☑ The two Conducting Chapters Twenty-One and Twenty-Two are preparation for this chapter on managing an efficient rehearsal. They will enable you to bring all of these tools to bear on effective Sunday worship.

Rehearsal Strategies

Long- and short-term rehearsal planning was introduced in Chapter Two, pp. 62-65.

Salvation Army music leaders in the various disciplines are all under time constraints as we encounter a variety of songs and brass scores from week to week. Here are a number of time-saving rehearsal strategies. They use the terminology of photographers and videographers to help the conductor visualize how to work more efficiently.

WAYS TO BEGIN WORK ON A NEW PIECE:

- **• SNAPSHOTS**
  Identify a few tricky spots, such as a dramatic change in tempo or key. Work these in-depth before attempting a full reading.

- **• SHORT**
  Isolate a short section to give the players or singers a taste of the piece. Work to get a convincing, initial impression of the song into the ensemble's ear.

Chapter 23 | **LISTEN AND RESPOND**

- **LANDSCAPES**
  Identify the principal sections of the piece. (Many Army compositions are in three sections.) Work each landscape individually. Many conductors consciously proceed from the back section to successfully overlap the essential transitions into each section. Conclude with a full reading across the entire landscape of the piece.

AS WORK PROGRESSES:

- **ZOOM–IN** on a characteristic phrase, transition, or trouble spot, and then **ZOOM–OUT** to place it in the wider context.

- **SLOW–MO**
  A technically challenging section is rehearsed slowly at first in exact rhythm, working gradually up to *tempo*, or with the *tempo* change required. If an extremely loud or soft dynamic is indicated, ease the dynamics a notch or two to facilitate the repetition, before requiring the proper dynamic as the passage becomes more secure.

- **SPLIT–TRACK**
  Rehearse separately the essential elements of the music. For instance, isolate the accompaniment from the main theme and countermelody, or vocals from the backing. Then build the other elements over the now firmly established accompaniment.

- **DIVIDE AND CONQUER**
  Valuable rehearsal time and focus are easily lost when working out trouble spots over and over with an isolated section. This leaves much of the ensemble not engaged. Splitting up for sectionals multiplies the learning across the various sections. This is a real time-saver, especially if the leader prepares a "hit list" of problem areas to focus on.

- **CLOSE–UP**
  Change formation in order to hear each other better. Stand in the round or face one another, even at close proximity.

- **CANDIDS**
  Make *legato* passages *staccato* to help feel the pulse. This exercise helps crystallize rhythmic precision and eliminates the margin of error in locating pitches. Singers can use a neutral syllable to establish an open vowel sound before adding the text, or can even remove the consonants to work on the color of vowel sounds.

More detail on rehearsing *legato* passages with *staccato* can be found in the Songster Chapter Thirteen, p. 269. This technique is also useful in band settings.

GETTING CLOSE TO A PERFORMANCE:

- **INSTANT REPLAY**
  A full reading is followed with "instant replay" work on any difficult transitions that didn't go well. This approach is especially useful as the song or piece nears a Sunday or performance date and rehearsal time is limited.

The Beat Goes On

*I Hear,
I Forget.
I See,
I Remember.
I Do,
I Know.*

—Chinese Proverb

- **SLIDE SHOW**
Play a set of pieces back to back in the order of the service or performance. This approach affirms required mood transitions, pace, and energy level. Missed details can be followed up after the run-through, usually with common consent.

Experience is the best teacher!

We cannot emphasize enough that **one learns to conduct by conducting**. The ability to listen well and respond quickly by communicating adjustments through our hands, arms, and faces is the difference between a good concert conductor and a musician who trains well. Too often conducting is taught as geometric gesturing in the air, devoid of a give-and-take connection with the sound of an ensemble.[60] Take every opportunity to be in front of an ensemble. "Gestures are a conductor's spontaneous immediate physical reactions to what he/she hears."[61]

Remember that every performance and rehearsal is an opportunity to "recreate" a piece. It should never sound exactly the same. Strive to *hear, see, and feel* something new in the music every time you conduct. A live performance lives in that moment and should have a life of its own appropriate to that moment!

Bring out the expressive element in a *cantabile* passage, but not at a tempo where your singers or players can't carry the phrase and run out of air. When a piece seems to be lagging, sometimes you can recapture excitement by moving the *tempo* early or accentuating a dramatic pause. On the other hand, be careful not to take things at an unplayable *tempo*. Vocal conductors need to be careful not to grimace, which causes the singers' jaws to tighten.[62]

The conductor's musical ability and knowledge of the score must be at a high level to make adjustments or handle mishaps with efficiency. When something doesn't go quite right, we learn not to panic. Experience teaches us to not only identify the problem by listening but also to respond with a remedy which satisfactorily moves the music forward.[63]

Moments of transcendent connection

"There are times when it does not seem to be the voice that sings, or the ears that listen, and what is beautiful leaves one's heart and enters the hearts of others, and before applause there is the breathless silence of knowing this was so. But it does not happen often, and it is never forgotten—or ever quite remembered as it was."

—From Awakened, Margaret Abrams

23 BARS REST

1. How often do you feel you take your ensemble to an expressive understanding beyond the correct notes and rhythm, and really get inside the music? Have you tried colorful analogies, exaggerated gestures, singing, or motions to enliven the core emotion of a piece?

2. What rehearsal techniques could you use to improve dynamic contrast and more effectively "color" pieces?

3. Do you think it would benefit your rehearsals and performance to memorize text, sections, or whole pieces, in an effort to get your head out of the score, and your ensemble further inside the piece?

4. In your current repertoire, identify places in the music where some of the suggested photo techniques might benefit your rehearsal process. Then find opportunities to try them.

5. The only way to learn to conduct is by conducting! **Take every opportunity** to coach or **get in front of an ensemble!**

REHEARSAL LEADERS' RESOURCES

Valuable insights into rehearsal strategy can be found in many of the books listed at the conclusion of Chapter Twenty, as well as the following:

Beyond the Downbeat, Sandra Willetts (Abingdon Press)
Choral Director's Rehearsal and Performance Guide, Lewis Gordon (Parker)
The Choral Director's Cookbook–Insights and Inspired Recipes for Beginners and Experts, Alan Gumm, editor (Meredith Music)
Classroom Management in the Music Room– "Pin-Drop Quiet" Classes and Rehearsals, David Newell (Neil Kjos Music Company)
Teaching Music with Promise, Peter Boonshaft (Meredith Music)
The Composer's Advocate, Erich Leinsdorf (Yale)
The Composer's Craft–A Practical Guide for Students and Teachers, Blake Henson and Gerald Custer (GIA Publications)
The Creative Director–Beginning and Intermediate Levels, Edward Lisk (Meredith Music)
This Idea Will Work! 136 Ways to Revitalize Your Music Ministry, Bob Burroughs (Lorenz)

It Ain't Over 'Til It's Over! —Yogi Berra

LAST chapter coming up ➤

POSTLUDE

PASSING THE BATON
The Beat Goes On!

The music in my heart I bore long after it was heard no more.
—William Wordsworth

A RACE INTO THE FUTURE!

At the crack of the gun the runner, with baton in hand, is off! The three other members of the relay team await their turn across the course of the track. Precisely at the moment that the approaching runner hits the mark, the outgoing runner starts to sprint. While running at full tilt, the approaching runner reaches forward in an upward motion, as the outgoing runner reaches back with her hand and receives the baton pass. The approaching runner runs through the pass, never slackening the pace in the exchange, while the outgoing runner sprints off, remaining in her lane. Speed, coordination, and teamwork are required through three baton passes to complete the race.

So it is in the race of faith. As the anchor leg runners approach the finish line, the cheers of the crowd swell into a mighty roar. The stands are filled with those looking down who have already won a crown, heroes of the faith who went before (Hebrews 12:1). The faces of Abraham, Sarah, Moses, Esther, David, and a host of prophets crowd the stands. Do I also spot Martin Luther, Catherine and William Booth, the Wesleys (Susannah, John, and Charles), Samuel Brengle, as well as Salvationist musicians extraordinaire—Richard Slater, Erik Leidzén, Richard Holz, Eric Ball, Leslie Condon, and Ray Steadman-Allen? These are the faces of the faithful through history who have known victories amid the throes of battle.

Yet they also know the travails and difficulties that Christian leaders face, and have set for us a high standard to carry. As an active, vibrant throng, they shout encouragement to those who now struggle to get out of the blocks in their own arena. They've passed the finish line, the race is over for them, and we are left to pick up the baton and run.[1]

In this closing chapter we:
- explore ways to influence and inspire future and emerging leaders
- consider the difficulties and challenges of an effective baton pass
- use Paul's baton pass to Timothy as a model to glean practical helps for the rising leader

Scenes from the funeral procession for William Booth, 1912.

On May 9, 1912, Salvation Army Founder William Booth spoke to more than 7,000 Salvationists packed into London's Royal Albert Hall. They heard what proved to be his historic farewell address:

> And now, comrades and friends, I must say goodbye. I am going into dry-dock for repairs, but the Army will not be allowed to suffer, either financially or spiritually, or in any other way by my absence.
>
> And in the long future I think it will be seen—I shall not be here to see, but you will—that the Army will answer every doubt and banish every fear and strangle every slander, and **by its marvelous success show to the world that it is the work of God** and that the General has been His servant.[2]

Three months later, a message was posted on the window of The Salvation Army International Headquarters, stating simply that "The General Has Laid Down His Sword."

Now over a hundred years later, God's work through The Salvation Army has been passed from one cheering generation to another, and **the beat goes on!** Considering that records are set and then broken time and time again, is any less expected of us today than what was expected from a former generation? Will it cost less in terms of hours of dedicated service than it did for those who came before? No, the same or even greater diligence and perseverance is required! These heroes cheer us on to endure with determination even when our bodies cry out for us to let up. In this race (in Greek, *agōn*, as in agony), we work to bring others after us to full maturity. As Paul says, "I toil and struggle, using the mighty strength that Christ supplies, which is at work in me." (Colossians 1:29, *TEV*)

Everyone who competes goes into strict training. They do it for a crown that will not last; we do it for a crown that will last forever. (1 Corinthians 9:25)

baton (*noun*) \be-'tən\ 1. A thin stick used by the conductor of an orchestra, choir, etc. to indicate rhythm or expression. 2. The hollow cylinder that is carried in turn by each member of a relay team in a running race and passed to the next team member.[3]

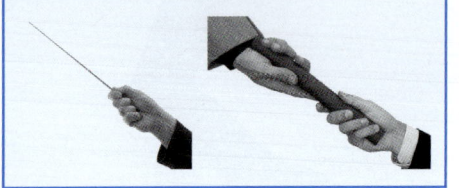

PASSING THE BATON TO THE NEXT GENERATION

Many an experienced leader hedges when asked about a succession plan. After decades of relentlessly pursuing a vision, they rightfully feel boxed into the only world they know. Feeling threatened, they hog the leadership table, don't want to let go, and simply refuse to move on. Others are more than ready to pass the baton, but fear that the one who follows won't share the passion that has been theirs for so long.

On the chessboard of world history, power struggles and wars have been fought to assure that a monarch's true heir assumes the crown. The shadow looms large and may seem insurmountable for those appointed to succeed accomplished conductors, executives, pastors, and coaches. More often than not, a founder leaves an enormous void. Speaking of his statesman-father Winston, Randolph Churchill said, "Nothing grows under the shadow of a great tree."

Postlude | PASSING THE BATON

Scripture is replete with a variegated latticework of baton passes. Consider what happened moving from Abraham to Isaac (born of faith), Elijah to Elisha (a thrown mantle), Saul to David (a chase scene), David to Solomon (a little rough and tumble), or Elizabeth to Mary (blessed among women). Moses was spoken to by God, and eventually handed command over to Joshua.

- Moses passed on a living faith, but, significantly, gave Joshua the ability to discern the voice of God for himself.
- Moses led the Israelites to freedom across a parted Red Sea, while Joshua had them step into the Jordan River in faith.
- Moses stood on a mountaintop with his arms raised, while Joshua walked around a city seven times.

We see two generations doing things in different ways, but both successfully leading God's people in obedience to God.[4]

Curiosity, courage, and resilience

Sociobiologists inform us that, "the genes of an individual may be arranged in such a way as to offer leadership traits." Leadership essentials, like sociability, conscientiousness, and courage, apparently reside within. "The structures do not determine whether the individual will *choose* to behave in a particular manner. They only enable the action should the individual choose to exercise the behavior."[5] The oft-heard expression, "She's a born leader" is not so far-fetched when we look at our genetic makeup.

In a loose paraphrase of God's bold declaration to the prophet Jeremiah (1:5), "I [God] formed you, therefore, I know what's inside of you. I [God] intend to set you apart to do something that is wrapped up in the purpose for your life." Even before you were knit together in your mother's womb (Psalm 139:13), God engineered the "chemistry" to fulfill His purpose in our lives. No one exists as a spectator, but rather we can *choose* to be set apart in this foreknowledge, or in Eugene Peterson's words "traitorously defect" from it.[6] To defect is to belittle God's design for our lives.

Any latent talent or gifting, then, lies dormant, unless it is tapped and nurtured. Scripture reminds us, "many are called, yet few are chosen." Like the roll call of the faithful found in Hebrews 12, deep within The Salvation Army DNA is a long history of men and women who exhibited the fire and perseverance to make a difference. We rightly ask how we can access and release the curiosity, courage, and resilience to inspire the next generation of leadership.

Some men's ambition is art.
Some men's ambition is fame.
Some men's ambition is gold.
My ambition is the souls of men.
Written by William Booth in King Edward VII's autograph book, 1904

The Beat Goes On

Curiosity

Thomas Edison tried 1,600 different materials before settling on carbon as a filament for the electric light bulb. Edison perfected his "phonograph" recording device over ten years, moving from a small, blunt pin touching tinfoil to a sapphire stylus balanced by an ingenious floating weight on a wax cylinder.[7] His unflinching **curiosity** revolutionized life within his generation. "How is a piece of music put together?" probes the inquisitive youngster. "How does one get that tone?" We take time to answer these questions and thereby sow the seeds of a future composer or conductor. We must never discourage inquiry. **The visionary leader, like Edison, asks seemingly countless "what if?" questions.**

Courage

When asked for the secret of his success, Walt Disney responded simply, "You do it by working." Disney garnered the **courage** to begin each day with fresh imagination and vigor. As musicians and artists, we progress from our first rudimentary solos to major works, which, step-by-step, measure our endless hours of preparation. Managing our nerves takes great courage, but with experience, we grow in confidence. **The leaders of today open as many doors as possible for the leaders of tomorrow, as they attempt to courageously advance their gifts.**

Resilience

Few have better demonstrated Ben Franklin's adage, "If at first you don't succeed, try, try again," than Oscar Hammerstein. Hammerstein bounced back from five shows that flopped before *Oklahoma* ran for 269 weeks, grossing a staggering, for its time, $7 million. In our generation, Steve Jobs rebounded from the exclusion of being fired from Apple while battling pancreatic cancer. In an address to Stanford graduates, Jobs shares how these events, coupled with his adoption in infancy (another rejection) "forced him into the wilderness, strengthened him and made him the innovator we know today."[8] Reflecting on his desert experiences, Jobs says, "Management is about persuading people to do things they do not want to do. Leadership is about inspiring people to do things they never thought they could do."[9] Leaders with resilience take failure in stride and bounce back from inevitable setbacks. A leader's first efforts may barely win the day, but "because you have been faithful with small things, the master will let you care for much greater things." The master bids us "share this happiness." (Matthew 25:23, NC) **Taking on leadership is a yearning of sorts, born from deep within, which never seems to go away and even intensifies over time.**

Leaders from all spheres of life, whether in churches, government, or business enterprises, struggle with an effective baton pass of leadership. Another computer pioneer, Michael Dell, comments, "Perhaps the best measure of a founder's success is not how bright the star shines while they are there—no doubt this is certainly an important trajectory—but what happens after they are long gone?" How is the DNA imprinted on a church or business maintained? What should the visionaries themselves do to prepare for that day when the company needs to go on growing without them? Is it possible to hand-pick a successor, or should there be a step-by-step process to choose a successor who will, hopefully, prove more creative than the founder?[10]

"Now THERE'S a Job for you!"

Postlude | PASSING THE BATON

Jesus was one who hand-picked and equipped His successors, the apostles, and they were the most unlikely candidates for leadership. He brought this unseemly assortment of twelve together for a brief three-year apprenticeship. How is it that a common fisherman named Simon emerged as the church's first leader? We know him today as Peter, the rock upon which Jesus predicted he would build His church. We chuckle sometimes as we observe Peter's precocious curiosity, yet we marvel at his unyielding resilience to bounce back from lapses, and even denials, of faith. Was it an inbred courage that helped Peter face a brutal death hung upside down on a cross? Peter's legacy teaches us that "if we are going to live (and lead) appropriately, **we must be aware that we are living in the middle of the story that was begun and will be concluded by another**. This other is God ... My identity is what God thinks of me."[11]

We can outwardly trace the history of the Church from Jesus teaching the apostles on a hillside, through the church reformers, like Luther, Wesley, and Booth, up to today's leaders of the faith community. God knew who those leaders would be long before they did. Before time began God knew them and knit them together. How marvelous to consider how God chose to uniquely equip our Salvationist forebears. The first bandmaster Fred Fry, the first head of the music department Richard Slater, and our visionary Founders, William and Catherine Booth, could hardly have imagined the worldwide magnitude of the Spirit's outpouring of music on The Salvation Army. Generation after generation, leaders have succeeded leaders, who have succeeded leaders. Consequently **the beat of Salvation Army music goes on!**

The Salvation Army International Congress, 1904 with General William Booth, front right.

SEARCHING FOR EAGLES

Let this mind be in you, which was in Christ Jesus. –Philippians 2:5, *KJV*

What does a future leader look like?

The church music leader must have a pastor's heart. He is **spiritually alert and sensitive** to the cultural perspective of his church community, particularly the ethnic and generational makeup. Through careful repertoire selection, the music director guards the theological perspective of the church and at the same time educates both the ensemble and congregation. As discussed in Chapter One, the music director is a proponent of spiritual formation within her sphere of influence, and a student of God's Word. Songster Leader Graeme Press speaks of "putting myself in places where God can speak to me."[13]

searching for eagles
(*metaphor*) the image of a young eagle is often used by a number of writers to identify emerging leaders.[12]

Back to the future...Can you identify these emerging leaders?

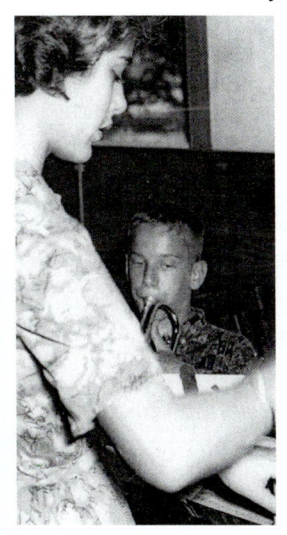

The Beat Goes On

Here they are as leaders today …

Ronald Waiksnoris
New York Staff Bandmaster (R)

Peggy Paton-Thomas
Norridge Citadel Bandmaster

William L. Rollins
Eastern Territorial Songsters Founding Conductor

Beatrice Hill-Holz, OF
Asbury College Professor (R)

Neil Smith
Western Territorial Music Secretary

Often officers and leaders come from other church backgrounds. They may bring with them liturgical underpinnings and the observant, listening music director can help strike a balance. Emerging music leaders **surround themselves with good music of many styles**, looking for the next great piece. Sometimes this can prove a stretch stylistically, forcing the ensemble out of its well-worn box.

Finally, the Salvationist music director needs to be **a skilled musician**. The time-honored adage "those who can, do; and those who can't, teach" is not always a formula for success. The next leader is not necessarily your premiere soloist, but has already led by example through consistency and musicianship. Another old saying has it, "When you see a turtle on the fencepost…you know he didn't get there by himself." The rising leader adeptly brings people and ideas along.

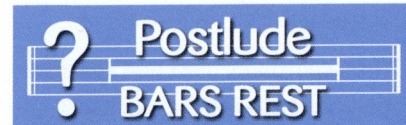

? Postlude — BARS REST

Consider these challenges:

1. What hinders us from seeing other people's potential?

2. Name some fears that prevent people from getting involved in ministry.

3. What remedies would you offer to dispel these fears?

4. Why are leaders sometimes hesitant to allow others to be included in their ministry?

ASSIMILATING THE HOW, WHEN AND WHY

While at the University of Michigan, Bill Himes sat under the baton of the legendary concert band conductor, William Revelli. Dr. Revelli was known for his intimidating and despotic demeanor on and off the podium. There really wasn't any wiggle room. You were there to make music **his** way. One entered the rehearsal room with fear and trembling, particularly as a novice underclassman. Bill explains that as the weeks and then years went by, one could almost anticipate **why** Revelli had stopped the band and **how** he would correct things. Revelli, in his fierce dedication to excellence, was raising

William Himes, OF
Chicago Staff Bandmaster (R)

the sights of each of the future band directors in his rehearsal room. Having encountered Revelli's passionate wellspring of musical knowledge every weekday afternoon from 3:30 to 5:30 for four years, Bill and the other future band directors in that rehearsal room couldn't help but begin to acquire the mind of William Revelli.[14]

We often set folks up for failure, or a discouraging experience, by not making sure emerging leaders know the how, when, and why of what is hoped they will achieve. Exposure and familiarity are good things, but understanding, like the transformation Bill Himes experienced, is accomplished when our future leaders can predict what we will do or say before we do it. One of the keys to the commanding influence of William Revelli on the life of Bill Himes was the daily regimen over a number of years. As we discussed in Chapter Four, to be empowered, our young eagles need to be engaged at the adult table and their lives influenced with regular intensity from a young age. Many Salvation Army leaders do this, and do it everyday, not as despots, but with the passion and vigor of a William Revelli.

> "Lord, I have asked for the mind of Christ, but right now He doesn't seem to have the answers."
> —student taking an exam

ROUND ONE:
More rhyme than reason

Over a few summers I experimented with teaching my leadership interns the principles of harmony through sung *solfeggio*. (*Solfeggio* was introduced in Chapter Six on pp. 136–137.) I devised a progression of learning steps to help them understand the ultimate end of why we have music theory; that is, to explain and appreciate the harmonies of hymns. Each student was provided a copy of the *Youth Songbook*, chosen because it resembles a hymnal in its words and music format. They were permitted to mark their songbooks liberally. We used a keyboard so that students always heard what they saw on the hymn pages. With practice, this would help them identify the harmonies as they unfolded.

We rarely wrote notes down, though, as is common in most theory methods. Instead, we sang them, limiting the use of our pencils to reminders of *solfege* syllables and identifications of chords. The result was a quiet rebellion against relegating the study of music theory to bookwork, where notes are rarely heard. In my wild idealism, I envisioned how this approach to theory instruction through ear-training would naturally segue these emerging leaders into score reading, steering them away from the "recall" of pieces through endless repetitions of sound recordings, and minimal reference to the printed score.

Day after day, we sang our way through harmonic progressions and inversions. Soon I began to see signs that we were moving too quickly for some, glossing over essential first steps. Most of the students really did not grasp the harmonic analysis, missed far too many *solfege* syllables, and seemed to retain only the more clever acronyms and aids to memorizing these principles.

Things got worse, as I found myself "feeding" the *solfege* syllables. I wondered if we needed to revert

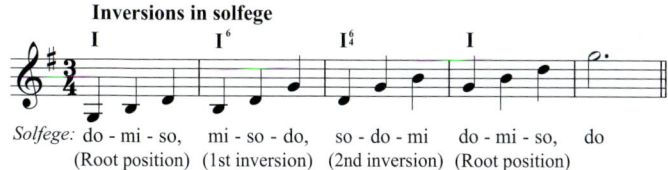

I-IV-V triads in solfege

Solfege: do - mi - so, fa - la - do, so - ti - re, do

Inversions in solfege

Solfege: do - mi - so, mi - so - do, so - do - mi, do - mi - so, do
(Root position) (1st inversion) (2nd inversion) (Root position)

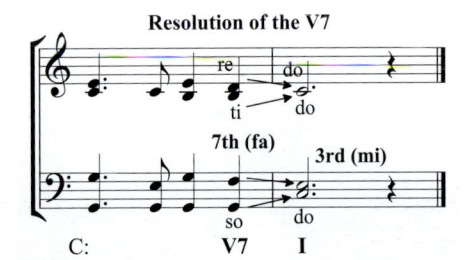

to a sight-singing book. In analyzing the relationships of harmonies to each other, answers were slow in coming, insinuating that a standard theory book might have proved a better course of action. After all the daily singing of syllables and sitting up until midnight analyzing hymns, somehow my students ultimately missed the grand intent of my method—to demonstrate that harmonic practice evolved over its long history because of "voices leading." Since the ear dictates the rules, we endeavored to always experience how each "voice" felt and led within a chord. I wondered if the students had any idea how desperately I wanted them to love the wonders of harmonic practice (and train their ears in the process).

To resolve the dominant seventh (V^7) to the tonic (I) chord, we sang: *so–do, ti–do, re–do, fa–mi*. As the students sang, they would feel what we call the "tonal magnetism" of *so* to *do*, *ti* up to *do*, *re* down to *do*, and *fa* resolving to *mi*. This demonstrated, by way of the ear, how the harmonic practice for resolving the dominant seventh evolved.

Over that summer, I learned that **there can be a gulf between teaching and real learning**. Both students and instructor worked feverishly to get the right answers. But we had missed the real meaning, that what we hear and anticipate in our inner ear "leads" the voices. I realized I had not asked enough times, "What do you hear?" or even better, "What does your ear tell you?" We can slog our way through pieces, scale studies, and method books attempting to get most of the notes or identify chords but ultimately miss out on the essence of the music. We discovered that this is why we repeat exercises, études, and even maxims of rules over and over, day in and day out. The notes, *solfege* syllables, and chord symbols are veiled representations of what we hear, but once embedded in our aural and motor memory, they unleash understanding.

Exposure to a subject and even familiarity through repetition or rehearsal are significant steps. But attaining a level of real understanding, as Bill Himes did with Dr. Revelli, is the place where our young eagles can anticipate what we will do or say. Instead, our minds outpace our words. We skip steps in our explanations, choose not to reiterate the essential steps, and despite our apparent enthusiasm, lose our students in the process.

ROUND TWO:
Singing with the understanding also

As I passed out those same hymnals the following summer, I was not surprised that a few returnees commented that they had never really understood what we were doing the previous summer. We agreed to slow the whole process down. After a series of refresher classes, the students discovered they could correctly render *solfege* syllables in *moveable do* (introduced in Chapter Six on p. 136), and recall more and more harmonic sequences. We sang over and over the catchy memory aids and once again analyzed into the night. (Staying up past curfew was permitted for theory homework.) The difference was that I waited, watched, and sometimes cajoled, with added diligence and discernment. I looked for signs in their eyes, voice, and body language that *each and every* step was being absorbed, and even enjoyed, by all!

This time our young eagles began to revel in the inner sanctum of music theory! We traded bewildered stares for looks of real comprehension. Some figured out that they needed to make charts of the basic chords in the different keys. They started checking each other's work, patiently explaining corrections. We joked about theory and *solfege* on our walks. There even was a skit about our class at the campfire circle!

We sang harmonic cadences outside of class and spotted what we were learning in other classes and rehearsals. We delighted in sharing our secret knowledge with each other. Especially in chorus, I would whisper from the piano, "Altos, do you see what's going on in measure 12?" An enthusiastic nod affirmed that they understood how their part worked. There was a glow of appreciation as a guitarist finally understood how a "sweet chord" he favored was put together. The class reached a point where they were so familiar with how I taught sight-singing and theory that they would enthusiastically anticipate the mantra or anecdote. They had learned to "sing with the understanding also." —1 Corinthians 14:15, *KJV*.

ROUND THREE:
Taking on the mind of ...

Elise, a summer leadership intern, recalls our grand experiment in blending harmonic practice through *solfege*. From her first years with us in Junior Conservatory, Music Camp, and Prep Band, Elise always seemed a step ahead of her peers. Admitting her to divisional band at age thirteen raised a few eyebrows. She relished every minute of her training her first summer as a leadership intern and returned in the same role the next summer. When I opened my computer to what appeared to her to be the same leadership slides, she legitimately asked, "Will this be the same as last summer?" In some ways it was the same. We met in the same location, with many of the same projected images, with a slightly enhanced curriculum. But because personalities on that team were so diverse, the conversation proved quite different. Elise cooperated with the repetition of the core concepts of the leadership apprenticeship and another happy summer passed.

By the third summer, Elise's playing and singing skills approached that of our counselor-instructors. But because she was a junior in high school, we could not move her on to the next level of our summer music leader's course. Once again, Elise respectfully absorbed the teaching, but this was the first year of our noble experiment unraveling the mysteries of harmonic practice through *solfeggio* and ear-training. In her words, "I didn't like theory at all, probably because I didn't understand much that first year," she said. Meanwhile, Elise was being trained to teach and conduct, so she transitioned to being the one who taught sight-singing and theory, gave private lessons, and warmed up the camp choruses. We began to see that excellent training at her high school and with us in the summers had equipped her with "the eyes of a teacher." She spoke enthusiastically about a teaching technique that really worked or suggested ways to improve a student's playing. **She had taken on the mind of a teacher**.

In the postscript to this story, Elise managed to skip her senior year and graduate from high school a year early. She headed off to university to study music. That summer, she was finally old enough to be a full-fledged counselor-instructor. I recall giving her an opening day assignment to do theory auditions, to which she enthusiastically responded, "Sure, I love theory." She waxed on

As teachers much of our world is our students and they indeed will speak for us, now and long after we are gone.

—Peter Boonshaft

Hymn Setting – Day by Day

No. 302

OSCAR AHNFELT
Arr. KATHRYN OPINA

and on of the joys of her music theory studies. We learned that Elise was at the head of her class in music theory, and had begun to pursue music composition as her concentration. Through those summers of attempting to unravel the mysteries of music theory, we never imagined Elise taking on the mind of her instructor, but so she had. She aspires to teach and write music.

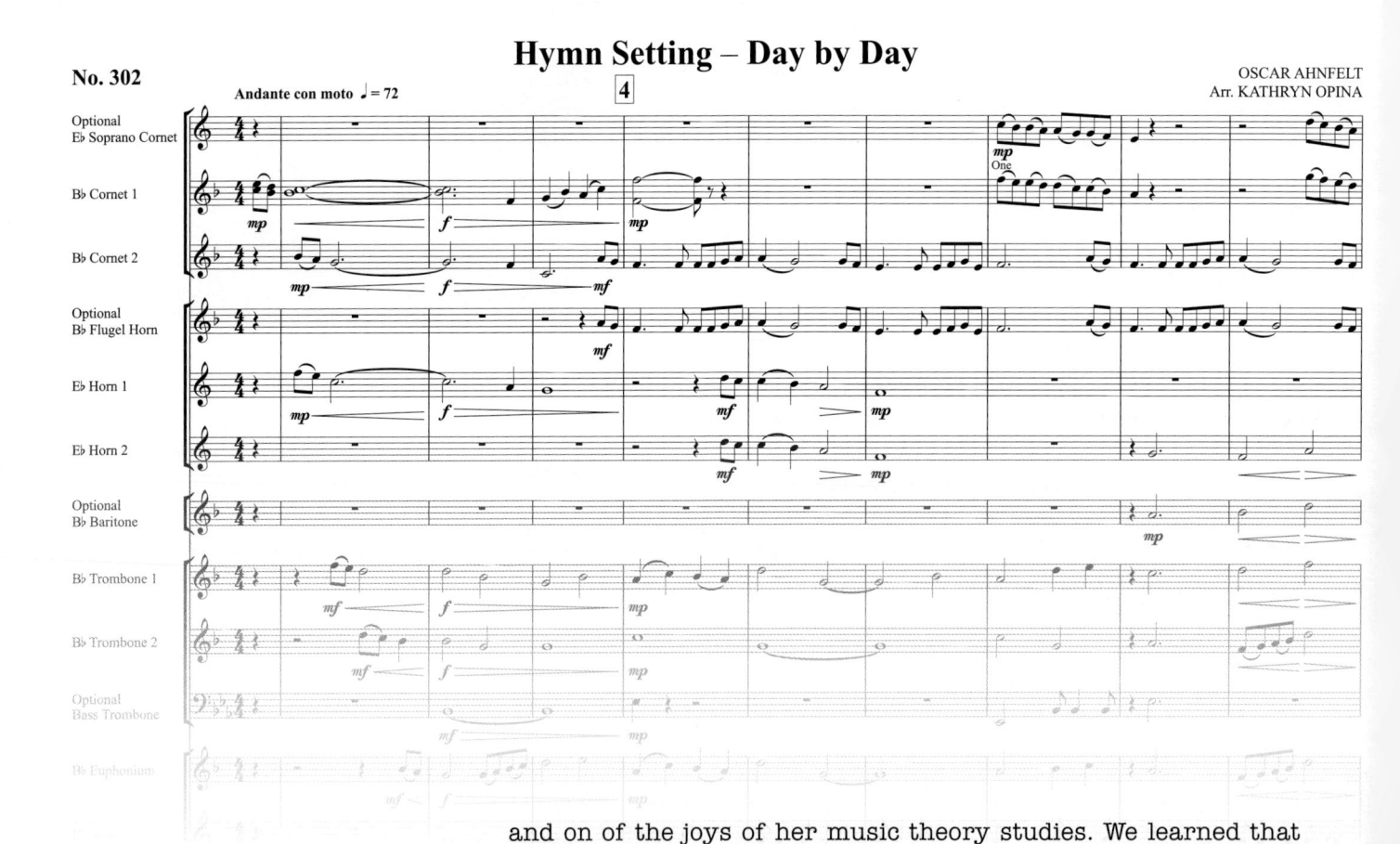

Postlude — BARS REST

A MUSIC LEADER'S SELF APPRAISAL[15]

1. **Servanthood**—How well do you follow? How did you respond the last time you were asked to serve out of the spotlight, behind the scenes? Do you find it difficult to place the needs of others ahead of your own?

2. **Gifting**—Do you feel that you are using your artistic gifts in your present congregation? Are you experiencing genuine community with a group of Christian artists?

3. **Perfectionism**—Do you entertain thoughts in your head that you're not good enough as an artist? Are you hard on yourself when you make a mistake? If you are a leader who is also an artist, do you experience tension between these two roles?

4. **Team–building**—How well do you feel folks follow you? How do you respond to constructive criticism? Do you think your group "buys into" your vision for them?

5. **Positive thinking**—Has anybody ever told you that you are negative or moody? Do you ever sense that you are being controlled by your emotions? How do you resolve conflict in your life?

6. **Spiritual discipline**—Do you have a regular devotional time with the Lord? Do you feel that you have a strong relationship with the Lord these days? Do you have anyone in your life to whom you are accountable for your spiritual walk?

7. **The present future**—Are you feeling fresh and challenged in your present leadership? Do you see opportunities to share some of your responsibilities? What did your predecessor give to you that you might pass on to your successor?

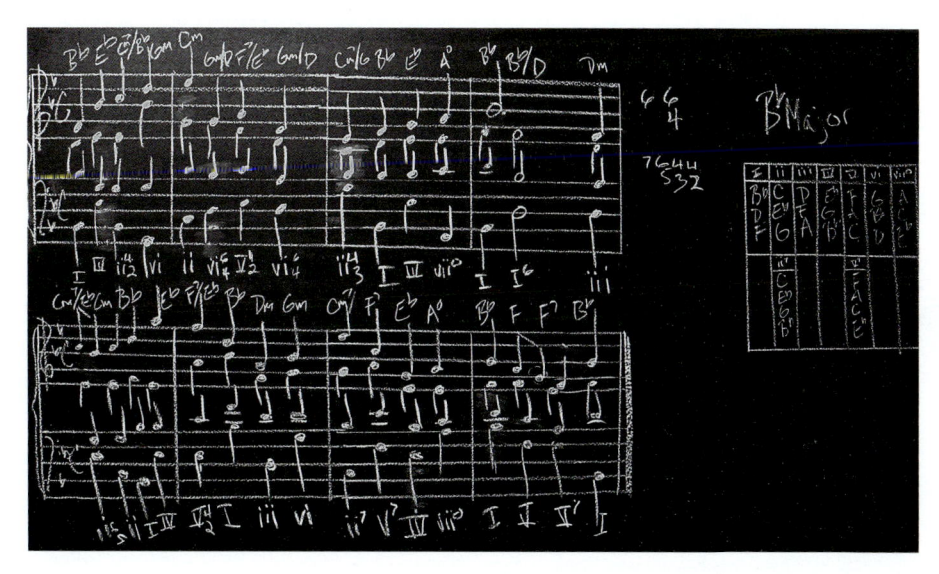

THE EMERGING LEADER'S TOOLBOX

PAUL PASSES THE BATON

Things I wish I had known before I stepped on this train!

We are fortunate to have Paul's instructions to "Timothy, my dear son" as a model of an effective baton pass. Paul's practical and forthright advice is God-directed, intentional, and ultimately, Kingdom-building. In Chapter One, we spoke of the "priesthood of the believers" and the fallacy that ministry is limited to those who are ordained. Throughout his letters, Paul leaves no doubt that each of us is called and gifted for ministry. He reminds Timothy to "guard well the splendid, God-given ability you received as a gift from the Holy Spirit who lives within you." —2 Timothy 1:14, *TLB*.

Paul passes the mantle to his beloved disciple with focused intentionality, and his voice resonates with deep love and affection. We learn much from observing his tenderness, sincerity, and wisdom. My hope is that some of these reflections from my own experience in music leadership may benefit another generation of Salvationist leaders.

Encouraging an emerging leader in Oruro, Bolivia, 2012.

Leaders not helpers

For this reason I remind you to fan into flame the gift of God, which is in you … For God did not give us a spirit of timidity, but a spirit of power, of love and of self discipline. —2 Timothy 1:6–7

Growing up, I was the shyest kid on the block. This suited me fine. I was happy to play sports with my brothers and give the remainder of my time to practicing my instrument. Even though I am a firstborn, I absolutely hated having to ask for anything. Yet years later, as a music director, I found myself having to approach people every day to do countless tasks.

Paul contends that timidity is overcome through God's Spirit. It is easy to picture Timothy holding back for fear of the crowds or the limelight if he steps forward. We can encourage potential leaders to identify and exercise their spiritual gifts. We consider their natural personalities and ask what opportunities in the corps will confirm their gifts to benefit the church body as a whole. Moses, generations ago, beseeched the Lord to *"establish the work of our hands for us—yes, establish the work of our hands"* —Psalm 90:17.

Larry Osborne advocates **selecting *leaders*, rather than *helpers***, not so much to lighten your load, but to broaden the ministry. Helpers increase the mentor's workload by constantly running to you for guidance. Too much talk drains the batteries quickly. Experience has taught that begging someone into the fold early in the game most often results in a quick letdown exit. Have the courage not to engage helpers now. Otherwise, you may later regret having to take the steps to remove them.[16]

When searching for leaders, keep an eye out for great people and **train** them. Start where a person is. Believe in them more than they believe in themselves. You can usually tutor someone in a skill, but it is far more difficult to teach character. Look for leaders who solve problems and recruit others around them. Educational initiatives, like the every day *El Sistema* regimen, (see p. 77) successfully utilize student-leaders in peer-to-peer teaching at young ages to activate their innate leadership and teaching skills.

Steps to empowerment

There are three steps to making the transition and empowering the next generation leader:

> **Selection**—Getting the right person in the right place.
> **Training**—Making sure every future leader knows when, how, and why we do what we do.
> **Empowerment**—Empowering future leaders for significant ministry and maximum impact.

There is little merit in worrying about today's assistant becoming tomorrow's competition. Rather our attitude can be, "Someday, I'm going to be able to say, I taught that guy!"[17] Your encouragement, prayers, and willingness to open doors allow the novice to see and learn from your strengths and weaknesses. Most importantly, teach them, by the power of God, how a leader can better follow Jesus.

From cross-training to empowerment

The things you have heard me say in the presence of many witnesses entrust to reliable people who will also be qualified to teach others. —2 Timothy 2:2

When young people ask me what it takes to become a music director, I half-kiddingly reply, "If you want my job, then learn to move equipment!" Most players and singers have little idea of the hours of meetings, preparation, instruction, loading, set-up and tear-down that make for a successful performance or Sunday meeting. In Chapter Eighteen, we suggested a rough equation of two hours of preparation to every hour of rehearsal. That is preceded by a sizeable investment of time given to repertoire selection and programming. What follows are unending contacts with the corps officer, secretary, boards, worship committee, librarian, drivers, tech folks, and many others.

One person takes the podium, but this surely is not a one-person show. Paul wisely counsels Timothy to *"entrust to reliable people."* Although it may seem easier to do things by yourself, assume that people do want to help or be put to work. My groups would not exist under my leadership without the people who surround me and shoulder much of the workload. Many do it without notice or applause. With time, there is less of a need for coaxing or guidance.

Great leaders **cross-train**. This means they safeguard the organization by being sure there are few tasks under their responsibility that only one person can do. This averts calamity when only one person knows how to fix something (or run the sound)![18] Besides, there will be those rare occasions when a leader is unable to make a rehearsal. Generous mentors give future conductors, songwriters, arrangers, and choreographers their initial opportunities to employ their gifts. Many a writer speaks graciously of the veteran who gave them their first words of encouragement and correction. Have a deputy and "assure that he or she is used at practice on a weekly basis...so they are encouraged to continue and broaden their musical education."[19] True empowerment permits the intern a safe place to make mistakes. There will be shortcomings, but there is no real substitute for experiencing face-to-face contact with an ensemble. Watching a novice take his first baby steps actually gives your group a better appreciation for the challenges of leadership.

Larry Osborne advises to "inspect what you expect." Check things out yourself—before, during, and after—not because you don't trust people, but because the intentions are not

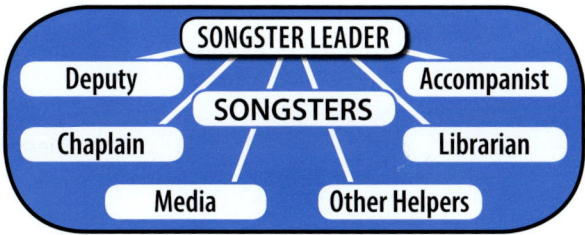

Two generations side-by side in a trombone feature. Left to right: son–father Will and Fred Clarke, father–daughter Judd and Katie Laidlaw.

always mutually understood. Conversely, if you "don't inspect, then don't expect." Trainees need encouragement and guidance. The tendency is to walk away too quickly and miss an opportunity to both evaluate and affirm the efforts.[20] Remember that "you can delegate authority, but you *cannot* delegate responsibility." Ultimately, the leader is still responsible for the deliverables of those we oversee.[21]

Shadowing

We've mentioned several times during the course of this book that we glean the majority of our perspective on music leadership from those under whom we've sung or played. In many ways we are what we remember. Memory proves to be a lens through which we view ourselves.[22] To actualize this process, encourage the journeyman conductor to lead next to or with an experienced mentor. According to Dr. Jack Stephenson, an effective baton pass follows a sequence of six stages of shadowing:

LEADERSHIP RAINBOW

Stage 3: **WE** do it together   Stage 4: **YOU** do it—**I** help

Stage 2: **I** do it—**YOU** help   Stage 5: **YOU** do it—**I** watch

Stage 1: **I** do it—**YOU** watch   Stage 6: **YOU** do it—**I** applaud!

I raise up another... **YOU** raise up another... A pot of gold [23]

One of the most produced writers of musical theatre in our time is Stephen Sondheim (*Company, Gypsy, Sweeney Todd, Sunday in the Park,* and *West Side Story*–lyrics only). During his formative years as a fifteen-year-old student at George School east of Philadelphia, Sondheim met and asked the veteran lyricist and writer Oscar Hammerstein to read his new musical, *By George.* Hammerstein told him it was awful, but he also told him why it was awful–and thus began an amazing mentorship that not only changed Sondheim's life but arguably, the course of the American musical. "Oscar was passing the baton," said Sondheim. "He caught me at just the right moment...at fifteen, you are clay." In an interview, while reflecting on Hammerstein's investment in him as a teenager, and Sondheim's current influence on the next generation of musical theatre writers, Sondheim quietly remarked, "I rarely say this in public, but I think Oscar would have been proud of me...I love passing on what Oscar passed on to me."[24]

Salvation Army Composers Gathering, Centennial Congress, London, 1965

Find us faithful

Learn to treasure the wisdom of the faithful who have gone before. Each year on Star Lake Musicamp Alumni Day, I relished receiving a nugget of assurance from the likes of Vernon Post, Norman Bearcroft, Derek Smith, or guests such as Len and Heather Ballantine. Martin Cordner speaks of his youth band leader giving up his podium to allow Martin to hear his first pieces, often taking time afterward to review the recording with helpful comments. At a music school in Chile, Joy Webb patiently listened to the first compositions of David Ayma.[25] Jim Curnow recalls his first attempts at composition under the watchful eye of Max Wood. Bill Himes, at age thirteen, shared a piano bench with an encouraging Eric Ball. Ron Waiksnoris speaks with admiration of the influence of trumpeter Carole Reinhart. Leslie Condon and Robert Redhead saw something in me as a fledgling songwriter and inspired me to keep writing. For the young and old, male or female, coming from a variety of ethnic backgrounds, Proverbs 16:21 advises us, "The wise in heart are called discerning and pleasant words promote instruction." An encouraging word goes a long way! Treasure it!

Establish high standards of excellence

Do your best to present yourself to God as one approved, a workman who does not need to be ashamed.
—2 Timothy 2:15

Salvation Army musicians embrace a spiritual mission, which, in the best of situations, is taken as seriously as the technical musical demands. The anointing is readily apparent to those receiving the blessing, either listening or within the group. Our ensemble members, and those waiting in the wings, must understand that their musical skills alone won't secure them a place. The ministry-driven leader spends more time interviewing prospective members in auditions than asking them to make music. The conversation touches on their life aspirations, why they want to be in the group, what's happening in their lives spiritually, their understanding of what will be expected of them, and how belonging to this group will help them grow.[26]

Paul reminds Timothy *"to present yourself to God as one approved."* This process allows you, the leader, to get to know your membership and what motivates them. It ultimately benefits the group's ministry as a whole. *Ad optimum* (meaning, for the highest) is the motto of the well-known Enfield Citadel Salvation Army band. **True excellence is not a perfect performance, but doing the best with what we have**. Knowing what we have is an essential first step. Remember these premises when you are being pressured by well-meaning parents, teachers, or other corps leadership to let someone into the group who does not reach the standard.

Nancy Beach reminds us that extreme perfectionism or overt competitiveness too often rears its ugly head in music and arts circles.[27] Paul correctly instructs Timothy, *"not to neglect his gift, by being diligent in these matters, giving himself wholly to them"* – 1 Timothy 4:14. This is not a call to baneful pride, but a call to practice, preparation, and training, while seeking wisdom and experience. It bears repeating that excellence is "doing the best with what you have."

Rightly, a leader should not be as concerned about a personal failure as about averting embarrassment for members on any given Sunday. A greater danger, however, may rest with a well-rendered performance, with all notes in place, that seems untouched by the Spirit of God, or one in which pride seems to supersede a spirit of humility. Worthy intentions should motivate a consistent investment in productive practices, which engenders trust, confidence, and ultimately, freedom in worship. "Well done, thou good and faithful servant" is not just a "pat on the back" after a Sunday morning. It reflects hours of diligent rehearsal, honest reflection, and effective team-building focused up to God and out to the needs of others. In other words, **it is ministry blended with discipleship**.

Absence is the enemy!

Keep coming back to your best intentions as the season progresses. Young people, in particular, thrive on consistent leadership. Be there! In exchange, expect full ("on time is late") attendance. Discipline yourself to finish on time.

> "Compromising people can't stand the sight of excellence."
> —Beth Moore

More on collaborating with the "artsy types" can be found back in Chapter Two, pp. 55–58.

Set clear guidelines for a courtesy call or message in the event of absence or lateness. Every music leader knows the frustration of rehashing music because of empty seats. Celebrate full attendance, as it saves precious rehearsal time. First Corinthians 12:19 reminds us, *"There are many parts, but one body."* With all members present we have a chance of making the full ensemble really jell.

Discover your group's identity...together
Continue in what you have learned and have become convinced of, because you know those from whom you learned it...the servant of God may be thoroughly equipped for every good work. —2 Timothy 3:14, 17, NIV

It took me a long time to figure out that if people dislike an activity, it is usually because not enough is expected of them. When asked about a sermon, Abraham Lincoln once replied, "It failed because it didn't ask us to do anything great."[28] Kids come back, not necessarily because they had fun, but because they learned something. Many are there primarily for their friends, so give them success with the music and they can continue to enjoy their friends. As we mentioned in Chapter Four, remember that kids know. They know if you know their name. They know if you love them. They know if you are doing this for the right reasons—they just know.

Armies, it is said, run on their stomachs. **Music and arts groups run on making music.** Avoid too much chat (from you and the members) in rehearsal and get down to the music. "Get lost" in the inner beauty of the music and words, and bring your team along. Work hard to schedule enough worthy performance opportunities, utilizing quality repertoire choices to grow into. It never works to say, "We will sing this song when it is ready." The world runs on deadlines, and we learn best when we have a deadline.[29] Set musical goals for concert dates, weekends, and trips, and watch your group rise to the occasion.

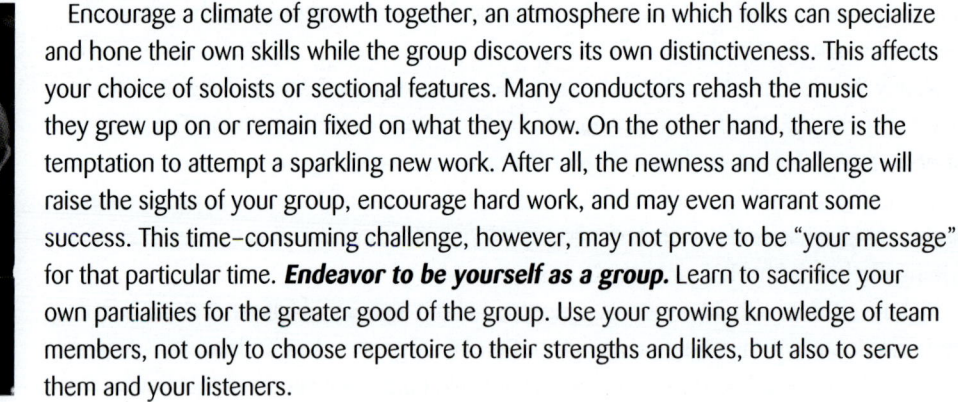

Encourage a climate of growth together, an atmosphere in which folks can specialize and hone their own skills while the group discovers its own distinctiveness. This affects your choice of soloists or sectional features. Many conductors rehash the music they grew up on or remain fixed on what they know. On the other hand, there is the temptation to attempt a sparkling new work. After all, the newness and challenge will raise the sights of your group, encourage hard work, and may even warrant some success. This time-consuming challenge, however, may not prove to be "your message" for that particular time. **Endeavor to be yourself as a group.** Learn to sacrifice your own partialities for the greater good of the group. Use your growing knowledge of team members, not only to choose repertoire to their strengths and likes, but also to serve them and your listeners.

Deliver more than you promise
Capitalize on the desire of a group to succeed by going public with dreams about new directions **we will take together.** Any message you are trying to convey must authentically contain a piece of you.[30] As the instigator of that vision, *strive to deliver more than you promise,* but take care not to attempt to deliver too much too quickly.[31] When you *make* a commitment, you create hope. When you *keep* a commitment, you create trust.[32] Remember to communicate, communicate, communicate with all parties, including parents, members, your staff, and your corps officer. Gladys Stern observed, "Silent gratitude isn't much good to anyone."[33] Commend success publicly and find excuses to celebrate. A vision fulfilled garners a growing trust in your leadership.

Body building

The Lord's servant...must be kind to everyone, able to teach, not resentful. —2 Timothy 2:24

Be prepared in season and out of season; correct, rebuke and encourage—with great patience and careful instruction. —2 Timothy 4:2

Encouragement beats nagging in motivating groups! Look for the good side in everybody by affirming strengths over weaknesses. Silly rules, unrealistic expectations, and subtle forms of micromanagement unravel *esprit de corps*. A corporate "we" pronoun goes further than a threatening "you." Caustic criticism compels members to become defensive and protective. Keep watch over your own personal strengths and weaknesses. Often, "it is better to swallow words, than to have to eat them later."[34] View everyone as unique and looking for your attention as well as your affirmation. Simple compliments in writing, which we sometimes call "luv notes," go far. It is hard to tell a friend what to do, so be a friendly leader, but remember that you cannot be everybody's friend.

We've all heard these expressions before: *"Find out what people want and help them get there...We are a part of all we've met...You can tell where they're going by where they've been."* Time in building bridges builds trust. "Knowing your choir" includes the compliment of a home visit, a long car ride together, or a cup of coffee with warm conversation. Chemistry is important. Do everything possible to allow the team to get to know one another. Time together will reap the benefits of improving understanding between each other.

> "If you want to walk fast, walk alone. If you want to walk far, walk with others."
> —African proverb

Beyond entitlement

Few things grate on leadership and create tension with membership more than the ever-burgeoning entitlement mindset. Discontentment with what we have promotes a feeling that the people around us, or even God, owe us something. This somehow validates anger when we are denied something. God's servant realizes that what *we really deserve is death* (Romans 6:23), yet through Christ's sacrifice, *we are "entitled to grace"*[35] (Ephesians 2:8-9), an escape route from escalating self-interest.

On mission trips, we meet impoverished people who "do so much with so little." Yet at home, we expect to be provided for with little inconvenience, expense, or sacrifice. Many are caught in a web of "cutting corners" in their commitments, in a vain effort to do it all! *"Better one handful with tranquility than two handfuls with toil and chasing after the wind,"* counsels the writer of Ecclesiastes (4:6).

Sports, school, or work can easily spread an individual far too thin. This can result in a lack of real commitment to any of what are in themselves worthy activities. The outward evidence of overcommitment is usually a lack of preparation, frequent lateness, and an early exit. There will be times when hard choices must be made, and the answer may simply be "No." You don't have the time or energy to do *all* of these things. Help folks, including well-meaning parents, make these difficult choices.

Quiet strength

Reflect on what I am saying, for the Lord will give you insight into all this. —2 Timothy 2:7

For years as the holiday season drew near, each of my four daughters would come into my study and ask, "Dad, what do you want for Christmas?" Habitually, their well-intentioned inquiry would be met with an uncomplicated response, "All I want is quiet." I was not referring to that moment, as though annoyed by the interruption. They knew that I thrive on being in the middle of a happening rehearsal with numerous elements

> "When I pause the longest, I make the most telling strokes."
> –Leonardo Da Vinci

to coordinate all around me. They also understood that as much as I feel energized by working a crowd and meeting new people, my spirit constantly longs for solitude.

Early mornings are reserved for reading and a solitary run, where I often process what I have read. As an arranger of music, I spend hours alone wrestling with my thoughts. I can easily shut off my phone or not respond to email for days. Time at the office, on the phone, or in meetings can clutter my thinking. On vacations, for me, the solace of an early morning canoe ride certainly surpasses a day on a crowded beach. There can never be enough quiet, at least in my life! In a joint letter written by Paul, Silas, and Timothy we read, *"Make it your ambition to lead a quiet life."* (1 Thessalonians 4:11a)

General William Booth once paraphrased the verse that precedes 2 Timothy 2:7 in a message to those under him: **"The tendency of fire is to go out; watch the fire on the altar of your heart. Keep the fire aglow."** The simplicity of Paul's wisdom links reflection to insight. Who of us does not want to make the best choices, whether in the moment or for the future? Sometimes we have to be man or woman enough to change course.

"In quietness and trust is your strength," writes Isaiah (30:15b). Many voices, even emails or phone messages, compete for your best attention. While there is a time for the input of others, many decisions are best made alone. Trust your instincts. Listen to yourself. Give attention to your second thoughts. Listen for God's still voice. Think, pray, and journal, searching for that inner compass that says, *"This is the way; walk in it."* (Isaiah 30:21)

Finishing Well

I have fought the good fight, I have finished the race,
I have kept the faith. —2 Timothy 4:7

Retired General John Gowans concludes his poignant autobiography *There's a boy here...* with a chapter recounting regrets at the end of his career. The sincerity of his confessions bespeaks a leader who lived his message and led the way he lived, a testament to finishing well:

> I regret very much that I did not give the early identification and development of leaders more attention. I am thinking ... of leadership at every level. In some parts of the world decline among us can be traced to the absence of lay leadership at the corps level ... The Salvation Army will never be better than its ... Spirit-filled leaders, Spirit-gifted leaders. The latent leadership of the Army needs to be recognized, liberated, developed and trained. The earlier it is identified the better. The gift must have the opportunity to grow, even if arrogance is a major danger among the gifted. Satan does not always demolish God's potential leaders. Why should he, if he can demobilize them, paralyze them with pride? The word "leader" should always be associated with the word "servant" in our vocabulary ... A be-ranked Salvationist needs to keep closely to the Army's master, who insisted that, in his Kingdom, the first shall be last.[36]

General John Gowans

Throughout this book, but particularly in Chapter Four, we suggested ways that officers and soldiers can intentionally cultivate the next generation of leaders, from the youngest age to the latest convert. Those in the twilight of their ministries can act as catalysts to spring the young eaglet into flight. Successors often ascend only to the level of genuine expectancy of a leader they respect.[37] If "leadership is a lifetime of God's lessons,"[38] then we must share our stories, particularly how our faith-walk moved us from a minstrel-performer to a minister-priest.

Postlude | PASSING THE BATON

We are compelled to find ways to go out of our way to carry on our love language of music. "An Army of One" is the U.S. Army's recruitment motto. How can one person constitute an army, you rightly ask? Real ministry involves transmission from Jesus to Paul, who passed on his ministry to Timothy, who imparted the message of love to others, who in turn have proved faithful in passing on the same legacy. Paul charges Timothy, *"You then, my son, be strong in the grace that is in Christ Jesus. And the things you have heard me say in the presence of many witnesses entrust to reliable people who will also be qualified to teach others."* (2 Timothy 2:1-2) Through the years, "one by one, by one," as the old chorus says, we pass the mantle onto our successors.

Heroes of the faith carry forth Salvation Army song
From the humble beginnings of the Fry Family quartet on a corner in Salisbury, England, in 1878, Salvation Army music-making has come into being on every continent with nearly a half million junior and senior musician members. Today brass bands alone number more than 2,400, comprising some 46,000 members.[39] We are not the last one standing, as Elijah naively thought. "We are surrounded with such a cloud of witnesses," or, as Eugene Peterson paraphrases it, "All these pioneers who blazed the way, all these veterans cheering us on? It means we'd better get on with it." Jesus began and finished this race we're in. Now it is our turn to pass the baton. "Let us run with perseverance the race set before us." (Hebrews 12:1, *NIV 1984*) **The extinction of Salvation Army music-making will always be a generation away until one person teaches another who teaches another.**[40] In this way our unique love language passes from generation to generation. Even those naysayers, who through rose-tinted glasses pine for the "good old days," recall with gratitude that they were the beneficiary of one person's time, love, and instruction. You may be that one!

While someone might expect *Salvo* music-making to carry on in the United Kingdom, the United States, and the countries Down Under, why should there still be brass bands and Salvation Army song in places like Haiti, Soweto, or Latin America? Every ounce of cultural fiber legislates against this anomaly. Yet, musicians in the thousands enliven weekly worship on the African continent, India, and in other places completely removed from Western culture. At the 1990 International Congress, 85-year-old Chinese Salvationist Major Yin Hung-Shun, in response to receiving The Order of the Founder, The Salvation Army's highest honor, "sang the chorus he had sung at the end of each day in the labor camp, that helped keep alive his faith and Salvationism: *"All my days and all my hours, all my will and all my powers...shall be thine, dear Lord."*[42] Even in the dark winters of repressive captivity, heroes of the faith carry forth Salvation Army song! There is hidden vigor in winter!

M. Scott Peck famously opens his book *The Road Less Traveled* declaring, "Life is difficult." The onset of hardships represents a reality we, in our humanness, try to resist. Peck reminds us, "Life really consists of solving problems of varying degrees of difficulty." In the same manner, real ministry is difficult. We often call looking for potential leaders as "searching for eagles," particularly because the eagle reaches its full capacity through facing adversity.[43]

Paul charges Timothy to "endure hardship as a good soldier of Jesus Christ." To illustrate this, he paints a trio of real-life pictures: the soldier who leaves all pursuits, the athlete who models discipline, and the hard-working farmer who gives us a pattern for

Can you identify each of these Salvation Heroes? Answers on page 552.

YP Band Leader Ken Luyk teaching future New York Staff Bandsman Ron Livingston

"If not you, then who? And if not now, when?"
—M. Scott Peck[41]

The Beat Goes On

perseverance. (2 Timothy 2:3–6) "Good soldiers (like runners) never look back," wrote Howard Davies. For the athlete, there are no quick fixes. "Buy now–pay later" deals tend to cheapen and cheat the life-journey of a leader. We accept responsibility for our use of time and our actions and feelings, without discrediting others or our surroundings.[44] God places us exactly where he needs us.

Seeds do sprout

Ministry is not a 9-to-5 endeavor. The farmer is prepared to work at any hour. At harvest time, he works from dawn to dusk, anxious to capture every ounce of daylight.[45] A teacher can teach and see little evidence of real learning over months. The preacher can sow the good seed of the Word into the minds and hearts of his parishioners and not see fruit for a long time. A bandmaster can prepare his musical forces week in and week out and still yearn for a breakthrough. When it seems no one is listening, really participating, or learning quickly enough, *persevere and keep teaching.* Like the soldier, runner, or farmer, we keep on, keep on...believing that someone will get it! In time your musicians will grow, lives will be changed, and the congregation will become inspired.[46]

It is an unfortunate reality that too few stay the course in their journey as leaders. Some stray and drop out. A majority plateau and merely get by. Like vocalists trying to maintain pitch over a series of repeated notes yet going flat, in our rapidly changing society, stationary actually represents a decline. But there are those valiant hearts who continue to "grow in the grace of our Lord Jesus Christ" and ultimately finish well.[47] They echo the words of the Apostle Paul, *"I do not consider myself yet to have taken hold of it. But one thing I do: Forgetting what is behind and straining toward what is ahead, I press on toward the goal to win the prize for which God has called me heavenward in Christ Jesus."* (Philippians 3:13–14)

The baton pass

A few years ago, I witnessed the public "baton pass" of leadership of the National Capitol Band from the ailing Bandmaster James Anderson to his successor Steve Kellner.[48] Jim had courageously prevailed in his illness long past the doctor's prognosis. His stellar, flag-waving Salvationism was on full display that day in his heartfelt choices of music and song. Jim recounted his journey from teaching in Scotland to Salvation Army music ministry in the United States. A musical tribute from Bandmaster William Himes referred to Jim's first published work, his endearing arrangement of "Jesus Loves Me," and his final piece, a simple setting of "Jesus is the Sweetest Name I Know."[49] Jim Anderson was, as we say in Salvation Army parlance, promoted to Glory a few months after that baton pass.

I have pondered the blessing of that day many times. Jim was a model Salvationist servant music leader. His teaching and music have already traversed to the next generation. Even when ill-disposed, he would call from his hospital bed and say he was praying for my family. With his hand out to his fellow man and his heart to God, Jim exemplified ministry—the Salvation Army way. Here was a good soldier who endured hardship! Like Jim Anderson, may we as Salvationist music leaders keep our eyes on the prize of the high calling of Jesus Christ (Philippians 3:13–14, paraphrase) because, by the grace of God, Salvationists continue to rejoice with buoyant musical strains, and **the beat goes on!**

> "Don't judge each day by the harvest you reap, but by the seeds you plant."
> –Robert Louis Stevenson

My baton pass?

Have you experienced an exhilarating performance, or perhaps time spent in God's presence? Reminiscent of a final curtain drop, as the last tones or thoughts fade, the original live impact has vanished forever. As available as all kinds of recordings are today, they cannot recreate the sensation of that moment in time! Like me, perhaps you have looked back, or listened hard for that which can never be recovered. After slugging through hours of practice and anticipation, all that remains is an emptying room and some notes on a page, which are lifeless until performed.

Privileged as I was to observe the actual baton pass by Jim Anderson, this was a rare anomaly. This watershed moment, something I may never experience again, taught me that it is much easier to pass the baton on with success when the ministry wholeheartedly belongs to God. Jim taught us to humbly view ourselves as stewards of the Lord's work for that season, limited as it may be by our circumstances.[50] Having shared in a number of retirement and farewell services where the successor is normally kept a week's distance away, I find myself pondering what my anchor-leg baton pass might be like a decade or so from now.

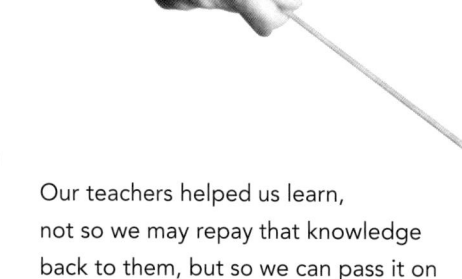

Our teachers helped us learn, not so we may repay that knowledge back to them, but so we can pass it on to others, who in turn may pass it on to still others.

—Peter Boonshaft

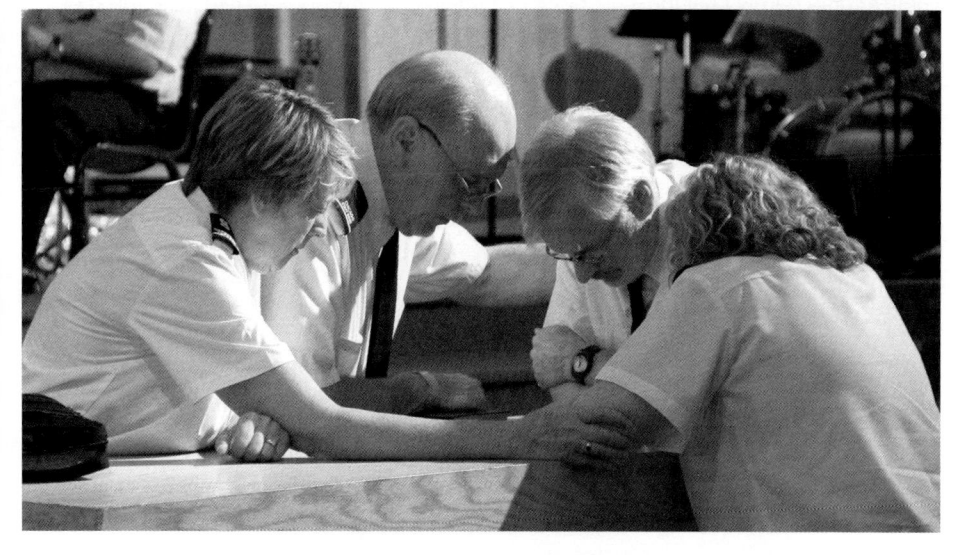

In the picture to the left, I was the recipient of a baton pass. Overwhelmed with the magnitude of becoming the territorial music secretary for the USA Central Territory, I felt compelled to offer my gifts afresh to the Lord's service. God has proven faithful in providing His strong hand of direction.

Sharing in the succession of leadership at the Soweto Central Corps, South Africa.

The Beat Goes On

The beat *will* go on!

"So I will very gladly spend for you everything I have and expend myself as well" (2 Corinthians 12:15a), states Paul in a passionate, paternal-sounding plea to the Corinthians. Having often pushed aside personal aspirations, I hold in the reservoir of my memory countless hours of prayer, preparation, planning, rehearsals, and services, which meant staying late, arriving early—and did I mention worrying?—on behalf of "my children." Then, having reached for the highest musical and spiritual intentions, too soon, we have to let "our children" go, hoping that they will reach beyond our expectations. Life teaches us that parenting is an incredibly inexact science, with numerous detours and diversions. The cycle of life continues, and somehow **the beat goes on ...**

Immersed in the moment, we hardly see how quickly time passes. I didn't notice my initial baton passes as I nudged novice music leaders, even divisional music directors, on with their first steps (and many more since). It has been a privilege to share musical instruction and curriculum overseas. Yet I earnestly yearn for any small influence, not just as a matter of stewardship, in circumstances where the Spirit of God glows fervently despite limited means. For me, this is something I have witnessed in my periodic visits to Argentina over several decades. And so **the beat goes on ...**

Circling another lap, one applauds the hard-working officers, some of whom in their youth I could hardly imagine in leadership. I applaud their efforts to carry the torch of music-making wherever they go. They replicate what they experienced as a child or teen, often rehashing the repertoire they learned with us as youngsters. I also commend those soldiers and officers who remain exemplary musician-ministers, some as staff bandsmen, military musicians, or musicians in cross-cultural settings far from their childhood environs. And so **the beat goes on ...**

It gives me great satisfaction to see those who have adopted a lifestyle of sharing their gifts musically from Sunday to Sunday, and of passing the baton on to another generation by teaching youngsters and assuming leadership of corps ensembles. Some also serve humanity as medical professionals, attorneys, social workers, and accountants. One works on Hollywood film scores while another can occasionally be spotted in a television commercial. And so **the beat goes on ...**

Sometimes with great intention and sometimes unwittingly, we pass on the heritage of Salvationist music-making in a multiplicity of guises, places, and times. Like Bandmaster Anderson, I am discovering that there are surprises along the way. Some might even call them miracles. Young people, by God's grace, are transformed out of severe and unkind circumstances, in some measure because of my obedient influence. In my spiritual near-sightedness, I never imagined my young intern Elise emerging as a composer-teacher. And so **the beat goes on ...**

How crucial is a convincing baton pass?

Even for one who attempts to live each day without regrets, there are dropped baton passes. Thankfully, there are also laps yet to run. I do wonder how to finish well. I suppose there will be a day when I will make that final baton pass. (Hopefully by then I will have learned how to cheer more enthusiastically, like the cloud of witnesses!) How I will miss wielding the baton, especially a few bars before a magical climax that goes beyond music. Yet these "here today-gone tomorrow" moments of live music-making do fade, never to be recovered. I believe William Wordsworth understood this when he wrote, "The music in my heart I bore long after it was heard no more."

> "The central question is, are the leaders of the future truly men and women of God, people with an ardent desire to dwell in God's presence, to listen to God's voice, to look at God's beauty, to touch God's incarnate Word and to taste fully God's infinite goodness?"
>
> –Henri Nouwen
> *In the Name of Jesus*

Postlude | **PASSING THE BATON**

Let us join those who *blazed the way* for us, in cheering on tomorrow's runners as we strive to pass on a stout-hearted influence to those who dare to stride the next laps. In the words of the apostle Paul,

> *I hope the test won't show that we have failed. But if it comes to that, we'd rather the test showed our failure than yours. We're rooting for the truth to win out in you. We couldn't possibly do otherwise. We don't just put up with our limitations; we celebrate them, and then go on to celebrate every strength, every triumph of the truth in you. We pray hard that it will all come together in your lives.* —2 Corinthians 13: 5–9, The Message

So the race of faith goes on … **As the anchor leg runners approach the finish line, the cheers of the crowd swell into a mighty roar** … It is the sound of a mighty Army. "Shout your praises to God, Everybody! Let loose and sing! Strike up the band! Feature trumpets and big trombones, Fill the air with praises to King God." (Psalm 98:4,6, *The Message*) Amid the cheers we hear a distant, yet insistent growing pulse from a ever swelling band of Salvation Army musicians … And so **the beat goes on!**

The Beat Goes On

Slowly, slowly, build the beat,
Clap your hands, move your feet,
Bang the drum and make it strong,
Feel the rhythm of the song.

Quickly, quickly, spread the word,
Good news means souls are stirred.
Sing of joy that can be found –
Take this message, pass it round.

Softly, softly, like a breeze,
Fear is spreading like disease.
Keep it back with faith and hope,
Cleansing doubt like holy soap!

Louder, louder, tell it out,
Spread the message, give a shout.
God's love is the song we sing,
Love that conquers anything!

—Kevin Sims

See Appendix 24.1 for the setting and recording of this poem, **The Beat Goes On**, arranged for singing company by the author.

The Beat Goes On

Leader Development Resources

Bringing Out the Best in People, Alan Loy McGinnis (Augsburg)
Developing the Leaders Around You, John C. Maxwell (Nelson)
Everyone Communicates, Few Connect, John C. Maxwell (Nelson)
Leadership on the Axis of Change, Chick Yuill (Crest Books)
Sticky Teams, Larry Osborne (Zondervan)
The 5 Levels of Leadership, John C. Maxwell (Center Street)
The Leadership Jump: Building Partnerships Between Existing and Emerging Christian Leaders, Jimmy Long (InterVarsity Press)
The Making of a Leader, J. Robert Clinton (NavPress)
The Present Future, Reggie McNeal (Jolley–Bass)

SALVATION HEROES

Salvation Heroes from left to right:

Samuel Logan Brengle was an American Salvation Army evangelist, principally known as an author and teacher on the doctrine of holiness. Brengle, today known as the Ambassador of Holiness, is pictured in the Prelude, p. 22.

Evangeline Booth, daughter of The Founder, often presented musical and dramatic presentations in colorful outfits. Evangeline Booth, the future U.S. National Commander and fourth General of The Salvation Army, is pictured at just fourteen years of age in the first Salvation Army songster brigade found on the first page of Chapter Twelve.

Elijah Cadman was instrumental in the militarization of The Salvation Army, including implementing the use of uniforms. At a diminutive five feet, Cadman traveled extensively with William Booth, and became known as "Fiery Elijah" because of his zeal for preaching.

George Scott Railton became known as William Booth's "spiritual son." In an age predating air travel, "the missionary to the world" amazingly pioneered the work or conducted spiritual campaigns in the US, Canada, South and West Africa, Europe, the Far East, Turkey, Russia and South America.

Joseph Garabed, better known as Joe the Turk, was an enthusiastic evangelist known for his zany antics to attract attention to the Gospel. In this book Joe the Turk is pictured playing his saxophone for a sizable crowd in Chapter One (p. 35) and also ministering to children at the conclusion of Chapter Six.

Eliza Shirley, at just 17 years of age, came to Philadelphia in 1879 to commence the work of The Salvation Army in America, utilizing vibrant preaching and her solo voice, accompanying herself on guitar. A mature Eliza Shirley is pictured in Chapter Four, p. 87.

ENDNOTES

Prelude:
THE LOVE LANGUAGE OF MUSIC

1. From "The Mission." Words and Music by Jon Mohr and Randall Dennis, © 1989 Feed and Seed Music/J.R. Dennis Music.
2. *Sing and Make Music: Orders and Regulations for Music Organizations in the USA,* The Salvation Army National Headquarters, 1998, p. 1. In December, 2004, *International Principles and Guidelines for Gospel Arts Groups* were released paralleling the long-standing Orders and Regulations for Bands and Songsters.
3. John Larsson. *The Officer,* The Salvation Army, November/December, 2005.
4. Reggie McNeal. *The Present Future: Six Tough Questions for the Church,* Jossey-Bass, p. xi.
5. Eric Metaxas. *Bonhoeffer: Pastor, Martyr, Prophet, Spy,* Thomas Nelson, 2011.
6. Meredith Willson. Lyric from *Banners and Bonnets,* © 1952 Plymouth Music Company, *Gems for Songsters 8,* Salvationist Publishing, p. 124.
7. Keith Getty and Stuart Townend. Lyric from *O Church, Arise!* Thankyou Music, © 2005.
8. William Himes. Lyric from *All That I Am.*
9. Jennifer Powell McNutt. "The Enduring Church," *Christianity Today,* January 2011, p. 47.
10. Gwenyth Redhead. "Holy ground ... holy hands," *Salvationist,* July 9, 2005, p. 16.
11. "Salvation Plus Music," *Newsweek,* December 15, 1941, p. 69.
12. These figures are from the November, 2014 *Disposition of Forces*—National Statistics. The author acknowledges the growing number of "praise bands" taking on the role of congregational song accompaniment, once the sole domain of senior bands and corps pianists.
13. William Barclay. *The Gospel of Matthew, Vol. 1,* Westminster Press, p. 356.
14. Samuel Logan Brengle. *Ancient Prophets and Modern Problems,* from Chapter 23, "The Future of The Salvation Army," Salvationist Publishing, 1930.
15. This poem by Kevin Sims and photo by Doug MacLellan are reprinted with permission, originally appearing as a back panel in The Salvation Army's *All the World* magazine, April-May, 2008, p. 20.

Part One: MUSIC MINISTERS

Chapter One:
FROM MINSTRELS TO MINISTERS

1. My first recollection of hearing the minstrel/ministry comparison was a conversation with then Lt. Colonel Jim Knaggs regarding an engagement that clearly was not ministry-driven. For that reason, we opted out. I inquired of the now retired Commissioner Knaggs as to his recollection of using these terms. He replied, "I can tell you without reservation that the idea did not come from reading anything I know of, but rather from our experience and particularly facilitated by your own witness among us." (From an email of August 16, 2011.)
2. *Webster's New Collegiate Dictionary,* Merriam, 1981.
3. From July 29, 2011 correspondence with jazz professor Paul Scott, professional bassist and Salvationist from Regent Hall, United Kingdom.
4. Douglas Stuart. *Mastering the Old Testament—Ezekiel,* Thomas Nelson, 2002, pp. 393-395.
5. John C. Maxwell. *Everyone Communicates, Few Connect,* Thomas Nelson, 2010, p. 62.
6. Richard Foster. *Prayer—Finding the Heart's True Home,* Harper, 1992, p. 1.
7. Richard Foster. *Celebration of Discipline,* Harper, 1998, p. 161.
8. Barry Liesch. *The New Worship,* Baker Books, 2002, p. 123.
9. Søren Kierkegaard. *Purity of Heart is To Will One Thing,* trans. Douglas Steere, Harper and Brothers, 1948. pp. 180-181.
10. Liesch, *The New Worship,* p. 123.
11. Morgenthaler, Sally. *Worship Evangelism: Inviting Unbelievers into the Presence of God,* Zondervan, 1999.
12. The "pew potato" phrase was gleaned from NC Baptists in Worship blog, *Renewing Worship,* September 9, 2010.
13. Morgenthaler, *Worship Evangelism.*
14. Philip Yancey. *Grace Notes—Daily Readings with a Fellow Pilgrim,* Zondervan, 2009, p. 74.
15. Diane Winston. *Red-Hot and Righteous: The Urban Religion of The Salvation Army,* Harvard University Press, 1999. p. 100.
16. The Salvation Army. *Sing and Make Music—Orders and Regulations for Music Organizations in the USA,* The Salvation Army National Headquarters, 1998, p. 1.
17. Stephen King. *On Writing: A Memoir of the Craft,* Scribner, 2010.
18. Gwenyth Redhead. Concert evaluation comments made during a presentation to the Eastern Territorial USA Music Committee in January, 2004.
19. Eugene Peterson. *Run with the Horses: The quest for life at its best,* InterVarsity Press, 1983, p. 137.

Chapter Two:
SUNDAY MORNING

1. Robert Street. *Called to Be God's People: The International Spiritual Life Commission—Its Report, Implications and Challenge,* Salvation Books, 1999, p. 10.
2. Nancy Beach. *An Hour on Sunday,* Zondervan, 2004, p. 21.
3. Richard Foster. *Celebration of Discipline,* Harper & Row, 1998 edition, p. 161.
4. Street, *Called to be God's People,* p. 10.
5. Beach, *An Hour on Sunday,* p. 23.
6. Foster, *Celebration of Discipline,* p. 172.
7. As quoted in Elton Trueblood, *The People Called Quakers,* Harper & Row, 1966, p. 91.
8. From lyrics by James Morgan from "The Quiet Heart," music by June Collin, *Gems 8 for Songsters,* p. 110-111, first published in *The Musical Salvationist,* April, 1968.
9. I am further indebted to Nancy Beach for the basic concepts of this section, drawn from pp. 23-34 of *An Hour on Sunday.* This quote is from p. 34.

10. John Piper. *Recovering Biblical Manhood and Womanhood,* Crossway Books, 1991, p. 16.
11. Gleaned from a teaching by Darlene Zschech titled, "Extravagant Worship" from the *Worship Leader's Toolkit 2,* Worship Institute, 2004.
12. Street, *Called to be God's People,* p. 9.
13. Dave Williamson. *God's Singers,* in:ciite media, 2010, pp. 111–112.
14. Beach, *An Hour on Sunday,* p. 25.
15. ibid., p. 59.
16. Thomas B. Bergler. *The Juvenilization of American Christianity,* Eerdmans, 2012.
17. Adapted from an email from Colonel Richard Munn, June 6, 2012.
18. John Ortberg. "Ponce de Leon on Steroids," *Christianity Today,* June 2012, p. 26.
19. Street, *Called to be God's People,* p. 11.
20. Richard Munn. "Worship–The Jewel on the Crest" Workshop notes, Territorial Worship Arts Convocation, USA East, Ladore Conference Center, January 20, 2007.
21. ibid.
22. Williamson, *God's Singers,* pp. 111–112.
23. Beach, *An Hour on Sunday,* pp. 175–176.
24. Rory Noland. *The Heart of the Artist,* Zondervan, pp. 13–14.
25. *We Are An Offering* CD jacket liner notes, Pendel Brass and Singers Soloists—Past and Present, PBS 12, 2005.
26. Donald P. Hustad. *Jubilate! Church Music in the Evangelical Tradition,* Hope, 1981, front flyleaf.
27. Mark Hood. "YS talks to Mark Hood," *Young Salvationist,* December, 2011, p. 16.
28. Eugene Peterson. *Run with the Horses,* InterVarsity Press, 1983, pp. 14–15.
29. From a conversation with Salvationist Carol Jaudes, a former Broadway artist, now Eastern Territorial Arts Ministries Director.
30. Larry Osborne. *Sticky Teams,* Zondervan, 2010, p. 110.
31. I am indebted to Australian Salvationist Graeme Press for this definition by American minister Kennan Birch. Graeme quoted Birch in an interview in *Theme Magazine,* published by The Salvation Army Canada Music Department, April–June, 2005, p. 12.
32. Quoted from a tribute written by Derick Kane, THQ–United Kingdom Music Ministries Newsletter, Issue 35: December, 2011.
33. Ken Gire. *Windows of the Soul,* Zondervan, 1996, p. 20.
34. Reuben Welch. *We Really Do Need Each Other: A Call to Community in the Church,* Impact Books, p. 10.
35. Peggy Thomas. From a Worship Arts Convocation workshop, Ladore Conference Center, April 6, 2013. Peggy attributes this concept to Constance Cherry, from her fine book on worship design entitled *The Worship Architect,* Baker Academic, 2010.
36. Robert Schaper. *In His Presence,* T. Nelson Publishers, 1984. Italics added for emphasis.
37. This four-fold worship-design "structure" is gleaned from Constance Cherry, *The Worship Architect,* Baker Academic, 2010, pp. 53–111.
38. I am indebted to Peggy Thomas for the two meeting outlines that follow, adapted to Salvation Army context, as presented in a Worship Arts Convocation workshop, Ladore Conference Center, April 6, 2013.
39. Beach, *An Hour on Sunday,* p. 168.
40. The Canadian Staff Band usually travels on the first weekend of each month. Therefore former bandmaster Brian Burditt managed his rehearsals over a four-week cycle to successfully be ready for these monthly outings.
41. I am indebted to Colonel Richard Munn for his provocative workshop title: "Worship–A Jewel on the Crest." It symbolically weds Tozer's missing gem of worship with a significant Salvation Army emblem.
42. Aiden Wilson Tozer. *Worship,* Christian Publications, n.d. pp. 12, 23–24.

Chapter Three:
HAND ME DOWN MY SILVER TRUMPET

1. Norman Davies. *Europe–A History,* Oxford, 1996, pp. 486-487.
2. William Booth. This "headline" title is derived from a sermon on "Good singing" delivered in 1877 by William Booth, then general superintendent of The Christian Mission. The actual text reads: "You must sing good tunes. Let it be a good tune to begin with. I don't care much whether you call it secular or sacred. I rather enjoy robbing the devil of his choicest tunes, and, after his subjects themselves, music is about the best commodity he possesses. It is like taking the enemy's guns and turning them against him."
3. Gordon Cox. *The Musical Salvationist, the World of Richard Slater (1854-1939), The Father of Salvation Army Music,* The Boydell Press, 2011, pp. 26-29.
4. William Booth. *Orders and Regulations for Field Officers,* 1917, p. 213.
5. ibid.
6. William Booth. "Musical Instruments from the General," *War Cry,* March 27, 1880.
7. Cox, *The Musical Salvationist,* p. 69.
8. Ronald Holz. *Brass Bands of the Salvation Army, Volume 1,* Egon Publishers, 2006, p. 100.
9. *Bandsman, Local Officer and Songster,* February 12, 1927, p. 57.
10. I was first introduced to this hammered trumpet concept at a workshop by Larry Osborne, *Finding, Developing and Empowering Leadership in Your Church,* National Pastor's Convention, San Diego, February 11-12, 1998.
11. Cox. *The Musical Salvationist,* p. 31.
12. *Webster's New Collegiate Dictionary,* Merriam, 1981.
13. George Barna. *Transforming Children into Spiritual Champions.* Regal Books, 2003, pp 77-78.
14. ibid., p. 98.
15. I learned of this entrance policy from Bandmaster William Himes, of his highly successful beginners' brass program at Oakbrook Terrace, IL Corps.
16. Connie Fortunato. *Children's Music Ministry,* David C. Cook, 1981.

Chapter Four:
WORKERS TOGETHER

1. Reggie McNeal. *The Present Future,* Jossey-Bass, 2003, p. xi.
2. Gwenyth and Robert Redhead. "Music and Arts," *Hallmarks of The Salvation Army,* Salvo Publications, 2009, pp. 88-89.
3. Edward McKinley. *Marching to Glory,* First Edition, Harper & Row, 1980, p. 42.
4. ibid., p. 42.
5. Larry Osborne. *Sticky Teams,* Zondervan, 2010, pp. 113-114.
6. Lyric by Oscar Hammerstein from *The Sound of Music.* © 1959 Oscar Hammerstein II/Williamson Music

7. Bruce D. Perry and Maia Szalavitz. *The Boy Who Was Raised as a Dog and Other Stories from a Child Psychiatrist's Notebook,* Basic Books, 2008, documents what happens when young children are traumatized. In the case of Leon (Chapter 5, pp. 99–124), his mother's systematic neglect from infancy on resulted in a total lack of remorse for a double murder he committed at age sixteen.
8. Dorothy Law Nolte's poem "Children Learn What They Live" (1972) is mounted conspicuously in lobbies of schools and doctor's offices. It is a challenging list of character development insights for parents, teachers, caregivers, and administrators alike. Nolte contrasts a long list of negative adult vices with what children learn to model. Here is a sampling: "If children live with criticism, they learn to condemn ... live with approval, like themselves ... live with recognition, they learn it is good to have a goal ... live with kindness and consideration, they learn respect ... live with encouragement, learn confidence ... [and importantly,] live with acceptance, they find love."
9. I am indebted to Rabbi Amy Scheinerman's commentary on Nolte's classic primer for this line of thinking found on her blog, *A Taste of Torah.*
10. James Dobson. *Dr. Dobson Answers Your Questions,* Tyndale House Publishers, 1982, p. 42.
11. The Barna Institute conducted research of over 1,000 adults in May 2001 on the probability of people accepting Jesus Christ as their Savior for a lifetime relationship with the following outcomes: 32% for children between 5 and 13 years old; 4% for those 14 to 18; and 6% for people 19 years and older, indicating five to eight times more impact to learn about God as a child. This study also showed that church attendance by children has a lifelong impact. 61% of adults who attended church as children still attend regularly. Only 20% who were not churched as children attend today. (Cited from Barna Research Online: *Adults Who Attended Church as Children Show Lifelong Effect.*)
12. Lorena Lance. "125 Years of the New York Staff Band: An Insider's View." NYSB Newsletter, Fall, 2012.
13. "A survey conducted by Natural Church Development of 1200 Christians yielded a shocking result: 80% of those surveyed had no idea what their spiritual gifts might be. Only 20% indicated that they knew what their spiritual gifts were and used them." Christian Scharwz, *The 3 Colors of Ministry,* ChurchSmart Resources, p. 42.
14. Dave Williamson. *God's Singers, Director's Edition,* in:ciite media, 2010, pp. 74, 79.
15. Henry Gariepy. *Christianity in Action: The Salvation Army in the USA Today,* Victor Books, 1990, p. 18.
16. Larry Osborne. *Sticky Teams,* p. 114.
17. ibid., p. 115.
18. There are numerous studies on high school and college-age attrition from the church. One example is a 2007 study by LifeWay Research which states that 70% of youth who attended church in high school will leave the faith in college. Only 35% eventually return. Seven in ten Protestants ages 18 to 30—both evangelical and mainline—who went to church regularly in high school said they quit attending by age 23. 34% of those said they had not returned, even sporadically, by age 30. That means about one in four Protestant young people have left the church.
19. Mark Dowds. "When the Old Armour Doesn't Fit," *Horizons,* January-February, 2003, p. 4.
20. John F. Kennedy delivered a speech in Indianapolis on April 12, 1959 famously saying: "When written in Chinese the word *crisis* is composed of two characters. One represents danger and the other represents opportunity." According to Chinese philologist Victor Mair, the more exact meaning of the dual characters is a "dangerous or perilous crucial point."
21. Eugene H. Peterson. *Run With the Horses: the Quest for Life at its Best,* InterVarsity Press, 1983.
22. Mark Dowds, "When the Old Armour Doesn't Fit," p. 5.
23. Peter Farthing. "Will the Army be Renewed?" *The Officer,* February, 1996, p. 57.
24. ibid., p. 58.
25. ibid., p. 59.
26. Andrew Vertigan. "You see bones–I see an Army–Part I," *The Salvationist,* October 22, 2011, p. 15.
27. Andrew Vertigan. "You see bones–I see an Army"–Part II, *The Salvationist,* October 29, 2011, p. 15.

Chapter Five:
THEN SINGS MY SOUL!

1. This humorous exchange was adapted from "40 Ways to Wreck a Meeting" by Lt. Colonel Ray Steadman-Allen from *The Officer,* SP&S, 1984.
2. Abraham Joshua Heschel. *The Insecurity of Freedom,* Schoken Books, 1959.
3. Alice Parker. *Melodious Accord,* Liturgy Training Publications, 1991, p. 84.
4. ibid., p. 84.
5. Brindley Boon. *Sing the Happy Song,* SP&S, 1978, pp. 1–2.
6. Robert Sandall. *The History of The Salvation Army, Volume II,* Thomas Nelson, 1950, p. 108.
7. ibid.
8. ibid., p. 109.
9. ibid., p. 121.
10. Boon, *Sing the Happy Song,* p. 7.
11. ibid., p. 8.
12. Sandall, *The History of The Salvation Army, Volume II,* p. 121.
13. Albert Edward Bailey. *The Gospel in Hymns,* Scribners, 1950, p. 313.
14. Don Hustad. *Jubilate, Church Music in the Evangelical Tradition,* Hope Publishing Company, 1981, p. 243.
15. The author was privileged to be a working member of the most recent Song Book Council which decided to put words in the piano tune book for all verses for songs of irregular meter.
16. Alison Stewart. *Worship Team Handbook,* InterVarsity Press, 1998, p. 126.
17. Adapted from "Technical Writing Tips for the Oil Patch," WordPress.com weblog, posted September 29, 2010.
18. I am grateful to Kim Garreffa (Canada) and Tom Scheibner (USA East) for the clarifications on CCLI, copyright, and public domain. Copyright extends for the life of the longest surviving author plus 70 years for works created *after* January 1, 1978. Works registered *before* January 1, 1978 carry secure copyright coverage for 95 years. Works registered *before* January 1, 1923 "have fallen into the public domain (PD)."
19. CCLI offers a Church Rehearsal License which allows legal copying and sharing of commercial recordings of songs as shared audio files via email, flash drives, or worship planning websites. It also covers copying of legally purchased digital downloads. These copies are intended for rehearsal purposes only, and are not to remain as

permanent copies for personal collections. This agreement does not cover duplication of rehearsal or performance recordings of copyrighted material or duplication of downloads from free streaming websites like YouTube.
20. These Song Book titles are courtesy of Major Christine Clement, editor of the 2015 *Song Book of The Salvation Army*.
21. This information is courtesy of Lt. Colonel Trevor Davis, music editor for the 2015 Tune Books.
22. I am indebted to an article from the *Band Training Correspondence Course* on the Metrical Index by Colonel Charles Skinner for much of this section's content.
23. Max Rudolf. *The Grammar of Conducting,* Third Edition, Schirmer, 1994, p. 7.

Part Two: YOUTH MUSIC MINISTRY

Chapter Six:
LET THE CHILDREN SING!

1. Most recent confirmation of this fact is available in Janet Louise Seale's Master of Music Thesis at the University of Calgary, "The Role of the Right Ear in Accurate Pitch Matching," January 1998.
2. Helen Kemp. *Children Sing His Praise–A Handbook for Children's Choir Directors,* edited by Donald Rotermund, 1985, Concordia. "Understanding and Developing the Child's Voice," p. 74.
3. These suggested low, high, and middle pitches are by Dr. Beatrice Holz.
4. This warm-up rhyme was learned in a workshop by Helen Kemp. Available in print in *Children Sing His Praise,* p. 77.
5. ibid., p. 71.
6. Ed Roseman. *Edly's Music Theory for Practical People,* Musical EdVentures, 1996, p. 63.
7. Sally K. Albrecht, ed. *The Choral Warm-Up Collection,* Alfred Publishing, 2003, p. 72.
8. ibid., p. 72.
9. ibid., p. 56.
10. Other possibilities for easy reading from the *Youth Songbook,* now available as *Songs of Praise,* (The Salvation Army, National Headquarters, 1988) include: *Fairest Lord Jesus* (YSB 59, in F); *Search Me, O God* (YSB 94, in F); *Break Thou the Bread of Life* (YSB 182, transpose voices from Eb down to C); *When I Survey* (YSB 48, in F); and *When Morning Gilds the Skies* (YSB 66, in C).

Chapter Seven:
THE RIGHT SONG FOR YOUR KIDS!

1. Nicholas Simmons-Smith. May 16, 2012 email to the author.
2. Helen Kemp. "10 Questions for Composer Helen Kemp," *The Chorister,* August/September 2012, p. 32.
3. A true "head voice tone" is now recognized acoustically and in fiberoptic photography by a very thin sound and the approximation, or closure, of the vocal cords along the edges only. But an optimal sound actually is a "blended" sound that includes not just the "chest" voice quality of speech but also a "mix" of head voice quality. Thus the term head-voice mix. (From a note from Dr. Beatrice Holz dated August 5, 2011.)
4. Adapted from an article by Keith Pate, "Song Teaching Tips (that work!)," *The Chorister,* August/September, 2012, p. 12–13.
5. "The Chorister's Prayer" was first published in 1934 by the School of English Church Music in the *Chorister's Pocket Book,* without an indication of its origin.

Chapter Eight:
ALL HAIL TO DANIEL'S BAND

1. I am indebted to Major Hollie Ruthberg for drawing my attention to the high priority given to the multi-generational musical training of the Levite musician-priests, even from a young age.
2. William Himes. *Lessons in Leadership, Part 1,* newsletter of the Salvation Army Central Territory Music Department, Opus 46, January/February 1990, p. 2.
3. Commentators place the Davidic census in 980 BC and Hezekiah's coming to power in 715 BC, leaving possibly 265 years between.
4. Quoted from an article by Elgar Howarth, *The Brass Herald,* October, 2011, p. 72 on Bram Wiggins who was trained in the Harlesden Citadel Junior Band and became one of Britain's most sought-after symphonic trumpeters.
5. Johann Fux. *The Study of Counterpoint–Gradus Ad Parnassum,* edited and translated by Alfred Mann. W. W. Norton, 1971, p. 48.
6. Young children can be exposed to music-making through a variety of games and songs, engaging their mind and body through a mixture of singing, dancing, and use of percussion instruments. The Orff Approach, as one example, utilizes an array of child-sized xylophones and metallophones, coupled with rhythm instruments like castanets, triangles, finger cymbals, maracas, and rhythm sticks.
7. Definition adapted from Philip Farkas, *The Art of Brass Playing,* Brass Publications, 1962, p. 5.
8. The Suzuki Method is based on the principle that all children possess ability. As easily as children learn to speak their language, other learned skills can be naturally nurtured. The essential elements of Suzuki's Talent Education are an early start (ages 3–4 is normal in most centers); *the importance of listening to quality music and sound;* learning to play before learning to read; the involvement of the parents; a nurturing and positive learning environment; the importance of producing a good sound and the use of a core repertoire, mostly learned by rote. (International Suzuki Association)
9. It will not be a surprise to anyone that there are preschoolers and elementary age children who do not have adequate use of grasping skills or upper body skills because of endless hours staring at a video screen. Yet as youthful consumers of art, they have convinced their parents that they want to play drums. A Suzuki teacher has her "Pre-Twinkle violin classes tapping each Twinkle rhythm on a small drum and then with a pair of rhythm sticks … Once perfected and up to tempo, the pre-Twinklers have had their fill of percussion instruments and look forward to their violin." (Cynthia Faisst in *Suzuki Forum,* November 9, 2009.)
10. Junior percussion kits include practice bells with a stand and mallets, a practice pad with snare drum sticks, all fitting nicely in a case, allowing for quiet home practice for years. Use of the lightweight (and economical) JPKs allows percussion students to start on both keyboard percussion and snare drum from the beginning. With

the bells, they can participate in melodic warm-ups during band rehearsal and learn note reading from an early age.
11. Bruce Pearson and Ryan Nowlin. *Teaching Band with Excellence,* Kjos Music Company, 2011, p. 294.

Chapter Nine:
GOD'S SPECIAL INSTRUMENTS

1. Don & Katie Fortune. *Discover Your God-Given Gifts,* Chosen Books, 2009, p. 97.
2. William Himes. "God in you, God in me," Hallelujah Chorus #79.
3. Dave Williamson. *God's Singers,* in:ciite media, 2010, p. 107.
4. Bruce Pearson and Ryan Nowlin. *Teaching Band with Excellence,* Kjos Music Company, 2011, p. 5.
5. ibid., p. 7.
6. Gleaned from helpful comments by Eric Dina.
7. Based on material by trombonist Cathy Hayes.
8. I am indebted to my former associate, Ronda Atwater, for these "Twelve Tips for Giving a Beginner Brass Lesson." She first organized them for our teaching training workshops and models them in private lessons week in and week out.
9. I am indebted to Bill Quick, a skilled percussionist and retired music educator, for his helpful review of these tips on snare drum instruction, as well as the corresponding photos.
10. For a comprehensive listing of Salvation Army solo collections, see Ronald Holz, *Brass Bands of The Salvation Army,* Volume II, Streets Publishing, pp. 60-63.

Part Three: ADULT MUSIC MINISTRY

Chapter Ten:
WHAT'S THE SCORE?

1. *Webster's New Collegiate Dictionary,* Merriam, 1981, p. 1028.
2. Donald Grout. *A History of Western Music,* Shorter/Revised Edition, Norton, 1973, p. 49.
3. Douglas Harper. *Online Etymology Dictionary,* 2001-2012.
4. ibid.
5. Adapted from *The Harvard Dictionary of Music,* Fourth Edition, p. 765.
6. I first learned of the threefold concept of the "imagined, ideal and real" sounds in hearing musical scores from choral conductor-clinician Jane Marshall.
7. Frank Battisti and Robert Garofalo. *Guide to Score Study for the Wind Band Conductor,* Meredith Music, 1990, p. 23.
8. Reprinted with permission from *Hallelujah Choruses,* The Salvation Army, 2000, Des Plaines, IL, HC#98, p. 63.
9. Timothy Sharp. *Precision Conducting,* Roger Dean Publishing Company, 2003. The steps listed here are extrapolated for use with vocal scores from a chapter of this book, pp. 17-20.
10. *Webster's New Collegiate Dictionary,* Merriam, p. 1213.
11. Chris Mallett. *Sing to the Lord,* London, SP&S, 2006, Vol. 13, Part 1, p. 8. "Come Home." Used with permission.
12. As with Score-Reading Exercise #2, I am again indebted to Timothy Sharp, *Precision Conducting,* pp. 19-20, for these introductory s core-reading exercises, in this case applied to band scores.

13. I first learned of this enjoyable introductory exercise in score study from composer Julie Giroux, in a compilation entitled *Composers on Composing for Band,* Volume Two, 2004, GIA Publications, pp. 77-78.

Chapter Eleven:
FROM SCORE READING TO SCORE STUDY

1. Willi Apel, and Ralph T. Daniel. *The Harvard Brief Dictionary of Music,* Washington Square Press, 1960, p. 297.
2. Louis C. Elson. *Elson's Pocket Music Dictionary,* Oliver Ditson Company, 1909, p. 142.
3. Peter Boonshaft. *Teaching Music with Passion,* Meredith Music, 2002, p. 55.
4. ibid., p. 77.
5. Elizabeth Green, as quoted in Frank Battisti, *On Becoming a Conductor,* Meredith Music, p. 38.

Chapter Twelve:
AWAKE MY VOICE AND SING!

1. Robert Shaw. "Letters to a Symphony Chorus," *The Choral Journal,* April 1986.
2. Robert Sandall. *The History of The Salvation Army,* Volume I, Thomas Nelson, 1947, p. 209.
3. Robert Sandall. *The History of The Salvation Army,* Volume II, Thomas Nelson, 1950, p. 106.
4. Henry Gariepy. *Songs in the Night,* Wm. B. Eerdmans Publishing, p. viii.
5. Gwenyth and Robert Redhead. *Hallmarks of The Salvation Army,* Australia South: Salvo Publishing, 2009, p. 89.
6. Reynolds Chapman. "Worship in Black and White," *Christianity Today,* March 2011, p. 28.
7. Gavin Whitehouse. From an article on the Sydney Staff Songster Tour of Canada in *Theme SA—Canada,* April 2005, p. 10. Songster Leader Whitehouse now resides in Philadelphia where he leads the Pendel Singers and the United States Eastern Territorial Songsters.
8. Len Ballantine. Quoted by permission from the Sydney Staff Songster 20th Anniversary booklet—*More Than a Song,* SA Australia East, p. 13.
9. These helpful insights are from interaction and correspondence with Dorothy Nancekievill, conductor of The International Staff Songsters.
10. A number of videos demonstrate physical gestures that work within the warm-up sequence, such as: *Daily Workout for a Beautiful Voice,* Charlotte Adams (Santa Barbara Music), *The Perfect Blend DVD,* Timothy Seelig (Shawnee Press) and *Ready, Set, Sing DVD,* Jefferson Johnson (Santa Barbara Publishing). In book form, *Making More Sense of How to Sing* by Alan Gumm (Meredith Music) and *The Perfect Blend* outline lots of ideas to reinforce good singing habits through physical gesture. The songster leader is encouraged to adapt these ideas to suit his or her brigade.
11. Sandra Willetts. *Beyond the Downbeat,* Abingdon Press, 2000. Choir formation diagrams extracted from pp. 56, 58, 64.
12. The vowel formation notes and associated hand gestures were gleaned over the years from various workshops and books

including *The Complete Choral Warm-up* by Russell Robinson and Jay Althouse (Alfred), *The Perfect Blend DVD,* Timothy Seelig (Shawnee Press) and two DVDs from Santa Barbara Music Publishing: *Daily Workout for a Beautiful Voice* by Charlotte Adams and *Ready, Set, Sing* by Jefferson Johnson, with helpful insights from Dr. Beatrice Holz. Chapter 5 of *Making More Sense of How to Sing* by Alan Gumm (Meredith Music) commences with a listing of vowel gestures. For ideas for creating your own vowel hand-gestures, consult the Resonance Exercises in these helpful resources.

13. "Eh," as in the word "red," creates an "open" sound. For a pure, long "A" sound without a diphthong, try the "long A," as in "chaotic."
14. This warm-up rhyme was learned in a workshop with renowned children's choir specialist Helen Kemp. Found in print in *Children Sing His Praise,* Donald Rotermund, ed. Concordia, 1985, p. 77.
15. James Jordan. *Evoking Sound–The Choral Warm-Up,* GIA, 2005, p. 15.
16. Jordan, ibid, p. 14.
17. In compiling this diction section, I have benefited particularly from two references: Madeline Marshall, *The Singer's Manual of English Diction* (Schirmer) and Sandra Willetts, *Beyond the Downbeat* (Abingdon Press), as well as helpful comments from Dr. Beatrice Holz.
18. Madeline Marshall. *The Singer's Manual of English Diction,* Schirmer, p. 139.
19. Willetts, *Downbeat,* p. 22.
20. Willetts, ibid, pp. 26–27.
21. Marshall, *Singer's Manual,* p. 64.
22. Willetts, *Downbeat,* pp. 28–29.

Chapter Thirteen:
THE EFFECTIVE SONGSTER REHEARSAL

1. *Psalms, Hymns and Spiritual Songs, Book I–No. 3,* The Salvation Army, New York. Used with permission.
2. Bettina Shepherd. *The Everything Singing Book,* Adams Media, 2008, p. 76.
3. *Songs of Praise* (formerly *Youth Song Book*) of The Salvation Army, The Salvation Army National Headquarters, 1988. Used by permission.

Chapter Fourteen:
STRIKE UP THE BAND!

1. Robert Sandall. *The History of The Salvation Army, Volume I,* Thomas Nelson, 1947, pp. 211–212.
2. Robert Sandall. *The History of the Salvation Army, Volume II,* Thomas Nelson, 1950, pp. 113–114.
3. Ronald Holz. *Brass Bands of The Salvation Army,* Streets Publishing, 2006. Adapted from the Foreword by Ray Steadman-Allen, p. vii.
4. John Philip Sousa. "Why the World Needs Bands," *Etude Magazine,* September 1930, p. 48.
5. William Himes. "The Brass Band: Dynamo or Dinosaur?" article first appeared in the 1980s.
6. A well-known exposé of the effect of Pythagorean comma on harmony is found in the first chapters of *The Craft of Musical Composition,* Associated Music Press, 1945, by Paul Hindemith. Pythagoras explored the relationship between numbers and harmony and demonstrated that one cannot tune a full circle of perfect fifths and end up on the note where you started. The small interval (or Pythagorean comma) exists between two enharmonically equivalent notes such as C or B#, amounting to roughly a quarter of a semitone.
7. David Cherniavsky. "Extract from Casals' Approach to Teaching the Cello," *Etude,* June 1953.
8. Edward Lisk. *The Creative Director,* Meredith Music Publications, 2001, p. 85.
9. Christopher Leuba. *A Study of Musical Intonation,* Prospect Publications, Sixth Printing, 1984, p. 32. This concept of perceived intonation is often identified as "pitch drift" and explained on pp. 29–30.
10. ibid., p. 34.
11. *60 Minutes* interview with Dan Rather, 1977.
12. Ronald Holz. *Brass Bands of The Salvation Army, Volume II,* Streets Publishing, 2006, p. 24.

Chapter Fifteen:
FROM SCORE STUDY TO REHEARSAL STRATEGY

1. Translation of this verse as rendered by Donald Hustad, *Jubilate,* Hope, 1981, p. 3.
2. *How Sweet the Name of Jesus Sounds,* with words by John Newton, to the tune "French," in a choral arrangement by Ronald Tremain as found in *Gems for Songsters,* No. 6, © 1960 Salvationist Publishing, p. 70.
3. The transcription for brass band by Donald Osgood of *How Sweet the Name of Jesus Sounds,* sometimes known as "French," is found in *General Series* 1491-2, © 1960 Salvationist Publishing. Reprinted in this book on pp. 6–9 of Chapter Fifteen with permission.
4. *Stella,* as arranged by Erik Silfverberg is published as *Triumph Series* 651 and in the *Favorite Triumph Series* No. 3–28, © 1964 Salvationist Publishing. Reprinted in this chapter as transposition examples and in full on pp. 11–21 with permission.

Part Four: WORSHIP LEADERSHIP

Chapter Sixteen:
PLAY ME A SONG. YOU'RE THE PIANO MAN!

1. I am grateful to Bandmaster William Himes for this helpful sequence in nurturing young pianists to play for worship, adapted from his "Keyboard Workshop" notes.
2. Some collections for beginning and intermediate level youth bands include parts for keyboard, like *First Things First* and *Unity Series* (SA, London) and the *American Instrumental Ensemble Series* (SA, USA South)
3. The "dead-weight" advice comes from Canadian Salvationist Kim Garreffa. This exercise has limited value on electronic keyboards lacking "weighted" keys, which offer little resistance to "dropped chords."
4. Ed Roseman. *Edly's Music Theory for Practical People,* Musical EdVentures, 1996, p. 55.

Chapter Seventeen:
KEYBOARD WORSHIP: THE MEETING PIANIST

1. Bram Rader. From the CD liner notes he wrote for his piano solo album, *Aspiration—To Be Like Jesus*, PBS 15, 2010.
2. I am indebted to Major Leonard Ballantine, and a presentation he titles "Piano Stylings for Worship," for this sequence of ways the keyboardist can enhance the worship experience. A written version of this presentation can be found in the Canadian Music Department's *Theme* magazine, April/May/June 2005, pp. 3–5, 9.
3. Expression used by William Himes.
4. This advice comes from Canadian Salvationist Kim Garreffa.
5. A number of these prayer meeting tips for pianists are gleaned from a Keyboard Workshop by William Himes.
6. Leonard Ballantine. "Piano Stylings for Worship," *Theme* magazine, Canadian Music Department, April/May/June 2005, p. 4.
7. Ed Roseman. *Edly's Music Theory for Practical People*, Musical Edventures, 1996, p. 47.
8. I am indebted to both Leonard Ballantine ("Piano Styling for Worship") and William Himes ("Keyboard Workshop") for this sequence of steps for modulation.
9. Himes, "Keyboard Workshop."

Chapter Eighteen:
MORE THAN A SONG

1. I have heard Bob Sorge speak on "watching the river of God flow." He also describes the same in his book *Exploring Worship*, Oasis House, 2001, pp. 87–88.
2. Ken Gire. *Windows of the Soul: Experiencing God in New Ways*, Zondervan, 1996.
3. These three test questions were adapted from Doug and Tami Flather, *The Praise and Worship Team Instant Tune-Up*, (Zondervan, 2002) pp. 46–57. The authors present similar questions as a progression: Tier 1–Atmosphere (appealing to emotions); Tier 2–Content (thoughts and themes), and Tier 3–Song direction (orientation up and/or out).
4. From a letter submitted by Benny Knoll, *Salvationist*, SP&S, December 17, 2011, p. 10.
5. Dave Williamson. *God's Singers,* in:ciite media, 2010, p. 260.
6. Sorge, *Exploring Worship,* p. 237.
7. Williamson, *God's Singers,* pp. 259–260.
8. Sorge, *Exploring Worship,* p. 239.
9. Flather, *The Praise and Worship Team Instant Tune-Up,* p. 65.
10. I am grateful to Canadian Salvationist worship leader Kim Garreffa for this series of illustrations of ways to color various verses.
11. These insights on orchestrating a worship band arrangement are gleaned from an email from Kim Garreffa, dated July 29, 2011.
12. These suggestions to enhance the stylistic approach to "arranging" come from Paul Scott, a professional bassist, professor of jazz, and soldier at the Regent Hall Corps in Britain.
13. This instrumental technique listing is adapted from *The Praise and Worship Team Instant Tune-Up,* Doug and Tami Flather, p. 67.
14. Steve Kranz. "Playing Together" http://www.themeonline.ca/e-worship-worship-team.
15. Some ideas on transitions in this section are taken from correspondence and an article by Kim Garreffa on *Transitions* at www.themeonline.ca/e-worship-worship-team, as well as from Doug and Tami Flather, *Instant Tune-Up*, pp. 68–76.
16. The essence of the discussion in this section on transitions in keys and tempos is based on Flather, *Instant Tune-Up*, p. 67–73, with specific comments on clapping found on page 73.
17. The essence of this step-by-step preparation for rehearsal planning is gleaned from Flather, *Instant Tune-Up*, pp. 98–99, combined with my own experience.
18. Sorge, *Exploring Worship*, p. 232.
19. From an email response from Richard Hayes, head of HighPower Productions, a sound reinforcement company. He also oversees installations of Salvation Army corps sound and projection systems.
20. Once again I am indebted to Doug and Tami Flather for their excellent chapter on running a worship team rehearsal found in *The Praise and Worship Team Instant Tune-Up*, pp. 103–108.

Chapter Nineteen:
THE HOLY HASSLE OF ANOTHER SUNDAY

1. Douglas R. and Tami Flather. *The Praise and Worship Instant Tune-Up,* Zondervan, 2002. Thanks also to Richard Hayes for help with this sound check sequence.
2. Richard Hayes adds: "In large rooms, the engineer may opt to put a microphone in front of the guitar cabinet, and bring the house speakers up to check the level. In smaller rooms, where the amp is simply too loud, it will need to be placed 'off-stage.' In this case, the microphone is placed in front of the now off-stage cabinet and a monitor is provided for the guitarist."
3. In-ear monitors give the front-of-house engineer or the praise band the ability to have exactly the monitor mix the band and vocalist requires, without concern for a stage monitor mix that overwhelms the vocalists or congregational singing. To facilitate this, the engineer sets up a pair of microphones directed at the congregation and brings this live component into the in-ear mix. This way the entire praise band stays connected to the worshipers.
4. Comments on "weighing the balance of levels" from an email response by Richard Hayes, dated September 14, 2012.
5. Comments from an email response by Kim Garreffa, dated October 31, 2012.
6. The use of the term, Christian Contemporary Music, or CCM is, for me, a regrettable label. Most of this genre is highly derivative from pop mediums and lacks the originality or freshness that the term "contemporary music" might connote. My hesitation is represented in the closing byline of a daily NPR radio feature "The Composer's Datebook," celebrating the birthdays of composers, which concludes, "remembering that all music was once new."
7. Much of this section on chords is gleaned from James Oestereich and Earl Pennington, *Improvising & Arranging on the Keyboard,* Prentice Hall, 1981, pp. 15–24.
8. These two details came from correspondence with British Salvationist and bass player Paul Scott.
9. Thanks to Kim Garreffa for this insight, from an email of October 31, 2012.
10. Flather, *Instant Tune-Up*, p. 26.
11. The chord box diagram format is adapted from Jake Johnson, *Chords for Kids,* Flame Tree Publishing, 2009. The author acknowledges that many guitarists also read the notated tablature, but chord boxes are used here as they give a better idea of chord shapes than tablature.

12. Garreffa, October 31, 2012 email.
13. Flather, *Instant Tune-Up,* p. 27.
14. *Songs of Fellowship,* "Guitar Chord Chart" Appendix, Kingsway Music, 1998, p. 2.
15. Thanks to Salvationist-songwriter Mark Hood for his help with the inversion and sus chord examples.
16. Dave Williamson. *God's Singers,* in:ciite media, 2010, pp. 212-213. I am indebted to Williamson's Chapter 20, titled "Head-Chart Harmony—What It Is, and How To Teach It," pp. 212-231 for the essence of these principles for singers harmonizing, as he calls them, "head-charts." To quote him, "with 'chart' being musician slang for 'arrangement,' and 'head' meaning that nothing is written down, you just make it up in your head." (p. 213)
17. Like most rules, there are exceptions. There is a trend to voice a sus chord using a 4th *with* the 3rd, such as: G, C, F, A, B. (Mark Levine, *The Jazz Piano Book,* p. 24.) Guitarists seem to prefer playing the added sus4 chords in the key of E or A.
18. Some concepts on addition and subtraction to chords given in this section are assimilated from Douglas R. and Tami Flather, *The Praise and Worship Team Instant Tune-Up,* pp. 14-25.

Part Five: THE CONDUCTOR'S TOOLBOX

Chapter Twenty:
WHERE'S THE BEAT?

1. Gunther Schuller. *Musings: The Musical Worlds of Gunther Schuller,* Oxford University Press, 1986, pp. 162-163.
2. This Riccardo Muti and the policeman story is used with permission by Maestro Muti's management, photographer Todd Rosenberg and quoted [with small bracketed adaptations for print] from an acceptance speech given in December of 2009, when Muti was recognized as *Musical America's* Musician of the Year. It is available on a You Tube clip at www.youtube.com/watch?v=SZ-G3qNmI0U.
3. Frank Battisti, *On Becoming a Conductor,* Meredith Music, 2007, p. vii.
4. ibid., p. xi.
5. Kenneth Phillips. *Basic Techniques of Conducting,* Second Edition, Oxford, 1997, pp. 39-40.
6. ibid. pp. 39-40.
7. I am indebted to Professor Gail Poch of Temple University for these images linked to the "Basic Effort Actions" (i.e. float, flick, punch) taught by Rudolf van Laban.
8. Timothy Sharp. *Precision Conducting,* Second Edition, Roger Dean, 2003, pp. 33.
9. Phillips, *Basic Techniques of Conducting,* pp. 10-11.
10. Brock McElheran. *Conducting Technique,* Oxford, 1966, p. 34.
11. ibid. pp. 31-32.
12. Sharp, *Precision Conducting,* p. x.
13. James Jordan. *Evoking Sound, Fundamentals of Choral Conducting and Rehearsing,* GIA Publications, 1996, p. 11.
14. Sharp, *Precision Conducting,* p. 34.
15. Jordan, *Evoking Sound,* p. 18.
16. Eugene Corporon. DVD *Evoking Sound,* 8:14' mark of track 2.
17. Jordan, *Evoking Sound,* p. 45.
18. James Jordan and Eugene Corporon. DVD, *The Anatomy of Conducting, Architecture and Essentials,* GIA, 2008, about the 14:05' mark.
19. Jordon, *Evoking Sound,* p. 62.
20. ibid., p. 63.
21. ibid., p. 64.
22. Sharp, *Precision Conducting,* p. 36.
23. Jordan, *Evoking Sound,* p. 18.
24. ibid., p. 95.
25. ibid., p. 73.
26. ibid., p. 73.
27. ibid., pp. 69-70.
28. ibid., pp. 70, 93-94.
29. McElheran, *Conducting Technique,* p. 8.
30. Jordon, *Evoking Sound,* p. 87.
31. James Jordon calls this a "released rebound gesture." *Evoking Sound,* p. 87.
32. *Webster's Ninth New Collegiate Dictionary,* 1990, Merriam-Webster, p. 596.
33. Tim Reynish. "The Technique of Directing," 2012 web posting.
34. Leonard Bernstein. *The Conductor's Art,* McGraw-Hill, 1965, p. 272.
35. Phillips, *Basic Techniques of Conducting,* p. 19.
36. Jordan, *Evoking Sound,* p. 72.
37. Jordan, *Evoking Sound,* p. 84.
38. McElheran, *Conducting Technique,* p. 18.
39. Jordan and Corporon, DVD, *The Anatomy of Conducting,* track 2, 1:47 mark.
40. McElheran, *Conducting Technique,* p. 32.

Chapter Twenty-One:
STICKS, STARTS, AND STOPS

1. Donald Grout. *A History of Western Music,* Third Edition, Norton, 1980, pp. 61.
2. Adapted from James Jordan. *Evoking Sound, Fundamentals of Choral Conducting and Rehearsing,* GIA Publications, 1996, p. 86.
3. Elizabeth Green. *The Modern Conductor,* Fourth Edition, Prentice Hall, 1987, p. 5.
4. ibid., p. 20.
5. This line of thinking is derived from Brock McElheran, *Conducting Technique,* Oxford, 1966, p. 13ff.
6. Frank Battisti. *On Becoming a Conductor,* Meredith Music, 2007, p. 72.
7. McElheran, *Conducting Technique,* p. 14.
8. Green, *The Modern Conductor,* pp. 6-7.
9. ibid., p. 7.
10. ibid., pp. 9-10.
11. ibid., p. 25.
12. McElheran, *Conducting Technique,* p. 14.
13. Green, *The Modern Conductor,* p. 25.
14. McElheran, *Conducting Technique,* p. 14.
15. Jordan, *Evoking Sound,* p. 153.
16. From a workshop by Jane Marshall.
17. Timothy Sharp. *Precision Conducting,* Second Edition, Roger Dean, 2003, p. 51.
18. ibid., p. 51.
19. Max Rudolph. *The Grammar of Conducting,* Third Edition, Schirmer, 1994, p. 98.
20. Sharp, *Precision Conducting,* p. 52.
21. Jordan, *Evoking Sound,* p. 131.

22. ibid., pp. 130–131.
23. ibid., p. 151.
24. *Harvard Dictionary of Music,* Fourth Edition, Harvard University/Belknap Press, 2003. p. 310.
25. McElheran, *Conducting Technique,* p. 85.
26. ibid., pp. 85–86.
27. ibid., pp. 86–87.
28. ibid., p. 87.
29. ibid., pp. 88–89.
30. ibid., p. 98.
31. ibid., p. 90.

Chapter Twenty-Two:
GESTURE AND EXPRESSION

1. James Jordan. *Evoking Sound: Fundamentals of Choral Conducting and Rehearsing,* GIA, 1996, pp. 105–106.
2. Wilhelm Ehmann. *Choral Directing,* Augsburg, p. 126.
3. Max Rudolph. *The Grammar of Conducting,* Third Edition, Schirmer, 1994, p. 359.
4. Frank Battisti. *On Becoming a Conductor,* Meredith Music, 2007, p. 98.
5. Rudolph, *The Grammar of Conducting,* p. 359.
6. Erich Leinsdorf. *The Composer's Advocate,* Yale University Press, 1997, p. 101.
7. Rudolph, *The Grammar of Conducting,* p. 258.
8. Elizabeth Green and Mark Gibson, *The Modern Conductor,* Seventh Edition, Pearson Education, 2004, pp. 69–70.
9. Rudolph, *The Grammar of Conducting,* p. 359.
10. ibid., p. 360.
11. ibid., p. 99.
12. Green and Gibson, *The Modern Conductor,* p. 32.
13. Tempos and definitions adapted from Timothy Sharp, *Precision Conducting,* Second Edition, Roger Dean, 2003, p. 45.
14. Brock McElheran. *Conducting Technique,* Oxford, 1966, p. 42.
15. ibid., p. 43.
16. Variations in tempo definitions adapted from Timothy Sharp, *Precision Conducting,* and Kenneth Phillips, *Basic Techniques of Conducting,* Second Edition, Oxford, 1997, p. 42.
17. McElheran, *Conducting Technique,* pp. 80–81.
18. Phillips, p. 202.
19. Rudolph, *The Grammar of Conducting,* p. 131.
20. McElheran, *Conducting Technique,* p. 76.
21. "More or less beats charts" adapted from Brock McElheran, *Conducting Technique,* p. 81.
22. These are three samples of what Rudolf van Laban calls "Basic Effort Actions," useful in describing gestural movements. Laban teaches that movement occurs in *space* and with an attitude toward *time,* and is accomplished with a degree of strength or *weight.* All of these components are executed with a degree of *flow* or control. By combining one aspect from each of the three elements of weight, space, and time, Laban formulated eight different full efforts. The other five are: Dab, Glide, Slash, Press, and Wring. From Conducting classnotes with Professor Gail Poch.
23. Jordan, *Evoking Sound,* p. vv.
24. McElheran, *Conducting Technique,* p. 43.
25. Rudolph, *The Grammar of Conducting,* p. 21.
26. Jordan, *Evoking Sound,* p. 193.
27. ibid., p. 103.
28. Sharp, *Precision Conducting,* p. 47.
29. "Character Terms" definitions adapted from Sharp, *Precision Conducting,* p. 50, and Phillips, *Basic Techniques of Conducting,* p. 71.
30. Rudolph, *The Grammar of Conducting,* p. 23.
31. Sharp, *Precision Conducting,* p. 48.
32. Phillips, *Basic Techniques of Conducting,* p. 202.
33. Green and Gibson, *The Modern Conductor,* p. 51.
34. Rudolph, *The Grammar of Conducting,* p. 16.
35. McElheran, *Conducting Technique,* p. 43.
36. Jordan, *Evoking Sound,* p. 103.
37. McElheran, *Conducting Technique,* p. 43.
38. Jordan, *Evoking Sound,* p. 193.
39. Green and Gibson, *The Modern Conductor,* p. 64.
40. Rudolph, *The Grammar of Conducting,* p. 13.
41. ibid., p. 86.
42. ibid., p. 185.
43. Jordan, *Evoking Sound,* p. 193.
44. McElheran, *Conducting Technique,* p. 43.
45. Sharp, *Precision Conducting,* p. 49.
46. Rudolph, *The Grammar of Conducting,* p. 86.
47. Sharp, *Precision Conducting,* p. 49.
48. ibid., p. 50.
49. McElheran, *Conducting Technique,* p. 37.
50. Green and Gibson, *The Modern Conductor,* p. 71.
51. McElheran, *Conducting Technique,* p. 37.
52. ibid., p. 37 and Green and Gibson, *The Modern Conductor,* p. 71.
53. Sharp, *Precision Conducting,* p. 36.
54. McElheran, *Conducting Technique,* p. 38.
55. Green and Gibson, *The Modern Conductor,* p. 72.
56. McElheran, *Conducting Technique,* p. 46.
57. ibid., p. 47.
58. This list is gleaned from Green and Gibson, *The Modern Conductor,* p. 74, and McElheran, *Conducting Technique,* p. 46.
59. *Harvard Dictionary of Music,* Fourth Edition, Harvard Press, p. 532.
60. Green and Gibson, *The Modern Conductor,* p. 75.
61. Phillips, *Basic Techniques of Conducting,* p. 203.
62. Green and Gibson, *The Modern Conductor,* p. 75.
63. Phillips, *Basic Techniques of Conducting,* p. 203.
64. Green and Gibson, *The Modern Conductor,* p. 53.
65. McElheran, *Conducting Technique,* p. 50.
66. Green and Gibson, *The Modern Conductor,* p. 54.
67. McElheran, *Conducting Technique,* p. 47, "Count to 10."
68. Green and Gibson, *The Modern Conductor,* p. 76, no. 5.
69. Battisti, *On Becoming a Conductor,* p. 101.
70. Jordan, *Evoking Sound,* p. 103.
71. McElheran, *Conducting Technique,* p. 39.
72. "Dynamic Terms" definitions from Phillips, *Basic Techniques of Conducting,* p. 60.
73. McElheran, *Conducting Technique,* p. 40.
74. "Changing Dynamic Terms" definitions from Phillips, *Basic Techniques of Conducting,* p. 61.
75. Rudolph, *The Grammar of Conducting,* p. 72.
76. Green and Gibson, *The Modern Conductor,* p. 73.
77. ibid., p. 73.
78. Rudolph, *The Grammar of Conducting,* p. 269.
79. McElheran, *Conducting Technique,* p. 42.
80. Rudolph, *The Grammar of Conducting,* p. 278.

81. Battisti, *On Becoming a Conductor,* p. 99.
82. Sharp, *Precision Conducting,* p. 49.
83. Phillips, *Basic Techniques of Conducting,* p. 136.
84. McElheran, *Conducting Technique,* p. 83.
85. Battisti, *On Becoming a Conductor,* p. 102.
86. McElheran, *Conducting Technique,* p. 44–45.
87. ibid., p. 42.
88. ibid.. p. 45.
89. ibid., p. 46.

Chapter Twenty-Three:
LISTEN AND RESPOND

1. Frank Battisti. *On Becoming a Conductor,* Meredith Music, 2007, p. 69.
2. Max Rudolph. *The Grammar of Conducting Technique,* The Third Edition. Schirmer, 1994, p. 323.
3. Webster's New Collegiate Dictionary.
4. Battisti, *On Becoming a Conductor,* p. 72.
5. Nadia Boulanger, as quoted in Don Campbell, *Master Teacher,* The Pastoral Press, 1984, p. 70.
6. Battisti, *On Becoming a Conductor,* p. 72.
7. Peter Boonshaft. *Teaching Music with Promise,* Meredith Music, 2009, p. 142. In this chapter Boonshaft also recommends walking around the ensemble during rehearsal, actually listening for what students hear from their seats.
8. James Jordan. *Evoking Sound: Fundamentals of Choral Conducting and Rehearsing,* GIA Publications, 1996, pp. 139–140.
9. McElheran, *Conducting Technique,* p. 95.
10. Battisti, *On Becoming a Conductor,* p. 126.
11. McElheran, *Conducting Technique,* p. 101.
12. ibid., p. 7.
13. ibid., pp. 7–9.
14. ibid., p. 8.
15. Jordan, *Evoking Sound,* pp. 139–141.
16. Question framed from a comment by Dennis Russell Davies in Jeannine Wager, *Conductors in Conversation,* G. K. Hall, 1991, p. 45.
17. Battisti, *On Becoming a Conductor,* p. 70.
18. ibid., p. 72.
19. ibid., p. 72.
20. ibid., p. 72.
21. ibid., p. 72.
22. Rudolph, *The Grammar of Conducting,* p. 332.
23. Peter Boonshaft. *Teaching Music with Promise,* Meredith Music, 2009, p. 98.
24. David Newell. *Classroom Management in the Music Room,* Kjos, p. 207.
25. Boonshaft, *Teaching Music with Promise,* pp. 92–93.
26. Newell, *Classroom Management in the Music Room,* p. 208.
27. The choirmaster was John Bertalot, teaching a workshop about his *Five Wheels to Sightsinging* book at Westminster Choir College. While he was applying the "absolutely correct" directive to positively affirm sight-reading passages, I have found it genuinely useful when pressing to get *all* the notes, as well as expression indicated below and above the staff.
28. Boonshaft, *Teaching Music with Promise,* p. 98.
29. ibid., pp. 105, 107.
30. ibid., p. 102.
31. ibid., p. 107.
32. Brock McElheran, in *Conducting Technique,* states that we need to drive home to our ensemble that the time to watch the conductor most is when sight-reading music for the first time (p. 107).
33. Rudolph, *The Grammar of Conducting,* p. 332.
34. ibid., p. 332.
35. ibid., p. 332.
36. ibid., p. 333.
37. ibid., p. 333.
38. ibid., p. 333.
39. McElheran, *Conducting Technique,* p. 107.
40. ibid., p. 107.
41. Rudolph, *The Grammar of Conducting,* p. 337.
42. McElheran, *Conducting Technique,* p. 40.
43. After years of not always responding very well to questions during my rehearsals, I came across a fine article by Kelsey Menehan, based on a survey of choral conductors, entitled "Is it okay to ask questions during rehearsals?" (*The Voice,* Winter 2012/13, pp. 28–31) from which I organized this segment.
44. McElheran, *Conducting Technique,* p. 103.
45. ibid., p. 104.
46. ibid., p. 104.
47. ibid., p. 104.
48. Rudolph, *The Grammar of Conducting,* p. 380.
49. McElheran, *Conducting Technique,* pp. 104–105.
50. Elizabeth Green. *The Modern Conductor,* Fourth Edition, Prentice-Hall, 1987, p. 219.
51. McElheran, *Conducting Technique,* p. 123.
52. Newell, *Classroom Management in the Music Room,* p. 208.
53. James Barnes workshop, Midwest Band and Orchestra Clinic, December, 1991.
54. Rudolph, *The Grammar of Conducting,* p. 324.
55. Green, *The Modern Conductor,* p. 219.
56. ibid., p. 219.
57. ibid., pp. 222–223.
58. ibid., pp. 220–221.
59. ibid., p. 223.
60. Jordan, *Evoking Sound,* p. 139.
61. Battisti, *On Becoming a Conductor,* p. 70.
62. McElheran, *Conducting Technique,* p. 124.
63. ibid., p. 126.

Postlude:
PASSING THE BATON

1. My thanks to Major Colin DeVault for his helpful thoughts on this passage from Hebrews.
2. As recorded by George Scott Railton, *General Booth,* quoted from *A Salvationist's Treasury,* Henry Gariepy, Crest Books, 2000, p. 301. These words of farewell from William Booth prefaced his famous "I'll Fight" speech.
3. *American Heritage Dictionary of the English Language,* Fourth Edition, Houghton-Mifflin, 2000.
4. Mark Dowds. "When the Old Armour Doesn't Fit," *Horizons,* Jan-Feb, 2003, p. 5.
5. George Goethals, ed. "Sociobiology of Leadership," *Encyclopedia of Leadership,* Volume 4, p. 1465–1466.

6. Eugene Peterson. *Run with the Horses,* InterVarsity Press, 1983, p. 40.
7. Matthew Josephson. *Edison,* McGraw-Hill, 1959, from the Readers' Digest Condensed Version, 1978, pp. 411–420.
8. Quoted from Paul Theroux. "How Apple Revolutionized the World," *Newsweek,* September 5, 2011, p. 36.
9. Quoted from John C. Maxwell. *Everyone Communicates, Few Connect,* Thomas Nelson, 2010, p. 205.
10. Jeffery Sonnenfield. Dell quote and this line of thought gleaned from, "The Genius Dilemma," *Newsweek,* January 31, 2011, pp. 13, 15.
11. Peterson, *Run with the Horses,* p. 37.
12. Maxwell, *Everyone Communicates, Few Connect,* pp. 110–111. Also Larry Osborne, *Sticky Teams,* Zondervan, 2010. Chapter 8 is entitled *Making Room at the Top: Why Young Eagles Don't Stay,* pp. 113–124.
13. From an interview with former Sydney Staff Songster Leader Graeme Press in *More Than a Song ... 20th Anniversary* brochure article "Seeking God's Face."
14. As related by Bill Himes at the Territorial Music Secretary's Conference, October 27, 2011. Dr. William Revelli served as Director of Bands at the University of Michigan from 1935–1971. He was a legendary figure in raising the standard of American school banding and music education.
15. These questions are adapted from Rory Noland, *The Heart of the Artist,* Zondervan, 1999.
16. Larry Osborne. *Finding, Developing and Empowering Leadership in Your Church* Seminar, Youth Specialties Conference, 2000.
17. Quote of Pastor Adam Henry, in Maxwell, *Everyone Communicates, Few Connect,* p. 203.
18. Osborne, *Finding, Developing and Empowering* Seminar.
19. Craig Buchan. "Leeds Central Band," *Music Ministries Unit Newsletter,* December 2012.
20. Osborne, *Finding, Developing and Empowering* Seminar.
21. Dr. Julie Reams, Director of Spiritual Formation, DC Metro Church, Alexandria, Virginia.
22. Gary Demarest. *The Communicator's Commentary, Volume 9* on 1, 2 Thessalonians, 1, 2 Timothy, and Titus, Word, 1984, p. 259.
23. The Leadership Rainbow used with permission of Dr. Jack Stephenson, senior pastor at Anona United Methodist Church, Anona, Florida.
24. From director's notes by Terry Nolan for *A Little Night Music,* Walnut Street Theater, Philadelphia, Spring 2013.
25. Joy Webb. *Bridge of Songs,* Salvation Army–United Kingdom, 2000, p. 122.
26. This line of questioning is gleaned from the interview process Graeme Press used with the Sydney Staff Songsters.
27. Nancy Beach. *An Hour on Sunday,* Zondervan, 2004, Ch. 8, p. 146.
28. Maxwell, *Everyone Communicates, Few Connect,* p. 205.
29. M. Scott Peck. *Further Along the Road Less Traveled,* Simon & Schuster, 1993, p. 62.
30. Maxwell, *Everyone Communicates, Few Connect,* p. 50.
31. Osborne, *Finding, Developing and Empowering* Seminar.
32. John C. Maxwell. *The 17 Indisputable Laws of Teamwork: Embrace Them and Empower Your Team,* Thomas Nelson, p. 112.
33. Maxwell, *Everyone Communicates, Few Connect,* p. 217.
34. Sam Horn. *Tongue Fu,* St. Martin's Press, 1996, p. 48.
35. These principles are gleaned from the "Pride" section of the DC Metro Church: Growth Track, 301: Freedom by Kathryn Luse.
36. John Gowans. *There's a boy here ...* The Salvation Army, 2002, Ch. 19, p. 128.
37. Bennie Goodwin. *The Effective Leader* booklet, Intervarsity Press.
38. J. Robert Clinton. *The Making of a Leader,* NavPress, 1988, p. 205.
39. These composite youth and senior band statistics are for the year 2014 from *The Salvation Army Year Book 2015,* The Salvation Army, International Headquarters, p. 20.
40. Adapted from Gary Demarest, *The Communicator's Commentary, Volume 9,* p. 253.
41. Peck, *Further Along the Road,* p. 98.
42. Henry Gariepy. *Mobilized by God–The History of The Salvation Army, Volume 8,* Eerdmans, 2000, p. 219.
43. *Character Sketches, Volume III,* 1985 Basic Institute for Youth Conflicts, p. 168.
44. Demarest, *Communicator's Commentary, Vol. 9,* p. 255.
45. William Barclay. *The Letters to Timothy, Titus and Philemon,* Revised Edition, Westminster Press, 1975, p. 163.
46. Sid Davis. "What I Know Now That I Wish I'd Known Then," *The Chorister,* Volume 57, Number 5, p. 13.
47. Clinton, *Making of A Leader,* p. 201.
48. The National Capitol Band is comprised of Salvationist musicians from the Washington, DC and Northern Virginia Division. This retirement service took place at the Alexandria, VA Corps on July 18, 2010.
49. "This I Know" based on Jim Anderson's setting of "Jesus Loves Me," in a paraphrase by William Himes was subsequently published by the USA East Territory in the *American Band Journal 66,* No. 286.
50. Comment by Kathryn Luse in an email to the author, dated March 13, 2013, speculating on General William Booth's Farewell Address, "where he speaks of 'the Army's marvelous success being the work of God, and that the General has been His servant.'"

| APPENDIX & RESOURCES

ONLINE APPENDIX AND AUDIO RESOURCES

The online appendix and audio files are organized in order of appearance within each chapter, and are found at [www.music.saconnects.org]. This permits the reader easy access to supporting reference materials and/or audio demonstrations of many of the musical examples while studying a chapter. In the course of the reading, these are indicated either in the body text or in the sidebar as helpful cross references. Not all chapters have appendix or audio supporting resources.

Appendix materials are identified by number. For instance, Appendix 8.5 is the fifth appendix reference for Chapter Eight. These titles appear in **bold**:

    Appendix 8.5 **Major and Minor Scale** sheets—Correlated by number for youth bands

Audio demonstrations of musical examples are indicated sequentially by title with the page(s) on which the printed music appears noted on the left margin of the listing below. These titles appear in ***bolded italic***:

Chapter Eight online audio demonstration:

    pp. 14–15 ***This Little Light of Mine*** (arr. Hollie Ruthberg) from *38 Sunday School Choruses for Young Bands*

Part One: MUSIC MINISTERS

Chapter Two:
SUNDAY MORNING

    Appendix 2.1 **Models of Worship Design**

Chapter Three:
HAND ME DOWN MY SILVER TRUMPET

    Appendix 3.1 **Entrance and Practice Policies**

Chapter Five:
THEN SINGS MY SOUL!

Chapter Five online audio accompaniments for song leading introduction:

    p. 119   ***Jesus Loves Me***, one verse only, no chorus
    p. 120   ***Boston***, first four bars only
                Lobe Den Herron, one full verse
    p. 121   ***Praise My Soul***, one full verse

Carolers' Favorites online audio accompaniments for practicing beat patterns:

    p. 122   ***Hark the Herald Angels***
                Angels from the Realms
                Angels We Have Heard on High
                Jingle Bells—just one chorus, no verse
    p. 123   ***Joy to the World***
                Deck the Halls
                Away in a Manger
                The First Noel
    p. 124   ***O Christmas Tree***
                Carolers' Favorites
                © 2006 The Salvation Army, USA Eastern Territory
                Used with permission

Part Two: YOUTH MUSIC MINISTRY

Chapter Six:
LET THE CHILDREN SING!

    Appendix 6.1 **Interval Reference Chart**
    Appendix 6.2 **Rhythmic Syllables Systems**
    Appendix 6.3 **Sequence of Voice Levels**
                        Six-level M.A.P. Voice Curriculum
    Appendix 6.4 **Let the Children Sing!**
                        Getting Started (video demonstration)

Chapter Seven:
THE RIGHT SONG FOR YOUR KIDS!

    Appendix 7.1 **Let the Children Sing!**
                        The Intermediate Group
                        (video introducing part-singing)

Chapter Seven online audio demonstrations on how to teach a singing company song:

    pp. 151–153 ***Win Them One by One*** (Harold Burgmayer)
                      from *Children's Praise*, Volume 13
                      © 2010 The Salvation Army, USA Southern Territory
                      Used with permission
    pp. 159–162 ***They Should Know*** (Ivor Bosanko) from
                      New Songs for Young People, March 1985
                      © 1985 Salvationist Supplies & Publishing
                      Used with permission

Chapter Eight:
ALL HAIL TO DANIEL'S BAND

Appendix 8.1	**M.A.P. Brass Guidelines** A six-level curriculum	
Appendix 8.2	**Rental/Loan Instrument Agreement**	
Appendix 8.3	**Sample Practice Contract**	
Appendix 8.4	**Home Practice Suggestions** *For parents and caregivers*—How you can help your children's progress on their instrument *For students*—Home practice suggestions	
Appendix 8.5	**Major and Minor Scale sheets**—Correlated by number for ease of use in youth band rehearsals	

Chapter Eight online audio demonstration:

pp. 178–179	**This Little Light of Mine** (arr. Hollie Ruthberg) from *38 Sunday School Choruses for Young Bands* © 2016 The Salvation Army, USA Eastern Territory Used with permission

Chapter Nine:
GOD'S SPECIAL INSTRUMENTS

Appendix 9.1	**Brass Treble Clef Fingering Chart**
Appendix 9.2	**Trombone Positions Charts** (for treble and bass clefs)
Appendix 9.3	**What's the Buzz About Buzzing?** (Bill Quick)
Appendix 9.4	**Major and Minor Scales** correlated by number (in Bb, Eb and C bass clef pitch) for use with ensembles
Appendix 9.5	**Matched Grip Hand Position** (Bill Quick)
Appendix 9.6	**Traditional Grip** (Bill Quick)
Appendix 9.7	**Snare Drum Rudiments** A six-level sequence (Bill Quick)
Appendix 9.8	**Arban's Companion**—An abridged compilation of 24 lessons organized sequentially from the *Arban's Complete Conservatory Method*.
Appendix 9.9	**Guide for Teaching and Rehearsing in Spanish-Speaking Cultures**

Part Three: ADULT MUSIC MINISTRY

Chapter Ten:
WHAT'S THE SCORE?

Chapter Ten online audio demonstrations on how to read a band and vocal score:

pp. 206–207	**Nothing But Thy Blood** introduction (Donna Peterson, arr. Wm. Himes) from *Hallelujah Choruses* No. 98 © 2000 The Salvation Army, Des Plaines, Illinois Used with permission
pp. 210–213	**Come Home**, verse three only (Chris Mallett) from *Sing to the Lord,* Volume 13, Part 1 © 2006 Salvationist Supplies & Publishing Used with permission Four examples for Step #4 and one for Step #5.
p. 215	**What a Friend**, cornet melody line, then melody line with euphonium countermelody.
p. 217	**What a Friend**, opening bars (Erik Leidzén) from *American Band Journal*, No. 52 © The Salvation Army, New York Used with permission
p. 218	**I'm in His Hands**, final refrain (Stanley Ditmer/Phil Laeger) from *Psalms, Hymns and Spiritual Songs* © 2006 The Salvation Army, New York Used with permission
pp. 220–221	**Trio to God's Children** (William Himes) from *Triumph Series,* No. 825 © 1978 Salvationist Supplies & Publishing Used with permission

Chapter Eleven:
FROM SCORE READING TO SCORE STUDY

Appendix 11.1	**Glossary of Salvation Army Musical Forms**

Chapter Eleven online audio demonstrations on developing score reading skills:

pp. 227–230	**God's Children**, full march (William Himes) from *Triumph Series,* No. 825 © 1978 Salvationist Supplies & Publishing Used with permission
pp. 233–235	**What a Friend**, three excerpts (Erik Leidzén) from *American Band Journal*, No. 52 © The Salvation Army, New York Used with permission
p. 237	**All for Thee** (Paul Kellner) from *The Musical Salvationist* © 1976 Salvationist Supplies & Publishing Used with permission

| APPENDIX & RESOURCES

pp. 238–240 **Come Home** (Chris Mallett)
verse three demonstration from
Sing to the Lord, Volume 13, Part 1
© 2006 Salvationist Supplies & Publishing
Used with permission

Chapter Twelve:
AWAKE MY VOICE AND SING!

Appendix 12.1 **International Phonetic Alphabet** (IPA)

Chapter Thirteen:
THE EFFECTIVE SONGSTER REHEARSAL

Appendix 13.1 **Fixes for Choir**

Chapter Thirteen online audio demonstration of:

pp. 273–277 **Only This I Ask** (Graeme Press) from *Psalms, Hymns and Spiritual Songs,* Book 1, No. 3
© 2006 The Salvation Army, New York
Used with permission

Appendix 13.2 **Rehearsal Plans for Songster Leaders**—
Emphasizing Elementary Music-Reading
When I Survey the Wondrous Cross
(Isasc Watts/Lowell Mason, tune: Boston)
A simple two-part "re-voicing" from *The Youth Songbook (Songs of Praise),* No. 48
© 1988 The Salvation Army, Verona, New Jersey
Used with permission
To God Be the Glory (Fanny Crosby/Donna Peterson) from *Psalms, Hymns and Spiritual Songs,* Book 1, No. 1
© 2006 The Salvation Army, New York
Used with permission
Outside Your Door (Janette Smart/Terry Camsey) from *Psalms, Hymns and Spiritual Songs,* Book 1, No. 4
© 2006 The Salvation Army, New York
Used with permission
Do Lord (Traditional, arr. Vernon Post) from *The Youth Songbook (Songs of Praise),* No. 239
© 1988 The Salvation Army, Verona, New Jersey
Used with permission

Appendix 13.3 **Summary of Voice Ranges and Tessitura**

Chapter Fourteen:
STRIKE UP THE BAND!

Appendix 14.1 **Technique Tips for Concert Percussion** (Bill Quick)
Appendix 14.2 **Alternate Fingerings/Positions**
Appendix 14.3 **Sample Subscription Form**

Chapter Fifteen:
FROM SCORE STUDY TO REHEARSAL STRATEGY

Chapter Fifteen online audio demonstration of:

p. 314 **How Sweet the Name**, choral version (Ronald Tremain) from *The Musical Salvationist*
© 1947 Salvationist Supplies & Publishing
Choral-organ recording from *The Majesty and Glory of Your Name* by the Chelmsford Songsters
Used with permission

pp. 318–321 **How Sweet the Name**, brass band version (Ronald Tremain, arr. Donald Osgood) from *General Series,* No. 1491(2)
© 1960 Salvationist Supplies & Publishing
Brass band recording from *Trumpet of Jesus* by Norridge Citadel Band
Used with permission

pp. 329–335 **Stella** (Erik Silfverberg) from *Triumph Series,* No. 651 or *Favorite Triumph Series* No. 2—No. 27
© 1964 Salvationist Supplies & Publishing
Used with permission

Appendix 15.1 **What a Friend** full brass band score for piano reduction. (Erik Leidzén) from *American Band Journal,* No. 52
© The Salvation Army, New York
Used with permission

Part Four: WORSHIP LEADERSHIP

Chapter Sixteen:
PLAY ME A SONG. YOU'RE THE PIANO MAN!

Chapter Sixteen online audio piano demonstrations by Eric Dina:

p. 340 **Fewster** (arr. Harold Burgmayer) demonstration of pedaling, first eight bars from *Encore* piano offertory album
© 2012 The Salvation Army, USA Western Territory
Used with permission

pp. 341–343 **Scales and Cadences** C scale with two hands, C scale in contrary motion, Using I-IV-V-I cadences, **The B-I-B-L-E** and **Yes, Jesus Loves Me**

Appendix 16.1 **Piano Scale Sheets with I-IV-V-I Cadences**

pp. 344–345 **Playing by Ear** sequence using **God is So Good**; I-IV-V chords in solfege

pp. 345–346 **Scales Expand into Triads** A third above (**Sweet Hour of Prayer**/*Scales in thirds*), A sixth below (**Boston**/*Scales in sixths*/**Joy to the World**)

pp. 347–348 **A Triad as Stacked Thirds** Scale in triads, **Joy to the World** in tenths, Parallel motion in sixths, Scales in triads, I-IV-I-V-I chord progressions

p. 349 **Chords Can Be Inverted** "Dead weight" drops, Scale triads in inversion, Harmonizing in parallel motion

Appendix 16.2 **Piano Chords in Inversions**

pp. 350–352	**Inversions Help Us "Voice-Lead"** Voice-lead by step, Substituting secondary chords, Alternative minor chords, **The Well is Deep, Oh Susannah, Hyfrydol** (in I-IV-V, with minor "cousin" chords), I-vi-ii-V-I in inversions
pp. 352–353	16 Bars Rest—**Basic Chord Progressions** **Be Thou My Vision** **Teach Me How to Love Thee**
pp. 353–354	**Dominant and Dominant Seventh (V^7) Chords** The dominant chord, The dominant seventh chord, Tendency tones, Resolution of the dominant seventh, Broken chord inversion of dominant sevenths, C major cadences in three inversions
Appendix 16.3	**V7 Chord in Cadences**
Appendix 16.4	**Inversion of V7 Chords**
Appendix 16.5	**How to Play from a Lead Sheet**
Appendix 16.6	**M.A.P. Piano Guidelines** A six-level piano curriculum

Chapter Seventeen:
KEYBOARD WORSHIP: THE MEETING PIANIST

Chapter Seventeen online audio piano demonstrations by Eric Dina:

pp. 357–358	**Piano Worship Examples**, Introduction, Adjusting the key, Reprise a meaningful phrase
pp. 358–359	**The Art of Piano PRAYing** using **Teach Me How to Love Thee**, Underscore for prayer, Seque out of prayer, Simplified transition, Chord pads, Male voice range underscore
pp. 360–363	**Hands On! Elaborating on the Piano Tune Book** Simple arpeggiation using **Fairest Lord Jesus**, Elaboration using **How Great Thou Art** and **Hendon**, Octave doubling using **It is Well, Joy in The Salvation Army** and **Make Me A Blessing, I Have Decided to Follow Jesus** (in four styles)
pp. 366–367	**Applying the Circle of Fifths at the Keyboard Morning Has Broken**, Chords "under the hands," I IV V I Cadence using **The Light Has Come**, Minor cousins using **Fairest Lord Jesus**
p. 367-368	**Added Sevenths** Diatonic seventh chords, Major sevenths, Minor sevenths, Dominant seventh, Diminished seventh, Voice-leading using seventh chords, Chord substitutions using major and minor sevenths
pp. 368–369	**Modulation** Modulating by fourths and fifths using **Spirit of the Living God/Spirit of God**, Modulating by whole and half steps using **Savior Like a Shepherd** and **Ottawa**, Use of the pivot chord, IV/V and mediant modulations
pp. 372–373	**Less is More** Accompanying soloists and songsters, Less pitches using **Make My Heart a Garden, Let Us With a Gladsome Mind** and **The Well is Deep**, Warmup modulation sequence
Appendix 17.1	**Choral Warm-Up Piano Accompaniments** Notated and audio versions

Chapter Eighteen:
MORE THAN A SONG

Chapter Eighteen online audio piano demonstrations by Eric Dina:

p. 384	**Bless His Holy Name** using "watered down" and "correct" chords
p. 386	**Lead Sheets** using **God is So Good** and **Love Round**
p. 388	Shifts to minor mode using **Praise to the Lord, the Almighty** and **Be Thou My Vision**
p. 390	**Link** between **How Great is Our God** with **How Great Thou Art**, and **Great is the Lord** with **He is Exalted**
p. 391	**Be Thou My Vision** in 4/4 time **Modulating by Half and Whole Steps**
Appendix 18.1	**Quick Reference Modulation Guide**

Chapter Nineteen:
THE HOLY HASSLE OF ANOTHER SUNDAY

Chapter Nineteen online audio piano demonstrations by Eric Dina:

p. 410–411	**Piano Stylings** examples [A to H]
p. 411	**Hearing the Color of Chords**, using major, minor, diminished and augmented chords, Suspensions, Seventh chords, Dominant seventh resolution in minor
Appendix 19.1	**M.A.P. Guitar** curriculum (six levels) **M.A.P. Ukulele** curriculum (Beginner Levels Primer and One only)
pp. 415-416	**Singing Harmonies** Voices in parallel motion using **Joyful, Joyful, Boogie Woogie Bugle Boy** and **Wade in the Water**, Gospel harmony (three excerpts), Rock and contemporary worship vocalizations based on **Be Thou My Vision**
pp. 419	**Vocal Stylings** using **Joy to the World**

Part Five: THE CONDUCTOR'S TOOLBOX

Chapter Twenty:
WHERE'S THE BEAT?

Chapter Twenty online audio hymn tune excerpts for practicing legato, staccato and marcato beat patterns:

p. 431	**Lathbury**, first four bars **In My Heart There Rings a Melody**, at chorus, first four bars **Sound the Battle Cry**, at chorus, first four bars
p. 433	The FOUR Pattern **Boston**, one verse **Standing on the Promises**, one verse with no chorus **Storm the Forts**, phrases 1, 2 and 4

pp. 434–435	The THREE Pattern	
	Slane, one verse	
	Ash Grove, one verse	
	Come Thou Almighty King, one verse	
pp. 436–437	The TWO Pattern	
	Count Your Blessings, verse only, no chorus	
	Praise Him! Praise Him! last eight bars of refrain	
	Praise My Soul, one verse	
pp. 438	The SIX Pattern	
	Healing Stream, one verse	
	Trusting As the Moments Fly, one verse and chorus	

Chapter Twenty-One:
STICKS, STARTS, AND STOPS

Chapter Twenty-One online audio examples of phrasal stops and fermatas:

p. 462	**Gift for His Altar** (Leslie Condon) pickup to A, first four bars only *General Series,* No. 1771
	© 1983 Salvationist Supplies & Publishing
	Used with permission
	Whiter Than the Snow (Mike Burn)
	© 1998 Daybreak Music
	Used with permission
p. 463	**Gift for His Altar**, pickup to fourth bar of F through two bars before G
	Gift for His Altar, pickup to three before letter I, fade at I
p. 464	**Gift for His Altar**, pickup to two before letter B, fade at bar 2 of B
	Gift for His Altar, pickup to two before letter F, fade at second bar of F

Chapter Twenty-Two:
GESTURE AND EXPRESSION

Chapter Twenty-Two online audio examples:

pp. 472–474	**Tempo transitions**
p. 488	**Canticle** (arr. Harold Burgmayer), measures 15 to 30
p. 489	**Triumph of Peace** (Eric Ball), 2 bars before A *Festival Series,* No. 130
	© 1939 Salvationist Supplies & Publishing
	Used with permission
p. 495	**Triumph of Peace**, Letter G, first two bars
p. 496	**The Well is Deep** (arr. Norman Bearcroft), Final phrase, *The Musical Salvationist,* April 1981
	© 1981 Salvationist Supplies & Publishing
	Used with permission
p. 498	**Be Still My Soul/Finlandia** (Jean Sibelius), first eight bars

Chapter Twenty-Three:
LISTEN AND RESPOND

Chapter Twenty-Three online audio examples:

p. 504	**Lord, Teach Us How to Pray** (James Curnow) four brief excerpts *The Musical Salvationist,* July 1978
	© 1981 Salvationist Supplies & Publishing
	Used with permission
Appendix 23.1	**Conducting Evaluation Form**
p. 518	**Sound Out the Proclamation** (Eric Ball) Letter M & Letter O, *General Series,* No. 1098
	© 1935 Salvationist Supplies & Publishing
	Used with permission
p. 519	**Praise** (Wilfred Heaton) Letter A, first 8 bars *Festival Series,* No. 163
	© 1949 Salvationist Supplies & Publishing
	Used with permission
	The Children's Friend (Erik Leidzén) Letter M to end *Festival Series,* No. 242
	© 1959 Salvationist Supplies & Publishing
	Used with permission
pp. 521–522	Excerpts from **Mourning Into Dancing** (Johnny Walker, arr. Len Ballantine)
	© 1992 Integrity's Praise
	Used with permission

Postlude:
PASSING THE BATON

Appendix 24.1	**The Beat Goes On!** (Words by Kevin Sims and Music by Harold Burgmayer) in audio and print version, **Children's Praise,** Volume 14
	© 2014 Salvationist Supplies & Publishing
	Reprinted with permission

SCRIPTURE INDEX

GENESIS
4:21, p. 57

EXODUS
31:1–5, p. 57
33:15, p. 378

NUMBERS
10:1–2, pp. 70–71
10:8, p. 71

JOSHUA
3:5, p. 57

1 SAMUEL
7:12, p. 107
16:7, p. 20

2 SAMUEL
24:24, p. 53

1 KINGS
19:14, p. 19
19:18, p. 19

1 CHRONICLES
6:31–32, p. 1
15:22, p. 313
25:6–7, p. 166
25:8, p. 166

2 CHRONICLES
29:26, p. 167
29:28, p. 167
29:35-36, p. 167
31:21, p. 168

PSALMS
8:2a, p. 127
24, p. 40
27, pp. 272, 273
27:4, p. 5
33:3, p. 53
46:4, p. 378
68:24–26, p. 27
69:9, p. 66
90:17, p. 540
92:4, p. 377
98:4, p. 551
98:6, p. 551
100:4, pp. 43, 49
136, p. 40
139:13, p. 531
139:14, p. 520
145:4, pp. 165, 167, 168
147:1, p. 103

PROVERBS
15:22, p. 60
16:21, p. 543

ECCLESIASTES
4:6, p. 545

SONG OF SOLOMON
1:3b, p. 316

ISAIAH
6:8, p. 19
6:13, p. 19
30:15b, p. 546
30:21, p. 546
52:7–10, p. 386

JEREMIAH
1:5, p. 531
6:16, p. 508
18:4b, p. 17

EZEKIEL
1:15–21, p. 379
1:20, p. 379
33:32, p. 29
37:10, p. 100
37:11, p. 99
43:5, p. 99
44, p. 29
44:13, p. 29
44:15, pp. 29, 30
47:1–9, p. 377
47:9a, p. 377

ZECHARIAH
4:10, p. 17

MATTHEW
5:20, p. 376
9:36, p. 21
9:37–38, p. 21
15:32, p. 94
18:5, p. 94
18:12, p. 94
25:23, p. 532

MARK
10:14, p. 127
10:43, p. 48

LUKE
14:13–14, p. 94
20:39–40, p. 516

JOHN
4, p. 381
7:37–38, p. 378
7:38, pp. 13, 22
8:12, p. 108
10:3b–4, p. 21
10:13, p. 393

ACTS
20, p. 37

ROMANS
6:23, p. 545
8:35, p. 22
8:37, p. 22
11:5–7, p. 19
12:1, pp. 29, 106
12:2, p. 106
12:6–8, p. 183
12:9–10, p. 18
12:10–12, p. 57
12:18, p. 18

1 CORINTHIANS
9:25, p. 530
12:7, p. 91
12:19, p. 544
12:22–23, p. 91
14:8, p. 287
14:15, pp. 394, 537
14:40, p. 380

2 CORINTHIANS
9:6–8, p. 74
9:10–12, p. 74
12:15a, p. 550

EPHESIANS
2:8–9, p. 545
3:20, pp. 69, 71, 82
4:2–3, p. 18
4:11–12, p. 96
4:12, p. 18
4:15, p. 51
4:29, p. 18
4:32, p. 18
5:19, p. 1

PHILIPPIANS
2:5, p. 533
2:5–11, p. 1
3:3, p. 379
3:4, p. 379
3:13–14, p. 548
4:8, p. 90

COLOSSIANS
1:29, p. 530
3:15–16, p. 247
3:16, p. 117

1 THESSALONIANS
4:11a, p. 546

1 TIMOTHY
4:12, p. 88
4:14, pp. 89, 543
4:15, p. 89

2 TIMOTHY
1:5, p. 89
1:6–7, p. 540
1:14, p. 540
2:1–2, p. 547
2:2, pp. 11, 541
2:3–6, p. 548
2:7, pp. 545, 546
2:15, p. 543
2:24, p. 545
3:14, p. 544
3:17, p. 544
4:2, p. 545
4:7, p. 546

HEBREWS
10:22, p. 107
10:22–25, p. 29
10:24, p. 31
10:25, p. 49
11:1, p. 16, 17
12:1, pp. 529, 547
13:15, p. 107

1 PETER
2:5, p. 28
4:10, p. 96
5:2–3, p. 83

1 JOHN
4:9, p. 16
4:13, p. 16

REVELATION
7:9–12, p. 1
22:1–2, p. 378

MUSIC INDEX

Bold page numbers (**283**) indicate definitions of musical terms. Italian musical terms (*a cappella*) appear in lower case italic.
An "n" following a page number (560n16) indicates an endnote reference number found on that page which further addresses a topic.

A
a cappella, **283**
a tempo, **471**
accelerando (accel.), **471**, 472
accidentals, 225–26, **316**, 358, 369
adagio, **469**
agitato, **477**
allargando (allarg.), **471**
allegretto, **469**
allegro, **469**
andante, **469**
andantino, **469**
animato, **477**, 506
arpeggio, **360**

B
baton, 450–53, **530**

C
cantabile, **450**, **477**, 526
capo, **383**, 413
chord, **344**
　adding and subtracting, 420–23
　arpeggiation, 360–61
　bar chords, 413
　beyond sevenths, 409, 421
　block chords, 348, 360
　broken chords, 360–61
　chord charts, 385
　circle of fifths, 363–68, **364**, 410
　color of, 411
　defined, 344
　dominant (V) chord, 353
　dominant seventh (V7) chord, 353–54, 367–68, 371, 409, 411
　guitar, **412**, 412–14, 560n16
　inversion, 348–54, 409, 414
　keyboard basics, 342–45, 348–54
　keyboard worship, 363–68
　open-voiced chords, 417
　pivot chord, 369–70
　power chord, 410, 413
　practicing sequences, 410
　progressions, 350–52
　secondary chords, 350–52
　secondary minor chords, 366
　seventh chords, 367–68, 408–9, 411
　slash notation, 370, 409
　smooth transitions, 350
　substitution, 366–68
　sus chords, 414, 560n16
　symbols, 408
　tonic (I) chord, 353
　types, 408
　for worship team, 407–11
click track, **387**
closed voicing, **328**

compound time, **436**
con bravura, **477**
con brio, **477**
con fuoco, **477**
con tenerezza, **477**
contrary motion, **350**
counterpoint, **316**
crescendo, **294**, **494**
　band training, 298
　conducting gestures, 494–96
　count-dynamics, 268
　inner rhythm and pulse, 294
　score marking, 235
cued notes, **315**

D
decrescendo, **494**, 495
descant, **315**
diminuendo, **294**, **494**
　band training, 297–98
　conducting gestures, 495–96
　count-dynamics, 268
　inner rhythm and pulse, 294
　score marking, 235
dolce, **477**

E
embouchure, **171**, 186
enharmonic tones, **301**
espressivo, **477**
expressive-legato beat, **476**

F
fermata, **462**, 462–65, 481
flam, **193**
forte, **493**, 495
forte-piano, **304**, **494**
fortissimo, 492, **493**
full score, 322
full-*staccato* beat, **479**

G
giocoso, **477**

I
ictus, **444**
l'istesso tempo, **471**

K
key, **225**, **368**
　brass band transpositions, 293, 322–28
　finding "do," 138, 368
　flexibility, 278–79
　modulation, 368–71, 391–92
　score study, 225–26

L

larghetto, **469**
largo, **469**
legato, **430, 477**
   in 2, 436, 437
   in 3, 434
   in 4, 433
   in 6, 438
   conducting gestures, 430–31, 476, 481, 497
   rehearsal strategies, 525
leggiero, **477**
lento, **469**

M

maestoso, **477**
marcato, **430, 477**
   in 2, 436
   in 3, 435
   in 4, 433
   conducting gestures, 430–31, 476, 480
   keyboard basics, 340
marcato beat, **480**
meno mosso, **471**
mezzo forte, **493**
mezzo piano, **493**
moderato, **469**
modulation, 147, 368–71, 391–92
molto legato, **477,** 478, 481
monitor speakers, **404**
motif, **224, 485**
motor memory, **341,** 414, 520

O

octavo, **202**
open voicing, **328**
orchestration, 322
orphan (literary term), **109**
overtone series, **302**

P

passaggio, 278
passing tones, **362**
pedal point, **330**
pedal tones, **189**
pesante, **477**
pianissimo, **493,** 496
piano (term), **493,** 495
piano reduction, **322**
   from band score, 322–28
      Stella, 322, 328–35
più allegro, **471**
più mosso, **471**
pivot chord, 369–70, **370**
placido, **506**
power chord, 410, **413**
preparatory beat, 119, 121, **295,** 454
prestissimo, **469**
presto, **469**
pulse, **294,** 294–96, 468–69
rallentando (rall.), **471**

rebound, 444, 445–46
rehearse, **505**. *see also* rehearsal *in topic index*
riff, **390**
ritenuto (rit.), **471**
rubato, **471**
ruff, **194**

S

score, **202**. *see also* score marking; score-reading *in topic index*
searching for eagles (metaphor), **533,** 533–34, 547
semplice, **477**
sforzando, **304,** 430, **494,** 496
short score, 322
single paradiddle, **194**
solfeggio/solfege, **131**
   establishing pitch, 269
   exercises, 131
   finding "do," 138, 368
   harmony instruction, 535–37
   invention of, 449
   reading stepwise melodies, 136–39
   tonal magnetism, 353, 536
sostenuto, **477**
sotto voce, **477,** 492
staccato, **430, 477**
   in 2, 436
   in 3, 435
   in 4, 433
   conducting gestures, 430–31, 476, 479, 481
   keyboard basics, 340
   rehearsal strategies, 525
   syllables, 269
stringendo, **471**
subito forte, **494**
subito piano, **494,** 496
syncopation, **225**

T

tempo, **224, 296**
   and beat patterns, 119
   changes in, 472–74
   conducting, 468–76
   fixed tempo indications, 469
   marches, 468
   merging, 474
   rehearsal, 515, 526
   score marking, 234, 235, 236
   score study, 224
   score-reading, 207, 216
   subdivision, 470–71, 474
   terms, 471
tempo primo, **471**
tenuto, 240, **315, 471,** 478, 481
tessitura, 278–79
timbre, **209,** 215
time-in, **128**
tonality, **300**. *see also* key
transposing notation, **290,** 290–93, 322
triad, **329, 347**
   dead weight, 349

inversion, 348–49, 352
modulation, 370–71
notation, 365
progression, 350–52
root position, 348
scales expanding into, 345–48
as stacked thirds, 347
tritone, **353,** 408

V

vivace, **469**
vivo, **477**
voice-leading, 350, **350,** 415

W

widow (literary term), **109**

TOPIC INDEX

Page numbers in italics (*480*) indicate photos or illustrations. Italian musical terms (*a tempo*) appear in lower case italic, while titles of musical pieces (*Above All*) or books appear in italics with initial capital letters. An "n" following a page number (563n48) indicates an endnote reference number found on that page which further addresses a topic.

A

a cappella, 283
a tempo, 471
abilities. *see* levels; skillfulness
ABJ. *see* American Band Journal
Above All, 414
Abrams, Margaret, 526
accelerando (accel.), 471, 472
accents, 480, *480*, 481–82
accidentals, 225–26, 316, 358, 369
accompaniment
    keyboard worship, 362–63, 371–74
    in song selection, 147
    style, 362–63
    unaccompanied songs, 39
    variation in, 41
acoustic "pyramid," 296–97, *297*
activate the breath (warm-up), 134
active tones, 353
ACTS (Adoration, Confession, Thanksgiving, Supplication), 383
adagio, 469
Adams, Bernard, 6
admission policies, 78, 172
adolescents. *see entries at* youth
Adoration, Confession, Thanksgiving, Supplication (ACTS), 383
African-American gospel choirs, 245–46, 415–16
AFS. *see* American Festival Series
after-school programs, 76, 79
age, and instrument choice, 171
age, and musical tastes, 50–51
agitato, 477
Ahnfelt, Oscar, 538
AIES. *see* The American Instrumental Ensemble Series
All Creatures of Our God and King, 112
All for Thee, 237, 253
All Things Are Possible, 394
allargando (allarg.), 471
allegretto, 469
allegro, 469
Alleluia, 137
Allen, Nancy, 140
alternative minor chords, 351
Amazing Grace, 113, 316
American Band Journal (ABJ), *309*, 309, 310, 311
American Festival Series (AFS), 308, *308*, 311
American Instrumental Ensemble Series (AIES), 170, 181, *181*, 307, *307*, 310, 311
And You Will Be My Witnesses, 253
andante, 469
andantino, 469
Anderson, James, 548–49, 563n48
Andrews Sisters, 415
Angels from the Realms, 122
Angels Watching Over Me, 148
Angels We Have Heard on High, 122

animato, 477, 506
Arlen, Harold, 411
arpeggiation, 360–61
arpeggio, 360
articulators, 256
artsy types, working with, 55–58
Asimakoupoulos, Greg, 107, 124
At Thy Feet I Bow Adoring, 112
Atlantic City, New Jersey, open air meeting (1927), *34*
attack, sustain, release, 295
attention, in children, 128
Atwater, Ronda, 9, 10
audience. *see* congregation
augmented chords, 408, 411
Augustine of Hippo, St., 13
Awakened, 526
Away in a Manger, 123
Ayma, David, 542
Azmon, 112

B

baby dedications, 90, *90*
Baird, Catherine, 105
Baker, Charles, 6
balance, 296–97, 302–3
Ball, Eric
    on challenges, 305
    on dynamics, 297
    on maintaining quality of sound, 298
    as mentor, 543
    on rhythm and pulse, 294
    Star Lake Musicamp, 6, *294*
    on transitions, 390
Ballantine, Leonard
    conceptual feedback, 9
    I Am Praying, 374
    influence on Burgmayer, 7
    on keyboard worship, 357
    Mourning into Dancing, 522
    on suspended tones, 361
    "tactile sense of home base," 366
    warm-ups, 253, 256, 257
    on worship-leading choir, 247
Baloche, Paul, 414
band corps. *see also* instrumental program, building
    history, 167, 287
    layering in, 388
    number of, 20, 70
    position of, during worship, 401–3
    score, 214–19
    seeing the conductor, 444, 453
bandmaster's rehearsal, 287–311
    attack, sustain, release, 295
    balance, 296–97
    band training, 293–98

band training techniques, 306
Booth and the birth of The Salvation Army Band, 287–88
brass band instruments, 290–93
brass band today, 288–90
brass level guidelines, 310
divide and conquer, 304
dynamics, 297
every note thoughtfully placed, 303
inner ear and sound, 296–98
inner rhythm and pulse, 294–96
maintaining quality of sound, 297–98
melody, 304
rehearsal, 303–4
rehearse beyond necessity, 303
sacrifice, 305
Salvation Army publications, 307–11
scales require tuning, 300–303
singing, 303
slurs, 295–96
tuning brass instruments, 298–300
work on deficiencies, 304
bandmaster's toolbox, 313–36
   from band score to piano reduction, 322–28
   from layers to rehearsal tactics, 317–22
   score preparation resources, 336
   from songster anthem to brass transcription, 313–16
   Stella by piano reduction, 328–36
bar chords, 413, *413*
Barclay, William, 88, 89
baritone, 171, 178, 186, *186*, 291, *291*
Barna, George, 72–73
Barna Institute, 555n11
Barney Family, *95*
Barrie, J. M., 164
bass, 211, 216–17
bass clef, 326, 327, 328
bass drum, 292, *292*
bass guitar, 389
bass trombone, 292, *292*, 323, 326, *326*, 328
bass tuba, 291, *291*
baton, 450–53
   basic grip, 451, *451–52*
   defined, 530
   exercises, 453
   light grip, 452, *452*
   myths, 450
   seeing the beat, 453, *453*
   selection, 451
   slips and fixes, 452
Battisti, Frank, 467, 492, 507
Batya, Naomi, 410
Baugh, William, 85
Bay Psalm Book, 105, *105*
Be Still, 39
Be Thou My Vision, 352, 388, 390, 434
Beach, Nancy
   An Hour on Sunday, 38, 43
   on perfectionism and competitiveness, 543
   on service, 44
   on transcendent moments, 45
   on worship planning, 48, 50

Bearcroft, Norman, 351, 373
beat, preparatory, 119, 121, 295, 454
The Beat Goes On (Sims), 22–23, 551
beat patterns, 119–20
   2/2 time, *436*, 436–37, *437*
   2/4 time, 119, 121, *436*, 436–37, *437*
   3/2 time, *434*, 434–35, *435*
   3/4 time, 119, 120, *434*, 434–35, *435*
   4/2 time, 432–33
   4/4 time, 119, 120, 432–33
   6/4 compound time, *437*, 437–39, *438*
   6/8 time, *436*, 436–37, *437*, 437–39, *438*
   9/8 time, *434*, 434–35, *435*
   12/8 time, 432–33
   conducting fundamentals, 430–39
   conducting starts and entrances, 454–61
   legato, staccato, and marcato conducting gestures, 430–31, *431*
   score marking, 236
Bedford Corps (UK), *167*
Beecher, Henry Ward, 104–5
Beethoven, Ludwig van, 485
"Beginning Brass—The Ultimate Challenge" (Himes), 166–67
Begler, Thomas, 50
Bender, Mark, 9
benediction, 359
Berlin, Irving, 410
Bernard of Clairvaux, St., 107
Berry, Douglas, 9
Bertalot, John, 562n27
BES (Brass Ensemble Series), 307
beyond seventh chords, 409, 421
Bezalel (artisan), 57
Bb baritone, 291, *291*, 323, *323*, 324, *324*, 327, 328
Bb bass tuba, 291, *291*
   key transposition, 323, *323*, 324, *324*, 326, *326*, 327, 328
Bb cornet, 291, *291*
   key transposition, 323, *323*, 324, *324*, 325, *325*, 327, *327*, 328
Bb euphonium, 291, *291*, 323, *323*, 324, *324*, 327, 328
Bb instruments
   in brass band, 291, *291*
   choosing an instrument, 171
   key transposition, 291, *291*, 293, *293*, 323–24, 327, *327*
   small group instruction, 173
   troubleshooting, 177
Bb key, 293
Bb trombone, 291, *291*
   key transposition, 323, *323*, 324, *324*, 325, *325*, 327, 328
Big Feet, 256
Birch, Kennan, 57
black church. *see* African-American gospel choirs
Blanchard, Richard, 49
Bless His Holy Name, 384, 395
Bless His Name, He Sets Me Free!, 85
Blessed Assurance, 107
Blessed Lord, in Thee Is Refuge, 104
block chords, 348, 360
BMYB. *see* Brass Music for Young Bands
Bonhoeffer, Dietrich, 243, 245–46
Boogie Woogie Bugle Boy, 415
Boon, Brindley, 104, 105
Boonshaft, Peter, 232, 538, 549

Booth, Catherine, 97
Booth, Evangeline, 105, *243*, 552
Booth, Herbert, 104, 105, 243
Booth, William
    on ambition, 531
    on choirs, 243
    concerns about music for music's sake, 84
    diary, 104
    farewell address, 530, 563n50
    founding Salvation Army, 97
    funeral procession, *530*
    heart as necessary for success, 21
    International Congress (1904), *533*
    on keeping the fire aglow, 546
    music evangelism, 35, 104, 105–6, 287
    portrait, *21*
    Salvation Army band, birth of, 287
    The Salvation Army Song Book, 113–14
    secular music, use of, 70, 84–85, 554n2
    songs by, 104, 105
Bosanko, Ivor
    Day of Victory, 374
    as mentor, 5, 6
    Pendel Division, 5, 6, *6*, 7
    They Should Know!, 154, 159–62
Bosanko, Janette, 5, 6, *6*
Boston, 346
bounce. *see* rebound
Bowen, Brian, 9
boys, vocal range, 130
Bradley, C. Randall, 380, 392
brass and drum instructor, 183–97
    advancing brass players, 189–91
    assembling the instrument, 185, *185*
    beginner brass lesson, 188–89
    blowing air, *186*, 186–87
    breathing, 190, *190*
    buzzing, 187, *187*, 188
    embouchure, 186, *186*
    getting started on brass instruments, 185–87
    getting started on the snare drum, 191–92
    high register, 190–91
    holding the horn, 186, *186*
    method books, 195
    mouthpieces, 185, *185*, 187, *187*
    posture, 185, *185*
    resonance, 190
    resources for instruction, 194–96
    snare drum routine, 192–94
    teaching as gift, 183–84
    trombone pointers, 187–88
    warm-ups, 190–91
brass band
    acoustical nature, 289
    continued usefulness, 288–89
    every note thoughtfully placed, 303
    inner ear and sound, 296–98
    level guidelines chart, 310
    number of, 547
    positioning, during worship, 401
    practicality, 289
    rehearsal tactics, 317
    Salvation Army publications, *307*, 307–11
    scales require tuning, 300–303
    training, 293–98
    versatility, 288–89
Brass Ensemble Series (BES), 307
brass instruments. *see also specific instruments*
    age suggestions, 171
    brights, 295, 315, 317, 319
    "centering" pitch, 301
    choosing the correct one for each student, 171
    embouchure, 171, *171*
    first band books, 181–82
    mellows, 295, 315, 317, 318
    mouthpieces, 172, *172*
    score shorthand, 233
    score-reading, 214–19
    transposing notation, 290–92
    tuning, 176, 298–300
    tuning notes, 299, *299*
Brass Music for Young Bands (BMYB), 307, 310, 311
break strain, 223–24, 278–79
Break Thou the Bread of Life, 431
breath control
    brass instruments, 190, *190*
    chant, 255
    conducting, 440, *440*, 443, *443*
    conducting gestures, 477, *477*, 497
    deep breathing exercises, 443, *443*
    group rehearsal techniques, 271
    imagery with props, 135
    phrasal stops, 462
    score marking, 235
    singing, 250, 462
    tone quality and, 302
    warm-ups, 133, *133*, 134
Brengle, Samuel Logan, 22, *22*, 115, 552
bridge, 108
brights (brass instruments), 295, 315, 317, 319. *see also* cornet;
    trombone
brilliant mixed voicings, 280
Broughton, Bruce, 6
Buckingham Palace, 15
Buechner, Frederick, 95, 376
Buenos Aires Central Songsters, 14, *14*
Bülow, Hans von, 231
Burditt, Brian, 554n40
Burgmayer, David (brother), *7*
Burgmayer, Harold
    baton pass, 549, *549*
    biography, 5–8
    calling, 18–19
    childhood, *5*, *7*
    with Henry Gariepy, *10*
    in Manhattan, 18–19
    mentors, 5–6, 502
    Pendel Brass 50th Anniversary (2014), *6*
    portrait, *5*
    with Priscilla, *8*

Burgmayer, Harold George (father), 5
Burgmayer, Naomi (mother), 6
Burgmayer, Paul (brother), *5*, *7*
Burgmayer, Priscilla (wife)
    in acknowledgments, 9, 10
    background, 5
    Boot Camp Basic Training, 132–35
    with Harold, *8*
    as mentor, 7
    Philadelphia Pioneer Corps, 7, 8
    youth singing companies, 150–51
Burgmayer-Duenke, Sarah (daughter), 10, *10*
Burgmayer Family, *10*, 95, *95*, 204–5
Burgmayer-Garcia, Carissa (daughter), 10, *10*
Burgmayer-Luse, Katie (daughter), 10, *10*
Burgmayer-Morgan, Erin (daughter), 10, *10*
buzzing, brass instruments, 187, *187*, 188

C

C pitch, 293
Caddy, Joe, 9
cadences, 343, 366
Cadman, Elijah, 552
call to worship
    children singing, 39, 149
    importance of, 43–45
    keyboard worship, 357, 359
    unison singing, 149
Called to Conquer (Prince), 18
calling, *18*, 18–19, 531
Calvin, John, 19
Camp Ladore, 8, *19*
Camsey, Terry, 57, *57*
Canadian Staff Band, 6, 554n40
cantabile, 450, 477, 526
capo, 383, 413, *413*
cardboard testimonies, 49
Carlson, William, 9
Carolers' Favorites (Christmas carol book), 121, 307, *307*, 375, *375*
Carroll, Lewis, 16
Carrow, Stimson, 8
Catherwood, David, 267
CCLI (Christian Copyright Licensing International), 111, 386, 555n19
CCM (Christian Contemporary Music), 559n6
Celebrate Jesus, 395
The Celebration Hymnal, 376
Celebration of Discipline (Foster), 29–30
Centennial Congress, London (1965), *542*
"centering" pitch, 301
Central Territory Worship Arts Seminar (2017), 9
chamber music, 315, 317, 320
Chambers, Oswald, 380
"Champagne Charlie Is My Name," 85
change, fear of, 97–98
Chapman, Reynolds, 245
Chelmsford Singing Company, 145
children. *see also* instrumental program; *entries at* youth
    baby dedications, 90, *90*
    benefits of music instruction, 170, 184
    bridges for leader interaction with, 91–94
    choosing an instrument, 171
    exposure to music-making, 556n6, 556nn8–9
    junior church, 51, *90*
    learning what they live, 89–91, 555nn7–8
    modeling appropriate behavior for, 88–91
    musical tastes, 50
    receptiveness to Gospel, 90, 555n11
    singing call to worship, 39
Children's Praise, 151, 164
chimes, 292, *292*
choir. *see also* song leader; songster leader
    breathing, 250
    color imagery, 253
    formations, 250, *250*
    gospel choirs, 245–46, 415–16
    posture, 250
    praise choruses, 245
    worship, 244–47
choral benediction, 359
choral reading, 209–14, 349
choral training. *see* song leader; songster leader; youth singing
chordal style, 362
chords
    adding and subtracting, 420–23
    arpeggiation, 360–61
    bar chords, 413, *413*
    beyond sevenths, 409, 421
    block chords, 348, 360
    broken chords, 360–61
    chord charts, 385
    circle of fifths, 363–68, *364*, 410
    color of, 411
    defined, 344
    dominant (V) chord, 353
    dominant seventh (V7) chord, 353–54, 367–68, 371, 409, 411
    guitar, *412*, 412–14, 560n16
    inversion, 348–54, 409, 414
    keyboard basics, 342–45, 348–54
    keyboard worship, 363–68
    open-voiced chords, 417
    pivot chord, 369–70
    power chord, 410, 413
    practicing sequences, 410
    progressions, 350–52
    secondary chords, 350–52
    secondary minor chords, 366
    seventh chords, 367–68, 408–9, 411
    slash notation, 370, 409
    smooth transitions, 350
    substitution, 366–68
    sus chords, 414, 560n16
    symbols, 408
    tonic (I) chord, 353
    types, 408
    for worship team, 407–11
Choristers' Prayer, 163
chorus, song structure, 107–8
Christian Contemporary Music (CCM), 559n6
Christian Copyright Licensing International (CCLI), 111, 386, 555n19
Christmas, worship planning, 41, 54

Christmas carols, 122–24, 375, *375*
Christmas Praise, 375, *375*
chromatic mirror warm-ups, 257
chromatic scale steps, 254
chromatic tuning and pitch memory, 257
Churchill, Randolph, 530
Churchill, Winston, 530
circle of fifths, 363–68, *364*, 366–68, 410
clapping, 133
Clarke, Fred, *542*
Clarke, Will, *542*
click track, 387
closed voicing, 328
A Closing Prayer, 149
C.M. (Common Meter), 113
Cobb, Stephen, *484*
code of ethics, 79
Coles, Bramwell, 49, *336*
Coller, Charles, 15
Collier, Joel, 9
Collier, Lisa, 9
Colon, Jamie, 10
color-coded phrases, 163
color of music, 218–19, 517–18
Come Home, 209–13, 238
Come Thou Almighty King, 435
Come Thou Fount of Every Blessing, 107
Common Meter (C.M.), 113
common time (4/4), 119, 120, 432–33
communication, 79, 91–94
compound time, 436
con bravura, 477
con brio, 477
con fuoco, 477
con tenerezza, 477
concentration, in children, 128
"concert pitch" key, 293, 322–24, 358
concerts, 34, 36, 41
Condon, Leslie, 6, 303, 543
conducting fundamentals, 427–65
   baton use, 450–53, *451*, *452*, *453*
   batter's box, 432, *432*
   beat patterns, 119–21, 430–39, 454–61
   body language, 439
   breathing, 440, *440*, 443, *443*
   conducting language, 439–43
   consonants, 462
   cut-offs, 461–65
   differences in approach, 502
   early and late beats, *446*, 446–47
   embracing the sound, 441, *441*
   entrance cues, 454–61
   entrances, preparing, 454–55
   entrances on a full beat, 454
   entrances on less than a half beat, 460
   entrances on the beat, 456–58
   entrances on the half beat, 459–60
   face and eyes, 441
   fermatas, 462–65
   final releases, 461–62

   four pattern, *432*, 432–33, *433*
   fundamentals, 427–65
   handling traffic or making music?, 429–30
   historical evolution, 449
   maestro as teacher, 429–30
   memorization, 240, 520
   muscle "release" exercises, 442, *442*
   pauses, 461–65
   phrasal stops, 462
   posture, 439–40, *440*
   practice, 465
   preparatory beat, 454
   preparatory upbeat, 445, *445*
   resources, 447
   seeing the beat, 453, *453*
   six pattern, *437*, 437–39, *438*
   starts, cues for, 454–61
   survival kit, 180
   three pattern, *434*, 434–35, *435*
   touching the sound, 441
   two pattern, *436*, 436–37, *437*
   variations in score-reading, 217–18
   vowel production, 251–52, 455, *455*, 558n13
conducting gestures, 467–99
   accents, 480, *480*, 481–82, 488–89, 492
   beat, 444–47
   beat patterns, altering, 471, 474
   breath, 477, *477*, 497
   character terms, 477
   cueing, 484–92
   cutoff, 461, *461*
   downbeat, 444, 445, *445*, 446, *446*
   dynamics, 492–96, *493*, *494*, 498–99
   expressive beat, 476–83, 561n22
   fermatas, 462–65, 481
   gestural contrasts diagram, 481
   left hand for cueing, 484–88, 490–91
   left hand for expression, 483–84
   left hand for phrasing, *497*, 497–98, *498*
   left hand indicating dynamics, *493*, *494*, 494–95, *495*
   legato, 430–31, *431*, 476, *476*, 481, 497
   light staccato, 479, *479*, 481
   loving the music, 498
   marcato, 430–31, *431*, 476, 480, *480*
   molto legato, 478, 481
   off-beat cues, 488–89, 491–92
   on-the-beat cues, *487*, 487–92
   phrasing, 496–99, *497*
   for singers, 455, *455*
   staccato, 430–31, *431*, 476, 479, *479*, 481
   syncopation, 488–89, *489*, 491–92
   tempo, 468–76
   tempo changes, 472–74
   tempo merging, 474
   tempo practice, 475–76
   tempo subdivision, 470–71, 474
   tenuto, 478, *478*, 481
congregation
   engagement, 246
   singing from, 40

teaching new songs, 41, 118
tuning in to, 50–52, 378, 396
Consolation, 254
consonants, 261, 262, 455, 462
contemporary songs, 46, 559n6
contrary motion, 350
Conty, Sophie, 410
Converse, C. C., 233
Coombes, Tommy, 33
copyright, 111, 386, 555nn18–19
Cordner, Martin, 542
cornet
  Bb, 291, *291*, *323*, 323–25, *324*, *325*, 327, *327*, 328
  choosing an instrument, 171
  Eb soprano, 292, *292*, 325, *325*, 327, *327*, 328
  holding the horn, 186, *186*
  key transposition, *323*, 323–25, *324*, *325*, 327, *327*, 328
  mouthpiece, 172
  score-reading, 215–17
  troubleshooting, 178
corporate devotions, 30
corporate song, 243–44
corps band. *see* band corps
corps leadership team, 83–100. *see also* leader development
  change, 97–99
  corps officer's role, 85–86
  music program support, 58–62, 91–94
  next generation needs, 96–100
  people of purpose, 84–86
  resources, 100
  as role models, 88–90, 93, 94
  young leaders, encouraging, 86–91, 96–97
  youth, bridges for interacting with, 91–94
Count Your Blessings, 436
count-dynamics, 268
countermelodies, 225
counterpoint, 316
count-singing, 268, 294
courage, 531, 532
Cox, André, 1, *1*
Cox, Sidney, 372, 468
crescendo
  band training, 298
  conducting gestures, *494*, 494–96, *495*
  count-dynamics, 268
  defined, 294, 494
  inner rhythm and pulse, 294
  score marking, 235
Crosby, Fanny, 48, 107
Crouch, Andraé, 384, 395
cued notes, 315
curiosity, 531, 532
Curnow, James, 6, 254, 268, 542
Curwen, John, 136
Curwen hand signs, 137, *137*, 269

D

Daggett, Ron, 7
Dailey, Darren, 505
dance instruction, 77

David, King of Israel, 53, 66, 165–66, 167, 556n3
Davies, Howard, 548
Davis, Margaret, 9
Day by Day, 538
Day of Victory, 374
D.C.M. (Double Common Meter), 113
Deck the Halls, 123
decrescendo, 494, 495
Deep and Wide, 468
Dell, Michael, 532
descant, 315
diction
  consonants, 261, 262
  group rehearsal techniques, 268
  mixed or blended vowels, 258–59
  pure vowels, 258
  "R," neutralizing or sounding, 259–60
  subordinate vowels, 258
  suggestions, 262
  warm-ups, 134
  youth singing groups, 156
diminished chords, 351, 408, 411
diminished seventh chord, 368, 409
diminuendo
  band training, 297–98
  conducting gestures, *495*, 495–96
  count-dynamics, 268
  defined, 294, 494
  inner rhythm and pulse, 294
  score marking, 235
Dina, Eric, 9
discipline, 81–82
Disney, Walt, 532
Ditmer, Stanley, 218
divine calling. *see* calling
Divisional Band, 169
Divisional Prep Band, 169
djembe (drum), 246, *246*
D.L.M. (Double Long Meter), 113
do-re-mi. *see* solfeggio/solfege
Doctor, John, 73, *166*
Doctor, Robert, 73, *166*
Doctor, Zachary, 73, *166*
dolce, 477
dominant (V) chord, 353
dominant seventh (V7) chord, 353–54, 367–68, 371, 409, 411
Double Common Meter (D.C.M.), 113
Double Long Meter (D.L.M.), 113
Double Short Meter (D.S.M.), 113
Dowds, Mark, 97–98
downbeat
  conducting, 119–20, *444*, 445, *445*, 446, *446*
  defined, 119
  gesture, *116*, 119
  song leader's toolbox, 119
  starts and entrance cues, 454, *454*, 456
doxology, 359
dream big, 71
"The Dream-maker's Prayer," 82
drum instructor. *see* brass and drum instructor

drums. *see also* snare drum
    holding sticks properly, 171–72, *191*, 191–92, *192*
    instructor's toolbox, 183–97
    instrumental techniques, 389
    notation, 292, *292*
    who should play them?, 171–72
D.S.M. (Double Short Meter), 113
duple time (2/4), 119, 121, *436*, 436–37, *437*
dynamics
    band training, 297
    conducting, 492–96, *493*, *494*
    conducting gestures, 498–99
    count-dynamics, 268
    in demanding passages, 518
    differences across time and styles, 492
    graded dynamics, 493
    gradual changes in, 494–95, 519
    group rehearsal techniques, 268
    rehearsal, 517–19
    role in gauging color of passage, 517–18
    score marking, 234
    score-reading, 216
    sudden changes in, 495–96, 519
    terms, 493, 494
    in vocal songs, 209

E

echo clapping, 133
Ecuador, Salvation Army music corps, 14, *14*
Edison, Thomas, 532
Edward VII, King, 531
Eb bass tuba, 291, *291*
    key transposition, 323, 325, *325*, 326, *326*, 327, *327*, 328
Eb horn, 291, *291*
    key transposition, 323, 325, *325*, 327, *327*, 328
Eb instruments
    choosing an instrument, 171
    key transposition, 291, *291*, 293, *293*, 325–28, *326*, *327*
    small group instruction, 173
    transposition to concert pitch key, 323, 325–26
    troubleshooting, 177
Eb key, 293
Eb soprano cornet, 292, *292*, 325, *325*, 327, *327*, 328
Einstein, Albert, 183
El es El Senor, 236
El Sistema model, 77, 172, 540
elaboration, 361–62
Elijah (prophet), 19, 547
embouchure, 171, *171*, 186, *186*
emerging leaders
    assimilating the how, when and why, 534–35
    characteristics, 533–34
    consistency, 543–44
    curiosity, courage, and resilience, 531–33
    deliver more than you promise, 544
    empowerment, 541–42
    group identity, discovering, 544
    group motivation, 545
    quiet strength, 545–46
    resources, 552

    search for, 533–34, 547
    shadowing, 542
    standards of excellence, 543–44
    toolbox, 540–51
    treasuring forebears, 542–43
Enfield Citadel Salvation Army band, 543
engineer
    recording studio, 387
    rehearsal attendance, 406
    sound adjustments during performance, 405–6
    sound check, 404, 405, 559nn2–3
    on worship team, 394, 404, 405–6
enharmonic tones, 301
enrollment policies, 78, 172
ensemble experience, 175
entitlement mindset, 545
espressivo, 477
ethics, 79
euphonium, 178, 186, *186*, 215–17, 291, *291*
Eutychus, 37
evangelism, music for, 33, 35–36
expression, 209, 216, 234
expressive-*legato* beat, 476
Ezekiel (prophet), 29

F

Face to Face recording session, *7*, 73
Fairest Lord Jesus, 367
faith, seeing and believing, 16–17
Falcon Street, 114
families
    baby dedications, 90, *90*
    role in youth ensembles, 72–73, 150, 174
    worshiping together, 40
Farrar, Siran, 10
Farrell, Jim, 74
Farthing, Peter, 9, 98
Fennel, Frederick, 510
fermatas, 462–65, 481
Festival Series, 308, *308*, 310, 311
Fielder, "Sailor," 85
Fifth Symphony (Beethoven), 485
The First Noel, 123
fixed-do, 136
flam, 193
flat keys, 138, 368
flat tire hiss (warm-up), 134
Flinn, Bill, 6, *6*
FLRRT (Focus, Level, Range, Rebound, Tension), 467, 512
flugelhorn, 291, *291*
fonts, 110
For the Beauty of the Earth, 107, 279–83
forte, 493, 495
forte-piano, 304
forte-piano, 494
fortissimo, 492, 493
Foster, Richard, 29–30, 44
Founder's Song. *see O Boundless Salvation*
Franklin, Ben, 532
French, 313, 315, 316, 318

French grip, 192, *192*
friendship, as magnet, 80
Fry, Bert, 105
Fry, Ernest, 105
Fry, Fred, *70*, 105, *243*
Fry Family, 105, 243, 287, *287*
FS. see Festival Series
full score, 322
full-*staccato* beat, 479
"The Future of The Salvation Army" (Brengle), 22
Fux, Johann, 169

G

Garabed, Joseph (Joe the Turk), *35*, *82*, 552
Gariepy, Henry, 10, *10*
Gariepy, Marjorie, 10
Garreffa, Kim, 9, 48, 363
General Series, 308, *308*, 310, 311
generational differences, 50–51
generational resonance, 52
German grip, 192, *192*
Getty, Keith, 18, 410
giocoso, 477
Gire, Ken, 57, 380
glockenspiel, 292, *292*
Glover, Sarah, 136, *136*
God is So Good, *137*, 385
God's Children
    harmonic layer, 225–26
    melodic layer, 225
    rhythmic layer, 224
    score, 220–21, 227–30
    score-reading, 218–19
    structural layer, 223–24
    text layer, 226
God's Soldier, 115
Goffin, Dean, 6
Goodin, Chuck, 9
Gordon method, 139
gospel song
    choirs, 245–46, 415–16
    harmonies, 415–16, 418, 419, 422
    song structure, 107
Gotrich, Jude, *271*
Gowans, John, 92, 105, 154, 159–62, 546, *546*
graded dynamics, 158, *158*, 493
Graham, Billy, 103, *103*
Graham, Peter, 236
Grandy, Bill, 7
Great is the Lord, 390
Green, Elizabeth
    baton basic grip, 451–52
    conducting exercises, 465
    on patterned rhythmic designs, 450
    safety checks, 522
    on score markings, 232
    on tempo, 469
Gregson, Bram, 503
Grey, Andrew, 10
Grimsby, 112

GS. see General Series
Gui, Vittorio, 428
Guido d'Arezzo, 449
Guigo I, 81
guitar
    age suggestions, 171
    capo, 383, 413, *413*
    chords, *412*, 412–14, 560n16
    flat keys, 391
    instrumental techniques, 389
    key choice, 410

H

Hallelujah Choruses series
    brass bands, 308, *308*, 310
    congregational song accompaniments, 118
    corps band use, 47, *47*
    difficulty level, 310, 311
    introductions, 115
    meeting pianist resources, 375, *375*
    songster leader resources, 284
    worship team resources, 67, 397, 423–24
Hallelujah Lassies, 104–5
Hammerstein, Oscar, 532, 542
Hammond, William, 254, 269
Handel, George F., 123
Hanover, 111
Harburg, E.Y., 411
Hark! the Herald Angels, 122
harmonies
    contemporary worship harmony, 417, 418, 419
    gospel harmony, 415–16, 418, 419, 422
    harmonic rhythm, 226
    harmonizing by ear, 415
    keyboard basics, 346, 350–51
    parallel motion, 415
    rock harmony, 416, 417, 418, 419
    score-reading, 203, 206–7, 216–17, 316
    singing, 415–20
    solfeggio/solfege, 535–37
    traditional, 416
    voice-leading, 415
Harris, Aaron, 9, 10
Harris, Rose, 9, 10
Havergal, Frances Ridley, 106
Hayes, Cathy, 9
Hayes, Richard, 9, 559n2
He Giveth More Grace, 435
He is Exalted, 390
head voice
    experiencing high, low, and middle, 129
    imagery with props, 135
    optimal sound, 556n3
    range extension, 133, 147
    "singing on the break," 278
    warm-ups, 133, 134, 251
Hedgren, Steve, 91, *91*
Here at the Cross, 49
Here I am to Worship, 108
Heschel, Abraham, 103

Hezekiah, King of Israel, 167, 168, 556n3
high, low, middle, 129–31
Hill, Henry, *70*
Hill-Holz, Beatrice, *533, 534*
Hillis, Margaret, 223
Himes, William, *288, 534*
    Anderson, tribute to, 548
    "Beginning Brass-The Ultimate Challenge," 166–67
    on brass band's usefulness, 288–89
    conceptual feedback, 9
    God's Children, 218–21, 223–30
    mentors, 534–35, 542–43
    Nothing But Thy Blood, 205
    works by, 6
Hine, Stuart K., 390
The History of The Salvation Army, Volume II (Sandall), 85
Hitler, Adolf, 18
holidays
    rehearsal planning, 62–63
    Salvation Army observances, 63
    worship planning, 41, 54
Holy Spirit
    as river of living water, 377–78
    worship leader tuned in to, 378–79, 399–400
Holz, Beatrice, 7, 9, 10, 237
Holz, Ronald, 6, 9, 300
Hood, Mark, 56, *56*
horizontal worship, 382
horn
    Eb horn, 291, *291*, 323, 325, *325*, 327, *327*, 328
    holding the horn, 186, *186*
    score-reading, 217
    troubleshooting, 178
An Hour on Sunday (Beach), 38, 43
house speakers, 404
How Beautiful Upon the Mountains, 268
How Great is Our God, 390
How Great Thou Art, 387–88, 390
How Sweet the Name
    arrangements, 313–14, 318–21
    brass score, 318–20
    harmonic layer, 316
    melodic layer, 316
    music only version, 314
    preparation warm-ups, 254
    rehearsal concerns, 317
    rhythmic layer, 315
    structural layer, 315
    text layer, 316
    vocal score, 314–15
Howard, Janice, 9
Hudson, Jim, 139
Hughes, Tim, 108
Hull, Bill, 98
Hulteen, Dave, Jr., 9, 10
Hustad, Donald, 339
Hyfrydol, 351
hymn stories, 115

hymns
    arrangement flexibility, 277–79
    re-voicing, 279–83
    song structure, 107
    strophic settings, 277–78

I

I am a Child of God, 226
I Am Praying, 374
I Have Decided to Follow Jesus, 363
Iambic meter, 113
ictus, 444
I'm in His Hands, 218, 395
The Imitation of Christ (Thomas à Kempis), 509
In Christ Alone, 410
"in-ear" monitors, 404
In My Heart There Rings a Melody, 431
In the Love of Jesus, 254, 269
In the Name of Jesus (Nouwen), 550
Ingersoll, Robert, 35
inner ear, and sound, 296–98
inner rhythm, 294–96
instructors. *see also* bandmaster; songster leader
    brass and percussion resources, 194–97
    expectations for, 173–74
    gift of teaching, 183
    locating, 173
    teaching life skills, 184
    touching lives, 184
Instrumental Music Index of Salvation Army Band Publications, 310, *310*
instrumental program, building, 165–82. *see also* entries at band
    admission policy, 172
    assessment of students, 171, 172
    benefits of, 170
    challenges, 166, 175
    choice of instrument, 171
    expectations for students, 173–74
    expectations for teachers, 174
    first band books, 181–82
    giving thanks, 180
    instrument preparation and repairs, 172–73
    instruments, obtaining, 173
    leader survival kit, 180
    leadership, 168
    lease/loan instrument agreement, 173
    legacy, 167
    locating instructors, 173
    long-term incentives, 169–70
    method book, 169–70
    as multigenerational, 165–68
    new pieces, 177
    policies, 172
    private or small-group session, 169
    ready equipment and music, 172–73
    recruitment, 171
    scheduling, 173
    scholarships, 170
    short-term goals, 169
    solo work, 170
    support staff, 173

teachable moments, 180
teamwork, 176
troubleshooting, 177–79
who should play drums?, 171–72
youth band rehearsal, 175–76
instrumentation, unaccompanied songs, 39
intentional bridging, 91–94
intermediate vocal group, 132–35
International Congress (1886), 243
International Congress (1904), *533*
International Congress (1990), 547
International Staff Band, 54
intervals, 139–40
intonation, 302–3
"invitation" preparatory beat, 119, 121
Isaiah (prophet), 19
l'istesso tempo, 471

J

Jacobs, Ruth Krehbiel, 100
James (disciple), 48
Jesus
    apostle selection, 533
    on belief in Him, 22
    on children, 71, 127
    defining greatness as being a servant of all, 48
    on living water, 378
    on righteousness, 376
    as shepherd, 21
    on shepherds, 21
Jesus is the Sweetest Name I Know, 548
Jesus Keep Me Near the Cross, 438
Jesus Loves Me, 85, 119, 120, 135, 136, 548
Jingle Bells, 122
Jobs, Steve, 532
Joe the Turk, *35*, *82*, 552
John (disciple), 48
Johnson, Keri, 9
Johnson, Linda, 9
Jones, Dean, 236
Jordan, James, 439, 443, 461, 476, 479, 508
Joy in The Salvation Army, 362
Joy to the World!, 123, 346, 349
Joyful, Joyful, We Adore Thee, 415
JPK. *see* junior percussion kit
Jubal (musician), 57
Jubilate (Hustad), 339
The Judd Street Collection, 308, *308*, 311
junior band. *see* brass and drum instructor; instrumental program
junior church, 51, *90*
junior percussion kit (JPK), 173, *173*, 556n10
Just As I Am, 381
juvenilization (of church), 50

K

Keller, Helen, 96
Kellner, Paul, 237, 253
Kellner, Steve, 548
Kelly, Chip, 9
Kelly, Thomas, 399

Kemp, Helen, 7, 129, 133, 134, 146–47
Kendrick, Graham, 410
Kennedy, John F., 555n20
Kensico (1931), *35*
Kerr, Jack, 10
key
    brass band transpositions, 293, 322–28
    defined, 225, 368
    finding "do," 138, 368
    flexibility, 278–79
    modulation, 368–71, 391–92
    score study, 225–26
keyboard basics, 339–55
    age suggestions, 171
    cadences, 343
    chording and playing by ear, 342–45
    chords can be inverted, 348–49
    contrary motion, 350
    dominant seventh (V7) chord, 353–54
    finding middle C, 339
    getting acquainted with the piano, 339–42
    hand positions, *339*, 339–40, *340*
    instrumental techniques, 389
    inversions help us "voice-lead," 350–53
    key choice, 410
    piano instruction resources, 355
    piano mentor, 341
    playing by ear, 344–45
    posture, 339
    as rehearsal reference, 504
    scale playing, 341
    scales, 341, 343
    scales expand into triads, 345–48
    secondary chords, 350–51
    in the service, 342
    striking the keys, 340, *340*
    sustain pedal, 340, *340*
    touch, 340
    worship service, 341, 342
keyboard worship (meeting pianist), 357–76
    accompaniment style, 362–63
    accompanying soloists and songsters, 371–74
    arpeggiation, 360–61
    art of piano praying, 358–59
    chord choices, 363–68
    circle of fifths, applying, 366–68
    circle of fifths and you, 363–66, *364*
    congregational songs, introductions to, 357–58
    elaboration, 361–62
    less is more, 371–75
    modulation, 368–71
    organ octaves, 362
    Piano Tune Book, elaborating on, 360–63
    piano worship, 357–60
    postlude, 359
    prayer accompaniment, 358–59, 360
    prelude music, 357
    resources, 375–76
    service transitions, 358–59, 360

tuning, 373
underscore for prayer, 358–59, 360
Khubvi (South Africa) Corps, 13, *14*
Kierkegaard, Søren, 31–32, 33, 56–57
Kierkegaard paradigm, 31–32, 33, 56–57
King, Martin Luther, Jr., 245
King James Bible, title page, *105*
King of Kings, 410
King's Kids recording session, *7*
Kise, Jane, 145
Kloos, Ted, 7
Knaggs, Jason, *8*
Knaggs, Jim, 553n1
Knaggs, Jonathan, *8*, 10
Known To You, 267
Kocher, Conrad, 107, 279–83
Kodaly, Zoltan, 138
Kodaly system, 138–39, 140, 147
Kostlin, Julius, 69
Kranz, Steve, 390
Krehbiel, Janeal, 139
Kroc Centers, 77
Kum Ba Yah, 148, 364

L

Laban, Rudolf van, 476, 478, 561n22
Laeger, Phil, 218, 395
Laidlaw, Judd, *542*
Laidlaw, Katie, 10, *542*
Lamm, Jane, 10
Lance, Derek, *8*, 9
larghetto, 469
largo, 469
Larsson, John, 16, *16*, *17*
Laudate Dominum, 112
layering, 387–90
lead sheets, 385–86
leader development, 529–52. *see also* corps leadership team
    assimilating the how, when and why, 534–35
    baton pass, 548–51
    consistency, 543–44
    courage, 531, 532
    cross-training, 541–42
    curiosity, 531, 532
    deliver more than you promise, 544
    emerging leader's toolbox, 540–51
    empowerment, 541–42
    encouragement and motivation, 545
    finishing well, 546–51
    future leaders, characteristics of, 533–34
    group identity, discovering, 544
    group motivation, 545
    leadership traits, 531–33
    passing the baton, 530–33
    quiet strength, 545–46
    race into the future, 529–30
    resilience, 531, 532–33
    resources, 552
    search for future leaders, 533–34, 547
    seeds do sprout, 548
    selection, 540, 541
    self appraisal, 539
    shadowing, 542
    standards of excellence, 543–44
    training, 540, 541
LeBlanc, Lenny, 414
legato
    in 2, 436, 437
    in 3, 434
    in 4, 433
    in 6, 438
    conducting gestures, 430–31, *431*, 476, 481, 497
    defined, 430, 477
    rehearsal strategies, 525
leggiero, 477
Leidzén, Erik
    American Band Journal, 309
    leadership courses, 8
    Star Lake Musicamp (1948), *336*
    works by, 6, 54, 214, 233–35, 336, *336*
Leinsdorf, Eric, 201
lento, 469
Let Us With a Gladsome Mind, 372
levels
    brass level guidelines, 310
    instrumental series, 311
    junior band program, 169–70
    sight-singing, 141
Lewis, C. S., 45
Liesch, Barry, 31–32
life calling. *see* calling
Life Together (Bonhoeffer), 243, 245–46
LifeKeys (Kise), 145
LifeWay Research, 555n18
light staccato, 479, *479*, 481
Liles, Dwight, 386
Lincoln, Abraham, 201, 544
Lip Trill Buzz, 256
Lisk, Edward, 302
Livingston, Ron, *547*
Lombardi, Vince, 132
Long Meter (L.M.), 112, 113
Longfellow, Henry Wadsworth, 243
loudspeakers, 404
love, as life of Salvation Army, 18, 22
Love Round, 385
Lully, Jean-Baptiste, 450
Luther, Martin, 21, *69*, 69–70, 101, 105, 106
Luyk, Ken, *547*
lyrics. *see* text

M

Mack, Valerie, 134
MacLellan, Doug, 22
maestoso, 477
Magnify (SA song book), 115, 118, 375, *375*
Mahler, Gustav, 305
Mair, Victor, 555n20
major chords, 408, 411, 420–21
major seventh (M7) chords, 367, 409, 410, 411

The Beat Goes On   587

Make Me a Blessing, 362
Make My Heart a Garden, 372
mallet percussion, 192, *192*, 197, 292, *292*
Mallett, Chris, 209-13, 238
M.A.P. (Music Arts Proficiency) Curriculum, 169-70
Maranatha! Music, 33
marcato
   in 2, 436
   in 3, 435
   in 4, 433
   conducting gestures, 430-31, *431*, 476, 480, *480*
   defined, 430, 477
   keyboard basics, 340
marcato beat, 480
marches, 223-24, 468
Marshall, Catherine, 29
Marshall, Jane, 467, 512
Marshall, Madeline, 262
Maxwell, John, 86, 96
Maynor, Cheryl, 9
Maynor, Kenneth, 9
McAllister, Dawson, 87
McCarthy, Ryan, 10
McElheran, Brock, 479, 508, 562n32
McLuhan, Marshall, 50
McNeal, Reggie, 17
McRae, Shirley, 371
meaning, score study, 226
mediant modulations, 370
Medin, Amber, 9
Meditation on Richmond, 336
Meditations (Guigo I), 81
meetings. *see* keyboard worship; worship design
mellows (brass instruments), 295, 315, 317, 318. *see also* horn; baritone; euphonium; tuba
melodic layer, 225, 272, 316
melodic visualization, 163
melody
   band rehearsal, 304
   learning a new song, 210-13
   score marking, 239-40
   score study, 225
   in song selection, 147
memorization
   conducting, 240, 520-21
   group rehearsal techniques, 267
   of new songs, 213, 240, 269
   rehearsal leader, 520-23
   steps, 521-22
   ways to memorize scores, 522-23
Mendelssohn, Felix, 122
meno mosso, 471
mentoring, 30, 341
meter, 112-14, 224
metronome, 224, *224*, 341, *341*, 387
mezzo forte, 493
mezzo piano, 493
middle C, finding, 339
A Mighty Fortress is Our God, *69*, 106, 111, 113
Miles, C. Austin, 151

The Mind of the Maker (Sayers), 265
minister, musician as, 28, 29
ministry-driven model, 98-99
minor chords, 351, 408, 411, 421
minor seventh (m7) chords, 367, 409
minstrel, musician as, 27-28, 29, 56
moderato, 469
modulation, 147, 368-71, 391-92
molto legato, 477, 478, 481
monitor speakers, 404
Montclair Citadel (New Jersey), 14, *14*, 36
Monteux, Pierre, 515
Moody, Dwight L., 103, *103*
Moore, Beth, 543
Morgenthaler, Sally, 33, 37, 61
Moses, 70-71, 540
Mother Teresa, 17
motifs, 224, 485
motions. *see also* conducting gestures
   Curwen hand signs, *269*
   to songs, 156-57
   songster leader, 406, *406*
   up-and-over range extension, 270
motor memory, 341, 414, 520
Mourning into Dancing, 521, 522
mouth formation, 132, 135
mouthpieces, 172, *172*, 185, *185*, 187, *187*
movable-do, 136
Mozart, Leopold, 468-69
Munn, Richard, 52-53
Murray, James R., 123
Music Arts Proficiency (M.A.P.) Curriculum, 169-70
The Music Man (musical), 205
music ministry, 27-42. *see also* entries at band; songster; youth
   congregational song, 41
   corporate devotions, 30
   daring to draw near, 29-31
   effective leaders, 21
   enhancing worship, 39-41
   history of, 104-6
   keeping alive and relevant, 99-100
   leaders' support for, 91-94
   meeting elements, 40
   multigenerational, 165-68
   music for evangelism, 35-36
   musician, as minister, 28, 29
   musician, as minstrel, 27, 29, 56
   one-on-one mentoring, 30
   as partnership, 58-62
   playing skillfully, 53-54
   resources, 42
   self appraisal, 539
   small groups, 30
   from spectator to participant, 31-34, 36
   spoken word, 40
   supreme purposes, 15
   toolbox, 37-39
   value of music, 15
   worship committee, *60*, 60-62

TOPIC INDEX

worship planning, 48, 50–55
worship team, 58–59
music notation, resources, 263
music reading, 139–42, 163, 556n10. *see also* score; sight-reading; sight-singing
musical fingers, 163
musician, as minister, 28, 29
musician, as minstrel, 27, 29, 56
MusicMakers class, 183
Muti, Riccardo, 427–29, 501

N

Nairobi Central Corps Songsters, *54*
Nancekievill, Dorothy, 9, *249*, 269, 371
National Capitol Band, 548, 563n48
Natural Church Development, 555n13
Nelson, C. Emil, *143*
New Christmas Praise, 307
new songs
  beginner brass lessons, 188
  "feeding" the words, 118
  introducing, 117–18
  memorization, 213, 240, 269
  rehearsal strategies, 524–26
  seven steps to learning, 209–14
  teaching congregation, 41, 118
  teaching youth singing company, 147, 150–53
  vocal score, 209–14
  vocal score, marking, 238–41
  from vocal score to rehearsal preparation, 272–77
  youth bands, 177
New Songs for Young People, 154
The New Worship (Liesch), 31–32
New York Sextet Series (SJ), 307, *307*
New York Staff Band, 5, 6, *15*, 35
Newsweek, 20
Newton, John, 316
Nolte, Dorothy Law, 555n8
note systems, 138. *see also* solfeggio/solfege
Nothing But Thy Blood, 205, 395
Nouwen, Henri, 550
Now Thank We All Our God, 115
nursery, 51

O

O, How I Love Jesus, 111
O Boundless Salvation (Founder's Song), 104, 388, 509
O Christmas Tree, 124
O Come Little Children, 140
O Come to My Heart, Lord Jesus, 147
O for a Thousand Tongues, 112
O Lord, Not More Verse! (Gowans), 92
O Worship the King, 111–12
octave compensation, 324
octave displacement, 324
octavo, 202
The Officer (magazine), 98
officers. *see* corps leadership team
Oh Susannah, 351
Oklahoma (musical), 532

Oliver, Gary, 395
one-on-one mentoring, 30, 90, 145, 341
Only This I Ask, 272–77
open air meetings, *34*
open voicing, 328
Opina, Kathryn, 538
orchestration, 322
Orders and Regulations for Band and Songster Brigades in the United States, 15
Orff Approach, 556n6
organ octaves, 362
organ pipes, 315, 317, 321
orphan (literary term), 109
Orsborn, Albert, 20, 21, *21*, 105, 378
Oruro, Bolivia, *67*
Osborne, Larry, 96, 540, 541–42
Osgood, Donald, 313
Our God reigns, 386
over on the top tones (warm-up), 134
overdubbing, 387
overtone series, 302
Overture to William Tell (Rossini), 224
owl at the window (warm-up), 134

P

Page-A-Week Club (P.A.W. Club), 169
Palermo, Argentina Corps Band, *17*
parallel motion, 346, 347–48
parents
  baby dedications, 90, *90*
  role in youth ensembles, 72–73, 150, 174
Park, Hannah, 10
Parker, Alice, 103
Parker, Charlie, 29
Parkins, Billie, *35*
part-singing
  four-part singing, 282
  re-voicing hymns, 279–83
  song selection, 146–47
  teaching, 148
  youth choirs, 147–50
Pasadena Tabernacle Band, *73*, *166*
Pascal, Blaise, 48
passaggio, 278
passing the baton. *see* leader development
passing tones, 362
Pastin, Abigail, 10
Paton-Thomas, Peggy, *533*, *534*
Paul (apostle)
  "Be devoted to one another," 57
  counsel to Corinthians, 74
  Eutychus and, 37
  on failure, 551
  on faithful, 19
  generosity toward Corinthians, 550
  on integrity, 88–89
  on love of Christ, 22
  pressing on toward goal, 548
  on quiet life, 546
  on strength of Christ, 530

Timothy and, 88–89, 540, 541, 543, 547–48
   on using one's gifts, 96
   on walking in manner worthy of your calling, 18
   on worship by the Spirit, 379
   on young, 88–89
P.A.W. Club (Page-A-Week Club), 169
Pearson, William, 243, 287
Peck, M. Scott, 547
pedal point, 330
pedal tones, 189
peer-to-peer partnering, 30, 145
Pelikan, Jaroslav, 45
Pendel Brass, 5, 6, *6*, *19*
Pendel Division, 7
Pendel Singers, *7*, 10, *73*
Pendel Youth Chorus, 10
Pennington, Isaac, 44
"Penny Song Book" (Salvation Army), 104
percussion instruments. *see also* drums; snare drum
   age suggestions, 171
   in brass band, 292, *292*
   children, exposure to music-making, 556n6
   junior percussion kit (JPK), 173, *173*, 556n10
   mallet percussion, 192, *192*, 197, 292, *292*
   matched grip, *191*, 191–92, *192*
   method books, 196
   notation, 194, *194*
   resources for instruction, 194, 196–97
   score shorthand, 233
   setting cadence, 176
   survival kit, 180
   transposing notation, 292, *292*
   troubleshooting, 178
Perrin, Wayne and Cathy, 395
pesante, 477
Peter (apostle), 28, 533
Peterson, Donna, 205, 395
Peterson, Eugene
   on change, 97
   on God helping you, 29
   on heroes of the faith, 547
   on life of faith, 56
   on life of purpose, 71
   spectator to participant, 42
   on Word of Christ in us, 247
   on worship by the Spirit, 379
pew potatoes, 32–33
Philadelphia Citadel Corps, 5, 6, *18*
Philadelphia Pioneer Corps, 5, 7, 8, 14
photocopying, 111, 384–85, 386, 555nn18–19
phrasing
   conducting gestures, 496–99, *497*
   hearing, 214–15
   score study, 226
   singing, 212
   vocal style, 418
pianissimo, 493, 496
piano (instrument). *see* keyboard basics; keyboard worship
piano (term), 493, 495

piano reduction
   from band score, 322–28
   defined, 322
   Stella, 322, 328–35
Piano Tune Book. see The Salvation Army Piano Tune Book
Pierpoint, Folliott Sandford, 107, 282
Pierpont, James, 122
Pierson, Meghan, 9
pitch
   "centering" pitch, 301
   establishing, 269
   group rehearsal techniques, 269
   pitch drift, 558n9
   pitch-matching, 128–29, 371
   repeated, 130
   resources for pitch reading methods, 142–43
   score-reading, 206
   skips, 130
   stepwise, 130–31
   tone deafness, 129
   unison pitch, 128–29
   untuned singers, 128
   in vocal songs, 209
più allegro, 471
più mosso, 471
pivot chord, 369–70
placido, 506
Plato, 71
playlist, for worship service
   arrangement, 386–90
   creating, 380–84
   praying, 379–80
   rehearsal preparation, 393–94
Poch, Gail, 8
pop songs, song structure, 108
Post, Dorothy, 9
posture
   brass instruments, 185, *185*
   chant, 255
   conducting, 439–40, *440*
   keyboard, 339
   singing, 250, 251, *251*
   tone quality and, 302
   training children for singing, 132, 133, *133*
   trombone, 188
   warm-ups, 133, *133*
Powell, Colin, 84
power chord, 410, 413
practice
   conducting, 465, 475–76
   expectations for students, 173–74
   practice sheets, 174
   scale playing, 341
   teaching *how* to practice, 189
Praise, My Soul, 112, 437
praise and worship songs, song structure, 107–8
praise choruses, 245
Praise Him! Praise Him!, 436
Praise to the Lord, the Almighty, 120, 388

prayer
  concert of, 41
  "The Dream-maker's Prayer," 82
  partners, 30
  piano accompaniment, 358–59, 360
  in rehearsals, 393
  youth ensembles, 79
preparatory beat, 119, 121, 295, 454
presbyter, 28
The Present Age, 303
present future, 84
The Present Future (McNeal), 17
Press, Graeme, 7, 272–77, *273*, 533
prestissimo, 469
presto, 469
priest, root of word, 28
Prince, Derek, 18
Pritchard, Joe, 10
private sessions, 77, 169
program-centered model, 98–99
projected text, 108–11, 115, 117, 402
projection (singing), 132
props, 135
pulse, 294–96, 468–69
puppets, 134, 135
pure vowels, 258
Pythagorean comma, 298, 558n6

Q
Quick, Bill, 10, 169, 175
Quicksilver, 236
quiet strength, 545–46

R
"R," neutralizing or sounding, 259–60
Rader, Bram, 10, 357
Rader, June, 90
Railton, George Scott, 104–5, 552
Raines, Reggie, 9
rallentando (rall.), 471
range extension, 129–30, 256, 270
Rather, Dan, 305
reading music, 139–42, 163, 556n10. *see also* score-reading; sight-reading; sight-singing
rebound, 444, *445*, 445–46
recitals, 73, 170, 341
recorder, as pre-instrument, 171
recording studio, 387
recruitment, 75, 85–86, 171
Redhead, Gwen, 244
Redhead, Robert, 6, 9, 236, 244, 543
Redman, Matt, 379
Reformation, 21, 69
Regent Hall Band (London), 14, *14*
rehearsal. *see also* rehearsal leader
  accompanists, 373–74
  active listening, 270
  agenda, 396
  aural aura, 270
  band corps, 175–76, 303–4
  breath control, 271
  count–dynamics, 268
  count–singing, 268
  defined, 505
  devotional thrust, 31
  diction clarity, 268
  expectations, 394
  functions, 511
  group rehearsal techniques, 267–71
  heads up, 269
  intentionality, 271
  new songs, 150
  pace, 180
  for performances, 150
  pitch, establishing, 269
  range extension, 270
  score preparation, 317, 394–95
  songster brigades, 150, 247–49
  staccato syllables, 269
  teamwork, 176
  text, absorbing, 267
  tune-up, 176
  vocal tuning, 270
  worship during, 30, 65
  worship leader's preparation, 393–97
  youth ensembles, 75–77, 150, 175–76
rehearsal leader, 501–27
  addressing errors, 503, 513–14
  calculating rehearsal time available, 63
  coloring by dynamics, 517–18
  conducting from memory, 520–21
  correctness, insisting on, 512
  discover ensemble's unique sound, 504
  dynamic levels, establishing, 518–19
  experience is the best teacher!, 526
  eye contact, 504, 512
  four-week plan grid, 64
  give instructions clearly, 503
  how do I get ensemble "inside" the music?, 517–23
  how do I get performers to watch me?, 512–13
  how do I know when and how to stop?, 513–17
  keyboard as reference, 504
  lessons in rehearsal routine, 503–5
  listening to ensemble and responding, 510–11
  listening to music, 505–9, 562n7
  memorizing pieces, 520–23
  mutual respect, 515
  new songs, 524–26
  overconducting, 517
  pace and order of pieces, 65
  questions from ensemble, 515–16
  rehearsal mechanics, 511
  rehearsal strategies, 524–26
  repeating passages, 514
  resources, 527
  responding, 510–11
  seasonal planning, 62–63
  six-week plan, 154–59
  from snapshots to slide shows, 524–27
  tempo, 515, 526

toolbox, 62–65
trust, establishing, 513
weekly planning, 63–64, 65
when to stop, 505
Reinhart, Carole, 543
repertoire selection
    contemporary songs, 46
    rehearsal planning, 64
    score study, 272
    seasonal planning, 62–63
    Sunday worship, 37, 45–49
    usefulness, 272
    youth bands, 177, 181–82
repose tones, 353
Repton, 113
re-reading, 231
resilience, 531, 532–33
resonance, 190
resonators, 255
resources
    brass instruction, 194–96
    choral training, 263
    conducting fundamentals, 447
    corps dynamics, 100
    keyboard basics, 355
    keyboard worship, 375–76
    leader development, 552
    music ministry, 42
    percussion instruction, 194, 196–97
    piano instruction, 355
    rehearsal leaders, 527
    score preparation, 336
    score study, 241
    score-reading, 219
    song leader, 124
    songster leader, 284
    worship design, 66–67
    worship team, 397, 423–24
    youth band, 181–82
    youth music leader, 82
    youth singers, 142–43
    youth singing company leader, 164
Revelli, William, 501, 534–35, 563n14
"Revival Songs" (Booth), 104
re-voicing hymns, 279–83
rhythm
    brass instruments, 188
    count-singing, 268
    group rehearsal techniques, 268
    harmonic rhythm, 226
    inner rhythm and pulse, 294–96
    score marking, 239
    score study, 224
    score-reading, 203, 205–6
    syllable systems, 138–39, 140
    training, 172, 178, 188, 203, 205–6
    in vocal songs, 209, 210
    vocal style, 418
Richmond, 112
Rickart, Martin, 115

riff, 390
righteousness, 376
Riley, Marissa, 10
ritardando, 472
ritenuto (rit.), 471
The Road Less Traveled (Peck), 547
Robinson, Robert, 16, 107
Rodeheaver, Homer, 103, *103*
roll rudiments, 193
Rollins, William L., 254, *533*, *534*
Roosevelt, Theodore, 82
Roseman, Ed, 353
Rossini, Gioacchino, 224
rubato, 471
Rudolf, Max, 119, 449, 454, 503
ruff, 194
Rupff, Conrad, 69, *69*
Ruthberg, Hollie, 9, 177–79

S

St. Anne (tune), 295
St Francis (tune), 112
Saleh, Nabi, 93
Sallie Salvos, 71–74
The Salvation Army
    Centennial Congress, London (1965), *542*
    choral publications, 104, 284
    Composers Gathering (1965), *542*
    decline, concerns about, 19, 20
    evangelism, 35–36
    heroes, 552
    history of music ministry, 70, 104–6
    International Congress (1886), 243
    International Congress (1904), *533*
    International Congress (1990), 547
    member recruitment and retention, 85–86
    mission, 71
    theology of worship, 52–53
    unique features, 52
The Salvation Army Piano Tune Book, 375, *375*
    chords in, 383, 384
    elaborating on, 360–63
    keyboard worship (meeting pianist), 358
    lyrics in, 106–7, 111, 555n15
    use in song selection, 383
    use with *Salvation Army Song Book*, 106–7, 111–12, 114
    use with *Salvation Army Tune Books*, 358
Salvation Army Song Book
    abbreviations for, 112
    Booth's foreword to, 113–14
    compared to online resources, 115
    compared to *Piano Tune Book*, 106–7
    finding and projecting the right words, 108–11
    history, *104*, 105, *105*
    index to songs, 109
    metrical index, 112–14
    Scripture index, 108
    structure of, 108–9, 111–12
    table of contents, 108
    thematic index, 108
    use with *Piano Tune Book*, 111–12, 114

Salvation Army Tune Books, 112, 307, *307*, 310, 311
The Salvation Soldier's Song Book, 105
Samuel (prophet), 20
sanctified amazement, 60
Sandall, Robert, 85, 287
Sankey, Ira, 103, *103*
SASB. see Salvation Army Song Book
SATB. see Salvation Army Tune Book
Satterlee, Allen, 9
Sayers, Dorothy, 265
SB. see Salvation Army Song Book
SBS. see Scripture-Based Songs collection
scale sheets, 176
scales. see also solfeggio/solfege
    expanding into triads, 345–48
    keyboard basics, 341, 343
    rehearsals, 176
    songster brigade, 254
    in thirds, 301–2
    tuning brass instruments and, 300–303
Schaper, Robert, 60
scholarships, 170
Schubert, Franz, 427–29
Schuller, Gunther, 427
score marking, 223–41
    brackets, asterisks, 233
    circles, underlines, highlights, 234
    harmonic layer, 225–26, 272, 316
    layers, 223–31, 272, 315–16
    marks on a score, 231–37
    melodic layer, 225, 272, 316
    overstriking, 235
    resources, 241
    rhythmic layer, 224, 272, 315
    steps for, 238–41
    structural layer, 223–24, 272, 315
    text layer, 226, 272, 316
    trouble spots, 394–95
score-reading, 201–21. see also bandmaster's toolbox
    aids, 202
    band score, 214–19
    brass instruments, 214–19
    color, dynamics, and expression, 207
    coloring the score, 218–19
    colors of vocal score, 208
    conducting variations, 217–18
    exercises, 205–8, 214–19, 241
    five lines, mystery of, 205–8, 214–19
    harmonic combinations, 203, 206–7
    hearing, 203, 206–7, 214–16
    internalizing the sound, 208, 214
    learning method, 204–5
    melodic patterns, 203
    pitch profiles, 206
    reasons for, 203–4
    resources, 219
    rhythmic movement, 203, 205–6
    score, defined, 202
    score, etymology, 201
    score study, move to, 231–32

    tempo, 207
    vocal score, 209–14
Scott, Paul, 9
Scripture-Based Songs collection, 115, 118, 308, *309*
Scriven, Joseph, 115
searching for eagles (metaphor), 533–34, 547
seasonal rehearsal planning, 62–63
seating formations
    choir formations, 250, *250*, 271
    youth band rehearsal, 175
    youth choir, 148–49
section leaders, 516
secular music, use of, 70, 84–85, 554n2
Select Children's Chorus, 7
semplice, 477
Señora (Ballantine), 257
service, flowing out of worship, 29–30
seventh chords, 367–68, 408–9, 411
sforzando, 304, 430, 494, 496
Shade, JoAnn, 9, 52
sharp keys, finding "do," 138, 368
Shaw, George Bernard, 267
Shaw, Robert, 243, 261
Shea, George Beverly, 103, *103*
Sheppard, Bettina, 278
Shirley, Eliza, 14, 87, *87*, 552
Short Meter (S.M.), 113
short score, 322
Shout Salvation (Redhead), 236
sighs for relaxation (warm-up), 134
sight-reading
    as aid to score reading, 202
    children, 147
    correctness, 562n27
    keyboard basics, 339
    snare drum, 192
    watching conductor and, 513, 562n32
    youth bands, 169
sight-singing
    children, 139–42, 147
    at rehearsals, 150
    resources, 142–43, 263
Silas (apostle), 546
Silfverberg, Erik, 322, 323, *323*, 332. see also Stella
Simmons-Smith, Nick, *145*, 145–46
Simplified Piano Tune Book, 341
Sims, Kevin, 22–23, 551
Sing the Happy Song (Boon), 104
singing. see entries at song; youth singing
Singing, Speaking and Praying Brigades, 243, *243*
"singing on the break," 278
single paradiddle, 194
El Sistema model, 77, 172, 540
60 Minutes (television show), 305
SJ (New York Sextet Series), 307, *307*
skillfulness, 53–54, 73–74, 80
Slane, 107
slash notation, 370, 409
Slater, Richard, 16, *16*, 70, *70*, 105, 205, *243*, 244
slurs, 295–96

S.M. (Short Meter), 113
small group instruction. *see* youth singing, small group instruction
Smart, Henry T., 122
Smart, Ronald, 7
Smith, Derek, 5, 6, 496
Smith, Neil, *533, 534*
Smith, Phil, 186
snare drum
    basic drum strokes, 193, *193*
    basics, 192
    establishing a routine, 192–94
    getting started, 191–92
    matched grip, *191,* 191–92
    method books, 196
    notation, 292
    readiness, 172
    rhythmic reading, 194
    rolls, 193
    rudiments, 193
    solo collections, 197
    traditional grip, 192, *192*
    warm-ups, 193–94
social work, youth ensembles as, 72, 168
Soldier's Hymn, 395
solfeggio/solfege
    chromatic scale, 137, *137,* 269
    defined, 131, 136
    establishing pitch, 269
    exercises, 131
    finding "do," 138, 368
    fixed-do, 136
    hand signs, 137, *137*
    harmony instruction, 535–37
    invention of, 449
    letter system, 138
    movable-do, 136
    number system, 138
    reading stepwise melodies, 136–39
    rhythmic syllables, 138–39
    tonal magnetism, 353, 536
    tree, 137, *137*
solo work
    music of the heart, 271
    as part of team, 415
    percussion collections, 197
    piano accompaniment, 371–74
    youth instrumental program, 170
Somewhere over the Rainbow, 411
Sondheim, Stephen, 150–51, 542
Song Book. see Salvation Army Song Book
Song Book Council, 555n15
The Song Book of The Salvation Army, 7, 105, *105*
song leader, 101–24
    be absolutely sure how the song starts, 115
    beat patterns, 119–21
    check the words with the tune, 114
    double-check projected text or song sheets, 115
    finding and projecting the right words, 108–11, 117
    finding the right tune, 111–14
    Hebrew tradition, 103
    before introducing a song, 114–15
    motions and signals, *116,* 116–17, *117*
    need for, 103–4
    new songs, 117–18
    outlining verses, 115
    resources, 124
    role of, 103
    Salvation Army tradition, 104–7
    script for, 116–17
    song structure, 107–8
    tempo, 115
    toolbox, 119–24
song selection. *see* repertoire selection
song sheets
    double-checking, 115
    making text readable, 108–11
    value of, 117
Songs of Fellowship, 376
Songs of Praise, 376, *376*
Songs of Salvation–ARC Songbook, 376, *376*
songster leader, 243–63
    accompanists, working with, 373–74
    choir formations, 250, *250*
    clothing choices, 248
    connect stylistically, 253
    diction, 258–62
    don't talk, sing!, 249
    engaging congregation, 246
    flexibility, 249
    folders for songsters, 248
    head-voice mix, 251
    honor the singer's time, 248
    linking hearts and voices, 247–49
    listening "chorally," 250
    make music, 248
    moment by moment, 243–44
    objectives, 248
    posture, 250, 251, *251*
    prep time, 247
    "preparation" warm-ups, 253–54
    rehearsal, 247–49 (*see also* songster rehearsal)
    repertoire selection, 246
    resources, 263
    room preparation, 248
    Salvation Army history, 243
    scale work, *252,* 252–53
    signals and cues, 406, *406*
    think, breathe, sing, 250–54
    vowel production, 251–52, *252,* 558n13
    warm-up, 249–50, 253–58, 557n10
    worshiping choir, 244–47
songster rehearsal, 265–85
    active listening, 270
    arrangement flexibility, 277–79
    aural aura, 270
    breath control, 271
    building beautiful sound, 267–71
    conducting, 266
    count-dynamics, 268
    count-singing, 268

diction clarity, 268
formations and focus, 271
group rehearsal techniques, 267–71
heads up, 269
intentionality, 271
memorization, 269
music of the heart, 271
pitch, establishing, 269
punctuality, 265
range extension, 270
rehearsal punctuality, 265
rehearsal techniques, 267–71
resources, 284–85
re-voicing hymns, 279–83
self-sabotage, 265–66
setting a spiritual standard, 271
staccato syllables, 269
text, absorbing, 267
toolbox, 265–85
from vocal score to rehearsal preparation, 272–77
vocal tuning, 270
Sorge, Bob, 378, 383, 393
sostenuto, 477
sotto voce, 477, 492
sound check, 404–5, 559nn2–3
Sound the Battle Cry!, 431
Sousa, John Philip, 287–88, 468
Soweto, South Africa, *15*, *549*
speakers (loudspeakers), 404
Spirit of God, Descend, 369
Spirit of the Living God, 369
spiritual gifts, 183, 555n13
spoken word, 40
St. Anne (tune), 295
St Francis (tune), 112
staccato
    in 2, 436
    in 3, 435
    in 4, 433
    conducting gestures, 430–31, *431*, 476, 479, *479*, 481
    defined, 430, 477
    keyboard basics, 340
    rehearsal strategies, 525
    syllables, 269
staff, use in teaching pitch, 130–31
Stand Up and Bless the Lord, 114
Standing on the Promises, 433
Star Lake Band, 6
Star Lake Musicamp, 3, 6, 7, *294*, *336*, 542
Star Lake Vocal School, 7
The Stars and Stripes Forever, 468
Stead, W. T., 104
Steadman-Allen, Ray, 6
Stella
    arrangements, 322, 323
    piano reduction, 322, 328–35
    score, 329–35
    transposition to concert pitch, 322–28
Stephenson, Jack, 542
stepwise melodies, 136–42

stepwise pitches, 130–31, 206
Stern, Gladys, 544
Stevenson, Robert Louis, 548
Sticky Teams (Osborne), 96
Stokowski, Leopold, 305
Storm the Forts, 433
Street, Robert, 44
street evangelism, 33, 35
Strehle, Kenneth, 5, 6
stress patterns, 112–13
stringendo, 471
strophic settings, 150, 277–78
structural layer, 223–24, 272, 315
Studd, C.T., 95
style, applying to score, 216, 235
Suarez, Stephany, 10
subito forte, 494
subito piano, 494, 496
subordinate vowels, 258
Sunday, Billy, 103, *103*
suspended chords, 408, 411, 414
suspended tones, 361–62
Sussex Chapel, Delaware Youth Band, 15, *15*
Suzuki Method, 556nn8–9
Sweet Hour of Prayer, 346
Sweet Little Jesus Boy, 140
syncopation, 225

T

Take My Life and Let It Be, 106
Taylor, Clifford, 8
TB. *see* Salvation Army Tune Book
Teach Me How to Love Thee, 39, 353
Teach Me to Dance, 410
teachers. *see* instructors
TEAM (Teaching, Equipping, Affirming, Multiplying), 9
teens. *see entries at* youth
Temple, 29
tempo
    and beat patterns, 119
    changes in, 472–74
    conducting, 468–76
    defined, 224, 296
    fixed tempo indications, 469
    marches, 468
    merging, 474
    rehearsal, 515, 526
    score marking, 234, 235, 236
    score study, 224
    score-reading, 207, 216
    subdivision, 470–71, 474
    terms, 471
tempo primo, 471
tendency tones, 353
tenuto, 240, 315, 471, 478, *478*, 481
Teresa, Mother, 17
tessitura, 278–79
testimonies, cardboard testimonies, 49
tetrachord, 343

text
- band rehearsals, 303
- checking with tune, 114
- finding and projecting, 108-11
- group rehearsal techniques, 267
- phrasing, 418
- projected text, 108-11, 115, 117, 402
- score study, 226, 272, 316
- in song selection, 146

themes
- score study, 225
- worship playlist, 381

There's a boy here... (Gowans), 546
They Should Know!, 150, 154-62
Thine Is the Glory, 149
This is My Father's World, 279
This Little Light of Mine, 177-79
Thomas, Peggy, 9, 60, 62
Thomas, Scott, 10
Thomas à Kempis, 509
Thompson, Steve, 410
Thompson, Will, 209-13
Through the Looking Glass (Carroll), 16
timbre, 209, 215
time-in, 128
time signature, 119
Timothy
- Paul and, 88-89, 540, 541, 543, 547-48
- on quiet life, 546

timpani, 192, *192*, 197, 292, *292*
To the Eden Above, 104
Tomlin, Chris, 390
tom-tom, 292, *292*
tonality, 300. *see also* key
tonally challenged singers, 149
tone deafness, 129
tone quality, tuning and, 302
tongue twisters, 134
tonic (I) chord, 353
Tonic Sol-Fa, 136, *136*
Townend, Stuart, 18, 410
Tozer, A.W., 65-66
Tracy, Ruth, 21
traditionalism, 45
transitions, 390-92, 395
transposing notation, 290-93, 322
Tremain, Ronald, 313, 314, 318
triads
- dead weight, 349
- defined, 329, 347
- inversion, 348-49, 352
- modulation, 370-71
- notation, 365
- progression, 350-52
- root position, 348
- scales expanding into, 345-48
- as stacked thirds, 347

trio (march section), 223-24
triple meter (3/4), 119, 120
tritone, 353, 408

Triumph Series (TS), 308-9, *309*, 310, 311
Triumphonic Series, 308, 311
trochaic meter, 112-13
trombone
- assembling, 187, *187*
- bass trombone, 292, *292*
- Bb, 291, *291*
- choosing an instrument, 171
- holding the trombone, 188, *188*
- lubricating the slide, 188, *188*
- mouthpiece, 172
- pointers, 187-88
- posture, 188
- score-reading, 217
- troubleshooting, 178
- tuning, 299, *299*

Trusting As the Moments Fly, 438
TS. *see* Triumph Series
tuba, 171, 178, 186, *186*, 291, *291*
tuning
- blend and, 302-3
- brass instruments, 298-300
- "centering" pitch, 301
- choir warm-up, 257
- songster rehearsal techniques, 270
- tuning note, 299, *299*
- youth band, 176

Turner, Josh, 9
two-part singing, 146-47

U

ukelele, as pre-instrument, 171
unaccompanied songs, 39
"Unfinished" Symphony (Schubert), 427-29
unison exercises, 173
unison pitch, 128-29
unison singing, 146-47
Unity Series (US), 307, *307*, 310, 311
untuned singers, 128
upbeat gesture, *116*
US. *see* The Unity Series

V

V7 chords. *see* dominant seventh (V7) chord
VASA (Sweden) Gospel Choir, *416*
Venables, Brindley, 9
verse, song structure, 107-8
vertical worship, 382
Vertigan, Andrew, 99
vibraphone, 292
vibrato, 302, 418
violin, age suggestions, 171
Violinschule (Mozart), 468-69
vivace, 469
vivo, 477
vocal conductor. *see* song leader; songster leader
vocal range of children, 129-30, 147
vocal score
- colors, 208
- dynamics, 209

elements, 209
expression, 209
layering, 387
marking, 237, 238–41, 394–95
pitch, 209
rhythm, 209, 210
teaching a new song, 209–14
words, 209
vocal style, elements of, 418
voice-leading, 350, 415
voicing, closed and open, 328
Votto, Antonino, 427
vowel color, 455, *455*
vowel diction, 258–59, 259–60, *441*
vowel production, *251*, 251–52, *252*, 254, 255, 258–59, 558n13

W

Wade in the Water, 415
Wagner, Richard, 468
Waiksnoris, Ronald, 3, *3*, 6, 9, *533*, *534*, 543
Walker, David, 371
Walker, Tommy, 522
Walther, Johann, 69, *69*
The War Cry, 85, 104, *104*
Wargo, Al, 7
warm-ups
   activate the breath, 134
   aural aura, 270
   brass instruments, 190–91
   children's vocal groups, 133–34
   diction chants, 134
   echo clapping, 133
   flat tire hiss, 134
   head-voice mix, 251
   nine-step choral warm-up, 254–58
   over on the top tones, 134
   owl at the window, 134
   posture "rap" and breathing test, 133, *133*
   sighs for relaxation, 134
   sight-singing, 139–40
   snare drum, 193–94
   songster brigades, 249–50, 253–58, 557n10
We Are an Offering (album), 55
We Are an Offering (song), 386
We Are Climbing Jacob's Ladder, 140
Webb, Joy, 148, 542
Welch, Reuben, 57
The Well is Deep, 351, 373
We'll Understand It Better By and By, 391
Wesley, Charles, 98, 103, *103*
Wesley, John, 103, *103*
What a Friend, 115, 214, 233–35, 336
What the Lord Has Done, 395
When I Look Into Your Holiness, 395
When I Survey the Wondrous Cross, 433
When We All Get to Heaven, 391
Whitehouse, Gavin, 246, *249*, 557n7
Whitfield, Frederick, 111
widow (literary term), 109
Wiggins, Bram, 556n4

Willetts, Sandra, 256, 262
Williams, Jim, 6
Williamson, Dave, 53, *53*, 381, 382, 415
Willson, Meredith, 18
Win Them One by One, 150–53
Windows of the Soul (Gire), 57
Wishful Thinking (Buechner), 376
Wonder, Stevie, 410
Wood, Max, 542
Wordsworth, William, 529, 550
worship design, 43–67. *see also* keyboard worship; music ministry; worship leader
   artists and performers, 55–58
   call to worship, 43–45
   cultivating the art of worship, 65–66
   elements, 59
   freedom in worship, 53
   God's presence, 60–61
   ministry as partnership, 58–62
   planning, 50–55, 58–60
   rehearsal leader's toolbox, 62–64
   rehearsal plan grid, 64
   resources, 66–67
   revelation and response, 60–61
   Salvation Army theology, 52–53
   seasonal rehearsal planning, 62–64
   templates, 61, 62
   themes, 58, 60
   tools for, 67
   weekly rehearsal plan, 65
   what word, what song?, 45–50
   worship committee, 60–62
   worship team, 58–59
worship leader, 377–424
   adjustments, on stage, 405–7
   band, positioning of, *401*, 401–3, *402*, *403*
   beyond the top five, 380
   chord charts, 385
   chords, 407–11
   chords, guitar, 412–14
   chords, subtracting and adding, 420–23
   flexibility during worship, 406
   flow of song set, 381, 382–83
   goal, 378
   layering music, 387–90
   lead sheets, 385–86
   leading the team, 377–97
   locating music and words, 384–86
   playlist, arrangement, 386–90
   playlist, creating, 380–84
   playlist, praying, 379–80
   preparation of the heart, 379–80
   rehearsal preparation, 393–97
   resources, 397, 423–24
   responsibility, 378–79
   singer selection, 415
   singing harmonies, 415–20
   song selection, aids for, 383
   sound check, 404–5, 559nn2–3
   technical difficulties, 399–400

testing flow, 395
testing timing, 395
toolbox, 399–424
transitions between songs, 390–92, 395
tuned in to congregation, 378, 396
tuned in to Holy Spirit, 378–79, 399–400
words only songbooks, 386
worship songs, song structure, 107–8
"Worship–The Jewel on the Crest" (Munn), 52–53
Wright, Maurice, 8

X

xylophone, 292, *292*

Y

Ya-ha-ha-ha!, 256
Yancey, Philip, 33
Yes, Jesus Loves Me. see *Jesus Loves Me*
Yin Hung-Shun, 547
youth
   bridges for leader interaction with, 91–94
   as entrepreneurial, 97–98
   including and finding roles for, 96–98
   leadership models, 88–90
   leadership training, 86–88
   leaving the church, 555n18
youth music ensembles. *see* brass and drum instructor; instrumental program; youth singing
youth music leader, 69–82
   after-school programs, 76, 79
   classroom discipline, 81–82
   code of ethics, 79
   communications, 79
   community-based model, 75
   consistency as magnet, 80
   dance instruction, 77
   enrollment schedule, 78
   friendship as magnet, 80
   goals, 74, 78
   Kroc Centers, 77
   leadership team, 78
   model structures, 75–77
   music education, 72
   parental involvement, 72–73, 76–77
   policies, 78–79
   prayer, 79
   private lesson studios, 77
   recitals, 73
   recognition, 79
   regional music schools, 76
   resources, 82
   sacrifice of praise, 72
   seven Sallie Salvos, 71–74
   as social work, 72
   special opportunities, 73
   standards, 73–74, 80
   starting and growing, 78–80
   structure, love, and prayer, 74
   student recruitment and retention, 75
   Sunday commuters, 76
   team thinking, 79
   toolbox, 80–82
   traditional flavor, 76
   yuppie model, 77
youth singing, small group instruction, 127–43
   beginner singers, 128
   breath control, 133, 134, 135
   concentration, 128
   diction, 134
   encouraging, 127
   experiencing high, low, middle, 129–31
   fear of failure, 128
   intermediate vocal group, 132–35
   mouth formation, 132, 135
   posture, 132, 133, *133*
   projection, 132
   props, 135
   range extension, 129–30
   resources, 142–43
   sight-singing, 139–42
   solfeggio, 136–39
   stepwise melodies, 136–42
   stepwise pitches, 130–31
   tone deafness, 129
   unison pitch, 128–29
   untuned singers, 128
   vocal range, 129–30
   warm-ups, 133–34
youth singing companies, 145–64
   Choristers' Prayer, 163
   color-coded phrases, 163
   leader's resources, 164
   leader's toolbox, 150–53
   melodic visualization, 163
   musical fingers, 163
   part-singing, 147–50
   performance preparation, 150
   seating formations, 148–49
   six-week rehearsal plan, 154–59
   song selection, 146–47
   teaching new songs, 147, 150–53
   two-part singing, 146–47
   unison singing, 146–47
   worship services, 149

Z

Zimbabwe, Salvation Army work in, 22, *23*
Zschech, Darlene, 46, 394